P9-DGK-563

EXECUTIVE OFFICE OF THE PRESIDENT
OFFICE OF MANAGEMENT AND BUDGET

NORTH AMERICAN INDUSTRY CLASSIFICATION SYSTEM

United States, 2002

Dedication

The Office of Management and Budget (OMB) is indebted to the many individuals and organizations whose vision, insights, and energies have made NAICS United States a reality.

This NAICS United States manual is dedicated to the memory of ***Linda M. Dill,*** *of the Social Security Administration, who worked on the Administrative and Maintenance Subcommittees until her death.*

This product is the result of collaboration and a partnership between Bernan and the Department of Commerce's National Technical Information Service (NTIS). Users of the product are advised that subsequent updates, additions and notifications of alteration with answers to frequently asked questions can be found on the site ⟨http://www.census.gov/naics⟩ as listed on each page of the publication. Additional copies may be conveniently ordered from Bernan, NTIS, or through most major book outlets.

Bernan, a division of The Kraus Organization Limited.

Published 2002
Printed in the United States of America

2003 2002 4 3 2 1

BERNAN
4611-F Assembly Drive
Lanham, MD 20706
(800) 274-4447
email: info@bernan.com
www.bernan.com

National Technical Information Service
5285 Port Royal Road
Springfield, VA 22161
(800) 553-6847
email: info@ntis.fedworld.gov
www.ntis.gov

This official product is released as available in these formats:

ISBN 0-934213-86-0 (NTIS Order Number: PB2002-101430)
CD-ROM version ISBN 0-934213-87-9 (NTIS Order Number: PB2002-502024)

Printed by Automated Graphic Systems, Inc., White Plains, MD, on acid-free paper that meets the American National Standards Institute Z39-48 standard.

Foreword

The Instituto Nacional de Estadística, Geografía e Informática (INEGI) of Mexico, Statistics Canada, and the United States Office of Management and Budget, through its Economic Classification Policy Committee, have jointly updated the system of classification of economic activities that makes the industrial statistics produced in the three countries comparable. The North American Industry Classification System (NAICS) revision for 2002 is scheduled to go into effect for reference year 2002 in Canada and the United States, and 2003 in Mexico. NAICS was originally developed to provide a consistent framework for the collection, analysis and dissemination of industrial statistics used by government policy analysts, by academics and researchers, by the business community, and by the public. Revisions for 2002 were made to account for our rapidly changing economies.

Classifications serve as a lens through which to view the data they classify. NAICS is the first industry classification system that was developed in accordance with a single principle of aggregation, the principle that producing units that use similar production processes should be grouped together. NAICS also reflects, in a much more explicit way, the enormous changes in technology and in the growth and diversification of services that have marked recent decades. Though NAICS differs from other industry classification systems, statistics compiled on NAICS are comparable with statistics compiled according to the latest revision of the United Nations' International Standard Industrial Classification (ISIC, Revision 3) for some 60 high level groupings.

The actual classification reveals only the tip of the work carried out by dedicated staff from INEGI, Statistics Canada, and U.S. statistical agencies. It is through their efforts, painstaking analysis, and spirit of accommodation that NAICS has emerged as a harmonized international classification of economic activities.

Preface

Statistics Canada, Mexico's Instituto Nacional de Estadística, Geografía e Informática (INEGI), and the Economic Classification Policy Committee (ECPC) of the United States, acting on behalf of the Office of Management and Budget, created a common classification system that replaced the existing classification of each country, the Standard Industrial Classification (1980) of Canada, the Mexican Classification of Activities and Products (1994), and the Standard Industrial Classification (1987) of the United States.

The North American Industry Classification System (NAICS) is unique among industry classifications in that it is constructed within a single conceptual framework. Economic units that have similar production processes are classified in the same industry, and the lines drawn between industries demarcate, to the extent practicable, differences in production processes. This supply-based, or production-oriented, economic concept was adopted for NAICS because an industry classification system is a framework for collecting and publishing information on both inputs and outputs, for statistical uses that require that inputs and outputs be used together and be classified consistently. Examples of such uses include measuring productivity, unit labor costs, and the capital intensity of production, estimating employment-output relationships, constructing input-output tables, and other uses that imply the analysis of production relationships in the economy. The classification concept for NAICS will produce data that facilitate such analyses.

In the design of NAICS, attention was given to developing production-oriented classifications for (a) new and emerging industries, (b) service industries in general, and (c) industries engaged in the production of advanced technologies. These special emphases are embodied in the particular features of NAICS, discussed below. These same areas of special emphasis account for many of the differences between the structure of NAICS and the structures of industry classification systems in use elsewhere. NAICS provides enhanced industry comparability among the three North American Free Trade Agreement (NAFTA) trading partners, while also increasing compatibility with the two-digit level of the International Standard Industrial Classification (ISIC, Rev. 3) of the United Nations.

NAICS divides the economy into 20 sectors. Industries within these sectors are grouped according to the production criterion. Though the goods/services distinction is not explicitly reflected in the structure of NAICS, four sectors are largely goods-producing and 16 are entirely services-producing industries.

A key feature of NAICS is the Information sector that groups industries that primarily create and disseminate a product subject to copyright. The NAICS Information sector brings together those activities that transform information into a commodity that is produced and distributed, and activities that provide the means for distributing those products, other than through traditional wholesale-retail distribution channels. A few of the new and important industries created in this sector for the 2002 revision include: Internet service providers and Web search portals, and Internet publishing and broadcasting. Also included in the Information sector are telecommunications; newspaper, book, and periodical publishing; motion picture and sound recording industries; libraries; and other information services.

Another feature of NAICS is a sector for Professional, Scientific, and Technical Services, that comprises establishments engaged in activities where human capital is the major input. The industries within this sector are each defined by the expertise and training of the service provider. The sector includes such industries as offices of lawyers, engineering services, architectural services, advertising agencies, and interior design services.

A sector for Arts, Entertainment, and Recreation greatly expands the number of industries providing services in these three areas.

Another key sector, Health Care and Social Assistance, recognizes the merging of the boundaries of health care and social assistance. The industries in this sector are arranged in an order that reflects the range and extent of health care and social assistance provided. Some important industries are family planning centers, outpatient mental health and substance abuse centers, and community care facilities for the elderly.

In the Manufacturing sector, an important subsector, Computer and Electronic Product Manufacturing, brings together industries producing electronic products and their components. Establishments that manufacture computers, communications equipment, and semiconductors, for example, are grouped into the same subsector because of the inherent technological similarities of their production processes, and the likelihood that these technologies will continue to converge in the future. The reproduction of packaged software is placed in this sector, rather than in the services sector, because the reproduction of packaged software is a manufacturing process, and the product moves through the wholesale and retail distribution systems like any other manufactured product. NAICS acknowledges the importance of these electronic industries, their rapid growth over the past several years and the likelihood that these industries will, in the future, become even more important in the economies of the three North American countries.

This NAICS structure reflects the levels at which data comparability was agreed upon by the three statistical agencies. The boundaries of all the sectors of NAICS have been delineated. In most sectors, NAICS provides for compatibility at the industry (five-digit) level. During the 2002 revision, five-digit comparability was obtained in the construction sector for all areas except one industry group. This was a major achievement and goal of the 2002 revision. However, for real estate, utilities, finance and insurance, and for three of the four subsectors in other services (except public administration), three-country compatibility will occur either at the industry group (four-digit) or subsector (three-digit) levels. For these sectors, differences in the economies of the three countries prevent full compatibility at the NAICS industry level. For wholesale trade, retail trade, and public administration, the three countries' statistical agencies have agreed, at this time, only on the boundaries of the sector (two-digit level). Below the agreed upon level of compatibility, each country may add additional detailed industries, as necessary to meet national needs, provided that this additional detail aggregates to the NAICS level.

The United States has adopted the revised classification in its statistical programs for reference years beginning on or after 2002. Agencies may adopt the 2002 NAICS earlier at their discretion.

Acknowledgments

The first revision of the North American Industry Classification System (NAICS) was an immense undertaking requiring the time, energy, creativity, and cooperation of numerous people and organizations throughout the three countries. The work that has been accomplished is a testament to the individual and collective willingness of many persons and organizations both inside and outside government to contribute to the development of NAICS. Within the United States, NAICS was revised under the guidance of the Office of Management and Budget by the Economic Classification Policy Committee (ECPC). Members of the ECPC were **John R. Kort** and **Kenneth Johnson,** Bureau of Economic Analysis, U.S. Department of Commerce; **Thomas L. Mesenbourg, Carole A. Ambler** (retired Chair), and **John B. Murphy** (current Chair), Bureau of the Census, U.S. Department of Commerce; and **George S. Werking,** Bureau of Labor Statistics, U.S. Department of Labor; and ex officio, **Paul Bugg**, Office of Management and Budget.

The ECPC established two U.S. interagency subcommittees to work with their counterparts in Canada and Mexico to revise specific portions of the structure of NAICS. Eight U.S. government agencies provided staff for these subcommittees. Their contributions were invaluable. The agencies that generously made their staff available to support this process were as follows: Bureau of the Census; Bureau of Economic Analysis; Bureau of Labor Statistics; International Trade Administration; International Trade Commission; Internal Revenue Service; National Agricultural Statistics Service; and the Social Security Administration.

NAICS Revision Subcommittees:

Construction—**Michael J. Zampogna** (retired), Chair, Bureau of the Census; **Barry Rappaport**, Chair, Bureau of the Census

Wholesale Trade—**John R. Trimble**, Chair, Bureau of the Census

The ECPC established an additional subcommittee to coordinate the maintenance and upkeep of the system within the U.S. and with Canada and Mexico. Membership in this U.S. Maintenance Subcommittee included the Bureau of the Census, the Bureau of Economic Analysis, the Bureau of Labor Statistics, and the Social Security Administration.

Maintenance Subcommittee:

Michael J. Zampogna (retired), Co-Chair; **Wanda K. Dougherty**, Chair, Bureau of the Census

John B. Murphy, former Co-Chair; **David Talan**, Bureau of Labor Statistics

Paula C. Young (retired); **Jeffrey H. Lowe**, Bureau of Economic Analysis

Linda M. Dill (deceased), Social Security Administration

In addition to the parties listed above, the ECPC would like to acknowledge the dedicated staff of the **Economic Product and Industry Classification Branch** at the Bureau of the Census. Their hard work and dedication was invaluable in the preparation of the NAICS United States, 2002 manuscript for publication.

Contents

	Page
Foreword	1
Preface	3
Explanation of Symbols	13
Introduction	15
NAICS United States Structure	27
Frequently Asked Questions About Economic Classifications	101
Directory of Selected Federal Government Agencies	103
Part I. Titles and Descriptions of Industries	109
Sector 11. Agriculture, Forestry, Fishing and Hunting	111
Subsector 111. Crop Production	111
Subsector 112. Animal Production	127
Subsector 113. Forestry and Logging	135
Subsector 114. Fishing, Hunting and Trapping	137
Subsector 115. Support Activities for Agriculture and Forestry	139
Sector 21. Mining	145
Subsector 211. Oil and Gas Extraction	146
Subsector 212. Mining (except Oil and Gas)	148
Subsector 213. Support Activities for Mining	161
Sector 22. Utilities	165
Subsector 221. Utilities	165
Sector 23. Construction	171
Subsector 236. Construction of Buildings	172
Subsector 237. Heavy and Civil Engineering Construction	177
Subsector 238. Specialty Trade Contractors	184
Sector 31-33. Manufacturing	199
Subsector 311. Food Manufacturing	201
Subsector 312. Beverage and Tobacco Product Manufacturing	232
Subsector 313. Textile Mills	237
Subsector 314. Textile Product Mills	243
Subsector 315. Apparel Manufacturing	247
Subsector 316. Leather and Allied Product Manufacturing	266
Subsector 321. Wood Product Manufacturing	272
Subsector 322. Paper Manufacturing	281
Subsector 323. Printing and Related Support Activities	294
Subsector 324. Petroleum and Coal Products Manufacturing	301
Subsector 325. Chemical Manufacturing	305

Subsector 326. Plastics and Rubber Products Manufacturing ... 326
Subsector 327. Nonmetallic Mineral Product Manufacturing ... 338
Subsector 331. Primary Metal Manufacturing ... 351
Subsector 332. Fabricated Metal Product Manufacturing ... 368
Subsector 333. Machinery Manufacturing ... 395
Subsector 334. Computer and Electronic Product Manufacturing ... 427
Subsector 335. Electrical Equipment, Appliance, and Component Manufacturing ... 445
Subsector 336. Transportation Equipment Manufacturing ... 461
Subsector 337. Furniture and Related Product Manufacturing ... 483
Subsector 339. Miscellaneous Manufacturing ... 491
Sector 42. Wholesale Trade ... 507
Subsector 423. Merchant Wholesalers, Durable Goods ... 508
Subsector 424. Merchant Wholesalers, Nondurable Goods ... 532
Subsector 425. Wholesale Electronic Markets and Agents and Brokers ... 549
Sector 44-45. Retail Trade ... 551
Subsector 441. Motor Vehicle and Parts Dealers ... 552
Subsector 442. Furniture and Home Furnishings Stores ... 558
Subsector 443. Electronics and Appliance Stores ... 561
Subsector 444. Building Material and Garden Equipment and Supplies Dealers ... 565
Subsector 445. Food and Beverage Stores ... 569
Subsector 446. Health and Personal Care Stores ... 574
Subsector 447. Gasoline Stations ... 578
Subsector 448. Clothing and Clothing Accessories Stores ... 579
Subsector 451. Sporting Goods, Hobby, Book, and Music Stores ... 586
Subsector 452. General Merchandise Stores ... 590
Subsector 453. Miscellaneous Store Retailers ... 594
Subsector 454. Nonstore Retailers ... 601
Sector 48-49. Transportation and Warehousing ... 607
Subsector 481. Air Transportation ... 608
Subsector 482. Rail Transportation ... 613
Subsector 483. Water Transportation ... 614
Subsector 484. Truck Transportation ... 618
Subsector 485. Transit and Ground Passenger Transportation ... 622

Subsector 486. Pipeline Transportation 629
Subsector 487. Scenic and Sightseeing Transportation.... 631
Subsector 488. Support Activities for Transportation 634
Subsector 491. Postal Service 642
Subsector 492. Couriers and Messengers 643
Subsector 493. Warehousing and Storage........................ 645
Sector 51. Information 649
Subsector 511. Publishing Industries (except Internet) 650
Subsector 512. Motion Picture and Sound
Recording Industries................................ 657
Subsector 515. Broadcasting (except Internet)................ 665
Subsector 516. Internet Publishing and Broadcasting...... 668
Subsector 517. Telecommunications 669
Subsector 518. Internet Service Providers, Web Search
Portals, and Data Processing Services..... 673
Subsector 519. Other Information Services..................... 676
Sector 52. Finance and Insurance.. 679
Subsector 521. Monetary Authorities-Central Bank......... 680
Subsector 522. Credit Intermediation and Related
Activities 681
Subsector 523. Securities, Commodity Contracts, and
Other Financial Investments and Related
Activities 689
Subsector 524. Insurance Carriers and Related Activities.... 696
Subsector 525. Funds, Trusts, and Other
Financial Vehicles.................................. 702
Sector 53. Real Estate and Rental and Leasing 707
Subsector 531. Real Estate.. 707
Subsector 532. Rental and Leasing Services................... 712
Subsector 533. Lessors of Nonfinancial Intangible
Assets (except Copyrighted Works)......... 722
Sector 54. Professional, Scientific, and Technical Services 725
Subsector 541. Professional, Scientific, and
Technical Services 725
Sector 55. Management of Companies and Enterprises 757
Subsector 551. Management of Companies and
Enterprises 757
Sector 56. Administrative and Support and Waste
Management and Remediation Services 761
Subsector 561. Administrative and Support Services 761
Subsector 562. Waste Management and Remediation
Services 784
Sector 61. Educational Services 793
Subsector 611. Educational Services 793
Sector 62. Health Care and Social Assistance 805
Subsector 621. Ambulatory Health Care Services 805

Subsector 622. Hospitals 820
Subsector 623. Nursing and Residential Care Facilities 822
Subsector 624. Social Assistance 827
Sector 71. Arts, Entertainment, and Recreation 833
Subsector 711. Performing Arts, Spectator Sports, and Related Industries 833
Subsector 712. Museums, Historical Sites, and Similar Institutions 843
Subsector 713. Amusement, Gambling, and Recreation Industries 845
Sector 72. Accommodation and Food Services 853
Subsector 721. Accommodation 853
Subsector 722. Food Services and Drinking Places 858
Sector 81. Other Services (except Public Administration) 867
Subsector 811. Repair and Maintenance 867
Subsector 812. Personal and Laundry Services 880
Subsector 813. Religious, Grantmaking, Civic, Professional, and Similar Organizations 889
Subsector 814. Private Households 899
Sector 92. Public Administration 901
Subsector 921. Executive, Legislative, and Other General Government Support 901
Subsector 922. Justice, Public Order, and Safety Activities 904
Subsector 923. Administration of Human Resource Programs 908
Subsector 924. Administration of Environmental Quality Programs 911
Subsector 925. Administration of Housing Programs, Urban Planning, and Community Development 913
Subsector 926. Administration of Economic Programs 914
Subsector 927. Space Research and Technology 917
Subsector 928. National Security and International Affairs 917
Part II. Numerical List of Short Titles 919
Abbreviations and Acronyms 964
Part III. Appendixes 965
A. 2002 NAICS United States Matched to 1997 NAICS United States (Changes Only) 967
B. 1997 NAICS United States Matched to 2002 NAICS United States (Changes Only) 995
Part IV. Alphabetic Index 1017

EXPLANATION OF SYMBOLS

In NAICS United States Structure

Symbol	Explanation
US	United States industry only.
CAN	United States and Canadian industries are comparable.
MEX	United States and Mexican industries are comparable.
[Blank]	[No superscript symbol] Canadian, Mexican, and United States industries are comparable.

In Part I, Titles and Descriptions

Symbol	Explanation
US	United States industry only.
CAN	United States and Canadian industries are comparable.
MEX	United States and Mexican industries are comparable.
[Blank]	[No superscript symbol] Canadian, Mexican, and United States industries are comparable.

In Appendix A

Symbol	Explanation
US	United States industry only.
CAN	United States and Canadian industries are comparable.
MEX	United States and Mexican industries are comparable.
[Blank]	[No superscript symbol] Canadian, Mexican, and United States industries are comparable.
*	Part of

In Appendix B

Symbol	Explanation
pt	Part of

Introduction

Background

In 1937, the Central Statistical Board established an Interdepartmental Committee on Industrial Classification "to develop a plan of classification of various types of statistical data by industries and to promote the general adoption of such classification as the standard classification of the Federal Government.[1]" The List of Industries for manufacturing was first available in 1938, with the List of Industries for nonmanufacturing following in 1939. These Lists of Industries became the first Standard Industrial Classification (SIC) for the United States.

The SIC was developed for use in the classification of establishments by type of activity in which they are primarily engaged; for purposes of facilitating the collection, tabulation, presentation, and analysis of data relating to establishments; and for promoting uniformity and comparability in the presentation of statistical data collected by various agencies of the United States Government, State agencies, trade associations, and private research organizations. The SIC covered the entire field of economic activities by defining industries in accordance with the composition and structure of the economy.

Since the inception of the SIC in the 1930s, the system has been periodically revised to reflect the economy's changing industrial composition and organization. The last revision of the SIC was in 1987.

Rapid changes in both the U.S. and world economies brought the SIC under increasing criticism. In 1991, an International Conference on the Classification of Economic Activities was convened in Williamsburg, Virginia, to provide a forum for responding to such criticism and to explore new approaches to classifying economic activity. In July 1992, the Office of Management and Budget (OMB) established the Economic Classification Policy Committee (ECPC) and charged it with a "fresh slate" examination of economic classifications for statistical purposes. The ECPC prepared a number of issue papers regarding classification, consulted with outside users, and ultimately joined with Mexico's Instituto Nacional de Estadística, Geografía e Informática (INEGI) and Statistics Canada to develop the North American Industry Classification System (NAICS), that replaced the 1987 U.S. SIC and the classification systems of Canada (1980 SIC) and Mexico (1994 Mexican Classification of Activities and Products (CMAP)).

The dynamic nature of world economies continues to impact classification systems. NAICS was revised in 2002 to achieve two main goals. The first goal was increased comparability among the three countries for selected areas. To that end, the construction sector has been revised and comparability has been achieved, for the most part, at the NAICS industry (five-digit) level. The second goal was to identify additional industries for new and emerging activities. In the United States,

[1] Pearce, Esther, History of the Standard Industrial Classification, Executive Office of the President, Office of Statistical Standards, U.S. Bureau of the Budget, Washington, DC, July 1957 (mimeograph).

industries were created for electronic shopping, electronic auctions, Web search portals, Internet service providers, and Internet publishing and broadcasting.

The impact of NAICS on various countries has brought about a renewed effort for additional convergence with the many industry classifications used throughout the world. Future revisions of NAICS will continue to strive for greater global comparability.

Purpose of NAICS

NAICS is an industry classification system that groups establishments into industries based on the activities in which they are primarily engaged. It is a comprehensive system covering the entire field of economic activities, producing and nonproducing. There are 20 sectors in NAICS and 1,179 industries in NAICS United States.

NAICS was initially developed and subsequently revised by Mexico's INEGI, Statistics Canada, and the U.S. ECPC (the latter acting on behalf of OMB) to provide common industry definitions for Canada, Mexico, and the United States that will facilitate economic analyses of the economies of the three North American countries. The statistical agencies in the three countries produce information on inputs and outputs, industrial performance, productivity, unit labor costs, and employment. NAICS, which is based on a production-oriented concept, ensures maximum usefulness of industrial statistics for these and similar purposes.

NAICS United States is used by U.S. statistical agencies to facilitate the collection, tabulation, presentation, and analysis of data relating to establishments; and to provide uniformity and comparability in the presentation of statistical data describing the U.S. economy. NAICS United States is designed for statistical purposes. Although the classification also may be used for various administrative, regulatory and taxation purposes, the requirements of government agencies that use it for nonstatistical purposes played no role in its development or subsequent revision.

Development of NAICS

The U.S. ECPC established by OMB in 1992 was chaired by the Bureau of Economic Analysis, U.S. Department of Commerce, with representatives from the Bureau of the Census, U.S. Department of Commerce, and the Bureau of Labor Statistics, U.S. Department of Labor. The ECPC was asked to examine economic classifications for statistical purposes and to determine the desirability of developing a new industry classification system for the United States based on a single economic concept. On March 31, 1993, OMB published a **Federal Register** notice (58FR16990–17004) announcing the intention to revise the SIC for 1997, the establishment of the ECPC, and the process for revising the SIC.

In July 1994, the OMB announced plans to develop a new industry classification system in cooperation with Mexico's INEGI and Statistics Canada. The new system—NAICS—replaces the current U.S. SIC. The concepts of the new system and the principles upon which NAICS was to be developed were announced in a July 26, 1994 **Federal Register** notice (59FR38092–38096) and were as follows:

1. NAICS will be erected on a production-oriented or supply-based conceptual framework. This means that producing units that use identical or similar production processes will be grouped together in NAICS.
2. The system will give special attention to developing production-oriented classifications for (a) new and emerging industries, (b) service industries in general, and (c) industries engaged in the production of advanced technologies.
3. Time series continuity will be maintained to the extent possible. However, changes in the economy and proposals from data users must be considered. In addition, adjustments will be required for sectors where the United States, Canada, and Mexico have incompatible industry classification definitions in order to produce a common industry system for all three North American countries.
4. The system will strive for compatibility with the two-digit level of the International Standard Industrial Classification of All Economic Activities (ISIC, Rev. 3) of the United Nations.

The structure of NAICS was developed in a series of meetings among the three countries. Public proposals for individual industries from all three countries were considered for acceptance if the proposed industry was based on the production-oriented concept of the system. In the United States, public comments also were solicited as groups of subsectors of NAICS were completed and agreed upon by the three countries. The ECPC published the proposed industries for those subsectors in a series of five successive **Federal Register** notices, in 1995 and 1996, asking for comments from interested data users.

Revision of NAICS for 2002

OMB published a notification of intention to complete portions of NAICS in a February 25, 1999, **Federal Register** notice (FR 64 9416–9419). This notice solicited comments on the advisability of revising the NAICS 1997 Structure for 2002 and solicited proposals for the creation of new industries in the Construction and Wholesale Trade Sectors, modifications to the national industries for department stores and non-store retailers, and changes necessary to NAICS 1997 identified during the implementation of NAICS 1997.

After considering all proposals from the public, consulting with a large number of U.S. data users and industry groups, and undertaking extensive discussions with Statistics Canada and Mexico's Instituto Nacional de Estadística, Geografía e Informática (INEGI), a revised industrial structure for NAICS was developed that would apply to all three North American countries. This includes a revised structure for both the Construction and Information sectors and additional U.S. industry detail in the Retail Trade sector. Statistics Canada and INEGI sought comments on the proposed revisions. Further discussions were held among the three countries to consider public comments received from all three countries. The United States has chosen to restructure the Wholesale Trade sector to more accurately reflect production function differences between those wholesalers that take title to goods and those that do not, and to better capture the rapidly-growing business-to-business electronic markets developing in the United States. These changes for the United States did not impact comparability among the three partners in NAICS. In an April 20, 2000 **Federal Register** notice (FR 65 21242–21282) OMB published the proposed structure of NAICS United States, 2002, and formalized adoption in a **Federal Register** notice (FR 66 3826–3827) on January 16, 2001.

Conceptual Framework

NAICS is erected on a production-oriented or supply-based conceptual framework that groups establishments into industries according to similarity in the processes used to produce goods or services. A production-oriented industry classification system ensures that statistical agencies in the three countries can produce information on inputs and outputs, industrial performance, productivity, unit labor costs, employment, and other statistics and structural changes occurring in each of the three economies.

When an industry is defined on a production-oriented concept, producing units within the industry's boundaries share a basic production process; they use closely similar technology. In the language of economics, producing units within an industry share the same production functions; producing units in different industries have different production functions. The boundaries between industries thus demarcate, in principle, differences in production processes and production technologies.

The reasoning behind the three countries' decision to base NAICS on a production-oriented concept is summarized as follows: An industry is a grouping of economic activities. Though it inevitably groups the products of the economic activities that are included in the industry definition, it is not solely a grouping of products; put another way, an industry groups producing units. Accordingly, an industry classification system provides a framework for collecting data on inputs and outputs together.

The uses of economic data that require that data on inputs and outputs be used together and be collected on the same basis, include production analyses, productivity measurement, and studying input usage and input intensities. The North American statistical agencies developed NAICS using a production-oriented concept as the framework for two reasons: (1) an industry classification system groups producing units, not products or services; and (2) groupings of producing units permit the collection of data on inputs and outputs on a comparable basis, which is required for production-oriented analysis, but do not facilitate a comprehensive collection of data on the total output of any particular good or service, which is required for market-oriented analysis. Thus, the efficient organizing concept of an industry classification system is production-oriented rather than market-oriented.

Structure of NAICS

The structure of NAICS is hierarchical. The first two digits of the structure designate the NAICS sectors that represent general categories of economic activities.

NAICS classifies all economic activities into 20 sectors. The NAICS sectors, their two-digit codes, and the distinguishing activities of each are:

11 Agriculture, Forestry, Fishing and Hunting—Activities of this sector are growing crops, raising animals, harvesting timber, and harvesting fish and other animals from farms, ranches, or the animals' natural habitats.

21 Mining—Activities of this sector are extracting naturally occurring mineral solids, such as coal and ore; liquid minerals, such as crude petroleum; and gases, such as natural gas; and beneficiating (e.g., crushing, screening, washing, and flotation) and other preparation at the mine site, or as part of mining activity.

22 Utilities—Activities of this sector are generating, transmitting, and/or distributing electricity, gas, steam, and water and removing sewage through a permanent infrastructure of lines, mains, and pipe.

23 Construction—Activities of this sector are erecting buildings and other structures (including additions); heavy construction other than buildings; and alterations, reconstruction, installation, and maintenance and repairs.

31-33 Manufacturing—Activities of this sector are the mechanical, physical, or chemical transformation of material, substances, or components into new products.

42 Wholesale Trade—Activities of this sector are selling or arranging for the purchase or sale of goods for resale; capital or durable nonconsumer goods; and raw and intermediate materials and supplies used in production, and providing services incidental to the sale of the merchandise.

44-45 Retail Trade—Activities of this sector are retailing merchandise generally in small quantities to the general public and providing services incidental to the sale of the merchandise.

48-49 Transportation and Warehousing—Activities of this sector are providing transportation of passengers and cargo, warehousing and storing goods, scenic and sightseeing transportation, and supporting these activities.

51 Information—Activities of this sector are distributing information and cultural products, providing the means to transmit or distribute these products as data or communications, and processing data.

52 Finance and Insurance—Activities of this sector involve the creation, liquidation, or change in ownership of financial assets (financial transactions) and/or facilitating financial transactions.

53 Real Estate and Rental and Leasing—Activities of this sector are renting, leasing, or otherwise allowing the use of tangible or intangible assets (except copyrighted works), and providing related services.

54 Professional, Scientific, and Technical Services—Activities of this sector are performing professional, scientific, and technical services for the operations of other organizations.

55 Management of Companies and Enterprises—Activities of this sector are the holding of securities of companies and enterprises, for the purpose of owning controlling interest or influencing their management decision, or administering, overseeing, and managing other establishments of the same company or enterprise and normally undertaking the strategic or organizational planning and decision making of the company or enterprise.

56 Administrative and Support and Waste Management and Remediation Services—Activities of this sector are performing routine support activities for the day-to-day operations of other organizations.

61 Educational Services—Activities of this sector are providing instruction and training in a wide variety of subjects.

62 Health Care and Social Assistance—Activities of this sector are providing health care and social assistance for individuals.

71 Arts, Entertainment, and Recreation—Activities of this sector are operating or providing services to meet varied cultural, entertainment, and recreational interests of their patrons.

72 Accommodation and Food Services—Activities of this sector are providing customers with lodging and/or preparing meals, snacks, and beverages for immediate consumption.

81 Other Services (except Public Administration)—Activities of this sector are providing services not elsewhere specified, including repairs, religious activities, grantmaking, advocacy, laundry, personal care, death care, and other personal services.

92 Public Administration—Activities of this sector are administration, management, and oversight of public programs by Federal, State, and local governments.

NAICS uses a six-digit coding system to identify particular industries and their placement in this hierarchical structure of the classification system. The first two digits of the code designate the sector, the third designates the subsector, the fourth digit designates the industry group, the fifth digit designates the NAICS industry, and the sixth digit designates the national industry. A zero as the sixth digit generally indicates that the NAICS industry and the U.S. industry are the same.

The subsectors, industry groups, and NAICS industries, in accord with the conceptual principle of NAICS, are production-oriented combinations of establishments. However, the production distinctions become more narrowly defined as one moves down the hierarchy.

NAICS agreements permit each country to designate detailed industries, below the level of a NAICS industry, to meet national needs. The United States has such industry detail in many places in the classification system to recognize large, important U.S. industries that cannot be recognized in the other countries because of size, specialization, or organization of the industry.

Typically the level at which comparable data will be available for Canada, Mexico, and the United States is the five-digit NAICS industry; for some sectors (or subsectors or industry groups) however, the three countries agreed upon the boundaries at a higher level of detail rather than the detailed industry structure (five-digit). Agreement was reached at the sector level for utilities; wholesale trade; retail trade; and public administration and at the subsector level for finance; personal and laundry services; religious, grantmaking, civic, and professional and similar organizations; and waste management and remediation services. For insurance and real estate, the three countries agreed on comparability at the industry group level. The 2002 revision effort obtained comparability at the five-digit level for most areas of the construction sector.

Differences in the economies of the three countries or time constraints necessitated these modifications. For each of these sectors, except wholesale trade and public administration, Canada and the United States have agreed upon an industry structure and hierarchy to ensure comparability of statistics between those two countries. Canada and the United States also have established the same national detail (six-digit) industries where possible, adopting the same codes to describe comparable industries. For this reason, the numbers of the U.S. industries may not be consecutive. In a few cases, it was necessary for the United States to use all of the numbers available to establish its six-digit detail so that the same six-digit codes do not represent comparable industries in the U.S. and Canada.

NAICS with U.S. detail will be known as NAICS United States (denoted by ''US'' in Appendix A and a superscript ''US'' at the end of the title in Part I) while Canada and Mexico will produce six-digit detail and will publish that detail as NAICS Canada and NAICS (SCIAN in Spanish) Mexico.

Definition of an Establishment

NAICS is a classification system for establishments. The establishment as a statistical unit is defined as the smallest operating entity for which records provide information on the cost of resources materials, labor, and capital employed to produce the units of output. The output may be sold to other establishments and receipts or sales recorded, or the output may be provided without explicit charge, that is, the good or service may be ''sold'' within the company itself.

The establishment, in NAICS United States, is generally a single physical location, where business is conducted or where services or industrial operations are performed (for example, a factory, mill, store, hotel, movie theater, mine, farm, airline terminal, sales office, warehouse, or central administrative office). There are cases where records identify distinct and separate economic activities performed at a single physical location (e.g., shops in a hotel). These retailing activities, operated out of the same physical location as the hotel, are identified as separate establishments and classified in retail trade while the hotel is classified in accommodations. In such cases, each activity is treated as a separate establishment provided:

(1) no one industry description in the classification includes such combined activities; (2) separate reports can be prepared on the number of employees, their wages and salaries, sales or receipts, and expenses; and (3) employment and output are significant for both activities.

Exceptions to the single location exist for physically dispersed operations, such as construction, transportation, and communication. For these activities the individual sites, projects, fields, networks, lines, or systems of such dispersed activities are not normally considered to be establishments. The establishment is represented by those relatively permanent main or branch offices, terminals, stations, and so forth, that are either (1) directly responsible for supervising such activities, or (2) the base from which personnel operate to carry out these activities.

Although an establishment may be identical with the enterprise (company), the two terms should not be confused. An enterprise (company) may consist of more than one establishment. Such multiunit enterprises may have establishments in more than one industry in NAICS. If such enterprises have a separate establishment primarily engaged in providing headquarters services, these establishments are classified in NAICS Sector 55, Management of Companies and Enterprises.

Although all establishments have output, they may or may not have receipts. In large enterprises it is not unusual for establishments to exist that solely serve other establishments of the same enterprise (auxiliary establishments). In such cases, these units often do not collect receipts from the establishments they serve. This type of support (captive) activity is found throughout the economy and involves goods producing activities as well as services. Units that carry out support activities for the enterprise to which they belong are classified, to the extent feasible, according to the NAICS code related to their own activity. This means that warehouses providing storage facilities for their own enterprise will be classified as warehouses.

Determining an Establishment's Industry Classification

An establishment is classified to an industry when its primary activity meets the definition for that industry. Because establishments may perform more than one activity, it is necessary to determine procedures for identifying the primary activity of the establishment.

In most cases, if an establishment is engaged in more than one activity, the industry code is assigned based on the establishment's principal product or group of products produced or distributed, or services rendered. Ideally, the principal good or service should be determined by its relative share of current production costs and capital investment at the establishment. In practice, however, it is often necessary to use other variables such as revenue, shipments, or employment as proxies for measuring significance.

There are two types of combined activities that are given special attention in NAICS. They are vertical integration and joint production. These combined activities have an economic basis and occur in both goods-producing and services-producing sectors. In some cases, there are efficiencies to be gained from combining certain activities in the same establishment. Some of these combinations occur so commonly or frequently that their combination can be treated as a third activity in its own right and explicitly classified in a specific industry.

One approach to classifying these activities would be to use the primary activity rule, that is, whichever activity is largest. However, the fundamental principle of NAICS is that establishments that employ the same production process should be classified in the same industry. If the premise that the combined activities correspond to a distinct third activity is accepted, then using the primary activity rule would place establishments performing the same combination of activities in different industries, thereby violating the production principle of NAICS. A second reason for NAICS recognizing combined activities is to improve the stability of establishment classification, both over time and among the various agencies that implement the classification. An establishment should remain classified in the same industry unless its production process changes, and different agencies should code the same establishment or type of establishment in the same way. A consistent treatment of establishments with combined activities is more likely if they are classified to a single industry.

Vertical integration involves consecutive stages of fabrication or production processes in which the output of one step is the input of the next. In general, establishments will be classified based on the final process in a vertically integrated production environment, unless specifically identified as classified in another industry. For example, paper may be produced either by establishments that first produce pulp and then consume that pulp to produce paper or by those establishments producing paper from purchased pulp. NAICS specifically specifies that both of these types of paper-producing processes should be classified in NAICS 32212, Paper Mills, the industry, or the final step in paper manufacturing, rather than in NAICS 32211, Pulp Mills. In other cases, NAICS specifies that vertically integrated establishments be classified in the industry representing the first stage of the manufacturing process. For example, steel mills that make steel and also perform other activities such as producing steel castings are classified in NAICS 33111, Iron and Steel Mills and Ferroalloy Manufacturing, the first stage of the manufacturing process.

The joint production of goods or services represents the second type of combined activities. For example, automobile dealers both sell and repair autos; automotive parts dealers may both sell parts and repair automobiles; and musical instrument stores may both sell and rent instruments. In the manufacturing sector, establishments may make two different products such as women's dresses and women's suits, activities that are classified in two different NAICS United States detailed industries. In general, receipts/sales and revenue data are used as a proxy to determine primary activity for these establishments. The assumption is that the activity generating the most receipts is also the activity using the most resources and most indicative of the production process.

In some cases, however, these combined activities have been assigned to a specific NAICS industry. Most of these activities involve either the sale and repair of goods or the sale and rental of goods in the same establishment. For example, establishments that both sell automobile parts and repair automobiles are classified in NAICS 44131, Automotive Parts and Accessories Stores, and those music stores that both sell and rent musical instruments are classified in NAICS 45114, Musical Instrument and Supplies Stores. In other cases, specific industries have been identified for these combined activities, such as NAICS 44711, Gasoline Stations with Convenience Stores.

Classification rules related to the agreement to permit individual country detail at the six-digit level for NAICS sometimes results in less comparable NAICS industries at the five-digit level and above. For example in NAICS, the assignment of the industry code is at the most detailed level of the classification (the six-digit U.S. detail code), except for agriculture. That is, if the value of an establishment's production consists of 30 percent from computers, 30 percent from computer storage devices, and 40 percent from semiconductors and related devices, it will be classified in U.S. detail industry 334413, Semiconductor and Related Device Manufacturing, that will be aggregated to NAICS 33441, Semiconductor and Other Electronic Component Manufacturing, the level that comparable information is shown for all three countries. If the classification for the above example were at the five-digit NAICS level, that establishment would be classified in NAICS 33411, Computer and Peripheral Equipment Manufacturing. There would then be more comparable information at the NAICS level, but it would be impossible to classify this establishment to a U.S. detail six-digit industry.

In agriculture, however, NAICS coding begins at the top of the structure and continues down to the most detailed level (the six-digit U.S. detail code). The existence of a 50 percent rule in agriculture, rather than the plurality rule used elsewhere, and the presence of combination industries based on families of related agricultural products with none accounting for 50 percent or more of production require a top down coding procedure rather than coding at the most detailed level first as is done in the balance of the classification.

Use of Reporting Units Other than Establishments

NAICS is based on the economic principle that establishments should be grouped together based on their production processes. The NAICS definition of the establishment ensures that, at some level, ''establishments'': (1) identify the most refined (generally smallest) individual entity possible; (2) can provide the information needed when surveying economic activity; and (3) when aggregated, approximate the statistical universe of economic activity. Each economic survey program, in practice, will need to determine whether the establishment is the most appropriate reporting unit to meet the three criteria listed above with respect to the program's objectives. If not, an alternative reporting unit may have to be identified.

For example, an economic survey of employment or wage data may choose the establishment—generally a physical location—as the reporting unit. Physical locations generally have records for the number of employees and their wages readily available. Therefore, it is reasonable to expect that separate wage and employment data would be available for each switching station in a multiunit telecommunications carrier enterprise and the physical location is a logical choice for the reporting unit.

If the economic survey collects output data, the individual switching stations would not have the total number of telephone calls or a complete accounting of inputs and outputs of the multiunit telecommunications carrier. If a telephone call is routed through three different switching stations and the price is determined at a fourth location, all of the related locations would need to be merged into an alternative reporting unit to measure the volume and value of the output. In this case, the physical location would not be an appropriate reporting unit. The level of aggregation of physical units required to create reporting units will vary greatly depending on the business activity being studied. To efficiently define reporting units, statistical surveys need to evaluate the characteristics of the activities being studied and the organizational structure of the entities producing goods or services. In some cases, the physical location is appropriate, sometimes units will need to be grouped based on homogeneous production characteristics or geographical groupings, and in other cases, the enterprise (company) may form the most appropriate reporting unit.

The practical variation in reporting unit definitions affects comparability of data. A count of units defined as physical locations will be different from a count of units defined based on the need for complete input and output records in the telecommunications industries. It is critical that each data provider clearly identifies the reporting unit definition used when presenting summary statistics. The analysis of statistical data from a variety of sources requires the transparency of clearly defined reporting units.

While the reporting unit definition can vary, NAICS is a classification system for establishments, and is based on grouping establishments with similar production function characteristics.

Comparison of NAICS to the International Standard Industrial Classification (ISIC)

Recognizing the need for international comparability of economic statistics, the United Nations (UN) first adopted an International Standard Industrial Classification (ISIC) system in 1948. Revisions to the ISIC structure and codes were adopted by the UN's Statistical Commission in 1958, 1968, and 1989.[2]

Similar to NAICS, ISIC was designed primarily to provide classifications for grouping activities (rather than enterprises or firms), and the primary focus for the ISIC classification system is the kind of activity in which establishments or other

---

[2] International Standard Industrial Classification of all Economic Activities, Statistical Papers, Series M., No. 4, Department of International Economic and Social Affairs, Statistical Office, United Nations, New York, 1958, International Standard Industrial Classification of All Economic Activities, Statistical Papers, Series M., No. 4, Rev. 2, Department of International Economic and Social Affairs, Statistical Office, United Nations, New York, 1968. International Standard Industrial Classification of All Economic Activities, Statistical Papers, Series M., No. 4., Rev. 3, Department of International Economic and Social Affairs, Statistical Office, United Nations, New York, 1990.

statistical entities are engaged. The main criteria employed in delineating divisions and groups (the two- and three-digit categories, respectively) of ISIC are: (a) the character of the goods and services produced; (b) the uses to which the goods and services are put; and (c) the inputs, the process, and the technology of production.

The third classification criterion of the ISIC is the conceptual foundation of NAICS, and thus, NAICS is aligned more closely with ISIC than was the 1987 SIC system. However, there are differences between the NAICS and ISIC classification schemes. Most important, perhaps, is the single (production process) conceptual framework of NAICS. As noted elsewhere, this is unique among industry classifications. Distinctions also were made during ISIC's development with regard to (1) select characteristics of goods and services produced; (2) the range of kinds of activity frequently carried out under the same ownership or control; (3) differences between enterprises in scale, organization of activities, capital requirements, and finance; and (4) the pattern of categories at various levels of classification in national classifications.

The ISIC, Rev. 3 groups economic activity into 17 broad Sections, 60 Divisions, 159 Groups, and 292 Classes. In the coding system, Sections are distinguished by the letters A through Q and the Divisions, Groups, and Classes are identified as the two-digit, three-digit, and four-digit groupings, respectively. NAICS United States groups economic activity into 20 sectors (two-digit), 100 subsectors (three-digit), 317 industry groups (four-digit), 725 NAICS industries (five-digit, of which 484 are comparable among all three countries), and 1,179 six-digit industries. Of the 1,179 six-digit industry codes, 669 identify an economic type unique to the United States (a U.S. industry), but within the general NAICS structure.

In the development and subsequent revision of NAICS industries, the statistical agencies of the three countries strove to create industries that did not cross ISIC two-digit boundaries. While this general goal was met in the initial development of NAICS, continuing efforts are underway to identify and evaluate the differences between NAICS and ISIC.

NAICS United States Structure

The following page contains a summary table of the NAICS United States structure. This table shows the counts of subsectors, industry groups, industries, and United States detail industries for each of the NAICS sectors.

Following the summary table is a complete numerical list of the NAICS United States structure. This list displays the codes and official full titles for the sectors, subsectors, industry groups, industries, and United States detail industries. It also indicates the comparability of the codes with NAICS Canada and NAICS Mexico.

Part II of this manual contains a numerical list of short titles that are recommended for use when space limitations preclude the use of the full titles for the dissemination of data classified to NAICS.

NAICS United States Structure

Sector	Name	Sub-sectors (3-digit)	Industry Groups (4-digit)	NAICS Industries (5-digit)	6-digit Industries		
					U.S. Detail	Same as 5-digit	Total
11	Agriculture, Forestry, Fishing and Hunting	5	19	42	32	32	64
21	Mining	3	5	10	28	1	29
22	Utilities	1	3	6	6	4	10
23	Construction	3	10	28	4	27	31
31-33	Manufacturing	21	86	184	408	65	473
42	Wholesale Trade	3	19	71	0	71	71
44-45	Retail Trade	12	27	61	24	51	75
48-49	Transportation and Warehousing	11	29	42	25	32	57
51	Information	7	16	30	12	24	36
52	Finance and Insurance	5	11	32	15	27	42
53	Real Estate and Rental and Leasing	3	8	19	9	15	24
54	Professional, Scientific, and Technical Services	1	9	35	17	30	47
55	Management of Companies and Enterprises	1	1	1	3	0	3
56	Administrative and Support and Waste Management and Remediation Services	2	11	29	23	20	43
61	Educational Services	1	7	12	7	10	17
62	Health Care and Social Assistance	4	18	30	16	23	39
71	Arts, Entertainment, and Recreation	3	9	23	3	22	25
72	Accommodation and Food Services	2	7	11	7	8	15
81	Other Services (except Public Administration)	4	14	30	30	19	49
92	Public Administration	8	8	29	0	29	29
	Total	100	317	725	669	510	1179

11 Agriculture, Forestry, Fishing and Hunting

111 Crop Production

1111 Oilseed and Grain Farming

11111 Soybean Farming
111110 Soybean Farming
11112 Oilseed (except Soybean) Farming
111120 Oilseed (except Soybean) Farming[CAN]
11113 Dry Pea and Bean Farming
111130 Dry Pea and Bean Farming[CAN]
11114 Wheat Farming
111140 Wheat Farming
11115 Corn Farming
111150 Corn Farming[CAN]
11116 Rice Farming
111160 Rice Farming
11119 Other Grain Farming
111191 Oilseed and Grain Combination Farming[US]
111199 All Other Grain Farming[US]

1112 Vegetable and Melon Farming

11121 Vegetable and Melon Farming
111211 Potato Farming[CAN]
111219 Other Vegetable (except Potato) and Melon Farming[CAN]

1113 Fruit and Tree Nut Farming

11131 Orange Groves
111310 Orange Groves
11132 Citrus (except Orange) Groves
111320 Citrus (except Orange) Groves[CAN]
11133 Noncitrus Fruit and Tree Nut Farming
111331 Apple Orchards[US]
111332 Grape Vineyards[US]
111333 Strawberry Farming[US]
111334 Berry (except Strawberry) Farming[US]
111335 Tree Nut Farming[US]
111336 Fruit and Tree Nut Combination Farming[US]
111339 Other Noncitrus Fruit Farming[US]

1114 Greenhouse, Nursery, and Floriculture Production

11141 Food Crops Grown Under Cover
111411 Mushroom Production[CAN]
111419 Other Food Crops Grown Under Cover[CAN]
11142 Nursery and Floriculture Production

111421 Nursery and Tree Production[CAN]
111422 Floriculture Production[CAN]

1119 Other Crop Farming

11191 Tobacco Farming
111910 Tobacco Farming
11192 Cotton Farming
111920 Cotton Farming
11193 Sugarcane Farming
111930 Sugarcane Farming
11194 Hay Farming
111940 Hay Farming[CAN]
11199 All Other Crop Farming
111991 Sugar Beet Farming[US]
111992 Peanut Farming[MEX]
111998 All Other Miscellaneous Crop Farming[US]

112 Animal Production

1121 Cattle Ranching and Farming

11211 Beef Cattle Ranching and Farming, including Feedlots
112111 Beef Cattle Ranching and Farming[US]
112112 Cattle Feedlots[US]
11212 Dairy Cattle and Milk Production
112120 Dairy Cattle and Milk Production
11213 Dual-Purpose Cattle Ranching and Farming[MEX]
112130 Dual-Purpose Cattle Ranching and Farming[MEX]

1122 Hog and Pig Farming

11221 Hog and Pig Farming
112210 Hog and Pig Farming[CAN]

1123 Poultry and Egg Production

11231 Chicken Egg Production
112310 Chicken Egg Production[CAN]
11232 Broilers and Other Meat Type Chicken Production
112320 Broilers and Other Meat Type Chicken Production
11233 Turkey Production
112330 Turkey Production
11234 Poultry Hatcheries
112340 Poultry Hatcheries
11239 Other Poultry Production
112390 Other Poultry Production[MEX]

1124 Sheep and Goat Farming

11241 Sheep Farming
112410 Sheep Farming[CAN]
11242 Goat Farming
112420 Goat Farming

1125 Animal Aquaculture

11251 Animal Aquaculture
112511 Finfish Farming and Fish Hatcheries[US]
112512 Shellfish Farming[US]
112519 Other Animal Aquaculture[US]

1129 Other Animal Production

11291 Apiculture
112910 Apiculture
11292 Horses and Other Equine Production
112920 Horses and Other Equine Production
11293 Fur-Bearing Animal and Rabbit Production
112930 Fur-Bearing Animal and Rabbit Production
11299 All Other Animal Production
112990 All Other Animal Production[MEX]

113 Forestry and Logging

1131 Timber Tract Operations

11311 Timber Tract Operations
113110 Timber Tract Operations

1132 Forest Nurseries and Gathering of Forest Products

11321 Forest Nurseries and Gathering of Forest Products
113210 Forest Nurseries and Gathering of Forest Products[CAN]

1133 Logging

11331 Logging
113310 Logging[MEX]

114 Fishing, Hunting and Trapping

1141 Fishing

11411 Fishing
114111 Finfish Fishing[US]
114112 Shellfish Fishing[US]
114119 Other Marine Fishing[US]

1142 Hunting and Trapping

11421 Hunting and Trapping
114210 Hunting and Trapping

115 Support Activities for Agriculture and Forestry

1151 Support Activities for Crop Production

11511 Support Activities for Crop Production
115111 Cotton Ginning[US]
115112 Soil Preparation, Planting, and Cultivating[US]
115113 Crop Harvesting, Primarily by Machine[US]
115114 Postharvest Crop Activities (except Cotton Ginning)[US]
115115 Farm Labor Contractors and Crew Leaders[US]
115116 Farm Management Services[US]

1152 Support Activities for Animal Production

11521 Support Activities for Animal Production
115210 Support Activities for Animal Production

1153 Support Activities for Forestry

11531 Support Activities for Forestry
115310 Support Activities for Forestry

21 Mining

211 Oil and Gas Extraction

2111 Oil and Gas Extraction

21111 Oil and Gas Extraction
211111 Crude Petroleum and Natural Gas Extraction[US]
211112 Natural Gas Liquid Extraction[US]

212 Mining (except Oil and Gas)

2121 Coal Mining

21211 Coal Mining
212111 Bituminous Coal and Lignite Surface Mining[US]
212112 Bituminous Coal Underground Mining[US]
212113 Anthracite Mining[US]

2122 Metal Ore Mining

21221 Iron Ore Mining
212210 Iron Ore Mining
21222 Gold Ore and Silver Ore Mining
212221 Gold Ore Mining[MEX]
212222 Silver Ore Mining[MEX]
21223 Copper, Nickel, Lead, and Zinc Mining
212231 Lead Ore and Zinc Ore Mining[CAN]
212234 Copper Ore and Nickel Ore Mining[US]
21229 Other Metal Ore Mining

212291 Uranium-Radium-Vanadium Ore Mining[CAN]
212299 All Other Metal Ore Mining[CAN]

2123 Nonmetallic Mineral Mining and Quarrying

21231 Stone Mining and Quarrying
212311 Dimension Stone Mining and Quarrying[US]
212312 Crushed and Broken Limestone Mining and Quarrying[US]
212313 Crushed and Broken Granite Mining and Quarrying[US]
212319 Other Crushed and Broken Stone Mining and Quarrying[US]
21232 Sand, Gravel, Clay, and Ceramic and Refractory Minerals Mining and Quarrying
212321 Construction Sand and Gravel Mining[MEX]
212322 Industrial Sand Mining[US]
212324 Kaolin and Ball Clay Mining[US]
212325 Clay and Ceramic and Refractory Minerals Mining[US]
21239 Other Nonmetallic Mineral Mining and Quarrying
212391 Potash, Soda, and Borate Mineral Mining[US]
212392 Phosphate Rock Mining[US]
212393 Other Chemical and Fertilizer Mineral Mining[US]
212399 All Other Nonmetallic Mineral Mining[US]

213 Support Activities for Mining

2131 Support Activities for Mining

21311 Support Activities for Mining
213111 Drilling Oil and Gas Wells
213112 Support Activities for Oil and Gas Operations[US]
213113 Support Activities for Coal Mining[US]
213114 Support Activities for Metal Mining[US]
213115 Support Activities for Nonmetallic Minerals (except Fuels) Mining[US]

22 Utilities

221 Utilities[CAN]

2211 Electric Power Generation, Transmission and Distribution

22111 Electric Power Generation[CAN]
221111 Hydroelectric Power Generation[CAN]
221112 Fossil Fuel Electric Power Generation[CAN]
221113 Nuclear Electric Power Generation[CAN]
221119 Other Electric Power Generation[CAN]

22112 Electric Power Transmission, Control, and Distribution[CAN]
221121 Electric Bulk Power Transmission and Control[CAN]
221122 Electric Power Distribution[CAN]

2212 Natural Gas Distribution[CAN]
22121 Natural Gas Distribution[CAN]
221210 Natural Gas Distribution[CAN]

2213 Water, Sewage and Other Systems[CAN]
22131 Water Supply and Irrigation Systems[CAN]
221310 Water Supply and Irrigation Systems[CAN]
22132 Sewage Treatment Facilities[CAN]
221320 Sewage Treatment Facilities[CAN]
22133 Steam and Air-Conditioning Supply[CAN]
221330 Steam and Air-Conditioning Supply[CAN]

23 Construction

236 Construction of Buildings

2361 Residential Building Construction
23611 Residential Building Construction
236115 New Single-Family Housing Construction (except Operative Builders)[US]
236116 New Multifamily Housing Construction (except Operative Builders)[US]
236117 New Housing Operative Builders [US]
236118 Residential Remodelers [US]

2362 Nonresidential Building Construction
23621 Industrial Building Construction
236210 Industrial Building Construction[CAN]
23622 Commercial and Institutional Building Construction
236220 Commercial and Institutional Building Construction[CAN]

237 Heavy and Civil Engineering Construction

2371 Utility System Construction
23711 Water and Sewer Line and Related Structures Construction
237110 Water and Sewer Line and Related Structures Construction[CAN]
23712 Oil and Gas Pipeline and Related Structures Construction

237120 Oil and Gas Pipeline and Related Structures Construction[CAN]
23713 Power and Communication Line and Related Structures Construction
237130 Power and Communication Line and Related Structures Construction[CAN]

2372 Land Subdivision

23721 Land Subdivision
237210 Land Subdivision[CAN]

2373 Highway, Street, and Bridge Construction

23731 Highway, Street, and Bridge Construction
237310 Highway, Street, and Bridge Construction[CAN]

2379 Other Heavy and Civil Engineering Construction

23799 Other Heavy and Civil Engineering Construction
237990 Other Heavy and Civil Engineering Construction[CAN]

238 Specialty Trade Contractors

2381 Foundation, Structure, and Building Exterior Contractors

23811 Poured Concrete Foundation and Structure Contractors[CAN]
238110 Poured Concrete Foundation and Structure Contractors[CAN]
23812 Structural Steel and Precast Concrete Contractors
238120 Structural Steel and Precast Concrete Contractors[CAN]
23813 Framing Contractors[CAN]
238130 Framing Contractors[CAN]
23814 Masonry Contractors[CAN]
238140 Masonry Contractors[CAN]
23815 Glass and Glazing Contractors[CAN]
238150 Glass and Glazing Contractors[CAN]
23816 Roofing Contractors[CAN]
238160 Roofing Contractors[CAN]
23817 Siding Contractors[CAN]
238170 Siding Contractors[CAN]
23819 Other Foundation, Structure, and Building Exterior Contractors[CAN]
238190 Other Foundation, Structure, and Building Exterior Contractors[CAN]

2382 Building Equipment Contractors

23821 Electrical Contractors
238210 Electrical Contractors

23822 Plumbing, Heating, and Air-Conditioning Contractors
238220 Plumbing, Heating, and Air-Conditioning Contractors[CAN]
23829 Other Building Equipment Contractors
238290 Other Building Equipment Contractors[MEX]

2383 Building Finishing Contractors

23831 Drywall and Insulation Contractors
238310 Drywall and Insulation Contractors[CAN]
23832 Painting and Wall Covering Contractors
238320 Painting and Wall Covering Contractors
23833 Flooring Contractors
238330 Flooring Contractors
23834 Tile and Terrazzo Contractors
238340 Tile and Terrazzo Contractors
23835 Finish Carpentry Contractors
238350 Finish Carpentry Contractors
23839 Other Building Finishing Contractors
238390 Other Building Finishing Contractors

2389 Other Specialty Trade Contractors

23891 Site Preparation Contractors
238910 Site Preparation Contractors
23899 All Other Specialty Trade Contractors
238990 All Other Specialty Trade Contractors[CAN]

31-33 Manufacturing

311 Food Manufacturing

3111 Animal Food Manufacturing

31111 Animal Food Manufacturing
311111 Dog and Cat Food Manufacturing[CAN]
311119 Other Animal Food Manufacturing[CAN]

3112 Grain and Oilseed Milling

31121 Flour Milling and Malt Manufacturing
311211 Flour Milling[CAN]
311212 Rice Milling[US]
311213 Malt Manufacturing[US]
31122 Starch and Vegetable Fats and Oils Manufacturing
311221 Wet Corn Milling[CAN]
311222 Soybean Processing[US]
311223 Other Oilseed Processing[US]
311225 Fats and Oils Refining and Blending[CAN]

31123 Breakfast Cereal Manufacturing
311230 Breakfast Cereal Manufacturing

3113 Sugar and Confectionery Product Manufacturing

31131 Sugar Manufacturing
311311 Sugarcane Mills[US]
311312 Cane Sugar Refining[US]
311313 Beet Sugar Manufacturing[US]
31132 Chocolate and Confectionery Manufacturing from Cacao Beans
311320 Chocolate and Confectionery Manufacturing from Cacao Beans
31133 Confectionery Manufacturing from Purchased Chocolate
311330 Confectionery Manufacturing from Purchased Chocolate
31134 Nonchocolate Confectionery Manufacturing
311340 Nonchocolate Confectionery Manufacturing

3114 Fruit and Vegetable Preserving and Specialty Food Manufacturing

31141 Frozen Food Manufacturing
311411 Frozen Fruit, Juice, and Vegetable Manufacturing[MEX]
311412 Frozen Specialty Food Manufacturing[MEX]
31142 Fruit and Vegetable Canning, Pickling, and Drying
311421 Fruit and Vegetable Canning[US]
311422 Specialty Canning[US]
311423 Dried and Dehydrated Food Manufacturing[US]

3115 Dairy Product Manufacturing

31151 Dairy Product (except Frozen) Manufacturing
311511 Fluid Milk Manufacturing[CAN]
311512 Creamery Butter Manufacturing[US]
311513 Cheese Manufacturing[US]
311514 Dry, Condensed, and Evaporated Dairy Product Manufacturing[US]
31152 Ice Cream and Frozen Dessert Manufacturing
311520 Ice Cream and Frozen Dessert Manufacturing

3116 Animal Slaughtering and Processing

31161 Animal Slaughtering and Processing
311611 Animal (except Poultry) Slaughtering[CAN]
311612 Meat Processed from Carcasses[US]
311613 Rendering and Meat Byproduct Processing[US]
311615 Poultry Processing[CAN]

3117 Seafood Product Preparation and Packaging

31171 Seafood Product Preparation and Packaging
311711 Seafood Canning[US]
311712 Fresh and Frozen Seafood Processing[US]

3118 Bakeries and Tortilla Manufacturing

31181 Bread and Bakery Product Manufacturing
311811 Retail Bakeries[CAN]
311812 Commercial Bakeries[US]
311813 Frozen Cakes, Pies, and Other Pastries Manufacturing[US]
31182 Cookie, Cracker, and Pasta Manufacturing
311821 Cookie and Cracker Manufacturing[CAN]
311822 Flour Mixes and Dough Manufacturing from Purchased Flour [CAN]
311823 Dry Pasta Manufacturing[CAN]
31183 Tortilla Manufacturing
311830 Tortilla Manufacturing

3119 Other Food Manufacturing

31191 Snack Food Manufacturing
311911 Roasted Nuts and Peanut Butter Manufacturing[CAN]
311919 Other Snack Food Manufacturing[CAN]
31192 Coffee and Tea Manufacturing
311920 Coffee and Tea Manufacturing[CAN]
31193 Flavoring Syrup and Concentrate Manufacturing
311930 Flavoring Syrup and Concentrate Manufacturing
31194 Seasoning and Dressing Manufacturing
311941 Mayonnaise, Dressing, and Other Prepared Sauce Manufacturing[US]
311942 Spice and Extract Manufacturing[US]
31199 All Other Food Manufacturing
311991 Perishable Prepared Food Manufacturing[US]
311999 All Other Miscellaneous Food Manufacturing[US]

312 Beverage and Tobacco Product Manufacturing

3121 Beverage Manufacturing

31211 Soft Drink and Ice Manufacturing
312111 Soft Drink Manufacturing[MEX]
312112 Bottled Water Manufacturing[MEX]
312113 Ice Manufacturing[MEX]
31212 Breweries
312120 Breweries
31213 Wineries
312130 Wineries[CAN]

31214 Distilleries
312140 Distilleries[CAN]

3122 Tobacco Manufacturing

31221 Tobacco Stemming and Redrying
312210 Tobacco Stemming and Redrying
31222 Tobacco Product Manufacturing
312221 Cigarette Manufacturing[MEX]
312229 Other Tobacco Product Manufacturing[US]

313 Textile Mills

3131 Fiber, Yarn, and Thread Mills

31311 Fiber, Yarn, and Thread Mills
313111 Yarn Spinning Mills[US]
313112 Yarn Texturizing, Throwing, and Twisting Mills[US]
313113 Thread Mills[MEX]

3132 Fabric Mills

31321 Broadwoven Fabric Mills
313210 Broadwoven Fabric Mills
31322 Narrow Fabric Mills and Schiffli Machine Embroidery
313221 Narrow Fabric Mills[US]
313222 Schiffli Machine Embroidery[US]
31323 Nonwoven Fabric Mills
313230 Nonwoven Fabric Mills
31324 Knit Fabric Mills
313241 Weft Knit Fabric Mills[US]
313249 Other Knit Fabric and Lace Mills[US]

3133 Textile and Fabric Finishing and Fabric Coating Mills

31331 Textile and Fabric Finishing Mills
313311 Broadwoven Fabric Finishing Mills[US]
313312 Textile and Fabric Finishing (except Broadwoven Fabric) Mills[US]
31332 Fabric Coating Mills
313320 Fabric Coating Mills

314 Textile Product Mills

3141 Textile Furnishings Mills

31411 Carpet and Rug Mills
314110 Carpet and Rug Mills
31412 Curtain and Linen Mills
314121 Curtain and Drapery Mills[US]
314129 Other Household Textile Product Mills[US]

3149 Other Textile Product Mills

31491 Textile Bag and Canvas Mills
314911 Textile Bag Mills[US]
314912 Canvas and Related Product Mills[US]
31499 All Other Textile Product Mills
314991 Rope, Cordage, and Twine Mills[US]
314992 Tire Cord and Tire Fabric Mills[US]
314999 All Other Miscellaneous Textile Product Mills[US]

315 Apparel Manufacturing

3151 Apparel Knitting Mills

31511 Hosiery and Sock Mills
315111 Sheer Hosiery Mills[US]
315119 Other Hosiery and Sock Mills[US]
31519 Other Apparel Knitting Mills
315191 Outerwear Knitting Mills[US]
315192 Underwear and Nightwear Knitting Mills[US]

3152 Cut and Sew Apparel Manufacturing

31521 Cut and Sew Apparel Contractors[CAN]
315211 Men's and Boys' Cut and Sew Apparel Contractors[US]
315212 Women's, Girls', and Infants' Cut and Sew Apparel Contractors[US]
31522 Men's and Boys' Cut and Sew Apparel Manufacturing[CAN]
315221 Men's and Boys' Cut and Sew Underwear and Nightwear Manufacturing[CAN]
315222 Men's and Boys' Cut and Sew Suit, Coat, and Overcoat Manufacturing[CAN]
315223 Men's and Boys' Cut and Sew Shirt (except Work Shirt) Manufacturing[US]
315224 Men's and Boys' Cut and Sew Trouser, Slack, and Jean Manufacturing[US]
315225 Men's and Boys' Cut and Sew Work Clothing Manufacturing[US]
315228 Men's and Boys' Cut and Sew Other Outerwear Manufacturing[US]
31523 Women's and Girls' Cut and Sew Apparel Manufacturing[CAN]
315231 Women's and Girls' Cut and Sew Lingerie, Loungewear, and Nightwear Manufacturing[CAN]
315232 Women's and Girls' Cut and Sew Blouse and Shirt Manufacturing[CAN]

315233 Women's and Girls' Cut and Sew Dress Manufacturing[CAN]
315234 Women's and Girls' Cut and Sew Suit, Coat, Tailored Jacket, and Skirt Manufacturing[CAN]
315239 Women's and Girls' Cut and Sew Other Outerwear Manufacturing[CAN]
31529 Other Cut and Sew Apparel Manufacturing[CAN]
315291 Infants' Cut and Sew Apparel Manufacturing[CAN]
315292 Fur and Leather Apparel Manufacturing[CAN]
315299 All Other Cut and Sew Apparel Manufacturing[CAN]

3159 Apparel Accessories and Other Apparel Manufacturing

31599 Apparel Accessories and Other Apparel Manufacturing
315991 Hat, Cap, and Millinery Manufacturing[MEX]
315992 Glove and Mitten Manufacturing[US]
315993 Men's and Boys' Neckwear Manufacturing[US]
315999 Other Apparel Accessories and Other Apparel Manufacturing[US]

316 Leather and Allied Product Manufacturing

3161 Leather and Hide Tanning and Finishing

31611 Leather and Hide Tanning and Finishing
316110 Leather and Hide Tanning and Finishing

3162 Footwear Manufacturing

31621 Footwear Manufacturing
316211 Rubber and Plastics Footwear Manufacturing[US]
316212 House Slipper Manufacturing[US]
316213 Men's Footwear (except Athletic) Manufacturing[US]
316214 Women's Footwear (except Athletic) Manufacturing[US]
316219 Other Footwear Manufacturing[US]

3169 Other Leather and Allied Product Manufacturing

31699 Other Leather and Allied Product Manufacturing
316991 Luggage Manufacturing[US]
316992 Women's Handbag and Purse Manufacturing[US]
316993 Personal Leather Good (except Women's Handbag and Purse) Manufacturing[US]
316999 All Other Leather Good Manufacturing[US]

321 Wood Product Manufacturing

3211 Sawmills and Wood Preservation

32111 Sawmills and Wood Preservation

321113 Sawmills[US]
321114 Wood Preservation[CAN]

3212 Veneer, Plywood, and Engineered Wood Product Manufacturing

32121 Veneer, Plywood, and Engineered Wood Product Manufacturing
321211 Hardwood Veneer and Plywood Manufacturing[CAN]
321212 Softwood Veneer and Plywood Manufacturing[CAN]
321213 Engineered Wood Member (except Truss) Manufacturing[US]
321214 Truss Manufacturing[US]
321219 Reconstituted Wood Product Manufacturing[US]

3219 Other Wood Product Manufacturing

32191 Millwork
321911 Wood Window and Door Manufacturing[CAN]
321912 Cut Stock, Resawing Lumber, and Planing[US]
321918 Other Millwork (including Flooring)[US]
32192 Wood Container and Pallet Manufacturing
321920 Wood Container and Pallet Manufacturing
32199 All Other Wood Product Manufacturing
321991 Manufactured Home (Mobile Home) Manufacturing[CAN]
321992 Prefabricated Wood Building Manufacturing[CAN]
321999 All Other Miscellaneous Wood Product Manufacturing[CAN]

322 Paper Manufacturing

3221 Pulp, Paper, and Paperboard Mills

32211 Pulp Mills
322110 Pulp Mills[MEX]
32212 Paper Mills
322121 Paper (except Newsprint) Mills[CAN]
322122 Newsprint Mills[CAN]
32213 Paperboard Mills
322130 Paperboard Mills[CAN]

3222 Converted Paper Product Manufacturing

32221 Paperboard Container Manufacturing
322211 Corrugated and Solid Fiber Box Manufacturing[CAN]
322212 Folding Paperboard Box Manufacturing[CAN]
322213 Setup Paperboard Box Manufacturing[US]
322214 Fiber Can, Tube, Drum, and Similar Products Manufacturing[US]
322215 Nonfolding Sanitary Food Container Manufacturing[US]

32222 Paper Bag and Coated and Treated Paper Manufacturing
322221 Coated and Laminated Packaging Paper and Plastics Film Manufacturing[US]
322222 Coated and Laminated Paper Manufacturing[US]
322223 Plastics, Foil, and Coated Paper Bag Manufacturing[US]
322224 Uncoated Paper and Multiwall Bag Manufacturing[US]
322225 Laminated Aluminum Foil Manufacturing for Flexible Packaging Uses[US]
322226 Surface-Coated Paperboard Manufacturing[US]
32223 Stationery Product Manufacturing
322231 Die-Cut Paper and Paperboard Office Supplies Manufacturing[US]
322232 Envelope Manufacturing[US]
322233 Stationery, Tablet, and Related Product Manufacturing[US]
32229 Other Converted Paper Product Manufacturing
322291 Sanitary Paper Product Manufacturing[CAN]
322299 All Other Converted Paper Product Manufacturing[CAN]

323 Printing and Related Support Activities

3231 Printing and Related Support Activities

32311 Printing
323110 Commercial Lithographic Printing[US]
323111 Commercial Gravure Printing[US]
323112 Commercial Flexographic Printing[US]
323113 Commercial Screen Printing[CAN]
323114 Quick Printing[CAN]
323115 Digital Printing[CAN]
323116 Manifold Business Forms Printing[CAN]
323117 Books Printing[US]
323118 Blankbook, Looseleaf Binders, and Devices Manufacturing[US]
323119 Other Commercial Printing[US]
32312 Support Activities for Printing
323121 Tradebinding and Related Work[US]
323122 Prepress Services[US]

324 Petroleum and Coal Products Manufacturing

3241 Petroleum and Coal Products Manufacturing

32411 Petroleum Refineries
324110 Petroleum Refineries

32412 Asphalt Paving, Roofing, and Saturated Materials Manufacturing
324121 Asphalt Paving Mixture and Block Manufacturing[CAN]
324122 Asphalt Shingle and Coating Materials Manufacturing[CAN]
32419 Other Petroleum and Coal Products Manufacturing
324191 Petroleum Lubricating Oil and Grease Manufacturing[MEX]
324199 All Other Petroleum and Coal Products Manufacturing[US]

325 Chemical Manufacturing

3251 Basic Chemical Manufacturing

32511 Petrochemical Manufacturing
325110 Petrochemical Manufacturing
32512 Industrial Gas Manufacturing
325120 Industrial Gas Manufacturing
32513 Synthetic Dye and Pigment Manufacturing
325131 Inorganic Dye and Pigment Manufacturing[US]
325132 Synthetic Organic Dye and Pigment Manufacturing[US]
32518 Other Basic Inorganic Chemical Manufacturing
325181 Alkalies and Chlorine Manufacturing[CAN]
325182 Carbon Black Manufacturing[US]
325188 All Other Basic Inorganic Chemical Manufacturing[US]
32519 Other Basic Organic Chemical Manufacturing
325191 Gum and Wood Chemical Manufacturing[US]
325192 Cyclic Crude and Intermediate Manufacturing[US]
325193 Ethyl Alcohol Manufacturing[US]
325199 All Other Basic Organic Chemical Manufacturing[US]

3252 Resin, Synthetic Rubber, and Artificial Synthetic Fibers and Filaments Manufacturing

32521 Resin and Synthetic Rubber Manufacturing
325211 Plastics Material and Resin Manufacturing[US]
325212 Synthetic Rubber Manufacturing[MEX]
32522 Artificial and Synthetic Fibers and Filaments Manufacturing
325221 Cellulosic Organic Fiber Manufacturing[US]
325222 Noncellulosic Organic Fiber Manufacturing[US]

3253 Pesticide, Fertilizer, and Other Agricultural Chemical Manufacturing

32531 Fertilizer Manufacturing
325311 Nitrogenous Fertilizer Manufacturing[US]
325312 Phosphatic Fertilizer Manufacturing[US]
325314 Fertilizer (Mixing Only) Manufacturing[CAN]
32532 Pesticide and Other Agricultural Chemical Manufacturing
325320 Pesticide and Other Agricultural Chemical Manufacturing

3254 Pharmaceutical and Medicine Manufacturing

32541 Pharmaceutical and Medicine Manufacturing
325411 Medicinal and Botanical Manufacturing[US]
325412 Pharmaceutical Preparation Manufacturing[US]
325413 In-Vitro Diagnostic Substance Manufacturing[US]
325414 Biological Product (except Diagnostic) Manufacturing[US]

3255 Paint, Coating, and Adhesive Manufacturing

32551 Paint and Coating Manufacturing
325510 Paint and Coating Manufacturing
32552 Adhesive Manufacturing
325520 Adhesive Manufacturing

3256 Soap, Cleaning Compound, and Toilet Preparation Manufacturing

32561 Soap and Cleaning Compound Manufacturing
325611 Soap and Other Detergent Manufacturing[US]
325612 Polish and Other Sanitation Good Manufacturing[US]
325613 Surface Active Agent Manufacturing[US]
32562 Toilet Preparation Manufacturing
325620 Toilet Preparation Manufacturing

3259 Other Chemical Product and Preparation Manufacturing

32591 Printing Ink Manufacturing
325910 Printing Ink Manufacturing
32592 Explosives Manufacturing
325920 Explosives Manufacturing
32599 All Other Chemical Product and Preparation Manufacturing
325991 Custom Compounding of Purchased Resins[CAN]
325992 Photographic Film, Paper, Plate, and Chemical Manufacturing[MEX]
325998 All Other Miscellaneous Chemical Product and Preparation Manufacturing[US]

326 Plastics and Rubber Products Manufacturing

3261 Plastics Product Manufacturing

32611 Plastics Packaging Materials and Unlaminated Film and Sheet Manufacturing
326111 Plastics Bag Manufacturing[CAN]
326112 Plastics Packaging Film and Sheet (including Laminated) Manufacturing[US]
326113 Unlaminated Plastics Film and Sheet (except Packaging) Manufacturing[US]
32612 Plastics Pipe, Pipe Fitting, and Unlaminated Profile Shape Manufacturing
326121 Unlaminated Plastics Profile Shape Manufacturing[CAN]
326122 Plastics Pipe and Pipe Fitting Manufacturing[CAN]
32613 Laminated Plastics Plate, Sheet (except Packaging), and Shape Manufacturing
326130 Laminated Plastics Plate, Sheet (except Packaging), and Shape Manufacturing
32614 Polystyrene Foam Product Manufacturing
326140 Polystyrene Foam Product Manufacturing
32615 Urethane and Other Foam Product (except Polystyrene) Manufacturing
326150 Urethane and Other Foam Product (except Polystyrene) Manufacturing
32616 Plastics Bottle Manufacturing
326160 Plastics Bottle Manufacturing
32619 Other Plastics Product Manufacturing
326191 Plastics Plumbing Fixture Manufacturing[CAN]
326192 Resilient Floor Covering Manufacturing[US]
326199 All Other Plastics Product Manufacturing[US]

3262 Rubber Product Manufacturing

32621 Tire Manufacturing
326211 Tire Manufacturing (except Retreading)[MEX]
326212 Tire Retreading[MEX]
32622 Rubber and Plastics Hoses and Belting Manufacturing
326220 Rubber and Plastics Hoses and Belting Manufacturing
32629 Other Rubber Product Manufacturing
326291 Rubber Product Manufacturing for Mechanical Use[US]
326299 All Other Rubber Product Manufacturing[US]

327 Nonmetallic Mineral Product Manufacturing

3271 Clay Product and Refractory Manufacturing

32711 Pottery, Ceramics, and Plumbing Fixture Manufacturing
327111 Vitreous China Plumbing Fixture and China and Earthenware Bathroom Accessories Manufacturing[US]
327112 Vitreous China, Fine Earthenware, and Other Pottery Product Manufacturing[US]
327113 Porcelain Electrical Supply Manufacturing[US]
32712 Clay Building Material and Refractories Manufacturing
327121 Brick and Structural Clay Tile Manufacturing[US]
327122 Ceramic Wall and Floor Tile Manufacturing[US]
327123 Other Structural Clay Product Manufacturing[US]
327124 Clay Refractory Manufacturing[US]
327125 Nonclay Refractory Manufacturing[US]

3272 Glass and Glass Product Manufacturing

32721 Glass and Glass Product Manufacturing
327211 Flat Glass Manufacturing[MEX]
327212 Other Pressed and Blown Glass and Glassware Manufacturing[US]
327213 Glass Container Manufacturing[US]
327215 Glass Product Manufacturing Made of Purchased Glass[CAN]

3273 Cement and Concrete Product Manufacturing

32731 Cement Manufacturing
327310 Cement Manufacturing
32732 Ready-Mix Concrete Manufacturing
327320 Ready-Mix Concrete Manufacturing
32733 Concrete Pipe, Brick, and Block Manufacturing
327331 Concrete Block and Brick Manufacturing[US]
327332 Concrete Pipe Manufacturing[US]
32739 Other Concrete Product Manufacturing
327390 Other Concrete Product Manufacturing[CAN]

3274 Lime and Gypsum Product Manufacturing

32741 Lime Manufacturing
327410 Lime Manufacturing
32742 Gypsum Product Manufacturing
327420 Gypsum Product Manufacturing

3279 Other Nonmetallic Mineral Product Manufacturing

32791 Abrasive Product Manufacturing
327910 Abrasive Product Manufacturing
32799 All Other Nonmetallic Mineral Product Manufacturing

327991 Cut Stone and Stone Product Manufacturing[US]
327992 Ground or Treated Mineral and Earth Manufacturing[US]
327993 Mineral Wool Manufacturing[US]
327999 All Other Miscellaneous Nonmetallic Mineral Product Manufacturing[US]

331 Primary Metal Manufacturing

3311 Iron and Steel Mills and Ferroalloy Manufacturing

33111 Iron and Steel Mills and Ferroalloy Manufacturing
331111 Iron and Steel Mills[US]
331112 Electrometallurgical Ferroalloy Product Manufacturing[US]

3312 Steel Product Manufacturing from Purchased Steel

33121 Iron and Steel Pipe and Tube Manufacturing from Purchased Steel
331210 Iron and Steel Pipe and Tube Manufacturing from Purchased Steel
33122 Rolling and Drawing of Purchased Steel
331221 Rolled Steel Shape Manufacturing[CAN]
331222 Steel Wire Drawing[CAN]

3313 Alumina and Aluminum Production and Processing

33131 Alumina and Aluminum Production and Processing
331311 Alumina Refining[US]
331312 Primary Aluminum Production[US]
331314 Secondary Smelting and Alloying of Aluminum[US]
331315 Aluminum Sheet, Plate, and Foil Manufacturing[US]
331316 Aluminum Extruded Product Manufacturing[US]
331319 Other Aluminum Rolling and Drawing[US]

3314 Nonferrous Metal (except Aluminum) Production and Processing

33141 Nonferrous Metal (except Aluminum) Smelting and Refining
331411 Primary Smelting and Refining of Copper[MEX]
331419 Primary Smelting and Refining of Nonferrous Metal (except Copper and Aluminum)[MEX]
33142 Copper Rolling, Drawing, Extruding, and Alloying
331421 Copper Rolling, Drawing, and Extruding[US]
331422 Copper Wire (except Mechanical) Drawing[US]
331423 Secondary Smelting, Refining, and Alloying of Copper[US]

33149 Nonferrous Metal (except Copper and Aluminum) Rolling, Drawing, Extruding, and Alloying
331491 Nonferrous Metal (except Copper and Aluminum) Rolling, Drawing, and Extruding[US]
331492 Secondary Smelting, Refining, and Alloying of Nonferrous Metal (except Copper and Aluminum)[US]

3315 Foundries

33151 Ferrous Metal Foundries
331511 Iron Foundries[CAN]
331512 Steel Investment Foundries[US]
331513 Steel Foundries (except Investment)[US]
33152 Nonferrous Metal Foundries
331521 Aluminum Die-Casting Foundries[US]
331522 Nonferrous (except Aluminum) Die-Casting Foundries[US]
331524 Aluminum Foundries (except Die-Casting)[US]
331525 Copper Foundries (except Die-Casting)[US]
331528 Other Nonferrous Foundries (except Die-Casting)[US]

332 Fabricated Metal Product Manufacturing

3321 Forging and Stamping

33211 Forging and Stamping
332111 Iron and Steel Forging[US]
332112 Nonferrous Forging[US]
332114 Custom Roll Forming[US]
332115 Crown and Closure Manufacturing[US]
332116 Metal Stamping[US]
332117 Powder Metallurgy Part Manufacturing[US]

3322 Cutlery and Handtool Manufacturing

33221 Cutlery and Handtool Manufacturing
332211 Cutlery and Flatware (except Precious) Manufacturing[US]
332212 Hand and Edge Tool Manufacturing[US]
332213 Saw Blade and Handsaw Manufacturing[US]
332214 Kitchen Utensil, Pot, and Pan Manufacturing[US]

3323 Architectural and Structural Metals Manufacturing

33231 Plate Work and Fabricated Structural Product Manufacturing
332311 Prefabricated Metal Building and Component Manufacturing[CAN]
332312 Fabricated Structural Metal Manufacturing[US]

332313 Plate Work Manufacturing[US]
33232 Ornamental and Architectural Metal Products Manufacturing
332321 Metal Window and Door Manufacturing[CAN]
332322 Sheet Metal Work Manufacturing[US]
332323 Ornamental and Architectural Metal Work Manufacturing[US]

3324 Boiler, Tank, and Shipping Container Manufacturing

33241 Power Boiler and Heat Exchanger Manufacturing
332410 Power Boiler and Heat Exchanger Manufacturing
33242 Metal Tank (Heavy Gauge) Manufacturing
332420 Metal Tank (Heavy Gauge) Manufacturing
33243 Metal Can, Box, and Other Metal Container (Light Gauge) Manufacturing
332431 Metal Can Manufacturing[CAN]
332439 Other Metal Container Manufacturing[CAN]

3325 Hardware Manufacturing

33251 Hardware Manufacturing
332510 Hardware Manufacturing

3326 Spring and Wire Product Manufacturing

33261 Spring and Wire Product Manufacturing
332611 Spring (Heavy Gauge) Manufacturing[CAN]
332612 Spring (Light Gauge) Manufacturing[US]
332618 Other Fabricated Wire Product Manufacturing[US]

3327 Machine Shops; Turned Product; and Screw, Nut, and Bolt Manufacturing

33271 Machine Shops
332710 Machine Shops
33272 Turned Product and Screw, Nut, and Bolt Manufacturing
332721 Precision Turned Product Manufacturing[US]
332722 Bolt, Nut, Screw, Rivet, and Washer Manufacturing[US]

3328 Coating, Engraving, Heat Treating, and Allied Activities

33281 Coating, Engraving, Heat Treating, and Allied Activities
332811 Metal Heat Treating[US]
332812 Metal Coating, Engraving (except Jewelry and Silverware), and Allied Services to Manufacturers[US]
332813 Electroplating, Plating, Polishing, Anodizing, and Coloring[US]

3329 Other Fabricated Metal Product Manufacturing

33291 Metal Valve Manufacturing
332911 Industrial Valve Manufacturing[US]
332912 Fluid Power Valve and Hose Fitting Manufacturing[US]
332913 Plumbing Fixture Fitting and Trim Manufacturing[US]
332919 Other Metal Valve and Pipe Fitting Manufacturing[US]
33299 All Other Fabricated Metal Product Manufacturing
332991 Ball and Roller Bearing Manufacturing
332992 Small Arms Ammunition Manufacturing[US]
332993 Ammunition (except Small Arms) Manufacturing[US]
332994 Small Arms Manufacturing[US]
332995 Other Ordnance and Accessories Manufacturing[US]
332996 Fabricated Pipe and Pipe Fitting Manufacturing[US]
332997 Industrial Pattern Manufacturing[US]
332998 Enameled Iron and Metal Sanitary Ware Manufacturing[US]
332999 All Other Miscellaneous Fabricated Metal Product Manufacturing[US]

333 Machinery Manufacturing

3331 Agriculture, Construction, and Mining Machinery Manufacturing

33311 Agricultural Implement Manufacturing
333111 Farm Machinery and Equipment Manufacturing[US]
333112 Lawn and Garden Tractor and Home Lawn and Garden Equipment Manufacturing[US]
33312 Construction Machinery Manufacturing
333120 Construction Machinery Manufacturing
33313 Mining and Oil and Gas Field Machinery Manufacturing
333131 Mining Machinery and Equipment Manufacturing[US]
333132 Oil and Gas Field Machinery and Equipment Manufacturing[US]

3332 Industrial Machinery Manufacturing

33321 Sawmill and Woodworking Machinery Manufacturing
333210 Sawmill and Woodworking Machinery Manufacturing

33322 Plastics and Rubber Industry Machinery Manufacturing
333220 Plastics and Rubber Industry Machinery Manufacturing
33329 Other Industrial Machinery Manufacturing
333291 Paper Industry Machinery Manufacturing[CAN]
333292 Textile Machinery Manufacturing[MEX]
333293 Printing Machinery and Equipment Manufacturing[MEX]
333294 Food Product Machinery Manufacturing[US]
333295 Semiconductor Machinery Manufacturing[US]
333298 All Other Industrial Machinery Manufacturing[US]

3333 Commercial and Service Industry Machinery Manufacturing

33331 Commercial and Service Industry Machinery Manufacturing
333311 Automatic Vending Machine Manufacturing[US]
333312 Commercial Laundry, Drycleaning, and Pressing Machine Manufacturing[US]
333313 Office Machinery Manufacturing[US]
333314 Optical Instrument and Lens Manufacturing[US]
333315 Photographic and Photocopying Equipment Manufacturing[US]
333319 Other Commercial and Service Industry Machinery Manufacturing[US]

3334 Ventilation, Heating, Air-Conditioning, and Commercial Refrigeration Equipment Manufacturing

33341 Ventilation, Heating, Air-Conditioning, and Commercial Refrigeration Equipment Manufacturing
333411 Air Purification Equipment Manufacturing[US]
333412 Industrial and Commercial Fan and Blower Manufacturing[US]
333414 Heating Equipment (except Warm Air Furnaces) Manufacturing[US]
333415 Air-Conditioning and Warm Air Heating Equipment and Commercial and Industrial Refrigeration Equipment Manufacturing[US]

3335 Metalworking Machinery Manufacturing

33351 Metalworking Machinery Manufacturing
333511 Industrial Mold Manufacturing[CAN]
333512 Machine Tool (Metal Cutting Types) Manufacturing[US]

333513 Machine Tool (Metal Forming Types) Manufacturing[US]
333514 Special Die and Tool, Die Set, Jig, and Fixture Manufacturing[US]
333515 Cutting Tool and Machine Tool Accessory Manufacturing[US]
333516 Rolling Mill Machinery and Equipment Manufacturing[US]
333518 Other Metalworking Machinery Manufacturing[US]

3336 Engine, Turbine, and Power Transmission Equipment Manufacturing

33361 Engine, Turbine, and Power Transmission Equipment Manufacturing
333611 Turbine and Turbine Generator Set Units Manufacturing[CAN]
333612 Speed Changer, Industrial High-Speed Drive, and Gear Manufacturing[US]
333613 Mechanical Power Transmission Equipment Manufacturing[US]
333618 Other Engine Equipment Manufacturing[US]

3339 Other General Purpose Machinery Manufacturing

33391 Pump and Compressor Manufacturing
333911 Pump and Pumping Equipment Manufacturing[US]
333912 Air and Gas Compressor Manufacturing[US]
333913 Measuring and Dispensing Pump Manufacturing[US]
33392 Material Handling Equipment Manufacturing
333921 Elevator and Moving Stairway Manufacturing[US]
333922 Conveyor and Conveying Equipment Manufacturing[US]
333923 Overhead Traveling Crane, Hoist, and Monorail System Manufacturing[US]
333924 Industrial Truck, Tractor, Trailer, and Stacker Machinery Manufacturing[US]
33399 All Other General Purpose Machinery Manufacturing
333991 Power-Driven Handtool Manufacturing[US]
333992 Welding and Soldering Equipment Manufacturing[US]
333993 Packaging Machinery Manufacturing[US]
333994 Industrial Process Furnace and Oven Manufacturing[US]
333995 Fluid Power Cylinder and Actuator Manufacturing[US]
333996 Fluid Power Pump and Motor Manufacturing[US]

333997 Scale and Balance (except Laboratory) Manufacturing[US]

333999 All Other Miscellaneous General Purpose Machinery Manufacturing[US]

334 Computer and Electronic Product Manufacturing

3341 Computer and Peripheral Equipment Manufacturing

33411 Computer and Peripheral Equipment Manufacturing

334111 Electronic Computer Manufacturing[US]

334112 Computer Storage Device Manufacturing[US]

334113 Computer Terminal Manufacturing[US]

334119 Other Computer Peripheral Equipment Manufacturing[US]

3342 Communications Equipment Manufacturing

33421 Telephone Apparatus Manufacturing

334210 Telephone Apparatus Manufacturing

33422 Radio and Television Broadcasting and Wireless Communications Equipment Manufacturing

334220 Radio and Television Broadcasting and Wireless Communications Equipment Manufacturing

33429 Other Communications Equipment Manufacturing

334290 Other Communications Equipment Manufacturing

3343 Audio and Video Equipment Manufacturing

334310 Audio and Video Equipment Manufacturing

334310 Audio and Video Equipment Manufacturing

3344 Semiconductor and Other Electronic Component Manufacturing

33441 Semiconductor and Other Electronic Component Manufacturing

334411 Electron Tube Manufacturing[US]

334412 Bare Printed Circuit Board Manufacturing[US]

334413 Semiconductor and Related Device Manufacturing[US]

334414 Electronic Capacitor Manufacturing[US]

334415 Electronic Resistor Manufacturing[US]

334416 Electronic Coil, Transformer, and Other Inductor Manufacturing[US]

334417 Electronic Connector Manufacturing[US]

334418 Printed Circuit Assembly (Electronic Assembly) Manufacturing[US]

334419 Other Electronic Component Manufacturing[US]

3345 Navigational, Measuring, Electromedical, and Control Instruments Manufacturing

33451 Navigational, Measuring, Electromedical, and Control Instruments Manufacturing

334510 Electromedical and Electrotherapeutic Apparatus Manufacturing[US]

334511 Search, Detection, Navigation, Guidance, Aeronautical, and Nautical System and Instrument Manufacturing[CAN]

334512 Automatic Environmental Control Manufacturing for Residential, Commercial, and Appliance Use[US]

334513 Instruments and Related Products Manufacturing for Measuring, Displaying, and Controlling Industrial Process Variables[US]

334514 Totalizing Fluid Meter and Counting Device Manufacturing[US]

334515 Instrument Manufacturing for Measuring and Testing Electricity and Electrical Signals[US]

334516 Analytical Laboratory Instrument Manufacturing[US]

334517 Irradiation Apparatus Manufacturing[US]

334518 Watch, Clock, and Part Manufacturing[US]

334519 Other Measuring and Controlling Device Manufacturing[US]

3346 Manufacturing and Reproducing Magnetic and Optical Media

33461 Manufacturing and Reproducing Magnetic and Optical Media

334611 Software Reproducing[US]

334612 Prerecorded Compact Disc (except Software), Tape, and Record Reproducing[US]

334613 Magnetic and Optical Recording Media Manufacturing[US]

335 Electrical Equipment, Appliance, and Component Manufacturing

3351 Electric Lighting Equipment Manufacturing

33511 Electric Lamp Bulb and Part Manufacturing

335110 Electric Lamp Bulb and Part Manufacturing

33512 Lighting Fixture Manufacturing

335121 Residential Electric Lighting Fixture Manufacturing[US]

335122 Commercial, Industrial, and Institutional Electric Lighting Fixture Manufacturing[US]

335129 Other Lighting Equipment Manufacturing[US]

3352 Household Appliance Manufacturing

33521 Small Electrical Appliance Manufacturing
335211 Electric Housewares and Household Fan Manufacturing[US]
335212 Household Vacuum Cleaner Manufacturing[US]
33522 Major Appliance Manufacturing
335221 Household Cooking Appliance Manufacturing[US]
335222 Household Refrigerator and Home Freezer Manufacturing[US]
335224 Household Laundry Equipment Manufacturing[US]
335228 Other Major Household Appliance Manufacturing[US]

3353 Electrical Equipment Manufacturing

33531 Electrical Equipment Manufacturing
335311 Power, Distribution, and Specialty Transformer Manufacturing[CAN]
335312 Motor and Generator Manufacturing[CAN]
335313 Switchgear and Switchboard Apparatus Manufacturing[US]
335314 Relay and Industrial Control Manufacturing[US]

3359 Other Electrical Equipment and Component Manufacturing

33591 Battery Manufacturing
335911 Storage Battery Manufacturing[US]
335912 Primary Battery Manufacturing[US]
33592 Communication and Energy Wire and Cable Manufacturing
335921 Fiber Optic Cable Manufacturing[US]
335929 Other Communication and Energy Wire Manufacturing[US]
33593 Wiring Device Manufacturing
335931 Current-Carrying Wiring Device Manufacturing[US]
335932 Noncurrent-Carrying Wiring Device Manufacturing[US]
33599 All Other Electrical Equipment and Component Manufacturing
335991 Carbon and Graphite Product Manufacturing[MEX]
335999 All Other Miscellaneous Electrical Equipment and Component Manufacturing[MEX]

336 Transportation Equipment Manufacturing

3361 Motor Vehicle Manufacturing

33611 Automobile and Light Duty Motor Vehicle Manufacturing

336111 Automobile Manufacturing[US]
336112 Light Truck and Utility Vehicle Manufacturing[US]
33612 Heavy Duty Truck Manufacturing
336120 Heavy Duty Truck Manufacturing

3362 Motor Vehicle Body and Trailer Manufacturing

33621 Motor Vehicle Body and Trailer Manufacturing
336211 Motor Vehicle Body Manufacturing[CAN]
336212 Truck Trailer Manufacturing[CAN]
336213 Motor Home Manufacturing[US]
336214 Travel Trailer and Camper Manufacturing[US]

3363 Motor Vehicle Parts Manufacturing

33631 Motor Vehicle Gasoline Engine and Engine Parts Manufacturing
336311 Carburetor, Piston, Piston Ring, and Valve Manufacturing[US]
336312 Gasoline Engine and Engine Parts Manufacturing[US]
33632 Motor Vehicle Electrical and Electronic Equipment Manufacturing
336321 Vehicular Lighting Equipment Manufacturing[US]
336322 Other Motor Vehicle Electrical and Electronic Equipment Manufacturing[US]
33633 Motor Vehicle Steering and Suspension Components (except Spring) Manufacturing
336330 Motor Vehicle Steering and Suspension Components (except Spring) Manufacturing
33634 Motor Vehicle Brake System Manufacturing
336340 Motor Vehicle Brake System Manufacturing
33635 Motor Vehicle Transmission and Power Train Parts Manufacturing
336350 Motor Vehicle Transmission and Power Train Parts Manufacturing
33636 Motor Vehicle Seating and Interior Trim Manufacturing
336360 Motor Vehicle Seating and Interior Trim Manufacturing
33637 Motor Vehicle Metal Stamping
336370 Motor Vehicle Metal Stamping
33639 Other Motor Vehicle Parts Manufacturing
336391 Motor Vehicle Air-Conditioning Manufacturing[US]
336399 All Other Motor Vehicle Parts Manufacturing[US]

3364 Aerospace Product and Parts Manufacturing

33641 Aerospace Product and Parts Manufacturing

336411 Aircraft Manufacturing[US]
336412 Aircraft Engine and Engine Parts Manufacturing[US]
336413 Other Aircraft Parts and Auxiliary Equipment Manufacturing[US]
336414 Guided Missile and Space Vehicle Manufacturing[US]
336415 Guided Missile and Space Vehicle Propulsion Unit and Propulsion Unit Parts Manufacturing[US]
336419 Other Guided Missile and Space Vehicle Parts and Auxiliary Equipment Manufacturing[US]

3365 Railroad Rolling Stock Manufacturing

33651 Railroad Rolling Stock Manufacturing
336510 Railroad Rolling Stock Manufacturing

3366 Ship and Boat Building

33661 Ship and Boat Building
336611 Ship Building and Repairing[CAN]
336612 Boat Building[CAN]

3369 Other Transportation Equipment Manufacturing

33699 Other Transportation Equipment Manufacturing
336991 Motorcycle, Bicycle, and Parts Manufacturing[US]
336992 Military Armored Vehicle, Tank, and Tank Component Manufacturing[US]
336999 All Other Transportation Equipment Manufacturing[US]

337 Furniture and Related Product Manufacturing

3371 Household and Institutional Furniture and Kitchen Cabinet Manufacturing

33711 Wood Kitchen Cabinet and Countertop Manufacturing
337110 Wood Kitchen Cabinet and Countertop Manufacturing
33712 Household and Institutional Furniture Manufacturing
337121 Upholstered Household Furniture Manufacturing[CAN]
337122 Nonupholstered Wood Household Furniture Manufacturing[US]
337124 Metal Household Furniture Manufacturing[US]
337125 Household Furniture (except Wood and Metal) Manufacturing[US]
337127 Institutional Furniture Manufacturing[CAN]

337129 Wood Television, Radio, and Sewing Machine Cabinet Manufacturing[US]

3372 Office Furniture (including Fixtures) Manufacturing

33721 Office Furniture (including Fixtures) Manufacturing
337211 Wood Office Furniture Manufacturing[US]
337212 Custom Architectural Woodwork and Millwork Manufacturing[US]
337214 Office Furniture (except Wood) Manufacturing[CAN]
337215 Showcase, Partition, Shelving, and Locker Manufacturing[CAN]

3379 Other Furniture Related Product Manufacturing

33791 Mattress Manufacturing
337910 Mattress Manufacturing
33792 Blind and Shade Manufacturing
337920 Blind and Shade Manufacturing

339 Miscellaneous Manufacturing

3391 Medical Equipment and Supplies Manufacturing

33911 Medical Equipment and Supplies Manufacturing
339111 Laboratory Apparatus and Furniture Manufacturing[US]
339112 Surgical and Medical Instrument Manufacturing[US]
339113 Surgical Appliance and Supplies Manufacturing[US]
339114 Dental Equipment and Supplies Manufacturing[US]
339115 Ophthalmic Goods Manufacturing[US]
339116 Dental Laboratories[US]

3399 Other Miscellaneous Manufacturing

33991 Jewelry and Silverware Manufacturing
339911 Jewelry (except Costume) Manufacturing[US]
339912 Silverware and Hollowware Manufacturing[US]
339913 Jewelers' Material and Lapidary Work Manufacturing[US]
339914 Costume Jewelry and Novelty Manufacturing[US]
33992 Sporting and Athletic Goods Manufacturing
339920 Sporting and Athletic Goods Manufacturing
33993 Doll, Toy, and Game Manufacturing
339931 Doll and Stuffed Toy Manufacturing[US]
339932 Game, Toy, and Children's Vehicle Manufacturing[US]
33994 Office Supplies (except Paper) Manufacturing
339941 Pen and Mechanical Pencil Manufacturing[US]
339942 Lead Pencil and Art Good Manufacturing[US]

339943 Marking Device Manufacturing[US]
339944 Carbon Paper and Inked Ribbon Manufacturing[US]
33995 Sign Manufacturing
339950 Sign Manufacturing
33999 All Other Miscellaneous Manufacturing
339991 Gasket, Packing, and Sealing Device Manufacturing[US]
339992 Musical Instrument Manufacturing[US]
339993 Fastener, Button, Needle, and Pin Manufacturing[US]
339994 Broom, Brush, and Mop Manufacturing[US]
339995 Burial Casket Manufacturing[MEX]
339999 All Other Miscellaneous Manufacturing[US]

42 Wholesale Trade

423 Merchant Wholesalers, Durable Goods[US]

4231 Motor Vehicle and Motor Vehicle Parts and Supplies Merchant Wholesalers[US]

42311 Automobile and Other Motor Vehicle Merchant Wholesalers[US]
423110 Automobile and Other Motor Vehicle Merchant Wholesalers[US]
42312 Motor Vehicle Supplies and New Parts Merchant Wholesalers[US]
423120 Motor Vehicle Supplies and New Parts Merchant Wholesalers[US]
42313 Tire and Tube Merchant Wholesalers[US]
423130 Tire and Tube Merchant Wholesalers[US]
42314 Motor Vehicle Parts (Used) Merchant Wholesalers[US]
423140 Motor Vehicle Parts (Used) Merchant Wholesalers[US]

4232 Furniture and Home Furnishing Merchant Wholesalers[US]

42321 Furniture Merchant Wholesalers[US]
423210 Furniture Merchant Wholesalers[US]
42322 Home Furnishing Merchant Wholesalers[US]
423220 Home Furnishing Merchant Wholesalers[US]

4233 Lumber and Other Construction Materials Merchant Wholesalers[US]

42331 Lumber, Plywood, Millwork, and Wood Panel Merchant Wholesalers[US]

423310 Lumber, Plywood, Millwork, and Wood Panel Merchant Wholesalers[US]

42332 Brick, Stone, and Related Construction Material Merchant Wholesalers[US]

423320 Brick, Stone, and Related Construction Material Merchant Wholesalers[US]

42333 Roofing, Siding, and Insulation Material Merchant Wholesalers[US]

423330 Roofing, Siding, and Insulation Material Merchant Wholesalers[US]

42339 Other Construction Material Merchant Wholesalers[US]

423390 Other Construction Material Merchant Wholesalers[US]

4234 Professional and Commercial Equipment and Supplies Merchant Wholesalers[US]

42341 Photographic Equipment and Supplies Merchant Wholesalers[US]

423410 Photographic Equipment and Supplies Merchant Wholesalers[US]

42342 Office Equipment Merchant Wholesalers[US]

423420 Office Equipment Merchant Wholesalers[US]

42343 Computer and Computer Peripheral Equipment and Software Merchant Wholesalers[US]

423430 Computer and Computer Peripheral Equipment and Software Merchant Wholesalers[US]

42344 Other Commercial Equipment Merchant Wholesalers[US]

423440 Other Commercial Equipment Merchant Wholesalers[US]

42345 Medical, Dental, and Hospital Equipment and Supplies Merchant Wholesalers[US]

423450 Medical, Dental, and Hospital Equipment and Supplies Merchant Wholesalers[US]

42346 Ophthalmic Goods Merchant Wholesalers[US]

423460 Ophthalmic Goods Merchant Wholesalers[US]

42349 Other Professional Equipment and Supplies Merchant Wholesalers[US]

423490 Other Professional Equipment and Supplies Merchant Wholesalers[US]

4235 Metal and Mineral (except Petroleum) Merchant Wholesalers[US]

42351 Metal Service Centers and Other Metal Merchant Wholesalers[US]

423510 Metal Service Centers and Other Metal Merchant Wholesalers[US]

42352 Coal and Other Mineral and Ore Merchant Wholesalers[US]

423520 Coal and Other Mineral and Ore Merchant Wholesalers[US]

4236 Electrical and Electronic Goods Merchant Wholesalers[US]

42361 Electrical Apparatus and Equipment, Wiring Supplies, and Related Equipment Merchant Wholesalers[US]

423610 Electrical Apparatus and Equipment, Wiring Supplies, and Related Equipment Merchant Wholesalers[US]

42362 Electrical and Electronic Appliance, Television, and Radio Set Merchant Wholesalers[US]

423620 Electrical and Electronic Appliance, Television, and Radio Set Merchant Wholesalers[US]

42369 Other Electronic Parts and Equipment Merchant Wholesalers[US]

423690 Other Electronic Parts and Equipment Merchant Wholesalers[US]

4237 Hardware, and Plumbing and Heating Equipment and Supplies Merchant Wholesalers[US]

42371 Hardware Merchant Wholesalers[US]

423710 Hardware Merchant Wholesalers[US]

42372 Plumbing and Heating Equipment and Supplies (Hydronics) Merchant Wholesalers[US]

423720 Plumbing and Heating Equipment and Supplies (Hydronics) Merchant Wholesalers[US]

42373 Warm Air Heating and Air-Conditioning Equipment and Supplies Merchant Wholesalers[US]

423730 Warm Air Heating and Air-Conditioning Equipment and Supplies Merchant Wholesalers[US]

42374 Refrigeration Equipment and Supplies Merchant Wholesalers[US]

423740 Refrigeration Equipment and Supplies Merchant Wholesalers[US]

4238 Machinery, Equipment, and Supplies Merchant Wholesalers[US]

42381 Construction and Mining (except Oil Well) Machinery and Equipment Merchant Wholesalers[US]

423810 Construction and Mining (except Oil Well) Machinery and Equipment Merchant Wholesalers[US]

42382 Farm and Garden Machinery and Equipment Merchant Wholesalers[US]

423820 Farm and Garden Machinery and Equipment Merchant Wholesalers[US]

42383 Industrial Machinery and Equipment Merchant Wholesalers[US]

423830 Industrial Machinery and Equipment Merchant Wholesalers[US]

42384 Industrial Supplies Merchant Wholesalers[US]

423840 Industrial Supplies Merchant Wholesalers[US]

42385 Service Establishment Equipment and Supplies Merchant Wholesalers[US]

423850 Service Establishment Equipment and Supplies Merchant Wholesalers[US]

42386 Transportation Equipment and Supplies (except Motor Vehicle) Merchant Wholesalers[US]

423860 Transportation Equipment and Supplies (except Motor Vehicle) Merchant Wholesalers[US]

4239 Miscellaneous Durable Goods Merchant Wholesalers[US]

42391 Sporting and Recreational Goods and Supplies Merchant Wholesalers[US]

423910 Sporting and Recreational Goods and Supplies Merchant Wholesalers[US]

42392 Toy and Hobby Goods and Supplies Merchant Wholesalers[US]

423920 Toy and Hobby Goods and Supplies Merchant Wholesalers[US]

42393 Recyclable Material Merchant Wholesalers[US]

423930 Recyclable Material Merchant Wholesalers[US]

42394 Jewelry, Watch, Precious Stone, and Precious Metal Merchant Wholesalers[US]

423940 Jewelry, Watch, Precious Stone, and Precious Metal Merchant Wholesalers[US]

42399 Other Miscellaneous Durable Goods Merchant Wholesalers[US]

423990 Other Miscellaneous Durable Goods Merchant Wholesalers[US]

424 Merchant Wholesalers, Nondurable Goods[US]

4241 Paper and Paper Product Merchant Wholesalers[US]

42411 Printing and Writing Paper Merchant Wholesalers[US]

424110 Printing and Writing Paper Merchant Wholesalers[US]
42412 Stationery and Office Supplies Merchant Wholesalers[US]
424120 Stationery and Office Supplies Merchant Wholesalers[US]
42413 Industrial and Personal Service Paper Merchant Wholesalers[US]
424130 Industrial and Personal Service Paper Merchant Wholesalers[US]

4242 Drugs and Druggists' Sundries Merchant Wholesalers[US]

42421 Drugs and Druggists' Sundries Merchant Wholesalers[US]
424210 Drugs and Druggists' Sundries Merchant Wholesalers[US]

4243 Apparel, Piece Goods, and Notions Merchant Wholesalers[US]

42431 Piece Goods, Notions, and Other Dry Goods Merchant Wholesalers[US]
424310 Piece Goods, Notions, and Other Dry Goods Merchant Wholesalers[US]
42432 Men's and Boys' Clothing and Furnishings Merchant Wholesalers[US]
424320 Men's and Boys' Clothing and Furnishings Merchant Wholesalers[US]
42433 Women's, Children's, and Infants' Clothing and Accessories Merchant Wholesalers[US]
424330 Women's, Children's, and Infants' Clothing and Accessories Merchant Wholesalers[US]
42434 Footwear Merchant Wholesalers[US]
424340 Footwear Merchant Wholesalers[US]

4244 Grocery and Related Product Merchant Wholesalers[US]

42441 General Line Grocery Merchant Wholesalers[US]
424410 General Line Grocery Merchant Wholesalers[US]
42442 Packaged Frozen Food Merchant Wholesalers[US]
424420 Packaged Frozen Food Merchant Wholesalers[US]
42443 Dairy Product (except Dried or Canned) Merchant Wholesalers[US]
424430 Dairy Product (except Dried or Canned) Merchant Wholesalers[US]
42444 Poultry and Poultry Product Merchant Wholesalers[US]
424440 Poultry and Poultry Product Merchant Wholesalers[US]

42445 Confectionery Merchant Wholesalers[US]
424450 Confectionery Merchant Wholesalers[US]
42446 Fish and Seafood Merchant Wholesalers[US]
424460 Fish and Seafood Merchant Wholesalers[US]
42447 Meat and Meat Product Merchant Wholesalers[US]
424470 Meat and Meat Product Merchant Wholesalers[US]
42448 Fresh Fruit and Vegetable Merchant Wholesalers[US]
424480 Fresh Fruit and Vegetable Merchant Wholesalers[US]
42449 Other Grocery and Related Products Merchant Wholesalers[US]
424490 Other Grocery and Related Products Merchant Wholesalers[US]

4245 Farm Product Raw Material Merchant Wholesalers[US]

42451 Grain and Field Bean Merchant Wholesalers[US]
424510 Grain and Field Bean Merchant Wholesalers[US]
42452 Livestock Merchant Wholesalers[US]
424520 Livestock Merchant Wholesalers[US]
42459 Other Farm Product Raw Material Merchant Wholesalers[US]
424590 Other Farm Product Raw Material Merchant Wholesalers[US]

4246 Chemical and Allied Products Merchant Wholesalers[US]

42461 Plastics Materials and Basic Forms and Shapes Merchant Wholesalers[US]
424610 Plastics Materials and Basic Forms and Shapes Merchant Wholesalers[US]
42469 Other Chemical and Allied Products Merchant Wholesalers[US]
424690 Other Chemical and Allied Products Merchant Wholesalers[US]

4247 Petroleum and Petroleum Products Merchant Wholesalers[US]

42471 Petroleum Bulk Stations and Terminals[US]
424710 Petroleum Bulk Stations and Terminals[US]
42472 Petroleum and Petroleum Products Merchant Wholesalers (except Bulk Stations and Terminals)[US]
424720 Petroleum and Petroleum Products Merchant Wholesalers (except Bulk Stations and Terminals)[US]

4248 Beer, Wine, and Distilled Alcoholic Beverage Merchant Wholesalers[US]

42481 Beer and Ale Merchant Wholesalers[US]
424810 Beer and Ale Merchant Wholesalers[US]
42482 Wine and Distilled Alcoholic Beverage Merchant Wholesalers[US]
424820 Wine and Distilled Alcoholic Beverage Merchant Wholesalers[US]

4249 Miscellaneous Nondurable Goods Merchant Wholesalers[US]

42491 Farm Supplies Merchant Wholesalers[US]
424910 Farm Supplies Merchant Wholesalers[US]
42492 Book, Periodical, and Newspaper Merchant Wholesalers[US]
424920 Book, Periodical, and Newspaper Merchant Wholesalers[US]
42493 Flower, Nursery Stock, and Florists' Supplies Merchant Wholesalers[US]
424930 Flower, Nursery Stock, and Florists' Supplies Merchant Wholesalers[US]
42494 Tobacco and Tobacco Product Merchant Wholesalers[US]
424940 Tobacco and Tobacco Product Merchant Wholesalers[US]
42495 Paint, Varnish, and Supplies Merchant Wholesalers[US]
424950 Paint, Varnish, and Supplies Merchant Wholesalers[US]
42499 Other Miscellaneous Nondurable Goods Merchant Wholesalers[US]
424990 Other Miscellaneous Nondurable Goods Merchant Wholesalers[US]

425 Wholesale Electronic Markets and Agents and Brokers[US]

4251 Wholesale Electronic Markets and Agents and Brokers[US]

42511 Business to Business Electronic Markets[US]
425110 Business to Business Electronic Markets[US]
42512 Wholesale Trade Agents and Brokers[US]
425120 Wholesale Trade Agents and Brokers[US]

44-45 Retail Trade

441 Motor Vehicle and Parts Dealers[CAN]

4411 Automobile Dealers[CAN]

44111 New Car Dealers[CAN]
441110 New Car Dealers[CAN]

44112 Used Car Dealers[CAN]
441120 Used Car Dealers[CAN]

4412 Other Motor Vehicle Dealers[CAN]

44121 Recreational Vehicle Dealers[CAN]
441210 Recreational Vehicle Dealers[CAN]
44122 Motorcycle, Boat, and Other Motor Vehicle Dealers[CAN]
441221 Motorcycle Dealers[US]
441222 Boat Dealers[US]
441229 All Other Motor Vehicle Dealers[US]

4413 Automotive Parts, Accessories, and Tire Stores[CAN]

44131 Automotive Parts and Accessories Stores[CAN]
441310 Automotive Parts and Accessories Stores[CAN]
44132 Tire Dealers[CAN]
441320 Tire Dealers[CAN]

442 Furniture and Home Furnishings Stores[CAN]

4421 Furniture Stores[CAN]

44211 Furniture Stores[CAN]
442110 Furniture Stores[CAN]

4422 Home Furnishings Stores[CAN]

44221 Floor Covering Stores[CAN]
442210 Floor Covering Stores[CAN]
44229 Other Home Furnishings Stores[CAN]
442291 Window Treatment Stores[CAN]
442299 All Other Home Furnishings Stores[US]

443 Electronics and Appliance Stores[CAN]

4431 Electronics and Appliance Stores[CAN]

44311 Appliance, Television, and Other Electronics Stores [CAN]
443111 Household Appliance Stores[US]
443112 Radio, Television, and Other Electronics Stores[US]
44312 Computer and Software Stores[CAN]
443120 Computer and Software Stores[CAN]
44313 Camera and Photographic Supplies Stores[CAN]
443130 Camera and Photographic Supplies Stores[CAN]

444 Building Material and Garden Equipment and Supplies Dealers[CAN]

4441 Building Material and Supplies Dealers[CAN]

44411 Home Centers[CAN]

444110 Home Centers[CAN]
44412 Paint and Wallpaper Stores[CAN]
444120 Paint and Wallpaper Stores[CAN]
44413 Hardware Stores[CAN]
444130 Hardware Stores[CAN]
44419 Other Building Material Dealers[CAN]
444190 Other Building Material Dealers[CAN]

4442 Lawn and Garden Equipment and Supplies Stores[CAN]

44421 Outdoor Power Equipment Stores[CAN]
444210 Outdoor Power Equipment Stores[CAN]
44422 Nursery, Garden Center, and Farm Supply Stores[CAN]
444220 Nursery, Garden Center, and Farm Supply Stores[CAN]

445 Food and Beverage Stores[CAN]

4451 Grocery Stores[CAN]

44511 Supermarkets and Other Grocery (except Convenience) Stores[CAN]
445110 Supermarkets and Other Grocery (except Convenience) Stores[CAN]
44512 Convenience Stores[CAN]
445120 Convenience Stores[CAN]

4452 Specialty Food Stores[CAN]

44521 Meat Markets[CAN]
445210 Meat Markets[CAN]
44522 Fish and Seafood Markets[CAN]
445220 Fish and Seafood Markets[CAN]
44523 Fruit and Vegetable Markets[CAN]
445230 Fruit and Vegetable Markets[CAN]
44529 Other Specialty Food Stores[CAN]
445291 Baked Goods Stores[CAN]
445292 Confectionery and Nut Stores[CAN]
445299 All Other Specialty Food Stores[CAN]

4453 Beer, Wine, and Liquor Stores[CAN]

44531 Beer, Wine, and Liquor Stores[CAN]
445310 Beer, Wine, and Liquor Stores[CAN]

446 Health and Personal Care Stores[CAN]

4461 Health and Personal Care Stores[CAN]

44611 Pharmacies and Drug Stores[CAN]
446110 Pharmacies and Drug Stores[CAN]

44612 Cosmetics, Beauty Supplies, and Perfume Stores[CAN]
446120 Cosmetics, Beauty Supplies, and Perfume Stores[CAN]
44613 Optical Goods Stores[CAN]
446130 Optical Goods Stores[CAN]
44619 Other Health and Personal Care Stores[CAN]
446191 Food (Health) Supplement Stores[CAN]
446199 All Other Health and Personal Care Stores[CAN]

447 Gasoline Stations[CAN]

4471 Gasoline Stations[CAN]

44711 Gasoline Stations with Convenience Stores[CAN]
447110 Gasoline Stations with Convenience Stores[CAN]
44719 Other Gasoline Stations[CAN]
447190 Other Gasoline Stations[CAN]

448 Clothing and Clothing Accessories Stores[CAN]

4481 Clothing Stores[CAN]

44811 Men's Clothing Stores[CAN]
448110 Men's Clothing Stores[CAN]
44812 Women's Clothing Stores[CAN]
448120 Women's Clothing Stores[CAN]
44813 Children's and Infants' Clothing Stores[CAN]
448130 Children's and Infants' Clothing Stores[CAN]
44814 Family Clothing Stores[CAN]
448140 Family Clothing Stores[CAN]
44815 Clothing Accessories Stores[CAN]
448150 Clothing Accessories Stores[CAN]
44819 Other Clothing Stores[CAN]
448190 Other Clothing Stores[US]

4482 Shoe Stores[CAN]

44821 Shoe Stores[CAN]
448210 Shoe Stores[CAN]

4483 Jewelry, Luggage, and Leather Goods Stores[CAN]

44831 Jewelry Stores[CAN]
448310 Jewelry Stores[CAN]
44832 Luggage and Leather Goods Stores[CAN]
448320 Luggage and Leather Goods Stores[CAN]

451 Sporting Goods, Hobby, Book, and Music Stores[CAN]

4511 Sporting Goods, Hobby, and Musical Instrument Stores[CAN]

45111 Sporting Goods Stores[CAN]
451110 Sporting Goods Stores[CAN]
45112 Hobby, Toy, and Game Stores[CAN]
451120 Hobby, Toy, and Game Stores[CAN]
45113 Sewing, Needlework, and Piece Goods Stores[CAN]
451130 Sewing, Needlework, and Piece Goods Stores[CAN]
45114 Musical Instrument and Supplies Stores[CAN]
451140 Musical Instrument and Supplies Stores[CAN]

4512 Book, Periodical, and Music Stores[CAN]

45121 Book Stores and News Dealers[CAN]
451211 Book Stores[US]
451212 News Dealers and Newsstands[US]
45122 Prerecorded Tape, Compact Disc, and Record Stores[CAN]
451220 Prerecorded Tape, Compact Disc, and Record Stores[CAN]

452 General Merchandise Stores[CAN]

4521 Department Stores[CAN]

45211 Department Stores[CAN]
452111 Department Stores (except Discount Department Stores)[US]
452112 Discount Department Stores[US]

4529 Other General Merchandise Stores[CAN]

45291 Warehouse Clubs and Supercenters[CAN]
452910 Warehouse Clubs and Supercenters[CAN]
45299 All Other General Merchandise Stores[CAN]
452990 All Other General Merchandise Stores[US]

453 Miscellaneous Store Retailers[CAN]

4531 Florists[CAN]

45311 Florists[CAN]
453110 Florists[CAN]

4532 Office Supplies, Stationery, and Gift Stores[CAN]

45321 Office Supplies and Stationery Stores[CAN]
453210 Office Supplies and Stationery Stores[CAN]
45322 Gift, Novelty, and Souvenir Stores[CAN]
453220 Gift, Novelty, and Souvenir Stores[CAN]

4533 Used Merchandise Stores[CAN]

45331 Used Merchandise Stores[CAN]
453310 Used Merchandise Stores[CAN]

4539 Other Miscellaneous Store Retailers[CAN]

45391 Pet and Pet Supplies Stores[CAN]
453910 Pet and Pet Supplies Stores[CAN]
45392 Art Dealers[CAN]
453920 Art Dealers[CAN]
45393 Manufactured (Mobile) Home Dealers[CAN]
453930 Manufactured (Mobile) Home Dealers[CAN]
45399 All Other Miscellaneous Store Retailers[CAN]
453991 Tobacco Stores[US]
453998 All Other Miscellaneous Store Retailers (except Tobacco Stores)[US]

454 Nonstore Retailers[CAN]

4541 Electronic Shopping and Mail-Order Houses[CAN]

45411 Electronic Shopping and Mail-Order Houses[CAN]
454111 Electronic Shopping[US]
454112 Electronic Auctions[US]
454113 Mail-Order Houses[US]

4542 Vending Machine Operators[CAN]

45421 Vending Machine Operators[CAN]
454210 Vending Machine Operators[CAN]

4543 Direct Selling Establishments[CAN]

45431 Fuel Dealers[CAN]
454311 Heating Oil Dealers[US]
454312 Liquefied Petroleum Gas (Bottled Gas) Dealers[US]
454319 Other Fuel Dealers[US]
45439 Other Direct Selling Establishments[CAN]
454390 Other Direct Selling Establishments[CAN]

48-49 Transportation and Warehousing

481 Air Transportation

4811 Scheduled Air Transportation

48111 Scheduled Air Transportation
481111 Scheduled Passenger Air Transportation[US]
481112 Scheduled Freight Air Transportation[US]

4812 Nonscheduled Air Transportation

48121 Nonscheduled Air Transportation
481211 Nonscheduled Chartered Passenger Air Transportation[US]

481212 Nonscheduled Chartered Freight Air Transportation[US]
481219 Other Nonscheduled Air Transportation[US]

482 Rail Transportation

4821 Rail Transportation

48211 Rail Transportation
482111 Line-Haul Railroads[US]
482112 Short Line Railroads[CAN]

483 Water Transportation

4831 Deep Sea, Coastal, and Great Lakes Water Transportation

48311 Deep Sea, Coastal, and Great Lakes Water Transportation
483111 Deep Sea Freight Transportation[US]
483112 Deep Sea Passenger Transportation[US]
483113 Coastal and Great Lakes Freight Transportation[US]
483114 Coastal and Great Lakes Passenger Transportation[US]

4832 Inland Water Transportation

48321 Inland Water Transportation
483211 Inland Water Freight Transportation[US]
483212 Inland Water Passenger Transportation[US]

484 Truck Transportation

4841 General Freight Trucking

48411 General Freight Trucking, Local
484110 General Freight Trucking, Local[CAN]
48412 General Freight Trucking, Long-Distance
484121 General Freight Trucking, Long-Distance, Truckload[CAN]
484122 General Freight Trucking, Long-Distance, Less Than Truckload[CAN]

4842 Specialized Freight Trucking

48421 Used Household and Office Goods Moving
484210 Used Household and Office Goods Moving
48422 Specialized Freight (except Used Goods) Trucking, Local
484220 Specialized Freight (except Used Goods) Trucking, Local[US]
48423 Specialized Freight (except Used Goods) Trucking, Long-Distance

484230 Specialized Freight (except Used Goods) Trucking, Long-Distance[US]

485 Transit and Ground Passenger Transportation

4851 Urban Transit Systems

48511 Urban Transit Systems
485111 Mixed Mode Transit Systems[US]
485112 Commuter Rail Systems[US]
485113 Bus and Other Motor Vehicle Transit Systems[US]
485119 Other Urban Transit Systems[US]

4852 Interurban and Rural Bus Transportation

48521 Interurban and Rural Bus Transportation
485210 Interurban and Rural Bus Transportation

4853 Taxi and Limousine Service

48531 Taxi Service
485310 Taxi Service[CAN]
48532 Limousine Service
485320 Limousine Service

4854 School and Employee Bus Transportation

48541 School and Employee Bus Transportation
485410 School and Employee Bus Transportation

4855 Charter Bus Industry

48551 Charter Bus Industry
485510 Charter Bus Industry

4859 Other Transit and Ground Passenger Transportation

48599 Other Transit and Ground Passenger Transportation
485991 Special Needs Transportation[US]
485999 All Other Transit and Ground Passenger Transportation[US]

486 Pipeline Transportation

4861 Pipeline Transportation of Crude Oil

48611 Pipeline Transportation of Crude Oil
486110 Pipeline Transportation of Crude Oil

4862 Pipeline Transportation of Natural Gas

48621 Pipeline Transportation of Natural Gas
486210 Pipeline Transportation of Natural Gas

4869 Other Pipeline Transportation

48691 Pipeline Transportation of Refined Petroleum Products
486910 Pipeline Transportation of Refined Petroleum Products
48699 All Other Pipeline Transportation
486990 All Other Pipeline Transportation

487 Scenic and Sightseeing Transportation

4871 Scenic and Sightseeing Transportation, Land

48711 Scenic and Sightseeing Transportation, Land
487110 Scenic and Sightseeing Transportation, Land

4872 Scenic and Sightseeing Transportation, Water

48721 Scenic and Sightseeing Transportation, Water
487210 Scenic and Sightseeing Transportation, Water

4879 Scenic and Sightseeing Transportation, Other

48799 Scenic and Sightseeing Transportation, Other
487990 Scenic and Sightseeing Transportation, Other

488 Support Activities for Transportation

4881 Support Activities for Air Transportation

48811 Airport Operations
488111 Air Traffic Control
488119 Other Airport Operations[CAN]
48819 Other Support Activities for Air Transportation
488190 Other Support Activities for Air Transportation

4882 Support Activities for Rail Transportation

48821 Support Activities for Rail Transportation
488210 Support Activities for Rail Transportation

4883 Support Activities for Water Transportation

48831 Port and Harbor Operations
488310 Port and Harbor Operations
48832 Marine Cargo Handling
488320 Marine Cargo Handling
48833 Navigational Services to Shipping
488330 Navigational Services to Shipping[MEX]
48839 Other Support Activities for Water Transportation
488390 Other Support Activities for Water Transportation

4884 Support Activities for Road Transportation

48841 Motor Vehicle Towing
488410 Motor Vehicle Towing
48849 Other Support Activities for Road Transportation

488490 Other Support Activities for Road Transportation[CAN]

4885 Freight Transportation Arrangement

48851 Freight Transportation Arrangement
488510 Freight Transportation Arrangement[US]

4889 Other Support Activities for Transportation

48899 Other Support Activities for Transportation
488991 Packing and Crating[US]
488999 All Other Support Activities for Transportation[US]

491 Postal Service

4911 Postal Service

49111 Postal Service
491110 Postal Service

492 Couriers and Messengers

4921 Couriers

49211 Couriers
492110 Couriers

4922 Local Messengers and Local Delivery

49221 Local Messengers and Local Delivery
492210 Local Messengers and Local Delivery

493 Warehousing and Storage

4931 Warehousing and Storage

49311 General Warehousing and Storage
493110 General Warehousing and Storage[CAN]
49312 Refrigerated Warehousing and Storage
493120 Refrigerated Warehousing and Storage
49313 Farm Product Warehousing and Storage
493130 Farm Product Warehousing and Storage
49319 Other Warehousing and Storage
493190 Other Warehousing and Storage

51 Information

511 Publishing Industries (except Internet)

5111 Newspaper, Periodical, Book, and Directory Publishers

51111 Newspaper Publishers
511110 Newspaper Publishers[CAN]
51112 Periodical Publishers
511120 Periodical Publishers[CAN]

51113 Book Publishers
511130 Book Publishers[CAN]
51114 Directory and Mailing List Publishers
511140 Directory and Mailing List Publishers[CAN]
51119 Other Publishers
511191 Greeting Card Publishers[US]
511199 All Other Publishers[US]

5112 Software Publishers

51121 Software Publishers
511210 Software Publishers

512 Motion Picture and Sound Recording Industries

5121 Motion Picture and Video Industries

51211 Motion Picture and Video Production
512110 Motion Picture and Video Production[CAN]
51212 Motion Picture and Video Distribution
512120 Motion Picture and Video Distribution
51213 Motion Picture and Video Exhibition
512131 Motion Picture Theaters (except Drive-Ins)[US]
512132 Drive-In Motion Picture Theaters[US]
51219 Postproduction Services and Other Motion Picture and Video Industries
512191 Teleproduction and Other Postproduction Services[US]
512199 Other Motion Picture and Video Industries[US]

5122 Sound Recording Industries

51221 Record Production
512210 Record Production
51222 Integrated Record Production/Distribution
512220 Integrated Record Production/Distribution
51223 Music Publishers
512230 Music Publishers
51224 Sound Recording Studios
512240 Sound Recording Studios
51229 Other Sound Recording Industries
512290 Other Sound Recording Industries

515 Broadcasting (except Internet)

5151 Radio and Television Broadcasting

51511 Radio Broadcasting
515111 Radio Networks[US]
515112 Radio Stations[US]
51512 Television Broadcasting
515120 Television Broadcasting

5152 Cable and Other Subscription Programming

51521 Cable and Other Subscription Programming
515210 Cable and Other Subscription Programming

516 Internet Publishing and Broadcasting

5161 Internet Publishing and Broadcasting

51611 Internet Publishing and Broadcasting
516110 Internet Publishing and Broadcasting

517 Telecommunications

5171 Wired Telecommunications Carriers

51711 Wired Telecommunications Carriers
517110 Wired Telecommunications Carriers

5172 Wireless Telecommunications Carriers (except Satellite)

51721 Wireless Telecommunications Carriers (except Satellite)
517211 Paging[US]
517212 Cellular and Other Wireless Telecommunications[US]

5173 Telecommunications Resellers

51731 Telecommunications Resellers
517310 Telecommunications Resellers

5174 Satellite Telecommunications

51741 Satellite Telecommunications
517410 Satellite Telecommunications

5175 Cable and Other Program Distribution

51751 Cable and Other Program Distribution
517510 Cable and Other Program Distribution

5179 Other Telecommunications

51791 Other Telecommunications
517910 Other Telecommunications

518 Internet Service Providers, Web Search Portals, and Data Processing Services

5181 Internet Service Providers and Web Search Portals

51811 Internet Service Providers and Web Search Portals
518111 Internet Service Providers[US]
518112 Web Search Portals[US]

5182 Data Processing, Hosting, and Related Services

51821 Data Processing, Hosting, and Related Services
518210 Data Processing, Hosting, and Related Services

519 Other Information Services

5191 Other Information Services

51911 News Syndicates
519110 News Syndicates
51912 Libraries and Archives
519120 Libraries and Archives[US]
51919 All Other Information Services
519190 All Other Information Services

52 Finance and Insurance

521 Monetary Authorities—Central Bank

5211 Monetary Authorities—Central Bank

52111 Monetary Authorities—Central Bank
521110 Monetary Authorities—Central Bank

522 Credit Intermediation and Related Activities

5221 Depository Credit Intermediation[CAN]

52211 Commercial Banking[US]
522110 Commercial Banking[US]
52212 Savings Institutions[US]
522120 Savings Institutions[US]
52213 Credit Unions[CAN]
522130 Credit Unions[CAN]
52219 Other Depository Credit Intermediation[CAN]
522190 Other Depository Credit Intermediation[CAN]

5222 Nondepository Credit Intermediation[CAN]

52221 Credit Card Issuing[CAN]
522210 Credit Card Issuing[CAN]
52222 Sales Financing[CAN]
522220 Sales Financing[CAN]
52229 Other Nondepository Credit Intermediation[CAN]
522291 Consumer Lending[CAN]
522292 Real Estate Credit[US]
522293 International Trade Financing[US]
522294 Secondary Market Financing[US]
522298 All Other Nondepository Credit Intermediation[US]

5223 Activities Related to Credit Intermediation[CAN]

52231 Mortgage and Nonmortgage Loan Brokers[CAN]
522310 Mortgage and Nonmortgage Loan Brokers[CAN]

52232 Financial Transactions Processing, Reserve, and Clearinghouse Activities[CAN]
522320 Financial Transactions Processing, Reserve, and Clearinghouse Activities[US]
52239 Other Activities Related to Credit Intermediation[CAN]
522390 Other Activities Related to Credit Intermediation[CAN]

523 Securities, Commodity Contracts, and Other Financial Investments and Related Activities

5231 Securities and Commodity Contracts Intermediation and Brokerage

52311 Investment Banking and Securities Dealing[CAN]
523110 Investment Banking and Securities Dealing[CAN]
52312 Securities Brokerage[CAN]
523120 Securities Brokerage[CAN]
52313 Commodity Contracts Dealing[CAN]
523130 Commodity Contracts Dealing[CAN]
52314 Commodity Contracts Brokerage[CAN]
523140 Commodity Contracts Brokerage[CAN]

5232 Securities and Commodity Exchanges

52321 Securities and Commodity Exchanges
523210 Securities and Commodity Exchanges

5239 Other Financial Investment Activities

52391 Miscellaneous Intermediation[CAN]
523910 Miscellaneous Intermediation[CAN]
52392 Portfolio Management[CAN]
523920 Portfolio Management[CAN]
52393 Investment Advice[CAN]
523930 Investment Advice[CAN]
52399 All Other Financial Investment Activities[CAN]
523991 Trust, Fiduciary, and Custody Activities[US]
523999 Miscellaneous Financial Investment Activities[US]

524 Insurance Carriers and Related Activities

5241 Insurance Carriers

52411 Direct Life, Health, and Medical Insurance Carriers[CAN]
524113 Direct Life Insurance Carriers[US]
524114 Direct Health and Medical Insurance Carriers[US]
52412 Direct Insurance (except Life, Health, and Medical) Carriers[CAN]

524126 Direct Property and Casualty Insurance Carriers[US]
524127 Direct Title Insurance Carriers[US]
524128 Other Direct Insurance (except Life, Health, and Medical) Carriers[US]
52413 Reinsurance Carriers[CAN]
524130 Reinsurance Carriers[US]

5242 Agencies, Brokerages, and Other Insurance Related Activities

52421 Insurance Agencies and Brokerages[CAN]
524210 Insurance Agencies and Brokerages[CAN]
52429 Other Insurance Related Activities[CAN]
524291 Claims Adjusting[CAN]
524292 Third Party Administration of Insurance and Pension Funds[US]
524298 All Other Insurance Related Activities[US]

525 Funds, Trusts, and Other Financial Vehicles[US]

5251 Insurance and Employee Benefit Funds[US]

52511 Pension Funds[US]
525110 Pension Funds[US]
52512 Health and Welfare Funds[US]
525120 Health and Welfare Funds[US]
52519 Other Insurance Funds[US]
525190 Other Insurance Funds[US]

5259 Other Investment Pools and Funds[US]

52591 Open-End Investment Funds[US]
525910 Open-End Investment Funds[US]
52592 Trusts, Estates, and Agency Accounts[US]
525920 Trusts, Estates, and Agency Accounts[US]
52593 Real Estate Investment Trusts[US]
525930 Real Estate Investment Trusts[US]
52599 Other Financial Vehicles[US]
525990 Other Financial Vehicles[US]

53 Real Estate and Rental and Leasing

531 Real Estate

5311 Lessors of Real Estate

53111 Lessors of Residential Buildings and Dwellings[CAN]
531110 Lessors of Residential Buildings and Dwellings[US]
53112 Lessors of Nonresidential Buildings (except Miniwarehouses)[CAN]

531120 Lessors of Nonresidential Buildings (except Miniwarehouses)[CAN]
53113 Lessors of Miniwarehouses and Self-Storage Units[CAN]
531130 Lessors of Miniwarehouses and Self-Storage Units[CAN]
53119 Lessors of Other Real Estate Property[CAN]
531190 Lessors of Other Real Estate Property[CAN]

5312 Offices of Real Estate Agents and Brokers

53121 Offices of Real Estate Agents and Brokers
531210 Offices of Real Estate Agents and Brokers

5313 Activities Related to Real Estate

53131 Real Estate Property Managers[CAN]
531311 Residential Property Managers[US]
531312 Nonresidential Property Managers[US]
53132 Offices of Real Estate Appraisers[CAN]
531320 Offices of Real Estate Appraisers[CAN]
53139 Other Activities Related to Real Estate[CAN]
531390 Other Activities Related to Real Estate[CAN]

532 Rental and Leasing Services

5321 Automotive Equipment Rental and Leasing

53211 Passenger Car Rental and Leasing
532111 Passenger Car Rental[CAN]
532112 Passenger Car Leasing[CAN]
53212 Truck, Utility Trailer, and RV (Recreational Vehicle) Rental and Leasing
532120 Truck, Utility Trailer, and RV (Recreational Vehicle) Rental and Leasing[CAN]

5322 Consumer Goods Rental

53221 Consumer Electronics and Appliances Rental
532210 Consumer Electronics and Appliances Rental
53222 Formal Wear and Costume Rental
532220 Formal Wear and Costume Rental
53223 Video Tape and Disc Rental
532230 Video Tape and Disc Rental
53229 Other Consumer Goods Rental
532291 Home Health Equipment Rental[US]
532292 Recreational Goods Rental[US]
532299 All Other Consumer Goods Rental[US]

5323 General Rental Centers

53231 General Rental Centers
532310 General Rental Centers

5324 Commercial and Industrial Machinery and Equipment Rental and Leasing

53241 Construction, Transportation, Mining, and Forestry Machinery and Equipment Rental and Leasing
532411 Commercial Air, Rail, and Water Transportation Equipment Rental and Leasing[US]
532412 Construction, Mining, and Forestry Machinery and Equipment Rental and Leasing[US]
53242 Office Machinery and Equipment Rental and Leasing
532420 Office Machinery and Equipment Rental and Leasing
53249 Other Commercial and Industrial Machinery and Equipment Rental and Leasing
532490 Other Commercial and Industrial Machinery and Equipment Rental and Leasing[CAN]

533 Lessors of Nonfinancial Intangible Assets (except Copyrighted Works)

5331 Lessors of Nonfinancial Intangible Assets (except Copyrighted Works)

53311 Lessors of Nonfinancial Intangible Assets (except Copyrighted Works)
533110 Lessors of Nonfinancial Intangible Assets (except Copyrighted Works)

54 Professional, Scientific, and Technical Services

541 Professional, Scientific, and Technical Services

5411 Legal Services

54111 Offices of Lawyers
541110 Offices of Lawyers
54112 Offices of Notaries
541120 Offices of Notaries
54119 Other Legal Services
541191 Title Abstract and Settlement Offices[US]
541199 All Other Legal Services[US]

5412 Accounting, Tax Preparation, Bookkeeping, and Payroll Services

54121 Accounting, Tax Preparation, Bookkeeping, and Payroll Services
541211 Offices of Certified Public Accountants[US]
541213 Tax Preparation Services[CAN]

541214 Payroll Services[US]
541219 Other Accounting Services[US]

5413 Architectural, Engineering, and Related Services

54131 Architectural Services
541310 Architectural Services
54132 Landscape Architectural Services
541320 Landscape Architectural Services
54133 Engineering Services
541330 Engineering Services
54134 Drafting Services
541340 Drafting Services
54135 Building Inspection Services
541350 Building Inspection Services
54136 Geophysical Surveying and Mapping Services
541360 Geophysical Surveying and Mapping Services
54137 Surveying and Mapping (except Geophysical) Services
541370 Surveying and Mapping (except Geophysical) Services
54138 Testing Laboratories
541380 Testing Laboratories

5414 Specialized Design Services

54141 Interior Design Services
541410 Interior Design Services
54142 Industrial Design Services
541420 Industrial Design Services
54143 Graphic Design Services
541430 Graphic Design Services
54149 Other Specialized Design Services
541490 Other Specialized Design Services

5415 Computer Systems Design and Related Services

54151 Computer Systems Design and Related Services
541511 Custom Computer Programming Services[US]
541512 Computer Systems Design Services[US]
541513 Computer Facilities Management Services[US]
541519 Other Computer Related Services[US]

5416 Management, Scientific, and Technical Consulting Services

54161 Management Consulting Services
541611 Administrative Management and General Management Consulting Services[CAN]
541612 Human Resources and Executive Search Consulting Services[CAN]

541613 Marketing Consulting Services[US]
541614 Process, Physical Distribution, and Logistics Consulting Services[US]
541618 Other Management Consulting Services[US]
54162 Environmental Consulting Services
541620 Environmental Consulting Services
54169 Other Scientific and Technical Consulting Services
541690 Other Scientific and Technical Consulting Services

5417 Scientific Research and Development Services

54171 Research and Development in the Physical, Engineering, and Life Sciences
541710 Research and Development in the Physical, Engineering, and Life Sciences[CAN]
54172 Research and Development in the Social Sciences and Humanities
541720 Research and Development in the Social Sciences and Humanities[CAN]

5418 Advertising and Related Services

54181 Advertising Agencies
541810 Advertising Agencies
54182 Public Relations Agencies
541820 Public Relations Agencies
54183 Media Buying Agencies
541830 Media Buying Agencies
54184 Media Representatives
541840 Media Representatives
54185 Display Advertising
541850 Display Advertising
54186 Direct Mail Advertising
541860 Direct Mail Advertising
54187 Advertising Material Distribution Services
541870 Advertising Material Distribution Services
54189 Other Services Related to Advertising
541890 Other Services Related to Advertising[MEX]

5419 Other Professional, Scientific, and Technical Services

54191 Marketing Research and Public Opinion Polling
541910 Marketing Research and Public Opinion Polling
54192 Photographic Services
541921 Photography Studios, Portrait[US]
541922 Commercial Photography[US]
54193 Translation and Interpretation Services

541930 Translation and Interpretation Services
54194 Veterinary Services
541940 Veterinary Services[CAN]
54199 All Other Professional, Scientific, and Technical Services
541990 All Other Professional, Scientific, and Technical Services

55 Management of Companies and Enterprises

551 Management of Companies and Enterprises

5511 Management of Companies and Enterprises

55111 Management of Companies and Enterprises
551111 Offices of Bank Holding Companies[US]
551112 Offices of Other Holding Companies[US]
551114 Corporate, Subsidiary, and Regional Managing Offices[CAN]

56 Administrative and Support and Waste Management and Remediation Services

561 Administrative and Support Services

5611 Office Administrative Services

56111 Office Administrative Services
561110 Office Administrative Services

5612 Facilities Support Services

56121 Facilities Support Services
561210 Facilities Support Services

5613 Employment Services

56131 Employment Placement Agencies
561310 Employment Placement Agencies
56132 Temporary Help Services
561320 Temporary Help Services
56133 Professional Employer Organizations
561330 Professional Employer Organizations

5614 Business Support Services

56141 Document Preparation Services
561410 Document Preparation Services
56142 Telephone Call Centers
561421 Telephone Answering Services[US]
561422 Telemarketing Bureaus[MEX]
56143 Business Service Centers
561431 Private Mail Centers[US]

561439 Other Business Service Centers (including Copy Shops)[US]
56144 Collection Agencies
561440 Collection Agencies
56145 Credit Bureaus
561450 Credit Bureaus
56149 Other Business Support Services
561491 Repossession Services[US]
561492 Court Reporting and Stenotype Services[US]
561499 All Other Business Support Services[US]

5615 Travel Arrangement and Reservation Services

56151 Travel Agencies
561510 Travel Agencies
56152 Tour Operators
561520 Tour Operators
56159 Other Travel Arrangement and Reservation Services
561591 Convention and Visitors Bureaus[US]
561599 All Other Travel Arrangement and Reservation Services[US]

5616 Investigation and Security Services

56161 Investigation, Guard, and Armored Car Services
561611 Investigation Services[CAN]
561612 Security Guards and Patrol Services[CAN]
561613 Armored Car Services[CAN]
56162 Security Systems Services
561621 Security Systems Services (except Locksmiths)[CAN]
561622 Locksmiths[CAN]

5617 Services to Buildings and Dwellings

56171 Exterminating and Pest Control Services
561710 Exterminating and Pest Control Services
56172 Janitorial Services
561720 Janitorial Services[MEX]
56173 Landscaping Services
561730 Landscaping Services
56174 Carpet and Upholstery Cleaning Services
561740 Carpet and Upholstery Cleaning Services
56179 Other Services to Buildings and Dwellings
561790 Other Services to Buildings and Dwellings[MEX]

5619 Other Support Services

56191 Packaging and Labeling Services
561910 Packaging and Labeling Services
56192 Convention and Trade Show Organizers

561920 Convention and Trade Show Organizers
56199 All Other Support Services
561990 All Other Support Services

562 Waste Management and Remediation Services

5621 Waste Collection[CAN]

56211 Waste Collection[CAN]
562111 Solid Waste Collection[US]
562112 Hazardous Waste Collection[US]
562119 Other Waste Collection[US]

5622 Waste Treatment and Disposal[CAN]

56221 Waste Treatment and Disposal[CAN]
562211 Hazardous Waste Treatment and Disposal[US]
562212 Solid Waste Landfill[US]
562213 Solid Waste Combustors and Incinerators[US]
562219 Other Nonhazardous Waste Treatment and Disposal[US]

5629 Remediation and Other Waste Management Services[CAN]

56291 Remediation Services[CAN]
562910 Remediation Services[CAN]
56292 Materials Recovery Facilities[CAN]
562920 Materials Recovery Facilities[CAN]
56299 All Other Waste Management Services[CAN]
562991 Septic Tank and Related Services[US]
562998 All Other Miscellaneous Waste Management Services[US]

61 Educational Services

611 Educational Services

6111 Elementary and Secondary Schools

61111 Elementary and Secondary Schools[CAN]
611110 Elementary and Secondary Schools[CAN]

6112 Junior Colleges

61121 Junior Colleges
611210 Junior Colleges[CAN]

6113 Colleges, Universities, and Professional Schools

61131 Colleges, Universities, and Professional Schools
611310 Colleges, Universities, and Professional Schools[CAN]

6114 Business Schools and Computer and Management Training

61141 Business and Secretarial Schools
611410 Business and Secretarial Schools^CAN
61142 Computer Training
611420 Computer Training^CAN
61143 Professional and Management Development Training
611430 Professional and Management Development Training^CAN

6115 Technical and Trade Schools

61151 Technical and Trade Schools
611511 Cosmetology and Barber Schools^US
611512 Flight Training^US
611513 Apprenticeship Training^US
611519 Other Technical and Trade Schools^US

6116 Other Schools and Instruction

61161 Fine Arts Schools
611610 Fine Arts Schools^CAN
61162 Sports and Recreation Instruction
611620 Sports and Recreation Instruction^CAN
61163 Language Schools
611630 Language Schools^CAN
61169 All Other Schools and Instruction
611691 Exam Preparation and Tutoring^US
611692 Automobile Driving Schools^US
611699 All Other Miscellaneous Schools and Instruction^US

6117 Educational Support Services

61171 Educational Support Services
611710 Educational Support Services

62 Health Care and Social Assistance

621 Ambulatory Health Care Services

6211 Offices of Physicians

62111 Offices of Physicians
621111 Offices of Physicians (except Mental Health Specialists)^US
621112 Offices of Physicians, Mental Health Specialists^US

6212 Offices of Dentists

62121 Offices of Dentists
621210 Offices of Dentists^CAN

6213 Offices of Other Health Practitioners

62131 Offices of Chiropractors
621310 Offices of Chiropractors[CAN]
62132 Offices of Optometrists
621320 Offices of Optometrists
62133 Offices of Mental Health Practitioners (except Physicians)
621330 Offices of Mental Health Practitioners (except Physicians)[CAN]
62134 Offices of Physical, Occupational and Speech Therapists, and Audiologists
621340 Offices of Physical, Occupational and Speech Therapists, and Audiologists[CAN]
62139 Offices of All Other Health Practitioners
621391 Offices of Podiatrists[US]
621399 Offices of All Other Miscellaneous Health Practitioners[US]

6214 Outpatient Care Centers

62141 Family Planning Centers
621410 Family Planning Centers[CAN]
62142 Outpatient Mental Health and Substance Abuse Centers
621420 Outpatient Mental Health and Substance Abuse Centers[CAN]
62149 Other Outpatient Care Centers
621491 HMO Medical Centers[US]
621492 Kidney Dialysis Centers[US]
621493 Freestanding Ambulatory Surgical and Emergency Centers[US]
621498 All Other Outpatient Care Centers[US]

6215 Medical and Diagnostic Laboratories

62151 Medical and Diagnostic Laboratories
621511 Medical Laboratories[US]
621512 Diagnostic Imaging Centers[US]

6216 Home Health Care Services

62161 Home Health Care Services
621610 Home Health Care Services

6219 Other Ambulatory Health Care Services

62191 Ambulance Services
621910 Ambulance Services[MEX]
62199 All Other Ambulatory Health Care Services
621991 Blood and Organ Banks[US]
621999 All Other Miscellaneous Ambulatory Health Care Services[US]

622 Hospitals

6221 General Medical and Surgical Hospitals

62211 General Medical and Surgical Hospitals
622110 General Medical and Surgical Hospitals[US]

6222 Psychiatric and Substance Abuse Hospitals

62221 Psychiatric and Substance Abuse Hospitals
622210 Psychiatric and Substance Abuse Hospitals[CAN]

6223 Specialty (except Psychiatric and Substance Abuse) Hospitals

62231 Specialty (except Psychiatric and Substance Abuse) Hospitals
622310 Specialty (except Psychiatric and Substance Abuse) Hospitals[CAN]

623 Nursing and Residential Care Facilities

6231 Nursing Care Facilities

62311 Nursing Care Facilities
623110 Nursing Care Facilities[CAN]

6232 Residential Mental Retardation, Mental Health and Substance Abuse Facilities

62321 Residential Mental Retardation Facilities
623210 Residential Mental Retardation Facilities[CAN]
62322 Residential Mental Health and Substance Abuse Facilities
623220 Residential Mental Health and Substance Abuse Facilities[US]

6233 Community Care Facilities for the Elderly

62331 Community Care Facilities for the Elderly
623311 Continuing Care Retirement Communities[US]
623312 Homes for the Elderly[US]

6239 Other Residential Care Facilities

62399 Other Residential Care Facilities
623990 Other Residential Care Facilities[US]

624 Social Assistance

6241 Individual and Family Services

62411 Child and Youth Services
624110 Child and Youth Services[CAN]
62412 Services for the Elderly and Persons with Disabilities

624120 Services for the Elderly and Persons with Disabilities[CAN]
62419 Other Individual and Family Services
624190 Other Individual and Family Services[CAN]

6242 Community Food and Housing, and Emergency and Other Relief Services

62421 Community Food Services
624210 Community Food Services[CAN]
62422 Community Housing Services
624221 Temporary Shelters[US]
624229 Other Community Housing Services[US]
62423 Emergency and Other Relief Services
624230 Emergency and Other Relief Services[CAN]

6243 Vocational Rehabilitation Services

62431 Vocational Rehabilitation Services
624310 Vocational Rehabilitation Services[CAN]

6244 Child Day Care Services

62441 Child Day Care Services
624410 Child Day Care Services[CAN]

71 Arts, Entertainment, and Recreation

711 Performing Arts, Spectator Sports, and Related Industries

7111 Performing Arts Companies

71111 Theater Companies and Dinner Theaters
711110 Theater Companies and Dinner Theaters[US]
71112 Dance Companies
711120 Dance Companies[CAN]
71113 Musical Groups and Artists
711130 Musical Groups and Artists[CAN]
71119 Other Performing Arts Companies
711190 Other Performing Arts Companies[CAN]

7112 Spectator Sports

71121 Spectator Sports
711211 Sports Teams and Clubs[CAN]
711212 Racetracks[US]
711219 Other Spectator Sports[US]

7113 Promoters of Performing Arts, Sports, and Similar Events

71131 Promoters of Performing Arts, Sports, and Similar Events with Facilities

711310 Promoters of Performing Arts, Sports, and Similar Events with Facilities[US]
71132 Promoters of Performing Arts, Sports, and Similar Events without Facilities
711320 Promoters of Performing Arts, Sports, and Similar Events without Facilities[MEX]

7114 Agents and Managers for Artists, Athletes, Entertainers, and Other Public Figures

71141 Agents and Managers for Artists, Athletes, Entertainers, and Other Public Figures
711410 Agents and Managers for Artists, Athletes, Entertainers, and Other Public Figures

7115 Independent Artists, Writers, and Performers

71151 Independent Artists, Writers, and Performers
711510 Independent Artists, Writers, and Performers

712 Museums, Historical Sites, and Similar Institutions

7121 Museums, Historical Sites, and Similar Institutions

71211 Museums
712110 Museums[US]
71212 Historical Sites
712120 Historical Sites
71213 Zoos and Botanical Gardens
712130 Zoos and Botanical Gardens[CAN]
71219 Nature Parks and Other Similar Institutions
712190 Nature Parks and Other Similar Institutions

713 Amusement, Gambling, and Recreation Industries

7131 Amusement Parks and Arcades

71311 Amusement and Theme Parks
713110 Amusement and Theme Parks[CAN]
71312 Amusement Arcades
713120 Amusement Arcades

7132 Gambling Industries

71321 Casinos (except Casino Hotels)
713210 Casinos (except Casino Hotels)
71329 Other Gambling Industries
713290 Other Gambling Industries[US]

7139 Other Amusement and Recreation Industries

71391 Golf Courses and Country Clubs
713910 Golf Courses and Country Clubs
71392 Skiing Facilities

713920 Skiing Facilities
71393 Marinas
713930 Marinas
71394 Fitness and Recreational Sports Centers
713940 Fitness and Recreational Sports Centers[CAN]
71395 Bowling Centers
713950 Bowling Centers
71399 All Other Amusement and Recreation Industries
713990 All Other Amusement and Recreation Industries[CAN]

72 Accommodation and Food Services

721 Accommodation

7211 Traveler Accommodation

72111 Hotels (except Casino Hotels) and Motels
721110 Hotels (except Casino Hotels) and Motels[US]
72112 Casino Hotels
721120 Casino Hotels
72119 Other Traveler Accommodation
721191 Bed-and-Breakfast Inns[CAN]
721199 All Other Traveler Accommodation[US]

7212 RV (Recreational Vehicle) Parks and Recreational Camps

72121 RV (Recreational Vehicle) Parks and Recreational Camps
721211 RV (Recreational Vehicle) Parks and Campgrounds[CAN]
721214 Recreational and Vacation Camps (except Campgrounds)[US]

7213 Rooming and Boarding Houses

72131 Rooming and Boarding Houses
721310 Rooming and Boarding Houses[CAN]

722 Food Services and Drinking Places

7221 Full-Service Restaurants

72211 Full-Service Restaurants
722110 Full-Service Restaurants[CAN]

7222 Limited-Service Eating Places

72221 Limited-Service Eating Places
722211 Limited-Service Restaurants[US]
722212 Cafeterias[US]
722213 Snack and Nonalcoholic Beverage Bars[US]

7223 Special Food Services

72231 Food Service Contractors
722310 Food Service Contractors
72232 Caterers
722320 Caterers
72233 Mobile Food Services
722330 Mobile Food Services

7224 Drinking Places (Alcoholic Beverages)

72241 Drinking Places (Alcoholic Beverages)
722410 Drinking Places (Alcoholic Beverages)[CAN]

81 Other Services (except Public Administration)

811 Repair and Maintenance

8111 Automotive Repair and Maintenance

81111 Automotive Mechanical and Electrical Repair and Maintenance
811111 General Automotive Repair[CAN]
811112 Automotive Exhaust System Repair[CAN]
811113 Automotive Transmission Repair[US]
811118 Other Automotive Mechanical and Electrical Repair and Maintenance[US]
81112 Automotive Body, Paint, Interior, and Glass Repair
811121 Automotive Body, Paint, and Interior Repair and Maintenance[CAN]
811122 Automotive Glass Replacement Shops[CAN]
81119 Other Automotive Repair and Maintenance
811191 Automotive Oil Change and Lubrication Shops[US]
811192 Car Washes[CAN]
811198 All Other Automotive Repair and Maintenance[US]

8112 Electronic and Precision Equipment Repair and Maintenance

81121 Electronic and Precision Equipment Repair and Maintenance
811211 Consumer Electronics Repair and Maintenance[MEX]
811212 Computer and Office Machine Repair and Maintenance[US]
811213 Communication Equipment Repair and Maintenance[US]
811219 Other Electronic and Precision Equipment Repair and Maintenance[US]

8113 Commercial and Industrial Machinery and Equipment (except Automotive and Electronic) Repair and Maintenance

81131 Commercial and Industrial Machinery and Equipment (except Automotive and Electronic) Repair and Maintenance

811310 Commercial and Industrial Machinery and Equipment (except Automotive and Electronic) Repair and Maintenance[CAN]

8114 Personal and Household Goods Repair and Maintenance

81141 Home and Garden Equipment and Appliance Repair and Maintenance

811411 Home and Garden Equipment Repair and Maintenance[CAN]

811412 Appliance Repair and Maintenance[CAN]

81142 Reupholstery and Furniture Repair

811420 Reupholstery and Furniture Repair

81143 Footwear and Leather Goods Repair

811430 Footwear and Leather Goods Repair

81149 Other Personal and Household Goods Repair and Maintenance

811490 Other Personal and Household Goods Repair and Maintenance[CAN]

812 Personal and Laundry Services

8121 Personal Care Services[CAN]

81211 Hair, Nail, and Skin Care Services[CAN]

812111 Barber Shops[US]

812112 Beauty Salons[US]

812113 Nail Salons[US]

81219 Other Personal Care Services[CAN]

812191 Diet and Weight Reducing Centers[US]

812199 Other Personal Care Services[US]

8122 Death Care Services[CAN]

81221 Funeral Homes and Funeral Services[CAN]

812210 Funeral Homes and Funeral Services[CAN]

81222 Cemeteries and Crematories[CAN]

812220 Cemeteries and Crematories[CAN]

8123 Drycleaning and Laundry Services[CAN]

81231 Coin-Operated Laundries and Drycleaners[CAN]

812310 Coin-Operated Laundries and Drycleaners[CAN]

81232 Drycleaning and Laundry Services (except Coin-Operated)[CAN]

812320 Drycleaning and Laundry Services (except Coin-Operated)[CAN]
81233 Linen and Uniform Supply[CAN]
812331 Linen Supply[US]
812332 Industrial Launderers[US]

8129 Other Personal Services[CAN]

81291 Pet Care (except Veterinary) Services[CAN]
812910 Pet Care (except Veterinary) Services[CAN]
81292 Photofinishing[CAN]
812921 Photofinishing Laboratories (except One-Hour)[CAN]
812922 One-Hour Photofinishing[CAN]
81293 Parking Lots and Garages[CAN]
812930 Parking Lots and Garages[CAN]
81299 All Other Personal Services[CAN]
812990 All Other Personal Services[CAN]

813 Religious, Grantmaking, Civic, Professional, and Similar Organizations

8131 Religious Organizations[CAN]

81311 Religious Organizations[CAN]
813110 Religious Organizations[CAN]

8132 Grantmaking and Giving Services[CAN]

81321 Grantmaking and Giving Services[CAN]
813211 Grantmaking Foundations[US]
813212 Voluntary Health Organizations[US]
813219 Other Grantmaking and Giving Services[US]

8133 Social Advocacy Organizations[CAN]

81331 Social Advocacy Organizations[CAN]
813311 Human Rights Organizations[US]
813312 Environment, Conservation and Wildlife Organizations[US]
813319 Other Social Advocacy Organizations[US]

8134 Civic and Social Organizations[CAN]

81341 Civic and Social Organizations[CAN]
813410 Civic and Social Organizations[CAN]

8139 Business, Professional, Labor, Political, and Similar Organizations[CAN]

81391 Business Associations[CAN]
813910 Business Associations[CAN]
81392 Professional Organizations[CAN]
813920 Professional Organizations[CAN]

81393 Labor Unions and Similar Labor Organizations[CAN]
813930 Labor Unions and Similar Labor Organizations[CAN]
81394 Political Organizations[CAN]
813940 Political Organizations[CAN]
81399 Other Similar Organizations (except Business, Professional, Labor, and Political Organizations)[CAN]
813990 Other Similar Organizations (except Business, Professional, Labor, and Political Organizations)[CAN]

814 Private Households

8141 Private Households

81411 Private Households
814110 Private Households

92 Public Administration

921 Executive, Legislative, and Other General Government Support[US]

9211 Executive, Legislative, and Other General Government Support[US]

92111 Executive Offices[US]
921110 Executive Offices[US]
92112 Legislative Bodies[US]
921120 Legislative Bodies[US]
92113 Public Finance Activities[US]
921130 Public Finance Activities[US]
92114 Executive and Legislative Offices, Combined[US]
921140 Executive and Legislative Offices, Combined[US]
92115 American Indian and Alaska Native Tribal Governments[US]
921150 American Indian and Alaska Native Tribal Governments[US]
92119 Other General Government Support[US]
921190 Other General Government Support[US]

922 Justice, Public Order, and Safety Activities[US]

9221 Justice, Public Order, and Safety Activities[US]

92211 Courts[US]
922110 Courts[US]
92212 Police Protection[US]
922120 Police Protection[US]
92213 Legal Counsel and Prosecution[US]

922130 Legal Counsel and Prosecution[US]
92214 Correctional Institutions[US]
922140 Correctional Institutions[US]
92215 Parole Offices and Probation Offices[US]
922150 Parole Offices and Probation Offices[US]
92216 Fire Protection[US]
922160 Fire Protection[US]
92219 Other Justice, Public Order, and Safety Activities[US]
922190 Other Justice, Public Order, and Safety Activities[US]

923 Administration of Human Resource Programs[US]

9231 Administration of Human Resource Programs[US]

92311 Administration of Education Programs[US]
923110 Administration of Education Programs[US]
92312 Administration of Public Health Programs[US]
923120 Administration of Public Health Programs[US]
92313 Administration of Human Resource Programs (except Education, Public Health, and Veterans' Affairs Programs)[US]
923130 Administration of Human Resource Programs (except Education, Public Health, and Veterans' Affairs Programs)[US]
92314 Administration of Veterans' Affairs[US]
923140 Administration of Veterans' Affairs[US]

924 Administration of Environmental Quality Programs[US]

9241 Administration of Environmental Quality Programs[US]

92411 Administration of Air and Water Resource and Solid Waste Management Programs[US]
924110 Administration of Air and Water Resource and Solid Waste Management Programs[US]
92412 Administration of Conservation Programs[US]
924120 Administration of Conservation Programs[US]

925 Administration of Housing Programs, Urban Planning, and Community Development[US]

9251 Administration of Housing Programs, Urban Planning, and Community Development[US]

92511 Administration of Housing Programs[US]
925110 Administration of Housing Programs[US]

92512 Administration of Urban Planning and Community and Rural Development[US]
925120 Administration of Urban Planning and Community and Rural Development[US]

926 Administration of Economic Programs[US]

9261 Administration of Economic Programs[US]

92611 Administration of General Economic Programs[US]
926110 Administration of General Economic Programs[US]
92612 Regulation and Administration of Transportation Programs[US]
926120 Regulation and Administration of Transportation Programs[US]
92613 Regulation and Administration of Communications, Electric, Gas, and Other Utilities[US]
926130 Regulation and Administration of Communications, Electric, Gas, and Other Utilities[US]
92614 Regulation of Agricultural Marketing and Commodities[US]
926140 Regulation of Agricultural Marketing and Commodities[US]
92615 Regulation, Licensing, and Inspection of Miscellaneous Commercial Sectors[US]
926150 Regulation, Licensing, and Inspection of Misccellaneous Commercial Sectors[US]

927 Space Research and Technology[US]

9271 Space Research and Technology[US]

92711 Space Research and Technology[US]
927110 Space Research and Technology[US]

928 National Security and International Affairs[US]

9281 National Security and International Affairs[US]

92811 National Security[US]
928110 National Security[US]
92812 International Affairs[US]
928120 International Affairs[US]

Frequently Asked Questions About Economic Classifications

1. What is the purpose of an industry classification system?
   - An industry classification system facilitates the collection, tabulation, presentation, and analysis of data relating to establishments and ensures that data about the U.S. economy published by U.S. statistical agencies are uniform and comparable. NAICS ensures that such data are uniform and comparable among the North American countries.
2. What is an establishment?
   - An establishment is generally a single, physical location at which economic activity occurs (e.g., store, factory, farm, etc.). An enterprise, on the other hand, may consist of more than one location performing the same or different types of economic activities. Each establishment of that enterprise is assigned a NAICS code.
3. In which industry is my company classified?
   - NAICS is an establishment classification system, not a company classification system. To determine in which industry each establishment of your company is classified, you should first identify the primary activity of each establishment and then go to the alphabetic list of activities in the NAICS United States Manual. Find that activity in the alphabetic index, turn to the industry description of the specified code, read the definition of the industry as printed in the description, and determine if that description fits the activities of your establishment. Electronic references are available at http://www.census.gov/naics.
4. How are NAICS codes assigned?
   - NAICS codes are assigned to each establishment of an enterprise based on the primary activity of that establishment. When a company applies for an Employer Identification Number (EIN), information about the type of activity in which that business is engaged is requested in order to assign a NAICS code. In addition, statistical programs such as those conducted by the Census Bureau and the Bureau of Labor Statistics assign NAICS codes based on information reported to them.
5. How do I apply for a NAICS code?
   - As explained above, NAICS codes are assigned based on the primary activity of the business establishment. You may contact the appropriate agency assigning codes for your particular need (see 4. Above).
6. Have the Small Business Administration's size standards been updated to reflect the NAICS 2002 codes?
   - You should contact the Office of Size Standards of the Small Business Administration, 409 Third Street SW, Washington, DC 20416 for this information. They can be reached at 202-205-6618.
7. How do the NAICS codes affect the Environmental Protection Agency's regulations?
   - You should contact the Environmental Protection Agency at 202-260-3071 for answers to those questions.

8. When will NAICS codes be used in Federal Procurement regulations?
   - You should contact the U.S. General Services Administration at 202-205-6618.
9. What are NAICS' principal advantages as compared with the SIC?
   - Relevance. NAICS is more relevant to today's economy, in which high-tech and services-producing industries are far more important than they were when the original structure of the SIC was established in the 1930s. NAICS identifies over 350 new industries and nine new service industry sectors.
   - Consistency. NAICS uses a consistent classification principle. Establishments that use similar production processes are grouped together.
   - Comparability among countries. NAICS will be used by the United States, Canada, and Mexico to produce comparable industry data.
   - Adaptability. NAICS will be reviewed every 5 years, so classifications can keep pace with the changing economy.
10. Will U.S. international trade data be available on a NAICS basis?
    - Data on international trade in goods are necessarily collected on a commodity basis, whereas NAICS, like SIC, data are on an establishment basis. Commodity groups approximating the NAICS categories have been developed, however, and have been published for the years 1997 through 1999. (These overlap with series for groups using SIC commodity group classifications in the year 1997.) It should be noted that some of the kinds of distinctions made in NAICS and other industry classifications cannot be made in commodity trade data. A notable example is printing and publishing. NAICS places publishing in the new Information industry and retains only printing in manufacturing. In commodity trade data, however, the entire value of imported and exported publications is included in the goods classification ''Printing, publishing and similar products.'' For additional information, please visit the Foreign Trade Statistics Web site at ⟨http://www.census.gov/foreign-trade⟩.
11. For some uses, market-based rather than production-based statistical classifications are more useful. Will NAICS be able to provide these?
    - A new North American Product Classification System (NAPCS) is under development, starting in nine service sectors.
12. How does NAICS 2002 differ from NAICS 1997?
    - Since NAICS 1997, there have been major changes in four sectors. Such changes are reflected in NAICS 2002.
    - The Construction sector has been reorganized to achieve greater comparability among the statistical systems of the United States, Canada, and Mexico.
    - The Information sector has also been reorganized.
    - For the United States, additional industry detail has been added in both Wholesale and Retail Trade.

For answers to other NAICS questions, you may visit the NAICS Web site at ⟨http://www.census.gov/naics⟩.

Directory of Selected Federal Government Agencies

Government agencies involved in the development of NAICS are listed below. Also listed are government agencies that use NAICS in the collection and dissemination of data, or in the implementation of their programs.

U.S. Economic Classification Policy Committee (ECPC)

Office of Management and Budget
Statistical Policy Branch
725 17th Street, NW
Washington, DC 20503
(202) 395-3093
fax (202) 395-7245
http://www.whitehouse.gov/omb/

Bureau of Economic Analysis, Department of Commerce
1441 L Street, NW
Washington, DC 20230
(202) 606-9219
fax (202) 606-5321
http://www.bea.gov

Bureau of Labor Statistics, Department of Labor
Division of Administrative Statistics and Labor Turnover
2 Massachusetts Avenue, NE
Room 4840
Washington, DC 20212
(202) 691-6567
fax: (202) 691-6645
email: naics_stf@bls.gov
http://www.bls.gov

Bureau of the Census, Department of Commerce
Service Sector Statistics Division
Suitland Federal Center
Washington, DC 20233
(301) 763-5172
http://www.census.gov/naics

Other Agencies Implementing NAICS

Department of Agriculture
http://www.usda.gov

National Agriculture Statistics Service
fax (202) 720-8738
http://www.usda.gov/nass/

Survey Administration Branch
1400 Independence Avenue, SW
Washington, DC 20250
(202) 720-2248
Agriculture Data and Classification Structure

Commodities Secretary
1400 Independence Avenue, SW
Washington, DC 20250
(202) 690-8747
Census of Agriculture Data

Economic Research Service
1800 M Street, NW
Washington, DC 20036-5831
(202) 694-5395
fax (202) 694-5757
http://www.ers.usda.gov

Forest Service
Research and Development Economist
P.O. Box 96090
Washington, DC 20090-6090
(703) 605-4887
fax (703) 605-5137
email ddarr@fs.fed.us
http://www.fs.fed.us

Department of Commerce
International Trade Administration
Office of Trade and Economic Analysis
14th Street and Constitution Avenue, NW
Washington, DC 20230
(202) 482-5145
fax (202) 482-4614
http://www.ita.doc.gov/td/industry/otea/

Department of Defense
Central Contractor Registration (CCR) Assistance Center
Defense Logistics Information Service
(888) 227-2423
(616) 961-4725
email dlis_support@dlis.dla.mil
http://www.ccr.gov

Department of Energy

Energy Information Administration
National Energy Information Center
1000 Independence Avenue, SW
Washington, DC 20585-0001
(202) 586-8800
fax (202) 586-0721
email infoctr@eia.doe.gov
http://www.eia.doe.gov

Department of the Interior

U.S. Geological Survey
Geological Division
Minerals Information Team
988 National Center
Reston, VA 22092
(703) 648-6410
fax (703) 648-4995
http://minerals.usgs.gov/minerals/

Department of Justice

Immigration and Naturalization Service
425 I Street, NW
Washington, DC 20536
(800) 375-5283
TTY: (800) 767-1833
http://www.ins.usdoj.gov

Department of Labor

Occupational Safety and Health Administration (OSHA)
Office of Statistics
200 Constitution Avenue, NW
Washington, DC 20210
(202) 693-1702
fax (202) 693-1631
http://www.osha.gov

Department of Transportation

Bureau of Transportation Statistics
Transportation Studies
400 7th Street, SW
Washington, DC 20590
(202) 366-1270
fax (202) 366-3640
http://www.bts.gov

Department of the Treasury
Internal Revenue Service
Statistics of Income Division
1111 Constitution Avenue, NW
Washington, DC 20224
(202) 874-0700
fax (202) 874-0964
http://www.irs.ustreas.gov/prod/taxstats/othsoi.html

Environmental Protection Agency
1200 Pennsylvania Avenue, NW
Washington, DC 20460
http://www.epa.gov

Office of Environmental Information
Environmental Data Registry
(202) 260-3071
http://www.epa.gov/edr/

Federal Reserve Board
Industrial Production
20th and C Streets, NW
Washington, DC 20551
(202) 452-3197
http://www.federalreserve.gov

General Services Administration
Federal Procurement Data Center
7th and D Street, SW, Room 5652
Washington, DC 20407
(202) 401-1529
fax (202) 401-1546
http://www.fpdc.gov

International Trade Commission
500 E Street, SW
Washington, DC 20436
http://www.usitc.gov

Office of Economics
(202) 205-3277
fax (202) 205-2340

Office of Industries
(202) 205-3296
fax (202) 205-3161

Office of Information Services
Statistical and Editorial Services Division
General Information
(202) 205-2513
fax (202) 205-2024

Small Business Administration
409 3rd Street, SW
Washington, DC 20416
email answerdesk@sba.gov
http://www.sba.gov

Office of Advocacy
(202) 205-6533
fax (202) 205-6928
http://www.sba.gov/ADVO/

Office of Government Contracting and Business Development
Size Standards Staff
(202) 205-6618
fax (202) 205-6390
sizestandards@sba.gov
http://www.sba.gov/size/

Part I

Titles and Descriptions of Industries

Sector 11—Agriculture, Forestry, Fishing and Hunting

The Sector as a Whole

The Agriculture, Forestry, Fishing and Hunting sector comprises establishments primarily engaged in growing crops, raising animals, harvesting timber, and harvesting fish and other animals from a farm, ranch, or their natural habitats.

The establishments in this sector are often described as farms, ranches, dairies, greenhouses, nurseries, orchards, or hatcheries. A farm may consist of a single tract of land or a number of separate tracts which may be held under different tenures. For example, one tract may be owned by the farm operator and another rented. It may be operated by the operator alone or with the assistance of members of the household or hired employees, or it may be operated by a partnership, corporation, or other type of organization. When a landowner has one or more tenants, renters, croppers, or managers, the land operated by each is considered a farm.

The sector distinguishes two basic activities: agricultural production and agricultural support activities. Agricultural production includes establishments performing the complete farm or ranch operation, such as farm owner-operators, tenant farm operators, and sharecroppers. Agricultural support activities include establishments that perform one or more activities associated with farm operation, such as soil preparation, planting, harvesting, and management, on a contract or fee basis.

Excluded from the Agriculture, Forestry, Hunting and Fishing sector are establishments primarily engaged in agricultural research and establishments primarily engaged in administering programs for regulating and conserving land, mineral, wildlife, and forest use. These establishments are classified in Industry 54171, Research and Development in the Physical, Engineering, and Life Sciences; and Industry 92412, Administration of Conservation Programs, respectively.

111 Crop Production

Industries in the Crop Production subsector grow crops mainly for food and fiber. The subsector comprises establishments, such as farms, orchards, groves, greenhouses, and nurseries, primarily engaged in growing crops, plants, vines, or trees and their seeds.

The industries in this subsector are grouped by similarity of production activity, including biological and physiological characteristics and economic requirements, the length of growing season, degree of crop rotation, extent of input specialization, labor requirements, and capital demands. The production process is typically completed when the raw product or commodity grown reaches the ''farm gate'' for market, that is, at the point of first sale or price determination.

US—United States industry only. CAN—United States and Canadian industries are comparable. MEX—United States and Mexican industries are comparable. Blank—Canadian, Mexican, and United States industries are comparable.

Establishments are classified to the crop production subsector when crop production (i.e., value of crops for market) accounts for one-half or more of the establishment's total agricultural production. Within the subsector, establishments are classified to a specific industry when a product or industry family of products (i.e., oilseed and grain farming, vegetable and melon farming, fruit and tree nut farming) account for one-half or more of the establishment's agricultural production. Establishments with one-half or more crop production with no one product or family of products of an industry accounting for one-half of the establishment's agricultural production are treated as general combination crop farming and are classified in Industry 11199, All Other Crop Farming.

Industries in the Crop Production subsector include establishments that own, operate, and manage and those that operate and manage. Those that manage only are classified in Subsector 115, Support Activities for Agriculture and Forestry.

1111 Oilseed and Grain Farming

This industry group comprises establishments primarily engaged in (1) growing oilseed and/or grain crops and/or (2) producing oilseed and grain seeds. These crops have an annual life cycle and are typically grown in open fields.

11111 Soybean Farming

See industry description for 111110 below.

111110 Soybean Farming

This industry comprises establishments primarily engaged in growing soybeans and/or producing soybean seeds.

Cross-References.

Establishments engaged in growing soybeans in combination with grain(s) with the soybeans or grain(s) not accounting for one-half of the establishment's agricultural production (value of crops for market) are classified in U.S. Industry 111191, Oilseed and Grain Combination Farming.

11112 Oilseed (except Soybean) Farming

See industry description for 111120 below.

111120 Oilseed (except Soybean) Farming[CAN]

This industry comprises establishments primarily engaged in growing fibrous oilseed producing plants and/or producing oilseed seeds, such as sunflower, safflower, flax, rape, canola, and sesame.

US—United States industry only. CAN—United States and Canadian industries are comparable. MEX—United States and Mexican industries are comparable. Blank—Canadian, Mexican, and United States industries are comparable.

Cross-References. Establishments primarily engaged in—

- Growing soybeans—are classified in Industry 111110, Soybean Farming; and
- Growing oilseed(s) in combination with grain(s) with no one oilseed (or family of oilseeds) or grain(s) (or family of grains) accounting for one-half of the establishment's agricultural production (value of crops for market)—are classified in U.S. Industry 111191, Oilseed and Grain Combination Farming.

11113 Dry Pea and Bean Farming

See industry description for 111130 below.

111130 Dry Pea and Bean Farming[CAN]

This industry comprises establishments primarily engaged in growing dry peas, beans, and/or lentils.

Cross-References.

Establishments primarily engaged in growing fresh green beans and peas are classified in U.S. Industry 111219, Other Vegetable (except Potato) and Melon Farming.

11114 Wheat Farming

See industry description for 111140 below.

111140 Wheat Farming

This industry comprises establishments primarily engaged in growing wheat and/or producing wheat seeds.

Cross-References.

Establishments growing wheat in combination with oilseed(s) with the wheat or oilseed(s) not accounting for one-half of the establishment's agricultural production (value of crops for market) are classified in U.S. Industry 111191, Oilseed and Grain Combination Farming.

11115 Corn Farming

See industry description for 111150 below.

US—United States industry only. CAN—United States and Canadian industries are comparable. MEX—United States and Mexican industries are comparable. Blank—Canadian, Mexican, and United States industries are comparable.

111150 Corn Farming[CAN]

This industry comprises establishments primarily engaged in growing corn (except sweet corn) and/or producing corn seeds.

Cross-References. Establishments primarily engaged in—

- Growing sweet corn—are classified in U.S. Industry 111219, Other Vegetable (except Potato) and Melon Farming; and
- Growing corn in combination with oilseed(s) with the corn or oilseed(s) not accounting for one-half of the establishment's production (value of crops for market)—are classified in U.S. Industry 111191, Oilseed and Grain Combination Farming.

11116 Rice Farming

See industry description for 111160 below.

111160 Rice Farming

This industry comprises establishments primarily engaged in growing rice (except wild rice) and/or producing rice seeds.

Cross-References. Establishments primarily engaged in—

- Growing wild rice—are classified in U.S. Industry 111199, All Other Grain Farming; and
- Engaged in growing rice in combination with oilseed(s) with the rice or oilseed(s) not accounting for one-half of the establishment's agricultural production (value of crops for market)—are classified in U.S. Industry 111191, Oilseed and Grain Combination Farming.

11119 Other Grain Farming

This industry comprises establishments primarily engaged in (1) growing grain(s) and/or producing grain seeds (except wheat, corn, and rice) or (2) growing a combination of grain(s) and oilseed(s) with no one grain (or family of grains) or oilseed (or family of oilseeds) accounting for one-half of the establishment's agriculture production (value of crops for market). Combination grain(s) and oilseed(s) establishments may produce oilseed(s) and grain(s) seeds and/or grow oilseed(s) and grain(s).

US—United States industry only. CAN—United States and Canadian industries are comparable. MEX—United States and Mexican industries are comparable. Blank—Canadian, Mexican, and United States industries are comparable.

Illustrative Examples:

Barley farming
Milo farming
Oat farming
Oilseed and grain combination farming
Rye farming
Sorghum farming
Wild rice farming

Cross-References. Establishments primarily engaged in—

- Growing wheat—are classified in U.S. Industry 11114, Wheat Farming;
- Growing corn (except sweet corn)—are classified in U.S. Industry 11115, Corn Farming;
- Growing sweet corn—are classified in U.S. Industry 11121, Vegetable and Melon Farming; and
- Growing rice (except wild rice)—are classified in U.S. Industry 11116, Rice Farming.

111191 Oilseed and Grain Combination Farming[US]

This U.S. industry comprises establishments engaged in growing a combination of oilseed(s) and grain(s) with no one oilseed (or family of oilseeds) or grain (or family of grains) accounting for one-half of the establishment's agricultural production (value of crops for market). These establishments may produce oilseed(s) and grain(s) seeds and/or grow oilseed(s) and grain(s).

Cross-References.

Establishments engaged in growing one grain (or family of grains) or oilseed (or family of oilseeds) accounting for one-half of the establishment's agriculture production (value of crops for market) are classified in Industry Group 1111, Oilseed and Grain Farming accordingly by the prominent grain(s) or oilseed(s) grown.

111199 All Other Grain Farming[US]

This U.S. industry comprises establishments primarily engaged in growing grains and/or producing grain(s) seeds (except wheat, corn, rice, and oilseed(s) and grain(s) combinations).

Illustrative Examples:

Barley farming
Oat farming
Rye farming
Sorghum farming
Wild Rice farming

US—United States industry only. CAN—United States and Canadian industries are comparable. MEX—United States and Mexican industries are comparable. Blank—Canadian, Mexican, and United States industries are comparable.

Cross-References. Establishments primarily engaged in—

- Growing wheat—are classified in Industry 111140, Wheat Farming;
- Growing corn—are classified in Industry 111150, Corn Farming;
- Growing rice (except wild rice)—are classified in Industry 111160, Rice Farming;
- Growing sweet corn—are classified in U.S. Industry 111219, Other Vegetable (except Potato) and Melon Farming; and
- Growing a combination of grain(s) and oilseed(s) with no one grain (or family of grains) or oilseed (or family of oilseeds) accounting for one-half of the establishment's agricultural production (value of crops for market)—are classified in U.S. Industry 111191, Oilseed and Grain Combination Farming.

1112 Vegetable and Melon Farming

This industry group comprises establishments primarily engaged in growing root and tuber crops (except sugar beets and peanuts) or edible plants and/or producing root and tuber or edible plant seeds. The crops included in this group have an annual growth cycle and are grown in open fields. Climate and cultural practices limit producing areas but often permit the growing of a combination of crops in a year.

11121 Vegetable and Melon Farming

This industry comprises establishments primarily engaged in one or more of the following: (1) growing vegetable and/or melon crops; (2) producing vegetable and melon seeds; and (3) growing vegetable and/or melon bedding plants.

Cross-References. Establishments primarily engaged in—

- Growing sugar beets—are classified in Industry 11199, All Other Crop Farming;
- Growing vegetables and melons under glass or protective cover—are classified in Industry 11141, Food Crops Grown Under Cover;
- Growing dry peas and beans—are classified in Industry 11113, Dry Pea and Bean Farming;
- Growing corn (except sweet corn)—are classified in Industry 11115, Corn Farming;
- Canning, pickling, and/or drying (artificially) vegetables—are classified in Industry 31142, Fruit and Vegetable Canning, Pickling and Drying; and

---

US—United States industry only. CAN—United States and Canadian industries are comparable. MEX—United States and Mexican industries are comparable. Blank—Canadian, Mexican, and United States industries are comparable.

- Growing fruit on trees and other fruit-bearing plants (except melons)—are classified in Industry Group 1113, Fruit and Tree Nut Farming.

111211 Potato Farming[CAN]

This U.S. industry comprises establishments primarily engaged in growing potatoes and/or producing seed potatoes (except sweet potatoes).

Cross-References. Establishments primarily engaged in—

- Growing sweet potatoes, cassava, and yams—are classified in U.S. Industry 111219, Other Vegetable (except Potato) and Melon Farming; and
- Canning or drying potatoes—are classified in Industry 31142, Fruit and Vegetable Canning, Pickling and Drying.

111219 Other Vegetable (except Potato) and Melon Farming[CAN]

This U.S. industry comprises establishments primarily engaged in one or more of the following: (1) growing melons and/or vegetables (except potatoes; dry peas; dry beans; field, silage, or seed corn; and sugar beets); (2) producing vegetable and/or melon seeds; and (3) growing vegetable and/or melon bedding plants.

Illustrative Examples:

Carrot farming
Green bean farming
Melon farming (e.g., cantaloupe, casaba, honeydew, watermelon)
Pepper farming (e.g., bell, chili, green, red, sweet peppers)
Squash farming
Sweet potato farming
Tomato farming
Vegetable (except potato) and melon farming
Watermelon farming

Cross-References. Establishments primarily engaged in—

- Growing potatoes—are classified in U.S. Industry 111211, Potato Farming;
- Growing sugar beets—are classified in U.S. Industry 111991, Sugar Beet Farming;
- Growing vegetables and melons under glass or protective cover—are classified in U.S. Industry 111419, Other Food Crops Grown Under Cover;
- Growing dry peas and beans—are classified in Industry 111130, Dry Pea and Bean Farming;
- Growing corn (except sweet corn)—are classified in Industry 111150, Corn Farming;

US—United States industry only. CAN—United States and Canadian industries are comparable. MEX—United States and Mexican industries are comparable. Blank—Canadian, Mexican, and United States industries are comparable.

- Canning, pickling, and/or drying (artificially) vegetables—are classified in Industry 31142, Fruit and Vegetable Canning, Pickling and Drying; and
- Growing fruit on trees and other fruit-bearing plants (except melons)—are classified in Industry Group 1113, Fruit and Tree Nut Farming.

1113 Fruit and Tree Nut Farming

This industry group comprises establishments primarily engaged in growing fruit and/or tree nut crops. The crops included in this industry group are generally not grown from seeds and have a perennial life cycle.

11131 Orange Groves

See industry description for 111310 below.

111310 Orange Groves

This industry comprises establishments primarily engaged in growing oranges.

11132 Citrus (except Orange) Groves

See industry description for 111320 below.

111320 Citrus (except Orange) Groves[CAN]

This industry comprises establishments primarily engaged in growing citrus fruits (except oranges).

Illustrative Examples:

Citrus groves (except oranges)
Grapefruit groves
Lemon groves
Mandarin groves
Tangelo groves
Tangerine groves

Cross-References.

Establishments primarily engaged in growing oranges are classified in Industry 111310, Orange Groves.

11133 Noncitrus Fruit and Tree Nut Farming

This industry comprises establishments primarily engaged in one or more of the following: (1) growing noncitrus fruits (e.g., apples, grapes, berries, peaches);

US—United States industry only. CAN—United States and Canadian industries are comparable. MEX—United States and Mexican industries are comparable. Blank—Canadian, Mexican, and United States industries are comparable.

(2) growing tree nuts (e.g., pecans, almonds, pistachios); or (3) growing a combination of fruit(s) and tree nut(s) with no one fruit (or family of fruit) or family of tree nuts accounting for one-half of the establishment's agriculture production (value of crops for market).

Cross-References. Establishments primarily engaged in—

- Harvesting berries or nuts from native and noncultivated plants—are classified in Industry 11321, Forest Nurseries and Gathering of Forest Products; and
- Canning and/or drying (artificially) fruit—are classified in Industry 31142, Fruit and Vegetable Canning, Pickling and Drying.

111331 Apple Orchards[US]

This U.S. industry comprises establishments primarily engaged in growing apples.

Cross-References.

Establishments engaged in growing apples in combination with tree nut(s) with the apples or family of tree nuts not accounting for one-half of the establishment's agriculture production (i.e., value of crops for market) are classified in U.S. Industry 111336, Fruit and Tree Nut Combination Farming.

111332 Grape Vineyards[US]

This U.S. industry comprises establishments primarily engaged in growing grapes and/or growing grapes to sun dry into raisins.

Cross-References. Establishments primarily engaged in—

- Drying grapes artificially—are classified in U.S. Industry 311423, Dried and Dehydrated Food Manufacturing; and
- Growing grapes in combination with tree nut(s) with the grapes or family of tree nuts not accounting for one-half of the establishment's agriculture production (i.e., value of crops for market)—are classified in U.S. Industry 111336, Fruit and Tree Nut Combination Farming.

111333 Strawberry Farming[US]

This U.S. industry comprises establishments primarily engaged in growing strawberries.

US—United States industry only. CAN—United States and Canadian industries are comparable. MEX—United States and Mexican industries are comparable. Blank—Canadian, Mexican, and United States industries are comparable.

Cross-References.

Establishments engaged in growing strawberries in combination with tree nut(s) with the strawberries or family of tree nuts not accounting for one-half of the establishment's agriculture production (i.e., value of crops for market) are classified in U.S. Industry 111336, Fruit and Tree Nut Combination Farming.

111334 Berry (except Strawberry) Farming[US]

This U.S. industry comprises establishments primarily engaged in growing berries.

Illustrative Examples:

Berry (except strawberries) farming
Blackberry farming
Blueberry farming
Cranberry farming
Currant farming
Raspberry farming

Cross-References. Establishments primarily engaged in—

- Growing strawberries—are classified in U.S. Industry 111333, Strawberry Farming;
- Harvesting berries from native and noncultivated bushes or vines—are classified in Industry 113210, Forest Nurseries and Gathering of Forest Products; and
- Growing berries in combination with tree nut(s) with the berries or family of tree nuts not accounting for one-half of the establishment's agriculture production (i.e., value of crops for market)—are classified in U.S. Industry 111336, Fruit and Tree Nut Combination Farming.

111335 Tree Nut Farming[US]

This U.S. industry comprises establishments primarily engaged in growing tree nuts.

Illustrative Examples:

Almond farming
Filbert farming
Macadamia farming
Pecan farming
Pistachio farming
Tree nut farming
Walnut farming

Cross-References. Establishments primarily engaged in—

- Growing coconut and coffee—are classified in U.S. Industry 111339, Other Noncitrus Fruit Farming; and

US—United States industry only. CAN—United States and Canadian industries are comparable. MEX—United States and Mexican industries are comparable. Blank—Canadian, Mexican, and United States industries are comparable.

- Growing tree nut(s) in combination with fruit(s) with no one fruit (or family of fruit or of tree nuts) accounting for one-half of the establishment's agriculture production (i.e., value of crops for market)—are classified in U.S. Industry 111336, Fruit and Tree Nut Combination Farming.

111336 Fruit and Tree Nut Combination Farming[US]

This U.S. industry comprises establishments primarily engaged in growing a combination of fruit(s) and tree nut(s) with no one fruit (or family of fruit) or family of tree nuts accounting for one-half of the establishment's agriculture production (i.e., value of crops for market).

Cross-References.

Establishments engaged in growing fruit(s) or the family of tree nut(s) accounting for one-half of the establishment's agriculture production (i.e., value of crops for market) are classified in Industry Group 1113, Fruit and Tree Nut Farming accordingly by the prominent fruit(s) or tree nut(s) grown.

111339 Other Noncitrus Fruit Farming[US]

This U.S. industry comprises establishments primarily engaged in growing noncitrus fruits (except apples, grapes, berries, and fruit(s) and tree nut(s) combinations).

Illustrative Examples:

Apricot farming
Banana farming
Cherry farming
Coffee farming
Date farming
Fig farming
Noncitrus fruit farming
Peach farming
Pineapple farming
Prune farming

Cross-References. Establishments primarily engaged in—

- Growing apples—are classified in U.S. Industry 111331, Apple Orchards;
- Growing grapes including sun drying of grapes into raisins—are classified in U.S. Industry 111332, Grape Vineyards;
- Growing strawberries—are classified in U.S. Industry 111333, Strawberry Farming;
- Growing berries (except strawberries)—are classified in U.S. Industry 111334, Berry (except Strawberry) Farming;

US—United States industry only. CAN—United States and Canadian industries are comparable. MEX—United States and Mexican industries are comparable. Blank—Canadian, Mexican, and United States industries are comparable.

- Drying fruit artificially—are classified in U.S. Industry 311423, Dried and Dehydrated Food Manufacturing; and
- Growing noncitrus fruit(s) in combination with tree nut(s) with no one fruit (or family of fruits) or family of tree nuts accounting for one-half of the establishment's agriculture production (i.e., value of crops for market)—are classified in U.S. Industry 111336, Fruit and Tree Nut Combination Farming.

1114 Greenhouse, Nursery, and Floriculture Production

This industry group comprises establishments primarily engaged in growing crops of any kind under cover and/or growing nursery stock and flowers. ''Under cover'' is generally defined as greenhouses, cold frames, cloth houses, and lath houses. The crops grown are removed at various stages of maturity and have annual and perennial life cycles. The nursery stock includes short rotation woody crops that have growth cycles of 10 years or less.

11141 Food Crops Grown Under Cover

This industry comprises establishments primarily engaged in growing food crops (e.g., fruits, melons, tomatoes) under glass or protective cover.

Cross-References.

Establishments primarily engaged in growing vegetable and melon bedding plants are classified in Industry 11121, Vegetable and Melon Farming.

111411 Mushroom Production[CAN]

This U.S. industry comprises establishments primarily engaged in growing mushrooms under cover in mines underground, or in other controlled environments.

111419 Other Food Crops Grown Under Cover[CAN]

This U.S. industry comprises establishments primarily engaged in growing food crops (except mushrooms) under glass or protective cover.

Illustrative Examples:

Alfalfa sprout farming, grown under cover
Fruit farming, grown under cover
Hydroponic crop farming
Melon farming, grown under cover
Vegetable farming, grown under cover

US—United States industry only. CAN—United States and Canadian industries are comparable. MEX—United States and Mexican industries are comparable. Blank—Canadian, Mexican, and United States industries are comparable.

Cross-References.

Establishments primarily engaged in growing mushrooms under cover are classified in U.S. Industry 111411, Mushroom Production.

11142 Nursery and Floriculture Production

This industry comprises establishments primarily engaged in (1) growing nursery and floriculture products (e.g., nursery stock, shrubbery, cut flowers, flower seeds, foliage plants) under cover or in open fields and/or (2) growing short rotation woody trees with a growing and harvesting cycle of 10 years or less for pulp or tree stock (e.g., cut Christmas trees, cottonwoods).

Cross-References. Establishments primarily engaged in—

- Growing vegetable and melon bedding plants—are classified in Industry 11121, Vegetable and Melon Farming;
- Operating timber tracts (i.e., growing cycle greater than 10 years)—are classified in Industry 11311, Timber Tract Operations; and
- Retailing nursery, tree stock, and floriculture products primarily purchased from others—are classified in Industry 44422, Nursery, Garden Center, and Farm Supply Stores.

111421 Nursery and Tree Production[CAN]

This U.S. industry comprises establishments primarily engaged in (1) growing nursery products, nursery stock, shrubbery, bulbs, fruit stock, sod, and so forth, under cover or in open fields and/or (2) growing short rotation woody trees with a growth and harvest cycle of 10 years or less for pulp or tree stock.

Cross-References. Establishments primarily engaged in—

- Growing vegetable and melon bedding plants—are classified in Industry 11121, Vegetable and Melon Farming;
- Operating timber tracts (i.e., growing cycle greater than 10 years)—are classified in Industry 113110, Timber Tract Operations; and
- Retailing nursery, tree stock, and floriculture products primarily purchased from others—are classified in Industry 444220, Nursery, Garden Center, and Farm Supply Stores.

111422 Floriculture Production[CAN]

This U.S. industry comprises establishments primarily engaged in growing and/ or producing floriculture products (e.g., cut flowers and roses, cut cultivated

US—United States industry only. CAN—United States and Canadian industries are comparable. MEX—United States and Mexican industries are comparable. Blank—Canadian, Mexican, and United States industries are comparable.

greens, potted flowering and foliage plants, and flower seeds) under cover and in open fields.

Cross-References.

Establishments primarily engaged in retailing floriculture products primarily purchased from others are classified in Industry 444220, Nursery, Garden Center, and Farm Supply Stores.

1119 Other Crop Farming

This industry group comprises establishments primarily engaged in (1) growing crops (except oilseed and/or grain; vegetable and/or melon; fruit and tree nut; and greenhouse, nursery, and/or floriculture products). These establishments grow crops, such as tobacco, cotton, sugarcane, hay, sugar beets, peanuts, agave, herbs and spices, and hay and grass seeds; or (2) growing a combination of crops (except a combination of oilseed(s) and grain(s) and a combination of fruit(s) and tree nut(s)).

11191 Tobacco Farming

See industry description for 111910 below.

111910 Tobacco Farming

This industry comprises establishments primarily engaged in growing tobacco.

11192 Cotton Farming

See industry description for 111920 below.

111920 Cotton Farming

This industry comprises establishments primarily engaged in growing cotton.

Cross-References.

Establishments primarily engaged in ginning cotton are classified in U.S. Industry 115111, Cotton Ginning.

11193 Sugarcane Farming

See industry description for 111930 below.

US—United States industry only. CAN—United States and Canadian industries are comparable. MEX—United States and Mexican industries are comparable. Blank—Canadian, Mexican, and United States industries are comparable.

111930 Sugarcane Farming

This industry comprises establishments primarily engaged in growing sugarcane.

11194 Hay Farming

See industry description for 111940 below.

111940 Hay Farming[CAN]

This industry comprises establishments primarily engaged in growing hay, alfalfa, clover, and/or mixed hay.

Cross-References. Establishments primarily engaged in—

- Growing grain hay—are classified in Industry Group 1111, Oilseed and Grain Farming; and
- Growing grass and hay seeds—are classified in U.S. Industry 111998, All Other Miscellaneous Crop Farming.

11199 All Other Crop Farming

This industry comprises establishments primarily engaged in (1) growing crops (except oilseeds and/or grains; vegetables and/or melons; fruits and/or tree nuts; greenhouse, nursery and/or floriculture products; tobacco; cotton; sugarcane; or hay) or (2) growing a combination of crops (except a combination of oilseed(s) and grain(s); and a combination of fruit(s) and tree nut(s)) with no one crop or family of crops accounting for one-half of the establishment's agricultural production (i.e., value of crops for market).

Illustrative Examples:

Agave farming
Algae farming
General combination crop farming (except oilseed and grain; vegetables and melons; fruit and nut combinations)
Grass seed farming
Hay seed farming
Maple sap gathering
Peanut farming
Spice farming
Sugar beet farming
Tea farming

Cross-References. Establishments primarily engaged in—

- Growing oilseeds and/or wheat, corn, rice, or other grains—are classified in Industry Group 1111, Oilseed and Grain Farming;
- Growing vegetables and/or melons—are classified in Industry Group 1112, Vegetable and Melon Farming;

US—United States industry only. CAN—United States and Canadian industries are comparable. MEX—United States and Mexican industries are comparable. Blank—Canadian, Mexican, and United States industries are comparable.

- Growing fruits and/or tree nuts—are classified in Industry Group 1113, Fruit and Tree Nut Farming;
- Growing greenhouse, nursery, and/or floriculture products—are classified in Industry Group 1114, Greenhouse, Nursery, and Floriculture Production;
- Growing tobacco—are classified in Industry 11191, Tobacco Farming;
- Growing cotton—are classified in Industry 11192, Cotton Farming;
- Growing sugarcane—are classified in Industry 11193, Sugarcane Farming; and
- Growing hay—are classified in Industry 11194, Hay Farming.

111991 Sugar Beet Farming[US]

This U.S. industry comprises establishments primarily engaged in growing sugar beets.

Cross-References.

Establishments primarily engaged in growing beets (except sugar beets) are classified in U.S. Industry 111219, Other Vegetable (except Potato) and Melon Farming.

111992 Peanut Farming[MEX]

This U.S. industry comprises establishments primarily engaged in growing peanuts.

111998 All Other Miscellaneous Crop Farming[US]

This U.S. industry comprises establishments primarily engaged in one of the following: (1) growing crops (except oilseeds and/or grains; vegetables and/or melons; fruits and/or tree nuts; greenhouse, nursery and/or floriculture products; tobacco; cotton; sugarcane; hay; sugar beets; or peanuts); (2) growing a combination of crops (except a combination of oilseed(s) and grain(s); and a combination of fruit(s) and tree nut(s)) with no one crop or family of crop(s) accounting for one-half of the establishment's agricultural production (i.e., value of crops for market); or (3) gathering tea or maple sap.

Illustrative Examples:

Agave farming
Algae farming
Grass seed farming
Hay seed farming

US—United States industry only. CAN—United States and Canadian industries are comparable. MEX—United States and Mexican industries are comparable. Blank—Canadian, Mexican, and United States industries are comparable.

General combination crop farming (except oilseed and grain; vegetables and melons; fruit and tree nut combinations)

Hop farming

Mint farming

Spice farming

Cross-References. Establishment primarily engaged in—

- Growing oilseeds and/or wheat, corn, rice, or other grains—are classified in Industry Group 1111, Oilseed and Grain Farming;
- Growing vegetables and/or melons—are classified in Industry Group 1112, Vegetable and Melon Farming;
- Growing fruits and/or tree nuts—are classified in Industry Group 1113, Fruit and Tree Nut Farming;
- Growing greenhouse, nursery and/or floriculture products—are classified in Industry Group 1114, Greenhouse, Nursery, and Floriculture Production;
- Growing tobacco—are classified in Industry 111910, Tobacco Farming;
- Growing cotton—are classified in Industry 111920, Cotton Farming;
- Growing sugarcane—are classified in Industry 111930, Sugarcane Farming;
- Growing hay—are classified in Industry 111940, Hay Farming;
- Growing sugar beets—-are classified in U.S. Industry 111991, Sugar Beet Farming; and
- Growing peanuts—are classified in U.S. Industry 111992, Peanut Farming.

112 Animal Production

Industries in the Animal Production subsector raise or fatten animals for the sale of animals or animal products. The subsector comprises establishments, such as ranches, farms, and feedlots primarily engaged in keeping, grazing, breeding, or feeding animals. These animals are kept for the products they produce or for eventual sale. The animals are generally raised in various environments, from total confinement or captivity to feeding on an open range pasture.

The industries in this subsector are grouped by important factors, such as suitable grazing or pasture land, specialized buildings, type of equipment, and the amount and types of labor required. Establishments are classified to the Animal Production subsector when animal production (i.e., value of animals for market) accounts for one-half or more of the establishment's total agricultural production. Establishments with one-half or more animal production with no one animal product or family of animal products of an industry accounting for one-half of the establishment's agricultural production are treated as combination animal farming classified to Industry 11299, All Other Animal Production.

US—United States industry only. CAN—United States and Canadian industries are comparable. MEX—United States and Mexican industries are comparable. Blank—Canadian, Mexican, and United States industries are comparable.

1121 Cattle Ranching and Farming

This industry group comprises establishments primarily engaged in raising cattle, milking dairy cattle, or feeding cattle for fattening.

11211 Beef Cattle Ranching and Farming, including Feedlots

This industry comprises establishments primarily engaged in raising cattle (including cattle for dairy herd replacements), or feeding cattle for fattening.

Cross-References. Establishments primarily engaged in—

- Milking dairy cattle—are classified in Industry 11212, Dairy Cattle and Milk Production; and
- Operating stockyards for transportation and not buying, selling, or auctioning livestock—are classified in Industry 48899, Other Support Activities for Transportation.

112111 Beef Cattle Ranching and Farming^US

This U.S. industry comprises establishments primarily engaged in raising cattle (including cattle for dairy herd replacements).

Cross-References.

Establishments primarily engaged in milking dairy cattle are classified in Industry 112120, Dairy Cattle and Milk Production.

112112 Cattle Feedlots^US

This U.S. industry comprises establishments primarily engaged in feeding cattle for fattening.

Cross-References.

Establishments primarily engaged in operating stockyards for transportation and not buying, selling, or auctioning livestock are classified in U.S. Industry 488999, All Other Support Activities for Transportation.

11212 Dairy Cattle and Milk Production

See industry description for 112120 below.

US—United States industry only. CAN—United States and Canadian industries are comparable. MEX—United States and Mexican industries are comparable. Blank—Canadian, Mexican, and United States industries are comparable.

112120 Dairy Cattle and Milk Production

This industry comprises establishments primarily engaged in milking dairy cattle.

Cross-References. Establishment primarily engaged in—

- Raising dairy herd replacements—are classified in U.S. Industry 112111, Beef Cattle Ranching and Farming; and
- Milking goats—are classified in Industry 112420, Goat Farming.

11213 Dual-Purpose Cattle Ranching and Farming[MEX]

See industry description for 112130 below.

112130 Dual-Purpose Cattle Ranching and Farming[MEX]

This industry comprises establishments primarily engaged in raising cattle for both milking and meat production.

Cross-References. Establishments primarily engaged in—

- Milking dairy cattle—are classified in Industry 11212, Dairy Cattle and Milk Production;
- Raising cattle or feeding cattle for fattening—are classified in Industry 11211, Beef Cattle Ranching and Farming, including Feedlots; and
- Operating stockyards for transportation and not buying, selling, or auctioning livestock—are classified in U.S. Industry 488999, All Other Support Activities for Transportation.

1122 Hog and Pig Farming

11221 Hog and Pig Farming

See industry description for 112210 below.

112210 Hog and Pig Farming[CAN]

This industry comprises establishments primarily engaged in raising hogs and pigs. These establishments may include farming activities, such as breeding, farrowing, and the raising of weanling pigs, feeder pigs, or market size hogs.

Cross-References.

Establishments primarily engaged in operating stockyards for transportation and not buying, selling, or auctioning livestock are classified in U.S. Industry 488999, All Other Support Activities for Transportation.

US—United States industry only. CAN—United States and Canadian industries are comparable. MEX—United States and Mexican industries are comparable. Blank—Canadian, Mexican, and United States industries are comparable.

1123 Poultry and Egg Production

This industry group comprises establishments primarily engaged in breeding, hatching, and raising poultry for meat or egg production.

11231 Chicken Egg Production

See industry description for 112310 below.

112310 Chicken Egg Production[CAN]

This industry comprises establishments primarily engaged in raising chickens for egg production. The eggs produced may be for use as table eggs or hatching eggs.

Cross-References.

Establishments primarily engaged in raising chickens for the production of meat are classified in Industry 112320, Broilers and Other Meat Type Chicken Production.

11232 Broilers and Other Meat Type Chicken Production

See industry description for 112320 below.

112320 Broilers and Other Meat Type Chicken Production

This industry comprises establishments primarily engaged in raising broilers, fryers, roasters, and other meat type chickens.

Cross-References.

Establishments primarily engaged in raising chickens for egg production are classified in Industry 112310, Chicken Egg Production.

11233 Turkey Production

See industry description for 112330 below.

112330 Turkey Production

This industry comprises establishments primarily engaged in raising turkeys for meat or egg production.

US—United States industry only. CAN—United States and Canadian industries are comparable. MEX—United States and Mexican industries are comparable. Blank—Canadian, Mexican, and United States industries are comparable.

11234 Poultry Hatcheries

See industry description for 112340 below.

112340 Poultry Hatcheries

This industry comprises establishments primarily engaged in hatching poultry of any kind.

11239 Other Poultry Production

See industry description for 112390 below.

112390 Other Poultry Production[MEX]

This industry comprises establishments primarily engaged in raising poultry (except chickens for meat or egg production and turkeys).

Illustrative Examples:

Duck production
Emu production
Geese production
Ostrich production
Pheasant production
Quail production

Cross-References. Establishments primarily engaged in—

- Raising aviary birds, such as parakeets, canaries, and love birds,—are classified in Industry 112990, All Other Animal Production;
- Raising chickens for egg production—are classified in Industry 112310, Chicken Egg Production;
- Raising broilers and other meat type chickens—are classified in Industry 112320, Broilers and Other Meat Type Chicken Production;
- Raising turkeys—are classified in Industry 112330, Turkey Production; and
- Raising swans, peacocks, flamingos or other ''adornment birds''—are classified in Industry 112990, All Other Animal Production.

1124 Sheep and Goat Farming

This industry group comprises establishments primarily engaged in raising sheep, lambs, and goats, or feeding lambs for fattening.

11241 Sheep Farming

See industry description for 112410 below.

US—United States industry only. CAN—United States and Canadian industries are comparable. MEX—United States and Mexican industries are comparable. Blank—Canadian, Mexican, and United States industries are comparable.

112410 Sheep Farming[CAN]

This industry comprises establishments primarily engaged in raising sheep and lambs, or feeding lambs for fattening. The sheep or lambs may be raised for sale or wool production.

Cross-References.

Establishments primarily engaged in operating stockyards for transportation and not buying, selling, or auctioning livestock are classified in U.S. Industry 488999, All Other Support Activities for Transportation.

11242 Goat Farming

See industry description for 112420 below.

112420 Goat Farming

This industry comprises establishments primarily engaged in raising goats.

1125 Animal Aquaculture

11251 Animal Aquaculture

This industry comprises establishments primarily engaged in the farm raising of finfish, shellfish, or any other kind of animal aquaculture. These establishments use some form of intervention in the rearing process to enhance production, such as holding in captivity, regular stocking, feeding, and protecting from predators.

Cross-References.

Establishments primarily engaged in the catching or taking of fish and other aquatic animals from their natural habitat are classified in Industry 11411, Fishing.

112511 Finfish Farming and Fish Hatcheries[US]

This U.S. industry comprises establishments primarily engaged in (1) farm raising finfish (e.g., catfish, trout, goldfish, tropical fish, minnows) and/or (2) hatching fish of any kind.

Cross-References.

Establishments primarily engaged in the catching or taking of finfish from their natural habitat are classified in U.S. Industry 114111, Finfish Fishing.

US—United States industry only. CAN—United States and Canadian industries are comparable. MEX—United States and Mexican industries are comparable. Blank—Canadian, Mexican, and United States industries are comparable.

112512 Shellfish Farming[US]

This U.S. industry comprises establishments primarily engaged in farm raising shellfish (e.g., crayfish, shrimp, oysters, clams, mollusks).

Cross-References.

Establishments primarily engaged in the catching or taking of shellfish from their natural habitat are classified in U.S. Industry 114112, Shellfish Fishing.

112519 Other Animal Aquaculture[US]

This U.S. industry comprises establishments primarily engaged in farm raising animal aquaculture (except finfish and shellfish). Alligator, frog, or turtle production is included in this industry.

Cross-References. Establishments primarily engaged in—

- Miscellaneous fishing activities, such as catching or taking of terrapins, turtles, and frogs in their natural habitat,—are classified in U.S. Industry 114119, Other Marine Fishing;
- Farm raising finfish—are classified in U.S. Industry 112511, Finfish Farming and Fish Hatcheries; and
- Farm raising shellfish—are classified in U.S. Industry 112512, Shellfish Farming.

1129 Other Animal Production

This industry group comprises establishments primarily engaged in raising animals and insects (except cattle, hogs and pigs, poultry, sheep and goats, animal aquaculture) for sale or product production. These establishments are primarily engaged in raising one of the following: bees, horses and other equines, rabbits and other fur-bearing animals, and so forth, and producing products, such as honey and other bee products. Establishments primarily engaged in raising a combination of animals with no one animal or family of animals accounting for one-half of the establishment's agricultural production (i.e., value of animals for market) are included in this industry group.

11291 Apiculture

See industry description for 112910 below.

US—United States industry only. CAN—United States and Canadian industries are comparable. MEX—United States and Mexican industries are comparable. Blank—Canadian, Mexican, and United States industries are comparable.

112910 Apiculture

This industry comprises establishments primarily engaged in raising bees. These establishments may collect and gather honey; and/or sell queen bees, packages of bees, royal jelly, bees' wax, propolis, venom, and/or other bee products.

11292 Horses and Other Equine Production

See industry description for 112920 below.

112920 Horses and Other Equine Production

This industry comprises establishments primarily engaged in raising horses, mules, donkeys, and other equines.

Cross-References.

- Establishments primarily engaged in equine boarding are classified in Industry 115210, Support Activities for Animal Production; and
- Equine owners entering horses in racing or other spectator sporting events are classified in U.S. Industry 711219, Other Spectator Sports.

11293 Fur-Bearing Animal and Rabbit Production

See industry description for 112930 below.

112930 Fur-Bearing Animal and Rabbit Production

This industry comprises establishments primarily engaged in raising fur-bearing animals including rabbits. These animals may be raised for sale or for their pelt production.

Cross-References.

Establishments primarily engaged in the trapping or hunting of wild fur-bearing animals are classified in Industry 114210, Hunting and Trapping.

11299 All Other Animal Production

See industry description for 112990 below.

112990 All Other Animal Production[MEX]

This industry comprises establishments primarily engaged in: (1) raising animals (except cattle, hogs and pigs, poultry, sheep and goats, animal aquaculture, apicul-

---

US—United States industry only. CAN—United States and Canadian industries are comparable. MEX—United States and Mexican industries are comparable. Blank—Canadian, Mexican, and United States industries are comparable.

ture, horses and other equines; and fur-bearing animals including rabbits); or (2) raising a combination of animals, with no one animal or family of animals accounting for one-half of the establishment's agricultural production (i.e., value of animals for market) are included in this industry.

Illustrative Examples:

Bird production (e.g., canaries, parakeets, parrots)
Combination animal farming (except dairy, poultry)
Companion animals production (e.g., cats, dogs)
Deer production
Laboratory animal production (e.g., rats, mice, guinea pigs)
Llama production
Worm production

Cross-References. Establishments primarily engaged in—

- Raising cattle, dairy cattle or feeding cattle for fattening—are classified in Industry Group 1121, Cattle Ranching and Farming;
- Raising hogs and pigs—are classified in Industry Group 1122, Hog and Pig Farming;
- Raising poultry and raising poultry for egg production—are classified in Industry Group 1123, Poultry and Egg Production;
- Raising sheep and goats—are classified in Industry Group 1124, Sheep and Goat Farming;
- Raising animal aquaculture—are classified in Industry Group 1125, Animal Aquaculture;
- Raising bees—are classified in Industry 112910, Apiculture;
- Raising horses and other equines—are classified in Industry 112920, Horses and Other Equine Production; and
- Raising fur-bearing animals including rabbits—are classified in Industry 112930, Fur-Bearing Animal and Rabbit Production.

113 Forestry and Logging

Industries in the Forestry and Logging subsector grow and harvest timber on a long production cycle (i.e., of 10 years or more). Long production cycles use different production processes than short production cycles, which require more horticultural interventions prior to harvest, resulting in processes more similar to those found in the Crop Production subsector. Consequently, Christmas tree production and other production involving production cycles of less than 10 years, are classified in the Crop Production subsector.

US—United States industry only. CAN—United States and Canadian industries are comparable. MEX—United States and Mexican industries are comparable. Blank—Canadian, Mexican, and United States industries are comparable.

Industries in this subsector specialize in different stages of the production cycle. Reforestation requires production of seedlings in specialized nurseries. Timber production requires natural forest or suitable areas of land that are available for a long duration. The maturation time for timber depends upon the species of tree, the climatic conditions of the region, and the intended purpose of the timber. The harvesting of timber (except when done on an extremely small scale) requires specialized machinery unique to the industry. Establishments gathering forest products, such as gums, barks, balsam needles, rhizomes, fibers, Spanish moss, and ginseng and truffles, are also included in this subsector.

1131 Timber Tract Operations

11311 Timber Tract Operations

See industry description for 113110 below.

113110 Timber Tract Operations

This industry comprises establishments primarily engaged in the operation of timber tracts for the purpose of selling standing timber.

Cross-References. Establishments primarily engaged in—

- Acting as lessors of land with trees as real estate property—are classified in Industry 53119, Lessors of Other Real Estate Property;
- Growing short rotation woody trees (i.e., growing and harvesting cycle is 10 years or less)—are classified in U.S. Industry 111421, Nursery and Tree Production; and
- Cutting timber—are classified in Industry 113310, Logging.

1132 Forest Nurseries and Gathering of Forest Products

11321 Forest Nurseries and Gathering of Forest Products

See industry description for 113210 below.

113210 Forest Nurseries and Gathering of Forest Products[CAN]

This industry comprises establishments primarily engaged in (1) growing trees for reforestation and/or (2) gathering forest products, such as gums, barks, balsam needles, rhizomes, fibers, Spanish moss, ginseng, and truffles.

US—United States industry only. CAN—United States and Canadian industries are comparable. MEX—United States and Mexican industries are comparable. Blank—Canadian, Mexican, and United States industries are comparable.

Cross-References. Establishments primarily engaged in—

- Gathering tea and maple sap—are classified in U.S. Industry 111998, All Other Miscellaneous Crop Farming; and
- Processing maple syrup into other products—are classified in Industry 31199, All Other Food Manufacturing.

1133 Logging

11331 Logging

See industry description for 113310 below.

113310 Logging[MEX]

This industry comprises establishments primarily engaged in one or more of the following: (1) cutting timber; (2) cutting and transporting timber; and (3) producing wood chips in the field.

Cross-References.

Establishments primarily engaged in trucking timber are classified in Industry 484220, Specialized Freight (except Used Goods) Trucking, Local.

114 Fishing, Hunting and Trapping

Industries in the Fishing, Hunting, and Trapping subsector harvest fish and other wild animals from their natural habitats and are dependent upon a continued supply of the natural resource. The harvesting of fish is the predominant economic activity of this subsector and it usually requires specialized vessels that, by the nature of their size, configuration and equipment, are not suitable for any other type of production, such as transportation.

Hunting and trapping activities utilize a wide variety of production processes and are classified in the same subsector as fishing because the availability of resources and the constraints imposed, such as conservation requirements and proper habitat maintenance, are similar.

1141 Fishing

11411 Fishing

This industry comprises establishments primarily engaged in the commercial catching or taking of finfish, shellfish, or miscellaneous marine products from a

---

US—United States industry only. CAN—United States and Canadian industries are comparable. MEX—United States and Mexican industries are comparable. Blank—Canadian, Mexican, and United States industries are comparable.

natural habitat, such as the catching of bluefish, eels, salmon, tuna, clams, crabs, lobsters, mussels, oysters, shrimp, frogs, sea urchins, and turtles.

Cross-References. Establishments primarily engaged in—

- Farm raising finfish, shellfish or other marine animals—are classified in Industry 11251, Animal Aquaculture; and
- Gathering and processing (known as ''floating factory ships'') seafood into canned seafood products—are classified in Industry 31171, Seafood Product Preparation and Packaging.

114111 Finfish Fishing[US]

This U.S. industry comprises establishments primarily engaged in the commercial catching or taking of finfish (e.g., bluefish, salmon, trout, tuna) from their natural habitat.

Cross-References. Establishments primarily engaged in—

- Farm raising finfish—are classified in U.S. Industry 112511, Finfish Farming and Fish Hatcheries; and
- Gathering and processing (known as ''floating factory ships'') seafood into canned seafood products—are classified in U.S. Industry 311711, Seafood Canning.

114112 Shellfish Fishing[US]

This U.S. industry comprises establishments primarily engaged in the commercial catching or taking of shellfish (e.g., clams, crabs, lobsters, mussels, oysters, sea urchins, shrimp) from their natural habitat.

Cross-References.

Establishments primarily engaged in farm raising shellfish are classified in U.S. Industry 112512, Shellfish Farming.

114119 Other Marine Fishing[US]

This U.S. industry comprises establishments primarily engaged in the commercial catching or taking of marine animals (except finfish and shellfish).

Cross-References. Establishments primarily engaged in—

- Raising animal aquaculture (except finfish and shellfish)—are classified in U.S. Industry 112519, Other Animal Aquaculture;

US—United States industry only. CAN—United States and Canadian industries are comparable. MEX—United States and Mexican industries are comparable. Blank—Canadian, Mexican, and United States industries are comparable.

- The commercial catching or taking of finfish from their natural habitat—are classified in U.S. Industry 114111, Finfish Fishing; and
- The commercial catching or taking of shellfish from their natural habitat—are classified in U.S. Industry 114112, Shellfish Fishing.

1142 Hunting and Trapping

11421 Hunting and Trapping

See industry description for 114210 below.

114210 Hunting and Trapping

This industry comprises establishments primarily engaged in one or more of the following: (1) commercial hunting and trapping; (2) operating commercial game preserves, such as game retreats; and (3) operating hunting preserves.

Cross-References. Establishments primarily engaged in—

- Operating nature preserves—are classified in Industry 712190, Nature Parks and Other Similar Institutions; and
- Farm raising rabbits and other fur-bearing animals—are classified in Industry 112930, Fur-Bearing Animal and Rabbit Production.

115 Support Activities for Agriculture and Forestry

Industries in the Support Activities for Agriculture and Forestry subsector provide support services that are an essential part of agricultural and forestry production. These support activities may be performed by the agriculture or forestry producing establishment or conducted independently as an alternative source of inputs required for the production process for a given crop, animal, or forestry industry. Establishments that primarily perform these activities independent of the agriculture or forestry producing establishment are in this subsector.

1151 Support Activities for Crop Production

11511 Support Activities for Crop Production

This industry comprises establishments primarily engaged in providing support activities for growing crops.

US—United States industry only. CAN—United States and Canadian industries are comparable. MEX—United States and Mexican industries are comparable. Blank—Canadian, Mexican, and United States industries are comparable.

Illustrative Examples:

Aerial dusting or spraying (i.e., using specialized or dedicated aircraft)
Cotton ginning
Cultivating services
Farm management services
Planting crops
Vineyard cultivation services

Cross-References. Establishments primarily engaged in—

- Performing crop production that are generally known as farms, orchards, groves, or vineyards (including sharecroppers and tenant farms)—are classified in the appropriate crop industry within Subsector 111, Crop Production;
- Providing support activities for forestry—are classified in Industry 11531, Support Activities for Forestry;
- Landscaping and horticultural services, such as lawn and maintenance care and ornamental shrub and tree services,—are classified in Industry 56173, Landscaping Services;
- Land clearing, land leveling, and earth moving for terracing, ponds, and irrigation—are classified in Industry 23891, Site Preparation Contractors;
- Artificially drying and dehydrating fruits and vegetables—are classified in Industry 31142, Fruit and Vegetable Canning, Pickling and Drying;
- Stemming and redrying tobacco—are classified in Industry 31221, Tobacco Stemming and Redrying;
- Providing water for irrigation—are classified in Industry 22131, Water Supply and Irrigation Systems; and
- Buying farm products, such as fruits or vegetables, for resale to other wholesalers or retailers, and preparing them for market or further processing—are classified in Industry 42448, Fresh Fruit and Vegetable Merchant Wholesalers.

115111 Cotton Ginning[US]

This U.S. industry comprises establishments primarily engaged in ginning cotton.

115112 Soil Preparation, Planting, and Cultivating[US]

This U.S. industry comprises establishments primarily engaged in performing a soil preparation activity or crop production service, such as plowing, fertilizing, seed bed preparation, planting, cultivating, and crop protecting services.

US—United States industry only. CAN—United States and Canadian industries are comparable. MEX—United States and Mexican industries are comparable. Blank—Canadian, Mexican, and United States industries are comparable.

Cross-References. Establishments primarily engaged in—

- Land clearing, land leveling, and earth moving for terracing, ponds, and irrigation—are classified in Industry 238910, Site Preparation Contractors; and
- Providing water for irrigation—are classified in Industry 221310, Water Supply and Irrigation Systems.

115113 Crop Harvesting, Primarily by Machine[US]

This U.S. industry comprises establishments primarily engaged in mechanical harvesting, picking, and combining of crops, and related activities. The machinery used is provided by the servicing establishment.

Cross-References. Establishments primarily engaged in—

- Providing personnel for manual harvesting—are classified in U.S. Industry 115115, Farm Labor Contractors and Crew Leaders; and
- Providing farm management services (i.e., a contract or fee basis) and arranging or contracting crop mechanical or manual harvesting operations for the farm(s) it manages—are classified in U.S. Industry 115116, Farm Management Services.

115114 Postharvest Crop Activities (except Cotton Ginning)[US]

This U.S. industry comprises establishments primarily engaged in performing services on crops, subsequent to their harvest, with the intent of preparing them for market or further processing. These establishments provide postharvest activities, such as crop cleaning, sun drying, shelling, fumigating, curing, sorting, grading, packing, and cooling.

Cross-References. Establishments primarily engaged in—

- Ginning cotton—are classified in U.S. Industry 115111, Cotton Ginning;
- Artificially drying and dehydrating fruits and vegetables—are classified in U.S. Industry 311423, Dried and Dehydrated Food Manufacturing;
- Stemming and redrying tobacco—are classified in Industry 312210, Tobacco Stemming and Redrying;
- Buying farm products for resale to other wholesalers or retailers and preparing them for market or further processing—are classified in Industry 424480, Fresh Fruit and Vegetable Merchant Wholesalers; and

US—United States industry only. CAN—United States and Canadian industries are comparable. MEX—United States and Mexican industries are comparable. Blank—Canadian, Mexican, and United States industries are comparable.

- Providing farm management services (i.e., a contract or fee basis) and arranging or contracting postharvesting crop activities for the farm(s) it manages—are classified in U.S. Industry 115116, Farm Management Services.

115115 Farm Labor Contractors and Crew Leaders[US]

This U.S. industry comprises establishments primarily engaged in supplying labor for agricultural production or harvesting.

Cross-References. Establishments primarily engaged in—

- Providing machine harvesting—are classified in U.S. Industry 115113, Crop Harvesting, Primarily by Machine; and
- Providing farm management services (i.e., a contract or fee basis) and arranging or contracting farm labor for the farm(s) it manages—are classified in U.S. Industry 115116, Farm Management Services.

115116 Farm Management Services[US]

This U.S. industry comprises establishments primarily engaged in providing farm management services on a contract or fee basis usually to citrus groves, orchards, or vineyards. These establishments always provide management and may arrange or contract for the partial or the complete operations of the farm establishment(s) it manages. Operational activities may include cultivating, harvesting, and/or other specialized agricultural support activities.

Cross-References.

Establishments primarily engaged in crop production that are generally known as farms, orchards, groves, or vineyards (including share croppers and tenant farms), are classified in the appropriate crop industry within Subsector 111, Crop Production.

1152 Support Activities for Animal Production

11521 Support Activities for Animal Production

See industry description for 115210 below.

115210 Support Activities for Animal Production

This industry comprises establishments primarily engaged in performing support activities related to raising livestock (e.g., cattle, goats, hogs, horses, poultry,

US—United States industry only. CAN—United States and Canadian industries are comparable. MEX—United States and Mexican industries are comparable. Blank—Canadian, Mexican, and United States industries are comparable.

sheep). These establishments may perform one or more of the following: (1) breeding services for animals, including companion animals (e.g., cats, dogs, pet birds); (2) pedigree record services; (3) boarding horses; (4) dairy herd improvement activities; (5) livestock spraying; and (6) sheep dipping and shearing.

1153 Support Activities for Forestry

11531 Support Activities for Forestry

See industry description for 115310 below.

115310 Support Activities for Forestry

This industry comprises establishments primarily engaged in performing particular support activities related to timber production, wood technology, forestry economics and marketing, and forest protection. These establishments may provide support activities for forestry, such as estimating timber, forest firefighting, forest pest control, and consulting on wood attributes and reforestation.

Cross-References.

Establishments primarily engaged in the public administration and conservation of forest lands are classified in Industry 924120, Administration of Conservation Programs.

US—United States industry only. CAN—United States and Canadian industries are comparable. MEX—United States and Mexican industries are comparable. Blank—Canadian, Mexican, and United States industries are comparable.

Sector 21—Mining

The Sector as a Whole

The Mining sector comprises establishments that extract naturally occurring mineral solids, such as coal and ores; liquid minerals, such as crude petroleum; and gases, such as natural gas. The term mining is used in the broad sense to include quarrying, well operations, beneficiating (e.g., crushing, screening, washing, and flotation), and other preparation customarily performed at the mine site, or as a part of mining activity.

The Mining sector distinguishes two basic activities: mine operation and mining support activities. Mine operation includes establishments operating mines, quarries, or oil and gas wells on their own account or for others on a contract or fee basis. Mining support activities include establishments that perform exploration (except geophysical surveying) and/or other mining services on a contract or fee basis (except mine site preparation and construction of oil/gas pipelines).

Establishments in the Mining sector are grouped and classified according to the natural resource mined or to be mined. Industries include establishments that develop the mine site, extract the natural resources, and/or those that beneficiate (i.e., prepare) the mineral mined. Beneficiation is the process whereby the extracted material is reduced to particles that can be separated into mineral and waste, the former suitable for further processing or direct use. The operations that take place in beneficiation are primarily mechanical, such as grinding, washing, magnetic separation, and centrifugal separation. In contrast, manufacturing operations primarily use chemical and electrochemical processes, such as electrolysis and distillation. However, some treatments, such as heat treatments, take place in both the beneficiation and the manufacturing (i.e., smelting/refining) stages. The range of preparation activities varies by mineral and the purity of any given ore deposit. While some minerals, such as petroleum and natural gas, require little or no preparation, others are washed and screened, while yet others, such as gold and silver, can be transformed into bullion before leaving the mine site.

Mining, beneficiating, and manufacturing activities often occur in a single location. Separate receipts will be collected for these activities whenever possible. When receipts cannot be broken out between mining and manufacturing, establishments that mine or quarry nonmetallic minerals, beneficiate the nonmetallic minerals into more finished manufactured products are classified based on the primary activity of the establishment. A mine that manufactures a small amount of finished products will be classified in Sector 21, Mining. An establishment that mines whose primary output is a more finished manufactured product will be classified in Sector 31-33, Manufacturing.

US—United States industry only. CAN—United States and Canadian industries are comparable. MEX—United States and Mexican industries are comparable. Blank—Canadian, Mexican, and United States industries are comparable.

211 Oil and Gas Extraction

Industries in the Oil and Gas Extraction subsector operate and/or develop oil and gas field properties. Such activities may include exploration for crude petroleum and natural gas; drilling, completing, and equipping wells; operating separators, emulsion breakers, desilting equipment, and field gathering lines for crude petroleum and natural gas; and all other activities in the preparation of oil and gas up to the point of shipment from the producing property. This subsector includes the production of crude petroleum, the mining and extraction of oil from oil shale and oil sands, and the production of natural gas, sulfur recovery from natural gas, and recovery of hydrocarbon liquids.

Establishments in this subsector include those that operate oil and gas wells on their own account or for others on a contract or fee basis. Establishments primarily engaged in providing support services, on a fee or contract basis, required for the drilling or operation of oil and gas wells (except geophysical surveying and mapping, mine site preparation, and construction of oil/gas pipelines) are classified in Subsector 213, Support Activities for Mining.

2111 Oil and Gas Extraction

21111 Oil and Gas Extraction

This industry comprises establishments primarily engaged in operating and/or developing oil and gas field properties and establishments primarily engaged in recovering liquid hydrocarbons from oil and gas field gases. Such activities may include exploration for crude petroleum and natural gas; drilling, completing, and equipping wells; operation of separators, emulsion breakers, desilting equipment, and field gathering lines for crude petroleum and natural gas; and all other activities in the preparation of oil and gas up to the point of shipment from the producing property. This industry includes the production of crude petroleum, the mining and extraction of oil from oil shale and oil sands, the production of natural gas, sulfur recovery from natural gas, and the recovery of hydrocarbon liquids from oil and gas field gases. Establishments in this industry operate oil and gas wells on their own account or for others on a contract or fee basis.

Cross-References. Establishments primarily engaged in—

- Performing oil field services for operators on a contract or fee basis—are classified in Industry 21311, Support Activities for Mining;
- Manufacturing acyclic and cyclic aromatic hydrocarbons from refined petroleum or liquid hydrocarbons—are classified in Industry 32511, Petrochemical Manufacturing;

US—United States industry only. CAN—United States and Canadian industries are comparable. MEX—United States and Mexican industries are comparable. Blank—Canadian, Mexican, and United States industries are comparable.

- Refining crude petroleum into refined petroleum and liquid hydrocarbons—are classified in Industry 32411, Petroleum Refineries; and
- Recovering helium from natural gas—are classified in Industry 32512, Industrial Gas Manufacturing.

211111 Crude Petroleum and Natural Gas Extraction[US]

This U.S. industry comprises establishments primarily engaged in (1) the exploration, development and/or the production of petroleum or natural gas from wells in which the hydrocarbons will initially flow or can be produced using normal pumping techniques or (2) the production of crude petroleum from surface shales or tar sands or from reservoirs in which the hydrocarbons are semisolids. Establishments in this industry operate oil and gas wells on their own account or for others on a contract or fee basis.

Cross-References. Establishments primarily engaged in—

- Performing oil field services for operators on a contract or fee basis—are classified in Industry 21311, Support Activities for Mining;
- Refining crude petroleum into refined petroleum and liquid hydrocarbons—are classified in Industry 324110, Petroleum Refineries; and
- Recovering helium from natural gas—are classified in Industry 325120, Industrial Gas Manufacturing.

211112 Natural Gas Liquid Extraction[US]

This U.S. industry comprises establishments primarily engaged in the recovery of liquid hydrocarbons from oil and gas field gases. Establishments primarily engaged in sulfur recovery from natural gas are included in this industry.

Cross-References. Establishments primarily engaged in—

- Manufacturing acyclic and cyclic aromatic hydrocarbons from refined petroleum or converting refined petroleum into liquid hydrocarbons (petrochemicals) and/or recovering liquid hydrocarbons—are classified in Industry 325110, Petrochemical Manufacturing;
- Refining crude petroleum into refined petroleum and liquid hydrocarbons—are classified in Industry 324110, Petroleum Refineries; and
- Recovering helium from natural gas—are classified in Industry 325120, Industrial Gas Manufacturing.

US—United States industry only. CAN—United States and Canadian industries are comparable. MEX—United States and Mexican industries are comparable. Blank—Canadian, Mexican, and United States industries are comparable.

212 Mining (except Oil and Gas)

Industries in the Mining (except Oil and Gas) subsector primarily engage in mining, mine site development, and beneficiating (i.e., preparing) metallic minerals and nonmetallic minerals, including coal. The term ''mining'' is used in the broad sense to include ore extraction, quarrying, and beneficiating (e.g., crushing, screening, washing, sizing, concentrating, and flotation), customarily done at the mine site.

Beneficiation is the process whereby the extracted material is reduced to particles which can be separated into mineral and waste, the former suitable for further processing or direct use. The operations that take place in beneficiation are primarily mechanical, such as grinding, washing, magnetic separation, centrifugal separation, and so on. In contrast, manufacturing operations primarily use chemical and electrochemical processes, such as electrolysis, distillation, and so on. However some treatments, such as heat treatments, take place in both stages: the beneficiation and the manufacturing (i.e., smelting/refining) stages. The range of preparation activities varies by mineral and the purity of any given ore deposit. While some minerals, such as petroleum and natural gas, require little or no preparation, others are washed and screened, while yet others, such as gold and silver, can be transformed into bullion before leaving the mine site.

Establishments in the Mining (except Oil and Gas) subsector include those that have complete responsibility for operating mines and quarries (except oil and gas wells) and those that operate mines and quarries (except oil and gas wells) for others on a contract or fee basis. Establishments primarily engaged in providing support services, on a contract or fee basis, required for the mining and quarrying of minerals are classified in Subsector 213, Support Activities for Mining.

2121 Coal Mining

21211 Coal Mining

This industry comprises establishments primarily engaged in one or more of the following: (1) mining bituminous coal, anthracite, and lignite by underground mining, auger mining, strip mining, culm bank mining, and other surface mining; (2) developing coal mine sites; and (3) beneficiating (i.e., preparing) coal (e.g., cleaning, washing, screening, and sizing coal).

Cross-References. Establishments primarily engaged in—

- Manufacturing code oven products in coke oven establishments—are classified in Industry 32419, Other Petroleum and Coal Products Manufacturing; and

US—United States industry only. CAN—United States and Canadian industries are comparable. MEX—United States and Mexican industries are comparable. Blank—Canadian, Mexican, and United States industries are comparable.

- Manufacturing coal products in steel mills—are classified in Industry 33111, Iron and Steel Mills and Ferroalloy Manufacturing.

212111 Bituminous Coal and Lignite Surface Mining[US]

This U.S. industry comprises establishments primarily engaged in one or more of the following: (1) surface mining of bituminous coal and lignite; (2) developing bituminous coal and lignite surface mine sites; (3) surface mining and beneficiating (e.g., cleaning. washing, screening, and sizing coal) of bituminous coal; or (4) beneficiating (e.g., cleaning, washing, screening, and sizing coal), but not mining, bituminous coal.

Cross-References. Establishments primarily engaged in—

- Manufacturing coke oven products in coke oven establishments—are classified in U.S. Industry 324199, All Other Petroleum and Coal Products Manufacturing;
- Underground mining of bituminous coal—are classified in U.S. Industry 212112, Bituminous Coal Underground Mining; and
- Mining and/or beneficiating anthracite coal—are classified in U.S. Industry 212113, Anthracite Mining.

212112 Bituminous Coal Underground Mining[US]

This U.S. industry comprises establishments primarily engaged in one or more of the following: (1) underground mining of bituminous coal; (2) developing bituminous coal underground mine sites; and (3) underground mining and beneficiating of bituminous coal (e.g., cleaning, washing, screening, and sizing coal).

Cross-References. Establishments primarily engaged in—

- Manufacturing coke oven products in coke oven establishments—are classified in U.S. Industry 324199, All Other Petroleum and Coal Products Manufacturing;
- Surface mining and/or beneficiating of bituminous coal or lignite—are classified in U.S. Industry 212111, Bituminous Coal and Lignite Surface Mining; and
- Mining and/or beneficiating anthracite coal—are classified in U.S. Industry 212113, Anthracite Mining.

212113 Anthracite Mining[US]

This U.S. industry comprises establishments primarily engaged in one or more of the following: (1) mining anthracite coal; (2) developing anthracite coal mine

US—United States industry only. CAN—United States and Canadian industries are comparable. MEX—United States and Mexican industries are comparable. Blank—Canadian, Mexican, and United States industries are comparable.

sites; and (3) beneficiating anthracite coal (e.g., cleaning, washing, screening, and sizing coal).

Cross-References. Establishments primarily engaged in—

- Manufacturing coke oven products in coke oven establishments—are classified in U.S. Industry 324199, All Other Petroleum and Coal Products Manufacturing;
- Surface mining and/or beneficiating bituminous coal or lignite—are classified in U.S. Industry 212111, Bituminous Coal and Lignite Surface Mining; and
- Underground mining of bituminous coal—are classified in U.S. Industry 212112, Bituminous Coal Underground Mining.

2122 Metal Ore Mining

This industry group comprises establishments primarily engaged in developing mine sites or mining metallic minerals, and establishments primarily engaged in ore dressing and beneficiating (i.e., preparing) operations, such as crushing, grinding, washing, drying, sintering, concentrating, calcining, and leaching. Beneficiating may be performed at mills operated in conjunction with the mines served or at mills, such as custom mills, operated separately.

21221 Iron Ore Mining

See industry description for 212210 below.

212210 Iron Ore Mining

This industry comprises establishments primarily engaged in (1) developing mine sites, mining, and/or beneficiating (i.e., preparing) iron ores and manganiferous ores valued chiefly for their iron content and/or (2) producing sinter iron ore (except iron ore produced in iron and steel mills) and other iron ore agglomerates.

Cross-References.

Establishments primarily engaged in manufacturing pig iron ore are classified in U.S. Industry 331111, Iron and Steel Mills.

21222 Gold Ore and Silver Ore Mining

This industry comprises establishments primarily engaged in developing the mine site, mining, and/or beneficiating (i.e., preparing) ores valued chiefly for their

US—United States industry only. CAN—United States and Canadian industries are comparable. MEX—United States and Mexican industries are comparable. Blank—Canadian, Mexican, and United States industries are comparable.

gold and or silver content. Establishments primarily engaged in the transformation of the gold and silver into bullion or dore bar in combination with mining activities are included in this industry.

Cross-References.

Establishments primarily engaged in manufacturing gold or silver bullion or dore bar without mining are classified in Industry 33141, Nonferrous Metal (except Aluminum) Smelting and Refining.

212221 Gold Ore Mining[MEX]

This U.S. industry comprises establishments primarily engaged in developing the mine site, mining, and/or beneficiating (i.e., preparing) ores valued chiefly for their gold content. Establishments primarily engaged in transformation of the gold into bullion or dore bar in combination with mining activities are included in this industry.

Cross-References.

Establishments primarily engaged in manufacturing gold bullion or dore bar without mining are classified in U.S. Industry 331419, Primary Smelting and Refining of Nonferrous Metal (except Copper and Aluminum).

212222 Silver Ore Mining[MEX]

This U.S. industry comprises establishments primarily engaged in developing the mine site, mining, and/or beneficiating (i.e., preparing) ores valued chiefly for their silver content. Establishments primarily engaged in transformation of the silver into bullion or dore bar in combination with mining activities are included in this industry.

Cross-References.

Establishments primarily engaged in manufacturing silver bullion or dore bar without mining are classified in U.S. Industry 331419, Primary Smelting and Refining of Nonferrous Metal (except Copper and Aluminum).

21223 Copper, Nickel, Lead, and Zinc Mining

This industry comprises establishments primarily engaged in developing the mine site, mining, and/or beneficiating (i.e., preparing) ores valued chiefly for their copper, nickel, lead, or zinc content. Beneficiating includes the transformation of ores into concentrates.

US—United States industry only. CAN—United States and Canadian industries are comparable. MEX—United States and Mexican industries are comparable. Blank—Canadian, Mexican, and United States industries are comparable.

Cross-References. Establishments primarily engaged in—

- Refining copper concentrates—are classified in Industry 33141, Nonferrous Metal (except Aluminum) Smelting and Refining; and
- Developing the mine site, mining, and/or beneficiating iron and manganiferous ores valued for their iron content—are classified in Industry 21221, Iron Ore Mining.

212231 Lead Ore and Zinc Ore Mining[CAN]

This U.S. industry comprises establishments primarily engaged in developing the mine site, mining, and/or beneficiating (i.e., preparing) lead ores, zinc ores, or lead-zinc ores.

212234 Copper Ore and Nickel Ore Mining[US]

This U.S. industry comprises establishments primarily engaged in: (1) developing the mine site, mining, and/or beneficiating (i.e, preparing) copper and/or nickel ores; and (2) recovering copper concentrates by the precipitation, leaching, or electrowinning of copper ore.

Cross-References.

Establishments primarily engaged in refining copper concentrates are classified in U.S. Industry 331411, Primary Smelting and Refining of Copper.

21229 Other Metal Ore Mining

This industry comprises establishments primarily engaged in developing the mine site, mining, and/or beneficiating (i.e., preparing) metal ores (except iron and manganiferous ores valued for their iron content, gold ore, silver ore, copper, nickel, lead, and zinc ore).

Illustrative Examples:

Antimony ores mining and/or beneficiating
Columbite ores mining and/or beneficiating
Ilmenite ores mining and/or beneficiating
Molybdenum ores mining and/or beneficiating
Tantalum ores mining and/or beneficiating
Tungsten ores mining and/or beneficiating
Uranium-radium-vanadium ores mining and/or beneficiating

US—United States industry only. CAN—United States and Canadian industries are comparable. MEX—United States and Mexican industries are comparable. Blank—Canadian, Mexican, and United States industries are comparable.

Cross-References. Establishments primarily engaged in—

- Developing the mine site, mining, and/or beneficiating iron and manganiferous ores valued chiefly for their iron content—are classified in Industry 21221, Iron Ore Mining;
- Developing the mine site, mining, and/or beneficiating ores valued chiefly for their gold or silver content—are classified in Industry 21222, Gold Ore and Silver Ore Mining;
- Developing the mine site, mining, and/or beneficiating ores valued chiefly for their copper, nickel, lead, or zinc content—are classified in Industry 21223, Copper, Nickel, Lead, and Zinc Mining; and
- Enriching uranium—are classified in Industry 32518, Other Basic Inorganic Chemical Manufacturing.

212291 Uranium-Radium-Vanadium Ore Mining[CAN]

This U.S. industry comprises establishments primarily engaged in developing the mine site, mining, and/or beneficiating (i.e., preparing) uranium-radium-vanadium ores.

Cross-References.

Establishments primarily engaged in enriching uranium are classified in U.S. Industry 325188, All Other Basic Inorganic Chemical Manufacturing.

212299 All Other Metal Ore Mining[CAN]

This U.S. industry comprises establishments primarily engaged in developing the mine site, mining, and/or beneficiating (i.e., preparing) metal ores (except iron and manganiferous ores valued for their iron content, gold ore, silver ore, copper, nickel, lead, zinc, and uranium-radium-vanadium ore).

Illustrative Examples:

Antimony ores mining and/or beneficiating
Columbite ores mining and/or beneficiating
Ilmenite ores mining and/or beneficiating
Molybdenum ores mining and/or beneficiating
Rare-earth metal ores mining and/or beneficiating
Tantalum ores mining and/or beneficiating
Tungsten ores mining and/or beneficiating

Cross-References. Establishments primarily engaged in—

- Developing the mine site, mining, and/or beneficiating iron and manganiferous ores valued for their iron content—are classified in Industry 212210, Iron Ore Mining;

US—United States industry only. CAN—United States and Canadian industries are comparable. MEX—United States and Mexican industries are comparable. Blank—Canadian, Mexican, and United States industries are comparable.

- Developing the mine site, mining, and/or beneficiating ores valued chiefly for their gold or silver content—are classified in Industry 21222, Gold Ore and Silver Ore Mining;
- Developing the mine site, mining, and/or beneficiating ores valued chiefly for their copper, nickel, lead, or zinc content—are classified in Industry 21223, Copper, Nickel, Lead, and Zinc Mining; and
- Developing the mine site, mining, and/or beneficiating uranium-radium-vanadium ores—are classified in U.S. Industry 212291, Uranium-Radium-Vanadium Ore Mining.

2123 Nonmetallic Mineral Mining and Quarrying

This industry group comprises establishments primarily engaged in developing mine sites, or in mining or quarrying nonmetallic minerals (except fuels). Also included are certain well and brine operations, and preparation plants primarily engaged in beneficiating (e.g., crushing, grinding, washing, and concentrating) nonmetallic minerals.

Beneficiation is the process whereby the extracted material is reduced to particles which can be separated into mineral and waste, the former suitable for further processing or direct use. The operations that take place in beneficiation are primarily mechanical, such as grinding, washing, magnetic separation, and centrifugal separation. In contrast, manufacturing operations primarily use chemical and electrochemical processes, such as electrolysis and distillation. However, some treatments, such as heat treatments, take place in both the beneficiation and the manufacturing (i.e., smelting/refining) stages. The range of preparation activities varies by mineral and the purity of any given ore deposit. While some minerals, such as petroleum and natural gas, require little or no preparation, others are washed and screened, while yet others, such as gold and silver, can be transformed into bullion before leaving the mine site.

21231 Stone Mining and Quarrying

This industry comprises (1) establishments primarily engaged in developing the mine site, mining or quarrying dimension stone (i.e., rough blocks and/or slabs of stone), or mining and quarrying crushed and broken stone and/or (2) preparation plants primarily engaged in beneficiating stone (e.g., crushing, grinding, washing, screening, pulverizing, and sizing).

Cross-References. Establishments primarily engaged in—

- Producing lime—are classified in Industry 32741, Lime Manufacturing; and

---

US—United States industry only. CAN—United States and Canadian industries are comparable. MEX—United States and Mexican industries are comparable. Blank—Canadian, Mexican, and United States industries are comparable.

- Quarrying and dressing dimension stone—are classified Industry 32799, All Other Nonmetallic Mineral Product Manufacturing.

212311 Dimension Stone Mining and Quarrying[US]

This U.S. industry comprises establishments primarily engaged in developing the mine site and/or mining or quarrying dimension stone (i.e., rough blocks and/ or slabs of stone).

Cross-References.

Establishments primarily engaged in dressing dimension stone and manufacturing stone products are classified in U.S. Industry 327991, Cut Stone and Stone Product Manufacturing.

212312 Crushed and Broken Limestone Mining and Quarrying[US]

This U.S. industry comprises (1) establishments primarily engaged in developing the mine site, mining or quarrying crushed and broken limestone (including related rocks, such as dolomite, cement rock, marl, travertine, and calcareous tufa); and (2) preparation plants primarily engaged in beneficiating limestone (e.g., grinding or pulverizing).

Cross-References. Establishments primarily engaged in—

- Producing lime—are classified in Industry 327410, Lime Manufacturing; and
- Mining or quarrying bituminous limestone—are classified U.S. Industry 212319, Other Crushed and Broken Stone Mining and Quarrying.

212313 Crushed and Broken Granite Mining and Quarrying[US]

This U.S. industry comprises: (1) establishments primarily engaged in developing the mine site, and/or mining or quarrying crushed and broken granite (including related rocks, such as gneiss, syenite, and diorite); and (2) preparation plants primarily engaged in beneficiating granite (e.g., grinding or pulverizing).

212319 Other Crushed and Broken Stone Mining and Quarrying[US]

This U.S. industry comprises: (1) establishments primarily engaged in developing the mine site and/or mining or quarrying crushed and broken stone (except limestone and granite); (2) preparation plants primarily engaged in beneficiating

US—United States industry only. CAN—United States and Canadian industries are comparable. MEX—United States and Mexican industries are comparable. Blank—Canadian, Mexican, and United States industries are comparable.

(e.g., grinding and pulverizing) stone (except limestone and granite); and (3) establishments primarily engaged in mining or quarrying bituminous limestone and bituminous sandstone.

Illustrative Examples:

Bituminous limestone mining and/or beneficiating
Bituminous sandstone mining and/or beneficiating
Marble crushed and broken stone mining and/or beneficiating
Sandstone crushed and broken stone mining and/or beneficiating

Cross-References. Establishments primarily engaged in—

- Mining or quarrying crushed and broken limestone—are classified in U.S. Industry 212312, Crushed and Broken Limestone Mining and Quarrying; and
- Mining or quarrying crushed and broken granite—are classified in U.S. Industry 212313, Crushed and Broken Granite Mining and Quarrying.

21232 Sand, Gravel, Clay, and Ceramic and Refractory Minerals Mining and Quarrying

This industry comprises (1) establishments primarily engaged in developing the mine site and/or mining, quarrying, dredging for sand and gravel, or mining clay, (e.g., china clay, paper clay and slip clay) and (2) preparation plants primarily engaged in beneficiating (e.g., washing, screening, and grinding) sand and gravel, clay, and ceramic and refractory minerals.

Cross-References. Establishments primarily engaged in—

- Calcining, dead burning, or otherwise processing (i.e., beyond basic preparation) clay or refractory minerals—are classified in Industry 32799, All Other Nonmetallic Mineral Product Manufacturing;
- Shaping, molding, baking, burning, or hardening nonclay ceramics, clay and nonclay refractories, and structural clay products—are classified in Industry 32712, Clay Building Material and Refractories Manufacturing; and
- Shaping, molding, glazing, and firing pottery, ceramics, and plumbing fixtures—are classified in Industry 32711, Pottery, Ceramics and Plumbing Fixture Manufacturing.

212321 Construction Sand and Gravel Mining[MEX]

This U.S. industry comprises establishments primarily engaged in one or more of the following: (1) operating commercial grade (i.e., construction) sand and

US—United States industry only. CAN—United States and Canadian industries are comparable. MEX—United States and Mexican industries are comparable. Blank—Canadian, Mexican, and United States industries are comparable.

gravel pits; (2) dredging for commercial grade sand and gravel; and (3) washing, screening, or otherwise preparing commercial grade sand and gravel.

Cross-References.

Establishments primarily engaged in mining industrial grade sand are classified in U.S. Industry 212322, Industrial Sand Mining.

212322 Industrial Sand Mining[US]

This U.S. industry comprises establishments primarily engaged in one or more of the following: (1) operating industrial grade sand pits; (2) dredging for industrial grade sand; and (3) washing, screening, or otherwise preparing industrial grade sand.

Cross-References.

Establishments primarily engaged in mining commercial (i.e., construction) grade gravel are classified in U.S. Industry 212321, Construction Sand and Gravel Mining.

212324 Kaolin and Ball Clay Mining[US]

This U.S. industry comprises (1) establishments primarily engaged in developing the mine site and/or mining kaolin or ball clay (e.g., china clay, paper clay, and slip clay) and (2) establishments primarily engaged in beneficiating (i.e., preparing) kaolin or ball clay.

Cross-References.

Establishments primarily engaged in calcining, dead burning, or otherwise processing (i.e., beyond basic preparation) kaolin and ball clay are classified in U.S. Industry 327992, Ground or Treated Mineral and Earth Manufacturing.

212325 Clay and Ceramic and Refractory Minerals Mining[US]

This U.S. industry comprises establishments primarily engaged in one or more of the following: (1) mining clay (except kaolin and ball), ceramic, or refractory minerals; (2) developing the mine site for clay, ceramic, or refractory minerals; and (3) beneficiating (i.e., preparing) clay (except kaolin and ball), ceramic, or refractory minerals.

Illustrative Examples:

Bentonite mining and/or beneficiating
Magnesite mining and/or beneficiating

US—United States industry only. CAN—United States and Canadian industries are comparable. MEX—United States and Mexican industries are comparable. Blank—Canadian, Mexican, and United States industries are comparable.

Common clay mining and/or beneficiating
Feldspar mining and/or beneficiating
Fire clay mining and/or beneficiating
Fuller's earth mining and/or beneficiating
Nepheline syenite mining and/or beneficiating
Shale (except oil shale) mining and/or beneficiating

Cross-References. Establishments primarily engaged in—

- Shaping, molding, baking, burning, or hardening clay and nonclay refractories, and structural clay products—are classified in Industry 32712, Clay Building Material and Refractories Manufacturing;
- Developing the mine site, mining, and/or beneficiating kaolin or ball clay—are classified in U.S. Industry 212324, Kaolin and Ball Clay Mining; and
- Shaping, molding, glazing, and firing pottery, ceramics, and plumbing fixtures—are classified in Industry 32711, Pottery, Ceramics and Plumbing Fixture Manufacturing.

21239 Other Nonmetallic Mineral Mining and Quarrying

This industry comprises establishments primarily engaged in developing the mine site, mining, and/or milling or otherwise beneficiating (i.e., preparing) nonmetallic minerals (except coal, stone, sand, gravel, clay, ceramic, and refractory minerals).

Illustrative Examples:

Barite mining and/or beneficiating
Borate, natural, mining and/or beneficiating
Peat mining and/or beneficiating
Phosphate rock mining and/or beneficiating
Potash mining and/or beneficiating
Rock salt mining and/or beneficiating

Cross-References. Establishments primarily engaged in—

- Mining or quarrying dimension stone—are classified in Industry 21231, Stone Mining and Quarrying;
- Mining or quarrying sand, gravel, clay and ceramic and refractory minerals—are classified in Industry 21232, Sand, Gravel, Clay, and Ceramic and Refractory Minerals Mining and Quarrying;
- Calcining, dead burning, or otherwise processing (i.e., beyond basic preparation) minerals, such as talc, mica, feldspar, barite, and soapstone—are classified in Industry 32799, All Other Nonmetallic Mineral Product Manufacturing;
- Manufacturing boron compounds and potassium salts—are classified in Industry 32518, Other Basic Inorganic Chemical Manufacturing;

US—United States industry only. CAN—United States and Canadian industries are comparable. MEX—United States and Mexican industries are comparable. Blank—Canadian, Mexican, and United States industries are comparable.

- Manufacturing table salt—are classified in Industry 31194, Seasoning and Dressing Manufacturing;
- Manufacturing salt (except table salt)—are classified in Industry 32599, All Other Chemical Product and Preparation Manufacturing; and
- Manufacturing phosphoric acid, superphosphates, or other phosphatic fertilizer materials—are classified in Industry 32531, Fertilizer Manufacturing.

212391 Potash, Soda, and Borate Mineral Mining[US]

This U.S. industry comprises establishments primarily engaged in developing the mine site, mining and/or milling, or otherwise beneficiating (i.e., preparing) natural potassium, sodium, or boron compounds. Drylake brine operations are included in this industry, as well as establishments engaged in producing the specified minerals from underground and open pit mines.

Cross-References. Establishments primarily engaged in—

- Manufacturing boron compounds and potassium salts—are classified in U.S. Industry 325188, All Other Basic Inorganic Chemical Manufacturing;
- Manufacturing sodium carbonate—are classified in U.S. Industry 325181, Alkalies and Chlorine Manufacturing; and
- Manufacturing table salt—are classified in U.S. Industry 311942, Spice and Extract Manufacturing.

212392 Phosphate Rock Mining[US]

This U.S. industry comprises establishments primarily engaged in developing the mine site, mining, milling, and/or drying or otherwise beneficiating (i.e., preparing) phosphate rock.

Cross-References.

Establishments primarily engaged in manufacturing phosphoric acid, superphosphates, or other phosphatic fertilizer materials are classified in U.S. Industry 325312, Phosphatic Fertilizer Manufacturing.

212393 Other Chemical and Fertilizer Mineral Mining[US]

This U.S. industry comprises establishments primarily engaged in developing the mine site, mining, milling, and/or drying or otherwise beneficiating (i.e., preparing) chemical or fertilizer mineral raw materials (except potash, soda, boron, and phosphate rock).

US—United States industry only. CAN—United States and Canadian industries are comparable. MEX—United States and Mexican industries are comparable. Blank—Canadian, Mexican, and United States industries are comparable.

Illustrative Examples:

Barite mining and/or beneficiating
Celestite mining and/or beneficiating
Fluorspar mining and/or beneficiating
Rock salt mining and/or beneficiating
Sulfur mining and/or beneficiating

Cross-References. Establishment primarily engaged in—

- Mining and/or milling or otherwise beneficiating natural potassium, sodium, or boron compounds—are classified in U.S. Industry 212391, Potash, Soda, and Borate Mineral Mining;
- Manufacturing industrial salt—are classified in U.S. Industry 325998, All Other Miscellaneous Chemical Product and Preparation Manufacturing;
- Mining, milling, drying, and/or sintering or otherwise beneficiating phosphate rock—are classified in U.S. Industry 212392, Phosphate Rock Mining; and
- Manufacturing table salt—are classified in U.S. Industry 311942, Spice and Extract Manufacturing.

212399 All Other Nonmetallic Mineral Mining[US]

This U.S. industry comprises establishments primarily engaged in developing the mine site, mining and/or milling or otherwise beneficiating (i.e., preparing) nonmetallic minerals (except stone, sand, gravel, clay, ceramic, refractory minerals, chemical and fertilizer minerals).

Illustrative Examples:

Gypsum mining and/or beneficiating
Mica mining and/or beneficiating
Pyrophyllite mining and/or beneficiating
Soapstone mining and/or beneficiating
Talc mining and/or beneficiating

Cross-References. Establishments primarily engaged in—

- Mining or quarrying dimension stone—are classified in Industry 21231, Stone Mining and Quarrying;
- Mining, quarrying, or beneficiating sand, gravel, clay, and ceramic and refractory minerals—are classified in Industry 21232, Sand, Gravel, Clay, and Ceramic and Refractory Minerals Mining and Quarrying;
- Mining, quarrying or beneficiating natural potash, soda, and borate—are classified in U.S. Industry 212391, Potash, Soda, and Borate Mineral Mining; and
- Mining and/or milling or otherwise beneficiating phosphate rock—are classified in U.S. Industry 212392, Phosphate Rock Mining.

US—United States industry only. CAN—United States and Canadian industries are comparable. MEX—United States and Mexican industries are comparable. Blank—Canadian, Mexican, and United States industries are comparable.

213 Support Activities for Mining

Industries in the Support Activities for Mining subsector group establishments primarily providing support services, on a contract or fee basis, required for the mining and quarrying of minerals and for the extraction of oil and gas. Establishments performing exploration (except geophysical surveying and mapping) for minerals, on a contract or fee basis, are included in this subsector. Exploration includes traditional prospecting methods, such as taking core samples and making geological observations at prospective sites.

The activities performed on a contract or fee basis by establishments in the Support Activities for Mining subsector are also often performed in-house by mining operators. These activities include: taking core samples, making geological observations at prospective sites, excavating slush pits and cellars, and such oil and gas operations as spudding in, drilling in, redrilling, directional drilling, well surveying; running, cutting, and pulling casings, tubes and rods; cementing wells, shooting wells; perforating well casings; acidizing and chemically treating wells; and cleaning out, bailing, and swabbing wells.

2131 Support Activities for Mining

21311 Support Activities for Mining

This industry comprises establishments primarily engaged in providing support services, on a contract or fee basis, required for the mining and quarrying of minerals and for the extraction of oil and gas. Drilling, taking core samples, and making geological observations at prospective sites (except geophysical surveying and mapping) for minerals, on a contract or fee basis, is included in this industry.

Cross-References. Establishments primarily engaged in—

- Performing geophysical surveying and mapping services for minerals (i.e., coal, metal ores, oil and gas, and nonmetallic minerals) on a contract or fee basis—are classified in Industry 54136, Geophysical Surveying and Mapping Services;
- Mining, quarrying, and/or beneficiating on a contract or fee basis—are classified in Subsector 212, Mining (except Oil and Gas) based on the mineral mined; and
- Operating oil and gas field properties on a contract or fee basis—are classified in Subsector 211, Oil and Gas Extraction based on the activity.

US—United States industry only. CAN—United States and Canadian industries are comparable. MEX—United States and Mexican industries are comparable. Blank—Canadian, Mexican, and United States industries are comparable.

213111 Drilling Oil and Gas Wells

This U.S. industry comprises establishments primarily engaged in drilling oil and gas wells for others on a contract or fee basis. This industry includes contractors that specialize in spudding in, drilling in, redrilling, and directional drilling.

Cross-References. Establishments primarily engaged in—

- Performing exploration (except geophysical surveying and mapping) services for oil and gas on a contract or fee basis—are classified in U.S. Industry 213112, Support Activities for Oil and Gas Operations; and
- Performing geophysical surveying and mapping services for oil and gas on a contract or fee basis—are classified in Industry 541360, Geophysical Surveying and Mapping Services.

213112 Support Activities for Oil and Gas Operations[US]

This U.S. industry comprises establishments primarily engaged in performing support activities on a contract or fee basis for oil and gas operations (except site preparation and related construction activities). Services included are exploration (except geophysical surveying and mapping); excavating slush pits and cellars, well surveying; running, cutting, and pulling casings, tubes, and rods; cementing wells, shooting wells; perforating well casings; acidizing and chemically treating wells; and cleaning out, bailing, and swabbing wells.

Cross-References. Establishments primarily engaged in—

- Contract drilling for oil and gas—are classified in U.S. Industry 213111, Drilling Oil and Gas Wells;
- Operating oil and gas field properties on a contract or fee basis—are classified in Subsector 211, Oil and Gas Extraction, based on the activity;
- Performing geophysical surveying and mapping services for oil and gas on a contract or fee basis—are classified in Industry 541360, Geophysical Surveying and Mapping Services;
- Oil and gas pipeline and related structures construction—are classified in Industry 237120, Oil and Gas Pipeline and Related Structures Construction; and
- Site preparation and related construction activities on a contract or fee basis—are classified in Industry 238910, Site Preparation Contractors.

213113 Support Activities for Coal Mining[US]

This U.S. industry comprises establishments primarily engaged in providing support activities for coal mining (except site preparation and related construction

US—United States industry only. CAN—United States and Canadian industries are comparable. MEX—United States and Mexican industries are comparable. Blank—Canadian, Mexican, and United States industries are comparable.

activities) on a contract or fee basis. Exploration for coal is included in this industry. Exploration includes traditional prospecting methods, such as taking core samples and making geological observations at prospective sites.

Cross-References. Establishments primarily engaged in—

- Performing geophysical surveying and mapping services for coal on a contract or fee basis—are classified in Industry 541360, Geophysical Surveying and Mapping Services;
- Operating coal mines or quarries on a contract or fee basis—are classified in Industry Group 2121, Coal Mining, based on the type of coal mined; and
- Site preparation and related construction activities on a contract or fee basis—are classified in Industry 238910, Site Preparation Contractors.

213114 Support Activities for Metal Mining[US]

This U.S. industry comprises establishments primarily engaged in providing support activities (except site preparation and related construction activities) on a contract or fee basis for the mining and quarrying of metallic minerals and for the extraction of metal ores. Exploration for minerals is included in this industry. Exploration (except geophysical surveying and mapping services) includes traditional prospecting methods, such as taking core samples and making geological observations at prospective sites.

Cross-References. Establishments primarily engaged in—

- Performing geophysical surveying and mapping services for metallic minerals on a contract or fee basis—are classified in Industry 541360, Geophysical Surveying and Mapping Services;
- Operating metallic mineral mines or quarries on a contract or fee basis—are classified in Industry Group 2122, Metal Ore Mining, based on the type of ore mined; and
- Site preparation and related construction activities on a contract or fee basis—are classified in Industry 238910, Site Preparation Contractors.

213115 Support Activities for Nonmetallic Minerals (except Fuels) Mining[US]

This U.S. industry comprises establishments primarily engaged in providing support activities, on a fee or contract basis, for the mining and quarrying of nonmetallic minerals (except fuel) and for the extraction of nonmetallic minerals (except site preparation and related construction activities). Exploration for miner-

US—United States industry only. CAN—United States and Canadian industries are comparable. MEX—United States and Mexican industries are comparable. Blank—Canadian, Mexican, and United States industries are comparable.

als is included in this industry. Exploration (except geophysical surveying and mapping services) includes traditional prospecting methods, such as taking core samples and making geological observations at prospective sites.

Cross-References. Establishments primarily engaged in—

- Performing geophysical surveying and mapping services for nonmetallic minerals on a contract or fee basis—are classified in Industry 541360, Geophysical Surveying and Mapping Services;
- Operating nonmetallic mineral mines or quarries on a contract or fee basis—are classified in Industry Group 2123, Nonmetallic Mineral Mining and Quarrying, based on the type of mineral mined or quarried; and
- Site preparation and related construction activities—are classified in Industry 238910, Site Preparation Contractors.

US—United States industry only. CAN—United States and Canadian industries are comparable. MEX—United States and Mexican industries are comparable. Blank—Canadian, Mexican, and United States industries are comparable.

Sector 22—Utilities

The Sector as a Whole

The Utilities sector comprises establishments engaged in the provision of the following utility services: electric power, natural gas, steam supply, water supply, and sewage removal. Within this sector, the specific activities associated with the utility services provided vary by utility: electric power includes generation, transmission, and distribution; natural gas includes distribution; steam supply includes provision and/or distribution; water supply includes treatment and distribution; and sewage removal includes collection, treatment, and disposal of waste through sewer systems and sewage treatment facilities.

Excluded from this sector are establishments primarily engaged in waste management services classified in Subsector 562, Waste Management and Remediation Services. These establishments also collect, treat, and dispose of waste materials; however, they do not use sewer systems or sewage treatment facilities.

221 Utilities[CAN]

Industries in the Utilities subsector provide electric power, natural gas, steam supply, water supply, and sewage removal through a permanent infrastructure of lines, mains, and pipes. Establishments are grouped together based on the utility service provided and the particular system or facilities required to perform the service.

2211 Electric Power Generation, Transmission and Distribution

This industry group comprises establishments primarily engaged in generating, transmitting, and/or distributing electric power. Establishments in this industry group may perform one or more of the following activities: (1) operate generation facilities that produce electric energy; (2) operate transmission systems that convey the electricity from the generation facility to the distribution system; and (3) operate distribution systems that convey electric power received from the generation facility or the transmission system to the final consumer.

22111 Electric Power Generation[CAN]

This industry comprises establishments primarily engaged in operating electric power generation facilities. These facilities convert other forms of energy, such as water power (i.e., hydroelectric), fossil fuels, nuclear power, and solar power,

US—United States industry only. CAN—United States and Canadian industries are comparable. MEX—United States and Mexican industries are comparable. Blank—Canadian, Mexican, and United States industries are comparable.

into electrical energy. The establishments in this industry produce electric energy and provide electricity to transmission systems or to electric power distribution systems.

Cross-References.

Establishments primarily engaged in operating trash incinerators that also generate electricity are classified in Industry 56221, Waste Treatment and Disposal.

221111 Hydroelectric Power Generation[CAN]

This U.S. industry comprises establishments primarily engaged in operating hydroelectric power generation facilities. These facilities use water power to drive a turbine and produce electric energy. The electric energy produced in these establishment is provided to electric power transmission systems or to electric power distribution systems.

221112 Fossil Fuel Electric Power Generation[CAN]

This U.S. industry comprises establishments primarily engaged in operating fossil fuel powered electric power generation facilities. These facilities use fossil fuels, such as coal, oil, or gas, in internal combustion or combustion turbine conventional steam process to produce electric energy. The electric energy produced in these establishments are provided to electric power transmission systems or to electric power distribution systems.

221113 Nuclear Electric Power Generation[CAN]

This U.S. industry comprises establishments primarily engaged in operating nuclear electric power generation facilities. These facilities use nuclear power to produce electric energy. The electric energy produced in these establishments are provided to electric power transmission systems or to electric power distribution systems.

221119 Other Electric Power Generation[CAN]

This U.S. industry comprises establishments primarily engaged in operating electric power generation facilities (except hydroelectric, fossil fuel, nuclear). These facilities convert other forms of energy, such as solar, wind, or tidal power, into electrical energy. The electric energy produced in these establishment is provided to electric power transmission systems or to electric power distribution systems.

US—United States industry only. CAN—United States and Canadian industries are comparable. MEX—United States and Mexican industries are comparable. Blank—Canadian, Mexican, and United States industries are comparable.

Cross-References. Establishments primarily engaged in—

- Operating trash disposal incinerators that also generate electricity—are classified in U.S. Industry 562213, Solid Waste Combustors and Incinerators;
- Operating hydroelectric power generation facilities—are classified in U.S. Industry 221111, Hydroelectric Power Generation;
- Operating fossil fuel powered electric power generation facilities—are classified in U.S. Industry 221112, Fossil Fuel Electric Power Generation; and
- Operating nuclear electric power generation facilities—are classified in U.S. Industry 221113, Nuclear Electric Power Generation.

22112 Electric Power Transmission, Control, and Distribution[CAN]

This industry comprises establishments primarily engaged in operating electric power transmission systems, controlling (i.e., regulating voltages) the transmission of electricity, and/or distributing electricity. The transmission system includes lines and transformer stations. These establishments arrange, facilitate, or coordinate the transmission of electricity from the generating source to the distribution centers, other electric utilities, or final consumers. The distribution system consists of lines, poles, meters, and wiring that deliver the electricity to final consumers.

Cross-References.

Establishments primarily engaged in generating electric energy are classified in Industry 22111, Electric Power Generation.

221121 Electric Bulk Power Transmission and Control[CAN]

This U.S. industry comprises establishments primarily engaged in operating electric power transmission systems and/or controlling (i.e., regulatory voltage) the transmission of electricity from the generating source to distribution centers or other electric utilities. The transmission system includes lines and transformer stations.

Cross-References. Establishments primarily engaged in—

- Generating electric energy—are classified in Industry 22111, Electric Power Generation; and
- Distributing electricity to final consumers—are classified in U.S. Industry 221122, Electric Power Distribution.

US—United States industry only. CAN—United States and Canadian industries are comparable. MEX—United States and Mexican industries are comparable. Blank—Canadian, Mexican, and United States industries are comparable.

221122 Electric Power Distribution[CAN]

This U.S. industry comprises electric power establishments primarily engaged in either (1) operating electric power distribution systems (i.e., consisting of lines, poles, meters, and wiring) or (2) operating as electric power brokers or agents that arrange the sale of electricity via power distribution systems operated by others.

Cross-References. Establishments primarily engaged in—

- Generating electric energy—are classified in Industry 22111, Electric Power Generation; and
- Transmitting electricity between generating sources or distribution centers—are classified in U.S. Industry 221121, Electric Bulk Power Transmission and Control.

2212 Natural Gas Distribution[CAN]

22121 Natural Gas Distribution[CAN]

See industry description for 221210 below.

221210 Natural Gas Distribution[CAN]

This industry comprises: (1) establishments primarily engaged in operating gas distribution systems (e.g., mains, meters); (2) establishments known as gas marketers that buy gas from the well and sell it to a distribution system; (3) establishments known as gas brokers or agents that arrange the sale of gas over gas distribution systems operated by others; and (4) establishments primarily engaged in transmitting and distributing gas to final consumers.

Cross-References. Establishments primarily engaged in—

- Pipeline transportation of natural gas from process plants to local distribution systems—are classified in Industry 486210, Pipeline Transportation of Natural Gas; and
- Retailing liquified petroleum (LP) gas via direct selling—are classified in U.S. Industry 454312, Liquefied Petroleum Gas (Bottled Gas) Dealers.

2213 Water, Sewage and Other Systems[CAN]

22131 Water Supply and Irrigation Systems[CAN]

See industry description for 221310 below.

US—United States industry only. CAN—United States and Canadian industries are comparable. MEX—United States and Mexican industries are comparable. Blank—Canadian, Mexican, and United States industries are comparable.

221310 Water Supply and Irrigation Systems[CAN]

This industry comprises establishments primarily engaged in operating water treatment plants and/or operating water supply systems. The water supply system may include pumping stations, aqueducts, and/or distribution mains. The water may be used for drinking, irrigation, or other uses.

22132 Sewage Treatment Facilities[CAN]

See industry description for 221320 below.

221320 Sewage Treatment Facilities[CAN]

This industry comprises establishments primarily engaged in operating sewer systems or sewage treatment facilities that collect, treat, and dispose of waste.

Cross-References. Establishments primarily engaged in—

- Operating waste treatment or disposal facilities (except sewer systems or sewage treatment facilities)—are classified in Industry 56221, Waste Treatment and Disposal;
- Pumping (i.e., cleaning) septic tanks and cesspools—are classified in U.S. Industry 562991, Septic Tank and Related Services; and
- Cleaning and rodding sewers and catch basins—are classified in U.S. Industry 562998, All Other Miscellaneous Waste Management Services.

22133 Steam and Air-Conditioning Supply[CAN]

See industry description for 221330 below.

221330 Steam and Air-Conditioning Supply[CAN]

This industry comprises establishments primarily engaged in providing steam, heated air, or cooled air. The steam distribution may be through mains.

US—United States industry only. CAN—United States and Canadian industries are comparable. MEX—United States and Mexican industries are comparable. Blank—Canadian, Mexican, and United States industries are comparable.

Sector 23—Construction

The Sector as a Whole

The construction sector comprises establishments primarily engaged in the construction of buildings or engineering projects (e.g., highways and utility systems). Establishments primarily engaged in the preparation of sites for new construction and establishments primarily engaged in subdividing land for sale as building sites also are included in this sector.

Construction work done may include new work, additions, alterations, or maintenance and repairs. Activities of these establishments generally are managed at a fixed place of business, but they usually perform construction activities at multiple project sites. Production responsibilities for establishments in this sector are usually specified in (1) contracts with the owners of construction projects (prime contracts) or (2) contracts with other construction establishments (subcontracts).

Establishments primarily engaged in contracts that include responsibility for all aspects of individual construction projects are commonly known as general contractors, but also may be known as design-builders, construction managers, turnkey contractors, or (in cases where two or more establishments jointly secure a general contract) joint-venture contractors. Construction managers that provide oversight and scheduling only (i.e., agency) as well as construction managers that are responsible for the entire project (i.e., at risk) are included as general contractor type establishments. Establishments of the ''general contractor type'' frequently arrange construction of separate parts of their projects through subcontracts with other construction establishments.

Establishments primarily engaged in activities to produce a specific component (e.g., masonry, painting, and electrical work) of a construction project are commonly known as specialty trade contractors. Activities of specialty trade contractors are usually subcontracted from other construction establishments but, especially in remodeling and repair construction, the work may be done directly for the owner of the property.

Establishments primarily engaged in activities to construct buildings to be sold on sites that they own are known as operative builders, but also may be known as speculative builders or merchant builders. Operative builders produce buildings in a manner similar to general contractors, but their production processes also include site acquisition and securing of financial backing. Operative builders are most often associated with the construction of residential buildings. Like general contractors, they may subcontract all or part of the actual construction work on their buildings.

There are substantial differences in the types of equipment, work force skills, and other inputs required by establishments in this sector. To highlight these differences and variations in the underlying production functions, this sector is divided into three subsectors.

US—United States industry only. CAN—United States and Canadian industries are comparable. MEX—United States and Mexican industries are comparable. Blank—Canadian, Mexican, and United States industries are comparable.

Subsector 236, Construction of Buildings, comprises establishments of the general contractor type and operative builders involved in the construction of buildings. Subsector 237, Heavy and Civil Engineering Construction, comprises establishments involved in the construction of engineering projects. Subsector 238, Specialty Trade Contractors, comprises establishments engaged in specialty trade activities generally needed in the construction of all types of buildings.

Force account construction is construction work performed by an enterprise primarily engaged in some business other than construction for its own account and use, using employees of the enterprise. This activity is not included in the construction sector unless the construction work performed is the primary activity of a separate establishment of the enterprise. The installation and the ongoing repair and maintenance of telecommunications and utility networks is excluded from construction when the establishments performing the work are not independent contractors. Although a growing proportion of this work is subcontracted to independent contractors in the Construction Sector, the operating units of telecommunications and utility companies performing this work are included with the telecommunications or utility activities.

236 Construction of Buildings

The Construction of Buildings subsector comprises establishments primarily responsible for the construction of buildings. The work performed may include new work, additions, alterations, or maintenance and repairs. The on-site assembly of precut, panelized, and prefabricated buildings and construction of temporary buildings are included in this subsector. Part or all of the production work for which the establishments in this sector have responsibility may be subcontracted to other construction establishments—usually specialty trade contractors.

Establishments in this subsector are classified based on the types of buildings they construct. This classification reflects variations in the requirements of the underlying production processes.

2361 Residential Building Construction

23611 Residential Building Construction

This Industry comprises establishments primarily responsible for the construction or remodeling and renovation of single-family and multifamily residential buildings. Included in this industry are residential housing general contractors (i.e., new construction, remodeling or renovating existing residential structures), operative builders and remodelers of residential structures, residential project construction management firms, and residential design-build firms.

US—United States industry only. CAN—United States and Canadian industries are comparable. MEX—United States and Mexican industries are comparable. Blank—Canadian, Mexican, and United States industries are comparable.

Cross-References. Establishments primarily engaged in—

- Performing specialized construction work on houses and other residential buildings, generally on a subcontract basis—are classified in Subsector 238, Specialty Trade Contractors;
- Performing manufactured (mobile) home setup and tie-down work—are classified in Industry 23899, All Other Specialty Trade Contractors; and
- Constructing and leasing residential buildings on their own account—are classified in Industry 53111, Lessors of Residential Buildings and Dwellings.

236115 New Single-Family Housing Construction (except Operative Builders)US

This U.S. industry comprises general contractor establishments primarily responsible for the entire construction of new single-family housing, such as single-family detached houses and town houses or row houses where each housing unit (1) is separated from its neighbors by a ground-to-roof wall and (2) has no housing units constructed above or below. This industry includes general contractors responsible for the on-site assembly of modular and prefabricated houses. Single-family housing design-build firms and single-family construction management firms acting as general contractors are included in this industry.

Cross-References. Establishments primarily engaged in—

- Building single-family houses on their own account for sale as operative or speculative builders—are classified in U.S. Industry 236117, New Housing Operative Builders;
- Remodeling or repairing existing houses and other residential buildings—are classified in U.S. Industry 236118, Residential Remodelers;
- Performing manufactured (mobile) home setup and tie-down work—are classified in Industry 238990, All Other Specialty Trade Contractors;
- Performing specialized construction work on houses and other residential buildings, generally on a subcontract basis—are classified in Subsector 238, Specialty Trade Contractors; and
- Constructing and leasing residential buildings on their own account—are classified in Industry 531110, Lessors of Residential Buildings and Dwellings.

236116 New Multifamily Housing Construction (except Operative Builders)US

This U.S. industry comprises general contractor establishments responsible for the construction of new multifamily residential housing units (e.g., high-rise,

US—United States industry only. CAN—United States and Canadian industries are comparable. MEX—United States and Mexican industries are comparable. Blank—Canadian, Mexican, and United States industries are comparable.

garden, and town house apartments and condominiums where each unit is not separated from its neighbors by a ground-to-roof wall). Multifamily design-build firms and multifamily housing construction management firms acting as general contractors are included in this industry.

Cross-References. Establishments primarily engaged in—

- Building multifamily buildings on their own account for sale as operative or speculative builders—are classified in U.S. Industry 236117, New Housing Operative Builders;
- Remodeling or repairing existing multifamily housing and other residential buildings—are classified in U.S. Industry 236118, Residential Remodelers;
- Performing specialized construction work on multifamily housing and other residential buildings, generally on a subcontract basis—are classified in Subsector 238, Specialty Trade Contractors; and
- Constructing and leasing residential buildings on their own account—are classified in Industry 531110, Lessors of Residential Buildings and Dwellings.

236117 New Housing Operative Builders[US]

This U.S. industry comprises operative builders primarily responsible for the entire construction of new houses and other residential buildings, single-family and multifamily, on their own account for sale. Operative builders are also known as speculative or merchant builders.

Cross-References. Establishments primarily engaged in—

- Building single-family houses for others as general contractors—are classified in U.S. Industry 236115, New Single-Family Housing Construction (except Operative Builders);
- Building multifamily residential buildings for others as general contractors—are classified in U.S. Industry 236116, New Multifamily Housing Construction (except Operative Builders);
- Remodeling or repairing existing houses and other residential buildings, either for others or on own account for sale—are classified in U.S. Industry 236118, Residential Remodelers;
- Performing specialized construction work on houses or other residential buildings, generally on a subcontract basis—are classified in Subsector 238, Specialty Trade Contractors; and

US—United States industry only. CAN—United States and Canadian industries are comparable. MEX—United States and Mexican industries are comparable. Blank—Canadian, Mexican, and United States industries are comparable.

- Constructing and leasing residential buildings on their own account—are classified in Industry 531110, Lessors of Residential Buildings and Dwellings.

236118 Residential Remodelers[US]

This U.S. industry comprises establishments primarily responsible for the remodeling construction (including additions, alterations, reconstruction, maintenance and repair work) of houses and other residential buildings, single-family and multifamily. Included in this industry are remodeling general contractors, operative remodelers, remodeling design-build firms, and remodeling project construction management firms.

Cross-References. Establishments primarily engaged in—

- Building single-family houses for others as general contractors—are classified in U.S. Industry 236115, New Single-Family Housing Construction (except Operative Builders);
- Building multifamily buildings for others as general contractors—are classified in U.S. Industry 236116, New Multifamily Housing Construction (except Operative Builders);
- Building houses or other residential buildings, on their own account for sale as operative or speculative builders—are classified in U.S. Industry 236117, New Housing Operative Builders;
- Remodeling nonresidential buildings—are classified in Industry Group 2362, Nonresidential Building Construction, based on the type of structure being remodeled;
- Performing specialized construction work on houses or other residential buildings generally on a subcontract basis—are classified in Subsector 238, Specialty Trade Contractors; and
- Constructing and leasing residential buildings on their own account—are classified in Industry 531110, Lessors of Residential Buildings and Dwellings.

2362 Nonresidential Building Construction

This industry group comprises establishments primarily responsible for the construction (including new work, additions, alterations, maintenance, and repairs) of nonresidential buildings. This industry group includes nonresidential general contractors, nonresidential operative builders, nonresidential design-build firms, and nonresidential project construction management firms.

US—United States industry only. CAN—United States and Canadian industries are comparable. MEX—United States and Mexican industries are comparable. Blank—Canadian, Mexican, and United States industries are comparable.

23621 Industrial Building Construction

See industry description for 236210 below.

236210 Industrial Building Construction[CAN]

This industry comprises establishments primarily responsible for the construction (including new work, additions, alterations, maintenance, and repairs) of industrial buildings (except warehouses). The construction of selected additional structures, whose production processes are similar to those for industrial buildings (e.g., incinerators, cement plants, blast furnaces, and similar nonbuilding structures), is included in this industry. Included in this industry are industrial building general contractors, industrial building operative builders, industrial building design-build firms, and industrial building construction management firms.

Illustrative Examples:

Assembly plant construction
Cannery construction
Cement plant construction
Chemical plant (except petrochemical) construction
Factory construction
Food processing plant construction
Furnace, industrial plant, construction
Mine loading and discharging station construction
Paper or pulp mill construction
Pharmaceutical manufacturing plant construction
Steel mill construction
Waste disposal plant (except sewage treatment) construction

Cross-References. Establishments primarily engaged in—

- Constructing oil refineries and petrochemical plant—are classified in Industry 237120, Oil and Gas Pipeline and Related Structures Construction;
- Constructing water treatment plants, sewage treatment plants, and pumping stations for water and sewer systems—are classified in Industry 237110, Water and Sewer Line and Related Structures Construction;
- Constructing power generation plants (except hydroelectric)—are classified in Industry 237130, Power and Communication Line and Related Structures Construction;
- Constructing industrial warehouses—are classified in Industry 236220, Commercial and Institutional Building Construction; and
- Performing specialized construction work on industrial buildings, generally on a subcontract basis—are classified in Subsector 238, Specialty Trade Contractors.

23622 Commercial and Institutional Building Construction

See industry description for 236220 below.

US—United States industry only. CAN—United States and Canadian industries are comparable. MEX—United States and Mexican industries are comparable. Blank—Canadian, Mexican, and United States industries are comparable.

236220 Commercial and Institutional Building Construction[CAN]

This industry comprises establishments primarily responsible for the construction (including new work, additions, alterations, maintenance, and repairs) of commercial and institutional buildings and related structures, such as stadiums, grain elevators, and indoor swimming pools. This industry includes establishments responsible for the on-site assembly of modular or prefabricated commercial and institutional buildings. Included in this industry are commercial and institutional building general contractors, commercial and institutional building operative builders, commercial and institutional building design-build firms, and commercial and institutional building project construction management firms.

Illustrative Examples:

Airport building construction
Arena construction
Barrack construction
Farm building construction
Fire station construction
Grain elevator construction
Hospital construction
Hotel construction
Indoor swimming pool construction
Office building construction
Parking garage construction
Prison construction
Radio and television broadcast studio construction
Religious building (e.g., church, synagogue, mosque, temple) construction
Restaurant construction
School building construction
Shopping mall construction
Warehouse construction (e.g., commercial, industrial, manufacturing, private)

Cross-References. Establishments primarily engaged in—

- Constructing structures that are integral parts of utility systems (e.g., storage tanks, pumping stations) or are used to produce products for these systems (e.g., power plants, refineries)—are classified in Industry Group 2371, Utility System Construction, based on type of construction project;
- Performing specialized construction work on commercial and institutional buildings generally on a subcontract basis—are classified in Subsector 238, Specialty Trade Contractors; and
- Constructing buildings on their own account for rent or lease—are classified in Industry Group 5311, Lessors of Real Estate.

237 Heavy and Civil Engineering Construction

The Heavy and Civil Engineering Construction subsector comprises establishments whose primary activity is the construction of entire engineering projects (e.g., highways and dams), and specialty trade contractors, whose primary activity

US—United States industry only. CAN—United States and Canadian industries are comparable. MEX—United States and Mexican industries are comparable. Blank—Canadian, Mexican, and United States industries are comparable.

is the production of a specific component for such projects. Specialty trade contractors in Heavy and Civil Engineering Construction generally are performing activities that are specific to heavy and civil engineering construction projects and are not normally performed on buildings. The work performed may include new work, additions, alterations, or maintenance and repairs.

Specialty trade activities are classified in this subsector if the skills and equipment present are specific to heavy or civil engineering construction projects. For example, specialized equipment is needed to paint lines on highways. This equipment is not normally used in building applications so the activity is classified in this subsector. Traffic signal installation, while specific to highways, uses much of the same skills and equipment that are needed for electrical work in building projects and is therefore classified in Subsector 238, Specialty Trade Contractors.

Construction projects involving water resources (e.g., dredging and land drainage) and projects involving open space improvement (e.g., parks and trails) are included in this subsector. Establishments whose primary activity is the subdivision of land into individual building lots usually perform various additional site-improvement activities (e.g., road building and utility line installation) and are included in this subsector.

Establishments in this subsector are classified based on the types of structures that they construct. This classification reflects variations in the requirements of the underlying production processes.

2371 Utility System Construction

This industry group comprises establishments primarily engaged in the construction of distribution lines and related buildings and structures for utilities (i.e., water, sewer, petroleum, gas, power, and communication). All structures (including buildings) that are integral parts of utility systems (e.g., storage tanks, pumping stations, power plants, and refineries) are included in this industry group.

23711 Water and Sewer Line and Related Structures Construction

See industry description for 237110 below.

237110 Water and Sewer Line and Related Structures Construction[CAN]

This industry comprises establishments primarily engaged in the construction of water and sewer lines, mains, pumping stations, treatment plants and storage tanks. The work performed may include new work, reconstruction, rehabilitation, and repairs. Specialty trade contractors are included in this group if they are engaged in activities primarily related to water and sewer line and related structures construction. All structures (including buildings) that are integral parts of water

---

US—United States industry only. CAN—United States and Canadian industries are comparable. MEX—United States and Mexican industries are comparable. Blank—Canadian, Mexican, and United States industries are comparable.

and sewer networks (e.g., storage tanks, pumping stations, water treatment plants, and sewage treatment plants) are included in this industry.

Illustrative Examples:

Distribution line, sewer and water, construction
Fire hydrant installation
Irrigation systems construction
Pumping station, water and sewage system, construction
Reservoir construction
Sewage disposal plant construction
Sewer main, pipe, and connection, construction
Storm sewer construction
Water main and line construction
Water system storage tank and tower construction
Water treatment plant construction
Water well drilling, digging, boring, or sinking (except water intake wells in oil and gas fields)

Cross-References.

Establishments primarily engaged in constructing marine facilities (e.g., ports), flood control structures, dams, or hydroelectric power generation facilities are classified in Industry 237990, Other Heavy and Civil Engineering Construction.

23712 Oil and Gas Pipeline and Related Structures Construction

See industry description for 237120 below.

237120 Oil and Gas Pipeline and Related Structures Construction[CAN]

This industry comprises establishments primarily engaged in the construction of oil and gas lines, mains, refineries, and storage tanks. The work performed may include new work, reconstruction, rehabilitation, and repairs. Specialty trade contractors are included in this group if they are engaged in activities primarily related to oil and gas pipeline and related structures construction. All structures (including buildings) that are integral parts of oil and gas networks (e.g., storage tanks, pumping stations, and refineries) are included in this industry.

Illustrative Examples:

Distribution line, gas and oil, construction
Gas main construction
Gathering line, gas and oil field, construction
Natural gas pipeline construction
Natural gas processing plant construction
Oil refinery construction
Petrochemical plant construction
Pumping station, gas and oil transmission, construction
Storage tank, natural gas or oil, tank farm or field, construction

US—United States industry only. CAN—United States and Canadian industries are comparable. MEX—United States and Mexican industries are comparable. Blank—Canadian, Mexican, and United States industries are comparable.

Cross-References.

Establishments primarily engaged in building chemical plants (except petrochemical) and similar process or batch facilities are classified in Industry 236210, Industrial Building Construction.

23713 Power and Communication Line and Related Structures Construction

See industry description for 237130 below.

237130 Power and Communication Line and Related Structures Construction[CAN]

This industry comprises establishments primarily engaged in the construction of power lines and towers, power plants, and radio, television, and telecommunications transmitting/receiving towers. The work performed may include new work, reconstruction, rehabilitation, and repairs. Specialty trade contractors are included in this group if they are engaged in activities primarily related to power and communication line and related structures construction. All structures (including buildings) that are integral parts of power and communication networks (e.g., transmitting towers, substations, and power plants) are included.

Illustrative Examples:

Alternative energy (e.g., geothermal, ocean wave, solar, wind) structure construction
Cellular phone tower construction
Co-generation plant construction
Communication tower construction
Electric light and power plant (except hydroelectric) construction
Electric power transmission line and tower construction
Nuclear power plant construction
Power line stringing
Radio transmitting tower construction
Satellite receiving station construction
Telephone line stringing
Transformer station and substation, electric power, construction
Underground cable (e.g., cable television, electricity, telephone) laying

Cross-References. Establishments primarily engaged in—

- Constructing hydroelectric generating facilities—are classified in Industry 237990, Other Heavy and Civil Engineering Construction;
- Constructing broadcast studios and similar nonresidential buildings—are classified in Industry 236220, Commercial and Institutional Building Construction;
- Performing electrical work within buildings—are classified in Industry 238210, Electrical Contractors;

US—United States industry only. CAN—United States and Canadian industries are comparable. MEX—United States and Mexican industries are comparable. Blank—Canadian, Mexican, and United States industries are comparable.

- Line slashing or cutting (except maintenance)—are classified in Industry 238910, Site Preparation Contractors;
- Installing and maintaining communication transmission lines performed by telecommunications companies—are classified in Subsector 517, Telecommunications;
- Locating underground utility lines prior to digging—are classified in Industry 561990, All Other Support Services; and
- Tree and brush trimming for overhead utility lines—are classified in Industry 561730, Landscaping Services.

2372 Land Subdivision

23721 Land Subdivision

See industry description for 237210 below.

237210 Land Subdivision[CAN]

This industry comprises establishments primarily engaged in servicing land and subdividing real property into lots, for subsequent sale to builders. Servicing of land may include excavation work for the installation of roads and utility lines. The extent of work may vary from project to project. Land subdivision precedes building activity and the subsequent building is often residential, but may also be commercial tracts and industrial parks. These establishments may do all the work themselves or subcontract the work to others. Establishments that perform only the legal subdivision of land are not included in this industry.

Cross-References. Establishments primarily engaged in—

- Constructing buildings, for sale, on lots they subdivide—are classified in Industry Group 2361, Residential Building Construction, or Industry Group 2362, Nonresidential Building Construction, based on the type of construction project;
- Installing roads on a subcontract basis for land subdividers—are classified in Industry 237310, Highway, Street, and Bridge Construction;
- Installing utilities on a subcontract basis for land subdividers—are classified in Industry Group 2371, Utility System Construction;
- Preparing land owned by others for building construction—are classified in Industry 238910, Site Preparation Contractors;
- Constructing buildings, for rent or own use, on lots they subdivide—are classified in Industry Group 5311, Lessors of Real Estate; and

---

US—United States industry only. CAN—United States and Canadian industries are comparable. MEX—United States and Mexican industries are comparable. Blank—Canadian, Mexican, and United States industries are comparable.

- Legal subdivision of land without land preparation—are classified elsewhere in the classification system based on the primary activity of the establishment.

2373 Highway, Street, and Bridge Construction

23731 Highway, Street, and Bridge Construction

See industry description for 237310 below.

237310 Highway, Street, and Bridge Construction[CAN]

This industry comprises establishments primarily engaged in the construction of highways (including elevated), streets, roads, airport runways, public sidewalks, or bridges. The work performed may include new work, reconstruction, rehabilitation, and repairs. Specialty trade contractors are included in this group if they are engaged in activities primarily related to highway, street, and bridge construction (e.g., installing guardrails on highways).

Illustrative Examples:

Airport runway construction
Causeway construction
Culverts, highway, road, and street, construction
Elevated highway construction
Guardrail construction
Highway line painting
Painting traffic lanes or parking lot
Pothole filling, highway, road, street, or bridge
Resurfacing, highway, road, street, or bridge
Sign erection, highway, road, street, or bridge

Cross-References. Establishments primarily engaged in—

- Constructing tunnels—are classified in Industry 237990, Other Heavy and Civil Engineering Construction;
- Highway lighting and signal installation—are classified in Industry 238210, Electrical Contractors;
- Painting bridges—are classified in Industry 238320, Painting and Wall Covering Contractors; and
- Constructing parking lots and private driveways and sidewalks, or erecting billboards—are classified in Industry 238990, All Other Specialty Trade Contractors.

2379 Other Heavy and Civil Engineering Construction

23799 Other Heavy and Civil Engineering Construction

See industry description for 237990 below.

US—United States industry only. CAN—United States and Canadian industries are comparable. MEX—United States and Mexican industries are comparable. Blank—Canadian, Mexican, and United States industries are comparable.

237990 Other Heavy and Civil Engineering Construction[CAN]

This industry comprises establishments primarily engaged in heavy and engineering construction projects (excluding highway, street, bridge, and distribution line construction). The work performed may include new work, reconstruction, rehabilitation, and repairs. Specialty trade contractors are included in this group if they are engaged in activities primarily related to engineering construction projects (excluding highway, street, bridge, distribution line, oil and gas structure, and utilities building and structure construction). Construction projects involving water resources (e.g., dredging and land drainage), development of marine facilities, and projects involving open space improvement (e.g., parks and trails) are included in this industry.

Illustrative Examples:

Channel construction
Dam construction
Dock construction
Dredging (e.g., canal, channel, ditch, waterway)
Earth retention system construction
Flood control project construction
Golf course construction
Horizontal drilling (e.g., cable, pipeline, sewer installation)
Hydroelectric generating station construction
Land drainage contractors
Marine construction
Microtunneling contractors
Nuclear waste disposal site construction
Park ground and recreational open space improvement construction
Railroad construction
Subway construction
Trenching, underwater
Tunnel construction

Cross-References. Establishments primarily engaged in—

- Constructing water mains, sewers, and related structures—are classified in Industry 237110, Water and Sewer Line and Related Structures Construction;
- Constructing oil and gas pipelines and related structures—are classified in Industry 237120, Oil and Gas Pipeline and Related Structures Construction;
- Constructing power and communication transmission lines and related structures—are classified in Industry 237130, Power and Communication Line and Related Structures Construction;
- Constructing highways, streets, and bridges—are classified in Industry 237310, Highway, Street, and Bridge Construction; and
- Trenching (except underwater)—are classified in U.S. Industry 238910, Site Preparation Contractors.

US—United States industry only. CAN—United States and Canadian industries are comparable. MEX—United States and Mexican industries are comparable. Blank—Canadian, Mexican, and United States industries are comparable.

238 Specialty Trade Contractors

The Specialty Trade Contractors subsector comprises establishments whose primary activity is performing specific activities (e.g., pouring concrete, site preparation, plumbing, painting, and electrical work) involved in building construction or other activities that are similar for all types of construction but that are not responsible for the entire project. The work performed may include new work, additions, alterations, maintenance, and repairs. The production work performed by establishments in this subsector is usually subcontracted from establishments of the general contractor type or operative builders but, especially in remodeling and repair construction, work also may be done directly for the owner of the property. Specialty trade contractors usually perform most of their work at the construction site, although they may have shops where they perform prefabrication and other work. Establishments primarily engaged in preparing sites for new construction are also included in this subsector.

There are substantial differences in types of equipment, work force skills, and other inputs required by specialty trade contractors. Establishments in this subsector are classified based on the underlying production function for the specialty trade in which they specialize. Throughout the Specialty Trade Contractors subsector, establishments commonly provide both the parts and labor required to complete work. For example, electrical contractors supply the current-carrying and noncurrent-carrying wiring devices that are required to install a circuit. Plumbing, Heating and Air-Conditioning contractors also supply the parts required to complete a contract.

Establishments that specialize in activities primarily related to heavy and civil engineering construction that are not normally performed on buildings, such as the painting of lines on highways are classified in Subsector 237, Heavy and Civil Engineering Construction.

Establishments that are primarily engaged in selling construction materials are classified in Sector 42, Wholesale Trade, or Sector 44-45, Retail Trade, based on the characteristics of the selling unit.

2381 Foundation, Structure, and Building Exterior Contractors

This industry group comprises establishments primarily engaged in the specialty trades needed to complete the basic structure (i.e., foundation, frame, and shell) of buildings. The work performed may include new work, additions, alterations, maintenance, and repairs.

23811 Poured Concrete Foundation and Structure Contractors[CAN]

See industry description for 238110 below.

US—United States industry only. CAN—United States and Canadian industries are comparable. MEX—United States and Mexican industries are comparable. Blank—Canadian, Mexican, and United States industries are comparable.

238110 Poured Concrete Foundation and Structure Contractors[CAN]

This industry comprises establishments primarily engaged in pouring and finishing concrete foundations and structural elements. This industry also includes establishments performing grout and shotcrete work. The work performed may include new work, additions, alterations, maintenance, and repairs.

Illustrative Examples:

Concrete work (except paving)
Concrete pouring and finishing
Concrete pumping (i.e., placement)
Footing and foundation concrete contractors
Gunite contractors
Mud-jacking contractors
Shotcrete contractors

Cross-References. Establishments primarily engaged in—

- Constructing or paving streets, highways, and public sidewalks—are classified in Industry 237310, Highway, Street, and Bridge Construction;
- Concrete sealing, coating, waterproofing, or dampproofing—are classified in Industry 238390, Other Building Finishing Contractors; and
- Paving residential driveways, commercial parking lots, and other private parking areas—are classified in Industry 238990, All Other Specialty Trade Contractors.

23812 Structural Steel and Precast Concrete Contractors

See industry description for 238120 below.

238120 Structural Steel and Precast Concrete Contractors[CAN]

This industry comprises establishments primarily engaged in: (1) erecting and assembling structural parts made from steel or precast concrete (e.g., steel beams, structural steel components, and similar products of precast concrete); and/or (2) assembling and installing other steel construction products (e.g., steel rods, bars, rebar, mesh, and cages) to reinforce poured-in-place concrete. The work performed may include new work, additions, alterations, maintenance, and repairs.

Illustrative Examples:

Concrete product (e.g., structural precast, structural prestressed) installation
Erecting structural steel
Precast concrete panel, slab, or form installation
Rebar contractors
Reinforcing steel contractors

US—United States industry only. CAN—United States and Canadian industries are comparable. MEX—United States and Mexican industries are comparable. Blank—Canadian, Mexican, and United States industries are comparable.

Placing and tying reinforcing rod at a construction site
Structural steel contractors

Cross-References.

Establishments primarily engaged in pouring concrete at the construction site for building foundations or structural elements are classified in Industry 238110, Poured Concrete Foundation and Structure Contractors.

23813 Framing Contractors[CAN]

See industry description for 238130 below.

238130 Framing Contractors[CAN]

This industry comprises establishments primarily engaged in structural framing and sheathing using materials other than structural steel or concrete. The work performed may include new work, additions, alterations, maintenance, and repairs.

Illustrative Examples:

Building framing (except structural steel)
Foundation, building, wood, contractors
Framing contractors
Post frame contractors
Steel framing contractors
Wood frame component (e.g., truss) fabrication on site

Cross-References. Establishments primarily engaged in—

- Finish carpentry—are classified in Industry 238350, Finish Carpentry Contractors; and
- Installing structural steel or precast concrete framing or structural elements—are classified in Industry 238120, Structural Steel and Precast Concrete Contractors.

23814 Masonry Contractors[CAN]

See industry description for 238140 below.

238140 Masonry Contractors[CAN]

This industry comprises establishments primarily engaged in masonry work, stone setting, brick laying, and other stone work. The work performed may include new work, additions, alterations, maintenance, and repairs.

US—United States industry only. CAN—United States and Canadian industries are comparable. MEX—United States and Mexican industries are comparable. Blank—Canadian, Mexican, and United States industries are comparable.

Illustrative Examples:

Block laying
Brick laying
Concrete block laying
Foundation (e.g., brick, block, stone), building, contractors
Marble, granite, and slate, exterior, contractors
Masonry pointing, cleaning, or caulking
Stucco contractors

Cross-References. Establishments primarily engaged in—

- Erecting the basic structure of buildings by pouring concrete—are classified in Industry 238110, Poured Concrete Foundation and Structure Contractors;
- Interior marble, granite and slate work—are classified in Industry 238340, Tile and Terrazzo Contractors; and
- Laying precast stones or bricks for patios, sidewalks, and driveways; or paving residential driveways, commercial parking lots and other private parking areas—are classified in Industry 238990, All Other Specialty Trade Contractors.

23815 Glass and Glazing Contractors[CAN]

See industry description for 238150 below.

238150 Glass and Glazing Contractors[CAN]

This industry comprises establishments primarily engaged in installing glass panes in prepared openings (i.e., glazing work) and other glass work for buildings. The work performed may include new work, additions, alterations, maintenance, and repairs.

Illustrative Examples:

Decorative glass and mirror installation
Glass cladding installation
Glass coating and tinting (except automotive) contractors
Glass installation (except automotive) contractors
Glazing contractors
Stained glass installation
Window pane or sheet installation

Cross-References. Establishments primarily engaged in—

- Installing prefabricated window units—are classified in Industry 238350, Finish Carpentry Contractors; and
- The replacement, repair, and/or tinting of automotive glass—are classified in U.S. Industry 811122, Automotive Glass Replacement Shops.

US—United States industry only. CAN—United States and Canadian industries are comparable. MEX—United States and Mexican industries are comparable. Blank—Canadian, Mexican, and United States industries are comparable.

23816 Roofing Contractors[CAN]

See industry description for 238160 below.

238160 Roofing Contractors[CAN]

This industry comprises establishments primarily engaged in roofing. This industry also includes establishments treating roofs (i.e., spraying, painting, or coating) and installing skylights. The work performed may include new work, additions, alterations, maintenance, and repairs.

Illustrative Examples:

Painting, spraying, or coating, roof
Shake and shingle, roof, installation
Sheet metal roofing installation
Skylight installation

Cross-References. Establishments primarily engaged in—

- Installing roof trusses and sheathing attached to trusses—are classified in Industry 238130, Framing Contractors; and
- Installing downspouts, gutters, fascia, and soffits—are classified in Industry 238170, Siding Contractors.

23817 Siding Contractors[CAN]

See industry description for 238170 below.

238170 Siding Contractors[CAN]

This industry comprises establishments primarily engaged in installing siding of wood, aluminum, vinyl or other exterior finish material (except brick, stone, stucco, or curtain wall). This industry also includes establishments installing gutters and downspouts. The work performed may include new work, additions, alterations, maintenance, and repairs.

Illustrative Examples:

Downspout, gutter, and gutter guard installation
Fascia and soffit installation
Siding (e.g., vinyl, wood, aluminum)

Cross-References. Establishments primarily engaged in—

- Installing brick, stone, or stucco building exterior finish materials—are classified in Industry 238140, Masonry Contractors;
- Installing curtain wall—are classified in Industry 238190, Other Foundation, Structure, and Building Exterior Contractors; and

---

US—United States industry only. CAN—United States and Canadian industries are comparable. MEX—United States and Mexican industries are comparable. Blank—Canadian, Mexican, and United States industries are comparable.

- Installing sheet metal duct work—are classified in Industry 238220, Plumbing, Heating, and Air-Conditioning Contractors.

23819 Other Foundation, Structure, and Building Exterior Contractors[CAN]

See industry description for 238190 below.

238190 Other Foundation, Structure, and Building Exterior Contractors[CAN]

This industry comprises establishments primarily engaged in building foundation and structure trades work (except poured concrete, structural steel, precast concrete, framing, masonry, glass and glazing, roofing, and siding). The work performed may include new work, additions, alterations, maintenance, and repairs.

Illustrative Examples:

Curtain wall, metal, installation
Decorative steel and wrought iron work installation
Fire escape installation
Forms for poured concrete, erecting and dismantling
Ornamental metal work installation
Welding, on site, contractors

Cross-References: Establishments primarily engaged in—

- Poured concrete foundation and structure work—are classified in Industry 238110, Poured Concrete Foundation and Structure Contractors;
- Installation of structural steel or precast concrete building components—are classified in Industry 238120, Structural Steel and Precast Concrete Contractors;
- Framing buildings—are classified in Industry 238130, Framing Contractors;
- Masonry work—are classified in Industry 238140, Masonry Contractors;
- Glass and glazing work—are classified in Industry 238150, Glass and Glazing Contractors;
- Installing or repairing roofs—are classified in Industry 238160, Roofing Contractors; and
- Installing siding—are classified in Industry 238170, Siding Contractors.

2382 Building Equipment Contractors

This industry group comprises establishments primarily engaged in installing or servicing equipment that forms part of a building mechanical system (e.g.,

US—United States industry only. CAN—United States and Canadian industries are comparable. MEX—United States and Mexican industries are comparable. Blank—Canadian, Mexican, and United States industries are comparable.

electricity, water, heating, and cooling). The work performed may include new work, additions, alterations, or maintenance and repairs. Contractors installing specialized building equipment, such as elevators, escalators, service station equipment, and central vacuum cleaning systems are also included.

23821 Electrical Contractors

See industry description for 238210 below.

238210 Electrical Contractors[CAN]

This industry comprises establishments primarily engaged in installing and servicing electrical wiring and equipment. Electrical contractors included in this industry may include both the parts and labor when performing work. Electrical contractors may perform new work, additions, alterations, maintenance, and repairs.

Illustrative Examples:

Airport runway lighting contractors
Alarm system (e.g., fire, burglar), electric, installation only
Audio equipment (except automotive) installation contractors
Cable television hookup contractors
Cable splicing, electrical or fiber optic
Computer and network cable installation
Environmental control system installation
Fiber optic cable (except transmission line) contractors
Highway, street, and bridge lighting and electrical signal installation
Home automation system installation
Lighting system installation
Telecommunication equipment and wiring (except transmission line) installation contractors
Traffic signal installation

Cross-References. Establishments primarily engaged in—

- Installing and maintaining telecommunications lines by telecommunications companies—are classified in Subsector 517, Telecommunications;
- Constructing power and communication transmission lines—are classified in Industry 237130, Power and Communication Line and Related Structures Construction; and
- Burglar and fire alarm installation combined with sales, maintenance, or monitoring services—are classified in U.S. Industry 561621, Security Systems Services (except Locksmiths).

23822 Plumbing, Heating, and Air-Conditioning Contractors

See industry description for 238220 below.

US—United States industry only. CAN—United States and Canadian industries are comparable. MEX—United States and Mexican industries are comparable. Blank—Canadian, Mexican, and United States industries are comparable.

238220 Plumbing, Heating, and Air-Conditioning Contractors[CAN]

This industry comprises establishments primarily engaged in installing and servicing plumbing, heating, and air-conditioning equipment. Contractors in this industry may provide both parts and labor when performing work. The work performed may include new work, additions, alterations, maintenance, and repairs.

Illustrative Examples:

Cooling tower installation
Duct work (e.g., cooling, dust collection, exhaust, heating, ventilation) installation
Fire sprinkler system installation
Fireplace, natural gas, installation
Furnace installation
Heating, ventilation, and air-conditioning (HVAC) contractors
Lawn sprinkler system installation
Mechanical contractors
Refrigeration system (e.g., commercial, industrial, scientific) installation
Sewer hook-up and connection, building

Cross-References. Establishments primarily engaged in—

- Installing electrical controls for HVAC systems—are classified in Industry 238210, Electrical Contractors; and
- Duct cleaning—are classified in Industry 561790, Other Services to Buildings and Dwellings.

23829 Other Building Equipment Contractors

See industry description for 238290 below.

238290 Other Building Equipment Contractors[US]

This industry comprises establishments primarily engaged in installing or servicing building equipment (except electrical; plumbing; heating, cooling, or ventilation equipment). The repair and maintenance of miscellaneous building equipment is included in this industry. The work performed may include new work, additions, alterations, maintenance, and repairs.

Illustrative Examples:

Automated and revolving door installation
Boiler and pipe insulation installation
Commercial-type door installation
Conveyor system installation
Dismantling large-scale machinery and equipment
Lightning protection equipment (e.g., lightning rod) installation
Machine rigging
Millwrights
Overhead door, commercial- or industrial-type, installation
Revolving door installation

US—United States industry only. CAN—United States and Canadian industries are comparable. MEX—United States and Mexican industries are comparable. Blank—Canadian, Mexican, and United States industries are comparable.

Elevator installation
Escalator installation
Gasoline pump, service station, installation
Satellite dish, household-type, installation
Vacuum cleaning system, built-in, installation

Cross-References. Establishments primarily engaged in—

- Manufacturing of industrial equipment with incidental installation—are classified in Sectors 31-33, Manufacturing; and
- Repair and maintenance of commercial refrigeration equipment or production equipment—are classified in Industry 811310, Commercial and Industrial Machinery and Equipment (except Automotive and Electronic) Repair and Maintenance.

2383 Building Finishing Contractors

This industry group comprises establishments primarily engaged in the specialty trades needed to finish buildings. The work performed may include new work, additions, alterations, or maintenance and repairs.

23831 Drywall and Insulation Contractors

See industry description for 238310 below.

238310 Drywall and Insulation Contractors[CAN]

This industry comprises establishments primarily engaged in drywall, plaster work, and building insulation work. Plaster work includes applying plain or ornamental plaster, and installation of lath to receive plaster. The work performed may include new work, additions, alterations, maintenance, and repairs.

Illustrative Examples:

Acoustical ceiling tile and panel installation
Drop ceiling installation
Drywall contractors
Fresco (i.e., decorative plaster finishing) contractors
Gypsum board installation
Lathing contractors
Plastering (i.e., ornamental, plain) contractors
Soundproofing contractors
Taping and finishing drywall
Wall cavity and attic space insulation installation

Cross-References. Establishments primarily engaged in—

- Applying stucco—are classified in Industry 238140, Masonry Contractors; and

US—United States industry only. CAN—United States and Canadian industries are comparable. MEX—United States and Mexican industries are comparable. Blank—Canadian, Mexican, and United States industries are comparable.

- Insulating pipes and boilers—are classified in Industry 238290, Other Building Equipment Contractors.

23832 Painting and Wall Covering Contractors

See industry description for 238320 below.

238320 Painting and Wall Covering Contractors[CAN]

This industry comprises establishments primarily engaged in interior or exterior painting or interior wall covering. The work performed may include new work, additions, alterations, maintenance, and repairs.

Illustrative Examples:

Bridge painting
House painting
Paint and wallpaper stripping
Paperhanging or removal contractors
Ship painting contractors
Wallpaper hanging and removal contractors

Cross-References. Establishments primarily engaged in—

- Painting lines on highways, streets, and parking lots—are classified in Industry 237310, Highway, Street, and Bridge Construction;
- Roof painting—are classified in Industry 238160, Roofing Contractors; and
- Installing wood paneling—are classified in Industry 238350, Finish Carpentry Contractors.

23833 Flooring Contractors

See industry description for 238330 below.

238330 Flooring Contractors[CAN]

This industry comprises establishments primarily engaged in the installation of resilient floor tile, carpeting, linoleum, and hard wood flooring. The work performed may include new work, additions, alterations, maintenance, and repairs.

Illustrative Examples:

Carpet, installation only
Floor laying, scraping, finishing, and refinishing
Hardwood flooring, installation only
Resilient floor tile or sheet (e.g., linoleum, rubber, vinyl), installation only
Resurfacing hardwood flooring
Vinyl flooring contractors

US—United States industry only. CAN—United States and Canadian industries are comparable. MEX—United States and Mexican industries are comparable. Blank—Canadian, Mexican, and United States industries are comparable.

Cross-References. Establishments primarily engaged in—

- Laying concrete flooring—are classified in Industry 238110, Poured Concrete Foundation and Structure Contractors;
- Installing stone or ceramic floor tile—are classified in Industry 238340, Tile and Terrazzo Contractors; and
- Selling and installing carpet and other flooring products as retail establishments—are classified in Sector 44-45, Retail Trade.

23834 Tile and Terrazzo Contractors

See industry description for 238340 below.

238340 Tile and Terrazzo Contractors[CAN]

This industry comprises establishments primarily engaged in setting and installing ceramic tile, stone (interior only), and mosaic and/or mixing marble particles and cement to make terrazzo at the job site. The work performed may include new work, additions, alterations, maintenance, and repairs.

Illustrative Examples:

Ceramic tile installation
Mantel, marble or stone, installation
Marble, granite, and slate, interior installation contractors
Mosaic work
Stone flooring installation
Tile (except resilient) laying and setting

Cross-References. Establishments primarily engaged in—

- Exterior marble, granite, and slate work—are classified in Industry 238140, Masonry Contractors;
- Manufacturing precast terrazzo products—are classified in Industry 327390, Other Concrete Product Manufacturing; and
- Installing, without selling resilient floor tile—are classified in Industry 238330, Flooring Contractors.

23835 Finish Carpentry Contractors

See industry description for 238350 below.

238350 Finish Carpentry Contractors[CAN]

This industry comprises establishments primarily engaged in finish carpentry work. The work performed may include new work, additions, alterations, maintenance, and repairs.

US—United States industry only. CAN—United States and Canadian industries are comparable. MEX—United States and Mexican industries are comparable. Blank—Canadian, Mexican, and United States industries are comparable.

Illustrative Examples:

Built-in wood cabinets constructed on site
Counter top, residential-type, installation
Door and window frame construction
Garage door, residential-type, installation
Millwork installation
Molding or trim, wood or plastic, installation
Paneling installation
Prefabricated kitchen and bath cabinet, residential-type, installation
Ship joinery contractors
Window and door, residential type, of any material, prefabricated, installation

Cross-References. Establishments primarily engaged in—

- Installing skylights—are classified in Industry 238160, Roofing Contractors;
- Framing—are classified in Industry 238130, Framing Contractors; and
- Building custom kitchen and bath cabinets (except free standing) in a shop are—classified in Industry 337110, Wood Kitchen Cabinet and Countertop Manufacturing.

23839 Other Building Finishing Contractors

See industry description for 238390 below.

238390 Other Building Finishing Contractors[CAN]

This industry comprises establishments primarily engaged in building finishing trade work (except drywall, plaster and insulation work; painting and wall covering work; flooring work; tile and terrazzo work; and finish carpentry work). The work performed may include new work, additions, alterations, or maintenance and repairs.

Illustrative Examples:

Bath tub refinishing on site
Closet organizer system installation
Concrete coating, glazing, or sealing
Countertop and cabinet, metal (except residential-type), installation
Drapery fixture (e.g., hardware, rods, tracks) installation
Fabricating metal cabinets or countertops on site
Modular furniture system attachment and installation
Trade show exhibit installation and dismantling
Waterproofing contractors
Window shade and blind installation

Cross-References. Establishments primarily engaged in—

- Installing drywall, plaster or insulation—are classified in Industry 238310, Drywall and Insulation Contractors;

US—United States industry only. CAN—United States and Canadian industries are comparable. MEX—United States and Mexican industries are comparable. Blank—Canadian, Mexican, and United States industries are comparable.

- Installing or removing paint or wall coverings—are classified in Industry 238320, Painting and Wall Covering Contractors;
- Installing or repairing wood floors, resilient flooring, and carpet—are classified in Industry 238330, Flooring Contractors;
- Setting tile or performing terrazzo work—are classified in Industry 238340, Tile and Terrazzo Contractors; and
- Finish carpentry—are classified in Industry 238350, Finish Carpentry Contractors.

2389 Other Specialty Trade Contractors

23891 Site Preparation Contractors

See industry description for 238910 below.

238910 Site Preparation Contractors[CAN]

This industry comprises establishments primarily engaged in site preparation activities, such as excavating and grading, demolition of buildings and other structures, septic system installation, and house moving. Earth moving and land clearing for all types of sites (e.g., building, nonbuilding, mining) is included in this industry. Establishments primarily engaged in construction equipment rental with operator (except cranes) are also included.

Illustrative Examples:

Blasting, building demolition
Concrete breaking and cutting for demolition
Cutting new rights of way
Demolition, building and structure
Dewatering contractors
Dirt moving for construction
Equipment rental (except crane), construction, with operator
Excavating, earthmoving, or land clearing contractors
Foundation digging (i.e., excavation)
Foundation drilling contractors
Grading construction sites
Line slashing or cutting (except maintenance)
Septic system contractors
Trenching (except underwater)
Underground tank (except hazardous) removal
Wrecking, building or other structure

Cross-References. Establishments primarily engaged in—

- Earth retention or underwater trenching—are classified in Industry 237990, Other Heavy and Civil Engineering Construction;
- Crane rental with operator—are classified in Industry 238990, All Other Specialty Trade Contractors;

US—United States industry only. CAN—United States and Canadian industries are comparable. MEX—United States and Mexican industries are comparable. Blank—Canadian, Mexican, and United States industries are comparable.

- Overburden removal as an activity prior to mineral removal from quarries or open pit mines—are classified in Sector 21, Mining;
- Drilling oil and gas field water intake wells—are classified in U.S. Industry 213111, Support Activities for Mining;
- Dismantling tanks in oil fields—are classified in U.S. Industry 213112, Drilling Oil and Gas Wells;
- Construction equipment rental without an operator—are classified in U.S. Industry 532412, Construction, Mining, and Forestry Machinery and Equipment Rental and Leasing;
- Tree and brush trimming for overhead utility lines—are classified in Industry 561730, Landscaping Services; and
- Nuclear power plant decommissioning and environmental remediation work, such as the removal of underground steel tanks for hazardous materials—are classified in Industry 562910, Remediation Services.

23899 All Other Specialty Trade Contractors

See industry description for 238990 below.

238990 All Other Specialty Trade Contractors[CAN]

This industry comprises establishments primarily engaged in specialized trades (except foundation, structure, and building exterior contractors; building equipment contractors; building finishing contractors; and site preparation contractors). The specialty trade work performed includes new work, additions, alterations, maintenance, and repairs.

Illustrative Examples:

Billboard erection
Crane rental with operator
Cleaning building interiors during and immediately after construction
Driveway paving or sealing
Fence installation
Interlocking brick and block installation
Manufactured (mobile) home, set up and tie-down
Outdoor swimming pool construction
Paver, brick (e.g., driveway, patio, sidewalk), installation
Paving, residential and commercial driveway and parking lot
Sandblasting building exteriors
Scaffold erecting and dismantling
Steeplejack work

Cross-References. Establishments primarily engaged in—

- Foundation, structure, and building exterior work—are classified in Industry Group 2381, Foundation, Structure, and Building Exterior Contractors;

US—United States industry only. CAN—United States and Canadian industries are comparable. MEX—United States and Mexican industries are comparable. Blank—Canadian, Mexican, and United States industries are comparable.

- Installing, repairing, or maintaining building mechanical systems—are classified in Industry Group 2382, Building Equipment Contractors;
- Finishing buildings—are classified in Industry Group 2383, Building Finishing Contractors;
- Paving public highways, streets, and roads—are classified in Industry 237310, Highway, Street, and Bridge Construction;
- Construction equipment rental with an operator (except cranes) or preparing land for building construction—are classified in Industry 238910, Site Preparation Contractors;
- Construction equipment rental without an operator—are classified in U.S. Industry 532412, Construction, Mining, and Forestry Machinery and Equipment Rental and Leasing;
- Radon testing—are classified in Industry 541380, Testing Laboratories;
- Power washing and other building exterior cleaning (except sandblasting)—are classified in Industry 561790, Other Services to Buildings and Dwellings; and
- Environmental remediation work, such as asbestos abatement—are classified in Industry 562910, Remediation Services.

US—United States industry only. CAN—United States and Canadian industries are comparable. MEX—United States and Mexican industries are comparable. Blank—Canadian, Mexican, and United States industries are comparable.

Sector 31-33—Manufacturing

The Sector as a Whole

The Manufacturing sector comprises establishments engaged in the mechanical, physical, or chemical transformation of materials, substances, or components into new products. The assembling of component parts of manufactured products is considered manufacturing, except in cases where the activity is appropriately classified in Sector 23, Construction.

Establishments in the Manufacturing sector are often described as plants, factories, or mills and characteristically use power-driven machines and materials-handling equipment. However, establishments that transform materials or substances into new products by hand or in the worker's home and those engaged in selling to the general public products made on the same premises from which they are sold, such as bakeries, candy stores, and custom tailors, may also be included in this sector. Manufacturing establishments may process materials or may contract with other establishments to process their materials for them. Both types of establishments are included in manufacturing.

The materials, substances, or components transformed by manufacturing establishments are raw materials that are products of agriculture, forestry, fishing, mining, or quarrying as well as products of other manufacturing establishments. The materials used may be purchased directly from producers, obtained through customary trade channels, or secured without recourse to the market by transferring the product from one establishment to another, under the same ownership.

The new product of a manufacturing establishment may be finished in the sense that it is ready for utilization or consumption, or it may be semifinished to become an input for an establishment engaged in further manufacturing. For example, the product of the alumina refinery is the input used in the primary production of aluminum; primary aluminum is the input to an aluminum wire drawing plant; and aluminum wire is the input for a fabricated wire product manufacturing establishment.

The subsectors in the Manufacturing sector generally reflect distinct production processes related to material inputs, production equipment, and employee skills. In the machinery area, where assembling is a key activity, parts and accessories for manufactured products are classified in the industry of the finished manufactured item when they are made for separate sale. For example, a replacement refrigerator door would be classified with refrigerators and an attachment for a piece of metal working machinery would be classified with metal working machinery. However, components, input from other manufacturing establishments, are classified based on the production function of the component manufacturer. For example, electronic components are classified in Subsector 334, Computer and Electronic Product Manufacturing and stampings are classified in Subsector 332, Fabricated Metal Product Manufacturing.

US—United States industry only. CAN—United States and Canadian industries are comparable. MEX—United States and Mexican industries are comparable. Blank—Canadian, Mexican, and United States industries are comparable.

Manufacturing establishments often perform one or more activities that are classified outside the Manufacturing sector of NAICS. For instance, almost all manufacturing has some captive research and development or administrative operations, such as accounting, payroll, or management. These captive services are treated the same as captive manufacturing activities. When the services are provided by separate establishments, they are classified to the NAICS sector where such services are primary, not in manufacturing.

The boundaries of manufacturing and the other sectors of the classification system can be somewhat blurry. The establishments in the manufacturing sector are engaged in the transformation of materials into new products. Their output is a new product. However, the definition of what constitutes a new product can be somewhat subjective. As clarification, the following activities are considered manufacturing in NAICS:

Milk bottling and pasteurizing;
Water bottling and processing;
Fresh fish packaging (oyster shucking, fish filleting);
Apparel jobbing (assigning of materials to contract factories or shops for fabrication or other contract operations) as well as contracting on materials owned by others;
Printing and related activities;
Ready-mixed concrete production;
Leather converting;
Grinding of lenses to prescription;
Wood preserving;
Electroplating, plating, metal heat treating, and polishing for the trade;
Lapidary work for the trade;
Fabricating signs and advertising displays;
Rebuilding or remanufacturing machinery (i.e., automotive parts)
Ship repair and renovation;
Machine shops; and
Tire retreading.

Conversely, there are activities that are sometimes considered manufacturing, but which for NAICS are classified in another sector (i.e., not classified as manufacturing). They include:

1. Logging, classified in Sector 11, Agriculture, Forestry, Fishing and Hunting is considered a harvesting operation;
2. The beneficiating of ores and other minerals, classified in Sector 21, Mining, is considered part of the activity of mining;
3. The construction of structures and fabricating operations performed at the site of construction by contractors, is classified in Sector 23, Construction;
4. Establishments engaged in breaking of bulk and redistribution in smaller lots, including packaging, repackaging, or bottling products, such as liquors or chemicals; the customized assembly of computers; sorting of scrap; mixing paints to customer order; and cutting metals to customer order, classified in Sector 42, Wholesale Trade or Sector 44-45, Retail Trade, produce a modified version of the same product, not a new product; and
5. Publishing and the combined activity of publishing and printing, classified in Sector 51, Information, perform the transformation of information into a

US—United States industry only. CAN—United States and Canadian industries are comparable. MEX—United States and Mexican industries are comparable. Blank—Canadian, Mexican, and United States industries are comparable.

product where as the value of the product to the consumer lies in the information content, not in the format in which it is distributed (i.e., the book or software diskette).

311 Food Manufacturing

Industries in the Food Manufacturing subsector transform livestock and agricultural products into products for intermediate or final consumption. The industry groups are distinguished by the raw materials (generally of animal or vegetable origin) processed into food products.

The food products manufactured in these establishments are typically sold to wholesalers or retailers for distribution to consumers, but establishments primarily engaged in retailing bakery and candy products made on the premises not for immediate consumption are included.

Establishments primarily engaged in manufacturing beverages are classified in Subsector 312, Beverage and Tobacco Product Manufacturing.

3111 Animal Food Manufacturing

31111 Animal Food Manufacturing

This industry comprises establishments primarily engaged in manufacturing food and feed for animals from ingredients, such as grains, oilseed mill products, and meat products.

Cross-References. Establishments primarily engaged in—

- Slaughtering animals for feed—are classified in Industry 31161, Animal Slaughtering and Processing; and
- Manufacturing vitamins and minerals for animals—are classified in Industry 32541, Pharmaceutical and Medicine Manufacturing.

311111 Dog and Cat Food Manufacturing[CAN]

This U.S. industry comprises establishments primarily engaged in manufacturing dog and cat food from ingredients, such as grains, oilseed mill products, and meat products.

Cross-References. Establishments primarily engaged in—

- Manufacturing food for animals (except dog and cat)—are classified in U.S. Industry 311119, Other Animal Food Manufacturing;

US—United States industry only. CAN—United States and Canadian industries are comparable. MEX—United States and Mexican industries are comparable. Blank—Canadian, Mexican, and United States industries are comparable.

- Slaughtering animals for feed—are classified in Industry 31161, Animal Slaughtering and Processing; and
- Manufacturing vitamins and minerals for dogs and cats—are classified in Industry 32541, Pharmaceutical and Medicine Manufacturing.

311119 Other Animal Food Manufacturing[CAN]

This U.S. industry comprises establishments primarily engaged in manufacturing animal food (except dog and cat) from ingredients, such as grains, oilseed mill products, and meat products.

Cross-References. Establishments primarily engaged in—

- Manufacturing dog and cat foods—are classified in U.S. Industry 311111, Dog and Cat Food Manufacturing;
- Slaughtering animals for feed—are classified in Industry 31161, Animal Slaughtering and Processing; and
- Manufacturing vitamins and minerals for animals—are classified in Industry 32541, Pharmaceutical and Medicine Manufacturing.

3112 Grain and Oilseed Milling

31121 Flour Milling and Malt Manufacturing

This industry comprises establishments primarily engaged in one or more of the following: (1) milling flour or meal from grains or vegetables; (2) preparing flour mixes or doughs from flour milled in the same establishment; (3) milling, cleaning, and polishing rice; and (4) manufacturing malt from barley, rye, or other grains.

Cross-References. Establishments primarily engaged in—

- Preparing breakfast cereals from flour milled in the same establishment—are classified in Industry 31123, Breakfast Cereal Manufacturing;
- Crushing soybeans or wet milling corn and vegetables—are classified in Industry 31122, Starch and Vegetable Fats and Oils Manufacturing;
- Manufacturing prepared flour mixes or doughs from flour ground elsewhere—are classified in Industry 31182, Cookie, Cracker, and Pasta Manufacturing;
- Brewing malt beverages—are classified in Industry 31212, Breweries;

US—United States industry only. CAN—United States and Canadian industries are comparable. MEX—United States and Mexican industries are comparable. Blank—Canadian, Mexican, and United States industries are comparable.

- Mixing purchased dried and dehydrated ingredients with purchased rice—are classified in Industry 31199, All Other Food Manufacturing;
- Drying and/or dehydrating ingredients and packaging them with purchased rice—are classified in Industry 31142, Fruit and Vegetable Canning, Pickling, and Drying; and
- Manufacturing malt extract and syrups—are classified in Industry 31194, Seasoning and Dressing Manufacturing.

311211 Flour Milling[CAN]

This U.S. industry comprises establishments primarily engaged in (1) milling flour or meal from grains (except rice) or vegetables and/or (2) milling flour and preparing flour mixes or doughs.

Cross-References. Establishments primarily engaged in—

- Preparing breakfast cereals from flour milled in the same establishment—are classified in Industry 311230, Breakfast Cereal Manufacturing;
- Manufacturing prepared flour mixes or doughs from flour ground elsewhere—are classified in U.S. Industry 311822, Flour Mixes and Dough Manufacturing from Purchased Flour;
- Milling rice or cleaning and polishing rice—are classified in U.S. Industry 311212, Rice Milling;
- Wet milling corn and vegetables—are classified in U.S. Industry, 311221, Wet Corn Milling; and
- Crushing soybean and extracting soybean oil—are classified in U.S. Industry 311222, Soybean Processing.

311212 Rice Milling[US]

This U.S. industry comprises establishments primarily engaged in one of the following: (1) milling rice; (2) cleaning and polishing rice; or (3) milling, cleaning, and polishing rice. The establishments in this industry may package the rice they mill with other ingredients.

Cross-References. Establishments primarily engaged in—

- Drying and/or dehydrating ingredients and packaging them with purchased rice—are classified in U.S. Industry 311423, Dried and Dehydrated Food Manufacturing; and

---

US—United States industry only. CAN—United States and Canadian industries are comparable. MEX—United States and Mexican industries are comparable. Blank—Canadian, Mexican, and United States industries are comparable.

- Mixing purchased dried and/or dehydrated ingredients with purchased rice—are classified in U.S. Industry 311999, All Other Miscellaneous Food Manufacturing.

311213 Malt Manufacturing[US]

This U.S. industry comprises establishments primarily engaged in manufacturing malt from barley, rye, or other grains.

Cross-References. Establishments primarily engaged in—

- Brewing malt beverages—are classified in Industry 312120, Breweries; and
- Manufacturing malt extract and syrups—are classified in U.S. Industry 311942, Spice and Extract Manufacturing.

31122 Starch and Vegetable Fats and Oils Manufacturing

This industry comprises establishments primarily engaged in one or more of the following: (1) wet milling corn and vegetables; (2) crushing oilseeds and tree nuts; (3) refining and/or blending vegetable oils; (4) manufacturing shortening and margarine; and (5) blending purchased animal fats with vegetable fats.

Cross-References. Establishments primarily engaged in—

- Manufacturing table syrups from corn syrup and starch base dessert powders—are classified in Industry 31199, All Other Food Manufacturing;
- Reducing maple sap to maple syrup—are classified in Industry 11199, All Other Crop Farming;
- Milling flour or meal from grains and vegetables—are classified in Industry 31121, Flour Milling and Malt Manufacturing;
- Wet milling corn to produce nonpotable ethyl alcohol—are classified in Industry 32519, Other Basic Organic Chemical Manufacturing;
- Rendering or refining animal fats and oils—are classified in Industry 31161, Animal Slaughtering and Processing; and
- Manufacturing laundry starches—are classified in Industry 32561, Soap and Cleaning Compound Manufacturing.

311221 Wet Corn Milling[CAN]

This U.S. industry comprises establishments primarily engaged in wet milling corn and other vegetables (except to make ethyl alcohol). Examples of products

---

US—United States industry only. CAN—United States and Canadian industries are comparable. MEX—United States and Mexican industries are comparable. Blank—Canadian, Mexican, and United States industries are comparable.

made in these establishments are corn sweeteners, such as glucose, dextrose, and fructose; corn oil; and starches (except laundry).

Cross-References. Establishments primarily engaged in—

- Refining and/or blending corn oil from purchased oils—are classified in U.S. Industry 311225, Fats and Oils Refining and Blending;
- Manufacturing sweetening syrups from corn syrup and starch base dessert powders—are classified in U.S. Industry 311999, All Other Miscellaneous Food Manufacturing;
- Reducing maple sap to maple syrup—are classified in U.S. Industry 111998, All Other Miscellaneous Crop Farming;
- Milling (except wet milling) corn—are classified in U.S. Industry 311211, Flour Milling;
- Wet milling corn to produce nonpotable ethyl alcohol—are classified in U.S. Industry 325193, Ethyl Alcohol Manufacturing; and
- Manufacturing laundry starches—are classified in U.S. Industry 325612, Polish and Other Sanitation Good Manufacturing.

311222 Soybean Processing[US]

This U.S. industry comprises establishments engaged in crushing soybeans. Examples of products produced in these establishments are soybean oil, soybean cake and meal, and soybean protein isolates and concentrates.

Cross-References. Establishments primarily engaged in—

- Refining and/or blending soybean oil from purchased oil—are classified in U.S. Industry 311225, Fats and Oils Refining and Blending;
- Wet milling corn and other vegetables—are classified in U.S. Industry 311221, Wet Corn Milling; and
- Crushing oilseeds (except soybeans) and tree nuts—are classified in U.S. Industry 311223, Other Oilseed Processing.

311223 Other Oilseed Processing[US]

This U.S. industry comprises establishments engaged in crushing oilseeds (except soybeans) and tree nuts, such as cottonseeds, linseeds, peanuts, and sunflower seeds.

Cross-References. Establishments primarily engaged in—

- Wet milling corn and other vegetables—are classified in U.S. Industry 311221, Wet Corn Milling;

US—United States industry only. CAN—United States and Canadian industries are comparable. MEX—United States and Mexican industries are comparable. Blank—Canadian, Mexican, and United States industries are comparable.

- Crushing soybeans—are classified in U.S. Industry 311222, Soybean Processing; and
- Refining and/or blending vegetable, oilseed, and tree nut oils from purchased oils—are classified in U.S. Industry 311225, Fats and Oils Refining and Blending.

311225 Fats and Oils Refining and Blending[CAN]

This U.S. industry comprises establishments primarily engaged in one or more of the following: (1) manufacturing shortening and margarine from purchased fats and oils; (2) refining and/or blending vegetable, oilseed, and tree nut oils from purchased oils; and (3) blending purchased animal fats with purchased vegetable fats.

Cross-References. Establishments primarily engaged in—

- Refining and/or blending soybean oil in soybean crushing mills—are classified in U.S. Industry 311222, Soybean Processing;
- Refining and/or blending corn oil made by wet corn milling—are classified in U.S. Industry 311221, Wet Corn Milling;
- Refining and/or blending oilseeds (except soybeans) and tree nuts in crushing mills—are classified in U.S. Industry 311223, Other Oilseed Processing; and
- Rendering or refining animal fats and oils—are classified in Industry 31161, Animal Slaughtering and Processing.

31123 Breakfast Cereal Manufacturing

See industry description for 311230 below.

311230 Breakfast Cereal Manufacturing

This industry comprises establishments primarily engaged in manufacturing breakfast cereal foods.

Cross-References. Establishments primarily engaged in—

- Manufacturing nonchocolate-coated granola bars and other types of breakfast bars—are classified in Industry 311340, Nonchocolate Confectionery Manufacturing;
- Manufacturing chocolate-coated granola bars from purchased chocolate—are classified in Industry 311330, Confectionery Manufacturing from Purchased Chocolate;

US—United States industry only. CAN—United States and Canadian industries are comparable. MEX—United States and Mexican industries are comparable. Blank—Canadian, Mexican, and United States industries are comparable.

- Manufacturing chocolate-coated granola bars from cacao beans—are classified in Industry 311320, Chocolate and Confectionery Manufacturing from Cacao Beans; and
- Manufacturing coffee substitutes from grain—are classified in Industry 311920, Coffee and Tea Manufacturing.

3113 Sugar and Confectionery Product Manufacturing

This industry group comprises (1) establishments that process agricultural inputs, such as sugarcane, beet, and cacao, to give rise to a new product (sugar or chocolate), and (2) those that begin with sugar and chocolate and process these further.

31131 Sugar Manufacturing

This industry comprises establishments primarily engaged in manufacturing raw sugar, liquid sugar, and refined sugar from sugarcane, raw cane sugar and sugarbeets.

Cross-References. Establishments primarily engaged in—

- Manufacturing corn sweeteners by wet milling corn—are classified in Industry 31122, Starch and Vegetable Fats and Oils Manufacturing;
- Manufacturing table syrups from corn syrup and starch base dessert powders—are classified in Industry 31199, All Other Food Manufacturing;
- Reducing maple sap to maple syrup—are classified in Industry 11199, All Other Crop Farming; and
- Manufacturing synthetic sweeteners (i.e., sweetening agents), such as saccharin and sugar substitutes (i.e., synthetic sweetener blended with other ingredients),—are classified in Subsector 325, Chemical Manufacturing.

311311 Sugarcane Mills[US]

This U.S. industry comprises establishments primarily engaged in processing sugarcane.

Cross-References. Establishments primarily engaged in—

- Manufacturing refined cane sugar from raw cane sugar—are classified in U.S. Industry 311312, Cane Sugar Refining;
- Manufacturing beet sugar—are classified in U.S. Industry 311313, Beet Sugar Manufacturing;

US—United States industry only. CAN—United States and Canadian industries are comparable. MEX—United States and Mexican industries are comparable. Blank—Canadian, Mexican, and United States industries are comparable.

- Manufacturing corn sweeteners by wet milling corn—are classified in U.S. Industry 311221, Wet Corn Milling;
- Manufacturing table syrups from corn syrup—are classified in U.S. Industry 311999, All Other Miscellaneous Food Manufacturing; and
- Manufacturing synthetic sweeteners (i.e., sweetening agents), such as saccharin and sugar substitutes (i.e., synthetic sweetener blended with other ingredients),—are classified in Subsector 325, Chemical Manufacturing.

311312 Cane Sugar Refining[US]

This U.S. industry comprises establishments primarily engaged in refining cane sugar from raw cane sugar.

Cross-References. Establishments primarily engaged in—

- Processing and refining sugarcane—are classified in U.S. Industry 311311, Sugarcane Mills;
- Manufacturing beet sugar—are classified in U.S. Industry 311313, Beet Sugar Manufacturing;
- Manufacturing corn sweeteners by wet milling corn—are classified in U.S. Industry 311221, Wet Corn Milling;
- Reducing maple sap to maple syrup—are classified in U.S. Industry 111998, All Other Miscellaneous Crop Farming;
- Manufacturing table syrups from corn syrup—are classified in U.S. Industry 311999, All Other Miscellaneous Food Manufacturing; and
- Manufacturing synthetic sweeteners (i.e., sweetening agents), such as saccharin and sugar substitutes (i.e., synthetic sweetener blended with other ingredients),—are classified in Subsector 325, Chemical Manufacturing.

311313 Beet Sugar Manufacturing[US]

This U.S. industry comprises establishments primarily engaged in manufacturing refined beet sugar from sugarbeets.

Cross-References. Establishments primarily engaged in—

- Manufacturing raw cane sugar and/or refined cane sugar from sugarcane—are classified in U.S. Industry 311311, Sugarcane Mills;
- Manufacturing refined cane sugar from raw cane sugar—are classified in U.S. Industry 311312, Cane Sugar Refining;

US—United States industry only. CAN—United States and Canadian industries are comparable. MEX—United States and Mexican industries are comparable. Blank—Canadian, Mexican, and United States industries are comparable.

- Manufacturing corn sweeteners by wet milling corn—are classified in U.S. Industry 311221, Wet Corn Milling;
- Manufacturing table syrups from corn syrup—are classified in U.S. Industry 311999, All Other Miscellaneous Food Manufacturing;
- Reducing maple sap to maple syrup—are classified in U.S. Industry 111998, All Other Miscellaneous Crop Farming; and
- Manufacturing synthetic sweeteners (i.e., sweetening agents), such as saccharin and sugar substitutes (i.e., synthetic sweetener blended with other ingredients),—are classified in Subsector 325, Chemical Manufacturing.

31132 Chocolate and Confectionery Manufacturing from Cacao Beans

See industry description for 311320 below.

311320 Chocolate and Confectionery Manufacturing from Cacao Beans

This industry comprises establishments primarily engaged in shelling, roasting, and grinding cacao beans and making chocolate cacao products and chocolate confectioneries.

Cross-References. Establishments primarily engaged in—

- Manufacturing, not for immediate consumption, chocolate confectioneries from chocolate made elsewhere—are classified in Industry 311330, Confectionery Manufacturing from Purchased Chocolate;
- Manufacturing, not for immediate consumption, nonchocolate candies—are classified in Industry 311340, Nonchocolate Confectionery Manufacturing;
- Preparing and selling confectioneries for immediate consumption—are classified in U.S. Industry 722213, Snack and Nonalcoholic Beverage Bars; and
- Retailing confectioneries not for immediate consumption made elsewhere—are classified in U.S. Industry 445292, Confectionery and Nut Stores.

31133 Confectionery Manufacturing from Purchased Chocolate

See industry description for 311330 below.

311330 Confectionery Manufacturing from Purchased Chocolate

This industry comprises establishments primarily engaged in manufacturing chocolate confectioneries from chocolate produced elsewhere. Included in this

US—United States industry only. CAN—United States and Canadian industries are comparable. MEX—United States and Mexican industries are comparable. Blank—Canadian, Mexican, and United States industries are comparable.

industry are establishments primarily engaged in retailing chocolate confectionery products not for immediate consumption made on the premises from chocolate made elsewhere.

Cross-References. Establishments primarily engaged in—

- Manufacturing chocolate confectioneries from cacao beans—are classified in Industry 311320, Chocolate and Confectionery Manufacturing from Cacao Beans;
- Manufacturing nonchocolate confectioneries—are classified in Industry 311340, Nonchocolate Confectionery Manufacturing;
- Retailing confectioneries not for immediate consumption made elsewhere—are classified in U.S. Industry 445292, Confectionery and Nut Stores; and
- Preparing and selling confectioneries for immediate consumption—are classified in U.S. Industry 722213, Snack and Nonalcoholic Beverage Bars.

31134 Nonchocolate Confectionery Manufacturing

See industry description for 311340 below.

311340 Nonchocolate Confectionery Manufacturing

This industry comprises establishments primarily engaged in manufacturing nonchocolate confectioneries. Included in this industry are establishments primary engaged in retailing nonchocolate confectionery products not for immediate consumption made on the premises.

Cross-References. Establishments primarily engaged in—

- Manufacturing chocolate confectioneries from cacao beans—are classified in Industry 311320, Chocolate and Confectionery Manufacturing from Cacao Beans;
- Manufacturing chocolate confectioneries from chocolate made elsewhere—are classified in Industry 311330, Confectionery Manufacturing from Purchased Chocolate;
- Retailing confectioneries not for immediate consumption made elsewhere—are classified in U.S. Industry 445292, Confectionery and Nut Stores;
- Preparing and selling confectioneries for immediate consumption—are classified in U.S. Industry 722213, Snack and Nonalcoholic Beverage Bars; and
- Roasting, salting, drying, cooking, or canning nuts and seeds—are classified in U.S. Industry 311911, Roasted Nuts and Peanut Butter Manufacturing.

US—United States industry only. CAN—United States and Canadian industries are comparable. MEX—United States and Mexican industries are comparable. Blank—Canadian, Mexican, and United States industries are comparable.

3114 Fruit and Vegetable Preserving and Specialty Food Manufacturing

This industry group includes (1) establishments that freeze food and (2) those that use preservation processes, such as pickling, canning, and dehydrating. Both types begin their production process with inputs of vegetable or animal origin.

31141 Frozen Food Manufacturing

This industry comprises establishments primarily engaged in manufacturing frozen fruit, frozen juices, frozen vegetables, and frozen specialty foods (except seafood), such as frozen dinners, entrees, and side dishes; frozen pizza; frozen whipped toppings; and frozen waffles, pancakes, and french toast.

Cross-References. Establishments primarily engaged in—

- Manufacturing frozen dairy specialties—are classified in Industry 31152, Ice Cream and Frozen Dessert Manufacturing;
- Manufacturing frozen bakery products—are classified in Industry 31181, Bread and Bakery Product Manufacturing;
- Manufacturing frozen seafood products—are classified in Industry 31171, Seafood Product Preparation and Packaging; and
- Manufacturing frozen meat products—are classified in Industry 31161, Animal Slaughtering and Processing.

311411 Frozen Fruit, Juice, and Vegetable Manufacturing[MEX]

This U.S. industry comprises establishments primarily engaged in manufacturing frozen fruits; frozen vegetables; and frozen fruit juices, ades, drinks, cocktail mixes and concentrates.

Cross-References.

Establishments primarily engaged in manufacturing frozen specialty foods are classified in U.S. Industry 311412, Frozen Specialty Food Manufacturing.

311412 Frozen Specialty Food Manufacturing[MEX]

This U.S. industry comprises establishments primarily engaged in manufacturing frozen specialty foods (except seafood), such as frozen dinners, entrees, and side dishes; frozen pizza; frozen whipped topping; and frozen waffles, pancakes, and french toast.

US—United States industry only. CAN—United States and Canadian industries are comparable. MEX—United States and Mexican industries are comparable. Blank—Canadian, Mexican, and United States industries are comparable.

Cross-References. Establishments primarily engaged in—

- Manufacturing frozen dairy specialties—are classified in Industry 311520, Ice Cream and Frozen Dessert Manufacturing;
- Manufacturing frozen bakery products—are classified in U.S. Industry 311813, Frozen Cakes, Pies, and Other Pastries Manufacturing;
- Manufacturing frozen fruits, frozen fruit juices, and frozen vegetables—are classified in U.S. Industry 311411, Frozen Fruit, Juice, and Vegetable Manufacturing;
- Manufacturing frozen meat products—are classified in Industry 31161, Animal Slaughtering and Processing; and
- Manufacturing frozen seafood products—are classified in U.S. Industry 311712, Fresh and Frozen Seafood Processing.

31142 Fruit and Vegetable Canning, Pickling, and Drying

This industry comprises establishments primarily engaged in manufacturing canned, pickled, and dried fruits, vegetables, and specialty foods. Establishments in this industry may package the dried or dehydrated ingredients they make with other purchased ingredients. Examples of products made by these establishments are canned juices; canned baby foods; canned soups (except seafood); canned dry beans; canned tomato-based sauces, such as catsup, salsa, chili, spaghetti, barbeque, and tomato paste, pickles, relishes, jams and jellies, dried soup mixes and bullions, and sauerkraut.

Cross-References. Establishments primarily engaged in—

- Manufacturing canned dairy products—are classified in Industry 31151, Dairy Product (except Frozen) Manufacturing;
- Manufacturing canned seafood soups and seafood products—are classified in Industry 31171, Seafood Product Preparation and Packaging;
- Manufacturing canned meat products—are classified in Industry 31161, Animal Slaughtering and Processing;
- Milling rice and packaging it with other ingredients or manufacturing vegetable flours and meals—are classified in Industry 31121, Flour Milling and Malt Manufacturing;
- Manufacturing dry pasta and packaging it with other ingredients—are classified in Industry 31182, Cookie, Cracker, and Pasta Manufacturing;
- Mixing purchased dried and/or dehydrated potatoes, rice, and pasta and packaging them with other purchased ingredients; mixing purchased dried

US—United States industry only. CAN—United States and Canadian industries are comparable. MEX—United States and Mexican industries are comparable. Blank—Canadian, Mexican, and United States industries are comparable.

and/or dehydrated ingredients for soup mixes and bouillon; and manufacturing canned puddings—are classified in Industry 31199, All Other Food Manufacturing;

- Manufacturing dry salad dressing and dry sauce mixes—are classified in Industry 31194, Seasoning and Dressing Manufacturing; and
- Manufacturing canned fruit and vegetable drinks, cocktails, and ades—are classified in Industry 31211, Soft Drink and Ice Manufacturing.

311421 Fruit and Vegetable Canning[US]

This U.S. industry comprises establishments primarily engaged in manufacturing canned, pickled, and brined fruits and vegetables. Examples of products made in these establishments are canned juices; canned jams and jellies; canned tomato-based sauces, such as catsup, salsa, chili, spaghetti, barbeque, and tomato paste; pickles, relishes, and sauerkraut.

Cross-References. Establishments primarily engaged in—

- Manufacturing canned baby foods, canned soups (except seafood), and canned specialty foods (except seafood)—are classified in U.S. Industry 311422, Specialty Canning;
- Manufacturing canned seafood soups and canned seafood products—are classified in U.S. Industry 311711, Seafood Canning;
- Manufacturing canned meat products—are classified in Industry 31161, Animal Slaughtering and Processing; and
- Manufacturing canned fruit and vegetable drinks, cocktails, and ades—are classified in U.S. Industry 312111, Soft Drink Manufacturing.

311422 Specialty Canning[US]

This U.S. industry comprises establishments primarily engaged in manufacturing canned specialty foods. Examples of products made in these establishments are canned baby food, canned baked beans, canned soups (except seafood), canned spaghetti, and other canned nationality foods.

Cross-References. Establishments primarily engaged in—

- Manufacturing canned dairy products—are classified in U.S. Industry 311514, Dry, Condensed, and Evaporated Dairy Product Manufacturing;
- Manufacturing canned fruits, canned vegetables, and canned juices—are classified in U.S. Industry 311421, Fruit and Vegetable Canning;

US—United States industry only. CAN—United States and Canadian industries are comparable. MEX—United States and Mexican industries are comparable. Blank—Canadian, Mexican, and United States industries are comparable.

- Manufacturing canned seafood soups and canned seafood products—are classified in U.S. Industry 311711, Seafood Canning;
- Manufacturing canned meat products—are classified in Industry 31161, Animal Slaughtering and Processing; and
- Manufacturing canned puddings—are classified in U.S. Industry 311999, All Other Miscellaneous Food Manufacturing.

311423 Dried and Dehydrated Food Manufacturing[US]

This U.S. industry comprises establishments primarily engaged in (1) drying (including freeze-dried) and/or dehydrating fruits, vegetables, and soup mixes and bouillon and/or (2) drying and/or dehydrating ingredients and packaging them with other purchased ingredients, such as rice and dry pasta.

Cross-References. Establishments primarily engaged in—

- Milling rice and packaging it with other ingredients—are classified in U.S. Industry 311212, Rice Milling;
- Manufacturing dry pasta and packaging it with other ingredients—are classified in U.S. Industry 311823, Dry Pasta Manufacturing;
- Manufacturing vegetable flours and meals—are classified in U.S. Industry 311211, Flour Milling;
- Mixing purchased dried and/or dehydrated potatoes, rice, and dry pasta, and packaging them with other purchased ingredients, and mixing purchased dried and/or dehydrated ingredients for soup mixes and bouillon—are classified in U.S. Industry 311999, All Other Miscellaneous Food Manufacturing; and
- Manufacturing dry salad dressing and dry sauce mixes—are classified in U.S. Industry 311942, Spice and Extract Manufacturing.

3115 Dairy Product Manufacturing

This industry group comprises establishments that manufacture dairy products from raw milk, processed milk, and dairy substitutes.

31151 Dairy Product (except Frozen) Manufacturing

This industry comprises establishments primarily engaged in one or more of the following: (1) manufacturing dairy products (except frozen) from raw milk and/or processed milk products; (2) manufacturing dairy substitutes (except frozen)

US—United States industry only. CAN—United States and Canadian industries are comparable. MEX—United States and Mexican industries are comparable. Blank—Canadian, Mexican, and United States industries are comparable.

from soybeans and other nondairy substances; and (3) manufacturing dry, condensed, concentrated, and evaporated dairy and dairy substitute products.

Cross-References. Establishments primarily engaged in—

- Manufacturing cheese-based salad dressings—are classified in Industry 31194, Seasoning and Dressing Manufacturing;
- Manufacturing margarine or margarine-butter blends—are classified in Industry 31122, Starch and Vegetable Fats and Oils Manufacturing;
- Manufacturing frozen whipped toppings—are classified in Industry 31141, Frozen Food Manufacturing; and
- Manufacturing ice cream, frozen yogurt, and other frozen dairy desserts—are classified in Industry 31152, Ice Cream and Frozen Dessert Manufacturing.

311511 Fluid Milk Manufacturing[CAN]

This U.S. industry comprises establishments primarily engaged in (1) manufacturing processed milk products, such as pasteurized milk or cream and sour cream and/or (2) manufacturing fluid milk dairy substitutes from soybeans and other nondairy substances.

Cross-References. Establishments primarily engaged in—

- Manufacturing dry mix whipped toppings, canned milk, and ultra high temperature milk— are classified in U.S. Industry 311514, Dry, Condensed, and Evaporated Dairy Product Manufacturing;
- Manufacturing frozen whipped toppings—are classified in U.S. Industry 311412, Frozen Specialty Food Manufacturing; and
- Manufacturing ice cream and frozen yogurt and other frozen desserts—are classified in Industry 311520, Ice Cream and Frozen Dessert Manufacturing.

311512 Creamery Butter Manufacturing[US]

This U.S. industry comprises establishments primarily engaged in manufacturing creamery butter from milk and/or processed milk products.

Cross-References.

Establishments primarily engaged in manufacturing margarine or margarine-butter blends are classified in U.S. Industry 311225, Fats and Oils Refining and Blending.

US—United States industry only. CAN—United States and Canadian industries are comparable. MEX—United States and Mexican industries are comparable. Blank—Canadian, Mexican, and United States industries are comparable.

311513 Cheese Manufacturing[US]

This U.S. industry comprises establishments primarily engaged in (1) manufacturing cheese products (except cottage cheese) from raw milk and/or processed milk products and/or (2) manufacturing cheese substitutes from soybean and other nondairy substances.

Cross-References. Establishments primarily engaged in—

- Manufacturing cheese-based salad dressings—are classified in U.S. Industry 311941, Mayonnaise, Dressing, and Other Prepared Sauce Manufacturing; and
- Manufacturing cottage cheese—are classified in U.S. Industry 311511, Fluid Milk Manufacturing.

311514 Dry, Condensed, and Evaporated Dairy Product Manufacturing[US]

This U.S. industry comprises establishments primarily engaged in manufacturing dry, condensed, and evaporated milk and dairy substitute products.

Cross-References. Establishments primarily engaged in—

- Manufacturing fluid milk products—are classified in U.S. Industry 311511, Fluid Milk Manufacturing;
- Manufacturing creamery butter—are classified in U.S. Industry 311512, Creamery Butter Manufacturing; and
- Manufacturing cheese products—are classified in U.S. Industry 311513, Cheese Manufacturing.

31152 Ice Cream and Frozen Dessert Manufacturing

See industry description for 311520 below.

311520 Ice Cream and Frozen Dessert Manufacturing

This industry comprises establishments primarily engaged in manufacturing ice cream, frozen yogurts, frozen ices, sherbets, frozen tofu, and other frozen desserts (except bakery products).

Cross-References. Establishments primarily engaged in—

- Manufacturing frozen bakery products—are classified in U.S. Industry 311813, Frozen Cakes, Pies, and Other Pastries Manufacturing; and

---

US—United States industry only. CAN—United States and Canadian industries are comparable. MEX—United States and Mexican industries are comparable. Blank—Canadian, Mexican, and United States industries are comparable.

- Manufacturing ice cream and ice milk mixes—are classified in U.S. Industry 311514, Dry, Condensed, and Evaporated Dairy Product Manufacturing.

3116 Animal Slaughtering and Processing

31161 Animal Slaughtering and Processing

This industry comprises establishments primarily engaged in one or more of the following: (1) slaughtering animals; (2) preparing processed meats and meat byproducts; and (3) rendering and/or refining animal fat, bones, and meat scraps. This industry includes establishments primarily engaged in assembly cutting and packing of meats (i.e., boxed meats) from purchased carcasses.

Cross-References. Establishments primarily engaged in—

- Manufacturing canned meat for baby food—are classified in Industry 31142, Fruit and Vegetable Canning, Pickling, and Drying;
- Manufacturing meat-based animal feeds from carcasses—are classified in Industry 31111, Animal Food Manufacturing;
- Blending purchased animal fats with vegetable fats—are classified in Industry 31122, Starch and Vegetable Fats and Oils Manufacturing;
- Manufacturing canned and frozen specialty foods containing meat, such as nationality foods (e.g., enchiladas, pizza, egg rolls) and frozen dinners,—are classified in Industry Group 3114, Fruit and Vegetable Preserving and Specialty Food Manufacturing;
- Drying, freezing, or breaking eggs—are classified in Industry 31199, All Other Food Manufacturing; and
- Cutting meat (except box meat)—are classified in Industry 42447, Meat and Meat Product Merchant Wholesalers.

311611 Animal (except Poultry) Slaughtering[CAN]

This U.S. industry comprises establishments primarily engaged in slaughtering animals (except poultry and small game). Establishments that slaughter and prepare meats are included in this industry.

Cross-References. Establishments primarily engaged in—

- Processing meat and meat byproducts (except poultry and small game) from purchased meats—are classified in U.S. Industry 311612, Meat Processed from Carcasses;

US—United States industry only. CAN—United States and Canadian industries are comparable. MEX—United States and Mexican industries are comparable. Blank—Canadian, Mexican, and United States industries are comparable.

- Slaughtering and/or processing poultry and small game—are classified in U.S. Industry 311615, Poultry Processing;
- Rendering lard and other animal fats and oils, animal fat, bones, and meat scraps—are classified in U.S. Industry 311613, Rendering and Meat Byproduct Processing; and
- Manufacturing canned and frozen specialty foods containing meat, such as nationality foods (e.g., enchiladas, egg rolls, pizza) and frozen dinners,—are classified in Industry Group 3114, Fruit and Vegetable Preserving and Specialty Food Manufacturing.

311612 Meat Processed from Carcasses[US]

This U.S. industry comprises establishments primarily engaged in processing or preserving meat and meat byproducts (except poultry and small game) from purchased meats. This industry includes establishments primarily engaged in assembly cutting and packing of meats (i.e., boxed meats) from purchased meats.

Cross-References. Establishments primarily engaged in—

- Slaughtering animals (except poultry and small game)—are classified in U.S. Industry 311611, Animal (except Poultry) Slaughtering;
- Slaughtering poultry and small game—are classified in U.S. Industry 311615, Poultry Processing;
- Rendering animal fat, bones, and meat scraps—are classified in U.S. Industry 311613, Rendering and Meat Byproduct Processing;
- Manufacturing canned meats for baby food—are classified in U.S. Industry 311422, Specialty Canning;
- Manufacturing meat-based animal feeds from carcasses—are classified in Industry 31111, Animal Food Manufacturing;
- Manufacturing canned and frozen specialty foods containing meat, such as nationality foods (e.g., enchiladas, egg rolls, pizza) and frozen dinners,—are classified in Industry Group 3114, Fruit and Vegetable Preserving and Specialty Food Manufacturing; and
- Cutting meat (except boxed meat)—are classified in U.S. Industry 424470, Meat and Meat Product Merchant Wholesalers.

311613 Rendering and Meat Byproduct Processing[US]

This U.S. industry comprises establishments primarily engaged in rendering animal fat, bones, and meat scraps.

US—United States industry only. CAN—United States and Canadian industries are comparable. MEX—United States and Mexican industries are comparable. Blank—Canadian, Mexican, and United States industries are comparable.

Cross-References.

Establishments primarily engaged in blending purchased animal fats with vegetable fats are classified in U.S. Industry 311225, Fats and Oils Refining and Blending.

311615 Poultry Processing[CAN]

This U.S. industry comprises establishments primarily engaged in (1) slaughtering poultry and small game and/or (2) preparing processed poultry and small game meat and meat byproducts.

Cross-References. Establishments primarily engaged in—

- Slaughtering animals (except poultry and small game) and/or preparing meats—are classified in U.S. Industry 311611, Animal (except Poultry) Slaughtering;
- Preparing meat and meat byproducts (except poultry and small game) from purchased meats—are classified in U.S. Industry 311612, Meat Processed from Carcasses;
- Rendering animal fat, bones, and meat scraps—are classified in U.S. Industry 311613, Rendering and Meat Byproduct Processing;
- Canning poultry and small game for baby food—are classified in U.S. Industry 311422, Specialty Canning;
- Producing meat-based animal feeds from carcasses—are classified in Industry 31111, Animal Food Manufacturing;
- Manufacturing canned and frozen meat products, such as nationality foods (e.g., enchiladas, egg rolls, pizza) and frozen dinners,—are classified in Industry Group 3114, Fruit and Vegetable Preserving and Specialty Food Manufacturing; and
- Drying, freezing, and breaking eggs—are classified in U.S. Industry 311999, All Other Miscellaneous Food Manufacturing.

3117 Seafood Product Preparation and Packaging

31171 Seafood Product Preparation and Packaging

This industry comprises establishments primarily engaged in one or more of the following: (1) canning seafood (including soup); (2) smoking, salting, and drying seafood; (3) eviscerating fresh fish by removing heads, fins, scales, bones, and entrails; (4) shucking and packing fresh shellfish; (5) processing marine fats and oils; and (6) freezing seafood. Establishments known as ‘‘floating factory

---

US—United States industry only. CAN—United States and Canadian industries are comparable. MEX—United States and Mexican industries are comparable. Blank—Canadian, Mexican, and United States industries are comparable.

ships'' that are engaged in the gathering and processing of seafood into canned seafood products are included in this industry.

311711 Seafood Canning[US]

This U.S. industry comprises establishments primarily engaged in (1) canning seafood (including soup) and marine fats and oils and/or (2) smoking, salting, and drying seafood. Establishments known as ''floating factory ships'' that are engaged in the gathering and processing of seafood into canned seafood products are included in this industry.

Cross-References.

Establishments primarily engaged in preparing fresh and frozen seafood and marine fats and oils are classified in U.S. Industry 311712, Fresh and Frozen Seafood Processing.

311712 Fresh and Frozen Seafood Processing[US]

This U.S. industry comprises establishments primarily engaged in one or more of the following: (1) eviscerating fresh fish by removing heads, fins, scales, bones, and entrails; (2) shucking and packing fresh shellfish; (3) manufacturing frozen seafood; and (4) processing fresh and frozen marine fats and oils.

Cross-References.

Establishments primarily engaged in canning and curing seafood are classified in U.S. Industry 311711, Seafood Canning.

3118 Bakeries and Tortilla Manufacturing

31181 Bread and Bakery Product Manufacturing

This industry comprises establishments primarily engaged in manufacturing fresh and frozen bread and other bakery products.

Cross-References. Establishments primarily engaged in—

- Manufacturing cookies and crackers—are classified in Industry 31182, Cookie, Cracker, and Pasta Manufacturing;
- Preparing and selling bakery products (e.g., cookies, pretzels) for immediate consumption—are classified in Industry 72221, Limited-Service Eating Places;

US—United States industry only. CAN—United States and Canadian industries are comparable. MEX—United States and Mexican industries are comparable. Blank—Canadian, Mexican, and United States industries are comparable.

- Retailing bakery products not for immediate consumption made elsewhere—are classified in Industry 44529, Other Specialty Food Stores; and
- Manufacturing pretzels (except soft)—are classified in Industry 31191, Snack Food Manufacturing.

311811 Retail Bakeries[CAN]

This U.S. industry comprises establishments primarily engaged in retailing bread and other bakery products not for immediate consumption made on the premises from flour, not from prepared dough.

Cross-References. Establishments primarily engaged in—

- Retailing bakery products not for immediate consumption made elsewhere—are classified in U.S. Industry 445291, Baked Goods Stores;
- Preparing and selling bakery products (e.g., cookies, pretzels) for immediate consumption—are classified in U.S. Industry 722213, Snack and Nonalcoholic Beverage Bars;
- Manufacturing fresh or frozen breads and other fresh bakery (except cookies and crackers) products—are classified in U.S. Industry 311812, Commercial Bakeries; and
- Manufacturing cookies and crackers—are classified in U.S. Industry 311821, Cookie and Cracker Manufacturing.

311812 Commercial Bakeries[US]

This U.S. industry comprises establishments primarily engaged in manufacturing fresh and frozen bread and bread-type rolls and other fresh bakery (except cookies and crackers) products.

Cross-References. Establishments primarily engaged in—

- Retailing bread and other bakery products not for immediate consumption made on the premises from flour, not from prepared dough—are classified in U.S. Industry 311811, Retail Bakeries;
- Manufacturing frozen bakery products (except bread)—are classified in U.S. Industry 311813, Frozen Cakes, Pies, and Other Pastries Manufacturing;
- Preparing and selling bakery products (e.g., cookies, pretzels) for immediate consumption—are classified in U.S. Industry 722213, Snack and Nonalcoholic Beverage Bars;

US—United States industry only. CAN—United States and Canadian industries are comparable. MEX—United States and Mexican industries are comparable. Blank—Canadian, Mexican, and United States industries are comparable.

- Retailing bakery products not for immediate consumption made elsewhere—are classified in U.S. Industry 445291, Baked Goods Stores;
- Manufacturing cookies and crackers—are classified in U.S. Industry 311821, Cookie and Cracker Manufacturing; and
- Manufacturing pretzels (except soft)—are classified in U.S. Industry 311919, Other Snack Food Manufacturing.

311813 Frozen Cakes, Pies, and Other Pastries Manufacturing[US]

This U.S. industry comprises establishments primarily engaged in manufacturing frozen bakery products (except bread), such as cakes, pies, and doughnuts.

Cross-References. Establishments primarily engaged in—

- Manufacturing frozen breads—are classified in U.S. Industry 311812, Commercial Bakeries;
- Retailing bakery products not for immediate consumption made on the premises from flour, not from prepared dough—are classified in U.S. Industry 311811, Retail Bakeries;
- Preparing and selling bakery products (e.g., cookies, pretzels) for immediate consumption—are classified in U.S. Industry 722213, Snack and Nonalcoholic Beverage Bars;
- Manufacturing cookies and crackers—are classified in U.S. Industry 311821, Cookie and Cracker Manufacturing; and
- Retailing bakery products not for immediate consumption made elsewhere—are classified in U.S. Industry 445291, Baked Goods Stores.

31182 Cookie, Cracker, and Pasta Manufacturing

This industry comprises establishments primarily engaged in one of the following: (1) manufacturing cookies and crackers; (2) preparing flour and dough mixes and dough from flour ground elsewhere; and (3) manufacturing dry pasta. The establishments in this industry may package the dry pasta they manufacture with other ingredients.

Cross-References. Establishments primarily engaged in—

- Preparing and selling bakery products (e.g., cookies, pretzels) for immediate consumption—are classified in Industry 72221, Limited-Service Eating Places;

US—United States industry only. CAN—United States and Canadian industries are comparable. MEX—United States and Mexican industries are comparable. Blank—Canadian, Mexican, and United States industries are comparable.

- Retailing bakery products not for immediate consumption made elsewhere—are classified in Industry 44529, Other Specialty Food Stores;
- Manufacturing bakery products (e.g., bread, cookies, pies)—are classified in Industry 31181, Bread and Bakery Product Manufacturing;
- Milling flour and preparing flour mixes or doughs—are classified in Industry 31121, Flour Milling and Malt Manufacturing;
- Manufacturing canned pasta specialties—are classified in Industry 31142, Fruit and Vegetable Canning, Pickling, and Drying;
- Manufacturing fresh pasta—are classified in Industry 31199, All Other Food Manufacturing;
- Manufacturing pretzels (except soft)—are classified in Industry 31191, Snack Food Manufacturing;
- Mixing purchased dried and/or dehydrated ingredients with purchased dry pasta—are classified in Industry 31199, All Other Food Manufacturing; and
- Drying and/or dehydrating ingredients and packaging them with purchased dry pasta—are classified in Industry 31142, Fruit and Vegetable Canning, Pickling, and Drying.

311821 Cookie and Cracker Manufacturing[CAN]

This U.S. industry comprises establishments primarily engaged in manufacturing cookies, crackers, and other products, such as ice cream cones.

Cross-References. Establishments primarily engaged in—

- Preparing and selling bakery products (e.g., cookies, pretzels) for immediate consumption—are classified in U.S. Industry 722213, Snack and Nonalcoholic Beverage Bars;
- Retailing bakery products not for immediate consumption made elsewhere—are classified in U.S. Industry 445291, Baked Goods Stores;
- Manufacturing bakery products (e.g., breads, cookies, pies)—are classified in Industry 31181, Bread and Bakery Product Manufacturing; and
- Manufacturing pretzels (except soft)—are classified in U.S. Industry 311919, Other Snack Food Manufacturing.

311822 Flour Mixes and Dough Manufacturing from Purchased Flour[CAN]

This U.S. industry comprises establishments primarily engaged in manufacturing prepared flour mixes or dough mixes from flour ground elsewhere.

US—United States industry only. CAN—United States and Canadian industries are comparable. MEX—United States and Mexican industries are comparable. Blank—Canadian, Mexican, and United States industries are comparable.

Cross-References.

Establishments primarily engaged in milling flour and preparing flour mixes or doughs are classified in U.S. Industry 311211, Flour Milling.

311823 Dry Pasta Manufacturing[CAN]

This U.S. industry comprises establishments primarily engaged in manufacturing dry pasta. The establishments in this industry may package the dry pasta they manufacture with other ingredients.

Cross-References. Establishments primarily engaged in—

- Manufacturing fresh pasta—are classified in U.S. Industry 311991, Perishable Prepared Food Manufacturing;
- Manufacturing pasta specialties—are classified in Industry Group 3114, Fruit and Vegetable Preserving and Specialty Food Manufacturing;
- Mixing purchased dried and/or dehydrated ingredients with purchased dry pasta—are classified in U.S. Industry 311999, All Other Miscellaneous Food Manufacturing; and
- Drying and/or dehydrating ingredients packaged with purchased dry pasta—are classified in U.S. Industry 311423, Dried and Dehydrated Food Manufacturing.

31183 Tortilla Manufacturing

See industry description for 311830 below.

311830 Tortilla Manufacturing

This industry comprises establishments primarily engaged in manufacturing tortillas.

Cross-References. Establishments primarily engaged in—

- Manufacturing canned nationality foods using tortillas—are classified in U.S. Industry 311422, Specialty Canning;
- Manufacturing frozen nationality foods using tortillas—are classified in U.S. Industry 311412, Frozen Specialty Food Manufacturing; and
- Manufacturing tortilla chips—are classified in U.S. Industry 311919, Other Snack Food Manufacturing.

US—United States industry only. CAN—United States and Canadian industries are comparable. MEX—United States and Mexican industries are comparable. Blank—Canadian, Mexican, and United States industries are comparable.

3119 Other Food Manufacturing

This industry group comprises establishments primarily engaged in manufacturing food (except animal food; grain and oilseed milling; sugar and confectionery products; preserved fruit, vegetable, and specialty foods; dairy products; meat products; seafood products; and bakeries and tortillas). The industry group includes industries with different productive processes, such as snack food manufacturing; coffee and tea manufacturing; concentrate, syrup, condiment, and spice manufacturing; and, in general, an entire range of other miscellaneous food product manufacturing.

31191 Snack Food Manufacturing

This industry comprises establishments primarily engaged in one or more of the following: (1) salting, roasting, drying, cooking, or canning nuts; (2) processing grains or seeds into snacks; (3) manufacturing peanut butter; and (4) manufacturing potato chips, corn chips, popped popcorn, pretzels (except soft), pork rinds, and similar snacks.

Cross-References. Establishments primarily engaged in—

- Manufacturing crackers—are classified in Industry 31182, Cookie, Cracker, and Pasta Manufacturing;
- Manufacturing unpopped popcorn—are classified in Industry 31199, All Other Food Manufacturing;
- Manufacturing chocolate or candy-coated nuts and candy-covered popcorn—are classified in Industry Group 3113, Sugar and Confectionery Product Manufacturing; and
- Manufacturing soft pretzels—are classified in Industry 31181, Bread and Bakery Product Manufacturing.

311911 Roasted Nuts and Peanut Butter Manufacturing[CAN]

This U.S. industry comprises establishments primarily engaged in one or more of the following: (1) salting, roasting, drying, cooking, or canning nuts; (2) processing grains or seeds into snacks; and (3) manufacturing peanut butter.

Cross-References.

Establishments primarily engaged in manufacturing chocolate or candy-coated nuts and candy-covered popcorn are classified in Industry Group 3113, Sugar and Confectionery Product Manufacturing.

US—United States industry only. CAN—United States and Canadian industries are comparable. MEX—United States and Mexican industries are comparable. Blank—Canadian, Mexican, and United States industries are comparable.

311919 Other Snack Food Manufacturing[CAN]

This U.S. industry comprises establishments primarily engaged in manufacturing snack foods (except roasted nuts and peanut butter).

Illustrative Examples:

Corn chips and related corn snacks manufacturing
Popped popcorn (except candy-covered) manufacturing
Pork rinds manufacturing
Potato chips manufacturing
Pretzels (except soft) manufacturing
Tortilla chips manufacturing

Cross-References. Establishments primarily engaged in—

- Manufacturing cookies and crackers—are classified in U.S. Industry 311821, Cookie and Cracker Manufacturing;
- Manufacturing candy covered popcorn and nonchocolate granola bars—are classified in Industry 311340, Nonchocolate Confectionery Manufacturing;
- Salting, roasting, drying, cooking, or canning nuts and seeds—are classified in U.S. Industry 311911, Roasted Nuts and Peanut Butter Manufacturing;
- Manufacturing unpopped popcorn—are classified in U.S. Industry 311999, All Other Miscellaneous Food Manufacturing; and
- Manufacturing soft pretzels—are classified in U.S. Industry 311812, Commercial Bakeries.

31192 Coffee and Tea Manufacturing

See industry description for 311920 below.

311920 Coffee and Tea Manufacturing[CAN]

This industry comprises establishments primarily engaged in one or more of the following: (1) roasting coffee; (2) manufacturing coffee and tea concentrates (including instant and freeze-dried); (3) blending tea; (4) manufacturing herbal tea; and (5) manufacturing coffee extracts, flavorings, and syrups.

Cross-References.

Establishments primarily engaged in bottling and canning iced tea are classified in U.S. Industry 312111, Soft Drink Manufacturing.

31193 Flavoring Syrup and Concentrate Manufacturing

See industry description for 311930 below.

US—United States industry only. CAN—United States and Canadian industries are comparable. MEX—United States and Mexican industries are comparable. Blank—Canadian, Mexican, and United States industries are comparable.

311930 Flavoring Syrup and Concentrate Manufacturing

This industry comprises establishments primarily engaged in manufacturing flavoring syrup drink concentrates and related products for soda fountain use or for the manufacture of soft drinks.

Cross-References. Establishments primarily engaged in—

- Manufacturing chocolate syrup—are classified in Industry 311320, Chocolate and Confectionery Manufacturing from Cacao Beans;
- Manufacturing flavoring extracts (except coffee and meat) and natural food colorings—are classified in U.S. Industry 311942, Spice and Extract Manufacturing;
- Manufacturing coffee extracts—are classified in Industry 311920, Coffee and Tea Manufacturing;
- Manufacturing meat extracts—are classified in Industry 31161, Animal Slaughtering and Processing;
- Manufacturing powdered drink mixes (except coffee, tea, chocolate, or milk-based) and table syrup from corn syrup—are classified in U.S. Industry 311999, All Other Miscellaneous Food Manufacturing;
- Reducing maple sap to maple syrup—are classified in U.S. Industry 111998, All Other Miscellaneous Crop Farming; and
- Manufacturing natural nonfood colorings—are classified in U.S. Industry 325199, All Other Basic Organic Chemical Manufacturing.

31194 Seasoning and Dressing Manufacturing

This industry comprises establishments primarily engaged in one or more of the following: (1) manufacturing dressings and sauces, such as mayonnaise, salad dressing, vinegar, mustard, horseradish, soy sauce, tarter sauce, Worcestershire sauce, and other prepared sauces (except tomato-based and gravies); (2) manufacturing spices, table salt, seasoning, and flavoring extracts (except coffee and meat), and natural food colorings; and (3) manufacturing dry mix food preparations, such as salad dressing mixes, gravy and sauce mixes, frosting mixes, and other dry mix preparations.

Cross-References. Establishments primarily engaged in—

- Manufacturing catsup and other tomato-based sauces—are classified in Industry 31142, Fruit and Vegetable Canning, Pickling, and Drying;

US—United States industry only. CAN—United States and Canadian industries are comparable. MEX—United States and Mexican industries are comparable. Blank—Canadian, Mexican, and United States industries are comparable.

- Mixing purchased dried and/or dehydrated potato, rice, and pasta and packaging them with other purchased ingredients, and manufacturing prepared frosting—are classified in Industry 31199, All Other Food Manufacturing;
- Drying and/or dehydrating ingredients for dry soup mixes and bouillon—are classified in Industry 31142, Fruit and Vegetable Canning, Pickling, and Drying;
- Mixing purchased dried and/or dehydrated ingredients for dry soup mixes and bouillon—are classified in Industry 31199, All Other Food Manufacturing;
- Manufacturing industrial salts—are classified in Industry 32599, Other Chemical Product and Preparation Manufacturing;
- Manufacturing flavoring syrups (except coffee)—are classified in Industry 31193, Flavoring Syrup and Concentrate Manufacturing;
- Manufacturing synthetic food colorings—are classified in Industry 32513, Synthetic Dye and Pigment Manufacturing;
- Manufacturing natural organic colorings for nonfood uses—are classified in Industry 32519, Other Basic Organic Chemical Manufacturing;
- Manufacturing coffee extracts—are classified in Industry 31192, Coffee and Tea Manufacturing;
- Manufacturing meat extracts—are classified in Industry 31161, Animal Slaughtering and Processing; and
- Manufacturing gravies—are classified in Industry 31199, All Other Food Manufacturing.

311941 Mayonnaise, Dressing, and Other Prepared Sauce Manufacturing[US]

This U.S. industry comprises establishments primarily engaged in manufacturing mayonnaise, salad dressing, vinegar, mustard, horseradish, soy sauce, tarter sauce, Worcestershire sauce, and other prepared sauces (except tomato-based and gravy).

Cross-References. Establishments primarily engaged in—

- Manufacturing catsup and similar tomato-based sauces—are classified in U.S. Industry 311421, Fruit and Vegetable Canning;
- Manufacturing dry salad dressing and dry sauce mixes—are classified in U.S. Industry 311942, Spice and Extract Manufacturing; and
- Manufacturing gravies—are classified in U.S. Industry 311999, All Other Miscellaneous Food Manufacturing.

US—United States industry only. CAN—United States and Canadian industries are comparable. MEX—United States and Mexican industries are comparable. Blank—Canadian, Mexican, and United States industries are comparable.

311942 Spice and Extract Manufacturing[US]

This U.S. industry comprises establishments primarily engaged in (1) manufacturing spices, table salt, seasonings, flavoring extracts (except coffee and meat), and natural food colorings and/or (2) manufacturing dry mix food preparations, such as salad dressing mixes, gravy and sauce mixes, frosting mixes, and other dry mix preparations.

Cross-References. Establishments primarily engaged in—

- Manufacturing catsup and other tomato-based sauces—are classified in U.S. Industry 311421, Fruit and Vegetable Canning;
- Manufacturing mayonnaise, dressings, and prepared nontomato-based sauces—are classified in U.S. Industry 311941, Mayonnaise, Dressing, and Other Prepared Sauce Manufacturing;
- Manufacturing industrial salts—are classified in U.S. Industry 325998, All Other Miscellaneous Chemical Product and Preparation Manufacturing;
- Drying and/or dehydrating ingredients for dry soup mixes and bouillon—are classified in U.S. Industry 311423, Dried and Dehydrated Food Manufacturing;
- Mixing purchased dried and/or dehydrated ingredients for dry soup mixes and bouillon—are classified in U.S. Industry 311999, All Other Miscellaneous Food Manufacturing;
- Manufacturing flavoring syrups (except coffee-based syrups)—are classified in Industry 311930, Flavoring Syrup and Concentrate Manufacturing;
- Manufacturing dried and dehydrated potato, rice, or dry pasta packaged with other ingredients, and prepared frostings—are classified in U.S. Industry 311999, All Other Miscellaneous Food Manufacturing;
- Manufacturing coffee extracts and/or coffee-based syrups—are classified in Industry 311920, Coffee and Tea Manufacturing;
- Manufacturing meat extracts—are classified in Industry 31161, Animal Slaughtering and Processing;
- Manufacturing synthetic food colorings—are classified in U.S. Industry 325132, Synthetic Organic Dye and Pigment Manufacturing; and
- Manufacturing natural organic colorings for nonfood uses—are classified in U.S. Industry 325199, All Other Basic Organic Chemical Manufacturing.

31199 All Other Food Manufacturing

This industry comprises establishments primarily engaged in manufacturing food (except animal food; grain and oilseed milling; sugar and confectionery

US—United States industry only. CAN—United States and Canadian industries are comparable. MEX—United States and Mexican industries are comparable. Blank—Canadian, Mexican, and United States industries are comparable.

products; preserved fruits, vegetables, and specialties; dairy products; meat products; seafood products; bakeries and tortillas; snack foods; coffee and tea; flavoring syrups and concentrates; seasonings; and dressings). Included in this industry are establishments primarily engaged in mixing purchased dried and/or dehydrated ingredients including those mixing purchased dried and/or dehydrated ingredients for soup mixes and bouillon.

Illustrative Examples:

Baking powder manufacturing
Cut or peeled fresh vegetables manufacturing
Dessert puddings manufacturing
Egg substitutes manufacturing
Fresh pasta manufacturing
Fresh pizza manufacturing
Honey processing
Popcorn (except popped) manufacturing
Powdered drink mixes (except chocolate, coffee, tea, or milk based) manufacturing
Sweetening syrups (except pure maple) manufacturing

Cross-References. Establishments primarily engaged in—

- Manufacturing animal foods—are classified in Industry Group 3111, Animal Food Manufacturing;
- Milling grain and oilseed—are classified in Industry Group 3112, Grain and Oilseed Milling;
- Manufacturing sugar and confectionery products—are classified in Industry Group 3113, Sugar and Confectionery Product Manufacturing;
- Preserving fruit, vegetables, and specialty foods—are classified in Industry Group 3114, Fruit and Vegetable Preserving and Specialty Food Manufacturing;
- Manufacturing dairy products—are classified in Industry Group 3115, Dairy Product Manufacturing;
- Manufacturing meat products—are classified in Industry Group 3116, Animal Slaughtering and Processing;
- Manufacturing seafood products—are classified in Industry Group 3117, Seafood Product Preparation and Packaging;
- Manufacturing bakery and tortilla products—are classified in Industry Group 3118, Bakeries and Tortilla Manufacturing;
- Manufacturing snack foods—are classified in Industry 31191, Snack Food Manufacturing;
- Manufacturing coffee and tea—are classified in Industry 31192, Coffee and Tea Manufacturing;
- Manufacturing flavoring syrups and concentrates—are classified in Industry 31193, Flavoring Syrup and Concentrate Manufacturing;

US—United States industry only. CAN—United States and Canadian industries are comparable. MEX—United States and Mexican industries are comparable. Blank—Canadian, Mexican, and United States industries are comparable.

- Manufacturing seasonings and dressings—are classified in Industry 31194, Seasoning and Dressing Manufacturing;
- Milling rice and packaging it with other ingredients—are classified in Industry 31121, Flour Milling and Malt Manufacturing;
- Manufacturing dry pasta and packaging it with other ingredients—are classified in Industry 31182, Cookie, Cracker, and Pasta Manufacturing; and
- Drying and/or dehydrating ingredients and packaging them with other purchased ingredients—are classified in Industry 31142, Fruit and Vegetable Canning, Pickling, and Drying.

311991 Perishable Prepared Food Manufacturing[US]

This U.S. industry comprises establishments primarily engaged in manufacturing perishable prepared foods, such as salads, sandwiches, prepared meals, fresh pizza, fresh pasta, and peeled or cut vegetables.

311999 All Other Miscellaneous Food Manufacturing[US]

This U.S. industry comprises establishments primarily engaged in manufacturing food (except animal food; grain and oilseed milling; sugar and confectionery products; preserved fruits, vegetables, and specialties; dairy products; meat products; seafood products; bakeries and tortillas; snack foods; coffee and tea; flavoring syrups and concentrates; seasonings and dressings; and perishable prepared food). Included in this industry are establishments primarily engaged in mixing purchased dried and/or dehydrated ingredients including those mixing purchased dried and/or dehydrated ingredients for soup mixes and bouillon.

Illustrative Examples:

Baking powder manufacturing
Cake frosting manufacturing
Dessert puddings manufacturing
Egg substitutes manufacturing
Gelatin dessert preparations manufacturing
Honey processing
Popcorn (except popped) manufacturing
Powdered drink mixes (except chocolate, coffee, tea, or milk based) manufacturing
Sweetening syrups (except pure maple) manufacturing
Yeast manufacturing

Cross-References. Establishments primarily engaged in—

- Manufacturing animal foods—are classified in Industry Group 3111, Animal Food Manufacturing;
- Milling grain and oilseed—are classified in Industry Group 3112, Grain and Oilseed Milling;

US—United States industry only. CAN—United States and Canadian industries are comparable. MEX—United States and Mexican industries are comparable. Blank—Canadian, Mexican, and United States industries are comparable.

- Manufacturing sugar and confectionery products—are classified in Industry Group 3113, Sugar and Confectionery Product Manufacturing;
- Preserving fruit, vegetable, and specialty foods—are classified in Industry Group 3114, Fruit and Vegetable Preserving and Specialty Food Manufacturing;
- Manufacturing dairy products—are classified in Industry Group 3115, Dairy Product Manufacturing;
- Manufacturing meat products—are classified in Industry Group 3116, Meat Product Manufacturing;
- Manufacturing seafood products—are classified in Industry Group 3117, Seafood Product Preparation and Packaging;
- Manufacturing bakery and tortilla products—are classified in Industry Group 3118, Bakeries and Tortilla Manufacturing;
- Manufacturing snack foods—are classified in Industry 31191, Snack Food Manufacturing;
- Manufacturing coffee and tea—are classified in Industry 31192, Coffee and Tea Manufacturing;
- Manufacturing flavoring syrups and concentrates—are classified in Industry 31193, Flavoring Syrup and Concentrate Manufacturing;
- Manufacturing seasonings and dressings—are classified in Industry 31194, Seasoning and Dressing Manufacturing;
- Manufacturing perishable prepared foods—are classified in U.S. Industry 311991, Perishable Prepared Food Manufacturing;
- Milling rice and packaging it with other ingredients—are classified in U.S. Industry 311212, Rice Milling;
- Manufacturing dry pasta and packaging it with ingredients—are classified in U.S. Industry 311823, Dry Pasta Manufacturing; and
- Drying and/or dehydrating ingredients and packaging them with other purchased ingredients—are classified in U.S. Industry 311423, Dried and Dehydrated Food Manufacturing.

312 Beverage and Tobacco Product Manufacturing

Industries in the Beverage and Tobacco Product Manufacturing subsector manufacture beverages and tobacco products. The industry group, Beverage Manufacturing, includes three types of establishments: (1) those that manufacture nonalcoholic beverages; (2) those that manufacture alcoholic beverages through the fermentation process; and (3) those that produce distilled alcoholic beverages. Ice manufacturing,

---

US—United States industry only. CAN—United States and Canadian industries are comparable. MEX—United States and Mexican industries are comparable. Blank—Canadian, Mexican, and United States industries are comparable.

while not a beverage, is included with nonalcoholic beverage manufacturing because it uses the same production process as water purification.

In the case of activities related to the manufacture of beverages, the structure follows the defined productive processes. Brandy, a distilled beverage, was not placed under distillery product manufacturing, but rather under the NAICS class for winery product manufacturing since the productive process used in the manufacturing of alcoholic grape-based beverages produces both wines (fermented beverage) and brandies (distilled beverage).

The industry group, Tobacco Manufacturing, includes two types of establishments: (1) those engaged in redrying and stemming tobacco and, (2) those that manufacture tobacco products, such as cigarettes and cigars.

3121 Beverage Manufacturing

31211 Soft Drink and Ice Manufacturing

This industry comprises establishments primarily engaged in one or more of the following: (1) manufacturing soft drinks; (2) manufacturing ice; and (3) purifying and bottling water.

Cross-References. Establishments primarily engaged in—

- Canning fruit and vegetable juices—are classified in Industry 31142, Fruit and Vegetable Canning, Pickling and Drying;
- Manufacturing soft drink bases—are classified in Industry 31193, Flavoring Syrup and Concentrate Manufacturing;
- Manufacturing nonalcoholic cider—are classified in Industry 31194, Seasoning and Dressing Manufacturing;
- Manufacturing dry ice—are classified in Industry 32512, Industrial Gas Manufacturing;
- Manufacturing milk-based drinks—are classified in Industry 31151, Dairy Product (except Frozen) Manufacturing;
- Manufacturing nonalcoholic beers—are classified in Industry 31212, Breweries;
- Manufacturing nonalcoholic wines—are classified in Industry 31213, Wineries; and
- Bottling purchased purified water—are classified in Industry 42449, Other Grocery and Related Products Merchant Wholesalers.

US—United States industry only. CAN—United States and Canadian industries are comparable. MEX—United States and Mexican industries are comparable. Blank—Canadian, Mexican, and United States industries are comparable.

312111 Soft Drink Manufacturing[MEX]

This U.S. industry comprises establishments primarily engaged in manufacturing soft drinks and artificially carbonated waters.

Cross-References. Establishments primarily engaged in—

- Canning fruit and vegetable juices—are classified in U.S. Industry 311421, Fruit and Vegetable Canning;
- Manufacturing fruit syrups for flavoring—are classified in Industry 31193, Flavoring Syrup and Concentrate Manufacturing;
- Manufacturing nonalcoholic cider—are classified in U.S. Industry 311941, All Other Miscellaneous Food Manufacturing;
- Purifying and bottling water (except artificially carbonated and flavored water)—are classified in U.S. Industry 312112, Bottled Water Manufacturing;
- Manufacturing milk-based drinks—are classified in U.S. Industry 311511, Fluid Milk Manufacturing;
- Manufacturing nonalcoholic beers—are classified in Industry 312120, Breweries; and
- Manufacturing nonalcoholic wines—are classified in Industry 312130, Wineries.

312112 Bottled Water Manufacturing[MEX]

This U.S. industry comprises establishments primarily engaged in purifying and bottling water (including naturally carbonated).

Cross-References. Establishments primarily engaged in—

- Manufacturing artificially carbonated waters—are classified in U.S. Industry 312111, Soft Drink Manufacturing; and
- Bottling purchased purified water— are classified in Industry 424490, Other Grocery and Related Products Merchant Wholesalers.

312113 Ice Manufacturing[MEX]

This U.S. industry comprises establishments primarily engaged in manufacturing ice.

US—United States industry only. CAN—United States and Canadian industries are comparable. MEX—United States and Mexican industries are comparable. Blank—Canadian, Mexican, and United States industries are comparable.

Cross-References.

Establishments primarily engaged in manufacturing dry ice are classified in Industry 325120, Industrial Gas Manufacturing.

31212 Breweries

See industry description for 312120 below.

312120 Breweries

This industry comprises establishments primarily engaged in brewing beer, ale, malt liquors, and nonalcoholic beer.

Cross-References. Establishments primarily engaged in—

- Bottling purchased malt beverages—are classified in Industry 424810, Beer and Ale Merchant Wholesalers; and
- Manufacturing malt—are classified in U.S. Industry 311213, Malt Manufacturing.

31213 Wineries

See industry description for 312130 below.

312130 Wineries[CAN]

This industry comprises establishments primarily engaged in one or more of the following: (1) growing grapes and manufacturing wine and brandies; (2) manufacturing wine and brandies from grapes and other fruits grown elsewhere; and (3) blending wines and brandies.

Cross-References.

Establishments primarily engaged in bottling purchased wines are classified in Industry 424820, Wine and Distilled Alcoholic Beverage Merchant Wholesalers.

31214 Distilleries

See industry description for 312140 below.

312140 Distilleries[CAN]

This industry comprises establishments primarily engaged in one or more of the following: (1) distilling potable liquors (except brandies); (2) distilling and blending liquors; and (3) blending and mixing liquors and other ingredients.

US—United States industry only. CAN—United States and Canadian industries are comparable. MEX—United States and Mexican industries are comparable. Blank—Canadian, Mexican, and United States industries are comparable.

Cross-References. Establishments primarily engaged in—

- Manufacturing nonpotable ethyl alcohol—are classified in U.S. Industry 325193, Ethyl Alcohol Manufacturing;
- Bottling liquors made elsewhere—are classified in Industry 424820, Wine and Distilled Alcoholic Beverage Merchant Wholesalers; and
- Manufacturing brandies—are classified in Industry 312130, Wineries.

3122 Tobacco Manufacturing

31221 Tobacco Stemming and Redrying

See industry description for 312210 below.

312210 Tobacco Stemming and Redrying

This industry comprises establishments primarily engaged in the stemming and redrying of tobacco.

Cross-References. Establishments primarily engaged in—

- Reconstituting tobacco—are classified in U.S. Industry 312229, Other Tobacco Product Manufacturing;
- Selling leaf tobacco as merchant wholesalers that also engage in stemming tobacco—are classified in Industry 424940, Tobacco and Tobacco Product Merchant Wholesalers; and
- Selling leaf tobacco as agents or brokers that also engage in stemming tobacco—are classified in Industry 425120, Wholesale Trade Agents and Brokers.

31222 Tobacco Product Manufacturing

This industry comprises establishments primarily engaged in manufacturing cigarettes, cigars, smoking and chewing tobacco, and reconstituted tobacco.

Cross-References.

Establishments primarily engaged in stemming and redrying tobacco are classified in Industry 31221, Tobacco Stemming and Redrying.

312221 Cigarette Manufacturing[MEX]

This U.S. industry comprises establishments primarily engaged in manufacturing cigarettes.

US—United States industry only. CAN—United States and Canadian industries are comparable. MEX—United States and Mexican industries are comparable. Blank—Canadian, Mexican, and United States industries are comparable.

Cross-References.

Establishments primarily engaged in manufacturing cigars, smoking tobacco, chewing tobacco, and reconstituted tobacco are classified in U.S. Industry 312229, Other Tobacco Product Manufacturing.

312229 Other Tobacco Product Manufacturing[US]

This U.S. industry comprises establishments primarily engaged in manufacturing tobacco products (except cigarettes).

Illustrative Examples:

Chewing tobacco manufacturing
Cigar manufacturing
Prepared pipe tobacco manufacturing
Reconstituting tobacco
Snuff manufacturing

Cross-References. Establishments primarily engaged in—

- Manufacturing cigarettes—are classified in U.S. Industry 312221, Cigarette Manufacturing; and
- Stemming and redrying tobacco—are classified in Industry 312210, Tobacco Stemming and Redrying.

313 Textile Mills

Industries in the Textile Mills subsector group establishments that transform a basic fiber (natural or synthetic) into a product, such as yarn or fabric, that is further manufactured into usable items, such as apparel, sheets towels, and textile bags for individual or industrial consumption. The further manufacturing may be performed in the same establishment and classified in this subsector, or it may be performed at a separate establishment and be classified elsewhere in manufacturing.

The main processes in this subsector include preparation and spinning of fiber, knitting or weaving of fabric, and the finishing of the textile. The NAICS structure follows and captures this process flow. Major industries in this flow, such as preparation of fibers, weaving of fabric, knitting of fabric, and fiber and fabric finishing, are uniquely identified. Texturizing, throwing, twisting, and winding of yarn contains aspects of both fiber preparation and fiber finishing and is classified with preparation of fibers rather than with finishing of fiber.

NAICS separates the manufacturing of primary textiles and the manufacturing of textile products (except apparel) when the textile product is produced from purchased primary textiles, such as fabric. The manufacturing of textile products (except apparel) from purchased fabric is classified in Subsector 314, Textile

---

US—United States industry only. CAN—United States and Canadian industries are comparable. MEX—United States and Mexican industries are comparable. Blank—Canadian, Mexican, and United States industries are comparable.

Product Mills, and apparel from purchased fabric is classified in Subsector 315, Apparel Manufacturing.

Excluded from this subsector are establishments that weave or knit fabric and make garments. These establishments are included in Subsector 315, Apparel Manufacturing.

3131 Fiber, Yarn, and Thread Mills

31311 Fiber, Yarn, and Thread Mills

This industry comprises establishments primarily engaged in one or more of the following: (1) spinning yarn; (2) manufacturing thread of any fiber; (3) texturizing, throwing, twisting, and winding purchased yarn or manmade fiber filaments; and (4) producing hemp yarn and further processing into rope or bags.

Cross-References.

Establishments primarily engaged in manufacturing artificial and synthetic fibers and filaments and texturizing these filaments are classified in Industry 32522, Artificial and Synthetic Fibers and Filaments Manufacturing.

313111 Yarn Spinning Mills[US]

This U.S. industry comprises establishments primarily engaged in spinning yarn from any fiber and/or producing hemp yarn and further processing into rope or bags.

313112 Yarn Texturizing, Throwing, and Twisting Mills[US]

This U.S. industry comprises establishments primarily engaged in texturizing, throwing, twisting, spooling, or winding purchased yarns or manmade fiber filaments.

Cross-References.

Establishments primarily engaged in manufacturing artificial and synthetic fiber and filament and texturizing these fibers and filaments are classified in Industry 32522, Artificial and Synthetic Fibers and Filaments Manufacturing.

313113 Thread Mills[MEX]

This U.S. industry comprises establishments primarily engaged in manufacturing thread (e.g., sewing, hand-knitting, crochet) of all fibers.

US—United States industry only. CAN—United States and Canadian industries are comparable. MEX—United States and Mexican industries are comparable. Blank—Canadian, Mexican, and United States industries are comparable.

3132 Fabric Mills

31321 Broadwoven Fabric Mills

See industry description for 313210 below.

313210 Broadwoven Fabric Mills

This industry comprises establishments primarily engaged in weaving broadwoven fabrics and felts (except tire fabrics and rugs). Establishments in this industry may weave only, weave and finish, or weave, finish, and further fabricate fabric products.

Cross-References. Establishments primarily engaged in—

- Weaving widths specifically constructed for cutting to narrow widths—are classified in U.S. Industry 313221, Narrow Fabric Mills;
- Weaving or tufting carpet and rugs—are classified in Industry 314110, Carpet and Rug Mills; and
- Making tire cord and tire fabrics—are classified in U.S. Industry 314992, Tire Cord and Tire Fabric Mills.

31322 Narrow Fabric Mills and Schiffli Machine Embroidery

This industry comprises establishments primarily engaged in one or more of the following: (1) weaving or braiding narrow fabrics; (2) manufacturing Schiffli machine embroideries; and (3) making fabric-covered elastic yarn and thread.

313221 Narrow Fabric Mills[US]

This U.S. industry comprises establishments primarily engaged in (1) weaving or braiding narrow fabrics in their final form or initially made in wider widths that are specially constructed for narrower widths and/or (2) making fabric-covered elastic yarn and thread. Establishments in this industry may weave only; weave and finish; or weave, finish, and further fabricate fabric products.

313222 Schiffli Machine Embroidery[US]

This U.S. industry comprises establishments primarily engaged in manufacturing Schiffli machine embroideries.

US—United States industry only. CAN—United States and Canadian industries are comparable. MEX—United States and Mexican industries are comparable. Blank—Canadian, Mexican, and United States industries are comparable.

31323 Nonwoven Fabric Mills

See industry description for 313230 below.

313230 Nonwoven Fabric Mills

This industry comprises establishments primarily engaged in manufacturing nonwoven fabrics and felts. Processes used include bonding and/or interlocking fibers by mechanical, chemical, thermal, or solvent means, or by combinations thereof.

31324 Knit Fabric Mills

This industry comprises establishments primarily engaged in one of the following: (1) knitting weft (i.e., circular) and warp (i.e., flat) fabric; (2) knitting and finishing weft and warp fabric; (3) manufacturing lace; or (4) manufacturing, dyeing, and finishing lace and lace goods. Establishments in this industry may knit only; knit and finish; or knit, finish, and further fabricate fabric products (except apparel).

Cross-References.

Establishments primarily engaged in knitting apparel are classified in Industry Group 3151, Apparel Knitting Mills.

313241 Weft Knit Fabric Mills[US]

This U.S. industry comprises establishments primarily engaged in knitting weft (i.e., circular) fabric or knitting and finishing weft fabric. Establishments in this industry may knit only; knit and finish; or knit, finish, and further fabricate fabric products (except apparel).

Cross-References.

Establishments primarily engaged in knitting apparel are classified in Industry Group 3151, Apparel Knitting Mills.

313249 Other Knit Fabric and Lace Mills[US]

This U.S. industry comprises establishments primarily engaged in one of the following: (1) knitting warp (i.e., flat) fabric; (2) knitting and finishing warp fabric; (3) manufacturing lace; or (4) manufacturing, dyeing, or finishing lace and lace goods. Establishments in this industry may knit only; knit and finish; or knit, finish, and further fabricate fabric products (except apparel).

US—United States industry only. CAN—United States and Canadian industries are comparable. MEX—United States and Mexican industries are comparable. Blank—Canadian, Mexican, and United States industries are comparable.

Cross-References.

Establishments primarily engaged in knitting apparel are classified in Industry Group 3151, Apparel Knitting Mills.

3133 Textile and Fabric Finishing and Fabric Coating Mills

31331 Textile and Fabric Finishing Mills

This industry comprises (1) establishments primarily engaged in finishing of textiles, fabrics, and apparel, and (2) establishments of converters who buy fabric goods in the grey, have them finished on contract, and sell at wholesale. Finishing operations include: bleaching, dyeing, printing (e.g., roller, screen, flock, plisse), stonewashing, and other mechanical finishing, such as preshrinking, shrinking, sponging, calendering, mercerizing, and napping; as well as cleaning, scouring, and the preparation of natural fibers and raw stock.

Cross-References. Establishments primarily engaged in—

- Coating or impregnating fabrics—are classified in Industry 31332, Fabric Coating Mills;
- Knitting or knitting and finishing fabric—are classified in Industry 31324, Knit Fabric Mills;
- Manufacturing and finishing apparel—are classified in Subsector 315, Apparel Manufacturing;
- Weaving and finishing fabrics—are classified in Industry Group 3132, Fabric Mills;
- Manufacturing and finishing rugs and carpets—are classified in Industry 31411, Carpet and Rug Mills; and
- Printing on apparel—are classified in Industry 32311, Printing.

313311 Broadwoven Fabric Finishing Mills[US]

This U.S. industry comprises (1) establishments primarily engaged in finishing broadwoven fabrics, and (2) establishments of converters who buy broadwoven fabrics in the grey, have them finished on contract, and sell at wholesale. Finishing operations include bleaching, dyeing, printing (roller, screen, flock, plisse), and other mechanical finishing, such as preshrinking, shrinking, sponging, calendering, mercerizing and napping.

US—United States industry only. CAN—United States and Canadian industries are comparable. MEX—United States and Mexican industries are comparable. Blank—Canadian, Mexican, and United States industries are comparable.

Cross-References. Establishments primarily engaged in—

- Coating or impregnating fabrics—are classified in Industry 313320, Fabric Coating Mills; and
- Weaving and finishing broadwoven fabrics—are classified in Industry 313210, Broadwoven Fabric Mills.

313312 Textile and Fabric Finishing (except Broadwoven Fabric) Mills[US]

This U.S. industry comprises (1) establishments primarily engaged in dyeing, bleaching, printing, and other finishing of textiles, apparel, and fabrics (except broadwoven) and (2) establishments of converters who buy fabrics (except broadwoven) in the grey, have them finished on contract, and sell at wholesale. Finishing operations include bleaching, dyeing, printing (e.g., roller, screen, flock, plisse), stonewashing, and other mechanical finishing, such as preshrinking, shrinking, sponging, calendering, mercerizing and napping; as well as cleaning, scouring, and the preparation of natural fibers and raw stock.

Cross-References. Establishments primarily engaged in—

- Knitting and finishing fabric—are classified in Industry 31324, Knit Fabric Mills;
- Finishing broadwoven fabric—are classified in U.S. Industry 313311, Broadwoven Fabric Finishing Mills;
- Weaving and finishing narrow woven fabric—are classified in U.S. Industry 313221, Narrow Fabric Mills;
- Manufacturing and finishing apparel—are classified in Subsector 315, Apparel Manufacturing;
- Coating or impregnating fabrics—are classified in Industry 313320, Fabric Coating Mills; and
- Printing on apparel—are classified in Industry 32311, Printing.

31332 Fabric Coating Mills

See industry description for 313320 below.

313320 Fabric Coating Mills

This industry comprises establishments primarily engaged in coating, laminating, varnishing, waxing, and rubberizing textiles and apparel.

US—United States industry only. CAN—United States and Canadian industries are comparable. MEX—United States and Mexican industries are comparable. Blank—Canadian, Mexican, and United States industries are comparable.

Cross-References.

Establishments primarily engaged in dyeing and finishing textiles are classified in Industry 31331, Textile and Fabric Finishing Mills.

314 Textile Product Mills

Industries in the Textile Product Mills subsector group establishments that make textile products (except apparel). With a few exceptions, processes used in these industries are generally cut and sew (i.e., purchasing fabric and cutting and sewing to make nonapparel textile products, such as sheets and towels).

3141 Textile Furnishings Mills

31411 Carpet and Rug Mills

See industry description for 314110 below.

314110 Carpet and Rug Mills

This industry comprises establishments primarily engaged in (1) manufacturing woven, tufted, and other carpets and rugs, such as art squares, floor mattings, needlepunch carpeting, and door mats and mattings, from textile materials or from twisted paper, grasses, reeds, sisal, jute, or rags and/or (2) finishing carpets and rugs.

31412 Curtain and Linen Mills

This industry comprises establishments primarily engaged in manufacturing household textile products, such as curtains, draperies, linens, bedspreads, sheets, tablecloths, towels, and shower curtains, from purchased materials.

Cross-References. Establishments primarily engaged in—

- Weaving broadwoven fabrics—are classified in Industry 31321, Broadwoven Fabric Mills;
- Manufacturing lace curtains on lace machines—are classified in Industry 31324, Knit Fabric Mills;
- Manufacturing textile blanket, wardrobe, and laundry bags—are classified in Industry 31491, Textile Bag and Canvas Mills; and
- Manufacturing mops—are classified in Industry 33999, All Other Miscellaneous Manufacturing.

US—United States industry only. CAN—United States and Canadian industries are comparable. MEX—United States and Mexican industries are comparable. Blank—Canadian, Mexican, and United States industries are comparable.

314121 Curtain and Drapery Mills[US]

This U.S. industry comprises establishments primarily engaged in manufacturing window curtains and draperies from purchased fabrics or sheet goods. The curtains and draperies may be made on a stock or custom basis for sale to individual retail customers.

Cross-References.

Establishments primarily engaged in manufacturing lace curtains on lace machines are classified in U.S. Industry 313249, Other Knit Fabric and Lace Mills.

314129 Other Household Textile Product Mills[US]

This U.S. industry comprises establishments primarily engaged in manufacturing household textile products (except window curtains and draperies), such as bedspreads, sheets, tablecloths, towels, and shower curtains, from purchased materials.

Cross-References. Establishments primarily engaged in—

- Weaving fabrics—are classified in Industry 313210, Broadwoven Fabric Mills;
- Manufacturing blanket, laundry, and wardrobe bags—are classified in U.S. Industry 314911, Textile Bag Mills;
- Manufacturing mops—are classified in U.S. Industry 339994, Broom, Brush, and Mop Manufacturing; and
- Manufacturing window curtains and draperies—are classified in U.S. Industry 314121, Curtain and Drapery Mills.

3149 Other Textile Product Mills

This industry group comprises establishments primarily engaged in making textile products, (except carpets and rugs, curtains and draperies, and other household textile products) from purchased materials.

31491 Textile Bag and Canvas Mills

This industry comprises establishments primarily engaged in manufacturing textile bags, awnings, tents, and related products from purchased textile fabrics.

Cross-References. Establishments primarily engaged in—

- Manufacturing plastic bags—are classified in Industry 32611, Plastics Packaging Materials and Unlaminated Film and Sheet Manufacturing;

US—United States industry only. CAN—United States and Canadian industries are comparable. MEX—United States and Mexican industries are comparable. Blank—Canadian, Mexican, and United States industries are comparable.

- Manufacturing canvas blinds and shades—are classified in Industry 33792, Blind and Shade Manufacturing;
- Manufacturing luggage—are classified in Industry 31699, Other Leather and Allied Product Manufacturing; and
- Manufacturing women's handbags and purses of leather or other material (except precious metal)—are classified in Industry 31699, Other Leather and Allied Product Manufacturing.

314911 Textile Bag Mills[US]

This U.S. industry comprises establishments primarily engaged in manufacturing bags from purchased textile fabrics or yarns.

Illustrative Examples:

Canvas bags manufacturing
Laundry bags made from purchased woven or knitted materials
Seed bags made from purchased woven or knitted materials
Textile bags made from purchased woven or knitted materials

Cross-References. Establishments primarily engaged in—

- Manufacturing plastics bags—are classified in U.S. Industry 326111, Plastics Bag Manufacturing;
- Manufacturing luggage—are classified in U.S. Industry 316991, Luggage Manufacturing; and
- Manufacturing women's handbags and purses of leather or other material, except precious metal—are classified in U.S. Industry 316992, Women's Handbag and Purse Manufacturing.

314912 Canvas and Related Product Mills[US]

This U.S. industry comprises establishments primarily engaged in manufacturing canvas and canvas-like products, such as awnings, sails, tarpaulins, and tents, from purchased fabrics.

Cross-References. Establishments primarily engaged in—

- Manufacturing canvas blinds and shades—are classified in Industry 337920, Blind and Shade Manufacturing; and
- Manufacturing canvas bags—are classified in U.S. Industry 314911, Textile Bag Mills.

US—United States industry only. CAN—United States and Canadian industries are comparable. MEX—United States and Mexican industries are comparable. Blank—Canadian, Mexican, and United States industries are comparable.

31499 All Other Textile Product Mills

This industry comprises establishments primarily engaged in manufacturing nonapparel textile products (except carpet, rugs, curtains, linens, bags, and canvas products) from purchased materials.

Illustrative Examples:

- Batts and batting (except nonwoven fabrics) manufacturing
- Carpet cutting and binding
- Diapers (except disposable) made from purchased fabric
- Dust cloths made from purchased fabric apparel) for the trade
- Fishing nets made from purchased materials
- Sleeping bags manufacturing
- Textile fire hoses made from purchased materials
- Weatherstripping made from purchased textiles

Cross-References. Establishments primarily engaged in—

- Manufacturing yarns and thread—are classified in Industry 31311, Fiber, Yarn, and Thread Mills;
- Manufacturing carpets and rugs—are classified in Industry 31411, Carpet and Rug Mills;
- Manufacturing apparel—are classified in Subsector 315, Apparel Manufacturing;
- Manufacturing curtains and linens—are classified in Industry 31412, Curtain and Linen Mills; and
- Manufacturing textile bags and canvas products—are classified in Industry 31491, Textile Bag and Canvas Mills.

314991 Rope, Cordage, and Twine Mills[US]

This U.S. industry comprises establishments primarily engaged in manufacturing rope, cable, cordage, twine, and related products from all materials (e.g., abaca, sisal, henequen, hemp, cotton, paper, jute, flax, manmade fibers including glass).

Cross-References.

Establishments primarily engaged in spinning yarns and filaments are classified in U.S. Industry 313111, Yarn Spinning Mills.

314992 Tire Cord and Tire Fabric Mills[US]

This U.S. industry comprises establishments primarily engaged in manufacturing cord and fabric of polyester, rayon, cotton, glass, steel, or other materials for use in reinforcing rubber tires, industrial belting, and similar uses.

US—United States industry only. CAN—United States and Canadian industries are comparable. MEX—United States and Mexican industries are comparable. Blank—Canadian, Mexican, and United States industries are comparable.

314999 All Other Miscellaneous Textile Product Mills[US]

This U.S. industry comprises establishments primarily engaged in manufacturing textile products (except carpets and rugs; curtains and linens; textile bags and canvas products; rope, cordage, and twine; and tire cords and tire fabrics) from purchased materials.

Illustrative Examples:

Batts and batting (except nonwoven fabrics) manufacturing
Carpet cutting and binding
Diapers (except disposable) made from purchased fabricDust cloths made from purchased fabric
Embroidering on textile products (except apparel) for the trade
Sleeping bags manufacturing
Textile fire hose made from purchased materials

Cross-References. Establishments primarily engaged in—

- Manufacturing yarns and thread—are classified in Industry 31311, Fiber, Yarn, and Thread Mills;
- Manufacturing carpets and rugs—are classified in Industry 314110, Carpet and Rug Mills;
- Manufacturing curtains and linens—are classified in Industry 31412, Curtain and Linen Mills;
- Manufacturing textile bags and canvas products—are classified in Industry 31491, Textile Bag and Canvas Mills;
- Manufacturing rope, cordage, and twine—are classified in U.S. Industry 314991, Rope, Cordage, and Twine Mills; and
- Manufacturing tire cords and tire fabrics—are classified in U.S. Industry 314992, Tire Cord and Tire Fabric Mills.

315 Apparel Manufacturing

Industries in the Apparel Manufacturing subsector group establishments with two distinct manufacturing processes: (1) cut and sew (i.e., purchasing fabric and cutting and sewing to make a garment), and (2) the manufacture of garments in establishments that first knit fabric and then cut and sew the fabric into a garment. The Apparel Manufacturing subsector includes a diverse range of establishments manufacturing full lines of ready-to-wear apparel and custom apparel: apparel contractors, performing cutting or sewing operations on materials owned by others; jobbers performing entrepreneurial functions involved in apparel manufacture; and tailors, manufacturing custom garments for individual clients are all included.

US—United States industry only. CAN—United States and Canadian industries are comparable. MEX—United States and Mexican industries are comparable. Blank—Canadian, Mexican, and United States industries are comparable.

Knitting, when done alone, is classified in the Textile Mills subsector, but when knitting is combined with the production of complete garments, the activity is classified in Apparel Manufacturing.

3151 Apparel Knitting Mills

This industry group comprises establishments primarily engaged in knitting apparel or knitting fabric and then manufacturing apparel. This industry group includes jobbers performing entrepreneurial functions involved in knitting apparel and accessories. Knitting fabric, without manufacturing apparel, is classified in Subsector 313, Textile Mills.

31511 Hosiery and Sock Mills

This industry comprises establishments primarily engaged in knitting or knitting and finishing hosiery and socks.

Cross-References. Establishments primarily engaged in—

- Manufacturing orthopedic hosiery—are classified in Industry 33911, Medical Equipment and Supplies Manufacturing;
- Manufacturing slipper socks from purchased socks—are classified in Industry 31621, Footwear Manufacturing; and
- Finishing apparel products only—are classified in Industry 31331, Textile and Fabric Finishing Mills.

315111 Sheer Hosiery Mills[US]

This U.S. industry comprises establishments primarily engaged in knitting or knitting and finishing women's, misses', and girls' full-length and knee-length sheer hosiery (except socks).

Cross-References. Establishments primarily engaged in—

- Knitting or knitting and finishing socks—are classified in U.S. Industry 315119, Other Hosiery and Sock Mills;
- Finishing apparel products only—are classified in U.S. Industry 313312, Textile and Fabric Finishing (except Broadwoven Fabric) Mills; and
- Manufacturing orthopedic hosiery—are classified in U.S. Industry 339113, Surgical Appliance and Supplies Manufacturing.

US—United States industry only. CAN—United States and Canadian industries are comparable. MEX—United States and Mexican industries are comparable. Blank—Canadian, Mexican, and United States industries are comparable.

315119 Other Hosiery and Sock Mills[US]

This U.S. industry comprises establishments primarily engaged in knitting or knitting and finishing hosiery (except women's, misses', and girls' sheer hosiery).

Cross-References. Establishments primarily engaged in—

- Knitting or knitting and finishing women's, misses', and girls' full-length and knee-length sheer hosiery—are classified in U.S. Industry 315111, Sheer Hosiery Mills;
- Manufacturing orthopedic hosiery—are classified in U.S. Industry 339113, Surgical Appliance and Supplies Manufacturing;
- Finishing apparel products only—are classified in U.S. Industry 313312, Textile and Fabric Finishing (except Broadwoven Fabric) Mills; and
- Manufacturing slipper socks from purchased socks—are classified in U.S. Industry 316212, House Slipper Manufacturing.

31519 Other Apparel Knitting Mills

This industry comprises establishments primarily engaged in one of the following: (1) knitting underwear, outerwear, and/or nightwear; (2) knitting fabric and manufacturing underwear, outerwear, and/or nightwear; or (3) knitting, manufacturing, and finishing knit underwear, outerwear, and/or nightwear.

Cross-References. Establishments primarily engaged in—

- Manufacturing outerwear, underwear, and nightwear from purchased fabric—are classified in Industry Group 3152, Cut and Sew Apparel Manufacturing; and
- Finishing apparel products only—are classified in Industry 31331, Textile and Fabric Finishing Mills.

315191 Outerwear Knitting Mills[US]

This U.S. industry comprises establishments primarily engaged in one or more of the following: (1) knitting outerwear; (2) knitting fabric and manufacturing outerwear; and (3) knitting, manufacturing, and finishing knit outerwear. Examples of products made in knit outerwear mills are shirts, shorts, sweat suits, sweaters, gloves, and pants.

Cross-References. Establishments primarily engaged in—

- Manufacturing outerwear from purchased fabric—are classified in Industry Group 3152, Cut and Sew Apparel Manufacturing;

US—United States industry only. CAN—United States and Canadian industries are comparable. MEX—United States and Mexican industries are comparable. Blank—Canadian, Mexican, and United States industries are comparable.

- Finishing apparel products only—are classified in U.S. Industry 313312, Textile and Fabric Finishing (except Broadwoven Fabric) Mills; and
- Knitting underwear and nightwear, knitting fabric and manufacturing underwear and nightwear, or knitting, manufacturing, and finishing knit underwear and nightwear—are classified in U.S. Industry 315192, Underwear and Nightwear Knitting Mills.

315192 Underwear and Nightwear Knitting Mills[US]

This U.S. industry comprises establishments primarily engaged in one of the following: (1) knitting underwear and nightwear; (2) knitting fabric and manufacturing underwear and nightwear; or (3) knitting, manufacturing, and finishing knit underwear and nightwear. Examples of products produced in underwear and nightwear knitting mills are briefs, underwear T-shirts, pajamas, nightshirts, foundation garments, and panties.

Cross-References. Establishments primarily engaged in—

- Manufacturing underwear and nightwear from purchased fabric—are classified in Industry Group 3152, Cut and Sew Apparel Manufacturing; and
- Finishing apparel products only—are classified in U.S. Industry 313312, Textile and Fabric Finishing (except Broadwoven Fabric) Mills.

3152 Cut and Sew Apparel Manufacturing

This industry group comprises establishments primarily engaged in manufacturing cut and sew apparel from woven fabric or purchased knit fabric. Included in this industry group is a diverse range of establishments manufacturing full lines of ready-to-wear apparel and custom apparel: apparel contractors, performing cutting or sewing operations on materials owned by others; jobbers performing entrepreneurial functions involved in apparel manufacture; and tailors, manufacturing custom garments for individual clients. Establishments weaving or knitting fabric, without manufacturing apparel, are classified in Subsector 313, Textile Mills.

31521 Cut and Sew Apparel Contractors[CAN]

This industry comprises establishments commonly referred to as contractors primarily engaged in (1) cutting materials owned by others for apparel and accessories and/or (2) sewing materials owned by others for apparel and accessories.

US—United States industry only. CAN—United States and Canadian industries are comparable. MEX—United States and Mexican industries are comparable. Blank—Canadian, Mexican, and United States industries are comparable.

Cross-References. Establishments primarily engaged in—

- Manufacturing men's and boys' apparel from purchased fabric—are classified in Industry 31522, Men's and Boys' Cut and Sew Apparel Manufacturing;
- Manufacturing women's and girls' apparel from purchased fabric—are classified in Industry 31523, Women's and Girls' Cut and Sew Apparel Manufacturing;
- Manufacturing infants' apparel and all other cut and sew apparel from purchased fabric—are classified in Industry 31529, Other Cut and Sew Apparel Manufacturing; and
- Manufacturing apparel accessories from purchased fabric—are classified in Industry 31599, Apparel Accessories and Other Apparel Manufacturing.

315211 Men's and Boys' Cut and Sew Apparel Contractors[US]

This U.S. industry comprises establishments commonly referred to as contractors primarily engaged in (1) cutting materials owned by others for men's and boys' apparel and/or (2) sewing materials owned by others for men's and boys' apparel.

Cross-References. Establishments primarily engaged in—

- Manufacturing men's and boys' apparel from purchased fabric—are classified in Industry 31522, Men's and Boys' Cut and Sew Apparel Manufacturing;
- Manufacturing infants' apparel from purchased fabric—are classified in U.S. Industry 315291, Infants' Cut and Sew Apparel Manufacturing; and
- Manufacturing men's and boys' apparel accessories from purchased fabric—are classified in Industry 31599, Apparel Accessories and Other Apparel Manufacturing.

315212 Women's, Girls', and Infants' Cut and Sew Apparel Contractors[US]

This U.S. industry comprises establishments commonly referred to as contractors primarily engaged in (1) cutting materials owned by others for women's, girls', and infants' apparel and accessories and/or (2) sewing materials owned by others for women's, girls', and infants' apparel and accessories.

Cross-References. Establishments primarily engaged in—

- Manufacturing women's and girls' apparel from purchased fabric—are classified in Industry 31523, Women's and Girls' Cut and Sew Apparel Manufacturing;

US—United States industry only. CAN—United States and Canadian industries are comparable. MEX—United States and Mexican industries are comparable. Blank—Canadian, Mexican, and United States industries are comparable.

- Manufacturing infants' apparel from purchased fabric—are classified in U.S. Industry 315291, Infants' Cut and Sew Apparel Manufacturing; and
- Manufacturing women's, girls', and infants' apparel accessories from purchased fabric—are classified in Industry 31599, Apparel Accessories and Other Apparel Manufacturing.

31522 Men's and Boys' Cut and Sew Apparel Manufacturing[CAN]

This industry comprises establishments primarily engaged in manufacturing men's and boys' cut and sew apparel from purchased fabric. Men's and boys' clothing jobbers, who perform entrepreneurial functions involved in apparel manufacture, including buying raw materials, designing and preparing samples, arranging for apparel to be made from their materials, and marketing finished apparel, are included.

Cross-References. Establishments primarily engaged in—

- Cutting and/or sewing materials owned by others for men's and boys' apparel—are classified in Industry 31521, Cut and Sew Apparel Contractors;
- Knitting men's and boys' apparel or knitting fabric and manufacturing men's and boys' apparel—are classified in Industry Group 3151, Apparel Knitting Mills; and
- Manufacturing fur or leather apparel and team athletic uniforms—are classified in Industry 31529, Other Cut and Sew Apparel Manufacturing.

315221 Men's and Boys' Cut and Sew Underwear and Nightwear Manufacturing[CAN]

This U.S. industry comprises establishments primarily engaged in manufacturing men's and boys' underwear and nightwear from purchased fabric. Men's and boys' underwear and nightwear jobbers, who perform entrepreneurial functions involved in apparel manufacture, including buying raw materials, designing and preparing samples, arranging for apparel to be made from their materials, and marketing finished apparel, are included. Examples of products made by these establishments are briefs, bathrobes, underwear T-shirts and shorts, nightshirts, and pajamas.

Cross-References. Establishments primarily engaged in—

- Knitting men's and boys' underwear and nightwear and/or knitting and manufacturing men's and boys' underwear and nightwear—are classified in U.S. Industry 315192, Underwear and Nightwear Knitting Mills; and

US—United States industry only. CAN—United States and Canadian industries are comparable. MEX—United States and Mexican industries are comparable. Blank—Canadian, Mexican, and United States industries are comparable.

- Cutting and/or sewing materials owned by others for men's and boys' underwear and nightwear—are classified in U.S. Industry 315211, Men's and Boys' Cut and Sew Apparel Contractors.

315222 Men's and Boys' Cut and Sew Suit, Coat, and Overcoat Manufacturing[CAN]

This U.S. industry comprises establishments primarily engaged in manufacturing men's and boys' suits, overcoats, sport coats, tuxedos, dress uniforms, and other tailored apparel (except fur and leather) from purchased fabric. Men's and boys' suit, coat, and overcoat jobbers, who perform entrepreneurial functions involved in apparel manufacture, including buying raw materials, designing and preparing samples, arranging for apparel to be made from their materials, and marketing finished apparel, are included.

Cross-References. Establishments primarily engaged in—

- Manufacturing men's and boys' nontailored coats and jackets such as down coats and windbreakers made from purchased fabric—are classified in U.S. Industry 315228, Men's and Boys' Cut and Sew Other Outerwear Manufacturing;
- Manufacturing fur and leather apparel—are classified in U.S. Industry 315292, Fur and Leather Apparel Manufacturing;
- Manufacturing men's and boys' washable service apparel from purchased fabric—are classified in U.S. Industry 315225, Men's and Boys' Cut and Sew Work Clothing Manufacturing;
- Manufacturing men's and boys' team athletic uniforms from purchased fabric—are classified in U.S. Industry 315299, All Other Cut and Sew Apparel Manufacturing; and
- Cutting and/or sewing materials owned by others for men's and boys' suits, coats, and overcoats—are classified in U.S. Industry 315211, Men's and Boys' Cut and Sew Apparel Contractors.

315223 Men's and Boys' Cut and Sew Shirt (except Work Shirt) Manufacturing[US]

This U.S. industry comprises establishments primarily engaged in manufacturing men's and boys' outerwear shirts from purchased fabric. Men's and boys' shirt (except work shirt) jobbers, who perform entrepreneurial functions involved in apparel manufacture, including buying raw materials, designing and preparing samples, arranging for apparel to be made from their materials, and marketing

US—United States industry only. CAN—United States and Canadian industries are comparable. MEX—United States and Mexican industries are comparable. Blank—Canadian, Mexican, and United States industries are comparable.

finished apparel, are included. Unisex outerwear shirts, such as T-shirts and sweatshirts that are sized without specific reference to gender (i.e., adult S, M, L, XL) are included in this industry.

Cross-References. Establishments primarily engaged in—

- Manufacturing men's and boys' work shirts from purchased fabric—are classified in U.S. Industry 315225, Men's and Boys' Cut and Sew Work Clothing Manufacturing;
- Manufacturing men's and boys' underwear T-shirts and underwear tank tops from purchased fabric—are classified in U.S. Industry 315221, Men's and Boys' Cut and Sew Underwear and Nightwear Manufacturing;
- Cutting and/or sewing materials owned by others for men's and boys' shirts—are classified in U.S. Industry 315211, Men's and Boys' Cut and Sew Apparel Contractors; and
- Knitting men's and boys' outerwear shirts or knitting fabric and manufacturing men's and boys' outerwear shirts—are classified in U.S. Industry 315191, Outerwear Knitting Mills.

315224 Men's and Boys' Cut and Sew Trouser, Slack, and Jean Manufacturing[US]

This U.S. industry comprises establishments primarily engaged in manufacturing men's and boys' jeans, dungarees, and other separate trousers and slacks (except work pants) from purchased fabric. Men's and boys' trouser, slack, and jean jobbers, who perform entrepreneurial functions involved in apparel manufacture, including buying raw materials, designing and preparing samples, arranging for apparel to be made from their materials, and marketing finished apparel, are included.

Cross-References. Establishments primarily engaged in—

- Manufacturing men's and boys' work pants from purchased fabric—are classified in U.S. Industry 315225, Men's and Boys' Cut and Sew Work Clothing Manufacturing;
- Manufacturing fur and leather apparel—are classified in U.S. Industry 315292, Fur and Leather Apparel Manufacturing;
- Manufacturing men's and boys' sweatpants and shorts from purchased fabric—are classified in U.S. Industry 315228, Men's and Boys' Cut and Sew Other Outerwear Manufacturing; and
- Cutting and/or sewing materials owned by others for men's and boys' separate trousers, slacks, and jeans—are classified in U.S. Industry 315211, Men's and Boys' Cut and Sew Apparel Contractors.

US—United States industry only. CAN—United States and Canadian industries are comparable. MEX—United States and Mexican industries are comparable. Blank—Canadian, Mexican, and United States industries are comparable.

315225 Men's and Boys' Cut and Sew Work Clothing Manufacturing[US]

This U.S. industry comprises establishments primarily engaged in manufacturing men's and boys' work shirts, work pants (excluding jeans and dungarees), other work clothing, and washable service apparel from purchased fabric. Men's and boys' work clothing jobbers, who perform entrepreneurial functions involved in apparel manufacture, including buying raw materials, designing and preparing samples, arranging for apparel to be made from their materials, and marketing finished apparel, are included. Examples of products made by these establishments are washable service apparel, laboratory coats, work shirts, work pants (except jeans and dungarees), and hospital apparel.

Cross-References. Establishments primarily engaged in—

- Manufacturing men's and boys' separate trousers, slacks, and pants, including jeans and dungarees from purchased fabric—are classified in U.S. Industry 315224, Men's and Boys' Cut and Sew Trouser, Slack, and Jean Manufacturing; and
- Cutting and/or sewing materials owned by others for men's and boys' work clothing—are classified in U.S. Industry 315211, Men's and Boys' Cut and Sew Apparel Contractors.

315228 Men's and Boys' Cut and Sew Other Outerwear Manufacturing[US]

This U.S. industry comprises establishments primarily engaged in manufacturing men's and boys' cut and sew outerwear from purchased fabric (except underwear, nightwear, shirts, suits, overcoats and tailored coats, separate trousers and slacks, and work clothing). Men's and boys' other outerwear jobbers, who perform entrepreneurial functions involved in apparel manufacture, including buying raw materials, designing and preparing samples, arranging for apparel to be made from their materials, and marketing finished apparel, are included. Unisex sweatpants and similar garments that are sized without specific reference to gender (i.e., adult S, M, L, XL) are also included in this industry. Examples of products made by these establishments are athletic clothing (except athletic uniforms), bathing suits, down coats, outerwear shorts, windbreakers and jackets, and jogging suits.

Cross-References. Establishments primarily engaged in—

- Manufacturing men's and boys' athletic uniforms from purchased fabric—are classified in U.S. Industry 315299, All Other Cut and Sew Apparel Manufacturing;

US—United States industry only. CAN—United States and Canadian industries are comparable. MEX—United States and Mexican industries are comparable. Blank—Canadian, Mexican, and United States industries are comparable.

- Manufacturing leather and fur apparel—are classified in U.S. Industry 315292, Fur and Leather Apparel Manufacturing;
- Knitting men's and boys' apparel or knitting fabric and manufacturing men's and boys' apparel—are classified in Industry Group 3151, Apparel Knitting Mills;
- Cutting and/or sewing materials owned by others for men's and boys' apparel—are classified in U.S. Industry 315211, Men's and Boys' Cut and Sew Apparel Contractors;
- Manufacturing men's and boys' underwear and nightwear from purchased fabric—are classified in U.S. Industry 315221, Men's and Boys' Cut and Sew Underwear and Nightwear Manufacturing;
- Manufacturing men's and boys' tailored suits, coats, and overcoats from purchased fabric—are classified in U.S. Industry 315222, Men's and Boys' Cut and Sew Suit, Coat and Overcoat Manufacturing;
- Manufacturing men's and boys' outerwear shirts (except work shirts) from purchased fabric—are classified in U.S. Industry 315223, Men's and Boys' Cut and Sew Shirt (except Work Shirt) Manufacturing;
- Manufacturing men's and boys' separate pants, trousers, and slacks from purchased fabric—are classified in U.S. Industry 315224, Men's and Boys' Cut and Sew Trouser, Slack, and Jean Manufacturing; and
- Manufacturing men's and boys' work clothing from purchased fabric—are classified in U.S. Industry 315225, Men's and Boys' Cut and Sew Work Clothing Manufacturing.

31523 Women's and Girls' Cut and Sew Apparel Manufacturing[CAN]

This industry comprises establishments primarily engaged in manufacturing women's and girls' apparel from purchased fabric. Women's and girls' clothing jobbers, who perform entrepreneurial functions involved in apparel manufacture, including buying raw materials, designing and preparing samples, arranging for apparel to be made from their materials, and marketing finished apparel, are included.

Cross-References. Establishments primarily engaged in—

- Knitting women's and girls' apparel or knitting fabric and manufacturing women's and girls' apparel—are classified in Industry Group 3151, Apparel Knitting Mills;
- Manufacturing unisex outerwear garments, such as T-shirts, sweatshirts, and sweatpants that are sized without reference to specific gender (i.e., adult S, M, L, XL),—are classified in Industry 31522, Men's and Boys' Cut and Sew Apparel Manufacturing;

US—United States industry only. CAN—United States and Canadian industries are comparable. MEX—United States and Mexican industries are comparable. Blank—Canadian, Mexican, and United States industries are comparable.

- Cutting and/or sewing materials owned by others for women's and girls' apparel—are classified in Industry 31521, Cut and Sew Apparel Contractors; and
- Manufacturing fur or leather apparel and team athletic uniforms—are classified in Industry 31529, Other Cut and Sew Apparel Manufacturing.

315231 Women's and Girls' Cut and Sew Lingerie, Loungewear, and Nightwear Manufacturing[CAN]

This U.S. industry comprises establishments primarily engaged in manufacturing women's and girls' bras, girdles, and other underwear; lingerie; loungewear; and nightwear from purchased fabric. Women's and girls' lingerie, loungewear, and nightwear jobbers, who perform entrepreneurial functions involved in apparel manufacture, including buying raw materials, designing and preparing samples, arranging for apparel to be made from their materials, and marketing finished apparel, are included. Examples of products made by these establishments are bathrobes, foundation garments, nightgowns, pajamas, panties, and slips.

Cross-References. Establishments primarily engaged in—

- Knitting women's and girls' underwear, nightwear, and lingerie or knitting fabric and manufacturing women's and girls' underwear, nightwear, and lingerie—are classified in U.S. Industry 315192, Underwear and Nightwear Knitting Mills; and
- Cutting and/or sewing materials owned by others for women's and girls' underwear, nightwear, and lingerie—are classified in U.S. Industry 315212, Women's, Girls', and Infants' Cut and Sew Apparel Contractors.

315232 Women's and Girls' Cut and Sew Blouse and Shirt Manufacturing[CAN]

This U.S. industry comprises establishments primarily engaged in manufacturing women's and girls' blouses and shirts from purchased fabric. Women's and girls' blouse and shirt jobbers, who perform entrepreneurial functions involved in apparel manufacture, including buying raw materials, designing and preparing samples, arranging for apparel to be made from their materials, and marketing finished apparel, are included.

Cross-References. Establishments primarily engaged in—

- Knitting women's and girls' blouses, shirts, and tops or knitting fabric and manufacturing women's and girls' blouses, shirts, and tops—are classified in U.S. Industry 315191, Outerwear Knitting Mills;

US—United States industry only. CAN—United States and Canadian industries are comparable. MEX—United States and Mexican industries are comparable. Blank—Canadian, Mexican, and United States industries are comparable.

- Manufacturing unisex outerwear shirts, such as T-shirts and sweatshirts that are sized without specific reference to gender (i.e., adult S, M, L, XL),—are classified in U.S. Industry 315223, Men's and Boys' Cut and Sew Shirt (except Work Shirt) Manufacturing; and
- Cutting and/or sewing materials owned by others for women's and girls' shirts and blouses—are classified in U.S. Industry 315212, Women's, Girls', and Infants' Cut and Sew Apparel Contractors.

315233 Women's and Girls' Cut and Sew Dress Manufacturing[CAN]

This U.S. industry comprises establishments primarily engaged in manufacturing women's and girls' dresses from purchased fabric. Women's and girls' dress jobbers, who perform entrepreneurial functions involved in apparel manufacture, including buying raw materials, designing and preparing samples, arranging for apparel to be made from their materials, and marketing finished apparel, are included.

Cross-References. Establishments primarily engaged in—

- Knitting women's and girls' dresses or knitting fabric and manufacturing women's and girls' dresses—are classified in U.S. Industry 315191, Outerwear Knitting Mills; and
- Cutting and/or sewing materials owned by others for women's and girls' dresses—are classified in U.S. Industry 315212, Women's, Girls', and Infants' Cut and Sew Apparel Contractors.

315234 Women's and Girls' Cut and Sew Suit, Coat, Tailored Jacket, and Skirt Manufacturing[CAN]

This U.S. industry comprises establishments primarily engaged in manufacturing women's and girls' suits, pantsuits, skirts, tailored jackets, vests, raincoats, and other tailored coats, (except fur and leather coats) from purchased fabric. Women's and girls' suit, coat, tailored jacket, and skirt jobbers, who perform entrepreneurial functions involved in apparel manufacture, including buying raw materials, designing and preparing samples, arranging for apparel to be made from their materials, and marketing finished apparel, are included.

Cross-References. Establishments primarily engaged in—

- Manufacturing women's and girls' team athletic uniforms from purchased fabric—are classified in U.S. Industry 315299, All Other Cut and Sew Apparel Manufacturing;

US—United States industry only. CAN—United States and Canadian industries are comparable. MEX—United States and Mexican industries are comparable. Blank—Canadian, Mexican, and United States industries are comparable.

- Manufacturing women's and girls' separate slacks, jeans, pants, and nontailored coats and jackets, such as down coats and windbreakers from purchased fabric,—are classified in U.S. Industry 315239, Women's and Girls' Cut and Sew Other Outerwear Manufacturing;
- Manufacturing fur and leather apparel—are classified in U.S. Industry 315292, Fur and Leather Apparel Manufacturing;
- Knitting women's and girls' tailored skirts, suits, vests, and coats or knitting fabric and manufacturing women's and girls' tailored skirts, suits, vests, and coats—are classified in U.S. Industry 315191, Outerwear Knitting Mills; and
- Cutting and/or sewing materials owned by others for women's and girls' suits, coats, tailored jackets, and skirts—are classified in U.S. Industry 315212, Women's, Girls', and Infants' Cut and Sew Apparel Contractors.

315239 Women's and Girls' Cut and Sew Other Outerwear Manufacturing[CAN]

This U.S. industry comprises establishments primarily engaged in manufacturing women's and girls' cut and sew apparel from purchased fabric (except underwear, lingerie, nightwear, blouses, shirts, dresses, suits, tailored coats, tailored jackets, and skirts). Women's and girls' other outerwear clothing jobbers, who perform entrepreneurial functions involved in apparel manufacture, including buying raw materials, designing and preparing samples, arranging for apparel to be made from their materials, and marketing finished apparel, are included. Examples of products made by these establishments are bathing suits, down coats, sweaters, jogging suits, outerwear pants and shorts, and windbreakers.

Cross-References. Establishments primarily engaged in—

- Manufacturing women's and girls' team athletic uniforms from purchased fabric—are classified in U.S. Industry 315299, All Other Cut and Sew Apparel Manufacturing;
- Knitting women's and girls' apparel or knitting fabric and manufacturing women's and girls' apparel—are classified in U.S. Industry 315191, Outerwear Knitting Mills;
- Manufacturing women's and girls' fur and leather apparel—are classified in U.S. Industry 315292, Fur and Leather Apparel Manufacturing;
- Cutting and/or sewing materials owned by others for women's and girls' apparel—are classified in U.S. Industry 315212, Women's, Girls', and Infants' Cut and Sew Apparel Contractors;
- Manufacturing women's and girls' lingerie, loungewear, and nightwear from purchased fabric—are classified in U.S. Industry 315231, Women's

US—United States industry only. CAN—United States and Canadian industries are comparable. MEX—United States and Mexican industries are comparable. Blank—Canadian, Mexican, and United States industries are comparable.

and Girls' Cut and Sew Lingerie, Loungewear, and Nightwear Manufacturing;

- Manufacturing women's and girls' blouses and outerwear shirts from purchased fabric—are classified in U.S. Industry 315232, Women's and Girls' Cut and Sew Blouse and Shirt Manufacturing;
- Manufacturing unisex sweatpants and similar outerwear garments that are sized without specific reference to gender (i.e., adult S, M, L, XL)—are classified in U.S. Industry 315228, Men's and Boys' Cut and Sew Other Outerwear Manufacturing;
- Manufacturing women's and girls' dresses from purchased fabric—are classified in U.S. Industry 315233, Women's and Girls' Cut and Sew Dress Manufacturing; and
- Manufacturing women's and girls' suits, skirts, and tailored coats and jackets from purchased fabric—are classified in U.S. Industry 315234, Women's and Girls' Cut and Sew Suit, Coat, Tailored Jacket, and Skirt Manufacturing.

31529 Other Cut and Sew Apparel Manufacturing[CAN]

This industry comprises establishments primarily engaged in manufacturing cut and sew apparel from purchased fabric (except men's, boys', women's, and girls' apparel). This industry includes establishments manufacturing apparel, such as fur apparel, leather apparel, infants' apparel, costumes, and clerical vestments.

Cross-References. Establishments primarily engaged in—

- Manufacturing men's and boys' apparel from purchased fabric—are classified in Industry 31522, Men's and Boys' Cut and Sew Apparel Manufacturing;
- Manufacturing women's and girls' apparel from purchased fabric—are classified in Industry 31523, Women's and Girls' Cut and Sew Apparel Manufacturing;
- Knitting apparel or knitting fabric and manufacturing apparel—are classified in Industry Group 3151, Apparel Knitting Mills;
- Cutting and/or sewing materials owned by others for apparel—are classified in Industry 31521, Cut and Sew Apparel Contractors;
- Manufacturing fur and leather mittens and gloves—are classified in Industry 31599, Apparel Accessories and Other Apparel Manufacturing; and
- Dyeing and dressing furs—are classified in Industry 31611, Leather and Hide Tanning and Finishing.

US—United States industry only. CAN—United States and Canadian industries are comparable. MEX—United States and Mexican industries are comparable. Blank—Canadian, Mexican, and United States industries are comparable.

315291 Infants' Cut and Sew Apparel Manufacturing[CAN]

This U.S. industry comprises establishments primarily engaged in manufacturing infants' dresses, blouses, shirts, and all other infants' wear from purchased fabric. Infants' clothing jobbers, who perform entrepreneurial functions involved in apparel manufacture, including buying raw materials, designing and preparing samples, arranging for apparel to be made from their materials, and marketing finished apparel, are included. For the purposes of classification, the term ''infants' apparel'' includes apparel for young children of an age not exceeding 24 months.

Cross-References. Establishments primarily engaged in—

- Knitting infants' apparel or knitting fabric and manufacturing infants' apparel—are classified in U.S. Industry 315191, Outerwear Knitting Mills; and
- Cutting and/or sewing materials owned by others for infants' apparel—are classified in U.S. Industry 315212, Women's, Girls', and Infants' Cut and Sew Apparel Contractors.

315292 Fur and Leather Apparel Manufacturing[CAN]

This U.S. industry comprises establishments primarily engaged in manufacturing cut and sew fur and leather apparel, and sheep-lined clothing. Fur and leather apparel jobbers, who perform entrepreneurial functions involved in apparel manufacture, including buying raw materials, designing and preparing samples, arranging for apparel to be made from their materials, and marketing finished apparel, are included.

Cross-References. Establishments primarily engaged in—

- Cutting and/or sewing materials owned by others for apparel—are classified in Industry 31521, Cut and Sew Apparel Contractors;
- Dyeing and dressing furs—are classified in Industry 316110, Leather and Hide Tanning and Finishing; and
- Manufacturing fur and leather mittens and gloves—are classified in U.S. Industry 315992, Glove and Mitten Manufacturing.

315299 All Other Cut and Sew Apparel Manufacturing[CAN]

This U.S. industry comprises establishments primarily engaged in manufacturing cut and sew apparel from purchased fabric (except cut and sew apparel contractors; men's and boys' cut and sew underwear, nightwear, suits, coats, shirts, trousers,

US—United States industry only. CAN—United States and Canadian industries are comparable. MEX—United States and Mexican industries are comparable. Blank—Canadian, Mexican, and United States industries are comparable.

work clothing, and other outerwear; women's and girls' lingerie, blouses, shirts, dresses, suits, coats, and other outerwear; infants' apparel; and fur and leather apparel). Clothing jobbers for these products, who perform entrepreneurial functions involved in apparel manufacture, including buying raw materials, designing and preparing samples, arranging for apparel to be made from their materials, and marketing finished apparel, are included. Examples of products made by these establishments are team athletic uniforms, band uniforms, academic caps and gowns, clerical vestments, and costumes.

Cross-References. Establishments primarily engaged in—

- Cutting and/or sewing materials owned by others for apparel—are classified in Industry 31521, Cut and Sew Apparel Contractors;
- Knitting apparel or knitting fabric and manufacturing apparel—are classified in Industry Group 3151, Apparel Knitting Mills;
- Manufacturing men's and boys' underwear and nightwear from purchased fabric—are classified in U.S. Industry 315221, Men's and Boys' Cut and Sew Underwear and Nightwear Manufacturing;
- Manufacturing men's and boys' suits, coats, and overcoats from purchased fabric—are classified in U.S. Industry 315222, Men's and Boys' Cut and Sew Suit, Coat and Overcoat Manufacturing;
- Manufacturing men's and boys' shirts (except work shirts) from purchased fabric—are classified in U.S. Industry 315223, Men's and Boys' Cut and Sew Shirt (except Work Shirt) Manufacturing;
- Manufacturing men's and boys' pants, slacks, trousers, and jeans from purchased fabric—are classified in U.S. Industry 315224, Men's and Boys' Cut and Sew Trouser, Slack, and Jean Manufacturing;
- Manufacturing men's and boys' work clothing from purchased fabric—are classified in U.S. Industry 315225, Men's and Boys' Cut and Sew Work Clothing Manufacturing;
- Manufacturing other men's and boys' outerwear from purchased fabric—are classified in U.S. Industry 315228, Men's and Boys' Cut and Sew Other Outerwear Manufacturing;
- Manufacturing women's and girls' lingerie and nightwear from purchased fabric—are classified in U.S. Industry 315231, Women's and Girls' Cut and Sew Lingerie, Loungewear, and Nightwear Manufacturing;
- Manufacturing women's and girls' blouses and shirts from purchased fabric—are classified in U.S. Industry 315232, Women's and Girls' Cut and Sew Blouse and Shirt Manufacturing;

US—United States industry only. CAN—United States and Canadian industries are comparable. MEX—United States and Mexican industries are comparable. Blank—Canadian, Mexican, and United States industries are comparable.

- Manufacturing women's and girls' dresses from purchased fabric—are classified in U.S. Industry 315233, Women's and Girls' Cut and Sew Dress Manufacturing;
- Manufacturing women's and girls' suits, tailored coats and jackets, and skirts from purchased fabric—are classified in U.S. Industry 315234, Women's and Girls' Cut and Sew Suit, Coat, Tailored Jacket, and Skirt Manufacturing;
- Manufacturing other women's and girls' outerwear from purchased fabric—are classified in U.S. Industry 315239, Women's and Girls' Cut and Sew Other Outerwear Manufacturing;
- Manufacturing infants' apparel from purchased fabric—are classified in U.S. Industry 315291, Infants' Cut and Sew Apparel Manufacturing; and
- Manufacturing fur and leather apparel—are classified in U.S. Industry 315292, Fur and Leather Apparel Manufacturing.

3159 Apparel Accessories and Other Apparel Manufacturing

This industry group comprises establishments primarily engaged in manufacturing apparel accessories and other apparel (except apparel knitting mills, apparel contractors, men's and boys' cut and sew apparel, women's and girls' cut and sew apparel, infants' cut and sew apparel, fur and leather apparel, and all other cut and sew apparel). This industry group includes jobbers performing entrepreneurial functions involved in manufacturing apparel accessories.

31599 Apparel Accessories and Other Apparel Manufacturing

This industry comprises establishments primarily engaged in manufacturing apparel and accessories (except apparel knitting mills, cut and sew apparel contractors, men's and boys' cut and sew apparel, women's and girls' cut and sew apparel, and other cut and sew apparel). Jobbers, who perform entrepreneurial functions involved in apparel accessories manufacture, including buying raw materials, designing and preparing samples, arranging for apparel accessories to be made from their materials, and marketing finished apparel accessories, are included. Examples of products made by these establishments are belts, caps, gloves (except medical, sporting, safety), hats, and neckties.

Cross-References. Establishments primarily engaged in—

- Cutting and/or sewing materials owned by others for apparel accessories—are classified in Industry 31521, Cut and Sew Apparel Contractors;

US—United States industry only. CAN—United States and Canadian industries are comparable. MEX—United States and Mexican industries are comparable. Blank—Canadian, Mexican, and United States industries are comparable.

- Manufacturing paper hats and caps—are classified in Industry 32229, Other Converted Paper Product Manufacturing;
- Manufacturing plastics or rubber hats and caps (except bathing caps)—are classified in Subsector 326, Plastics and Rubber Products Manufacturing;
- Manufacturing athletic gloves, such as boxing gloves, baseball gloves, golf gloves, batting gloves, and racquetball gloves,—are classified in Industry 33992, Sporting and Athletic Goods Manufacturing;
- Manufacturing metal fabric, metal mesh, or rubber gloves—are classified in Industry 33911, Medical Equipment and Supplies Manufacturing;
- Knitting apparel, mittens, gloves, hats, and caps or knitting fabric and manufacturing apparel, mittens, gloves, hats, and caps—are classified in Industry Group 3151, Apparel Knitting Mills;
- Cutting and/or sewing materials owned by others for apparel—are classified in Industry 31521, Cut and Sew Apparel Contractors;
- Manufacturing men's and boys' underwear and outerwear from purchased fabric—are classified in Industry 31522, Men's and Boys' Cut and Sew Apparel Manufacturing;
- Manufacturing women's and girls' underwear and outerwear from purchased fabric—are classified in Industry 31523, Women's and Girls' Cut and Sew Apparel Manufacturing; and
- Manufacturing other apparel from purchased fabric and manufacturing fur and leather apparel, hats, and caps—are classified in Industry 31529, Other Cut and Sew Apparel Manufacturing.

315991 Hat, Cap, and Millinery Manufacturing[MEX]

This U.S. industry comprises establishments primarily engaged in manufacturing cut and sew hats, caps, millinery, and hat bodies from purchased fabric. Jobbers, who perform entrepreneurial functions involved in hat, cap, and millinery manufacture, including buying raw materials, designing and preparing samples, arranging for hats, caps, and millinery to be made from their materials, and marketing finished hats, caps, and millinery, are included.

Cross-References. Establishments primarily engaged in—

- Cutting and/or sewing materials owned by others for hats, caps, and millinery—are classified in Industry 31521, Cut and Sew Apparel Contractors;
- Manufacturing paper hats and caps—are classified in U.S. Industry 322299, All Other Converted Paper Product Manufacturing;

US—United States industry only. CAN—United States and Canadian industries are comparable. MEX—United States and Mexican industries are comparable. Blank—Canadian, Mexican, and United States industries are comparable.

- Manufacturing plastics or rubber hats and caps (except bathing caps)—are classified in Subsector 326, Plastics and Rubber Products Manufacturing; and
- Manufacturing fur and leather hats and caps—are classified in U.S. Industry 315292, Fur and Leather Apparel Manufacturing.

315992 Glove and Mitten Manufacturing[US]

This U.S. industry comprises establishments primarily engaged in manufacturing cut and sew gloves (except rubber, metal, and athletic gloves) and mittens from purchased fabric, fur, leather, or from combinations of fabric, fur, or leather. Jobbers, who perform entrepreneurial functions involved in glove and mitten manufacture, including buying raw materials, designing and preparing samples, arranging for gloves and mittens to be made from their materials, and marketing finished gloves and mittens, are included.

Cross-References. Establishments primarily engaged in—

- Cutting and/or sewing materials owned by others for gloves and mittens—are classified in Industry 31521, Cut and Sew Apparel Contractors;
- Knitting mittens and gloves or knitting fabric and manufacturing mittens and gloves—are classified in U.S. Industry 315191, Outerwear Knitting Mills;
- Manufacturing athletic gloves, such as boxing gloves, baseball gloves, golf gloves, batting gloves, and racquetball gloves—are classified in Industry 339920, Sporting and Athletic Goods Manufacturing; and
- Manufacturing metal fabric, metal mesh, or rubber gloves—are classified in U.S. Industry 339113, Surgical Appliance and Supplies Manufacturing.

315993 Men's and Boys' Neckwear Manufacturing[US]

This U.S. industry comprises establishments primarily engaged in manufacturing men's and boys' cut and sew neckties, scarves, and mufflers from purchased fabric, leather, or from combinations of leather and fabric. Men's and boys' neckwear jobbers, who perform entrepreneurial functions involved in neckwear manufacture, including buying raw materials, designing and preparing samples, arranging for neckwear to be made from their materials, and marketing finished neckwear, are included.

Cross-References.

Establishments primarily engaged in cutting and/or sewing materials owned by others for men's and boys' neckwear are classified in U.S. Industry 315211, Men's and Boys' Cut and Sew Apparel Contractors.

US—United States industry only. CAN—United States and Canadian industries are comparable. MEX—United States and Mexican industries are comparable. Blank—Canadian, Mexican, and United States industries are comparable.

315999 Other Apparel Accessories and Other Apparel Manufacturing[US]

This U.S. industry comprises establishments primarily engaged in manufacturing apparel and apparel accessories (except apparel knitting mills; cut and sew apparel contractors; cut and sew apparel; hats and caps; mittens and gloves; and men's and boys' neckwear). Jobbers for these products, who perform entrepreneurial functions involved in other apparel and accessory manufacture, including buying raw materials, designing and preparing samples, arranging for other apparel and accessories to be made from their materials, and marketing finished other apparel and accessories, are included. Examples of products made by these establishments are apparel trimmings and findings, belts, women's scarves, and suspenders.

Cross-References. Establishments primarily engaged in—

- Knitting apparel or knitting fabric and manufacturing apparel—are classified in Industry Group 3151, Apparel Knitting Mills;
- Cutting and/or sewing materials owned by others for apparel—are classified in Industry 31521, Cut and Sew Apparel Contractors;
- Manufacturing men's and boys' cut and sew underwear and outerwear from purchased fabric—are classified in Industry 31522, Men's and Boys' Cut and Sew Apparel Manufacturing;
- Manufacturing women's and girls' cut and sew underwear and outerwear from purchased fabric—are classified in Industry 31523, Women's and Girls' Cut and Sew Apparel Manufacturing;
- Manufacturing infants' cut and sew apparel from purchased fabric—are classified in U.S. Industry 315291, Infants' Cut and Sew Apparel Manufacturing;
- Manufacturing fur and leather apparel—are classified in U.S. Industry 315292, Fur and Leather Apparel Manufacturing;
- Manufacturing hats, caps, and millinery—are classified in U.S. Industry 315991, Hat, Cap, and Millinery Manufacturing;
- Manufacturing gloves and mittens—are classified in U.S. Industry 315992, Glove and Mitten Manufacturing; and
- Manufacturing men's and boys' neckwear—are classified in U.S. Industry 315993, Men's and Boys' Neckwear Manufacturing.

316 Leather and Allied Product Manufacturing

Establishments in the Leather and Allied Product Manufacturing subsector transform hides into leather by tanning or curing and fabricating the leather into products

US—United States industry only. CAN—United States and Canadian industries are comparable. MEX—United States and Mexican industries are comparable. Blank—Canadian, Mexican, and United States industries are comparable.

for final consumption. It also includes the manufacture of similar products from other materials, including products (except apparel) made from "leather substitutes," such as rubber, plastics, or textiles. Rubber footwear, textile luggage, and plastics purses or wallets are examples of "leather substitute" products included in this group. The products made from leather substitutes are included in this subsector because they are made in similar ways leather products are made (e.g., luggage). They are made in the same establishments, so it is not practical to separate them.

The inclusion of leather making in this subsector is partly because leather tanning is a relatively small industry that has few close neighbors as a production process, partly because leather is an input to some of the other products classified in this subsector and partly for historical reasons.

3161 Leather and Hide Tanning and Finishing

31611 Leather and Hide Tanning and Finishing

See industry description for 316110 below.

316110 Leather and Hide Tanning and Finishing

This industry comprises establishments primarily engaged in one or more of the following: (1) tanning, currying, and finishing hides and skins; (2) having others process hides and skins on a contract basis; and (3) dyeing or dressing furs.

3162 Footwear Manufacturing

31621 Footwear Manufacturing

This industry comprises establishments primarily engaged in manufacturing footwear (except orthopedic extension footwear).

Cross-References.

Establishments primarily engaged in manufacturing orthopedic extension footwear are classified in Industry 33911, Medical Equipment and Supplies Manufacturing.

316211 Rubber and Plastics Footwear Manufacturing[US]

This U.S. industry comprises establishments primarily engaged in manufacturing rubber and plastics footwear with vulcanized rubber or plastics soles, molded or cemented to rubber, plastics, or fabric uppers, and rubber and plastics protective footwear.

US—United States industry only. CAN—United States and Canadian industries are comparable. MEX—United States and Mexican industries are comparable. Blank—Canadian, Mexican, and United States industries are comparable.

Cross-References. Establishments primarily engaged in—

- Manufacturing house slippers with fabric uppers and rubber or plastics soles—are classified in U.S. Industry 316212, House Slipper Manufacturing;
- Manufacturing men's footwear (except athletic) with leather or vinyl uppers, regardless of sole material—are classified in U.S. Industry 316213, Men's Footwear (except Athletic) Manufacturing;
- Manufacturing women's footwear (except athletic) with leather or vinyl uppers, regardless of sole material—are classified in U.S. Industry 316214, Women's Footwear (except Athletic) Manufacturing; and
- Manufacturing youths' children's and infants' footwear and athletic footwear with leather or vinyl uppers, regardless of sole material—are classified in U.S. Industry 316219, Other Footwear Manufacturing.

316212 House Slipper Manufacturing[US]

This U.S. industry comprises establishments primarily engaged in manufacturing house slippers and slipper socks, regardless of material.

316213 Men's Footwear (except Athletic) Manufacturing[US]

This U.S. industry comprises establishments primarily engaged in manufacturing men's footwear designed primarily for dress, street, and work. This industry includes men's shoes with rubber or plastics soles and leather or vinyl uppers.

Cross-References. Establishments primarily engaged in—

- Manufacturing men's footwear with fabric uppers and rubber or plastics soles—are classified in U.S. Industry 316211, Rubber and Plastics Footwear Manufacturing;
- Manufacturing orthopedic extension footwear—are classified in U.S. Industry 339113, Surgical Appliance and Supplies Manufacturing; and
- Manufacturing men's leather or vinyl upper athletic footwear and youths' and boys' footwear—are classified in U.S. Industry 316219, Other Footwear Manufacturing.

316214 Women's Footwear (except Athletic) Manufacturing[US]

This U.S. industry comprises establishments primarily engaged in manufacturing women's footwear designed for dress, street, and work. This industry includes women's shoes with rubber or plastics soles and leather or vinyl uppers.

US—United States industry only. CAN—United States and Canadian industries are comparable. MEX—United States and Mexican industries are comparable. Blank—Canadian, Mexican, and United States industries are comparable.

Cross-References. Establishments primarily engaged in—

- Manufacturing women's footwear with fabric uppers and rubber or plastics soles and rubber or plastics sandals—are classified in U.S. Industry 316211, Rubber and Plastics Footwear Manufacturing;
- Manufacturing orthopedic extension footwear—are classified in U.S. Industry 339113, Surgical Appliance and Supplies Manufacturing; and
- Manufacturing women's leather or vinyl upper athletic footwear and youths' and girls' footwear—are classified in U.S. Industry 316219, Other Footwear Manufacturing.

316219 Other Footwear Manufacturing[US]

This U.S. industry comprises establishments primarily engaged in manufacturing other footwear (except rubber and plastics footwear; house slippers; men's footwear (except athletic); and women's footwear (except athletic)).

Illustrative Examples:

Athletic shoes (except rubber-soled, fabric upper) manufacturing
Ballet slippers manufacturing
Children's shoes (except plastics and rubber footwear and orthopedic extension shoes) manufacturing
Cleated athletic shoes manufacturing
Infants' shoes (except plastics and rubber footwear) manufacturing

Cross-References. Establishments primarily engaged in—

- Manufacturing rubber and plastics footwear with fabric uppers—are classified in U.S. Industry 316211, Rubber and Plastics Footwear Manufacturing;
- Manufacturing house slippers—are classified in U.S. Industry 316212, House Slipper Manufacturing;
- Manufacturing men's footwear (except athletic)—are classified in U.S. Industry 316213, Men's Footwear (except Athletic) Manufacturing;
- Manufacturing orthopedic extension footwear—are classified in Industry 339113, Surgical Appliance and Supplies Manufacturing; and
- Manufacturing women's footwear (except athletic)—are classified in U.S. Industry 316214, Women's Footwear (except Athletic) Manufacturing.

US—United States industry only. CAN—United States and Canadian industries are comparable. MEX—United States and Mexican industries are comparable. Blank—Canadian, Mexican, and United States industries are comparable.

3169 Other Leather and Allied Product Manufacturing

31699 Other Leather and Allied Product Manufacturing

This industry comprises establishments primarily engaged in manufacturing leather products (except footwear and apparel) from purchased leather or leather substitutes (e.g., fabric, plastics).

Illustrative Examples:

Billfolds, all materials, manufacturing
Boot and shoe cut stock and findings, leather, manufacturing
Dog furnishings (e.g., collars, leashes, harnesses, muzzles), manufacturing
Luggage, all materials, manufacturing
Purses, women's, all materials (except metal), manufacturing
Shoe soles, leather, manufacturing
Toilet kits and cases (except metal) manufacturing
Watchbands (except metal) manufacturing
Welders' jackets, leggings, and sleeves, leather, manufacturing

Cross-References. Establishments primarily engaged in—

- Manufacturing leather apparel—are classified in Industry 31529, Other Cut and Sew Apparel Manufacturing;
- Manufacturing leather gloves, mittens, belts, and apparel accessories—are classified in Industry 31599, Apparel Accessories and Other Apparel Manufacturing;
- Manufacturing footwear—are classified in Industry 31621, Footwear Manufacturing;
- Manufacturing nonleather soles—are classified elsewhere based on the primary input material;
- Manufacturing small articles made of metal carried on or about the person made of metal—are classified in Industry 33991, Jewelry and Silverware Manufacturing; and
- Manufacturing leather gaskets—are classified in Industry 33999, All Other Miscellaneous Manufacturing.

316991 Luggage Manufacturing[US]

This U.S. industry comprises establishments primarily engaged in manufacturing luggage of any material.

US—United States industry only. CAN—United States and Canadian industries are comparable. MEX—United States and Mexican industries are comparable. Blank—Canadian, Mexican, and United States industries are comparable.

316992 Women's Handbag and Purse Manufacturing[US]

This U.S. industry comprises establishments primarily engaged in manufacturing women's handbags and purses of any material (except precious metal).

Cross-References.

Establishments primarily engaged in manufacturing precious metal handbags and purses are classified in U.S. Industry 339911, Jewelry (except Costume) Manufacturing.

316993 Personal Leather Good (except Women's Handbag and Purse) Manufacturing[US]

This U.S. industry comprises establishments primarily engaged in manufacturing personal leather goods (i.e., small articles of any material (except metal) normally carried on or about the person or in a handbag). Examples of personal leather goods made by these establishments are billfolds, coin purses, key cases, toilet kits, and watchbands (except metal).

Cross-References. Establishments primarily engaged in—

- Manufacturing personal goods of precious metal—are classified in U.S. Industry 339911, Jewelry (except Costume) Manufacturing; and
- Manufacturing personal goods of metal (except precious)—are classified in U.S. Industry 339914, Costume Jewelry and Novelty Manufacturing.

316999 All Other Leather Good Manufacturing[US]

This U.S. industry comprises establishments primarily engaged in manufacturing leather goods (except footwear, luggage, handbags, purses, and personal leather goods).

Illustrative Examples:

Boot and shoe cut stock and findings, leather, manufacturing
Dog furnishings (e.g., collars, leashes, harnesses, muzzles) manufacturing
Leather belting for machinery (e.g., flat, solid, twisted, built-up) manufacturing
Shoe soles, leather, manufacturing
Welders' jackets, leggings, and sleeves, leather, manufacturing

Cross-References. Establishments primarily engaged in—

- Manufacturing leather gloves or mittens—are classified in U.S. Industry 315992, Glove and Mitten Manufacturing;

US—United States industry only. CAN—United States and Canadian industries are comparable. MEX—United States and Mexican industries are comparable. Blank—Canadian, Mexican, and United States industries are comparable.

- Manufacturing leather apparel belts—are classified in U.S. Industry 315999, Other Apparel Accessories and Other Apparel Manufacturing;
- Manufacturing footwear—are classified in Industry 31621, Footwear Manufacturing;
- Manufacturing luggage of any material—are classified in U.S. Industry 316991, Luggage Manufacturing;
- Manufacturing handbags and purses—are classified in U.S. Industry 316992, Women's Handbag and Purse Manufacturing;
- Manufacturing personal leather goods, such as wallets and key cases, of all materials (except metal)—are classified in U.S. Industry 316993, Personal Leather Good (except Women's Handbag and Purse) Manufacturing;
- Manufacturing nonleather soles—are classified elsewhere based on the primary input material;
- Manufacturing leather apparel—are classified in U.S. Industry 315292, Fur and Leather Apparel Manufacturing; and
- Manufacturing leather gaskets—are classified in U.S. Industry 339991, Gasket, Packing, and Sealing Device Manufacturing.

321 Wood Product Manufacturing

Industries in the Wood Product Manufacturing subsector manufacture wood products, such as lumber, plywood, veneers, wood containers, wood flooring, wood trusses, manufactured homes (i.e., mobile home), and prefabricated wood buildings. The production processes of the Wood Product Manufacturing subsector include sawing, planing, shaping, laminating, and assembling of wood products starting from logs that are cut into bolts, or lumber that then may be further cut, or shaped by lathes or other shaping tools. The lumber or other transformed wood shapes may also be subsequently planed or smoothed, and assembled into finished products, such as wood containers. The Wood Product Manufacturing subsector includes establishments that make wood products from logs and bolts that are sawed and shaped, and establishments that purchase sawed lumber and make wood products. With the exception of sawmills and wood preservation establishments, the establishments are grouped into industries mainly based on the specific products manufactured.

3211 Sawmills and Wood Preservation

This industry group comprises establishments whose primary production process begins with logs or bolts that are transformed into boards, dimension lumber, beams, timbers, poles, ties, shingles, shakes, siding, and wood chips. Establishments

US—United States industry only. CAN—United States and Canadian industries are comparable. MEX—United States and Mexican industries are comparable. Blank—Canadian, Mexican, and United States industries are comparable.

that cut and treat round wood and/or treat wood products made in other establishments to prevent rotting by impregnation with creosote or other chemical compounds are also included in this industry group.

32111 Sawmills and Wood Preservation

This industry comprises establishments primarily engaged in one or more of the following: (1) sawing dimension lumber, boards, beams, timber, poles, ties, shingles, shakes, siding, and wood chips from logs or bolts; (2) sawing round wood poles, pilings, and posts and treating them with preservatives; and (3) treating wood sawed, planed, or shaped in other establishments with creosote or other preservatives to prevent decay and to protect against fire and insects. Sawmills may plane the rough lumber that they make with a planing machine to achieve smoothness and uniformity of size.

Cross-References. Establishments primarily engaged in—

- Operating portable chipper mills in the field—are classified in Industry 11331, Logging;
- Manufacturing wood products (except round wood poles, pilings, and posts) and treating them with preservatives—are classified elsewhere in Subsector 321, Wood Product Manufacturing, based on the related production process;
- Manufacturing veneer from logs and bolts or manufacturing engineered lumber and structural members other than solid wood—are classified in Industry 32121, Veneer, Plywood, and Engineered Wood Product Manufacturing; and
- Planing purchased lumber or manufacturing cut stock or dimension stock (i.e., shapes) from logs or bolts—are classified in Industry 32191, Millwork.

321113 Sawmills[US]

This U.S. industry comprises establishments primarily engaged in sawing dimension lumber, boards, beams, timbers, poles, ties, shingles, shakes, siding, and wood chips from logs or bolts. Sawmills may plane the rough lumber that they make with a planing machine to achieve smoothness and uniformity of size.

Cross-References. Establishments primarily engaged in—

- Planing purchased lumber or manufacturing cut stock or dimension stock (i.e., shapes) from logs or bolts—are classified in Industry 32191, Millwork;
- Manufacturing veneer from logs or bolts—are classified in Industry 32121, Veneer, Plywood, and Engineered Wood Product Manufacturing; and

---

US—United States industry only. CAN—United States and Canadian industries are comparable. MEX—United States and Mexican industries are comparable. Blank—Canadian, Mexican, and United States industries are comparable.

- Operating portable chipper mills in the field—are classified in Industry 113310, Logging.

321114 Wood Preservation[CAN]

This U.S. industry comprises establishments primarily engaged in (1) treating wood sawed, planed, or shaped in other establishments with creosote or other preservatives, such as chromated copper arsenate, to prevent decay and to protect against fire and insects and/or (2) sawing round wood poles, pilings, and posts and treating them with preservatives.

Cross-References.

Establishments primarily engaged in manufacturing wood products (except round wood poles, pilings, and posts) and treating them with preservatives are classified elsewhere in Subsector 321, Wood Product Manufacturing, based on the related production process.

3212 Veneer, Plywood, and Engineered Wood Product Manufacturing

32121 Veneer, Plywood, and Engineered Wood Product Manufacturing

This industry comprises establishments primarily engaged in one or more of the following: (1) manufacturing veneer and/or plywood; (2) manufacturing engineered wood members; and (3) manufacturing reconstituted wood products. This industry includes manufacturing plywood from veneer made in the same establishment or from veneer made in other establishments, and manufacturing plywood faced with nonwood materials, such as plastics or metal.

Illustrative Examples:

Fabricated structural wood members manufacturing
Laminated structural wood members manufacturing
Medium density fiberboard (MDF) manufacturing
Oriented strandboard (OSB) manufacturing
Particleboard manufacturing
Plywood manufacturing
Reconstituted wood sheets and boards manufacturing
Roof trusses, wood, manufacturing
Veneer mills
Waferboard manufacturing

Cross-References. Establishments primarily engaged in—

- Manufacturing veneer and further processing that veneer into wood containers or wood container parts in the same establishment—are classified in Industry 32192, Wood Container and Pallet Manufacturing;

US—United States industry only. CAN—United States and Canadian industries are comparable. MEX—United States and Mexican industries are comparable. Blank—Canadian, Mexican, and United States industries are comparable.

- Manufacturing prefabricated wood buildings or wood sections, and panels for buildings—are classified in Industry 32199, All Other Wood Product Manufacturing; and
- Manufacturing solid wood structural members, such as dimension lumber and timber from logs or bolts in sawmills—are classified in Industry 32111, Sawmills and Wood Preservation.

321211 Hardwood Veneer and Plywood Manufacturing[CAN]

This U.S. industry comprises establishments primarily engaged in manufacturing hardwood veneer and/or hardwood plywood.

Cross-References. Establishments primarily engaged in—

- Manufacturing veneer and further processing that veneer into wood containers or wood container parts—are classified in Industry 321920, Wood Container and Pallet Manufacturing;
- Manufacturing softwood veneer and softwood plywood—are classified in U.S. Industry 321212, Softwood Veneer and Plywood Manufacturing; and
- Manufacturing reconstituted wood sheets and boards—are classified in U.S. Industry 321219, Reconstituted Wood Product Manufacturing.

321212 Softwood Veneer and Plywood Manufacturing[CAN]

This U.S. industry comprises establishments primarily engaged in manufacturing softwood veneer and/or softwood plywood.

Cross-References. Establishments primarily engaged in—

- Manufacturing veneer and further processing that veneer into wood containers or wood container parts—are classified in Industry 321920, Wood Container and Pallet Manufacturing;
- Manufacturing hardwood veneer and hardwood plywood—are classified in U.S. Industry 321211, Hardwood Veneer and Plywood Manufacturing; and
- Manufacturing reconstituted wood sheets and boards—are classified in U.S. Industry 321219, Reconstituted Wood Product Manufacturing.

321213 Engineered Wood Member (except Truss) Manufacturing[US]

This U.S. industry comprises establishments primarily engaged in manufacturing fabricated or laminated wood arches and/or other fabricated or laminated wood structural members.

US—United States industry only. CAN—United States and Canadian industries are comparable. MEX—United States and Mexican industries are comparable. Blank—Canadian, Mexican, and United States industries are comparable.

Illustrative Examples:

Finger joint lumber manufacturing
I-joists, wood, fabricating
Laminated veneer lumber (LVL) manufacturing
Parallel strand lumber manufacturing
Timbers, structural, glue laminated or pre-engineered wood, manufacturing

Cross-References. Establishments primarily engaged in—

- Manufacturing prefabricated wood buildings, or wood sections, and panels for buildings—are classified in U.S. Industry 321992, Prefabricated Wood Building Manufacturing;
- Manufacturing wood trusses—are classified in U.S. Industry 321214, Truss Manufacturing; and
- Manufacturing solid wood structural members, such as dimension lumber and timber from logs or bolts,—are classified in U.S. Industry 321113, Sawmills.

321214 Truss Manufacturing[US]

This U.S. industry comprises establishments primarily engaged in manufacturing laminated or fabricated wood roof and floor trusses.

Cross-References.

Establishments primarily engaged in manufacturing wood I-joists are classified in U.S. Industry 321213, Engineered Wood Member (except Truss) Manufacturing.

321219 Reconstituted Wood Product Manufacturing[US]

This U.S. industry comprises establishments primarily engaged in manufacturing reconstituted wood sheets and boards.

Illustrative Examples:

Medium density fiberboard (MDF) manufacturing
Oriented strandboard (OSB) manufacturing
Particleboard manufacturing
Reconstituted wood sheets and boards manufacturing
Waferboard manufacturing

Cross-References. Establishments primarily engaged in—

- Manufacturing softwood plywood—are classified in U.S. Industry 321212, Softwood Veneer and Plywood Manufacturing; and

US—United States industry only. CAN—United States and Canadian industries are comparable. MEX—United States and Mexican industries are comparable. Blank—Canadian, Mexican, and United States industries are comparable.

- Manufacturing hardwood plywood—are classified in U.S. Industry 321211, Hardwood Veneer and Plywood Manufacturing.

3219 Other Wood Product Manufacturing

This industry group comprises establishments primarily engaged in manufacturing wood products (except establishments operating sawmills and wood preservation facilities; and establishments manufacturing veneer, plywood, or engineered wood products).

32191 Millwork

This industry comprises establishments primarily engaged in manufacturing hardwood and softwood cut stock and dimension stock (i.e., shapes); wood windows and wood doors; and other millwork including wood flooring. Dimension stock or cut stock is defined as lumber and worked wood products cut or shaped to specialized sizes. These establishments generally use woodworking machinery, such as jointers, planers, lathes, and routers to shape wood.

Cross-References. Establishments primarily engaged in—

- Manufacturing dimension lumber, boards, beams, timbers, poles, ties, shingles, shakes, siding, and wood chips from logs and bolts—are classified in Industry 32111, Sawmills and Wood Preservation;
- Fabricating millwork at the construction site—are classified in Industry 23835, Finish Carpentry Contractors; and
- Manufacturing wood furniture frames and finished wood furniture parts—are classified in Industry 33721, Office Furniture (including Fixtures) Manufacturing.

321911 Wood Window and Door Manufacturing[CAN]

This U.S. industry comprises establishments primarily engaged in manufacturing window and door units, sash, window and door frames, and doors from wood or wood clad with metal or plastics.

Cross-References.

Establishments primarily engaged in fabricating wood windows or wood doors at the construction site are classified in Industry 238350, Finish Carpentry Contractors.

US—United States industry only. CAN—United States and Canadian industries are comparable. MEX—United States and Mexican industries are comparable. Blank—Canadian, Mexican, and United States industries are comparable.

321912 Cut Stock, Resawing Lumber, and Planing[US]

This U.S. industry comprises establishments primarily engaged in one or more of the following: (1) manufacturing dimension lumber from purchased lumber; (2) manufacturing dimension stock (i.e., shapes) or cut stock; (3) resawing the output of sawmills; and (4) planing purchased lumber. These establishments generally use woodworking machinery, such as jointers, planers, lathes, and routers to shape wood.

Cross-References. Establishments primarily engaged in—

- Manufacturing dimension lumber, boards, beams, timbers, poles, ties, shingles, shakes, siding, and wood chips from logs or bolts—are classified in U.S. Industry 321113, Sawmills;
- Manufacturing wood stairwork, wood molding, wood trim, and other millwork—are classified in U.S. Industry 321918, Other Millwork (including Flooring); and
- Manufacturing wood furniture frames and finished wood furniture parts—are classified in U.S. Industry 337215, Showcase, Partition, Shelving, and Locker Manufacturing.

321918 Other Millwork (including Flooring)[US]

This U.S. industry comprises establishments primarily engaged in manufacturing millwork (except wood windows, wood doors, and cut stock).

Illustrative Examples:

Clear and finger joint wood moldings manufacturing
Decorative wood moldings (e.g., base, chair rail, crown, shoe) manufacturing
Ornamental woodwork (e.g., cornices, mantel) manufacturing
Planing mills, millwork
Stairwork (e.g., newel posts, railings, stairs, staircases), wood, manufacturing
Wood flooring manufacturing
Wood shutters manufacturing

Cross-References. Establishments primarily engaged in—

- Manufacturing wood windows and doors—are classified in U.S. Industry 321911, Wood Window and Door Manufacturing; and
- Manufacturing cut stock, resawing lumber, and/or planing purchased lumber—are classified in U.S. Industry 321912, Cut Stock, Resawing Lumber, and Planing.

US—United States industry only. CAN—United States and Canadian industries are comparable. MEX—United States and Mexican industries are comparable. Blank—Canadian, Mexican, and United States industries are comparable.

32192 Wood Container and Pallet Manufacturing

See industry description for 321920 below.

321920 Wood Container and Pallet Manufacturing

This industry comprises establishments primarily engaged in manufacturing wood pallets, wood box shook, wood boxes, other wood containers, and wood parts for pallets and containers.

Cross-References.

Establishments primarily engaged in manufacturing wood burial caskets are classified in U.S. Industry 339995, Burial Casket Manufacturing.

32199 All Other Wood Product Manufacturing

This industry comprises establishments primarily engaged in manufacturing wood products (except establishments operating sawmills and wood preservation facilities; and establishments manufacturing veneer, plywood, engineered wood products, millwork, wood containers, or pallets).

Illustrative Examples:

Mobile home manufacturing
Panels, prefabricated wood building, manufacturing
Prefabricated wood buildings
Sections, prefabricated wood building, manufacturing
Wood dowels manufacturing
Wood handles (e.g., broom, handtool, mop), manufacturing

Cross-References. Establishments primarily engaged in—

- Operating sawmills or preserving wood—are classified in Industry 32111, Sawmills and Wood Preservation;
- Manufacturing veneer, plywood, and engineered wood products—are classified in Industry 32121, Veneer, Plywood, and Engineered Wood Product Manufacturing;
- Manufacturing millwork—are classified in Industry 32191, Millwork;
- Manufacturing wood containers, pallets, and wood container parts—are classified in Industry 32192, Wood Container and Pallet Manufacturing;
- Manufacturing travel trailers with self-contained facilities for storage of water and waste—are classified in Industry 33621, Motor Vehicle Body and Trailer Manufacturing; and

---

US—United States industry only. CAN—United States and Canadian industries are comparable. MEX—United States and Mexican industries are comparable. Blank—Canadian, Mexican, and United States industries are comparable.

- Fabricating of wood buildings or wood sections and panels for buildings at the construction site—are classified in Sector 23, Construction.

321991 Manufactured Home (Mobile Home) Manufacturing[CAN]

This U.S. industry comprises establishments primarily engaged in making manufactured homes (i.e., mobile homes) and nonresidential mobile buildings. Manufactured homes are designed to accept permanent water, sewer, and utility connections and although equipped with wheels, they are not intended for regular highway movement.

Cross-References. Establishments primarily engaged in—

- Manufacturing prefabricated wood buildings not equipped with wheels—are classified in U.S. Industry 321992, Prefabricated Wood Building Manufacturing; and
- Manufacturing travel trailers with self-contained facilities for storage of water and waste—are classified in U.S. Industry 336214, Travel Trailer and Camper Manufacturing.

321992 Prefabricated Wood Building Manufacturing[CAN]

This U.S. industry comprises establishments primarily engaged in manufacturing prefabricated wood buildings and wood sections and panels for prefabricated wood buildings.

Cross-References. Establishments primarily engaged in—

- Fabricating wood buildings or wood sections and panels for buildings at the construction site—are classified in Sector 23, Construction; and
- Making manufactured homes (i.e., mobile homes)—are classified in U.S. Industry 321991, Manufactured Home (Mobile Home) Manufacturing.

321999 All Other Miscellaneous Wood Product Manufacturing[CAN]

This U.S. industry comprises establishments primarily engaged in manufacturing wood products (except establishments operating sawmills and preservation facilities; establishments manufacturing veneer, engineered wood products, millwork, wood containers, pallets, and wood container parts; and establishments making manufactured homes (i.e., mobile homes) and prefabricated buildings and components).

US—United States industry only. CAN—United States and Canadian industries are comparable. MEX—United States and Mexican industries are comparable. Blank—Canadian, Mexican, and United States industries are comparable.

Illustrative Examples:

Cork products (except gaskets) manufacturing
Kiln drying lumber
Shoe trees manufacturing
Wood dowels manufacturing
Wood extension ladders manufacturing
Wood handles (e.g., broom, handtool, mop), manufacturing
Wood kitchenware manufacturing
Wood stepladders manufacturing
Wood toilet seats manufacturing
Wood toothpicks manufacturing

Cross-References. Establishments primarily engaged in—

- Operating sawmills and preserving wood—are classified in Industry 32111, Sawmills and Wood Preservation;
- Manufacturing veneer and engineered wood products—are classified in Industry 32121, Veneer, Plywood, and Engineered Wood Product Manufacturing;
- Manufacturing millwork—are classified in Industry 32191, Millwork;
- Manufacturing boxes, box shook, wood containers, pallets, and wood parts for containers—are classified in Industry 321920, Wood Container and Pallet Manufacturing;
- Making manufactured homes (i.e., mobile homes)—are classified in U.S. Industry 321991, Manufactured Home (Mobile Home) Manufacturing; and
- Manufacturing prefabricated wood buildings or wood sections and panels for buildings—are classified in U.S. Industry 321992, Prefabricated Wood Building Manufacturing.

322 Paper Manufacturing

Industries in the Paper Manufacturing subsector make pulp, paper, or converted paper products. The manufacturing of these products is grouped together because they constitute a series of vertically connected processes. More than one is often carried out in a single establishment. There are essentially three activities. The manufacturing of pulp involves separating the cellulose fibers from other impurities in wood or used paper. The manufacturing of paper involves matting these fibers into a sheet. Converted paper products are made from paper and other materials by various cutting and shaping techniques and includes coating and laminating activities.

The Paper Manufacturing subsector is subdivided into two industry groups, the first for the manufacturing of pulp and paper and the second for the manufacturing of converted paper products. Paper making is treated as the core activity of the subsector. Therefore, any establishment that makes paper (including paperboard), either alone or in combination with pulp manufacturing or paper converting, is classified as a paper or paperboard mill. Establishments that make pulp without

---

US—United States industry only. CAN—United States and Canadian industries are comparable. MEX—United States and Mexican industries are comparable. Blank—Canadian, Mexican, and United States industries are comparable.

making paper are classified as pulp mills. Pulp mills, paper mills and paperboard mills comprise the first industry group.

Establishments that make products from purchased paper and other materials make up the second industry group, Converted Paper Product Manufacturing. This general activity is then subdivided based, for the most part, on process distinctions. Paperboard container manufacturing uses corrugating, cutting, and shaping machinery to form paperboard into containers. Paper bag and coated and treated paper manufacturing establishments cut and coat paper and foil. Stationery product manufacturing establishments make a variety of paper products used for writing, filing, and similar applications. Other converted paper product manufacturing includes, in particular, the conversion of sanitary paper stock into such things as tissue paper and disposable diapers.

An important process used in the Paper Bag and Coated and Treated Paper Manufacturing industry is lamination, often combined with coating. Lamination and coating makes a composite material with improved properties of strength, impermeability, and so on. The laminated materials may be paper, metal foil, or plastics film. While paper is often one of the components, it is not always. Lamination of plastics film to plastics film is classified in the NAICS Subsector 326, Plastics and Rubber Products Manufacturing, because establishments that do this often first make the film. The same situation holds with respect to bags. The manufacturing of bags from plastics only, whether or not laminated, is classified in Subsector 326, Plastics and Rubber Products Manufacturing, but all other bag manufacturing is classified in this subsector.

Excluded from this subsector are photosensitive papers. These papers are chemically treated and are classified in Industry 32599, All Other Chemical Product and Preparation Manufacturing.

3221 Pulp, Paper, and Paperboard Mills

This industry group comprises establishments primarily engaged in manufacturing pulp, paper, or paperboard.

32211 Pulp Mills

See industry description for 322110 below.

322110 Pulp Mills[MEX]

This industry comprises establishments primarily engaged in manufacturing pulp without manufacturing paper or paperboard. The pulp is made by separating the cellulose fibers from the other impurities in wood or other materials, such as used or recycled rags, linters, scrap paper, and straw.

US—United States industry only. CAN—United States and Canadian industries are comparable. MEX—United States and Mexican industries are comparable. Blank—Canadian, Mexican, and United States industries are comparable.

Cross-References. Establishments primarily engaged in—

- Manufacturing both pulp and paper—are classified in Industry 32212, Paper Mills; and
- Manufacturing both pulp and paperboard—are classified in Industry 322130, Paperboard Mills.

32212 Paper Mills

This industry comprises establishments primarily engaged in manufacturing paper from pulp. These establishments may manufacture or purchase pulp. In addition, the establishments may convert the paper they make. The activity of making paper classifies an establishment into this industry regardless of the output.

Cross-References. Establishments primarily engaged in—

- Manufacturing pulp without manufacturing paper—are classified in Industry 32211, Pulp Mills;
- Manufacturing paperboard—are classified in Industry 32213, Paperboard Mills;
- Converting paper without manufacturing paper—are classified in Industry Group 3222, Converted Paper Product Manufacturing; and
- Manufacturing photographic sensitized paper—are classified in Industry 32599, All Other Chemical Product and Preparation Manufacturing.

322121 Paper (except Newsprint) Mills[CAN]

This U.S. industry comprises establishments primarily engaged in manufacturing paper (except newsprint and uncoated groundwood paper) from pulp. These establishments may manufacture or purchase pulp. In addition, the establishments may also convert the paper they make.

Cross-References. Establishments primarily engaged in—

- Manufacturing newsprint and uncoated groundwood paper—are classified in U.S. Industry 322122, Newsprint Mills;
- Converting paper without manufacturing paper—are classified in Industry Group 3222, Converted Paper Product Manufacturing;
- Manufacturing paperboard—are classified in Industry 322130, Paperboard Mills;
- Manufacturing pulp without manufacturing paper—are classified in Industry 322110, Pulp Mills; and

---

US—United States industry only. CAN—United States and Canadian industries are comparable. MEX—United States and Mexican industries are comparable. Blank—Canadian, Mexican, and United States industries are comparable.

- Manufacturing photographic sensitized paper from purchased paper—are classified in U.S. Industry 325992, Photographic Film, Paper, Plate, and Chemical Manufacturing.

322122 Newsprint Mills[CAN]

This U.S. industry comprises establishments primarily engaged in manufacturing newsprint and uncoated groundwood paper from pulp. These establishments may manufacture or purchase pulp. In addition, the establishments may also convert the paper they make.

Cross-References. Establishments primarily engaged in—

- Manufacturing paper (except newsprint and uncoated groundwood)—are classified in U.S. Industry 322121, Paper (except Newsprint) Mills;
- Converting paper without manufacturing paper—are classified in Industry Group 3222, Converted Paper Product Manufacturing;
- Manufacturing paperboard—are classified in Industry 322130, Paperboard Mills; and
- Manufacturing pulp without manufacturing paper—are classified in Industry 322110, Pulp Mills.

32213 Paperboard Mills

See industry description for 322130 below.

322130 Paperboard Mills[CAN]

This industry comprises establishments primarily engaged in manufacturing paperboard from pulp. These establishments may manufacture or purchase pulp. In addition, the establishments may also convert the paperboard they make.

Cross-References. Establishments primarily engaged in—

- Manufacturing pulp without manufacturing paperboard—are classified in Industry 322110, Pulp Mills;
- Converting paperboard without manufacturing paperboard—are classified in Industry Group 3222, Converted Paper Product Manufacturing; and
- Manufacturing insulation board and other reconstituted wood fiberboard—are classified in U.S. Industry 321219, Reconstituted Wood Product Manufacturing.

US—United States industry only. CAN—United States and Canadian industries are comparable. MEX—United States and Mexican industries are comparable. Blank—Canadian, Mexican, and United States industries are comparable.

3222 Converted Paper Product Manufacturing

This industry group comprises establishments primarily engaged in converting paper or paperboard without manufacturing paper or paperboard.

32221 Paperboard Container Manufacturing

This industry comprises establishments primarily engaged in converting paperboard into containers without manufacturing paperboard. These establishments use corrugating, cutting, and shaping machinery to form paperboard into containers. Products made by these establishments include boxes; corrugated sheets, pads, and pallets; paper dishes; and fiber drums and reels.

Cross-References. Establishments primarily engaged in—

- Manufacturing similar items of plastics materials—are classified in Industry Group 3261, Plastics Product Manufacturing;
- Manufacturing paperboard and converting paperboard into containers—are classified in Industry 32213, Paperboard Mills;
- Manufacturing egg cartons, food trays, and other food containers from molded pulp—are classified in Industry 32229, Other Converted Paper Product Manufacturing;
- Manufacturing paper and converting paper into containers—are classified in Industry 32212, Paper Mills; and
- Manufacturing paper bags without manufacturing paper—are classified in Industry 32222, Paper Bag and Coated and Treated Paper Manufacturing.

322211 Corrugated and Solid Fiber Box Manufacturing[CAN]

This U.S. industry comprises establishments primarily engaged in laminating purchased paper or paperboard into corrugated or solid fiber boxes and related products, such as pads, partitions, pallets, and corrugated paper without manufacturing paperboard. These boxes are generally used for shipping.

Cross-References. Establishments primarily engaged in—

- Manufacturing setup paperboard boxes (except corrugated or laminated solid fiber boxes)—are classified in U.S. Industry 322213, Setup Paperboard Box Manufacturing;
- Manufacturing folding paperboard boxes (except corrugated or laminated solid fiber boxes)—are classified in U.S. Industry 322212, Folding Paperboard Box Manufacturing; and

US—United States industry only. CAN—United States and Canadian industries are comparable. MEX—United States and Mexican industries are comparable. Blank—Canadian, Mexican, and United States industries are comparable.

- Manufacturing paperboard and converting paperboard into boxes—are classified in Industry 322130, Paperboard Mills.

322212 Folding Paperboard Box Manufacturing[CAN]

This U.S. industry comprises establishments primarily engaged in converting paperboard (except corrugated) into folding paperboard boxes without manufacturing paper and paperboard.

Cross-References. Establishments primarily engaged in—

- Manufacturing setup paperboard boxes (except corrugated)—are classified in U.S. Industry 322213, Setup Paperboard Box Manufacturing;
- Manufacturing corrugated and solid fiber boxes—are classified in U.S. Industry 322211, Corrugated and Solid Fiber Box Manufacturing;
- Manufacturing paperboard and converting paperboard into containers—are classified in Industry 322130, Paperboard Mills;
- Manufacturing paper and converting paper into containers—are classified in Industry 32212, Paper Mills;
- Manufacturing milk cartons—are classified in U.S. Industry 322215, Nonfolding Sanitary Food Container Manufacturing; and
- Manufacturing paper bags—are classified in Industry 32222, Paper Bag and Coated and Treated Paper Manufacturing.

322213 Setup Paperboard Box Manufacturing[US]

This U.S. industry comprises establishments primarily engaged in converting paperboard into setup paperboard boxes (i.e., rigid-sided boxes not shipped flat) without manufacturing paperboard.

Cross-References. Establishments primarily engaged in—

- Manufacturing folding paperboard boxes (except corrugated)—are classified in U.S. Industry 322212, Folding Paperboard Box Manufacturing;
- Manufacturing corrugated and solid fiber boxes—are classified in U.S. Industry 322211, Corrugated and Solid Fiber Box Manufacturing; and
- Manufacturing paperboard and converting paperboard into containers—are classified in Industry 322130, Paperboard Mills.

US—United States industry only. CAN—United States and Canadian industries are comparable. MEX—United States and Mexican industries are comparable. Blank—Canadian, Mexican, and United States industries are comparable.

322214 Fiber Can, Tube, Drum, and Similar Products Manufacturing[US]

This U.S. industry comprises establishments primarily engaged in converting paperboard into fiber cans, tubes, drums, and similar products without manufacturing paperboard.

Cross-References.

Establishments engaged in manufacturing paperboard and converting paperboard into containers are classified in Industry 322130, Paperboard Mills.

322215 Nonfolding Sanitary Food Container Manufacturing[US]

This U.S. industry comprises establishments primarily engaged in converting sanitary foodboard into food containers (except folding).

Cross-References. Establishments primarily engaged in—

- Manufacturing sanitary food containers of solely plastics materials—are classified in Industry Group 3261, Plastics Product Manufacturing;
- Manufacturing egg cartons, food trays, and other food containers from molded pulp—are classified in U.S. Industry 322299, All Other Converted Paper Product Manufacturing; and
- Manufacturing folding sanitary cartons—are classified in U.S. Industry 322212, Folding Paperboard Box Manufacturing.

32222 Paper Bag and Coated and Treated Paper Manufacturing

This industry comprises establishments primarily engaged in one or more of the following: (1) cutting and coating paper and paperboard; (2) cutting and laminating paper and paperboard and other flexible materials (except plastics film to plastics film); (3) manufacturing bags or multiwall bags or sacks of paper, metal foil, coated paper, or laminates or coated combinations of paper and foil with plastics film; (4) manufacturing laminated aluminum and other converted metal foils from purchased foils; and (5) surface coating paper or paperboard.

Cross-References. Establishments primarily engaged in—

- Manufacturing paper from pulp—are classified in Industry 32212, Paper Mills;
- Manufacturing photographic sensitized paper—are classified in Industry 32599, All Other Chemical Product and Preparation Manufacturing;

US—United States industry only. CAN—United States and Canadian industries are comparable. MEX—United States and Mexican industries are comparable. Blank—Canadian, Mexican, and United States industries are comparable.

- Manufacturing textile bags—are classified in Industry 31491, Textile Bag and Canvas Mills;
- Manufacturing single and multiwall plastics bags or plastics laminated bags—are classified in Industry 32611, Plastics Packaging Materials and Unlaminated Film and Sheet Manufacturing;
- Making aluminum and aluminum foil—are classified in Industry 33131, Alumina and Aluminum Production and Processing; and
- Cutting purchased aluminum foil into smaller lengths and widths—are classified in Industry 33299, All Other Fabricated Metal Product Manufacturing.

322221 Coated and Laminated Packaging Paper and Plastics Film Manufacturing[US]

This U.S. industry comprises establishments primarily engaged in performing one or more of the following activities associated with the manufacturing of packaging materials: (1) cutting and coating paper; and (2) cutting and laminating paper with other flexible materials (except plastics to plastics or foil to paper laminates). The products made in this industry are made from purchased sheet materials and may be printed in the same establishment.

Cross-References. Establishments primarily engaged in—

- Manufacturing coated or laminated paper for nonpackaging purposes—are classified in U.S. Industry 322222, Coated and Laminated Paper Manufacturing;
- Manufacturing unsupported plastics film—are classified in U.S. Industry 326113, Unlaminated Plastics Film and Sheet (except Packaging) Manufacturing;
- Manufacturing laminated aluminum foil for flexible packaging uses—are classified in U.S. Industry 322225, Laminated Aluminum Foil Manufacturing for Flexible Packaging Uses;
- Making aluminum and aluminum foil—are classified in Industry 33131, Alumina and Aluminum Production and Processing;
- Cutting purchased aluminum foil into smaller lengths and widths—are classified in U.S. Industry 332999, All Other Miscellaneous Fabricated Metal Product Manufacturing; and
- Manufacturing paper from pulp—are classified in Industry 32212, Paper Mills.

US—United States industry only. CAN—United States and Canadian industries are comparable. MEX—United States and Mexican industries are comparable. Blank—Canadian, Mexican, and United States industries are comparable.

322222 Coated and Laminated Paper Manufacturing[US]

This U.S. industry comprises establishments primarily engaged in performing one or more of the following activities associated with making products designed for purposes other than packaging: (1) cutting and coating paper; (2) cutting and laminating paper and other flexible materials (except plastics film to plastics film); and (3) laminating aluminum and other metal foils for nonpackaging uses from purchased foils. The products made in this industry are made from purchased sheet materials and may be printed in the same establishment.

Illustrative Examples:

Book paper made by coating purchased paper
Gift wrap, laminated, made from purchased paper
Gummed paper products (e.g., labels sheets, tapes) made from purchased paper
Tapes, gummed (e.g., cellophane, masking, pressure sensitive) made from purchased paper or other structures
Wallpaper made from purchased papers or other materials

Cross-References. Establishments primarily engaged in—

- Manufacturing coated and laminated paper for packaging uses—are classified in U.S. Industry 322221, Coated and Laminated Packaging Paper and Plastics Film Manufacturing;
- Manufacturing photographic sensitized paper—are classified in U.S. Industry 325992, Photographic Film, Paper, Plate, and Chemical Manufacturing;
- Making aluminum and aluminum foil—are classified in Industry 33131, Alumina and Aluminum Production and Processing;
- Cutting purchased aluminum foil into smaller lengths and widths—are classified in U.S. Industry 332999, All Other Miscellaneous Fabricated Metal Product Manufacturing; and
- Manufacturing laminated aluminum foil for flexible packaging uses—are classified in U.S. Industry 322225, Laminated Aluminum Foil Manufacturing for Flexible Packaging Uses.

322223 Plastics, Foil, and Coated Paper Bag Manufacturing[US]

This U.S. industry comprises establishments primarily engaged in manufacturing bags of coated paper, of metal foil, or of laminated or coated combinations of plastics, foil, and paper, whether or not printed.

US—United States industry only. CAN—United States and Canadian industries are comparable. MEX—United States and Mexican industries are comparable. Blank—Canadian, Mexican, and United States industries are comparable.

Cross-References. Establishments primarily engaged in—

- Manufacturing uncoated paper bags and multiwall bags and sacks—are classified in U.S. Industry 322224, Uncoated Paper and Multiwall Bag Manufacturing;
- Manufacturing textile bags—are classified in U.S. Industry 314911, Textile Bag Mills; and
- Manufacturing single and multiwall plastics bags—are classified in U.S. Industry 326111, Plastics Bag Manufacturing.

322224 Uncoated Paper and Multiwall Bag Manufacturing[US]

This U.S. industry comprises establishments primarily engaged in manufacturing uncoated paper bags or multiwall bags and sacks.

Cross-References. Establishments primarily engaged in—

- Manufacturing single wall and multiwall bags from plastics unsupported film—are classified in U.S. Industry 326111, Plastics Bag Manufacturing;
- Manufacturing bags of coated paper, of metal foil, or of laminated or coated combinations of plastics, foil, and paper bags—are classified in U.S. Industry 322223, Plastics, Foil, and Coated Paper Bag Manufacturing; and
- Manufacturing textile bags—are classified in U.S. Industry 314911, Textile Bag Mills.

322225 Laminated Aluminum Foil Manufacturing for Flexible Packaging Uses[US]

This U.S. industry comprises establishments primarily engaged in laminating aluminum and other metal foil into products with flexible packaging uses or gift wrap and other packaging wrap applications.

Cross-References. Establishments primarily engaged in—

- Manufacturing plain aluminum foil—are classified in U.S. Industry 331315, Aluminum Sheet, Plate, and Foil Manufacturing;
- Manufacturing laminated aluminum bags and liners—are classified in U.S. Industry 322223, Plastics, Foil, and Coated Paper Bag Manufacturing;
- Manufacturing converted aluminum and other metal foils for nonpackaging uses from purchased foils—are classified in U.S. Industry 322222, Coated and Laminated Paper Manufacturing; and

---

US—United States industry only. CAN—United States and Canadian industries are comparable. MEX—United States and Mexican industries are comparable. Blank—Canadian, Mexican, and United States industries are comparable.

- Manufacturing cookware, dinnerware, and other semirigid metal containers—are classified in U.S. Industry 332999, All Other Miscellaneous Fabricated Metal Product Manufacturing.

322226 Surface-Coated Paperboard Manufacturing[US]

This U.S. industry comprises establishments primarily engaged in laminating, lining, or surface coating purchased paperboard to make other paperboard products.

32223 Stationery Product Manufacturing

This industry comprises establishments primarily engaged in converting paper or paperboard into products used for writing, filing, art work, and similar applications.

Illustrative Examples:

Die-cut paper products for office use made from purchased paper or paperboard
Envelopes (i.e., mailing, stationery) made from any material
Tapes (e.g., adding machines, calculator, cash register) made from purchased paper
Stationery made from purchased paper
Tablets (e.g., memo, note, writing) made from purchased paper

Cross-References.

Establishments primarily engaged in manufacturing die-cut paper and paperboard products other than office supplies are classified in U.S. Industry 322299, All Other Converted Paper Product Manufacturing.

322231 Die-Cut Paper and Paperboard Office Supplies Manufacturing[US]

This U.S. industry comprises establishments primarily engaged in converting paper rollstock or paperboard into die-cut paper or paperboard office supplies. For the purpose of this industry, office supplies are defined as office products, such as filing folders, index cards, rolls for adding machines, file separators and dividers, tabulating cards, and other paper and paperboard office supplies.

Cross-References. Establishments primarily engaged in—

- Manufacturing die-cut paper and paperboard products (except office supplies)—are classified in U.S. Industry 322299, All Other Converted Paper Product Manufacturing; and

US—United States industry only. CAN—United States and Canadian industries are comparable. MEX—United States and Mexican industries are comparable. Blank—Canadian, Mexican, and United States industries are comparable.

- Manufacturing paper and paperboard products used for writing and similar applications (e.g., looseleaf fillers, notebooks, pads, stationery, tablets)—are classified in U.S. Industry 322233, Stationery, Tablet, and Related Product Manufacturing.

322232 Envelope Manufacturing[US]

This U.S. industry comprises establishments primarily engaged in manufacturing envelopes for mailing or stationery of any material including combinations.

Cross-References.

Establishments primarily engaged in manufacturing stationery are classified in U.S. Industry 322233, Stationery, Tablet, and Related Product Manufacturing.

322233 Stationery, Tablet, and Related Product Manufacturing[US]

This U.S. industry comprises establishments primarily engaged in converting paper and paperboard into products used for writing and similar applications (e.g., looseleaf fillers, notebooks, pads, stationery, tablets).

Cross-References. Establishments primarily engaged in—

- Manufacturing envelopes—are classified in U.S. Industry 322232, Envelope Manufacturing; and
- Manufacturing die-cut paper and paperboard office supplies—are classified in U.S. Industry 322231, Die-Cut Paper and Paperboard Office Supplies Manufacturing.

32229 Other Converted Paper Product Manufacturing

This industry comprises establishments primarily engaged in (1) converting paper and paperboard into products (except containers, bags, coated and treated paper and paperboard, and stationery products), or (2) converting pulp into pulp products, such as disposable diapers, or molded pulp egg cartons, food trays, and dishes. Processes used include laminating or lining purchased paper or paperboard.

Illustrative Examples:

Crepe paper made from purchased paper
Die-cut paper products (except for office use) made from purchased paper or paperboard
Paper novelties made from purchased paper

US—United States industry only. CAN—United States and Canadian industries are comparable. MEX—United States and Mexican industries are comparable. Blank—Canadian, Mexican, and United States industries are comparable.

Molded pulp products (e.g., egg cartons, food containers, food trays) manufacturing

Sanitary products made from purchased sanitary paper stock

Cross-References. Establishments primarily engaged in—

- Manufacturing pulp from wood or from other materials—are classified in Industry 32211, Pulp Mills;
- Manufacturing paper from pulp or making pulp and manufacturing paper—are classified in Industry 32212, Paper Mills;
- Manufacturing paperboard from pulp or making pulp and manufacturing paperboard—are classified in Industry 32213, Paperboard Mills;
- Manufacturing paperboard containers—are classified in Industry 32221, Paperboard Container Manufacturing;
- Manufacturing bags of coated, laminated, or uncoated paper, of metal foil, or combinations thereof—are classified in Industry 32222, Paper Bag and Coated and Treated Paper Manufacturing; and
- Manufacturing stationery and other related office supplies—are classified in Industry 32223, Stationery Product Manufacturing.

322291 Sanitary Paper Product Manufacturing[CAN]

This U.S. industry comprises establishments primarily engaged in converting purchased sanitary paper stock or wadding into sanitary paper products, such as facial tissues and handkerchiefs, table napkins, toilet paper, towels, disposable diapers, sanitary napkins, and tampons.

322299 All Other Converted Paper Product Manufacturing[CAN]

This U.S. industry comprises establishments primarily engaged in converting paper or paperboard into products (except containers, bags, coated and treated paper, stationery products, and sanitary paper products) or converting pulp into pulp products, such as egg cartons, food trays, and other food containers from molded pulp.

Illustrative Examples:

Crepe paper made from purchased paper

Die-cut paper products (except for office use) made from purchased paper or paperboard

Molded pulp products (e.g., egg cartons, food containers, food trays) manufacturing

Paper novelties made from purchased paper

US—United States industry only. CAN—United States and Canadian industries are comparable. MEX—United States and Mexican industries are comparable. Blank—Canadian, Mexican, and United States industries are comparable.

Cross-References. Establishments primarily engaged in—

- Manufacturing pulp from wood or from other materials—are classified in Industry 322110, Pulp Mills;
- Manufacturing paper from pulp or making pulp and manufacturing paper—are classified in Industry 32212, Paper Mills;
- Manufacturing paperboard from pulp or making pulp and manufacturing paperboard—are classified in Industry 322130, Paperboard Mills;
- Manufacturing paperboard containers—are classified in Industry 32221, Paperboard Container Manufacturing;
- Manufacturing bags of coated, laminated, or uncoated paper, of metal foil, or combinations thereof—are classified in Industry 32222, Paper Bag and Coated and Treated Paper Manufacturing; and
- Manufacturing stationery and other related office supplies—are classified in Industry 32223, Stationery Product Manufacturing.

323 Printing and Related Support Activities

Industries in the Printing and Related Support Activities subsector print products, such as newspapers, books, labels, business cards, stationery, business forms, and other materials, and perform support activities, such as data imaging, platemaking services, and bookbinding. The support activities included here are an integral part of the printing industry, and a product (a printing plate, a bound book, or a computer disk or file) that is an integral part of the printing industry is almost always provided by these operations.

Processes used in printing include a variety of methods used to transfer an image from a plate, screen, film, or computer file to some medium, such as paper, plastics, metal, textile articles, or wood. The most prominent of these methods is to transfer the image from a plate or screen to the medium (lithographic, gravure, screen, and flexographic printing). A rapidly growing new technology uses a computer file to directly ''drive'' the printing mechanism to create the image and new electrostatic and other types of equipment (digital or nonimpact printing).

In contrast to many other classification systems that locate publishing of printed materials in manufacturing, NAICS classifies the publishing of printed products in Subsector 511, Publishing Industries (except Internet). Though printing and publishing are often carried out by the same enterprise (a newspaper, for example), it is less and less the case that these distinct activities are carried out in the same establishment. When publishing and printing are done in the same establishment, the establishment is classified in Sector 51, Information, in the appropriate NAICS industry even if the receipts for printing exceed those for publishing.

This subsector includes printing on clothing because the production process for that activity is printing, not clothing manufacturing. For instance, the printing of

---

US—United States industry only. CAN—United States and Canadian industries are comparable. MEX—United States and Mexican industries are comparable. Blank—Canadian, Mexican, and United States industries are comparable.

T-shirts is included in this subsector. In contrast, printing on fabric (or grey goods) is not included. This activity is part of the process of finishing the fabric and is included in the NAICS Textile Mills subsector in Industry 31331, Textile and Fabric Finishing Mills.

3231 Printing and Related Support Activities

32311 Printing

This industry comprises establishments primarily engaged in printing on apparel and textile products, paper, metal, glass, plastics, and other materials, except fabric (grey goods). The printing processes employed include, but are not limited to, lithographic, gravure, screen, flexographic, digital, and letterpress. Establishments in this industry do not manufacture the stock that they print but may perform postprinting activities, such as folding, cutting, or laminating the materials they print, and mailing.

Cross-References. Establishments primarily engaged in—

- Providing photocopying service on nondigital photocopy equipment without performing traditional printing activities—are classified in Industry 56143, Business Service Centers;
- Printing on grey goods—are classified in Industry 31331, Textile and Fabric Finishing Mills;
- Printing and publishing, known as publishers,—are classified in Subsector 511, Publishing Industries (except Internet); and
- Performing prepress or postpress services without performing traditional printing activities—are classified in Industry 32312, Support Services for Printing.

323110 Commercial Lithographic Printing[US]

This U.S. industry comprises establishments primarily engaged in lithographic (i.e., offset) printing without publishing (except books, grey goods, and manifold business forms). This industry includes establishments engaged in lithographic printing on purchased stock materials, such as stationery, letterhead, invitations, labels, and similar items, on a job order basis.

Cross-References. Establishments primarily engaged in—

- Quick printing—are classified in U.S. Industry 323114, Quick Printing;
- Printing on grey goods—are classified in Industry 31331, Textile and Fabric Finishing Mills;

US—United States industry only. CAN—United States and Canadian industries are comparable. MEX—United States and Mexican industries are comparable. Blank—Canadian, Mexican, and United States industries are comparable.

- Printing books and pamphlets—are classified in U.S. Industry 323117, Books Printing;
- Printing manifold business forms including checkbooks—are classified in U.S. Industry 323116, Manifold Business Forms Printing;
- Manufacturing printed stationery, invitations, labels, and similar items—are classified in Subsector 322, Paper Manufacturing; and
- Printing and publishing, known as publishers,—are classified in Subsector 511, Publishing Industries (except Internet).

323111 Commercial Gravure Printing[US]

This U.S. industry comprises establishments primarily engaged in gravure printing without publishing (except books, grey goods, and manifold business forms). This industry includes establishments engaged in gravure printing on purchased stock materials, such as stationery, letterhead, invitations, labels, and similar items, on a job order basis.

Cross-References. Establishments primarily engaged in—

- Printing on grey goods—are classified in Industry 31331, Textile and Fabric Finishing Mills;
- Printing books and pamphlets—are classified in U.S. Industry 323117, Book Printing;
- Printing manifold business forms including checkbooks—are classified in U.S. Industry 323116, Manifold Business Form Printing;
- Manufacturing printed stationery, invitations, labels, and similar items—are classified in Subsector 322, Paper Manufacturing; and
- Printing and publishing, known as publishers,—are classified in Subsector 511, Publishing Industries (except Internet).

323112 Commercial Flexographic Printing[US]

This U.S. industry comprises establishments primarily engaged in flexographic printing without publishing (except books, grey goods, and manifold business forms). This industry includes establishments engaged in flexographic printing on purchased stock materials, such as stationery, invitations, labels, and similar items, on a job order basis.

Cross-References. Establishments primarily engaged in—

- Printing on grey goods—are classified in Industry 31331, Textile and Fabric Finishing Mills;

US—United States industry only. CAN—United States and Canadian industries are comparable. MEX—United States and Mexican industries are comparable. Blank—Canadian, Mexican, and United States industries are comparable.

- Printing books and pamphlets—are classified in U.S. Industry 323117, Books Printing;
- Printing manifold business forms including checkbooks—are classified in U.S. Industry 323116, Manifold Business Forms Printing;
- Manufacturing printed stationery, invitations, labels, and similar items—are classified elsewhere in Subsector 322, Manufacturing; and
- Printing and publishing, known as publishers,—are classified in Subsector 511, Publishing Industries (except Internet).

323113 Commercial Screen Printing[CAN]

This U.S. industry comprises establishments primarily engaged in screen printing without publishing (except books, grey goods, and manifold business forms). This industry includes establishments engaged in screen printing on purchased stock materials, such as stationery, invitations, labels, and similar items, on a job order basis. Establishments primarily engaged in printing on apparel and textile products, such as T-shirts, caps, jackets, towels, and napkins, are included in this industry.

Cross-References. Establishments primarily engaged in—

- Printing on grey goods—are classified in Industry 31331, Textile and Fabric Finishing Mills;
- Printing books and pamphlets—are classified in U.S. Industry 323117, Books Printing;
- Printing manifold business forms including checkbooks—are classified in U.S. Industry 323116, Manifold Business Forms Printing;
- Manufacturing printed stationery, invitations, labels, and similar items—are classified in Subsector 322, Paper Manufacturing; and
- Printing and publishing, known as publishers,—are classified in Subsector 511, Publishing Industries (except Internet).

323114 Quick Printing[CAN]

This U.S. industry comprises establishments primarily engaged in traditional printing activities, such as short-run offset printing or prepress services, in combination with providing document photocopying service. Prepress services include receiving documents in electronic format and directly duplicating from the electronic file and formatting, colorizing, and otherwise modifying the original docu-

US—United States industry only. CAN—United States and Canadian industries are comparable. MEX—United States and Mexican industries are comparable. Blank—Canadian, Mexican, and United States industries are comparable.

ment to improve presentation. These establishments, known as quick printers, generally provide short-run printing and copying with fast turnaround times.

Cross-References. Establishments primarily engaged in—

- Providing photocopying service on nondigital photocopy equipment without performing traditional printing activities—are classified in U.S. Industry 561439, Other Business Service Centers (including Copy Shops);
- Printing with lithographic equipment known as commercial lithographic printers—are classified in U.S. Industry 323110, Commercial Lithographic Printing; and
- Digital printing on graphical material—are classified in U.S. Industry 323115, Digital Printing.

323115 Digital Printing[CAN]

This U.S. industry comprises establishments primarily engaged in printing graphical materials using digital printing equipment. Establishments known as digital printers typically provide sophisticated prepress services including using scanners to input images and computers to manipulate and format the graphic images prior to printing.

Cross-References.

Establishments primarily engaged in printing with ''up front'' computer files on conventional-type printing equipment are classified to books, manifold business forms, or based on the type of printing equipment (e.g., lithographic, flexographic, screen) being used.

323116 Manifold Business Forms Printing[CAN]

This U.S. industry comprises establishments primarily engaged in printing special forms, including checkbooks, for use in the operation of a business. The forms may be in single and multiple sets, including carbonized, interleaved with carbon, or otherwise processed for multiple reproduction.

Cross-References.

Establishments primarily engaged in manufacturing single layered continuous computer paper and similar products are classified in U.S. Industry 322231, Die-Cut Paper and Paperboard Office Supplies Manufacturing.

US—United States industry only. CAN—United States and Canadian industries are comparable. MEX—United States and Mexican industries are comparable. Blank—Canadian, Mexican, and United States industries are comparable.

323117 Books Printing[US]

This U.S. industry comprises establishments primarily engaged in printing or printing and binding books and pamphlets without publishing.

Cross-References. Establishments primarily engaged in—

- Printing and publishing, known as book publishers,—are classified in Subsector 511, Publishing Industries (except Internet); and
- Binding books without printing in the same establishment—are classified in U.S. Industry 323121, Tradebinding and Related Work.

323118 Blankbook, Looseleaf Binders, and Devices Manufacturing[US]

This U.S. industry comprises establishments primarily engaged in manufacturing blankbooks, looseleaf devices, and binders. Establishments in this industry may print or print and bind.

Cross-References. Establishments primarily engaged in—

- Checkbook printing—are classified in U.S. Industry 323116, Manifold Business Form Printing; and
- Binding books without printing in the same establishment—are classified in U.S. Industry 323121, Tradebinding and Related Work.

323119 Other Commercial Printing[US]

This U.S. industry comprises establishments primarily engaged in commercial printing (except lithographic, gravure, screen, or flexographic printing) without publishing (except books, grey goods, and manifold business forms). Printing processes included in this industry are letterpress printing and engraving printing. This industry includes establishments engaged in commercial printing on purchased stock materials, such as stationery, invitations, labels, and similar items, on a job order basis.

Cross-References. Establishments primarily engaged in—

- Lithographic, gravure, screen, or flexographic printing on purchased stock materials (except books, grey goods, and manifold business forms)—are classified in Industry 32311, Printing, by printing process employed;
- Printing on grey goods—are classified in Industry 31331, Textile and Fabric Finishing Mills;

US—United States industry only. CAN—United States and Canadian industries are comparable. MEX—United States and Mexican industries are comparable. Blank—Canadian, Mexican, and United States industries are comparable.

- Quick printing—are classified in U.S. Industry 323114, Quick Printing;
- Digital printing on graphical materials—are classified in U.S. Industry 323115, Digital Printing;
- Printing books and pamphlets—are classified in U.S. Industry 323117, Books Printing;
- Printing manifold business forms including checkbooks—are classified in U.S. Industry 323116, Manifold Business Forms Printing;
- Manufacturing printed stationery, invitations, labels, and similar items—are classified in Subsector 322, Paper Manufacturing; and
- Printing and publishing, known as book publishers,—are classified in Subsector 511, Publishing Industries (except Internet).

32312 Support Activities for Printing

This industry comprises establishments primarily engaged in performing prepress (e.g., platemaking, typesetting) and postpress services (e.g., book binding) in support of printing activities.

Cross-References. Establishments primarily engaged in—

- Engraving of the type done on metal—are classified in Industry 33281, Coating, Engraving, Heat Treating, and Allied Activities;
- Manufacturing photosensitive plates for printing—are classified in Industry 32599, All Other Chemical Product and Preparation Manufacturing;
- Manufacturing blank plates for printing—are classified in Industry 33329, Other Industrial Machinery Manufacturing; and
- Printing books or printing and binding books—are classified in Industry 32311, Printing.

323121 Tradebinding and Related Work[US]

This U.S. industry comprises establishments primarily engaged in one or more of the following: (1) tradebinding; (2) sample mounting; and (3) postpress services (e.g., book or paper bronzing, die-cutting, edging, embossing, folding, gilding, gluing, indexing).

Cross-References.

Establishments primarily engaged in printing books or printing and binding books are classified in U.S. Industry 323117, Books Printing.

US—United States industry only. CAN—United States and Canadian industries are comparable. MEX—United States and Mexican industries are comparable. Blank—Canadian, Mexican, and United States industries are comparable.

323122 Prepress Services[US]

This U.S. industry comprises (1) establishments primarily engaged in prepress services, such as imagesetting or typesetting, for printers and (2) establishments primarily engaged in preparing film or plates for printing purposes.

Cross-References. Establishments primarily engaged in—

- Engraving of the type done on metal—are classified in U.S. Industry 332812, Metal Coating, Engraving (except jewelry and silverware), and Allied Services to Manufacturers;
- Manufacturing blank plates (except photosensitive plates) for printing—are classified in U.S. Industry 333293, Printing Machinery and Equipment Manufacturing; and
- Manufacturing photosensitive plates for printing—are classified in U.S. Industry 325992, Photographic Film, Paper, Plate, and Chemical Manufacturing.

324 Petroleum and Coal Products Manufacturing

The Petroleum and Coal Products Manufacturing subsector is based on the transformation of crude petroleum and coal into usable products. The dominant process is petroleum refining that involves the separation of crude petroleum into component products through such techniques as cracking and distillation.

In addition, this subsector includes establishments that primarily further process refined petroleum and coal products and produce products, such as asphalt coatings and petroleum lubricating oils. However, establishments that manufacture petrochemicals from refined petroleum are classified in Industry 32511, Petrochemical Manufacturing.

3241 Petroleum and Coal Products Manufacturing

32411 Petroleum Refineries

See industry description for 324110 below.

324110 Petroleum Refineries

This industry comprises establishments primarily engaged in refining crude petroleum into refined petroleum. Petroleum refining involves one or more of the following activities: (1) fractionation; (2) straight distillation of crude oil; and (3) cracking.

US—United States industry only. CAN—United States and Canadian industries are comparable. MEX—United States and Mexican industries are comparable. Blank—Canadian, Mexican, and United States industries are comparable.

Cross-References. Establishments primarily engaged in—

- Manufacturing asphalt paving, roofing, and saturated materials from refined petroleum—are classified in Industry 32412, Asphalt Paving, Roofing, and Saturated Materials Manufacturing;
- Manufacturing paper mats and felts and saturating them with asphalt or tar into rolls and sheets—are classified in U.S. Industry 322121, Paper (except Newsprint) Mills;
- Blending or compounding refined petroleum to make lubricating oils and greases and/or re-refining used petroleum lubricating oils—are classified in U.S. Industry 324191, Petroleum Lubricating Oil and Grease Manufacturing;
- Manufacturing synthetic lubricating oils and greases—are classified in U.S. Industry 325998, All Other Miscellaneous Chemical Product and Preparation Manufacturing;
- Recovering natural gasoline and/or liquid hydrocarbons from oil and gas field gases—are classified in Industry 21111, Oil and Gas Extraction;
- Manufacturing acyclic and cyclic aromatic hydrocarbons (i.e., petrochemicals) from refined petroleum or liquid hydrocarbons—are classified in Industry 325110, Petrochemical Manufacturing;
- Manufacturing cyclic and acyclic chemicals (except petrochemicals)—are classified in Industry 32519, Other Basic Organic Chemical Manufacturing;
- Manufacturing coke oven products in steel mills—are classified in U.S. Industry 331111, Iron and Steel Mills; and
- Manufacturing coke oven products in coke oven establishments—are classified in U.S. Industry, 324199, All Other Petroleum and Coal Products Manufacturing.

32412 Asphalt Paving, Roofing, and Saturated Materials Manufacturing

This industry comprises establishments primarily engaged in (1) manufacturing asphalt and tar paving mixtures and blocks and roofing cements and coatings from purchased asphaltic materials and/or (2) saturating purchased mats and felts with asphalt or tar from purchased asphaltic materials.

Cross-References. Establishments primarily engaged in—

- Refining crude petroleum and manufacturing asphalt and tar paving, roofing, and saturated materials—are classified in Industry 324110, Petroleum Refineries; and

US—United States industry only. CAN—United States and Canadian industries are comparable. MEX—United States and Mexican industries are comparable. Blank—Canadian, Mexican, and United States industries are comparable.

- Manufacturing paper mats and felts and saturating them with asphalt or tar—are classified in Industry 32212, Paper Mills.

324121 Asphalt Paving Mixture and Block Manufacturing[CAN]

This U.S. industry comprises establishments primarily engaged in manufacturing asphalt and tar paving mixtures and blocks from purchased asphaltic materials.

Cross-References.

Establishments primarily engaged in refining crude petroleum and manufacturing asphalt and tar paving mixtures and blocks are classified in Industry 324110, Petroleum Refineries.

324122 Asphalt Shingle and Coating Materials Manufacturing[CAN]

This U.S. industry comprises establishments primarily engaged in (1) saturating purchased mats and felts with asphalt or tar from purchased asphaltic materials and (2) manufacturing asphalt and tar and roofing cements and coatings from purchased asphaltic materials.

Cross-References. Establishments primarily engaged in—

- Refining crude petroleum and saturating purchased mats and felts with asphalt or tar into rolls and sheets and/or refining crude petroleum and manufacturing asphalt and tar roofing cements and coatings—are classified in Industry 324110, Petroleum Refineries; and
- Manufacturing paper mats and felts and saturating them with asphalt or tar into rolls and sheets—are classified in U.S. Industry 322121, Paper (except Newsprint) Mills.

32419 Other Petroleum and Coal Products Manufacturing

This industry comprises establishments primarily engaged in manufacturing petroleum products (except asphalt paving, roofing and saturated materials) from refined petroleum or coal products made in coke ovens not integrated with a steel mill.

Illustrative Examples:

Coke oven products (e.g., coke, gases, tars) made in coke oven establishments
Petroleum brake fluids made from refined petroleum
Petroleum lubricating oils and greases made from refined petroleum
Petroleum waxes made from refined petroleum

US—United States industry only. CAN—United States and Canadian industries are comparable. MEX—United States and Mexican industries are comparable. Blank—Canadian, Mexican, and United States industries are comparable.

Petroleum briquettes made from refined petroleum
Petroleum jelly made from refined petroleum
Re-refined used petroleum lubricating oils

Cross-References. Establishments primarily engaged in—

- Manufacturing petroleum products by refining crude petroleum—are classified in Industry 32411, Petroleum Refineries;
- Manufacturing asphalt and tar paving, roofing, and saturated materials from refined petroleum—are classified in Industry 32412, Asphalt Paving, Roofing, and Saturated Materials Manufacturing;
- Manufacturing coke oven products in steel mills—are classified in Industry 33111, Iron and Steel Mills and Ferroalloy Manufacturing;
- Manufacturing acyclic and cyclic aromatic hydrocarbons (i.e., petrochemicals) from refined petroleum or liquid hydrocarbons—are classified in Industry 32511, Petrochemical Manufacturing;
- Manufacturing cyclic and acyclic organic chemicals (except petrochemicals)—are classified in Industry 32519, Other Basic Organic Chemical Manufacturing; and
- Manufacturing synthetic lubricating oils and greases—are classified in Industry 32599, All Other Chemical Product and Preparation Manufacturing.

324191 Petroleum Lubricating Oil and Grease Manufacturing[MEX]

This U.S. industry comprises establishments primarily engaged in blending or compounding refined petroleum to make lubricating oils and greases and/or re-refining used petroleum lubricating oils.

Cross-References. Establishments primarily engaged in—

- Refining crude petroleum and manufacturing lubricating oils and greases—are classified in Industry 324110, Petroleum Refineries; and
- Manufacturing synthetic lubricating oils and greases—are classified in U.S. Industry 325998, All Other Miscellaneous Chemical Product and Preparation Manufacturing.

324199 All Other Petroleum and Coal Products Manufacturing[US]

This U.S. industry comprises establishments primarily engaged in manufacturing petroleum products (except asphalt paving, roofing, and saturated materials and

US—United States industry only. CAN—United States and Canadian industries are comparable. MEX—United States and Mexican industries are comparable. Blank—Canadian, Mexican, and United States industries are comparable.

lubricating oils and greases) from refined petroleum and coal products made in coke ovens not integrated with a steel mill.

Illustrative Examples:

Coke oven products (e.g., coke, gases, tars) made in coke oven establishments
Petroleum briquettes made from refined petroleum
Petroleum jelly made from refined petroleum
Petroleum waxes made from refined petroleum

Cross-References. Establishments primarily engaged in—

- Manufacturing petroleum products by refining crude petroleum—are classified in Industry 324110, Petroleum Refineries;
- Manufacturing asphalt paving and roofing materials from refined petroleum—are classified in Industry 32412, Asphalt Paving, Roofing, and Saturated Materials Manufacturing;
- Blending and compounding petroleum lubricating oils and greases and/or re-refining used petroleum lubrication oils and greases—are classified in U.S. Industry 324191, Petroleum Lubricating Oil and Grease Manufacturing;
- Manufacturing coke oven products in steel mills—are classified in U.S. Industry 331111, Iron and Steel Mills;
- Manufacturing acyclic and cyclic aromatic hydrocarbons (i.e., petrochemicals) from refined petroleum or liquid hydrocarbons—are classified in Industry 325110, Petrochemical Manufacturing; and
- Manufacturing cyclic and acyclic organic chemicals (except petrochemicals)—are classified in Industry 32519, Other Basic Organic Chemical Manufacturing.

325 Chemical Manufacturing

The Chemical Manufacturing subsector is based on the transformation of organic and inorganic raw materials by a chemical process and the formulation of products. This subsector distinguishes the production of basic chemicals that comprise the first industry group from the production of intermediate and end products produced by further processing of basic chemicals that make up the remaining industry groups.

This subsector does not include all industries transforming raw materials by a chemical process. It is common for some chemical processing to occur during mining operations. These beneficiating operations, such as copper concentrating, are classified in Sector 21, Mining. Furthermore, the refining of crude petroleum is included in Subsector 324, Petroleum and Coal Products Manufacturing. In

US—United States industry only. CAN—United States and Canadian industries are comparable. MEX—United States and Mexican industries are comparable. Blank—Canadian, Mexican, and United States industries are comparable.

addition, the manufacturing of aluminum oxide is included in Subsector 331, Primary Metal Manufacturing; and beverage distilleries are classified in Subsector 312, Beverage and Tobacco Product Manufacturing. As in the case of these two activities, the grouping of industries into subsectors may take into account the association of the activities performed with other activities in the subsector.

3251 Basic Chemical Manufacturing

This industry group comprises establishments primarily engaged in manufacturing chemicals using basic processes, such as thermal cracking and distillation. Chemicals manufactured in this industry group are usually separate chemical elements or separate chemically-defined compounds.

32511 Petrochemical Manufacturing

See industry description for 325110 below.

325110 Petrochemical Manufacturing

This industry comprises establishments primarily engaged in (1) manufacturing acyclic (i.e., aliphatic) hydrocarbons such as ethylene, propylene, and butylene made from refined petroleum or liquid hydrocarbon and/or (2) manufacturing cyclic aromatic hydrocarbons such as benzene, toluene, styrene, xylene, ethyl benzene, and cumene made from refined petroleum or liquid hydrocarbons.

Cross-References. Establishments primarily engaged in—

- Manufacturing petrochemicals by refining crude petroleum—are classified in Industry 324110, Petroleum Refineries;
- Manufacturing acetylene—are classified in Industry 325120, Industrial Gas Manufacturing;
- Manufacturing basic organic chemicals (except petrochemicals)—are classified in Industry 32519, Other Basic Organic Chemical Manufacturing; and
- Recovering liquid hydrocarbons from oil and gas field gases—are classified in Industry 211110, Oil and Gas Extraction.

32512 Industrial Gas Manufacturing

See industry description for 325120 below.

325120 Industrial Gas Manufacturing

This industry comprises establishments primarily engaged in manufacturing industrial organic and inorganic gases in compressed, liquid, and solid forms.

US—United States industry only. CAN—United States and Canadian industries are comparable. MEX—United States and Mexican industries are comparable. Blank—Canadian, Mexican, and United States industries are comparable.

Cross-References. Establishments primarily engaged in—

- Manufacturing chlorine gas—are classified in U.S. Industry 325181, Alkalies and Chlorine Manufacturing; and
- Manufacturing ethane and butane gases made from refined petroleum or liquid hydrocarbons—are classified in Industry 325110, Petrochemical Manufacturing.

32513 Synthetic Dye and Pigment Manufacturing

This industry comprises establishments primarily engaged in manufacturing synthetic organic and inorganic dyes and pigments, such as lakes and toners (except electrostatic and photographic).

Cross-References. Establishments primarily engaged in—

- Manufacturing wood byproducts used as dying materials—are classified in Industry 32519, Other Basic Organic Chemical Manufacturing;
- Manufacturing carbon, bone, and lamp black—are classified in Industry 32518, Other Basic Inorganic Chemical Manufacturing;
- Manufacturing electrostatic and photographic toners—are classified in Industry 32599, All Other Chemical Product and Preparation Manufacturing;
- Manufacturing natural food colorings—are classified in Industry 31193, Flavoring Syrup and Concentrate Manufacturing; and
- Manufacturing natural organic colorings for nonfood uses—are classified in Industry 32519, Other Basic Organic Chemical Manufacturing.

325131 Inorganic Dye and Pigment Manufacturing[US]

This U.S. industry comprises establishments primarily engaged in manufacturing inorganic dyes and pigments.

Cross-References. Establishments primarily engaged in—

- Manufacturing wood byproducts used as dyeing materials—are classified in U.S. Industry 325191, Gum and Wood Chemical Manufacturing;
- Manufacturing organic synthetic dyes and pigments—are classified in U.S. Industry 325132, Synthetic Organic Dye and Pigment Manufacturing;
- Manufacturing carbon, bone, and lamp black—are classified in U.S. Industry 325182, Carbon Black Manufacturing; and
- Manufacturing natural food colorings—are classified in Industry 311930, Flavoring Syrup and Concentrate Manufacturing.

US—United States industry only. CAN—United States and Canadian industries are comparable. MEX—United States and Mexican industries are comparable. Blank—Canadian, Mexican, and United States industries are comparable.

325132 Synthetic Organic Dye and Pigment Manufacturing[US]

This U.S. industry comprises establishments primarily engaged in manufacturing synthetic organic dyes and pigments, such as lakes and toners (except electrostatic and photographic).

Cross-References. Establishments primarily engaged in—

- Manufacturing wood byproducts used as dyeing materials—are classified in U.S. Industry 325191, Gum and Wood Chemical Manufacturing;
- Manufacturing inorganic dyes and pigments—are classified in U.S. Industry 325131, Inorganic Dye and Pigment Manufacturing;
- Manufacturing electrostatic and photographic toners—are classified in U.S. Industry 325992, Photographic Film, Paper, Plate, and Chemical Manufacturing;
- Manufacturing natural food colorings—are classified in Industry 311930, Flavoring Syrup and Concentrate Manufacturing; and
- Manufacturing natural organic colorings for nonfood uses (except wood byproducts)—are classified in U.S. Industry 325199, All Other Basic Organic Chemical Manufacturing.

32518 Other Basic Inorganic Chemical Manufacturing

This industry comprises establishments primarily engaged in manufacturing basic inorganic chemicals (except industrial gases and synthetic dyes and pigments).

Illustrative Examples:

Alkalies manufacturing
Aluminum compounds, not specified elsewhere by process, manufacturing
Carbides (e.g., baron, calcium, silium, tungsten) manufacturing
Carbon black manufacturing
Chlorine manufacturing
Hydrochloric acid manufacturing
Potassium inorganic compounds, not specified elsewhere by process, manufacturing
Radioactive isotopes manufacturing
Sulfides and sulfites manufacturing
Sulfuric acid manufacturing

Cross-References. Establishments primarily engaged in—

- Manufacturing industrial gases—are classified in Industry 32512, Industrial Gas Manufacturing;
- Manufacturing inorganic dyes and pigments—are classified in Industry 32513, Synthetic Dye and Pigment Manufacturing;
- Manufacturing household bleaches—are classified in Industry 32561, Soap and Cleaning Compound Manufacturing;

US—United States industry only. CAN—United States and Canadian industries are comparable. MEX—United States and Mexican industries are comparable. Blank—Canadian, Mexican, and United States industries are comparable.

- Mining and/or beneficiating alkalies—are classified in Industry 21239, Other Nonmetallic Mineral Mining and Quarrying;
- Manufacturing chlorine preparations (e.g., for swimming pools)—are classified in Industry 32599, All Other Chemical Product and Preparation Manufacturing;
- Manufacturing nitrogenous and phosphoric fertilizers and fertilizer materials—are classified in Industry 32531, Fertilizer Manufacturing;
- Manufacturing aluminum oxide (alumina)—are classified in Industry 33131, Alumina and Aluminum Production and Processing;
- Manufacturing inorganic insecticidal, herbicidal, fungicidal and pesticidal preparations—are classified in Industry 32532, Pesticide and Other Agricultural Chemical Manufacturing; and
- Manufacturing photographic chemicals—are classified in Industry 32599, All Other Chemical Product and Preparation Manufacturing.

325181 Alkalies and Chlorine Manufacturing[CAN]

This U.S. industry comprises establishments primarily engaged in manufacturing chlorine, sodium hydroxide (i.e., caustic soda), and other alkalies often using an electrolysis process.

Cross-References. Establishments primarily engaged in—

- Mining and beneficiating alkalies—are classified in U.S. Industry 212391, Potash, Soda, and Borate Mineral Mining;
- Manufacturing chlorine preparations (e.g., for swimming pools)—are classified in U.S. Industry 325998, All Other Miscellaneous Chemical Product and Preparation Manufacturing;
- Manufacturing industrial bleaches—are classified in U.S. Industry 325188, All Other Basic Inorganic Chemical Manufacturing; and
- Manufacturing household bleaches—are classified in U.S. Industry 325612, Polish and Other Sanitation Good Manufacturing.

325182 Carbon Black Manufacturing[US]

This U.S. industry comprises establishments primarily engaged in manufacturing carbon black, bone black, and lamp black.

Cross-References. Establishments primarily engaged in manufacturing pigments are classified in Industry 32513, Synthetic Dye and Pigment Manufacturing.

US—United States industry only. CAN—United States and Canadian industries are comparable. MEX—United States and Mexican industries are comparable. Blank—Canadian, Mexican, and United States industries are comparable.

325188 All Other Basic Inorganic Chemical Manufacturing[US]

This U.S. industry comprises establishments primarily engaged in manufacturing basic inorganic chemicals (except industrial gases, inorganic dyes and pigments, alkalies and chlorine, and carbon black).

Illustrative Examples:

Aluminum compounds, not specified elsewhere by process, manufacturing
Carbides (e.g., baron, calcium, silicon, tungsten) manufacturing
Fluorine manufacturing
Hydrochloric acid manufacturing
Potassium inorganic compounds, not specified elsewhere by process, manufacturing
Sodium inorganic compounds, not specified elsewhere by process, manufacturing
Sulfides and sulfites manufacturing
Sulfuric acid manufacturing

Cross-References. Establishments primarily engaged in—

- Manufacturing industrial gases—are classified in Industry 325120, Industrial Gas Manufacturing;
- Manufacturing inorganic dyes and pigments—are classified in U.S. Industry 325131, Inorganic Dye and Pigment Manufacturing;
- Manufacturing alkalies and chlorine—are classified in U.S. Industry 325181, Alkalies and Chlorine Manufacturing;
- Manufacturing carbon black—are classified in U.S. Industry 325182, Carbon Black Manufacturing;
- Manufacturing household bleaches—are classified in U.S. Industry 325612, Polish and Other Sanitation Good Manufacturing;
- Manufacturing nitrogenous and phosphoric fertilizers and fertilizer material—are classified in Industry 32531, Fertilizer Manufacturing;
- Manufacturing aluminum oxide (i.e., alumina)—are classified in U.S. Industry 331311, Alumina Refining;
- Manufacturing inorganic insecticidal, herbicidal, fungicidal, and pesticidal preparations—are classified in Industry 325320, Pesticide and Other Agriculture Chemical Manufacturing; and
- Manufacturing photographic chemicals—are classified in U.S. Industry 325992, Photographic Film, Paper, Plate, and Chemical Manufacturing.

US—United States industry only. CAN—United States and Canadian industries are comparable. MEX—United States and Mexican industries are comparable. Blank—Canadian, Mexican, and United States industries are comparable.

32519 Other Basic Organic Chemical Manufacturing

This industry comprises establishments primarily engaged in manufacturing basic organic chemicals (except petrochemicals, industrial gases, and synthetic dyes and pigments).

Illustrative Examples:

Carbon organic compounds, not specified elsewhere by process, manufacturing
Cyclic intermediates made from refined petroleum or natural gas
Enzyme proteins (i.e., basic synthetic chemicals) (except pharmaceutical use) manufacturing
Fatty acids (e.g., margaric, oleic, stearic) manufacturing
Gum and wood chemicals manufacturing
Organo-inorganic compound manufacturing
Plasticizers (i.e., basic synthetic chemical) manufacturing
Silicone (except resins) manufacturing
Synthetic sweeteners (i.e., sweetening agents) manufacturing

Cross-References. Establishments primarily engaged in—

- Manufacturing petrochemicals from refined petroleum or liquid hydrocarbons—are classified in Industry 32511, Petrochemical Manufacturing;
- Manufacturing petrochemicals by refining crude petroleum—are classified in Industry 32411, Petroleum Refineries;
- Manufacturing organic industrial gases—are classified in Industry 32512, Industrial Gas Manufacturing;
- Manufacturing synthetic organic dyes and pigments—are classified in Industry 32513, Synthetic Dye and Pigment Manufacturing;
- Manufacturing natural glycerin—are classified in Industry 32561, Soap and Cleaning Compound Manufacturing;
- Manufacturing activated charcoal—are classified in Industry 32599, All Other Chemical Product and Preparation Manufacturing;
- Manufacturing organic insecticidal, herbicidal, fungicidal, and pesticidal preparations—are classified in Industry 32532, Pesticide and Other Agriculture Chemical Manufacturing;
- Manufacturing elastomers—are classified in Industry 32521, Resin and Synthetic Rubber Manufacturing;
- Manufacturing urea—are classified in Industry 32531, Fertilizer Manufacturing;
- Manufacturing coal tar crudes in integrated steel mills with coke ovens—are classified in Industry 33111, Iron and Steel Mills and Ferroalloy Manufacturing;

US—United States industry only. CAN—United States and Canadian industries are comparable. MEX—United States and Mexican industries are comparable. Blank—Canadian, Mexican, and United States industries are comparable.

- Manufacturing coal tar crudes in coke ovens not integrated with steel mills and fuel briquettes from refined petroleum—are classified in Industry 32419, Other Petroleum and Coal Products Manufacturing; and
- Manufacturing natural food colorings—are classified in Industry 31194, Seasoning and Dressing Manufacturing.

325191 Gum and Wood Chemical Manufacturing[US]

This U.S. industry comprises establishments primarily engaged in (1) distilling wood or gum into products, such as tall oil and wood distillates, and (2) manufacturing wood or gum chemicals, such as naval stores, natural tanning materials, charcoal briquettes, and charcoal (except activated).

Cross-References. Establishments primarily engaged in—

- Manufacturing activated charcoal—are classified in U.S. Industry 325998, All Other Miscellaneous Chemical Product and Preparation Manufacturing; and
- Manufacturing fuel briquettes from refined petroleum—are classified in U.S. Industry 324199, All Other Petroleum and Coal Products Manufacturing.

325192 Cyclic Crude and Intermediate Manufacturing[US]

This U.S. industry comprises establishments primarily engaged in (1) distilling coal tars and/or (2) manufacturing cyclic crudes or, cyclic intermediates (i.e., hydrocarbons, except aromatic petrochemicals) from refined petroleum or natural gas.

Cross-References. Establishments primarily engaged in—

- Manufacturing cyclic chemicals (except aromatic and intermediates)—are classified in U.S. Industry 325199, All Other Basic Organic Chemical Manufacturing;
- Manufacturing aromatic petrochemicals from refined petroleum or natural gas—are classified in Industry 325110, Petrochemical Manufacturing;
- Manufacturing aromatic petrochemicals by refining crude petroleum—are classified in Industry 324110, Petroleum Refineries;
- Distilling wood products—are classified in U.S. Industry 325191, Gum and Wood Chemical Manufacturing;
- Manufacturing coal tar crudes in steel mills with coke ovens—are classified in U.S. Industry 331111, Iron and Steel Mills; and

US—United States industry only. CAN—United States and Canadian industries are comparable. MEX—United States and Mexican industries are comparable. Blank—Canadian, Mexican, and United States industries are comparable.

- Manufacturing coal tar crudes in coke oven establishments and fuel briquettes from refined petroleum—are classified in U.S. Industry 324199, All Other Petroleum and Coal Products Manufacturing.

325193 Ethyl Alcohol Manufacturing[US]

This U.S. industry comprises establishments primarily engaged in manufacturing nonpotable ethyl alcohol.

Cross-References. Establishments primarily engaged in—

- Distilling liquors (except brandy)—are classified in Industry 312140, Distilleries; and
- Manufacturing brandies—are classified in Industry 312130, Wineries.

325199 All Other Basic Organic Chemical Manufacturing[US]

This U.S. industry comprises establishments primarily engaged in manufacturing basic organic chemical products (except aromatic petrochemicals, industrial gases, synthetic organic dyes and pigments, gum and wood chemicals, cyclic crudes and intermediates, and ethyl alcohol).

Illustrative Examples:

Calcium organic compounds, not specified elsewhere by process, manufacturing
Carbon organic compounds, not specified elsewhere by process, manufacturing
Enzyme proteins (i.e., basic synthetic chemicals) (except pharmaceutical use) manufacturing
Fatty acids (e.g., margaric, oleic, stearic) manufacturing
Organo-inorganic compound manufacturing
Plasticizers (i.e., basic synthetic chemical) manufacturing
Silicone (except resins) manufacturing
Synthetic sweeteners (i.e., sweetening agents) manufacturing

Cross-References. Establishments primarily engaged in—

- Manufacturing aromatic petrochemicals from refined petroleum or natural gas—are classified in Industry 325110, Petrochemical Manufacturing;
- Manufacturing aromatic petrochemicals by refining crude petroleum—are classified in Industry 324110, Petroleum Refineries;
- Manufacturing organic industrial gases—are classified in Industry 325120, Industrial Gas Manufacturing;

US—United States industry only. CAN—United States and Canadian industries are comparable. MEX—United States and Mexican industries are comparable. Blank—Canadian, Mexican, and United States industries are comparable.

- Manufacturing synthetic organic dyes and pigments—are classified in U.S. Industry 325132, Synthetic Organic Dye and Pigment Manufacturing;
- Manufacturing ethyl alcohol—are classified in U.S. Industry 325193, Ethyl Alcohol Manufacturing;
- Manufacturing organic insecticidal, herbicidal, fungicidal, and pesticidal preparations—are classified in Industry 325320, Pesticide and Other Agriculture Chemical Manufacturing;
- Manufacturing elastomers—are classified in Industry 325210, Resin and Synthetic Rubber Manufacturing;
- Manufacturing urea—are classified in U.S. Industry 325311, Nitrogenous Fertilizer Manufacturing;
- Manufacturing natural glycerin—are classified in U.S. Industry 325611, Soap and Other Detergent Manufacturing; and
- Manufacturing natural food colorings—are classified in U.S. Industry 311942, Spice and Extract Manufacturing.

3252 Resin, Synthetic Rubber, and Artificial Synthetic Fibers and Filaments Manufacturing

32521 Resin and Synthetic Rubber Manufacturing

This industry comprises establishments primarily engaged in one or more of the following: (1) manufacturing synthetic resins, plastics materials, and nonvulcanizable elastomers and mixing and blending resins on a custom basis; (2) manufacturing noncustomized synthetic resins; and (3) manufacturing synthetic rubber.

Cross-References. Establishments primarily engaged in—

- Manufacturing plastics resins and converting resins into plastics products—are classified in Industry Group 3261, Plastics Product Manufacturing;
- Processing natural, synthetic, or reclaimed rubber into intermediate or final products—are classified in Industry Group 3262, Rubber Product Manufacturing;
- Custom compounding resins made elsewhere—are classified in Industry 32599, All Other Chemical Product and Preparation Manufacturing; and
- Manufacturing resin adhesives—are classified in Industry 32552, Adhesive Manufacturing.

US—United States industry only. CAN—United States and Canadian industries are comparable. MEX—United States and Mexican industries are comparable. Blank—Canadian, Mexican, and United States industries are comparable.

325211 Plastics Material and Resin Manufacturing[US]

This U.S. industry comprises establishments primarily engaged in (1) manufacturing resins, plastics materials, and nonvulcanizable thermoplastic elastomers and mixing and blending resins on a custom basis and/or (2) manufacturing noncustomized synthetic resins.

Cross-References. Establishments primarily engaged in—

- Manufacturing plastics resins and converting the resins into plastics products—are classified in 3261, Plastics Product Manufacturing;
- Custom compounding resins made elsewhere—are classified in U.S. Industry 325991, Custom Compounding of Purchased Resins; and
- Manufacturing plastics adhesives—are classified in Industry 325520, Adhesive Manufacturing.

325212 Synthetic Rubber Manufacturing[MEX]

This U.S. industry consists of establishments primarily engaged in manufacturing synthetic rubber.

Cross-References. Establishments primarily engaged in—

- Processing natural, synthetic, or reclaimed rubber into intermediate or final products (except adhesives)—are classified in Industry Group 3262, Rubber Product Manufacturing; and
- Manufacturing rubber adhesives—are classified Industry 325520, Adhesive Manufacturing.

32522 Artificial and Synthetic Fibers and Filaments Manufacturing

This industry comprises establishments primarily engaged in (1) manufacturing cellulosic (i.e., rayon and acetate) and noncellulosic (i.e., nylon, polyolefin, and polyester) fibers and filaments in the form of monofilament, filament yarn, staple, or tow or (2) manufacturing and texturing cellulosic and noncellulosic fibers and filaments.

Cross-References. Establishments primarily engaged in—

- Texturizing cellulosic and noncellulosic fiber and filament made elsewhere—are classified in Industry 31311, Fiber, Yarn, and Thread Mills; and
- Manufacturing textile glass fibers—are classified in Industry 32721, Glass and Glass Product Manufacturing.

US—United States industry only. CAN—United States and Canadian industries are comparable. MEX—United States and Mexican industries are comparable. Blank—Canadian, Mexican, and United States industries are comparable.

325221 Cellulosic Organic Fiber Manufacturing[US]

This U.S. industry comprises establishments primarily engaged in (1) manufacturing cellulosic (i.e., rayon and acetate) fibers and filaments in the form of monofilament, filament yarn, staple, or tow or (2) manufacturing and texturizing cellulosic fibers and filaments.

Cross-References. Establishments primarily engaged in—

- Texturizing cellulosic fibers and filaments made elsewhere—are classified in U.S. Industry 313112, Yarn Texturing, Throwing, and Twisting Mills; and
- Manufacturing noncellulosic fibers and filaments—are classified in U.S. Industry 325222, Noncellulosic Organic Fiber Manufacturing.

325222 Noncellulosic Organic Fiber Manufacturing[US]

This U.S. industry consists of establishments primarily engaged in (1) manufacturing noncellulosic (i.e., nylon, polyolefin, and polyester) fibers and filaments in the form of monofilament, filament yarn, staple, or tow, or (2) manufacturing and texturizing noncellulosic fibers and filaments.

Cross-References. Establishments primarily engaged in—

- Texturizing noncellulosic fibers—are classified in U.S. Industry 313112, Yarn Texturing, Throwing, and Twisting Mills;
- Manufacturing cellulose fibers—are classified in U.S. Industry 325221, Cellulosic Organic Fiber Manufacturing; and
- Manufacturing textile glass fibers—are classified in U.S. Industry 327212, Other Pressed and Blown Glass and Glassware Manufacturing.

3253 Pesticide, Fertilizer, and Other Agricultural Chemical Manufacturing

32531 Fertilizer Manufacturing

This industry comprises establishments primarily engaged in one or more of the following: (1) manufacturing nitrogenous or phosphatic fertilizer materials; (2) manufacturing fertilizers from sewage or animal waste; (3) manufacturing nitrogenous or phosphatic materials and mixing with other ingredients into fertilizers; and (4) mixing ingredients made elsewhere into fertilizers.

US—United States industry only. CAN—United States and Canadian industries are comparable. MEX—United States and Mexican industries are comparable. Blank—Canadian, Mexican, and United States industries are comparable.

325311 Nitrogenous Fertilizer Manufacturing[US]

This U.S. industry comprises establishments primarily engaged in one or more of the following: (1) manufacturing nitrogenous fertilizer materials and mixing ingredients into fertilizers; (2) manufacturing fertilizers from sewage or animal waste; and (3) manufacturing nitrogenous materials and mixing them into fertilizers.

Cross-References.

Establishments primarily engaged in mixing ingredients made elsewhere into nitrogenous fertilizers are classified in U.S. Industry 325314, Fertilizer (Mixing Only) Manufacturing.

325312 Phosphatic Fertilizer Manufacturing[US]

This U.S. industry comprises establishments primarily engaged in (1) manufacturing phosphatic fertilizer materials or (2) manufacturing phosphatic materials and mixing them into fertilizers.

Cross-References.

Establishments primarily engaged in mixing ingredients made elsewhere into phosphatic fertilizers are classified in U.S. Industry 325314, Fertilizer (Mixing Only) Manufacturing.

325314 Fertilizer (Mixing Only) Manufacturing[CAN]

This U.S. industry comprises establishments primarily engaged in mixing ingredients made elsewhere into fertilizers.

Cross-References. Establishments primarily engaged in—

- Manufacturing nitrogenous fertilizer materials or fertilizer materials from sewage or animal waste and mixing these ingredients into nitrogenous fertilizers—are classified in U.S. Industry 325311, Nitrogenous Fertilizer Manufacturing; and
- Manufacturing phosphatic fertilizer materials and mixing ingredients into fertilizers—are classified in U.S. Industry 325312, Phosphatic Fertilizer Manufacturing.

32532 Pesticide and Other Agricultural Chemical Manufacturing

See industry description for 325320 below.

US—United States industry only. CAN—United States and Canadian industries are comparable. MEX—United States and Mexican industries are comparable. Blank—Canadian, Mexican, and United States industries are comparable.

325320 Pesticide and Other Agricultural Chemical Manufacturing

This industry comprises establishments primarily engaged in the formulation and preparation of agricultural and household pest control chemicals (except fertilizers).

Cross-References. Establishments primarily engaged in—

- Manufacturing basic chemicals requiring further processing before use as agriculture chemicals—are classified in Industry Group 3251, Basic Chemical Manufacturing;
- Manufacturing fertilizers—are classified in Industry 325310, Fertilizer Manufacturing; and
- Manufacturing agricultural lime products—are classified in Industry 327410, Lime Manufacturing.

3254 Pharmaceutical and Medicine Manufacturing

32541 Pharmaceutical and Medicine Manufacturing

This industry comprises establishments primarily engaged in one or more of the following: (1) manufacturing biological and medicinal products; (2) processing (i.e., grading, grinding, and milling) botanical drugs and herbs; (3) isolating active medicinal principals from botanical drugs and herbs; and (4) manufacturing pharmaceutical products intended for internal and external consumption in such forms as ampoules, tablets, capsules, vials, ointments, powders, solutions, and suspensions.

325411 Medicinal and Botanical Manufacturing[US]

This U.S. industry comprises establishments primarily engaged in (1) manufacturing uncompounded medicinal chemicals and their derivatives (i.e., generally for use by pharmaceutical preparation manufacturers) and/or (2) grading, grinding, and milling uncompounded botanicals.

Cross-References. Establishments primarily engaged in—

- Manufacturing packaged compounded medicinals and botanicals—are classified in U.S. Industry 325412, Pharmaceutical Preparation Manufacturing; and
- Manufacturing vaccines, toxoids, blood fractions, and culture media of plant or animal origin (except for diagnostic use)—are classified in U.S. Industry 325414, Biological Product (except Diagnostic) Manufacturing.

US—United States industry only. CAN—United States and Canadian industries are comparable. MEX—United States and Mexican industries are comparable. Blank—Canadian, Mexican, and United States industries are comparable.

325412 Pharmaceutical Preparation Manufacturing[US]

This U.S. industry comprises establishments primarily engaged in manufacturing in-vivo diagnostic substances and pharmaceutical preparations (except biological) intended for internal and external consumption in dose forms, such as ampoules, tablets, capsules, vials, ointments, powders, solutions, and suspensions.

Cross-References. Establishments primarily engaged in—

- Manufacturing uncompounded medicinal chemicals and their derivatives—are classified in U.S. Industry 325411, Medicinal and Botanical Manufacturing;
- Manufacturing in-vitro diagnostic substances—are classified in U.S. Industry 325413; In-Vitro Diagnostic Substance Manufacturing; and
- Manufacturing vaccines, toxoids, blood fractions, and culture media of plant or animal origin (except for diagnostic use)—are classified in U.S. Industry 325414, Biological Product (except Diagnostic) Manufacturing.

325413 In-Vitro Diagnostic Substance Manufacturing[US]

This U.S. industry comprises establishments primarily engaged in manufacturing in-vitro (i.e., not taken internally) diagnostic substances, such as chemical, biological, or radioactive substances. The substances are used for diagnostic tests that are performed in test tubes, petri dishes, machines, and other diagnostic test-type devices.

Cross-References.

Establishments primarily engaged in manufacturing in-vivo diagnostic substances are classified in U.S. Industry 325412, Pharmaceutical Preparation Manufacturing.

325414 Biological Product (except Diagnostic) Manufacturing[US]

This U.S. industry comprises establishments primarily engaged in manufacturing vaccines, toxoids, blood fractions, and culture media of plant or animal origin (except diagnostic).

Cross-References. Establishments primarily engaged in—

- Manufacturing in-vitro diagnostic substances—are classified in U.S. Industry 325413, In-Vitro Diagnostic Substance Manufacturing; and

US—United States industry only. CAN—United States and Canadian industries are comparable. MEX—United States and Mexican industries are comparable. Blank—Canadian, Mexican, and United States industries are comparable.

- Manufacturing pharmaceutical preparations, (except biological and in-vivo diagnostic substances)—are classified in U.S. Industry 325412, Pharmaceutical Preparation Manufacturing.

3255 Paint, Coating, and Adhesive Manufacturing

32551 Paint and Coating Manufacturing

See industry description for 325510 below.

325510 Paint and Coating Manufacturing

This industry comprises establishments primarily engaged in (1) mixing pigments, solvents, and binders into paints and other coatings, such as stains, varnishes, lacquers, enamels, shellacs, and water repellant coatings for concrete and masonry, and/or (2) manufacturing allied paint products, such as putties, paint and varnish removers, paint brush cleaners, and frit.

Cross-References. Establishments primarily engaged in—

- Manufacturing creosote—are classified in Industry 32519, Other Basic Organic Chemical Manufacturing;
- Manufacturing caulking compounds and sealants—are classified in Industry 325520, Adhesive Manufacturing;
- Manufacturing artists' paints—are classified in U.S. Industry 339942, Lead Pencil and Art Good Manufacturing; and
- Manufacturing turpentine—are classified in U.S. Industry 325191, Gum and Wood Chemical Manufacturing.

32552 Adhesive Manufacturing

See industry description for 325520 below.

325520 Adhesive Manufacturing

This industry comprises establishments primarily engaged in manufacturing adhesives, glues, and caulking compounds.

Cross-References. Establishments primarily engaged in—

- Manufacturing asphalt and tar roofing cements from purchased asphaltic materials—are classified in Industry 324122, Asphalt Shingle and Coating Materials Manufacturing; and

---

US—United States industry only. CAN—United States and Canadian industries are comparable. MEX—United States and Mexican industries are comparable. Blank—Canadian, Mexican, and United States industries are comparable.

- Manufacturing gypsum based caulking compounds—are classified in Industry 327420, Gypsum Product Manufacturing.

3256 Soap, Cleaning Compound, and Toilet Preparation Manufacturing

32561 Soap and Cleaning Compound Manufacturing

This industry comprises establishments primarily engaged in manufacturing and packaging soap and other cleaning compounds, surface active agents, and textile and leather finishing agents used to reduce tension or speed the drying process.

Cross-References. Establishments primarily engaged in—

- Manufacturing synthetic glycerin—are classified in Industry 32519, Other Basic Organic Chemical Manufacturing;
- Manufacturing industrial bleaches—are classified in Industry 32518 Other Basic Inorganic Chemical Manufacturing; and
- Manufacturing shampoos and shaving preparations—are classified in Industry 32562, Toilet Preparation Manufacturing.

325611 Soap and Other Detergent Manufacturing^US

This U.S. industry comprises establishments primarily engaged in manufacturing and packaging soaps and other detergents, such as laundry detergents; dishwashing detergents; toothpaste gels, and tooth powders; and natural glycerin.

Cross-References. Establishments primarily engaged in—

- Manufacturing synthetic glycerin—are classified in U.S. Industry 325199, All Other Basic Organic Chemical Manufacturing; and
- Manufacturing shampoos and shaving preparations—are classified in Industry 325620, Toilet Preparation Manufacturing.

325612 Polish and Other Sanitation Good Manufacturing^US

This U.S. industry comprises establishments primarily engaged in manufacturing and packaging polishes and specialty cleaning preparations.

Cross-References.

Establishments primarily engaged in manufacturing chlorine dioxide (i.e., industrial bleaching agent) are classified in U.S. Industry 325188, All Other Basic Inorganic Chemical Manufacturing.

US—United States industry only. CAN—United States and Canadian industries are comparable. MEX—United States and Mexican industries are comparable. Blank—Canadian, Mexican, and United States industries are comparable.

325613 Surface Active Agent Manufacturing[US]

This U.S. industry comprises establishments primarily engaged in (1) manufacturing bulk surface active agents for use as wetting agents, emulsifiers, and penetrants, and/or (2) manufacturing textiles and leather finishing agents used to reduce tension or speed the drying process.

32562 Toilet Preparation Manufacturing

See industry description for 325620 below.

325620 Toilet Preparation Manufacturing

This industry comprises establishments primarily engaged in preparing, blending, compounding, and packaging toilet preparations, such as perfumes, shaving preparations, hair preparations, face creams, lotions (including sunscreens), and other cosmetic preparations.

Cross-References.

Establishments primarily engaged in manufacturing toothpaste are classified in U.S. Industry 325611, Soap and Other Detergent Manufacturing.

3259 Other Chemical Product and Preparation Manufacturing

This industry group comprises establishments primarily engaged in manufacturing chemical products (except basic chemicals; resins, synthetic rubber, cellulosic and noncellulosic fibers and filaments; pesticides, fertilizers, and other agricultural chemicals; pharmaceuticals and medicines; paints, coatings, and adhesives; soaps and cleaning compounds; and toilet preparations).

32591 Printing Ink Manufacturing

See industry description for 325910 below.

325910 Printing Ink Manufacturing

This industry comprises establishments primarily engaged in manufacturing printing and inkjet inks and inkjet cartridges.

Cross-References. Establishments primarily engaged in—

- Recycling inkjet cartridges—are classified in U.S. Industry 811212, Computer and Office Machine Repair and Maintenance;

US—United States industry only. CAN—United States and Canadian industries are comparable. MEX—United States and Mexican industries are comparable. Blank—Canadian, Mexican, and United States industries are comparable.

- Manufacturing writing, drawing, and stamping ink—are classified in U.S. Industry 325998, All Other Miscellaneous Chemical Product and Preparation Manufacturing; and
- Manufacturing toners and toner cartridges for photocopiers, fax machines, computer printers and similar office machines—are classified in U.S. Industry 325992, Photographic Film, Paper, Plate, and Chemical Manufacturing.

32592 Explosives Manufacturing

See industry description for 325920 below.

325920 Explosives Manufacturing

This industry comprises establishments primarily engaged in manufacturing explosives.

Cross-References. Establishments primarily engaged in—

- Manufacturing ammunition, ammunition detonators, and percussion caps—are classified in U.S. Industry 332992, Small Arms Ammunition Manufacturing; and
- Manufacturing pyrotechnics—are classified in U.S. Industry 325998, All Other Miscellaneous Chemical Product and Preparation Manufacturing.

32599 All Other Chemical Product and Preparation Manufacturing

This industry comprises establishments primarily engaged in manufacturing chemical products (except basic chemicals, resins, and synthetic rubber; cellulosic and noncellulosic fibers and filaments; pesticides, fertilizers, and other agricultural chemicals; pharmaceuticals and medicines; paints, coatings, and adhesives; and soaps, cleaning compounds, and toilet preparations; printing inks; and explosives).

Illustrative Examples:

Activated carbon and charcoal manufacturing
Antifreeze preparations manufacturing
Custom compounding (i.e., blending and mixing) of purchased plastics resins
Industrial salt manufacturing
Sugar substitutes (i.e., synthetic sweeteners blended with other ingredients) made from purchased synthetic sweeteners
Swimming pool chemical preparations manufacturing

US—United States industry only. CAN—United States and Canadian industries are comparable. MEX—United States and Mexican industries are comparable. Blank—Canadian, Mexican, and United States industries are comparable.

Matches and matchbook manufacturing
Photographic chemicals manufacturing
Pyrotechnics (e.g., flares, flashlight bombs, signals) manufacturing
Writing inks and fluids manufacturing

Cross-References. Establishments primarily engaged in—

- Manufacturing basic chemicals—are classified in Industry Group 3251, Basic Chemical Manufacturing;
- Manufacturing resins, synthetic rubber, and artificial synthetic fibers and filaments—are classified in Industry Group 3252, Resin, Synthetic Rubber, and Artificial Synthetic Fibers and Filaments Manufacturing;
- Manufacturing pesticides, fertilizers, and other agricultural chemicals—are classified in Industry Group 3253, Pesticide, Fertilizer, and Other Agriculture Chemical Manufacturing;
- Manufacturing pharmaceuticals and medicine including medicinal vegetable gelatin (i.e., agar-agar)—are classified in Industry Group 3254, Pharmaceutical and Medicine Manufacturing;
- Manufacturing paints, coatings, and adhesives—are classified in Industry Group 3255, Paint, Coating, and Adhesive Manufacturing;
- Manufacturing soaps and cleaning compounds—are classified in Industry Group 3256, Soap, Cleaning Compound, and Toilet Preparation Manufacturing;
- Manufacturing printing and inkjet inks—are classified in Industry 32591, Printing Ink Manufacturing;
- Manufacturing explosives—are classified in Industry 32592, Explosives Manufacturing;
- Manufacturing photographic paper stock (i.e., unsensitized) and paper mats, mounts, easels, and folders for photographic use—are classified in Subsector 322, Paper Manufacturing;
- Manufacturing dessert gelatins—are classified in Industry 31199, All Other Miscellaneous Food Manufacturing; and
- Manufacturing medicinal gelatins—are classified in Industry 32541, Pharmaceutical and Medicine Manufacturing.

325991 Custom Compounding of Purchased Resins[CAN]

This industry comprises establishments primarily engaged in (1) custom mixing and blending plastics resins made elsewhere or (2) reformulating plastics resins from recycled plastics products.

US—United States industry only. CAN—United States and Canadian industries are comparable. MEX—United States and Mexican industries are comparable. Blank—Canadian, Mexican, and United States industries are comparable.

Cross-References.

Establishments primarily engaged in manufacturing synthetic resins and custom mixing and blending resins are classified in U.S. Industry 325211, Plastics Material and Resin Manufacturing.

325992 Photographic Film, Paper, Plate, and Chemical Manufacturing[MEX]

This U.S. industry comprises establishments primarily engaged in manufacturing sensitized film, sensitized paper, sensitized cloth, sensitized plates, toners (i.e., for photocopiers, laser printers, and similar electrostatic printing devices), toner cartridges, and photographic chemicals.

Cross-References.

Establishments primarily engaged in manufacturing photographic paper stock (i.e., unsensitized) and paper mats, mounts, easels, and folders for photographic use—are classified in Subsector 322, Paper Manufacturing.

325998 All Other Miscellaneous Chemical Product and Preparation Manufacturing[US]

This U.S. industry comprises establishments primarily engaged in manufacturing chemical products (except basic chemicals, resins, synthetic rubber; cellulosic and noncellulosic fiber and filaments; pesticides, fertilizers, and other agricultural chemicals; pharmaceuticals and medicines; paints, coatings and adhesives; soap, cleaning compounds, and toilet preparations; printing inks; explosives; custom compounding of purchased resins; and photographic films, papers, plates, and chemicals).

Illustrative Examples:

Activated carbon and charcoal manufacturing
Antifreeze preparations manufacturing
Industrial salt manufacturing
Lighter fluids (e.g., charcoal, cigarette) manufacturing
Matches and matchbook manufacturing
Pyrotechnics (e.g., flares, flashlight bombs, signals) manufacturing
Sugar substitutes (i.e., synthetic sweeteners blended with other ingredients) made from purchased synthetic sweeteners manufacturing
Swimming pool chemical preparations manufacturing
Writing inks manufacturing

US—United States industry only. CAN—United States and Canadian industries are comparable. MEX—United States and Mexican industries are comparable. Blank—Canadian, Mexican, and United States industries are comparable.

Cross-References. Establishments primarily engaged in—

- Manufacturing basic chemicals—are classified in Industry Group 3251, Basic Chemical Manufacturing;
- Manufacturing resins, synthetic rubber, and artificial synthetic fibers and filaments—are classified in Industry Group 3252, Resin, Synthetic Rubber, and Artificial Synthetic Fibers and Filaments Manufacturing;
- Manufacturing pesticides, fertilizers, and other agricultural chemicals—are classified in Industry Group 3253, Pesticide, Fertilizer, and Other Agriculture Chemical Manufacturing;
- Manufacturing pharmaceuticals and medicines including medicinal vegetable gelatin (i.e., agar-agar)—are classified in Industry Group 3254, Pharmaceutical and Medicine Manufacturing;
- Manufacturing paints, coatings, and adhesives—are classified in Industry Group 3255, Paint, Coating, and Adhesive Manufacturing;
- Manufacturing soaps and cleaning compounds—are classified in Industry Group 3256, Soap, Cleaning Compound, and Toilet Preparation Manufacturing;
- Manufacturing printing and inkjet inks—are classified in Industry 325910, Printing Ink Manufacturing;
- Manufacturing explosives—are classified in Industry 325920, Explosives Manufacturing;
- Custom compounding purchased plastics resins—are classified in U.S. Industry 325991, Custom Compounding of Purchased Resins;
- Manufacturing photographic films, papers, plates, and chemicals—are classified in U.S. Industry 325992, Photographic Film, Paper, Plate, and Chemical Manufacturing; and
- Manufacturing dessert gelatin—are classified in U.S. Industry 311999, All Other Miscellaneous Food Manufacturing.

326 Plastics and Rubber Products Manufacturing

Industries in the Plastics and Rubber Products Manufacturing subsector make goods by processing plastics materials and raw rubber. The core technology employed by establishments in this subsector is that of plastics or rubber product production. Plastics and rubber are combined in the same subsector because plastics are increasingly being used as a substitute for rubber; however the subsector is generally restricted to the production of products made of just one material, either solely plastics or rubber.

US—United States industry only. CAN—United States and Canadian industries are comparable. MEX—United States and Mexican industries are comparable. Blank—Canadian, Mexican, and United States industries are comparable.

Many manufacturing activities use plastics or rubber, for example the manufacture of footwear, or furniture. Typically, the production process of these products involves more than one material. In these cases, technologies that allow disparate materials to be formed and combined are of central importance in describing the manufacturing activity. In NAICS, such activities (the footwear and furniture manufacturing) are not classified in the Plastics and Rubber Products Manufacturing subsector because the core technologies for these activities are diverse and involve multiple materials.

Within the Plastics and Rubber Products Manufacturing subsector, a distinction is made between plastics and rubber products at the industry group level, although it is not a rigid distinction, as can be seen from the definition of Industry 32622, Rubber and Plastics Hoses and Belting Manufacturing. As materials technology progresses, plastics are increasingly being used as a substitute for rubber; and eventually, the distinction may disappear as a basis for establishment classification.

In keeping with the core technology focus of plastics, lamination of plastics film to plastics film as well as the production of bags from plastics only is classified in this subsector. Lamination and bag production involving plastics and materials other than plastics are classified in the NAICS Subsector 322, Paper Manufacturing.

3261 Plastics Product Manufacturing

This industry group comprises establishments primarily engaged in processing new or spent (i.e., recycled) plastics resins into intermediate or final products, using such processes as compression molding; extrusion molding; injection molding; blow molding; and casting. Within most of these industries, the production process is such that a wide variety of products can be made.

32611 Plastics Packaging Materials and Unlaminated Film and Sheet Manufacturing

This industry comprises establishments primarily engaged in (1) converting plastics resins into unsupported plastics film and sheet and/or (2) forming, coating or laminating plastics film and sheet into plastics bags.

Cross-References. Establishments primarily engaged in—

- Laminating plastics sheet (except for packaging)—are classified in Industry 32613, Laminated Plastics Plate, Sheet (except Packaging), and Shape Manufacturing;

US—United States industry only. CAN—United States and Canadian industries are comparable. MEX—United States and Mexican industries are comparable. Blank—Canadian, Mexican, and United States industries are comparable.

- Manufacturing plastics blister and bubble packaging—are classified in Industry 32619, Other Plastics Product Manufacturing; and
- Coating or laminating combinations of plastics, foils and paper (except plastics film to plastics film) into film, sheet or bags—are classified in Industry 32222, Paper Bag and Coated and Treated Paper Manufacturing.

326111 Plastics Bag Manufacturing[CAN]

This U.S. industry comprises establishments primarily engaged in (1) converting plastics resins into plastics bags or (2) forming, coating or laminating plastics film and sheet into single wall or multiwall plastics bags. Establishments in this industry may print on the bags they manufacture.

Cross-References. Establishments primarily engaged in—

- Manufacturing laminated or coated combinations of plastics, foils and paper (except plastics film to plastics film) materials into single wall bags—are classified in U.S. Industry 322223, Plastics, Foil, and Coated Paper Bag Manufacturing; and
- Manufacturing laminated or coated combinations of plastics, foils and paper (except plastics film to plastics film) into multiwalled bags—are classified in U.S. Industry 322224, Uncoated Paper and Multiwall Bag Manufacturing.

326112 Plastics Packaging Film and Sheet (including Laminated) Manufacturing[US]

This U.S. industry comprises establishments primarily engaged in converting plastics resins into plastics packaging (flexible) film and packaging sheet.

Cross-References. Establishments primarily engaged in—

- Converting plastics resins into plastics film and unlaminated sheet (except packaging)—are classified in U.S. Industry 326113, Unlaminated Plastics Film and Sheet (except Packaging) Manufacturing;
- Laminating or coating packaging combinations of plastics, foils and paper (except plastics film to plastics film) film and sheet—are classified in U.S. Industry 322221, Coated and Laminated Packaging Paper and Plastics Film Manufacturing;
- Laminating or coating combinations of plastics, foils, and paper (except plastics film to plastics film) nonpackaging film and sheet—are classified in U.S. Industry 322222, Coated and Laminated Paper Manufacturing;

US—United States industry only. CAN—United States and Canadian industries are comparable. MEX—United States and Mexican industries are comparable. Blank—Canadian, Mexican, and United States industries are comparable.

- Laminating plastics sheet (except for packaging)—are classified in Industry 326130, Laminated Plastics Plate, Sheet (except Packaging), and Shape Manufacturing; and
- Manufacturing plastics bags—are classified in U.S. Industry 326111, Plastics Bag Manufacturing.

326113 Unlaminated Plastics Film and Sheet (except Packaging) Manufacturing[US]

This U.S. industry comprises establishments primarily engaged in converting plastics resins into plastics film and unlaminated sheet (except packaging).

Cross-References. Establishments primarily engaged in—

- Converting plastics resins into plastics packaging film and unlaminated packaging sheet—are classified in U.S. Industry 326112, Plastics Packaging Film and Sheet (including Laminated) Manufacturing;
- Laminating plastics sheet (except for packaging)—are classified in Industry 326130, Laminated Plastics Plate, Sheet (except Packaging), and Shape Manufacturing;
- Laminating or coating a combination of plastics, foils, and paper (except plastics film to plastics film) nonpackaging film and sheet—are classified in U.S. Industry 322222, Coated and Laminated Paper Manufacturing; and
- Manufacturing plastics bags—are classified in U.S. Industry 326111, Plastics Bag Manufacturing.

32612 Plastics Pipe, Pipe Fitting, and Unlaminated Profile Shape Manufacturing

This industry comprises establishments primarily engaged in manufacturing plastics pipes and pipe fittings, and plastics profile shapes such as rod, tube, and sausage casings.

Cross-References. Establishments primarily engaged in—

- Manufacturing plastics hose—are classified in Industry 32622, Rubber and Plastics Hoses and Belting Manufacturing;
- Manufacturing noncurrent carrying plastics conduit—are classified in Industry 33593, Wiring Device Manufacturing;
- Manufacturing plastics plumbing fixtures—are classified in Industry 32619, Other Plastics Product Manufacturing; and

US—United States industry only. CAN—United States and Canadian industries are comparable. MEX—United States and Mexican industries are comparable. Blank—Canadian, Mexican, and United States industries are comparable.

- Manufacturing plastics film, plastics unlaminated sheet, and plastics bags—are classified in Industry 32611, Plastics Packaging Materials and Unlaminated Film and Sheet Manufacturing.

326121 Unlaminated Plastics Profile Shape Manufacturing[CAN]

This U.S. industry comprises establishments primarily engaged in converting plastics resins into nonrigid plastics profile shapes (except film, sheet and bags), such as rod, tube, and sausage casings.

Cross-References. Establishments primarily engaged in—

- Manufacturing plastics film, plastics unlaminated sheet, and plastics bags—are classified in Industry 32611, Plastics Packaging Materials and Unlaminated Film and Sheet Manufacturing; and
- Manufacturing plastics hoses—are classified in Industry 326220, Rubber and Plastics Hoses and Belting Manufacturing.

326122 Plastics Pipe and Pipe Fitting Manufacturing[CAN]

This U.S. industry comprises establishments primarily engaged in converting plastics resins into rigid plastics pipes and pipe fittings.

Cross-References. Establishments primarily engaged in—

- Manufacturing plastics hose—are classified in Industry 326220, Rubber and Plastics Hoses and Belting Manufacturing;
- Manufacturing noncurrent-carrying plastics conduit—are classified in U.S. Industry 335932, Noncurrent-Carrying Wiring Device Manufacturing; and
- Manufacturing plastics plumbing fixtures—are classified in U.S. Industry 326191, Plastics Plumbing Fixture Manufacturing.

32613 Laminated Plastics Plate, Sheet (except Packaging), and Shape Manufacturing

See industry description for 326130 below.

326130 Laminated Plastics Plate, Sheet (except Packaging), and Shape Manufacturing

This industry comprises establishments primarily engaged in laminating plastics profile shapes such as plate, sheet (except packaging), and rod. The lamination

---

US—United States industry only. CAN—United States and Canadian industries are comparable. MEX—United States and Mexican industries are comparable. Blank—Canadian, Mexican, and United States industries are comparable.

process generally involves bonding or impregnating profiles with plastics resins and compressing them under heat.

Cross-References. Establishments primarily engaged in—

- Manufacturing plastics film, plastics unlaminated sheet, and plastics bags—are classified in Industry 32611, Plastics Packaging Materials and Unlaminated Film and Sheet Manufacturing;
- Coating or laminating nonplastics film, sheet, or bags with plastics—are classified in Industry 32222, Paper Bag and Coated and Treated Paper Manufacturing; and
- Manufacturing plastics bags—are classified in U.S. Industry 326111, Plastics Bag Manufacturing.

32614 Polystyrene Foam Product Manufacturing

See industry description for 326140 below.

326140 Polystyrene Foam Product Manufacturing

This industry comprises establishments primarily engaged in manufacturing polystyrene foam products.

Cross-References.

Establishments primarily engaged in manufacturing plastics foam products (except polystyrene) are classified in Industry 326150, Urethane and Other Foam Product (except Polystyrene) Manufacturing.

32615 Urethane and Other Foam Product (except Polystyrene) Manufacturing

See industry description for 326150 below.

326150 Urethane and Other Foam Product (except Polystyrene) Manufacturing

This industry comprises establishments primarily engaged in manufacturing plastics foam products (except polystyrene).

Cross-References.

Establishments primarily engaged in manufacturing polystyrene foam products are classified in Industry 326140, Polystyrene Foam Product Manufacturing.

US—United States industry only. CAN—United States and Canadian industries are comparable. MEX—United States and Mexican industries are comparable. Blank—Canadian, Mexican, and United States industries are comparable.

32616 Plastics Bottle Manufacturing

See industry description for 32616 below.

326160 Plastics Bottle Manufacturing

This industry comprises establishments primarily engaged in manufacturing plastics bottles.

Cross-References.

Establishments primarily engaged in manufacturing plastics containers (except bottles) are classified in U.S. Industry 326199, All Other Plastics Product Manufacturing.

32619 Other Plastics Product Manufacturing

This industry comprises establishments primarily engaged in manufacturing resilient floor covering and other plastics products (except film, sheet, bags, profile shapes, pipes, pipe fittings, laminates, foam products, and bottles).

Illustrative Examples:

Inflatable plastics boats manufacturing
Plastics bowls and bowl covers manufacturing
Plastics cups (except foam) manufacturing
Plastics dinnerware (except foam) manufacturing
Plastics gloves manufacturing
Plastics hardware manufacturing
Plastics or fiberglass plumbing fixtures (e.g., toilets, shower stalls, urinals) manufacturing
Plastics siding manufacturing
Plastics trash containers manufacturing
Resilient floor coverings (e.g., sheet, tiles) manufacturing

Cross-References. Establishments primarily engaged in—

- Manufacturing plastics film, plastics unlaminated sheet, and plastics bags—are classified in Industry 32611, Plastics Packaging Materials and Unlaminated Film and Sheet Manufacturing;
- Manufacturing plastics pipes, pipe fittings and plastics profile shapes (except films, sheet, bags)—are classified in Industry 32612, Plastics Pipe, Pipe Fitting, and Unlaminated Profile Shape Manufacturing;
- Laminating plastics profile shapes, such as plate, sheet and rod,—are classified in Industry 32613, Laminated Plastics Plate, Sheet (except packaging) and Shape Manufacturing;
- Manufacturing polystyrene foam products—are classified in Industry 32614, Polystyrene Foam Product Manufacturing;

US—United States industry only. CAN—United States and Canadian industries are comparable. MEX—United States and Mexican industries are comparable. Blank—Canadian, Mexican, and United States industries are comparable.

- Manufacturing foam products (except polystyrene)—are classified in Industry 32615 Urethane and Other Foam Product (except Polystyrene) Manufacturing;
- Manufacturing plastics bottles—are classified in Industry 32616, Plastics Bottle Manufacturing;
- Manufacturing plastics furniture parts—are classified in Industry 33721, Office Furniture (including Fixtures) Manufacturing;
- Assembling plastics components into plumbing fixture fittings, such as faucets,—are classified in Industry 33291, Metal Valve Manufacturing; and
- Manufacturing rubber floor mats and rubber treads—are classified in Industry 32629, Other Rubber Product Manufacturing.

326191 Plastics Plumbing Fixture Manufacturing[CAN]

This U.S. industry comprises establishments primarily engaged in manufacturing plastics or fiberglass plumbing fixtures. Examples of products made by these establishments are plastics or fiberglass bathtubs, hot tubs, portable toilets, and shower stalls.

Cross-References. Establishments primarily engaged in—

- Assembling plastics components into plumbing fixture fittings, such as faucets,—are classified in U.S. Industry 332913, Plumbing Fixture Fitting and Trim Manufacturing; and
- Manufacturing plastics pipe and pipe fittings—are classified in U.S. Industry 326122, Plastics Pipe and Pipe Fitting Manufacturing.

326192 Resilient Floor Covering Manufacturing[US]

This U.S. industry comprises establishments primarily engaged in manufacturing resilient floor coverings for permanent installation.

Cross-References.

Establishments primarily engaged in manufacturing rubber floor mats and rubber treads are classified in U.S. Industry 326299, All Other Rubber Product Manufacturing.

326199 All Other Plastics Product Manufacturing[US]

This U.S. industry comprises establishments primarily engaged in manufacturing plastics products (except film, sheet, bags, profile shapes, pipes, pipe fittings, laminates, foam products, bottles, plumbing fixtures, and resilient floor coverings).

US—United States industry only. CAN—United States and Canadian industries are comparable. MEX—United States and Mexican industries are comparable. Blank—Canadian, Mexican, and United States industries are comparable.

Illustrative Examples:

Inflatable plastics boats manufacturing
Plastics air mattresses manufacturing
Plastics bowls and bowl covers manufacturing
Plastics clothes hangers manufacturing
Plastics cups (except foam) manufacturing
Plastics dinnerware (except foam) manufacturing
Plastics gloves manufacturing
Plastics hardware manufacturing
Plastics siding manufacturing
Plastics trash containers manufacturing

Cross-References. Establishments primarily engaged in—

- Manufacturing plastics film, plastics unlaminated sheet, and plastics bags—are classified in Industry 32611, Plastics Packaging Materials and Unlaminated Film and Sheet Manufacturing;
- Manufacturing plastics pipes, pipe fittings, and plastics profile shapes (except film, sheet, bags)—are classified in Industry 32612, Plastics Pipe, Pipe Fitting, and Unlaminated Profile Shape Manufacturing;
- Manufacturing plastic pipes and pipe fittings—are classified in U.S. Industry 326122, Plastics Pipe and Pipe Fitting Manufacturing;
- Laminating plastics profile shapes, such as plate, sheet, and rod,—are classified in Industry 326130, Laminated Plastics Plate, Sheet (except Packaging), and Shapes Manufacturing;
- Manufacturing polystyrene foam products—are classified in Industry 326140, Polystyrene Foam Product Manufacturing;
- Manufacturing foam (except polystyrene) products—are classified in Industry 326150, Urethane and Other Foam Product (except Polystyrene) Manufacturing;
- Manufacturing plastics bottles—are classified in Industry 326160, Plastics Bottle Manufacturing;
- Manufacturing plastics furniture parts and components—are classified in U.S. Industry 337215, Showcase, Partition, Shelving, and Locker Manufacturing;
- Manufacturing plastics plumbing fixtures—are classified in U.S. Industry 326191, Plastics Plumbing Fixture Manufacturing;
- Manufacturing resilient floor coverings—are classified in U.S. Industry 326192, Resilient Floor Covering Manufacturing; and
- Assembling plastics components into plumbing fixtures fittings such as faucets—are classified in U.S. Industry 332913, Plumbing Fixture Fitting and Trim Manufacturing.

US—United States industry only. CAN—United States and Canadian industries are comparable. MEX—United States and Mexican industries are comparable. Blank—Canadian, Mexican, and United States industries are comparable.

3262 Rubber Product Manufacturing

This industry group comprises establishments primarily engaged in processing natural, and synthetic or reclaimed rubber materials into intermediate or final products using processes such as vulcanizing, cementing, molding, extruding, and lathe-cutting.

32621 Tire Manufacturing

This industry comprises establishments primarily engaged in manufacturing tires and inner tubes from natural and synthetic rubber and retreading or rebuilding tires.

Cross-References. Establishments primarily engaged in—

- Repairing tires, such as plugging,—are classified in Industry 81119, Other Automotive Repair and Maintenance; and
- Retailing tires—are classified in the Industry 44132, Tire Dealers.

326211 Tire Manufacturing (except Retreading)[MEX]

This U.S. industry comprises establishments primarily engaged in manufacturing tires and inner tubes from natural and synthetic rubber.

Cross-References.

Establishments primarily engaged in retreading or rebuilding tires are classified in U.S. Industry 326212, Tire Retreading.

326212 Tire Retreading[MEX]

This U.S. industry comprises establishments primarily engaged in retreading, or rebuilding tires.

Cross-References. Establishments primarily engaged in—

- Repairing tires, such as pluggings—are classified in U.S. Industry 811198, All Other Automotive Repair and Maintenance;
- Retailing tires—are classified in Industry 441320, Tire Dealers; and
- Manufacturing tires and inner tubes from natural and synthetic rubber—are classified in U.S. Industry 326211, Tire Manufacturing (except Retreading).

US—United States industry only. CAN—United States and Canadian industries are comparable. MEX—United States and Mexican industries are comparable. Blank—Canadian, Mexican, and United States industries are comparable.

32622 Rubber and Plastics Hoses and Belting Manufacturing

See industry description for 326220 below.

326220 Rubber and Plastics Hoses and Belting Manufacturing

This industry comprises establishments primarily engaged in manufacturing rubber hose and/or plastics (reinforced) hose and belting from natural and synthetic rubber and/or plastics resins. Establishments manufacturing garden hoses from purchased hose are included in this industry.

Cross-References. Establishments primarily engaged in—

- Manufacturing rubber tubing—are classified in U.S. Industry 326299, All Other Rubber Product Manufacturing;
- Manufacturing plastics tubing—are classified in U.S. Industry 326121, Unlaminated Plastics Profile Shape Manufacturing; and
- Manufacturing fluid power hose assemblies—are classified in U.S. Industry 332912, Fluid Power Valve and Hose Fitting Manufacturing.

32629 Other Rubber Product Manufacturing

This industry comprises establishments primarily engaged in manufacturing rubber products (except tires, hoses, and belting) from natural and synthetic rubber.

Illustrative Examples:

Birth control devices (e.g., diaphragms, prophylactics) manufacturing
Latex foam rubber manufacturing
Mechanical rubber goods (i.e., molded, extruded, lathe-cut) manufacturing
Reclaiming rubber from waste and scrap
Rubber balloons manufacturing
Rubberbands manufacturing
Rubber floor mats (e.g., door, bath) manufacturing
Rubber hair care products (e.g., combs, curlers) manufacturing
Rubber tubing (except extruded, lathe-cut, molded) manufacturing

Cross-References. Establishments primarily engaged in—

- Manufacturing tires and inner tubes—are classified in Industry 32621, Tire Manufacturing;
- Manufacturing rubber hoses and belting—are classified in Industry 32622, Rubber and Plastics Hoses and Belting Manufacturing;
- Rubberizing fabric—are classified in Industry 31332, Fabric Coating Mills;
- Manufacturing rubber gaskets, packing and sealing devices—are classified in Industry 33999, All Other Miscellaneous Manufacturing;

US—United States industry only. CAN—United States and Canadian industries are comparable. MEX—United States and Mexican industries are comparable. Blank—Canadian, Mexican, and United States industries are comparable.

- Manufacturing rubber gloves—are classified in Industry 33911, Medical Equipment and Supplies Manufacturing;
- Manufacturing rubber clothing accessories (e.g., bathing caps)—are classified in Industry 31599, Apparel Accessories and Other Apparel Manufacturing; and
- Manufacturing rubber toys—are classified in Industry 33993, Doll, Toy, and Game Manufacturing.

326291 Rubber Product Manufacturing for Mechanical Use[US]

This U.S. industry comprises establishments primarily engaged in molding, extruding or lathe- cutting rubber to manufacture rubber goods (except tubing) for mechanical applications. Products of this industry are generally parts for motor vehicles, machinery, and equipment.

Cross-References.

Establishments primarily engaged in manufacturing rubber tubing from natural and synthetic rubber and manufacturing rubber products for mechanical applications using a process other than molding, extruding or lathe-cutting are classified in U.S. Industry 326299, All Other Rubber Product Manufacturing.

326299 All Other Rubber Product Manufacturing[US]

This U.S. industry comprises establishments primarily engaged in manufacturing rubber products (except tires; hoses and belting; and molded, extruded, and lathe-cut rubber goods for mechanical applications) from natural and synthetic rubber.

Illustrative Examples:

Birth control devices (i.e., diaphragms, prophylactics) manufacturing
Inflatable rubber life rafts manufacturing
Latex foam rubber manufacturing
Reclaiming rubber from waste and scrap
Rubber balloons manufacturing
Rubberbands manufacturing
Rubber floor mats (e.g., door, bath) manufacturing
Rubber hair care products (e.g., combs, curlers) manufacturing
Rubber tubing (except extruded, lathe-cut, molded) manufacturing

Cross-References. Establishments primarily engaged in—

- Manufacturing tires and inner tubes and tire rebuilding—are classified in Industry 32621, Tire Manufacturing;
- Manufacturing rubber hoses and belting—are classified in Industry 326220, Rubber and Plastics Hoses and Belting Manufacturing;

US—United States industry only. CAN—United States and Canadian industries are comparable. MEX—United States and Mexican industries are comparable. Blank—Canadian, Mexican, and United States industries are comparable.

- Molding, extruding, and lathe-cutting rubber to manufacture rubber goods (except tubing) for mechanical applications—are classified in Industry 326291, Rubber Product Manufacturing for Mechanical Use;
- Rubberizing fabrics—are classified in Industry 313320, Fabric Coating Mills;
- Manufacturing rubber gaskets, packing and sealing devices—are classified in U.S. Industry 339991, Gasket, Packing, and Sealing Device Manufacturing;
- Manufacturing rubber toys—are classified in Industry 33993, Doll, Toy, and Game Manufacturing;
- Manufacturing rubber gloves—are classified in U.S. Industry 339113, Surgical Appliance and Supplies Manufacturing; and
- Manufacturing rubber clothing accessories (e.g., bathing caps)—are classified in U.S. Industry 315999, Other Apparel Accessories and Other Apparel Manufacturing.

327 Nonmetallic Mineral Product Manufacturing

The Nonmetallic Mineral Product Manufacturing subsector transforms mined or quarried nonmetallic minerals, such as sand, gravel, stone, clay, and refractory materials, into products for intermediate or final consumption. Processes used include grinding, mixing, cutting, shaping, and honing. Heat often is used in the process and chemicals are frequently mixed to change the composition, purity, and chemical properties for the intended product. For example, glass is produced by heating silica sand to the melting point (sometimes combined with cullet or recycled glass) and then drawn, floated, or blow molded to the desired shape or thickness. Refractory materials are heated and then formed into bricks or other shapes for use in industrial applications.

The Nonmetallic Mineral Product Manufacturing subsector includes establishments that manufacture products, such as bricks, refractories, ceramic products, and glass and glass products, such as plate glass and containers. Also included are cement and concrete products, lime, gypsum and other nonmetallic mineral products including abrasive products, ceramic plumbing fixtures, statuary, cut stone products, and mineral wool. The products are used in a wide range of activities from construction and heavy and light manufacturing to articles for personal use.

Mining, beneficiating, and manufacturing activities often occur in a single location. Separate receipts will be collected for these activities whenever possible. When receipts cannot be broken out between mining and manufacturing, establishments that mine or quarry nonmetallic minerals, beneficiate the nonmetallic minerals and further process the nonmetallic minerals into a more finished manufactured product are classified based on the primary activity of the establishment. A mine that manufactures a small amount of finished products will be classified in Sector

US—United States industry only. CAN—United States and Canadian industries are comparable. MEX—United States and Mexican industries are comparable. Blank—Canadian, Mexican, and United States industries are comparable.

21, Mining. An establishment that mines whose primary output is a more-finished manufactured product will be classified in the Manufacturing Sector.

Excluded from the Nonmetallic Mineral Product Manufacturing subsector are establishments that primarily beneficiate mined nonmetallic minerals. Beneficiation is the process whereby the extracted material is reduced to particles that can be separated into mineral and waste, the former suitable for further processing or direct use. Beneficiation establishments are included in Sector 21, Mining.

3271 Clay Product and Refractory Manufacturing

32711 Pottery, Ceramics, and Plumbing Fixture Manufacturing

This industry comprises establishments primarily engaged in shaping, molding, glazing, and firing pottery, ceramics, and plumbing fixtures made entirely or partly of clay or other ceramic materials.

Cross-References. Establishments primarily engaged in—

- Manufacturing ferrite microwave devices and electronic components—are classified in Subsector 334, Computer and Electronic Product Manufacturing;
- Manufacturing enameled iron and steel plumbing fixtures—are classified in Industry 33299, All Other Fabricated Metal Product Manufacturing;
- Manufacturing metal bathroom accessories—are classified in Subsector 332, Fabricated Metal Product Manufacturing;
- Manufacturing plastic bathroom accessories, cultured marble, and other plastic plumbing fixtures—are classified in Industry 32619, Other Plastics Product Manufacturing; and
- Manufacturing clay building materials, such as ceramic tile, bricks, and clay roofing tiles, and refractories—are classified in Industry 32712, Clay Building Material and Refractories Manufacturing.

327111 Vitreous China Plumbing Fixture and China and Earthenware Bathroom Accessories Manufacturing[US]

This U.S. industry comprises establishments primarily engaged in manufacturing vitreous china plumbing fixtures and china and earthenware bathroom accessories, such as faucet handles, towel bars, and soap dishes.

Cross-References. Establishments primarily engaged in—

- Manufacturing enameled iron and steel plumbing fixtures—are classified in U.S. Industry 332998, Enameled Iron and Metal Sanitary Ware Manufacturing;

US—United States industry only. CAN—United States and Canadian industries are comparable. MEX—United States and Mexican industries are comparable. Blank—Canadian, Mexican, and United States industries are comparable.

- Manufacturing metal bathroom accessories—are classified in Subsector 332, Fabricated Metal Product Manufacturing;
- Manufacturing plastic bathroom accessories—are classified in U.S. Industry 326199, All Other Plastics Product Manufacturing;
- Manufacturing cultured marble and other plastic plumbing fixtures—are classified in U.S. Industry 326191, Plastics Plumbing Fixture Manufacturing; and
- Manufacturing china and earthenware products (except bathroom fixtures and accessories)— are classified in U.S. Industry 327112, Vitreous China, Fine Earthenware, and Other Pottery Product Manufacturing.

327112 Vitreous China, Fine Earthenware, and Other Pottery Product Manufacturing[US]

This U.S. industry comprises establishments primarily engaged in manufacturing table and kitchen articles, art and ornamental items, and similar vitreous china, fine earthenware, stoneware, coarse earthenware, and pottery products.

Illustrative Examples:

Chemical stoneware (i.e., pottery products) manufacturing
Clay and ceramic statuary manufacturing
Cooking ware (e.g., stoneware, coarse earthenware, pottery) manufacturing
Earthenware table and kitchen articles, coarse, manufacturing
Florists' articles, red earthenware, manufacturing
Vases, pottery (e.g., china, earthenware, stoneware), manufacturing

Cross-References. Establishments primarily engaged in—

- Manufacturing vitreous china plumbing fixtures—are classified in U.S. Industry 327111, Vitreous China Plumbing Fixture and China and Earthenware Bathroom Accessories Manufacturing;
- Manufacturing porcelain and ceramic electrical products, such as insulators,—are classified in U.S. Industry 327113, Porcelain Electrical Supply Manufacturing; and
- Manufacturing clay building materials, such as ceramic tile, bricks, and clay roofing tiles, and refractories,—are classified in Industry 32712, Clay Building Material and Refractories Manufacturing.

327113 Porcelain Electrical Supply Manufacturing[US]

This U.S. industry comprises establishments primarily engaged in manufacturing porcelain electrical insulators, molded porcelain parts for electrical devices, ferrite

US—United States industry only. CAN—United States and Canadian industries are comparable. MEX—United States and Mexican industries are comparable. Blank—Canadian, Mexican, and United States industries are comparable.

or ceramic magnets, and electronic and electrical supplies from nonmetallic minerals, such as clay and ceramic materials.

Cross-References.

Establishments primarily engaged in manufacturing ferrite microwave devices and electronic components are classified in Subsector 334, Computer and Electronic Product Manufacturing.

32712 Clay Building Material and Refractories Manufacturing

This industry comprises establishments primarily engaged in shaping, molding, baking, burning, or hardening clay refractories, nonclay refractories, ceramic tile, structural clay tile, brick, and other structural clay building materials.

Cross-References. Establishments primarily engaged in—

- Manufacturing glass blocks—are classified in Industry 32721, Glass and Glass Product Manufacturing;
- Manufacturing concrete brick and block—are classified in Industry 32733, Concrete Pipe, Brick, and Block Manufacturing; and
- Manufacturing resilient flooring—are classified in Industry 32619, Other Plastics Product Manufacturing.

327121 Brick and Structural Clay Tile Manufacturing[US]

This U.S. industry comprises establishments primarily engaged in manufacturing brick and structural clay tiles.

Cross-References. Establishments primarily engaged in—

- Manufacturing clay fire brick (i.e., refractories)—are classified in U.S. Industry 327124, Clay Refractory Manufacturing;
- Manufacturing nonclay fire brick (i.e., refractories)—are classified in U.S. Industry 327125, Nonclay Refractory Manufacturing;
- Manufacturing glass brick—are classified in Industry 32721, Glass and Glass Product Manufacturing;
- Manufacturing concrete bricks—are classified in U.S. Industry 327331, Concrete Block and Brick Manufacturing; and
- Manufacturing adobe bricks or clay roofing tiles—are classified in U.S. Industry 327123, Other Structural Clay Product Manufacturing.

US—United States industry only. CAN—United States and Canadian industries are comparable. MEX—United States and Mexican industries are comparable. Blank—Canadian, Mexican, and United States industries are comparable.

327122 Ceramic Wall and Floor Tile Manufacturing[US]

This U.S. industry comprises establishments primarily engaged in manufacturing ceramic wall and floor tiles.

Cross-References. Establishments primarily engaged in—

- Manufacturing structural clay tiles—are classified in U.S. Industry 327121, Brick and Structural Clay Tile Manufacturing;
- Manufacturing clay drain tiles—are classified in U.S. Industry 327123, Other Structural Clay Product Manufacturing; and
- Manufacturing resilient flooring and asphalt floor tiles—are classified in U.S. Industry 326192, Resilient Floor Covering Manufacturing.

327123 Other Structural Clay Product Manufacturing[US]

This U.S. industry comprises establishments primarily engaged in manufacturing clay sewer pipe, drain tile, flue lining tile, architectural terra-cotta, and other structural clay products.

Cross-References. Establishments primarily engaged in—

- Manufacturing bricks and structural clay tiles—are classified in U.S. Industry 327121, Brick and Structural Clay Tile Manufacturing;
- Manufacturing ceramic floor and wall tiles—are classified in U.S. Industry 327122, Ceramic Wall and Floor Tile Manufacturing;
- Manufacturing clay refractories—are classified in U.S. Industry 327124, Clay Refractory Manufacturing; and
- Manufacturing nonclay refractories—are classified in U.S. Industry 327125, Nonclay Refractory Manufacturing.

327124 Clay Refractory Manufacturing[US]

This U.S. industry comprises establishments primarily engaged in manufacturing clay refractory, mortar, brick, block, tile, and fabricated clay refractories, such as melting pots. A refractory is a material that will retain its shape and chemical identity when subjected to high temperatures and is used in applications that require extreme resistance to heat, such as furnace linings.

Cross-References.

Establishments primarily engaged in manufacturing nonclay refractories are classified in U.S. Industry 327125, Nonclay Refractory Manufacturing.

US—United States industry only. CAN—United States and Canadian industries are comparable. MEX—United States and Mexican industries are comparable. Blank—Canadian, Mexican, and United States industries are comparable.

327125 Nonclay Refractory Manufacturing[US]

This U.S. industry comprises establishments primarily engaged in manufacturing nonclay refractory, mortar, brick, block, tile, and fabricated nonclay refractories such as graphite, magnesite, silica, or alumina crucibles. A refractory is a material that will retain its shape and chemical identity when subjected to high temperatures and is used in applications that require extreme resistance to heat, such as furnace linings.

Cross-References.

Establishments primarily engaged in manufacturing clay refractories are classified in U.S. Industry 327124, Clay Refractory Manufacturing.

3272 Glass and Glass Product Manufacturing

32721 Glass and Glass Product Manufacturing

This industry comprises establishments primarily engaged in manufacturing glass and/or glass products. Establishments in this industry may manufacture glass and/or glass products by melting silica sand or cullet, or purchasing glass.

Cross-References. Establishments primarily engaged in—

- Manufacturing glass wool (i.e., fiberglass) insulation products—are classified in Industry 32799, All Other Nonmetallic Mineral Product Manufacturing;
- Manufacturing optical lenses (except ophthalmic), such as magnifying, photographic, and projection lenses,—are classified in Industry 33331, Commercial and Service Industry Machinery Manufacturing;
- Grinding ophthalmic (i.e., eyeglass) lenses for the trade—are classified in Industry 33911, Medical Equipment and Supplies Manufacturing; and
- Manufacturing fiber optic cable from purchased fiber optic strand—are classified in Industry 33592, Communication and Energy Wire and Cable Manufacturing.

327211 Flat Glass Manufacturing[MEX]

This U.S. industry comprises establishments primarily engaged in (1) manufacturing flat glass by melting silica sand or cullet or (2) manufacturing both flat glass and laminated glass by melting silica sand or cullet.

US—United States industry only. CAN—United States and Canadian industries are comparable. MEX—United States and Mexican industries are comparable. Blank—Canadian, Mexican, and United States industries are comparable.

Cross-References.

Establishments primarily engaged in manufacturing laminated glass from purchased flat glass are classified in U.S. Industry 327215, Glass Product Manufacturing Made of Purchased Glass.

327212 Other Pressed and Blown Glass and Glassware Manufacturing[US]

This U.S. industry comprises establishments primarily engaged in manufacturing glass by melting silica sand or cullet and making pressed, blown, or shaped glass or glassware (except glass packaging containers).

Cross-References. Establishments primarily engaged in—

- Manufacturing flat glass—are classified in U.S. Industry 327211, Flat Glass Manufacturing;
- Manufacturing glass packaging containers in glassmaking operations—are classified in U.S. Industry 327213, Glass Container Manufacturing;
- Manufacturing glass wool (i.e., fiberglass) insulation—are classified in U.S. Industry 327993, Mineral Wool Manufacturing;
- Manufacturing glassware from purchased glass—are classified in U.S. Industry 327215, Glass Product Manufacturing Made of Purchased Glass; and
- Manufacturing fiber optic cable—are classified in U.S. Industry 335921, Fiber Optic Cable Manufacturing.

327213 Glass Container Manufacturing[US]

This U.S. industry comprises establishments primarily engaged in manufacturing glass packaging containers.

327215 Glass Product Manufacturing Made of Purchased Glass[CAN]

This U.S. industry comprises establishments primarily engaged in coating, laminating, tempering, or shaping purchased glass.

Cross-References. Establishments primarily engaged in—

- Manufacturing optical lenses (except ophthalmic), such as magnifying, photographic and projection lenses,—are classified in U.S. Industry 333314, Optical Instrument and Lens Manufacturing;

US—United States industry only. CAN—United States and Canadian industries are comparable. MEX—United States and Mexican industries are comparable. Blank—Canadian, Mexican, and United States industries are comparable.

- Manufacturing ophthalmic (i.e., eyeglass) lenses—are classified in U.S. Industry 339115, Ophthalmic Goods Manufacturing; and
- Manufacturing fiber optic cable from purchased fiber optic strand—are classified in U.S. Industry 335921, Fiber Optic Cable Manufacturing.

3273 Cement and Concrete Product Manufacturing

32731 Cement Manufacturing

See industry description for 327310 below.

327310 Cement Manufacturing

This industry comprises establishments primarily engaged in manufacturing portland, natural, masonry, pozzalanic, and other hydraulic cements. Cement manufacturing establishments may calcine earths or mine, quarry, manufacture, or purchase lime.

Cross-References. Establishments primarily engaged in—

- Mining or quarrying limestone—are classified in U.S. Industry 212312, Crushed and Broken Limestone Mining and Quarrying;
- Manufacturing lime—are classified in Industry 327410, Lime Manufacturing;
- Manufacturing ready-mix concrete—are classified in Industry 327320, Ready-Mix Concrete Manufacturing; and
- Manufacturing dry mix concrete—are classified in U.S. Industry 327999, All Other Miscellaneous Nonmetallic Mineral Product Manufacturing.

32732 Ready-Mix Concrete Manufacturing

See industry description for 327320 below.

327320 Ready-Mix Concrete Manufacturing

This industry comprises establishments, such as batch plants or mix plants, primarily engaged in manufacturing concrete delivered to a purchaser in a plastic and unhardened state. Ready-mix concrete manufacturing establishments may mine, quarry, or purchase sand and gravel.

Cross-References. Establishments primarily engaged in—

- Operating sand or gravel pits—are classified in U.S. Industry 212321, Construction Sand and Gravel Mining; and

---

US—United States industry only. CAN—United States and Canadian industries are comparable. MEX—United States and Mexican industries are comparable. Blank—Canadian, Mexican, and United States industries are comparable.

- Manufacturing dry mix concrete—are classified in U.S. Industry 327999, All Other Miscellaneous Nonmetallic Mineral Product Manufacturing.

32733 Concrete Pipe, Brick, and Block Manufacturing

This industry comprises establishments primarily engaged in manufacturing concrete pipe, brick, and block.

Cross-References.

Establishments primarily engaged in manufacturing concrete products (except brick, block, and pipe) are classified in Industry 32739, Other Concrete Product Manufacturing.

327331 Concrete Block and Brick Manufacturing[US]

This U.S. industry comprises establishments primarily engaged in manufacturing concrete block and brick.

327332 Concrete Pipe Manufacturing[US]

This U.S. industry comprises establishments primarily engaged in manufacturing concrete pipe.

32739 Other Concrete Product Manufacturing

See industry description for 327390 below.

327390 Other Concrete Product Manufacturing[CAN]

This industry comprises establishments primarily engaged in manufacturing concrete products (except block, brick, and pipe).

Cross-References. Establishments primarily engaged in—

- Manufacturing concrete brick and block—are classified in U.S. Industry 327331, Concrete Block and Brick Manufacturing; and
- Manufacturing concrete pipe—are classified in U.S. Industry 327332, Concrete Pipe Manufacturing.

3274 Lime and Gypsum Product Manufacturing

32741 Lime Manufacturing

See industry description for 327410 below.

US—United States industry only. CAN—United States and Canadian industries are comparable. MEX—United States and Mexican industries are comparable. Blank—Canadian, Mexican, and United States industries are comparable.

327410 Lime Manufacturing

This industry comprises establishments primarily engaged in manufacturing lime from calcitic limestone, dolomitic limestone, or other calcareous materials, such as coral, chalk, and shells. Lime manufacturing establishments may mine, quarry, collect, or purchase the sources of calcium carbonate.

Cross-References.

Establishments primarily engaged in manufacturing dolomite refractories are classified in U.S. Industry 327125, Nonclay Refractory Manufacturing.

32742 Gypsum Product Manufacturing

See industry description for 327420 below.

327420 Gypsum Product Manufacturing

This industry comprises establishments primarily engaged in manufacturing gypsum products such as wallboard, plaster, plasterboard, molding, ornamental moldings, statuary, and architectural plaster work. Gypsum product manufacturing establishments may mine, quarry, or purchase gypsum.

Cross-References.

Establishments primarily engaged in operating gypsum mines or quarries are classified in U.S. Industry 212399, All Other Nonmetallic Mineral Mining.

3279 Other Nonmetallic Mineral Product Manufacturing

The Other Nonmetallic Mineral Product Manufacturing industry group comprises establishments manufacturing nonmetallic mineral products (except clay products, refractory products, glass products, cement and concrete products, lime, and gypsum products).

32791 Abrasive Product Manufacturing

See industry description for 327910 below.

327910 Abrasive Product Manufacturing

This industry comprises establishments primarily engaged in manufacturing abrasive grinding wheels of natural or synthetic materials, abrasive-coated products, and other abrasive products.

US—United States industry only. CAN—United States and Canadian industries are comparable. MEX—United States and Mexican industries are comparable. Blank—Canadian, Mexican, and United States industries are comparable.

Illustrative Examples:

Aluminum oxide (fused) abrasives manufacturing
Buffing and polishing wheels, abrasive and nonabrasive, manufacturing
Diamond dressing wheels manufacturing
Sandpaper manufacturing
Silicon carbide abrasives manufacturing
Whetstones manufacturing

Cross-References. Establishments primarily engaged in—

- Mining and cutting grindstones, pulpstones, and whetstones—are classified in U.S. Industry 212399, All Other Nonmetallic Mineral Mining;
- Manufacturing plastic scouring pads—are classified in U.S. Industry 326199, All Other Plastics Product Manufacturing; and
- Manufacturing metallic scouring sponges and soap impregnated scouring pads—are classified in U.S. Industry 332999, All Other Miscellaneous Fabricated Metal Product Manufacturing.

32799 All Other Nonmetallic Mineral Product Manufacturing

This industry comprises establishments primarily engaged in manufacturing nonmetallic mineral products (except pottery, ceramics, and plumbing fixtures; clay building materials and refractories; glass and glass products; cement; ready-mix concrete; concrete products; lime; gypsum products; and abrasive products).

Cross-References. Establishments primarily engaged in—

- Manufacturing pottery, ceramics, and plumbing fixtures—are classified in Industry 32711, Pottery, Ceramics, and Plumbing Fixture Manufacturing;
- Mining or quarrying stone, earth, or other nonmetallic minerals—are classified in Industry Group 2123, Nonmetallic Mineral Mining and Quarrying;
- Buying and selling semifinished monuments and tombstones with no work other than polishing, lettering, or shaping to custom order—are classified in Sector 42, Wholesale Trade or Sector 44-45, Retail Trade;
- Manufacturing clay building materials and refractories—are classified in Industry 32712, Clay Building Material and Refractories Manufacturing;
- Manufacturing glass and glass products—are classified in Industry 32721, Glass and Glass Product Manufacturing;
- Manufacturing cement—are classified in Industry 32731, Cement Manufacturing;
- Mixing and delivering ready-mix concrete—are classified in Industry 32732, Ready-Mix Concrete Manufacturing;

US—United States industry only. CAN—United States and Canadian industries are comparable. MEX—United States and Mexican industries are comparable. Blank—Canadian, Mexican, and United States industries are comparable.

- Manufacturing concrete pipe, brick, and block—are classified in Industry 32733, Concrete Pipe, Brick, and Block Manufacturing;
- Manufacturing concrete products (except pipe, brick, and block)—are classified in Industry 32739, Other Concrete Product Manufacturing;
- Manufacturing lime—are classified in Industry 32741, Lime Manufacturing;
- Manufacturing gypsum products—are classified in Industry 32742, Gypsum Product Manufacturing;
- Manufacturing abrasive products—are classified in Industry 32791, Abrasive Product Manufacturing; and
- Manufacturing metallic scouring pads and steel wool—are classified in Industry 33299, All Other Fabricated Metal Product Manufacturing.

327991 Cut Stone and Stone Product Manufacturing[US]

This U.S. industry comprises establishments primarily engaged in cutting, shaping, and finishing granite, marble, limestone, slate, and other stone for building and miscellaneous uses. Stone product manufacturing establishments may mine, quarry, or purchase stone.

Cross-References. Establishments primarily engaged in—

- Mining or quarrying stone—are classified in Industry Group 2123, Nonmetallic Mineral Mining and Quarrying; and
- Buying and selling semifinished monuments and tombstones with no work other than polishing, lettering, or shaping to custom order—are classified in Sector 42, Wholesale Trade or Sector 44-45, Retail Trade.

327992 Ground or Treated Mineral and Earth Manufacturing[US]

This U.S. industry comprises establishments primarily engaged in calcining, dead burning, or otherwise processing beyond beneficiation, clays, ceramic and refractory minerals, barite, and miscellaneous nonmetallic minerals.

Cross-References.

Establishments primarily engaged in crushing, grinding, pulverizing, washing, screening, sizing, or otherwise beneficiating mined clays, ceramics and refractory, and other miscellaneous nonmetallic minerals are classified in Industry Group 2123, Nonmetallic Mineral Mining and Quarrying.

US—United States industry only. CAN—United States and Canadian industries are comparable. MEX—United States and Mexican industries are comparable. Blank—Canadian, Mexican, and United States industries are comparable.

327993 Mineral Wool Manufacturing[US]

This U.S. industry comprises establishments primarily engaged in manufacturing mineral wool and mineral wool (i.e., fiberglass) insulation products made of such siliceous materials as rock, slag, and glass or combinations thereof.

Cross-References.

Establishments primarily engaged in manufacturing metallic scouring pads and steel wool are classified in U.S. Industry 332999, All Other Miscellaneous Fabricated Metal Product Manufacturing.

327999 All Other Miscellaneous Nonmetallic Mineral Product Manufacturing[US]

This U.S. industry comprises establishments primarily engaged in manufacturing nonmetallic mineral products (except pottery, ceramics, and plumbing fixtures; clay building materials and refractories; glass and glass products; cement; ready-mix concrete; concrete products; lime; gypsum products; abrasive products; cut stone and stone products; ground and treated minerals and earth; and mineral wool).

Illustrative Examples:

Dry mix concrete manufacturing
Mica products manufacturing
Synthetic stones, for gem stones and industrial use, manufacturing
Stucco and stucco products manufacturing

Cross-References. Establishments primarily engaged in—

- Manufacturing pottery, ceramics, and plumbing fixtures—are classified in Industry 32711, Pottery, Ceramics, and Plumbing Fixture Manufacturing;
- Manufacturing clay building materials and refractories—are classified in Industry 32712, Clay Building Material and Refractories Manufacturing;
- Manufacturing glass and glass products—are classified in Industry 32721, Glass and Glass Product Manufacturing;
- Manufacturing cement—are classified in Industry 327310, Cement Manufacturing;
- Mixing and delivering ready-mix concrete—are classified in Industry 327320, Ready-Mix Concrete Manufacturing;
- Manufacturing concrete pipe, brick, and block—are classified in Industry 32733, Concrete Pipe, Brick, and Block Manufacturing;

US—United States industry only. CAN—United States and Canadian industries are comparable. MEX—United States and Mexican industries are comparable. Blank—Canadian, Mexican, and United States industries are comparable.

- Manufacturing concrete products (except pipe, brick, and block)—are classified in Industry 327390, Other Concrete Product Manufacturing;
- Manufacturing lime—are classified in Industry 327410, Lime Manufacturing;
- Manufacturing gypsum products—are classified in Industry 327420, Gypsum Product Manufacturing;
- Manufacturing abrasives and abrasive products—are classified in Industry 327910, Abrasive Product Manufacturing;
- Manufacturing cut stone and stone products—are classified in U.S. Industry 327991, Cut Stone and Stone Product Manufacturing;
- Manufacturing ground and treated minerals and earth (i.e., not at the mine site)—are classified in U.S. Industry 327992, Ground or Treated Mineral and Earth Manufacturing; and
- Manufacturing mineral wool and fiberglass insulation products—are classified in U.S. Industry 327993, Mineral Wool Manufacturing.

331 Primary Metal Manufacturing

Industries in the Primary Metal Manufacturing subsector smelt and/or refine ferrous and nonferrous metals from ore, pig or scrap, using electrometallurgical and other process metallurgical techniques. Establishments in this subsector also manufacture metal alloys and superalloys by introducing other chemical elements to pure metals. The output of smelting and refining, usually in ingot form, is used in rolling, drawing, and extruding operations to make sheet, strip, bar, rod, or wire, and in molten form to make castings and other basic metal products.

Primary manufacturing of ferrous and nonferrous metals begins with ore or concentrate as the primary input. Establishments manufacturing primary metals from ore and/or concentrate remain classified in the primary smelting, primary refining, or iron and steel mill industries regardless of the form of their output. Establishments primarily engaged in secondary smelting and/or secondary refining recover ferrous and nonferrous metals from scrap and/or dross. The output of the secondary smelting and/or secondary refining industries is limited to shapes, such as ingot or billet, that will be further processed. Recovery of metals from scrap often occurs in establishments that are primarily engaged in activities, such as rolling, drawing, extruding, or similar processes.

Excluded from the Primary Metal Manufacturing subsector are establishments primarily engaged in manufacturing ferrous and nonferrous forgings (except ferrous forgings made in steel mills) and stampings. Although forging, stamping, and casting are all methods used to make metal shapes, forging and stamping do not use molten metals and are included in Subsector 332, Fabricated Metal Product

US—United States industry only. CAN—United States and Canadian industries are comparable. MEX—United States and Mexican industries are comparable. Blank—Canadian, Mexican, and United States industries are comparable.

Manufacturing. Establishments primarily engaged in operating coke ovens are classified in Industry 32419, Other Petroleum and Coal Products Manufacturing.

3311 Iron and Steel Mills and Ferroalloy Manufacturing

33111 Iron and Steel Mills and Ferroalloy Manufacturing

This industry comprises establishments primarily engaged in one or more of the following: (1) direct reduction of iron ore; (2) manufacturing pig iron in molten or solid form; (3) converting pig iron into steel; (4) manufacturing ferroalloys; (5) making steel; (6) making steel and manufacturing shapes (e.g., bar, plate, rod, sheet, strip, wire); and (7) making steel and forming pipe and tube.

Cross-References. Establishments primarily engaged in—

- Manufacturing nonferrous superalloys, such as cobalt or nickel-based superalloys,—are classified in Industry 33149, Nonferrous Metal (except Copper and Aluminum) Rolling, Drawing, Extruding, and Alloying; and
- Operating coke ovens—are classified in Industry 32419, Other Petroleum and Coal Products Manufacturing.

331111 Iron and Steel Mills[US]

This U.S. industry comprises establishments primarily engaged in one or more of the following: (1) direct reduction of iron ore; (2) manufacturing pig iron in molten or solid form; (3) converting pig iron into steel; (4) making steel; (5) making steel and manufacturing shapes (e.g., bar, plate, rod, sheet, strip, wire); and (6) making steel and forming tube and pipe.

Cross-References. Establishments primarily engaged in—

- Manufacturing ferroalloys (i.e., alloying elements used to improve, strengthen, or otherwise alter the characteristics of steel)—are classified in U.S. Industry 331112, Electrometallurgical Ferroalloy Product Manufacturing; and
- Operating coke ovens—are classified in U.S. Industry 324199, All Other Petroleum and Coal Products Manufacturing.

331112 Electrometallurgical Ferroalloy Product Manufacturing[US]

This U.S. industry comprises establishments primarily engaged in manufacturing electrometallurgical ferroalloys. Ferroalloys add critical elements, such as silicon

US—United States industry only. CAN—United States and Canadian industries are comparable. MEX—United States and Mexican industries are comparable. Blank—Canadian, Mexican, and United States industries are comparable.

and manganese for carbon steel and chromium, vanadium, tungsten, titanium, and molybdenum for low- and high-alloy metals. Ferroalloys include iron-rich alloys and more pure forms of elements added during the steel manufacturing process that alter or improve the characteristics of the metal being made.

Cross-References. Establishments primarily engaged in—

- Manufacturing electrometallurgical steel and iron-based superalloys—are classified in U.S. Industry 331111, Iron and Steel Mills; and
- Manufacturing nonferrous superalloys, such as cobalt or nickel-based superalloys,—are classified in U.S. Industry 331492, Secondary Smelting, Refining, and Alloying of Nonferrous Metal (except Copper and Aluminum).

3312 Steel Product Manufacturing from Purchased Steel

This industry group comprises establishments primarily engaged in manufacturing iron and steel tube and pipe, drawing steel wire, and rolling or drawing shapes from purchased iron or steel.

33121 Iron and Steel Pipe and Tube Manufacturing from Purchased Steel

See industry description for 331210 below.

331210 Iron and Steel Pipe and Tube Manufacturing from Purchased Steel

This industry comprises establishments primarily engaged in manufacturing welded, riveted, or seamless pipe and tube from purchased iron or steel.

Cross-References.

Establishments primarily engaged in making steel and further processing the steel into steel pipe and tube are classified in U.S. Industry 331111, Iron and Steel Mills.

33122 Rolling and Drawing of Purchased Steel

This industry comprises establishments primarily engaged in rolling and/or drawing steel shapes, such as plate, sheet, strip, rod, and bar, from purchased steel.

Cross-References. Establishments primarily engaged in—

- Making steel and rolling and/or drawing steel—are classified in Industry 33111, Iron and Steel Mills and Ferroalloy Manufacturing; and

US—United States industry only. CAN—United States and Canadian industries are comparable. MEX—United States and Mexican industries are comparable. Blank—Canadian, Mexican, and United States industries are comparable.

- Manufacturing wire products from purchased wire—are classified in Industry 33261, Spring and Wire Product Manufacturing.

331221 Rolled Steel Shape Manufacturing[CAN]

This U.S. industry comprises establishments primarily engaged in rolling or drawing shapes (except wire), such as plate, sheet, strip, rod, and bar, from purchased steel.

Cross-References. Establishments primarily engaged in—

- Making steel and rolling or drawing steel shapes—are classified in U.S. Industry 331111, Iron and Steel Mills; and
- Drawing wire from purchased steel—are classified in U.S. Industry 331222, Steel Wire Drawing.

331222 Steel Wire Drawing[CAN]

This U.S. industry comprises establishments primarily engaged in drawing wire from purchased steel.

Cross-References. Establishments primarily engaged in—

- Making steel and drawing steel wire—are classified in U.S. Industry 331111, Iron and Steel Mills; and
- Manufacturing wire products, such as nails, spikes, and paper clips, from purchased steel wire—are classified in Industry 33261, Spring and Wire Product Manufacturing.

3313 Alumina and Aluminum Production and Processing

33131 Alumina and Aluminum Production and Processing

This industry comprises establishments primarily engaged in one or more of the following: (1) refining alumina; (2) making (i.e., the primary production) aluminum from alumina; (3) recovering aluminum from scrap or dross; (4) alloying purchased aluminum; and (5) manufacturing aluminum primary forms (e.g., bar, foil, pipe, plate, rod, sheet, tube, wire).

Cross-References. Establishments primarily engaged in—

- Manufacturing aluminum oxide abrasives and refractories—are classified in Subsector 327, Nonmetallic Mineral Product Manufacturing;

US—United States industry only. CAN—United States and Canadian industries are comparable. MEX—United States and Mexican industries are comparable. Blank—Canadian, Mexican, and United States industries are comparable.

- Sorting and breaking up scrap aluminum metal without also smelting or refining—are classified in Sector 42, Wholesale Trade; and
- Operating facilities where commingled recyclable materials, such as paper, plastics, used beverage cans, and metals are sorted into distinct categories without also smelting or refining—are classified in Industry 56292, Materials Recovery Facilities.

331311 Alumina Refining[US]

This U.S. industry comprises establishments primarily engaged in refining alumina (i.e., aluminum oxide) generally from bauxite.

Cross-References. Establishments primarily engaged in—

- Manufacturing aluminum oxide abrasives and refractories—are classified in Subsector 327, Nonmetallic Mineral Product Manufacturing; and
- Making aluminum from alumina—are classified in U.S. Industry 331312, Primary Aluminum Production.

331312 Primary Aluminum Production[US]

This U.S. industry comprises establishments primarily engaged in (1) making aluminum from alumina and/or (2) making aluminum from alumina and rolling, drawing, extruding, or casting the aluminum they make into primary forms (e.g., bar, billet, ingot, plate, rod, sheet, strip). Establishments in this industry may make primary aluminum or aluminum-based alloys from alumina.

Cross-References. Establishments primarily engaged in—

- Refining alumina—are classified in U.S. Industry 331311, Alumina Refining; and
- Recovering aluminum from scrap or alloying purchased aluminum—are classified in U.S. Industry 331314, Secondary Smelting and Alloying of Aluminum.

331314 Secondary Smelting and Alloying of Aluminum[US]

This U.S. industry comprises establishments primarily engaged in (1) recovering aluminum and aluminum alloys from scrap and/or dross (i.e., secondary smelting) and making billet or ingot (except by rolling) and/or (2) manufacturing alloys, powder, paste, or flake from purchased aluminum.

US—United States industry only. CAN—United States and Canadian industries are comparable. MEX—United States and Mexican industries are comparable. Blank—Canadian, Mexican, and United States industries are comparable.

Cross-References. Establishments primarily engaged in—

- Making aluminum and/or aluminum alloys from alumina—are classified in U.S. Industry 331312, Primary Aluminum Production;
- Refining alumina—are classified in U.S. Industry 331311, Alumina Refining;
- Manufacturing aluminum sheet, plate, and foil from purchased aluminum or by recovering aluminum from scrap and flat rolling or continuous casting—are classified in U.S. Industry 331315, Aluminum Sheet, Plate, and Foil Manufacturing;
- Manufacturing aluminum extruded products from purchased aluminum or by recovering aluminum from scrap and extruding—are classified in U.S. Industry 331316, Aluminum Extruded Product Manufacturing;
- Manufacturing rolled ingot or billet from purchased aluminum or by recovering aluminum from scrap and rolling or drawing—are classified in U.S. Industry 331319, Other Aluminum Rolling and Drawing;
- Sorting and breaking up scrap metal without also smelting or refining—are classified in Industry 423930, Recyclable Material Merchant Wholesalers; and
- Operating facilities where commingled recyclable materials, such as paper, plastics, used beverage cans, and metals, are sorted into distinct categories without also smelting or refining—are classified in Industry 562920, Materials Recovery Facilities.

331315 Aluminum Sheet, Plate, and Foil Manufacturing[US]

This U.S. industry comprises establishments primarily engaged in (1) flat rolling or continuous casting sheet, plate, foil and welded tube from purchased aluminum; and/or (2) recovering aluminum from scrap and flat rolling or continuous casting sheet, plate, foil, and welded tube in integrated mills.

Cross-References.

Establishments primarily engaged in making aluminum from alumina and flat rolling or continuous casting aluminum sheet, plate, foil, and welded tube are classified in U.S. Industry 331312, Primary Aluminum Production.

331316 Aluminum Extruded Product Manufacturing[US]

This U.S. industry comprises establishments primarily engaged in (1) extruding aluminum bar, pipe, and tube blooms or extruding or drawing tube from purchased

US—United States industry only. CAN—United States and Canadian industries are comparable. MEX—United States and Mexican industries are comparable. Blank—Canadian, Mexican, and United States industries are comparable.

aluminum; and/or (2) recovering aluminum from scrap and extruding bar, pipe, and tube blooms or drawing tube in integrated mills.

Cross-References.

Establishments primarily engaged in making aluminum from alumina and extruding aluminum bar, pipe, tube or tube blooms are classified in U.S. Industry 331312, Primary Aluminum Production.

331319 Other Aluminum Rolling and Drawing[US]

This U.S. Industry comprises establishments primarily engaged in (1) rolling, drawing, or extruding shapes (except flat rolled sheet, plate, foil, and welded tube; extruded rod, bar, pipe, and tube blooms; and drawn or extruded tube) from purchased aluminum and/or (2) recovering aluminum from scrap and rolling, drawing or extruding shapes (except flat rolled sheet, plate, foil, and welded tube; extruded rod, bar, pipe, and tube blooms; and drawn or extruded tube) in integrated mills.

Cross-References. Establishments primarily engaged in—

- Flat rolling sheet, plate, foil, and welded tube from either purchased aluminum or by recovering aluminum from scrap and flat rolling or continuous casting—are classified in U.S. Industry 331315, Aluminum Sheet, Plate, and Foil Manufacturing;
- Extruding rod, bar, pipe, tube and tube blooms or drawing tube from purchased aluminum or by recovering aluminum from scrap and extruding—are classified in U.S. Industry 331316, Aluminum Extruded Product Manufacturing; and
- Making aluminum from alumina and making aluminum shapes—are classified in U.S. Industry 331312, Primary Aluminum Production.

3314 Nonferrous Metal (except Aluminum) Production and Processing

33141 Nonferrous Metal (except Aluminum) Smelting and Refining

This industry comprises establishments primarily engaged in (1) smelting ores into nonferrous metals and/or (2) the primary refining of nonferrous metals (except aluminum) using electrolytic or other processes.

US—United States industry only. CAN—United States and Canadian industries are comparable. MEX—United States and Mexican industries are comparable. Blank—Canadian, Mexican, and United States industries are comparable.

Cross-References. Establishments primarily engaged in—

- Making aluminum from alumina or recovery of aluminum from scrap—are classified in Industry 33131, Alumina and Aluminum Production and Processing;
- Recovering copper or copper alloys from scrap or dross and/or alloying, rolling, drawing, and extruding purchased copper—are classified in Industry 33142, Copper Rolling, Drawing, Extruding, and Alloying;
- Recovering nonferrous metals (except copper and aluminum) from scrap and/or alloying, rolling, drawing, and extruding purchased nonferrous metals (except copper and aluminum)—are classified in Industry 33149, Nonferrous Metal (except Copper and Aluminum) Rolling, Drawing, Extruding, and Alloying;
- Mining and making copper and other nonferrous concentrates (including gold and silver bullion) using processes, such as solvent extraction or electrowinning,—are classified in Industry Group 2122, Metal Ore Mining;
- Sorting and breaking up scrap metal without also smelting or refining—are classified in Sector 42, Wholesale Trade; and
- Operating facilities where commingled recyclable materials, such as paper, plastics, used beverage cans, and metals, are sorted into distinct categories without also smelting or refining—are classified in Industry 56292, Materials Recovery Facilities.

331411 Primary Smelting and Refining of Copper[MEX]

This U.S. industry comprises establishments primarily engaged in (1) smelting copper ore and/or (2) the primary refining of copper by electrolytic methods or other processes. Establishments in this industry make primary copper and copper-based alloys, such as brass and bronze, from ore or concentrates.

Cross-References. Establishments primarily engaged in—

- Recovering copper or copper alloys from scrap and making primary forms and/or alloying purchased copper—are classified in U.S. Industry 331423, Secondary Smelting, Refining, and Alloying of Copper;
- Mining and making copper concentrates by processes, such as solvent extraction or electrowinning,—are classified in U.S. Industry 212234, Copper Ore and Nickel Ore Mining;
- Drawing copper wire (except mechanical) from purchased copper or recovering copper from scrap and drawing wire (except mechanical)—are classified in U.S. Industry 331422, Copper Wire (except Mechanical) Drawing; and

US—United States industry only. CAN—United States and Canadian industries are comparable. MEX—United States and Mexican industries are comparable. Blank—Canadian, Mexican, and United States industries are comparable.

- Rolling, drawing, or extruding copper shapes (except communication and energy wire) from purchased copper or recovering copper from scrap and rolling, drawing, and extruding copper shapes—are classified in U.S. Industry 331421, Copper Rolling, Drawing, and Extruding.

331419 Primary Smelting and Refining of Nonferrous Metal (except Copper and Aluminum)[MEX]

This U.S. industry comprises establishments primarily engaged in (1) making (i.e., the primary production) nonferrous metals by smelting ore and/or (2) the primary refining of nonferrous metals by electrolytic methods or other processes.

Cross-References. Establishments primarily engaged in—

- Recovering nonferrous metals (except copper and aluminum) from scrap and making primary forms and/or alloying purchased nonferrous metals (except copper and aluminum)—are classified in U.S. Industry 331492, Secondary Smelting, Refining, and Alloying of Nonferrous Metal (except Copper and Aluminum);
- Making aluminum from alumina—are classified in U.S. Industry 331312, Primary Aluminum Production;
- Primary smelting and primary refining of copper—are classified in U.S. Industry 331411, Primary Smelting and Refining of Copper;
- Mining and making copper and other nonferrous concentrates (including gold and silver bullion), by processes, such as solvent extraction or electrowinning,—are classified in Industry Group 2122, Metal Ore Mining; and
- Rolling, drawing, and/or extruding nonferrous metal shapes (except copper and aluminum) from purchased nonferrous metals (except copper and aluminum) or by recovering nonferrous metals (except copper and aluminum) and rolling, drawing, or extruding—are classified in U.S. Industry 331491, Nonferrous Metal (except Copper and Aluminum) Rolling, Drawing, and Extruding.

33142 Copper Rolling, Drawing, Extruding, and Alloying

This industry comprises establishments primarily engaged in one or more of the following: (1) recovering copper or copper alloys from scraps; (2) alloying purchased copper; (3) rolling, drawing, or extruding shapes, (e.g., bar, plate, sheet, strip, tube, wire) from purchased copper; and (4) recovering copper or copper alloys from scrap and rolling drawing, or extruding shapes (e.g., bar, plate, sheet, strip, tube, wire).

US—United States industry only. CAN—United States and Canadian industries are comparable. MEX—United States and Mexican industries are comparable. Blank—Canadian, Mexican, and United States industries are comparable.

Cross-References. Establishments primarily engaged in—

- Smelting copper ore, primary copper refining, and/or rolling, drawing or extruding primary copper made in the same establishment—are classified in Industry 33141, Nonferrous Metal (except Aluminum) Smelting and Refining;
- Manufacturing wire products from purchased wire—are classified in Industry 33261, Spring and Wire Product Manufacturing;
- Insulating purchased copper wire—are classified in Industry 33592, Communication and Energy Wire and Cable Manufacturing;
- Sorting and breaking up scrap metal without also smelting or refining—are classified in Sector 42, Wholesale Trade;
- Operating facilities where commingled recyclable materials, such as paper, plastics, used beverage cans, and metals, are sorted into distinct categories without also smelting or refining—are classified in Industry 56292, Materials Recovery Facilities;
- Die-casting purchased copper—are classified in Industry 33152, Nonferrous Metal Foundries; and
- Recovering nonferrous metals (except copper and aluminum) from scrap, and/or rolling, drawing, extruding, or alloying purchased nonferrous metals (except copper and aluminum)—are classified in Industry 33149, Nonferrous Metal (except Copper and Aluminum) Rolling, Drawing, Extruding, and Alloying.

331421 Copper Rolling, Drawing, and Extruding[US]

This U.S. industry comprises establishments primarily engaged in (1) rolling, drawing, and/or extruding shapes (e.g., bar, plate, sheet, strip, tube (except bare or insulated copper communication or energy wire), from purchased copper; and/or (2) recovering copper from scrap and rolling, drawing, and/or extruding shapes (e.g., bar, plate, sheet, strip, tube (except bare or insulated copper communication or energy wire, in integrated mills.))

Cross-References. Establishments primarily engaged in—

- Recovering copper or copper alloys from scrap and making primary forms and/or alloying purchased copper—are classified in U.S. Industry 331423, Secondary Smelting, Refining, and Alloying of Copper;
- Drawing copper wire (except mechanical) from purchased copper or recovering copper from scrap and drawing copper wire (except mechanical)—are classified in U.S. Industry 331422, Copper Wire (except Mechanical) Drawing;

US—United States industry only. CAN—United States and Canadian industries are comparable. MEX—United States and Mexican industries are comparable. Blank—Canadian, Mexican, and United States industries are comparable.

- Die-casting purchased copper—are classified in U.S. Industry 331522, Nonferrous (except Aluminum) Die-Casting Foundries;
- Making primary copper and rolling, drawing, and/or extruding copper shapes (e.g., bar, plate, rod, sheet, strip)—are classified in U.S. Industry 331411, Primary Smelting and Refining of Copper; and
- Rolling, drawing, or extruding shapes from purchased nonferrous metal (except copper and aluminum) or recovering nonferrous metals (except copper and aluminum) from scrap and rolling, drawing or extruding—are classified in U.S. Industry 331491, Nonferrous Metal (except Copper and Aluminum) Rolling, Drawing, and Extruding.

331422 Copper Wire (except Mechanical) Drawing[US]

This U.S. industry comprises establishments primarily engaged in drawing or drawing and insulating communication and energy wire and cable from purchased copper or in integrated secondary smelting and wire drawing plants.

Cross-References. Establishments primarily engaged in—

- Manufacturing copper mechanical wire from purchased copper or by recovering copper from scrap and drawing or extruding—are classified in U.S. Industry 331421, Copper Rolling, Drawing, and Extruding;
- Insulating purchased copper wire—are classified in U.S. Industry 335929, Other Communication and Energy Wire Manufacturing;
- Making primary copper and drawing copper wire—are classified in U.S. Industry 331411, Primary Smelting and Refining of Copper; and
- Manufacturing wire products from purchased copper wire—are classified in Industry 33261, Spring and Wire Product Manufacturing.

331423 Secondary Smelting, Refining, and Alloying of Copper[US]

This U.S. industry comprises establishments primarily engaged in (1) recovering copper and copper alloys from scrap and/or (2) alloying purchased copper. Establishments in this industry make primary forms, such as ingot, wire bar, cake, and slab from copper or copper alloys, such as brass and bronze.

Cross-References. Establishments primarily engaged in—

- Sorting and breaking up scrap metal without also smelting or refining—are classified in Industry 423930, Recyclable Material Merchant Wholesalers;
- Operating facilities where commingled recyclable materials, such as paper, plastics, used beverage cans, and metals, are sorted into distinct categories

US—United States industry only. CAN—United States and Canadian industries are comparable. MEX—United States and Mexican industries are comparable. Blank—Canadian, Mexican, and United States industries are comparable.

without also smelting or refining—are classified in Industry 562920, Materials Recovery Facilities;

- Smelting copper ore and/or the primary refining of copper—are classified in U.S. Industry 331411, Primary Smelting and Refining of Copper;
- Recovering copper and copper alloys from scrap and rolling, drawing, or extruding shapes—are classified in U.S. Industry 331421, Copper Rolling, Drawing, and Extruding;
- Recovering copper and copper alloys from scrap and drawing wire (except mechanical)—are classified in U.S. Industry 331422, Copper Wire (except Mechanical) Drawing; and
- Recovering nonferrous metals (except copper, aluminum) from scrap and making primary forms and/or alloying purchased nonferrous metals (except copper and aluminum)—are classified in U.S. Industry 331492, Secondary Smelting, Refining, and Alloying of Nonferrous Metal (except Copper and Aluminum).

33149 Nonferrous Metal (except Copper and Aluminum) Rolling, Drawing, Extruding, and Alloying

This industry comprises establishments primarily engaged in one or more of the following: (1) recovering nonferrous metals (except copper and aluminum) and nonferrous metal alloys from scrap; (2) alloying purchased nonferrous metals (except copper and aluminum); (3) rolling, drawing, and extruding shapes from purchased nonferrous metals (except copper and aluminum); and (4) recovering nonferrous metals from scrap (except copper and aluminum) and rolling, drawing, or extruding shapes in integrated facilities.

Cross-References. Establishments primarily engaged in—

- Rolling, drawing, and/or extruding aluminum or secondary smelting and alloying of aluminum—are classified in Industry 33131, Alumina and Aluminum Production and Processing;
- Recovering copper and copper alloys from scrap, alloying purchased copper, rolling, drawing, or extruding shapes from purchased copper, and recovering copper or copper alloys from scrap and rolling, drawing, or extruding shapes in integrated mills—are classified in Industry 33142, Copper Rolling, Drawing, Extruding, and Alloying;
- Insulating purchased nonferrous wire—are classified in Industry 33592, Communication and Energy Wire and Cable Manufacturing;
- Making primary nonferrous metals and rolling, drawing, or extruding nonferrous metal shapes—are classified in Industry 33141, Nonferrous Metal (except Aluminum) Smelting and Refining;

US—United States industry only. CAN—United States and Canadian industries are comparable. MEX—United States and Mexican industries are comparable. Blank—Canadian, Mexican, and United States industries are comparable.

- Manufacturing products from purchased wire—are classified in Industry 33261, Spring and Wire Product Manufacturing;
- Sorting and breaking up scrap metal without also smelting or refining—are classified in Sector 42, Wholesale Trade; and
- Operating facilities where commingled recyclable materials, such as paper, plastics, used beverage cans, and metals, are sorted into distinct categories without also smelting or refining—are classified in Industry 56292, Materials Recovery Facilities.

331491 Nonferrous Metal (except Copper and Aluminum) Rolling, Drawing, and Extruding[US]

This U.S. industry comprises establishments primarily engaged in (1) rolling, drawing, or extruding shapes (e.g., bar, plate, sheet, strip, tube) from purchased nonferrous metals) and/or (2) recovering nonferrous metals from scrap and rolling, drawing, and/or extruding shapes (e.g., bar, plate, sheet, strip, tube) in integrated mills.

Cross-References. Establishments primarily engaged in—

- Rolling, drawing, and/or extruding shapes from purchased copper or recovering copper from scrap and rolling, drawing, or extruding shapes—are classified in U.S. Industry 331421, Copper Rolling, Drawing, and Extruding;
- Recovering nonferrous metals (except copper and aluminum) from scrap and making primary forms and/or alloying purchased nonferrous metals—are classified in U.S. Industry 331492, Secondary Smelting, Refining, and Alloying of Nonferrous Metal (except Copper and Aluminum);
- Rolling, drawing, and/or extruding aluminum—are classified in Industry 33131, Alumina and Aluminum Production and Processing;
- Making primary nonferrous metals and rolling, drawing, or extruding nonferrous metal shapes—are classified in U.S. Industry 331419, Primary Smelting and Refining of Nonferrous Metal (except Copper and Aluminum); and
- Insulating purchased nonferrous wire—are classified in U.S. Industry 335929, Other Communication and Energy Wire Manufacturing.

331492 Secondary Smelting, Refining, and Alloying of Nonferrous Metal (except Copper and Aluminum)[US]

This U.S. industry comprises establishments primarily engaged in (1) alloying purchased nonferrous metals and/or (2) recovering nonferrous metals from scrap.

US—United States industry only. CAN—United States and Canadian industries are comparable. MEX—United States and Mexican industries are comparable. Blank—Canadian, Mexican, and United States industries are comparable.

Establishments in this industry make primary forms (e.g., bar, billet, bloom, cake, ingot, slab, slug, wire) using smelting or refining processes.

Cross-References. Establishments primarily engaged in—

- Recovering aluminum and aluminum alloys from scrap and/or alloying purchased aluminum—are classified in U.S. Industry 331314, Secondary Smelting and Alloying of Aluminum;
- Sorting and breaking up scrap metal without also smelting or refining—are classified in Industry 423930, Recyclable Material Merchant Wholesalers;
- Recovering nonferrous metals from scrap and rolling, drawing, or extruding shapes in integrated facilities—are classified in U.S. Industry 331491, Nonferrous Metal (except Copper and Aluminum) Rolling, Drawing, and Extruding;
- Operating facilities where commingled recyclable materials, such as paper, plastics, used beverage cans, and metals, are sorted into distinct categories without also smelting or refining—are classified in Industry 562920, Materials Recovery Facilities; and
- Recovering copper and copper alloys from scrap and making primary forms; and/or alloying purchased copper—are classified in U.S. Industry 331423, Secondary Smelting, Refining, and Alloying of Copper.

3315 Foundries

This industry group comprises establishments primarily engaged in pouring molten metal into molds or dies to form castings. Establishments making castings and further manufacturing, such as machining or assembling, a specific manufactured product are classified in the industry of the finished product. Foundries may perform operations, such as cleaning and deburring, on the castings they manufacture. More involved processes, such as tapping, threading, milling, or machining to tight tolerances, that transform castings into more finished products are classified elsewhere in the manufacturing sector based on the product being made.

Establishments in this industry group make castings from purchased metals or in integrated secondary smelting and casting facilities. When the production of primary metals is combined with making castings, the establishment is classified in 331 with the primary metal being made.

33151 Ferrous Metal Foundries

This industry comprises establishments primarily engaged in pouring molten iron and steel into molds of a desired shape to made castings. Establishments in this industry purchase iron and steel made in other establishments.

US—United States industry only. CAN—United States and Canadian industries are comparable. MEX—United States and Mexican industries are comparable. Blank—Canadian, Mexican, and United States industries are comparable.

Cross-References.

Establishments primarily engaged in manufacturing iron or steel castings and further manufacturing them into finished products are classified based on the specific finished product.

331511 Iron Foundries[CAN]

This U.S. industry comprises establishments primarily engaged in pouring molten pig iron or iron alloys into molds to manufacture castings, (e.g., cast iron manhole covers, cast iron pipe, cast iron skillets). Establishments in this industry purchase iron made in other establishments.

Cross-References.

Establishments primarily engaged in manufacturing iron castings and further manufacturing them into finished products are classified based on the specific finished product.

331512 Steel Investment Foundries[US]

This U.S. industry comprises establishments primarily engaged in manufacturing steel investment castings. Investment molds are formed by covering a wax shape with a refractory slurry. After the refractory slurry hardens, the wax is melted, leaving a seamless mold. Investment molds provide highly detailed, consistent castings. Establishments in this industry purchase steel made in other establishments.

Cross-References. Establishments primarily engaged in—

- Manufacturing steel castings (except steel investment castings)—are classified in U.S. Industry 331513, Steel Foundries (except Investment); and
- Manufacturing steel investment castings and further manufacturing them into finished products—are classified based on the specific finished product.

331513 Steel Foundries (except Investment)[US]

This U.S. industry comprises establishments primarily engaged in manufacturing steel castings (except steel investment castings). Establishments in this industry purchase steel made in other establishments.

Cross-References. Establishments primarily engaged in—

- Manufacturing steel investment castings—are classified in U.S. Industry 331512, Steel Investment Foundries; and

---

US—United States industry only. CAN—United States and Canadian industries are comparable. MEX—United States and Mexican industries are comparable. Blank—Canadian, Mexican, and United States industries are comparable.

- Manufacturing steel castings and further manufacturing them into finished products—are classified based on the specific finished product.

33152 Nonferrous Metal Foundries

This industry comprises establishments primarily engaged in pouring and/or introducing molten nonferrous metal, under high pressure, into metal molds or dies to manufacture castings. Establishments in this industry purchase nonferrous metals made in other establishments.

Cross-References. Establishments primarily engaged in—

- Manufacturing iron or steel castings—are classified in Industry 33151, Ferrous Metal Foundries; and
- Manufacturing nonferrous metal castings and further manufacturing them into finished products—are classified based on the specific finished product.

331521 Aluminum Die-Casting Foundries[US]

This U.S. industry comprises establishments primarily engaged in introducing molten aluminum, under high pressure, into molds or dies to make aluminum die-castings. Establishments in this industry purchase aluminum made in other establishments.

Cross-References. Establishments primarily engaged in—

- Pouring molten aluminum into molds to manufacture aluminum castings—are classified in U.S. Industry 331524, Aluminum Foundries (except Die-Casting); and
- Manufacturing aluminum die-castings and further manufacturing them into finished products—are classified based on the specific finished product.

331522 Nonferrous (except Aluminum) Die-Casting Foundries[US]

This U.S. industry comprises establishments primarily engaged in introducing molten nonferrous metal (except aluminum), under high pressure, into molds to make nonferrous metal die-castings. Establishments in this industry purchase nonferrous metals made in other establishments.

Cross-References. Establishments primarily engaged in—

- Manufacturing aluminum die-castings—are classified in U.S. Industry 331521, Aluminum Die-Casting Foundries;

US—United States industry only. CAN—United States and Canadian industries are comparable. MEX—United States and Mexican industries are comparable. Blank—Canadian, Mexican, and United States industries are comparable.

- Pouring molten aluminum into molds to manufacture aluminum castings—are classified in U.S. Industry 331524, Aluminum Foundries (except Die-Casting);
- Pouring molten copper into molds to manufacture copper castings—are classified in U.S. Industry 331525, Copper Foundries (except Die-Casting);
- Pouring molten nonferrous metal (except copper and aluminum) into molds to manufacture nonferrous (except copper and aluminum) castings—are classified in U.S. Industry 331528, Other Nonferrous Foundries (except Die-Casting); and
- Manufacturing nonferrous die-castings and further manufacturing them into finished products—are classified based on the specific finished product.

331524 Aluminum Foundries (except Die-Casting)[US]

This U.S. industry comprises establishments primarily engaged in pouring molten aluminum into molds to manufacture aluminum castings. Establishments in this industry purchase aluminum made in other establishments.

Cross-References. Establishments primarily engaged in—

- Manufacturing aluminum die-castings—are classified in U.S. Industry 331521, Aluminum Die-Casting Foundries; and
- Manufacturing aluminum or aluminum alloy castings and further manufacturing them into finished products—are classified based on the specific finished product.

331525 Copper Foundries (except Die-Casting)[US]

This U.S. industry comprises establishments primarily engaged in pouring molten copper into molds to manufacture copper castings. Establishments in this industry purchase copper made in other establishments.

Cross-References. Establishments primarily engaged in—

- Manufacturing copper die-castings—are classified in U.S. Industry 331522, Nonferrous (except Aluminum) Die-Casting Foundries; and
- Manufacturing copper castings and further manufacturing them into finished products—are classified based on the specific finished product.

331528 Other Nonferrous Foundries (except Die-Casting)[US]

This U.S. industry comprises establishments primarily engaged in pouring molten nonferrous metals (except aluminum and copper) into molds to manufacture

US—United States industry only. CAN—United States and Canadian industries are comparable. MEX—United States and Mexican industries are comparable. Blank—Canadian, Mexican, and United States industries are comparable.

nonferrous castings (except aluminum die-castings, nonferrous (except aluminum) die-castings, aluminum castings, and copper castings). Establishments in this industry purchase nonferrous metals, such as nickel, lead, and zinc, made in other establishments.

Cross-References. Establishments primarily engaged in—

- Manufacturing aluminum die-castings—are classified in U.S. Industry 331521, Aluminum Die-Casting Foundries;
- Manufacturing nonferrous (except aluminum) die-castings—are classified in U.S. Industry 331522, Nonferrous (except Aluminum) Die-Casting Foundries;
- Pouring molten aluminum into molds to manufacture aluminum castings—are classified in U.S. Industry 331524, Aluminum Foundries (except Die-Casting);
- Manufacturing copper castings—are classified in U.S. Industry 331525, Copper Foundries (except Die-Casting); and
- Manufacturing nonferrous castings and further manufacturing them into finished products—are classified based on the specific finished product.

332 Fabricated Metal Product Manufacturing

Industries in the Fabricated Metal Product Manufacturing subsector transform metal into intermediate or end products, other than machinery, computers and electronics, and metal furniture or treating metals and metal formed products fabricated elsewhere. Important fabricated metal processes are forging, stamping, bending, forming, and machining, used to shape individual pieces of metal; and other processes, such as welding and assembling, used to join separate parts together. Establishments in this subsector may use one of these processes or a combination of these processes.

The NAICS structure for this subsector distinguishes the forging and stamping processes in a single industry. The remaining industries, in the subsector, group establishments based on similar combinations of processes used to make products.

The manufacturing performed in the Fabricated Metal Product Manufacturing subsector begins with manufactured metal shapes. The establishments in this sector further fabricate the purchased metal shapes into a product. For instance, the Spring and Wire Product Manufacturing industry starts with wire and fabricates such items.

Within manufacturing there are other establishments that make the same products made by this subsector; only these establishments begin production further back in the production process. These establishments have a more integrated operation. For instance, one establishment may manufacture steel, draw it into wire, and

---

US—United States industry only. CAN—United States and Canadian industries are comparable. MEX—United States and Mexican industries are comparable. Blank—Canadian, Mexican, and United States industries are comparable.

make wire products in the same establishment. Such operations are classified in the Primary Metal Manufacturing subsector.

3321 Forging and Stamping

33211 Forging and Stamping

This industry comprises establishments primarily engaged in one or more of the following: (1) manufacturing forgings from purchased metals; (2) manufacturing metal custom roll forming products; (3) manufacturing metal stamped and spun products (except automotive, cans, coins); and (4) manufacturing powder metallurgy products. Establishments making metal forgings, metal stampings, and metal spun products and further manufacturing (e.g., machining, assembling) a specific manufactured product are classified in the industry of the finished product. Metal forging, metal stamping, and metal spun products establishments may perform surface finishing operations, such as cleaning and deburring, on the products they manufacture.

Cross-References. Establishments primarily engaged in—

- Manufacturing metal forgings in integrated primary metal establishments—are classified in Subsector 331, Primary Metal Manufacturing;
- Stamping automotive stampings—are classified in Industry 33637, Motor Vehicle Metal Stamping;
- Manufacturing and installing rolled formed seamless gutters at construction sites—are classified in Industry 23839, Other Building Finishing Contractors; and
- Stamping coins—are classified in Industry 33991, Jewelry and Silverware Manufacturing.

332111 Iron and Steel Forging[US]

This U.S. industry comprises establishments primarily engaged in manufacturing iron and steel forgings from purchased iron and steel by hammering mill shapes. Establishments making iron and steel forgings and further manufacturing (e.g., machining, assembling) a specific manufactured product are classified in the industry of the finished product. Iron and steel forging establishments may perform surface finishing operations, such as cleaning and deburring, on the forgings they manufacture.

US—United States industry only. CAN—United States and Canadian industries are comparable. MEX—United States and Mexican industries are comparable. Blank—Canadian, Mexican, and United States industries are comparable.

Cross-References. Establishments primarily engaged in—

- Manufacturing iron and steel forgings in integrated iron and steel mills—are classified in U.S. Industry 331111, Iron and Steel Mills; and
- Manufacturing nonferrous forgings—are classified in U.S. Industry 332112, Nonferrous Forging.

332112 Nonferrous Forging[US]

This U.S. industry comprises establishments primarily engaged in manufacturing nonferrous forgings from purchased nonferrous metals by hammering mill shapes. Establishments making nonferrous forgings and further manufacturing (e.g., machining, assembling) a specific manufactured product are classified in the industry of the finished product. Nonferrous forging establishments may perform surface finishing operations, such as cleaning and deburring, on the forgings they manufacture.

Cross-References. Establishments primarily engaged in—

- Manufacturing iron and steel forgings—are classified in U.S. Industry 332111, Iron and Steel Forging; and
- Manufacturing nonferrous forgings in integrated primary or secondary nonferrous metal production facilities—are classified in Subsector 331, Primary Metal Manufacturing.

332114 Custom Roll Forming[US]

This U.S. industry comprises establishments primarily engaged in custom roll forming metal products by use of rotary motion of rolls with various contours to bend or shape the products.

Cross-References.

Establishments primarily engaged in manufacturing and installing rolled formed seamless gutters at construction sites are classified in Industry 238390, Other Building Finishing Contractors.

332115 Crown and Closure Manufacturing[US]

This U.S. industry comprises establishments primarily engaged in stamping metal crowns and closures, such as bottle caps and home canning lids and rings.

US—United States industry only. CAN—United States and Canadian industries are comparable. MEX—United States and Mexican industries are comparable. Blank—Canadian, Mexican, and United States industries are comparable.

332116 Metal Stamping[US]

This U.S. industry comprises establishments primarily engaged in manufacturing unfinished metal stampings and spinning unfinished metal products (except crowns, cans, closures, automotive, and coins). Establishments making metal stampings and metal spun products and further manufacturing (e.g., machining, assembling) a specific product are classified in the industry of the finished product. Metal stamping and metal spun products establishments may perform surface finishing operations, such as cleaning and deburring, on the products they manufacture.

Cross-References. Establishments primarily engaged in—

- Stamping automotive stampings—are classified in Industry 336370, Motor Vehicle Metal Stamping;
- Stamping metal crowns and closures—are classified in U.S. Industry 332115, Crown and Closure Manufacturing;
- Manufacturing metal cans—are classified in U.S. Industry 332431, Metal Can Manufacturing; and
- Stamping coins—are classified in U.S. Industry 339911, Jewelry (except Costume) Manufacturing.

332117 Powder Metallurgy Part Manufacturing[US]

This U.S. industry comprises establishments primarily engaged in manufacturing powder metallurgy products by compacting them in a shaped die and sintering. Establishments in this industry generally make a wide range of parts on a job or order basis.

3322 Cutlery and Handtool Manufacturing

33221 Cutlery and Handtool Manufacturing

This industry comprises establishments primarily engaged in one or more of the following: (1) manufacturing nonprecious and precious plated metal cutlery and flatware; (2) manufacturing nonpowered hand and edge tools; (3) manufacturing nonpowered handsaws; (4) manufacturing saw blades, all types (including those for sawing machines); and (5) manufacturing metal kitchen utensils (except cutting-type) and pots and pans (except those manufactured by casting (e.g., cast iron skillets) or stamped without further fabrication).

US—United States industry only. CAN—United States and Canadian industries are comparable. MEX—United States and Mexican industries are comparable. Blank—Canadian, Mexican, and United States industries are comparable.

Cross-References. Establishments primarily engaged in—

- Manufacturing precious (except precious plated) metal cutlery and flatware—are classified in Industry 33991, Jewelry and Silverware Manufacturing;
- Manufacturing electric razors and hair clippers for use on humans—are classified in Industry 33521, Small Electrical Appliance Manufacturing;
- Manufacturing power hedge shears and trimmers and electric hair clippers for use on animals—are classified in Industry 33311, Agricultural Implement Manufacturing;
- Manufacturing metal cutting dies, attachments, and accessories for machine tools—are classified in Industry 33351, Metalworking Machinery Manufacturing;
- Manufacturing handheld power-driven handtools—are classified in Industry 33399, All Other General Purpose Machinery Manufacturing; and
- Manufacturing finished cast iron kitchen utensils (i.e., cast iron skillets) and castings for kitchen utensils, pots, and pans—are classified in Industry Group 3315, Foundries.

332211 Cutlery and Flatware (except Precious) Manufacturing[US]

This U.S. industry comprises establishments primarily engaged in manufacturing nonprecious and precious plated metal cutlery and flatware.

Cross-References. Establishments primarily engaged in—

- Manufacturing precious (except precious plated) metal cutlery and flatware—are classified in U.S. Industry 339912, Silverware and Hollowware Manufacturing;
- Manufacturing electric razors and hair clippers for use on humans and housewares—are classified in U.S. Industry 335211, Electric Housewares and Household Fan Manufacturing;
- Manufacturing power hedge shears and trimmers and electric hair clippers for animal use— are classified in U.S. Industry 333112, Lawn and Garden Tractor and Home Lawn and Garden Equipment Manufacturing; and
- Manufacturing nonelectric hair clippers for use on animals—are classified in U.S. Industry 332212, Hand and Edge Tool Manufacturing.

332212 Hand and Edge Tool Manufacturing[US]

This industry comprises establishments primarily engaged in manufacturing nonpowered hand and edge tools (except saws).

US—United States industry only. CAN—United States and Canadian industries are comparable. MEX—United States and Mexican industries are comparable. Blank—Canadian, Mexican, and United States industries are comparable.

Cross-References. Establishments primarily engaged in—

- Manufacturing saw blades and handsaws—are classified in U.S. Industry 332213, Saw Blade and Handsaw Manufacturing;
- Manufacturing metal cutting dies, attachments, and accessories for machine tools—are classified in Industry 33351, Metalworking Machinery Manufacturing;
- Manufacturing handheld power-driven handtools—are classified in U.S. Industry 333991, Power-Driven Handtool Manufacturing;
- Manufacturing electric razors and hair clippers for use on humans—are classified in U.S. Industry 335211, Electric Housewares and Household Fan Manufacturing;
- Manufacturing electric hair clippers for use on animals—are classified in U.S. Industry 333111, Farm Machinery and Equipment Manufacturing; and
- Manufacturing nonelectric household-type scissors and shears—are classified in U.S. Industry 332211, Cutlery and Flatware (except Precious) Manufacturing.

332213 Saw Blade and Handsaw Manufacturing[US]

This U.S. industry comprises establishments primarily engaged in (1) manufacturing nonpowered handsaws and/or (2) manufacturing saw blades, all types (including those for power sawing machines).

Cross-References.

Establishments primarily engaged in manufacturing handheld powered saws are classified in U.S. Industry 333991, Power-Driven Handtool Manufacturing.

332214 Kitchen Utensil, Pot, and Pan Manufacturing[US]

This U.S. industry comprises establishments primarily engaged in manufacturing metal kitchen utensils (except cutting-type), pots, and pans (except those manufactured by casting (e.g., cast iron skillets) or stamped without further fabrication).

Cross-References. Establishments primarily engaged in—

- Manufacturing finished cast metal kitchen utensils or castings for kitchen utensils—are classified in Industry Group 3315, Foundries;
- Manufacturing stampings for kitchen utensils, pots, and pans—are classified in U.S. Industry 332116, Metal Stamping; and

US—United States industry only. CAN—United States and Canadian industries are comparable. MEX—United States and Mexican industries are comparable. Blank—Canadian, Mexican, and United States industries are comparable.

- Manufacturing metal cutting-type kitchen utensils—are classified in U.S. Industry 332211, Cutlery and Flatware (except Precious) Manufacturing.

3323 Architectural and Structural Metals Manufacturing

33231 Plate Work and Fabricated Structural Product Manufacturing

This industry comprises establishments primarily engaged in manufacturing one or more of the following: (1) prefabricated metal buildings, panels and sections; (2) structural metal products; and (3) metal plate work products.

Cross-References. Establishments primarily engaged in—

- Making manufactured homes (i.e., mobile homes) and prefabricated wood buildings—are classified in Industry 32199, All Other Wood Product Manufacturing;
- Constructing buildings, bridges, and other heavy construction projects on site—are classified in Sector 23, Construction;
- Building ships, boats and barges—are classified in Industry 33661, Ship and Boat Building;
- Manufacturing power boilers and heat exchangers—are classified in Industry 33241, Power Boiler and Heat Exchanger Manufacturing;
- Manufacturing heavy gauge tanks—are classified in Industry 33242, Metal Tank (Heavy Gauge) Manufacturing;
- Manufacturing metal plate cooling towers—are classified in Industry 33341, Ventilation, Heating, Air-Conditioning, and Commercial Refrigeration Equipment Manufacturing; and
- Manufacturing metal windows, doors, and studs—are classified in Industry 33232, Ornamental and Architectural Metal Products Manufacturing.

332311 Prefabricated Metal Building and Component Manufacturing[CAN]

This U.S. industry comprises establishments primarily engaged in manufacturing prefabricated metal buildings, panels, and sections.

Cross-References. Establishments primarily engaged in—

- Making manufactured homes (i.e., mobile homes) and prefabricated wood buildings—are classified in Industry 32199, All Other Wood Product Manufacturing;

US—United States industry only. CAN—United States and Canadian industries are comparable. MEX—United States and Mexican industries are comparable. Blank—Canadian, Mexican, and United States industries are comparable.

- Constructing prefabricated buildings on site—are classified in Subsector 236, Construction of Buildings; and
- Manufacturing metal windows and doors—are classified in U.S. Industry 332321, Metal Window and Door Manufacturing.

332312 Fabricated Structural Metal Manufacturing[US]

This U.S. industry comprises establishments primarily engaged in fabricating structural metal products, such as concrete reinforcing bars and fabricated bar joists.

Cross-References. Establishments primarily engaged in—

- Manufacturing metal windows and doors—are classified in U.S. Industry 332321, Metal Window and Door Manufacturing;
- Manufacturing metal studs—are classified in U.S. Industry 332322, Sheet Metal Work Manufacturing;
- Constructing buildings, bridges, and other heavy construction projects on site—are classified in Sector 23, Construction;
- Building ships, boats and barges—are classified in Industry 33661, Ship and Boat Building; and
- Prefabricating metal buildings, panels, and sections—are classified in U.S. Industry 332311, Prefabricated Metal Building and Component Manufacturing.

332313 Plate Work Manufacturing[US]

This industry comprises establishments primarily engaged in manufacturing fabricated metal plate work by cutting, punching, bending, shaping, and welding purchased metal plate.

Cross-References. Establishments primarily engaged in—

- Manufacturing power boilers and heat exchangers—are classified in Industry 332410, Power Boiler and Heat Exchanger Manufacturing;
- Manufacturing heavy gauge tanks—are classified in Industry 332420, Metal Tank (Heavy Gauge) Manufacturing; and
- Manufacturing metal plate cooling towers—are classified in U.S. Industry 333415, Air-Conditioning and Warm Air Heating Equipment and Commercial and Industrial Refrigeration Equipment Manufacturing.

US—United States industry only. CAN—United States and Canadian industries are comparable. MEX—United States and Mexican industries are comparable. Blank—Canadian, Mexican, and United States industries are comparable.

33232 Ornamental and Architectural Metal Products Manufacturing

This industry comprises establishments primarily engaged in manufacturing one or more of the following: (1) metal framed windows (i.e., typically using purchased glass) and metal doors; (2) sheet metal work; and (3) ornamental and architectural metal products.

Cross-References. Establishments primarily engaged in—

- Manufacturing metal covered (i.e., clad) wood windows and doors—are classified in Industry 32191, Millwork;
- Manufacturing bins, cans, vats, and light tanks of sheet metal—are classified in Industry 33243, Metal Can, Box, and Other Metal Container (Light Gauge) Manufacturing;
- Manufacturing prefabricated metal buildings, panels, and sections—are classified in Industry 33231, Plate Work and Fabricated Structural Product Manufacturing;
- Fabricating sheet metal work on site—are classified in Subsector 238, Specialty Trade Contractors;
- Manufacturing metal stampings (except automotive, coins) and custom roll forming products—are classified in Industry 33211, Forging and Stamping;
- Manufacturing automotive stampings—are classified in Industry 33637, Motor Vehicle Metal Stamping; and
- Stamping coins—are classified in Industry 33991, Jewelry and Silverware Manufacturing.

332321 Metal Window and Door Manufacturing[CAN]

This U.S. industry comprises establishments primarily engaged in manufacturing metal framed windows (i.e., typically using purchased glass) and metal doors. Examples of products made by these establishments are metal door frames; metal framed window and door screens; and metal molding and trim (except automotive).

Cross-References. Establishments primarily engaged in—

- Manufacturing wood or metal covered (i.e., clad) wood framed windows and doors—are classified in U.S. Industry 321911, Wood Window and Door Manufacturing; and
- Manufacturing metal automotive molding and trim—are classified in Industry 336370, Motor Vehicle Metal Stamping.

US—United States industry only. CAN—United States and Canadian industries are comparable. MEX—United States and Mexican industries are comparable. Blank—Canadian, Mexican, and United States industries are comparable.

332322 Sheet Metal Work Manufacturing[US]

This U.S. industry comprises establishments primarily engaged in manufacturing sheet metal work (except stampings).

Cross-References. Establishments primarily engaged in—

- Manufacturing sheet metal bins, vats, and light tanks of sheet metal—are classified in U.S. Industry 332439, Other Metal Container Manufacturing;
- Manufacturing metal cans, lids, and ends—are classified in U.S. Industry 332431, Metal Can Manufacturing;
- Fabricating sheet metal work on site—are classified in Subsector 238, Specialty Trade Contractors;
- Manufacturing metal stampings (except automotive, coins) and custom roll forming products—are classified in Industry 33211, Forging and Stamping;
- Manufacturing automotive stampings—are classified in Industry 336370, Motor Vehicle Metal Stamping; and
- Stamping coins—are classified in U.S. Industry 339911, Jewelry (except Costume) Manufacturing.

332323 Ornamental and Architectural Metal Work Manufacturing[US]

This U.S. industry comprises establishments primarily engaged in manufacturing ornamental and architectural metal work, such as staircases, metal open steel flooring, fire escapes, railings, and scaffolding.

Cross-References.

Establishments primarily engaged in manufacturing prefabricated metal buildings, panels, and sections are classified in U.S. Industry 332311, Prefabricated Metal Building and Component Manufacturing.

3324 Boiler, Tank, and Shipping Container Manufacturing

33241 Power Boiler and Heat Exchanger Manufacturing

See industry description for 332410 below.

332410 Power Boiler and Heat Exchanger Manufacturing

This industry comprises establishments primarily engaged in manufacturing power boilers and heat exchangers. Establishments in this industry may perform installation in addition to manufacturing power boilers and heat exchangers.

US—United States industry only. CAN—United States and Canadian industries are comparable. MEX—United States and Mexican industries are comparable. Blank—Canadian, Mexican, and United States industries are comparable.

Cross-References. Establishments primarily engaged in—

- Manufacturing heavy gauge metal tanks—are classified in Industry 332420, Metal Tank (Heavy Gauge) Manufacturing;
- Manufacturing steam or hot water low pressure heating boilers—are classified in U.S. Industry 333414, Heating Equipment (except Warm Air Furnaces) Manufacturing; and
- Installing power boilers and heat exchanges without manufacturing—are classified in Industry 238220, Plumbing, Heating, and Air-Conditioning Contractors.

33242 Metal Tank (Heavy Gauge) Manufacturing

See industry description for 332420 below.

332420 Metal Tank (Heavy Gauge) Manufacturing

This industry comprises establishments primarily engaged in cutting, forming, and joining heavy gauge metal to manufacture tanks, vessels, and other containers.

Cross-References. Establishments primarily engaged in—

- Manufacturing power boilers—are classified in Industry 332410, Power Boiler and Heat Exchanger Manufacturing;
- Manufacturing light gauge metal containers—are classified in Industry 33243, Metal Can, Box, and Other Metal Container (Light Gauge) Manufacturing; and
- Installing heavy gauge metal tanks without manufacturing—are classified in Industry 238120, Structural Steel and Precast Concrete Contractors.

33243 Metal Can, Box, and Other Metal Container (Light Gauge) Manufacturing

This industry comprises establishments primarily engaged in forming light gauge metal containers.

Cross-References. Establishments primarily engaged in—

- Manufacturing foil containers—are classified in Industry 33299, All Other Fabricated Metal Product Manufacturing;
- Reconditioning barrels and drums—are classified in Industry 81131, Commercial and Industrial Machinery and Equipment (except Automotive and Electronic) Repair and Maintenance; and

US—United States industry only. CAN—United States and Canadian industries are comparable. MEX—United States and Mexican industries are comparable. Blank—Canadian, Mexican, and United States industries are comparable.

- Manufacturing heavy gauge metal containers—are classified in Industry 33242, Metal Tank (Heavy Gauge) Manufacturing.

332431 Metal Can Manufacturing[CAN]

This U.S. industry comprises establishments primarily engaged in manufacturing metal cans, lids, and ends.

Cross-References. Establishments primarily engaged in—

- Manufacturing foil containers—are classified in U.S. Industry 332999, All Other Miscellaneous Fabricated Metal Product Manufacturing; and
- Manufacturing light gauge metal containers (except cans)—are classified in U.S. Industry 332439, Other Metal Container Manufacturing.

332439 Other Metal Container Manufacturing[CAN]

This U.S. industry comprises establishments primarily engaged in manufacturing metal (light gauge) containers (except cans).

Illustrative Examples:

Light gauge metal bins manufacturing
Light gauge metal drums manufacturing
Light gauge metal garbage cans manufacturing
Light gauge metal lunch boxes manufacturing
Light gauge metal mailboxes manufacturing
Light gauge metal tool boxes manufacturing
Light gauge metal vats manufacturing
Metal air cargo containers manufacturing
Metal barrels manufacturing
Vacuum bottles and jugs manufacturing

Cross-References. Establishments primarily engaged in—

- Manufacturing foil containers—are classified in U.S. Industry 332999, All Other Miscellaneous Fabricated Metal Product Manufacturing;
- Manufacturing metal cans—are classified in U.S. Industry 332431, Metal Can Manufacturing;
- Reconditioning barrels and drums—are classified in Industry 811310, Commercial and Industrial Machinery and Equipment (except Automotive and Electronic) Repair and Maintenance; and
- Manufacturing heavy gauge metal containers—are classified in Industry 332420, Metal Tank (Heavy Gauge) Manufacturing.

US—United States industry only. CAN—United States and Canadian industries are comparable. MEX—United States and Mexican industries are comparable. Blank—Canadian, Mexican, and United States industries are comparable.

3325 Hardware Manufacturing

33251 Hardware Manufacturing

See industry description for 332510 below.

332510 Hardware Manufacturing

This industry comprises establishments primarily engaged in manufacturing metal hardware, such as metal hinges, metal handles, keys, and locks (except coin-operated, time locks).

Cross-References. Establishments primarily engaged in—

- Manufacturing bolts, nuts, screws, rivets, washers, hose clamps, and turnbuckles—are classified in U.S. Industry 332722, Bolt, Nut, Screw, Rivet, and Washer Manufacturing;
- Manufacturing nails and spikes from wire drawn elsewhere—are classified in U.S. Industry 332618, Other Fabricated Wire Product Manufacturing;
- Manufacturing metal furniture parts (except hardware)—are classified in U.S. Industry 337215, Showcase, Partition, Shelving, and Locker Manufacturing;
- Drawing wire and manufacturing nails and spikes—are classified in Subsector 331, Primary Metal Manufacturing;
- Manufacturing pole line and transmission hardware—are classified in U.S. Industry 335932, Noncurrent-Carrying Wiring Device Manufacturing;
- Manufacturing coin-operated locking mechanisms—are classified in U.S. Industry 333311, Automatic Vending Machine Manufacturing;
- Manufacturing time locks—are classified in U.S. Industry 334518, Watch, Clock, and Part Manufacturing;
- Manufacturing fireplace fixtures and equipment, traps, handcuffs and leg irons, ladder jacks, and other like metal products—are classified in U.S. Industry 332999, All Other Miscellaneous Fabricated Metal Product Manufacturing;
- Manufacturing fire hose nozzles and couplings—are classified in U.S. Industry 332919, Other Metal Valve and Pipe Fitting Manufacturing; and
- Manufacturing luggage and utility racks—are classified in U.S. Industry 336399, All Other Motor Vehicle Parts Manufacturing.

US—United States industry only. CAN—United States and Canadian industries are comparable. MEX—United States and Mexican industries are comparable. Blank—Canadian, Mexican, and United States industries are comparable.

3326 Spring and Wire Product Manufacturing

33261 Spring and Wire Product Manufacturing

This industry comprises establishments primarily engaged in (1) manufacturing steel springs by forming, such as cutting, bending, and heat winding, metal rod or strip stock and/or (2) manufacturing wire springs and fabricated wire products from wire drawn elsewhere (except watch and clock springs).

Cross-References. Establishments primarily engaged in—

- Manufacturing watch and clock springs from purchased wire—are classified in Industry 33451, Navigational, Measuring, Electromedical, and Control Instruments Manufacturing;
- Drawing wire and manufacturing wire products—are classified in Subsector 331, Primary Metal Manufacturing; and
- Manufacturing nonferrous insulated wire from wire drawn elsewhere—are classified in Industry 33592, Communication and Energy Wire and Cable Manufacturing.

332611 Spring (Heavy Gauge) Manufacturing[CAN]

This U.S. industry comprises establishments primarily engaged in manufacturing heavy gauge springs by forming, such as cutting, bending, and heat winding, rod or strip stock.

Cross-References. Establishments primarily engaged in—

- Manufacturing light gauge springs from purchased wire or strip—are classified in U.S. Industry 332612, Spring (Light Gauge) Manufacturing; and
- Drawing wire and manufacturing wire spring—are classified in Subsector 331, Primary Metal Manufacturing.

332612 Spring (Light Gauge) Manufacturing[US]

This U.S. industry comprises establishments primarily engaged in manufacturing light gauge springs from purchased wire or strip.

Cross-References. Establishments primarily engaged in—

- Manufacturing watch and clock springs—are classified in U.S. Industry 334518, Watch, Clock, and Part Manufacturing;

US—United States industry only. CAN—United States and Canadian industries are comparable. MEX—United States and Mexican industries are comparable. Blank—Canadian, Mexican, and United States industries are comparable.

- Manufacturing heavy gauge springs—are classified in U.S. Industry 332611, Spring (Heavy Gauge) Manufacturing; and
- Drawing wire and manufacturing wire spring—are classified in Subsector 331, Primary Metal Manufacturing.

332618 Other Fabricated Wire Product Manufacturing[US]

This U.S.industry comprises establishments primarily engaged in manufacturing fabricated wire products (except springs) made from purchased wire.

Illustrative Examples:

Barbed wire made from purchased wire
Chain link fencing and fence gates made from purchased wire
Metal baskets made from purchased wire
Nails, brads, and staples made from purchased wire
Noninsulated wire cable made from purchased wire
Paper clips made from purchased wire
Woven wire cloth made from purchased wire

Cross-References. Establishments primarily engaged in—

- Drawing wire and manufacturing wire products—are classified in Subsector 331, Primary Metal Manufacturing;
- Manufacturing heavy gauge springs—are classified in U.S. Industry 332611, Spring (Heavy Gauge) Manufacturing;
- Manufacturing light gauge springs from purchased wire or strip—are classified in U.S. Industry 332612, Spring (Light Gauge) Manufacturing; and
- Insulating nonferrous wire from wire drawn elsewhere—are classified in U.S. Industry 335929, Other Communication and Energy Wire Manufacturing.

3327 Machine Shops; Turned Product; and Screw, Nut, and Bolt Manufacturing

33271 Machine Shops

See industry description for 332710 below.

332710 Machine Shops

This industry comprises establishments known as machine shops primarily engaged in machining metal parts on a job or order basis. Generally machine shop jobs are low volume using machine tools, such as lathes (including computer

US—United States industry only. CAN—United States and Canadian industries are comparable. MEX—United States and Mexican industries are comparable. Blank—Canadian, Mexican, and United States industries are comparable.

numerically controlled); automatic screw machines; and machines for boring, grinding, and milling.

Cross-References. Establishments primarily engaged in—

- Repairing industrial machinery and equipment—are classified in Industry 811310, Commercial and Industrial Machinery and Equipment (except Automotive and Electronic) Repair and Maintenance; and
- Manufacturing parts (except on a job or order basis) for machinery and equipment—are generally classified in the same manufacturing industry that makes complete machinery and equipment.

33272 Turned Product and Screw, Nut, and Bolt Manufacturing

This industry comprises establishments primarily engaged in (1) machining precision turned products or (2) manufacturing metal bolts, nuts, screws, rivets, and other industrial fasteners. Included in this industry are establishments primarily engaged in manufacturing parts for machinery and equipment on a customized basis.

Cross-References.

Establishments primarily engaged in manufacturing plastics fasteners are classified in Industry 32619, Other Plastics Product Manufacturing.

332721 Precision Turned Product Manufacturing[US]

This U.S. industry comprises establishments known as precision turned manufacturers primarily engaged in machining precision products of all materials on a job or order basis. Generally precision turned product jobs are large volume using machines, such as automatic screw machines, rotary transfer machines, computer numerically controlled (CNC) lathes, or turning centers.

Cross-References.

Establishments primarily engaged in manufacturing metal bolts, nuts, screws, rivets, washers, and other industrial fasteners on machines, such as headers, threaders, and nut forming machines, are classified in U.S. Industry 332722, Bolt, Nut, Screw, Rivet, and Washer Manufacturing.

332722 Bolt, Nut, Screw, Rivet, and Washer Manufacturing[US]

This U.S. industry comprises establishments primarily engaged in manufacturing metal bolts, nuts, screws, rivets, and washers, and other industrial fasteners using machines, such as headers, threaders, and nut forming machines.

US—United States industry only. CAN—United States and Canadian industries are comparable. MEX—United States and Mexican industries are comparable. Blank—Canadian, Mexican, and United States industries are comparable.

Cross-References. Establishments primarily engaged in—

- Manufacturing precision turned products—are classified in U.S. Industry 332721, Precision Turned Product Manufacturing; and
- Plastics fasteners—are classified in U.S. Industry 326199, All Other Plastics Product Manufacturing.

3328 Coating, Engraving, Heat Treating, and Allied Activities

33281 Coating, Engraving, Heat Treating, and Allied Activities

This industry comprises establishments primarily engaged in one or more of the following: (1) heat treating metals and metal products; (2) enameling, lacquering, and varnishing metals and metal products; (3) hot dip galvanizing metals and metal products; (4) engraving, chasing, or etching metals and metal products (except jewelry; personal goods carried on or about the person, such as compacts and cigarette cases; precious metal products (except precious plated flatware and other plated ware); and printing plates); (5) powder coating metals and metal products; (6) electroplating, plating, anodizing, coloring, and finishing metals and metal products; and (7) providing other metal surfacing services for the trade. Establishments in this industry coat engravings and heat treat metals and metal formed products fabricated elsewhere.

Cross-References. Establishments primarily engaged in—

- Engraving, chasing or etching jewelry, metal personal goods, or precious (except precious plated) metal flatware and other plated ware—are classified in Industry 33991, Jewelry and Silverware Manufacturing;
- Engraving, chasing or etching printing plates—are classified in Industry 32312, Support Activities for Printing; and
- Both fabricating and coating, engraving, and heat treating metals and metal products—are classified in manufacturing according to the product made.

332811 Metal Heat Treating[US]

This U.S. industry comprises establishments primarily engaged in heat treating, such as annealing, tempering, and brazing, metals and metal products for the trade.

Cross-References.

Establishments primarily engaged in both fabricating and heat treating metal products are classified in the Manufacturing sector according to the product made.

US—United States industry only. CAN—United States and Canadian industries are comparable. MEX—United States and Mexican industries are comparable. Blank—Canadian, Mexican, and United States industries are comparable.

332812 Metal Coating, Engraving (except Jewelry and Silverware), and Allied Services to Manufacturers[US]

This U.S. industry comprises establishments primarily engaged in one or more of the following: (1) enameling, lacquering, and varnishing metals and metal products; (2) hot dip galvanizing metals and metal products; (3) engraving, chasing, or etching metals and metal products (except jewelry; personal goods carried on or about the person, such as compacts and cigarette cases; precious metal products (except precious plated flatware and other plated ware); and printing plates); (4) powder coating metals and metal products; and (5) providing other metal surfacing services for the trade.

Cross-References. Establishments primarily engaged in—

- Both fabricating and coating and engraving products—are classified in the Manufacturing sector according to the product made;
- Engraving, chasing or etching jewelry, metal personal goods, or precious metal products (except precious plated metal flatware and other plated ware)—are classified in Industry 33991, Jewelry and Silverware Manufacturing; and
- Engraving, chasing or etching printing plates—are classified in U.S. Industry 323122, Prepress Services.

332813 Electroplating, Plating, Polishing, Anodizing, and Coloring[US]

This U.S. industry comprises establishments primarily engaged in electroplating, plating, anodizing, coloring, buffing, polishing, cleaning, and sandblasting metals and metal products for the trade.

Cross-References.

Establishments primarily engaged in both fabricating and electroplating, plating, polishing, anodizing, and coloring products are classified in the Manufacturing sector according to the product made.

3329 Other Fabricated Metal Product Manufacturing

This industry group comprises establishments primarily engaged in manufacturing fabricated metal products (except forgings and stampings, cutlery and handtools, architectural and structural metals, boilers, tanks, shipping containers, hardware, spring and wire products, machine shop products, turned products, screws, and nuts and bolts).

33291 Metal Valve Manufacturing

This industry comprises establishments primarily engaged in manufacturing one or more of the following metal valves: (1) industrial valves; (2) fluid power valves

---

US—United States industry only. CAN—United States and Canadian industries are comparable. MEX—United States and Mexican industries are comparable. Blank—Canadian, Mexican, and United States industries are comparable.

and hose fittings; (3) plumbing fixture fittings and trim; and (4) other metal valves and pipe fittings.

Cross-References. Establishments primarily engaged in—

- Manufacturing fluid power cylinder and pumps—are classified in Industry 33399, All Other General Purpose Machinery Manufacturing;
- Manufacturing intake and exhaust valves for internal combustion engines—are classified in Industry 33631, Motor Vehicle Gasoline Engine and Engine Parts Manufacturing;
- Manufacturing metal shower rods and metal couplings from purchased metal pipe—are classified in Industry 33299, All Other Fabricated Metal Product Manufacturing;
- Manufacturing plastics aerosol spray nozzles—are classified in Industry 32619, Other Plastics Product Manufacturing;
- Casting iron pipe fittings and couplings without machining—are classified in Industry 33151, Ferrous Metal Foundries; and
- Manufacturing plastics pipe fittings and couplings—are classified in Industry 32612, Plastics Pipe, Pipe Fitting, and Unlaminated Profile Shape Manufacturing.

332911 Industrial Valve Manufacturing[US]

This U.S. industry comprises establishments primarily engaged in manufacturing industrial valves and valves for water works and municipal water systems.

Illustrative Examples:

Complete fire hydrants manufacturing
Industrial-type ball valves manufacturing
Industrial-type butterfly valves manufacturing
Industrial-type check valves manufacturing
Industrial-type gate valves manufacturing
Industrial-type globe valves manufacturing
Industrial-type plug valves manufacturing
Industrial-type solenoid valves (except fluid power) manufacturing
Industrial-type steam traps manufacturing
Valves for nuclear applications manufacturing

Cross-References. Establishments primarily engaged in—

- Manufacturing fluid power valves—are classified in U.S. Industry 332912, Fluid Power Valve and Hose Fitting Manufacturing; and

US—United States industry only. CAN—United States and Canadian industries are comparable. MEX—United States and Mexican industries are comparable. Blank—Canadian, Mexican, and United States industries are comparable.

- Manufacturing plumbing and heating valves—are classified in U.S. Industry 332919, Other Metal Valve and Pipe Fitting Manufacturing.

332912 Fluid Power Valve and Hose Fitting Manufacturing[US]

This U.S. industry comprises establishments primarily engaged in manufacturing fluid power valves and hose fittings.

Illustrative Examples:

Fluid power aircraft subassemblies
Hydraulic and pneumatic hose and tube
Hose assemblies for fluid power systems fittings
Hydraulic and pneumatic valves

Cross-References. Establishments primarily engaged in—

- Manufacturing fluid power cylinders—are classified in U.S. Industry 333995, Fluid Power Cylinder and Actuator Manufacturing;
- Manufacturing fluid power pumps—are classified in U.S. Industry 333996, Fluid Power Pump and Motor Manufacturing;
- Manufacturing intake and exhaust valves for internal combustion engines—are classified in U.S. Industry 336311, Carburetor, Piston, Piston Ring, and Valve Manufacturing;
- Manufacturing industrial-type valves—are classified in U.S. Industry 332911, Industrial Valve Manufacturing; and
- Manufacturing plumbing and heating valves—are classified in U.S. Industry 332919, Other Metal Valve and Pipe Fitting Manufacturing.

332913 Plumbing Fixture Fitting and Trim Manufacturing[US]

This U.S. industry comprises establishments primarily engaged in manufacturing metal and plastics plumbing fixture fittings and trim, such as faucets, flush valves, and shower heads.

Cross-References. Establishments primarily engaged in—

- Manufacturing metal shower rods—are classified in U.S. Industry 332999, All Other Miscellaneous Fabricated Metal Product Manufacturing; and
- Manufacturing fire hose nozzles, lawn hose nozzles, water traps, and couplings—are classified in U.S. Industry 332919, Other Metal Valve and Pipe Fitting Manufacturing.

US—United States industry only. CAN—United States and Canadian industries are comparable. MEX—United States and Mexican industries are comparable. Blank—Canadian, Mexican, and United States industries are comparable.

332919 Other Metal Valve and Pipe Fitting Manufacturing[US]

This U.S. industry comprises establishments primarily engaged in manufacturing metal valves (except industrial valves, fluid power valves, fluid power hose fittings, and plumbing fixture fittings and trim).

Illustrative Examples:

Aerosol valves manufacturing
Firefighting nozzles manufacturing
Lawn hose nozzles manufacturing
Lawn sprinklers manufacturing
Metal hose couplings (except fluid power) manufacturing
Metal pipe flanges and flange unions manufacturing
Plumbing and heating in-line valves (e.g., check, cutoff, stop) manufacturing

Cross-References. Establishments primarily engaged in—

- Manufacturing fluid power valves and hose fittings—are classified in U.S. Industry 332912, Fluid Power Valve and Hose Fitting Manufacturing;
- Manufacturing industrial valves—are classified in U.S. Industry 332911, Industrial Valve Manufacturing;
- Manufacturing plastics aerosol spray nozzles—are classified in U.S. Industry 326199, All Other Plastics Product Manufacturing;
- Casting iron pipe fittings and couplings without machining—are classified in U.S. Industry 331511, Iron Foundries;
- Manufacturing metal couplings from purchased metal pipe—are classified in U.S. Industry 332996, Fabricated Pipe and Pipe Fitting Manufacturing; and
- Manufacturing plastics pipe fittings and couplings—are classified in U.S. Industry 326122, Plastics Pipe and Pipe Fitting Manufacturing.

33299 All Other Fabricated Metal Product Manufacturing

This industry comprises establishments primarily engaged in manufacturing fabricated metal products (except forgings and stampings, cutlery and handtools, architectural and structural metal products, boilers, tanks, shipping containers, hardware, spring and wire products, machine shop products, turned products, screws, nuts and bolts, and metal valves).

Illustrative Examples:

Ammunition manufacturing
Ball and roller bearing manufacturing
Industrial pattern manufacturing
Metal safes manufacturing

US—United States industry only. CAN—United States and Canadian industries are comparable. MEX—United States and Mexican industries are comparable. Blank—Canadian, Mexican, and United States industries are comparable.

Enameled iron and metal sanitary ware manufacturing
Fabricated pipe and pipe fittings made from purchased metal pipe
Foil container (except bags) manufacturing
Portable metal ladder manufacturing
Small arms and other ordnance manufacturing
Steel wool manufacturing

Cross-References. Establishments primarily engaged in—

- Manufacturing forging and stamping and powder metallurgy parts—are classified in Industry 33211, Forging and Stamping;
- Manufacturing cutlery and handtools—are classified in Industry 33221, Cutlery and Handtool Manufacturing;
- Manufacturing architectural and structural metals—are classified in Industry Group 3323, Architectural and Structural Metals Manufacturing;
- Manufacturing boilers, tanks, and shipping containers—are classified in Industry Group 3324, Boiler, Tank, and Shipping Container Manufacturing;
- Manufacturing hardware and safe and vault locks—are classified in Industry 33251, Hardware Manufacturing;
- Manufacturing spring and wire products—are classified in Industry 33261, Spring and Wire Product Manufacturing;
- Manufacturing machine shop products, turned products, screws, and nuts and bolts—are classified in Industry Group 3327, Machine Shops; Turned Product; and Screw, Nut, and Bolt Manufacturing;
- Coating, engraving, heat treating and allied activities—are classified in Industry 33281, Coating, Engraving, Heat Treating, and Allied Activities;
- Manufacturing plain bearings—are classified in Industry 33361, Engine, Turbine, and Power Transmission Equipment Manufacturing;
- Manufacturing military tanks—are classified in Industry 33699, Other Transportation Equipment Manufacturing;
- Manufacturing guided missiles—are classified in Industry 33641, Aerospace Product and Parts Manufacturing;
- Manufacturing cast iron pipe and fittings—are classified in Industry 33151, Ferrous Metal Foundries;
- Manufacturing pipe system fittings (except cast iron couplings and couplings made from purchased pipe) and metal aerosol spray nozzles—are classified in Industry 33291, Metal Valve Manufacturing;
- Manufacturing welded and seamless steel pipes from purchased steel—are classified in Industry 33121, Iron and Steel Pipe and Tube Manufacturing from Purchased Steel;

US—United States industry only. CAN—United States and Canadian industries are comparable. MEX—United States and Mexican industries are comparable. Blank—Canadian, Mexican, and United States industries are comparable.

- Manufacturing plastics plumbing fixtures and plastics portable chemical toilets—are classified in Industry 32619, Other Plastics Product Manufacturing;
- Manufacturing vitreous and semivitreous pottery sanitary ware—are classified in Industry 32711, Pottery, Ceramics, and Plumbing Fixture Manufacturing;
- Manufacturing blasting caps, detonating caps, and safety fuses—are classified in Industry 32592, Explosives Manufacturing;
- Manufacturing fireworks—are classified in Industry 32599, All Other Chemical Product and Preparation Manufacturing;
- Manufacturing metal furniture frames—are classified in Industry 33721, Office Furniture (including Fixtures) Manufacturing;
- Manufacturing nonprecious metal trophies—are classified in Industry 33991, Jewelry and Silverware Manufacturing;
- Manufacturing metal mechanically refrigerated drinking fountains—are classified in Industry 33341, Ventilation, Heating, Air-Conditioning, and Commercial Refrigeration Equipment Manufacturing;
- Manufacturing metal foil bags—are classified in Industry 32222, Paper Bag and Coated and Treated Paper Manufacturing;
- Manufacturing aluminum foil—are classified in Industry 33131, Alumina and Aluminum Production and Processing;
- Manufacturing metal foil (except aluminum)—are classified in Industry Group 3314, Nonferrous Metal (except Aluminum) Production and Processing; and
- Manufacturing metal burial vaults—are classified in Industry 33999, All Other Miscellaneous Manufacturing.

332991 Ball and Roller Bearing Manufacturing

This U.S. industry comprises establishments primarily engaged in manufacturing ball and roller bearings of all materials.

Cross-References.

Establishments primarily engaged in manufacturing plain bearings are classified in U.S. Industry 333613, Mechanical Power Transmission Equipment Manufacturing.

332992 Small Arms Ammunition Manufacturing[US]

This U.S. industry comprises establishments primarily engaged in manufacturing small arms ammunition.

US—United States industry only. CAN—United States and Canadian industries are comparable. MEX—United States and Mexican industries are comparable. Blank—Canadian, Mexican, and United States industries are comparable.

Cross-References. Establishments primarily engaged in—

- Manufacturing ammunition (except small arms)—are classified in U.S. Industry 332993, Ammunition (except Small Arms) Manufacturing;
- Manufacturing blasting and detonating caps and safety fuses—are classified in Industry 325920, Explosives Manufacturing; and
- Manufacturing fireworks—are classified in U.S. Industry 325998, All Other Miscellaneous Chemical Product and Preparation Manufacturing.

332993 Ammunition (except Small Arms) Manufacturing[US]

This U.S. industry comprises establishments primarily engaged in manufacturing ammunition (except small arms). Examples of products made by these establishments are bombs, depth charges, rockets (except guided missiles), grenades, mines, and torpedoes.

Cross-References. Establishments primarily engaged in—

- Manufacturing small arms ammunition—are classified in U.S. Industry 332992, Small Arms Ammunition Manufacturing;
- Manufacturing blasting and detonating caps and safety fuses—are classified in Industry 325920, Explosives Manufacturing;
- Manufacturing fireworks—are classified in U.S. Industry 325998, All Other Miscellaneous Chemical Product and Preparation Manufacturing; and
- Manufacturing guided missiles—are classified in U.S. Industry 336414, Guided Missile and Space Vehicle Manufacturing.

332994 Small Arms Manufacturing[US]

This U.S. industry comprises establishments primarily engaged in manufacturing small firearms that are carried and fired by the individual.

Cross-References.

Establishments primarily engaged in manufacturing firearms (except small) are classified in U.S. Industry 332995, Other Ordnance and Accessories Manufacturing.

332995 Other Ordnance and Accessories Manufacturing[US]

This U.S. industry comprises establishments primarily engaged in manufacturing ordnance (except small arms) and accessories.

US—United States industry only. CAN—United States and Canadian industries are comparable. MEX—United States and Mexican industries are comparable. Blank—Canadian, Mexican, and United States industries are comparable.

Cross-References. Establishments primarily engaged in—

- Manufacturing small arms—are classified in U.S. Industry 332994, Small Arms Manufacturing;
- Manufacturing military tanks—are classified in U.S. Industry 336992, Military Armored Vehicle, Tank, and Tank Component Manufacturing; and
- Manufacturing guided missiles—are classified in U.S. Industry 336414, Guided Missile and Space Vehicle Manufacturing.

332996 Fabricated Pipe and Pipe Fitting Manufacturing[US]

This U.S. industry comprises establishments primarily engaged in fabricating, such as cutting, threading and bending metal pipes and pipe fittings made from purchased metal pipe.

Cross-References. Establishments primarily engaged in—

- Manufacturing cast iron pipe and fittings—are classified in U.S. Industry 331511, Iron Foundries;
- Manufacturing pipe system fittings (except cast iron couplings)—are classified in U.S. Industry 332919, Other Metal Valve and Pipe Fitting Manufacturing; and
- Manufacturing welded and seamless steel pipes from purchased steel—are classified in Industry 331210, Iron and Steel Pipe and Tube Manufacturing from Purchased Steel.

332997 Industrial Pattern Manufacturing[US]

This U.S. industry comprises establishments primarily engaged in manufacturing industrial patterns.

332998 Enameled Iron and Metal Sanitary Ware Manufacturing[US]

This U.S. industry comprises establishments primarily engaged in manufacturing enameled iron and metal sanitary ware.

Cross-References. Establishments primarily engaged in—

- Manufacturing plastics plumbing fixtures—are classified in U.S. Industry 326191, Plastics Plumbing Fixture Manufacturing;

US—United States industry only. CAN—United States and Canadian industries are comparable. MEX—United States and Mexican industries are comparable. Blank—Canadian, Mexican, and United States industries are comparable.

- Manufacturing vitreous and semivitreous pottery sanitary ware—are classified in U.S. Industry 327111, Vitreous China Plumbing Fixture and China and Earthenware Bathroom Accessories Manufacturing;
- Manufacturing plastics portable chemical toilets—are classified in U.S. Industry 326199, All Other Plastics Product Manufacturing; and
- Manufacturing metal mechanically refrigerated drinking fountains—are classified in U.S. Industry 333415, Air-Conditioning and Warm Air Heating Equipment and Commercial and Industrial Refrigeration Equipment Manufacturing.

332999 All Other Miscellaneous Fabricated Metal Product Manufacturing[US]

This U.S. industry comprises establishments primarily engaged in manufacturing fabricated metal products (except forgings and stampings, cutlery and handtools, architectural and structural metals, boilers, tanks, shipping containers, hardware, spring and wire products, machine shop products, turned products, screws, nuts and bolts, metal valves, ball and roller bearings, ammunition, small arms and other ordnances, fabricated pipes and pipe fittings, industrial patterns, and enameled iron and metal sanitary ware).

Illustrative Examples:

Foil containers (except bags) manufacturing
Metal hair curlers manufacturing
Metal ironing boards manufacturing
Metal pipe hangers and supports manufacturing
Metal pallets manufacturing
Metal safes manufacturing
Metal vaults (except burial) manufacturing
Permanent metallic magnets manufacturing
Portable metal ladders manufacturing
Steel wool manufacturing

Cross-References. Establishments primarily engaged in—

- Manufacturing forgings and stampings—are classified in Industry 33211, Forging and Stamping;
- Manufacturing cutlery and handtools—are classified in Industry 33221, Cutlery and Handtool Manufacturing;
- Manufacturing architectural and structural metals—are classified in Industry Group 3323, Architectural and Structural Metals Manufacturing;
- Manufacturing boilers, tanks, and shipping containers—are classified in Industry Group 3324, Boiler, Tank, and Shipping Container Manufacturing;
- Manufacturing hardware and safe and vault locks—are classified in Industry 332510, Hardware Manufacturing;

US—United States industry only. CAN—United States and Canadian industries are comparable. MEX—United States and Mexican industries are comparable. Blank—Canadian, Mexican, and United States industries are comparable.

- Manufacturing spring and wire products—are classified in Industry 33261, Spring and Wire Product Manufacturing;
- Manufacturing machine shop products, turned products, screws, and nut and bolt—are classified in Industry Group 3327, Machine Shops; Turned Product; and Screw Nut, and Bolt Manufacturing;
- Coating, engraving, heat treating and allied activities—are classified in Industry 33281, Coating, Engraving, Heat Treating, and Allied Activities;
- Manufacturing ball and roller bearings—are classified in U.S. Industry 332991, Ball and Roller Bearing Manufacturing;
- Manufacturing small arms ammunition—are classified in U.S. Industry 332992, Small Arms Ammunition Manufacturing;
- Manufacturing ammunition (except small arms)—are classified in U.S. Industry 332993, Ammunition (except Small Arms) Manufacturing;
- Manufacturing small firearms that are carried and fired by the individual—are classified in U.S. Industry 332994, Small Arms Manufacturing;
- Manufacturing ordnances (except small) and accessories—are classified in U.S. Industry 332995, Other Ordnance and Accessories Manufacturing;
- Manufacturing metal pipes and pipe fittings from metal pipe produced elsewhere—are classified in U.S. Industry 332996, Fabricated Pipe and Pipe Fitting Manufacturing;
- Manufacturing cast iron pipe and fittings—are classified in U.S. Industry 331511, Iron Foundries;
- Manufacturing welded and seamless steel pipes from purchased steel—are classified in Industry 331210, Iron and Steel Pipe and Tube Manufacturing from Purchased Steel;
- Manufacturing metal furniture frames—are classified in U.S. Industry 337215, Showcase, Partition, Shelving, and Locker Manufacturing;
- Manufacturing powder metallurgy parts—are classified in U.S. Industry 332117, Powder Metallurgy Part Manufacturing;
- Manufacturing metal boxes—are classified in U.S. Industry 332439, Other Metal Container Manufacturing;
- Manufacturing metal nozzles, hose couplings, and aerosol valves—are classified in U.S. Industry 332919, Other Metal Valve and Pipe Fitting Manufacturing;
- Manufacturing nonprecious metal trophies—are classified in U.S. Industry 339914, Costume Jewelry and Novelty Manufacturing;
- Manufacturing metal foil bags—are classified in U.S. Industry 322223, Plastics, Foil, and Coated Paper Bag Manufacturing;

US—United States industry only. CAN—United States and Canadian industries are comparable. MEX—United States and Mexican industries are comparable. Blank—Canadian, Mexican, and United States industries are comparable.

- Manufacturing aluminum foil—are classified in Industry 33131, Alumina and Aluminum Production and Processing;
- Manufacturing metal foil (except aluminum)—are classified in Industry Group 3314, Nonferrous Metal (except Aluminum) Production and Processing; and
- Manufacturing metal burial vaults—are classified in U.S. Industry 339995, Burial Casket Manufacturing.

333 Machinery Manufacturing

Industries in the Machinery Manufacturing subsector create end products that apply mechanical force, for example, the application of gears and levers, to perform work. Some important processes for the manufacture of machinery are forging, stamping, bending, forming, and machining that are used to shape individual pieces of metal. Processes, such as welding and assembling are used to join separate parts together. Although these processes are similar to those used in metal fabricating establishments, machinery manufacturing is different because it typically employs multiple metal forming processes in manufacturing the various parts of the machine. Moreover, complex assembly operations are an inherent part of the production process.

In general, design considerations are very important in machinery production. Establishments specialize in making machinery designed for particular applications. Thus, design is considered to be part of the production process for the purpose of implementing NAICS. The NAICS structure reflects this by defining industries and industry groups that make machinery for different applications. A broad distinction exists between machinery that is generally used in a variety of industrial applications (i.e., general purpose machinery) and machinery that is designed to be used in a particular industry (i.e., special purpose machinery). Three industry groups consist of special purpose machinery—Agricultural, Construction, and Mining Machinery Manufacturing; Industrial Machinery Manufacturing; and Commercial and Service Industry Machinery Manufacturing. The other industry groups make general-purpose machinery: Ventilation, Heating, Air Conditioning, and Commercial Refrigeration Equipment Manufacturing; Metalworking Machinery Manufacturing; Engine, Turbine, and Power Transmission Equipment Manufacturing; and Other General Purpose Machinery Manufacturing.

3331 Agriculture, Construction, and Mining Machinery Manufacturing

33311 Agricultural Implement Manufacturing

This industry comprises establishments primarily engaged in manufacturing farm machinery and equipment, powered mowing equipment and other powered home lawn and garden equipment.

US—United States industry only. CAN—United States and Canadian industries are comparable. MEX—United States and Mexican industries are comparable. Blank—Canadian, Mexican, and United States industries are comparable.

Illustrative Examples:

Combines (i.e., harvester-threshers) manufacturing
Cotton ginning machinery manufacturing
Farm tractors and attachments manufacturing
Farm-type fertilizing machinery manufacturing
Haying machines manufacturing
Milking machines manufacturing
Powered lawnmowers manufacturing
Planting machines, farm-type, manufacturing
Poultry brooders, feeders, and waterers manufacturing
Residential-type snowblowers and throwers manufacturing

Cross-References. Establishments primarily engaged in—

- Manufacturing agricultural handtools and nonpowered lawnmowers—are classified in Industry 33221, Cutlery and Handtool Manufacturing;
- Manufacturing farm conveyors—are classified in Industry 33392, Material Handling Equipment Manufacturing; and
- Manufacturing forestry machinery and equipment, such as brush, limb and log chippers; log splitters; and equipment—are classified in Industry 33312, Construction Machinery Manufacturing.

333111 Farm Machinery and Equipment Manufacturing[US]

This U.S. industry comprises establishments primarily engaged in manufacturing agricultural and farm machinery and equipment, and other turf and grounds care equipment, including planting, harvesting, and grass mowing equipment (except lawn and garden-type).

Illustrative Examples:

Combines (i.e., harvester-threshers) manufacturing
Cotton ginning machinery manufacturing
Farm-type feed processing equipment manufacturing
Farm-type fertilizing machinery manufacturing
Farm-type planting machines manufacturing
Farm-type plows manufacturing
Farm-type tractors and attachments manufacturing
Haying machines manufacturing
Milking machines manufacturing
Poultry brooders, feeders, and waterers manufacturing

Cross-References. Establishments primarily engaged in—

- Manufacturing farm conveyors—are classified in U.S. Industry 333922, Conveyor and Conveying Equipment Manufacturing;

US—United States industry only. CAN—United States and Canadian industries are comparable. MEX—United States and Mexican industries are comparable. Blank—Canadian, Mexican, and United States industries are comparable.

- Manufacturing tractors and lawnmowers for home lawn and garden care—are classified in U.S. Industry 333112, Lawn and Garden Tractor and Home Lawn and Garden Equipment Manufacturing; and
- Manufacturing construction-type tractors—are classified in Industry 333120, Construction Machinery Manufacturing.

333112 Lawn and Garden Tractor and Home Lawn and Garden Equipment Manufacturing[US]

This U.S. industry comprises establishments primarily engaged in manufacturing powered lawnmowers, lawn and garden tractors, and other home lawn and garden equipment, such as tillers, shredders, and yard vacuums and blowers.

Cross-References. Establishments primarily engaged in—

- Manufacturing commercial mowing and other turf and grounds care equipment—are classified in U.S. Industry 333111, Farm Machinery and Equipment Manufacturing; and
- Manufacturing nonpowered lawn and garden shears, edgers, pruners, and lawnmowers— are classified in U.S. Industry 332212, Hand and Edge Tool Manufacturing.

33312 Construction Machinery Manufacturing

See industry description for 333120 below.

333120 Construction Machinery Manufacturing

This industry comprises establishments primarily engaged in manufacturing construction machinery, surface mining machinery, and logging equipment.

Illustrative Examples:

Backhoes manufacturing
Bulldozers manufacturing
Construction and surface mining-type rock drill bits manufacturing
Construction-type tractors and attachments manufacturing
Off-highway trucks manufacturing
Pile-driving equipment manufacturing
Portable crushing, pulverizing, and screening machinery manufacturing
Powered post hole diggers manufacturing
Road graders manufacturing
Surface mining machinery (except drilling) manufacturing

Cross-References. Establishments primarily engaged in—

- Manufacturing drilling and underground mining machinery and equipment—are classified in Industry 33313, Mining and Oil and Gas Field Machinery Manufacturing;

US—United States industry only. CAN—United States and Canadian industries are comparable. MEX—United States and Mexican industries are comparable. Blank—Canadian, Mexican, and United States industries are comparable.

- Manufacturing industrial plant overhead traveling cranes, hoists, truck-type cranes and hoists, winches, aerial work platforms, and automotive wrecker hoists—are classified in Industry 33392, Material Handling Equipment Manufacturing; and
- Manufacturing rail layers, ballast distributors and other railroad track-laying equipment— are classified in Industry 336510, Railroad Rolling Stock Manufacturing.

33313 Mining and Oil and Gas Field Machinery Manufacturing

This industry comprises establishments primarily engaged in manufacturing oil and gas field and underground mining machinery and equipment.

Illustrative Examples:

Coal breakers, cutters, and pulverizers manufacturing
Core drills, underground mining-type, manufacturing
Mineral processing and beneficiating machinery manufacturing
Mining cars manufacturing
Oil and gas field-type derricks manufacturing
Oil and gas field-type drilling machinery and equipment (except offshore floating platforms) manufacturing
Stationary rock crushing machinery manufacturing
Water well drilling machinery manufacturing

Cross-References. Establishments primarily engaged in—

- Manufacturing offshore oil and gas well drilling and production floating platforms—are classified in Industry 33661, Ship and Boat Building;
- Manufacturing surface mining machinery and equipment—are classified in Industry 33312, Construction Machinery Manufacturing;
- Manufacturing coal and ore conveyors—are classified in Industry 33392, Material Handling Equipment Manufacturing;
- Manufacturing underground mining locomotives—are classified in Industry 33651, Railroad Rolling Stock Manufacturing; and
- Manufacturing pumps and pumping equipment—are classified in Industry 33391, Pump and Compressor Manufacturing.

333131 Mining Machinery and Equipment Manufacturing[US]

This U.S. industry comprises establishments primarily engaged in (1) manufacturing underground mining machinery and equipment, such as coal breakers,

US—United States industry only. CAN—United States and Canadian industries are comparable. MEX—United States and Mexican industries are comparable. Blank—Canadian, Mexican, and United States industries are comparable.

mining cars, core drills, coal cutters, rock drills and (2) manufacturing mineral beneficiating machinery and equipment used in surface or underground mines.

Cross-References. Establishments primarily engaged in—

- Manufacturing surface mining machinery and equipment—are classified in Industry 333120, Construction Machinery Manufacturing;
- Manufacturing well-drilling machinery—are classified in U.S. Industry 333132, Oil and Gas Field Machinery and Equipment Manufacturing;
- Manufacturing coal and ore conveyors—are classified in U.S. Industry 333922, Conveyor and Conveying Equipment Manufacturing; and
- Manufacturing underground mining locomotives—are classified in Industry 336510, Railroad Rolling Stock Manufacturing.

333132 Oil and Gas Field Machinery and Equipment Manufacturing[US]

This U.S. industry comprises establishments primarily engaged in (1) manufacturing oil and gas field machinery and equipment, such as oil and gas field drilling machinery and equipment; oil and gas field production machinery and equipment; and oil and gas field derricks and (2) manufacturing water well drilling machinery.

Cross-References. Establishments primarily engaged in—

- Manufacturing offshore oil and gas well drilling and production floating platforms—are classified in U.S. Industry 336611, Ship Building and Repairing;
- Manufacturing underground mining drills—are classified in U.S. Industry 333131, Mining Machinery and Equipment Manufacturing; and
- Manufacturing pumps and pumping equipment—are classified in U.S. Industry 333911, Pump and Pumping Equipment Manufacturing.

3332 Industrial Machinery Manufacturing

33321 Sawmill and Woodworking Machinery Manufacturing

See industry description for 333210 below.

333210 Sawmill and Woodworking Machinery Manufacturing

This industry comprises establishments primarily engaged in manufacturing sawmill and woodworking machinery (except handheld), such as circular and band sawing equipment, planing machinery, and sanding machinery.

US—United States industry only. CAN—United States and Canadian industries are comparable. MEX—United States and Mexican industries are comparable. Blank—Canadian, Mexican, and United States industries are comparable.

Cross-References. Establishments primarily engaged in—

- Manufacturing planes, axes, drawknives, and handsaws—are classified in Industry 33221, Cutlery and Handtool Manufacturing; and
- Manufacturing power-driven handtools—are classified in U.S. Industry 333991, Power-Driven Handtool Manufacturing.

33322 Plastics and Rubber Industry Machinery Manufacturing

See industry description for 333220 below.

333220 Plastics and Rubber Industry Machinery Manufacturing

This industry comprises establishments primarily engaged in manufacturing plastics and rubber products making machinery, such as plastics compression, extrusion and injection molding machinery and equipment, and tire building and recapping machinery and equipment.

Cross-References.

Establishments primarily engaged in manufacturing industrial metal molds for plastics and rubber products making machinery are classified in U.S. Industry 333511, Industrial Mold Manufacturing.

33329 Other Industrial Machinery Manufacturing

This industry comprises establishments primarily engaged in manufacturing industrial machinery (except agricultural and farm-type, construction, mining, sawmill and woodworking, and plastics and rubber products making machinery).

Illustrative Examples:

Bakery ovens manufacturing
Chemical processing machinery and equipment manufacturing
Glass making machinery (e.g., blowing, forming, molding) manufacturing
Paper making machinery manufacturing
Petroleum refinery machinery manufacturing
Printing presses (except textile) manufacturing
Semiconductor making machinery manufacturing
Sewing machines (including household-type) manufacturing
Tannery machinery manufacturing
Textile making machinery (except sewing machines) manufacturing

Cross-References. Establishments primarily engaged in—

- Manufacturing agricultural and farm-type, construction, and mining machinery—are classified in Industry Group 3331, Agriculture, Construction, and Mining Machinery Manufacturing;

US—United States industry only. CAN—United States and Canadian industries are comparable. MEX—United States and Mexican industries are comparable. Blank—Canadian, Mexican, and United States industries are comparable.

- Manufacturing sawmill and woodworking machinery—are classified in Industry 33321, Sawmill and Woodworking Machinery Manufacturing;
- Manufacturing plastics and rubber products making machinery—are classified in Industry 33322, Plastics and Rubber Industry Machinery Manufacturing;
- Manufacturing food and beverage packaging machinery—are classified in Industry 33399, All Other General Purpose Machinery Manufacturing;
- Manufacturing commercial and industrial refrigeration and freezer equipment—are classified in Industry 33341, Ventilation, Heating, Air-Conditioning, and Commercial Refrigeration Equipment Manufacturing;
- Manufacturing commercial-type cooking and food warming equipment, automotive maintenance equipment (except mechanics' handtools) and photocopiers—are classified in Industry 33331, Commercial and Service Industry Machinery Manufacturing; and
- Manufacturing mechanics' handtools—are classified in Industry 33221, Cutlery and Handtool Manufacturing.

333291 Paper Industry Machinery Manufacturing[CAN]

This U.S. industry comprises establishments primarily engaged in manufacturing paper industry machinery for making paper and paper products, such as pulp making machinery, paper and paperboard making machinery, and paper and paperboard converting machinery.

Cross-References.

Establishments primarily engaged in manufacturing printing machinery are classified in U.S. Industry 333293, Printing Machinery and Equipment Manufacturing.

333292 Textile Machinery Manufacturing[MEX]

This U.S. industry comprises establishments primarily engaged in manufacturing textile machinery for making thread, yarn, and fiber.

Illustrative Examples:

Drawing machinery for textiles manufacturing
Extruding machinery for yarn manufacturing
Finishing machinery for textiles manufacturing
Knitting machinery manufacturing
Spinning machinery for textiles manufacturing
Texturizing machinery for textiles manufacturing
Weaving machinery manufacturing

US—United States industry only. CAN—United States and Canadian industries are comparable. MEX—United States and Mexican industries are comparable. Blank—Canadian, Mexican, and United States industries are comparable.

Cross-References.

Establishments primarily engaged in manufacturing sewing machines are classified in U.S. Industry 333298, All Other Industrial Machinery Manufacturing.

333293 Printing Machinery and Equipment Manufacturing[MEX]

This U.S. industry comprises establishments primarily engaged in manufacturing printing and bookbinding machinery and equipment, such as printing presses, typesetting machinery, and bindery machinery.

Cross-References. Establishments primarily engaged in—

- Manufacturing textile printing machinery—are classified in U.S. Industry 333292, Textile Machinery Manufacturing; and
- Manufacturing photocopiers—are classified in U.S. Industry 333315, Photographic and Photocopying Equipment Manufacturing.

333294 Food Product Machinery Manufacturing[US]

This U.S. industry comprises establishments primarily engaged in manufacturing food and beverage manufacturing-type machinery and equipment, such as dairy product plant machinery and equipment (e.g., homogenizers, pasteurizers, ice cream freezers), bakery machinery and equipment (e.g., dough mixers, bake ovens, pastry rolling machines), meat and poultry processing and preparation machinery, and other commercial food products machinery (e.g., slicers, choppers, and mixers).

Cross-References. Establishments primarily engaged in—

- Manufacturing food and beverage packaging machinery—are classified in U.S. Industry 333993, Packaging Machinery Manufacturing;
- Manufacturing commercial and industrial refrigeration and freezer equipment—are classified in U.S. Industry 333415, Air Conditioning and Warm Air Heating Equipment and Commercial and Industrial Refrigeration Equipment Manufacturing; and
- Manufacturing commercial-type cooking and food warming equipment—are classified in U.S. Industry 333319, Other Commercial and Service Industry Machinery Manufacturing.

333295 Semiconductor Machinery Manufacturing[US]

This U.S. industry comprises establishments primarily engaged in manufacturing wafer processing equipment, semiconductor assembly and packaging equipment, and other semiconductor making machinery.

US—United States industry only. CAN—United States and Canadian industries are comparable. MEX—United States and Mexican industries are comparable. Blank—Canadian, Mexican, and United States industries are comparable.

Cross-References. Establishments primarily engaged in—

- Manufacturing printed circuit board manufacturing machinery—are classified in U.S. Industry 333298, All Other Industrial Machinery Manufacturing; and
- Manufacturing semiconductor testing instruments—are classified in U.S. Industry 334515, Instrument Manufacturing for Measuring and Testing Electricity and Electrical Signals.

333298 All Other Industrial Machinery Manufacturing[US]

This U.S. industry comprises establishments primarily engaged in manufacturing industrial machinery (except agricultural and farm-type, construction and mining machinery, sawmill and woodworking machinery, plastics and rubber making machinery, paper and paperboard making machinery, textile machinery, printing machinery and equipment, food manufacturing-type machinery, and semiconductor making machinery).

Illustrative Examples:

Chemical processing machinery and equipment manufacturing
Cigarette making machinery manufacturing
Circuit board making machinery manufacturing
Glass making machinery (e.g., blowing, forming, molding) manufacturing
Light bulb and tube (i.e., electric lamp) machinery manufacturing
Petroleum refining machinery manufacturing
Sewing machines (including household-type) manufacturing
Shoe making and repairing machinery manufacturing
Tannery machinery manufacturing
Wire and cable insulating machinery manufacturing

Cross-References. Establishments primarily engaged in—

- Manufacturing agricultural and farm-type, construction, and mining machinery—are classified in Industry Group 3331, Agriculture, Construction, and Mining Machinery Manufacturing;
- Manufacturing sawmill and woodworking machinery—are classified in Industry 333210, Sawmill and Woodworking Machinery Manufacturing;
- Manufacturing plastics and rubber products making machinery—are classified in Industry 333220, Plastics and Rubber Industry Machinery Manufacturing;
- Manufacturing paper and paperboard making machinery—are classified in U.S. Industry 333291, Paper Industry Machinery Manufacturing;
- Manufacturing textile machinery—are classified in U.S. Industry 333292, Textile Machinery Manufacturing;

US—United States industry only. CAN—United States and Canadian industries are comparable. MEX—United States and Mexican industries are comparable. Blank—Canadian, Mexican, and United States industries are comparable.

- Manufacturing printing and bookbinding machinery and equipment—are classified in U.S. Industry 333293, Printing Machinery and Equipment Manufacturing;
- Manufacturing food and beverage manufacturing-type machinery—are classified in U.S. Industry 333294, Food Product Machinery Manufacturing;
- Manufacturing semiconductor making machinery—are classified in U.S. Industry 333295, Semiconductor Machinery Manufacturing;
- Manufacturing automotive maintenance equipment (except mechanics' handtools)—are classified in U.S. Industry 333319, Other Commercial and Service Industry Machinery Manufacturing; and
- Manufacturing mechanics' handtools—are classified in U.S. Industry 332212, Hand and Edge Tool Manufacturing.

3333 Commercial and Service Industry Machinery Manufacturing

33331 Commercial and Service Industry Machinery Manufacturing

This industry comprises establishments primarily engaged in manufacturing commercial and service machinery, such as automatic vending machinery, commercial laundry and dry-cleaning machinery, office machinery, photographic and photocopying machinery, optical instruments and machinery, automotive maintenance equipment (except mechanic's handtools), industrial vacuum cleaners, and commercial-type cooking equipment.

Cross-References. Establishments primarily engaged in—

- Manufacturing household-type appliances—are classified in Industry Group 3352, Household Appliance Manufacturing;
- Manufacturing computer and peripheral equipment (including point-of-sale terminals and funds transfer devices (ATMs))—are classified in Industry 33411, Computer and Peripheral Equipment Manufacturing;
- Manufacturing facsimile equipment—are classified in Industry 33421, Telephone Apparatus Manufacturing;
- Manufacturing timeclocks, timestamps, and electron and proton microscopes—are classified in Industry 33451, Navigational, Measuring, Electromedical, and Control Instruments Manufacturing;
- Manufacturing pencil sharpeners and staplers—are classified in Industry 33994, Office Supplies (except Paper) Manufacturing;
- Manufacturing sensitized film, paper, cloth, and plates, and prepared photographic chemicals—are classified in Industry 32599, All Other Chemical Product and Preparation Manufacturing;

US—United States industry only. CAN—United States and Canadian industries are comparable. MEX—United States and Mexican industries are comparable. Blank—Canadian, Mexican, and United States industries are comparable.

- Manufacturing ophthalmic focus lenses—are classified in Industry 33911, Medical Equipment and Supplies Manufacturing;
- Manufacturing television, video, and digital cameras—are classified in Subsector 334, Computer and Electronic Product Manufacturing;
- Manufacturing coin-operated arcade games—are classified in Industry 33999, All Other Miscellaneous Manufacturing;
- Manufacturing mechanics' handtools—are classified in Industry 33221, Cutlery and Handtool Manufacturing;
- Manufacturing molded plastics lens blanks—are classified in Industry 32619, Other Plastics Product Manufacturing; and
- Manufacturing molded glass lens blanks—are classified in Industry 32721, Glass and Glass Product Manufacturing.

333311 Automatic Vending Machine Manufacturing[US]

This U.S. industry comprises establishments primarily engaged in (1) manufacturing coin, token, currency or magnetic card operated vending machines and/or (2) manufacturing coin operated mechanism for machines, such as vending machines, lockers, and laundry machines.

Cross-References.

Establishments primarily engaged in manufacturing coin-operated arcade games are classified in U.S. Industry 339999, All Other Miscellaneous Manufacturing.

333312 Commercial Laundry, Drycleaning, and Pressing Machine Manufacturing[US]

This U.S. industry comprises establishments primarily engaged in manufacturing commercial and industrial laundry and drycleaning equipment and pressing machines.

Cross-References.

Establishments primarily engaged in manufacturing household-type laundry equipment are classified in U.S. Industry 335224, Household Laundry Equipment Manufacturing.

333313 Office Machinery Manufacturing[US]

This U.S. industry comprises establishments primarily engaged in manufacturing office machinery (except computers and photocopying equipment), such as mail-

US—United States industry only. CAN—United States and Canadian industries are comparable. MEX—United States and Mexican industries are comparable. Blank—Canadian, Mexican, and United States industries are comparable.

handling machinery and equipment, calculators, typewriters, and dedicated word processing equipment.

Cross-References. Establishments primarily engaged in—

- Manufacturing computers and peripheral (including point-of-sale terminals and automatic teller machines (ATMs)) equipment—are classified in Industry 33411, Computer and Peripheral Equipment Manufacturing;
- Manufacturing photocopy equipment—are classified in U.S. Industry 333315, Photographic and Photocopying Equipment Manufacturing;
- Manufacturing facsimile equipment—are classified in Industry 334210, Telephone Apparatus Manufacturing;
- Manufacturing timeclocks and timestamps—are classified in U.S. Industry 334518, Watch, Clock, and Part Manufacturing; and
- Manufacturing pencil sharpeners, staplers, staple removers, hand paper punches, cutters, trimmers, and other hand office equipment—are classified in U.S. Industry 339942, Lead Pencil and Art Good Manufacturing.

333314 Optical Instrument and Lens Manufacturing[US]

This U.S. industry comprises establishments primarily engaged in one or more of the following: (1) manufacturing optical instruments and lens, such as binoculars, microscopes (except electron, proton), telescopes, prisms, and lenses (except ophthalmic); (2) coating or polishing lenses (except ophthalmic); and (3) mounting lenses (except ophthalmic).

Cross-References. Establishments primarily engaged in—

- Manufacturing ophthalmic focus lenses—are classified in U.S. Industry 339115, Ophthalmic Goods Manufacturing;
- Manufacturing electron and proton microscopes—are classified in U.S. Industry 334516, Analytical Laboratory Instrument Manufacturing;
- Manufacturing molded plastics lens blanks—are classified in U.S. Industry 326199, All Other Plastics Product Manufacturing; and
- Manufacturing molded glass lens blanks—are classified in U.S. Industry 327212, Other Pressed and Blown Glass and Glassware Manufacturing.

333315 Photographic and Photocopying Equipment Manufacturing[US]

This U.S. industry comprises establishments primarily engaged in manufacturing photographic and photocopying equipment, such as cameras (except television,

---

US—United States industry only. CAN—United States and Canadian industries are comparable. MEX—United States and Mexican industries are comparable. Blank—Canadian, Mexican, and United States industries are comparable.

video and digital) projectors , film developing equipment, photocopying equipment, and microfilm equipment.

Cross-References. Establishments primarily engaged in—

- Manufacturing sensitized film, paper, cloth, and plates, and prepared photographic chemicals—are classified in U.S. Industry 325992, Photographic Film, Paper, Plate, and Chemical Manufacturing;
- Manufacturing photographic lenses—are classified in U.S. Industry 333314, Optical Instrument and Lens Manufacturing; and
- Manufacturing television, video, and digital cameras—are classified in Subsector 334, Computer and Electronic Product Manufacturing.

333319 Other Commercial and Service Industry Machinery Manufacturing[US]

This U.S. industry comprises establishments primarily engaged in manufacturing commercial and service industry equipment (except automatic vending machines, commercial laundry, drycleaning and pressing machines, office machinery, optical instruments and lenses, and photographic and photocopying equipment).

Illustrative Examples:

Carnival and amusement park rides manufacturing
Carwashing machinery manufacturing
Commercial-type coffee makers and urns manufacturing
Commercial-type cooking equipment (i.e., fryers, microwave ovens, ovens, ranges) manufacturing
Industrial and commercial-type vacuum cleaners manufacturing
Mechanical carpet sweepers manufacturing
Motor vehicle alignment equipment manufacturing
Power washer cleaning equipment manufacturing
Teaching machines (e.g., flight simulators) manufacturing
Water treatment equipment manufacturing

Cross-References. Establishments primarily engaged in—

- Manufacturing automatic vending machines—are classified in U.S. Industry 333311, Automatic Vending Machine Manufacturing;
- Manufacturing commercial laundry drycleaning and pressing machines—are classified in U.S. Industry 333312, Commercial Laundry, Drycleaning, and Pressing Machine Manufacturing;
- Manufacturing office machinery—are classified in U.S. Industry 333313, Office Machinery Manufacturing;

US—United States industry only. CAN—United States and Canadian industries are comparable. MEX—United States and Mexican industries are comparable. Blank—Canadian, Mexican, and United States industries are comparable.

- Manufacturing optical instruments and lenses—are classified in U.S. Industry 333314, Optical Instrument and Lens Manufacturing;
- Manufacturing photographic and photocopying equipment—are classified in U.S. Industry 333315, Photographic and Photocopying Equipment Manufacturing;
- Manufacturing household-type appliances—are classified in Industry Group 3352, Household Appliance Manufacturing; and
- Manufacturing mechanics' handtools—are classified in U.S. Industry 332212, Hand and Edge Tool Manufacturing.

3334 Ventilation, Heating, Air-Conditioning, and Commercial Refrigeration Equipment Manufacturing

33341 Ventilation, Heating, Air-Conditioning, and Commercial Refrigeration Equipment Manufacturing

This industry comprises establishments primarily engaged in manufacturing ventilating, heating, air-conditioning, and commercial and industrial refrigeration and freezer equipment.

Illustrative Examples:

Air-conditioning and warm air heating combination units manufacturing
Air-conditioner filters manufacturing
Attic fans manufacturing
Dust and fume collecting equipment manufacturing
Gas fireplaces manufacturing
Heating boilers manufacturing
Industrial and commercial-type fans manufacturing
Refrigerated counter and display cases manufacturing
Refrigerated drinking fountains manufacturing
Space heaters (except portable electric) manufacturing

Cross-References. Establishments primarily engaged in—

- Manufacturing household-type fans (except attic), portable electric space heaters, humidifiers, dehumidifiers, and air purification equipment—are classified in Industry 33521, Small Electrical Appliance Manufacturing;
- Manufacturing household-type appliances, such as cooking stoves, ranges, refrigerators, and freezers—are classified in Industry 33522, Major Appliance Manufacturing;
- Manufacturing commercial-type cooking equipment—are classified in Industry 33329, Other Industrial Machinery Manufacturing;

US—United States industry only. CAN—United States and Canadian industries are comparable. MEX—United States and Mexican industries are comparable. Blank—Canadian, Mexican, and United States industries are comparable.

- Manufacturing industrial, power, and marine boilers—are classified in Industry 33241, Power Boiler and Heat Exchanger Manufacturing;
- Manufacturing industrial process furnaces and ovens—are classified in Industry 33399, All Other General Purpose Machinery Manufacturing; and
- Manufacturing motor vehicle air-conditioning systems and compressors—are classified in Industry 33639, Other Motor Vehicle Parts Manufacturing.

333411 Air Purification Equipment Manufacturing[US]

This U.S. industry comprises establishments primarily engaged in manufacturing stationary air purification equipment, such as industrial dust and fume collection equipment, electrostatic precipitation equipment, warm air furnace filters, air washers, and other dust collection equipment.

Cross-References. Establishments primarily engaged in—

- Manufacturing air-conditioning units (except motor vehicle)—are classified in U.S. Industry 333415, Air-Conditioning and Warm Air Heating Equipment and Commercial and Industrial Refrigeration Equipment Manufacturing;
- Manufacturing motor vehicle air-conditioning systems and compressors—are classified in U.S. Industry 336391, Motor Vehicle Air-Conditioning Manufacturing;
- Manufacturing household-type fans (except attic) and portable air purification equipment—are classified in U.S. Industry 335211, Electric Housewares and Household Fan Manufacturing; and
- Manufacturing industrial and commercial blowers, industrial and commercial exhaust and ventilating fans, and attic fans—are classified in U.S. Industry 333412, Industrial and Commercial Fan and Blower Manufacturing.

333412 Industrial and Commercial Fan and Blower Manufacturing[US]

This U.S. industry comprises establishments primarily engaged in manufacturing attic fans and industrial and commercial fans and blowers, such as commercial exhaust fans and commercial ventilating fans.

Cross-References. Establishments primarily engaged in—

- Manufacturing air-conditioning units (except motor vehicle)—are classified in U.S. Industry 333415, Air-Conditioning and Warm Air Heating Equipment and Commercial and Industrial Refrigeration Equipment Manufacturing;

US—United States industry only. CAN—United States and Canadian industries are comparable. MEX—United States and Mexican industries are comparable. Blank—Canadian, Mexican, and United States industries are comparable.

- Manufacturing motor vehicle air-conditioning systems and compressors—are classified in U.S. Industry 336391, Motor Vehicle Air-Conditioning Manufacturing;
- Manufacturing household-type fans (except attic) and portable air purification equipment—are classified in U.S. Industry 335211, Electric Housewares and Household Fan Manufacturing; and
- Manufacturing stationary air purification equipment—are classified in U.S. Industry 333411, Air Purification Equipment Manufacturing.

333414 Heating Equipment (except Warm Air Furnaces) Manufacturing[US]

This U.S. industry comprises establishments primarily engaged in manufacturing heating equipment (except electric and warm air furnaces), such as heating boilers, heating stoves, floor and wall furnaces, and wall and baseboard heating units.

Cross-References. Establishments primarily engaged in—

- Manufacturing warm air furnaces—are classified in U.S. Industry 333415, Air-Conditioning and Warm Air Heating Equipment and Commercial and Industrial Refrigeration Equipment Manufacturing;
- Manufacturing electric space heaters—are classified in U.S. Industry 335211, Electric Housewares and Household Fan Manufacturing;
- Manufacturing household-type cooking stoves and ranges—are classified in U.S. Industry 335221, Household Cooking Appliance Manufacturing;
- Manufacturing industrial, power, and marine boilers—are classified in Industry 332410, Power Boiler and Heat Exchanger Manufacturing;
- Manufacturing industrial process furnaces and ovens—are classified in U.S. Industry 333994, Industrial Process Furnace and Oven Manufacturing; and
- Manufacturing commercial-type cooking equipment—are classified in U.S. Industry 333319, Other Commercial and Service Industry Machinery Manufacturing.

333415 Air-Conditioning and Warm Air Heating Equipment and Commercial and Industrial Refrigeration Equipment Manufacturing[US]

This U.S. industry comprises establishments primarily engaged in (1) manufacturing air-conditioning (except motor vehicle) and warm air furnace equipment and/or (2) manufacturing commercial and industrial refrigeration and freezer equipment.

US—United States industry only. CAN—United States and Canadian industries are comparable. MEX—United States and Mexican industries are comparable. Blank—Canadian, Mexican, and United States industries are comparable.

Illustrative Examples:

Air-conditioning and warm air heating combination units manufacturing
Air-conditioning compressors (except motor vehicle) manufacturing
Air-conditioning condensers and condensing units manufacturing
Dehumidifiers (except portable electric) manufacturing
Heat pumps manufacturing
Humidifying equipment (except portable) manufacturing
Refrigerated counter and display cases manufacturing
Refrigerated drinking fountains manufacturing
Soda fountain cooling and dispensing equipment manufacturing
Snow making machinery manufacturing

Cross-References. Establishments primarily engaged in—

- Manufacturing motor vehicle air-conditioning systems and compressors—are classified in U.S. Industry 336391, Motor Vehicle Air-Conditioning Manufacturing;
- Manufacturing household-type refrigerators and freezers—are classified in U.S. Industry 335222, Household Refrigerator and Home Freezer Manufacturing;
- Manufacturing portable electric space heaters, humidifiers, and dehumidifiers—are classified in U.S. Industry 335211, Electric Housewares and Household Fan Manufacturing;
- Manufacturing heating boilers, heating stoves, floor and wall mount furnaces, and electric wall and baseboard heating units—are classified in U.S. Industry 333414, Heating Equipment (except Warm Air Furnaces) Manufacturing; and
- Manufacturing furnace air filters—are classified in U.S. Industry 333411, Air Purification Equipment Manufacturing.

3335 Metalworking Machinery Manufacturing

33351 Metalworking Machinery Manufacturing

This industry comprises establishments primarily engaged in manufacturing metalworking machinery, such as metal cutting and metal forming machine tools; cutting tools; and accessories for metalworking machinery; special dies, tools, jigs, and fixtures; industrial molds; rolling mill machinery; assembly machinery; coil handling, conversion, or straightening equipment; and wire drawing and fabricating machines.

Cross-References. Establishments primarily engaged in—

- Manufacturing handtools (except power-driven), cutting dies (except metal cutting), sawblades, and handsaws—are classified in Industry 33221, Cutlery and Handtool Manufacturing;

US—United States industry only. CAN—United States and Canadian industries are comparable. MEX—United States and Mexican industries are comparable. Blank—Canadian, Mexican, and United States industries are comparable.

- Manufacturing casting molds for heavy steel ingots—are classified in Industry 33151, Ferrous Metal Foundries; and
- Manufacturing power-driven handtools and welding and soldering equipment—are classified in Industry 33399, All Other General Purpose Machinery Manufacturing.

333511 Industrial Mold Manufacturing[CAN]

This U.S. industry comprises establishments primarily engaged in manufacturing industrial molds for casting metals or forming other materials, such as plastics, glass, or rubber.

Cross-References.

Establishments primarily engaged in manufacturing casting molds for steel ingots are classified in U.S. Industry 331511, Iron Foundries.

333512 Machine Tool (Metal Cutting Types) Manufacturing[US]

This U.S. industry comprises establishments primarily engaged in manufacturing metal cutting machine tools (except handtools).

Illustrative Examples:

Home workshop metal cutting machine tools (except handtools, welding equipment) manufacturing
Metalworking boring machines manufacturing
Metalworking buffing and polishing machines manufacturing
Metalworking drilling machines manufacturing
Metalworking grinding machines manufacturing
Metalworking lathes manufacturing
Metalworking milling machines manufacturing

Cross-References. Establishments primarily engaged in—

- Manufacturing welding and soldering equipment—are classified in U.S. Industry 333992, Welding and Soldering Equipment Manufacturing;
- Manufacturing metal-forming machine tools—are classified in U.S. Industry 333513, Machine Tool (Metal Forming Types) Manufacturing;
- Manufacturing power-driven metal cutting handtools—are classified in U.S. Industry 333991, Power-Driven Handtool Manufacturing; and
- Manufacturing accessories and attachments for metal cutting machine tools—are classified in U.S. Industry 333515, Cutting Tool and Machine Tool Accessory Manufacturing.

US—United States industry only. CAN—United States and Canadian industries are comparable. MEX—United States and Mexican industries are comparable. Blank—Canadian, Mexican, and United States industries are comparable.

333513 Machine Tool (Metal Forming Types) Manufacturing[US]

This U.S. industry comprises establishments primarily engaged in manufacturing metal forming machine tools (except handtools), such as punching, sheering, bending, forming, pressing, forging and die-casting machines.

Cross-References. Establishments primarily engaged in—

- Manufacturing welding and soldering equipment—are classified in U.S. Industry 333992, Welding and Soldering Equipment Manufacturing;
- Manufacturing metal-cutting machine tools—are classified in U.S. Industry 333512, Machine Tool (Metal Cutting Types) Manufacturing;
- Manufacturing power-driven handtools—are classified in U.S. Industry 333991, Power-Driven Handtool Manufacturing;
- Manufacturing rolling mill machinery and equipment—are classified in U.S. Industry 333516, Rolling Mill Machinery and Equipment Manufacturing; and
- Manufacturing accessories and attachments for metal forming machine tools—are classified in U.S. Industry 333515, Cutting Tool and Machine Tool Accessory Manufacturing.

333514 Special Die and Tool, Die Set, Jig, and Fixture Manufacturing[US]

This U.S. industry comprises establishments, known as tool and die shops, primarily engaged in manufacturing special tools and fixtures, such as cutting dies and jigs.

Cross-References. Establishments primarily engaged in—

- Manufacturing molds for die-casting and foundry casting; and metal molds for plaster working, rubber working, plastics working, and glass working machinery—are classified in U.S. Industry 333511, Industrial Mold Manufacturing;
- Manufacturing molds for heavy steel ingots—are classified in U.S. Industry 331511, Iron Foundries; and
- Manufacturing cutting dies for materials other than metal—are classified in U.S. Industry 332212, Hand and Edge Tool Manufacturing.

333515 Cutting Tool and Machine Tool Accessory Manufacturing[US]

This U.S. industry comprises establishments primarily engaged in manufacturing accessories and attachments for metal cutting and metal forming machine tools.

US—United States industry only. CAN—United States and Canadian industries are comparable. MEX—United States and Mexican industries are comparable. Blank—Canadian, Mexican, and United States industries are comparable.

Illustrative Examples:

Knives and bits for metalworking lathes, planers, and shapers manufacturing
Measuring attachments (e.g., sine bars) for machine tool manufacturing
Metalworking drill bits
Taps and dies (i.e., machine tool accessories) manufacturing

Cross-References. Establishments primarily engaged in—

- Manufacturing accessories and attachments for cutting and forming machines (except metal cutting, metal forming machinery)—are classified in U.S. Industry 332212, Hand and Edge Tool Manufacturing; and
- Manufacturing saw blades and handsaws—are classified in U.S. Industry 332213, Saw Blade and Handsaw Manufacturing.

333516 Rolling Mill Machinery and Equipment Manufacturing[US]

This U.S. industry comprises establishments primarily engaged in manufacturing rolling mill machinery and equipment for metal production.

333518 Other Metalworking Machinery Manufacturing[US]

This U.S. industry comprises establishments primarily engaged in manufacturing metal working machinery (except industrial molds; metal cutting machine tools; metal forming machine tools; special dies and tools, die sets, jigs, and fixtures; cutting tools and machine tool accessories; and rolling mill machinery and equipment).

Illustrative Examples:

Assembly machines manufacturing
Cradle assemblies machinery (i.e., wire making equipment) manufacturing
Metalworking coil winding and cutting machinery manufacturing
Wire drawing and fabricating machinery and equipment (except dies) manufacturing

Cross-References. Establishments primarily engaged in—

- Manufacturing industrial molds—are classified in U.S. Industry 333511, Industrial Mold Manufacturing;
- Manufacturing metal cutting machinery—are classified in U.S. Industry 333512, Machine Tool (Metal Cutting Types) Manufacturing;
- Manufacturing metal forming machinery—are classified in U.S. Industry 333513, Machine Tool (Metal Forming Types) Manufacturing;

US—United States industry only. CAN—United States and Canadian industries are comparable. MEX—United States and Mexican industries are comparable. Blank—Canadian, Mexican, and United States industries are comparable.

- Manufacturing special dies and tools, die sets, jigs, and fixtures—are classified in U.S. Industry 333514, Special Die and Tool, Die Set, Jig, and Fixture Manufacturing;
- Manufacturing cutting tools and machine tool accessories—are classified in U.S. Industry 333515, Cutting Tool and Machine Tool Accessory Manufacturing; and
- Manufacturing rolling mill machinery—are classified in U.S. Industry 333516, Rolling Mill Machinery and Equipment Manufacturing.

3336 Engine, Turbine, and Power Transmission Equipment Manufacturing

33361 Engine, Turbine, and Power Transmission Equipment Manufacturing

This industry comprises establishments primarily engaged in manufacturing turbines, power transmission equipment, and internal combustion engines (except automotive gasoline and aircraft).

Illustrative Examples:

Clutches and brakes (except electromagnetic industrial controls, motor vehicle) manufacturing
Diesel and semidiesel engines manufacturing
Electric outboard motors manufacturing
Plain bearings (except internal combustion engine) manufacturing
Plain bushings (except internal combustion engine) manufacturing
Power transmission pulleys manufacturing
Speed changers (i.e., power transmission equipment) manufacturing
Speed reducers (i.e., power transmission equipment) manufacturing
Turbine generator set units manufacturing
Universal joints (except aircraft, motor vehicle) manufacturing

Cross-References. Establishments primarily engaged in—

- Manufacturing motor vehicle power transmission equipment—are classified in Industry 33635, Motor Vehicle Transmission and Power Train Parts Manufacturing;
- Manufacturing aircraft engines and aircraft power transmission equipment—are classified in Industry 33641, Aerospace Product and Parts Manufacturing;
- Manufacturing ball and roller bearings—are classified in Industry 33299, All Other Fabricated Metal Product Manufacturing;

US—United States industry only. CAN—United States and Canadian industries are comparable. MEX—United States and Mexican industries are comparable. Blank—Canadian, Mexican, and United States industries are comparable.

- Manufacturing automotive engines (except diesel)—are classified in Industry 33631, Motor Vehicle Gasoline Engine and Engine Parts Manufacturing; and
- Manufacturing electric power transmission, electric power distribution equipment, generators, or prime mover generator sets (except turbines)—are classified in Industry 33531, Electrical Equipment Manufacturing.

333611 Turbine and Turbine Generator Set Units Manufacturing[CAN]

This U.S. industry comprises establishments primarily engaged in manufacturing turbines (except aircraft); and complete turbine generator set units, such as steam, hydraulic, gas, and wind.

Cross-References. Establishments primarily engaged in—

- Manufacturing aircraft turbines—are classified in U.S. Industry 336412, Aircraft Engine and Engine Parts Manufacturing; and
- Manufacturing generators or prime mover generator sets (except turbines)—are classified in U.S. Industry 335312, Motor and Generator Manufacturing.

333612 Speed Changer, Industrial High-Speed Drive, and Gear Manufacturing[US]

This U.S. industry comprises establishments primarily engaged in manufacturing gears, speed changers, and industrial high-speed drives (except hydrostatic).

Cross-References. Establishments primarily engaged in—

- Manufacturing motor vehicle power transmission equipment—are classified in Industry 336350, Motor Vehicle Transmission and Power Train Parts Manufacturing;
- Manufacturing aircraft power transmission equipment—are classified in U.S. Industry 336413, Other Aircraft Parts and Auxiliary Equipment Manufacturing; and
- Manufacturing industrial hydrostatic transmissions—are classified in U.S. Industry 333996, Fluid Power Pump and Motor Manufacturing.

333613 Mechanical Power Transmission Equipment Manufacturing[US]

This U.S. industry comprises establishments primarily engaged in manufacturing mechanical power transmission equipment (except motor vehicle and aircraft), such as plain bearings, clutches (except motor vehicle and electromagnetic industrial control), couplings, joints, and drive chains.

US—United States industry only. CAN—United States and Canadian industries are comparable. MEX—United States and Mexican industries are comparable. Blank—Canadian, Mexican, and United States industries are comparable.

Cross-References. Establishments primarily engaged in—

- Manufacturing motor vehicle power transmission equipment—are classified in Industry 336350, Motor Vehicle Transmission and Power Train Parts Manufacturing;
- Manufacturing aircraft power transmission equipment—are classified in U.S. Industry 336413, Other Aircraft Parts and Auxiliary Equipment Manufacturing;
- Manufacturing ball and roller bearings—are classified in U.S. Industry 332991, Ball and Roller Bearing Manufacturing; and
- Manufacturing gears, speed changers, and industrial high-speed drives (except hydrostatic)—are classified in U.S. Industry 333612, Speed Changer, Industrial High-Speed Drive, and Gear Manufacturing.

333618 Other Engine Equipment Manufacturing[US]

This U.S. industry comprises establishments primarily engaged in manufacturing internal combustion engines (except automotive gasoline and aircraft).

Cross-References. Establishments primarily engaged in—

- Manufacturing gasoline motor vehicle engines and motor vehicle transmissions—are classified in Industry Group 3363, Motor Vehicle Parts Manufacturing;
- Manufacturing gasoline aircraft engines and aircraft transmissions—are classified in Industry 33641, Aerospace Product and Parts Manufacturing;
- Manufacturing turbine and turbine generator sets units—are classified in U.S. Industry 333611, Turbine and Turbine Generator Set Units Manufacturing;
- Manufacturing speed changers and industrial high-speed drivers and gears—are classified in U.S. Industry 333612, Speed Changer, Industrial High-Speed Drive, and Gear Manufacturing; and
- Manufacturing mechanical power transmission equipment (except motor vehicle and aircraft)—are classified in U.S. Industry 333613, Mechanical Power Transmission Equipment Manufacturing.

3339 Other General Purpose Machinery Manufacturing

33391 Pump and Compressor Manufacturing

This industry comprises establishments primarily engaged in manufacturing pumps and compressors, such as general purpose air and gas compressors, nonagri-

US—United States industry only. CAN—United States and Canadian industries are comparable. MEX—United States and Mexican industries are comparable. Blank—Canadian, Mexican, and United States industries are comparable.

cultural spraying and dusting equipment, general purpose pumps and pumping equipment (except fluid power pumps and motors), and measuring and dispensing pumps.

Cross-References. Establishments primarily engaged in—

- Manufacturing fluid power pumps and motors and handheld pneumatic spray guns—are classified in Industry 33399, All Other General Purpose Machinery Manufacturing;
- Manufacturing agricultural spraying and dusting equipment—are classified in Industry 33311, Agricultural Implement Manufacturing;
- Manufacturing laboratory vacuum pumps—are classified in Industry 33911, Medical Equipment and Supplies Manufacturing;
- Manufacturing pumps and air-conditioning systems and compressors for motor vehicles—are classified in Industry Group 3363, Motor Vehicle Parts Manufacturing; and
- Manufacturing air-conditioning systems and compressors (except motor vehicle)—are classified in Industry 33341, Ventilation, Heating, Air-Conditioning, and Commercial Refrigeration Equipment Manufacturing.

333911 Pump and Pumping Equipment Manufacturing[US]

This U.S. industry comprises establishments primarily engaged in manufacturing general purpose pumps and pumping equipment (except fluid power pumps and motors), such as reciprocating pumps, turbine pumps, centrifugal pumps, rotary pumps, diaphragm pumps, domestic water system pumps, oil well and oil field pumps and sump pumps.

Cross-References. Establishments primarily engaged in—

- Manufacturing fluid power pumps and motors—are classified in U.S. Industry 333996, Fluid Power Pump and Motor Manufacturing;
- Manufacturing measuring and dispensing pumps—are classified in U.S. Industry 333913, Measuring and Dispensing Pump Manufacturing;
- Manufacturing vacuum pumps (except laboratory)—are classified in U.S. Industry 333912, Air and Gas Compressor Manufacturing;
- Manufacturing laboratory vacuum pumps—are classified in U.S. Industry 339111, Laboratory Apparatus and Furniture Manufacturing; and
- Manufacturing fluid pumps for motor vehicles, such as oil pumps, water pumps, and power steering pumps—are classified in Industry Group 3363, Motor Vehicle Parts Manufacturing.

US—United States industry only. CAN—United States and Canadian industries are comparable. MEX—United States and Mexican industries are comparable. Blank—Canadian, Mexican, and United States industries are comparable.

333912 Air and Gas Compressor Manufacturing[US]

This U.S. industry comprises establishments primarily engaged in manufacturing general purpose air and gas compressors, such as reciprocating compressors, centrifugal compressors, vacuum pumps (except laboratory), and nonagricultural spraying and dusting compressors and spray gun units.

Cross-References. Establishments primarily engaged in—

- Manufacturing refrigeration and air-conditioning (except motor vehicle) systems and compressors—are classified in U.S. Industry 333415, Air-Conditioning and Warm Air Heating Equipment and Commercial and Industrial Refrigeration Equipment Manufacturing;
- Manufacturing motor vehicle air-conditioning systems and compressors—are classified in U.S. Industry 336391, Motor Vehicle Air-Conditioning Manufacturing;
- Manufacturing fluid power pumps and motors—are classified in U.S. Industry 333996, Fluid Power Pump and Motor Manufacturing;
- Manufacturing agricultural spraying and dusting equipment—are classified in U.S. Industry 333111, Farm Machinery and Equipment Manufacturing;
- Manufacturing laboratory vacuum pumps—are classified in U.S. Industry 339111, Laboratory Apparatus and Furniture Manufacturing; and
- Manufacturing handheld pneumatic spray guns—are classified in U.S. Industry 333991, Power-Driven Handtool Manufacturing.

333913 Measuring and Dispensing Pump Manufacturing[US]

This U.S. industry comprises establishments primarily engaged in manufacturing measuring and dispensing pumps, such as gasoline pumps and lubricating oil measuring and dispensing pumps.

Cross-References.

Establishments primarily engaged in manufacturing pumps and pumping equipment for general industrial use are classified in U.S. Industry 333911, Pump and Pumping Equipment Manufacturing.

33392 Material Handling Equipment Manufacturing

This industry comprises establishments primarily engaged in manufacturing material handling equipment, such as elevators and moving stairs; conveyors and

US—United States industry only. CAN—United States and Canadian industries are comparable. MEX—United States and Mexican industries are comparable. Blank—Canadian, Mexican, and United States industries are comparable.

conveying equipment; overhead traveling cranes, hoists, and monorail systems; and industrial trucks, tractors, trailers, and stacker machinery.

Cross-References. Establishments primarily engaged in—

- Manufacturing motor vehicle-type trailers—are classified in Industry 33621, Motor Vehicle Body and Trailer Manufacturing;
- Manufacturing farm-type tractors—are classified in Industry 33311, Agricultural Implement Manufacturing;
- Manufacturing construction-type tractors and cranes—are classified in Industry 33312, Construction Machinery Manufacturing; and
- Manufacturing power transmission pulleys—are classified in Industry 33361, Engine, Turbine, and Power Transmission Equipment Manufacturing.

333921 Elevator and Moving Stairway Manufacturing[US]

This U.S. industry comprises establishments primarily engaged in manufacturing elevators and moving stairways.

Illustrative Examples:

Automobile lifts (i.e., garage-type, service station) manufacturing
Escalators manufacturing
Moving walkways manufacturing
Passenger and freight elevators manufacturing

Cross-References.

Establishments primarily engaged in manufacturing commercial conveyor systems and equipment are classified in U.S. Industry 333922, Conveyor and Conveying Equipment Manufacturing.

333922 Conveyor and Conveying Equipment Manufacturing[US]

This U.S. industry comprises establishments primarily engaged in manufacturing conveyors and conveying equipment, such as gravity conveyors, trolley conveyors, tow conveyors, pneumatic tube conveyors, carousel conveyors, farm conveyors, and belt conveyors.

Cross-References. Establishments primarily engaged in—

- Manufacturing passenger or freight elevators, dumbwaiters, and moving stairways—are classified in U.S. Industry 333921, Elevator and Moving Stairway Manufacturing; and

US—United States industry only. CAN—United States and Canadian industries are comparable. MEX—United States and Mexican industries are comparable. Blank—Canadian, Mexican, and United States industries are comparable.

- Manufacturing overhead traveling cranes and monorail systems—are classified in U.S. Industry 333923, Overhead Traveling Crane, Hoist, and Monorail System Manufacturing.

333923 Overhead Traveling Crane, Hoist, and Monorail System Manufacturing[US]

This U.S. industry comprises establishments primarily engaged in manufacturing overhead traveling cranes, hoists, and monorail systems.

Illustrative Examples:

Aerial work platforms manufacturing
Automobile wrecker (i.e., tow truck) hoists manufacturing
Block and tackle manufacturing
Metal pulleys (except power transmission) manufacturing
Winches manufacturing

Cross-References. Establishments primarily engaged in—

- Manufacturing construction-type cranes—are classified in Industry 333120, Construction Machinery Manufacturing;
- Manufacturing aircraft loading hoists—are classified in U.S. Industry 333924, Industrial Truck, Tractor, Trailer, and Stacker Machinery Manufacturing; and
- Manufacturing power transmission pulleys—are classified in U.S. Industry 333613, Mechanical Power Transmission Equipment Manufacturing.

333924 Industrial Truck, Tractor, Trailer, and Stacker Machinery Manufacturing[US]

This U.S. industry comprises establishments primarily engaged in manufacturing industrial trucks, tractors, trailers, and stackers (i.e., truck-type), such as forklifts, pallet loaders and unloaders, and portable loading docks.

Cross-References. Establishments primarily engaged in—

- Manufacturing motor vehicle-type trailers—are classified in U.S. Industry 336212, Truck Trailer Manufacturing;
- Manufacturing farm-type tractors—are classified in U.S. Industry 333111, Farm Machinery and Equipment Manufacturing; and
- Manufacturing construction-type tractors—are classified in Industry 333120, Construction Machinery Manufacturing.

US—United States industry only. CAN—United States and Canadian industries are comparable. MEX—United States and Mexican industries are comparable. Blank—Canadian, Mexican, and United States industries are comparable.

33399 All Other General Purpose Machinery Manufacturing

This industry comprises establishments primarily engaged in manufacturing general purpose machinery (except ventilation, heating, air-conditioning, and commercial refrigeration equipment; metal working machinery; engines, turbines, and power transmission equipment; pumps and compressors; and material handling equipment).

Illustrative Examples:

Automatic fire sprinkler systems manufacturing
Bridge and gate lifting machinery manufacturing
Fluid power cylinders manufacturing
Fluid power pumps manufacturing
Hydraulic and pneumatic jacks manufacturing
Industrial-type furnaces manufacturing
Packaging machinery manufacturing
Power-driven handtools manufacturing
Scales (except laboratory-type) manufacturing
Welding equipment manufacturing

Cross-References. Establishments primarily engaged in—

- Manufacturing ventilating, heating, air-conditioning (except motor vehicle), commercial refrigeration, and furnace filters—are classified in Industry 33341, Ventilation, Heating, Air-Conditioning, and Commercial Refrigeration Equipment Manufacturing;
- Manufacturing metalworking machinery—are classified in Industry Group 3335, Metalworking Machinery Manufacturing;
- Manufacturing engine, turbine, and power transmission equipment—are classified in Industry Group 3336, Engine, Turbine, and Power Transmission Equipment Manufacturing;
- Manufacturing pumps and compressors—are classified in Industry 33391, Pump and Compressor Manufacturing;
- Manufacturing material handling equipment—are classified in Industry 33392, Material Handling Equipment Manufacturing;
- Manufacturing motor vehicle air-conditioning systems and compressors, engine filters, and pumps—are classified in Industry Group 3363, Motor Vehicle Parts Manufacturing;
- Manufacturing laboratory scales, balances, ovens, and furnaces—are classified in Industry 33911, Medical Equipment and Supplies Manufacturing;
- Manufacturing metal cutting and metal forming machinery—are classified in Industry 33351, Metalworking Machinery Manufacturing;

US—United States industry only. CAN—United States and Canadian industries are comparable. MEX—United States and Mexican industries are comparable. Blank—Canadian, Mexican, and United States industries are comparable.

- Manufacturing power driven heavy construction and mining hand operated tools, such as tampers and augers—are classified in Industries 33312, Construction Machinery Manufacturing and 33313, Mining and Oil and Gas Field Machinery Manufacturing;
- Manufacturing bakery ovens and industrial kilns, such as cement, wood, and chemical—are classified in Industry 33329, Other Industrial Machinery Manufacturing;
- Manufacturing mechanical jacks, handheld soldering irons, countersink bits, drill bits, router bits, milling cutters, and other machine tools for woodcutting—are classified in Industry 33221, Cutlery and Handtool Manufacturing;
- Manufacturing carnival amusement park equipment, automotive maintenance equipment, and coin-operated vending machines—are classified in Industry 33331, Commercial and Service Industry Machinery Manufacturing; and
- Manufacturing transformers for arc-welding—are classified in Industry 33531, Electrical Equipment Manufacturing.

333991 Power-Driven Handtool Manufacturing[US]

This U.S. industry comprises establishments primarily engaged in manufacturing power-driven (e.g., battery, corded, pneumatic) handtools, such as drills, screwguns, circular saws, chain saws, staplers, and nailers.

Cross-References. Establishments primarily engaged in—

- Manufacturing metal cutting-type and metal forming-type machines (including home workshop)—are classified in Industry 33351, Metalworking Machinery Manufacturing;
- Manufacturing countersink bits, drill bits, router bits, milling cutters, and other machine tools for woodcutting—are classified in U.S. Industry 332212, Hand and Edge Tool Manufacturing;
- Manufacturing power-driven heavy construction or mining hand operated tools, such as tampers, jackhammers, and augers—are classified in Industries 333120, Construction Machinery Manufacturing and 33313, Mining and Oil and Gas Field Machinery Manufacturing; and
- Manufacturing powered home lawn and garden equipment—are classified in U.S. Industry 333112, Lawn and Garden Tractor and Home Lawn and Garden Equipment Manufacturing.

333992 Welding and Soldering Equipment Manufacturing[US]

This U.S. industry comprises establishments primarily engaged in manufacturing welding and soldering equipment and accessories (except transformers), such as

US—United States industry only. CAN—United States and Canadian industries are comparable. MEX—United States and Mexican industries are comparable. Blank—Canadian, Mexican, and United States industries are comparable.

arc, resistance, gas, plasma, laser, electron beam, and ultrasonic welding equipment; welding electrodes; coated or cored welding wire; and soldering equipment (except handheld).

Cross-References. Establishments primarily engaged in—

- Manufacturing handheld soldering irons—are classified in U.S. Industry 332212, Hand and Edge Tool Manufacturing; and
- Manufacturing transformers for arc-welding—are classified in U.S. Industry 335311, Power, Distribution, and Specialty Transformer Manufacturing.

333993 Packaging Machinery Manufacturing[US]

This U.S. industry comprises establishments primarily engaged in manufacturing packaging machinery, such as wrapping, bottling, canning, and labeling machinery.

333994 Industrial Process Furnace and Oven Manufacturing[US]

This U.S. Industry comprises establishments primarily engaged in manufacturing industrial process furnaces, ovens, induction and dielectric heating equipment, and kilns (except cement, chemical, wood).

Cross-References. Establishments primarily engaged in—

- Manufacturing bakery ovens—are classified in U.S. Industry 333294, Food Product Machinery Manufacturing;
- Manufacturing cement, wood, and chemical kilns—are classified in U.S. Industry 333298, All Other Industrial Machinery Manufacturing;
- Manufacturing cremating ovens—are classified in U.S. Industry 333999, All Other Miscellaneous General Purpose Machinery Manufacturing; and
- Manufacturing laboratory furnaces and ovens—are classified in U.S. Industry 339111, Laboratory Apparatus and Furniture Manufacturing.

333995 Fluid Power Cylinder and Actuator Manufacturing[US]

This U.S. industry comprises establishments primarily engaged in manufacturing fluid power (i.e., hydraulic and pneumatic) cylinders and actuators.

333996 Fluid Power Pump and Motor Manufacturing[US]

This U.S. industry comprises establishments primarily engaged in manufacturing fluid power (i.e., hydraulic and pneumatic) pumps and motors.

US—United States industry only. CAN—United States and Canadian industries are comparable. MEX—United States and Mexican industries are comparable. Blank—Canadian, Mexican, and United States industries are comparable.

Cross-References. Establishments primarily engaged in—

- Manufacturing fluid pumps for motor vehicles, such as oil pumps, water pumps, and power steering pumps—are classified in Industry Group 3363, Motor Vehicle Parts Manufacturing;
- Manufacturing general purpose pumps (except fluid power)—are classified in U.S. Industry 333911, Pump and Pumping Equipment Manufacturing; and
- Manufacturing air compressors—are classified in U.S. Industry 333912, Air and Gas Compressor Manufacturing.

333997 Scale and Balance (except Laboratory) Manufacturing[US]

This U.S. industry comprises establishments primarily engaged in manufacturing scales and balances (except laboratory).

Cross-References.

Establishments primarily engaged in manufacturing laboratory scales and balances are classified in U.S. Industry 339111, Laboratory Apparatus and Furniture Manufacturing.

333999 All Other Miscellaneous General Purpose Machinery Manufacturing[US]

This U.S. industry comprises establishments primarily engaged in manufacturing general purpose machinery (except ventilating, heating, air-conditioning, and commercial refrigeration equipment; metal working machinery; engines, turbines, and power transmission equipment; pumps and compressors; material handling equipment; power-driven handtools; welding and soldering equipment; packaging machinery; industrial process furnaces and ovens; fluid power cylinders and actuators; fluid power pumps and motors; and scales and balances).

Illustrative Examples:

Automatic fire sprinkler systems manufacturing
Baling machinery (e.g., paper, scrap metal) manufacturing
Bridge and gate lifting machinery manufacturing
Cremating ovens manufacturing
General purpose-type sieves and screening equipment manufacturing
Hydraulic and pneumatic jacks manufacturing
Industrial and general line filters (except internal combustion engine, warm air furnace) manufacturing
Industrial-type centrifuges manufacturing

US—United States industry only. CAN—United States and Canadian industries are comparable. MEX—United States and Mexican industries are comparable. Blank—Canadian, Mexican, and United States industries are comparable.

Cross-References. Establishments primarily engaged in—

- Manufacturing ventilating, heating, air-conditioning (except motor vehicle), and commercial refrigeration—are classified in Industry 33341, Ventilation, Heating, Air-Conditioning, and Commercial Refrigeration Equipment Manufacturing;
- Manufacturing motor vehicle air-conditioning systems and compressors—are classified in U.S. Industry 336391, Motor Vehicle Air-Conditioning Manufacturing;
- Manufacturing metalworking machinery—are classified in Industry Group 3335, Metalworking Machinery Manufacturing;
- Manufacturing engine, turbine, and power transmission equipment—are classified in Industry Group 3336, Engine, Turbine, and Power Transmission Equipment Manufacturing;
- Manufacturing pumps and compressors—are classified in Industry 33391, Pump and Compressor Manufacturing;
- Manufacturing material handling equipment—are classified in Industry 33392, Material Handling Equipment Manufacturing;
- Manufacturing power-driven handtools—are classified in U.S. Industry 333991, Power-Driven Handtool Manufacturing;
- Manufacturing welding and soldering equipment (except handheld soldering irons)—are classified in U.S. Industry 333992, Welding and Soldering Equipment Manufacturing;
- Manufacturing packaging machinery—are classified in U.S. Industry 333993, Packaging Machinery Manufacturing;
- Manufacturing bakery ovens and cement, wood, and chemical kilns—are classified in U.S. Industry 333298, All Other Industrial Machinery Manufacturing;
- Manufacturing industrial process furnaces and ovens (except bakery)—are classified in U.S. Industry 333994, Industrial Process Furnace and Oven Manufacturing;
- Manufacturing fluid power cylinders and actuators—are classified in U.S. Industry 333995, Fluid Power Cylinder and Actuator Manufacturing;
- Manufacturing fluid power pumps and motors—are classified in U.S. Industry 333996, Fluid Power Pump and Motor Manufacturing;
- Manufacturing scales and balances (except laboratory)—are classified in U.S. Industry 333997, Scale and Balance (except Laboratory) Manufacturing;

US—United States industry only. CAN—United States and Canadian industries are comparable. MEX—United States and Mexican industries are comparable. Blank—Canadian, Mexican, and United States industries are comparable.

- Manufacturing carnival and amusement park equipment, automotive maintenance equipment and coin-operated vending machines—are classified in Industry 33331, Commercial and Service Industry Machinery Manufacturing;
- Manufacturing motor vehicle engine filters and pumps—are classified in Industry Group 3363, Motor Vehicle Parts Manufacturing; and
- Manufacturing mechanical jacks—are classified in U.S. Industry 332212, Hand and Edge Tool Manufacturing.

334 Computer and Electronic Product Manufacturing

Industries in the Computer and Electronic Product Manufacturing subsector group establishments that manufacture computers, computer peripherals, communications equipment, and similar electronic products, and establishments that manufacture components for such products. The Computer and Electronic Product Manufacturing industries have been combined in the hierarchy of NAICS because of the economic significance they have attained. Their rapid growth suggests that they will become even more important to the economies of all three North American countries in the future, and in addition their manufacturing processes are fundamentally different from the manufacturing processes of other machinery and equipment. The design and use of integrated circuits and the application of highly specialized miniaturization technologies are common elements in the production technologies of the computer and electronic subsector. Convergence of technology motivates this NAICS subsector. Digitalization of sound recording, for example, causes both the medium (the compact disc) and the equipment to resemble the technologies for recording, storing, transmitting, and manipulating data. Communications technology and equipment have been converging with computer technology. When technologically-related components are in the same sector, it makes it easier to adjust the classification for future changes, without needing to redefine its basic structure. The creation of the Computer and Electronic Product Manufacturing subsector will assist in delineating new and emerging industries because the activities that will serve as the probable sources of new industries, such as computer manufacturing and communications equipment manufacturing, or computers and audio equipment, are brought together. As new activities emerge, they are less likely therefore, to cross the subsector boundaries of the classification.

3341 Computer and Peripheral Equipment Manufacturing

33411 Computer and Peripheral Equipment Manufacturing

This industry comprises establishments primarily engaged in manufacturing and/or assembling electronic computers, such as mainframes, personal computers,

US—United States industry only. CAN—United States and Canadian industries are comparable. MEX—United States and Mexican industries are comparable. Blank—Canadian, Mexican, and United States industries are comparable.

workstations, laptops, and computer servers; and computer peripheral equipment, such as storage devices, printers, monitors, input/output devices and terminals. Computers can be analog, digital, or hybrid. Digital computers, the most common type, are devices that do all of the following: (1) store the processing program or programs and the data immediately necessary for the execution of the program; (2) can be freely programmed in accordance with the requirements of the user; (3) perform arithmetical computations specified by the user; and (4) execute, without human intervention, a processing program that requires the computer to modify its execution by logical decision during the processing run. Analog computers are capable of simulating mathematical models and comprise at least analog, control, and programming elements.

Cross-References. Establishments primarily engaged in—

- Manufacturing digital telecommunications switches, local area network and wide area network communications equipment, such as bridges, routers, and gateways—are classified in Industry 33421, Telephone Apparatus Manufacturing;
- Manufacturing blank magnetic and optical recording media—are classified in Industry 33461, Manufacturing and Reproducing Magnetic and Optical Media;
- Manufacturing machinery or equipment that incorporate electronic computers for operation or control purposes and embedded control applications—are classified in the Manufacturing sector based on the classification of the complete machinery or equipment;
- Manufacturing external audio speakers for computer use—are classified in Industry 33431, Audio and Video Equipment Manufacturing;
- Manufacturing internal loaded printed circuit board devices, such as sound, video, controller, and network interface cards; internal and external computer modems; and semiconductor storage devices—are classified in Industry 33441, Semiconductor and Other Electronic Component Manufacturing; and
- Manufacturing other parts, such as casings, stampings, cable sets, and switches, for computers, storage devices and other peripheral equipment—are classified in the Manufacturing sector based on their associated production processes.

334111 Electronic Computer Manufacturing[US]

This U.S. industry comprises establishments primarily engaged in manufacturing and/or assembling electronic computers, such as mainframes, personal computers, workstations, laptops, and computer servers. Computers can be analog, digital, or

US—United States industry only. CAN—United States and Canadian industries are comparable. MEX—United States and Mexican industries are comparable. Blank—Canadian, Mexican, and United States industries are comparable.

hybrid. Digital computers, the most common type, are devices that do all of the following: (1) store the processing program or programs and the data immediately necessary for the execution of the program; (2) can be freely programmed in accordance with the requirements of the user; (3) perform arithmetical computations specified by the user; and (4) execute, without human intervention, a processing program that requires the computer to modify its execution by logical decision during the processing run. Analog computers are capable of simulating mathematical models and contain at least analog, control, and programming elements. The manufacture of computers includes the assembly or integration of processors, coprocessors, memory, storage, and input/output devices into a user-programmable final product.

Cross-References. Establishments primarily engaged in—

- Manufacturing digital telecommunications switches, local area network and wide area network communication equipment, such as bridges, routers, and gateways—are classified in Industry 334210, Telephone Apparatus Manufacturing;
- Manufacturing blank magnetic and optical recording media—are classified in U.S. Industry 334613, Magnetic and Optical Recording Media Manufacturing;
- Manufacturing machinery or equipment that incorporates electronic computers for operation or control purposes and embedded control applications—are classified in the Manufacturing sector based on the classification of the complete machinery or equipment;
- Manufacturing internal, loaded, printed circuit board devices, such as sound, video, controller, and network interface cards; internal and external computer modems; and solid state storage devices for computers—are classified in Industry 33441, Semiconductor and Other Electronic Component Manufacturing;
- Manufacturing other parts, such as casings, stampings, cable sets, and switches, for computers—are classified in the Manufacturing sector based on their associated production processes; and
- Retail sale of computers with on-site assembly is classified in Industry 443120, Computer and Software Stores.

334112 Computer Storage Device Manufacturing[US]

This U.S. industry comprises establishments primarily engaged in manufacturing computer storage devices that allow the storage and retrieval of data from a phase change, magnetic, optical, or magnetic/optical media. Examples of products made

US—United States industry only. CAN—United States and Canadian industries are comparable. MEX—United States and Mexican industries are comparable. Blank—Canadian, Mexican, and United States industries are comparable.

by these establishments are CD-ROM drives, floppy disk drives, hard disk drives, and tape storage and backup units.

Cross-References. Establishments primarily engaged in—

- Manufacturing blank magnetic and optical recording media—are classified in U.S. Industry 334613, Magnetic and Optical Recording Media Manufacturing;
- Manufacturing semiconductor storage devices, such as memory chips—are classified in U.S. Industry 334413, Semiconductor and Related Device Manufacturing;
- Manufacturing drive controller cards, internal or external to the storage device—are classified in U.S. Industry 334418, Printed Circuit Assembly (Electronic Assembly) Manufacturing; and
- Manufacturing other parts, such as casings, stampings, cable sets, and switches, for computer storage devices—are classified in the Manufacturing sector based on their associated production processes.

334113 Computer Terminal Manufacturing[US]

This U.S. industry comprises establishments primarily engaged in manufacturing computer terminals. Computer terminals are input/output devices that connect with a central computer for processing.

Cross-References. Establishments primarily engaged in—

- Manufacturing point-of-sale terminals, funds transfer, automatic teller machines, and monitors—are classified in U.S. Industry 334119, Other Computer Peripheral Equipment Manufacturing;
- Manufacturing internal loaded printed circuit board devices, such as sound, video, controller, and network interface cards for computer terminals—are classified in U.S. Industry 334418, Printed Circuit Assembly (Electronic Assembly) Manufacturing; and
- Manufacturing other parts, such as casings, stampings, cable sets, and switches, for computer terminals—are classified in the Manufacturing sector based on their associated production processes.

334119 Other Computer Peripheral Equipment Manufacturing[US]

This U.S. industry comprises establishments primarily engaged in manufacturing computer peripheral equipment (except storage devices and computer terminals).

US—United States industry only. CAN—United States and Canadian industries are comparable. MEX—United States and Mexican industries are comparable. Blank—Canadian, Mexican, and United States industries are comparable.

Illustrative Examples:

Automatic teller machines (ATM) manufacturing
Joystick devices manufacturing
Keyboards, computer peripheral equipment, manufacturing
Monitors, computer peripheral equipment, manufacturing
Mouse devices, computer peripheral equipment, manufacturing
Optical readers and scanners manufacturing
Plotters, computer, manufacturing
Point-of-sale terminals, manufacturing
Printers, computer, manufacturing

Cross-References. Establishments primarily engaged in—

- Manufacturing local area network and wide area network communications equipment, such as bridges, routers, and gateways—are classified in Industry 334210, Telephone Apparatus Manufacturing;
- Manufacturing computer storage devices—are classified in U.S. Industry 334112, Computer Storage Device Manufacturing;
- Manufacturing computer terminals—are classified in U.S. Industry 334113, Computer Terminal Manufacturing;
- Manufacturing external audio speakers for computer use—are classified in Industry 334310, Audio and Video Equipment Manufacturing;
- Manufacturing internal, loaded, printed circuit board devices, such as sound, video, controller, and network interface cards; and internal and external computer modems used as computer peripherals—are classified in U.S. Industry 334418, Printed Circuit Assembly (Electronic Assembly) Manufacturing; and
- Manufacturing other parts, such as casings, stampings, cable sets, and switches, for computer peripheral equipment—are classified in the Manufacturing sector based on their associated production processes.

3342 Communications Equipment Manufacturing

33421 Telephone Apparatus Manufacturing

See industry description for 334210 below.

334210 Telephone Apparatus Manufacturing

This industry comprises establishments primarily engaged in manufacturing wire telephone and data communications equipment. These products may be standalone or board-level components of a larger system. Examples of products made by these establishments are central office switching equipment, cordless telephones (except cellular), PBX equipment, telephones, telephone answering machines, LAN

US—United States industry only. CAN—United States and Canadian industries are comparable. MEX—United States and Mexican industries are comparable. Blank—Canadian, Mexican, and United States industries are comparable.

modems, multi-user modems, and other data communications equipment, such as bridges, routers, and gateways.

Cross-References. Establishments primarily engaged in—

- Manufacturing internal and external computer modems, single-user fax/modems and electronic components used in telephone apparatus—are classified in Industry 33441, Semiconductor and Other Electronic Component Manufacturing; and
- Manufacturing cellular telephones—are classified in Industry 334220, Radio and Television Broadcasting and Wireless Communications Equipment Manufacturing.

33422 Radio and Television Broadcasting and Wireless Communications Equipment Manufacturing

See industry description for 334220 below.

334220 Radio and Television Broadcasting and Wireless Communications Equipment Manufacturing

This industry comprises establishments primarily engaged in manufacturing radio and television broadcast and wireless communications equipment. Examples of products made by these establishments are: transmitting and receiving antennas, cable television equipment, GPS equipment, pagers, cellular phones, mobile communications equipment, and radio and television studio and broadcasting equipment.

Cross-References. Establishments primarily engaged in—

- Manufacturing household-type audio and video equipment, such as televisions and radio sets—are classified in Industry 334310, Audio and Video Equipment Manufacturing; and
- Manufacturing wired and nonwired intercommunications equipment (i.e., intercoms)—are classified in Industry 334290, Other Communications Equipment Manufacturing.

33429 Other Communications Equipment Manufacturing

See industry description for 334290 below.

334290 Other Communications Equipment Manufacturing

This industry comprises establishments primarily engaged in manufacturing communications equipment (except telephone apparatus, and radio and television broadcast, and wireless communications equipment).

US—United States industry only. CAN—United States and Canadian industries are comparable. MEX—United States and Mexican industries are comparable. Blank—Canadian, Mexican, and United States industries are comparable.

Illustrative Examples:

Fire detection and alarm systems manufacturing
Intercom systems and equipment manufacturing
Signals (e.g., highway, pedestrian, railway, traffic) manufacturing

Cross-References. Establishments primarily engaged in—

- Manufacturing telephone apparatus—are classified in Industry 334210, Telephone Apparatus Manufacturing;
- Manufacturing radio and television broadcast and wireless communication equipment—are classified in Industry 334220, Radio and Television Broadcasting and Wireless Communications Equipment Manufacturing; and
- Manufacturing automobile audio and related equipment—are classified in Industry 334310, Audio and Video Equipment Manufacturing.

3343 Audio and Video Equipment Manufacturing

33431 Audio and Video Equipment Manufacturing

See industry description for 334310 below.

334310 Audio and Video Equipment Manufacturing

This industry comprises establishments primarily engaged in manufacturing electronic audio and video equipment for home entertainment, motor vehicle, public address and musical instrument amplifications. Examples of products made by these establishments are video cassette recorders, televisions, stereo equipment, speaker systems, household-type video cameras, jukeboxes, and amplifiers for musical instruments and public address systems.

Cross-References. Establishments primarily engaged in—

- Manufacturing telephone answering machines—are classified in Industry 334210, Telephone Apparatus Manufacturing;
- Manufacturing photographic (i.e., still and motion picture) equipment—are classified in U.S. Industry 333315, Photographic and Photocopying Equipment Manufacturing;
- Manufacturing phonograph needles and cartridges—are classified in Industry 33441, Semiconductor and Other Electronic Component Manufacturing;
- Manufacturing auto theft alarms—are classified in Industry 334290, Other Communications Equipment Manufacturing; and

US—United States industry only. CAN—United States and Canadian industries are comparable. MEX—United States and Mexican industries are comparable. Blank—Canadian, Mexican, and United States industries are comparable.

- Manufacturing mobile radios, such as citizens band and FM transceivers for household or motor vehicle uses; studio and broadcast video cameras; and cable decoders and satellite television equipment—are classified in Industry 334220, Radio and Television Broadcasting and Wireless Communications Equipment Manufacturing.

3344 Semiconductor and Other Electronic Component Manufacturing

33441 Semiconductor and Other Electronic Component Manufacturing

This industry comprises establishments primarily engaged in manufacturing semiconductors and other components for electronic applications. Examples of products made by these establishments are capacitors, resistors, microprocessors, bare and loaded printed circuit boards, electron tubes, electronic connectors, and computer modems.

Cross-References. Establishments primarily engaged in—

- Manufacturing X-ray tubes—are classified in Industry 33451, Navigational, Measuring, Electromedical, and Control Instruments Manufacturing;
- Manufacturing glass blanks for electron tubes—are classified in Industry 32721, Glass and Glass Product Manufacturing;
- Manufacturing telephone system components or modules—are classified in Industry 33421, Telephone Apparatus Manufacturing;
- Manufacturing finished products that incorporate loaded printed circuit boards—are classified in the Manufacturing sector based on the production process of making the final product;
- Manufacturing communications antennas—are classified in Industry 33422, Radio and Television Broadcasting and Wireless Communications Equipment Manufacturing; and
- Manufacturing coils, switches, transformers, connectors, capacitors, rheostats, and similar devices for electrical applications—are classified in Subsector 335, Electrical Equipment, Appliance, and Component Manufacturing.

334411 Electron Tube Manufacturing[US]

This U.S. industry comprises establishments primarily engaged in manufacturing electron tubes and parts (except glass blanks). Examples of products made by

US—United States industry only. CAN—United States and Canadian industries are comparable. MEX—United States and Mexican industries are comparable. Blank—Canadian, Mexican, and United States industries are comparable.

these establishments are cathode ray tubes (i.e., picture tubes), klystron tubes, magnetron tubes, and traveling wave tubes.

Cross-References. Establishments primarily engaged in—

- Manufacturing X-ray tubes—are classified in U.S. Industry 334517, Irradiation Apparatus Manufacturing; and
- Manufacturing glass blanks for electron tubes—are classified in Industry 32721, Glass and Glass Product Manufacturing.

334412 Bare Printed Circuit Board Manufacturing[US]

This U.S. industry comprises establishments primarily engaged in manufacturing bare (i.e., rigid or flexible) printed circuit boards without mounted electronic components. These establishments print, perforate, plate, screen, etch, or photoprint interconnecting pathways for electric current on laminates.

Cross-References. Establishments primarily engaged in—

- Loading components onto printed circuit boards, or whose output is loaded printed circuit boards—are classified in U.S. Industry 334418, Printed Circuit Assembly (Electronic Assembly) Manufacturing; and
- Manufacturing printed circuit laminates—are classified in U.S. Industry 334419, Other Electronic Component Manufacturing.

334413 Semiconductor and Related Device Manufacturing[US]

This U.S. industry comprises establishments primarily engaged in manufacturing semiconductors and related solid state devices. Examples of products made by these establishments are integrated circuits, memory chips, microprocessors, diodes, transistors, solar cells and other optoelectronic devices.

334414 Electronic Capacitor Manufacturing[US]

This U.S. industry comprises establishments primarily engaged in manufacturing electronic fixed and variable capacitors and condensers.

Cross-References.

Establishments primarily engaged in manufacturing electrical capacitors for power generation and distribution, heavy industrial equipment, induction heating and melting, and similar industrial applications are classified in U.S. Industry

US—United States industry only. CAN—United States and Canadian industries are comparable. MEX—United States and Mexican industries are comparable. Blank—Canadian, Mexican, and United States industries are comparable.

335999, All Other Miscellaneous Electrical Equipment and Component Manufacturing.

334415 Electronic Resistor Manufacturing[US]

This U.S. industry comprises establishments primarily engaged in manufacturing electronic resistors, such as fixed and variable resistors, resistor networks, thermistors, and varistors.

Cross-References.

Establishments primarily engaged in manufacturing electronic rheostats are classified in U.S. Industry 334419, Other Electronic Component Manufacturing.

334416 Electronic Coil, Transformer, and Other Inductor Manufacturing[US]

This U.S. industry comprises establishments primarily engaged in manufacturing electronic inductors, such as coils and transformers.

Cross-References.

Establishments primarily engaged in manufacturing electrical transformers used in the generation, storage, transmission, transformation, distribution, and utilization of electrical energy are classified in U.S. Industry 335311, Power, Distribution, and Specialty Transformer Manufacturing.

334417 Electronic Connector Manufacturing[US]

This U.S. industry comprises establishments primarily engaged in manufacturing electronic connectors, such as coaxial, cylindrical, rack and panel, pin and sleeve, printed circuit and fiber optic.

Cross-References.

Establishments primarily engaged in manufacturing electrical connectors, such as plugs, bus bars, twist on wire connectors and terminals, are classified in U.S. Industry 335931, Current-Carrying Wiring Device Manufacturing.

334418 Printed Circuit Assembly (Electronic Assembly) Manufacturing[US]

This U.S. industry comprises establishments primarily engaged in loading components onto printed circuit boards or who manufacture and ship loaded printed

US—United States industry only. CAN—United States and Canadian industries are comparable. MEX—United States and Mexican industries are comparable. Blank—Canadian, Mexican, and United States industries are comparable.

circuit boards. Also known as printed circuit assemblies, electronics assemblies, or modules, these products are printed circuit boards that have some or all of the semiconductor and electronic components inserted or mounted and are inputs to a wide variety of electronic systems and devices.

Cross-References. Establishments primarily engaged in—

- Manufacturing printed circuit laminates—are classified in U.S. Industry 334419, Other Electronic Component Manufacturing;
- Manufacturing bare printed circuit boards—are classified in U.S. Industry 334412, Bare Printed Circuit Board Manufacturing;
- Manufacturing telephone system components or modules—are classified in Industry 334210, Telephone Apparatus Manufacturing; and
- Manufacturing finished products that incorporate loaded printed circuit boards—are classified in the Manufacturing sector based on the production process of making the final product.

334419 Other Electronic Component Manufacturing[US]

This U.S. industry comprises establishments primarily engaged in manufacturing electronic components (except electron tubes; bare printed circuit boards; semiconductors and related devices; electronic capacitors; electronic resistors; coils, transformers and other inductors; connectors; and loaded printed circuit boards).

Illustrative Examples:

Crystals and crystal assemblies, electronic, manufacturing
LCD (liquid crystal display) unit screens manufacturing
Microwave components manufacturing
Piezolelectric devices manufacturing
Printed circuit laminates manufacturing
Switches for electronic applications manufacturing
Transducers (except pressure) manufacturing

Cross-References. Establishments primarily engaged in—

- Manufacturing electron tubes—are classified in U.S. Industry 334411, Electron Tube Manufacturing;
- Manufacturing bare printed circuit boards—are classified in U.S. Industry 334412, Bare Printed Circuit Board Manufacturing;
- Manufacturing semiconductors and related devices—are classified in U.S. Industry 334413, Semiconductor and Related Device Manufacturing;
- Manufacturing electronic capacitors—are classified in U.S. Industry 334414, Electronic Capacitor Manufacturing;

US—United States industry only. CAN—United States and Canadian industries are comparable. MEX—United States and Mexican industries are comparable. Blank—Canadian, Mexican, and United States industries are comparable.

- Manufacturing electronic resistors—are classified in U.S. Industry 334415, Electronic Resistor Manufacturing;
- Manufacturing electronic inductors—are classified in U.S. Industry 334416, Electronic Coil, Transformer, and Other Inductor Manufacturing;
- Manufacturing electronic connectors—are classified in U.S. Industry 334417, Electronic Connector Manufacturing;
- Loading components onto printed circuit boards or whose output is loaded printed circuit boards—are classified in U.S. Industry 334418, Printed Circuit Assembly (Electronic Assembly) Manufacturing; and
- Manufacturing communications antennas—are classified in Industry 334220, Radio and Television Broadcasting and Wireless Communications Equipment Manufacturing.

3345 Navigational, Measuring, Electromedical, and Control Instruments Manufacturing

33451 Navigational, Measuring, Electromedical, and Control Instruments Manufacturing

This industry comprises establishments primarily engaged in manufacturing navigational, measuring, electromedical, and control instruments. Examples of products made by these establishments are aeronautical instruments, appliance regulators and controls (except switches), laboratory analytical instruments, navigation and guidance systems, and physical properties testing equipment.

Cross-References. Establishments primarily engaged in—

- Manufacturing global positioning system (GPS) equipment—are classified in Industry 33422, Radio and Television Broadcasting and Wireless Communications Equipment Manufacturing;
- Manufacturing motor control switches and relays (including timing relays)—are classified in Industry 33531, Electrical Equipment Manufacturing;
- Manufacturing switches for appliances—are classified in Industry 33593, Wiring Device Manufacturing;
- Manufacturing optical instruments—are classified in Industry 33331, Commercial and Service Industry Machinery Manufacturing;
- Manufacturing equipment for measuring and testing communications signals—are classified in Industry Group 3342, Communications Equipment Manufacturing;

US—United States industry only. CAN—United States and Canadian industries are comparable. MEX—United States and Mexican industries are comparable. Blank—Canadian, Mexican, and United States industries are comparable.

- Manufacturing glass watch and clock crystals—are classified in Industry 32721, Glass and Glass Product Manufacturing;
- Manufacturing plastics watch and clock crystals—are classified in Industry 32619, Other Plastics Product Manufacturing; and
- Manufacturing medical thermometers and other nonelectrical medical apparatus—are classified in Industry Group 3391, Medical Equipment and Supplies Manufacturing.

334510 Electromedical and Electrotherapeutic Apparatus Manufacturing[US]

This U.S. industry comprises establishments primarily engaged in manufacturing electromedical and electrotherapeutic apparatus, such as magnetic resonance imaging equipment, medical ultrasound equipment, pacemakers, hearing aids, electrocardiographs, and electromedical endoscopic equipment.

Cross-References. Establishments primarily engaged in—

- Manufacturing medical irradiation apparatus—are classified in U.S. Industry 334517, Irradiation Apparatus Manufacturing; and
- Manufacturing nonelectrical medical and therapeutic apparatus—are classified in Industry Group 3391, Medical Equipment and Supplies Manufacturing.

334511 Search, Detection, Navigation, Guidance, Aeronautical, and Nautical System and Instrument Manufacturing[CAN]

This U.S. industry comprises establishments primarily engaged in manufacturing search, detection, navigation, guidance, aeronautical, and nautical systems and instruments. Examples of products made by these establishments are aircraft instruments (except engine), flight recorders, navigational instruments and systems, radar systems and equipment, and sonar systems and equipment.

Cross-References. Establishments primarily engaged in—

- Manufacturing global positioning system (GPS) equipment—are classified in Industry 334220, Radio and Television Broadcasting and Wireless Communications Equipment Manufacturing; and
- Manufacturing aircraft engine instruments and meteorological systems and equipment—are classified in U.S. Industry 334519, Other Measuring and Controlling Device Manufacturing.

US—United States industry only. CAN—United States and Canadian industries are comparable. MEX—United States and Mexican industries are comparable. Blank—Canadian, Mexican, and United States industries are comparable.

334512 Automatic Environmental Control Manufacturing for Residential, Commercial, and Appliance Use[US]

This U.S. industry comprises establishments primarily engaged in manufacturing automatic controls and regulators for applications, such as heating, air-conditioning, refrigeration and appliances.

Cross-References. Establishments primarily engaged in—

- Manufacturing industrial process controls—are classified in U.S. Industry 334513, Instruments and Related Products Manufacturing for Measuring, Displaying, and Controlling Industrial Process Variables;
- Manufacturing motor control switches and relays—are classified in U.S. Industry 335314, Relay and Industrial Control Manufacturing;
- Manufacturing switches for appliances—are classified in U.S. Industry 335931, Current-Carrying Wiring Device Manufacturing; and
- Manufacturing appliance timers—are classified in U.S. Industry 334518, Watch, Clock, and Part Manufacturing.

334513 Instruments and Related Products Manufacturing for Measuring, Displaying, and Controlling Industrial Process Variables[US]

This U.S. industry comprises establishments primarily engaged in manufacturing instruments and related devices for measuring, displaying, indicating, recording, transmitting, and controlling industrial process variables. These instruments measure, display or control (monitor, analyze, and so forth) industrial process variables, such as temperature, humidity, pressure, vacuum, combustion, flow, level, viscosity, density, acidity, concentration, and rotation.

Cross-References. Establishments primarily engaged in—

- Manufacturing instruments for measuring or testing of electricity and electrical signals—are classified in U.S. Industry 334515, Instrument Manufacturing for Measuring and Testing Electricity and Electrical Signals;
- Manufacturing medical thermometers—are classified in U.S. Industry 339112, Surgical and Medical Instrument Manufacturing;
- Manufacturing glass hydrometers and thermometers for other nonmedical uses—are classified in U.S. Industry 334519, Other Measuring and Controlling Device Manufacturing;
- Manufacturing instruments and instrumentation systems for laboratory analysis of samples—are classified in U.S. Industry 334516, Analytical Laboratory Instrument Manufacturing; and

US—United States industry only. CAN—United States and Canadian industries are comparable. MEX—United States and Mexican industries are comparable. Blank—Canadian, Mexican, and United States industries are comparable.

- Manufacturing optical alignment and display instruments, optical comparators, and optical test and inspection equipment—are classified in U.S. Industry 333314, Optical Instrument and Lens Manufacturing.

334514 Totalizing Fluid Meter and Counting Device Manufacturing[US]

This U.S. industry comprises establishments primarily engaged in manufacturing totalizing (i.e., registering) fluid meters and counting devices. Examples of products made by these establishments are gas consumption meters, water consumption meters, parking meters, taxi meters, motor vehicle gauges, and fare collection equipment.

Cross-References. Establishments primarily engaged in—

- Manufacturing integrating meters and counters for measuring the characteristics of electricity and electrical signals—are classified in U.S. Industry 334515, Instrument Manufacturing for Measuring and Testing Electricity and Electrical Signals; and
- Manufacturing instruments and devices that measure, display, or control (i.e., monitor or analyze) related industrial process variables—are classified in U.S. Industry 334513, Instruments and Related Products Manufacturing for Measuring, Displaying, and Controlling Industrial Process Variables.

334515 Instrument Manufacturing for Measuring and Testing Electricity and Electrical Signals[US]

This U.S. industry comprises establishments primarily engaged in manufacturing instruments for measuring and testing the characteristics of electricity and electrical signals. Examples of products made by these establishments are circuit and continuity testers, volt meters, ohm meters, wattmeters, multimeters, and semiconductor test equipment.

Cross-References. Establishments primarily engaged in—

- Manufacturing electronic monitoring, evaluating, and other electronic support equipment for navigational, radar, and sonar systems—are classified in U.S. Industry 334511, Search, Detection, Navigation, Guidance, Aeronautical, and Nautical System and Instrument Manufacturing; and
- Manufacturing equipment for measuring and testing communications signals—are classified in Industry Group 3342, Communications Equipment Manufacturing.

US—United States industry only. CAN—United States and Canadian industries are comparable. MEX—United States and Mexican industries are comparable. Blank—Canadian, Mexican, and United States industries are comparable.

334516 Analytical Laboratory Instrument Manufacturing[US]

This U.S. industry comprises establishments primarily engaged in manufacturing instruments and instrumentation systems for laboratory analysis of the chemical or physical composition or concentration of samples of solid, fluid, gaseous, or composite material.

Cross-References. Establishments primarily engaged in—

- Manufacturing instruments for monitoring and analyzing continuous samples from medical patients—are classified in U.S. Industry 334510, Electromedical and Electrotherapeutic Apparatus Manufacturing; and
- Manufacturing instruments and related devices that measure, display, or control (i.e., monitor or analyze) industrial process variables—are classified in U.S. Industry 334513, Instruments and Related Products Manufacturing for Measuring, Displaying, and Controlling Industrial Process Variables.

334517 Irradiation Apparatus Manufacturing[US]

This U.S. industry comprises establishments primarily engaged in manufacturing irradiation apparatus and tubes for applications, such as medical diagnostic, medical therapeutic, industrial, research and scientific evaluation. Irradiation can take the form of beta-rays, gamma-rays, X-rays, or other ionizing radiation.

334518 Watch, Clock, and Part Manufacturing[US]

This U.S. industry comprises establishments primarily engaged in manufacturing and/or assembling: clocks; watches; timing mechanisms for clockwork operated devices; time clocks; time and date recording devices; and clock and watch parts (except crystals), such as springs, jewels, and modules.

Cross-References. Establishments primarily engaged in—

- Manufacturing glass watch and clock crystals—are classified in Industry 32721, Glass and Glass Product Manufacturing;
- Manufacturing plastics watch and clock crystals—are classified in U.S. Industry 326199, All Other Plastics Product Manufacturing; and
- Manufacturing timing relays—are classified in U.S. Industry 335314, Relay and Industrial Control Manufacturing.

334519 Other Measuring and Controlling Device Manufacturing[US]

This U.S. industry comprises establishments primarily engaged in manufacturing measuring and controlling devices (except search, detection, navigation, guidance,

US—United States industry only. CAN—United States and Canadian industries are comparable. MEX—United States and Mexican industries are comparable. Blank—Canadian, Mexican, and United States industries are comparable.

aeronautical, and nautical instruments and systems; automatic environmental controls for residential, commercial, and appliance use; instruments for measurement, display, and control of industrial process variables; totalizing fluid meters and counting devices; instruments for measuring and testing electricity and electrical signals; analytical laboratory instruments; watches, clocks, and parts; irradiation equipment; and electromedical and electrotherapeutic apparatus).

Illustrative Examples:

Aircraft engine instruments manufacturing
Automotive emissions testing equipment manufacturing
Meteorological instruments manufacturing
Physical properties testing and inspection equipment manufacturing
Polygraph machines manufacturing
Radiation detection and monitoring instruments manufacturing
Surveying instruments manufacturing
Thermometers liquid-in-glass and bimetal types (except medical), manufacturing

Cross-References. Establishments primarily engaged in—

- Manufacturing medical thermometers—are classified in U.S. Industry 339112, Surgical and Medical Instrument Manufacturing;
- Manufacturing search, detection, navigation, guidance, aeronautical, and nautical systems and instruments—are classified in U.S. Industry 334511, Search, Detection, Navigation, Guidance, Aeronautical, and Nautical System and Instrument Manufacturing;
- Manufacturing automatic controls and regulators for applications, such as heating, air-conditioning, refrigeration and appliances—are classified in U.S. Industry 334512, Automatic Environmental Control Manufacturing for Residential, Commercial, and Appliance Use;
- Manufacturing instruments and related devices that measure, display, or control (i.e., monitor or analyze) industrial process variables—are classified in U.S. Industry 334513, Instruments and Related Products Manufacturing for Measuring, Displaying, and Controlling Industrial Process Variables;
- Manufacturing totalizing (i.e., registering) fluid meters and counting devices, including motor vehicle gauges—are classified in U.S. Industry 334514, Totalizing Fluid Meter and Counting Device Manufacturing;
- Manufacturing instruments for measuring and testing the characteristics of electricity and electrical signals—are classified in U.S. Industry 334515, Instrument Manufacturing for Measuring and Testing Electricity and Electrical Signals;
- Manufacturing instruments for laboratory analysis of the physical composition or concentration of samples of solid, fluid, gaseous, or composite materials—are classified in U.S. Industry 334516, Analytical Laboratory Instrument Manufacturing;

US—United States industry only. CAN—United States and Canadian industries are comparable. MEX—United States and Mexican industries are comparable. Blank—Canadian, Mexican, and United States industries are comparable.

- Manufacturing and/or assembling watches, clocks, or parts—are classified in U.S. Industry 334518, Watch, Clock, and Part Manufacturing;
- Manufacturing X-ray apparatus, tubes, or related irradiation apparatus—are classified in U.S. Industry 334517, Irradiation Apparatus Manufacturing; and
- Manufacturing electromedical and electrotherapeutic apparatus—are classified in U.S. Industry 334510, Electromedical and Electrotherapeutic Apparatus Manufacturing.

3346 Manufacturing and Reproducing Magnetic and Optical Media

33461 Manufacturing and Reproducing Magnetic and Optical Media

This industry comprises establishments primarily engaged in (1) manufacturing optical and magnetic media, such as blank audio tape, blank video tape, and blank diskettes and/or (2) mass duplicating (i.e., making copies) audio, video, software, and other data on magnetic, optical, and similar media.

Cross-References. Establishments primarily engaged in—

- Designing, developing, and publishing prepackaged software—are classified in Industry 51121, Software Publishers; and
- Audio, motion picture and/or video production and/or distribution—are classified in Subsector 512, Motion Picture and Sound Recording Industries.

334611 Software Reproducing[US]

This U.S. industry comprises establishments primarily engaged in mass reproducing computer software. These establishments do not generally develop any software, they mass reproduce data and programs on magnetic media, such as diskettes, tapes, or cartridges. Establishments in this industry mass reproduce products, such as CD-ROMs and game cartridges.

Cross-References.

Establishments primarily engaged in designing, developing, and publishing prepackaged software are classified in Industry 511210, Software Publishers.

334612 Prerecorded Compact Disc (except Software), Tape, and Record Reproducing[US]

This U.S. industry comprises establishments primarily engaged in mass reproducing audio and video material on magnetic or optical media. Examples of

US—United States industry only. CAN—United States and Canadian industries are comparable. MEX—United States and Mexican industries are comparable. Blank—Canadian, Mexican, and United States industries are comparable.

products mass reproduced by these establishments are audio compact discs, prerecorded audio and video cassettes, and laser discs.

Cross-References. Establishments primarily engaged in—

- Designing, developing, and publishing prepackaged software—are classified in Industry 511210, Software Publishers;
- Audio, motion picture and/or video production and/or distribution—are classified in Subsector 512, Motion Picture and Sound Recording Industries; and
- Manufacturing blank audio and video tape, blank diskettes, and blank optical discs—are classified in U.S. Industry 334613, Magnetic and Optical Recording Media Manufacturing.

334613 Magnetic and Optical Recording Media Manufacturing[US]

This U.S. industry comprises establishments primarily engaged in manufacturing magnetic and optical recording media, such as blank magnetic tape, blank diskettes, blank optical discs, hard drive media, and blank magnetic tape cassettes.

Cross-References. Establishments primarily engaged in—

- Mass reproducing computer software—are classified in U.S. Industry 334611, Software Reproducing; and
- Mass reproducing audio and video material—are classified in U.S. Industry 334612, Prerecorded Compact Disc (Except Software), Tape, and Record Reproducing.

335 Electrical Equipment, Appliance, and Component Manufacturing

Industries in the Electrical Equipment, Appliance, and Component Manufacturing subsector manufacture products that generate, distribute and use electrical power. Electric Lighting Equipment Manufacturing establishments produce electric lamp bulbs, lighting fixtures, and parts. Household Appliance Manufacturing establishments make both small and major electrical appliances and parts. Electrical Equipment Manufacturing establishments make goods, such as electric motors, generators, transformers, and switchgear apparatus. Other Electrical Equipment and Component Manufacturing establishments make devices for storing electrical power (e.g., batteries), for transmitting electricity (e.g., insulated wire), and wiring devices (e.g., electrical outlets, fuse boxes, and light switches).

US—United States industry only. CAN—United States and Canadian industries are comparable. MEX—United States and Mexican industries are comparable. Blank—Canadian, Mexican, and United States industries are comparable.

3351 Electric Lighting Equipment Manufacturing

33511 Electric Lamp Bulb and Part Manufacturing

See industry description for 335110 below.

335110 Electric Lamp Bulb and Part Manufacturing

This industry comprises establishments primarily engaged in manufacturing electric light bulbs and tubes, and parts and components (except glass blanks for electric light bulbs).

Cross-References. Establishments primarily engaged in—

- Manufacturing glass blanks for electric light bulbs—are classified in U.S. Industry 327212, Other Pressed and Blown Glass and Glassware Manufacturing;
- Manufacturing vehicular lighting fixtures—are classified in U.S. Industry 336321, Vehicular Lighting Equipment Manufacturing;
- Manufacturing light emitting diodes (LEDs)—are classified in U.S. Industry 334413, Semiconductor and Related Device Manufacturing; and
- Manufacturing other lighting fixtures (except vehicular)—are classified in Industry 33512, Lighting Fixture Manufacturing.

33512 Lighting Fixture Manufacturing

This industry comprises establishments primarily engaged in manufacturing electric lighting fixtures (except vehicular), nonelectric lighting equipment, lamp shades (except glass and plastics), and lighting fixture components (except current-carrying wiring devices).

Cross-References. Establishments primarily engaged in—

- Manufacturing vehicular lighting fixtures—are classified in Industry 33632, Motor Vehicle Electrical and Electronic Equipment Manufacturing;
- Manufacturing electric light bulbs, tubes, and parts—are classified in Industry 33511, Electric Lamp Bulb and Part Manufacturing;
- Manufacturing current-carrying wiring devices for lighting fixtures—are classified in Industry 33593, Wiring Device Manufacturing;
- Manufacturing ceiling fans or bath fans with integrated lighting fixtures—are classified in Industry 33521, Small Electrical Appliance Manufacturing;

US—United States industry only. CAN—United States and Canadian industries are comparable. MEX—United States and Mexican industries are comparable. Blank—Canadian, Mexican, and United States industries are comparable.

- Manufacturing plastics lamp shades—are classified in Industry 32619, Other Plastics Product Manufacturing;
- Manufacturing glassware and glass parts for lighting fixtures—are classified in Industry 32721, Glass and Glass Product Manufacturing; and
- Manufacturing signaling devices that incorporate electric light bulbs, such as traffic and railway signals—are classified in Industry 33429, Other Communications Equipment Manufacturing.

335121 Residential Electric Lighting Fixture Manufacturing[US]

This U.S. industry comprises establishments primarily engaged in manufacturing fixed or portable residential electric lighting fixtures and lamp shades of metal, paper, or textiles. Residential electric lighting fixtures include those for use both inside and outside the residence.

Illustrative Examples:

Ceiling lighting fixtures, residential, manufacturing
Chandeliers, residential, manufacturing
Table lamps (i.e., lighting fixtures) manufacturing

Cross-References. Establishments primarily engaged in—

- Manufacturing glassware for residential lighting fixtures—are classified in Industry 32721, Glass and Glass Product Manufacturing;
- Manufacturing plastics lamp shades—are classified in U.S. Industry 326199, All Other Plastics Product Manufacturing;
- Manufacturing electric light bulbs, tubes, and parts—are classified in Industry 335110, Electric Lamp Bulb and Part Manufacturing;
- Manufacturing ceiling fans or bath fans with integrated lighting fixtures—are classified in U.S. Industry 335211, Electric Housewares and Household Fan Manufacturing;
- Manufacturing current-carrying wiring devices for lighting fixtures—are classified in U.S. Industry 335931, Current-Carrying Wiring Device Manufacturing;
- Manufacturing commercial, industrial, and institutional electric lighting fixtures—are classified in U.S. Industry 335122, Commercial, Industrial, and Institutional Electric Lighting Fixture Manufacturing; and
- Manufacturing other lighting fixtures, such as street lights, flashlights, and nonelectric lighting fixtures—are classified in U.S. Industry 335129, Other Lighting Equipment Manufacturing.

US—United States industry only. CAN—United States and Canadian industries are comparable. MEX—United States and Mexican industries are comparable. Blank—Canadian, Mexican, and United States industries are comparable.

335122 Commercial, Industrial, and Institutional Electric Lighting Fixture Manufacturing[US]

This U.S. industry comprises establishments primarily engaged in manufacturing commercial, industrial, and institutional electric lighting fixtures.

Cross-References. Establishments primarily engaged in—

- Manufacturing glassware for commercial, industrial, and institutional electric lighting fixtures—are classified in Industry 32721, Glass and Glass Product Manufacturing;
- Manufacturing residential electric lighting fixtures—are classified in U.S. Industry 335121, Residential Electric Lighting Fixture Manufacturing;
- Manufacturing current-carrying wiring devices for lighting fixtures—are classified in U.S. Industry 335931, Current-Carrying Wiring Device Manufacturing;
- Manufacturing vehicular lighting fixtures—are classified in U.S. Industry 336321, Vehicular Lighting Equipment Manufacturing;
- Manufacturing electric light bulbs, tubes, and parts—are classified in Industry 335110, Electric Lamp Bulb and Part Manufacturing; and
- Manufacturing other lighting fixtures, such as street lights, flashlights, and nonelectric lighting equipment—are classified in U.S. Industry 335129, Other Lighting Equipment Manufacturing.

335129 Other Lighting Equipment Manufacturing[US]

This U.S. industry comprises establishments primarily engaged in manufacturing electric lighting fixtures (except residential, commercial, industrial, institutional, and vehicular electric lighting fixtures) and nonelectric lighting equipment.

Illustrative Examples:

Christmas tree lighting sets, electric, manufacturing
Fireplace logs, electric, manufacturing
Flashlights manufacturing
Insect lamps, electric, manufacturing
Lanterns (e.g., carbide, electric, gas, gasoline, kerosene) manufacturing
Spotlights (except vehicular) manufacturing
Street lighting fixtures (except traffic signals) manufacturing

Cross-References. Establishments primarily engaged in—

- Manufacturing glassware for lighting fixtures—are classified in Industry 32721, Glass and Glass Product Manufacturing;

US—United States industry only. CAN—United States and Canadian industries are comparable. MEX—United States and Mexican industries are comparable. Blank—Canadian, Mexican, and United States industries are comparable.

- Manufacturing electric light bulbs, tubes, and parts—are classified in Industry 335110, Electric Lamp Bulb and Part Manufacturing;
- Manufacturing current-carrying wiring devices for lighting fixtures—are classified in U.S. Industry 335931, Current-Carrying Wiring Device Manufacturing;
- Manufacturing residential electric lighting fixtures—are classified in U.S. Industry 335121, Residential Electric Lighting Fixture Manufacturing;
- Manufacturing commercial, industrial, and institutional electric lighting fixtures—are classified in U.S. Industry 335122, Commercial, Industrial, and Institutional Electric Lighting Fixture Manufacturing;
- Manufacturing vehicular lighting fixtures—are classified in U.S. Industry 336321, Vehicular Lighting Equipment Manufacturing; and
- Manufacturing signaling devices that incorporate electric light bulbs, such as traffic and railway signals—are classified in Industry 334290, Other Communications Equipment Manufacturing.

3352 Household Appliance Manufacturing

33521 Small Electrical Appliance Manufacturing

This industry comprises establishments primarily engaged in manufacturing small electric appliances and electric housewares, household-type fans, household-type vacuum cleaners, and other electric household-type floor care machines.

Cross-References. Establishments primarily engaged in—

- Manufacturing room air-conditioners, attic fans, wall and baseboard heating units for permanent installation, and commercial ventilation and exhaust fans—are classified in Industry 33341, Ventilation, Heating, Air-Conditioning, and Commercial Refrigeration Equipment Manufacturing;
- Manufacturing commercial, industrial, and institutional vacuum cleaners, and mechanical carpet sweepers—are classified in Industry 33331, Commercial and Service Industry Machinery Manufacturing;
- Manufacturing major household-type appliances, such as washing machines, dryers, stoves, and hot water heaters—are classified in Industry 33522, Major Appliance Manufacturing; and
- Installing central vacuum cleaning systems—are classified in Industry 23829, Other Building Equipment Contractors.

US—United States industry only. CAN—United States and Canadian industries are comparable. MEX—United States and Mexican industries are comparable. Blank—Canadian, Mexican, and United States industries are comparable.

335211 Electric Housewares and Household Fan Manufacturing[US]

This U.S. industry comprises establishments primarily engaged in manufacturing small electric appliances and electric housewares for heating, cooking, and other purposes, and electric household-type fans (except attic fans).

Illustrative Examples:

Bath fans, residential, manufacturing
Ceiling fans, residential, manufacturing
Curling irons, household-type electric, manufacturing
Electronic blankets manufacturing
Portable cooking appliances (except microwave, convection ovens), household-type electric, manufacturing
Portable electric space heaters manufacturing
Portable hair dryers, electric, manufacturing
Portable humidifiers and dehumidifiers manufacturing
Scissors, electric, manufacturing
Ventilating and exhaust fans (except attic fans), household-type, manufacturing

Cross-References. Establishments primarily engaged in—

- Manufacturing attic fans—are classified in U.S. Industry 333412, Industrial and Commercial Fan and Blower Manufacturing;
- Manufacturing wall and baseboard heating units for permanent installation—are classified in U.S. Industry 333414, Heating Equipment (except Warm Air Furnaces) Manufacturing;
- Manufacturing room air-conditioners—are classified in U.S. Industry 333415, Air-Conditioning and Warm Air Heating Equipment and Commercial and Industrial Refrigeration Equipment Manufacturing; and
- Manufacturing microwave and convection ovens—are classified in U.S. Industry 335221, Household Cooking Appliance Manufacturing.

335212 Household Vacuum Cleaner Manufacturing[US]

This U.S. industry comprises establishments primarily engaged in manufacturing electric vacuum cleaners, electric floor waxing machines, and other electric floor care machines typically for household use.

Cross-References. Establishments primarily engaged in—

- Manufacturing electric vacuum cleaners for commercial, industrial, and institutional uses, and mechanical carpet sweepers—are classified in U.S. Industry 333319, Other Commercial and Service Industry Machinery Manufacturing; and

---

US—United States industry only. CAN—United States and Canadian industries are comparable. MEX—United States and Mexican industries are comparable. Blank—Canadian, Mexican, and United States industries are comparable.

- Installing central vacuum cleaning systems—are classified in Industry 238290, Other Building Equipment Contractors.

33522 Major Appliance Manufacturing

This industry comprises establishments primarily engaged in manufacturing household-type cooking appliances, household-type laundry equipment, household-type refrigerators, upright and chest freezers, and other electrical and nonelectrical major household-type appliances, such as dishwashers, water heaters, and garbage disposal units.

Cross-References. Establishments primarily engaged in—

- Manufacturing small electric appliances and electric housewares, such as hot plates, griddles, toasters, and electric irons—are classified in Industry 33521, Small Electrical Appliance Manufacturing;
- Manufacturing commercial and industrial refrigerators and freezers—are classified in Industry 33341, Ventilation, Heating, Air-Conditioning, and Commercial Refrigeration Equipment Manufacturing;
- Manufacturing commercial-type cooking equipment and commercial-type laundry, drycleaning, and pressing equipment—are classified in Industry 33331, Commercial and Service Industry Machinery Manufacturing; and
- Manufacturing household-type sewing machines—are classified in Industry 33329, Other Industrial Machinery Manufacturing.

335221 Household Cooking Appliance Manufacturing[US]

This U.S. industry comprises establishments primarily engaged in manufacturing household-type electric and nonelectric cooking equipment (except small electric appliances and electric housewares).

Cross-References. Establishments primarily engaged in—

- Manufacturing small electric appliances and electric housewares used for cooking, such as electric skillets, electric hot plates, electric griddles, toasters, and percolators—are classified in U.S. Industry 335211, Electric Housewares and Household Fan Manufacturing; and
- Manufacturing commercial-type cooking equipment—are classified in U.S. Industry 333319, Other Commercial and Service Industry Machinery Manufacturing.

US—United States industry only. CAN—United States and Canadian industries are comparable. MEX—United States and Mexican industries are comparable. Blank—Canadian, Mexican, and United States industries are comparable.

335222 Household Refrigerator and Home Freezer Manufacturing[US]

This U.S. industry comprises establishments primarily engaged in manufacturing household-type refrigerators and upright and chest freezers.

Cross-References.

Establishments primarily engaged in manufacturing commercial and industrial refrigeration equipment, such as refrigerators and freezers, are classified in U.S. Industry 333415, Air-Conditioning and Warm Air Heating Equipment and Commercial and Industrial Refrigeration Equipment Manufacturing.

335224 Household Laundry Equipment Manufacturing[US]

This U.S. industry comprises establishments primarily engaged in manufacturing household-type laundry equipment.

Cross-References. Establishments primarily engaged in—

- Manufacturing portable electric irons—are classified in U.S. Industry 335211, Electric Housewares and Household Fan Manufacturing; and
- Manufacturing commercial-type laundry and drycleaning equipment—are classified in U.S. Industry 333312, Commercial Laundry, Dry Cleaning, and Pressing Machine Manufacturing.

335228 Other Major Household Appliance Manufacturing[US]

This U.S. industry comprises establishments primarily engaged in manufacturing electric and nonelectric major household-type appliances (except cooking equipment, refrigerators, upright and chest freezers, and household-type laundry equipment).

Illustrative Examples:

Dishwashers, household-type, manufacturing
Garbage disposal units, household-type, manufacturing
Hot water heaters (including nonelectric), household-type, manufacturing
Trash and garbage compactors, household-type, manufacturing

Cross-References. Establishments primarily engaged in—

- Manufacturing household-type cooking equipment—are classified in U.S. Industry 335221, Household Cooking Appliance Manufacturing;

US—United States industry only. CAN—United States and Canadian industries are comparable. MEX—United States and Mexican industries are comparable. Blank—Canadian, Mexican, and United States industries are comparable.

- Manufacturing household-type sewing machines—are classified in U.S. Industry 333298, All Other Industrial Machinery Manufacturing;
- Manufacturing household-type refrigerators and upright and chest freezers—are classified in U.S. Industry 335222, Household Refrigerator and Home Freezer Manufacturing; and
- Manufacturing small electric appliances—are classified in U.S. Industry 335211, Electric Housewares and Household Fan Manufacturing.

3353 Electrical Equipment Manufacturing

33531 Electrical Equipment Manufacturing

This industry comprises establishments primarily engaged in manufacturing power, distribution, and specialty transformers; electric motors, generators, and motor generator sets; switchgear and switchboard apparatus; relays; and industrial controls.

Cross-References. Establishments primarily engaged in—

- Manufacturing turbine generator set units and electric outboard motors—are classified in Industry 33361, Engine, Turbine, and Power Transmission Equipment Manufacturing;
- Manufacturing electronic component-type transformers and switches—are classified in Industry 33441, Semiconductor and Other Electronic Component Manufacturing;
- Manufacturing environmental controls and industrial process control instruments—are classified in Industry 33451, Navigational, Measuring, Electromedical, and Control Instruments Manufacturing;
- Manufacturing switches for electrical circuits, such as pushbutton and snap switches—are classified in Industry 33593, Wiring Device Manufacturing;
- Manufacturing complete for welding and soldering equipment—are classified in Industry 33399, All Other General Purpose Machinery Manufacturing; and
- Manufacturing starting motors and generators for internal combustion engines—are classified in Industry 33632, Motor Vehicle Electrical and Electronic Equipment Manufacturing.

335311 Power, Distribution, and Specialty Transformer Manufacturing[CAN]

This U.S. industry comprises establishments primarily engaged in manufacturing power, distribution, and specialty transformers (except electronic components).

US—United States industry only. CAN—United States and Canadian industries are comparable. MEX—United States and Mexican industries are comparable. Blank—Canadian, Mexican, and United States industries are comparable.

Industrial-type and consumer-type transformers in this industry vary (e.g., step up or step down) voltage but do not convert alternating to direct or direct to alternating current.

Illustrative Examples:

Distribution transformers, electric, manufacturing
Fluorescent ballasts (i.e., transformers) manufacturing
Substation transformers, electric power distribution, manufacturing
Transmission and distribution voltage regulators manufacturing

Cross-References.

Establishments primarily engaged in manufacturing electronic component-type transformers are classified in U.S. Industry 334416, Electronic Coil, Transformer, and Other Inductor Manufacturing.

335312 Motor and Generator Manufacturing[CAN]

This U.S. industry comprises establishments primarily engaged in manufacturing electric motors (except internal combustion engine starting motors), power generators (except battery charging alternators for internal combustion engines), and motor generator sets (except turbine generator set units). This industry includes establishments rewinding armatures on a factory basis.

Cross-References. Establishments primarily engaged in—

- Manufacturing electric outboard motors—are classified in U.S. Industry 333618, Other Engine Equipment Manufacturing;
- Manufacturing gas, steam, or hydraulic turbine generator set units—are classified in U.S. Industry 333611, Turbine and Turbine Generator Set Units Manufacturing;
- Manufacturing starting motors and battery charging alternators for internal combustion engines—are classified in U.S. Industry 336322, Other Motor Vehicle Electrical and Electronic Equipment Manufacturing;
- Rewinding armatures, not on a factory basis—are classified in Industry 811310, Commercial and Industrial Machinery and Equipment (except Automotive and Electronic) Repair and Maintenance; and
- Manufacturing complete welding and soldering equipment—are classified in U.S. Industry 333992, Welding and Soldering Equipment Manufacturing.

335313 Switchgear and Switchboard Apparatus Manufacturing[US]

This U.S. industry comprises establishments primarily engaged in manufacturing switchgear and switchboard apparatus.

US—United States industry only. CAN—United States and Canadian industries are comparable. MEX—United States and Mexican industries are comparable. Blank—Canadian, Mexican, and United States industries are comparable.

Illustrative Examples:

Circuit breakers, power, manufacturing
Control panels, electric power distribution, manufacturing
Duct for electrical switchboard apparatus manufacturing
Fuses, electric, manufacturing
Power switching equipment manufacturing
Switches, electric power (except pushbutton, snap, solenoid, tumbler), manufacturing

Cross-References. Establishments primarily engaged in—

- Manufacturing relays—are classified in U.S. Industry 335314, Relay and Industrial Control Manufacturing;
- Manufacturing switches for electronic applications—are classified in U.S. Industry 334419, Other Electronic Component Manufacturing; and
- Manufacturing snap, pushbutton, and similar switches for electrical circuits—are classified in U.S. Industry 335931, Current-Carrying Wiring Device Manufacturing.

335314 Relay and Industrial Control Manufacturing[US]

This U.S. industry comprises establishments primarily engaged in manufacturing relays, motor starters and controllers, and other industrial controls and control accessories.

Cross-References. Establishments primarily engaged in—

- Manufacturing environmental and appliance control equipment—are classified in U.S. Industry 334512, Automatic Environmental Control Manufacturing for Residential, Commercial, and Appliance Use; and
- Manufacturing instruments for controlling industrial process variables—are classified in U.S. Industry 334513, Instruments and Related Products Manufacturing for Measuring, Displaying, and Controlling Industrial Process Variables.

3359 Other Electrical Equipment and Component Manufacturing

This industry group comprises establishments manufacturing electrical equipment and components (except electric lighting equipment, household-type appliances, transformers, switchgear, relays, motors, and generators).

33591 Battery Manufacturing

This industry comprises establishments primarily engaged in manufacturing primary and storage batteries.

US—United States industry only. CAN—United States and Canadian industries are comparable. MEX—United States and Mexican industries are comparable. Blank—Canadian, Mexican, and United States industries are comparable.

335911 Storage Battery Manufacturing[US]

This U.S. industry comprises establishments primarily engaged in manufacturing storage batteries.

Illustrative Examples:

Lead acid storage batteries manufacturing

Rechargeable nickel cadmium (NICAD) batteries manufacturing

Cross-References.

Establishments primarily engaged in manufacturing primary batteries are classified in U.S. Industry 335912, Primary Battery Manufacturing.

335912 Primary Battery Manufacturing[US]

This U.S. industry comprises establishments primarily engaged in manufacturing wet or dry primary batteries.

Illustrative Examples:

Disposable flashlight batteries manufacturing

Dry cells, primary (e.g., AAA, AA, C, D 9V), manufacturing

Lithium batteries, primary, manufacturing

Watch batteries manufacturing

Cross-References.

Establishments primarily engaged in manufacturing storage batteries are classified in U.S. Industry 335911, Storage Battery Manufacturing.

33592 Communication and Energy Wire and Cable Manufacturing

This industry comprises establishments insulating fiber-optic cable, and manufacturing insulated nonferrous wire and cable from nonferrous wire drawn in other establishments.

Cross-References. Establishments primarily engaged in—

- Drawing nonferrous wire—are classified in Subsector 331, Primary Metal Manufacturing;
- Manufacturing cable sets consisting of insulated wire and various connectors for electronic applications—are classified in Industry 33441, Semiconductor and Other Electronic Component Manufacturing;

US—United States industry only. CAN—United States and Canadian industries are comparable. MEX—United States and Mexican industries are comparable. Blank—Canadian, Mexican, and United States industries are comparable.

- Manufacturing extension cords, appliance cords, and similar electrical cord sets from purchased, insulated wire or cable—are classified in Industry 33599, All Other Electrical Equipment and Component Manufacturing; and
- Manufacturing unsheathed fiber-optic materials—are classified in Industry 32721, Glass and Glass Product Manufacturing.

335921 Fiber Optic Cable Manufacturing[US]

This U.S. industry comprises establishments primarily engaged in manufacturing insulated fiber-optic cable from purchased fiber-optic strand.

Cross-References. Establishments primarily engaged in—

- Manufacturing unsheathed fiber-optic materials—are classified in Industry 32721, Glass and Glass Product Manufacturing; and
- Manufacturing insulated nonferrous wire and cable from purchased wire—are classified in U.S. Industry 335929, Other Communication and Energy Wire Manufacturing.

335929 Other Communication and Energy Wire Manufacturing[US]

This U.S. industry comprises establishments primarily engaged in manufacturing insulated wire and cable of nonferrous metals from purchased wire.

Cross-References. Establishments primarily engaged in—

- Manufacturing cable sets consisting of insulated wire and various connectors for electronic applications—are classified in U.S. Industry 334419, Other Electronic Component Manufacturing;
- Manufacturing extension cords, appliance cords, and similar electrical cord sets from purchased insulated wire—are classified in U.S. Industry 335999, All Other Miscellaneous Electrical Equipment and Component Manufacturing;
- Drawing and insulating copper wire in the same establishment—are classified in U.S. Industry 331422, Copper Wire (except Mechanical) Drawing;
- Drawing and insulating aluminum wire in the same establishment—are classified in U.S. Industry 331319, Other Aluminum Rolling and Drawing; and
- Drawing nonferrous wire (except copper and aluminum)—are classified in U.S. Industry 331491, Nonferrous Metal (except Copper and Aluminum) Rolling, Drawing, and Extruding.

US—United States industry only. CAN—United States and Canadian industries are comparable. MEX—United States and Mexican industries are comparable. Blank—Canadian, Mexican, and United States industries are comparable.

33593 Wiring Device Manufacturing

This industry comprises establishments primarily engaged in manufacturing current-carrying wiring devices and noncurrent-carrying wiring devices for wiring electrical circuits.

Cross-References. Establishments primarily engaged in—

- Manufacturing ceramic and glass insulators—are classified in Subsector 327, Nonmetallic Mineral Product Manufacturing; and
- Manufacturing electronic component-type connectors, sockets, and switches—are classified in Industry 33441, Semiconductor and Other Electronic Component Manufacturing.

335931 Current-Carrying Wiring Device Manufacturing[US]

This U.S. industry comprises establishments primarily engaged in manufacturing current-carrying wiring devices.

Illustrative Examples:

Bus bars, electrical conductors (except switchgear-type), manufacturing
GFCI (ground fault circuit interrupters) manufacturing
Lamp holders manufacturing
Lightning arrestors and coils manufacturing
Receptacles (i.e., outlets), electrical, manufacturing
Switches for electrical wiring (e.g., pressure, pushbutton, snap, tumbler) manufacturing

Cross-References. Establishments primarily engaged in—

- Manufacturing electronic component-type connectors—are classified in U.S. Industry 334417, Electronic Connector Manufacturing;
- Manufacturing noncurrent-carrying wiring devices—are classified in U.S. Industry 335932, Noncurrent-Carrying Wiring Device Manufacturing; and
- Manufacturing electronic component-type sockets and switches—are classified in U.S. Industry 334419, Other Electronic Component Manufacturing.

335932 Noncurrent-Carrying Wiring Device Manufacturing[US]

This U.S. industry comprises establishments primarily engaged in manufacturing noncurrent-carrying wiring devices.

US—United States industry only. CAN—United States and Canadian industries are comparable. MEX—United States and Mexican industries are comparable. Blank—Canadian, Mexican, and United States industries are comparable.

Illustrative Examples:

Boxes, electrical wiring (e.g., junction, outlet, switch), manufacturing
Conduits and fittings, electrical, manufacturing
Face plates (i.e., outlet or switch covers) manufacturing
Transmission pole and line hardware manufacturing

Cross-References. Establishments primarily engaged in—

- Manufacturing porcelain and ceramic insulators—are classified in U.S. Industry 327113, Porcelain Electrical Supply Manufacturing;
- Manufacturing current-carrying wiring devices—are classified in U.S. Industry 335931, Current-Carrying Wiring Device Manufacturing; and
- Manufacturing glass insulators—are classified in Industry 32721, Glass and Glass Product Manufacturing.

33599 All Other Electrical Equipment and Component Manufacturing

This industry comprises establishments primarily engaged in manufacturing electrical equipment (except electric lighting equipment, household-type appliances, transformers, motors, generators, switchgear, relays, industrial controls, batteries, communication and energy wire and cable, and wiring devices).

Illustrative Examples:

Carbon and graphite electrodes and brushes manufacturing
Extension cords made from purchased insulated wire
Surge suppressors manufacturing

Cross-References. Establishments primarily engaged in—

- Manufacturing lighting equipment—are classified in Industry Group 3351, Electric Lighting Equipment Manufacturing;
- Manufacturing household-type appliances—are classified in Industry Group 3352, Household Appliance Manufacturing;
- Manufacturing transformers, motors, generators, switchgear, relays, and industrial controls—are classified in Industry 33531, Electrical Equipment Manufacturing;
- Manufacturing batteries—are classified in Industry 33591, Battery Manufacturing;
- Manufacturing communication and energy wire—are classified in Industry 33592, Communication and Energy Wire and Cable Manufacturing;

US—United States industry only. CAN—United States and Canadian industries are comparable. MEX—United States and Mexican industries are comparable. Blank—Canadian, Mexican, and United States industries are comparable.

- Manufacturing current-carrying and noncurrent-carrying wiring devices—are classified in Industry 33593, Wiring Device Manufacturing;
- Manufacturing carbon or graphite gaskets—are classified in Industry 33999, All Other Miscellaneous Manufacturing;
- Manufacturing electronic component-type rectifiers, voltage regulating integrated circuits, power converting integrated circuits, electronic capacitors, electronic resistors, and similar devices—are classified in Industry 33441, Semiconductor and Other Electronic Component Manufacturing; and
- Manufacturing equipment incorporating lasers—are classified in various subsectors of manufacturing based on the associated production process of the finished equipment.

335991 Carbon and Graphite Product Manufacturing[MEX]

This U.S. industry comprises establishments primarily engaged in manufacturing carbon, graphite, and metal-graphite brushes and brush stock; carbon or graphite electrodes for thermal and electrolytic uses; carbon and graphite fibers; and other carbon, graphite, and metal-graphite products.

Cross-References.

Establishments primarily engaged in manufacturing carbon or graphite gaskets are classified in U.S. Industry 339991, Gasket, Packing, and Sealing Device Manufacturing.

335999 All Other Miscellaneous Electrical Equipment and Component Manufacturing[MEX]

This U.S. industry comprises establishments primarily engaged in manufacturing industrial and commercial electric apparatus and other equipment (except lighting equipment, household appliances, transformers, motors, generators, switchgear, relays, industrial controls, batteries, communication and energy wire and cable, wiring devices, and carbon and graphite products). This industry includes power converters (i.e., AC to DC and DC to AC), power supplies, surge suppressors, and similar equipment for industrial-type and consumer-type equipment.

Illustrative Examples:

Appliance cords made from purchased insulated wire
Battery chargers, solid-state, manufacturing
Extension cords made from purchased insulated wire
Inverters manufacturing
Surge suppressers manufacturing

US—United States industry only. CAN—United States and Canadian industries are comparable. MEX—United States and Mexican industries are comparable. Blank—Canadian, Mexican, and United States industries are comparable.

Door opening and closing devices, electrical, manufacturing
Electric bells manufacturing
Uninterruptible power supplies (UPS) manufacturing

Cross-References. Establishments primarily engaged in—

- Manufacturing lighting equipment—are classified in Industry Group 3351, Electric Lighting Equipment Manufacturing;
- Manufacturing household-type appliances—are classified in Industry Group 3352, Household Appliance Manufacturing;
- Manufacturing transformers, motors, generators, switchgear, relays, and industrial controls—are classified in Industry 33531, Electrical Equipment Manufacturing;
- Manufacturing primary and storage batteries—are classified in Industry 33591, Battery Manufacturing;
- Manufacturing communication and energy wire and cable from purchased wire or fiber-optic strand—are classified in Industry 33592, Communication and Energy Wire and Cable Manufacturing;
- Manufacturing current-carrying and noncurrent-carrying wiring devices—are classified in Industry 33593, Wiring Device Manufacturing;
- Manufacturing electronic component-type rectifiers (except semiconductor)—are classified in U.S. Industry 334419, Other Electronic Component Manufacturing;
- Manufacturing semiconductor rectifiers, voltage regulating integrated circuits, power converting integrated circuits, and similar semiconductor devices—are classified in U.S. Industry 334413, Semiconductor and Related Device Manufacturing;
- Manufacturing electronic component-type capacitors and condensers—are classified in U.S. Industry 334414, Electronic Capacitor Manufacturing;
- Manufacturing carbon and graphite products—are classified in U.S. Industry 335991, Carbon and Graphite Product Manufacturing; and
- Manufacturing equipment incorporating lasers—are classified in various manufacturing subsectors based on the associated production process of the finished equipment.

336 Transportation Equipment Manufacturing

Industries in the Transportation Equipment Manufacturing subsector produce equipment for transporting people and goods. Transportation equipment is a type

US—United States industry only. CAN—United States and Canadian industries are comparable. MEX—United States and Mexican industries are comparable. Blank—Canadian, Mexican, and United States industries are comparable.

of machinery. An entire subsector is devoted to this activity because of the significance of its economic size in all three North American countries.

Establishments in this subsector utilize production processes similar to those of other machinery manufacturing establishments—bending, forming, welding, machining, and assembling metal or plastic parts into components and finished products. However, the assembly of components and subassemblies and their further assembly into finished vehicles tends to be a more common production process in this subsector than in the Machinery Manufacturing subsector.

NAICS has industry groups for the manufacture of equipment for each mode of transport—road, rail, air and water. Parts for motor vehicles warrant a separate industry group because of their importance and because parts manufacture requires less assembly, and the establishments that manufacture only parts are not as vertically integrated as those that make complete vehicles.

Land use motor vehicle equipment not designed for highway operation (e.g., agricultural equipment, construction equipment, and materials handling equipment) is classified in the appropriate NAICS subsector based on the type and use of the equipment.

3361 Motor Vehicle Manufacturing

33611 Automobile and Light Duty Motor Vehicle Manufacturing

This industry comprises establishments primarily engaged in (1) manufacturing complete automobile and light duty motor vehicles (i.e., body and chassis or unibody) or (2) manufacturing chassis only.

Cross-References.

Establishments primarily engaged in manufacturing car, truck, and bus bodies and assembling vehicles on a purchased chassis and manufacturing kit cars for highway use are classified in Industry 33621, Motor Vehicle Body and Trailer Manufacturing.

336111 Automobile Manufacturing[US]

This U.S. industry comprises establishments primarily engaged in (1) manufacturing complete automobiles (i.e., body and chassis or unibody) or (2) manufacturing automobile chassis only.

Cross-References.

Establishments primarily engaged in manufacturing car bodies and assembling vehicles on a purchased chassis and manufacturing kit cars for highway use are classified in U.S. Industry 336211, Motor Vehicle Body Manufacturing.

US—United States industry only. CAN—United States and Canadian industries are comparable. MEX—United States and Mexican industries are comparable. Blank—Canadian, Mexican, and United States industries are comparable.

336112 Light Truck and Utility Vehicle Manufacturing[US]

This U.S. industry comprises establishments primarily engaged in (1) manufacturing complete light trucks and utility vehicles (i.e., body and chassis) or (2) manufacturing light truck and utility vehicle chassis only. Vehicles made include light duty vans, pick-up trucks, minivans, and sport utility vehicles.

Cross-References.

Establishments primarily engaged in manufacturing truck and bus bodies and assembling vehicles on a purchased chassis are classified in U.S. Industry 336211, Motor Vehicle Body Manufacturing.

33612 Heavy Duty Truck Manufacturing

See industry description for 336120 below.

336120 Heavy Duty Truck Manufacturing

This industry comprises establishments primarily engaged in (1) manufacturing heavy duty truck chassis and assembling complete heavy duty trucks, buses, heavy duty motor homes, and other special purpose heavy duty motor vehicles for highway use or (2) manufacturing heavy duty truck chassis only.

Cross-References. Establishments primarily engaged in—

- Manufacturing truck and bus bodies and assembling vehicles on a purchased chassis—are classified in U.S. Industry 336211, Motor Vehicle Body Manufacturing;
- Manufacturing motor homes on purchased chassis—are classified in U.S. Industry 336213, Motor Home Manufacturing;
- Manufacturing vans, minivans, and light trucks—are classified in U.S. Industry 336112, Light Truck and Utility Vehicle Manufacturing;
- Manufacturing military armored vehicles—are classified in U.S. Industry 336992, Military Armored Vehicle, Tank, and Tank Component Manufacturing; and
- Manufacturing off highway construction equipment—are classified in Industry 333120, Construction Machinery Manufacturing.

3362 Motor Vehicle Body and Trailer Manufacturing

33621 Motor Vehicle Body and Trailer Manufacturing

This industry comprises establishments primarily engaged in (1) manufacturing motor vehicle bodies and cabs or (2) manufacturing truck, automobile and utility

---

US—United States industry only. CAN—United States and Canadian industries are comparable. MEX—United States and Mexican industries are comparable. Blank—Canadian, Mexican, and United States industries are comparable.

trailers, truck trailer chassis, detachable trailer bodies, and detachable trailer chassis. The products made may be sold separately or may be assembled on purchased chassis and sold as complete vehicles.

Motor homes are units where the motor and the living quarters are contained in the same integrated unit, while travel trailers are designed to be towed by a motor unit, such as an automobile or a light truck.

Illustrative Examples:

Bodies and cabs, truck, manufacturing
Camper unit, slide-in, for pick-up trucks, manufacturing
Motor homes, self-contained, assembling on purchased chassis
Pickup canopies, caps, or covers manufacturing
Travel trailers, recreational, manufacturing
Semitrailer manufacturing

Cross-References. Establishments primarily engaged in—

- Making manufactured homes (i.e., mobile homes)—are classified in Industry 32199, All Other Wood Product Manufacturing;
- Customizing automotive vehicle and trailer interiors (i.e., van conversions) on an individual basis—are classified in Industry 81112, Automotive Body, Paint, Interior, and Glass Repair;
- Manufacturing light duty motor home chassis and assembling complete motor homes—are classified in Industry 33611, Automobile and Light Duty Motor Vehicle Manufacturing; and
- Manufacturing heavy duty truck chassis and assembling heavy duty trucks, buses, motor homes, and other special purpose heavy duty motor vehicles for highway use—are classified in Industry 33612, Heavy Duty Truck Manufacturing.

336211 Motor Vehicle Body Manufacturing[CAN]

This U.S. industry comprises establishments primarily engaged in manufacturing truck and bus bodies and cabs and automobile bodies. The products made may be sold separately or may be assembled on purchased chassis and sold as complete vehicles.

Cross-References.

Establishments primarily engaged in manufacturing heavy duty chassis and assembling heavy duty trucks, buses, motor homes, and other special purpose heavy duty motor vehicles for highway use are classified in Industry 336120, Heavy Duty Truck Manufacturing.

US—United States industry only. CAN—United States and Canadian industries are comparable. MEX—United States and Mexican industries are comparable. Blank—Canadian, Mexican, and United States industries are comparable.

336212 Truck Trailer Manufacturing[CAN]

This U.S. industry comprises establishments primarily engaged in manufacturing truck trailers, truck trailer chassis, cargo container chassis, detachable trailer bodies, and detachable trailer chassis for sale separately.

Cross-References.

Establishments primarily engaged in manufacturing utility trailers, light-truck trailers, and travel trailers are classified in U.S. Industry 336214, Travel Trailer and Camper Manufacturing.

336213 Motor Home Manufacturing[US]

This U.S. industry comprises establishments primarily engaged in (1) manufacturing motor homes on purchased chassis and/or (2) manufacturing conversion vans on an assembly line basis. Motor homes are units where the motor and the living quarters are integrated in the same unit.

Cross-References. Establishments primarily engaged in—

- Manufacturing light duty motor homes chassis and assembling complete motor homes—are classified in U.S. Industry 336112, Light Truck and Utility Vehicle Manufacturing;
- Customizing automotive vehicle and trailer interiors (i.e., van conversions) on an individual basis—are classified in U.S. Industry 811121, Automotive Body, Paint, and Interior Repair and Maintenance; and
- Producing manufactured homes (i.e., mobile homes)—are classified in U.S. Industry 321991, Manufactured Home (Mobile Home) Manufacturing.

336214 Travel Trailer and Camper Manufacturing[US]

This U.S. industry comprises establishments primarily engaged in one or more of the following: (1) manufacturing travel trailers and campers designed to attach to motor vehicles; (2) manufacturing pickup coaches (i.e., campers) and caps (i.e., covers) for mounting on pickup trucks; and (3) manufacturing automobile, utility and light-truck trailers. Travel trailers do not have their own motor but are designed to be towed by a motor unit, such as an automobile or a light truck.

Illustrative Examples:

Automobile transporter trailers, single car, manufacturing

Travel trailers, recreational, manufacturing

US—United States industry only. CAN—United States and Canadian industries are comparable. MEX—United States and Mexican industries are comparable. Blank—Canadian, Mexican, and United States industries are comparable.

Camping trailers and chassis manufacturing
Horse trailers (except fifth wheel type) manufacturing
Utility trailers manufacturing

Cross-References.

Establishments primarily engaged in making manufactured homes (i.e., mobile homes) designed to accept permanent water, sewer, and utility connections and equipped with wheels, but not intended for regular highway use, are classified in U.S. Industry 321991, Manufactured Home (Mobile Home) Manufacturing.

3363 Motor Vehicle Parts Manufacturing

33631 Motor Vehicle Gasoline Engine and Engine Parts Manufacturing

This industry comprises establishments primarily engaged in manufacturing and/or rebuilding motor vehicle gasoline engines, and engine parts, whether or not for vehicular use.

Illustrative Examples:

Carburetors, all types, manufacturing
Crankshaft assemblies, automotive and truck gasoline engine, manufacturing
Cylinder heads, automotive and truck gasoline engine, manufacturing
Fuel injection systems and parts, automotive and truck gasoline engine, manufacturing
Manifolds (i.e., intake and exhaust), automotive and truck gasoline engine, manufacturing
Pistons and piston rings manufacturing
Pumps (e.g., fuel, oil, water), mechanical automotive and truck gasoline engine (except power steering), manufacturing
Timing gears and chains, automotive and truck gasoline engine, manufacturing
Valves, engine, intake and exhaust, manufacturing

Cross-References. Establishments primarily engaged in—

- Manufacturing wiring harnesses and other vehicular electrical and electronic equipment—are classified in Industry 33632, Motor Vehicle Electrical and Electronic Equipment Manufacturing;
- Manufacturing transmission and power train equipment—are classified in Industry 33635, Motor Vehicle Transmission and Power Train Parts Manufacturing;
- Manufacturing radiators—are classified in Industry 33639, Other Motor Vehicle Parts Manufacturing;

US—United States industry only. CAN—United States and Canadian industries are comparable. MEX—United States and Mexican industries are comparable. Blank—Canadian, Mexican, and United States industries are comparable.

- Manufacturing steering and suspension components—are classified in Industry 33633, Motor Vehicle Steering and Suspension Components (except Spring) Manufacturing;
- Manufacturing parts for machine repair and equipment parts (except electric) on a job or shop basis—are classified in Industry 33271, Machine Shops;
- Manufacturing rubber and plastic belts and hoses without fittings—are classified in Industry 32622, Rubber and Plastics Hoses and Belting Manufacturing; and
- Manufacturing stationary and diesel engines—are classified in Industry 33361, Engine, Turbine, and Power Transmission Equipment Manufacturing.

336311 Carburetor, Piston, Piston Ring, and Valve Manufacturing[US]

This U.S. industry comprises establishments primarily engaged in manufacturing and/or rebuilding carburetors, pistons, piston rings, and engine intake and exhaust valves.

Cross-References.

Establishments primarily engaged in manufacturing parts for machine repair and equipment parts (except electric) on a job or shop basis are classified in Industry 332710, Machine Shops.

336312 Gasoline Engine and Engine Parts Manufacturing[US]

This U.S. industry comprises establishments primarily engaged in manufacturing and/or rebuilding gasoline motor vehicle engines and gasoline motor vehicle engine parts, excluding carburetors, pistons, piston rings, and valves.

Illustrative Examples:

Crankshaft assemblies, automotive and truck gasoline engine, manufacturing
Flywheels and ring gears, automotive and truck gasoline engine, manufacturing
Fuel injection systems and parts, automotive and truck gasoline engine, manufacturing
Manifolds (i.e., intake and exhaust), automotive and truck gasoline engine, manufacturing
Positive crankcase ventilation (PCV) valves, engine, manufacturing
Pumps (e.g., fuel, oil, water), mechanical, automotive and truck gasoline engine (except power steering), manufacturing
Timing gears and chains, automotive and truck gasoline engine, manufacturing

---

US—United States industry only. CAN—United States and Canadian industries are comparable. MEX—United States and Mexican industries are comparable. Blank—Canadian, Mexican, and United States industries are comparable.

Cross-References. Establishments primarily engaged in—

- Manufacturing carburetors, pistons, piston rings, and valves—are classified in U.S. Industry 336311, Carburetor, Piston, Piston Ring, and Valve Manufacturing;
- Manufacturing wiring harnesses and other vehicular electrical and electronic equipment—are classified in U.S. Industry 336322, Other Motor Vehicle Electrical and Electronic Equipment Manufacturing;
- Manufacturing transmission and power train equipment—are classified in Industry 336350, Motor Vehicle Transmission and Power Train Parts Manufacturing;
- Manufacturing radiators—are classified in U.S. Industry 336399, All Other Motor Vehicle Parts Manufacturing;
- Manufacturing steering and suspension components—are classified in Industry 336330, Motor Vehicle Steering and Suspension Components (except Spring) Manufacturing;
- Manufacturing rubber and plastic belts and hoses without fittings—are classified in Industry 326220, Rubber and Plastics Hoses and Belting Manufacturing; and
- Manufacturing stationary and diesel engines—are classified in U.S. Industry 333618, Other Engine Equipment Manufacturing.

33632 Motor Vehicle Electrical and Electronic Equipment Manufacturing

This industry comprises establishments primarily engaged in (1) manufacturing vehicular lighting and/or (2) manufacturing and/or rebuilding motor vehicle electrical and electronic equipment. The products made can be used for all types of transportation equipment (i.e., aircraft, automobiles, trains, ships).

Illustrative Examples:

Alternators and generators for internal combustion engines manufacturing
Automotive lighting fixtures manufacturing
Coils, ignition, internal combustion engines, manufacturing
Distributors for internal combustion engines manufacturing
Electrical ignition cable sets for internal combustion engines manufacturing
Generators for internal combustion engines manufacturing
Ignition wiring harness for internal combustion engines manufacturing
Instrument control panels (i.e., assembling purchased gauges), automotive, truck, and bus, manufacturing
Spark plugs for internal combustion engines manufacturing
Windshield washer pumps, automotive, truck, and bus, manufacturing

US—United States industry only. CAN—United States and Canadian industries are comparable. MEX—United States and Mexican industries are comparable. Blank—Canadian, Mexican, and United States industries are comparable.

Cross-References. Establishments primarily engaged in—

- Manufacturing automotive lamps—are classified in Industry 33511, Electric Lamp Bulb and Part Manufacturing;
- Manufacturing batteries—are classified in Industry 33591, Battery Manufacturing;
- Manufacturing electric motors for motor vehicles (including electric vehicles)—are classified in Industry 33531, Electrical Equipment Manufacturing;
- Manufacturing railway traffic control signals and passenger car alarms—are classified in Industry 33429, Other Communications Equipment Manufacturing; and
- Manufacturing car stereos—are classified in Industry 33431, Audio and Video Equipment Manufacturing.

336321 Vehicular Lighting Equipment Manufacturing[US]

This U.S. industry comprises establishments primarily engaged in manufacturing vehicular lighting fixtures.

Cross-References.

Establishments primarily engaged in manufacturing automotive lamps (i.e., bulbs) are classified in Industry 335110, Electric Lamp Bulb and Part Manufacturing.

336322 Other Motor Vehicle Electrical and Electronic Equipment Manufacturing[US]

This U.S. industry comprises establishments primarily engaged in manufacturing and/or rebuilding electrical and electronic equipment for motor vehicles and internal combustion engines.

Illustrative Examples:

Alternators and generators for internal combustion engines manufacturing
Coils, ignition, internal combustion engines, manufacturing
Distributors for internal combustion engines manufacturing
Electrical ignition cable sets for internal combustion engines manufacturing
Generators for internal combustion engines manufacturing
Ignition wiring harness for internal combustion engines manufacturing
Instrument control panel (i.e., assembling purchased gauges), automotive, truck, and bus, manufacturing
Spark plugs for internal combustion engines manufacturing
Windshield washer pumps, automotive, truck, and bus, manufacturing

US—United States industry only. CAN—United States and Canadian industries are comparable. MEX—United States and Mexican industries are comparable. Blank—Canadian, Mexican, and United States industries are comparable.

Cross-References. Establishments primarily engaged in—

- Manufacturing vehicular lighting equipment—are classified in U.S. Industry 336321, Vehicular Lighting Equipment Manufacturing;
- Manufacturing automotive lamps—are classified in Industry 335110, Electric Lamp Bulb and Part Manufacturing;
- Manufacturing batteries—are classified in U.S. Industry 335911, Storage Battery Manufacturing;
- Manufacturing electric motors for electric vehicles—are classified in U.S. Industry 335312, Motor and Generator Manufacturing;
- Manufacturing railway traffic control signals and passenger car alarms—are classified in Industry 334290, Other Communications Equipment Manufacturing; and
- Manufacturing car stereos—are classified in Industry 334310, Audio and Video Equipment Manufacturing.

33633 Motor Vehicle Steering and Suspension Components (except Spring) Manufacturing

See industry description for 336330 below.

336330 Motor Vehicle Steering and Suspension Components (except Spring) Manufacturing

This industry comprises establishments primarily engaged in manufacturing and/or rebuilding motor vehicle steering mechanisms and suspension components (except springs).

Illustrative Examples:

Rack and pinion steering assemblies manufacturing
Shock absorbers, automotive, truck, and bus, manufacturing
Steering columns, automotive, truck, and bus, manufacturing
Steering wheels, automotive, truck, and bus, manufacturing
Struts, automotive, truck, and bus, manufacturing

Cross-References.

Establishments primarily engaged in manufacturing springs are classified in Industry 33261, Spring and Wire Product Manufacturing.

33634 Motor Vehicle Brake System Manufacturing

See industry description for 336340 below.

US—United States industry only. CAN—United States and Canadian industries are comparable. MEX—United States and Mexican industries are comparable. Blank—Canadian, Mexican, and United States industries are comparable.

336340 Motor Vehicle Brake System Manufacturing

This industry comprises establishments primarily engaged in manufacturing and/or rebuilding motor vehicle brake systems and related components.

Illustrative Examples:

- Brake cylinders, master and wheel, automotive, truck, and bus, manufacturing
- Brake drums, automotive, truck, and bus, manufacturing
- Brake hose assemblies manufacturing
- Brake pads and shoes, automotive, truck, and bus, manufacturing
- Calipers, brake, automotive, truck, and bus, manufacturing

Cross-References.

Establishments primarily engaged in manufacturing rubber and plastics belts and hoses without fittings are classified in Industry 326220, Rubber and Plastics Hoses and Belting Manufacturing.

33635 Motor Vehicle Transmission and Power Train Parts Manufacturing

See industry description for 336350 below.

336350 Motor Vehicle Transmission and Power Train Parts Manufacturing

This industry comprises establishments primarily engaged in manufacturing and/or rebuilding motor vehicle transmission and power train parts.

Illustrative Examples:

- Automatic transmissions, automotive, truck, and bus, manufacturing
- Axle bearings, automotive, truck, and bus, manufacturing
- Constant velocity joints, automotive, truck, and bus, manufacturing
- Differential and rear axle assemblies, automotive, truck, and bus, manufacturing
- Torque converters, automotive, truck, and bus, manufacturing
- Universal joints, automotive, truck, and bus, manufacturing

33636 Motor Vehicle Seating and Interior Trim Manufacturing

See industry description for 336360 below.

336360 Motor Vehicle Seating and Interior Trim Manufacturing

This industry comprises establishments primarily engaged in manufacturing motor vehicle seating, seats, seat frames, seat belts, and interior trimmings.

US—United States industry only. CAN—United States and Canadian industries are comparable. MEX—United States and Mexican industries are comparable. Blank—Canadian, Mexican, and United States industries are comparable.

Cross-References.

Establishments primarily engaged in manufacturing convertible tops for vehicles and those manufacturing air bags are classified in U.S. Industry 336399, All Other Motor Vehicle Parts Manufacturing.

33637 Motor Vehicle Metal Stamping

See industry description for 336370 below.

336370 Motor Vehicle Metal Stamping

This industry comprises establishments primarily engaged in manufacturing motor vehicle stampings, such as fenders, tops, body parts, trim, and molding.

Cross-References. Establishments primarily engaged in—

- Manufacturing stampings and further processing the stampings—are classified according to the process of the specific product made; and
- Manufacturing stampings (except motor vehicle)—are classified in U.S. Industry 332116 Metal Stamping.

33639 Other Motor Vehicle Parts Manufacturing

This industry comprises establishments primarily engaged in manufacturing and/or rebuilding motor vehicle parts and accessories (except motor vehicle gasoline engines and engine parts, motor vehicle electrical and electronic equipment, motor vehicle steering and suspension components, motor vehicle brake systems, motor vehicle transmission and power train parts, motor vehicle seating and interior trim, and motor vehicle stampings).

Illustrative Examples:

Air bag assemblies manufacturing
Air-conditioners, motor vehicle, manufacturing
Catalytic converters, engine exhaust, automotive, truck, and bus, manufacturing
Mufflers and resonators, motor vehicle, manufacturing
Radiators and cores manufacturing
Wheels (i.e., rims), automotive, truck, and bus, manufacturing

Cross-References. Establishments primarily engaged in—

- Manufacturing motor vehicle gasoline engines and engine parts—are classified in Industry 33631, Motor Vehicle Gasoline Engine and Engine Parts Manufacturing;

US—United States industry only. CAN—United States and Canadian industries are comparable. MEX—United States and Mexican industries are comparable. Blank—Canadian, Mexican, and United States industries are comparable.

- Manufacturing motor vehicle electrical and electronic equipment—are classified in Industry 33632, Motor Vehicle Electrical and Electronic Equipment Manufacturing;
- Manufacturing motor vehicle steering and suspension components—are classified in Industry 33633, Motor Vehicle Steering and Suspension Components (except Spring) Manufacturing;
- Manufacturing motor vehicle brake systems—are classified in Industry 33634, Motor Vehicle Brake System Manufacturing;
- Manufacturing motor vehicle transmission and power train parts—are classified in Industry 33635, Motor Vehicle Transmission and Power Train Parts Manufacturing;
- Manufacturing motor vehicle seating and interior trim—are classified in Industry 33636, Motor Vehicle Seating and Interior Trim Manufacturing;
- Manufacturing motor vehicle stampings—are classified in Industry 33637, Motor Vehicle Metal Stamping; and
- Manufacturing air-conditioning systems and compressors (except motor vehicle air-conditioning systems)—are classified in Industry 33341, Ventilation, Heating, Air-Conditioning, and Commercial Refrigeration Equipment Manufacturing.

336391 Motor Vehicle Air-Conditioning Manufacturing[US]

This U.S. industry comprises establishments primarily engaged in manufacturing air-conditioning systems and compressors for motor vehicles, such as automobiles, trucks, buses, aircraft, farm machinery, construction machinery, and other related vehicles.

Cross-References.

Establishments primarily engaged in manufacturing air-conditioning systems and compressors (except motor vehicle air-conditioning systems) are classified in U.S. Industry 333415, Air-Conditioning and Warm Air Heating Equipment and Commercial and Industrial Refrigeration Equipment Manufacturing.

336399 All Other Motor Vehicle Parts Manufacturing[US]

This U.S. industry comprises establishments primarily engaged in manufacturing and/or rebuilding motor vehicle parts and accessories (except motor vehicle gasoline engines and engine parts, motor vehicle electrical and electronic equipment, motor vehicle steering and suspension components, motor vehicle brake systems,

US—United States industry only. CAN—United States and Canadian industries are comparable. MEX—United States and Mexican industries are comparable. Blank—Canadian, Mexican, and United States industries are comparable.

motor vehicle transmission and power train parts, motor vehicle seating and interior trim, motor vehicle stampings, and motor vehicle air-conditioning systems and compressors).

Illustrative Examples:

Air bag assemblies manufacturing
Air-filters, automotive, truck, and bus, manufacturing
Catalytic converters, engine exhaust, automotive, truck, and bus, manufacturing
Mufflers and resonators, motor vehicle, manufacturing
Radiators and cores manufacturing
Wheels (i.e., rims), automotive, truck, and bus, manufacturing

Cross-References. Establishments primarily engaged in—

- Manufacturing motor vehicle gasoline engines and engine parts—are classified in Industry 33631, Motor Vehicle Gasoline Engine and Engine Parts Manufacturing;
- Manufacturing motor vehicle electrical and electronic equipment—are classified in Industry 33632, Motor Vehicle Electrical and Electronic Equipment Manufacturing;
- Manufacturing motor vehicle steering and suspension components—are classified in Industry 336330, Motor Vehicle Steering and Suspension Components (except Spring) Manufacturing;
- Manufacturing motor vehicle brake systems—are classified in Industry 336340, Motor Vehicle Brake System Manufacturing;
- Manufacturing motor vehicle transmission and power train parts—are classified in Industry 336350, Motor Vehicle Transmission and Power Train Parts Manufacturing;
- Manufacturing motor vehicle seating and interior trim—are classified in Industry 336360, Motor Vehicle Seating and Interior Trim Manufacturing;
- Manufacturing motor vehicle stampings—are classified in Industry 336370, Motor Vehicle Metal Stamping; and
- Manufacturing motor vehicle air-conditioning systems and compressors—are classified in U.S. Industry 336391, Motor Vehicle Air-Conditioning Manufacturing.

3364 Aerospace Product and Parts Manufacturing

33641 Aerospace Product and Parts Manufacturing

This industry comprises establishments primarily engaged in one or more of the following: (1) manufacturing complete aircraft, missiles, or space vehicles;

US—United States industry only. CAN—United States and Canadian industries are comparable. MEX—United States and Mexican industries are comparable. Blank—Canadian, Mexican, and United States industries are comparable.

(2) manufacturing aerospace engines, propulsion units, auxiliary equipment or parts; (3) developing and making prototypes of aerospace products; (4) aircraft conversion (i.e., major modifications to systems); and (5) complete aircraft or propulsion systems overhaul and rebuilding (i.e., periodic restoration of aircraft to original design specifications).

Cross-References.

- Establishments primarily engaged in manufacturing space satellites are classified in Industry 33422, Radio and Television Broadcasting and Wireless Communications Equipment Manufacturing;
- Establishments primarily engaged in the repair of aircraft or aircraft engines (except overhauling, conversion, and rebuilding) are classified in Industry 48819, Other Support Activities for Air Transportation;
- Research and development establishments primarily engaged in aerospace R&D (except prototype production) are classified in Industry 54171, Research and Development in the Physical, Engineering, and Life Sciences;
- Establishments primarily engaged in manufacturing aircraft engine intake and exhaust valves, pistons, or engine filters are classified in Industry 33631, Motor Vehicle Gasoline Engine and Engine Parts Manufacturing;
- Establishments primarily engaged in manufacturing of aircraft seating are classified in Industry 33636, Motor Vehicle Seating and Interior Trim Manufacturing;
- Establishments primarily engaged in manufacturing aeronautical, navigational, and guidance systems and instruments are classified in Industry 33451, Navigational, Measuring, Electromedical, and Control Instruments Manufacturing;
- Establishment primarily engaged in manufacturing aircraft engine electrical (aeronautical electrical) equipment or aircraft lighting fixtures are classified in Industry 33632, Motor Vehicle Electrical and Electronic Equipment Manufacturing; and
- Establishments primarily engaged in manufacturing of aircraft fluid power subassemblies are classified in Industry 33291, Metal Valve Manufacturing.

336411 Aircraft Manufacturing[US]

This U.S. industry comprises establishments primarily engaged in one or more of the following: (1) manufacturing or assembling complete aircraft; (2) developing and making aircraft prototypes; (3) aircraft conversion (i.e., major modifications to systems); and (4) complete aircraft overhaul and rebuilding (i.e., periodic restoration of aircraft to original design specifications).

US—United States industry only. CAN—United States and Canadian industries are comparable. MEX—United States and Mexican industries are comparable. Blank—Canadian, Mexican, and United States industries are comparable.

Cross-References.

- Establishments primarily engaged in manufacturing guided missiles and space vehicles are classified in U.S. Industry 336414, Guided Missile and Space Vehicle Manufacturing;
- Establishments primarily engaged in the repair of aircraft (except overhauling, conversion, and rebuilding) are classified in Industry 488190, Other Support Activities for Air Transportation; and
- Research and development establishments primarily engaged in aircraft R&D (except prototype production) are classified in Industry 541710, Research and Development in the Physical, Engineering, and Life Sciences.

336412 Aircraft Engine and Engine Parts Manufacturing[US]

This U.S. industry comprises establishments primarily engaged in one or more of the following: (1) manufacturing aircraft engines and engine parts; (2) developing and making prototypes of aircraft engines and engine parts; (3) aircraft propulsion system conversion (i.e., major modifications to systems); and (4) aircraft propulsion systems overhaul and rebuilding (i.e., periodic restoration of aircraft propulsion system to original design specifications).

Cross-References.

- Establishments primarily engaged in manufacturing guided missile and space vehicle propulsion units and parts are classified in U.S. Industry 336415, Guided Missile and Space Vehicle Propulsion Unit and Propulsion Unit Parts Manufacturing;
- Establishments primarily engaged in manufacturing aircraft intake and exhaust valves and pistons are classified in U.S. Industry 336311, Carburetor, Piston, Piston Ring, and Valve Manufacturing;
- Establishments primarily engaged in manufacturing aircraft internal combustion engine filters are classified in U.S. Industry 336312, Gasoline Engine and Engine Parts Manufacturing;
- Establishments primarily engaged in the repair of aircraft engines (except overhauling, conversion, and rebuilding) are classified in Industry 488190, Other Support Activities for Air Transportation;
- Research and development establishments primarily engaged in aircraft engine and engine parts R&D (except prototype production) are classified in Industry 541710, Research and Development in the Physical, Engineering, and Life Sciences; and
- Establishments primarily engaged in manufacturing aeronautical instruments are classified in U.S. Industry 334511, Search, Detection, Navigation,

US—United States industry only. CAN—United States and Canadian industries are comparable. MEX—United States and Mexican industries are comparable. Blank—Canadian, Mexican, and United States industries are comparable.

Guidance, Aeronautical, and Nautical System and Instrument Manufacturing.

336413 Other Aircraft Parts and Auxiliary Equipment Manufacturing[US]

This U.S. industry comprises establishment primarily engaged in (1) manufacturing aircraft parts or auxiliary equipment (except engines and aircraft fluid power subassemblies) and/or (2) developing and making prototypes of aircraft parts and auxiliary equipment. Auxiliary equipment includes such items as crop dusting apparatus, armament racks, inflight refueling equipment, and external fuel tanks.

Cross-References.

- Establishments primarily engaged in manufacturing aircraft engines and engine parts are classified in U.S. Industry 336412, Aircraft Engine and Engine Parts Manufacturing;
- Establishments primarily engaged in manufacturing aeronautical instruments are classified in U.S. Industry 334511, Search, Detection, Navigation, Guidance, Aeronautical, and Nautical System and Instrument Manufacturing;
- Establishments primarily engaged in manufacturing aircraft lighting fixtures are classified in U.S. Industry 336321, Vehicular Lighting Equipment Manufacturing;
- Establishments primarily engaged in manufacturing aircraft engine electrical (aeronautical electrical) equipment are classified in U.S. Industry 336322, Other Motor Vehicle Electrical and Electronic Equipment Manufacturing;
- Establishments primarily engaged in manufacturing guided missile and space vehicle parts and auxiliary equipment are classified in U.S. Industry 336419, Other Guided Missile and Space Vehicle Parts and Auxiliary Equipment Manufacturing;
- Establishments primarily engaged in manufacturing of aircraft fluid power subassemblies are classified in U.S. Industry 332912, Fluid Power Valve and Hose Fitting Manufacturing;
- Establishments primarily engaged in manufacturing of aircraft seating are classified in Industry 336360, Motor Vehicle Seating and Interior Trim Manufacturing; and
- Research and development establishments primarily engaged in aircraft parts and auxiliary equipment R&D (except prototype production) are classified in

US—United States industry only. CAN—United States and Canadian industries are comparable. MEX—United States and Mexican industries are comparable. Blank—Canadian, Mexican, and United States industries are comparable.

Industry 541710, Research and Development in the Physical, Engineering, and Life Sciences.

336414 Guided Missile and Space Vehicle Manufacturing[US]

This U.S. industry comprises establishments primarily engaged in (1) manufacturing complete guided missiles and space vehicles and/or (2) developing and making prototypes of guided missile or space vehicles.

Cross-References.

- Establishments primarily engaged in manufacturing space satellites are classified in Industry 334220, Radio and Television Broadcasting and Wireless Communications Equipment Manufacturing; and
- Research and development establishments primarily engaged in guided missile and space vehicle R&D (except prototype production) are classified in Industry 541710, Research and Development in the Physical, Engineering, and Life Sciences.

336415 Guided Missile and Space Vehicle Propulsion Unit and Propulsion Unit Parts Manufacturing[US]

This U.S. industry comprises establishments primarily engaged in (1) manufacturing guided missile and/or space vehicle propulsion units and propulsion unit parts and/or (2) developing and making prototypes of guided missile and space vehicle propulsion units and propulsion unit parts.

Cross-References.

Research and development establishments primarily engaged in guided missile and space propulsion unit and propulsion unit parts R&D (except prototype production) are classified in Industry 541710, Research and Development in the Physical, Engineering, and Life Sciences.

336419 Other Guided Missile and Space Vehicle Parts and Auxiliary Equipment Manufacturing[US]

This U.S. Industry comprises establishments primarily engaged in (1) manufacturing guided missile and space vehicle parts and auxiliary equipment (except guided missile and space vehicle propulsion units and propulsion unit parts) and/or (2) developing and making prototypes of guided missile and space vehicle parts and auxiliary equipment.

US—United States industry only. CAN—United States and Canadian industries are comparable. MEX—United States and Mexican industries are comparable. Blank—Canadian, Mexican, and United States industries are comparable.

Cross-References.

- Establishments primarily engaged in manufacturing navigational and guidance systems are classified in U.S. Industry 334511, Search, Detection, Navigation, Guidance, Aeronautical, and Nautical System and Instrument Manufacturing;
- Establishments primarily engaged in manufacturing guided missile and space vehicle propulsion units and propulsion unit parts are classified in U.S. Industry 336415, Guided Missile and Space Vehicle Propulsion Unit and Propulsion Unit Parts Manufacturing; and
- Research and development establishments primarily engaged in guided missile and space vehicle parts and auxiliary equipment R&D (except prototype production) are classified in Industry 541710, Research and Development in the Physical, Engineering, and Life Sciences.

3365 Railroad Rolling Stock Manufacturing

33651 Railroad Rolling Stock Manufacturing

See industry description for 336510 below.

336510 Railroad Rolling Stock Manufacturing

This industry comprises establishments primarily engaged in one or more of the following: (1) manufacturing and/or rebuilding locomotives, locomotive frames and parts; (2) manufacturing railroad, street, and rapid transit cars and car equipment for operation on rails for freight and passenger service; and (3) manufacturing rail layers, ballast distributors, rail tamping equipment and other railway track maintenance equipment.

Cross-References.

- Establishments primarily engaged in manufacturing mining rail cars are classified in U.S. Industry 333131, Mining Machinery and Equipment Manufacturing;
- Establishments primarily engaged in manufacturing locomotive fuel lubricating or cooling medium pumps are classified in U.S. Industry 333911, Pump and Pumping Equipment Manufacturing;
- Repair establishments of railroad and local transit companies primarily engaged in repairing railroad and transit cars are classified in Industry 488210, Support Activities for Rail Transportation; and
- Establishments not owned by railroad or local transit companies primarily engaged in repairing railroad cars and locomotive engines are classified in

US—United States industry only. CAN—United States and Canadian industries are comparable. MEX—United States and Mexican industries are comparable. Blank—Canadian, Mexican, and United States industries are comparable.

Industry 811310, Commercial and Industrial Machinery and Equipment (except Automotive and Electronic) Repair and Maintenance.

3366 Ship and Boat Building

33661 Ship and Boat Building

This industry comprises establishments primarily engaged in operating shipyards or boat yards (i.e., ship or boat manufacturing facilities). Shipyards are fixed facilities with drydocks and fabrication equipment capable of building a ship, defined as watercraft typically suitable or intended for other than personal or recreational use. Boats are defined as watercraft typically suitable or intended for personal use. Activities of shipyards include the construction of ships, their repair, conversion and alteration, the production of prefabricated ship and barge sections, and specialized services, such as ship scaling.

Illustrative Examples:

- Barge building
- Boat yards (i.e., boat manufacturing facilities)
- Cargo ship building
- Drilling and production platforms, floating, oil and gas, building
- Passenger ship building
- Rowboats manufacturing

Cross-References. Establishments primarily engaged in—

- Manufacturing rubber boats—are classified in Industry 32629, Other Rubber Product Manufacturing;
- Manufacturing nonrigid (i.e., inflatable) plastics boats—are classified in Industry 32619, Other Plastics Product Manufacturing;
- Fabricating structural assemblies or components for ships, or subcontractors engaged in ship painting, joinery, carpentry work, and electrical wiring installation—are classified based on the production process used; and
- Ship repairs performed in floating drydocks—are classified in Industry 48839, Other Support Activities for Water Transportation.

336611 Ship Building and Repairing[CAN]

This U.S. industry comprises establishments primarily engaged in operating a shipyard. Shipyards are fixed facilities with drydocks and fabrication equipment capable of building a ship, defined as watercraft typically suitable or intended for other than personal or recreational use. Activities of shipyards include the construction of ships, their repair, conversion and alteration, the production of prefabricated ship and barge sections, and specialized services, such as ship scaling.

US—United States industry only. CAN—United States and Canadian industries are comparable. MEX—United States and Mexican industries are comparable. Blank—Canadian, Mexican, and United States industries are comparable.

Illustrative Examples:

Barge building
Cargo ship building
Drilling and production platforms, floating, oil and gas, building
Passenger ship building
Submarine building

Cross-References. Establishments primarily engaged in—

- Fabricating structural assemblies or components for ships, or subcontractors engaged in ship painting, joinery, carpentry work, and electrical wiring installation—are classified based on the production process used; and
- Ship repairs performed in floating drydocks—are classified in Industry 488390, Other Support Activities for Water Transportation.

336612 Boat Building[CAN]

This U.S. industry comprises establishments primarily engaged in building boats. Boats are defined as watercraft not built in shipyards and typically of the type suitable or intended for personal use.

Illustrative Examples:

Dinghy (except inflatable rubber) manufacturing
Motorboats, inboard or outboard, building
Rowboats manufacturing
Sailboat building, not done in shipyards
Yacht building, not done in shipyards

Cross-References. Establishments primarily engaged in—

- Ship building or ship repairs performed in a shipyard—are classified in U.S. Industry 336611, Ship Building and Repairing;
- Manufacturing rubber boats and life rafts—are classified in U.S. Industry 326299, All Other Rubber Product Manufacturing; and
- Manufacturing nonrigid (i.e., inflatable) plastics boats—are classified in U.S. Industry 326199, All Other Plastics Product Manufacturing.

3369 Other Transportation Equipment Manufacturing

This industry group comprises establishments primarily engaged in manufacturing transportation equipment (except motor vehicles and parts, aerospace products and parts, railroad rolling stock, ship building, and boat manufacturing).

US—United States industry only. CAN—United States and Canadian industries are comparable. MEX—United States and Mexican industries are comparable. Blank—Canadian, Mexican, and United States industries are comparable.

33699 Other Transportation Equipment Manufacturing

This industry comprises establishments primarily engaged in manufacturing motorcycles, bicycles, metal tricycles, complete military armored vehicles, tanks, self-propelled weapons, vehicles pulled by draft animals, and other transportation equipment (except motor vehicles, boats, ships, railroad rolling stock, and aerospace products), including parts thereof.

Cross-References. Establishments primarily engaged in—

- Manufacturing ships and boats—are classified in Industry 33661, Ship and Boat Building;
- Manufacturing aerospace products and parts—are classified in Industry 33641, Aerospace Product and Parts Manufacturing;
- Manufacturing motor vehicle parts—are classified in Industry Group 3363, Motor Vehicle Parts Manufacturing;
- Manufacturing children's vehicles (except bicycles and metal tricycles)—are classified in Industry 33993, Doll, Toy, and Game Manufacturing;
- Manufacturing railroad rolling stock—are classified in Industry 33651, Railroad Rolling Stock Manufacturing; and
- Manufacturing motor vehicles—are classified in Industry Group 3361, Motor Vehicle Manufacturing.

336991 Motorcycle, Bicycle, and Parts Manufacturing[US]

This U.S. industry comprises establishments primarily engaged in manufacturing motorcycles, bicycles, tricycles and similar equipment, and parts.

Cross-References. Establishments primarily engaged in—

- Manufacturing children's vehicles (except bicycles and metal tricycles)—are classified in U.S. Industry 339932, Game, Toy, and Children's Vehicle Manufacturing; and
- Manufacturing golf carts and other similar personnel carriers—are classified in U.S. Industry 336999, All Other Transportation Equipment Manufacturing.

336992 Military Armored Vehicle, Tank, and Tank Component Manufacturing[US]

This U.S. industry comprises establishments primarily engaged in manufacturing complete military armored vehicles, combat tanks, specialized components for combat tanks, and self-propelled weapons.

US—United States industry only. CAN—United States and Canadian industries are comparable. MEX—United States and Mexican industries are comparable. Blank—Canadian, Mexican, and United States industries are comparable.

Cross-References.

Establishments primarily engaged in manufacturing nonarmored military universal carriers are classified in U.S. Industry 336112, Light Truck and Utility Vehicle Manufacturing.

336999 All Other Transportation Equipment Manufacturing[US]

This U.S. industry comprises establishments primarily engaged in manufacturing transportation equipment (except motor vehicles, motor vehicle parts, boats, ships, railroad rolling stock, aerospace products, motorcycles, bicycles, armored vehicles and tanks).

Illustrative Examples:

All-terrain vehicles (ATVs), wheeled or tracked, manufacturing
Animal-drawn vehicles and parts manufacturing
Gocarts (except children's) manufacturing
Golf carts and similar motorized passenger carriers manufacturing
Race cars manufacturing
Snowmobiles and parts manufacturing

Cross-References. Establishments primarily engaged in—

- Manufacturing motorcycles, bicycles and parts—are classified in U.S. Industry 336991, Motorcycle, Bicycle, and Parts Manufacturing;
- Manufacturing military armored vehicles, tanks, and tank components—are classified in U.S. Industry 336992, Military Armored Vehicle, Tank, and Tank Component Manufacturing;
- Manufacturing ships and boats—are classified in Industry 33661, Ship and Boat Building;
- Manufacturing aerospace products and parts—are classified in Industry 33641, Aerospace Product and Parts Manufacturing;
- Manufacturing motor vehicle parts—are classified in Industry Group 3363, Motor Vehicle Parts Manufacturing;
- Manufacturing railroad rolling stock—are classified in Industry 336510, Railroad Rolling Stock Manufacturing; and
- Manufacturing motor vehicles—are classified in Industry Group 3361, Motor Vehicle Manufacturing.

337 Furniture and Related Product Manufacturing

Industries in the Furniture and Related Product Manufacturing subsector make furniture and related articles, such as mattresses, window blinds, cabinets, and

US—United States industry only. CAN—United States and Canadian industries are comparable. MEX—United States and Mexican industries are comparable. Blank—Canadian, Mexican, and United States industries are comparable.

fixtures. The processes used in the manufacture of furniture include the cutting, bending, molding, laminating, and assembly of such materials as wood, metal, glass, plastics, and rattan. However, the production process for furniture is not solely bending metal, cutting and shaping wood, or extruding and molding plastics. Design and fashion trends play an important part in the production of furniture. The integrated design of the article for both esthetic and functional qualities is also a major part of the process of manufacturing furniture. Design services may be performed by the furniture establishment's work force or may be purchased from industrial designers.

Furniture may be made of any material, but the most common ones used in North America are metal and wood. Furniture manufacturing establishments may specialize in making articles primarily from one material. Some of the equipment required to make a wooden table, for example, is different from that used to make a metal one. However, furniture is usually made from several materials. A wooden table might have metal brackets, and a wooden chair a fabric or plastics seat. Therefore, in NAICS, furniture initially is classified based on the type of furniture (application for which it is designed) rather than the material used. For example, an upholstered sofa is treated as household furniture, although it may also be used in hotels or offices.

When classifying furniture according to the component material from which it is made, furniture made from more than one material is classified based on the material used in the frame, or if there is no frame, the predominant component material. Upholstered household furniture (excluding kitchen and dining room chairs with upholstered seats) is classified without regard to the frame material. Kitchen or dining room chairs with upholstered seats are classified according to the frame material.

Furniture may be made on a stock or custom basis and may be shipped assembled or unassembled (i.e., knockdown). The manufacture of furniture parts and frames is included in this subsector.

Some of the processes used in furniture manufacturing are similar to processes that are used in other segments of manufacturing. For example, cutting and assembly occurs in the production of wood trusses that are classified in Subsector 321, Wood Product Manufacturing. However, the multiple processes that distinguish wood furniture manufacturing from wood product manufacturing warrant inclusion of wooden furniture manufacturing in the Furniture and Related Product Manufacturing subsector. Metal furniture manufacturing uses techniques that are also employed in the manufacturing of roll-formed products classified in Subsector 332, Fabricated Metal Product Manufacturing. The molding process for plastics furniture is similar to the molding of other plastics products. However, plastics furniture producing establishments tend to specialize in furniture.

NAICS attempts to keep furniture manufacturing together, but there are two notable exceptions: seating for transportation equipment and laboratory and hospital furniture. These exceptions are related to that fact that some of the aspects of the

---

US—United States industry only. CAN—United States and Canadian industries are comparable. MEX—United States and Mexican industries are comparable. Blank—Canadian, Mexican, and United States industries are comparable.

production process for these products, primarily the design, are highly integrated with that of other manufactured goods, namely motor vehicles and health equipment.

3371 Household and Institutional Furniture and Kitchen Cabinet Manufacturing

This industry group comprises establishments manufacturing household-type furniture, such as living room, kitchen and bedroom furniture and institutional (i.e., public building) furniture, such as furniture for schools, theaters, and churches.

33711 Wood Kitchen Cabinet and Countertop Manufacturing

See industry description for 337110 below.

337110 Wood Kitchen Cabinet and Countertop Manufacturing

This industry comprises establishments primarily engaged in manufacturing wood or plastics laminated on wood kitchen cabinets, bathroom vanities, and countertops (except freestanding). The cabinets and counters may be made on a stock or custom basis.

Cross-References. Establishments primarily engaged in—

- Manufacturing metal kitchen and bathroom cabinets (except freestanding)—are classified in U.S. Industry 337124, Metal Household Furniture Manufacturing;
- Manufacturing plastics countertops—are classified in U.S. Industry 326199, All Other Plastics Product Manufacturing;
- Manufacturing stone countertops—are classified in U.S. Industry 327991, Cut Stone and Stone Product Manufacturing; and
- Manufacturing wood or plastics laminated on wood countertops (except kitchen and bathroom)—are classified in U.S. Industry 337215, Showcase, Partition, Shelving, and Locker Manufacturing.

33712 Household and Institutional Furniture Manufacturing

This industry comprises establishments primarily engaged in manufacturing household-type and public building furniture (i.e., library, school, theater, and church furniture). The furniture may be made on a stock or custom basis and may be assembled or unassembled (i.e., knockdown).

US—United States industry only. CAN—United States and Canadian industries are comparable. MEX—United States and Mexican industries are comparable. Blank—Canadian, Mexican, and United States industries are comparable.

Cross-References. Establishments primarily engaged in—

- Manufacturing laboratory and hospital furniture—are classified in Industry 33911, Medical Equipment and Supplies Manufacturing;
- Manufacturing wood or plastics laminated on wood kitchen cabinets, bathroom vanities, and countertops (except freestanding)—are classified in Industry 33711, Wood Kitchen Cabinet and Countertop Manufacturing;
- Manufacturing office-type furniture and/or office or store fixtures—are classified in Industry 33721, Office Furniture (including Fixtures) Manufacturing; and
- Repairing or refinishing furniture—are classified in Industry 81142, Reupholstery and Furniture Repair.

337121 Upholstered Household Furniture Manufacturing[CAN]

This U.S. industry comprises establishments primarily engaged in manufacturing upholstered household-type furniture. The furniture may be made on a stock or custom basis.

Cross-References. Establishments primarily engaged in—

- Reupholstering furniture or upholstering frames to individual order—are classified in Industry 811420, Reupholstery and Furniture Repair;
- Wood kitchen and dining room chairs with upholstered seats or backs—are classified in U. S. Industry 337122, Nonupholstered Wood Household Furniture Manufacturing;
- Metal kitchen and dining room chairs with upholstered seats or backs—are classified in U.S. Industry 337124, Metal Household Furniture Manufacturing; and
- Kitchen and dining room chairs (except wood and metal) with upholstered seats or backs— are classified in U.S. Industry 337125, Household Furniture (except Wood and Metal) Manufacturing.

337122 Nonupholstered Wood Household Furniture Manufacturing[US]

This U.S. industry comprises establishments primarily engaged in manufacturing nonupholstered wood household-type furniture and freestanding cabinets (except television, radio, and sewing machine cabinets). The furniture may be made on a stock or custom basis and may be assembled or unassembled (i.e., knockdown).

US—United States industry only. CAN—United States and Canadian industries are comparable. MEX—United States and Mexican industries are comparable. Blank—Canadian, Mexican, and United States industries are comparable.

Cross-References. Establishments primarily engaged in—

- Manufacturing reed, rattan, plastics and similar furniture—are classified in U.S. Industry 337125, Household Furniture (except Wood and Metal) Manufacturing;
- Manufacturing wood or plastics laminated on wood kitchen cabinets, bathroom vanities, and countertops (except freestanding)—are classified in Industry 337110, Wood Kitchen Cabinet and Countertop Manufacturing;
- Manufacturing wood television, stereo, loudspeaker, and sewing machine cabinets (i.e., housings)—are classified in U.S. Industry 337129, Wood Television, Radio, and Sewing Machine Cabinet Manufacturing; and
- Repairing or refinishing furniture—are classified in Industry 811420, Reupholstery and Furniture Repair.

337124 Metal Household Furniture Manufacturing[US]

This U.S. industry comprises establishments primarily engaged in manufacturing metal household-type furniture and freestanding cabinets. The furniture may be made on a stock or custom basis and may be assembled or unassembled (i.e., knockdown).

Cross-References.

Establishments primarily engaged in manufacturing metal laboratory and hospital furniture including beds are classified in Industry 33911, Medical Equipment and Supplies Manufacturing.

337125 Household Furniture (except Wood and Metal) Manufacturing[US]

This U.S. industry comprises establishments primarily engaged in manufacturing household-type furniture of materials other than wood or metal, such as plastics, reed, rattan, wicker, and fiberglass. The furniture may be made on a stock or custom basis and may be assembled or unassembled (i.e., knockdown).

Cross-References. Establishments primarily engaged in—

- Manufacturing concrete, ceramic, or stone furniture—are classified in Subsector 327, Nonmetallic Mineral Product Manufacturing, according to the materials used;
- Manufacturing upholstered household-type furniture—are classified in U.S. Industry 337121, Upholstered Household Furniture Manufacturing;

US—United States industry only. CAN—United States and Canadian industries are comparable. MEX—United States and Mexican industries are comparable. Blank—Canadian, Mexican, and United States industries are comparable.

- Manufacturing metal household-type furniture—are classified in U.S. Industry 337124, Metal Household Furniture Manufacturing; and
- Manufacturing nonupholstered wood household-type furniture—are classified in U.S. Industry 337122, Nonupholstered Wood Household Furniture Manufacturing.

337127 Institutional Furniture Manufacturing[CAN]

This U.S. industry comprises establishments primarily engaged in manufacturing institutional-type furniture (e.g., library, school, theater, and church furniture). The furniture may be made on a stock or custom basis and may be assembled or unassembled (i.e., knockdown).

Cross-References. Establishments primarily engaged in—

- Manufacturing laboratory and hospital furniture—are classified in Industry 33911, Medical Equipment and Supplies Manufacturing;
- Manufacturing wood kitchen cabinets, wood bathroom vanities, and countertops designed for permanent installation—are classified in Industry 337110, Wood Kitchen Cabinet and Countertop Manufacturing;
- Manufacturing office-type furniture and/or office or store fixtures—are classified in Industry 33721, Office Furniture (including Fixtures) Manufacturing; and
- Repairing or refinishing furniture—are classified in Industry 811420, Reupholstery and Furniture Repair.

337129 Wood Television, Radio, and Sewing Machine Cabinet Manufacturing[US]

This U.S. industry comprises establishments primarily engaged in manufacturing wood cabinets used as housings by television, stereo, loudspeaker, and sewing machine manufacturers.

Cross-References. Establishments primarily engaged in—

- Manufacturing plastics housings used by television, stereo, loudspeaker, and sewing machine manufacturers—are classified in U.S. Industry 326199, All Other Plastics Product Manufacturing;
- Manufacturing metal housings used by television, stereo, loudspeaker, and sewing machine manufacturers—are classified in U.S. Industry 332322, Sheet Metal Work Manufacturing;

US—United States industry only. CAN—United States and Canadian industries are comparable. MEX—United States and Mexican industries are comparable. Blank—Canadian, Mexican, and United States industries are comparable.

- Manufacturing freestanding wood household-type cabinets (e.g., entertainment centers, stands) for consumer electronics—are classified in U.S. Industry 337122, Nonupholstered Wood Household Furniture Manufacturing;
- Manufacturing freestanding metal household-type cabinets (e.g., entertainment centers, stands) for consumer electronics—are classified in U.S. Industry 337124, Metal Household Furniture Manufacturing; and
- Manufacturing freestanding household-type cabinets (e.g., entertainment centers, stands) (except wood and metal) for consumer electronics—are classified in U.S. Industry 337125, Household Furniture (except Wood and Metal) Manufacturing.

3372 Office Furniture (including Fixtures) Manufacturing

33721 Office Furniture (including Fixtures) Manufacturing

This industry comprises establishments primarily engaged in manufacturing office furniture and/or office and store fixtures. The furniture may be made on a stock or custom basis and may be assembled or unassembled (i.e., knockdown).

Cross-References. Establishments primarily engaged in—

- Manufacturing millwork on a factory basis—are classified in Industry 32191, Millwork;
- Manufacturing household-type and institutional-type furniture—are classified in Industry 33712, Household and Institutional Furniture Manufacturing;
- Manufacturing refrigerated cabinets, showcases, and display cases—are classified in Industry 33341, Ventilation, Heating, Air-Conditioning, and Commercial Refrigeration Equipment Manufacturing; and
- Manufacturing metal safes and vaults—are classified in Industry 33299, All Other Fabricated Metal Product Manufacturing.

337211 Wood Office Furniture Manufacturing[US]

This U.S. industry comprises establishments primarily engaged in manufacturing wood office-type furniture. The furniture may be made on a stock or custom basis and may be assembled or unassembled (i.e., knockdown).

337212 Custom Architectural Woodwork and Millwork Manufacturing[US]

This U.S. industry comprises establishments primarily engaged in manufacturing custom designed interiors consisting of architectural woodwork and fixtures utiliz-

US—United States industry only. CAN—United States and Canadian industries are comparable. MEX—United States and Mexican industries are comparable. Blank—Canadian, Mexican, and United States industries are comparable.

ing wood, wood products, and plastics laminates. All of the industry output is made to individual order on a job shop basis and requires skilled craftsmen as a labor input. A job might include custom manufacturing of display fixtures, gondolas, wall shelving units, entrance and window architectural detail, sales and reception counters, wall paneling, and matching furniture.

Cross-References. Establishments primarily engaged in—

- Manufacturing millwork on a factory basis—are classified in U.S. Industry 321918, Other Millwork (including Flooring);
- Manufacturing wood office-type furniture on a stock or custom basis—are classified in U.S. Industry 337211, Wood Office Furniture Manufacturing; and
- Manufacturing wood office-type furniture and store fixtures on a stock basis—are classified in U.S. Industry 337215, Showcase, Partition, Shelving, and Locker Manufacturing.

337214 Office Furniture (except Wood) Manufacturing[CAN]

This U.S. industry comprises establishments primarily engaged in manufacturing nonwood office-type furniture. The furniture may be made on a stock or custom basis and may be assembled or unassembled (i.e., knockdown).

337215 Showcase, Partition, Shelving, and Locker Manufacturing[CAN]

This U.S. industry comprises establishments primarily engaged in manufacturing wood and nonwood office and store fixtures, shelving, lockers, frames, partitions, and related fabricated products of wood and nonwood materials, including plastics laminated fixture tops. The products are made on a stock basis and may be assembled or unassembled (i.e., knockdown). Establishments exclusively making furniture parts (e.g., frames) are included in this industry.

Cross-References. Establishments primarily engaged in—

- Manufacturing refrigerated cabinets, showcases, and display cases—are classified in U.S. Industry 333415, Air-Conditioning and Warm Air Heating Equipment and Commercial and Industrial Refrigeration Equipment Manufacturing;
- Manufacturing metal safes and vaults—are classified in U.S. Industry 332999, All Other Miscellaneous Fabricated Metal Product Manufacturing; and
- Manufacturing wood or plastics laminated kitchen and bathroom countertops—are classified in Industry 337110, Wood Kitchen Cabinet and Countertop Manufacturing.

US—United States industry only. CAN—United States and Canadian industries are comparable. MEX—United States and Mexican industries are comparable. Blank—Canadian, Mexican, and United States industries are comparable.

3379 Other Furniture Related Product Manufacturing

This industry group comprises establishments manufacturing furniture related products, such as mattresses, blinds, and shades.

33791 Mattress Manufacturing

See industry description for 337910 below.

337910 Mattress Manufacturing

This industry comprises establishments primarily engaged in manufacturing innerspring, box spring, and noninnerspring mattresses, including mattresses for waterbeds.

Cross-References. Establishments primarily engaged in—

- Manufacturing individual wire springs—are classified in Industry 33261, Spring and Wire Product Manufacturing; and
- Manufacturing inflatable mattresses—are classified in Subsector 326, Plastics and Rubber Products Manufacturing.

33792 Blind and Shade Manufacturing

See industry description for 337920 below.

337920 Blind and Shade Manufacturing

This industry comprises establishments primarily engaged in manufacturing one or more of the following: venetian blinds, other window blinds, shades; curtain and drapery rods, poles; and/or curtain and drapery fixtures. The blinds and shades may be made on a stock or custom basis and may be made of any material.

Cross-References. Establishments primarily engaged in—

- Manufacturing canvas awnings—are classified in U.S. Industry 314912, Canvas and Related Product Mills; and
- Manufacturing curtains and draperies—are classified in U.S. Industry 314121, Curtain and Drapery Mills.

339 Miscellaneous Manufacturing

Industries in the Miscellaneous Manufacturing subsector make a wide range of products that cannot readily be classified in specific NAICS subsectors in

US—United States industry only. CAN—United States and Canadian industries are comparable. MEX—United States and Mexican industries are comparable. Blank—Canadian, Mexican, and United States industries are comparable.

manufacturing. Processes used by these establishments vary significantly, both among and within industries. For example, a variety of manufacturing processes are used in manufacturing sporting and athletic goods that include products, such as tennis racquets and golf balls. The processes for these products differ from each other, and the processes differ significantly from the fabrication processes used in making dolls or toys, the melting and shaping of precious metals to make jewelry, and the bending, forming, and assembly used in making medical products.

The industries in this subsector are defined by what is made rather than how it is made. Although individual establishments might be appropriately classified elsewhere in the NAICS structure, for historical continuity, these product-based industries were maintained. In most cases, no one process or material predominates for an industry.

Establishments in this subsector manufacture products as diverse as medical equipment and supplies, jewelry, sporting goods, toys, and office supplies.

3391 Medical Equipment and Supplies Manufacturing

33911 Medical Equipment and Supplies Manufacturing

This industry comprises establishments primarily engaged in manufacturing medical equipment and supplies. Examples of products made by these establishments are laboratory apparatus and furniture, surgical and medical instruments, surgical appliances and supplies, dental equipment and supplies, orthodontic goods, dentures, and orthodontic appliances.

Cross-References. Establishments primarily engaged in—

- Manufacturing laboratory instruments, X-ray apparatus, electromedical apparatus (including electronic hearing aids), and thermometers (except medical)—are classified in Industry 33451, Navigational, Measuring, Electromedical, and Control Instruments Manufacturing;
- Manufacturing molded glass lens blanks—are classified in Industry 32721, Glass and Glass Product Manufacturing;
- Manufacturing molded plastics lens blanks—are classified in Industry 32619, Other Plastics Product Manufacturing;
- Retailing and grinding prescription eyeglasses—are classified in Industry 44613, Optical Goods Stores; and
- Manufacturing sporting goods helmets and protective equipment—are classified in Industry, 33992 Sporting and Athletic Goods Manufacturing.

339111 Laboratory Apparatus and Furniture Manufacturing[US]

This U.S. industry comprises establishments primarily engaged in manufacturing laboratory apparatus and laboratory and hospital furniture (except dental). Exam-

US—United States industry only. CAN—United States and Canadian industries are comparable. MEX—United States and Mexican industries are comparable. Blank—Canadian, Mexican, and United States industries are comparable.

ples of products made by these establishments are hospital beds, operating room tables, laboratory balances and scales, furnaces, ovens, centrifuges, cabinets, cases, benches, tables, and stools.

Cross-References. Establishments primarily engaged in—

- Manufacturing dental laboratory apparatus and furniture—are classified in U.S. Industry 339114, Dental Equipment and Supplies Manufacturing; and
- Manufacturing laboratory instruments—are classified in U.S. Industry 334516, Analytical Laboratory Instrument Manufacturing.

339112 Surgical and Medical Instrument Manufacturing[US]

This U.S. industry comprises establishments primarily engaged in manufacturing medical, surgical, ophthalmic, and veterinary instruments and apparatus (except electrotherapeutic, electromedical and irradiation apparatus). Examples of products made by these establishments are syringes, hypodermic needles, anesthesia apparatus, blood transfusion equipment, catheters, surgical clamps, and medical thermometers.

Cross-References. Establishments primarily engaged in—

- Manufacturing electromedical and electrotherapeutic apparatus—are classified in U.S. Industry 334510, Electromedical and Electrotherapeutic Apparatus Manufacturing;
- Manufacturing irradiation apparatus—are classified in U.S. Industry 334517, Irradiation Apparatus Manufacturing;
- Manufacturing surgical and orthopedic appliances—are classified in U.S. Industry 339113 Surgical Appliance and Supplies Manufacturing;
- Manufacturing dental equipment, dental supplies, dental laboratory apparatus, and dental laboratory furniture—are classified in U.S. Industry 339114, Dental Equipment and Supplies Manufacturing;
- Manufacturing laboratory apparatus and laboratory and hospital furniture (except dental)—are classified in U.S. Industry 339111, Laboratory Apparatus and Furniture Manufacturing; and
- Manufacturing thermometers (except medical)—are classified in U.S. Industry 334519, Other Measuring and Controlling Device Manufacturing.

339113 Surgical Appliance and Supplies Manufacturing[US]

This U.S. industry comprises establishments primarily engaged in manufacturing surgical appliances and supplies. Examples of products made by these establish-

---

US—United States industry only. CAN—United States and Canadian industries are comparable. MEX—United States and Mexican industries are comparable. Blank—Canadian, Mexican, and United States industries are comparable.

ments are orthopedic devices, prosthetic appliances, surgical dressings, crutches, surgical sutures, and personal industrial safety devices (except protective eyewear).

Cross-References. Establishments primarily engaged in—

- Manufacturing dental equipment, dental supplies, dental laboratory apparatus, and dental laboratory furniture—are classified in U.S. Industry 339114, Dental Equipment and Supplies Manufacturing;
- Manufacturing laboratory apparatus and laboratory and hospital furniture (except dental)—are classified in U.S. Industry 339111, Laboratory Apparatus and Furniture Manufacturing;
- Manufacturing electronic hearing aids—are classified in U.S. Industry 334510, Electromedical and Electrotherapeutic Apparatus Manufacturing;
- Manufacturing industrial protective eyewear—are classified in U.S. Industry 339115, Ophthalmic Goods Manufacturing; and
- Manufacturing sporting goods helmets and protective equipment—are classified in Industry 339920, Sporting and Athletic Goods Manufacturing.

339114 Dental Equipment and Supplies Manufacturing[US]

This U.S. industry comprises establishments primarily engaged in manufacturing dental equipment and supplies used by dental laboratories and offices of dentists, such as dental chairs, dental instrument delivery systems, dental hand instruments, and dental impression material and dental cements.

Cross-References. Establishments primarily engaged in—

- Manufacturing dentures, crowns, bridges, and orthodontic appliances customized for individual application—are classified in U.S. Industry 339116, Dental Laboratories; and
- Manufacturing laboratory apparatus and laboratory and hospital furniture (except dental)—are classified in U.S. Industry 339111, Laboratory Apparatus and Furniture Manufacturing.

339115 Ophthalmic Goods Manufacturing[US]

This U.S. industry comprises establishments primarily engaged in manufacturing ophthalmic goods. Examples of products made by these establishments are prescription eyeglasses (except manufactured in a retail setting), contact lenses, sunglasses, eyeglass frames, and reading glasses made to standard powers, and protective eyewear.

US—United States industry only. CAN—United States and Canadian industries are comparable. MEX—United States and Mexican industries are comparable. Blank—Canadian, Mexican, and United States industries are comparable.

Cross-References. Establishments primarily engaged in—

- Manufacturing molded glass lens blanks—are classified in U.S. Industry 327212, Other Pressed and Blown Glass and Glassware Manufacturing;
- Manufacturing molded plastics lens blanks—are classified in U.S. Industry 326199, All Other Plastics Product Manufacturing; and
- Retailing and grinding prescription eyeglasses—are classified in Industry 446130, Optical Goods Stores.

339116 Dental Laboratories[US]

This U.S. industry comprises establishments primarily engaged in manufacturing dentures, crowns, bridges, and orthodontic appliances customized for individual application.

Cross-References.

Establishments primarily engaged in manufacturing dental equipment and supplies are classified in U.S. Industry 339114, Dental Equipment and Supplies Manufacturing.

3399 Other Miscellaneous Manufacturing

33991 Jewelry and Silverware Manufacturing

This industry comprises establishments primarily engaged in one or more of the following: (1) manufacturing, engraving, chasing, or etching jewelry; (2) manufacturing metal personal goods (i.e., small articles carried on or about the person, such as compacts or cigarette cases); (3) manufacturing, engraving, chasing, or etching precious metal solid, precious metal clad, or pewter cutlery and flatware; (4) manufacturing, engraving, chasing, or etching personal metal goods (i.e., small articles carried on or about the person, such as compacts or cigarette cases); (5) stamping coins; (6) manufacturing unassembled jewelry parts and stock shop products, such as sheet, wire, and tubing; (7) cutting, slabbing, tumbling, carving, engraving, polishing, or faceting precious or semiprecious stones and gems; (8) recutting, repolishing, and setting gem stones; and (9) drilling, sawing, and peeling cultured and costume pearls.

Cross-References. Establishments primarily engaged in—

- Manufacturing nonprecious and precious plated metal cutlery and flatware—are classified in Industry 33221, Cutlery and Handtool Manufacturing;

US—United States industry only. CAN—United States and Canadian industries are comparable. MEX—United States and Mexican industries are comparable. Blank—Canadian, Mexican, and United States industries are comparable.

- Manufacturing nonprecious plated ware (except cutlery, flatware)—are classified in Industry 33299, All Other Fabricated Metal Product Manufacturing;
- Engraving, chasing, or etching nonprecious and precious plated metal flatware and other plated ware and plated jewelry—are classified in Industry 33281, Coating, Engraving, Heat Treating, and Allied Activities;
- Manufacturing synthetic stones or gem stones—are classified in Industry 32799, All Other Nonmetallic Mineral Product Manufacturing; and
- Manufacturing personal goods (except metal) carried on or about the person, such as compacts and cigarette cases—are classified in Industry 31699, Other Leather and Allied Product Manufacturing.

339911 Jewelry (except Costume) Manufacturing[US]

This U.S. industry comprises establishments primarily engaged in one or more of the following: (1) manufacturing, engraving, chasing, or etching precious metal solid or precious metal clad jewelry; (2) manufacturing, engraving, chasing, or etching personal goods (i.e., small articles carried on or about the person, such as compacts or cigarette cases) made of precious solid or clad metal; and (3) stamping coins.

Cross-References. Establishments primarily engaged in—

- Manufacturing, engraving, chasing, or etching costume jewelry and nonprecious metal personal goods—are classified in U.S. Industry 339914, Costume Jewelry and Novelty Manufacturing;
- Manufacturing jewelers' materials or performing lapidary work—are classified in U.S. Industry 339913, Jewelers' Material and Lapidary Work Manufacturing; and
- Plating jewelry—are classified in U.S. Industry 332813, Electroplating, Plating, Polishing, Anodizing and Coloring.

339912 Silverware and Hollowware Manufacturing[US]

This U.S. industry comprises establishments primarily engaged in manufacturing, engraving, chasing, or etching precious metal solid, precious metal clad, or pewter flatware and other hollowware.

Cross-References. Establishments primarily engaged in—

- Manufacturing nonprecious and precious plated metal cutlery and flatware—are classified in U.S. Industry 332211, Cutlery and Flatware (except Precious) Manufacturing;

US—United States industry only. CAN—United States and Canadian industries are comparable. MEX—United States and Mexican industries are comparable. Blank—Canadian, Mexican, and United States industries are comparable.

- Manufacturing nonprecious metal plated ware (except cutlery and flatware)—are classified in U.S. Industry 332999, All Other Miscellaneous Fabricated Metal Product Manufacturing;
- Engraving, chasing, or etching nonprecious and precious plated metal cutlery, flatware and other plated ware—are classified in U.S. Industry 332812, Metal Coating, Engraving (except Jewelry and Silverware), and Allied Services to Manufactures; and
- Manufacturing, engraving, chasing, or etching precious (except precious plated) metal jewelry and personal goods—are classified in U.S. Industry 339911, Jewelry (except Costume) Manufacturing.

339913 Jewelers' Material and Lapidary Work Manufacturing[US]

This U.S. industry comprises establishments primarily engaged in one or more of the following: (1) manufacturing unassembled jewelry parts and stock shop products, such as sheet, wire, and tubing; (2) cutting, slabbing, tumbling, carving, engraving, polishing or faceting precious or semiprecious stones and gems; (3) recutting, repolishing, and setting gem stones; and (4) drilling, sawing, and peeling cultured pearls.

Cross-References. Establishments primarily engaged in—

- Manufacturing synthetic stones—are classified in Industry U.S. 327999, All Other Miscellaneous Nonmetallic Mineral Product Manufacturing; and
- Manufacturing costume pearls—are classified in U.S. Industry 339914, Costume Jewelry and Novelty Manufacturing.

339914 Costume Jewelry and Novelty Manufacturing[US]

This U.S. industry comprises establishments primarily engaged in (1) manufacturing, engraving, chasing, and etching costume jewelry; and/or (2) manufacturing, engraving, chasing, or etching nonprecious metal personal goods (i.e., small articles carried on or about the person, such as compacts or cigarette cases). This industry includes establishments primarily engaged in manufacturing precious plated jewelry and precious plated personal goods.

Cross-References. Establishments primarily engaged in—

- Manufacturing, engraving, chasing, or etching precious (except precious plated) metal jewelry and novelties—are classified in U.S. Industry 339911, Jewelry (except Costume) Manufacturing;

US—United States industry only. CAN—United States and Canadian industries are comparable. MEX—United States and Mexican industries are comparable. Blank—Canadian, Mexican, and United States industries are comparable.

- Manufacturing personal goods (except metal) carried on or about the person, such as compacts and cigarette cases—are classified in U.S. Industry 316993, Personal Leather Goods (except Women's Handbag and Purse) Manufacturing; and
- Manufacturing synthetic stones—are classified in U.S. Industry 327999, All Other Miscellaneous Nonmetallic Mineral Product Manufacturing.

33992 Sporting and Athletic Goods Manufacturing

See industry description for 339920 below.

339920 Sporting and Athletic Goods Manufacturing

This industry comprises establishments primarily engaged in manufacturing sporting and athletic goods (except apparel and footwear).

Cross-References. Establishments primarily engaged in—

- Manufacturing athletic apparel—are classified in Subsector 315, Apparel Manufacturing;
- Manufacturing athletic footwear—are classified in U.S. Industry 316219, Other Footwear Manufacturing; and
- Manufacturing small arms and small arms ammunition—are classified in Industry 33299, All Other Fabricated Metal Product Manufacturing.

33993 Doll, Toy, and Game Manufacturing

This industry comprises establishments primarily engaged in manufacturing dolls, toys, and games, such as complete dolls, doll parts, doll clothes, action figures, toys, games (including electronic), hobby kits, and children's vehicles (except metal bicycles and tricycles).

Cross-References. Establishments primarily engaged in—

- Manufacturing bicycles and metal tricycles—are classified in Industry 33699, Other Transportation Equipment Manufacturing;
- Manufacturing sporting and athletic goods—are classified in Industry 33992, Sporting and Athletic Goods Manufacturing;
- Manufacturing coin-operated game machines—are classified in Industry 33999, All Other Miscellaneous Manufacturing; and
- Manufacturing electronic video game cartridges and reproducing video game software—are classified in Industry 33461, Manufacturing and Reproducing Magnetic and Optical Media.

US—United States industry only. CAN—United States and Canadian industries are comparable. MEX—United States and Mexican industries are comparable. Blank—Canadian, Mexican, and United States industries are comparable.

339931 Doll and Stuffed Toy Manufacturing[US]

This U.S. industry comprises establishments primarily engaged in manufacturing complete dolls, doll parts, and doll clothes, action figures, and stuffed toys.

Cross-References.

Establishments primarily engaged in manufacturing toys (except stuffed) are classified in U.S. Industry 339932, Game, Toy, and Children's Vehicle Manufacturing.

339932 Game, Toy, and Children's Vehicle Manufacturing[US]

This U.S. industry comprises establishments primarily engaged in manufacturing games (including electronic), toys, and children's vehicles (except bicycles and metal tricycles).

Cross-References. Establishments primarily engaged in—

- Manufacturing dolls and stuffed toys—are classified in U.S. Industry 339931, Doll and Stuffed Toy Manufacturing;
- Manufacturing metal tricycles and bicycles—are classified in U.S. Industry 336991, Motorcycle, Bicycle, and Parts Manufacturing;
- Manufacturing sporting and athletic goods—are classified in Industry 339920, Sporting and Athletic Goods Manufacturing;
- Manufacturing coin-operated game machines—are classified in U.S. Industry 339999, All Other Miscellaneous Manufacturing; and
- Mass reproducing electronic video game cartridges—are classified in U.S. Industry 334611, Software Reproducing.

33994 Office Supplies (except Paper) Manufacturing

This industry comprises establishments primarily engaged in manufacturing office supplies. Examples of products made by these establishments are pens, pencils, felt tip markers, crayons, chalk, pencil sharpeners, staplers, hand operated stamps, modeling clay, and inked ribbons.

Cross-References. Establishments primarily engaged in—

- Manufacturing writing, drawing, and india inks—are classified in Industry 32599, All Other Chemical Product and Preparation Manufacturing;

US—United States industry only. CAN—United States and Canadian industries are comparable. MEX—United States and Mexican industries are comparable. Blank—Canadian, Mexican, and United States industries are comparable.

- Manufacturing drafting tables and boards—are classified in Industry 33712, Household and Institutional Furniture Manufacturing;
- Manufacturing rubber erasers—are classified in Industry 32629, Other Rubber Product Manufacturing;
- Manufacturing paper office supplies—are classified in Subsector 322, Paper Manufacturing;
- Manufacturing manifold business forms, blankbooks, and looseleaf binders—are classified in Industry 32311, Printing; and
- Manufacturing inkjet cartridges—are classified in Industry 32591, Printing Ink Manufacturing.

339941 Pen and Mechanical Pencil Manufacturing[US]

This U.S. industry comprises establishments primarily engaged in manufacturing pens, ballpoint pen refills and cartridges, mechanical pencils, and felt tipped markers.

Cross-References. Establishments primarily engaged in—

- Manufacturing nonmechanical pencils and pencil leads—are classified in U.S. Industry 339942, Lead Pencil and Art Good Manufacturing;
- Manufacturing writing, drawing, and india inks—are classified in U.S. Industry 325998, All Other Miscellaneous Chemical Product and Preparation Manufacturing; and
- Manufacturing rubber erasers—are classified in U.S. Industry 326299, All Other Rubber Product Manufacturing.

339942 Lead Pencil and Art Good Manufacturing[US]

This U.S. industry comprises establishments primarily engaged in manufacturing nonmechanical pencils, and art goods. Examples of products made by these establishments are pencil leads, crayons, chalk, framed blackboards, pencil sharpeners, staplers, artists' palettes and paints, and modeling clay.

Cross-References. Establishments primarily engaged in—

- Manufacturing mechanical pencils—are classified in U.S. Industry 339941, Pen and Mechanical Pencil Manufacturing;
- Manufacturing writing, drawing, and india inks—are classified in U.S. Industry 325998, All Other Miscellaneous Chemical Product and Preparation Manufacturing;

US—United States industry only. CAN—United States and Canadian industries are comparable. MEX—United States and Mexican industries are comparable. Blank—Canadian, Mexican, and United States industries are comparable.

- Manufacturing rubber erasers—are classified in U.S. Industry 326299, All Other Rubber Product Manufacturing;
- Manufacturing paper office supplies—are classified in Subsector 322, Paper Manufacturing;
- Printing manifold business forms and manufacturing blankbooks and looseleaf binders and devices—are classified in Industry 32311, Printing; and
- Manufacturing drafting tables and boards—are classified in U.S. Industry 337127, Institutional Furniture Manufacturing.

339943 Marking Device Manufacturing[US]

This U.S. industry comprises establishments primarily engaged in manufacturing marking devices, such as hand operated stamps, embossing stamps, stamp pads, and stencils.

Cross-References.

Establishments primarily engaged in manufacturing felt tipped markers are classified in U.S. Industry 339941, Pen and Mechanical Pencil Manufacturing.

339944 Carbon Paper and Inked Ribbon Manufacturing[US]

This U.S. industry comprises establishments primarily engaged in manufacturing carbon paper and inked ribbons.

Cross-References. Establishments primarily engaged in manufacturing inkjet cartridges are classified in Industry 325910, Printing Ink Manufacturing.

33995 Sign Manufacturing

See industry description for 339950 below.

339950 Sign Manufacturing

This industry comprises establishments primarily engaged in manufacturing signs and related displays of all materials (except printing paper and paperboard signs, notices, displays).

Cross-References. Establishments primarily engaged in—

- Printing advertising specialties or printing paper and paperboard signs, notices, and displays—are classified in Industry 32311, Printing;

US—United States industry only. CAN—United States and Canadian industries are comparable. MEX—United States and Mexican industries are comparable. Blank—Canadian, Mexican, and United States industries are comparable.

- Manufacturing and printing advertising specialties—are classified in the manufacturing sector according to products manufactured;
- Manufacturing die-cut paperboard displays—are classified in U.S. Industry 322299, All Other Converted Paper Product Manufacturing; and
- Sign lettering and painting—are classified in Industry 541890, Other Services Related to Advertising.

33999 All Other Miscellaneous Manufacturing

This industry comprises establishments primarily engaged in miscellaneous manufacturing (except medical equipment and supplies, jewelry and flatware, sporting and athletic goods, dolls, toys, games, office supplies (except paper), and signs).

Illustrative Examples:

Artificial Christmas trees manufacturing
Burial caskets and cases manufacturing
Candles manufacturing
Coin-operated amusement machines (except jukebox) manufacturing
Fasteners, buttons, needles, and pins (except precious metals or precious and semiprecious stones and gems) manufacturing
Floor and dust mops manufacturing
Gasket, packing, and sealing devices manufacturing
Musical instruments (except toy) manufacturing
Portable fire extinguishers manufacturing
Umbrellas manufacturing

Cross-References. Establishments primarily engaged in—

- Manufacturing medical equipment and supplies—are classified in Industry Group 3391; Medical Equipment and Supplies Manufacturing;
- Manufacturing jewelry and flatware—are classified in Industry 33991, Jewelry and Silverware Manufacturing;
- Manufacturing sporting and athletic goods—are classified in Industry 33992, Sporting and Athletic Goods Manufacturing;
- Manufacturing dolls, toys, and games—are classified in Industry 33993, Doll, Toy, and Game Manufacturing;
- Manufacturing office supplies (except paper)—are classified in Industry 33994, Office Supplies (except Paper) Manufacturing;
- Manufacturing signs—are classified in Industry 33995, Sign Manufacturing;
- Manufacturing concrete burial vaults—are classified in Industry 32739, Other Concrete Product Manufacturing;

US—United States industry only. CAN—United States and Canadian industries are comparable. MEX—United States and Mexican industries are comparable. Blank—Canadian, Mexican, and United States industries are comparable.

- Manufacturing Christmas tree glass ornaments and glass lamp shades—are classified in Industry 32721, Glass and Glass Product Manufacturing;
- Manufacturing Christmas tree lighting sets—are classified in Industry 33512, Lighting Fixture Manufacturing;
- Manufacturing beauty and barber chairs—are classified in Industry 33712, Household and Institutional Furniture Manufacturing;
- Manufacturing burnt wood articles—are classified in Industry 32199, All Other Wood Product Manufacturing;
- Dressing and bleaching furs—are classified in Industry 31611, Leather and Hide Tanning and Finishing;
- Manufacturing paper, textile, and metal lamp shades—are classified in Industry 33512, Lighting Fixture Manufacturing;
- Manufacturing plastics lamp shades—are classified in Industry 32619, Other Plastics Product Manufacturing;
- Manufacturing matches—are classified in Industry 32599, All Other Chemical Product and Preparation Manufacturing;
- Manufacturing metal products, such as metal combs and hair curlers—are classified in Industry 33299, All Other Fabricated Metal Product Manufacturing;
- Manufacturing plastics products, such as plastics combs and hair curlers—are classified in Industry 32619, Other Plastics Product Manufacturing; and
- Manufacturing electric hair clippers for use on humans—are classified in Industry 33521, Small Electrical Appliance Manufacturing.

339991 Gasket, Packing, and Sealing Device Manufacturing[US]

This U.S. industry comprises establishments primarily engaged in manufacturing gaskets, packing, and sealing devices of all materials.

339992 Musical Instrument Manufacturing[US]

This U.S. industry comprises establishments primarily engaged in manufacturing musical instruments (except toys).

Cross-References.

Establishments primarily engaged in manufacturing toy musical instruments are classified in U.S. Industry 339932, Game, Toy, and Children's Vehicle Manufacturing.

US—United States industry only. CAN—United States and Canadian industries are comparable. MEX—United States and Mexican industries are comparable. Blank—Canadian, Mexican, and United States industries are comparable.

339993 Fastener, Button, Needle, and Pin Manufacturing[US]

This U.S. industry comprises establishments primarily engaged in manufacturing fasteners, buttons, needles, pins, and buckles (except precious metals or precious and semiprecious stones and gems).

Cross-References. Establishments primarily engaged in—

- Manufacturing buttons, pins, and buckles made of precious metals or precious and semiprecious stones and gems—are classified in U.S. Industry 339911, Jewelry (except Costume) Manufacturing;
- Manufacturing hypodermic and suture needles—are classified in U.S. Industry 339112, Surgical and Medical Instrument Manufacturing; and
- Manufacturing phonograph and styli needles—are classified in U.S. Industry 334419, Other Electronic Component Manufacturing.

339994 Broom, Brush, and Mop Manufacturing[US]

This U.S. industry comprises establishments primarily engaged in manufacturing brooms, mops, and brushes.

339995 Burial Casket Manufacturing[MEX]

This U.S. industry comprises establishments primarily engaged in manufacturing burial caskets, cases, and vaults (except concrete).

Cross-References.

Establishments primarily engaged in manufacturing concrete burial vaults are classified in Industry 327390, Other Concrete Product Manufacturing.

339999 All Other Miscellaneous Manufacturing[US]

This U.S. industry comprises establishments primarily engaged in miscellaneous manufacturing (except medical equipment and supplies, jewelry and flatware, sporting and athletic goods, dolls, toys, games, office supplies (except paper), musical instruments, fasteners, buttons, needles, pins, brooms, brushes, mops, and burial caskets).

Illustrative Examples:

Artificial Christmas trees manufacturing
Candles manufacturing
Hair pieces (e.g., wigs, toupees, wiglets) manufacturing

US—United States industry only. CAN—United States and Canadian industries are comparable. MEX—United States and Mexican industries are comparable. Blank—Canadian, Mexican, and United States industries are comparable.

Christmas tree ornaments (except glass and electric) manufacturing
Cigarette lighters (except precious metal) manufacturing
Coin-operated amusement machines (except jukebox) manufacturing
Portable fire extinguishers manufacturing
Potpourri manufacturing
Tobacco pipes manufacturing
Umbrellas manufacturing

Cross-References. Establishments primarily engaged in—

- Manufacturing medical equipment and supplies—are classified in Industry Group 3391, Medical Equipment and Supplies Manufacturing;
- Manufacturing jewelry and flatware—are classified in Industry 33991, Jewelry and Silverware Manufacturing;
- Manufacturing sporting and athletic goods—are classified in Industry 339920, Sporting and Athletic Goods Manufacturing;
- Manufacturing dolls, toys, and games—are classified in Industry 33993, Doll, Toy, and Game Manufacturing;
- Manufacturing office supplies (except paper)—are classified in Industry 33994, Office Supplies (except Paper) Manufacturing;
- Manufacturing signs—are classified in Industry 33995, Sign Manufacturing;
- Manufacturing gasket, packing, and sealing devices—are classified in U.S. Industry 339991, Gasket, Packing, and Sealing Device Manufacturing;
- Manufacturing musical instruments—are classified in U.S. Industry 339992, Musical Instrument Manufacturing;
- Manufacturing fasteners, buttons, needles, and pins—are classified in U.S. Industry 339993, Fastener, Button, Needle, and Pin Manufacturing;
- Manufacturing brooms, brushes, and mops—are classified in U.S. Industry 339994, Broom, Brush, and Mop Manufacturing;
- Manufacturing burial caskets—are classified in U.S. Industry 339995, Burial Casket Manufacturing;
- Manufacturing Christmas tree glass ornaments and glass lamp shades—are classified in U.S. Industry 327215, Glass Product Manufacturing Made of Purchased Glass;
- Manufacturing Christmas tree lighting sets—are classified in U.S. Industry 335129, Other Lighting Equipment Manufacturing;
- Manufacturing beauty and barber chairs—are classified in U.S. Industry 337127, Institutional Furniture Manufacturing;
- Manufacturing burnt wood articles—are classified in U.S. Industry 321999, All Other Miscellaneous Wood Product Manufacturing;

US—United States industry only. CAN—United States and Canadian industries are comparable. MEX—United States and Mexican industries are comparable. Blank—Canadian, Mexican, and United States industries are comparable.

- Dressing and bleaching furs—are classified in Industry 316110, Leather and Hide Tanning and Finishing;
- Manufacturing paper, textile, and metal lamp shades—are classified in U.S. Industry 335121, Residential Electric Lighting Fixture Manufacturing;
- Manufacturing plastics lamp shades—are classified in U.S. Industry 326199, All Other Plastics Product Manufacturing;
- Manufacturing matches—are classified in U.S. Industry 325998, All Other Miscellaneous Chemical Product and Preparation Manufacturing;
- Manufacturing metal products, such as metal combs and hair curlers—are classified in U.S. Industry 332999, All Other Miscellaneous Fabricated Metal Product Manufacturing;
- Manufacturing plastics products, such as plastics combs and hair curlers—are classified in U.S. Industry 326199, All Other Plastics Product Manufacturing; and
- Manufacturing electric hair clippers for use on humans—are classified in U.S. Industry 335211, Electric Housewares and Household Fan Manufacturing.

US—United States industry only. CAN—United States and Canadian industries are comparable. MEX—United States and Mexican industries are comparable. Blank—Canadian, Mexican, and United States industries are comparable.

Sector 42—Wholesale Trade

The Sector as a Whole

The Wholesale Trade sector comprises establishments engaged in wholesaling merchandise, generally without transformation, and rendering services incidental to the sale of merchandise. The merchandise described in this sector includes the outputs of agriculture, mining, manufacturing, and certain information industries, such as publishing.

The wholesaling process is an intermediate step in the distribution of merchandise. Wholesalers are organized to sell or arrange the purchase or sale of (a) goods for resale (i.e., goods sold to other wholesalers or retailers), (b) capital or durable nonconsumer goods, and (c) raw and intermediate materials and supplies used in production.

Wholesalers sell merchandise to other businesses and normally operate from a warehouse or office. These warehouses and offices are characterized by having little or no display of merchandise. In addition, neither the design nor the location of the premises is intended to solicit walk-in traffic. Wholesalers do not normally use advertising directed to the general public. Customers are generally reached initially via telephone, in-person marketing, or by specialized advertising that may include Internet and other electronic means. Follow-up orders are either vendor-initiated or client-initiated, generally based on previous sales, and typically exhibit strong ties between sellers and buyers. In fact, transactions are often conducted between wholesalers and clients that have long-standing business relationships.

This sector comprises two main types of wholesalers: merchant wholesalers that sell goods on their own account and business to business electronic markets, agents, and brokers that arrange sales and purchases for others generally for a commission or fee.

(1) Establishments that sell goods on their own account are known as wholesale merchants, distributors, jobbers, drop shippers, and import/export merchants. Also included as wholesale merchants are sales offices and sales branches (but not retail stores) maintained by manufacturing, refining, or mining enterprises apart from their plants or mines for the purpose of marketing their products. Merchant wholesale establishments typically maintain their own warehouse, where they receive and handle goods for their customers. Goods are generally sold without transformation, but may include integral functions, such as sorting, packaging, labeling, and other marketing services.

(2) Establishments arranging for the purchase or sale of goods owned by others or purchasing goods, generally on a commission basis are known as business to business electronic markets, agents and brokers, commission merchants, import/export agents and brokers, auction companies, and manufacturers' representatives. These establishments operate from offices and generally do not own or handle the goods they sell.

US—United States industry only. CAN—United States and Canadian industries are comparable. MEX—United States and Mexican industries are comparable. Blank—Canadian, Mexican, and United States industries are comparable.

Some wholesale establishments may be connected with a single manufacturer and promote and sell the particular manufacturers' products to a wide range of other wholesalers or retailers. Other wholesalers may be connected to a retail chain, or limited number of retail chains, and only provide a variety of products needed by that particular retail operation(s). These wholesalers may obtain the products from a wide range of manufacturers. Still other wholesalers may not take title to the goods, but act as agents and brokers for a commission.

Although, in general, wholesaling normally denotes sales in large volumes, durable nonconsumer goods may be sold in single units. Sales of capital or durable nonconsumer goods used in the production of goods and services, such as farm machinery, medium and heavy duty trucks, and industrial machinery, are always included in wholesale trade.

423 Merchant Wholesalers, Durable Goods[US]

Industries in the Merchant Wholesalers, Durable Goods subsector sell capital or durable goods to other businesses. Merchant wholesalers generally take title to the goods that they sell; in other words, they buy and sell goods on their own account. Durable goods are new or used items generally with a normal life expectancy of three years or more. Durable goods merchant wholesale trade establishments are engaged in wholesaling products, such as motor vehicles, furniture, construction materials, machinery and equipment (including household-type appliances), metals and minerals (except petroleum), sporting goods, toys and hobby goods, recyclable materials, and parts.

Business-to-business electronic markets, agents, and brokers primarily engaged in wholesaling durable goods, generally on a commission or fee basis, are classified in Subsector 425, Wholesale Electronic Markets and Agents and Brokers.

4231 Motor Vehicle and Motor Vehicle Parts and Supplies Merchant Wholesalers[US]

This industry group comprises establishments primarily engaged in the merchant wholesale distribution of automobiles and other motor vehicles, motor vehicle supplies, tires, and new and used parts.

42311 Automobile and Other Motor Vehicle Merchant Wholesalers[US]

See industry description for 423110 below.

423110 Automobile and Other Motor Vehicle Merchant Wholesalers[US]

This industry comprises establishments primarily engaged in the merchant wholesale distribution of new and used passenger automobiles, trucks, trailers, and other motor vehicles, such as motorcycles, motor homes, and snowmobiles.

US—United States industry only. CAN—United States and Canadian industries are comparable. MEX—United States and Mexican industries are comparable. Blank—Canadian, Mexican, and United States industries are comparable.

42312 Motor Vehicle Supplies and New Parts Merchant Wholesalers[US]

See industry description for 423120 below.

423120 Motor Vehicle Supplies and New Parts Merchant Wholesalers[US]

This industry comprises establishments primarily engaged in the merchant wholesale distribution of motor vehicle supplies, accessories, tools, and equipment; and new motor vehicle parts (except new tires and tubes).

Cross-References. Establishments primarily engaged in—

- Merchant wholesale distribution of new and/or used tires and tubes—are classified in Industry 423130, Tire and Tube Merchant Wholesalers;
- Merchant wholesale distribution of automotive chemicals (except lubricating oils and greases)—are classified in Industry 424690, Other Chemical and Allied Products Merchant Wholesalers;
- Merchant wholesale distribution of lubricating oils and greases—are classified in Industry 424720, Petroleum and Petroleum Products Merchant Wholesalers (except Bulk Stations and Terminals); and
- Merchant wholesale distribution of used motor vehicle parts—are classified in Industry 423140, Motor Vehicle Parts (Used) Merchant Wholesalers.

42313 Tire and Tube Merchant Wholesalers[US]

See industry description for 423130 below.

423130 Tire and Tube Merchant Wholesalers[US]

This industry comprises establishments primarily engaged in the merchant wholesale distribution of new and/or used tires and tubes for passenger and commercial vehicles.

Cross-References. Establishments primarily engaged in—

- Merchant wholesale distribution of other new automobile parts and accessories—are classified in Industry 423120, Motor Vehicle Supplies and New Parts Merchant Wholesalers; and
- Merchant wholesale distribution of other used automobile parts and accessories—are classified in Industry 423140, Motor Vehicle Parts (Used) Merchant Wholesalers.

US—United States industry only. CAN—United States and Canadian industries are comparable. MEX—United States and Mexican industries are comparable. Blank—Canadian, Mexican, and United States industries are comparable.

42314 Motor Vehicle Parts (Used) Merchant Wholesalers[US]

See industry description for 423140 below.

423140 Motor Vehicle Parts (Used) Merchant Wholesalers[US]

This industry comprises establishments primarily engaged in the merchant wholesale distribution of used motor vehicle parts (except used tires and tubes) and establishments primarily engaged in dismantling motor vehicles for the purpose of selling the parts.

Cross-References. Establishments primarily engaged in—

- Dismantling motor vehicles for the purpose of selling scrap—are classified in Industry 423930, Recyclable Material Merchant Wholesalers; and
- Merchant wholesale distribution of new and/or used tires and tubes—are classified in Industry 423130, Tire and Tube Merchant Wholesalers.

4232 Furniture and Home Furnishing Merchant Wholesalers[US]

42321 Furniture Merchant Wholesalers[US]

See industry description for 423210 below.

423210 Furniture Merchant Wholesalers[US]

This industry comprises establishments primarily engaged in the merchant wholesale distribution of furniture (except hospital beds, medical furniture, and drafting tables).

Illustrative Examples:

Household-type furniture merchant wholesalers
Mattresses merchant wholesalers
Office furniture merchant wholesalers
Outdoor furniture merchant wholesalers
Public building furniture merchant wholesalers
Religious furniture merchant wholesalers

Cross-References. Establishments primarily engaged in—

- Merchant wholesale distribution of partitions, shelving, lockers, and store fixtures—are classified in Industry 423440, Other Commercial Equipment Merchant Wholesalers;
- Merchant wholesale distribution of hospital beds and medical furniture—are classified in Industry 423450, Medical, Dental, and Hospital Equipment and Supplies Merchant Wholesalers; and

US—United States industry only. CAN—United States and Canadian industries are comparable. MEX—United States and Mexican industries are comparable. Blank—Canadian, Mexican, and United States industries are comparable.

- Merchant wholesale distribution of drafting tables—are classified in Industry 423490, Other Professional Equipment and Supplies Merchant Wholesalers.

42322 Home Furnishing Merchant Wholesalers[US]

See industry description for 423220 below.

423220 Home Furnishing Merchant Wholesalers[US]

This industry comprises establishments primarily engaged in the merchant wholesale distribution of home furnishings and/or housewares.

Illustrative Examples:

Carpet merchant wholesalers
Chinaware merchant wholesalers
Curtain merchant wholesalers
Drapery merchant wholesalers
Floor covering merchant wholesalers
Glassware merchant wholesalers
Household-type cooking utensil merchant wholesalers
Lamp merchant wholesalers
Linen (e.g., bath, bed, table) merchant wholesalers
Window blind and shade merchant wholesalers

Cross-References. Establishments primarily engaged in—

- Merchant wholesale distribution of electrical household-type goods—are classified in Industry 423620, Electrical and Electronic Appliance, Television, and Radio Set Merchant Wholesalers; and
- Merchant wholesale distribution of precious metal flatware—are classified in Industry 423940, Jewelry, Watch, Precious Stone, and Precious Metal Merchant Wholesalers.

4233 Lumber and Other Construction Materials Merchant Wholesalers[US]

42331 Lumber, Plywood, Millwork, and Wood Panel Merchant Wholesalers[US]

See industry description for 423310 below.

423310 Lumber, Plywood, Millwork, and Wood Panel Merchant Wholesalers[US]

This industry comprises establishments primarily engaged in the merchant wholesale distribution of lumber; plywood; reconstituted wood fiber products;

US—United States industry only. CAN—United States and Canadian industries are comparable. MEX—United States and Mexican industries are comparable. Blank—Canadian, Mexican, and United States industries are comparable.

wood fencing; doors and windows and their frames (all materials); wood roofing and siding; and/or other wood or metal millwork.

Cross-References. Establishments primarily engaged in—

- Merchant wholesale distribution of nonwood roofing and siding materials—are classified in Industry 423330, Roofing, Siding, and Insulation Material Merchant Wholesalers; and
- Merchant wholesale distribution of timber and timber products, such as railroad ties, logs, firewood, and pulpwood,—are classified in Industry 423990, Other Miscellaneous Durable Goods Merchant Wholesalers.

42332 Brick, Stone, and Related Construction Material Merchant Wholesalers[US]

See industry description for 423320 below.

423320 Brick, Stone, and Related Construction Material Merchant Wholesalers[US]

This industry comprises establishments primarily engaged in the merchant wholesale distribution of stone, cement, lime, construction sand, and gravel; brick; asphalt and concrete mixtures; and/or concrete, stone, and structural clay products.

Cross-References. Establishments primarily engaged in—

- Merchant wholesale distribution of refractory brick and other refractory products—are classified in Industry 423840, Industrial Supplies Merchant Wholesalers; and
- Selling ready-mix concrete—are classified in Industry 327320, Ready-Mix Concrete Manufacturing.

42333 Roofing, Siding, and Insulation Material Merchant Wholesalers[US]

See industry description for 423330 below.

423330 Roofing, Siding, and Insulation Material Merchant Wholesalers[US]

This industry comprises establishments primarily engaged in the merchant wholesale distribution of nonwood roofing and nonwood siding and insulation materials.

US—United States industry only. CAN—United States and Canadian industries are comparable. MEX—United States and Mexican industries are comparable. Blank—Canadian, Mexican, and United States industries are comparable.

Cross-References.

Establishments primarily engaged in the merchant wholesale distribution of wood roofing and wood siding are classified in Industry 423310, Lumber, Plywood, Millwork, and Wood Panel Merchant Wholesalers.

42339 Other Construction Material Merchant Wholesalers[US]

See industry description for 423390 below.

423390 Other Construction Material Merchant Wholesalers[US]

This industry comprises (1) establishments primarily engaged in the merchant wholesale distribution of manufactured homes (i.e., mobile homes) and/or prefabricated buildings and (2) establishments primarily engaged in the merchant wholesale distribution of construction materials (except lumber, plywood, millwork, wood panels, brick, stone, roofing, siding, electrical and wiring supplies, and insulation materials).

Illustrative Examples:

Flat glass merchant wholesalers
Ornamental ironwork merchant wholesalers
Plate glass merchant wholesalers
Prefabricated buildings (except wood) merchant wholesalers
Wire fencing and fencing accessories merchant wholesalers

Cross-References. Establishments primarily engaged in—

- Merchant wholesale distribution of products of the primary metals industries—are classified in Industry 423510, Metal Service Centers and Other Metal Merchant Wholesalers;
- Merchant wholesale distribution of lumber; plywood; reconstituted wood fiber products; wood fencing; doors, windows, and their frames; wood roofing and wood siding; and other wood or metal millwork—are classified in Industry 423310, Lumber, Plywood, Millwork, and Wood Panel Merchant Wholesalers;
- Merchant wholesale distribution of stone, cement, lime, construction sand and gravel; brick; asphalt and concrete mixtures (except ready-mix concrete); and/or concrete, stone, and structural clay products—are classified in Industry 423320, Brick, Stone, and Related Construction Material Merchant Wholesalers;
- Merchant wholesale distribution of nonwood roofing, nonwood siding and insulation materials—are classified in Industry 423330, Roofing, Siding, and Insulation Material Merchant Wholesalers;

US—United States industry only. CAN—United States and Canadian industries are comparable. MEX—United States and Mexican industries are comparable. Blank—Canadian, Mexican, and United States industries are comparable.

- Merchant wholesale distribution of electrical supplies and wiring supplies—are classified in Industry 423610, Electrical Apparatus and Equipment, Wiring Supplies, and Related Equipment Merchant Wholesalers; and
- Selling ready-mix concrete—are classified in Industry 327320, Ready-Mix Concrete Manufacturing.

4234 Professional and Commercial Equipment and Supplies Merchant Wholesalers[US]

This industry group comprises establishments primarily engaged in the merchant wholesale distribution of photographic equipment and supplies; office, computer, and computer peripheral equipment; and medical, dental, hospital, ophthalmic, and other commercial and professional equipment and supplies.

42341 Photographic Equipment and Supplies Merchant Wholesalers[US]

See industry description for 423410 below.

423410 Photographic Equipment and Supplies Merchant Wholesalers[US]

This industry comprises establishments primarily engaged in the merchant wholesale distribution of photographic equipment and supplies (except office equipment).

Illustrative Examples:

Photofinishing equipment merchant wholesalers
Photographic camera equipment and supplies merchant wholesalers
Photographic film merchant wholesalers
Television cameras merchant wholesalers
Video cameras (except household-type) merchant wholesalers

Cross-References. Establishments primarily engaged in—

- Merchant wholesale distribution of household-type video cameras—are classified in Industry 423620, Electrical and Electronic Appliance, Television, and Radio Set Merchant Wholesalers; and
- Merchant wholesale distribution of office equipment, such as photocopy and microfilm equipment—are classified in Industry 423420, Office Equipment Merchant Wholesalers.

US—United States industry only. CAN—United States and Canadian industries are comparable. MEX—United States and Mexican industries are comparable. Blank—Canadian, Mexican, and United States industries are comparable.

42342 Office Equipment Merchant Wholesalers[US]

See industry description for 423420 below.

423420 Office Equipment Merchant Wholesalers[US]

This industry comprises establishments primarily engaged in the merchant wholesale distribution of office machines and related equipment (except computers and computer peripheral equipment).

Illustrative Examples:

Accounting machines merchant wholesalers
Calculator and calculating machines merchant wholesalers
Cash register merchant wholesalers
Copying machine merchant wholesalers
Mailing machine merchant wholesalers
Microfilm equipment and supplies merchant wholesalers
Security safe merchant wholesalers

Cross-References. Establishments primarily engaged in—

- Merchant wholesale distribution of office furniture—are classified in Industry 423210, Furniture Merchant Wholesalers;
- Merchant wholesale distribution of computers and computer peripheral equipment—are classified in Industry 423430, Computer and Computer Peripheral Equipment and Software Merchant Wholesalers; and
- Merchant wholesale distribution of office supplies—are classified in Industry 424120, Stationery and Office Supplies Merchant Wholesalers.

42343 Computer and Computer Peripheral Equipment and Software Merchant Wholesalers[US]

See industry description for 423430 below.

423430 Computer and Computer Peripheral Equipment and Software Merchant Wholesalers[US]

This industry comprises establishments primarily engaged in the merchant wholesale distribution of computers, computer peripheral equipment, loaded computer boards, and/or computer software.

Cross-References. Establishments primarily engaged in—

- Merchant wholesale distribution of modems and other electronic communications equipment—are classified in Industry 423690, Other Electronic Parts and Equipment Merchant Wholesalers; and

US—United States industry only. CAN—United States and Canadian industries are comparable. MEX—United States and Mexican industries are comparable. Blank—Canadian, Mexican, and United States industries are comparable.

- Selling, planning, and designing computer systems that integrate computer hardware, software, and communication technologies—are classified in U.S. Industry 541512, Computer Systems Design Services.

42344 Other Commercial Equipment Merchant Wholesalers[US]

See industry description for 423440 below.

423440 Other Commercial Equipment Merchant Wholesalers[US]

This industry comprises establishments primarily engaged in the merchant wholesale distribution of commercial and related machines and equipment (except photographic equipment and supplies; office equipment; and computers and computer peripheral equipment and software) generally used in restaurants and stores.

Illustrative Examples:

Balances and scales (except laboratory) merchant wholesalers
Coin-operated merchandising machine merchant wholesalers
Commercial chinaware merchant wholesalers
Commercial cooking equipment merchant wholesalers
Commercial shelving merchant wholesalers
Electrical sign merchant wholesalers
Partitions merchant wholesalers
Store fixture (except refrigerated) merchant wholesalers

Cross-References. Establishments primarily engaged in—

- Merchant wholesale distribution of photographic equipment and supplies—are classified in Industry 423410, Photographic Equipment and Supplies Merchant Wholesalers;
- Merchant wholesale distribution of office machines and related equipment—are classified in Industry 423420, Office Equipment Merchant Wholesalers;
- Merchant wholesale distribution of computers, computer peripheral equipment, and computer software—are classified in Industry 423430, Computer and Computer Peripheral Equipment and Software Merchant Wholesalers;
- Merchant wholesale distribution of laboratory scales and balances (except medical and dental)—are classified in Industry 423490, Other Professional Equipment and Supplies Merchant Wholesalers; and
- Merchant wholesale distribution of refrigerated store fixtures—are classified in Industry 423740, Refrigeration Equipment and Supplies Merchant Wholesalers.

42345 Medical, Dental, and Hospital Equipment and Supplies Merchant Wholesalers[US]

See industry description for 423450 below.

US—United States industry only. CAN—United States and Canadian industries are comparable. MEX—United States and Mexican industries are comparable. Blank—Canadian, Mexican, and United States industries are comparable.

423450 Medical, Dental, and Hospital Equipment and Supplies Merchant Wholesalers[US]

This industry comprises establishments primarily engaged in the merchant wholesale distribution of professional medical equipment, instruments, and supplies (except ophthalmic equipment and instruments and goods used by ophthalmologists, optometrists, and opticians).

Illustrative Examples:

- Dental equipment and supplies merchant wholesalers
- Electromedical equipment merchant wholesalers
- Hospital beds merchant wholesalers
- Hospital furniture merchant wholesalers
- Medical and dental X-ray machine merchant wholesalers
- Medical dressings merchant wholesalers
- Patient monitoring equipment merchant wholesalers
- Prosthetic appliance and supplies merchant wholesalers
- Surgical instrument and apparatus merchant wholesalers

Cross-References.

Establishments primarily engaged in the merchant wholesale distribution of professional equipment, instruments and/or goods sold, prescribed, or used by ophthalmologists, optometrists, and opticians are classified in Industry 423460, Ophthalmic Goods Merchant Wholesalers.

42346 Ophthalmic Goods Merchant Wholesalers[US]

See industry description for 423460 below.

423460 Ophthalmic Goods Merchant Wholesalers[US]

This industry comprises establishments primarily engaged in the merchant wholesale distribution of professional equipment, instruments, and/or goods sold, prescribed, or used by ophthalmologists, optometrists, and opticians.

Illustrative Examples:

- Binocular merchant wholesalers
- Ophthalmic frame merchant wholesalers
- Ophthalmic lenses merchant wholesalers
- Optometric equipment and supplies merchant wholesalers
- Sunglasses merchant wholesalers

42349 Other Professional Equipment and Supplies Merchant Wholesalers[US]

See industry description for 423490 below.

US—United States industry only. CAN—United States and Canadian industries are comparable. MEX—United States and Mexican industries are comparable. Blank—Canadian, Mexican, and United States industries are comparable.

423490 Other Professional Equipment and Supplies Merchant Wholesalers[US]

This industry comprises establishments primarily engaged in the merchant wholesale distribution of professional equipment and supplies (except ophthalmic goods and medical, dental, and hospital equipment and supplies).

Illustrative Examples:

Church supplies (except silverware, plated ware) merchant wholesalers
Drafting tables and instruments merchant wholesalers
Laboratory equipment (except medical, dental) merchant wholesalers
School equipment and supplies (except books, furniture) merchant wholesalers
Scientific instruments merchant wholesalers
Surveying equipment and supplies merchant wholesalers

Cross-References. Establishments primarily engaged in—

- Merchant wholesale distribution of professional equipment, instruments, and/or goods sold, prescribed, or used by ophthalmologists, optometrists, and opticians, such as ophthalmic frames and lenses, and sunglasses—are classified in Industry 423460, Ophthalmic Goods Merchant Wholesalers;
- Merchant wholesale distribution of medical professional equipment, instruments, and supplies used by medical and dental practitioners (except ophthalmic equipment, instruments, and goods used by ophthalmologists, optometrists, and opticians) and medical facilities—are classified in Industry 423450, Medical, Dental, and Hospital Equipment and Supplies Merchant Wholesalers;
- Merchant wholesale distribution of silverware and plated flatware—are classified in Industry 423940, Jewelry, Watch, Precious Stone, and Precious Metal Merchant Wholesalers;
- Merchant wholesale distribution of books—are classified in Industry 424920, Book, Periodical, and Newspaper Merchant Wholesalers; and
- Merchant wholesale distribution of school furniture—are classified in Industry 423210, Furniture Merchant Wholesalers.

4235 Metal and Mineral (except Petroleum) Merchant Wholesalers[US]

42351 Metal Service Centers and Other Metal Merchant Wholesalers[US]

See industry description for 423510 below.

US—United States industry only. CAN—United States and Canadian industries are comparable. MEX—United States and Mexican industries are comparable. Blank—Canadian, Mexican, and United States industries are comparable.

423510 Metal Service Centers and Other Metal Merchant Wholesalers[US]

This industry comprises establishments primarily engaged in the merchant wholesale distribution of products of the primary metals industries. Service centers maintain inventory and may perform functions, such as sawing, shearing, bending, leveling, cleaning, or edging, on a custom basis as part of sales transactions.

Illustrative Examples:

Cast iron pipe merchant wholesalers
Metal bars (except precious) merchant wholesalers
Metal ingots (except precious) merchant wholesalers
Metal pipe merchant wholesalers
Metal plate merchant wholesalers
Metal rod merchant wholesalers
Metal sheet merchant wholesalers
Metal spike merchant wholesalers
Nail merchant wholesalers
Noninsulated wire merchant wholesalers

Cross-References. Establishments primarily engaged in—

- Merchant wholesale distribution of gold, silver, and platinum—are classified in Industry 423940, Jewelry, Watch, Precious Stone, and Precious Metal Merchant Wholesalers;
- Merchant wholesale distribution of automotive, industrial, and other recyclable metal scrap—are classified in Industry 423930, Recyclable Material Merchant Wholesalers; and
- Merchant wholesale distribution of insulated wire—are classified in Industry 423610, Electrical Apparatus and Equipment, Wiring Supplies, and Related Equipment Merchant Wholesalers.

42352 Coal and Other Mineral and Ore Merchant Wholesalers[US]

See industry description for 423520 below.

423520 Coal and Other Mineral and Ore Merchant Wholesalers[US]

This industry comprises establishments primarily engaged in the merchant wholesale distribution of coal, coke, metal ores, and/or nonmetallic minerals (except precious and semiprecious stones and minerals used in construction, such as sand and gravel).

Cross-References. Establishments primarily engaged in—

- Merchant wholesale distribution of nonmetallic minerals used in construction, such as sand and gravel—are classified in Industry 423320, Brick, Stone, and Related Construction Material Merchant Wholesalers;

US—United States industry only. CAN—United States and Canadian industries are comparable. MEX—United States and Mexican industries are comparable. Blank—Canadian, Mexican, and United States industries are comparable.

- Merchant wholesale distribution of crude petroleum—are classified in Industry Group 4247, Petroleum and Petroleum Products Merchant Wholesalers; and
- Merchant wholesale distribution of precious and semiprecious stones and metals—are classified in Industry 423940, Jewelry, Watch, Precious Stone, and Precious Metal Merchant Wholesalers.

4236 Electrical and Electronic Goods Merchant Wholesalers[US]

42361 Electrical Apparatus and Equipment, Wiring Supplies, and Related Equipment Merchant Wholesalers[US]

See industry description for 423610 below.

423610 Electrical Apparatus and Equipment, Wiring Supplies, and Related Equipment Merchant Wholesalers[US]

This industry comprises establishments primarily engaged in the merchant wholesale distribution of electrical construction materials; wiring supplies; electric light fixtures; light bulbs; and/or electrical power equipment for the generation, transmission, distribution, or control of electric energy.

42362 Electrical and Electronic Appliance, Television, and Radio Set Merchant Wholesalers[US]

See industry description for 423620 below.

423620 Electrical and Electronic Appliance, Television, and Radio Set Merchant Wholesalers[US]

This industry comprises establishments primarily engaged in the merchant wholesale distribution of household-type electrical appliances, room air-conditioners, gas and electric clothes dryers, and/or household-type audio or video equipment.

Illustrative Examples:

- Electric water heater merchant wholesalers
- Household-type radio (including automotive) merchant wholesalers
- Household-type refrigerator merchant wholesalers
- Household-type sewing machine merchant wholesalers
- Household-type video camera merchant wholesalers
- Television set merchant wholesalers

US—United States industry only. CAN—United States and Canadian industries are comparable. MEX—United States and Mexican industries are comparable. Blank—Canadian, Mexican, and United States industries are comparable.

Cross-References. Establishments primarily engaged in—

- Merchant wholesale distribution of gas household-type appliances (except gas clothes dryers)—are classified in Industry 423720, Plumbing and Heating Equipment and Supplies (Hydronics) Merchant Wholesalers; and
- Merchant wholesale distribution of nonhousehold-type video cameras—are classified in Industry 423410, Photographic Equipment and Supplies Merchant Wholesalers.

42369 Other Electronic Parts and Equipment Merchant Wholesalers[US]

See industry description for 423690 below.

423690 Other Electronic Parts and Equipment Merchant Wholesalers[US]

This industry comprises establishments primarily engaged in the merchant wholesale distribution of electronic parts and equipment (except electrical apparatus and equipment, wiring supplies and construction material; and electrical appliances, television and radio sets).

Illustrative Examples:

Blank audio tape merchant wholesalers
Blank diskette merchant wholesalers
Blank video tape merchant wholesalers
Broadcasting equipment merchant wholesalers
Communications equipment merchant wholesalers
Radar equipment merchant wholesalers
Telegraph equipment merchant wholesalers
Telephone equipment merchant wholesalers
Unloaded computer board merchant wholesalers

Cross-References. Establishments primarily engaged in—

- Merchant wholesale distribution of household-type electrical appliances, and television and radio sets—are classified in Industry 423620, Electrical and Electronic Appliance, Television, and Radio Set Merchant Wholesalers;
- Merchant wholesale distribution of computers, computer peripheral equipment, and loaded computer boards—are classified in Industry 423430, Computer and Computer Peripheral Equipment and Software Merchant Wholesalers; and
- Merchant wholesale distribution of electrical construction materials, wiring supplies, electric light fixtures, light bulbs; and/or electrical power equipment for generation, transmission, distribution, or control of electric

US—United States industry only. CAN—United States and Canadian industries are comparable. MEX—United States and Mexican industries are comparable. Blank—Canadian, Mexican, and United States industries are comparable.

energy—are classified in Industry 423610, Electrical Apparatus and Equipment, Wiring Supplies, and Related Equipment Merchant Wholesalers.

4237 Hardware, and Plumbing and Heating Equipment and Supplies Merchant Wholesalers[US]

42371 Hardware Merchant Wholesalers[US]

See industry description for 423710 below.

423710 Hardware Merchant Wholesalers[US]

This industry comprises establishments primarily engaged in the merchant wholesale distribution of hardware, knives, or handtools.

Illustrative Examples:

Brads merchant wholesalers
Cutlery merchant wholesalers
Fasteners (e.g., bolts, nuts, rivets, screws) merchant wholesalers
Handtools (except motor vehicle, machinists' precision) merchant wholesalers
Knives (except disposable plastics) merchant wholesalers
Power handtools (e.g., drills, saws, sanders) merchant wholesalers
Staples merchant wholesalers
Tacks merchant wholesalers

Cross-References. Establishments primarily engaged in—

- Merchant wholesale distribution of nails, noninsulated wire, and screening—are classified in Industry 423510, Metal Service Centers and Other Metal Merchant Wholesalers;
- Merchant wholesale distribution of motor vehicle handtools and equipment—are classified in Industry 423120, Motor Vehicle Supplies and New Parts Merchant Wholesalers;
- Merchant wholesale distribution of machinists' precision handtools—are classified in Industry 423830, Industrial Machinery and Equipment Merchant Wholesalers; and
- Merchant wholesale distribution of disposable plastics knives and eating utensils—are classified in Industry 424130, Industrial and Personal Service Paper Merchant Wholesalers.

42372 Plumbing and Heating Equipment and Supplies (Hydronics) Merchant Wholesalers[US]

See industry description for 423720 below.

US—United States industry only. CAN—United States and Canadian industries are comparable. MEX—United States and Mexican industries are comparable. Blank—Canadian, Mexican, and United States industries are comparable.

423720 Plumbing and Heating Equipment and Supplies (Hydronics) Merchant Wholesalers[US]

This industry comprises establishments primarily engaged in the merchant wholesale distribution of plumbing equipment, hydronic heating equipment, household-type gas appliances (except gas clothes dryers), and/or supplies.

Cross-References. Establishments primarily engaged in—

- Selling and installing plumbing, heating and air conditioning equipment—are classified in Industry 238220, Plumbing, Heating, and Air-Conditioning Contractors;
- Merchant wholesale distribution of warm air heating and air-conditioning equipment—are classified in Industry 423730, Warm Air Heating and Air-Conditioning Equipment and Supplies Merchant Wholesalers; and
- Merchant wholesale distribution of household-type electrical appliances, room air-conditioners, gas clothes dryers, and/or household-type audio or video equipment—are classified in Industry 423620, Electrical and Electronic Appliance, Television, and Radio Set Merchant Wholesalers.

42373 Warm Air Heating and Air-Conditioning Equipment and Supplies Merchant Wholesalers[US]

See industry description for 423730 below.

423730 Warm Air Heating and Air-Conditioning Equipment and Supplies Merchant Wholesalers[US]

This industry comprises establishments primarily engaged in the merchant wholesale distribution of warm air heating and air-conditioning equipment and supplies.

Illustrative Examples:

Air pollution control equipment and supplies merchant wholesalers
Air-conditioning equipment (except room units) merchant wholesalers
Automotive air-conditioners merchant wholesalers
Nonportable electric baseboard heaters merchant wholesalers
Warm-air central heating equipment merchant wholesalers

Cross-References. Establishments primarily engaged in—

- Merchant wholesale distribution of household-type electrical appliances and room air-conditioners—are classified in Industry 423620, Electrical and Electronic Appliance, Television, and Radio Set Merchant Wholesalers;

US—United States industry only. CAN—United States and Canadian industries are comparable. MEX—United States and Mexican industries are comparable. Blank—Canadian, Mexican, and United States industries are comparable.

- Merchant wholesale distribution of hydronic heating equipment—are classified in Industry 423720, Plumbing and Heating Equipment and Supplies (Hydronics) Merchant Wholesalers; and
- Selling and installing warm air heating and air-conditioning equipment—are classified in Industry 238220, Plumbing, Heating, and Air-Conditioning Contractors.

42374 Refrigeration Equipment and Supplies Merchant Wholesalers[US]

See industry description for 423740 below.

423740 Refrigeration Equipment and Supplies Merchant Wholesalers[US]

This industry comprises establishments primarily engaged in the merchant wholesale distribution of refrigeration equipment (except household-type refrigerators, freezers, and air-conditioners).

Illustrative Examples:

Cold storage machinery merchant wholesalers
Commercial refrigerators merchant wholesalers
Refrigerated display cases merchant wholesalers
Water coolers merchant wholesalers

Cross-References. Establishments primarily engaged in—

- Merchant wholesale distribution of household-type refrigerators, freezers, and room air-conditioners—are classified in Industry 423620, Electrical and Electronic Appliance, Television, and Radio Set Merchant Wholesalers; and
- Merchant wholesale distribution of air-conditioning equipment (except room units)—are classified Industry 423730, Warm Air Heating and Air-Conditioning Equipment and Supplies Merchant Wholesalers.

4238 Machinery, Equipment, and Supplies Merchant Wholesalers[US]

This industry group comprises establishments primarily engaged in the merchant wholesale distribution of construction, mining, farm, garden, industrial, service establishment, and transportation machinery, equipment and supplies.

42381 Construction and Mining (except Oil Well) Machinery and Equipment Merchant Wholesalers[US]

See industry description for 423810 below.

US—United States industry only. CAN—United States and Canadian industries are comparable. MEX—United States and Mexican industries are comparable. Blank—Canadian, Mexican, and United States industries are comparable.

423810 Construction and Mining (except Oil Well) Machinery and Equipment Merchant Wholesalers[US]

This industry comprises establishments primarily engaged in the merchant wholesale distribution of specialized machinery, equipment, and related parts generally used in construction, mining (except oil well) and logging activities.

Illustrative Examples:

- Excavating machinery and equipment merchant wholesalers
- Forestry machinery and equipment merchant wholesalers
- Mining cranes merchant wholesalers
- Road construction and maintenance machinery merchant wholesalers
- Scaffolding merchant wholesalers

Cross-References.

Establishments primarily engaged in the merchant wholesale distribution of oil well machinery and equipment are classified in Industry 423830, Industrial Machinery and Equipment Merchant Wholesalers.

42382 Farm and Garden Machinery and Equipment Merchant Wholesalers[US]

See industry description for 423820 below.

423820 Farm and Garden Machinery and Equipment Merchant Wholesalers[US]

This industry comprises establishments primarily engaged in the merchant wholesale distribution of specialized machinery, equipment, and related parts generally used in agricultural, farm, and lawn and garden activities.

Illustrative Examples:

- Animal feeders merchant wholesalers
- Harvesting machinery and equipment merchant wholesalers
- Lawnmowers merchant wholesalers
- Milking machinery and equipment merchant wholesalers
- Planting machinery and equipment merchant wholesalers

42383 Industrial Machinery and Equipment Merchant Wholesalers[US]

See industry description for 423830 below.

US—United States industry only. CAN—United States and Canadian industries are comparable. MEX—United States and Mexican industries are comparable. Blank—Canadian, Mexican, and United States industries are comparable.

423830 Industrial Machinery and Equipment Merchant Wholesalers[US]

This industry comprises establishments primarily engaged in the merchant wholesale distribution of specialized machinery, equipment, and related parts generally used in manufacturing, oil well, and warehousing activities.

Illustrative Examples:

Fluid power transmission equipment merchant wholesalers
Food-processing machinery and equipment merchant wholesalers
Materials handling machinery and equipment merchant wholesalers
Metalworking machinery and equipment merchant wholesalers
Oil well machinery and equipment merchant wholesalers

Cross-References. Establishments primarily engaged in—

- Merchant wholesale distribution of specialized machinery, equipment, and related parts generally used in construction, mining (except oil well), and logging activities—are classified in Industry 423810, Construction and Mining (except Oil Well) Machinery and Equipment Merchant Wholesalers; and
- Merchant wholesale distribution of supplies used in machinery and equipment generally used in manufacturing, oil well, and warehousing activities—are classified in Industry 423840, Industrial Supplies Merchant Wholesalers.

42384 Industrial Supplies Merchant Wholesalers[US]

See industry description for 423840 below.

423840 Industrial Supplies Merchant Wholesalers[US]

This industry comprises establishments primarily engaged in the merchant wholesale distribution of supplies for machinery and equipment generally used in manufacturing, oil well, and warehousing activities.

Illustrative Examples:

Industrial containers merchant wholesalers
Industrial diamonds merchant wholesalers
Printing inks merchant wholesalers
Refractory materials (e.g., brick, blocks, shapes) merchant wholesalers
Welding supplies (except welding gases) merchant wholesalers

US—United States industry only. CAN—United States and Canadian industries are comparable. MEX—United States and Mexican industries are comparable. Blank—Canadian, Mexican, and United States industries are comparable.

Cross-References. Establishments primarily engaged in—

- Merchant wholesale distribution of hydraulic and pneumatic (fluid power) pumps, motors, pistons, and valves—are classified in Industry 423830, Industrial Machinery and Equipment Merchant Wholesalers; and
- Merchant wholesale distribution of welding gases—are classified in Industry 424690, Other Chemical and Allied Products Merchant Wholesalers.

42385 Service Establishment Equipment and Supplies Merchant Wholesalers[US]

See industry description for 423850 below.

423850 Service Establishment Equipment and Supplies Merchant Wholesalers[US]

This industry comprises establishments primarily engaged in the merchant wholesale distribution of specialized equipment and supplies of the type used by service establishments (except specialized equipment and supplies used in offices, stores, hotels, restaurants, schools, health and medical facilities, photographic facilities, and specialized equipment used in transportation and construction activities).

Illustrative Examples:

Amusement park equipment merchant wholesalers
Beauty parlor equipment and supplies merchant wholesalers
Car wash equipment and supplies merchant wholesalers
Drycleaning equipment and supplies merchant wholesalers
Janitorial equipment and supplies merchant wholesalers
Undertakers' equipment and supplies merchant wholesalers
Upholsterers' equipment and supplies (except fabrics) merchant wholesalers

Cross-References. Establishments primarily engaged in—

- Merchant wholesale distribution of janitorial and automotive chemicals—are classified in Industry 424690, Other Chemical and Allied Products Merchant Wholesalers;
- Merchant wholesale distribution of piece goods, fabrics, knitting yarns (except industrial), thread and other notions—are classified in Industry 424310, Piece Goods, Notions, and Other Dry Goods Merchant Wholesalers; and
- Merchant wholesale distribution of industrial yarns—are classified in Industry 424990, Other Miscellaneous Nondurable Goods Merchant Wholesalers.

US—United States industry only. CAN—United States and Canadian industries are comparable. MEX—United States and Mexican industries are comparable. Blank—Canadian, Mexican, and United States industries are comparable.

42386 Transportation Equipment and Supplies (except Motor Vehicle) Merchant Wholesalers[US]

See industry description for 423860 below.

423860 Transportation Equipment and Supplies (except Motor Vehicle) Merchant Wholesalers[US]

This industry comprises establishments primarily engaged in the merchant wholesale distribution of transportation equipment and supplies (except marine pleasure craft and motor vehicles).

Illustrative Examples:

Aircraft merchant wholesalers
Motorized passenger golf carts merchant wholesalers
Railroad cars merchant wholesalers
Ships merchant wholesalers

Cross-References. Establishments primarily engaged in—

- Merchant wholesale distribution of motor vehicles and motor vehicle parts—are classified in Industry Group 4231, Motor Vehicle and Motor Vehicle Parts and Supplies Merchant Wholesalers; and
- Merchant wholesale distribution of marine pleasure craft—are classified in Industry 423910, Sporting and Recreational Goods and Supplies Merchant Wholesalers.

4239 Miscellaneous Durable Goods Merchant Wholesalers[US]

This industry group comprises establishments primarily engaged in the merchant wholesale distribution of sporting, recreational, toy, hobby, and jewelry goods and supplies, and precious stones and metals.

42391 Sporting and Recreational Goods and Supplies Merchant Wholesalers[US]

See industry description for 423910 below.

423910 Sporting and Recreational Goods and Supplies Merchant Wholesalers[US]

This industry comprises establishments primarily engaged in the merchant wholesale distribution of sporting goods and accessories; billiard and pool supplies; sporting firearms and ammunition; and/or marine pleasure craft, equipment, and supplies.

US—United States industry only. CAN—United States and Canadian industries are comparable. MEX—United States and Mexican industries are comparable. Blank—Canadian, Mexican, and United States industries are comparable.

Cross References. Establishments primarily engaged in—

- Merchant wholesale distribution of motor vehicles and trailers—are classified in Industry 423110, Automobile and Other Motor Vehicle Merchant Wholesalers;
- Merchant wholesale distribution of motorized passenger golf carts—are classified in Industry 423860, Transportation Equipment and Supplies (except Motor Vehicle) Merchant Wholesalers; and
- Merchant wholesale distribution of athletic apparel and athletic footwear—are classified in Industry Group 4243, Apparel, Piece Goods, and Notions Merchant Wholesalers.

42392 Toy and Hobby Goods and Supplies Merchant Wholesalers[US]

See industry description for 423920 below.

423920 Toy and Hobby Goods and Supplies Merchant Wholesalers[US]

This industry comprises establishments primarily engaged in the merchant wholesale distribution of games, toys, fireworks, playing cards, hobby goods and supplies, and/or related goods.

42393 Recyclable Material Merchant Wholesalers[US]

See industry description for 423930 below.

423930 Recyclable Material Merchant Wholesalers[US]

This industry comprises establishments primarily engaged in the merchant wholesale distribution of automotive scrap, industrial scrap, and other recyclable materials. Included in this industry are auto wreckers primarily engaged in dismantling motor vehicles for the purpose of wholesaling scrap.

Cross-References. Establishments primarily engaged in—

- Dismantling motor vehicles for the purpose of selling used parts—are classified in Industry 423140, Motor Vehicle Parts (Used) Merchant Wholesalers; and
- Operating facilities where commingled recyclable materials, such as paper, plastics, used beverage cans, and metals are sorted into distinct categories—are classified in Industry 562920, Materials Recovery Facilities.

42394 Jewelry, Watch, Precious Stone, and Precious Metal Merchant Wholesalers[US]

See industry description for 423940 below.

US—United States industry only. CAN—United States and Canadian industries are comparable. MEX—United States and Mexican industries are comparable. Blank—Canadian, Mexican, and United States industries are comparable.

423940 Jewelry, Watch, Precious Stone, and Precious Metal Merchant Wholesalers[US]

This industry comprises establishments primarily engaged in the merchant wholesale distribution of jewelry, precious and semiprecious stones, precious metals and metal flatware, costume jewelry, watches, clocks, silverware, and/or jewelers' findings.

Cross-References. Establishments primarily engaged in—

- Merchant wholesale distribution of precious metal ores or concentrates—are classified in Industry 423520, Coal and Other Mineral and Ore Merchant Wholesalers; and
- Merchant wholesale distribution of nonprecious flatware—are classified in Industry 423220, Home Furnishing Merchant Wholesalers.

42399 Other Miscellaneous Durable Goods Merchant Wholesalers[US]

See industry description for 423990 below.

423990 Other Miscellaneous Durable Goods Merchant Wholesalers[US]

This industry comprises establishments primarily engaged in the merchant wholesale distribution of durable goods (except motor vehicle and motor vehicle parts and supplies; furniture and home furnishings; lumber and other construction materials; professional and commercial equipment and supplies; metals and minerals (except petroleum); electrical goods; hardware, and plumbing and heating equipment and supplies; machinery, equipment and supplies; sporting and recreational goods and supplies; toy and hobby goods and supplies; recyclable materials; and jewelry, watches, precious stones and precious metals).

Illustrative Examples:

Musical instruments merchant wholesalers
Phonograph records merchant wholesalers
Prerecorded audio and video cassettes merchant wholesalers
Prerecorded audio and video tapes and discs merchant wholesalers
Prerecorded compact discs (CDs) merchant wholesalers
Timber and timber products (except lumber) merchant wholesalers

Cross-References. Establishments primarily engaged in—

- Merchant wholesale distribution of automobiles and other motor vehicles, motor vehicle supplies, tires, and new and used parts—are classified in

US—United States industry only. CAN—United States and Canadian industries are comparable. MEX—United States and Mexican industries are comparable. Blank—Canadian, Mexican, and United States industries are comparable.

Industry Group 4231, Motor Vehicle and Motor Vehicle Parts and Supplies Merchant Wholesalers;

- Merchant wholesale distribution of furniture and home furnishings—are classified in Industry Group 4232, Furniture and Home Furnishing Merchant Wholesalers;
- Merchant wholesale distribution of lumber, plywood, millwork, wood panels, brick, stone, roofing, siding, and other nonelectrical construction materials—are classified in Industry Group 4233, Lumber and Other Construction Materials Merchant Wholesalers;
- Merchant wholesale distribution of photographic; office; computer and computer peripheral; medical, dental, hospital, ophthalmic; and other commercial and professional equipment and supplies—are classified in Industry Group 4234, Professional and Commercial Equipment and Supplies Merchant Wholesalers;
- Merchant wholesale distribution of coal and other minerals and ores and semifinished metal products—are classified in Industry Group 4235, Metal and Mineral (except Petroleum) Merchant Wholesalers;
- Merchant wholesale distribution of electrical goods—are classified in Industry Group 4236, Electrical and Electronic Goods Merchant Wholesalers;
- Merchant wholesale distribution of hardware, and plumbing, heating, air conditioning, and refrigeration equipment and supplies—are classified in Industry Group 4237, Hardware, and Plumbing and Heating Equipment and Supplies Merchant Wholesalers;
- Merchant wholesale distribution of construction, mining, farm, garden, industrial, service establishment, and transportation machinery, equipment and supplies—are classified in Industry Group 4238, Machinery, Equipment, and Supplies Merchant Wholesalers;
- Merchant wholesale distribution of sporting goods and accessories; billiard and pool supplies; sporting firearms and ammunition; and/or marine pleasure craft, equipment, and supplies—are classified in Industry 423910, Sporting and Recreational Goods and Supplies Merchant Wholesalers;
- Merchant wholesale distribution of toys, fireworks, playing cards, hobby goods and supplies and/or related goods—are classified in Industry 423920, Toy and Hobby Goods and Supplies Merchant Wholesalers;
- Merchant wholesale distribution of automotive, industrial, and other recyclable materials—are classified in Industry 423930, Recyclable Material Merchant Wholesalers; and
- Merchant wholesale distribution of jewelry, precious and semiprecious stones, precious metals and metal flatware, costume jewelry, watches,

US—United States industry only. CAN—United States and Canadian industries are comparable. MEX—United States and Mexican industries are comparable. Blank—Canadian, Mexican, and United States industries are comparable.

clocks, silverware, and/or jewelers' findings—are classified in Industry 423940, Jewelry, Watch, Precious Stone, and Precious Metal Merchant Wholesalers.

424 Merchant Wholesalers, Nondurable Goods[US]

Industries in the Merchant Wholesalers, Nondurable Goods subsector sell nondurable goods to other businesses. Nondurable goods are items generally with a normal life expectancy of less than three years. Nondurable goods merchant wholesale trade establishments are engaged in wholesaling products, such as paper and paper products, chemicals and chemical products, drugs, textiles and textile products, apparel, footwear, groceries, farm products, petroleum and petroleum products, alcoholic beverages, books, magazines, newspapers, flowers and nursery stock, and tobacco products.

The detailed industries within the subsector are organized in the classification structure based on the products sold.

Business to business electronic markets, agents, and brokers primarily engaged in wholesaling nondurable goods, generally on a commission or fee basis, are classified in Subsector 425, Wholesale Electronic Markets and Agents and Brokers.

4241 Paper and Paper Product Merchant Wholesalers[US]

42411 Printing and Writing Paper Merchant Wholesalers[US]

See industry description for 424110 below.

424110 Printing and Writing Paper Merchant Wholesalers[US]

This industry comprises establishments primarily engaged in the merchant wholesale distribution of bulk printing and/or writing paper generally on rolls for further processing.

Illustrative Examples:

- Bulk envelope paper merchant wholesalers
- Bulk groundwood paper merchant wholesalers
- Bulk paper (e.g., fine, printing, writing) merchant wholesalers

Cross-References.

Establishments primarily engaged in the merchant wholesale distribution of stationery are classified in Industry 424120, Stationery and Office Supplies Merchant Wholesalers.

US—United States industry only. CAN—United States and Canadian industries are comparable. MEX—United States and Mexican industries are comparable. Blank—Canadian, Mexican, and United States industries are comparable.

42412 Stationery and Office Supplies Merchant Wholesalers[US]

See industry description for 424120 below.

424120 Stationery and Office Supplies Merchant Wholesalers[US]

This industry comprises establishments primarily engaged in the merchant wholesale distribution of stationery, office supplies and/or gift wrap.

Illustrative Examples:

- Computer paper supplies merchant wholesalers
- Envelope merchant wholesalers
- File cards and folders merchant wholesalers
- Greeting cards merchant wholesalers
- Pencils merchant wholesalers
- Photocopy supplies merchant wholesalers
- Social stationery merchant wholesalers
- Typewriter paper merchant wholesalers
- Writing pens merchant wholesalers

Cross-References.

Establishments primarily engaged in the merchant wholesale distribution of bulk printing and/or writing paper are classified in Industry 424110, Printing and Writing Paper Merchant Wholesalers.

42413 Industrial and Personal Service Paper Merchant Wholesalers[US]

See industry description for 424130 below.

424130 Industrial and Personal Service Paper Merchant Wholesalers[US]

This industry comprises establishments primarily engaged in the merchant wholesale distribution of kraft wrapping and other coarse paper, paperboard, converted paper (except stationery and office supplies), and/or related disposable plastics products.

Illustrative Examples:

- Disposable plastics eating utensils merchant wholesalers
- Paper and disposable plastics dishes merchant wholesalers
- Paper and disposable plastics shipping supplies merchant wholesalers
- Paper bags merchant wholesalers
- Paper napkins merchant wholesalers
- Paperboard and disposable plastics boxes merchant wholesalers
- Plastics bags merchant wholesalers
- Sanitary paper products merchant wholesalers

US—United States industry only. CAN—United States and Canadian industries are comparable. MEX—United States and Mexican industries are comparable. Blank—Canadian, Mexican, and United States industries are comparable.

Cross-References.

Establishments primarily engaged in the merchant wholesale distribution of stationery, office supplies, and/or gift wrap are classified in Industry 424120, Stationery and Office Supplies Merchant Wholesalers.

4242 Drugs and Druggists' Sundries Merchant Wholesalers[US]

42421 Drugs and Druggists' Sundries Merchant Wholesalers[US]

See industry description for 424210 below.

424210 Drugs and Druggists' Sundries Merchant Wholesalers[US]

This industry comprises establishments primarily engaged in the merchant wholesale distribution of biological and medical products; botanical drugs and herbs; and pharmaceutical products intended for internal and external consumption in such forms as ampoules, tablets, capsules, vials, ointments, powders, solutions, and suspensions.

Illustrative Examples:

- Antibiotics merchant wholesalers
- Blood derivatives merchant wholesalers
- Botanicals merchant wholesalers
- Cosmetics merchant wholesalers
- Endocrine substances merchant wholesalers
- In-vitro and in-vivo diagnostics merchant wholesalers
- Vaccines merchant wholesalers
- Vitamins merchant wholesalers

Cross-References.

Establishments primarily engaged in the merchant wholesale distribution of surgical, dental, and hospital equipment are classified in Industry 423450, Medical, Dental, and Hospital Equipment and Supplies Merchant Wholesalers.

4243 Apparel, Piece Goods, and Notions Merchant Wholesalers[US]

42431 Piece Goods, Notions, and Other Dry Goods Merchant Wholesalers[US]

See industry description for 424310 below.

424310 Piece Goods, Notions, and Other Dry Goods Merchant Wholesalers[US]

This industry comprises establishments primarily engaged in the merchant wholesale distribution of piece goods, fabrics, knitting yarns (except industrial), thread and other notions, and/or hair accessories.

US—United States industry only. CAN—United States and Canadian industries are comparable. MEX—United States and Mexican industries are comparable. Blank—Canadian, Mexican, and United States industries are comparable.

Cross-References.

- Establishments primarily engaged as converters who buy fabric goods in the grey, have them finished on a contract basis, and sell at wholesale are classified in Industry 31331, Textile and Fabric Finishing Mills.
- Establishments primarily engaged in merchant wholesale distribution of industrial yarns are classified in Industry 424990, Other Miscellaneous Nondurable Goods Merchant Wholesalers.

42432 Men's and Boys' Clothing and Furnishings Merchant Wholesalers[US]

See industry description for 424320 below.

424320 Men's and Boys' Clothing and Furnishings Merchant Wholesalers[US]

This industry comprises establishments primarily engaged in the merchant wholesale distribution of men's and/or boys' clothing and furnishings.

Illustrative Examples:

Men's and boys' hosiery merchant wholesalers
Men's and boys' nightwear merchant wholesalers
Men's and boys' sportswear merchant wholesalers
Men's and boys' suits merchant wholesalers
Men's and boys' underwear merchant wholesalers
Men's and boys' work clothing merchant wholesalers

Cross-References.

Establishments primarily engaged in the merchant wholesale distribution of unisex clothing and men's fur clothing are classified in Industry 424330, Women's, Children's, and Infants' Clothing and Accessories Merchant Wholesalers.

42433 Women's, Children's, and Infants' Clothing and Accessories Merchant Wholesalers[US]

See industry description for 424330 below.

424330 Women's, Children's, and Infants' Clothing and Accessories Merchant Wholesalers[US]

This industry comprises establishments primarily engaged in the merchant wholesale distribution of (1) women's, children's, infants', and/or unisex clothing and accessories and/or (2) fur clothing.

US—United States industry only. CAN—United States and Canadian industries are comparable. MEX—United States and Mexican industries are comparable. Blank—Canadian, Mexican, and United States industries are comparable.

Illustrative Examples:

Dresses merchant wholesalers
Fur clothing merchant wholesalers
Lingerie merchant wholesalers
Millinery merchant wholesalers
Women's, children's, and infants' hosiery merchant wholesalers

42434 Footwear Merchant Wholesalers[US]

See industry description for 424340 below.

424340 Footwear Merchant Wholesalers[US]

This industry comprises establishments primarily engaged in the merchant wholesale distribution of footwear (including athletic) of leather, rubber, and other materials.

4244 Grocery and Related Product Merchant Wholesalers[US]

42441 General Line Grocery Merchant Wholesalers[US]

See industry description for 424410 below.

424410 General Line Grocery Merchant Wholesalers[US]

This industry comprises establishments primarily engaged in the merchant wholesale distribution of a general line (wide range) of groceries.

Cross-References.

Establishments primarily engaged in the merchant wholesale distribution of a specialized line of groceries are classified elsewhere in Sector 42, Wholesale Trade, according to the product sold.

42442 Packaged Frozen Food Merchant Wholesalers[US]

See industry description for 424420 below.

424420 Packaged Frozen Food Merchant Wholesalers[US]

This industry comprises establishments primarily engaged in the merchant wholesale distribution of packaged frozen foods (except dairy products).

Illustrative Examples:

Frozen bakery products merchant wholesalers
Packaged frozen meats merchant wholesalers

US—United States industry only. CAN—United States and Canadian industries are comparable. MEX—United States and Mexican industries are comparable. Blank—Canadian, Mexican, and United States industries are comparable.

Frozen juices merchant wholesalers
Frozen vegetables merchant wholesalers
Packaged frozen fish merchant wholesalers
Packaged frozen poultry merchant wholesalers

Cross-References.

Establishments primarily engaged in the merchant wholesale distribution of frozen dairy products are classified in Industry 424430, Dairy Product (except Dried or Canned) Merchant Wholesalers.

42443 Dairy Product (except Dried or Canned) Merchant Wholesalers[US]

See industry description for 424430 below.

424430 Dairy Product (except Dried or Canned) Merchant Wholesalers[US]

This industry comprises establishments primarily engaged in the merchant wholesale distribution of dairy products (except dried or canned).

Illustrative Examples:

Butter merchant wholesalers
Cheese merchant wholesalers
Cream merchant wholesalers
Fluid milk (except canned) merchant wholesalers
Ice cream and ices merchant wholesalers
Yogurt merchant wholesalers

Cross-References. Establishments primarily engaged in—

- Merchant wholesale distribution of dried or canned dairy products and dairy substitutes—are classified in Industry 424490, Other Grocery and Related Products Merchant Wholesalers; and
- Pasteurizing and bottling milk—are classified in U.S. Industry 311511, Fluid Milk Manufacturing.

42444 Poultry and Poultry Product Merchant Wholesalers[US]

See industry description for 424440 below.

424440 Poultry and Poultry Product Merchant Wholesalers[US]

This industry comprises establishments primarily engaged in the merchant wholesale distribution of poultry and/or poultry products (except canned and packaged frozen).

US—United States industry only. CAN—United States and Canadian industries are comparable. MEX—United States and Mexican industries are comparable. Blank—Canadian, Mexican, and United States industries are comparable.

Cross-References. Establishments primarily engaged in—

- Merchant wholesale distribution of packaged frozen poultry—are classified in Industry 424420, Packaged Frozen Food Merchant Wholesalers;
- Merchant wholesale distribution of canned poultry—are classified in Industry 424490, Other Grocery and Related Products Merchant Wholesalers; and
- Slaughtering and dressing poultry—are classified in U.S. Industry 311615, Poultry Processing.

42445 Confectionery Merchant Wholesalers[US]

See industry description for 424450 below.

424450 Confectionery Merchant Wholesalers[US]

This industry comprises establishments primarily engaged in the merchant wholesale distribution of confectioneries; salted or roasted nuts; popcorn; potato, corn, and similar chips; and/or fountain fruits and syrups.

Cross-References. Establishments primarily engaged in—

- Merchant wholesale distribution of frozen pretzels—are classified in Industry 424420, Packaged Frozen Food Merchant Wholesalers; and
- Merchant wholesale distribution of pretzels (except frozen)—are classified in Industry 424490, Other Grocery and Related Products Merchant Wholesalers.

42446 Fish and Seafood Merchant Wholesalers[US]

See industry description for 424460 below.

424460 Fish and Seafood Merchant Wholesalers[US]

This industry comprises establishments primarily engaged in the merchant wholesale distribution of fish and seafood (except canned or packaged frozen).

Cross-References. Establishments primarily engaged in—

- Merchant wholesale distribution of packaged frozen fish and seafood—are classified in Industry 424420, Packaged Frozen Food Merchant Wholesalers;
- Merchant wholesale distribution of canned fish and seafood—are classified in Industry 424490, Other Grocery and Related Products Merchant Wholesalers; and

US—United States industry only. CAN—United States and Canadian industries are comparable. MEX—United States and Mexican industries are comparable. Blank—Canadian, Mexican, and United States industries are comparable.

- Canning, smoking, salting, drying, or freezing seafood and shucking and packing fresh shellfish—are classified in Industry 31171, Seafood Product Preparation and Packaging.

42447 Meat and Meat Product Merchant Wholesalers[US]

See industry description for 424470 below.

424470 Meat and Meat Product Merchant Wholesalers[US]

This industry comprises establishments primarily engaged in the merchant wholesale distribution of meats and meat products (except canned and packaged frozen) and/or lard.

Cross-References. Establishments primarily engaged in—

- Merchant wholesale distribution of packaged frozen meats—are classified in Industry 424420, Packaged Frozen Food Merchant Wholesalers;
- Merchant wholesale distribution of canned meats—are classified in Industry 424490, Other Grocery and Related Products Merchant Wholesalers; and
- Preparing boxed beef—are classified in U.S. Industry 311612, Meat Processed from Carcasses.

42448 Fresh Fruit and Vegetable Merchant Wholesalers[US]

See industry description for 424480 below.

424480 Fresh Fruit and Vegetable Merchant Wholesalers[US]

This industry comprises establishments primarily engaged in the merchant wholesale distribution of fresh fruits and vegetables.

42449 Other Grocery and Related Products Merchant Wholesalers[US]

See industry description for 424490 below.

424490 Other Grocery and Related Products Merchant Wholesalers[US]

This industry comprises establishments primarily engaged in the merchant wholesale distribution of groceries and related products (except a general line of groceries; packaged frozen food; dairy products (except dried and canned); poultry products (except canned); confectioneries; fish and seafood (except canned); meat

US—United States industry only. CAN—United States and Canadian industries are comparable. MEX—United States and Mexican industries are comparable. Blank—Canadian, Mexican, and United States industries are comparable.

products (except canned); and fresh fruits and vegetables). Included in this industry are establishments primarily engaged in the bottling and merchant wholesale distribution of spring and mineral waters processed by others.

Illustrative Examples:

Bakery products (except frozen) merchant wholesalers
Canned fish merchant wholesalers
Canned fruits merchant wholesalers
Canned meats merchant wholesalers
Canned milk merchant wholesalers
Canned seafood merchant wholesalers
Canned vegetables merchant wholesalers
Dried milk merchant wholesalers
Soft drinks merchant wholesalers

Cross-References. Establishments primarily engaged in—

- Merchant wholesale distribution of grains, field beans, livestock, and other farm product raw materials—are classified in Industry Group 4245, Farm Product Raw Material Merchant Wholesalers;
- Merchant wholesale distribution of beer, wine, and distilled alcoholic beverages—are classified in Industry Group 4248, Beer, Wine, and Distilled Alcoholic Beverage Merchant Wholesalers;
- Bottling soft drinks—are classified in Industry 31211, Soft Drink and Ice Manufacturing;
- Merchant wholesale distribution of a general line of groceries—are classified in Industry 424410, General Line Grocery Merchant Wholesalers;
- Merchant wholesale distribution of packaged frozen foods (except dairy)—are classified in Industry 424420, Packaged Frozen Food Merchant Wholesalers;
- Merchant wholesale distribution of dairy products—are classified in Industry 424430, Dairy Product (except Dried or Canned) Merchant Wholesalers;
- Merchant wholesale distribution of poultry and poultry products (except canned and packaged frozen)—are classified in Industry 424440, Poultry and Poultry Product Merchant Wholesalers;
- Merchant wholesale distribution of confectioneries; salted or roasted nuts; popcorn; potato, corn, and similar chips; and/or fountain fruits and syrups—are classified in Industry 424450, Confectionery Merchant Wholesalers;
- Merchant wholesale distribution of fish and seafoods (except canned and packaged frozen)—are classified in Industry 424460, Fish and Seafood Merchant Wholesalers;
- Merchant wholesale distribution of meats (except canned and packaged frozen)—are classified in Industry 424470, Meat and Meat Product Merchant Wholesalers;

US—United States industry only. CAN—United States and Canadian industries are comparable. MEX—United States and Mexican industries are comparable. Blank—Canadian, Mexican, and United States industries are comparable.

- Merchant wholesale distribution of fresh fruits and vegetables—are classified in Industry 424480, Fresh Fruit and Vegetable Merchant Wholesalers; and
- Roasting coffee—are classified in Industry 311920, Coffee and Tea Manufacturing.

4245 Farm Product Raw Material Merchant Wholesalers[US]

This industry group comprises establishments primarily engaged in the merchant wholesale distribution of agricultural products (except raw milk, live poultry, and fresh fruit and vegetables), such as grains, field beans, livestock, and other farm product raw materials (excluding seeds).

42451 Grain and Field Bean Merchant Wholesalers[US]

See industry description for 424510 below.

424510 Grain and Field Bean Merchant Wholesalers[US]

This industry comprises establishments primarily engaged in the merchant wholesale distribution of grains, such as corn, wheat, oats, barley, and unpolished rice; dry beans; and soybeans and other inedible beans. Included in this industry are establishments primarily engaged in operating country or terminal grain elevators primarily for the purpose of wholesaling.

Cross-References. Establishments primarily engaged in—

- Merchant wholesale distribution of field and garden seeds—are classified in Industry 424910, Farm Supplies Merchant Wholesalers; and
- Operating grain elevators for storage only—are classified in Industry 493130, Farm Product Warehousing and Storage.

42452 Livestock Merchant Wholesalers[US]

See industry description for 424520 below.

424520 Livestock Merchant Wholesalers[US]

This industry comprises establishments primarily engaged in the merchant wholesale distribution of livestock (except horses and mules).

Illustrative Examples:

Cattle merchant wholesalers
Goats merchant wholesalers
Hogs merchant wholesalers
Sheep merchant wholesalers

US—United States industry only. CAN—United States and Canadian industries are comparable. MEX—United States and Mexican industries are comparable. Blank—Canadian, Mexican, and United States industries are comparable.

Cross-References.

Establishments primarily engaged in the merchant wholesale distribution of horses and mules are classified in Industry 424590, Other Farm Product Raw Material Merchant Wholesalers.

42459 Other Farm Product Raw Material Merchant Wholesalers[US]

See industry description for 424590 below.

424590 Other Farm Product Raw Material Merchant Wholesalers[US]

This industry comprises establishments primarily engaged in the merchant wholesale distribution of farm products (except grain and field beans, livestock, raw milk, live poultry, and fresh fruits and vegetables).

Illustrative Examples:

Chicks merchant wholesalers
Hides merchant wholesalers
Horses merchant wholesalers
Leaf tobacco merchant wholesalers
Mules merchant wholesalers
Raw cotton merchant wholesalers
Raw pelts merchant wholesalers

Cross-References. Establishments primarily engaged in—

- Merchant wholesale distribution of raw milk—are classified in Industry 424430, Dairy Product (except Dried or Canned) Merchant Wholesalers;
- Merchant wholesale distribution of live poultry (except chicks)—are classified in Industry 424440, Poultry and Poultry Product Merchant Wholesalers;
- Merchant wholesale distribution of grain, dry beans, and soybeans and other inedible beans—are classified in Industry 424510, Grain and Field Bean Merchant Wholesalers;
- Merchant wholesale distribution of livestock (except horses and mules), such as cattle, hogs, sheep, and goats—are classified in Industry 424520, Livestock Merchant Wholesalers; and
- Merchant wholesale distribution of fresh fruits and vegetables—are classified in Industry 424480, Fresh Fruit and Vegetable Merchant Wholesalers.

4246 Chemical and Allied Products Merchant Wholesalers[US]

This industry group comprises establishments primarily engaged in the merchant wholesale distribution of chemicals; plastics materials and basic forms and shapes; and allied products.

US—United States industry only. CAN—United States and Canadian industries are comparable. MEX—United States and Mexican industries are comparable. Blank—Canadian, Mexican, and United States industries are comparable.

42461 Plastics Materials and Basic Forms and Shapes Merchant Wholesalers[US]

See industry description for 424610 below.

424610 Plastics Materials and Basic Forms and Shapes Merchant Wholesalers[US]

This industry comprises establishments primarily engaged in the merchant wholesale distribution of plastics materials and resins, and unsupported plastics film, sheet, sheeting, rod, tube, and other basic forms and shapes.

42469 Other Chemical and Allied Products Merchant Wholesalers[US]

See industry description for 424690 below.

424690 Other Chemical and Allied Products Merchant Wholesalers[US]

This industry comprises establishments primarily engaged in the merchant wholesale distribution of chemicals and allied products (except agricultural and medicinal chemicals, paints and varnishes, fireworks, and plastics materials and basic forms and shapes).

Illustrative Examples:

Acids merchant wholesalers
Automotive chemicals (except lubricating oils and greases) merchant wholesalers
Dyestuffs merchant wholesalers
Explosives (except ammunition and fireworks) merchant wholesalers
Industrial chemicals merchant wholesalers
Industrial salts merchant wholesalers
Rosins merchant wholesalers
Turpentine merchant wholesalers

Cross-References. Establishments primarily engaged in—

- Merchant wholesale distribution of ammunition—are classified in Industry Group 4239, Miscellaneous Durable Goods Merchant Wholesalers;
- Merchant wholesale distribution of biological and medical products; botanical drugs and herbs; and pharmaceutical products intended for internal and external consumption in such forms as ampoules, tablets, capsules, vials, ointments, powders, solutions, and suspensions—are classified in Industry 424210, Drugs and Druggists' Sundries Merchant Wholesalers;
- Merchant wholesale distribution of farm supplies, such as animal feeds, fertilizers, agricultural chemicals, pesticides, seeds and plant bulbs—are classified in Industry 424910, Farm Supplies Merchant Wholesalers;

US—United States industry only. CAN—United States and Canadian industries are comparable. MEX—United States and Mexican industries are comparable. Blank—Canadian, Mexican, and United States industries are comparable.

- Merchant wholesale distribution of paints, and varnishes and similar coatings, pigments, wallpaper, and supplies, such as paint brushes and rollers—are classified in Industry 424950, Paint, Varnish, and Supplies Merchant Wholesalers;
- Merchant wholesale distribution of lubricating oils and greases—are classified in Industry 424720, Petroleum and Petroleum Products Merchant Wholesalers (except Bulk Stations and Terminals);
- Merchant wholesale distribution of fireworks—are classified in Industry 423920, Toy and Hobby Goods and Supplies Merchant Wholesalers; and
- Merchant wholesale distribution of plastics materials and resins, and unsupported plastics film, sheet, sheeting, rod, tube, and other basic forms and shapes—are classified in Industry 424610, Plastics Materials and Basic Forms and Shapes Merchant Wholesalers.

4247 Petroleum and Petroleum Products Merchant Wholesalers[US]

42471 Petroleum Bulk Stations and Terminals[US]

See industry description for 424710 below.

424710 Petroleum Bulk Stations and Terminals[US]

This industry comprises establishments with bulk liquid storage facilities primarily engaged in the merchant wholesale distribution of crude petroleum and petroleum products, including liquefied petroleum gas.

Cross-References.

Establishments primarily engaged in bulk storage of petroleum are classified in Industry 493190, Other Warehousing and Storage.

42472 Petroleum and Petroleum Products Merchant Wholesalers (except Bulk Stations and Terminals)[US]

See industry description for 424720 below.

424720 Petroleum and Petroleum Products Merchant Wholesalers (except Bulk Stations and Terminals)[US]

This industry comprises establishments primarily engaged in the merchant wholesale distribution of petroleum and petroleum products (except from bulk liquid storage facilities).

US—United States industry only. CAN—United States and Canadian industries are comparable. MEX—United States and Mexican industries are comparable. Blank—Canadian, Mexican, and United States industries are comparable.

Illustrative Examples:

- Bottled liquid petroleum gas merchant wholesalers
- Fuel oil merchant wholesalers (except bulk stations, terminals)
- Gasoline merchant wholesalers (except bulk stations, terminals)
- Lubricating oil and grease merchant wholesalers (except bulk stations, terminals)

Cross-References.

Establishments primarily engaged in the merchant wholesale distribution of crude petroleum and petroleum products from bulk liquid storage facilities are classified in Industry 424710, Petroleum Bulk Stations and Terminals.

4248 Beer, Wine, and Distilled Alcoholic Beverage Merchant Wholesalers[US]

42481 Beer and Ale Merchant Wholesalers[US]

See industry description for 424810 below.

424810 Beer and Ale Merchant Wholesalers[US]

This industry comprises establishments primarily engaged in the merchant wholesale distribution of beer, ale, porter, and other fermented malt beverages.

42482 Wine and Distilled Alcoholic Beverage Merchant Wholesalers[US]

See industry description for 424820 below.

424820 Wine and Distilled Alcoholic Beverage Merchant Wholesalers[US]

This industry comprises establishments primarily engaged in the merchant wholesale distribution of wine, distilled alcoholic beverages, and/or neutral spirits and ethyl alcohol used in blended wines and distilled liquors.

4249 Miscellaneous Nondurable Goods Merchant Wholesalers[US]

This industry group comprises establishments primarily engaged in the merchant wholesale distribution of nondurable goods, such as farm supplies; books, periodicals and newspapers; flowers; nursery stock; paints; varnishes; tobacco and tobacco

US—United States industry only. CAN—United States and Canadian industries are comparable. MEX—United States and Mexican industries are comparable. Blank—Canadian, Mexican, and United States industries are comparable.

products; and other miscellaneous nondurable goods, such as cut Christmas trees and pet supplies.

42491 Farm Supplies Merchant Wholesalers[US]

See industry description for 424910 below.

424910 Farm Supplies Merchant Wholesalers[US]

This industry comprises establishments primarily engaged in the merchant wholesale distribution of farm supplies, such as animal feeds, fertilizers, agricultural chemicals, pesticides, plant seeds, and plant bulbs.

Cross-References. Establishments primarily engaged in—

- Merchant wholesale distribution of pet food—are classified in Industry 424490, Other Grocery and Related Products Merchant Wholesalers;
- Merchant wholesale distribution of grains—are classified in Industry 424510, Grain and Field Bean Merchant Wholesalers;
- Merchant wholesale distribution of pet supplies—are classified in Industry 424990, Other Miscellaneous Nondurable Goods Merchant Wholesalers; and
- Merchant wholesale distribution of nursery stock (except seeds and plant bulbs)—are classified in Industry 424930, Flower, Nursery Stock, and Florists' Supplies Merchant Wholesalers.

42492 Book, Periodical, and Newspaper Merchant Wholesalers[US]

See industry description for 424920 below.

424920 Book, Periodical, and Newspaper Merchant Wholesalers[US]

This industry comprises establishments primarily engaged in the merchant wholesale distribution of books, periodicals, and newspapers.

42493 Flower, Nursery Stock, and Florists' Supplies Merchant Wholesalers[US]

See industry description for 424930 below.

424930 Flower, Nursery Stock, and Florists' Supplies Merchant Wholesalers[US]

This industry comprises establishments primarily engaged in the merchant wholesale distribution of flowers, florists' supplies, and/or nursery stock (except plant seeds and plant bulbs).

US—United States industry only. CAN—United States and Canadian industries are comparable. MEX—United States and Mexican industries are comparable. Blank—Canadian, Mexican, and United States industries are comparable.

Cross-References. Establishments primarily engaged in—

- Merchant wholesale distribution of cut Christmas trees—are classified in Industry 424990, Other Miscellaneous Nondurable Goods Merchant Wholesalers; and
- Merchant wholesale distribution of plant seeds and plant bulbs—are classified in Industry 424910, Farm Supplies Merchant Wholesalers.

42494 Tobacco and Tobacco Product Merchant Wholesalers[US]

See industry description for 424940 below.

424940 Tobacco and Tobacco Product Merchant Wholesalers[US]

This industry comprises establishments primarily engaged in the merchant wholesale distribution of tobacco products, such as cigarettes, snuff, cigars, and pipe tobacco.

Cross-References.

Establishments primarily engaged in the merchant wholesale distribution of leaf tobacco are classified in Industry 424590, Other Farm Product Raw Material Merchant Wholesalers.

42495 Paint, Varnish, and Supplies Merchant Wholesalers[US]

See industry description for 424950 below.

424950 Paint, Varnish, and Supplies Merchant Wholesalers[US]

This industry comprises establishments primarily engaged in the merchant wholesale distribution of paints, varnishes, and similar coatings; pigments; wallpaper; and supplies, such as paint brushes and rollers.

Cross-References.

Establishments primarily engaged in the merchant wholesale distribution of artists' paints are classified in Industry 424990, Other Miscellaneous Nondurable Goods Merchant Wholesalers.

42499 Other Miscellaneous Nondurable Goods Merchant Wholesalers[US]

See industry description for 424990 below.

US—United States industry only. CAN—United States and Canadian industries are comparable. MEX—United States and Mexican industries are comparable. Blank—Canadian, Mexican, and United States industries are comparable.

424990 Other Miscellaneous Nondurable Goods Merchant Wholesalers[US]

This industry comprises establishments primarily engaged in the merchant wholesale distribution of nondurable goods (except printing and writing paper; stationery and office supplies; industrial and personal service paper; drugs and druggists' sundries; apparel, piece goods, and notions; grocery and related products; farm product raw materials; chemical and allied products; petroleum and petroleum products; beer, wine, and distilled alcoholic beverages; farm supplies; books, periodicals and newspapers; flower, nursery stock and florists' supplies; tobacco and tobacco products; and paint, varnishes, wallpaper, and supplies).

Illustrative Examples:

Artists' supplies merchant wholesalers
Burlap merchant wholesalers
Christmas trees merchant wholesalers
Pet supplies (except pet food) merchant wholesalers
Statuary goods (except religious) merchant wholesalers
Textile bags merchant wholesalers
Industrial yarn merchant wholesalers

Cross-References. Establishments primarily engaged in—

- Distribution of advertising specialties—are classified in Industry 541890, Other Services Related to Advertising;
- Merchant wholesale distribution of farm supplies—are classified in Industry 424910, Farm Supplies Merchant Wholesalers;
- Merchant wholesale distribution of books, periodicals, and newspapers—are classified in Industry 424920, Book, Periodical, and Newspaper Merchant Wholesalers;
- Merchant wholesale distribution of flowers, nursery stock, and florists' supplies—are classified in Industry 424930, Flower, Nursery Stock, and Florists' Supplies Merchant Wholesalers;
- Merchant wholesale distribution of tobacco and its products—are classified in Industry 424940, Tobacco and Tobacco Product Merchant Wholesalers;
- Merchant wholesale distribution of paints, varnishes, and similar coatings; pigments; wallpaper; and supplies—are classified in Industry 424950, Paint, Varnish, and Supplies Merchant Wholesalers;
- Merchant wholesale distribution of bulk printing and/or writing paper—are classified in Industry 424110, Printing and Writing Paper Merchant Wholesalers;
- Merchant wholesale distribution of stationery, office supplies, and/or gift wrap—are classified in Industry 424120, Stationery and Office Supplies Merchant Wholesalers;

US—United States industry only. CAN—United States and Canadian industries are comparable. MEX—United States and Mexican industries are comparable. Blank—Canadian, Mexican, and United States industries are comparable.

- Merchant wholesale distribution of wrapping and other coarse paper, paperboard, converted paper (except stationery and office supplies), and related disposable plastics products—are classified in Industry 424130, Industrial and Personal Service Paper Merchant Wholesalers;
- Merchant wholesale distribution of biological and medical products; botanical drugs and herbs; and pharmaceutical products intended for internal and external consumption—are classified in Industry 424210, Drugs and Druggists' Sundries Merchant Wholesalers;
- Merchant wholesale distribution of clothing and accessories, footwear, piece goods, yard goods, notions, and/or hair accessories—are classified in Industry Group 4243, Apparel, Piece Goods, and Notions Merchant Wholesalers;
- Merchant wholesale distribution of meat, poultry, seafood, confectioneries, fruits and vegetables; and other groceries—are related products are classified in Industry Group 4244, Grocery and Related Product Merchant Wholesalers;
- Merchant wholesale distribution of grains, field beans, livestock, and other farm product raw materials—are classified in Industry Group 4245, Farm Product Raw Material Merchant Wholesalers;
- Merchant wholesale distribution of chemicals; plastics materials and basic forms and shapes; and allied products—are classified in Industry Group 4246, Chemical and Allied Products Merchant Wholesalers;
- Merchant wholesale distribution of petroleum and petroleum products—are classified in Industry Group 4247, Petroleum and Petroleum Products Merchant Wholesalers;
- Merchant wholesale distribution of beer, ale, wine, and distilled alcoholic beverages—are classified Industry Group 4248, Beer, Wine, and Distilled Alcoholic Beverage Merchant Wholesalers;
- Merchant wholesale distribution of pet foods—are classified in Industry 424490, Other Grocery and Related Products Merchant Wholesalers;
- Merchant wholesale distribution of religious statuary—are classified in Industry 423990, Other Miscellaneous Durable Goods Merchant Wholesalers; and
- Merchant wholesale distribution of knitting yarns (except industrial)—are classified in Industry 424310 Piece Goods, Notions, and Other Dry Goods Merchant Wholesalers.

425 Wholesale Electronic Markets and Agents and Brokers[US]

Industries in the Wholesale Electronic Markets and Agents and Brokers subsector arrange for the sale of goods owned by others, generally on a fee or commission

US—United States industry only. CAN—United States and Canadian industries are comparable. MEX—United States and Mexican industries are comparable. Blank—Canadian, Mexican, and United States industries are comparable.

basis. They act on behalf of the buyers and sellers of goods. This subsector contains agents and brokers as well as business to business electronic markets that facilitate wholesale trade.

4251 Wholesale Electronic Markets and Agents and Brokers[US]

42511 Business to Business Electronic Markets[US]

See industry description for 425110 below.

425110 Business to Business Electronic Markets[US]

This industry comprises business-to-business electronic markets bringing together buyers and sellers of goods using the Internet or other electronic means and generally receiving a commission or fee for the service. Business-to-business electronic markets for durable and nondurable goods are included in this industry.

Cross-References.

Establishments primarily engaged in bringing together buyers and sellers of goods using the Internet in a business-to-consumer or consumer-to-consumer environment are classified in Industry 45411, Electronic Shopping and Mail-Order Houses.

42512 Wholesale Trade Agents and Brokers[US]

See industry description for 425120 below.

425120 Wholesale Trade Agents and Brokers[US]

This industry comprises wholesale trade agents and brokers acting on behalf of buyers or sellers in the wholesale distribution of goods. Agents and brokers do not take title to the goods being sold but rather receive a commission or fee for their service. Agents and brokers for all durable and nondurable goods are included in this industry.

Illustrative Examples:

- Independent sales representatives
- Manufacturers' sales representatives

Cross-References.

Establishments acting in the capacity of agents or brokers that operate using the Internet or other electronic means instead of a sales force are classified in Industry 425110, Business to Business Electronic Markets.

US—United States industry only. CAN—United States and Canadian industries are comparable. MEX—United States and Mexican industries are comparable. Blank—Canadian, Mexican, and United States industries are comparable.

Sector 44-45—Retail Trade

The Sector as a Whole

The Retail Trade sector comprises establishments engaged in retailing merchandise, generally without transformation, and rendering services incidental to the sale of merchandise.

The retailing process is the final step in the distribution of merchandise; retailers are, therefore, organized to sell merchandise in small quantities to the general public. This sector comprises two main types of retailers: store and nonstore retailers.

1. Store retailers operate fixed point-of-sale locations, located and designed to attract a high volume of walk-in customers. In general, retail stores have extensive displays of merchandise and use mass-media advertising to attract customers. They typically sell merchandise to the general public for personal or household consumption, but some also serve business and institutional clients. These include establishments, such as office supply stores, computer and software stores, building materials dealers, plumbing supply stores, and electrical supply stores. Catalog showrooms, gasoline services stations, automotive dealers, and mobile home dealers are treated as store retailers.

   In addition to retailing merchandise, some types of store retailers are also engaged in the provision of after-sales services, such as repair and installation. For example, new automobile dealers, electronic and appliance stores, and musical instrument and supply stores often provide repair services. As a general rule, establishments engaged in retailing merchandise and providing after-sales services are classified in this sector.

   The first eleven subsectors of retail trade are store retailers. The establishments are grouped into industries and industry groups typically based on one or more of the following criteria:

   (a) The merchandise line or lines carried by the store; for example, specialty stores are distinguished from general-line stores.

   (b) The usual trade designation of the establishments. This criterion applies in cases where a store type is well recognized by the industry and the public, but difficult to define strictly in terms of commodity lines carried; for example, pharmacies, hardware stores, and department stores.

   (c) Capital requirements in terms of display equipment; for example, food stores have equipment requirements not found in other retail industries.

   (d) Human resource requirements in terms of expertise; for example, the staff of an automobile dealer requires knowledge in financing, registering, and licensing issues that are not necessary in other retail industries.

US—United States industry only. CAN—United States and Canadian industries are comparable. MEX—United States and Mexican industries are comparable. Blank—Canadian, Mexican, and United States industries are comparable.

2. Nonstore retailers, like store retailers, are organized to serve the general public, but their retailing methods differ. The establishments of this subsector reach customers and market merchandise with methods, such as the broadcasting of "infomercials," the broadcasting and publishing of direct-response advertising, the publishing of paper and electronic catalogs, door-to-door solicitation, in-home demonstration, selling from portable stalls (street vendors, except food), and distribution through vending machines. Establishments engaged in the direct sale (nonstore) of products, such as home heating oil dealers and home delivery newspaper routes are included here.

The buying of goods for resale is a characteristic of retail trade establishments that particularly distinguishes them from establishments in the agriculture, manufacturing, and construction industries. For example, farms that sell their products at or from the point of production are not classified in retail, but rather in agriculture. Similarly, establishments that both manufacture and sell their products to the general public are not classified in retail, but rather in manufacturing. However, establishments that engage in processing activities incidental to retailing are classified in retail. This includes establishments, such as optical goods stores that do in-store grinding of lenses, and meat and seafood markets.

Wholesalers also engage in the buying of goods for resale, but they are not usually organized to serve the general public. They typically operate from a warehouse or office and neither the design nor the location of these premises is intended to solicit a high volume of walk-in traffic. Wholesalers supply institutional, industrial, wholesale, and retail clients; their operations are, therefore, generally organized to purchase, sell, and deliver merchandise in larger quantities. However, dealers of durable nonconsumer goods, such as farm machinery and heavy duty trucks, are included in wholesale trade even if they often sell these products in single units.

441 Motor Vehicle and Parts Dealers[CAN]

Industries in the Motor Vehicle and Parts Dealers subsector retail motor vehicles and parts from fixed point-of-sale locations. Establishments in this subsector typically operate from a showroom and/or an open lot where the vehicles are on display. The display of vehicles and the related parts require little by way of display equipment. The personnel generally include both the sales and sales support staff familiar with the requirements for registering and financing a vehicle as well as a staff of parts experts and mechanics trained to provide repair and maintenance services for the vehicles. Specific industries have been included in this subsector to identify the type of vehicle being retailed.

Sales of capital or durable nonconsumer goods, such as medium and heavy-duty trucks, are always included in wholesale trade. These goods are virtually never sold through retail methods.

US—United States industry only. CAN—United States and Canadian industries are comparable. MEX—United States and Mexican industries are comparable. Blank—Canadian, Mexican, and United States industries are comparable.

4411 Automobile Dealers[CAN]

This industry group comprises establishments primarily engaged in retailing new and used automobiles and light trucks, such as sport utility vehicles, and passenger and cargo vans.

44111 New Car Dealers[CAN]

See industry description for 441110 below.

441110 New Car Dealers[CAN]

This industry comprises establishments primarily engaged in retailing new automobiles and light trucks, such as sport utility vehicles, and passenger and cargo vans, or retailing these new vehicles in combination with activities, such as repair services, retailing used cars, and selling replacement parts and accessories.

Illustrative Examples:

Automobile dealers, new only, or new and used

Light utility truck dealers, new only, or new and used

Cross-References. Establishments primarily engaged in—

- Retailing used automobiles and light trucks without retailing new automobiles and light trucks—are classified in Industry 441120, Used Car Dealers.
- Providing automotive repair services without retailing new automotive vehicles—are classified in Industry Group 8111, Automotive Repair and Maintenance.

44112 Used Car Dealers[CAN]

See industry description for 441120 below.

441120 Used Car Dealers[CAN]

This industry comprises establishments primarily engaged in retailing used automobiles and light trucks, such as sport utility vehicles, and passenger and cargo vans.

Illustrative Examples:

Antique auto dealers

Automobile dealers, used only

Light truck dealers, used only

US—United States industry only. CAN—United States and Canadian industries are comparable. MEX—United States and Mexican industries are comparable. Blank—Canadian, Mexican, and United States industries are comparable.

Cross-References.

Establishments primarily engaged in retailing new automobiles and light trucks are classified in Industry 441110, New Car Dealers.

4412 Other Motor Vehicle Dealers[CAN]

This industry group comprises establishments primarily engaged in retailing new and used vehicles (except automobiles, light trucks, such as sport utility vehicles, and passenger and cargo vans).

44121 Recreational Vehicle Dealers[CAN]

See industry description for 441210 below.

441210 Recreational Vehicle Dealers[CAN]

This industry comprises establishments primarily engaged in retailing new and/or used recreational vehicles commonly referred to as RVs or retailing these new vehicles in combination with activities, such as repair services and selling replacement parts and accessories.

Illustrative Examples:

Motor home dealers
Recreational vehicle (RV) dealers
Recreational vehicle parts and accessories stores
Travel trailer dealers

Cross-References. Establishments primarily engaged in—

- Retailing new or used boat trailers and utility trailers—are classified in Industry 44122, Motorcycle, Boat, and Other Motor Vehicle Dealers; and
- Retailing manufactured homes (i.e., mobile homes), parts, and equipment—are classified in Industry 453930, Manufactured (Mobile) Home Dealers.

44122 Motorcycle, Boat, and Other Motor Vehicle Dealers[CAN]

This industry comprises establishments primarily engaged in retailing new and used motorcycles, boats, and other vehicles (except automobiles, light trucks, and recreational vehicles), or retailing these new vehicles in combination with activities, such as repair services and selling replacement parts and accessories.

Illustrative Examples:

Aircraft dealers
All-terrain vehicle (ATV) dealers
Boat dealers, new and used
Motorcycle dealers
Utility trailer dealers

US—United States industry only. CAN—United States and Canadian industries are comparable. MEX—United States and Mexican industries are comparable. Blank—Canadian, Mexican, and United States industries are comparable.

Cross-References. Establishments primarily engaged in—

- Retailing new nonmotorized bicycles, surfboards, or wind sail boards—are classified in Industry 45111, Sporting Goods Stores;
- Retailing used nonmotorized bicycles, surfboards, or wind sail boards—are classified in Industry 45331, Used Merchandise Stores;
- Retailing new or used automobiles and light trucks—are classified in Industry Group 4411, Automotive Dealers;
- Retailing new or used recreational vehicles, such as travel trailers— are classified in Industry 44121, Recreational Vehicle Dealers;
- Providing repair services for vehicles without retailing new vehicles— are classified in the appropriate industry for the repair services and in Sector 81, Other Services (except Public Administration); and
- Retailing fuel and marine supplies at a marina—are classified in Industry 71393, Marinas.

441221 Motorcycle Dealers[US]

This U.S. industry comprises establishments primarily engaged in retailing new and/or used motorcycles, motor scooters, motor bikes, mopeds, off-road all-terrain vehicles, and personal watercraft, or retailing these new vehicles in combination with repair services and selling replacement parts and accessories.

Illustrative Examples:

All-terrain vehicle (ATV) dealers
Moped dealers
Motorcycle dealers
Motorcycle parts and accessories dealers
Personal watercraft dealers

Cross-References. Establishments primarily engaged in—

- Providing motorcycle repair services without retailing new motorcycles—are classified in Industry 811490, Other Personal and Household Goods Repair and Maintenance;
- Retailing new nonmotorized bicycles—are classified in Industry 451110, Sporting Goods Stores;
- Retailing used nonmotorized bicycles—are classified in Industry 453310, Used Merchandise Stores; and
- Retailing new or used boats—are classified in U.S. Industry 441222, Boat Dealers.

US—United States industry only. CAN—United States and Canadian industries are comparable. MEX—United States and Mexican industries are comparable. Blank—Canadian, Mexican, and United States industries are comparable.

441222 Boat Dealers[US]

This U.S. industry comprises establishments primarily engaged in (1) retailing new and/or used boats or retailing new boats in combination with activities, such as repair services and selling replacement parts and accessories, and/or (2) retailing new and/or used outboard motors, boat trailers, marine supplies, parts, and accessories.

Illustrative Examples:

Boat dealers (e.g., powerboats, rowboats, sailboats)
Marine supply dealers
Outboard motor dealers

Cross-References. Establishments primarily engaged in—

- Retailing new surfboards or wind sail boards—are classified in Industry 451110, Sporting Goods Stores;
- Retailing used surfboards or wind sail boards—are classified in Industry 453310, Used Merchandise Stores;
- Providing boat repair services without retailing new boats—are classified in Industry 811490, Other Personal and Household Goods Repair and Maintenance;
- Retailing new or used personal watercraft—are classified in U.S. Industry 441221, Motorcycle Dealers; and
- Operating docking and/or storage facilities for pleasure craft owners—are classified in Industry 713930, Marinas.

441229 All Other Motor Vehicle Dealers[US]

This U.S. industry comprises establishments primarily engaged in retailing new and/or used utility trailers and vehicles (except automobiles, light trucks, recreational vehicles, motorcycles, boats, motor scooters, motorbikes, off-road all-terrain vehicles, and personal watercraft) or retailing these new vehicles in combination with activities, such as repair services and selling replacement parts and accessories.

Illustrative Examples:

Aircraft dealers
Powered golf cart dealers
Snowmobile dealers
Utility trailer dealers

Cross-References. Establishments primarily engaged in—

- Retailing new automobiles and light trucks—are classified in Industry 441110, New Car Dealers;

US—United States industry only. CAN—United States and Canadian industries are comparable. MEX—United States and Mexican industries are comparable. Blank—Canadian, Mexican, and United States industries are comparable.

- Retailing used automobiles and light trucks—are classified in Industry 441120, Used Car Dealers;
- Retailing new or used recreational vehicles, such as travel trailers—are classified in Industry 441210, Recreational Vehicle Dealers;
- Retailing new or used motorcycles, motor scooters, motorbikes, off-road all-terrain vehicles, and personal watercraft—are classified in U.S. Industry 441221, Motorcycle Dealers;
- Retailing new or used boats, outboard motors, boat trailers, and marine supplies—are classified in U.S. Industry 441222, Boat Dealers; and
- Providing vehicle repair services without retailing new vehicles—are classified in the appropriate industry for the repair services.

4413 Automotive Parts, Accessories, and Tire Stores[CAN]

44131 Automotive Parts and Accessories Stores[CAN]

See industry description for 441310 below.

441310 Automotive Parts and Accessories Stores[CAN]

This industry comprises one or more of the following: (1) establishments known as automotive supply stores primarily engaged in retailing new, used, and/or rebuilt automotive parts and accessories; (2) automotive supply stores that are primarily engaged in both retailing automotive parts and accessories and repairing automobiles; and (3) establishments primarily engaged in retailing and installing automotive accessories.

Illustrative Examples:

Automotive parts and supply stores
Automotive stereo stores
Speed shops
Truck cap stores
Used automotive parts stores

Cross-References. Establishments primarily engaged in—

- Retailing automotive parts and accessories via electronic home shopping, mail-order, or direct sale—are classified in Subsector 454, Nonstore Retailers;
- Retailing new or used tires—are classified in Industry 441320, Tire Dealers; and
- Repairing and replacing automotive parts, such as transmissions, mufflers, and brake linings (except establishments known as automotive supply

US—United States industry only. CAN—United States and Canadian industries are comparable. MEX—United States and Mexican industries are comparable. Blank—Canadian, Mexican, and United States industries are comparable.

stores)—are classified in Industry 81111, Automotive Mechanical and Electrical Repair and Maintenance.

44132 Tire Dealers[CAN]

See industry description for 441320 below.

441320 Tire Dealers[CAN]

This industry comprises establishments primarily engaged in retailing new and/or used tires and tubes or retailing new tires in combination with automotive repair services.

Cross-References. Establishments primarily engaged in—

- Retailing tires via electronic home shopping, mail-order, or direct sale—are classified in Subsector 454, Nonstore Retailers; and
- Providing automotive repair services without retailing new tires—are classified in U.S. Industry 811198, All Other Automotive Repair and Maintenance.

442 Furniture and Home Furnishings Stores[CAN]

Industries in the Furniture and Home Furnishings Stores subsector retail new furniture and home furnishings from fixed point-of-sale locations. Establishments in this subsector usually operate from showrooms and have substantial areas for the presentation of their products. Many offer interior decorating services in addition to the sale of products.

4421 Furniture Stores[CAN]

44211 Furniture Stores[CAN]

See industry description for 442110 below.

442110 Furniture Stores[CAN]

This industry comprises establishments primarily engaged in retailing new furniture, such as household furniture (e.g., baby furniture box springs and mattresses) and outdoor furniture; office furniture (except those sold in combination with office supplies and equipment); and/or furniture sold in combination with major appliances, home electronics, home furnishings, or floor coverings.

US—United States industry only. CAN—United States and Canadian industries are comparable. MEX—United States and Mexican industries are comparable. Blank—Canadian, Mexican, and United States industries are comparable.

Cross-References. Establishments primarily engaged in—

- Retailing furniture via electronic home shopping, mail-order, or direct sale—are classified in Subsector 454, Nonstore Retailers;
- Retailing used furniture—are classified in Industry 453310, Used Merchandise Stores;
- Retailing custom furniture made on premises—are classified in Subsector 337, Furniture and Related Product Manufacturing; and
- Retailing new office furniture and a range of new office equipment and supplies—are classified in Industry 453210, Office Supplies and Stationery Stores.

4422 Home Furnishings Stores[CAN]

This industry group comprises establishments primarily engaged in retailing new home furnishings (except furniture).

44221 Floor Covering Stores[CAN]

See industry description for 442210 below.

442210 Floor Covering Stores[CAN]

This industry comprises establishments primarily engaged in retailing new floor coverings, such as rugs and carpets, vinyl floor coverings, and floor tile (except ceramic or wood only); or retailing new floor coverings in combination with installation and repair services.

Cross-References. Establishments primarily engaged in—

- Retailing floor coverings via electronic home shopping, mail-order, or direct sale—are classified in Subsector 454, Nonstore Retailers;
- Installing floor coverings without retailing new floor coverings—are classified in Industry 238330, Flooring Contractors;
- Retailing ceramic floor tile or wood floor coverings only—are classified in Industry 444190, Other Building Material Dealers; and
- Retailing used rugs and carpets—are classified in Industry 453310, Used Merchandise Stores.

44229 Other Home Furnishings Stores[CAN]

This industry comprises establishments primarily engaged in retailing new home furnishings (except furniture and floor coverings).

US—United States industry only. CAN—United States and Canadian industries are comparable. MEX—United States and Mexican industries are comparable. Blank—Canadian, Mexican, and United States industries are comparable.

Illustrative Examples:

Bath shops
Chinaware stores
Glassware stores
Kitchenware stores
Window treatment stores

Cross-References. Establishments primarily engaged in—

- Retailing home furnishings via electronic home shopping, mail-order, or direct sale—are classified in Subsector 454, Nonstore Retailers;
- Retailing custom curtains and draperies made on premises—are classified in Industry 31412, Curtain and Linen Mills;
- Retailing new mirrored glass, lighting fixtures, and new ceramic floor tile or wood floor coverings only—are classified in Industry 44419, Other Building Material Dealers;
- Retailing new furniture—are classified in Industry 44211, Furniture Stores;
- Retailing new floor coverings (except ceramic or wood only)—are classified in Industry 44221, Floor Covering Stores; and
- Retailing used home furnishings—are classified in Industry 45331, Used Merchandise Stores.

442291 Window Treatment Stores[CAN]

This U.S. industry comprises establishments primarily engaged in retailing new window treatments, such as curtains, drapes, blinds, and shades.

Cross-References. Establishments primarily engaged in—

- Retailing window treatments via electronic home shopping, mail-order, or direct sale—are classified in Subsector 454, Nonstore Retailers; and
- Retailing custom curtains and draperies made on premises—are classified in U.S. Industry 314121, Curtain and Drapery Mills.

442299 All Other Home Furnishings Stores[US]

This U.S. industry comprises establishments primarily engaged in retailing new home furnishings (except floor coverings, furniture, and window treatments).

Illustrative Examples:

Bath shops
Chinaware stores
Electric lamp shops
Kitchenware stores
Linen stores
Picture frame stores

US—United States industry only. CAN—United States and Canadian industries are comparable. MEX—United States and Mexican industries are comparable. Blank—Canadian, Mexican, and United States industries are comparable.

Glassware stores
Houseware stores
Wood-burning stove stores

Cross-References. Establishments primarily engaged in—

- Selling home furnishings via electronic home shopping, mail-order, or direct sale—are classified in Subsector 454, Nonstore Retailers;
- Retailing new mirrored glass or lighting fixtures—are classified in Industry 444190, Other Building Material Dealers;
- Retailing new furniture—are classified in Industry 442110, Furniture Stores;
- Retailing new floor coverings—are classified in Industry 442210, Floor Covering Stores;
- Retailing new window treatments—are classified in U.S. Industry 442291, Window Treatment Stores; and
- Retailing used home furnishings—are classified in Industry 453310, Used Merchandise Stores.

443 Electronics and Appliance Stores[CAN]

Industries in the Electronics and Appliance Stores subsector retail new electronics and appliances from point-of-sale locations. Establishments in this subsector often operate from locations that have special provisions for floor displays requiring special electrical capacity to accommodate the proper demonstration of the products. The staff includes sales personnel knowledgeable in the characteristics and warranties of the line of goods retailed and may also include trained repair persons to handle the maintenance and repair of the electronic equipment and appliances. The classifications within this subsector are made principally on the type of product and knowledge required to operate each type of store.

4431 Electronics and Appliance Stores[CAN]

This industry group comprises establishments primarily engaged in retailing the following new products: household-type appliances, cameras, computers, and other electronic goods.

44311 Appliance, Television, and Other Electronics Stores[CAN]

This industry comprises establishments primarily engaged in retailing one of the following: (1) retailing an array of new household-type appliances and consumer-type electronic products, such as radios, televisions, and computers; (2) specializing

US—United States industry only. CAN—United States and Canadian industries are comparable. MEX—United States and Mexican industries are comparable. Blank—Canadian, Mexican, and United States industries are comparable.

in retailing a single line of new consumer-type electronic products (except computers); and (3) retailing these new products in combination with repair services.

Illustrative Examples:

Appliance stores
Consumer electronics stores
Radio and television stores

Cross-References. Establishments primarily engaged in—

- Retailing new electronic products via electronic home shopping, mail-order, or direct sale—are classified in Subsector 454, Nonstore Retailers;
- Retailing new computers, computer peripherals, and prepackaged computer software without retailing other consumer-type electronic products or office equipment, office furniture, and office supplies; or retailing these products in combination with repair services—are classified in Industry 44312, Computer and Software Stores;
- Retailing new computers, computer peripherals, and prepackaged software in combination with retailing new office equipment, office furniture, and office supplies—are classified in Industry 45321, Office Supplies and Stationery Stores;
- Retailing new sewing machines in combination with selling new sewing supplies, fabrics, patterns, yarns, and other needlework accessories—are classified in Industry 45113, Sewing, Needlework, and Piece Goods Stores;
- Retailing new electronic toys—are classified in Industry 45112, Hobby, Toy, and Game Stores;
- Providing television or other electronic equipment repair services without retailing new televisions or electronic equipment—are classified in Industry 81121, Electronic and Precision Equipment Repair and Maintenance;
- Providing household-type appliance repair services without retailing new appliances—are classified in Industry 81141, Home and Garden Equipment and Appliance Repair and Maintenance;
- Retailing used appliance and electronic products—are classified in Industry 45331, Used Merchandise Stores;
- Retailing new still and motion picture cameras—are classified in Industry 44313, Camera and Photographic Supplies Stores; and
- Retailing automotive electronic sound systems—are classified in Industry 44131, Automotive Parts and Accessories Stores.

443111 Household Appliance Stores[US]

This U.S. industry comprises establishments known as appliance stores primarily engaged in retailing an array of new household appliances, such as refrigerators,

US—United States industry only. CAN—United States and Canadian industries are comparable. MEX—United States and Mexican industries are comparable. Blank—Canadian, Mexican, and United States industries are comparable.

dishwashers, ovens, irons, coffeemakers, hair dryers, electric razors, room air-conditioners, microwave ovens, sewing machines, and vacuum cleaners, or retailing new appliances in combination with appliance repair services.

Cross-References. Establishments primarily engaged in—

- Retailing household appliances via electronic home shopping, mail-order, or direct sale—are classified in Subsector 454, Nonstore Retailers;
- Retailing new sewing machines in combination with selling new sewing supplies, fabrics, patterns, yarns, and other needlework accessories—are classified in Industry 451130, Sewing, Needlework, and Piece Goods Stores;
- Providing household-type appliance repair services without retailing new appliances—are classified in U.S. Industry 811412, Appliance Repair and Maintenance; and
- Retailing used appliances—are classified in Industry 453310, Used Merchandise Stores.

443112 Radio, Television, and Other Electronics Stores[US]

This U.S. industry comprises: (1) establishments known as consumer electronics stores primarily engaged in retailing a general line of new consumer-type electronic products; (2) establishments specializing in retailing a single line of consumer-type electronic products (except computers); or (3) establishments primarily engaged in retailing these new electronic products in combination with repair services.

Illustrative Examples:

Consumer electronic stores
Radio and television stores
Stereo stores (except automotive)
Telephone stores (including cellular)

Cross-References. Establishments primarily engaged in—

- Retailing electronic goods via electronic home shopping, mail-order, or direct sale—are classified in Subsector 454, Nonstore Retailers;
- Retailing automotive electronic sound systems—are classified in Industry 441310, Automotive Parts and Accessories Stores;
- Retailing new computers, computer peripherals, and prepackaged computer software without retailing other consumer-type electronic products or office equipment, office furniture and office supplies; or retailing these new computer products in combination with repair services—are classified in Industry 443120, Computer and Software Stores;
- Retailing new computers, computer peripherals, and prepackaged software in combination with retailing new office equipment, office furniture, and

US—United States industry only. CAN—United States and Canadian industries are comparable. MEX—United States and Mexican industries are comparable. Blank—Canadian, Mexican, and United States industries are comparable.

office supplies—are classified in Industry 453210, Office Supplies and Stationery Stores;

- Retailing new still and motion picture cameras—are classified in Industry 443130, Camera and Photographic Supplies Stores;
- Providing television or other electronic equipment repair services without retailing new televisions or electronic products—are classified in Industry 81121, Electronic and Precision Equipment Repair and Maintenance;
- Retailing new electronic toys—are classified in Industry 451120, Hobby, Toy, and Game Stores; and
- Retailing used electronics—are classified in Industry 453310, Used Merchandise Stores.

44312 Computer and Software Stores[CAN]

See industry description for 443120 below.

443120 Computer and Software Stores[CAN]

This industry comprises establishments primarily engaged in retailing new computers, computer peripherals, and prepackaged computer software without retailing other consumer-type electronic products or office equipment, office furniture and office supplies; or retailing these new products in combination with repair and support services.

Cross-References. Establishments primarily engaged in—

- Retailing computers and software via electronic home shopping, mail-order, or direct sale—are classified in Subsector 454, Nonstore Retailers;
- Retailing new electronic toys, such as video games and handheld electronic games—are classified in Industry 451120, Hobby, Toy, and Game Stores;
- Providing computer repair services without retailing new computers—are classified in U.S. Industry 811212, Computer and Office Machine Repair and Maintenance;
- Retailing new computers, computer peripherals, and prepackaged software in combination with retailing new office equipment, office furniture, and office supplies—are classified in Industry 453210, Office Supplies and Stationery Stores;
- Retailing a general line of new electronic products or specializing in retailing a single line of consumer-type electronic products (except computers)—are classified in U.S. Industry 443112, Radio, Television, and Other Electronics Stores; and

US—United States industry only. CAN—United States and Canadian industries are comparable. MEX—United States and Mexican industries are comparable. Blank—Canadian, Mexican, and United States industries are comparable.

- Retailing used computers, computer software, video games, and handheld electronic games—are classified in Industry 453310, Used Merchandise Stores.

44313 Camera and Photographic Supplies Stores[CAN]

See industry description for 443130 below.

443130 Camera and Photographic Supplies Stores[CAN]

This industry comprises establishments primarily engaged in either retailing new cameras, photographic equipment, and photographic supplies or retailing new cameras and photographic equipment in combination with activities, such as repair services and film developing.

Cross-References. Establishments primarily engaged in—

- Retailing camera and photographic supplies via electronic home shopping, mail-order, or direct sale—are classified in Subsector 454, Nonstore Retailers;
- Retailing new video cameras—are classified in U.S. Industry 443112, Radio, Television, and Other Electronics Stores;
- One-hour film developing without retailing a range of new photographic equipment and supplies—are classified in U.S. Industry 812922, One-Hour Photofinishing;
- Providing repair services for photographic equipment without retailing new photographic equipment—are classified in U.S. Industry 811211, Consumer Electronics Repair and Maintenance;
- Developing film and/or producing photographic prints, slides, and enlargements (except one-hour photofinishing labs)—are classified in U.S. Industry 812921, Photofinishing Laboratories (except One-Hour); and
- Retailing used cameras and photographic equipment—are classified in Industry 453310, Used Merchandise Stores.

444 Building Material and Garden Equipment and Supplies Dealers[CAN]

Industries in the Building Material and Garden Equipment and Supplies Dealers subsector retail new building material and garden equipment and supplies from fixed point-of-sale locations. Establishments in this subsector have display equipment designed to handle lumber and related products and garden equipment and

US—United States industry only. CAN—United States and Canadian industries are comparable. MEX—United States and Mexican industries are comparable. Blank—Canadian, Mexican, and United States industries are comparable.

supplies that may be kept either indoors or outdoors under covered areas. The staff is usually knowledgeable in the use of the specific products being retailed in the construction, repair, and maintenance of the home and associated grounds.

4441 Building Material and Supplies Dealers[CAN]

This industry group comprises establishments primarily engaged in retailing new building materials and supplies.

44411 Home Centers[CAN]

See industry description for 444110 below.

444110 Home Centers[CAN]

This industry comprises establishments known as home centers primarily engaged in retailing a general line of new home repair and improvement materials and supplies, such as lumber, plumbing goods, electrical goods, tools, housewares, hardware, and lawn and garden supplies, with no one merchandise line predominating. The merchandise lines are normally arranged in separate departments.

44412 Paint and Wallpaper Stores[CAN]

See industry description for 444120 below.

444120 Paint and Wallpaper Stores[CAN]

This industry comprises establishments known as paint and wallpaper stores primarily engaged in retailing paint, wallpaper, and related supplies.

44413 Hardware Stores[CAN]

See industry description for 444130 below.

444130 Hardware Stores[CAN]

This industry comprises establishments known as hardware stores primarily engaged in retailing a general line of new hardware items, such as tools and builders' hardware.

Cross-References. Establishments primarily engaged in—

- Retailing hardware items via electronic home shopping, mail order, or direct sale—are classified in Subsector 454, Nonstore Retailers;

US—United States industry only. CAN—United States and Canadian industries are comparable. MEX—United States and Mexican industries are comparable. Blank—Canadian, Mexican, and United States industries are comparable.

- Retailing a general line of home repair and improvement materials and supplies, known as home centers—are classified in Industry 444110, Home Centers; and
- Retailing used hardware items—are classified in Industry 453310, Used Merchandise Stores.

44419 Other Building Material Dealers[CAN]

See industry description for 444190 below.

444190 Other Building Material Dealers[CAN]

This industry comprises establishments (except those known as home centers, paint and wallpaper stores, and hardware stores) primarily engaged in retailing specialized lines of new building materials, such as lumber, fencing, glass, doors, plumbing fixtures and supplies, electrical supplies, prefabricated buildings and kits, and kitchen and bath cabinets and countertops to be installed.

Illustrative Examples:

Electrical supply stores
Fencing dealers
Floor covering stores, wood or ceramic tile only
Glass stores
Garage door dealers
Kitchen cabinet (except custom) stores
Lumber yards, retail
Plumbing supply stores
Prefabricated building dealers

Cross-References. Establishments primarily engaged in—

- Retailing building materials via electronic home shopping, mail-order, or direct sale—are classified in Subsector 454, Nonstore Retailers;
- Retailing used building materials—are classified in Industry 453310, Used Merchandise Stores;
- Providing carpentry/installation services for products—are classified in Industry 238350, Finish Carpentry Contractors;
- Installing plumbing fixtures and supplies—are classified in Industry 238220, Plumbing, Heating, and Air-Conditioning Contractors;
- Installing electrical supplies, such as lighting fixtures and ceiling fans—are classified in Industry 238210, Electrical Contractors;
- Making custom furniture (e.g., kitchen cabinets)—are classified in Subsector 337, Furniture and Related Product Manufacturing;
- Retailing a general line of new hardware items, known as hardware stores—are classified in Industry 444130, Hardware Stores;

US—United States industry only. CAN—United States and Canadian industries are comparable. MEX—United States and Mexican industries are comparable. Blank—Canadian, Mexican, and United States industries are comparable.

- Retailing paint and wallpaper, known as paint and wallpaper stores—are classified in Industry 444120, Paint and Wallpaper Stores; and
- Retailing a general line of home repair and improvement materials and supplies, known as home centers—are classified in Industry 444110, Home Centers.

4442 Lawn and Garden Equipment and Supplies Stores[CAN]

This industry group comprises establishments primarily engaged in retailing new lawn and garden equipment and supplies.

44421 Outdoor Power Equipment Stores[CAN]

See industry description for 444210 below.

444210 Outdoor Power Equipment Stores[CAN]

This industry comprises establishments primarily engaged in retailing new outdoor power equipment or retailing new outdoor power equipment in combination with activities, such as repair services and selling replacement parts.

Cross-References. Establishments primarily engaged in—

- Retailing outdoor power equipment via electronic home shopping, mail-order, or direct sale—are classified in Subsector 454, Nonstore Retailers;
- Providing outdoor power equipment repair services without retailing new outdoor power equipment—are classified in U.S. Industry 811411, Home and Garden Equipment Repair and Maintenance; and
- Retailing used outdoor power equipment—are classified in Industry 453310, Used Merchandise Stores.

44422 Nursery, Garden Center, and Farm Supply Stores[CAN]

See industry description for 444220 below.

444220 Nursery, Garden Center, and Farm Supply Stores[CAN]

This industry comprises establishments primarily engaged in retailing nursery and garden products, such as trees, shrubs, plants, seeds, bulbs, and sod, that are predominantly grown elsewhere. These establishments may sell a limited amount of a product they grow themselves.

US—United States industry only. CAN—United States and Canadian industries are comparable. MEX—United States and Mexican industries are comparable. Blank—Canadian, Mexican, and United States industries are comparable.

Cross-References. Establishments primarily engaged in—

- Retailing nursery and garden products via electronic home shopping, mail-order, or direct sale—are classified in Subsector 454, Nonstore Retailers;
- Providing landscaping services—are classified in Industry 561730, Landscaping Services; and
- Growing and retailing nursery stock—are classified in U.S. Industry 111421, Nursery and Tree Production.

445 Food and Beverage Stores[CAN]

Industries in the Food and Beverage Stores subsector usually retail food and beverages merchandise from fixed point-of-sale locations. Establishments in this subsector have special equipment (e.g., freezers, refrigerated display cases, refrigerators) for displaying food and beverage goods. They have staff trained in the processing of food products to guarantee the proper storage and sanitary conditions required by regulatory authority.

4451 Grocery Stores[CAN]

This industry group comprises establishments primarily engaged in retailing a general line of food products.

44511 Supermarkets and Other Grocery (except Convenience) Stores[CAN]

See industry description for 445110 below.

445110 Supermarkets and Other Grocery (except Convenience) Stores[CAN]

This industry comprises establishments generally known as supermarkets and grocery stores primarily engaged in retailing a general line of food, such as canned and frozen foods; fresh fruits and vegetables; and fresh and prepared meats, fish, and poultry. Included in this industry are delicatessen-type establishments primarily engaged in retailing a general line of food.

Cross-References. Establishments primarily engaged in—

- Retailing automotive fuels in combination with a convenience store or food mart—are classified in Industry 447110, Gasoline Stations with Convenience Stores;

US—United States industry only. CAN—United States and Canadian industries are comparable. MEX—United States and Mexican industries are comparable. Blank—Canadian, Mexican, and United States industries are comparable.

- Retailing a limited line of goods, known as convenience stores or food marts (except those with fuel pumps)—are classified in Industry 445120, Convenience Stores;
- Retailing frozen food and freezer plans via direct sales to residential customers—are classified in Industry 454390, Other Direct Selling Establishments;
- Providing food services in delicatessen-type establishments—are classified in U.S. Industry 722211, Limited-Service Restaurants; and
- Retailing fresh meat in delicatessen-type establishments—are classified in Industry 445210, Meat Markets.

44512 Convenience Stores[CAN]

See industry description for 445120 below.

445120 Convenience Stores[CAN]

This industry comprises establishments known as convenience stores or food marts (except those with fuel pumps) primarily engaged in retailing a limited line of goods that generally includes milk, bread, soda, and snacks.

Cross-References. Establishments primarily engaged in—

- Retailing a general line of food, known as supermarkets and grocery stores—are classified in Industry 445110, Supermarkets and Other Grocery (except Convenience) Stores; and
- Retailing automotive fuels in combination with a convenience store or food mart—are classified in Industry 447110, Gasoline Stations with Convenience Stores.

4452 Specialty Food Stores[CAN]

This industry group comprises establishments primarily engaged in retailing specialized lines of food.

44521 Meat Markets[CAN]

See industry description for 445210 below.

445210 Meat Markets[CAN]

This industry comprises establishments primarily engaged in retailing fresh, frozen, or cured meats and poultry. Delicatessen-type establishments primarily engaged in retailing fresh meat are included in this industry.

US—United States industry only. CAN—United States and Canadian industries are comparable. MEX—United States and Mexican industries are comparable. Blank—Canadian, Mexican, and United States industries are comparable.

Illustrative Examples:

Baked ham stores
Butcher shops
Frozen meat shops
Meat markets
Poultry dealers

Cross-References. Establishments primarily engaged in—

- Retailing meat and poultry via electronic home shopping, mail-order, or direct sale—are classified in Subsector 454, Nonstore Retailers;
- Retailing a general line of food, known as supermarkets and grocery stores—are classified in Industry 445110, Supermarkets and Other Grocery (except Convenience) Stores; and
- Providing food services in delicatessen-type establishments—are classified in U.S. Industry 722211, Limited-Service Restaurants.

44522 Fish and Seafood Markets[CAN]

See industry description for 445220 below.

445220 Fish and Seafood Markets[CAN]

This industry comprises establishments primarily engaged in retailing fresh, frozen, or cured fish and seafood products.

Cross-References.

Establishments primarily engaged in retailing fish and seafood products via electronic home shopping, mail-order, or direct sale are classified in Subsector 454, Nonstore Retailers.

44523 Fruit and Vegetable Markets[CAN]

See industry descriptions for 445230 below.

445230 Fruit and Vegetable Markets[CAN]

This industry comprises establishments primarily engaged in retailing fresh fruits and vegetables.

Cross-References. Establishments primarily engaged in—

- Retailing fruits and vegetables via electronic home shopping, mail-order, or direct sale—are classified in Subsector 454, Nonstore Retailers; and

---

US—United States industry only. CAN—United States and Canadian industries are comparable. MEX—United States and Mexican industries are comparable. Blank—Canadian, Mexican, and United States industries are comparable.

- Growing and selling vegetables and/or fruits at roadside stands—are classified in Subsector 111, Crop Production.

44529 Other Specialty Food Stores[CAN]

This industry comprises establishments primarily engaged in retailing specialty foods (except meat, fish, seafood, and fruits and vegetables) not for immediate consumption and not made on premises.

Illustrative Examples:

Baked goods stores (except immediate consumption)
Coffee and tea (i.e., packaged) stores
Confectionery (i.e., packaged) stores
Dairy product stores
Gourmet food stores
Nut (i.e., packaged) stores

Cross-References. Establishments primarily engaged in—

- Retailing specialty foods via electronic home shopping, mail-order, or direct sale—are classified in Subsector 454, Nonstore Retailers;
- Retailing baked goods made on the premises, but not for immediate consumption—are classified in Industry 31181, Bread and Bakery Product Manufacturing;
- Retailing fresh, frozen, or cured meats and poultry—are classified in Industry 44521, Meat Markets;
- Retailing fresh, frozen, or cured fish and seafood products—are classified in Industry 44522, Fish and Seafood Markets;
- Retailing fresh fruits and vegetables—are classified in Industry 44523, Fruit and Vegetable Markets;
- Retailing candy and confectionery products not for immediate consumption and not made on premises—are classified in Industry Group 3113, Sugar and Confectionery Product Manufacturing; and
- Selling snack foods (e.g., doughnuts, bagels, ice cream, popcorn) for immediate consumption—are classified in Subsector 722, Food Services and Drinking Places.

445291 Baked Goods Stores[CAN]

This U.S. industry comprises establishments primarily engaged in retailing baked goods not for immediate consumption and not made on the premises.

US—United States industry only. CAN—United States and Canadian industries are comparable. MEX—United States and Mexican industries are comparable. Blank—Canadian, Mexican, and United States industries are comparable.

Cross-References. Establishments primarily engaged in—

- Retailing baked goods via electronic home shopping, mail-order, or direct sale—are classified in Subsector 454, Nonstore Retailers;
- Selling snack foods (e.g., doughnuts, bagels, ice cream, popcorn) for immediate consumption—are classified in U.S. Industry 722213, Snack and Nonalcoholic Beverage Bars; and
- Retailing baked goods made on the premises but not for immediate consumption—are classified in Industry 311811, Retail Bakeries.

445292 Confectionery and Nut Stores[CAN]

This U.S. industry comprises establishments primarily engaged in retailing candy and other confections, nuts, and popcorn not for immediate consumption and not made on the premises.

Cross-References. Establishments primarily engaged in—

- Retailing confectionery goods and nuts via electronic home shopping, mail-order, or direct sale—are classified in Subsector 454, Nonstore Retailers;
- Retailing confectionery goods and nuts made on premises and not packaged for immediate consumption—are classified in Industry Group 3113, Sugar and Confectionery Product Manufacturing;
- Selling snack foods (e.g., doughnuts, bagels, ice cream, popcorn) for immediate consumption—are classified in U.S. Industry 722213, Snack and Nonalcoholic Beverage Bars; and
- Retailing baked goods made on the premises but not for immediate consumption—are classified in Industry 311811, Retail Bakeries.

445299 All Other Specialty Food Stores[CAN]

This U.S. industry comprises establishments primarily engaged in retailing miscellaneous specialty foods (except meat, fish, seafood, fruit and vegetables, confections, nuts, popcorn, and baked goods) not for immediate consumption and not made on the premises.

Illustrative Examples:

Coffee and tea (i.e., packaged) stores
Dairy product stores
Gourmet food stores
Soft drink (i.e., bottled) stores
Spice stores
Water (i.e., bottled) stores

US—United States industry only. CAN—United States and Canadian industries are comparable. MEX—United States and Mexican industries are comparable. Blank—Canadian, Mexican, and United States industries are comparable.

Cross-References. Establishments primarily engaged in—

- Retailing specialty foods via electronic home shopping, mail-order, or direct sale—are classified in Subsector 454, Nonstore Retailers;
- Selling snack foods (e.g., doughnuts, bagels, ice cream, popcorn) for immediate consumption—are classified in U.S. Industry 722213, Snack and Nonalcoholic Beverage Bars;
- Retailing fresh, frozen, or cured meats and poultry—are classified in Industry 445210, Meat Markets;
- Retailing fresh, frozen, or cured fish and seafood products—are classified in Industry 445220, Fish and Seafood Markets;
- Retailing fresh fruits and vegetables—are classified in Industry 445230, Fruit and Vegetable Markets;
- Retailing candy and other confections, nuts, and popcorn not for immediate consumption and not made on the premises—are classified in U.S. Industry 445292, Confectionery and Nut Stores; and
- Retailing baked goods not for immediate consumption and not made on the premises—are classified in U.S. Industry 445291, Baked Goods Stores.

4453 Beer, Wine, and Liquor Stores[CAN]

44531 Beer, Wine, and Liquor Stores[CAN]

See industry description for 445310 below.

445310 Beer, Wine, and Liquor Stores[CAN]

This industry comprises establishments primarily engaged in retailing packaged alcoholic beverages, such as ale, beer, wine, and liquor.

Cross-References.

Establishments primarily engaged in retailing packaged liquor in combination with providing prepared drinks for immediate consumption on the premises are classified in Industry 722410, Drinking Places (Alcoholic Beverages).

446 Health and Personal Care Stores[CAN]

Industries in the Health and Personal Care Stores subsector retail health and personal care merchandise from fixed point-of-sale locations. Establishments in this subsector are characterized principally by the products they retail, and some

US—United States industry only. CAN—United States and Canadian industries are comparable. MEX—United States and Mexican industries are comparable. Blank—Canadian, Mexican, and United States industries are comparable.

health and personal care stores may have specialized staff trained in dealing with the products. Staff may include pharmacists, opticians, and other professionals engaged in retailing, advising customers, and/or fitting the product sold to the customer's needs.

4461 Health and Personal Care Stores[CAN]

This industry group comprises establishments primarily engaged in retailing health and personal care products.

44611 Pharmacies and Drug Stores[CAN]

See industry description for 446110 below.

446110 Pharmacies and Drug Stores[CAN]

This industry comprises establishments known as pharmacies and drug stores engaged in retailing prescription or nonprescription drugs and medicines.

Cross-References. Establishments primarily engaged in—

- Retailing food supplement products, such as vitamins, nutrition supplements, and body enhancing supplements—are classified in U.S. Industry 446191, Food (Health) Supplement Stores; and
- Retailing prescription and nonprescription drugs via electronic home shopping, mail-order, or direct sale—are classified in Subsector 454, Nonstore Retailers.

44612 Cosmetics, Beauty Supplies, and Perfume Stores[CAN]

See industry description for 446120 below.

446120 Cosmetics, Beauty Supplies, and Perfume Stores[CAN]

This industry comprises establishments known as cosmetic or perfume stores or beauty supply shops primarily engaged in retailing cosmetics, perfumes, toiletries, and personal grooming products.

Cross-References. Establishments primarily engaged in—

- Providing beauty parlor services—are classified in U.S. Industry 812112, Beauty Salons; and

---

US—United States industry only. CAN—United States and Canadian industries are comparable. MEX—United States and Mexican industries are comparable. Blank—Canadian, Mexican, and United States industries are comparable.

- Retailing perfumes, cosmetics, and beauty supplies via electronic home shopping, mail-order, or direct sale—are classified in Subsector 454, Nonstore Retailers.

44613 Optical Goods Stores[CAN]

See industry description for 446130 below.

446130 Optical Goods Stores[CAN]

This industry comprises establishments primarily engaged in one or more of the following: (1) retailing and fitting prescription eyeglasses and contact lenses; (2) retailing prescription eyeglasses in combination with the grinding of lenses to order on the premises; and (3) selling nonprescription eyeglasses.

Cross-References. Establishments primarily engaged in—

- Grinding lenses without retailing lenses—are classified in U.S. Industry 339115, Ophthalmic Goods Manufacturing;
- The private or group practice of optometry, even though glasses and contact lenses are sold at these establishments—are classified in Industry 621320, Offices of Optometrists; and
- Retailing eyeglasses and contact lenses via mail-order—are classified in U.S. Industry 454113, Mail-Order Houses.

44619 Other Health and Personal Care Stores[CAN]

This industry comprises establishments primarily engaged in retailing health and personal care items (except drugs, medicines, optical goods, perfumes, cosmetics, and beauty supplies).

Illustrative Examples:

Convalescent supply stores
Food (i.e., health) supplement stores
Hearing aid stores
Prosthetic stores
Sick room supply stores

Cross-References. Establishments primarily engaged in—

- Retailing health and personal care items via electronic home shopping, mail-order, or direct sale—are classified in Subsector 454, Nonstore Retailers;
- Retailing orthopedic shoes—are classified in Industry 44821, Shoe Stores;

US—United States industry only. CAN—United States and Canadian industries are comparable. MEX—United States and Mexican industries are comparable. Blank—Canadian, Mexican, and United States industries are comparable.

- Retailing orthopedic and prosthetic appliances that are made on premises—are classified in Industry 33911, Medical Equipment and Supplies Manufacturing;
- Retailing prescription and nonprescription drugs and medicines—are classified in Industry 44611, Pharmacies and Drug Stores;
- Retailing eyeglasses and contact lenses—are classified in Industry 44613, Optical Goods Stores;
- Retailing perfumes, cosmetics, and beauty supplies—are classified in Industry 44612, Cosmetics, Beauty Supplies, and Perfume Stores; and
- Retailing naturally organic foods, such as fruits and vegetables, dairy products, and cereals and grains—are classified in Subsector 445, Food and Beverage Stores.

446191 Food (Health) Supplement Stores[CAN]

This U.S. industry comprises establishments primarily engaged in retailing food supplement products, such as vitamins, nutrition supplements, and body enhancing supplements.

Cross-References. Establishments primarily engaged in—

- Retailing food supplement products via electronic home shopping, mail-order, or direct sale—are classified in Subsector 454, Nonstore Retailers;
- Retailing prescription and nonprescription drugs and medicines—are classified in Industry 446110, Pharmacies and Drug Stores; and
- Retailing naturally organic foods, such as fruits and vegetables, dairy products, and cereals and grains—are classified in Subsector 445, Food and Beverage Stores.

446199 All Other Health and Personal Care Stores[CAN]

This U.S. industry comprises establishments primarily engaged in retailing specialized lines of health and personal care merchandise (except drugs, medicines, optical goods, cosmetics, beauty supplies, perfume, and food supplement products).

Illustrative Examples:

Convalescent supply stores
Hearing aid stores
Prosthetic stores
Sick room supply stores

US—United States industry only. CAN—United States and Canadian industries are comparable. MEX—United States and Mexican industries are comparable. Blank—Canadian, Mexican, and United States industries are comparable.

Cross-References. Establishments primarily engaged in—

- Retailing specialized health and personal care merchandise via electronic home shopping, mail-order, or direct sale—are classified in Subsector 454, Nonstore Retailers;
- Retailing food supplement products—are classified in U.S. Industry 446191, Food (Health) Supplement Stores;
- Retailing prescription or nonprescription drugs and medicines—are classified in Industry 446110, Pharmacies and Drug Stores;
- Retailing eyeglasses and contact lenses—are classified in Industry 446130, Optical Goods Stores;
- Retailing perfumes, cosmetics, and beauty supplies—are classified in Industry 446120, Cosmetics, Beauty Supplies, and Perfume Stores;
- Retailing orthopedic shoes—are classified in Industry 448210, Shoe Stores; and
- Retailing orthopedic and prosthetic appliances that are made on premises—are classified in U.S. Industry 339113, Surgical Appliance and Supplies Manufacturing.

447 Gasoline Stations[CAN]

Industries in the Gasoline Stations subsector group establishments retailing automotive fuels (e.g., gasoline, diesel fuel, gasohol) and automotive oils and retailing these products in combination with convenience store items. These establishments have specialized equipment for the storage and dispensing of automotive fuels.

4471 Gasoline Stations[CAN]

44711 Gasoline Stations with Convenience Stores[CAN]

See industry description for 447110 below.

447110 Gasoline Stations with Convenience Stores[CAN]

This industry comprises establishments engaged in retailing automotive fuels (e.g., diesel fuel, gasohol, gasoline) in combination with convenience store or food mart items. These establishments can either be in a convenience store (i.e., food mart) setting or a gasoline station setting. These establishments may also provide automotive repair services.

US—United States industry only. CAN—United States and Canadian industries are comparable. MEX—United States and Mexican industries are comparable. Blank—Canadian, Mexican, and United States industries are comparable.

Cross-References. Establishments primarily engaged in—

- Retailing automotive fuels without a convenience store—are classified in Industry 447190, Other Gasoline Stations; and
- Retailing a limited line of goods, known as convenience stores or food marts (except those with fuel pumps)—are classified in Industry 445120, Convenience Stores.

44719 Other Gasoline Stations[CAN]

See industry description for 447190 below.

447190 Other Gasoline Stations[CAN]

This industry comprises establishments known as gasoline stations (except those with convenience stores) primarily engaged in one of the following: (1) retailing automotive fuels (e.g., diesel fuel, gasohol, gasoline) or (2) retailing these fuels in combination with activities, such as providing repair services; selling automotive oils, replacement parts, and accessories; and/or providing food services.

Illustrative Examples:

Gasoline stations without convenience stores
Marine service stations
Truck stops

Cross-References. Establishments primarily engaged in—

- Repairing motor vehicles without retailing automotive fuels—are classified in Industry 81111, Automotive Mechanical and Electrical Repair and Maintenance; and
- Retailing automotive fuels in combination with a convenience store or food mart—are classified in Industry 447110, Gasoline Stations with Convenience Stores.

448 Clothing and Clothing Accessories Stores[CAN]

Industries in the Clothing and Clothing Accessories Stores subsector retailing new clothing and clothing accessories merchandise from fixed point-of-sale locations. Establishments in this subsector have similar display equipment and staff that is knowledgeable regarding fashion trends and the proper match of styles, colors, and combinations of clothing and accessories to the characteristics and tastes of the customer.

US—United States industry only. CAN—United States and Canadian industries are comparable. MEX—United States and Mexican industries are comparable. Blank—Canadian, Mexican, and United States industries are comparable.

4481 Clothing Stores[CAN]

This industry group comprises establishments primarily engaged in retailing new clothing.

44811 Men's Clothing Stores[CAN]

See industry descriptions for 448110 below.

448110 Men's Clothing Stores[CAN]

This industry comprises establishments primarily engaged in retailing a general line of new men's and boys' clothing. These establishments may provide basic alterations, such as hemming, taking in or letting out seams, or lengthening or shortening sleeves.

Cross-References. Establishments primarily engaged in—

- Retailing men's and boys' clothing via electronic home shopping, mail-order, or direct sale—are classified in Subsector 454, Nonstore Retailers;
- Retailing custom men's clothing made on the premises—are classified in Industry Group 3152, Cut and Sew Apparel Manufacturing;
- Retailing new men's and boys' accessories—are classified in Industry 448150, Clothing Accessories Stores;
- Retailing specialized new apparel, such as raincoats, leather coats, fur apparel, and swimwear—are classified in Industry 448190, Other Clothing Stores;
- Retailing new clothing for all genders and age groups—are classified in Industry 448140, Family Clothing Stores;
- Retailing secondhand clothes—are classified in Industry 453310, Used Merchandise Stores; and
- Providing clothing alterations and repair—are classified in Industry 811490, Other Personal and Household Goods Repair and Maintenance.

44812 Women's Clothing Stores[CAN]

See industry description for 448120 below.

448120 Women's Clothing Stores[CAN]

This industry comprises establishments primarily engaged in retailing a general line of new women's, misses'; and juniors' clothing, including maternity wear.

US—United States industry only. CAN—United States and Canadian industries are comparable. MEX—United States and Mexican industries are comparable. Blank—Canadian, Mexican, and United States industries are comparable.

These establishments may provide basic alterations, such as hemming, taking in or letting out seams, or lengthening or shortening sleeves.

Cross-References. Establishments primarily engaged in—

- Retailing women's clothing via electronic home shopping, mail-order, or direct sale—are classified in Subsector 454, Nonstore Retailers;
- Retailing custom women's clothing made on premises—are classified in Industry Group 3152, Cut and Sew Apparel Manufacturing;
- Retailing new women's accessories—are classified in Industry 448150, Clothing Accessories Stores;
- Retailing new clothing for all genders and age groups—are classified in Industry 448140, Family Clothing Stores;
- Retailing specialized new apparel, such as bridal gowns, raincoats, leather coats, fur apparel, and swimwear—are classified in Industry 448190, Other Clothing Stores;
- Retailing secondhand clothes—are classified in Industry 453310, Used Merchandise Stores; and
- Providing clothing alterations and repair—are classified in Industry 811490, Other Personal and Household Goods Repair and Maintenance.

44813 Children's and Infants' Clothing Stores[CAN]

See industry description for 448130 below.

448130 Children's and Infants' Clothing Stores[CAN]

This industry comprises establishments primarily engaged in retailing a general line of new children's and infants' clothing. These establishments may provide basic alterations, such as hemming, taking in or letting out seams, or lengthening or shortening sleeves.

Cross-References. Establishments primarily engaged in—

- Retailing children's and infants' clothing via electronic home shopping, mail-order, or direct sale—are classified in Subsector 454, Nonstore Retailers;
- Retailing new children's and infants' accessories—are classified in Industry 448150, Clothing Accessories Stores;
- Retailing new clothing for all genders or age groups—are classified in Industry 448140, Family Clothing Stores;

US—United States industry only. CAN—United States and Canadian industries are comparable. MEX—United States and Mexican industries are comparable. Blank—Canadian, Mexican, and United States industries are comparable.

- Retailing secondhand clothes—are classified in Industry 453310, Used Merchandise Stores; and
- Providing clothing alterations and repair—are classified in Industry 811490, Other Personal and Household Goods Repair and Maintenance.

44814 Family Clothing Stores[CAN]

See industry description for 448140 below.

448140 Family Clothing Stores[CAN]

This industry comprises establishments primarily engaged in retailing a general line of new clothing for men, women, and children, without specializing in sales for an individual gender or age group. These establishments may provide basic alterations, such as hemming, taking in or letting out seams, or lengthening or shortening sleeves.

Cross-References. Establishments primarily engaged in—

- Retailing clothing for all genders via electronic home shopping, mail-order, or direct sale—are classified in Subsector 454, Nonstore Retailers;
- Retailing new men's and boys' clothing—are classified in Industry 448110, Men's Clothing Stores;
- Retailing new women's, misses', and juniors' clothing—are classified in Industry 448120, Women's Clothing Stores;
- Retailing new children's and infants' clothing—are classified in Industry 448130, Children's and Infants' Clothing Stores;
- Retailing specialized new apparel, such as raincoats, bridal gowns, leather coats, fur apparel, and swimwear—are classified in Industry 448190, Other Clothing Stores;
- Providing clothing alterations and repair—are classified in Industry 811490, Other Personal and Household Goods Repair and Maintenance; and
- Retailing secondhand clothes—are classified in Industry 453310, Used Merchandise Stores.

44815 Clothing Accessories Stores[CAN]

See industry descriptions for 448150 below.

448150 Clothing Accessories Stores[CAN]

This industry comprises establishments primarily engaged in retailing single or combination lines of new clothing accessories, such as hats and caps, costume jewelry, gloves, handbags, ties, wigs, toupees, and belts.

US—United States industry only. CAN—United States and Canadian industries are comparable. MEX—United States and Mexican industries are comparable. Blank—Canadian, Mexican, and United States industries are comparable.

Illustrative Examples:

Costume jewelry stores
Neckwear stores
Wig and hairpiece stores

Cross-References. Establishments primarily engaged in—

- Retailing specialized lines of clothing via electronic home shopping, mail-order, or direct sale—are classified in Subsector 454, Nonstore Retailers;
- Retailing precious jewelry and watches—are classified in Industry 448310, Jewelry Stores;
- Retailing used clothing accessories—are classified in Industry 453310, Used Merchandise Stores;
- Retailing luggage, briefcases, trunks, or these products in combination with a general line of leather items (except leather apparel), known as luggage and leather goods stores—are classified in Industry 448320, Luggage and Leather Goods Stores; and
- Retailing leather apparel—are classified in Industry 448190, Other Clothing Stores.

44819 Other Clothing Stores[CAN]

See industry description for 448190 below.

448190 Other Clothing Stores[US]

This industry comprises establishments primarily engaged in retailing specialized lines of new clothing (except general lines of men's, women's, children's, infants', and family clothing). These establishments may provide basic alterations, such as hemming, taking in or letting out seams, or lengthening or shortening sleeves.

Illustrative Examples:

Bridal gown (except custom) shops
Costume shops
Fur apparel stores
Hosiery stores
Leather coat stores
Lingerie stores
Swimwear stores
Uniform (except athletic) stores

Cross-References. Establishments primarily engaged in—

- Retailing specialized apparel via electronic home shopping, mail-order, or direct sale—are classified in Subsector 454, Nonstore Retailers;
- Retailing custom apparel and accessories made on the premises—are classified in Subsector 315, Apparel Manufacturing;

US—United States industry only. CAN—United States and Canadian industries are comparable. MEX—United States and Mexican industries are comparable. Blank—Canadian, Mexican, and United States industries are comparable.

- Retailing new men's and boys' clothing—are classified in Industry 448110, Men's Clothing Stores;
- Retailing new women's, misses', and juniors' clothing, including maternity wear—are classified in Industry 448120, Women's Clothing Stores;
- Retailing new children's and infants' clothing—are classified in Industry 448130, Children's and Infants' Clothing Stores;
- Retailing new clothing for all genders or age groups—are classified in Industry 448140, Family Clothing Stores;
- Retailing athletic uniforms—are classified in Industry 451110, Sporting Goods Stores;
- Retailing secondhand clothes—are classified in Industry 453310, Used Merchandise Stores;
- Retailing luggage, briefcases, trunks, or these products in combination with a general line of leather items (except leather apparel), known as luggage and leather good stores—are classified in Industry 448320, Luggage and Leather Goods Stores; and
- Providing clothing alterations and repair—are classified in Industry 811490, Other Personal Household Goods Repair and Maintenance.

4482 Shoe Stores[CAN]

44821 Shoe Stores[CAN]

See industry description for 448210 below.

448210 Shoe Stores[CAN]

This industry comprises establishments primarily engaged in retailing all types of new footwear (except hosiery and specialty sports footwear, such as golf shoes, bowling shoes, and spiked shoes). Establishments primarily engaged in retailing new tennis shoes or sneakers are included in this industry.

Cross-References. Establishments primarily engaged in—

- Retailing footwear via electronic home shopping, mail-order, or direct sale—are classified in Subsector 454, Nonstore Retailers;
- Retailing hosiery—are classified in Industry 448190, Other Clothing Stores;
- Retailing new specialty sports footwear (e.g., bowling shoes, golf shoes, spiked shoes)—are classified in Industry 451110, Sporting Goods Stores; and

US—United States industry only. CAN—United States and Canadian industries are comparable. MEX—United States and Mexican industries are comparable. Blank—Canadian, Mexican, and United States industries are comparable.

- Retailing used footwear—are classified in Industry 453310, Used Merchandise Stores.

4483 Jewelry, Luggage, and Leather Goods Stores[CAN]

This industry group comprises establishments primarily engaged in retailing new jewelry (except costume jewelry); new silver and plated silverware; new watches and clocks; and new luggage with or without a general line of new leather goods and accessories, such as hats, gloves, handbags, ties, and belts.

44831 Jewelry Stores[CAN]

See industry descriptions for 448310 below.

448310 Jewelry Stores[CAN]

This industry comprises establishments primarily engaged in retailing one or more of the following items: (1) new jewelry (except costume jewelry); (2) new sterling and plated silverware; and (3) new watches and clocks. Also included are establishments retailing these new products in combination with lapidary work and/or repair services.

Cross-References. Establishments primarily engaged in—

- Retailing new costume jewelry—are classified in Industry 448150, Clothing Accessories Stores;
- Retailing jewelry via electronic home shopping, mail-order, or direct sale—are classified in Subsector 454, Nonstore Retailers;
- Retailing antiques or used jewelry, silverware, and watches and clocks—are classified in Industry 453310, Used Merchandise Stores;
- Providing jewelry or watch and clock repair without retailing new jewelry or watches and clocks—are classified in Industry 811490, Other Personal and Household Goods Repair and Maintenance; and
- Cutting and setting gem stones—are classified in U.S. Industry 339913, Jewelers' Material and Lapidary Work Manufacturing.

44832 Luggage and Leather Goods Stores[CAN]

See industry descriptions for 448320 below.

448320 Luggage and Leather Goods Stores[CAN]

This industry comprises establishments known as luggage and leather goods stores primarily engaged in retailing new luggage, briefcases, trunks, or these new

US—United States industry only. CAN—United States and Canadian industries are comparable. MEX—United States and Mexican industries are comparable. Blank—Canadian, Mexican, and United States industries are comparable.

products in combination with a general line of leather items (except leather apparel), such as belts, gloves, and handbags.

Cross-References. Establishments primarily engaged in—

- Retailing luggage and leather goods via electronic home shopping, mail-order, or direct sale—are classified in Subsector 454, Nonstore Retailers;
- Retailing used luggage and leather goods—are classified in Industry 453310, Used Merchandise Stores;
- Retailing single or combination lines of new clothing accessories (e.g., gloves, handbags, or leather belts)—are classified in Industry 448150, Clothing Accessories Stores; and
- Retailing new leather coats—are classified in Industry 448190, Other Clothing Stores.

451 Sporting Goods, Hobby, Book, and Music Stores[CAN]

Industries in the Sporting Goods, Hobby, Book, and Music Stores subsector are engaged in retailing and providing expertise on use of sporting equipment or other specific leisure activities, such as needlework and musical instruments. Book stores are also included in this subsector.

4511 Sporting Goods, Hobby, and Musical Instrument Stores[CAN]

This industry group comprises establishments primarily engaged in retailing new sporting goods, games and toys, and musical instruments.

45111 Sporting Goods Stores[CAN]

See industry description for 451110 below.

451110 Sporting Goods Stores[CAN]

This industry comprises establishments primarily engaged in retailing new sporting goods, such as bicycles and bicycle parts; camping equipment; exercise and fitness equipment; athletic uniforms; specialty sports footwear; and sporting goods, equipment, and accessories.

Illustrative Examples:

Athletic uniform supply stores
Bicycle (except motorized) shops
Golf pro shops
Saddlery stores

US—United States industry only. CAN—United States and Canadian industries are comparable. MEX—United States and Mexican industries are comparable. Blank—Canadian, Mexican, and United States industries are comparable.

Bowling equipment and supply stores
Diving equipment stores
Exercise equipment stores
Fishing supply stores
Sporting goods (e.g., scuba, skiing, outdoor) stores
Sporting gun shops

Cross-References. Establishments primarily engaged in—

- Retailing sporting goods via electronic home shopping, mail order, or direct sale—are classified in Subsector 454, Nonstore Retailers;
- Retailing new or used campers (pickup coaches) and camping trailers—are classified in Industry 441210, Recreational Vehicle Dealers;
- Retailing new or used snowmobiles, motorized bicycles, and motorized golf carts—are classified in Industry 44122, Motorcycle, Boat, and Other Motor Vehicle Dealers;
- Retailing new shoes (except specialty sports footwear, such as golf shoes, bowling shoes, and spiked shoes)—are classified in Industry 448210, Shoe Stores;
- Repairing or servicing sporting goods, without retailing new sporting goods—are classified in Industry 811490, Other Personal and Household Goods Repair and Maintenance; and
- Retailing used sporting goods and used bicycles—are classified in Industry 453310, Used Merchandise Stores.

45112 Hobby, Toy, and Game Stores[CAN]

See industry description for 451120 below.

451120 Hobby, Toy, and Game Stores[CAN]

This industry comprises establishments primarily engaged in retailing new toys, games, and hobby and craft supplies (except needlecraft).

Cross-References. Establishments primarily engaged in—

- Retailing toys, games, and hobby and craft supplies via electronic home shopping, mail-order, or direct sale—are classified in Subsector 454, Nonstore Retailers;
- Retailing artists' supplies or collectors' items, such as coins, stamps, autographs, and cards—are classified in U.S. Industry 453998, All Other Miscellaneous Store Retailers (except Tobacco Stores);
- Retailing new computer software (e.g., game software)—are classified in Industry 443120, Computer and Software Stores;

US—United States industry only. CAN—United States and Canadian industries are comparable. MEX—United States and Mexican industries are comparable. Blank—Canadian, Mexican, and United States industries are comparable.

- Retailing used toys, games, and hobby supplies—are classified in Industry 453310, Used Merchandise Stores; and
- Retailing new sewing supplies, fabrics, and needlework accessories—are classified in Industry 451130, Sewing, Needlework, and Piece Goods Stores.

45113 Sewing, Needlework, and Piece Goods Stores[CAN]

See industry description for 451130 below.

451130 Sewing, Needlework, and Piece Goods Stores[CAN]

This industry comprises establishments primarily engaged in retailing new sewing supplies, fabrics, patterns, yarns, and other needlework accessories or retailing these products in combination with selling new sewing machines.

Illustrative Examples:

Fabric shops
Needlecraft sewing supply stores
Sewing supply stores
Upholstery materials stores

Cross-References. Establishments primarily engaged in—

- Retailing sewing supplies via electronic home shopping, mail-order, or direct sale—are classified in Subsector 454, Nonstore Retailers;
- Retailing new sewing machines only and in combination with retailing other new appliances—are classified in U.S. Industry 443111, Household Appliance Stores; and
- Retailing used sewing, needlework, and piece goods—are classified in Industry 453310, Used Merchandise Stores.

45114 Musical Instrument and Supplies Stores[CAN]

See industry description for 451140 below.

451140 Musical Instrument and Supplies Stores[CAN]

This industry comprises establishments primarily engaged in retailing new musical instruments, sheet music, and related supplies; or retailing these new products in combination with musical instrument repair, rental, or music instruction.

Illustrative Examples:

Music instrument stores
Piano stores
Sheet music stores

US—United States industry only. CAN—United States and Canadian industries are comparable. MEX—United States and Mexican industries are comparable. Blank—Canadian, Mexican, and United States industries are comparable.

Cross-References. Establishments primarily engaged in—

- Retailing musical instruments, sheet music, and related supplies via electronic home shopping, mail-order, or direct sale—are classified in Subsector 454, Nonstore Retailers;
- Retailing new musical recordings—are classified in Industry 451220, Prerecorded Tape, Compact Disc, and Record Stores; and
- Retailing used musical instruments, sheet music, and related supplies—are classified in Industry 453310, Used Merchandise Stores.

4512 Book, Periodical, and Music Stores[CAN]

This industry group comprises establishments primarily engaged in retailing new books, newspapers, magazines, and prerecorded audio and video media.

45121 Book Stores and News Dealers[CAN]

This industry comprises establishments primarily engaged in retailing new books, newspapers, magazines, and other periodicals.

Cross-References. Establishments primarily engaged in—

- Retailing newspapers, magazines, and other periodicals via electronic home shopping, mail-order, or direct sale—are classified in Subsector 454, Nonstore Retailers;
- Home delivery of newspapers—are classified in Industry 45439, Other Direct Selling Establishments; and
- Retailing used books, newspapers, magazines, and other periodicals—are classified in Industry 45331, Used Merchandise Stores.

451211 Book Stores[US]

This U.S. industry comprises establishments primarily engaged in retailing new books.

Cross-References. Establishments primarily engaged in—

- Retailing books via electronic home shopping, mail-order, or direct sale—are classified in Subsector 454, Nonstore Retailers; and
- Retailing used books—are classified in Industry 453310, Used Merchandise Stores.

US—United States industry only. CAN—United States and Canadian industries are comparable. MEX—United States and Mexican industries are comparable. Blank—Canadian, Mexican, and United States industries are comparable.

451212 News Dealers and Newsstands[US]

This U.S. industry comprises establishments primarily engaged in retailing current newspapers, magazines, and other periodicals.

Cross-References. Establishments primarily engaged in—

- Home delivery of newspapers—are classified in Industry 454390, Other Direct Selling Establishments;
- Retailing newspapers and periodicals by mail-order—are classified in Industry 454113, Mail-Order Houses; and
- Retailing used newspapers, magazines, and other periodicals—are classified in Industry 453310, Used Merchandise Stores.

45122 Prerecorded Tape, Compact Disc, and Record Stores[CAN]

See industry description for 451220 below.

451220 Prerecorded Tape, Compact Disc, and Record Stores[CAN]

This industry comprises establishments primarily engaged in retailing new prerecorded audio and video tapes, compact discs (CDs), digital video discs (DVDs), and phonograph records.

Cross-References. Establishments primarily engaged in—

- Retailing new computer software—are classified in Industry 443120, Computer and Software Stores;
- Retailing prerecorded tapes, compact discs, digital video discs (DVDs), and records by mail-order—are classified in Industry 454113, Mail-Order Houses;
- Retailing used phonograph records and prerecorded audio and video tapes and discs—are classified in Industry 453310, Used Merchandise Stores; and
- Retailing new audio sound equipment (except automotive)—are classified in U.S. Industry 443112, Radio, Television, and Other Electronics Stores.

452 General Merchandise Stores[CAN]

Industries in the General Merchandise Stores subsector retail new general merchandise from fixed point-of-sale locations. Establishments in this subsector are unique in that they have the equipment and staff capable of retailing a large variety

---

US—United States industry only. CAN—United States and Canadian industries are comparable. MEX—United States and Mexican industries are comparable. Blank—Canadian, Mexican, and United States industries are comparable.

of goods from a single location. This includes a variety of display equipment and staff trained to provide information on many lines of products.

4521 Department Stores[CAN]

45211 Department Stores[CAN]

This industry comprises establishments known as department stores primarily engaged in retailing a wide range of the following new products with no one merchandise line predominating: apparel, furniture, appliances and home furnishings; and selected additional items, such as paint, hardware, toiletries, cosmetics, photographic equipment, jewelry, toys, and sporting goods. Merchandise lines are normally arranged in separate departments.

Cross-References. Establishments primarily engaged in—

- Retailing packaged grocery items in combination with general lines of merchandise with no one merchandise line predominating—are classified in Industry 45291, Warehouse Clubs and Supercenters;
- Retailing apparel without a significant amount of housewares or general merchandise—are classified in Subsector 448, Clothing and Clothing Accessories Stores;
- Retailing general lines of merchandise via electronic home shopping, mail-order, or direct sale—are classified in Subsector 454, Nonstore Retailers; and
- Retailing used merchandise—are classified in Industry 45331, Used Merchandise Stores.

452111 Department Stores (except Discount Department Stores)[US]

This U.S. industry comprises establishments known as department stores that have separate departments for various merchandise lines, such as apparel, jewelry, home furnishings, and linens, each with separate cash registers and sales associates. Department stores in this industry generally do not have central customer checkout and cash register facilities.

Cross-References. Establishments primarily engaged in—

- Retailing apparel without a significant amount of housewares or general merchandise—are classified in Subsector 448, Clothing and Clothing Accessories Stores;

US—United States industry only. CAN—United States and Canadian industries are comparable. MEX—United States and Mexican industries are comparable. Blank—Canadian, Mexican, and United States industries are comparable.

- Retailing a wide variety of general merchandise in department stores with central customer checkout and cash register facilities—are classified in U.S. Industry 452112, Discount Department Stores; and
- Retailing a wide variety of general merchandise in combination with a general line of perishable groceries, such as fresh meat, vegetable, and dairy products—are classified in Industry 452910, Warehouse Clubs and Supercenters.

452112 Discount Department Stores[US]

This U.S. industry comprises establishments known as department stores that have central customer checkout areas, generally in the front of the store, and that may have additional cash registers located in one or more individual departments. Department stores in this industry sell a wide range of general merchandise (except fresh, perishable foods).

Cross-References. Establishments primarily engaged in—

- Retailing apparel without a significant amount of housewares or general merchandise—are classified in Subsector 448, Clothing and Clothing Accessories Stores;
- Retailing a wide variety of general merchandise in department stores with separate cash registers and sales associates for each department—are classified in U.S. Industry 452111, Department Stores (except Discount Department Stores); and
- Retailing a wide variety of general merchandise in combination with a general line of perishable groceries, such as fresh meat, vegetable, and dairy products—are classified in Industry 452910, Warehouse Clubs and Supercenters.

4529 Other General Merchandise Stores[CAN]

This industry group comprises establishments primarily engaged in retailing new goods in general merchandise stores (except department stores).

45291 Warehouse Clubs and Supercenters[CAN]

See industry description for 452910 below.

452910 Warehouse Clubs and Supercenters[CAN]

This industry comprises establishments known as warehouse clubs, superstores or supercenters primarily engaged in retailing a general line of groceries in combina-

US—United States industry only. CAN—United States and Canadian industries are comparable. MEX—United States and Mexican industries are comparable. Blank—Canadian, Mexican, and United States industries are comparable.

tion with general lines of new merchandise, such as apparel, furniture, and appliances.

Cross-References. Establishments primarily engaged in—

- Retailing general lines of merchandise via electronic home shopping, mail-order, or direct sale—are classified in Subsector 454, Nonstore Retailers;
- Retailing a general line of food, generally known as supermarkets and grocery stores—are classified in Industry 445110, Supermarkets and Other Grocery (except Convenience) Stores;
- Retailing general lines of new merchandise with little grocery item sales—are classified in Industry 452990, All Other General Merchandise Stores;
- Retailing new merchandise in discount department stores—are classified in U.S. Industry 452112, Discount Department Stores; and
- Retailing new merchandise in department stores other than discount department stores—are classified in U.S. Industry 452111, Department Stores (except Discount Department Stores); and
- Retailing used merchandise—are classified in Industry 453310, Used Merchandise Stores.

45299 All Other General Merchandise Stores[CAN]

See industry description for 452990 below.

452990 All Other General Merchandise Stores[US]

This industry comprises establishments primarily engaged in retailing new goods in general merchandise stores (except department stores, warehouse clubs, superstores, and supercenters). These establishments retail a general line of new merchandise, such as apparel, automotive parts, dry goods, hardware, groceries, housewares or home furnishings, and other lines in limited amounts, with none of the lines predominating.

Illustrative Examples:

Dollar stores
General merchandise catalog showrooms (except catalog mail-order)
General stores
General merchandise trading posts
Home and auto supply stores
Variety stores

Cross-References. Establishments primarily engaged in—

- Retailing general lines of merchandise via electronic home shopping, mail-order, or direct sale—are classified in Subsector 454, Nonstore Retailers;

US—United States industry only. CAN—United States and Canadian industries are comparable. MEX—United States and Mexican industries are comparable. Blank—Canadian, Mexican, and United States industries are comparable.

- Retailing automotive parts—are classified in Industry 441310, Automotive Parts and Accessories Stores;
- Retailing merchandise in department stores—are classified in U.S. Industry 452111, Department Stores (except Discount Department Stores);
- Retailing merchandise in warehouse clubs, superstores, or supercenters—are classified in Industry 452910, Warehouse Clubs and Supercenters;
- Retailing merchandise in catalogue showrooms of mail-order houses—are classified in U.S. Industry 454113, Mail-Order Houses;
- Retailing a general line of new hardware items, known as hardware stores—are classified in Industry 444130, Hardware Stores;
- Retailing a general line of new home repair and improvement materials and supplies, known as home centers—are classified in Industry 444110, Home Centers; and
- Retailing used merchandise—are classified in Industry 453310, Used Merchandise Stores.

453 Miscellaneous Store Retailers[CAN]

Industries in the Miscellaneous Store Retailers subsector retail merchandise from fixed point-of-sale locations (except new or used motor vehicles and parts; new furniture and house furnishings; new appliances and electronic products; new building materials; and garden equipment and supplies; food and beverages; health and personal care goods; gasoline; new clothing and accessories; and new sporting goods, hobby goods, books, and music). Establishments in this subsector include stores with unique characteristics like florists, used merchandise stores, and pet and pet supply stores as well as other store retailers.

4531 Florists[CAN]

45311 Florists[CAN]

See industry description for 453110 below.

453110 Florists[CAN]

This industry comprises establishments known as florists primarily engaged in retailing cut flowers, floral arrangements, and potted plants purchased from others. These establishments usually prepare the arrangements they sell.

Cross-References. Establishments primarily engaged in—

- Retailing flowers or nursery stock grown on premises—are classified in Industry 11142, Nursery and Floriculture Production;

US—United States industry only. CAN—United States and Canadian industries are comparable. MEX—United States and Mexican industries are comparable. Blank—Canadian, Mexican, and United States industries are comparable.

- Retailing trees, shrubs, plants, seeds, bulbs, and sod grown elsewhere—are classified in Industry 444220, Nursery, Garden Center and Farm Supply Stores; and
- Retailing flowers via electronic home shopping, mail-order, or direct sale—are classified in Subsector 454, Nonstore Retailers.

4532 Office Supplies, Stationery, and Gift Stores[CAN]

45321 Office Supplies and Stationery Stores[CAN]

See industry description for 453210 below.

453210 Office Supplies and Stationery Stores[CAN]

This industry comprises establishments primarily engaged in one or more of the following: (1) retailing new stationery, school supplies, and office supplies; (2) selling a combination of new office equipment, furniture, and supplies; and (3) selling new office equipment, furniture, and supplies in combination with selling new computers.

Cross-References. Establishments primarily engaged in—

- Retailing stationery, school supplies, and office supplies via electronic shopping, mail-order, or direct sale—are classified in Subsector 454, Nonstore Retailers;
- Retailing greeting cards—are classified in Industry 453220, Gift, Novelty, and Souvenir Stores;
- Retailing new typewriters—are classified in U.S. Industry 443112, Radio, Television, and Other Electronics Stores;
- Retailing new computers without retailing other consumer-type electronic products or office equipment, furniture, and supplies—are classified in Industry 443120, Computer and Software Stores;
- Printing business forms—are classified in Industry 32311, Printing;
- Retailing new office furniture—are classified in Industry 442110, Furniture Stores; and
- Retailing used office supplies—are classified in Industry 453310, Used Merchandise Stores.

45322 Gift, Novelty, and Souvenir Stores[CAN]

See industry description for 453220 below.

US—United States industry only. CAN—United States and Canadian industries are comparable. MEX—United States and Mexican industries are comparable. Blank—Canadian, Mexican, and United States industries are comparable.

453220 Gift, Novelty, and Souvenir Stores[CAN]

This industry comprises establishments primarily engaged in retailing new gifts, novelty merchandise, souvenirs, greeting cards, seasonal and holiday decorations, and curios.

Illustrative Examples:

Balloon shops
Christmas stores
Curio shops
Gift shops
Greeting card shops
Novelty shops
Souvenir shops

Cross-References. Establishments primarily engaged in—

- Retailing gifts and novelties via electronic home shopping, mail-order, or direct sale—are classified in Subsector 454, Nonstore Retailers;
- Retailing stationery—are classified in Industry 453210, Office Supplies and Stationery Stores; and
- Retailing used curios and novelties—are classified in Industry 453310, Used Merchandise Stores.

4533 Used Merchandise Stores[CAN]

45331 Used Merchandise Stores[CAN]

See industry description for 453310 below.

453310 Used Merchandise Stores[CAN]

This industry comprises establishments primarily engaged in retailing used merchandise, antiques, and secondhand goods (except motor vehicles, such as automobiles, RVs, motorcycles, and boats; motor vehicle parts; tires; and mobile homes).

Illustrative Examples:

Antique shops
Used book stores
Used clothing stores
Used household-type appliance stores
Used merchandise thrift shops
Used sporting goods stores

Cross-References. Establishments primarily engaged in—

- Retailing used merchandise via electronic home shopping, mail-order, or direct sale—are classified in Subsector 454, Nonstore Retailers;

US—United States industry only. CAN—United States and Canadian industries are comparable. MEX—United States and Mexican industries are comparable. Blank—Canadian, Mexican, and United States industries are comparable.

- Operating pawnshops—are classified in U.S. Industry 522298, All Other Nondepository Credit Intermediation;
- Retailing used automobiles—are classified in Industry 441120, Used Car Dealers;
- Retailing used automobile parts (except tires and tubes)—are classified in Industry 441310, Automotive Parts and Accessories Stores;
- Retailing used tires—are classified in Industry 441320, Tire Dealers;
- Retailing used mobile homes—are classified in Industry 453930, Manufactured (Mobile) Home Dealers;
- Retailing used motorcycles—are classified in U.S. Industry 441221, Motorcycle Dealers;
- Retailing used recreational vehicles—are classified in Industry 441210, Recreational Vehicle Dealers;
- Retailing used boats—are classified in U.S. Industry 441222, Boat Dealers;
- Retailing used aircraft, snowmobiles, and utility trailers—are classified in U.S. Industry 441229, All Other Motor Vehicle Dealers; and
- Retailing a general line of used merchandise on an auction basis (except electronic auctions)—are classified in U.S. Industry 453998, All Other Miscellaneous Store Retailers (except Tobacco Stores).

4539 Other Miscellaneous Store Retailers[CAN]

This industry group comprises establishments primarily engaged in retailing new miscellaneous specialty store merchandise (except motor vehicle and parts dealers; furniture and home furnishings stores; consumer-type electronics and appliance stores; building material and garden equipment and supplies dealers; food and beverage stores; health and personal care stores; gasoline stations; clothing and clothing accessories stores; sporting goods, hobby, book, and music stores; general merchandise stores; florists; office supplies, stationery, and gift stores; and used merchandise stores).

45391 Pet and Pet Supplies Stores[CAN]

See industry descriptions for 453910 below.

453910 Pet and Pet Supplies Stores[CAN]

This industry comprises establishments primarily engaged in retailing pets, pet foods, and pet supplies.

US—United States industry only. CAN—United States and Canadian industries are comparable. MEX—United States and Mexican industries are comparable. Blank—Canadian, Mexican, and United States industries are comparable.

Cross References. Establishments primarily engaged in—

- Retailing pets, pet foods, and pet supplies via electronic home shopping, mail-order, or direct sale—are classified in Subsector 454, Nonstore Retailers;
- Providing pet grooming and boarding services—are classified in Industry 812910, Pet Care (except Veterinary) Services; and
- Providing veterinary services—are classified in Industry 541940, Veterinary Services.

45392 Art Dealers[CAN]

See industry descriptions for 453920 below.

453920 Art Dealers[CAN]

This industry comprises establishments primarily engaged in retailing original and limited edition art works. Included in this industry are establishments primarily engaged in displaying works of art for retail sale in art galleries.

Cross-References. Establishments primarily engaged in—

- Retailing original and limited edition art works via electronic home shopping, mail-order, or direct sale—are classified in Subsector 454, Nonstore Retailers;
- Retailing art reproductions (except limited editions)—are classified in U.S. Industry 442299, All Other Home Furnishings Stores;
- Retailing artists' supplies—are classified in U.S. Industry 453998, All Other Miscellaneous Store Retailers (except Tobacco Stores); and
- Displaying works of art not for retail sale in art galleries—are classified in Industry 712110, Museums.

45393 Manufactured (Mobile) Home Dealers[CAN]

See industry description for 453930 below.

453930 Manufactured (Mobile) Home Dealers[CAN]

This industry comprises establishments primarily engaged in retailing new and/or used manufactured homes (i.e., mobile homes), parts, and equipment.

Cross-References. Establishments primarily engaged in—

- Retailing new or used motor homes, campers, and travel trailers—are classified in Industry 441210, Recreational Vehicle Dealers; and

US—United States industry only. CAN—United States and Canadian industries are comparable. MEX—United States and Mexican industries are comparable. Blank—Canadian, Mexican, and United States industries are comparable.

- Retailing prefabricated buildings and kits without construction—are classified in Industry 444190, Other Building Material Dealers.

45399 All Other Miscellaneous Store Retailers[CAN]

This industry comprises establishments primarily engaged in retailing specialized lines of merchandise (except motor vehicle and parts dealers; furniture and home furnishings stores; electronic and appliance stores; building material and garden equipment and supplies dealers; food and beverage stores; health and personal care stores; gasoline stations; clothing and clothing accessories stores; sporting goods, hobby, book, and music stores; general merchandise stores; florists; office supplies, stationery and gift stores; used merchandise stores; pet and pet supplies; art dealers; and manufactured home (i.e., mobile home) dealers). This industry also includes establishments primarily engaged in retailing a general line of new and used merchandise on an auction basis (except electronic auctions).

Illustrative Examples:

Art supply stores
Cemetery memorial (e.g., markers, headstones, vaults) dealers
Cigar stores
Swimming pool supply stores, new
Tobacco stores

Cross-References. Establishments primarily engaged in—

- Retailing merchandise via electronic home shopping, mail-order, or direct sale—are classified in Subsector 454, Nonstore Retailers;
- Auctioning on the location of others as independent auctioneers—are classified in Industry 56199, All Other Support Services;
- Retailing pets and pet supplies—are classified in Industry 45391, Pet and Pet Supplies Stores;
- Retailing original and limited edition art works—are classified in Industry 45392, Art Dealers;
- Retailing manufactured homes (i.e., mobile homes)—are classified in Industry 45393, Manufactured (Mobile) Home Dealers;
- Retailing new books—are classified in Industry 45121, Book Stores and News Dealers;
- Retailing new jewelry (except costume jewelry)—are classified in Industry 44831, Jewelry Stores;
- Retailing new costume jewelry—are classified in Industry 44815, Clothing Accessories Stores; and

US—United States industry only. CAN—United States and Canadian industries are comparable. MEX—United States and Mexican industries are comparable. Blank—Canadian, Mexican, and United States industries are comparable.

- Retailing used merchandise (except automobiles, RVs, mobile homes, motorcycles, boats, motor vehicle parts, and tires)—are classified in Industry 453310, Used Merchandise Stores.

453991 Tobacco Stores[US]

This U.S. industry comprises establishments primarily engaged in retailing cigarettes, cigars, tobacco, pipes, and other smokers' supplies.

Illustrative Examples:

Cigar stores
Cigarette stands (i.e., permanent)
Smokers' supply stores
Tobacco stores

Cross-References.

Establishments primarily engaged in retailing tobacco products and supplies via electronic home shopping, mail-order, or direct sale are classified in Subsector 454, Nonstore Retailers.

453998 All Other Miscellaneous Store Retailers (except Tobacco Stores)[US]

This U.S. industry comprises establishments primarily engaged in retailing specialized lines of merchandise (except motor vehicle and parts dealers; furniture and home furnishings stores; electronic and appliance stores; building material and garden equipment and supplies dealers; food and beverage stores; health and personal care stores; gasoline stations; clothing and clothing accessories stores; sporting goods, hobby, book and music stores; general merchandise stores; florists; office supplies, stationery and gift stores; used merchandise stores; pet and pet supplies stores; art dealers; manufactured home (i.e., mobile homes) dealers; and tobacco stores). This industry also includes establishments primarily engaged in retailing a general line of new and used merchandise on an auction basis.

Illustrative Examples:

Art supply stores
Candle shops
Cemetery memorial (e.g., headstones, markers, vaults) dealers
Collectors' items (e.g., autograph, coin, card, stamp) shops
Fireworks shops (permanent location)
Flower shops, artificial or dried
General merchandise auction houses
Home security equipment stores
Hot tub stores
Swimming pool supply stores
Trophy (e.g., awards and plaques) shops

US—United States industry only. CAN—United States and Canadian industries are comparable. MEX—United States and Mexican industries are comparable. Blank—Canadian, Mexican, and United States industries are comparable.

Cross-References. Establishments primarily engaged in—

- Retailing specialized lines of merchandise via electronic home shopping, mail-order, or direct sale—are classified in Subsector 454, Nonstore Retailers;
- Retailing merchandise via electronic auctions—are classified in Industry 454112, Electronic Auctions;
- Auctioning (i.e., on the location of others as independent auctioneers)—are classified in Industry 561990, All Other Support Services;
- Retailing pets and pet supplies—are classified in Industry 453910, Pet and Pet Supplies Stores;
- Retailing original and limited edition art works—are classified in Industry 453920, Art Dealers;
- Retailing manufactured homes (i.e., mobile homes)—are classified in Industry 453930, Manufactured (Mobile) Home Dealers;
- Retailing cigarettes, cigars, tobacco, pipes, and other smokers' supplies—are classified in U.S. Industry 453991, Tobacco Stores;
- Retailing antiques—are classified in Industry 453310, Used Merchandise Stores;
- Retailing new books—are classified in Industry 451211, Book Stores;
- Retailing new jewelry (except costume jewelry)—are classified in Industry 448310, Jewelry Stores; and
- Retailing new costume jewelry—are classified in Industry 448150, Clothing Accessories Stores.

454 Nonstore Retailers[CAN]

Industries in the Nonstore Retailers subsector retail merchandise using methods, such as the broadcasting of infomercials, the broadcasting and publishing of direct-response advertising, the publishing of paper and electronic catalogs, door-to-door solicitation, in-home demonstration, selling from portable stalls and distribution through vending machines. Establishments in this subsector include mail-order houses, vending machine operators, home delivery sales, door-to-door sales, party plan sales, electronic shopping, and sales through portable stalls (e.g., street vendors, except food). Establishments engaged in the direct sale (i.e., nonstore) of products, such as home heating oil dealers and newspaper delivery are included in this subsector.

4541 Electronic Shopping and Mail-Order Houses[CAN]

45411 Electronic Shopping and Mail-Order Houses[CAN]

This industry comprises establishments primarily engaged in retailing all types of merchandise using non-store means, such as catalogs, toll free telephone num-

---

US—United States industry only. CAN—United States and Canadian industries are comparable. MEX—United States and Mexican industries are comparable. Blank—Canadian, Mexican, and United States industries are comparable.

bers, or electronic media, such as interactive television or computer. Included in this industry are establishments primarily engaged in retailing from catalog showrooms of mail-order houses.

Illustrative Examples:

- Catalog (i.e., order-taking) office of mail- order house
- Collectors' items, mail-order houses
- Computer software, mail-order houses
- Home shopping television orders
- Mail-order book clubs (not publishing)
- Mail-order houses
- Web retailers
- Internet auction sites, retail

Cross-References. Establishments primarily engaged in—

- Store retailing or a combination of store retailing and non-store retailing in the same establishment—are classified in Sector 44-45, Retail Trade, based on the classification of the store portion of the activity;
- Facilitating business to business electronic sales of new and used merchandise on an auction basis using the Internet—are classified in Industry 42511, Business to Business Electronic Markets; and
- Providing telemarketing (e.g., telephone marketing) services for others—are classified in Industry 56142, Telephone Call Centers.

454111 Electronic Shopping[US]

This U.S. Industry comprises establishments engaged in retailing all types of merchandise using the Internet.

Cross-References. Establishments primarily engaged in—

- Store retailing or a combination of store retailing and Internet retailing in the same establishment—are classified in NAICS 44-45, Retail Trade, based on the classification of the store portion of the activity; and
- Retailing all types of merchandise using catalogs or television to generate clients and display merchandise—are classified in U.S. Industry 454113, Mail-Order Houses.

454112 Electronic Auctions[US]

This U.S. Industry comprises establishments engaged in providing sites for and facilitating consumer-to-consumer or business-to-consumer trade in new and used goods, on an auction basis, using the Internet. Establishments in this industry provide the electronic location for retail auctions, but do not take title to the goods being sold.

US—United States industry only. CAN—United States and Canadian industries are comparable. MEX—United States and Mexican industries are comparable. Blank—Canadian, Mexican, and United States industries are comparable.

Cross-References. Establishments primarily engaged in—

- Retailing a general line of new and used merchandise on an auction basis from physical auction sites—are classified in U.S. Industry 453998, All Other Miscellaneous Store Retailers (except Tobacco Stores);
- Facilitating business-to-business sales of new and used merchandise on an auction basis using the Internet—are classified in U.S. Industry 425110, Business to Business Electronic Markets; and
- A combination of Internet auction and auction house sales in the same establishment—are classified in NAICS 44-45, Retail Trade, based on the classification of the auction house portion of the activity

454113 Mail-Order Houses[US]

This U.S. industry comprises establishments primarily engaged in retailing all types of merchandise using mail catalogs or television to generate clients and display merchandise. Included in this industry are establishments primarily engaged in retailing from catalog showrooms of mail-order houses as well as establishments providing a combination of Internet and mail-order sales.

Illustrative Examples:

Catalog (i.e., order-taking) offices of mail-order houses
Home shopping television orders
Mail-order book clubs (not publishing)
Collectors' items, mail-order houses
Mail-order houses
Computer software, mail-order houses

Cross-References. Establishments primarily engaged in—

- Providing telemarketing (e.g., telephone marketing) services for others—are classified in U.S. Industry 561422, Telemarketing Bureaus; and
- Retailing merchandise using store and nonstore methods at the same establishment—are classified in Store retail activities based on the store portion of the activity.

4542 Vending Machine Operators[CAN]

45421 Vending Machine Operators[CAN]

See industry description for 454210 below.

454210 Vending Machine Operators[CAN]

This industry comprises establishments primarily engaged in retailing merchandise through vending machines that they service.

US—United States industry only. CAN—United States and Canadian industries are comparable. MEX—United States and Mexican industries are comparable. Blank—Canadian, Mexican, and United States industries are comparable.

Cross-References. Establishments primarily engaged in—

- Selling insurance policies through vending machines—are classified in Subsector 524, Insurance Carriers and Related Activities;
- Supplying and servicing coin-operated photobooths, restrooms, and lockers—are classified in Industry 812990, All Other Personal Services; and
- Supplying and servicing coin-operated amusement and gambling devices in places of business operated by others—are classified in Subsector 713, Amusement, Gambling, and Recreation Industries.

4543 Direct Selling Establishments[CAN]

This industry group comprises establishments primarily engaged in nonstore retailing (except electronic, mail-order, or vending machine sales). These establishments typically go to the customers' location rather than the customer coming to them (e.g., door-to-door sales, home parties). Examples of establishments in this industry are home delivery newspaper routes; home delivery of heating oil, liquefied petroleum (LP) gas, and other fuels; locker meat provisioners; frozen food and freezer plan providers; coffee-break services providers; and bottled water or water softener services.

45431 Fuel Dealers[CAN]

This industry comprises establishments primarily engaged in retailing heating oil, liquefied petroleum (LP) gas, and other fuels via direct selling.

Cross-References. Establishments primarily engaged in—

- Providing oil burner repair services—are classified in Industry 81141, Home and Garden Equipment and Appliance Repair and Maintenance; and
- Installing oil burners—are classified in Industry 23822, Plumbing, Heating, and Air-Conditioning Contractors.

454311 Heating Oil Dealers[US]

This U.S. industry comprises establishments primarily engaged in retailing heating oil via direct selling.

Cross-References. Establishments primarily engaged in—

- Providing oil burner repair services—are classified in U.S. Industry 811411, Home and Garden Equipment Repair and Maintenance; and

US—United States industry only. CAN—United States and Canadian industries are comparable. MEX—United States and Mexican industries are comparable. Blank—Canadian, Mexican, and United States industries are comparable.

- Installing oil burners—are classified in Industry 238220, Plumbing, Heating, and Air-Conditioning Contractors.

454312 Liquefied Petroleum Gas (Bottled Gas) Dealers[US]

This U.S. industry comprises establishments primarily engaged in retailing liquefied petroleum (LP) gas via direct selling.

454319 Other Fuel Dealers[US]

This U.S. industry comprises establishments primarily engaged in retailing fuels (except liquefied petroleum gas and heating oil) via direct selling.

45439 Other Direct Selling Establishments[CAN]

See industry description for 454390 below.

454390 Other Direct Selling Establishments[CAN]

This industry comprises establishments primarily engaged in retailing merchandise (except food for immediate consumption and fuel) via direct sale to the customer by means, such as in-house sales (i.e., party plan merchandising), truck or wagon sales, and portable stalls (i.e., street vendors).

Illustrative Examples:

Direct selling bottled water providers
Direct selling coffee-break service providers
Direct selling frozen food and freezer plan providers
Direct selling home delivery newspaper routes
Direct selling party plan merchandisers
Direct selling locker meat provisioners

Cross-References. Establishments primarily engaged in—

- Preparing and selling meals and snacks for immediate consumption from motorized vehicles or nonmotorized carts catering a route—are classified in Industry 722330, Mobile Food Services;
- Retailing heating oil via direct sale—are classified in U.S. Industry 454311, Heating Oil Dealers;
- Retailing liquefied petroleum (LP) gas via direct sale—are classified in U.S. Industry 454312, Liquefied Petroleum Gas (Bottled Gas) Dealers; and
- Retailing other fuels, such as coal or wood, via direct sale—are classified in U.S. Industry 454319, Other Fuel Dealers.

US—United States industry only. CAN—United States and Canadian industries are comparable. MEX—United States and Mexican industries are comparable. Blank—Canadian, Mexican, and United States industries are comparable.

Sector 48-49—Transportation and Warehousing

The Sector as a Whole

The Transportation and Warehousing sector includes industries providing transportation of passengers and cargo, warehousing and storage for goods, scenic and sightseeing transportation, and support activities related to modes of transportation. Establishments in these industries use transportation equipment or transportation related facilities as a productive asset. The type of equipment depends on the mode of transportation. The modes of transportation are air, rail, water, road, and pipeline.

The Transportation and Warehousing sector distinguishes three basic types of activities: subsectors for each mode of transportation, a subsector for warehousing and storage, and a subsector for establishments providing support activities for transportation. In addition, there are subsectors for establishments that provide passenger transportation for scenic and sightseeing purposes, postal services, and courier services.

A separate subsector for support activities is established in the sector because, first, support activities for transportation are inherently multimodal, such as freight transportation arrangement, or have multimodal aspects. Secondly, there are production process similarities among the support activity industries.

One of the support activities identified in the support activity subsector is the routine repair and maintenance of transportation equipment (e.g., aircraft at an airport, railroad rolling stock at a railroad terminal, or ships at a harbor or port facility). Such establishments do not perform complete overhauling or rebuilding of transportation equipment (i.e., periodic restoration of transportation equipment to original design specifications) or transportation equipment conversion (i.e., major modification to systems). An establishment that primarily performs factory (or shipyard) overhauls, rebuilding, or conversions of aircraft, railroad rolling stock, or a ship is classified in Subsector 336, Transportation Equipment Manufacturing according to the type of equipment.

Many of the establishments in this sector often operate on networks, with physical facilities, labor forces, and equipment spread over an extensive geographic area.

Warehousing establishments in this sector are distinguished from merchant wholesaling in that the warehouse establishments do not sell the goods.

Excluded from this sector are establishments primarily engaged in providing travel agent services that support transportation and other establishments, such as hotels, businesses, and government agencies. These establishments are classified in Sector 56, Administrative and Support and Waste Management and Remediation Services. Also, establishments primarily engaged in providing rental and leasing of transportation equipment without operator are classified in Subsector 532, Rental and Leasing Services.

US—United States industry only. CAN—United States and Canadian industries are comparable. MEX—United States and Mexican industries are comparable. Blank—Canadian, Mexican, and United States industries are comparable.

481 Air Transportation

Industries in the Air Transportation subsector provide air transportation of passengers and/or cargo using aircraft, such as airplanes and helicopters. The subsector distinguishes scheduled from nonscheduled air transportation. Scheduled air carriers fly regular routes on regular schedules and operate even if flights are only partially loaded. Nonscheduled carriers often operate during nonpeak time slots at busy airports. These establishments have more flexibility with respect to choice of airport, hours of operation, load factors, and similar operational characteristics. Nonscheduled carriers provide chartered air transportation of passengers, cargo, or specialty flying services. Specialty flying services establishments use general-purpose aircraft to provide a variety of specialized flying services.

Scenic and sightseeing air transportation and air courier services are not included in this subsector but are included in Subsector 487, Scenic and Sightseeing Transportation and in Subsector 492, Couriers and Messengers. Although these activities may use aircraft, they are different from the activities included in air transportation. Air sightseeing does not usually involve place-to-place transportation; the passenger's flight (e.g., balloon ride, aerial sightseeing) typically starts and ends at the same location. Courier services (individual package or cargo delivery) include more than air transportation; road transportation is usually required to deliver the cargo to the intended recipient.

4811 Scheduled Air Transportation

48111 Scheduled Air Transportation

This industry comprises establishments primarily engaged in providing air transportation of passengers and/or cargo over regular routes and on regular schedules. Establishments in this industry operate flights even if partially loaded. Establishments primarily engaged in providing scheduled air transportation of mail on a contract basis are included in this industry.

Illustrative Examples:

Air commuter carriers, scheduled
Scheduled air cargo carriers (except air couriers)
Scheduled air passenger carriers
Scheduled helicopter passenger carriers

Cross-References. Establishments primarily engaged in—

- Providing air courier services—are classified in Industry 49211, Couriers;
- Providing air transportation of passengers, cargo, or specialty flying services with no regular routes and regular schedules—are classified in Industry 48121, Nonscheduled Air Transportation; and

---

US—United States industry only. CAN—United States and Canadian industries are comparable. MEX—United States and Mexican industries are comparable. Blank—Canadian, Mexican, and United States industries are comparable.

- Providing helicopter rides for scenic and sightseeing transportation—are classified in Industry 48799, Scenic and Sightseeing Transportation, Other.

481111 Scheduled Passenger Air Transportation[US]

This U.S. industry comprises establishments primarily engaged in providing air transportation of passengers or passengers and freight over regular routes and on regular schedules. Establishments in this industry operate flights even if partially loaded. Scheduled air passenger carriers including commuter and helicopter carriers (except scenic and sightseeing) are included in this industry.

Cross-References. Establishments primarily engaged in—

- Providing air transportation of passengers or passengers and cargo with no regular routes and regular schedules—are classified in U.S. Industry 481211, Nonscheduled Chartered Passenger Air Transportation;
- Providing helicopter rides for scenic and sightseeing transportation—are classified in Industry 487990, Scenic and Sightseeing Transportation, Other; and
- Providing air transportation of cargo (without transporting passengers) over regular routes and on regular schedules—are classified in U.S. Industry 481112, Scheduled Freight Air Transportation.

481112 Scheduled Freight Air Transportation[US]

This U.S. industry comprises establishments primarily engaged in providing air transportation of cargo without transporting passengers over regular routes and on regular schedules. Establishments in this industry operate flights even if partially loaded. Establishments primarily engaged in providing scheduled air transportation of mail on a contract basis are included in this industry.

Cross-References. Establishments primarily engaged in—

- Providing air courier services—are classified in Industry 492110, Couriers;
- Providing air transportation of cargo with no regular routes and regular schedules—are classified in U.S. Industry 481212, Nonscheduled Chartered Freight Air Transportation; and
- Providing air transportation of passengers or passengers and cargo over regular routes and on regular schedules—are classified in U.S. Industry 481111, Scheduled Passenger Air Transportation.

US—United States industry only. CAN—United States and Canadian industries are comparable. MEX—United States and Mexican industries are comparable. Blank—Canadian, Mexican, and United States industries are comparable.

4812 Nonscheduled Air Transportation

48121 Nonscheduled Air Transportation

This industry comprises establishments primarily engaged in (1) providing air transportation of passengers and/or cargo with no regular routes and regular schedules or (2) providing specialty flying services with no regular routes and regular schedules using general purpose aircraft. These establishments have more flexibility with respect to choice of airports, hours of operation, load factors, and similar operational characteristics.

Illustrative Examples:

Air taxi services
Aircraft charter services
Nonscheduled air freight transportation services
Nonscheduled air passenger transportation services

Cross-References. Establishments primarily engaged in—

- Crop dusting using specialized aircraft—are classified in Industry 11511, Support Activities for Crop Production;
- Fighting forest fires using specialized water bombers—are classified in Industry 11531, Support Activities for Forestry;
- Providing air transportation of passengers and/or cargo over regular routes and on regular schedules—are classified in Industry 48111, Scheduled Air Transportation;
- Providing specialized air sightseeing services—are classified in Industry 48799, Scenic and Sightseeing Transportation, Other;
- Aerial gathering of geophysical data—are classified in Industry 54136, Geophysical Surveying and Mapping Services;
- Providing aerial and/or other surveying and mapping services—are classified in Industry 54137, Surveying and Mapping (except Geophysical) Services;
- Providing air ambulance services using specialized equipment—are classified in Industry 62191, Ambulance Services;
- Operating specialized flying schools, including all training for commercial pilots—are classified in Industry 61151, Technical and Trade Schools;
- Operating recreation aviation clubs—are classified in Industry 71399, All Other Amusement and Recreation Industries;
- Operating advocacy aviation clubs—are classified in U.S. Industry 81331, Social Advocacy Organizations; and
- Providing air courier services—are classified in Industry 49211, Couriers.

US—United States industry only. CAN—United States and Canadian industries are comparable. MEX—United States and Mexican industries are comparable. Blank—Canadian, Mexican, and United States industries are comparable.

481211 Nonscheduled Chartered Passenger Air Transportation[US]

This U.S. industry comprises establishments primarily engaged in providing air transportation of passengers or passengers and cargo with no regular routes and regular schedules.

Cross-References. Establishments primarily engaged in—

- Providing specialty air transportation or flying services with no regular routes and regular schedules using general purpose aircraft—are classified in U.S. Industry 481219, Other Nonscheduled Air Transportation;
- Providing specialized air sightseeing services—are classified in Industry 487990, Scenic and Sightseeing Transportation, Other;
- Providing air transportation of passengers or passengers and cargo over regular routes and on regular schedules—are classified in U.S. Industry 481111, Scheduled Passenger Air Transportation; and
- Providing air transportation of cargo (without transporting passengers) with no regular routes and schedules—are classified in U.S. Industry 481212, Nonscheduled Chartered Freight Air Transportation.

481212 Nonscheduled Chartered Freight Air Transportation[US]

This U.S. industry comprises establishments primarily engaged in providing air transportation of cargo without transporting passengers with no regular routes and regular schedules.

Cross-References. Establishments primarily engaged in—

- Providing specialty air transportation or flying services with no regular routes and regular schedules using general purpose aircraft—are classified in U.S. Industry 481219, Other Nonscheduled Air Transportation;
- Providing air courier services—are classified in Industry 492110, Couriers;
- Providing air transportation of cargo without transporting passengers over regular routes and on regular schedules—are classified in U.S. Industry 481112, Scheduled Freight Air Transportation; and
- Providing air transportation of cargo and passengers with no regular routes and schedules—are classified in U.S. Industry 481211, Nonscheduled Chartered Passenger Air Transportation.

481219 Other Nonscheduled Air Transportation[US]

This U.S. industry comprises establishments primarily engaged in providing air transportation with no regular routes and regular schedules (except nonscheduled

US—United States industry only. CAN—United States and Canadian industries are comparable. MEX—United States and Mexican industries are comparable. Blank—Canadian, Mexican, and United States industries are comparable.

chartered passenger and/or cargo air transportation). These establishments provide a variety of specialty air transportation or flying services based on individual customer needs using general purpose aircraft.

Illustrative Examples:

Aircraft charter services (i.e., general purpose aircraft used for a variety of specialty air and flying services)

Aviation clubs providing a variety of air transportation activities to the general public

Cross-References. Establishments primarily engaged in—

- Providing air transportation of passengers or passengers and cargo with no regular routes and regular schedules—are classified in U.S. Industry 481211, Nonscheduled Chartered Passenger Air Transportation;
- Providing air transportation of cargo without transporting passengers with no regular routes and regular schedules—are classified in U.S. Industry 481212, Nonscheduled Chartered Freight Air Transportation;
- Crop dusting using specialized aircraft—are classified in U.S. Industry 115112, Soil Preparation, Planting, and Cultivating;
- Fighting forest fires using specialized water bombers—are classified in Industry 115310, Support Activities for Forestry;
- Providing specialized air sightseeing services—are classified in Industry 487990, Scenic and Sightseeing Transportation, Other;
- Operating specialized flying schools, including all training for commercial pilots—are classified in U.S. Industry 611512, Flight Training;
- Providing specialized air ambulance services using specialized equipment—are classified in U.S. Industry 621999, All Other Miscellaneous Ambulatory Health Care Services;
- Operating recreation aviation clubs—are classified in Industry 713990, All Other Amusement and Recreation Industries;
- Operating advocacy aviation clubs—are classified in U.S. Industry 813319, Other Social Advocacy Organizations;
- Aerial gathering of geophysical data for surveying and mapping—are classified in Industry 541360, Geophysical Surveying and Mapping Services; and
- Providing aerial and/or other surveying and mapping services—are classified in Industry 541370, Surveying and Mapping (except Geophysical) Services.

US—United States industry only. CAN—United States and Canadian industries are comparable. MEX—United States and Mexican industries are comparable. Blank—Canadian, Mexican, and United States industries are comparable.

482 Rail Transportation

Industries in the Rail Transportation subsector provide rail transportation of passengers and/or cargo using railroad rolling stock. The railroads in this subsector primarily either operate on networks, with physical facilities, labor force, and equipment spread over an extensive geographic area, or operate over a short distance on a local rail line.

Scenic and sightseeing rail transportation and street railroads, commuter rail, and rapid transit are not included in this subsector but are included in Subsector 487, Scenic and Sightseeing Transportation, and Subsector 485, Transit and Ground Passenger Transportation, respectively. Although these activities use railroad rolling stock, they are different from the activities included in rail transportation. Sightseeing and scenic railroads do not usually involve place-to-place transportation; the passenger's trip typically starts and ends at the same location. Commuter railroads operate in a manner more consistent with local and urban transit and are often part of integrated transit systems.

4821 Rail Transportation

48211 Rail Transportation

This industry comprises establishments primarily engaged in operating railroads (except street railroads, commuter rail, urban rapid transit, and scenic and sightseeing trains). Line-haul rail roads and short line railroads are included in this industry.

Cross-References. Establishments primarily engaged in—

- Operating street railroads, commuter rail, and urban rapid transit systems—are classified in Industry Group 4851, Urban Transit Systems;
- Operating scenic and sightseeing trains—are classified in Industry 48711, Scenic and Sightseeing Transportation, Land; and
- Operating switching and terminal facilities as separate establishments—are classified in Industry 48821, Support Activities for Rail Transportation.

482111 Line-Haul Railroads[US]

This U.S. industry comprises establishments known as line-haul railroads primarily engaged in operating railroads for the transport of passengers and/or cargo over a long distance within a rail network. These establishments provide for the intercity movement of trains between the terminals and stations on main and branch lines of a line-haul rail network (except for local switching services).

US—United States industry only. CAN—United States and Canadian industries are comparable. MEX—United States and Mexican industries are comparable. Blank—Canadian, Mexican, and United States industries are comparable.

Cross-References. Establishments primarily engaged in—

- Operating switching and terminal facilities as separate establishments—are classified in Industry 488210, Support Activities for Rail Transportation;
- Operating railroads over a short distance on local rail lines—are classified in U.S. Industry 482112, Short Line Railroads; and
- Operating commuter rail systems—are classified in U.S. Industry 485112, Commuter Rail Systems.

482112 Short Line Railroads[CAN]

This U.S. industry comprises establishments known as short line railroads primarily engaged in operating railroads for the transport of cargo over a short distance on local rail lines not part of a rail network.

Cross-References. Establishments primarily engaged in—

- Operating street railroads, commuter rail, and urban rapid transit systems—are classified in Industry Group 4851, Urban Transit Systems;
- Operating scenic and sightseeing trains—are classified in Industry 487110, Scenic and Sightseeing Transportation, Land;
- Operating switching and terminal facilities as separate establishments—are classified in Industry 488210, Support Activities for Rail Transportation; and
- Operating railroads for the transport of passengers and/or cargo over a long distance—are classified in U.S. Industry 482111, Line-Haul Railroads.

483 Water Transportation

Industries in the Water Transportation subsector provide water transportation of passengers and cargo using water craft, such as ships, barges, and boats.

The subsector is composed of two industry groups: (1) one for deep sea, coastal, and Great Lakes; and (2) one for inland water transportation. This split typically reflects the difference in equipment used.

Scenic and sightseeing water transportation services are not included in this subsector but are included in Subsector 487, Scenic and Sightseeing Transportation. Although these activities use water craft, they are different from the activities included in water transportation. Water sightseeing does not usually involve place-to-place transportation; the passenger's trip starts and ends at the same location.

US—United States industry only. CAN—United States and Canadian industries are comparable. MEX—United States and Mexican industries are comparable. Blank—Canadian, Mexican, and United States industries are comparable.

4831 Deep Sea, Coastal, and Great Lakes Water Transportation

48311 Deep Sea, Coastal, and Great Lakes Water Transportation

This industry comprises establishments primarily engaged in providing deep sea, coastal, Great Lakes, and St. Lawrence Seaway water transportation. Marine transportation establishments using the facilities of the St. Lawrence Seaway Authority Commission are considered to be using the Great Lakes Water Transportation System.

Cross-References. Establishments primarily engaged in—

- Providing inland water transportation on lakes, rivers, or intracoastal waterways (except on the Great Lakes System)—are classified in Industry 48321, Inland Water Transportation;
- Providing scenic and sightseeing water transportation, such as harbor cruises—are classified in Industry 48721, Scenic and Sightseeing Transportation, Water; and
- Operating floating casinos (i.e., gambling cruises, river boat gambling casinos)—are classified in Industry 71321, Casinos (except Casino Hotels).

483111 Deep Sea Freight Transportation[US]

This U.S. industry comprises establishments primarily engaged in providing deep sea transportation of cargo to or from foreign ports.

Cross-References.

Establishments primarily engaged in providing deep sea transportation of cargo to and from domestic ports are classified in U.S. Industry 483113, Coastal and Great Lakes Freight Transportation.

483112 Deep Sea Passenger Transportation[US]

This U.S. industry comprises establishments primarily engaged in providing deep sea transportation of passengers to or from foreign ports.

Cross-References. Establishments primarily engaged in—

- Providing deep sea transportation of passengers to and from domestic ports—are classified in U.S. Industry 483114, Coastal and Great Lakes Passenger Transportation; and

---

US—United States industry only. CAN—United States and Canadian industries are comparable. MEX—United States and Mexican industries are comparable. Blank—Canadian, Mexican, and United States industries are comparable.

- Operating floating casinos (i.e., gambling cruises)—are classified in Industry 713210, Casinos (except Casino Hotels).

483113 Coastal and Great Lakes Freight Transportation[US]

This U.S. industry comprises establishments primarily engaged in providing water transportation of cargo in coastal waters, on the Great Lakes System, or deep seas between ports of the United States, Puerto Rico, and United States island possessions or protectorates. Marine transportation establishments using the facilities of the St. Lawrence Seaway Authority Commission are considered to be using the Great Lakes Water Transportation System. Establishments primarily engaged in providing coastal and/or Great Lakes barge transportation services are included in this industry.

Cross-References. Establishments primarily engaged in—

- Providing deep sea transportation of cargo to or from foreign ports—are classified in U.S. Industry 483111, Deep Sea Freight Transportation; and
- Providing inland water transportation of cargo on lakes, rivers, or intracoastal waterways (except on the Great Lakes System)—are classified in U.S. Industry 483211, Inland Water Freight Transportation.

483114 Coastal and Great Lakes Passenger Transportation[US]

This U.S. industry comprises establishments primarily engaged in providing water transportation of passengers in coastal waters, the Great Lakes System, or deep seas between ports of the United States, Puerto Rico, and United States island possessions and protectorates. Marine transportation establishments using the facilities of the St. Lawrence Seaway Authority Commission are considered to be using the Great Lakes Water Transportation System.

Cross-References. Establishments primarily engaged in—

- Providing inland water transportation of passengers on lakes, rivers or intracoastal waterways (except on the Great Lakes System)—are classified in U.S. Industry 483212, Inland Water Passenger Transportation;
- Providing scenic and sightseeing water transportation, such as harbor cruises—are classified in Industry 487210, Scenic and Sightseeing Transportation, Water; and
- Operating floating casinos (i.e., gambling cruises)—are classified in Industry 713210, Casinos (except Casino Hotels).

US—United States industry only. CAN—United States and Canadian industries are comparable. MEX—United States and Mexican industries are comparable. Blank—Canadian, Mexican, and United States industries are comparable.

4832 Inland Water Transportation

48321 Inland Water Transportation

This industry comprises establishments primarily engaged in providing inland water transportation of passengers and/or cargo on lakes, rivers, or intracoastal waterways (except on the Great Lakes System).

Cross-References. Establishments primarily engaged in—

- Providing water transportation in deep sea, coastal, or on the Great Lakes System—are classified in Industry Group 4831, Deep Sea, Coastal and Great Lakes Water Transportation;
- Providing scenic and sightseeing water transportation, such as harbor cruises—are classified in Industry 48721, Scenic and Sightseeing Transportation, Water; and
- Operating floating casinos (i.e., gambling cruises, river boat gambling casinos)—are classified in Industry 71321, Casinos (except Casino Hotels).

483211 Inland Water Freight Transportation[US]

This U.S. industry comprises establishments primarily engaged in providing inland water transportation of cargo on lakes, rivers, or intracoastal waterways (except on the Great Lakes System).

Cross-References. Establishments primarily engaged in—

- Providing deep sea transportation of cargo to and from foreign ports—are classified in U.S. Industry 483111, Deep Sea Freight Transportation; and
- Providing water transportation of cargo in coastal waters or on the Great Lakes System—are classified in U.S. Industry 483113, Coastal and Great Lakes Freight Transportation.

483212 Inland Water Passenger Transportation[US]

This U.S. industry comprises establishments primarily engaged in providing inland water transportation of passengers on lakes, rivers, or intracoastal waterways (except on the Great Lakes System).

Cross-References. Establishments primarily engaged in—

- Providing deep sea transportation of passengers to and from foreign ports—are classified in U.S. Industry 483112, Deep Sea Passenger Transportation;

US—United States industry only. CAN—United States and Canadian industries are comparable. MEX—United States and Mexican industries are comparable. Blank—Canadian, Mexican, and United States industries are comparable.

- Operating cruise ships or ferries in coastal waters or on the Great Lakes System—are classified in U.S. Industry 483114, Coastal and Great Lakes Passenger Transportation; and
- Providing scenic and sightseeing water transportation,such as harbor cruises—are classified in Industry 487210, Scenic and Sightseeing Transportation, Water.

484 Truck Transportation

Industries in the Truck Transportation subsector provide over-the-road transportation of cargo using motor vehicles,such as trucks and tractor trailers. The subsector is subdivided into general freight trucking and specialized freight trucking. This distinction reflects differences in equipment used, type of load carried, scheduling, terminal, and other networking services. General freight transportation establishments handle a wide variety of general commodities, generally palletized, and transported in a container or van trailer. Specialized freight transportation is the transportation of cargo that, because of size, weight, shape, or other inherent characteristics require specialized equipment for transportation.

Each of these industry groups is further subdivided based on distance traveled. Local trucking establishments primarily carry goods within a single metropolitan area and its adjacent nonurban areas. Long distance trucking establishments carry goods between metropolitan areas.

The Specialized Freight Trucking industry group includes a separate industry for Used Household and Office Goods Moving. The household and office goods movers are separated because of the substantial network of establishments that has developed to deal with local and long-distance moving and the associated storage. In this area, the same establishment provides both local and long-distance services, while other specialized freight establishments generally limit their services to either local or long-distance hauling.

4841 General Freight Trucking

This industry group comprises establishments primarily engaged in providing general freight trucking. General freight establishments handle a wide variety of commodities, generally palletized, and transported in a container or van trailer. The establishments of this industry group provide a combination of the following network activities: local pickup, local sorting and terminal operations, line-haul, destination sorting and terminal operations, and local delivery.

48411 General Freight Trucking, Local

See industry description for 484110 below.

US—United States industry only. CAN—United States and Canadian industries are comparable. MEX—United States and Mexican industries are comparable. Blank—Canadian, Mexican, and United States industries are comparable.

484110 General Freight Trucking, Local[CAN]

This industry comprises establishments primarily engaged in providing local general freight trucking. General freight establishments handle a wide variety of commodities, generally palletized and transported in a container or van trailer. Local general freight trucking establishments usually provide trucking within a metropolitan area which may cross state lines. Generally the trips are same-day return.

Cross-References. Establishments primarily engaged in—

- Operating independent trucking terminals—are classified in Industry 488490, Other Support Activities for Road Transportation; and
- Providing general freight long—distance trucking including all North American international travel—are classified in Industry 48412, General Freight Trucking, Long-Distance.

48412 General Freight Trucking, Long-Distance

This industry comprises establishments primarily engaged in providing long-distance general freight trucking. General freight establishments handle a wide variety of commodities, generally palletized and transported in a container or van trailer. Long-distance general freight trucking establishments usually provide trucking between metropolitan areas which may cross North American country borders. Included in this industry are establishments operating as truckload (TL) or less than truckload (LTL) carriers.

Cross-References. Establishments primarily engaged in—

- Providing courier services—are classified in Industry 49211, Couriers;
- Providing warehousing services of general freight—are classified in Industry 49311, General Warehousing and Storage;
- Providing specialized freight trucking—are classified in Industry Group 4842, Specialized Freight Trucking;
- Operating independent trucking terminals—are classified in Industry 48849, Other Support Activities for Road Transportation; and
- Providing local general freight trucking services—are classified in Industry 48411, General Freight Trucking, Local.

484121 General Freight Trucking, Long-Distance, Truckload[CAN]

This U.S. industry comprises establishments primarily engaged in providing long-distance general freight truckload (TL) trucking. These long-distance general

US—United States industry only. CAN—United States and Canadian industries are comparable. MEX—United States and Mexican industries are comparable. Blank—Canadian, Mexican, and United States industries are comparable.

freight truckload carrier establishments provide full truck movement of freight from origin to destination. The shipment of freight on a truck is characterized as a full single load not combined with other shipments.

Cross-References. Establishments primarily engaged in—

- Providing general freight long-distance, less than truckload trucking—are classified in U.S. Industry 484122, General Freight Trucking, Long-Distance, Less Than Truckload;
- Providing specialized freight trucking—are classified in Industry Group 4842, Specialized Freight Trucking;
- Operating independent trucking terminals—are classified in Industry 488490, Other Support Activities for Road Transportation; and
- Providing local general freight trucking services—are classified in Industry 484110, General Freight Trucking, Local.

484122 General Freight Trucking, Long-Distance, Less Than Truckload[CAN]

This U.S. industry comprises establishments primarily engaged in providing long-distance, general freight, less than truckload (LTL) trucking. LTL carriage is characterized as multiple shipments combined onto a single truck for multiple deliveries within a network. These establishments are generally characterized by the following network activities: local pickup, local sorting and terminal operations, line-haul, destination sorting and terminal operations, and local delivery.

Cross-References. Establishments primarily engaged in—

- Providing courier services—are classified in Industry 492110, Couriers;
- Providing warehousing services of general freight—are classified in Industry 493110, General Warehousing and Storage;
- Providing specialized freight trucking—are classified in Industry Group 4842, Specialized Freight Trucking;
- Operating independent trucking terminals—are classified in Industry 488490, Other Support Activities for Road Transportation;
- Providing general freight long-distance truckload trucking—are classified in U.S. Industry 484121, General Freight Trucking, Long-Distance, Truckload; and
- Providing local general freight trucking services—are classified in Industry 484110, General Freight Trucking, Local.

US—United States industry only. CAN—United States and Canadian industries are comparable. MEX—United States and Mexican industries are comparable. Blank—Canadian, Mexican, and United States industries are comparable.

4842 Specialized Freight Trucking

This industry group comprises establishments primarily engaged in providing local or long-distance specialized freight trucking. The establishments of this industry are primarily engaged in the transportation of freight which, because of size, weight, shape, or other inherent characteristics, requires specialized equipment,such as flatbeds, tankers, or refrigerated trailers. This industry includes the transportation of used household, institutional, and commercial furniture and equipment.

48421 Used Household and Office Goods Moving

See industry description for 484210 below.

484210 Used Household and Office Goods Moving

This industry comprises establishments primarily engaged in providing local or long-distance trucking of used household, used institutional, or used commercial furniture and equipment. Incidental packing and storage activities are often provided by these establishments.

48422 Specialized Freight (except Used Goods) Trucking, Local

See industry description for 484220 below.

484220 Specialized Freight (except Used Goods) Trucking, Local[US]

This industry comprises establishments primarily engaged in providing local, specialized trucking. Local trucking establishments provide trucking within a metropolitan area that may cross state lines. Generally the trips are same-day return.

Illustrative Examples:

Local agricultural products trucking
Local boat hauling
Local bulk liquids trucking
Local dump trucking (e.g., gravel, sand, top-soil)
Local livestock trucking

Cross-References. Establishments primarily engaged in—

- Providing long-distance specialized freight (except used goods) trucking including all North American international travel—are classified in Industry 48423, Specialized Freight (except Used Goods) Trucking, Long-Distance;
- Providing local general freight trucking—are classified in U.S. Industry 484110, General Freight Trucking, Local;

US—United States industry only. CAN—United States and Canadian industries are comparable. MEX—United States and Mexican industries are comparable. Blank—Canadian, Mexican, and United States industries are comparable.

- Providing trucking of used household and office goods—are classified in Industry 484210, Used Household and Office Goods Moving; and
- Providing waste collection—are classified in Industry Group 5621, Waste Collection.

48423 Specialized Freight (except Used Goods) Trucking, Long-Distance

See industry description for 484230 below.

484230 Specialized Freight (except Used Goods) Trucking, Long-Distance[US]

This industry comprises establishments primarily engaged in providing long-distance specialized trucking. These establishments provide trucking between metropolitan areas that may cross North American country borders.

Illustrative Examples:

Long-distance automobile carrier trucking
Long-distance bulk liquid trucking
Long-distance hazardous material trucking
Long-distance refrigerated product trucking
Long-distance trucking of waste

Cross-References. Establishments primarily engaged in—

- Providing local specialized freight trucking (except used goods)—are classified in Industry 484220, Specialized Freight (except Used Goods) Trucking, Local;
- Providing long-distance general freight trucking including all North American international travel—are classified in Industry 48412, General Freight Trucking, Long-Distance;
- Providing trucking of used household and office goods—are classified in Industry 484210, Used Household and Office Goods Moving; and
- Collecting and/or hauling hazardous waste, nonhazardous waste, and/or recyclable materials within a local area—are classified in Industry 56211, Waste Collection.

485 Transit and Ground Passenger Transportation

Industries in the Transit and Ground Passenger Transportation subsector include a variety of passenger transportation activities, such as urban transit systems; char-

---

US—United States industry only. CAN—United States and Canadian industries are comparable. MEX—United States and Mexican industries are comparable. Blank—Canadian, Mexican, and United States industries are comparable.

tered bus, school bus, and interurban bus transportation; and taxis. These activities are distinguished based primarily on such production process factors as vehicle types, routes, and schedules.

In this subsector, the principal splits identify scheduled transportation as separate from nonscheduled transportation. The scheduled transportation industry groups are Urban Transit Systems, Interurban and Rural Bus Transportation, and School and Employee Bus Transportation. The nonscheduled industry groups are the Charter Bus Industry and Taxi and Limousine Service. The Other Transit and Ground Passenger Transportation Industry group includes both scheduled and nonscheduled transportation.

Scenic and sightseeing ground transportation services are not included in this subsector but are included in Subsector 487, Scenic and Sightseeing Transportation. Sightseeing does not usually involve place-to-place transportation; the passenger's trip starts and ends at the same location.

4851 Urban Transit Systems

48511 Urban Transit Systems

This industry comprises establishments primarily engaged in operating local and suburban passenger transit systems over regular routes and on regular schedules within a metropolitan area and its adjacent nonurban areas. Such transportation systems involve the use of one or more modes of transport including light rail, commuter rail, subways, streetcars, as well as buses and other motor vehicles.

Cross-References. Establishments primarily engaged in—

- Providing scenic and sightseeing transportation—are classified in Industry 48711, Scenic and Sightseeing Transportation, Land;
- Providing support services to transit and ground transportation—are classified in Industry Group 4884, Support Activities for Road Transportation; and
- Providing interurban and rural bus transportation—are classified in Industry 48521, Interurban and Rural Bus Transportation.

485111 Mixed Mode Transit Systems[US]

This U.S. industry comprises establishments primarily engaged in operating local and suburban ground passenger transit systems using more than one mode of transport over regular routes and on regular schedules within a metropolitan area and its adjacent nonurban areas.

US—United States industry only. CAN—United States and Canadian industries are comparable. MEX—United States and Mexican industries are comparable. Blank—Canadian, Mexican, and United States industries are comparable.

Cross-References. Establishments primarily engaged in—

- Operating local and suburban passenger transit systems using only one mode of transportation—are classified according to the mode of transport; and
- Providing support services to transit and ground passenger transportation—are classified in Industry Group 4884, Support Activities for Road Transportation.

485112 Commuter Rail Systems[US]

This U.S. industry comprises establishments primarily engaged in operating local and suburban commuter rail systems over regular routes and on a regular schedule within a metropolitan area and its adjacent nonurban areas. Commuter rail is usually characterized by reduced fares, multiple ride, and commutation tickets and mostly used by passengers during the morning and evening peak periods.

Cross-References. Establishments primarily engaged in—

- Operating local and suburban mass passenger transit systems using both commuter rail and another mode of transport—are classified in U.S. Industry 485111, Mixed Mode Transit Systems;
- Operating a subway system—are classified in U.S. Industry 485119, Other Urban Transit Systems; and
- Providing scenic and sightseeing transportation on land—are classified in Industry 487110, Scenic and Sightseeing Transportation, Land.

485113 Bus and Other Motor Vehicle Transit Systems[US]

This U.S. industry comprises establishments primarily engaged in operating local and suburban passenger transportation systems using buses or other motor vehicles over regular routes and on regular schedules within a metropolitan area and its adjacent nonurban areas.

Cross-References. Establishments primarily engaged in—

- Operating local and suburban passenger transportation systems using both a bus or other motor vehicle and another mode of transport—are classified in U.S. Industry 485111, Mixed Mode Transit Systems;
- Providing interurban and rural bus transportation—are classified in Industry 485210, Interurban and Rural Bus Transportation; and
- Providing scenic and sightseeing transportation using buses or other motor vehicles—are classified in Industry 487110, Scenic and Sightseeing Transportation, Land.

US—United States industry only. CAN—United States and Canadian industries are comparable. MEX—United States and Mexican industries are comparable. Blank—Canadian, Mexican, and United States industries are comparable.

485119 Other Urban Transit Systems[US]

This U.S. industry comprises establishments primarily engaged in operating local and suburban ground passenger transit systems (except mixed mode transit systems, commuter rail systems, and buses and other motor vehicles) over regular routes and on regular schedules within a metropolitan area and its adjacent nonurban areas.

Illustrative Examples:

Commuter cable car systems (i.e., stand-alone)
Commuter tramway systems (i.e., stand-alone)
Commuter trolley systems (i.e., stand-alone)
Light rail systems (i.e., stand-alone)
Monorail transit systems (i.e., stand-alone)

Cross-References. Establishment primarily engaged in—

- Operating local and suburban ground passenger transit systems using more than one mode of transport—are classified in U.S. Industry 485111, Mixed Mode Transit Systems;
- Providing local and suburban passenger transportation using commuter rail systems—are classified in U.S. Industry 485112, Commuter Rail Systems; and
- Operating local and suburban bus transit systems—are classified in U.S. Industry 485113, Bus and Other Motor Vehicle Transit Systems.

4852 Interurban and Rural Bus Transportation

48521 Interurban and Rural Bus Transportation

See industry description for 485210 below.

485210 Interurban and Rural Bus Transportation

This industry comprises establishments primarily engaged in providing bus passenger transportation over regular routes and on regular schedules, principally outside a single metropolitan area and its adjacent nonurban areas.

Cross-References. Establishments primarily engaged in—

- Providing scenic and sightseeing transportation using buses—are classified in Industry 487110, Scenic and Sightseeing Transportation, Land;
- Providing buses for charter—are classified in Industry 485510, Charter Bus Industry;

US—United States industry only. CAN—United States and Canadian industries are comparable. MEX—United States and Mexican industries are comparable. Blank—Canadian, Mexican, and United States industries are comparable.

- Operating local and suburban bus transit systems—are classified in U.S. Industry 485113, Bus and Other Motor Vehicle Transit Systems; and
- Operating independent bus terminals—are classified in Industry 488490, Other Support Activities for Road Transportation.

4853 Taxi and Limousine Service

48531 Taxi Service

See industry description for 485310 below.

485310 Taxi Service[CAN]

This industry comprises establishments primarily engaged in providing passenger transportation by automobile or van, not operated over regular routes and on regular schedules. Establishments of taxicab owner/operators, taxicab fleet operators, or taxicab organizations are included in this industry.

Cross-References. Establishments primarily engaged in—

- Providing special needs transportation services (except to and from school or work) for the infirm, elderly, or handicapped—are classified in U.S. Industry 485991, Special Needs Transportation;
- Providing limousine services—are classified in Industry 485320, Limousine Service; and
- Providing scheduled shuttle services between hotels, airports, or other destination points—are classified in U.S. Industry 485999, All Other Transit and Ground Passenger Transportation.

48532 Limousine Service

See industry description for 485320 below.

485320 Limousine Service

This industry comprises establishments primarily engaged in providing an array of specialty and luxury passenger transportation services via limousine or luxury sedans generally on a reserved basis. These establishments do not operate over regular routes and on regular schedules.

Cross-References. Establishments primarily engaged in—

- Providing taxi services—are classified in Industry 485310, Taxi Service; and

---

US—United States industry only. CAN—United States and Canadian industries are comparable. MEX—United States and Mexican industries are comparable. Blank—Canadian, Mexican, and United States industries are comparable.

- Providing scheduled shuttle services between hotels, airports, or other destination points—are classified in U.S. Industry 485999, All Other Transit and Ground Passenger Transportation.

4854 School and Employee Bus Transportation

48541 School and Employee Bus Transportation

See industry description for 485410 below.

485410 School and Employee Bus Transportation

This industry comprises establishments primarily engaged in providing buses and other motor vehicles to transport pupils to and from school or employees to and from work.

Cross-References. Establishments primarily engaged in—

- Operating local and suburban bus transit systems—are classified in U.S. Industry, 485113 Bus and Other Motor Vehicle Transit Systems;
- Providing interurban and rural bus transportation—are classified in Industry 485210, Interurban and Rural Bus Transportation; and
- Providing buses for charter—are classified in Industry 485510, Charter Bus Industry.

4855 Charter Bus Industry

48551 Charter Bus Industry

See industry description for 485510 below.

485510 Charter Bus Industry

This industry comprises establishments primarily engaged in providing buses for charter. These establishments provide bus services to meet customers' road transportation needs and generally do not operate over fixed routes and on regular schedules.

Cross-References. Establishments primarily engaged in—

- Providing scenic and local sightseeing transportation using buses—are classified in Industry 487110, Scenic and Sightseeing Transportation, Land; and

---

US—United States industry only. CAN—United States and Canadian industries are comparable. MEX—United States and Mexican industries are comparable. Blank—Canadian, Mexican, and United States industries are comparable.

- Providing interurban and rural bus transportation—are classified in Industry 485210, Interurban and Rural Bus Transportation.

4859 Other Transit and Ground Passenger Transportation

48599 Other Transit and Ground Passenger Transportation

This industry comprises establishments primarily engaged in providing other transit and ground passenger transportation (except urban transit systems, interurban and rural bus transportation, taxi services, school and employee bus transportation, charter bus services, and limousine services (except shuttle services)). Shuttle services (except employee bus) and special needs transportation services are included in this industry. Shuttle services establishments generally travel within a metropolitan area and its adjacent nonurban areas on regular routes, on regular schedules and provide services between hotels, airports, or other destination points. Special needs transportation establishments provide passenger transportation to the infirm, elderly, or handicapped. These establishments may use specially equipped vehicles to provide passenger transportation.

Cross-References. Establishments primarily engaged in—

- Providing school or employee bus transportation for the infirm, elderly, or handicapped—are classified in Industry 48541, School and Employee Bus Transportation;
- Providing ambulance services for emergency and medical purposes—are classified in Industry 62191, Ambulance Services;
- Operating urban transit systems—are classified in Industry Group 4851, Urban Transit Systems;
- Providing interurban and rural bus transportation—are classified in Industry 48521, Interurban and Rural Bus Transportation;
- Providing taxi services and/or limousine services (except shuttle services)—are classified in Industry Group 4853; Taxi and Limousine Service; and
- Providing buses for charter—are classified in Industry 48551, Charter Bus Industry.

485991 Special Needs Transportation[US]

This U.S. industry comprises establishments primarily engaged in providing special needs transportation (except to and from school or work) to the infirm, elderly, or handicapped. These establishments may use specially equipped vehicles to provide passenger transportation.

US—United States industry only. CAN—United States and Canadian industries are comparable. MEX—United States and Mexican industries are comparable. Blank—Canadian, Mexican, and United States industries are comparable.

Cross-References. Establishments primarily engaged in—

- Providing school or employee bus transportation for the infirm, elderly, or handicapped—are classified in Industry 485410, School and Employee Bus Transportation; and
- Providing ambulance services for emergency and medical purposes—are classified in Industry 62191, Ambulance Services.

485999 All Other Transit and Ground Passenger Transportation[US]

This U.S. industry comprises establishments primarily engaged in providing ground passenger transportation (except urban transit systems; interurban and rural bus transportation, taxi and/or limousine services (except shuttle services), school and employee bus transportation, charter bus services, and special needs transportation). Establishments primarily engaged in operating shuttle services and vanpools are included in this industry. Shuttle services establishments generally provide travel on regular routes and on regular schedules between hotels, airports, or other destination points.

Cross-References. Establishments primarily engaged in—

- Providing urban transit systems—are classified in Industry Group 4851, Urban Transit Systems;
- Providing interurban and rural bus transportation—are classified in Industry 485210, Interurban and Rural Bus Transportation;
- Providing taxi and/or limousine services (except shuttle services)—are classified in Industry Group 4853, Taxi and Limousine Service;
- Providing school and employee bus transportation (including for the infirm, elderly, or handicapped)—are classified in Industry 485410, School and Employee Bus Transportation;
- Providing buses for charter—are classified in Industry 485510, Charter Bus Industry;
- Providing special needs transportation (except to and from school or work) for the infirm, elderly, or handicapped—are classified in Industry 485991, Special Needs Transportation; and
- Providing ambulance services for emergency and medical purposes—are classified in Industry 621910, Ambulance Services.

486 Pipeline Transportation

Industries in the Pipeline Transportation subsector use transmission pipelines to transport products,such as crude oil, natural gas, refined petroleum products,

---

US—United States industry only. CAN—United States and Canadian industries are comparable. MEX—United States and Mexican industries are comparable. Blank—Canadian, Mexican, and United States industries are comparable.

and slurry. Industries are identified based on the products transported (i.e., pipeline transportation of crude oil, natural gas, refined petroleum products, and other products).

The Pipeline Transportation of Natural Gas industry includes the storage of natural gas because the storage is usually done by the pipeline establishment and because a pipeline is inherently a network in which all the nodes are interdependent.

4861 Pipeline Transportation of Crude Oil

48611 Pipeline Transportation of Crude Oil

See industry description for 486110 below.

486110 Pipeline Transportation of Crude Oil

This industry comprises establishments primarily engaged in the pipeline transportation of crude oil.

Cross-References. Establishments primarily engaged in—

- Providing the pipeline transportation of natural gas—are classified in Industry 486210, Pipeline Transportation of Natural Gas; and
- Providing the pipeline transportation of refined petroleum products—are classified in Industry 486910, Pipeline Transportation of Refined Petroleum Products.

4862 Pipeline Transportation of Natural Gas

48621 Pipeline Transportation of Natural Gas

See industry description for 486210 below.

486210 Pipeline Transportation of Natural Gas

This industry comprises establishments primarily engaged in the pipeline transportation of natural gas from processing plants to local distribution systems.

Cross-References.

Establishments primarily engaged in providing natural gas to the end consumer are classified in Industry 221210, Natural Gas Distribution.

US—United States industry only. CAN—United States and Canadian industries are comparable. MEX—United States and Mexican industries are comparable. Blank—Canadian, Mexican, and United States industries are comparable.

4869 Other Pipeline Transportation

This industry group comprises establishments primarily engaged in the pipeline transportation of products (except crude oil and natural gas).

48691 Pipeline Transportation of Refined Petroleum Products

See industry description for 486910 below.

486910 Pipeline Transportation of Refined Petroleum Products

This industry comprises establishments primarily engaged in the pipeline transportation of refined petroleum products.

48699 All Other Pipeline Transportation

See industry description for 486990 below.

486990 All Other Pipeline Transportation

This industry comprises establishments primarily engaged in the pipeline transportation of products except crude oil, natural gas, and refined petroleum products.

Cross-References. Establishments primarily engaged in—

- Providing pipeline transportation of crude oil—are classified in Industry 486110, Pipeline Transportation of Crude Oil;
- Providing pipeline transportation of natural gas—are classified in Industry 486210, Pipeline Transportation of Natural Gas;
- Providing pipeline transportation of refined petroleum products—are classified in Industry 486910, Pipeline Transportation of Refined Petroleum Products; and
- Providing pipeline transportation of water—are classified in Industry 221310, Water Supply and Irrigation Systems.

487 Scenic and Sightseeing Transportation

Industries in the Scenic and Sightseeing Transportation subsector utilize transportation equipment to provide recreation and entertainment. These activities have a production process distinct from passenger transportation carried out for the purpose of other types of for-hire transportation. This process does not emphasize efficient transportation; in fact, such activities often use obsolete vehicles, such as

---

US—United States industry only. CAN—United States and Canadian industries are comparable. MEX—United States and Mexican industries are comparable. Blank—Canadian, Mexican, and United States industries are comparable.

steam trains, to provide some extra ambience. The activity is local in nature, usually involving a same-day return to the point of departure.

The Scenic and Sightseeing Transportation subsector is separated into three industries based on the mode: land, water, and other.

Activities that are recreational in nature and involve participation by the customer,such as white-water rafting, are generally excluded from this subsector, unless they impose an impact on part of the transportation system. Charter boat fishing, for example, is included in the Scenic and Sightseeing Transportation, Water industry.

4871 Scenic and Sightseeing Transportation, Land

48711 Scenic and Sightseeing Transportation, Land

See industry description for 487110 below.

487110 Scenic and Sightseeing Transportation, Land

This industry comprises establishments primarily engaged in providing scenic and sightseeing transportation on land, such as sightseeing buses and trolleys, steam train excursions, and horse-drawn sightseeing rides. The services provided are usually local and involve same-day return to place of origin.

Cross-References. Establishments primarily engaged in—

- Operating aerial trams or aerial cable cars—are classified in Industry 487990, Scenic and Sightseeing Transportation, Other;
- Providing sporting services, such as pack trains—are classified in Industry 713990, All Other Amusement and Recreation Industries;
- Providing intercity and rural bus transportation—are classified in Industry 485210, Interurban and Rural Bus Transportation;
- Providing buses for charter—are classified in Industry 485510, Charter Bus Industry;
- Operating local and suburban passenger transit systems—are classified in Industry 48511, Urban Transit Systems; and
- Providing passenger travel arrangements and tours—are classified in Industry Group 5615, Travel Arrangement and Reservation Services.

4872 Scenic and Sightseeing Transportation, Water

48721 Scenic and Sightseeing Transportation, Water

See industry description for 487210 below.

US—United States industry only. CAN—United States and Canadian industries are comparable. MEX—United States and Mexican industries are comparable. Blank—Canadian, Mexican, and United States industries are comparable.

487210 Scenic and Sightseeing Transportation, Water

This industry comprises establishments primarily engaged in providing scenic and sightseeing transportation on water. The services provided are usually local and involve same-day return to place of origin.

Illustrative Examples:

- Airboat (i.e., swamp buggy) operation
- Charter fishing boat services
- Dinner cruises
- Excursion boat operation
- Harbor sightseeing tours

Cross-References. Establishments primarily engaged in—

- Providing recreation services, such as fishing guides, white-water rafting, parasailing, and water skiing—are classified in Industry 713990, All Other Amusement and Recreation Industries;
- Providing water taxi services—are classified in Industry 48321, Inland Water Transportation;
- Providing water transportation of passengers—are classified in Subsector 483, Water Transportation;
- Operating floating casinos (i.e., gambling cruises or river boat casinos)—are classified in Industry 713210, Casinos (except Casino Hotels); and
- Providing boat rental without operators—are classified in U.S. Industry 532292, Recreational Goods Rental.

4879 Scenic and Sightseeing Transportation, Other

48799 Scenic and Sightseeing Transportation, Other

See industry description for 487990 below.

487990 Scenic and Sightseeing Transportation, Other

This industry comprises establishments primarily engaged in providing scenic and sightseeing transportation (except on land and water). The services provided are usually local and involve same-day return to place of departure.

Illustrative Examples:

- Aerial tramways, scenic and sightseeing operation
- Aerial cablecars, scenic and sightseeing operation
- Glider excursions
- Helicopter rides, scenic and sightseeing operation
- Hot air balloon rides, scenic and sightseeing operation

US—United States industry only. CAN—United States and Canadian industries are comparable. MEX—United States and Mexican industries are comparable. Blank—Canadian, Mexican, and United States industries are comparable.

Cross-References. Establishments primarily engaged in—

- Providing recreational activities, such as hang gliding—are classified in Industry 713990, All Other Amusement and Recreation Industries; and
- Providing scheduled or nonscheduled air transportation of passengers or specialty flying services—are classified in Subsector 481, Air Transportation.

488 Support Activities for Transportation

Industries in the Support Activities for Transportation subsector provide services which support transportation. These services may be provided to transportation carrier establishments or to the general public. This subsector includes a wide array of establishments, including air traffic control services, marine cargo handling, and motor vehicle towing.

The Support Activities for Transportation subsector includes services to transportation but is separated by type of mode serviced. The Support Activities for Rail Transportation industry includes services to the rail industry (e.g., railroad switching and terminal establishments).

Ship repair and maintenance not done in a shipyard are included in Other Support Activities for Water Transportation. An example would be floating drydock services in a harbor.

Excluded from this subsector are establishments primarily engaged in providing factory conversion and overhaul of transportation equipment, which are classified in Subsector 336, Transportation Equipment Manufacturing. Also, establishments primarily engaged in providing rental and leasing of transportation equipment without operator are classified in Subsector 532, Rental and Leasing Services.

4881 Support Activities for Air Transportation

This industry group comprises establishments primarily engaged in providing services to the air transportation industry. These services include airport operation, servicing, repairing (except factory conversion and overhaul of aircraft), maintaining and storing aircraft, and ferrying aircraft.

48811 Airport Operations

This industry comprises establishments primarily engaged in (1) operating international, national, or civil airports or public flying fields or (2) supporting airport operations (except special food services contractors), such as rental of hangar space, air traffic control services, baggage handling services, and cargo handling services.

US—United States industry only. CAN—United States and Canadian industries are comparable. MEX—United States and Mexican industries are comparable. Blank—Canadian, Mexican, and United States industries are comparable.

Cross-References. Establishments primarily engaged in—

- Providing factory conversion, overhaul, and rebuilding of aircraft—are classified in Industry 33641, Aerospace Product and Parts Manufacturing;
- Wholesaling fuel at airports—are classified in Industry 424720, Petroleum and Petroleum Products Merchant Wholesalers (except Bulk Stations and Terminals);
- Providing airport janitorial services—are classified in Industry 56172, Janitorial Services; and
- Providing food services at airports on a contractual arrangement (i.e., food service contractors)—are classified in Industry 72231, Food Service Contractors.

488111 Air Traffic Control

This U.S. industry comprises establishments primarily engaged in providing air traffic control services to regulate the flow of air traffic.

488119 Other Airport Operations[CAN]

This U.S. industry comprises establishments primarily engaged in (1) operating international, national, or civil airports, or public flying fields or (2) supporting airport operations, such as rental of hangar space, and providing baggage handling and/or cargo handling services.

Cross-References. Establishments primarily engaged in—

- Providing air traffic control services—are classified in U.S. Industry 488111, Air Traffic Control;
- Providing factory conversion, overhaul, and rebuilding of aircraft—are classified in Industry 33641, Aerospace Product and Parts Manufacturing;
- Wholesaling fuel at airports—are classified in Industry 424720, Petroleum and Petroleum Products Merchant Wholesalers (except Bulk Stations and Terminals);
- Providing airport janitorial services—are classified in Industry 561720, Janitorial Services; and
- Providing food services at airports on a contractual arrangement—are classified in Industry 722310, Food Service Contractors.

48819 Other Support Activities for Air Transportation

See industry description for 488190 below.

US—United States industry only. CAN—United States and Canadian industries are comparable. MEX—United States and Mexican industries are comparable. Blank—Canadian, Mexican, and United States industries are comparable.

488190 Other Support Activities for Air Transportation

This industry comprises establishments primarily engaged in providing specialized services for air transportation (except air traffic control and other airport operations).

Illustrative Examples:

Aircraft services
Aircraft maintenance and repair services (except factory conversions, overhauls, rebuilding
Aircraft testing services

Cross-References. Establishments primarily engaged in—

- Wholesaling fuel at airports—are classified in Industry 424720, Petroleum and Petroleum Products Merchant Wholesalers (except Bulk Stations and Terminals);
- Providing aircraft janitorial services—are classified in Industry 561720, Janitorial Services;
- Providing air traffic control services—are classified in U.S. Industry 488111, Air Traffic Control;
- Providing airport operations (except air traffic control)—are classified in U.S. Industry 488119, Other Airport Operations;
- Providing factory conversion, overhaul, and rebuilding of aircraft—are classified in Industry 33641, Aerospace Product and Parts Manufacturing; and
- Providing food services to airlines on a contractual arrangement—are classified in Industry 722310, Food Service Contractors.

4882 Support Activities for Rail Transportation

48821 Support Activities for Rail Transportation

See industry description for 488210 below.

488210 Support Activities for Rail Transportation

This industry comprises establishments primarily engaged in providing specialized services for railroad transportation including servicing, routine repairing (except factory conversion, overhaul or rebuilding of rolling stock), and maintaining rail cars; loading and unloading rail cars; and operating independent terminals.

US—United States industry only. CAN—United States and Canadian industries are comparable. MEX—United States and Mexican industries are comparable. Blank—Canadian, Mexican, and United States industries are comparable.

Cross-References. Establishments primarily engaged in—

- Providing railroad car rental—are classified in U.S. Industry 532411, Commercial Air, Rail, and Water Transportation Equipment Rental and Leasing;
- Factory conversion, overhaul, or rebuilding of railroad rolling stock—are classified in Industry 336510, Railroad Rolling Stock Manufacturing;
- Providing rail car janitorial services—are classified in Industry 561720, Janitorial Services; and
- Providing dredging services—are classified in Industry 237990, Other Heavy and Civil Engineering Construction.

4883 Support Activities for Water Transportation

48831 Port and Harbor Operations

See industry description for 488310 below.

488310 Port and Harbor Operations

This industry comprises establishments primarily engaged in operating ports, harbors (including docking and pier facilities), or canals.

Cross-References. Establishments primarily engaged in—

- Providing stevedoring and other marine cargo handling services—are classified in Industry 488320, Marine Cargo Handling;
- Providing navigational services to shipping—are classified in Industry 488330, Navigational Services to Shipping; and
- Operating docking and/or storage facilities and commonly known as marinas—are classified in Industry 713930, Marinas.

48832 Marine Cargo Handling

See industry description for 488320 below.

488320 Marine Cargo Handling

This industry comprises establishments primarily engaged in providing stevedoring and other marine cargo handling services (except warehousing).

Cross-References. Establishments primarily engaged in—

- Preparing freight for transportation—are classified in U.S. Industry 488991, Packing and Crating;

US—United States industry only. CAN—United States and Canadian industries are comparable. MEX—United States and Mexican industries are comparable. Blank—Canadian, Mexican, and United States industries are comparable.

- Operating general merchandise, refrigerated, or other warehousing and storage facilities—are classified in Subsector 493, Warehousing and Storage; and
- Operating docking and pier facilities—are classified in Industry 488310, Port and Harbor Operations.

48833 Navigational Services to Shipping

See industry description for 488330 below.

488330 Navigational Services to Shipping[MEX]

This industry comprises establishments primarily engaged in providing navigational services to shipping. Marine salvage establishments are included in this industry.

Illustrative Examples:

Docking and undocking marine vessel services
Marine vessel traffic reporting services
Piloting services, water transportation
Tugboat services, harbor operation

Cross-References. Establishments primarily engaged in—

- Providing water transportation of barges (except coastal or Great Lakes barge transportation services)—are classified in U.S. Industry 483211, Inland Water Freight Transportation; and
- Providing coastal and/or Great Lakes barge transportation services—are classified in U.S. Industry 483113, Coastal and Great Lakes Freight Transportation.

48839 Other Support Activities for Water Transportation

See industry description for 488390 below.

488390 Other Support Activities for Water Transportation

This industry comprises establishments primarily engaged in providing services to water transportation (except port and harbor operations; marine cargo handling services; and navigational services to shipping).

Illustrative Examples:

Floating drydocks (i.e., maintenance and routine repairs for ships)
Marine cargo checkers and surveyors
Ship scaling services

US—United States industry only. CAN—United States and Canadian industries are comparable. MEX—United States and Mexican industries are comparable. Blank—Canadian, Mexican, and United States industries are comparable.

Cross-References. Establishments primarily engaged in—

- Ship painting—are classified in Industry 238320, Painting and Wall Covering Contractors;
- Providing ship janitorial services—are classified in Industry 561720, Janitorial Services;
- Operating port, harbor, or canal facilities—are classified in Industry 488310, Port and Harbor Operations;
- Providing stevedoring and other marine cargo handling services—are classified in Industry 488320, Marine Cargo Handling;
- Providing navigational services to shipping—are classified in Industry 488330, Navigational Services to Shipping; and
- Providing ship overhauling or repairs in a shipyard—are classified in U.S. Industry 336611, Ship Building and Repairing.

4884 Support Activities for Road Transportation

48841 Motor Vehicle Towing

See industry description for 488410 below.

488410 Motor Vehicle Towing

This industry comprises establishments primarily engaged in towing light or heavy motor vehicles, both local and long distance. These establishments may provide incidental services, such as storage and emergency road repair services.

Cross-References. Establishments primarily engaged in—

- Operating gasoline stations—are classified in Industry Group 4471, Gasoline Stations;
- Providing automotive repair and maintenance—are classified in Industry Group 8111, Automotive Repair and Maintenance; and
- Both retailing automotive parts and accessories, and repairing automobiles and known as automotive supply stores—are classified in Industry 441310, Automotive Parts and Accessories Stores.

48849 Other Support Activities for Road Transportation

See industry description for 488490 below.

US—United States industry only. CAN—United States and Canadian industries are comparable. MEX—United States and Mexican industries are comparable. Blank—Canadian, Mexican, and United States industries are comparable.

488490 Other Support Activities for Road Transportation[CAN]

This industry comprises establishments primarily engaged in providing services (except motor vehicle towing) to road network users.

Illustrative Examples:

Bridge, tunnel, and highway operations
Driving services (e.g., automobile, truck delivery)
Pilot car services (i.e., wide load warning services)
Truck or weighing station operations

Cross-References. Establishments primarily engaged in—

- Providing automotive repair and maintenance—are classified in Industry Group 8111, Automotive Repair and Maintenance;
- Providing towing services to motor vehicles—are classified in Industry 488410, Motor Vehicle Towing;
- Providing a network for busing in combination with providing terminal services—are classified in Industry 485210, Interurban and Rural Bus Transportation; and
- Providing a network for trucking in combination with providing terminal services—are classified in Subsector 484, Truck Transportation.

4885 Freight Transportation Arrangement

48851 Freight Transportation Arrangement

See industry description for 488510 below.

488510 Freight Transportation Arrangement[US]

This industry comprises establishments primarily engaged in arranging transportation of freight between shippers and carriers. These establishments are usually known as freight forwarders, marine shipping agents, or customs brokers and offer a combination of services spanning transportation modes.

Cross-References.

Establishments primarily engaged in tariff and freight rate consulting services are classified in U.S. Industry 541614, Process, Physical Distribution, and Logistics Consulting Services.

US—United States industry only. CAN—United States and Canadian industries are comparable. MEX—United States and Mexican industries are comparable. Blank—Canadian, Mexican, and United States industries are comparable.

4889 Other Support Activities for Transportation

48899 Other Support Activities for Transportation

This industry comprises establishments primarily engaged in providing support activities to transportation (except for air transportation; rail transportation; water transportation; road transportation; and freight transportation arrangement).

Illustrative Examples:

Arrangement of vanpools or carpools
Independent pipeline terminal facilities
Stockyards (i.e., not for fattening or selling livestock)

Cross-References. Establishments primarily engaged in—

- Providing support activities for air transportation—are classified in Industry Group 4881, Support Activities for Air Transportation;
- Providing support activities for rail transportation—are classified in Industry Group 4882, Support Activities for Rail Transportation;
- Providing support activities for water transportation—are classified in Industry Group 4883, Support Activities for Water Transportation;
- Providing support activities for road transportation—are classified in Industry Group 4884, Support Activities for Road Transportation;
- Arranging transportation of freight between shippers and carriers—are classified in Industry 48851, Freight Transportation Arrangement;
- Providing tariff and freight rate consulting services—are classified in Industry 54161, Management Consulting Services;
- Operating stockyards for fattening livestock—are classified in Subsector 112, Animal Production; and
- Providing packaging and labeling services—are classified in Industry 56191, Packaging and Labeling Services.

488991 Packing and Crating[US]

This U.S. industry comprises establishments primarily engaged in packing, crating, and otherwise preparing goods for transportation.

Cross-References.

Establishments primarily engaged in providing packaging and labeling services are classified in Industry 561910, Packaging and Labeling Services.

US—United States industry only. CAN—United States and Canadian industries are comparable. MEX—United States and Mexican industries are comparable. Blank—Canadian, Mexican, and United States industries are comparable.

488999 All Other Support Activities for Transportation[US]

This U.S. industry comprises establishments primarily engaged in providing support activities to transportation (except for air transportation; rail transportation; water transportation; road transportation; freight transportation arrangement; and packing and crating).

Illustrative Examples:

Arrangement of vanpools or carpools
Independent pipeline terminal facilities
Stockyards (i.e., not for fattening or selling livestock)

Cross-References. Establishments primarily engaged in—

- Operating stockyards for fattening livestock—are classified in Subsector 112, Animal Production;
- Providing tariff and freight rate consulting services—are classified in U.S. Industry 541614, Process, Physical Distribution, and Logistics Consulting Services;
- Providing packing and crating services for transportation—are classified in U.S. Industry 488991, Packing and Crating;
- Providing support activities for air transportation—are classified in Industry Group 4881, Support Activities for Air Transportation;
- Providing support activities for rail transportation—are classified in Industry 488210, Support Activities for Rail Transportation;
- Providing support activities for water transportation—are classified in Industry Group 4883, Support Activities for Water Transportation;
- Providing support activities for road transportation—are classified in Industry Group 4884, Support Activities for Road Transportation; and
- Arranging transportation of freight between shippers and carriers—are classified in Industry 488510, Freight Transportation Arrangement.

491 Postal Service

The Postal Service subsector includes the activities of the National Post Office and its subcontractors in delivering letters and small parcels, normally without pick-up at the sender's location. These articles can be described as those that can be handled by one person without using special equipment. This allows the collection, pick-up, and delivery operations to be done with limited labor costs and minimal equipment. Sorting and transportation activities, where necessary, are generally mechanized. The restriction to small parcels distinguishes these establishments from those in the transportation industries.

US—United States industry only. CAN—United States and Canadian industries are comparable. MEX—United States and Mexican industries are comparable. Blank—Canadian, Mexican, and United States industries are comparable.

The traditional activity of the National Postal Service is described in this subsector. Subcontractors include rural Post Offices on contract to the Postal Service.

Bulk transportation of mail on contract to the Postal Service is not included here, because it is usually done by transportation establishments that carry other customers' cargo as well.

4911 Postal Service

49111 Postal Service

See industry description for 491110 below.

491110 Postal Service

This industry comprises establishments primarily engaged in operating the National Postal Service. Establishments primarily engaged in performing one or more postal services, such as sorting, routing, and/or delivery, on a contract basis (except the bulk transportation of mail) are included in this industry.

Cross-References. Establishments primarily engaged in—

- Providing bulk transportation of mail on a contract basis to and from postal service establishments—are classified in Industry Group 4841, General Freight Trucking;
- Providing courier services—are classified in Industry 492110, Couriers;
- Providing mailbox services along with other business services—are classified in U.S. Industry 561431, Private Mail Centers; and
- Providing local messenger and delivery services—are classified in Industry 492210, Local Messengers and Local Delivery.

492 Couriers and Messengers

Industries in the Couriers and Messengers subsector provide intercity and/or local delivery of parcels. These articles can be described as those that may be handled by one person without using special equipment. This allows the collection, pick-up, and delivery operations to be done with limited labor costs and minimal equipment. Sorting and transportation activities, where necessary, are generally mechanized. The restriction to small parcels partly distinguishes these establishments from those in the transportation industries. The complete network of courier services establishments also distinguishes these transportation services from local messenger and delivery establishments in this subsector. This includes the establishments that perform intercity transportation as well as establishments that, under

US—United States industry only. CAN—United States and Canadian industries are comparable. MEX—United States and Mexican industries are comparable. Blank—Canadian, Mexican, and United States industries are comparable.

contract to them, perform local pick-up and delivery. Messengers, which usually deliver within a metropolitan or single urban area, may use bicycle, foot, small truck, or van.

4921 Couriers

49211 Couriers

See industry description for 492110 below.

492110 Couriers

This industry comprises establishments primarily engaged in providing air, surface, or combined courier delivery services of parcels generally between metropolitan areas or urban centers. The establishments of this industry form a network including courier local pick-up and delivery to serve their customers' needs.

Cross-References. Establishments primarily engaged in—

- Providing messenger and delivery services within a metropolitan area or within an urban center—are classified in Industry 492210, Local Messengers and Local Delivery; and
- Providing the truck transportation of palletized general freight—are classified in Industry Group 4841, General Freight Trucking.

4922 Local Messengers and Local Delivery

49221 Local Messengers and Local Delivery

See industry description for 492210 below.

492210 Local Messengers and Local Delivery

This industry comprises establishments primarily engaged in providing local messenger and delivery services of small items within a single metropolitan area or within an urban center. These establishments generally provide point-to-point pickup and delivery and do not operate as part of an intercity courier network.

Illustrative Examples:

Alcoholic beverages delivery services
Grocery delivery services (i.e., independent service from grocery store)
Letters, documents, or small parcel local delivery services
Restaurant meals delivery services (i.e., independent service from restaurant)

US—United States industry only. CAN—United States and Canadian industries are comparable. MEX—United States and Mexican industries are comparable. Blank—Canadian, Mexican, and United States industries are comparable.

Cross-References. Establishments primarily engaged in—

- Providing local letter and parcel delivery services as part of an intercity courier network—are classified in Industry 492110, Couriers;
- Operating the National Postal Service or providing postal services on a contract basis (except the bulk transportation of mail)—are classified in Industry 491110, Postal Service; and
- Providing the bulk transportation of mail on a contract basis to and from Postal Service establishments—are classified in Industry Group 4841, General Freight Trucking.

493 Warehousing and Storage

Industries in the Warehousing and Storage subsector are primarily engaged in operating warehousing and storage facilities for general merchandise, refrigerated goods, and other warehouse products. These establishments provide facilities to store goods. They do not sell the goods they handle. These establishments take responsibility for storing the goods and keeping them secure. They may also provide a range of services, often referred to as logistics services, related to the distribution of goods. Logistics services can include labeling, breaking bulk, inventory control and management, light assembly, order entry and fulfillment, packaging, pick and pack, price marking and ticketing, and transportation arrangement. However, establishments in this industry group always provide warehousing or storage services in addition to any logistic services. Furthermore, the warehousing or storage of goods must be more than incidental to the performance of services, such as price marking.

Bonded warehousing and storage services and warehouses located in free trade zones are included in the industries of this subsector.

4931 Warehousing and Storage

49311 General Warehousing and Storage

See industry description for 493110 below.

493110 General Warehousing and Storage[CAN]

This industry comprises establishments primarily engaged in operating merchandise warehousing and storage facilities. These establishments generally handle goods in containers, such as boxes, barrels, and/or drums, using equipment, such as forklifts, pallets, and racks. They are not specialized in handling bulk products of any particular type, size, or quantity of goods or products.

US—United States industry only. CAN—United States and Canadian industries are comparable. MEX—United States and Mexican industries are comparable. Blank—Canadian, Mexican, and United States industries are comparable.

Cross-References. Establishments primarily engaged in—

- Renting or leasing space for self storage—are classified in Industry 531130, Lessors of Miniwarehouses and Self-Storage Units; and
- Selling in combination with handling and/or distributing goods to other wholesale or retail establishments—are classified in Sector 42, Wholesale Trade.

49312 Refrigerated Warehousing and Storage

See industry description for 493120 below.

493120 Refrigerated Warehousing and Storage

This industry comprises establishments primarily engaged in operating refrigerated warehousing and storage facilities. Establishments primarily engaged in the storage of furs for the trade are included in this industry. The services provided by these establishments include blast freezing, tempering, and modified atmosphere storage services.

Cross-References.

Establishments primarily engaged in storing furs (except for the trade) and garments are classified in Industry 812320, Drycleaning and Laundry Services (except Coin-Operated).

49313 Farm Product Warehousing and Storage

See industry description for 493130 below.

493130 Farm Product Warehousing and Storage

This industry comprises establishments primarily engaged in operating bulk farm product warehousing and storage facilities (except refrigerated). Grain elevators primarily engaged in storage are included in this industry.

Cross-References. Establishments primarily engaged in—

- Operating refrigerated warehousing and storage facilities—are classified in Industry 493120, Refrigerated Warehousing and Storage; and
- Storing grains and field beans (i.e., grain elevators) as an incidental activity to sales—are classified in Industry 424510, Grain and Field Bean Merchant Wholesalers.

US—United States industry only. CAN—United States and Canadian industries are comparable. MEX—United States and Mexican industries are comparable. Blank—Canadian, Mexican, and United States industries are comparable.

49319 Other Warehousing and Storage

See industry description for 493190 below.

493190 Other Warehousing and Storage

This industry comprises establishments primarily engaged in operating warehousing and storage facilities (except general merchandise, refrigerated, and farm product warehousing and storage).

Illustrative Examples:

Bulk petroleum storage
Lumber storage terminals
Whiskey warehousing

Cross-References. Establishments primarily engaged in—

- Renting or leasing space for self storage—are classified in Industry 531130, Lessors of Miniwarehouses and Self-Storage Units;
- Storing hazardous materials for treatment and disposal—are classified in U.S. Industry 562211, Hazardous Waste Treatment and Disposal;
- Operating general warehousing and storage facilities—are classified in Industry 493110, General Warehousing and Storage;
- Operating refrigerated warehousing and storage facilities—are classified in Industry 493120, Refrigerated Warehousing and Storage; and
- Operating farm product warehousing and storage facilities—are classified in Industry 493130, Farm Product Warehousing and Storage.

US—United States industry only. CAN—United States and Canadian industries are comparable. MEX—United States and Mexican industries are comparable. Blank—Canadian, Mexican, and United States industries are comparable.

Sector 51—Information

The Sector as a Whole

The Information sector comprises establishments engaged in the following processes: (a) producing and distributing information and cultural products, (b) providing the means to transmit or distribute these products as well as data or communications, and (c) processing data.

The main components of this sector are the publishing industries, including software publishing, and both traditional publishing and publishing exclusively on the Internet; the motion picture and sound recording industries; the broadcasting industries, including traditional broadcasting and those broadcasting exclusively over the Internet; the telecommunications industries; the industries known as Internet service providers and Web search portals, data processing industries, and the information services industries.

The expressions ''information age'' and ''global information economy'' are used with considerable frequency today. The general idea of an ''information economy'' includes both the notion of industries primarily producing, processing, and distributing information, as well as the idea that every industry is using available information and information technology to reorganize and make themselves more productive.

For the purpose of developing NAICS, it is the transformation of information into a commodity that is produced and distributed by a number of growing industries that is at issue. The Information sector groups three types of establishments: (1) those engaged in producing and distributing information and cultural products; (2) those that provide the means to transmit or distribute these products as well as data or communications; and (3) those that process data. Cultural products are those that directly express attitudes, opinions, ideas, values, and artistic creativity; provide entertainment; or offer information and analysis concerning the past and present. Included in this definition are popular, mass-produced, products as well as cultural products that normally have a more limited audience, such as poetry books, literary magazines, or classical records.

The unique characteristics of information and cultural products, and of the processes involved in their production and distribution, distinguish the Information sector from the goods-producing and service-producing sectors. Some of these characteristics are:

1. Unlike traditional goods, an ''information or cultural product,'' such as a newspaper on-line or television program, does not necessarily have tangible qualities, nor is it necessarily associated with a particular form. A movie can be shown at a movie theater, on a television broadcast, through video-on-demand or rented at a local video store. A sound recording can be aired on radio, embedded in multimedia products, or sold at a record store.

2. Unlike traditional services, the delivery of these products does not require direct contact between the supplier and the consumer.

US—United States industry only. CAN—United States and Canadian industries are comparable. MEX—United States and Mexican industries are comparable. Blank—Canadian, Mexican, and United States industries are comparable.

3. The value of these products to the consumer lies in their informational, educational, cultural, or entertainment content, not in the format in which they are distributed. Most of these products are protected from unlawful reproduction by copyright laws.
4. The intangible property aspect of information and cultural products makes the processes involved in their production and distribution very different from goods and services. Only those possessing the rights to these works are authorized to reproduce, alter, improve, and distribute them. Acquiring and using these rights often involves significant costs. In addition, technology is revolutionizing the distribution of these products. It is possible to distribute them in a physical form, via broadcast, or on-line.
5. Distributors of information and cultural products can easily add value to the products they distribute. For instance, broadcasters add advertising not contained in the original product. This capacity means that unlike traditional distributors, they derive revenue not from sale of the distributed product to the final consumer, but from those who pay for the privilege of adding information to the original product. Similarly, a directory and mailing list publisher can acquire the rights to thousands of previously published newspaper and periodical articles and add new value by providing search and software and organizing the information in a way that facilitates research and retrieval. These products often command a much higher price than the original information.

The distribution modes for information commodities may either eliminate the necessity for traditional manufacture, or reverse the conventional order of manufacture-distribute: A newspaper distributed on-line, for example, can be printed locally or by the final consumer. Similarly, it is anticipated that packaged software, which today is mainly bought through the traditional retail channels, will soon be available mainly on-line. The NAICS Information sector is designed to make such economic changes transparent as they occur, or to facilitate designing surveys that will monitor the new phenomena and provide data to analyze the changes.

Many of the industries in the NAICS Information sector are engaged in producing products protected by copyright law, or in distributing them (other than distribution by traditional wholesale and retail methods). Examples are traditional publishing industries, software and directory and mailing list publishing industries, and film and sound industries. Broadcasting and telecommunications industries and information providers and processors are also included in the Information sector, because their technologies are so closely linked to other industries in the Information sector.

511 Publishing Industries (except Internet)

Industries in the Publishing Industries (except Internet) subsector group establishments engaged in the publishing of newspapers, magazines, other periodicals,

US—United States industry only. CAN—United States and Canadian industries are comparable. MEX—United States and Mexican industries are comparable. Blank—Canadian, Mexican, and United States industries are comparable.

and books, as well as directory and mailing list and software publishing. In general, these establishments, which are known as publishers, issue copies of works for which they usually possess copyright. Works may be in one or more formats including traditional print form, CD-ROM, or proprietary electronic networks. Publishers may publish works originally created by others for which they have obtained the rights and/or works that they have created in-house. Software publishing is included here because the activity, creation of a copyrighted product and bringing it to market, is equivalent to the creation process for other types of intellectual products.

In NAICS, publishing—the reporting, writing, editing, and other processes that are required to create an edition of a newspaper—is treated as a major economic activity in its own right, rather than as a subsidiary activity to a manufacturing activity, printing. Thus, publishing is classified in the Information sector; whereas, printing remains in the NAICS Manufacturing sector. In part, the NAICS classification reflects the fact that publishing increasingly takes place in establishments that are physically separate from the associated printing establishments. More crucially, the NAICS classification of book and newspaper publishing is intended to portray their roles in a modern economy, in which they do not resemble manufacturing activities.

Music publishers are not included in the Publishing Industries (except Internet) subsector, but are included in the Motion Picture and Sound Recording Industries subsector. Reproduction of prepackaged software is treated in NAICS as a manufacturing activity; on-line distribution of software products is in the Information sector, and custom design of software to client specifications is included in the Professional, Scientific, and Technical Services sector. These distinctions arise because of the different ways that software is created, reproduced, and distributed.

The Publishing Industries (except Internet) subsector does not include establishments that publish exclusively on the Internet. Establishments publishing exclusively on the Internet are included in Subsector 516, Internet Publishing and Broadcasting. The Publishing Industries (except Internet) subsector also excludes products, such as manifold business forms. Information is not the essential component of these items. Establishments producing these items are included in Subsector 323, Printing and Related Support Activities.

5111 Newspaper, Periodical, Book, and Directory Publishers

This industry group comprises establishments primarily engaged in publishing newspapers, magazines, other periodicals, books, directories and mailing lists, and other works, such as calendars, greeting cards, and maps. These works are characterized by the intellectual creativity required in their development and are usually protected by copyright. Publishers distribute or arrange for the distribution of these works.

US—United States industry only. CAN—United States and Canadian industries are comparable. MEX—United States and Mexican industries are comparable. Blank—Canadian, Mexican, and United States industries are comparable.

Publishing establishments may create the works in-house, contract for, purchase, or compile works that were originally created by others. These works may be published in one or more formats, such as print and/or electronic form, including proprietary electronic networks. Establishments in this industry may print, reproduce, or offer direct access to the works themselves or may arrange with others to carry out such functions.

Establishments that both print and publish may fill excess capacity with commercial or job printing. However, the publishing activity is still considered to be the primary activity of these establishments.

51111 Newspaper Publishers

See industry description for 511110 below.

511110 Newspaper Publishers[CAN]

This industry comprises establishments known as newspaper publishers. Establishments in this industry carry out operations necessary for producing and distributing newspapers, including gathering news; writing news columns, feature stories, and editorials; and selling and preparing advertisements. These establishments may publish newspapers in print or electronic form.

Cross-References.

- Establishments publishing newspapers exclusively on the Internet are classified in Industry 516110, Internet Publishing and Broadcasting;
- Establishments primarily engaged in printing newspapers without publishing are classified in Industry 32311, Printing;
- Establishments, such as trade associations, schools and universities, and social welfare organizations that publish newsletters for distribution to their membership, but that are not commonly known as newspaper publishers, are classified according to their primary activity designation;
- Establishments primarily engaged in supplying the news media with information, such as news, reports, and pictures, are classified in Industry 519110, News Syndicates; and
- Establishments of independent representatives primarily engaged in selling advertising space are classified in Industry 541840, Media Representatives.

51112 Periodical Publishers

See industry description for 511120 below.

US—United States industry only. CAN—United States and Canadian industries are comparable. MEX—United States and Mexican industries are comparable. Blank—Canadian, Mexican, and United States industries are comparable.

511120 Periodical Publishers[CAN]

This industry comprises establishments known either as magazine publishers or periodical publishers. These establishments carry out the operations necessary for producing and distributing magazines and other periodicals, such as gathering, writing, and editing articles, and selling and preparing advertisements. These establishments may publish magazines and other periodicals in print or electronic form.

Illustrative Examples:

- Comic book publishers (except Internet)
- Magazine publishers (except Internet)
- Newsletter publishers (except Internet)
- Radio and television guide publishers (except Internet)
- Scholarly journal publishers (except Internet)
- Trade journal publishers (except Internet)

Cross-References.

- Establishments publishing periodicals exclusively on the Internet are classified in Industry 516110, Internet Publishing and Broadcasting;
- Establishments primarily engaged in printing periodicals without publishing are classified in Industry 32311, Printing;
- Establishments, such as trade associations, schools and universities, and social welfare organizations, that publish magazines and periodicals for distribution to their membership, but that are not commonly known as periodical publishers, are classified according to their primary activity designation;
- Establishments primarily engaged in publishing directories and mailing lists are classified in Industry 511140, Directory and Mailing List Publishers; and
- Establishments of independent representatives primarily engaged in selling advertising space are classified in Industry 541840, Media Representatives.

51113 Book Publishers

See industry description for 511130 below.

511130 Book Publishers[CAN]

This industry comprises establishments known as book publishers. Establishments in this industry carry out design, editing, and marketing activities necessary for producing and distributing books. These establishments may publish books in print, electronic, or audio form.

US—United States industry only. CAN—United States and Canadian industries are comparable. MEX—United States and Mexican industries are comparable. Blank—Canadian, Mexican, and United States industries are comparable.

Illustrative Examples:

Atlas publishers (except Internet)
Book publishers (except Internet)
Encyclopedia publishers (except Internet)
Map publishers (except Internet)
Religious book publishers (except Internet)
School textbook publishers (except Internet)
Technical manual publishers (except Internet)
Travel guide book publishers (except Internet)

Cross-References.

- Establishments publishing books on the Internet exclusively are classified in Industry 516110, Internet Publishing and Broadcasting;
- Establishments primarily engaged in printing books without publishing are classified in Industry 32311, Printing;
- Establishments known as music publishers are classified in Industry 512230, Music Publishers;
- Establishments, such as trade associations, schools and universities, and social welfare organizations, that publish books for distribution to their membership, that are not commonly known as book publishers, are classified according to their primary activity designation; and
- Book clubs primarily engaged in direct sales activities without publishing are classified in Industry 454390, Other Direct Selling Establishments.

51114 Directory and Mailing List Publishers

See industry description for 511140 below.

511140 Directory and Mailing List Publishers^{CAN}

This industry comprises establishments primarily engaged in publishing directories, mailing lists, and collections or compilations of fact. The products are typically protected in their selection, arrangement and/or presentation. Examples are lists of mailing addresses, telephone directories, directories of businesses, collections or compilations of proprietary drugs or legal case results, compilations of public records, etc. These establishments may publish directories and mailing lists in print or electronic form.

Illustrative Examples:

Business directory publishers (except Internet)
Directory publishers (except Internet)
Mailing list publishers (except Internet)
Telephone directory publishers (except Internet)

US—United States industry only. CAN—United States and Canadian industries are comparable. MEX—United States and Mexican industries are comparable. Blank—Canadian, Mexican, and United States industries are comparable.

Cross-References. Establishments primarily engaged in—

- Developing and publishing, exclusively on the Internet, collections or compilations of creative works or facts—are classified in Industry 516110, Internet Publishing and Broadcasting;
- Compiling mailing lists in conjunction with providing direct mail advertising services—are classified in Industry 541860, Direct Mail Advertising;
- Printing without publishing directories and mailing lists—are classified in Industry 32311, Printing;
- Operating Web search portals—are classified in U.S. Industry 518112, Web Search Portals;
- Publishing computer software—are classified in Industry 511210, Software Publishers;
- Creating and publishing encyclopedias and similar collections of creative works in print and/or electronic media—are classified in Industry 511130, Book Publishers; and
- Creating and publishing collections of creative works that are periodically updated—are classified in Industry 511120, Periodical Publishers.

51119 Other Publishers

This industry comprises establishments known as publishers (except newspaper, magazine, book, directory, mailing list, and music publishers). These establishments may publish works in print or electronic form.

Illustrative Examples:

Art print publishers (except Internet)
Calendar publishers (except Internet)
Greeting card publishers (except Internet)

Cross-References.

- Establishments publishing exclusively on the Internet are classified in Industry 51611, Internet Publishing and Broadcasting;
- Establishments known as newspaper publishers are classified in Industry 51111, Newspaper Publishers;
- Establishments known as magazine and other periodical publishers are classified in Industry 51112, Periodical Publishers;
- Establishments known as book publishers are classified in Industry 51113, Book Publishers;
- Establishments primarily engaged in publishing directories and mailing lists are classified in Industry 51114, Directory and Mailing List Publishers;

US—United States industry only. CAN—United States and Canadian industries are comparable. MEX—United States and Mexican industries are comparable. Blank—Canadian, Mexican, and United States industries are comparable.

- Establishments known as music publishers are classified in Industry 51223, Music Publishers; and
- Establishments primarily engaged in manufacturing manifold business forms are classified in Industry 32311, Printing.

511191 Greeting Card Publishers[US]

This U.S. industry comprises establishments primarily engaged in publishing greeting cards.

Cross-References. Establishments primarily engaged in—

- Publishing greeting cards exclusively on the Internet—are classified in Industry 516110, Internet Publishing and Broadcasting; and
- Printing greeting cards without publishing—are classified in Industry 32311, Printing.

511199 All Other Publishers[US]

This U.S. industry comprises establishments generally known as publishers (except newspaper, magazine, book, directory, database, music, and greeting card publishers). These establishments may publish works in print or electronic form.

Illustrative Examples:

Art print publishers (except Internet)

Calendar publishers (except Internet)

Cross-References.

- Establishments publishing exclusively on the Internet are classified in Industry 516110, Internet Publishing and Broadcasting;
- Establishments known as newspaper publishers are classified in Industry 511110, Newspaper Publishers;
- Establishments known as magazine or other periodical publishers are classified in Industry 511120, Periodical Publishers;
- Establishments known as book publishers are classified in Industry 511130, Book Publishers;
- Establishments primarily engaged in publishing directories and mailing lists are classified in Industry 511140, Directory and Mailing List Publishers;
- Establishments primarily engaged in greeting card publishing are classified in U.S. Industry 511191, Greeting Card Publishers;

US—United States industry only. CAN—United States and Canadian industries are comparable. MEX—United States and Mexican industries are comparable. Blank—Canadian, Mexican, and United States industries are comparable.

- Establishments known as music publishers are classified in Industry 512230, Music Publishers;
- Establishments primarily engaged in manufacturing manifold business forms are classified in U.S. Industry 323116, Manifold Business Forms Printing; and
- Establishments primarily engaged in manufacturing day schedulers are classified in U.S. Industry 323118, Blankbooks, Looseleaf Binders, and Devices Manufacturing.

5112 Software Publishers

51121 Software Publishers

See industry description for 511210 below.

511210 Software Publishers[CAN]

This industry comprises establishments primarily engaged in computer software publishing or publishing and reproduction. Establishments in this industry carry out operations necessary for producing and distributing computer software, such as designing, providing documentation, assisting in installation, and providing support services to software purchasers. These establishments may design, develop, and publish, or publish only.

Cross-References. Establishments primarily engaged in—

- Reselling packaged software—are classified in Sector 42, Wholesale Trade or Sector 44-45, Retail Trade;
- Providing access to software for clients from a central host site—are classified in Industry 518210, Data Processing, Hosting, and Related Services;
- Designing software to meet the needs of specific users—are classified in U.S. Industry 541511, Custom Computer Programming Services; and
- Mass duplication of software—are classified in U.S. Industry 334611, Software Reproducing.

512 Motion Picture and Sound Recording Industries

Industries in the Motion Picture and Sound Recording Industries subsector group establishments involved in the production and distribution of motion pictures and sound recordings. While producers and distributors of motion pictures and sound recordings issue works for sale as traditional publishers do, the processes are

US—United States industry only. CAN—United States and Canadian industries are comparable. MEX—United States and Mexican industries are comparable. Blank—Canadian, Mexican, and United States industries are comparable.

sufficiently different to warrant placing establishments engaged in these activities in a separate subsector. Production is typically a complex process that involves several distinct types of establishments that are engaged in activities, such as contracting with performers, creating the film or sound content, and providing technical postproduction services. Film distribution is often to exhibitors, such as theaters and broadcasters, rather than through the wholesale and retail distribution chain. When the product is in a mass-produced form, NAICS treats production and distribution as the major economic activity as it does in the Publishing Industries subsector, rather than as a subsidiary activity to the manufacture of such products.

This subsector does not include establishments primarily engaged in the wholesale distribution of videocassettes and sound recordings, such as compact discs and audio tapes; these establishments are included in the Wholesale Trade sector. Reproduction of videocassettes and sound recordings that is carried out separately from establishments engaged in production and distribution is treated in NAICS as a manufacturing activity.

5121 Motion Picture and Video Industries

This industry group comprises establishments primarily engaged in the production and/or distribution of motion pictures, videos, television programs, or commercials; in the exhibition of motion pictures; or in the provision of postproduction and related services.

51211 Motion Picture and Video Production

See industry description for 512110 below.

512110 Motion Picture and Video Production[CAN]

This industry comprises establishments primarily engaged in producing, or producing and distributing motion pictures, videos, television programs, or television commercials.

Cross-References. Establishments primarily engaged in—

- Producing motion pictures and videos on contract as independent producers—are classified in Industry 711510, Independent Artists, Writers, and Performers;
- Providing teleproduction and other postproduction services—are classified in U.S. Industry 512191, Teleproduction and Other Postproduction Services;
- Providing video taping of weddings, special events, and/or business inventories—are classified in Industry 54192, Photographic Services;

US—United States industry only. CAN—United States and Canadian industries are comparable. MEX—United States and Mexican industries are comparable. Blank—Canadian, Mexican, and United States industries are comparable.

- Providing motion picture laboratory services—are classified in U.S. Industry 512199, Other Motion Picture and Video Industries;
- Providing mass duplication and packaging of video tapes—are classified in U.S. Industry 334612, Prerecorded Compact Disc (except Software), Tape, and Record Reproducing; and
- Acquiring distribution rights and distributing motion pictures and videos—are classified in Industry 512120, Motion Picture and Video Distribution.

51212 Motion Picture and Video Distribution

See industry description for 512120 below.

512120 Motion Picture and Video Distribution[CAN]

This industry comprises establishments primarily engaged in acquiring distribution rights and distributing film and video productions to motion picture theaters, television networks and stations, and exhibitors.

Cross-References. Establishments primarily engaged in—

- Producing and distributing motion pictures and videos—are classified in Industry 512110, Motion Picture and Video Production;
- Merchant wholesale distribution of blank video cassette tapes and discs—are classified in Industry 423690, Other Electronic Parts and Equipment Merchant Wholesalers;
- Merchant wholesale distribution of prerecorded video cassette tapes and discs—are classified in Industry 423990, Other Miscellaneous Durable Goods Merchant Wholesalers;
- Providing mass duplication and packaging of video tapes—are classified in U.S. Industry 334612, Prerecorded Compact Disc (except Software), Tape, and Record Reproducing;
- Providing motion picture footage (via film libraries) to producers—are classified in U.S. Industry 512199, Other Motion Picture and Video Industries;
- Renting video tapes and discs to the general public—are classified in Industry 532230, Video Tape and Disc Rental; and
- Selling video cassettes and discs to the general public—are classified in Industry 451220, Prerecorded Tape, Compact Disc and Record Stores.

51213 Motion Picture and Video Exhibition

This industry comprises establishments primarily engaged in operating motion picture theaters and/or exhibiting motion pictures or videos at film festivals, and so forth.

US—United States industry only. CAN—United States and Canadian industries are comparable. MEX—United States and Mexican industries are comparable. Blank—Canadian, Mexican, and United States industries are comparable.

512131 Motion Picture Theaters (except Drive-Ins)[US]

This U.S. industry comprises establishments primarily engaged in operating motion picture theaters (except drive-ins) and/or exhibiting motion pictures or videos at film festivals, and so forth.

512132 Drive-In Motion Picture Theaters[US]

This U.S. industry comprises establishments primarily engaged in operating drive-in motion picture theaters.

51219 Postproduction Services and Other Motion Picture and Video Industries

This industry comprises establishments primarily engaged in providing postproduction services and other services to the motion picture industry, including specialized motion picture or video postproduction services, such as editing, film/tape transfers, titling, subtitling, credits, closed captioning, and computer-produced graphics, animation and special effects, as well as developing and processing motion picture film.

Illustrative Examples:

Motion picture film laboratories
Postproduction facilities
Stock footage film libraries
Teleproduction services

Cross-References. Establishments primarily engaged in—

- Mass duplicating video tapes and film—are classified in Industry 33461, Manufacturing and Reproducing Magnetic and Optical Media;
- Providing audio services for film, television, and video productions—are classified in Industry 51224, Sound Recording Studios;
- Renting wardrobes and costumes for motion picture production—are classified in Industry 53222, Formal Wear and Costume Rental;
- Renting studio equipment—are classified in Industry 53249, Other Commercial and Industrial Machinery and Equipment Rental and Leasing; and
- Casting actors and actresses with production companies—are classified in Industry 56131, Employment Placement Agencies.

512191 Teleproduction and Other Postproduction Services[US]

This U.S. industry comprises establishments primarily engaged in providing specialized motion picture or video postproduction services, such as editing, film/

US—United States industry only. CAN—United States and Canadian industries are comparable. MEX—United States and Mexican industries are comparable. Blank—Canadian, Mexican, and United States industries are comparable.

tape transfers, subtitling, credits, closed captioning, and animation and special effects.

Cross-References. Establishments primarily engaged in—

- Mass duplicating video tapes and film—are classified in Industry 33461, Manufacturing and Reproducing Magnetic and Optical Media;
- Developing and processing motion picture film—are classified in U.S. Industry 512199, Other Motion Picture and Video Industries;
- Providing audio services for film, television, and video productions—are classified in Industry 512240, Sound Recording Studios; and
- Acquiring distribution rights and distributing film and video productions to motion picture theaters, television networks and stations, and exhibitors—are classified in Industry 512120, Motion Picture and Video Distribution.

512199 Other Motion Picture and Video Industries[US]

This U.S. industry comprises establishments primarily engaged in providing motion picture and video services (except motion picture and video production, distribution, exhibition, and teleproduction and other postproduction services).

Illustrative Examples:

Motion picture film laboratories

Stock footage film libraries

Cross-References. Establishments primarily engaged in—

- Renting wardrobes and costumes for motion picture production—are classified in Industry 532220, Formal Wear and Costume Rental;
- Renting studio equipment—are classified in Industry 532490, Other Commercial and Industrial Machinery and Equipment Rental and Leasing;
- Casting actors and actresses with production companies—are classified in Industry 561310, Employment Placement Agencies;
- Motion picture and video production—are classified in Industry 512110, Motion Picture and Video Production;
- Motion picture and video distribution—are classified in Industry 512120, Motion Picture and Video Distribution;
- Teleproduction and other postproduction services—are classified in U.S. Industry 512191, Teleproduction and Other Postproduction Services; and
- Motion picture and video exhibition—are classified in Industry 51213, Motion Picture and Video Exhibition.

US—United States industry only. CAN—United States and Canadian industries are comparable. MEX—United States and Mexican industries are comparable. Blank—Canadian, Mexican, and United States industries are comparable.

5122 Sound Recording Industries

This industry group comprises establishments primarily engaged in producing and distributing musical recordings, in publishing music, or in providing sound recording and related services.

51221 Record Production

See industry description for 512210 below.

512210 Record Production[CAN]

This industry comprises establishments primarily engaged in record production (e.g., tapes, CDs). These establishments contract with artists and arrange and finance the production of original master recordings. Establishments in this industry hold the copyright to the master recording and derive most of their revenues from the sales, leasing, and licensing of master recordings. Establishments in this industry do not have their own duplication or distribution capabilities.

Cross-References. Establishments primarily engaged in—

- Releasing, promoting, and distributing recordings—are classified in Industry 512220, Integrated Record Production/Distribution;
- Promoting and authorizing the use of musical works in various media—are classified in Industry 512230, Music Publishers;
- Mass duplication services—are classified in U.S. Industry 334612, Prerecorded Compact Disc (except Software), Tape, and Record Reproducing;
- Merchant wholesale distribution of blank audio cassettes, tapes, and discs—are classified in Industry 423690, Other Electronic Parts and Equipment Merchant Wholesalers;
- Merchant wholesale distribution of prerecorded audio cassettes, tapes, and discs—are classified in Industry 423990, Other Miscellaneous Durable Goods Merchant Wholesalers;
- Managing the careers of artists—are classified in Industry 711410, Agents and Managers for Artists, Athletes, Entertainers and Other Public Figures;
- Providing facilities and technical expertise for recording musical performances—are classified in Industry 512240, Sound Recording Studios; and
- Producing albums on contract as independent producers—are classified in Industry 711510, Independent Artists, Writers, and Performers.

51222 Integrated Record Production/Distribution

See industry description for 512220 below.

US—United States industry only. CAN—United States and Canadian industries are comparable. MEX—United States and Mexican industries are comparable. Blank—Canadian, Mexican, and United States industries are comparable.

512220 Integrated Record Production/Distribution[CAN]

This industry comprises establishments primarily engaged in releasing, promoting, and distributing sound recordings. These establishments manufacture or arrange for the manufacture of recordings, such as audio tapes/cassettes and compact discs, and promote and distribute these products to wholesalers, retailers, or directly to the public. Establishments in this industry produce master recordings themselves, or obtain reproduction and distribution rights to master recordings produced by record production companies or other integrated record companies.

Cross-References. Establishments primarily engaged in—

- Contracting with musical artists, arranging for the production of master recordings, and marketing the reproduction rights—are classified in Industry 512210, Record Production;
- Providing facilities and technical expertise for recording musical performances—are classified in Industry 512240, Sound Recording Studios;
- Mass duplication of recorded products—are classified in U.S. Industry 334612, Prerecorded Compact Disc (except Software), Tape, and Record Reproducing;
- Merchant wholesale distribution of prerecorded audio cassettes, tapes, and discs—are classified in Industry 423990, Other Miscellaneous Durable Goods Merchant Wholesalers; and
- Retailing records, tapes, and compact discs without producing recordings—are classified in Sector 44-45, Retail Trade.

51223 Music Publishers

See industry description for 512230 below.

512230 Music Publishers[CAN]

This industry comprises establishments primarily engaged in acquiring and registering copyrights for musical compositions in accordance with law and promoting and authorizing the use of these compositions in recordings, radio, television, motion pictures, live performances, print, or other media. Establishments in this industry represent the interests of the songwriter or other owners of musical compositions to produce revenues from the use of such works, generally through licensing agreements. These establishments may own the copyright or act as administrator of the music copyrights on behalf of copyright owners. Publishers of music books and sheet music are included in this industry.

US—United States industry only. CAN—United States and Canadian industries are comparable. MEX—United States and Mexican industries are comparable. Blank—Canadian, Mexican, and United States industries are comparable.

Cross-References.

Establishments primarily engaged as independent songwriters who act as their own publishers are classified in Industry 711510, Independent Artists, Writers, and Performers.

51224 Sound Recording Studios

See industry description for 512240 below.

512240 Sound Recording Studios[CAN]

This industry comprises establishments primarily engaged in providing the facilities and technical expertise for sound recording in a studio. This industry includes establishments that provide audio production and postproduction services to produce master recordings. These establishments may provide audio services for film, television, and video productions.

Cross-References. Establishments primarily engaged in—

- Releasing, promoting, and distributing sound recordings—are classified in Industry 512220, Integrated Record Production/Distribution;
- Providing mass duplication of recorded products—are classified in U.S. Industry 334612, Prerecorded Compact Disc (except Software), Tape, and Record Reproducing; and
- Contracting with musical artists, arranging for the production of master recordings, and marketing the reproduction rights—are classified in Industry 512210, Record Production.

51229 Other Sound Recording Industries

See industry description for 512290 below.

512290 Other Sound Recording Industries[CAN]

This industry comprises establishments primarily engaged in providing sound recording services (except record production, distribution, music publishing, and sound recording in a studio). Establishments in this industry provide services, such as the audio recording of meetings and conferences.

Cross-References. Establishments primarily engaged in—

- Producing records, including contracting with musical artists, arranging and financing the production of master recordings, and marketing the reproduction rights—are classified in Industry 512210, Record Production;

US—United States industry only. CAN—United States and Canadian industries are comparable. MEX—United States and Mexican industries are comparable. Blank—Canadian, Mexican, and United States industries are comparable.

- Releasing, promoting, and distributing sound recordings—are classified in Industry 512220, Integrated Record Production/Distribution;
- Promoting and authorizing the use of musical works in various media—are classified in Industry 512230, Music Publishers;
- Providing facilities and expertise for recording musical performance—are classified in Industry 512240, Sound Recording Studios;
- Providing mass duplication of recorded products—are classified in U.S. Industry 334612, Prerecorded Compact Disc (except Software), Tape, and Record Reproducing; and
- Organizing and promoting the presentation of performing arts productions—are classified in Industry Group 7113, Promoters of Performing Arts, Sports and Similar Events.

515 Broadcasting (except Internet)

Industries in the Broadcasting (except Internet) subsector include establishments that create content or acquire the right to distribute content and subsequently broadcast the content. The industry groups (Radio and Television Broadcasting and Cable and Other Subscription Programming) are based on differences in the methods of communication and the nature of services provided. The Radio and Television Broadcasting industry group includes establishments that operate broadcasting studios and facilities for over the air or satellite delivery of radio and television programs of entertainment, news, talk, and the like. These establishments are often engaged in the production and purchase of programs and generating revenues from the sale of air time to advertisers and from donations, subsidies, and/or the sale of programs. The Cable and Other Subscription Programming industry group includes establishments operating studios and facilities for the broadcasting of programs that are typically narrowcast in nature (limited format, such as news, sports, education, and youth-oriented programming) on a subscription or fee basis.

The distribution of cable and other subscription programming is included in Subsector 517, Telecommunications. Establishments that broadcast exclusively on the Internet are included in Subsector 516, Internet Publishing and Broadcasting.

5151 Radio and Television Broadcasting

This industry group comprises establishments primarily engaged in operating broadcast studios and facilities for over-the-air or satellite delivery of radio and television programs. These establishments are often engaged in the production or purchase of programs or generate revenues from the sale of air time to advertisers, from donations and subsidies, or from the sale of programs.

US—United States industry only. CAN—United States and Canadian industries are comparable. MEX—United States and Mexican industries are comparable. Blank—Canadian, Mexican, and United States industries are comparable.

51511 Radio Broadcasting

This industry comprises establishments primarily engaged in broadcasting audio signals. These establishments operate radio broadcasting studios and facilities for the transmission of aural programming by radio to the public, to affiliates, or to subscribers. The radio programs may include entertainment, news, talk shows, business data, or religious services.

Cross-References. Establishments primarily engaged in—

- Broadcasting exclusively on the Internet—are classified in Industry 51611, Internet Publishing and Broadcasting; and
- Producing taped radio programming—are classified in Industry 51229, Other Sound Recording Industries.

515111 Radio Networks[US]

This U.S. industry comprises establishments primarily engaged in assembling and transmitting aural programming to their affiliates or subscribers via over-the-air broadcasts, cable, or satellite. The programming covers a wide variety of material, such as news services, religious programming, weather, sports, or music.

Cross-References. Establishments primarily engaged in—

- Broadcasting exclusively on the Internet—are classified in Industry 516110, Internet Publishing and Broadcasting; and
- Producing taped radio programming—are classified in Industry 512290, Other Sound Recording Industries.

515112 Radio Stations[US]

This U.S. industry comprises establishments primarily engaged in broadcasting aural programs by radio to the public. Programming may originate in their own studio, from an affiliated network, or from external sources.

51512 Television Broadcasting

See industry description for 515120 below.

515120 Television Broadcasting[CAN]

This industry comprises establishments primarily engaged in broadcasting images together with sound. These establishments operate television broadcasting

US—United States industry only. CAN—United States and Canadian industries are comparable. MEX—United States and Mexican industries are comparable. Blank—Canadian, Mexican, and United States industries are comparable.

studios and facilities for the programming and transmission of programs to the public. These establishments also produce or transmit visual programming to affiliated broadcast television stations, which in turn broadcast the programs to the public on a predetermined schedule. Programming may originate in their own studio, from an affiliated network, or from external sources.

Cross-References. Establishments primarily engaged in—

- Broadcasting exclusively on the Internet—are classified in Industry 516110, Internet Publishing and Broadcasting;
- Producing taped television program materials—are classified in Industry 512110, Motion Picture and Video Production;
- Furnishing cable and other pay television services—are classified in Industry 517510, Cable and Other Program Distribution; and
- Producing and broadcasting television programs for cable and satellite television systems—are classified in Industry 515210, Cable and Other Subscription Programming.

5152 Cable and Other Subscription Programming

51521 Cable and Other Subscription Programming

See industry description for 515210 below.

515210 Cable and Other Subscription Programming[CAN]

This industry comprises establishments primarily engaged in operating studios and facilities for the broadcasting of programs on a subscription or fee basis. The broadcast programming is typically narrowcast in nature (e.g., limited format, such as news, sports, education, or youth-oriented). These establishments produce programming in their own facilities or acquire programming from external sources. The programming material is usually delivered to a third party, such as cable systems or direct-to-home satellite systems, for transmission to viewers.

Cross-References. Establishments primarily engaged in—

- Producing taped television program material—are classified in Industry 512110, Motion Picture and Video Production;
- Producing and transmitting television programs to affiliated stations—are classified in Industry 515120, Television Broadcasting;
- Furnishing cable and other pay television services—are classified in Industry 517510, Cable and Other Program Distribution; and

US—United States industry only. CAN—United States and Canadian industries are comparable. MEX—United States and Mexican industries are comparable. Blank—Canadian, Mexican, and United States industries are comparable.

- Retailing merchandise by electronic media, such as television—are classified in Industry 45411, Electronic Shopping and Mail-Order Houses.

516 Internet Publishing and Broadcasting

Industries in the Internet Publishing and Broadcasting subsector group establishments that publish and/or broadcast content exclusively for the Internet. The unique combination of text, audio, video, and interactive features present in informational or cultural products on the Internet justifies the separation of Internet publishers and broadcasters from more traditional publishers included in subsector 511, Publishing Industries (except Internet) and subsector 515, Broadcasting (except Internet).

5161 Internet Publishing and Broadcasting

51611 Internet Publishing and Broadcasting

See industry description for 516110 below.

516110 Internet Publishing and Broadcasting[CAN]

This industry comprises establishments engaged in publishing and/or broadcasting content on the Internet exclusively. These establishments do not provide traditional (non-Internet) versions of the content that they publish or broadcast. Establishments in this industry provide textual, audio, and/or video content of general or specific interest on the Internet.

Illustrative Examples:

Internet book publishers
Internet entertainment sites
Internet game sites
Internet news publishers
Internet periodical publishers
Internet radio stations
Internet sports sites
Internet video broadcast sites

Cross-References. Establishments primarily engaged in—

- Providing Internet access, known as Internet Service Providers—are classified in U.S. Industry 518111, Internet Service Providers;
- Providing both Internet publishing and other print or electronic (e.g., CD-ROM, diskette) editions in the same establishment or using proprietary networks to distribute content—are classified in Subsector 511, Publishing Industries (except Internet) based on the materials produced;
- Operating web search portals—are classified in U.S. Industry 518112, Web Search Portals;

US—United States industry only. CAN—United States and Canadian industries are comparable. MEX—United States and Mexican industries are comparable. Blank—Canadian, Mexican, and United States industries are comparable.

- Providing streaming services on content owned by others—are classified in Industry 518210, Data Processing, Hosting, and Related Services;
- Wholesaling goods on the Internet—are classified in Sector 42, Wholesale Trade;
- Retailing goods on the Internet—are classified in Sector 44-45, Retail Trade; and
- Operating stock brokerages, travel reservation systems, purchasing services, and similar activities using the Internet rather than traditional methods—are classified with the more traditional establishments providing these services.

517 Telecommunications

Industries in the Telecommunications subsector include establishments providing telecommunications and the services related to that activity. The Telecommunications subsector is primarily engaged in operating, maintaining, and/or providing access to facilities for the transmission of voice, data, text, sound, and video. A transmission facility may be based on a single technology or a combination of technologies. Establishments primarily engaged as independent contractors in the maintenance and installation of broadcasting and telecommunications systems are classified in Sector 23, Construction.

5171 Wired Telecommunications Carriers

This industry group comprises establishments primarily engaged in operating, maintaining or providing access to facilities for the transmission of voice, data, text, sound, and video using wired telecommunications networks. Transmission facilities may be based on a single technology or a combination of technologies.

51711 Wired Telecommunications Carriers

See industry description for 517110 below.

517110 Wired Telecommunications Carriers[CAN]

This industry comprises establishments engaged in (1) operating and maintaining switching and transmission facilities to provide point-to-point communications via landlines, microwave, or a combination of landlines and satellite linkups or (2) furnishing telegraph and other non-vocal communications using their own facilities.

US—United States industry only. CAN—United States and Canadian industries are comparable. MEX—United States and Mexican industries are comparable. Blank—Canadian, Mexican, and United States industries are comparable.

Cross-References. Establishments primarily engaged in—

- Distributing scheduled television programs via cable or satellite facilities on a subscription or fee basis—are classified in Industry 517510, Cable and Other Program Distribution;
- Providing coin-operated pay telephones—are classified in Industry 812990, All Other Personal Services;
- Operating and maintaining wireless networks—are classified in Industry 51721, Wireless Telecommunications Carriers (except Satellite);
- Reselling telecommunications, without operating a network—are classified in Industry 517310, Telecommunications Resellers;
- Publishing telephone directories—are classified in Industry 511140, Directory and Mailing List Publishers; and
- Maintaining and installing wired telecommunication systems as independent contractors—are classified in Sector 23, Construction.

5172 Wireless Telecommunications Carriers (except Satellite)

This industry group comprises establishments primarily engaged in operating, maintaining or providing access to facilities for the transmission of voice, data, text, sound, and video using wireless telecommunications networks. Transmission facilities may be based on a single technology or a combination of technologies.

51721 Wireless Telecommunications Carriers (except Satellite)

This industry comprises establishments primarily engaged in operating and maintaining switching and transmission facilities that provide omni-directional communications via airwaves. Included in this industry are establishments providing wireless telecommunications network services, such as cellular telephone or paging services.

Cross-Reference.

Establishments primarily engaged in providing telephone answering services using pagers are classified in Industry 56142, Telephone Call Centers.

517211 Paging[US]

This U.S. industry comprises establishments primarily engaged in operating paging networks. The establishments of this industry may also supply and maintain equipment used to receive signals.

US—United States industry only. CAN—United States and Canadian industries are comparable. MEX—United States and Mexican industries are comparable. Blank—Canadian, Mexican, and United States industries are comparable.

Cross-Reference.

Establishments primarily engaged in providing telephone answering services using pagers are classified in U.S. Industry 561421, Telephone Answering Services.

517212 Cellular and Other Wireless Telecommunications[US]

This U.S. industry comprises establishments primarily engaged in operating cellular telecommunications and other wireless telecommunications networks (except paging).

Cross-Reference.

Establishments primarily engaged in operating paging networks are classified in U.S. Industry 517211, Paging.

5173 Telecommunications Resellers

51731 Telecommunications Resellers

See industry description for 517310 below.

517310 Telecommunications Resellers[CAN]

This industry comprises establishments primarily engaged in purchasing access and network capacity from owners and operators of the networks and reselling wired and wireless telecommunications services (except satellite) to businesses and households. Establishments in this industry resell telecommunications; they do not operate and maintain telecommunications switching and transmission facilities.

Cross-References. Establishments primarily engaged in—

- Operating and maintaining wired telecommunications networks—are classified in Industry 517110, Wired Telecommunications Carriers;
- Reselling satellite telecommunications services—are classified in Industry 517410, Satellite Telecommunications; and
- Operating and maintaining wireless telecommunications—are classified in Industry 51721, Wireless Telecommunications Carriers (except Satellite).

5174 Satellite Telecommunications

51741 Satellite Telecommunications

See industry description for 517410 below.

US—United States industry only. CAN—United States and Canadian industries are comparable. MEX—United States and Mexican industries are comparable. Blank—Canadian, Mexican, and United States industries are comparable.

517410 Satellite Telecommunications[CAN]

This industry comprises establishments primarily engaged in providing point-to-point telecommunications services to other establishments in the telecommunications and broadcasting industries by forwarding and receiving communications signals via a system of satellites or reselling satellite telecommunications.

Cross-Reference.

Establishments primarily engaged in providing direct-to-home satellite television systems to individual households or consumers are classified in Industry 517510, Cable and Other Program Distribution.

5175 Cable and Other Program Distribution

51751 Cable and Other Program Distribution

See industry description for 517510 below.

517510 Cable and Other Program Distribution[CAN]

This industry comprises establishments primarily engaged as third-party distribution systems for broadcast programming. The establishments of this industry deliver visual, aural, or textual programming received from cable networks, local television stations, or radio networks to consumers via cable or direct-to-home satellite systems on a subscription or fee basis. These establishments do not generally originate programming material.

Cross-References. Establishments primarily engaged in—

- Producing and broadcasting television programs for cable and satellite television systems—are classified in Industry 515210, Cable and Other Subscription Programming; and
- Maintenance and installation of cable systems as independent contractors—are classified in Sector 23, Construction.

5179 Other Telecommunications

51791 Other Telecommunications

See industry description for 517910 below.

US—United States industry only. CAN—United States and Canadian industries are comparable. MEX—United States and Mexican industries are comparable. Blank—Canadian, Mexican, and United States industries are comparable.

517910 Other Telecommunications[CAN]

This industry comprises establishments primarily engaged in (1) providing specialized telecommunications applications, such as satellite tracking, communications telemetry, and radar station operations; or (2) providing satellite terminal stations and associated facilities operationally connected with one or more terrestrial communications systems and capable of transmitting telecommunications to or receiving telecommunications from satellite systems.

Cross-References. Establishments primarily engaged in—

- Providing satellite telecommunications—are classified in Industry 517410, Satellite Telecommunications; and
- Providing custom design, programming, or facilities management services for integrated computer and telecommunications systems or operations—are classified in Industry 54151, Computer Systems Design and Related Services.

518 Internet Service Providers, Web Search Portals, and Data Processing Services

Industries in the Internet Service Providers, Web Search Portals, and Data Processing Services subsector group establishments that provide: (1) access to the Internet; (2) search facilities for the Internet; and (3) data processing, hosting, and related services. The industry groups (Internet Service Providers and Web Search Portals, Data Processing Hosting, and Related Services) are based on differences in the processes used to access information and process information. The Internet Service Providers and Web Search Portals industry group includes establishments that are providing access to the Internet or aiding in navigation on the Internet. The Data Processing, Hosting, and Related Services industry group includes establishments that process data. These establishments can transform data, prepare data for dissemination, or place data or content on the Internet for others. In addition, the shared use of computer resources is included in the Data Processing, Hosting, and Related Services industry group.

Establishments that are publishing exclusively on the Internet are included in Subsector 516, Internet Publishing and Broadcasting and establishments that are retailing goods using the Internet are included in Sector 44-45, Retail Trade.

5181 Internet Service Providers and Web Search Portals

51811 Internet Service Providers and Web Search Portals

This industry comprises establishments known as Internet service providers or known as Web search portals. Establishments in this industry provide clients access

US—United States industry only. CAN—United States and Canadian industries are comparable. MEX—United States and Mexican industries are comparable. Blank—Canadian, Mexican, and United States industries are comparable.

to the Internet or operate Web sites that use a search engine to provide Internet search services. Establishments in this industry generally provide related services, such as Web hosting, Web page design, and related advice and assistance. Web search portals often provide additional Internet services, such as e-mail, connections to other Web sites, auctions, news, and other limited content, and serve as a home base for Internet users.

Cross-References. Establishments primarily engaged in—

- Publishing or broadcasting exclusively on the Internet—are classified in Industry 51611, Internet Publishing and Broadcasting;
- Web hosting—are classified in Industry 51821, Data Processing, Hosting, and Related Services;
- Designing Web sites for others on a fee basis—are classified in Industry 54151, Computer Systems Design and Related Services;
- Providing telecommunications related consulting services—are classified in Industry 54161, Management Consulting Services;
- Wholesaling goods on the Internet—are classified in Sector 42, Wholesale Trade;
- Retailing goods on the Internet—are classified in Sector 44-45, Retail Trade; and
- Operating stock brokerages, travel reservation systems, purchasing services, and similar activities using the Internet rather than traditional methods—are classified with the more traditional establishments providing these services.

518111 Internet Service Providers[US]

This U.S. industry comprises establishments known as Internet service providers. Establishments in this industry provide clients access to the Internet and generally provide related services such as Web hosting, Web page designing, and hardware or software consulting related to Internet connectivity. Establishments in this industry may provide local, regional, or national coverage for clients or provide backbone services (except telecommunications carriers) for other Internet service providers. Internet service providers have the equipment and telecommunication network access required for a point-of-presence on the Internet.

Cross References. Establishments primarily engaged in—

- Publishing or broadcasting exclusively on the Internet—are classified in Industry 516110;
- Web hosting—are classified in Industry 518210, Data Processing, Hosting, and Related Services;

US—United States industry only. CAN—United States and Canadian industries are comparable. MEX—United States and Mexican industries are comparable. Blank—Canadian, Mexican, and United States industries are comparable.

- Designing Web sites for others on a fee basis—are classified in U.S. Industry 541511, Custom Computer Programming Services; and
- Providing telecommunications related consulting services—are classified in U.S. Industry 541618, Other Management Consulting Services.

518112 Web Search Portals[US]

This U.S. industry comprises establishments known as Web search portals. Establishments in this industry operate Web sites that use a search engine to generate and maintain extensive databases of Internet addresses and content in an easily searchable format. Web search portals often provide additional Internet services, such as e-mail, connections to other Web sites, auctions, news, and other limited content, and serve as a home base for Internet users.

Cross-References. Establishments primarily engaged in—

- Publishing or broadcasting exclusively on the Internet—are classified in Industry 516110;
- Providing Internet access, known as Internet Service Providers—are classified in U.S. Industry 518111, Internet Service Providers;
- Wholesaling goods on the Internet—are classified in Sector 42, Wholesale Trade;
- Retailing goods on the Internet—are classified in Sector 44-45, Retail Trade; and
- Operating stock brokerages, travel reservation systems, purchasing services, and similar activities using the Internet rather than traditional methods—are classified with the more traditional establishments providing these services.

5182 Data Processing, Hosting, and Related Services

51821 Data Processing, Hosting, and Related Services

See industry description for 518210 below

518210 Data Processing, Hosting, and Related Services[CAN]

This industry comprises establishments primarily engaged in providing infrastructure for hosting or data processing services. These establishments may provide specialized hosting activities, such as Web hosting, streaming services or application hosting, provide application service provisioning, or may provide general time-share mainframe facilities to clients. Data processing establishments provide com-

---

US—United States industry only. CAN—United States and Canadian industries are comparable. MEX—United States and Mexican industries are comparable. Blank—Canadian, Mexican, and United States industries are comparable.

plete processing and specialized reports from data supplied by clients or provide automated data processing and data entry services.

Illustrative Examples:

Application hosting
Application service providers
Computer input preparation services
Computer time rental
Microfilm imaging services
Optical scanning services
Web hosting

Cross-References. Establishments primarily engaged in—

- Providing text processing and related document preparation activities—are classified in Industry 561410, Document Preparation Services;
- Providing on-site management and operation of a clients' data-processing facilities—are classified in U.S. Industry 541513, Computer Facilities Management Services;
- Providing Internet access services in combination with Web hosting—are classified in U.S. Industry 518111, Internet Service Providers;
- Operating Web search portals—are classified in U.S. Industry 518112, Web Search Portals;
- Providing access to computers and office equipment, as well as other office support services—are classified in Industry 56143, Business Service Centers;
- Processing financial transactions, such as credit card transactions—are classified in Industry 522320, Financial Transactions Processing, Reserve, and Clearinghouse Activities; and
- Providing payroll processing services—are classified in U.S. Industry 541214, Payroll Services.

519 Other Information Services

Industries in the Other Information Services subsector group establishments supplying information, storing information, providing access to information, and searching and retrieving information. The main components of the subsector are news syndicates, libraries, and archives.

5191 Other Information Services

51911 News Syndicates

See industry description for 519110 below.

US—United States industry only. CAN—United States and Canadian industries are comparable. MEX—United States and Mexican industries are comparable. Blank—Canadian, Mexican, and United States industries are comparable.

519110 News Syndicates[CAN]

This industry comprises establishments primarily engaged in supplying information, such as news reports, articles, pictures, and features, to the news media.

Cross-Reference.

Independent writers and journalists (including photojournalists) are classified in Industry 711510, Independent Artists, Writers, and Performers.

51912 Libraries and Archives

See industry description for 519120 below.

519120 Libraries and Archives[US]

This industry comprises establishments primarily engaged in providing library or archive services. These establishments are engaged in maintaining collections of documents (e.g., books, journals, newspapers, and music) and facilitating the use of such documents (recorded information regardless of its physical form and characteristics) as are required to meet the informational, research, educational, or recreational needs of their user. These establishments may also acquire, research, store, preserve, and generally make accessible to the public historical documents, photographs, maps, audio material, audiovisual material, and other archival material of historical interest. All or portions of these collections may be accessible electronically.

Cross-References. Establishments primarily engaged in—

- Providing stock footage (via motion picture and video tape libraries) to the media, multimedia, and advertising industries—are classified in U.S. Industry 512199, Other Motion Picture and Video Industries; and
- Distributing film and video productions to motion picture theaters, television networks and stations, and exhibitors—are classified in Industry 512120, Motion Picture and Video Distribution.

51919 All Other Information Services

See industry description for 519190 below.

519190 All Other Information Services[CAN]

This industry comprises establishments primarily engaged in providing other information services (except news syndicates and libraries and archives).

US—United States industry only. CAN—United States and Canadian industries are comparable. MEX—United States and Mexican industries are comparable. Blank—Canadian, Mexican, and United States industries are comparable.

Illustrative Examples:

News clipping services
Stock photo agencies
Telephone-based information services

Cross-References. Establishments primarily engaged in—

- Providing Internet access—are classified in U.S. Industry 518111, Internet Service Providers;
- Operating Web search portals—are classified in U.S. Industry 518112, Web Search Portals,
- Publishing (except exclusively on the Internet)—are classified in Subsector 511, Publishing Industries (except Internet)
- Publishing or broadcasting exclusively on the Internet—are classified in Industry 516110, Internet Publishing and Broadcasting;
- Operating news syndicates—are classified in Industry 519110, News Syndicates; and
- Operating libraries and archives—are classified in Industry 519120, Libraries and Archives.

US—United States industry only. CAN—United States and Canadian industries are comparable. MEX—United States and Mexican industries are comparable. Blank—Canadian, Mexican, and United States industries are comparable.

Sector 52—Finance and Insurance

The Sector as a Whole

The Finance and Insurance sector comprises establishments primarily engaged in financial transactions (transactions involving the creation, liquidation, or change in ownership of financial assets) and/or in facilitating financial transactions. Three principal types of activities are identified:

1. Raising funds by taking deposits and/or issuing securities and, in the process, incurring liabilities. Establishments engaged in this activity use raised funds to acquire financial assets by making loans and/or purchasing securities. Putting themselves at risk, they channel funds from lenders to borrowers and transform or repackage the funds with respect to maturity, scale, and risk. This activity is known as financial intermediation.
2. Pooling of risk by underwriting insurance and annuities. Establishments engaged in this activity collect fees, insurance premiums, or annuity considerations; build up reserves; invest those reserves; and make contractual payments. Fees are based on the expected incidence of the insured risk and the expected return on investment.
3. Providing specialized services facilitating or supporting financial intermediation, insurance, and employee benefit programs.

In addition, monetary authorities charged with monetary control are included in this sector.

The subsectors, industry groups, and industries within the NAICS Finance and Insurance sector are defined on the basis of their unique production processes. As with all industries, the production processes are distinguished by their use of specialized human resources and specialized physical capital. In addition, the way in which these establishments acquire and allocate financial capital, their source of funds, and the use of those funds provides a third basis for distinguishing characteristics of the production process. For instance, the production process in raising funds through deposit-taking is different from the process of raising funds in bond or money markets. The process of making loans to individuals also requires different production processes than does the creation of investment pools or the underwriting of securities.

Most of the Finance and Insurance subsectors contain one or more industry groups of (1) intermediaries with similar patterns of raising and using funds and (2) establishments engaged in activities that facilitate, or are otherwise related to, that type of financial or insurance intermediation. Industries within this sector are defined in terms of activities for which a production process can be specified, and many of these activities are not exclusive to a particular type of financial institution.

US—United States industry only. CAN—United States and Canadian industries are comparable. MEX—United States and Mexican industries are comparable. Blank—Canadian, Mexican, and United States industries are comparable.

To deal with the varied activities taking place within existing financial institutions, the approach is to split these institutions into components performing specialized services. This requires defining the units engaged in providing those services and developing procedures that allow for their delineation. These units are the equivalents for finance and insurance of the establishments defined for other industries.

The output of many financial services, as well as the inputs and the processes by which they are combined, cannot be observed at a single location and can only be defined at a higher level of the organizational structure of the enterprise. Additionally, a number of independent activities that represent separate and distinct production processes may take place at a single location belonging to a multilocation financial firm. Activities are more likely to be homogeneous with respect to production characteristics than are locations, at least in financial services. The classification defines activities broadly enough that it can be used both by those classifying by location and by those employing a more top-down approach to the delineation of the establishment.

Establishments engaged in activities that facilitate, or are otherwise related to, the various types of intermediation have been included in individual subsectors, rather than in a separate subsector dedicated to services alone because these services are performed by intermediaries, as well as by specialist establishments, the extent to which the activity of the intermediaries can be separately identified is not clear.

The Finance and Insurance sector has been defined to encompass establishments primarily engaged in financial transactions; that is, transactions involving the creation, liquidation, change in ownership of financial assets; or in facilitating financial transactions. Financial industries are extensive users of electronic means for facilitating the verification of financial balances, authorizing transactions, transferring funds to and from transactors' accounts, notifying banks (or credit card issuers) of the individual transactions, and providing daily summaries. Since these transaction processing activities are integral to the production of finance and insurance services, establishments that principally provide a financial transaction processing service are classified to this sector, rather than to the data processing industry in the Information sector.

Legal entities that hold portfolios of assets on behalf of others are significant and data on them are required for a variety of purposes. Thus for NAICS, these funds, trusts, and other financial vehicles are the fifth subsector of the Finance and Insurance sector. These entities earn interest, dividends, and other property income, but have little or no employment and no revenue from the sale of services. Separate establishments and employees devoted to the management of funds are classified in Industry Group 5239, Other Financial Investment Activities.

521 Monetary Authorities-Central Bank

The Monetary Authorities-Central Bank subsector groups establishments that engage in performing central banking functions, such as issuing currency, managing

US—United States industry only. CAN—United States and Canadian industries are comparable. MEX—United States and Mexican industries are comparable. Blank—Canadian, Mexican, and United States industries are comparable.

the Nation's money supply and international reserves, holding deposits that represent the reserves of other banks and other central banks, and acting as a fiscal agent for the central government.

5211 Monetary Authorities-Central Bank

52111 Monetary Authorities-Central Bank

See industry description for 521110 below.

521110 Monetary Authorities-Central Bank

This industry comprises establishments primarily engaged in performing central banking functions, such as issuing currency, managing the Nation's money supply and international reserves, holding deposits that represent the reserves of other banks and other central banks, and acting as a fiscal agent for the central government.

Cross-References.

Establishments of the Board of Governors of the Federal Reserve System are classified in Industry 921130, Public Finance Activities.

522 Credit Intermediation and Related Activities

Industries in the Credit Intermediation and Related Activities subsector group establishments that (1) lend funds raised from depositors; (2) lend funds raised from credit market borrowing; or (3) facilitate the lending of funds or issuance of credit by engaging in such activities as mortgage and loan brokerage, clearinghouse and reserve services, and check cashing services.

5221 Depository Credit Intermediation[CAN]

This industry group comprises establishments primarily engaged in accepting deposits (or share deposits) and in lending funds from these deposits. Within this group, industries are defined on the basis of differences in the types of deposit liabilities assumed and in the nature of the credit extended.

52211 Commercial Banking[US]

See industry description for 522110 below.

US—United States industry only. CAN—United States and Canadian industries are comparable. MEX—United States and Mexican industries are comparable. Blank—Canadian, Mexican, and United States industries are comparable.

522110 Commercial Banking[US]

This industry comprises establishments primarily engaged in accepting demand and other deposits and making commercial, industrial, and consumer loans. Commercial banks and branches of foreign banks are included in this industry.

Cross-References.

- Establishments primarily engaged in credit card banking are classified in Industry 522210, Credit Card Issuing;
- Establishments known as industrial banks and primarily engaged in accepting deposits are classified in Industry 522190, Other Depository Credit Intermediation; and
- Establishments of depository institutions primarily engaged in trust activities are classified in U.S. Industry 523991, Trust, Fiduciary, and Custody Activities.

52212 Savings Institutions[US]

See industry description for 522120 below.

522120 Savings Institutions[US]

This U.S. industry comprises establishments primarily engaged in accepting time deposits, making mortgage and real estate loans, and investing in high-grade securities. Savings and loan associations and savings banks are included in this industry.

Cross-References.

Establishments primarily engaged in accepting demand and other deposits and making all types of loans are classified in Industry 522110, Commercial Banking.

52213 Credit Unions[CAN]

See industry description for 522130 below.

522130 Credit Unions[CAN]

This industry comprises establishments primarily engaged in accepting members' share deposits in cooperatives that are organized to offer consumer loans to their members.

US—United States industry only. CAN—United States and Canadian industries are comparable. MEX—United States and Mexican industries are comparable. Blank—Canadian, Mexican, and United States industries are comparable.

52219 Other Depository Credit Intermediation[CAN]

See industry description for 522190 below.

522190 Other Depository Credit Intermediation[CAN]

This industry comprises establishments primarily engaged in accepting deposits and lending funds (except commercial banking, savings institutions, and credit unions). Establishments known as industrial banks or Morris Plans and primarily engaged in accepting deposits, and private banks (i.e., unincorporated banks) are included in this industry.

Cross-References.

- Establishments primarily engaged in accepting demand and other deposits and making all types of loans are classified in Industry 522110, Commercial Banking;
- Establishments primarily engaged in accepting time deposits are classified in Industry 522120, Savings Institutions;
- Establishments primarily engaged in accepting members' share deposits in cooperatives are classified in Industry 522130, Credit Unions; and
- Establishments known as industrial banks and Morris Plans and are primarily engaged in providing nondepository credit are classified in U.S. Industry 522298, All Other Nondepository Credit Intermediation.

5222 Nondepository Credit Intermediation[CAN]

This industry group comprises establishments, both public (government-sponsored enterprises) and private, primarily engaged in extending credit or lending funds raised by credit market borrowing, such as issuing commercial paper or other debt instruments or by borrowing from other financial intermediaries. Within this group, industries are defined on the basis of the type of credit being extended.

52221 Credit Card Issuing[CAN]

See industry description for 522210 below.

522210 Credit Card Issuing[CAN]

This industry comprises establishments primarily engaged in providing credit by issuing credit cards. Credit card issuance provides the funds required to purchase goods and services in return for payment of the full balance or payments on an installment basis. Credit card banks are included in this industry.

US—United States industry only. CAN—United States and Canadian industries are comparable. MEX—United States and Mexican industries are comparable. Blank—Canadian, Mexican, and United States industries are comparable.

Cross-References.

Establishments primarily engaged in issuing cards that contain a stored prepaid value are classified with the industry providing the service represented by the cards, such as transit fare cards, in Subsector 482, Rail Transportation, and long-distance telephone cards in Subsector 517, Telecommunications.

52222 Sales Financing[CAN]

See industry description for 522220 below.

522220 Sales Financing[CAN]

This industry comprises establishments primarily engaged in sales financing or sales financing in combination with leasing. Sales financing establishments are primarily engaged in lending money for the purpose of providing collateralized goods through a contractual installment sales agreement, either directly from or through arrangements with dealers.

Cross-References.

Establishments not engaged in sales financing, but primarily engaged in providing leases for equipment and other assets are classified in Subsector 532, Rental and Leasing Services.

52229 Other Nondepository Credit Intermediation[CAN]

This industry comprises establishments primarily engaged in making cash loans or extending credit through credit instruments (except credit cards and sales finance agreements).

Illustrative Examples:

Consumer finance companies (i.e., unsecured cash loans)
International trade financing
Mortgage companies
Secondary market financing

Cross-References. Establishments primarily engaged in—

- Providing credit sales by issuing credit cards—are classified in Industry 52221, Credit Card Issuing;
- Providing leases for equipment and other assets without sales financing—are classified in Subsector 532, Rental and Leasing Services;
- Accepting deposits and lending funds from these deposits—are classified in Industry Group 5221, Depository Credit Intermediation;

US—United States industry only. CAN—United States and Canadian industries are comparable. MEX—United States and Mexican industries are comparable. Blank—Canadian, Mexican, and United States industries are comparable.

- Arranging loans for others on a commission or fee basis—are classified Industry 52231, Mortgage and Nonmortgage Loan Brokers; and
- Guaranteeing international trade loans—are classified in Industry 52412, Direct Insurance (except Life, Health, and Medical) Carriers.

522291 Consumer Lending[CAN]

This U.S. industry comprises establishments primarily engaged in making unsecured cash loans to consumers.

Illustrative Examples:

Finance companies (i.e., unsecured cash loans)
Loan companies (i.e., consumer, personal, student, small)
Personal credit institutions (i.e., unsecured cash loans)
Student loans companies

Cross-References. Establishments primarily engaged in—

- Accepting deposits and lending funds from these deposits—are classified in Industry Group 5221, Depository Credit Intermediation; and
- Arranging loans for others on a commission or fee basis—are classified Industry 522310, Mortgage and Nonmortgage Loan Brokers.

522292 Real Estate Credit[US]

This U.S. industry comprises establishments primarily engaged in lending funds with real estate as collateral.

Illustrative Examples:

Home equity credit lending
Mortgage banking (i.e., nondepository mortgage lending)
Mortgage companies

Cross-References. Establishments primarily engaged in—

- Servicing loans—are classified in Industry 522390, Other Activities Related to Credit Intermediation;
- Arranging loans for others on a commission or fee basis—are classified in Industry 522310, Mortgage and Nonmortgage Loan Brokers; and
- Accepting deposits and lending funds secured by real estate—are classified in Industry Group 5221, Depository Credit Intermediation.

US—United States industry only. CAN—United States and Canadian industries are comparable. MEX—United States and Mexican industries are comparable. Blank—Canadian, Mexican, and United States industries are comparable.

522293 International Trade Financing[US]

This U.S. industry comprises establishments primarily engaged in providing one or more of the following: (1) working capital funds to U.S. exporters; (2) lending funds to foreign buyers of U.S. goods; and/or (3) lending funds to domestic buyers of imported goods.

Illustrative Examples:

Agreement corporations (i.e., international trade financing)
Edge Act corporations (i.e., international trade financing)
Export-Import banks
Trade banks (i.e., international trade financing)

Cross-References. Establishments primarily engaged in—

- Guaranteeing international trade loans—are classified in U.S. Industry 524126, Direct Property and Casualty Insurance Carriers;
- Brokering international trade loans—are classified in Industry 522310, Mortgage and Nonmortgage Loan Brokers; and
- Accepting deposits and lending funds from these deposits—are classified in Industry Group 5221, Depository Credit Intermediation.

522294 Secondary Market Financing[US]

This U.S. industry comprises establishments primarily engaged in buying, pooling, and repackaging loans for sale to others on the secondary market.

Illustrative Examples:

Federal Home Loan Mortgage Corporation (FHLMC)
Federal National Mortgage Association (FNMA)
Government National Mortgage Association (GNMA)
Student Loan Marketing Association (SLMA)

522298 All Other Nondepository Credit Intermediation[US]

This U.S. industry comprises establishments primarily engaged in providing nondepository credit (except credit card issuing, sales financing, consumer lending, real estate credit, international trade financing, and secondary market financing). Examples of types of lending in this industry are: short-term inventory credit, agricultural lending (except real estate and sales financing) and consumer cash lending secured by personal property.

US—United States industry only. CAN—United States and Canadian industries are comparable. MEX—United States and Mexican industries are comparable. Blank—Canadian, Mexican, and United States industries are comparable.

Illustrative Examples:

- Commodity Credit Corporation
- Factoring accounts receivable
- Industrial banks (i.e., known as), nondepository
- Morris Plans (i.e., known as), nondepository
- Pawnshops

Cross-References.

- Establishments primarily engaged in providing credit sales funding are classified in Industry 522210, Credit Card Issuing;
- Establishments primarily engaged in sales financing or sales financing in combination with leasing are classified in Industry 522220, Sales Financing;
- Establishments primarily engaged in making unsecured cash loans to consumers are classified in U.S. Industry 522291, Consumer Lending;
- Establishments primarily engaged in lending funds with real estate as collateral are classified in U.S. Industry 522292, Real Estate Credit;
- Establishments primarily engaged in international trade financing are classified in U.S. Industry 522293, International Trade Financing;
- Establishments primarily engaged in buying, pooling, and repackaging loans for sale to others on the secondary market are classified in U.S. Industry 522294, Secondary Market Financing; and
- Establishments known as industrial banks or Morris Plans and are primarily engaged in accepting deposits are classified in Industry 522190, Other Depository Credit Intermediation.

5223 Activities Related to Credit Intermediation[CAN]

This industry group comprises establishments primarily engaged in facilitating credit intermediation by performing activities, such as arranging loans by bringing borrowers and lenders together and clearing checks and credit card transactions.

52231 Mortgage and Nonmortgage Loan Brokers[CAN]

See industry description for 522310 below.

522310 Mortgage and Nonmortgage Loan Brokers[CAN]

This industry comprises establishments primarily engaged in arranging loans by bringing borrowers and lenders together on a commission or fee basis.

Cross-References. Establishments primarily engaged in—

- Lending funds with real estate as collateral—are classified in U.S. Industry 522292, Real Estate Credit; and

---

US—United States industry only. CAN—United States and Canadian industries are comparable. MEX—United States and Mexican industries are comparable. Blank—Canadian, Mexican, and United States industries are comparable.

- Servicing loans—are classified in Industry 522390, Other Activities Related to Credit Intermediation.

52232 Financial Transactions Processing, Reserve, and Clearinghouse Activities[CAN]

See industry description for 522320 below.

522320 Financial Transactions Processing, Reserve, and Clearinghouse Activities[US]

This industry comprises establishments primarily engaged in providing one or more of the following: (1) financial transaction processing (except central bank); (2) reserve and liquidity services (except central bank); and/or (3) check or other financial instrument clearinghouse services (except central bank).

Illustrative Examples:

Automated clearinghouses, bank or check (except central bank)
Check clearing services (except central bank)
Credit card processing services
Electronic funds transfer services

Cross-References.

- Establishments primarily engaged in nonfinancial data and electronic transaction processing are classified in Industry Group 5182, Data Processing, Hosting, and Related Services; and
- Establishments of the central bank primarily engaged in check clearing and other financial transaction processing are classified in Industry 521110, Monetary Authorities-Central Bank.

52239 Other Activities Related to Credit Intermediation[CAN]

See industry description for 522390 below.

522390 Other Activities Related to Credit Intermediation[CAN]

This industry comprises establishments primarily engaged in facilitating credit intermediation (except mortgage and loan brokerage; and financial transactions processing, reserve, and clearinghouse activities).

Illustrative Examples:

Check cashing services
Loan servicing
Money order issuance services
Travelers' check issuance services

US—United States industry only. CAN—United States and Canadian industries are comparable. MEX—United States and Mexican industries are comparable. Blank—Canadian, Mexican, and United States industries are comparable.

Cross-References. Establishments primarily engaged in—

- Arranging loans for others on a commission or fee basis—are classified in Industry 522310, Mortgage and Nonmortgage Loan Brokers;
- Providing financial transactions processing, reserve, and clearinghouse activities—are classified in Industry 522320, Financial Transactions Processing, Reserve, and Clearinghouse Activities;
- Foreign currency exchange dealing—are classified in Industry 523130, Commodity Contracts Dealing; and
- Providing escrow services (except real estate)—are classified in U.S. Industry 523991, Trust, Fiduciary, and Custody Activities.

523 Securities, Commodity Contracts, and Other Financial Investments and Related Activities

Industries in the Securities, Commodity Contracts, and Other Financial Investments and Related Activities subsector group establishments that are primarily engaged in one of the following: (1) underwriting securities issues and/or making markets for securities and commodities; (2) acting as agents (i.e., brokers) between buyers and sellers of securities and commodities; (3) providing securities and commodity exchange services; and (4) providing other services, such as managing portfolios of assets; providing investment advice; and trust, fiduciary, and custody services.

5231 Securities and Commodity Contracts Intermediation and Brokerage

This industry group comprises establishments primarily engaged in putting capital at risk in the process of underwriting securities issues or in making markets for securities and commodities; and those acting as agents and/or brokers between buyers and sellers of securities and commodities, usually charging a commission.

52311 Investment Banking and Securities Dealing[CAN]

See industry description for 523110 below.

523110 Investment Banking and Securities Dealing[CAN]

This industry comprises establishments primarily engaged in underwriting, originating, and/or maintaining markets for issues of securities. Investment bankers act as principals (i.e., investors who buy or sell on their own account) in firm commit-

US—United States industry only. CAN—United States and Canadian industries are comparable. MEX—United States and Mexican industries are comparable. Blank—Canadian, Mexican, and United States industries are comparable.

ment transactions or act as agents in best effort and standby commitments. This industry also includes establishments acting as principals in buying or selling securities generally on a spread basis, such as securities dealers or stock option dealers.

Illustrative Examples:

Bond dealing (i.e., acting as a principal in dealing securities to investors)
Securities underwriting
Stock option dealing

Cross-References.

- Establishments primarily engaged in acting as agents (i.e., brokers) in buying or selling securities on a commission or transaction fee basis are classified in Industry 523120, Securities Brokerage; and
- Investment clubs or individual investors primarily engaged in buying or selling financial contracts (e.g., securities) on their own account are classified in Industry 523910, Miscellaneous Intermediation.

52312 Securities Brokerage[CAN]

See industry description for 523120 below.

523120 Securities Brokerage[CAN]

This industry comprises establishments primarily engaged in acting as agents (i.e., brokers) between buyers and sellers in buying or selling securities on a commission or transaction fee basis.

Illustrative Examples:

Mutual fund agencies (i.e., brokerages)
Securities brokerages
Stock brokerages

Cross-References.

Establishments primarily engaged in investment banking and securities dealing (i.e., buying or selling securities on their own account) are classified in Industry 523110, Investment Banking and Securities Dealing.

52313 Commodity Contracts Dealing[CAN]

See industry description for 523130 below.

523130 Commodity Contracts Dealing[CAN]

This industry comprises establishments primarily engaged in acting as principals (i.e., investors who buy or sell for their own account) in buying or selling spot or

---

US—United States industry only. CAN—United States and Canadian industries are comparable. MEX—United States and Mexican industries are comparable. Blank—Canadian, Mexican, and United States industries are comparable.

futures commodity contracts or options, such as precious metals, foreign currency, oil, or agricultural products, generally on a spread basis.

Cross-References. Establishments primarily engaged in—

- Acting as agents (i.e., brokers) in buying or selling spot or future commodity contracts on a commission or transaction fee basis—are classified in Industry 523140, Commodity Contracts Brokerage; and
- Buying and selling physical commodities for resale to other than the general public—are classified in Sector 42, Wholesale Trade.

52314 Commodity Contracts Brokerage[CAN]

See industry description for 523140 below.

523140 Commodity Contracts Brokerage[CAN]

This industry comprises establishments primarily engaged in acting as agents (i.e., brokers) in buying or selling spot or future commodity contracts or options on a commission or transaction fee basis.

Illustrative Examples:

Commodity contracts brokerages
Commodity futures brokerages
Financial futures brokerages

Cross-References. Establishments primarily engaged in—

- Acting as principals in buying or selling spot or futures commodity contracts generally on a spread basis—are classified in Industry 523130, Commodity Contracts Dealing; and
- Buying and selling physical commodities for resale to other than the general public—are classified in Sector 42, Wholesale Trade.

5232 Securities and Commodity Exchanges

52321 Securities and Commodity Exchanges

See industry description for 523210 below.

523210 Securities and Commodity Exchanges

This industry comprises establishments primarily engaged in furnishing physical or electronic marketplaces for the purpose of facilitating the buying and selling of stocks, stock options, bonds, or commodity contracts.

US—United States industry only. CAN—United States and Canadian industries are comparable. MEX—United States and Mexican industries are comparable. Blank—Canadian, Mexican, and United States industries are comparable.

Cross-References.

Establishments primarily engaged in investment banking, and securities dealing, securities brokering commodity contracts dealing, or commodity contracts brokering are classified in Industry Group 5231, Securities and Commodity Contracts Intermediation and Brokerage.

5239 Other Financial Investment Activities

This industry group comprises establishments primarily engaged in one of the following: (1) acting as principals in buying or selling financial contracts (except investment bankers, securities dealers, and commodity contracts dealers); (2) acting as agents (i.e., brokers) (except securities brokerages and commodity contracts brokerages) in buying or selling financial contracts; or (3) providing other investment services (except securities and commodity exchanges), such as portfolio management; investment advice; and trust, fiduciary, and custody services.

52391 Miscellaneous Intermediation[CAN]

See industry description for 523910 below.

523910 Miscellaneous Intermediation[CAN]

This industry comprises establishments primarily engaged in acting as principals (except investment bankers, securities dealers, and commodity contracts dealers) in buying or selling of financial contracts generally on a spread basis. Principals are investors that buy or sell for their own account.

Illustrative Examples:

Investment clubs
Mineral royalties or leases dealing (i.e., acting as a principal in dealing royalties or leases to investors)
Tax liens dealing (i.e., acting as a principal in dealing tax liens to investors)
Venture capital companies

Cross-References.

Establishments primarily engaged in investment banking, securities dealing, securities brokering, commodity contracts dealing, or commodity contracts brokering are classified in Industry Group 5231, Securities and Commodity Contracts Intermediation and Brokerage.

52392 Portfolio Management[CAN]

See industry description for 523920 below.

US—United States industry only. CAN—United States and Canadian industries are comparable. MEX—United States and Mexican industries are comparable. Blank—Canadian, Mexican, and United States industries are comparable.

523920 Portfolio Management[CAN]

This industry comprises establishments primarily engaged in managing the portfolio assets (i.e., funds) of others on a fee or commission basis. Establishments in this industry have the authority to make investment decisions, and they derive fees based on the size and/or overall performance of the portfolio.

Illustrative Examples:

Managing trusts
Mutual fund managing
Pension fund managing
Portfolio fund managing

Cross-References.

Establishments primarily engaged in investment banking and securities dealing, securities brokering, commodity contracts dealing, or commodity contracts brokering are classified in Industry Group 5231, Securities and Commodity Contracts Intermediation and Brokerage.

52393 Investment Advice[CAN]

See industry description for 523930 below.

523930 Investment Advice[CAN]

This industry comprises establishments primarily engaged in providing customized investment advice to clients on a fee basis, but do not have the authority to execute trades. Primary activities performed by establishments in this industry are providing financial planning advice and investment counseling to meet the goals and needs of specific clients.

Illustrative Examples:

Financial investment advice services, customized, fees paid by client
Financial planning services, customized, fees paid by client
Investment advisory services, customized, fees paid by client

Cross-References.

- Establishments providing investment advice in conjunction with their primary activity, such as portfolio management, or the sale of stocks, bonds, annuities, and real estate, are classified according to their primary activity; and

---

US—United States industry only. CAN—United States and Canadian industries are comparable. MEX—United States and Mexican industries are comparable. Blank—Canadian, Mexican, and United States industries are comparable.

- Establishments known as publishers providing generalized investment information to subscribers are classified in Subsector 511, Publishing Industries (except Internet) or Subsector 516, Internet Publishing and Broadcasting.

52399 All Other Financial Investment Activities[CAN]

This industry comprises establishments primarily engaged in acting as agents or brokers (except securities brokerages and commodity contracts brokerages) in buying and selling financial contracts providing financial investment activities (except securities and commodity exchanges, portfolio management, and investment advice).

Illustrative Examples:

Bank trust offices	Fiduciary agencies (except real estate)
Escrow agencies (except real estate)	Stock quotation services

Cross-References. Establishments primarily engaged in—

- Investment banking and securities dealing, securities brokerage, commodity contracts dealing, or commodity contracts brokering—are classified in Industry Group 5231, Securities and Commodity Contracts Intermediation and Brokerage;
- Acting as principals (except investment bankers, securities dealers, and commodity contracts dealers) in buying or selling financial contracts (except securities or commodity contracts)—are classified in Industry 52391, Miscellaneous Intermediation;
- Furnishing physical or electronic marketplaces for the purpose of facilitating the buying and selling of securities and commodities—are classified in Industry 52321, Securities and Commodity Exchanges;
- Managing the portfolio assets (i.e., funds) of others—are classified in Industry 52392, Portfolio Management;
- Providing customized investment advice—are classified in Industry 52393, Investment Advice;
- Awarding grants from trust funds—are classified in Industry 81321, Grantmaking and Giving Services;
- Performing real estate escrow or real estate fiduciary activities—are classified in Industry 53139, Other Activities Related to Real Estate; and
- Financial transactions processing, reserve, and clearinghouse activities—are classified in Industry 52232, Financial Transactions Processing, Reserve, and Clearinghouse Activities.

US—United States industry only. CAN—United States and Canadian industries are comparable. MEX—United States and Mexican industries are comparable. Blank—Canadian, Mexican, and United States industries are comparable.

523991 Trust, Fiduciary, and Custody Activities[US]

This U.S. industry comprises establishments primarily engaged in providing trust, fiduciary, and custody services to others, as instructed, on a fee or contract basis, such as bank trust offices and escrow agencies (except real estate).

Cross-References. Establishments primarily engaged in—

- Managing the portfolio assets (i.e., funds) of others—are classified in Industry 523920, Portfolio Management;
- Performing real estate escrow or real estate fiduciary activities—are classified in Industry 531390, Other Activities Related to Real Estate; and
- Awarding grants from trust funds—are classified in Industry 81321, Grantmaking and Giving Services.

523999 Miscellaneous Financial Investment Activities[US]

This U.S. industry comprises establishments primarily engaged in acting as agents and/or brokers (except securities brokerages and commodity contracts brokerages) in buying or selling financial contracts and those providing financial investment services (except securities and commodity exchanges; portfolio management; investment advice; and trust, fiduciary, and custody services) on a fee or commission basis.

Illustrative Examples:

Exchange clearinghouses, commodities or securities

Gas lease brokers' offices

Stock quotation services

Cross-References. Establishments primarily engaged in—

- Investment banking and securities dealing, securities brokering, commodity contracts dealing, or commodity contracts brokering—are classified in Industry Group 5231, Securities and Commodity Contracts Intermediation and Brokerage;
- Acting as principals (except investment bankers, securities dealers, and commodity contracts dealers) in buying or selling financial contracts—are classified in Industry 523910, Miscellaneous Intermediation;
- Furnishing physical or electrical marketplaces for the purpose of facilitating the buying and selling of securities and commodities—are classified in Industry 523210, Securities and Commodity Exchanges;
- Managing the portfolio assets (i.e., funds) of others—are classified in Industry 523920, Portfolio Management;

US—United States industry only. CAN—United States and Canadian industries are comparable. MEX—United States and Mexican industries are comparable. Blank—Canadian, Mexican, and United States industries are comparable.

- Providing customized investment advice—are classified in Industry 523930, Investment Advice;
- Providing trust, fiduciary, and custody services to others—are classified in U.S. Industry 523991, Trust, Fiduciary, and Custody Activities; and
- Financial transactions processing, reserve, and clearinghouse activities—are classified in Industry 522320, Financial Transactions Processing, Reserve, and Clearinghouse Activities.

524 Insurance Carriers and Related Activities

Industries in the Insurance Carriers and Related Activities subsector group establishments that are primarily engaged in one of the following: (1) underwriting (assuming the risk, assigning premiums, and so forth) annuities and insurance policies or (2) facilitating such underwriting by selling insurance policies, and by providing other insurance and employee-benefit related services.

5241 Insurance Carriers

This industry group comprises establishments primarily engaged in underwriting (assuming the risk, assigning premiums, and so forth) annuities and insurance policies and investing premiums to build up a portfolio of financial assets to be used against future claims. Direct insurance carriers are establishments that are primarily engaged in initially underwriting and assuming the risk of annuities and insurance policies. Reinsurance carriers are establishments that are primarily engaged in assuming all or part of the risk associated with an existing insurance policy (or set of policies) originally underwritten by another insurance carrier.

Industries are defined in terms of the type of risk being insured against, such as death, loss of employment because of age or disability, and/or property damage. Contributions and premiums are set on the basis of actuarial calculations of probable payouts based on risk factors from experience tables and expected investment returns on reserves.

52411 Direct Life, Health, and Medical Insurance Carriers[CAN]

This industry comprises establishments primarily engaged in initially underwriting (i.e., assuming the risk and assigning premiums) annuities and life insurance policies, disability income insurance policies, accidental death and dismemberment insurance policies, and health and medical insurance policies.

Cross-References.

- Establishments primarily engaged in reinsuring life insurance policies are classified in Industry 52413, Reinsurance Carriers;

US—United States industry only. CAN—United States and Canadian industries are comparable. MEX—United States and Mexican industries are comparable. Blank—Canadian, Mexican, and United States industries are comparable.

- Legal entities (i.e., funds, plans, and/or programs) organized to provide insurance and employee benefits exclusively for the sponsor, firm, or its employees or members are classified in Industry Group 5251, Insurance and Employee Benefit Funds; and
- HMO establishments providing health care services are classified in Industry 62149, Other Outpatient Care Centers.

524113 Direct Life Insurance Carriers[US]

This U.S. industry comprises establishments primarily engaged in initially underwriting (i.e., assuming the risk and assigning premiums) annuities and life insurance policies, disability income insurance policies, and accidental death and dismemberment insurance policies.

Cross-References.

- Establishments primarily engaged in reinsuring life insurance policies, disability income insurance policies, and accidental death and dismemberment insurance policies are classified in Industry 524130, Reinsurance Carriers; and
- Legal entities (i.e., funds, plans, and/or programs) organized to provide insurance and employee benefits exclusively for the sponsor, firm, or its employees or members are classified in Industry Group 5251, Insurance and Employee Benefit Funds.

524114 Direct Health and Medical Insurance Carriers[US]

This U.S. industry comprises establishments primarily engaged in initially underwriting (i.e., assuming the risk and assigning premiums) health and medical insurance policies. Group hospitalization plans and HMO establishments (except those providing health care services) that provide health and medical insurance policies without providing health care services are included in this industry.

Cross-References.

- HMO establishments that provide both health care services and underwrite health and medical insurance are classified in U.S. Industry 621491, HMO Medical Centers;
- Establishments primarily engaged in reinsuring health insurance policies are classified in Industry 524130, Reinsurance Carriers; and
- Legal entities (i.e., funds, plans, and/or programs) organized to provide health- and welfare-related employee benefits exclusively for the sponsor's employees or members are classified in Industry 525120, Health and Welfare Funds.

US—United States industry only. CAN—United States and Canadian industries are comparable. MEX—United States and Mexican industries are comparable. Blank—Canadian, Mexican, and United States industries are comparable.

52412 Direct Insurance (except Life, Health, and Medical) Carriers[CAN]

This industry comprises establishments primarily engaged in initially underwriting (i.e., assuming the risk and assigning premiums) various types of insurance policies (except life, disability income, accidental death and dismemberment, and health and medical insurance policies).

Illustrative Examples:

Automobile insurance carriers, direct
Bank deposit insurance carriers, direct
Mortgage guaranty insurance carriers, direct
Property and casualty insurance carriers, direct
Title insurance carriers, real estate, direct
Warranty insurance carriers (e.g., appliance, automobile, homeowners, product), direct

Cross-References.

- Establishments primarily engaged in reinsuring insurance policies are classified in Industry 524130, Reinsurance Carriers;
- Legal entities (i.e., funds, plans, and/or programs) organized to provide insurance and employee benefits exclusively for the sponsor, firm, or its employees or members are classified in Industry Group 5251, Insurance and Employee Benefit Funds; and
- Establishments primarily engaged in initially underwriting annuities and life insurance policies, disability income insurance policies, accidental death and dismemberment insurance policies, and health and medical insurance policies are classified in Industry 52411, Direct Life, Health, and Medical Insurance Carriers.

524126 Direct Property and Casualty Insurance Carriers[US]

This U.S. industry comprises establishments primarily engaged in initially underwriting (i.e., assuming the risk and assigning premiums) insurance policies that protect policyholders against losses that may occur as a result of property damage or liability.

Illustrative Examples:

Automobile insurance carriers, direct
Fidelity insurance carriers, direct
Homeowners insurance carriers, direct
Liability insurance carriers, direct
Malpractice insurance carriers, direct
Mortgage guaranty insurance carriers, direct
Surety insurance carriers, direct

US—United States industry only. CAN—United States and Canadian industries are comparable. MEX—United States and Mexican industries are comparable. Blank—Canadian, Mexican, and United States industries are comparable.

Cross-References.

Establishments primarily engaged in reinsuring property and casualty insurance policies are classified in Industry 524130, Reinsurance Carriers.

524127 Direct Title Insurance Carriers[US]

This U.S. industry comprises establishments primarily engaged in initially underwriting (i.e., assuming the risk and assigning premiums) insurance policies to protect the owners of real estate or real estate creditors against loss sustained by reason of any title defect to real property.

Cross-References.

Establishments primarily engaged in reinsuring title insurance policies are classified in Industry 524130, Reinsurance Carriers.

524128 Other Direct Insurance (except Life, Health, and Medical) Carriers[US]

This U.S. industry comprises establishments primarily engaged in initially underwriting (e.g., assuming the risk, assigning premiums) insurance policies (except life, disability income, accidental death and dismemberment, health and medical, property and casualty, and title insurance policies).

Illustrative Examples:

Bank deposit insurance carriers, direct
Deposit or share insurance carriers, direct
Product warranty insurance carriers, direct
Warranty insurance carriers (e.g., appliance, automobile, homeowners, product), direct

Cross-References. Establishments primarily engaged in—

- Reinsuring insurance policies—are classified in Industry 524130, Reinsurance Carriers;
- Initially underwriting annuities and life insurance policies, disability income insurance policies, and accidental death and dismemberment insurance policies—are classified in U.S. Industry 524113, Direct Life Insurance Carriers;
- Initially underwriting health and medical insurance policies—are classified in U.S. Industry 524114, Direct Health and Medical Insurance Carriers;
- Initially underwriting property and casualty insurance policies—are classified in U.S. Industry 524126, Direct Property and Casualty Insurance Carriers; and

---

US—United States industry only. CAN—United States and Canadian industries are comparable. MEX—United States and Mexican industries are comparable. Blank—Canadian, Mexican, and United States industries are comparable.

- Initially underwriting title insurance policies—are classified in U.S. Industry 524127, Direct Title Insurance Carriers.

52413 Reinsurance Carriers[CAN]

See industry description for 524130 below.

524130 Reinsurance Carriers[US]

This industry comprises establishments primarily engaged in assuming all or part of the risk associated with existing insurance policies originally underwritten by other insurance carriers.

Cross-References. Establishments primarily engaged in—

- Initially underwriting annuities and life insurance policies, disability income insurance policies, accidental death and dismemberment insurance policies, and health and medical insurance policies—are classified in Industry 52411, Direct Life, Health, and Medical Insurance Carriers; and
- Initially underwriting various types of insurance policies (except life, disability income, accidental death and dismemberment, and health and medical insurance policies)—are classified in Industry 52412, Direct Insurance (except Life, Health, and Medical) Carriers.

5242 Agencies, Brokerages, and Other Insurance Related Activities

This industry group comprises establishments primarily engaged in (1) acting as agents (i.e., brokers) in selling annuities and insurance policies or (2) providing other employee benefits and insurance related services, such as claims adjustment and third party administration.

52421 Insurance Agencies and Brokerages[CAN]

See industry description for 524210 below.

524210 Insurance Agencies and Brokerages[CAN]

This industry comprises establishments primarily engaged in acting as agents (i.e., brokers) in selling annuities and insurance policies.

Cross-References.

Establishments primarily engaged in underwriting annuities and insurance policies are classified in Industry Group 5241, Insurance Carriers.

US—United States industry only. CAN—United States and Canadian industries are comparable. MEX—United States and Mexican industries are comparable. Blank—Canadian, Mexican, and United States industries are comparable.

52429 Other Insurance Related Activities[CAN]

This industry comprises establishments primarily engaged in providing services related to insurance (except insurance agencies and brokerages).

Illustrative Examples:

Claims adjusting
Insurance adjusting
Insurance plan administrative services

Cross-References. Establishments primarily engaged in—

- Managing the portfolio assets (i.e., funds) of others—are classified in Industry 52392, Portfolio Management;
- Acting as agents (i.e., brokers) in selling annuities and insurance policies—are classified in Industry 52421, Insurance Agencies and Brokerages; and
- Providing actuarial consulting services—are classified in Industry 54161, Management Consulting Services.

524291 Claims Adjusting[CAN]

This industry comprises establishments primarily engaged in investigating, appraising, and settling insurance claims.

524292 Third Party Administration of Insurance and Pension Funds[US]

This U.S. industry comprises establishments primarily engaged in providing third party administration services of insurance and pension funds, such as claims processing and other administrative services to insurance carriers, employee-benefit plans, and self-insurance funds.

Cross-References. Establishments primarily engaged in—

- Managing the portfolio assets (i.e., funds) of others—are classified in Industry 523920, Portfolio Management; and
- Providing actuarial consulting services—are classified in U.S. Industry 541612, Human Resources and Executive Search Consulting Services.

524298 All Other Insurance Related Activities[US]

This U.S. industry comprises establishments primarily engaged in providing insurance services on a contract or fee basis (except insurance agencies and broker-

US—United States industry only. CAN—United States and Canadian industries are comparable. MEX—United States and Mexican industries are comparable. Blank—Canadian, Mexican, and United States industries are comparable.

ages, claims adjusting, and third party administration). Insurance advisory services and insurance ratemaking services are included in this industry.

Cross-References. Establishments primarily engaged in—

- Providing actuarial consulting services—are classified in U.S. Industry 541612, Human Resources Management and Executive Search Consulting Services;
- Acting as agents (i.e., brokers) in selling annuities and insurance policies—are classified in Industry 524210, Insurance Agencies and Brokerages;
- Insurance claims adjusting—are classified in U.S. Industry 524291, Claims Adjusting; and
- Third party administration services of insurance and pension funds—are classified in U.S. Industry 524292, Third Party Administration of Insurance and Pension Funds.

525 Funds, Trusts, and Other Financial Vehicles[US]

Industries in the Funds, Trusts, and Other Financial Vehicles subsector are comprised of legal entities (i.e., funds, plans, and/or programs) organized to pool securities or other assets on behalf of shareholders or beneficiaries of employee benefit or other trust funds. The portfolios are customized to achieve specific investment characteristics, such as diversification, risk, rate of return, and price volatility. These entities earn interest, dividends, and other property income, but have little or no employment and no revenue from the sale of services. Establishments with employees devoted to the management of funds are classified in Industry Group 5239, Other Financial Investment Activities.

Establishments primarily engaged in holding the securities of (or other equity interests in) other firms are classified in Sector 55, Management of Companies and Enterprises.

5251 Insurance and Employee Benefit Funds[US]

This industry group comprises legal entities (i.e., funds, plans, and/or programs) organized to provide insurance and employee benefits exclusively for the sponsor, firm, or its employees or members.

52511 Pension Funds[US]

See industry description for 525110 below.

US—United States industry only. CAN—United States and Canadian industries are comparable. MEX—United States and Mexican industries are comparable. Blank—Canadian, Mexican, and United States industries are comparable.

525110 Pension Funds[US]

This industry comprises legal entities (i.e., funds, plans, and/or programs) organized to provide retirement income benefits exclusively for the sponsor's employees or members.

Illustrative Examples:

Employee benefit plans
Pension funds and plans
Retirement plans

Cross-References. Establishments primarily engaged in—

- Managing portfolios of pension funds—are classified in Industry 523920, Portfolio Management; and
- Initially underwriting annuities—are classified in U.S. Industry 524113, Direct Life Insurance Carriers.

52512 Health and Welfare Funds[US]

See industry description for 525120 below.

525120 Health and Welfare Funds[US]

This industry comprises legal entities (i.e., funds, plans, and/or programs) organized to provide medical, surgical, hospital, vacation, training, and other health- and welfare-related employee benefits exclusively for the sponsor's employees or members.

Cross-References. Establishments primarily engaged in—

- Managing portfolios of health and welfare funds—are classified in Industry 523920, Portfolio Management; and
- Third party claims administration of health and welfare plans—are classified in U.S. Industry 524292, Third Party Administration of Insurance and Pension Funds.

52519 Other Insurance Funds[US]

See industry description for 525190 below.

525190 Other Insurance Funds[US]

This industry comprises legal entities (i.e., funds (except pension, and health- and welfare-related employee benefit funds)) organized to provide insurance exclu-

US—United States industry only. CAN—United States and Canadian industries are comparable. MEX—United States and Mexican industries are comparable. Blank—Canadian, Mexican, and United States industries are comparable.

sively for the sponsor, firm, or its employees or members. Self-insurance funds (except employee benefit funds) and workers' compensation insurance funds are included in this industry.

Cross-References.

- Legal entities (i.e., funds, plans, and/or programs) organized to provide retirement income benefits exclusively for the sponsor's employees or members are classified in Industry 525110, Pension Funds;
- Legal entities (i.e., funds, plans, and/or programs) organized to provide health- and welfare-related employee benefits exclusively for the sponsor's employees or members are classified in Industry 525120, Health and Welfare Funds;
- Establishments primarily engaged in managing portfolios of insurance funds are classified in Industry 523920, Portfolio Management;
- Establishments primarily engaged in third party claims administration of insurance, and other employee benefit funds are classified in U.S. Industry 524292, Third Party Administration of Insurance and Pension Funds; and
- Establishments primarily engaged in providing insurance on a fee or contract basis are classified in Industry Group 5241, Insurance Carriers.

5259 Other Investment Pools and Funds[US]

This industry group comprises legal entities (i.e., investment pools and/or funds) organized to pool securities or other assets (except insurance and employee-benefit funds) on behalf of shareholders, unitholders, or beneficiaries.

52591 Open-End Investment Funds[US]

See industry description for 525910 below.

525910 Open-End Investment Funds[US]

This industry comprises legal entities (i.e., open-end investment funds) organized to pool assets that consist of securities or other financial instruments. Shares in these pools are offered to the public in an initial offering with additional shares offered continuously and perpetually and redeemed at a specific price determined by the net asset value.

Illustrative Examples:

Investment funds, open-ended

Money market mutual funds, open-ended

US—United States industry only. CAN—United States and Canadian industries are comparable. MEX—United States and Mexican industries are comparable. Blank—Canadian, Mexican, and United States industries are comparable.

52592 Trusts, Estates, and Agency Accounts[US]

See industry description for 525920 below.

525920 Trusts, Estates, and Agency Accounts[US]

This industry comprises legal entities, trusts, estates, or agency accounts, administered on behalf of the beneficiaries under the terms of a trust agreement, will, or agency agreement.

Illustrative Examples:

Bankruptcy estates
Personal investment trusts
Private estates (i.e., administering on behalf of beneficiaries)
Testamentary trusts

Cross-References. Establishments primarily engaged in—

- Managing portfolios of trusts—are classified in Industry 523920, Portfolio Management;
- Administering personal estates—are classified in U.S. Industry 523991, Trust, Fiduciary, and Custody Activities; and
- Operating businesses of trusts and bankruptcy estates—are classified according to the kind of business operated.

52593 Real Estate Investment Trusts[US]

See industry description for 525930 below.

525930 Real Estate Investment Trusts[US]

This industry comprises legal entities that are Real Estate Investment Trusts (REITs).

Cross-References.

- Legal entities of mortgage-backed investment funds that are not REITs are classified elsewhere in the Funds, Trusts, and Other Financial Vehicles subsector based on the types of funds; and
- Legal entities of investments in real estate that are not REITs are classified in Industry Group 5311, Lessors of Real Estate.

52599 Other Financial Vehicles[US]

See industry description for 525990 below.

US—United States industry only. CAN—United States and Canadian industries are comparable. MEX—United States and Mexican industries are comparable. Blank—Canadian, Mexican, and United States industries are comparable.

525990 Other Financial Vehicles[US]

This industry comprises legal entities (i.e., funds (except insurance and employee benefit funds; open-end investment funds; trusts, estates, and agency accounts; and Real Estate Investment Trusts (REITs)).

Illustrative Examples:

Closed-end investment funds (except REITs)
Collateralized Mortgage Obligations (CMOs)
Face-amount certificate funds
Real Estate Mortgage Investment Conduits (REMICs)
Special purpose vehicles
Unit investment trust funds

Cross-References.

- Legal entities (i.e., funds, plans, and programs) that provide insurance and employee benefits exclusively for the sponsor, firm, or its employees or members are classified in Industry Group 5251, Insurance and Employee Benefit Funds;
- Legal entities (i.e., open-end investment funds) organized to pool assets that consist of securities or other financial instruments, where the pools are offered to the public in an initial offering with additional shares offered continuously and perpetually at a specific price determined by the net asset value, are classified in Industry 525910, Open-End Investment Funds;
- Legal entities (i.e., trusts, estates, or agency accounts) administered on behalf of the beneficiaries under the terms of a trust agreement, will, or agency agreement are classified in Industry 525920, Trusts, Estates, and Agency Accounts; and
- Legal entities that are Real Estate Investment Trusts (REITs) are classified in Industry 525930, Real Estate Investment Trusts.

US—United States industry only. CAN—United States and Canadian industries are comparable. MEX—United States and Mexican industries are comparable. Blank—Canadian, Mexican, and United States industries are comparable.

Sector 53—Real Estate and Rental and Leasing

The Sector as a Whole

The Real Estate and Rental and Leasing sector comprises establishments primarily engaged in renting, leasing, or otherwise allowing the use of tangible or intangible assets, and establishments providing related services. The major portion of this sector comprises establishments that rent, lease, or otherwise allow the use of their own assets by others. The assets may be tangible, as is the case of real estate and equipment, or intangible, as is the case with patents and trademarks.

This sector also includes establishments primarily engaged in managing real estate for others, selling, renting and/or buying real estate for others, and appraising real estate. These activities are closely related to this sector's main activity, and it was felt that from a production basis they would best be included here. In addition, a substantial proportion of property management is self-performed by lessors.

The main components of this sector are the real estate lessors industries; equipment lessors industries (including motor vehicles, computers, and consumer goods); and lessors of nonfinancial intangible assets (except copyrighted works).

Excluded from this sector are real estate investment trusts (REITS) and establishments primarily engaged in renting or leasing equipment with operators. REITS are classified in Subsector 525, Funds, Trusts, and Other Financial Vehicles, because they are considered investment vehicles. Establishments renting or leasing equipment with operators are classified in various subsectors of NAICS depending on the nature of the services provided (e.g., transportation, construction, agriculture). These activities are excluded from this sector because the client is paying for the expertise and knowledge of the equipment operator, in addition to the rental of the equipment. In many cases, such as the rental of heavy construction equipment, the operator is essential to operate the equipment.

531 Real Estate

Industries in the Real Estate subsector group establishments that are primarily engaged in renting or leasing real estate to others; managing real estate for others; selling, buying, or renting real estate for others; and providing other real estate related services, such as appraisal services.

Establishments primarily engaged in subdividing and developing unimproved real estate and constructing buildings for sale are classified in Subsector 236, Construction of Buildings. Establishments primarily engaged in subdividing and improving raw land for subsequent sale to builders are classified in Subsector 237, Heavy and Civil Engineering Construction.

Real Estate Investment Trusts (REITS) are classified in Subsector 525, Funds, Trusts, and Other Financial Vehicles, because they are considered investment vehicles.

US—United States industry only. CAN—United States and Canadian industries are comparable. MEX—United States and Mexican industries are comparable. Blank—Canadian, Mexican, and United States industries are comparable.

5311 Lessors of Real Estate

53111 Lessors of Residential Buildings and Dwellings[CAN]

See industry description for 531110 below.

531110 Lessors of Residential Buildings and Dwellings[US]

This industry comprises establishments primarily engaged in acting as lessors of buildings used as residences or dwellings, such as single-family homes, apartment buildings, and town homes. Included in this industry are owner-lessors and establishments renting real estate and then acting as lessors in subleasing it to others. The establishments in this industry may manage the property themselves or have another establishment manage it for them.

Cross-References.

Establishments primarily engaged in managing residential real estate for others are classified in U.S. Industry 531311, Residential Property Managers.

53112 Lessors of Nonresidential Buildings (except Miniwarehouses)[CAN]

See industry description for 531120 below.

531120 Lessors of Nonresidential Buildings (except Miniwarehouses)[CAN]

This industry comprises establishments primarily engaged in acting as lessors of buildings (except miniwarehouses and self-storage units) that are not used as residences or dwellings. Included in this industry are: (1) owner-lessors of nonresidential buildings; (2) establishments renting real estate and then acting as lessors in subleasing it to others; and (3) establishments providing full service office space, whether on a lease or service contract basis. The establishments in this industry may manage the property themselves or have another establishment manage it for them.

Cross-References. Establishments primarily engaged in—

- Acting as lessors of buildings used as residences or dwellings—are classified in Industry 531110, Lessors of Residential Buildings and Dwellings;
- Renting or leasing space for self-storage—are classified in Industry 531130, Lessors of Miniwarehouses and Self-Storage Units;

US—United States industry only. CAN—United States and Canadian industries are comparable. MEX—United States and Mexican industries are comparable. Blank—Canadian, Mexican, and United States industries are comparable.

- Managing nonresidential real estate for others—are classified in U.S. Industry 531312, Nonresidential Property Managers;
- Providing a range of office support services, such as mailbox rental, other postal and mailing (except direct mail advertising) services, document copying services, facsimile services, word processing services or on-site personal computer rental, that are not providing office space—are classified in Industry 56143, Business Service Centers;
- Managing and operating arenas, stadiums, theaters, or other related facilities and promoting and organizing performing arts productions, sports events, and similar events at those facilities—are classified in Industry 711310, Promoters of Performing Arts, Sports, and Similar Events with Facilities; and
- Operating public and contract general merchandise warehousing and storage facilities—are classified in Industry 493110, General Warehousing and Storage.

53113 Lessors of Miniwarehouses and Self-Storage Units[CAN]

See industry description for 531130 below.

531130 Lessors of Miniwarehouses and Self-Storage Units[CAN]

This industry comprises establishments primarily engaged in renting or leasing space for self-storage. These establishments provide secure space (i.e., rooms, compartments, lockers, containers, or outdoor space) where clients can store and retrieve their goods.

Cross-References. Establishments primarily engaged in—

- Operating public and contract general merchandise warehousing and storage facilities—are classified in Industry 493110, General Warehousing and Storage; and
- Operating coin-operated lockers—are classified in Industry 812990, All Other Personal Services.

53119 Lessors of Other Real Estate Property[CAN]

See industry description for 531190 below.

531190 Lessors of Other Real Estate Property[CAN]

This industry comprises establishments primarily engaged in acting as lessors of real estate (except buildings), such as manufactured home (i.e., mobile home) sites, vacant lots, and grazing land.

US—United States industry only. CAN—United States and Canadian industries are comparable. MEX—United States and Mexican industries are comparable. Blank—Canadian, Mexican, and United States industries are comparable.

Cross-References. Establishments primarily engaged in—

- Acting as lessors of buildings used as residences or dwellings including manufactured (mobile) homes on-site—are classified in Industry 531110, Lessors of Residential Buildings and Dwellings;
- Acting as lessors of buildings (except miniwarehouses and self-storage units) that are not used as residences or dwellings—are classified in Industry 531120, Lessors of Nonresidential Buildings (except Miniwarehouses); and
- Renting or leasing space for self-storage—are classified in Industry 531130, Lessors of Miniwarehouses and Self-Storage Units.

5312 Offices of Real Estate Agents and Brokers

53121 Offices of Real Estate Agents and Brokers

See industry description for 531210 below.

531210 Offices of Real Estate Agents and Brokers

This industry comprises establishments primarily engaged in acting as agents and/or brokers in one or more of the following: (1) selling real estate for others; (2) buying real estate for others; and (3) renting real estate for others.

5313 Activities Related to Real Estate

This industry group comprises establishments primarily engaged in providing real estate services (except lessors of real estate and offices of real estate agents and brokers). Included in this industry group are establishments primarily engaged in activities, such as managing real estate for others and appraising real estate.

53131 Real Estate Property Managers[CAN]

This industry comprises establishments primarily engaged in managing real property for others. Management includes ensuring that various activities associated with the overall operation of the property are performed, such as collecting rents, and overseeing other services (e.g., maintenance, security, trash removal.)

Cross-References.

- Establishments primarily engaged in acting as lessors of real estate are classified in Industry Group 5311, Lessors of Real Estate; and

---

US—United States industry only. CAN—United States and Canadian industries are comparable. MEX—United States and Mexican industries are comparable. Blank—Canadian, Mexican, and United States industries are comparable.

- Establishments formed on behalf of individual condominium owners or homeowners are classified in Industry 81399, Other Similar Organizations (except Business, Professional, Labor, and Political Organizations).

531311 Residential Property Managers[US]

This U.S. industry comprises establishments primarily engaged in managing residential real estate for others.

Cross-References.

- Establishments primarily engaged in managing nonresidential real estate for others are classified in U.S. Industry 531312, Nonresidential Property Managers;
- Establishments primarily engaged in acting as lessors of buildings used as residences or dwellings are classified in Industry 531110, Lessors of Residential Buildings and Dwellings; and
- Establishments formed on behalf of individual residential condominium owners or homeowners are classified in Industry 81399, Other Similar Organizations (except Business, Professional, Labor, and Political Organizations).

531312 Nonresidential Property Managers[US]

This U.S. industry comprises establishments primarily engaged in managing nonresidential real estate for others.

Cross-References.

- Establishments primarily engaged in managing residential real estate for others are classified in U.S. Industry 531311, Residential Property Managers;
- Establishments primarily engaged in acting as lessors of buildings (except miniwarehouses and self storage units) that are not used as residences or dwellings are classified in Industry 531120, Lessors of Nonresidential Buildings (except Miniwarehouses);
- Establishments primarily engaged in renting or leasing space for self-storage are classified in Industry 531130, Lessors of Miniwarehouses and Self-Storage Units; and
- Establishments formed on behalf of individual nonresidential condominium owners are classified in Industry 81399, Other Similar Organizations (except Business, Professional, Labor, and Political Organizations).

US—United States industry only. CAN—United States and Canadian industries are comparable. MEX—United States and Mexican industries are comparable. Blank—Canadian, Mexican, and United States industries are comparable.

53132 Offices of Real Estate Appraisers[CAN]

See industry description for 531320 below.

531320 Offices of Real Estate Appraisers[CAN]

This industry comprises establishments primarily engaged in estimating the fair market value of real estate.

53139 Other Activities Related to Real Estate[CAN]

See industry description for 531390 below.

531390 Other Activities Related to Real Estate[CAN]

This industry comprises establishments primarily engaged in performing real estate related services (except lessors of real estate, offices of real estate agents and brokers, real estate property managers, and offices of real estate appraisers).

Illustrative Examples:

Real estate escrow agencies
Real estate fiduciaries' offices
Real estate listing services

Cross-References. Establishments primarily engaged in—

- Acting as lessors of real estate—are classified in Industry Group 5311, Lessors of Real Estate;
- Selling, buying, and/or renting real estate for others—are classified in Industry 531210, Offices of Real Estate Agents and Brokers;
- Managing real estate for others—are classified in Industry 53131, Real Estate Property Managers;
- Estimating fair market value of real estate—are classified in Industry 531320, Offices of Real Estate Appraisers; and
- Researching public land records for ownership of titles and/or conveying real estate titles—are classified in U.S. Industry 541191, Title Abstract and Settlement Offices.

532 Rental and Leasing Services

Industries in the Rental and Leasing Services subsector include establishments that provide a wide array of tangible goods, such as automobiles, computers, consumer goods, and industrial machinery and equipment, to customers in return for a periodic rental or lease payment.

US—United States industry only. CAN—United States and Canadian industries are comparable. MEX—United States and Mexican industries are comparable. Blank—Canadian, Mexican, and United States industries are comparable.

The subsector includes two main types of establishments: (1) those that are engaged in renting consumer goods and equipment and (2) those that are engaged in leasing machinery and equipment often used for business operations. The first type typically operates from a retail-like or store-front facility and maintains inventories of goods that are rented for short periods of time. The latter type typically does not operate from retail-like locations or maintain inventories, and offers longer term leases. These establishments work directly with clients to enable them to acquire the use of equipment on a lease basis, or they work with equipment vendors or dealers to support the marketing of equipment to their customers under lease arrangements. Equipment lessors generally structure lease contracts to meet the specialized needs of their clients and use their remarketing expertise to find other users for previously leased equipment. Establishments that provide operating and capital (i.e., finance) leases are included in this subsector.

Establishments primarily engaged in leasing in combination with providing loans are classified in Sector 52, Finance and Insurance. Establishments primarily engaged in leasing real property are classified in Subsector 531, Real Estate. Those establishments primarily engaged in renting or leasing equipment with operators are classified in various subsectors of NAICS depending on the nature of the services provided (e.g., Transportation, Construction, Agriculture). These activities are excluded from this subsector since the client is paying for the expertise and knowledge of the equipment operator, in addition to the rental of the equipment. In many cases, such as the rental of heavy construction equipment, the operator is essential to operate the equipment. Likewise, since the provision of crop harvesting services includes both the equipment and operator, it is included in the agriculture subsector. The rental or leasing of copyrighted works is classified in Sector 51, Information, and the rental or leasing of assets, such as patents, trademarks, and/or licensing agreements is classified in Subsector 533, Lessors of Nonfinancial Intangible Assets (except Copyrighted Works).

5321 Automotive Equipment Rental and Leasing

This industry group comprises establishments primarily engaged in renting or leasing the following types of vehicles: passenger cars and trucks without drivers, and utility trailers. These establishments generally operate from a retail-like facility. Some establishments offer only short-term rental, others only longer-term leases, and some provide both type of services.

53211 Passenger Car Rental and Leasing

This industry comprises establishments primarily engaged in renting or leasing passenger cars without drivers.

US—United States industry only. CAN—United States and Canadian industries are comparable. MEX—United States and Mexican industries are comparable. Blank—Canadian, Mexican, and United States industries are comparable.

Cross-References. Establishments primarily engaged in—

- Renting or leasing passenger cars with drivers (e.g., limousines, hearses, taxis)—are classified in Industry Group 4853, Taxi and Limousine Service;
- Retailing passenger cars through sales or lease arrangements—are classified in Industry Group 4411, Automobile Dealers; and
- Leasing passenger cars in combination with providing loans to buyers of such vehicles—are classified in Sector 52, Finance and Insurance.

532111 Passenger Car Rental[CAN]

This industry comprises establishments primarily engaged in renting passenger cars without drivers, generally for short periods of time.

Cross-References. Establishments primarily engaged in—

- Leasing passenger cars without drivers, generally for long periods of time—are classified in U.S. Industry 532112, Passenger Car Leasing; and
- Renting or leasing passenger cars with drivers (e.g., limousines, hearses, taxis)—are classified in Industry Group 4853, Taxi and Limousine Service.

532112 Passenger Car Leasing[CAN]

This industry comprises establishments primarily engaged in leasing passenger cars without drivers, generally for long periods of time.

Cross-References. Establishments primarily engaged in—

- Renting passenger cars without drivers, generally for short periods of time—are classified in U.S. Industry 532111, Passenger Car Rental;
- Renting or leasing passenger cars with drivers (e.g., limousines, hearses, taxis)—are classified in Industry Group 4853, Taxi and Limousine Service;
- Retailing passenger cars through sales or lease arrangements—are classified in Industry Group 4411, Automobile Dealers; and
- Leasing passenger cars in combination with providing loans to buyers of such vehicles—are classified in Sector 52, Finance and Insurance.

53212 Truck, Utility Trailer, and RV (Recreational Vehicle) Rental and Leasing

See industry description for 532120 below.

US—United States industry only. CAN—United States and Canadian industries are comparable. MEX—United States and Mexican industries are comparable. Blank—Canadian, Mexican, and United States industries are comparable.

532120 Truck, Utility Trailer, and RV (Recreational Vehicle) Rental and Leasing[CAN]

This industry comprises establishments primarily engaged in renting or leasing, without drivers, one or more of the following: trucks, truck tractors or buses: semitrailers, utility trailers, or RVs (recreational vehicles).

Cross-References. Establishments primarily engaged in—

- Renting recreational goods, such as pleasure boats, canoes, motorcycles, mopeds, or bicycles—are classified in Industry 53229, Other Consumer Goods Rental;
- Renting or leasing farm tractors, industrial equipment, and industrial trucks, such as forklifts and other materials handling equipment—are classified in Industry 532490, Other Commercial and Industrial Machinery Equipment Rental and Leasing;
- Renting or leasing mobile home sites—are classified in Industry 53119, Lessors of Other Real Estate Property;
- Retailing vehicles commonly referred to as RVs through sales or lease arrangements—are classified in Industry 44121, Recreational Vehicle Dealers; and
- Leasing trucks, utility trailers, and RVs in combination with providing loans to buyers of such vehicles—are classified in Sector 52, Finance and Insurance.

5322 Consumer Goods Rental

This industry group comprises establishments primarily engaged in renting personal and household-type goods. Establishments classified in this industry group generally provide short-term rental although in some instances, the goods may be leased for longer periods of time. These establishments often operate from a retail-like or store-front facility.

53221 Consumer Electronics and Appliances Rental

See industry description for 532210 below.

532210 Consumer Electronics and Appliances Rental

This industry comprises establishments primarily engaged in renting consumer electronics equipment and appliances, such as televisions, stereos, and refrigerators. Included in this industry are appliance rental centers.

US—United States industry only. CAN—United States and Canadian industries are comparable. MEX—United States and Mexican industries are comparable. Blank—Canadian, Mexican, and United States industries are comparable.

Cross-References. Establishments primarily engaged in—

- Renting or leasing computers—are classified in Industry 532420, Office Machinery and Equipment Rental and Leasing; and
- Renting a range of consumer, commercial, and industrial equipment, such as lawn and garden equipment, home repair tools, and party and banquet equipment—are classified in Industry 532310, General Rental Centers.

53222 Formal Wear and Costume Rental

See industry description for 532220 below.

532220 Formal Wear and Costume Rental

This industry comprises establishments primarily engaged in renting clothing, such as formal wear, costumes (e.g., theatrical), or other clothing (except laundered uniforms and work apparel).

Cross-References.

Establishments primarily engaged in laundering and supplying uniforms and other work apparel are classified in Industry 81233, Linen and Uniform Supply.

53223 Video Tape and Disc Rental

See industry description for 532230 below.

532230 Video Tape and Disc Rental

This industry comprises establishments primarily engaged in renting prerecorded video tapes and discs for home electronic equipment.

Cross-References. Establishments primarily engaged in—

- Theatrical distribution of motion pictures and videos—are classified in Subsector 512, Motion Picture and Sound Recording Industries;
- Renting video recorders and players—are classified in Industry 532210, Consumer Electronics and Appliances Rental; and
- Retailing prerecorded video tapes and discs—are classified in Industry 451220, Prerecorded Tape, Compact Disc, and Record Stores.

53229 Other Consumer Goods Rental

This industry comprises establishments primarily engaged in renting consumer goods (except consumer electronics and appliances, formal wear and costumes, and prerecorded video tapes).

US—United States industry only. CAN—United States and Canadian industries are comparable. MEX—United States and Mexican industries are comparable. Blank—Canadian, Mexican, and United States industries are comparable.

Illustrative Examples:

Furniture rental centers
Party rental supply centers
Sporting goods rental

Cross-References. Establishments primarily engaged in—

- Renting consumer electronics and appliances—are classified in Industry 53221, Consumer Electronics and Appliances Rental;
- Renting formal wear and costumes—are classified in Industry 53222, Formal Wear and Costume Rental;
- Renting prerecorded video tapes and discs—are classified in Industry 53223, Video Tape and Disc Rental;
- Renting a general line of products, such as lawn and garden equipment, home repair tools, and party and banquet equipment—are classified in Industry 53231, General Rental Centers;
- Renting medical equipment (except home health equipment), such as electromedical and electrotherapeutic apparatus—are classified in Industry 53249, Other Commercial and Industrial Machinery and Equipment Rental and Leasing;
- Providing home health care services and home health equipment—are classified in Industry 62161, Home Health Care Services; and
- Retailing and renting musical instruments—are classified in Industry 45114, Musical Instrument and Supplies Stores.

532291 Home Health Equipment Rental[US]

This U.S. industry comprises establishments primarily engaged in renting home-type health and invalid equipment, such as wheel chairs, hospital beds, oxygen tanks, walkers, and crutches.

Cross-References. Establishments primarily engaged in—

- Renting medical equipment (except home health equipment), such as electromedical and electrotherapeutic apparatus—are classified in Industry 532490, Other Commercial and Industrial Machinery and Equipment Rental and Leasing; and
- Providing home health care services and home health equipment—are classified in Industry 62161, Home Health Care Services.

532292 Recreational Goods Rental[US]

This U.S. industry comprises establishments primarily engaged in renting recreational goods, such as bicycles, canoes, motorcycles, skis, sailboats, beach chairs, and beach umbrellas.

US—United States industry only. CAN—United States and Canadian industries are comparable. MEX—United States and Mexican industries are comparable. Blank—Canadian, Mexican, and United States industries are comparable.

532299 All Other Consumer Goods Rental[US]

This U.S. industry comprises establishments primarily engaged in renting consumer goods and products (except consumer electronics and appliances; formal wear and costumes; prerecorded video tapes and discs for home electronic equipment; home health furniture and equipment; and recreational goods). Included in this industry are furniture rental centers and party rental supply centers.

Cross-References. Establishments primarily engaged in—

- Renting consumer electronics and appliances—are classified in Industry 532210, Consumer Electronics and Appliances Rental;
- Renting formal wear and costumes—are classified in Industry 532220, Formal Wear and Costume Rental;
- Renting video tapes and discs—are classified in Industry 532230, Video Tape and Disc Rental;
- Renting home health furniture and equipment—are classified in U.S. Industry 532291, Home Health Equipment Rental;
- Renting recreational goods—are classified in U.S. Industry 532292, Recreational Goods Rental;
- Retailing and renting musical instruments—are classified in Industry 451140, Musical Instrument and Supplies Stores; and
- Renting a range of consumer, commercial, and industrial equipment, such as lawn and garden equipment, home repair tools, and party and banquet equipment—are classified in Industry 532310, General Rental Centers.

5323 General Rental Centers

53231 General Rental Centers

See industry description for 532310 below.

532310 General Rental Centers

This industry comprises establishments primarily engaged in renting a range of consumer, commercial, and industrial equipment. Establishments in this industry typically operate from conveniently located facilities where they maintain inventories of goods and equipment that they rent for short periods of time. The type of equipment that establishments in this industry provide often includes, but is not limited to: audio visual equipment, contractors' and builders' tools and equipment, home repair tools, lawn and garden equipment, moving equipment and supplies, and party and banquet equipment and supplies.

US—United States industry only. CAN—United States and Canadian industries are comparable. MEX—United States and Mexican industries are comparable. Blank—Canadian, Mexican, and United States industries are comparable.

Cross-References. Establishments primarily engaged in—

- Renting trucks and trailers without drivers—are classified in Industry 532120, Truck, Utility Trailer, and RV (Recreational Vehicle) Rental and Leasing;
- Renting party and banquet equipment—are classified in Industry 53229, Other Consumer Goods Rental;
- Renting heavy construction equipment without operators—are classified in U.S. Industry 532412, Construction, Mining, and Forestry Machinery and Equipment Rental and Leasing; and
- Renting specialized types of commercial and industrial equipment, such as garden tractors or public address systems—are classified in Industry 532490, Other Commercial and Industrial Machinery and Equipment Rental and Leasing.

5324 Commercial and Industrial Machinery and Equipment Rental and Leasing

This industry group comprises establishments primarily engaged in renting or leasing commercial-type and industrial-type machinery and equipment. The types of establishments included in this industry group are generally involved in providing capital or investment-type equipment that clients use in their business operations. These establishments typically cater to a business clientele and do not generally operate a retail-like or store-front facility.

53241 Construction, Transportation, Mining, and Forestry Machinery and Equipment Rental and Leasing

This industry comprises establishments primarily engaged in renting or leasing one or more of the following without operators: heavy construction, off-highway transportation, mining, and forestry machinery and equipment. Establishments in this industry may rent or lease products, such as aircraft, railroad cars, steamships, tugboats, bulldozers, earthmoving equipment, well-drilling machinery and equipment, or cranes.

Cross-References. Establishments primarily engaged in—

- Renting or leasing automobiles or trucks without operators—are classified in Industry Group 5321, Automotive Equipment Rental and Leasing;
- Renting or leasing air, rail, highway, and water transportation equipment with operators—are classified in Sector 48-49, Transportation and Warehousing, based on their primary activity;

US—United States industry only. CAN—United States and Canadian industries are comparable. MEX—United States and Mexican industries are comparable. Blank—Canadian, Mexican, and United States industries are comparable.

- Renting or leasing heavy construction equipment with operators—are classified in Industry 2389, Other Specialty Trade Contractors;
- Renting or leasing heavy equipment for mining with operators—are classified in Industry 21311, Support Activities for Mining;
- Renting or leasing heavy equipment for forestry with operators—are classified in Industry Group 1153, Support Activities for Forestry; and
- Leasing heavy equipment in combination with providing loans to buyers of such equipment—are classified in Sector 52, Finance and Insurance.

532411 Commercial Air, Rail, and Water Transportation Equipment Rental and Leasing[US]

This U.S. industry comprises establishments primarily engaged in renting or leasing off-highway transportation equipment without operators, such as aircraft, railroad cars, steamships, or tugboats.

Cross-References. Establishments primarily engaged in—

- Renting or leasing air, rail, highway, and water transportation equipment with operators—are classified in Sector 48-49, Transportation and Warehousing, based on their primary activity;
- Renting pleasure boats—are classified in U.S. Industry 532292, Recreational Goods Rental; and
- Renting or leasing automobiles or trucks without drivers—are classified in Industry Group 5321, Automotive Equipment Rental and Leasing.

532412 Construction, Mining, and Forestry Machinery and Equipment Rental and Leasing[US]

This U.S. industry comprises establishments primarily engaged in renting or leasing heavy equipment without operators that may be used for construction, mining, or forestry, such as bulldozers, earthmoving equipment, well-drilling machinery and equipment, or cranes.

Cross-References. Establishments primarily engaged in—

- Renting or leasing heavy construction equipment with operators—are classified in Industry 23499, All Other Heavy Construction;
- Renting or leasing heavy equipment for mining with operators—are classified in Industry 21311, Support Activities for Mining;
- Renting or leasing heavy equipment for forestry with operators—are classified in Industry Group 1153, Support Activities for Forestry; and

US—United States industry only. CAN—United States and Canadian industries are comparable. MEX—United States and Mexican industries are comparable. Blank—Canadian, Mexican, and United States industries are comparable.

- Leasing heavy equipment in combination with providing loans to buyers of such equipment—are classified in Sector 52, Finance and Insurance.

53242 Office Machinery and Equipment Rental and Leasing

See industry description for 532420 below.

532420 Office Machinery and Equipment Rental and Leasing

This industry comprises establishments primarily engaged in renting or leasing office machinery and equipment, such as computers, office furniture, duplicating machines (i.e., copiers), or facsimile machines.

Cross-References. Establishments primarily engaged in—

- Renting or leasing residential furniture—are classified in Industry 53229, Other Consumer Goods Rental; and
- Leasing office machinery and equipment in combination with providing loans to buyers of such equipment—are classified in Sector 52, Finance and Insurance.

53249 Other Commercial and Industrial Machinery and Equipment Rental and Leasing

See industry description for 532490 below.

532490 Other Commercial and Industrial Machinery and Equipment Rental and Leasing[CAN]

This industry comprises establishments primarily engaged in renting or leasing nonconsumer-type machinery and equipment (except heavy construction, transportation, mining, and forestry machinery and equipment without operators; and office machinery and equipment). Establishments in this industry rent or lease products, such as manufacturing equipment; metalworking, telecommunications, motion picture, or theatrical machinery and equipment; institutional (i.e., public building) furniture, such as furniture for schools, theaters, or buildings; or agricultural equipment without operators.

Cross-References. Establishments primarily engaged in—

- Renting or leasing heavy equipment without operators—are classified in Industry 53241, Construction, Transportation, Mining, and Forestry Machinery and Equipment Rental and Leasing;

US—United States industry only. CAN—United States and Canadian industries are comparable. MEX—United States and Mexican industries are comparable. Blank—Canadian, Mexican, and United States industries are comparable.

- Renting or leasing office machinery and equipment—are classified in Industry 532420, Office Machinery and Equipment Rental and Leasing;
- Renting or leasing agricultural machinery and equipment with operators—are classified in Subsector 115, Support Activities for Agriculture and Forestry;
- Renting home furniture or medical equipment for home use—are classified in Industry 53229, Other Consumer Goods Rental; and
- Leasing nonconsumer machinery and equipment in combination with providing loans to buyers of such equipment—are classified in Sector 52, Finance and Insurance.

533 Lessors of Nonfinancial Intangible Assets (except Copyrighted Works)

Industries in the Lessors of Nonfinancial Intangible Assets (except Copyrighted Works) subsector include establishments that are primarily engaged in assigning rights to assets, such as patents, trademarks, brand names, and/or franchise agreements for which a royalty payment or licensing fee is paid to the asset holder. Establishments in this subsector own the patents, trademarks, and/or franchise agreements that they allow others to use or reproduce for a fee and may or may not have created those assets.

Establishments that allow franchisees the use of the franchise name, contingent on the franchisee buying products or services from the franchisor, are classified elsewhere.

Excluded from this subsector are establishments primarily engaged in leasing real property and establishments primarily engaged in leasing tangible assets, such as automobiles, computers, consumer goods, and industrial machinery and equipment. These establishments are classified in Subsector 531, Real Estate and Subsector 532, Rental and Leasing Services, respectively.

5331 Lessors of Nonfinancial Intangible Assets (except Copyrighted Works)

53311 Lessors of Nonfinancial Intangible Assets (except Copyrighted Works)

See industry description for 533110 below.

533110 Lessors of Nonfinancial Intangible Assets (except Copyrighted Works)

This industry comprises establishments primarily engaged in assigning rights to assets, such as patents, trademarks, brand names, and/or franchise agreements for which a royalty payment or licensing fee is paid to the asset holder.

US—United States industry only. CAN—United States and Canadian industries are comparable. MEX—United States and Mexican industries are comparable. Blank—Canadian, Mexican, and United States industries are comparable.

Cross-References.

- Establishments primarily engaged in producing, reproducing, and/or distributing copyrighted works are classified in Sector 51, Information;
- Independent artists, writers, and performers primarily engaged in creating copyrighted works are classified in Industry 711510, Independent Artists, Writers, and Performers;
- Establishments primarily engaged in leasing real property are classified in Subsector 531, Real Estate;
- Establishments primarily engaged in leasing tangible assets, such as automobiles, computers, consumer goods, and industrial machinery and equipment, are classified in Subsector 532, Rental and Leasing Services; and
- Establishments that allow franchisees the use of the franchise name, contingent on the franchisee buying products or services from the franchisor are classified elsewhere.

US—United States industry only. CAN—United States and Canadian industries are comparable. MEX—United States and Mexican industries are comparable. Blank—Canadian, Mexican, and United States industries are comparable.

Sector 54—Professional, Scientific, and Technical Services

The Sector as a Whole

The Professional, Scientific, and Technical Services sector comprises establishments that specialize in performing professional, scientific, and technical activities for others. These activities require a high degree of expertise and training. The establishments in this sector specialize according to expertise and provide these services to clients in a variety of industries and, in some cases, to households. Activities performed include: legal advice and representation; accounting, bookkeeping, and payroll services; architectural, engineering, and specialized design services; computer services; consulting services; research services; advertising services; photographic services; translation and interpretation services; veterinary services; and other professional, scientific, and technical services.

This sector excludes establishments primarily engaged in providing a range of day-to-day office administrative services, such as financial planning, billing and recordkeeping, personnel, and physical distribution and logistics. These establishments are classified in Sector 56, Administrative and Support and Waste Management and Remediation Services.

541 Professional, Scientific, and Technical Services

Industries in the Professional, Scientific, and Technical Services subsector group establishments engaged in processes where human capital is the major input. These establishments make available the knowledge and skills of their employees, often on an assignment basis, where an individual or team is responsible for the delivery of services to the client. The individual industries of this subsector are defined on the basis of the particular expertise and training of the services provider.

The distinguishing feature of the Professional, Scientific, and Technical Services subsector is the fact that most of the industries grouped in it have production processes that are almost wholly dependent on worker skills. In most of these industries, equipment and materials are not of major importance, unlike health care, for example, where ''high tech'' machines and materials are important collaborating inputs to labor skills in the production of health care. Thus, the establishments classified in this subsector sell expertise. Much of the expertise requires degrees, though not in every case.

5411 Legal Services

54111 Offices of Lawyers

See industry description for 541110 below.

US—United States industry only. CAN—United States and Canadian industries are comparable. MEX—United States and Mexican industries are comparable. Blank—Canadian, Mexican, and United States industries are comparable.

541110 Offices of Lawyers

This industry comprises offices of legal practitioners known as lawyers or attorneys (i.e., counselors-at-law) primarily engaged in the practice of law. Establishments in this industry may provide expertise in a range or in specific areas of law, such as criminal law, corporate law, family and estate law, patent law, real estate law, or tax law.

Cross-References.

Establishments of legal practitioners (except lawyers or attorneys) primarily engaged in providing specialized legal or paralegal services are classified in Industry 54119, Other Legal Services.

54112 Offices of Notaries

See industry description for 541120 below.

541120 Offices of Notaries

This industry comprises establishments (except offices of lawyers and attorneys) primarily engaged in drafting, approving, and executing legal documents, such as real estate transactions, wills, and contracts; and in receiving, indexing, and storing such documents.

Cross-References.

- Establishments of lawyers and attorneys primarily engaged in the practice of law are classified in Industry 541110, Offices of Lawyers; and
- Establishments of notaries public engaged in activities, such as administering oaths and taking affidavits and depositions, witnessing and certifying signatures on documents, but not empowered to draw and approve legal documents and contracts, are classified in U.S. Industry 541199, All Other Legal Services

54119 Other Legal Services

This industry comprises establishments of legal practitioners (except lawyers and attorneys) primarily engaged in providing specialized legal or paralegal services.

Illustrative Examples:

Notary public services
Paralegal services
Process serving services
Real estate settlement offices

US—United States industry only. CAN—United States and Canadian industries are comparable. MEX—United States and Mexican industries are comparable. Blank—Canadian, Mexican, and United States industries are comparable.

Patent agent services (i.e., patent filing and searching services)

Real estate title abstract companies

Cross-References.

- Establishments of lawyers and attorneys primarily engaged in the practice of law are classified in Industry 54111, Offices of Lawyers; and
- Establishments (except offices of lawyers, attorneys, and paralegals) primarily engaged in providing arbitration and conciliation services are classified in Industry 54199, All Other Professional, Scientific, and Technical Services.

541191 Title Abstract and Settlement Offices[US]

This U.S. industry comprises establishments (except offices of lawyers and attorneys) primarily engaged in one or more of the following activities: (1) researching public land records to gather information relating to real estate titles; (2) preparing documents necessary for the transfer of the title, financing, and settlement; (3) conducting final real estate settlements and closings; and (4) filing legal and other documents relating to the sale of real estate. Real estate settlement offices, title abstract companies, and title search companies are included in this industry.

Cross-References.

Establishments of lawyers and attorneys primarily engaged in the practice of law are classified in Industry 541110, Offices of Lawyers.

541199 All Other Legal Services[US]

This U.S. industry comprises establishments of legal practitioners (except offices of lawyers and attorneys, settlement offices, and title abstract offices). These establishments are primarily engaged in providing specialized legal or paralegal services.

Illustrative Examples:

Notary public services
Paralegal services
Patent agent services (i.e., patent filing and searching services)
Process serving services

Cross-References.

- Establishments of lawyers and attorneys primarily engaged in the practice of law are classified in Industry 541110, Offices of Lawyers;

US—United States industry only. CAN—United States and Canadian industries are comparable. MEX—United States and Mexican industries are comparable. Blank—Canadian, Mexican, and United States industries are comparable.

- Establishments (except offices of lawyers and attorneys) primarily engaged in researching public land records for ownership or title; preparing documents necessary for the transfer of the title, financing, and settlement; conducting final real estate settlements and closings; and/or filing legal and other documents relating to the sale of real estate are classified in U.S. Industry 541191, Title Abstract and Settlement Offices; and
- Establishments (except offices of lawyers, attorneys, and paralegals) primarily engaged in providing arbitration and conciliation services are classified in Industry 541990, All Other Professional, Scientific, and Technical Services.

5412 Accounting, Tax Preparation, Bookkeeping, and Payroll Services

54121 Accounting, Tax Preparation, Bookkeeping, and Payroll Services

This industry comprises establishments primarily engaged in providing services, such as auditing of accounting records, designing accounting systems, preparing financial statements, developing budgets, preparing tax returns, processing payrolls, bookkeeping, and billing.

Illustrative Examples:

Accountants' offices
Bookkeeping services
Payroll processing services
Tax return preparation services

541211 Offices of Certified Public Accountants[US]

This U.S. industry comprises establishments of accountants that are certified to audit the accounting records of public and private organizations and to attest to compliance with generally accepted accounting practices. Offices of certified public accountants (CPAs) may provide one or more of the following accounting services: (1) auditing financial statements; (2) designing accounting systems; (3) preparing financial statements; (4) developing budgets; and (5) providing advice on matters related to accounting. These establishments may also provide related services, such as bookkeeping, tax return preparation, and payroll processing.

Cross-References. Establishments of non-CPAs engaged in—

- Providing tax return preparation services only—are classified in U.S. Industry 541213, Tax Preparation Services;
- Providing payroll processing services only—are classified in U.S. Industry 541214, Payroll Services; and

US—United States industry only. CAN—United States and Canadian industries are comparable. MEX—United States and Mexican industries are comparable. Blank—Canadian, Mexican, and United States industries are comparable.

- Providing accounting, bookkeeping, and billing services—are classified in U.S. Industry 541219, Other Accounting Services.

541213 Tax Preparation Services[CAN]

This U.S. industry comprises establishments (except offices of CPAs) engaged in providing tax return preparation services without also providing accounting, bookkeeping, billing, or payroll processing services. Basic knowledge of tax law and filing requirements is required.

Cross-References.

- Establishments of CPAs are classified in U.S. Industry 541211, Offices of Certified Public Accountants;
- Establishments of non-CPAs providing payroll services along with tax return preparation services are classified in U.S. Industry 541214, Payroll Services;
- Establishments of non-CPAs providing accounting, bookkeeping, or billing services along with tax return preparation services are classified in U.S. Industry 541219, Other Accounting Services; and
- Establishments providing computer data processing services at their own facility for others are classified in Industry 518210, Data Processing, Hosting, and Related Services.

541214 Payroll Services[US]

This U.S. industry comprises establishments (except offices of CPAs) engaged in the following without also providing accounting, bookkeeping, or billing services: (1) collecting information on hours worked, pay rates, deductions, and other payroll-related data from their clients and (2) using that information to generate paychecks, payroll reports, and tax filings. These establishments may use data processing and tabulating techniques as part of providing their services.

Cross-References.

- Establishments of CPAs are classified in U.S. Industry 541211, Offices of Certified Public Accountants;
- Establishments of non-CPAs providing tax return preparation services only are classified in U.S. Industry 541213, Tax Preparation Services; and
- Establishments of non-CPAs providing accounting, bookkeeping, or billing services along with payroll services are classified in U.S. Industry 541219, Other Accounting Services.

US—United States industry only. CAN—United States and Canadian industries are comparable. MEX—United States and Mexican industries are comparable. Blank—Canadian, Mexican, and United States industries are comparable.

541219 Other Accounting Services[US]

This U.S. industry comprises establishments (except offices of CPAs) engaged in providing accounting services (except tax return preparation services only or payroll services only). These establishments may also provide tax return preparation or payroll services. Accountant (except CPA) offices, bookkeeper offices, and billing offices are included in this industry.

Cross-References.

- Establishments of CPAs are classified in U.S. Industry 541211, Offices of Certified Public Accountants;
- Establishments of non-CPAs engaged in providing tax return preparation services only are classified in U.S. Industry 541213, Tax Preparation Services; and
- Establishments of non-CPAs engaged in providing payroll services only are classified in U.S. Industry 541214, Payroll Services.

5413 Architectural, Engineering, and Related Services

54131 Architectural Services

See industry description for 541310 below.

541310 Architectural Services

This industry comprises establishments primarily engaged in planning and designing residential, institutional, leisure, commercial, and industrial buildings and structures by applying knowledge of design, construction procedures, zoning regulations, building codes, and building materials.

Cross-References. Establishments primarily engaged in—

- Planning and designing the development of land areas—are classified in Industry 541320, Landscape Architectural Services; and
- Both the design and construction of buildings, highways, or other structures or in managing construction projects—are classified Sector 23, Construction, according to the type of project.

54132 Landscape Architectural Services

See industry description for 541320 below.

US—United States industry only. CAN—United States and Canadian industries are comparable. MEX—United States and Mexican industries are comparable. Blank—Canadian, Mexican, and United States industries are comparable.

541320 Landscape Architectural Services

This industry comprises establishments primarily engaged in planning and designing the development of land areas for projects, such as parks and other recreational areas; airports; highways; hospitals; schools; land subdivisions; and commercial, industrial, and residential areas, by applying knowledge of land characteristics, location of buildings and structures, use of land areas, and design of landscape projects.

Illustrative Examples:

Garden planning services
Golf course or ski area design services
Industrial land use planning services
Landscape architects' offices
Landscape consulting services
Landscape design services

Cross-References.

Establishments primarily engaged in providing landscape care and maintenance services and/or installing trees, shrubs, plants, lawns, or gardens along with the design of landscape plans are classified in Industry 561730, Landscaping Services.

54133 Engineering Services

See industry description for 541330 below.

541330 Engineering Services

This industry comprises establishments primarily engaged in applying physical laws and principles of engineering in the design, development, and utilization of machines, materials, instruments, structures, processes, and systems. The assignments undertaken by these establishments may involve any of the following activities: provision of advice, preparation of feasibility studies, preparation of preliminary and final plans and designs, provision of technical services during the construction or installation phase, inspection and evaluation of engineering projects, and related services.

Illustrative Examples:

Civil engineering services
Construction engineering services
Engineers' offices
Environmental engineering services
Mechanical engineering services

Cross-References. Establishments primarily engaged in—

- Planning and designing computer systems that integrate computer hardware, software, and communication technologies—are classified in U.S. Industry 541512, Computer Systems Design Services;

US—United States industry only. CAN—United States and Canadian industries are comparable. MEX—United States and Mexican industries are comparable. Blank—Canadian, Mexican, and United States industries are comparable.

- Performing surveying and mapping services of the surface of the earth, including the sea floor—are classified in Industry 541370, Surveying and Mapping (except Geophysical) Services;
- Gathering, interpreting, and mapping geophysical data—are classified in Industry 541360, Geophysical Surveying and Mapping Services;
- Creating and developing designs and specifications that optimize the use, value, and appearance of products—are classified in Industry 541420, Industrial Design Services;
- Providing advice and assistance to others on environmental issues, such as the control of environmental contamination from pollutants, toxic substances, and hazardous materials—are classified in Industry 541620, Environmental Consulting Services; and
- Both the design and construction of buildings, highways, and other structures or in managing construction projects—are classified in Sector 23, Construction, according to the type of project.

54134 Drafting Services

See industry description for 541340 below.

541340 Drafting Services

This industry comprises establishments primarily engaged in drawing detailed layouts, plans, and illustrations of buildings, structures, systems, or components from engineering and architectural specifications.

54135 Building Inspection Services

See industry description for 541350 below.

541350 Building Inspection Services

This industry comprises establishments primarily engaged in providing building inspection services. These establishments typically evaluate all aspects of the building structure and component systems and prepare a report on the physical condition of the property, generally for buyers or others involved in real estate transactions. Building inspection bureaus and establishments providing home inspection services are included in this industry.

Cross-References. Establishments primarily engaged in—

- Inspecting buildings for termites and other pests—are classified in Industry 561710, Exterminating and Pest Control Services;

US—United States industry only. CAN—United States and Canadian industries are comparable. MEX—United States and Mexican industries are comparable. Blank—Canadian, Mexican, and United States industries are comparable.

- Inspecting buildings for hazardous materials—are classified in Industry 541620, Environmental Consulting Services; and
- Conducting inspections and enforcing public building codes and standards—are classified in Industry 925110, Administration of Housing Programs.

54136 Geophysical Surveying and Mapping Services

See industry description for 541360 below.

541360 Geophysical Surveying and Mapping Services

This industry comprises establishments primarily engaged in gathering, interpreting, and mapping geophysical data. Establishments in this industry often specialize in locating and measuring the extent of subsurface resources, such as oil, gas, and minerals but they may also conduct surveys for engineering purposes. Establishments in this industry use a variety of surveying techniques depending on the purpose of the survey, including magnetic surveys, gravity surveys, seismic surveys, or electrical and electromagnetic surveys.

Cross-References.

Establishments primarily engaged in taking core samples, drilling test wells, or other mine development activities (except geophysical surveying and mapping) on a contract basis for others are classified in Industry 21311, Support Activities for Mining.

54137 Surveying and Mapping (except Geophysical) Services

See industry description for 541370 below.

541370 Surveying and Mapping (except Geophysical) Services

This industry comprises establishments primarily engaged in performing surveying and mapping services of the surface of the earth, including the sea floor. These services may include surveying and mapping of areas above or below the surface of the earth, such as the creation of view easements or segregating rights in parcels of land by creating underground utility easements.

Illustrative Examples:

Cadastral surveying services
Cartographic surveying services
Geodetic surveying services
Mapping (except geophysical) services
Topographic surveying services

US—United States industry only. CAN—United States and Canadian industries are comparable. MEX—United States and Mexican industries are comparable. Blank—Canadian, Mexican, and United States industries are comparable.

Cross-References. Establishments primarily engaged in—

- Providing geophysical surveying and mapping services—are classified in Industry 541360, Geophysical Surveying and Mapping Services; and
- Publishing atlases and maps, except for exclusive Internet publishing—are classified in U.S. Industry 511130, Book Publishers; and
- Publishing atlases and maps exclusively on the Internet—are classified in U.S. Industry 516110, Internet Publishing and Broadcasting.

54138 Testing Laboratories

See industry description for 541380 below.

541380 Testing Laboratories

This industry comprises establishments primarily engaged in performing physical, chemical, and other analytical testing services, such as acoustics or vibration testing, assaying, biological testing (except medical and veterinary), calibration testing, electrical and electronic testing, geotechnical testing, mechanical testing, nondestructive testing, or thermal testing. The testing may occur in a laboratory or on-site.

Cross-References. Establishments primarily engaged in—

- Laboratory testing for the medical profession—are classified in Industry 62151, Medical and Diagnostic Laboratories;
- Veterinary testing services—are classified in Industry 541940, Veterinary Services; and
- Auto emissions testing—are classified in U.S. Industry 811198, All Other Automotive Repair and Maintenance.

5414 Specialized Design Services

This industry group comprises establishments providing specialized design services (except architectural, engineering, and computer systems design).

54141 Interior Design Services

See industry description for 541410 below.

541410 Interior Design Services

This industry comprises establishments primarily engaged in planning, designing, and administering projects in interior spaces to meet the physical and aesthetic

US—United States industry only. CAN—United States and Canadian industries are comparable. MEX—United States and Mexican industries are comparable. Blank—Canadian, Mexican, and United States industries are comparable.

needs of people using them, taking into consideration building codes, health and safety regulations, traffic patterns and floor planning, mechanical and electrical needs, and interior fittings and furniture. Interior designers and interior design consultants work in areas, such as hospitality design, health care design, institutional design, commercial and corporate design, and residential design. This industry also includes interior decorating consultants engaged exclusively in providing aesthetic services associated with interior spaces.

54142 Industrial Design Services

See industry description for 541420 below.

541420 Industrial Design Services

This industry comprises establishments primarily engaged in creating and developing designs and specifications that optimize the use, value, and appearance of their products. These services can include the determination of the materials, construction, mechanisms, shape, color, and surface finishes of the product, taking into consideration human characteristics and needs, safety, market appeal, and efficiency in production, distribution, use, and maintenance. Establishments providing automobile or furniture industrial design services or industrial design consulting services are included in this industry.

Cross-References. Establishments primarily engaged in—

- Applying physical laws and principles of engineering in the design, development, and utilization of machines, materials, instruments, structures, processes, and systems—are classified in Industry 541330, Engineering Services; and
- Designing clothing, shoes, or jewelry—are classified in Industry 541490, Other Specialized Design Services.

54143 Graphic Design Services

See industry description for 541430 below.

541430 Graphic Design Services

This industry comprises establishments primarily engaged in planning, designing, and managing the production of visual communication in order to convey specific messages or concepts, clarify complex information, or project visual identities. These services can include the design of printed materials, packaging, advertising, signage systems, and corporate identification (logos). This industry also

---

US—United States industry only. CAN—United States and Canadian industries are comparable. MEX—United States and Mexican industries are comparable. Blank—Canadian, Mexican, and United States industries are comparable.

includes commercial artists engaged exclusively in generating drawings and illustrations requiring technical accuracy or interpretative skills.

Illustrative Examples:

Commercial art studios
Corporate identification (i.e., logo) design services
Graphic design consulting services
Independent commercial or graphic artists
Medical art or illustration services

Cross-References.

- Establishments primarily engaged in creating and/or placing public display advertising material are classified in Industry 541850, Display Advertising; and
- Independent artists primarily engaged in creating and selling visual artwork for noncommercial use and independent cartoonists are classified in Industry 711510, Independent Artists, Writers, and Performers.

54149 Other Specialized Design Services

See industry description for 541490 below.

541490 Other Specialized Design Services

This industry comprises establishments primarily engaged in providing professional design services (except architectural, landscape architecture, engineering, interior, industrial, graphic, and computer system design).

Illustrative Examples:

Costume design services (except independent theatrical costume designers)
Fashion design services
Float design services
Fur design services
Jewelry design services
Shoe design services
Textile design services

Cross-References. Establishments primarily engaged in—

- Providing architectural design services—are classified in Industry 541310, Architectural Services;
- Providing landscape architecture design services—are classified in Industry 541320, Landscape Architectural Services;
- Providing engineering design services—are classified in Industry 541330, Engineering Services;

US—United States industry only. CAN—United States and Canadian industries are comparable. MEX—United States and Mexican industries are comparable. Blank—Canadian, Mexican, and United States industries are comparable.

- Providing interior design services—are classified in Industry 541410, Interior Design Services;
- Providing industrial design services—are classified in Industry 541420, Industrial Design Services;
- Providing graphic design services—are classified in Industry 541430, Graphic Design Services;
- Providing computer systems design services—are classified in U.S. Industry 541512, Computer Systems Design Services; and
- Operating as independent theatrical designers—are classified in Industry 711510, Independent Artists, Writers, and Performers.

5415 Computer Systems Design and Related Services

See industry description for 54151 below.

54151 Computer Systems Design and Related Services

This industry comprises establishments primarily engaged in providing expertise in the field of information technologies through one or more of the following activities: (1) writing, modifying, testing, and supporting software to meet the needs of a particular customer; (2) planning and designing computer systems that integrate computer hardware, software, and communication technologies; (3) on-site management and operation of clients' computer systems and/or data processing facilities; and (4) other professional and technical computer-related advice and services.

Illustrative Examples:

Computer facilities management services
Computer hardware or software consulting services
Computer systems integration design services
Custom computer programming services
Software installation services

Cross-References. Establishments primarily engaged in—

- Selling computer hardware or software products from retail-like locations and providing supporting services, such as customized assembly of personal computers—are classified in Industry 44312, Computer and Software Stores;
- Wholesaling computer hardware or software products and providing supporting services, such as customized assembly of personal computers—are classified in Industry 423430, Computer and Computer Peripheral Equipment and Software Merchant Wholesalers;

US—United States industry only. CAN—United States and Canadian industries are comparable. MEX—United States and Mexican industries are comparable. Blank—Canadian, Mexican, and United States industries are comparable.

- Publishing packaged software—are classified in Industry 51121, Software Publishers; and
- Providing computer data processing services at their own facility for others—are classified in Industry 518210, Data Processing, Hosting, and Related Services.

541511 Custom Computer Programming Services[US]

This U.S. industry comprises establishments primarily engaged in writing, modifying, testing, and supporting software to meet the needs of a particular customer.

Cross-References. Establishments primarily engaged in—

- Publishing packaged software—are classified in Industry 511210, Software Publishers; and
- Planning and designing computer systems that integrate computer hardware, software, and communication technologies, even though such establishments may provide custom software as an integral part of their services—are classified in U.S. Industry 541512, Computer Systems Design Services.

541512 Computer Systems Design Services[US]

This U.S. industry comprises establishments primarily engaged in planning and designing computer systems that integrate computer hardware, software, and communication technologies. The hardware and software components of the system may be provided by this establishment or company as part of integrated services or may be provided by third parties or vendors. These establishments often install the system and train and support users of the system.

Illustrative Examples:

Computer systems integration design consulting services
Information management computer systems integration design services
Local area network (LAN) computer systems integration design services
Office automation computer systems integration design services

Cross-References. Establishments primarily engaged in—

- Selling computer hardware or software products and systems from retail-like locations, and providing supporting services, such as customized assembly of personal computers—are classified in Industry 443120, Computer and Software Stores; and
- Wholesaling computer hardware or software products and providing supporting services, such as customized assembly of personal computers—

US—United States industry only. CAN—United States and Canadian industries are comparable. MEX—United States and Mexican industries are comparable. Blank—Canadian, Mexican, and United States industries are comparable.

are classified in Industry 423430, Computer and Computer Peripheral Equipment and Software Merchant Wholesalers.

541513 Computer Facilities Management Services[US]

This U.S. industry comprises establishments primarily engaged in providing on-site management and operation of clients' computer systems and/or data processing facilities. Establishments providing computer systems or data processing facilities support services are included in this industry.

Cross-References.

Establishments primarily engaged in providing computer data processing services at their own facility for others are classified in Industry 518210, Data Processing, Hosting, and Related Services.

541519 Other Computer Related Services[US]

This U.S. industry comprises establishments primarily engaged in providing computer related services (except custom programming, systems integration design, and facilities management services). Establishments providing computer disaster recovery services or software installation services are included in this industry.

Cross-References. Establishments primarily engaged in—

- Providing custom computer programming services—are classified in U.S. Industry 541511, Custom Computer Programming Services;
- Providing computer systems integration design services—are classified in U.S. Industry 541512, Computer Systems Design Services; and
- Providing computer systems and/or data processing facilities management services—are classified in U.S. Industry 541513, Computer Facilities Management Services.

5416 Management, Scientific, and Technical Consulting Services

54161 Management Consulting Services

This industry comprises establishments primarily engaged in providing advice and assistance to businesses and other organizations on management issues, such as strategic and organizational planning; financial planning and budgeting; marketing objectives and policies; human resource policies, practices, and planning; production scheduling; and control planning.

US—United States industry only. CAN—United States and Canadian industries are comparable. MEX—United States and Mexican industries are comparable. Blank—Canadian, Mexican, and United States industries are comparable.

Illustrative Examples:

Actuarial, benefit, and compensation consulting services
Administrative and general management consulting services
Human resources and executive search consulting services
Marketing consulting services
Process, physical distribution, and logistics consulting services

Cross-References.

- Establishments primarily engaged in providing a range of day-to-day office administrative services, such as financial planning, billing and recordkeeping, personnel, and physical distribution and logistics, are classified in Industry 56111, Office Administrative Services;
- Establishments primarily engaged in administering, overseeing, and managing other establishments of the company or enterprise (except government establishments) are classified in Industry 55111, Management of Companies and Enterprises;
- Government establishments primarily engaged in administering, overseeing, and managing governmental programs are classified in Sector 92, Public Administration;
- Establishments primarily engaged in professional and management development training are classified in Industry 61143, Professional and Management Development Training;
- Establishments primarily engaged in listing employment vacancies and in selecting, referring, and placing applicants in employment are classified in Industry 56131, Employment Placement Agencies;
- Establishments primarily engaged in developing and implementing public relations plans are classified in Industry 54182, Public Relations Agencies;
- Establishments primarily engaged in developing and conducting marketing research or public opinion polling are classified in Industry 54191, Marketing Research and Public Opinion Polling;
- Establishments primarily engaged in planning and designing industrial processes and systems are classified in Industry 54133, Engineering Services;
- Establishments primarily engaged in planning and designing computer systems are classified in Industry 54151, Computer Systems Design and Related Services; and
- Establishments primarily engaged in providing financial investment advice services are classified in Industry 52393, Investment Advice.

US—United States industry only. CAN—United States and Canadian industries are comparable. MEX—United States and Mexican industries are comparable. Blank—Canadian, Mexican, and United States industries are comparable.

541611 Administrative Management and General Management Consulting Services[CAN]

This U.S. industry comprises establishments primarily engaged in providing operating advice and assistance to businesses and other organizations on administrative management issues, such as financial planning and budgeting, equity and asset management, records management, office planning, strategic and organizational planning, site selection, new business startup, and business process improvement. This industry also includes establishments of general management consultants that provide a full range of administrative; human resource; marketing; process, physical distribution, and logistics; or other management consulting services to clients.

Illustrative Examples:

Administrative management consulting services
Financial management (except investment advice) consulting services
General management consulting services
Site selection consulting services
Strategic planning consulting services

Cross-References.

- Establishments primarily engaged in providing a range of day-to-day office administrative services, such as financial planning, billing and recordkeeping, personnel, and physical distribution and logistics, are classified in Industry 561110, Office Administrative Services;
- Establishments primarily engaged in administering, overseeing, and managing other establishments of the company or enterprise (except government establishments) are classified in U.S. Industry 551114, Corporate, Subsidiary, and Regional Managing Offices;
- Government establishments primarily engaged in administering, overseeing, and managing governmental programs are classified in Sector 92, Public Administration; and
- Establishments primarily engaged in providing investment advice are classified in Industry 523930, Investment Advice.

541612 Human Resources and Executive Search Consulting Services[CAN]

This U.S. industry comprises establishments primarily engaged in providing advice and assistance to businesses and other organizations in one or more of the following areas: (1) human resource and personnel policies, practices, and procedures; (2) employee benefits planning, communication, and administration;

US—United States industry only. CAN—United States and Canadian industries are comparable. MEX—United States and Mexican industries are comparable. Blank—Canadian, Mexican, and United States industries are comparable.

(3) compensation systems planning; (4) wage and salary administration; and (5) executive search and recruitment.

Illustrative Examples:

Benefit or compensation consulting services
Employee assessment consulting services
Executive placement or search consulting services
Human resources consulting services
Personnel management consulting services

Cross-References. Establishments primarily engaged in—

- Professional and management development training—are classified in Industry 611430, Professional and Management Development Training; and
- Listing employment vacancies and in selecting, referring, and placing applicants in employment—are classified in Industry 561310, Employment Placement Agencies.

541613 Marketing Consulting Services[US]

This U.S. industry comprises establishments primarily engaged in providing operating advice and assistance to businesses and other organizations on marketing issues, such as developing marketing objectives and policies, sales forecasting, new product developing and pricing, licensing and franchise planning, and marketing planning and strategy.

Illustrative Examples:

Customer services management consulting services
Marketing management consulting services
New product development consulting services
Sales management consulting services

Cross-References. Establishment primarily engaged in—

- Developing and implementing public relations plans—are classified in Industry 541820, Public Relations Agencies; and
- Developing and conducting marketing research or public opinion polling—are classified in Industry 541910, Marketing Research and Public Opinion Polling.

541614 Process, Physical Distribution, and Logistics Consulting Services[US]

This U.S. industry comprises establishments primarily engaged in providing operating advice and assistance to businesses and other organizations in areas,

US—United States industry only. CAN—United States and Canadian industries are comparable. MEX—United States and Mexican industries are comparable. Blank—Canadian, Mexican, and United States industries are comparable.

such as: (1) manufacturing operations improvement; (2) productivity improvement; (3) production planning and control; (4) quality assurance and quality control; (5) inventory management; (6) distribution networks; (7) warehouse use, operations, and utilization; (8) transportation and shipment of goods and materials; and (9) materials management and handling.

Illustrative Examples:

Freight rate or tariff rate consulting services
Inventory planning and control management consulting services
Manufacturing management consulting services
Productivity improvement consulting services
Transportation management consulting services

Cross-References. Establishments primarily engaged in—

- Planning and designing industrial processes and systems—are classified in Industry 541330, Engineering Services; and
- Providing computer systems integration design services—are classified in U.S. Industry 541512, Computer Systems Design Services.

541618 Other Management Consulting Services[US]

This U.S. industry comprises establishments primarily engaged in providing management consulting services (except administrative and general management consulting; human resources consulting; marketing consulting; or process, physical distribution, and logistics consulting). Establishments providing telecommunications or utilities management consulting services are included in this industry.

Cross-References. Establishments primarily engaged in—

- Providing administrative and general management consulting services—are classified in U.S. Industry 541611, Administrative Management and General Management Consulting Services;
- Providing human resources and executive search consulting services—are classified in U.S. Industry 541612, Human Resources and Executive Search Consulting Services;
- Providing marketing consulting services—are classified in U.S. Industry 541613, Marketing Consulting Services; and
- Providing process, physical distribution, and logistics consulting services—are classified in U.S. Industry 541614, Process, Physical Distribution, and Logistics Consulting Services.

US—United States industry only. CAN—United States and Canadian industries are comparable. MEX—United States and Mexican industries are comparable. Blank—Canadian, Mexican, and United States industries are comparable.

54162 Environmental Consulting Services

See industry description for 541620 below.

541620 Environmental Consulting Services

This industry comprises establishments primarily engaged in providing advice and assistance to businesses and other organizations on environmental issues, such as the control of environmental contamination from pollutants, toxic substances, and hazardous materials. These establishments identify problems (e.g., inspect buildings for hazardous materials), measure and evaluate risks, and recommend solutions. They employ a multidisciplined staff of scientists, engineers, and other technicians with expertise in areas, such as air and water quality, asbestos contamination, remediation, and environmental law. Establishments providing sanitation or site remediation consulting services are included in this industry.

Cross-References. Establishments primarily engaged in—

- Environmental remediation—are classified in Industry 562910, Remediation Services; and
- Providing environmental engineering services—are classified in Industry 541330, Engineering Services.

54169 Other Scientific and Technical Consulting Services

See industry description for 541690 below.

541690 Other Scientific and Technical Consulting Services

This industry comprises establishments primarily engaged in providing advice and assistance to businesses and other organizations on scientific and technical issues (except environmental).

Illustrative Examples:

Agricultural consulting services
Biological consulting services
Chemical consulting services
Economic consulting services
Energy consulting services
Motion picture consulting services
Physics consulting services
Radio consulting services
Safety consulting services
Security consulting services

Cross-References.

Establishments primarily engaged in environmental consulting are classified in Industry 541620, Environmental Consulting Services.

US—United States industry only. CAN—United States and Canadian industries are comparable. MEX—United States and Mexican industries are comparable. Blank—Canadian, Mexican, and United States industries are comparable.

5417 Scientific Research and Development Services

This industry group comprises establishments engaged in conducting original investigation undertaken on a systematic basis to gain new knowledge (research) and/or the application of research findings or other scientific knowledge for the creation of new or significantly improved products or processes (experimental development). The industries within this industry group are defined on the basis of the domain of research; that is, on the scientific expertise of the establishment.

54171 Research and Development in the Physical, Engineering, and Life Sciences

See industry description for 541710 below.

541710 Research and Development in the Physical, Engineering, and Life Sciences[CAN]

This industry comprises establishments primarily engaged in conducting research and experimental development in the physical, engineering, and life sciences, such as agriculture, electronics, environmental, biology, botany, biotechnology, computers, chemistry, food, fisheries, forests, geology, health, mathematics, medicine, oceanography, pharmacy, physics, veterinary, and other allied subjects.

Cross-References. Establishments primarily engaged in—

- Providing physical, chemical, or other analytical testing services (except medical or veterinary)—are classified in Industry 541380, Testing Laboratories;
- Providing medical laboratory testing for humans—are classified in U.S. Industry 621511, Medical Laboratories; and
- Providing veterinary testing services—are classified in Industry 541940, Veterinary Services.

54172 Research and Development in the Social Sciences and Humanities

See industry description for 541720 below.

541720 Research and Development in the Social Sciences and Humanities[CAN]

This industry comprises establishments primarily engaged in conducting research and analyses in cognitive development, sociology, psychology, language, behavior, economic, and other social science and humanities research.

US—United States industry only. CAN—United States and Canadian industries are comparable. MEX—United States and Mexican industries are comparable. Blank—Canadian, Mexican, and United States industries are comparable.

Cross-References.

Establishments primarily engaged in marketing research are classified in Industry 541910, Marketing Research and Public Opinion Polling.

5418 Advertising and Related Services

54181 Advertising Agencies

See industry description for 541810 below.

541810 Advertising Agencies

This industry comprises establishments primarily engaged in creating advertising campaigns and placing such advertising in periodicals, newspapers, radio and television, or other media. These establishments are organized to provide a full range of services (i.e., through in-house capabilities or subcontracting), including advice, creative services, account management, production of advertising material, media planning, and buying (i.e., placing advertising).

Cross-References. Establishments primarily engaged in—

- Purchasing advertising space from media outlets and reselling it directly to advertising agencies or individual companies—are classified in Industry 541830, Media Buying Agencies;
- Conceptualizing and producing artwork or graphic designs without providing other advertising agency services—are classified in Industry 541430, Graphic Design Services;
- Creating direct mail advertising campaigns—are classified in Industry 541860, Direct Mail Advertising;
- Providing marketing consulting services—are classified in U.S. Industry 541613, Marketing Consulting Services; and
- Selling media time or space for media owners as independent representatives—are classified in Industry 541840, Media Representatives.

54182 Public Relations Agencies

See industry description for 541820 below.

541820 Public Relations Agencies

This industry comprises establishments primarily engaged in designing and implementing public relations campaigns. These campaigns are designed to pro-

US—United States industry only. CAN—United States and Canadian industries are comparable. MEX—United States and Mexican industries are comparable. Blank—Canadian, Mexican, and United States industries are comparable.

mote the interests and image of their clients. Establishments providing lobbying, political consulting, or public relations consulting are included in this industry.

54183 Media Buying Agencies

See industry description for 541830 below.

541830 Media Buying Agencies

This industry comprises establishments primarily engaged in purchasing advertising time or space from media outlets and reselling it to advertising agencies or individual companies directly.

Cross-References. Establishments primarily engaged in—

- Selling time and space to advertisers for media owners as independent representatives—are classified in Industry 541840, Media Representatives; and
- Creating advertising campaigns and placing such advertising in media—are classified in Industry 541810, Advertising Agencies.

54184 Media Representatives

See industry description for 541840 below.

541840 Media Representatives

This industry comprises establishments of independent representatives primarily engaged in selling media time or space for media owners.

Illustrative Examples:

Newspaper advertising representatives (i.e., independent of media owners)
Publishers' advertising representatives (i.e., independent of media owners)
Radio advertising representatives (i.e., independent of media owners)
Television advertising representatives (i.e., independent of media owners)

Cross-References. Establishments primarily engaged in—

- Purchasing advertising time or space from media outlets and reselling it directly to advertising agencies or individual companies—are classified in Industry 541830, Media Buying Agencies; and
- Creating advertising campaigns and placing such advertising in media—are classified in Industry 541810, Advertising Agencies.

US—United States industry only. CAN—United States and Canadian industries are comparable. MEX—United States and Mexican industries are comparable. Blank—Canadian, Mexican, and United States industries are comparable.

54185 Display Advertising

See industry description for 541850 below.

541850 Display Advertising

This industry comprises establishments primarily engaged in creating and designing public display advertising, campaign materials, such as printed, painted, or electronic displays, and/or placing such displays on indoor or outdoor billboards and panels, or on or within transit vehicles or facilities, shopping malls, retail (in-store) displays, and other display structures or sites.

Cross-References. Establishments primarily engaged in—

- Providing sign lettering and painting services—are classified in Industry 541890, Other Services Related to Advertising;
- Printing paper on paperboard signs—are classified in Industry 32311, Printing;
- Erecting display boards—are classified in Sector 238990, All Other Specialty Trade Contractors; and
- Manufacturing electrical, mechanical, or plate signs and point-of-sale advertising displays—are classified in Industry 339950, Sign Manufacturing.

54186 Direct Mail Advertising

See industry description for 541860 below.

541860 Direct Mail Advertising

This industry comprises establishments primarily engaged in (1) creating and designing advertising campaigns for the purpose of distributing advertising materials (e.g., coupons, flyers, samples) or specialties (e.g., key chains, magnets, pens with customized messages imprinted) by mail or other direct distribution; and/or (2) preparing advertising materials or specialties for mailing or other direct distribution. These establishments may also compile, maintain, sell, and rent mailing lists.

Cross-References. Establishments primarily engaged in—

- The direct distribution or delivery (e.g., door-to-door, windshield placement) of advertisements or samples—are classified in Industry 541870, Advertising Material Distribution Services;

US—United States industry only. CAN—United States and Canadian industries are comparable. MEX—United States and Mexican industries are comparable. Blank—Canadian, Mexican, and United States industries are comparable.

- Distributing advertising specialties for clients who wish to use such materials for promotional purposes—are classified in Industry 541890, Other Services Related to Advertising;
- Creating advertising campaigns and placing such advertising in media—are classified in Industry 541810, Advertising Agencies;
- Compiling and selling mailing lists without providing direct mail advertising services—are classified in Industry 511140, Directory and Mailing List Publishers; and
- Broadcasting exclusively on the Internet—are classified in Industry 516110, Internet Publishing and Broadcasting.

54187 Advertising Material Distribution Services

See industry description for 541870 below.

541870 Advertising Material Distribution Services

This industry comprises establishments primarily engaged in the direct distribution or delivery of advertisements (e.g., circulars, coupons, handbills) or samples. Establishments in this industry use methods, such as delivering advertisements or samples door-to-door, placing flyers or coupons on car windshields in parking lots, or handing out samples in retail stores.

Cross-References. Establishments primarily engaged in—

- Creating and designing advertising campaigns for the purpose of distributing advertising materials or samples through the mail—are classified in Industry 541860, Direct Mail Advertising;
- Publishing newspapers or operating television stations or on-line information services—are classified in Sector 51, Information; and
- Distributing advertising specialties (e.g., key chains, magnets, or pens with customized messages imprinted) to clients who wish to use such materials for promotional purposes—are classified in Industry 541890, Other Services Related to Advertising.

54189 Other Services Related to Advertising

See industry description for 541890 below.

541890 Other Services Related to Advertising[MEX]

This industry comprises establishments primarily engaged in providing advertising services (except advertising agency services, public relations agency services,

US—United States industry only. CAN—United States and Canadian industries are comparable. MEX—United States and Mexican industries are comparable. Blank—Canadian, Mexican, and United States industries are comparable.

media buying agency services, media representative services, display advertising services, direct mail advertising services, advertising material distribution services, and marketing consulting services).

Illustrative Examples:

Advertising specialties (e.g., key chains, magnets, pens) distribution services (except direct mail)
Display lettering services
Mannequin decorating services
Merchandise demonstration services
Sign lettering and painting services
Store window dressing or trimming services
Welcoming services (i.e., advertising services)

Cross-References. Establishments primarily engaged in—

- Creating advertising campaigns and placing such advertising in newspapers, television, or other media—are classified in Industry 541810, Advertising Agencies;
- Designing and implementing public relations campaigns—are classified in Industry 541820, Public Relations Agencies;
- Purchasing advertising time or space from media outlets and reselling it directly to advertising agencies or individual companies—are classified in Industry 541830, Media Buying Agencies;
- Selling media time or space for media owners as independent representatives—are classified in Industry 541840, Media Representatives;
- Providing display advertising services (except aerial)—are classified in Industry 541850, Display Advertising;
- Providing direct distribution or delivery (e.g., door-to-door, windshield placement) of advertisements or samples—are classified in Industry 541870, Advertising Material Distribution Services;
- Providing direct mail advertising services—are classified in Industry 541860, Direct Mail Advertising;
- Publishing newspapers or operating television stations or on-line information services—are classified in Sector 51, Information; and
- Providing marketing consulting services—are classified in U.S. Industry 541613, Marketing Consulting Services.

5419 Other Professional, Scientific, and Technical Services

This industry group comprises establishments engaged in professional, scientific, and technical services (except legal services; accounting, tax preparation, book-

US—United States industry only. CAN—United States and Canadian industries are comparable. MEX—United States and Mexican industries are comparable. Blank—Canadian, Mexican, and United States industries are comparable.

keeping, and related services; architectural, engineering, and related services; specialized design services; computer systems design and related services; management, scientific, and technical consulting services; scientific research and development services; and advertising and related services).

54191 Marketing Research and Public Opinion Polling

See industry description for 541910 below.

541910 Marketing Research and Public Opinion Polling

This industry comprises establishments primarily engaged in systematically gathering, recording, tabulating, and presenting marketing and public opinion data.

Illustrative Examples:

Broadcast media rating services
Marketing analysis or research services
Opinion research services
Political opinion polling services
Statistical sampling services

Cross-References. Establishments primarily engaged in—

- Providing research and analysis in economics, sociology, and related fields—are classified in Industry 541720, Research and Development in the Social Sciences and Humanities; and
- Providing advice and counsel on marketing strategies—are classified in U.S. Industry 541613, Marketing Consulting Services.

54192 Photographic Services

This industry comprises establishments primarily engaged in providing still, video, or digital photography services. These establishments may specialize in a particular field of photography, such as commercial and industrial photography, portrait photography, and special events photography. Commercial or portrait photography studios are included in this industry.

Cross-References. Establishments primarily engaged in—

- Producing film and videotape for commercial exhibition or sale—are classified in Industry 51211, Motion Picture and Video Production;
- Developing still photographs—are classified in Industry 81292, Photofinishing;
- Developing motion picture film—are classified in Industry 51219, Postproduction Services and Other Motion Picture and Video Industries;

US—United States industry only. CAN—United States and Canadian industries are comparable. MEX—United States and Mexican industries are comparable. Blank—Canadian, Mexican, and United States industries are comparable.

- Taking, developing, and selling artistic, news, or other types of photographs on a freelance basis, such as photojournalists—are classified in Industry 71151, Independent Artists, Writers, and Performers; and
- Supplying and servicing automatic photography machines in places of business operated by others—are classified in Industry 81299, All Other Personal Services.

541921 Photography Studios, Portrait[US]

This U.S. industry comprises establishments known as portrait studios primarily engaged in providing still, video, or digital portrait photography services.

Illustrative Examples:

Home photography services
Passport photography services
School photography services
Videotaping services for special events (e.g., weddings)

Cross-References. Establishments primarily engaged in—

- Producing film and videotape for commercial exhibition or sale—are classified in Industry 512110, Motion Picture and Video Production;
- Developing still photographs—are classified in Industry 81292, Photofinishing;
- Developing motion picture film—are classified in U.S. Industry 512199, Other Motion Picture and Video Industries;
- Taking, developing, and selling artistic, news, or other types of photographs on a freelance basis, such as photojournalists—are classified in Industry 711510, Independent Artists, Writers, and Performers; and
- Supplying and servicing automatic photography machines in places of business operated by others—are classified in Industry 812990, All Other Personal Services.

541922 Commercial Photography[US]

This U.S. industry comprises establishments primarily engaged in providing commercial photography services, generally for advertising agencies, publishers, and other business and industrial users.

Cross-References. Establishments primarily engaged in—

- Producing film and videotape for commercial exhibition or sale—are classified in Industry 512110, Motion Picture and Video Production;

US—United States industry only. CAN—United States and Canadian industries are comparable. MEX—United States and Mexican industries are comparable. Blank—Canadian, Mexican, and United States industries are comparable.

- Developing still photographs—are classified in Industry 81292, Photofinishing;
- Developing motion picture film—are classified in U.S. Industry 512199, Other Motion Picture and Video Industries;
- Taking, developing, and selling artistic, news, or other types of photographs on a freelance basis, such as photojournalists—are classified in Industry 711510, Independent Artists, Writers, and Performers; and
- Supplying and servicing coin-operated photography machines in places of business operated by others—are classified in Industry 812990, All Other Personal Services.

54193 Translation and Interpretation Services

See industry description for 541930 below.

541930 Translation and Interpretation Services

This industry comprises establishments primarily engaged in translating written material and interpreting speech from one language to another and establishments primarily engaged in providing sign language services.

Cross-References. Establishments primarily engaged in—

- Providing transcription services—are classified in Industry 561410, Document Preparation Services;
- Providing real-time (i.e., simultaneous) closed captioning services for live television performances, at meetings and conferences—are classified in U.S. Industry 561492, Court Reporting and Stenotype Services;
- Providing film or tape closed captioning services—are classified in U.S. Industry 512191, Teleproduction and Other Postproduction Services; and
- Analyzing handwriting—are classified in Industry 541990, All Other Professional, Scientific, and Technical Services.

54194 Veterinary Services

See industry description for industry 541940 below.

541940 Veterinary Services[CAN]

This industry comprises establishments of licensed veterinary practitioners primarily engaged in the practice of veterinary medicine, dentistry, or surgery for

---

US—United States industry only. CAN—United States and Canadian industries are comparable. MEX—United States and Mexican industries are comparable. Blank—Canadian, Mexican, and United States industries are comparable.

animals; and establishments primarily engaged in providing testing services for licensed veterinary practitioners.

Illustrative Examples:

Animal hospitals
Veterinarians' offices
Veterinary clinics
Veterinary testing laboratories

Cross-References. Establishments primarily engaged in—

- Providing veterinary research and development services—are classified in Industry 541710, Research and Development in the Physical, Engineering, and Life Sciences;
- Providing nonveterinary pet care services, such as boarding or grooming pets—are classified in Industry 812910, Pet Care (except Veterinary) Services;
- Providing animal breeding services or boarding horses—are classified in Industry 115210, Support Activities for Animal Production; and
- Transporting pets—are classified in U.S. Industry 485991, Special Needs Transportation.

54199 All Other Professional, Scientific, and Technical Services

See industry description for 541990 below.

541990 All Other Professional, Scientific, and Technical Services

This industry comprises establishments primarily engaged in the provision of professional, scientific, or technical services (except legal services; accounting, tax preparation, bookkeeping, and related services; architectural, engineering, and related services; specialized design services; computer systems design and related services; management, scientific, and technical consulting services; scientific research and development services; advertising and related services; market research and public opinion polling; photographic services; translation and interpretation services; and veterinary services).

Illustrative Examples:

Appraisal (except real estate) services
Arbitration and conciliation services (except by lawyer, attorney, or paralegal offices)
Commodity inspector services
Consumer credit counseling services
Handwriting analysis services
Marine surveyor (i.e., appraiser) services
Patent broker services (i.e., patent marketing services)
Pipeline or power line inspection (i.e., visual) services
Weather forecasting services

US—United States industry only. CAN—United States and Canadian industries are comparable. MEX—United States and Mexican industries are comparable. Blank—Canadian, Mexican, and United States industries are comparable.

Cross-References. Establishments primarily engaged in—

- Providing legal services—are classified in Industry Group 5411, Legal Services;
- Providing accounting, tax preparation, bookkeeping, and payroll services—are classified in Industry Group 5412, Accounting, Tax Preparation, Bookkeeping, and Payroll Services;
- Providing architectural, engineering, and related services—are classified in Industry Group 5413, Architectural, Engineering, and Related Services;
- Providing specialized design services—are classified in Industry Group 5414, Specialized Design Services;
- Providing computer systems design and related services—are classified in Industry Group 5415, Computer Systems Design and Related Services;
- Providing management, scientific, and technical consulting services—are classified in Industry Group 5416, Management, Scientific, and Technical Consulting Services;
- Providing scientific research and development services—are classified in Industry Group 5417, Scientific Research and Development Services;
- Providing advertising and related services—are classified in Industry Group 5418, Advertising and Related Services;
- Providing marketing research and public opinion polling—are classified in Industry 541910, Marketing Research and Public Opinion Polling;
- Providing photographic services—are classified in Industry 54192, Photographic Services;
- Providing translation and interpretation services—are classified in Industry 541930, Translation and Interpretation Services;
- Providing veterinary services—are classified in Industry 541940, Veterinary Services; and
- Providing real estate appraisal services—are classified in Industry 531320, Offices of Real Estate Appraisers.

US—United States industry only. CAN—United States and Canadian industries are comparable. MEX—United States and Mexican industries are comparable. Blank—Canadian, Mexican, and United States industries are comparable.

Sector 55—Management of Companies and Enterprises

The Sector as a Whole

The Management of Companies and Enterprises sector comprises (1) establishments that hold the securities of (or other equity interests in) companies and enterprises for the purpose of owning a controlling interest or influencing management decisions or (2) establishments (except government establishments) that administer, oversee, and manage establishments of the company or enterprise and that normally undertake the strategic or organizational planning and decisionmaking role of the company or enterprise. Establishments that administer, oversee, and manage may hold the securities of the company or enterprise.

Establishments in this sector perform essential activities that are often undertaken, in-house, by establishments in many sectors of the economy. By consolidating the performance of these activities of the enterprise at one establishment, economies of scale are achieved.

Government establishments primarily engaged in administering, overseeing, and managing governmental programs are classified in Sector 92, Public Administration. Establishments primarily engaged in providing a range of day-to-day office administrative services, such as financial planning, billing and recordkeeping, personnel, and physical distribution and logistics are classified in Industry 56111, Office Administrative Services.

551 Management of Companies and Enterprises

Industries in the Management of Companies and Enterprises subsector include three main types of establishments: (1) those that hold the securities of (or other equity interests in) companies and enterprises; (2) those (except government establishments) that administer, oversee, and manage other establishments of the company or enterprise but do not hold the securities of these establishments; and (3) those that both administer, oversee, and manage other establishments of the company or enterprise and hold the securities of (or other equity interests in) these establishments. Those establishments that administer, oversee, and manage normally undertake the strategic or organizational planning and decisionmaking role of the company or enterprise.

5511 Management of Companies and Enterprises

55111 Management of Companies and Enterprises

This industry comprises (1) establishments primarily engaged in holding the securities of (or other equity interests in) companies and enterprises for the purpose

US—United States industry only. CAN—United States and Canadian industries are comparable. MEX—United States and Mexican industries are comparable. Blank—Canadian, Mexican, and United States industries are comparable.

of owning a controlling interest or influencing the management decisions or (2) establishments (except government establishments) that administer, oversee, and manage other establishments of the company or enterprise and that normally undertake the strategic or organizational planning and decisionmaking role of the company or enterprise. Establishments that administer, oversee, and manage may hold the securities of the company or enterprise.

Cross-References.

- Establishments primarily engaged in holding the securities of companies or enterprises and operating these entities are classified according to the business operated;
- Establishments primarily engaged in holding the securities of depository banks and operating these entities are classified in Industry Group 5221, Depository Credit Intermediation;
- Establishments primarily engaged in providing a single service to other establishments of the company or enterprise, such as trucking, warehousing, research and development, and data processing are classified according to the service provided; and
- Government establishments primarily engaged in administering, overseeing, and managing governmental programs are classified in Sector 92, Public Administration.

551111 Offices of Bank Holding Companies[US]

This U.S. industry comprises legal entities known as bank holding companies primarily engaged in holding the securities of (or other equity interests in) companies and enterprises for the purpose of owning a controlling interest or influencing the management decisions of these firms. The holding companies in this industry do not administer, oversee, and manage other establishments of the company or enterprise whose securities they hold.

Cross-References. Establishments primarily engaged in—

- Holding the securities of (or other equity interests in) a company or enterprise and administering, overseeing, and managing establishments of the company or enterprise whose securities they hold—are classified in U.S. Industry 551114, Corporate, Subsidiary, and Regional Managing Offices; and
- Holding the securities of depository banks and operating these entities—are classified in Industry Group 5221, Depository Credit Intermediation.

US—United States industry only. CAN—United States and Canadian industries are comparable. MEX—United States and Mexican industries are comparable. Blank—Canadian, Mexican, and United States industries are comparable.

551112 Offices of Other Holding Companies[US]

This U.S. industry comprises legal entities known as holding companies (except bank holding) primarily engaged in holding the securities of (or other equity interests in) companies and enterprises for the purpose of owning a controlling interest or influencing the management decisions of these firms. The holding companies in this industry do not administer, oversee, and manage other establishments of the company or enterprise whose securities they hold.

Cross-References. Establishments primarily engaged in—

- Holding the securities of (or other equity interests in) depository banks for the purpose of owning a controlling interest or influencing the management decisions of these firms—are classified in U.S. Industry 551111, Offices of Bank Holding Companies;
- Holding the securities of (or other equity interests in) a company or enterprise and administering, overseeing, and managing establishments of the company or enterprise whose securities they hold—are classified in U.S. Industry 551114, Corporate, Subsidiary, and Regional Managing Offices; and
- Holding the securities of companies or enterprises and operating these entities—are classified according to the business operated.

551114 Corporate, Subsidiary, and Regional Managing Offices[CAN]

This U.S. industry comprises establishments (except government establishments) primarily engaged in administering, overseeing, and managing other establishments of the company or enterprise. These establishments normally undertake the strategic or organizational planning and decisionmaking role of the company or enterprise. Establishments in this industry may hold the securities of the company or enterprise.

Illustrative Examples:

Centralized administrative offices
Corporate offices
District and regional offices
Head offices
Holding companies that manage
Subsidiary management offices

Cross-References.

- Government establishments primarily engaged in administering, overseeing, and managing governmental programs are classified in Sector 92, Public Administration;
- Legal entities known as bank holding companies that do not administer, oversee, and manage other establishments of the companies or enterprises

US—United States industry only. CAN—United States and Canadian industries are comparable. MEX—United States and Mexican industries are comparable. Blank—Canadian, Mexican, and United States industries are comparable.

whose securities they hold are classified in U.S. Industry 551111, Offices of Bank Holding Companies; and

- Legal entities known as holding companies(except bank holding) that do not administer, oversee, and manage other establishments of the companies or enterprises whose securities they hold are classified in U.S. Industry 551112, Offices of Other Holding Companies.

US—United States industry only. CAN—United States and Canadian industries are comparable. MEX—United States and Mexican industries are comparable. Blank—Canadian, Mexican, and United States industries are comparable.

Sector 56—Administrative and Support and Waste Management and Remediation Services

The Sector as a Whole

The Administrative and Support and Waste Management and Remediation Services sector comprises establishments performing routine support activities for the day-to-day operations of other organizations. These essential activities are often undertaken in-house by establishments in many sectors of the economy. The establishments in this sector specialize in one or more of these support activities and provide these services to clients in a variety of industries and, in some cases, to households. Activities performed include: office administration, hiring and placing of personnel, document preparation and similar clerical services, solicitation, collection, security and surveillance services, cleaning, and waste disposal services.

The administrative and management activities performed by establishments in this sector are typically on a contract or fee basis. These activities may also be performed by establishments that are part of the company or enterprise. However, establishments involved in administering, overseeing, and managing other establishments of the company or enterprise, are classified in Sector 55, Management of Companies and Enterprises. These establishments normally undertake the strategic and organizational planning and decision making role of the company or enterprise. Government establishments engaged in administering, overseeing, and managing governmental programs are classified in Sector 92, Public Administration.

561 Administrative and Support Services

Industries in the Administrative and Support Services subsector group establishments engaged in activities that support the day-to-day operations of other organizations. The processes employed in this sector (e.g., general management, personnel administration, clerical activities, cleaning activities) are often integral parts of the activities of establishments found in all sectors of the economy. The establishments classified in this subsector have specialized in one or more of these activities and can, therefore, provide services to clients in a variety of industries and, in some cases, to households. The individual industries of this subsector are defined on the basis of the particular process that they are engaged in and the particular services they provide.

Many of the activities performed in this subsector are ongoing routine support functions that all businesses and organizations must do and that they have traditionally done for themselves. Recent trends, however, are to contract or purchase such services from businesses that specialize in such activities and can, therefore, provide the services more efficiently.

US—United States industry only. CAN—United States and Canadian industries are comparable. MEX—United States and Mexican industries are comparable. Blank—Canadian, Mexican, and United States industries are comparable.

The industries in this subsector cannot be viewed as strictly "support." The Travel Arrangement and Reservation Services industry group, includes travel agents, tour operators, and providers of other travel arrangement services, such as hotel and restaurant reservations and arranging the purchase of tickets, serves many types of clients, including individual consumers. This group was placed in this subsector because the services are often of the "support" nature (e.g., travel arrangement) and businesses and other organizations are increasingly the ones purchasing such services.

The administrative and management activities performed by establishments in this sector are typically on a contract or fee basis. These activities may also be performed by establishments that are part of the company or enterprise. However, establishments involved in administering, overseeing, and managing other establishments of the company or enterprise, are classified in Sector 55, Management of Companies and Enterprises. These establishments normally undertake the strategic and organizational planning and decisionmaking role of the company or enterprise. Government establishments engaged in administering, overseeing and managing governmental programs are classified in Sector 92, Public Administration.

5611 Office Administrative Services

56111 Office Administrative Services

See industry description for 561110 below.

561110 Office Administrative Services

This industry comprises establishments primarily engaged in providing a range of day-to-day office administrative services, such as financial planning; billing and recordkeeping; personnel; and physical distribution and logistics for others on a contract or fee basis. These establishments do not provide operating staff to carry out the complete operations of a business.

Cross-References. Establishments primarily engaged in—

- Holding the securities or financial assets of companies and enterprises for the purpose of controlling them and influencing their management decisions—are classified in U.S. Industry 551111, Offices of Bank Holding Companies or U.S. Industry 551112, Offices of Other Holding Companies;
- Administering, overseeing, and managing other establishments of the company or enterprise (except government establishments)—are classified in U.S. Industry 551114, Corporate, Subsidiary, and Regional Managing Offices;

US—United States industry only. CAN—United States and Canadian industries are comparable. MEX—United States and Mexican industries are comparable. Blank—Canadian, Mexican, and United States industries are comparable.

- Government establishments primarily engaged in administering, overseeing, and managing governmental programs—are classified in Sector 92, Public Administration;
- Providing computer facilities management—are classified in U.S. Industry 541513, Computer Facilities Management Services;
- Providing construction management—are classified in Sector 23, Construction, by type of construction project managed;
- Providing farm management—are classified in U.S. Industry 115116, Farm Management Services;
- Managing real property for others—are classified in Industry 53131, Real Estate Property Managers;
- Providing food services management at institutional, governmental, commercial, or industrial locations—are classified in Industry 722310, Food Service Contractors;
- Providing management advice without day-to-day management—are classified in Industry 54161, Management Consulting Services;
- Providing both management and operating staff for the complete operation of a client's business, such as a hotel, restaurant, mine site, or hospital—are classified according to the industry of the establishment operated; and
- Providing only one of the support services (e.g., accounting services) that establishments in this industry provide—are classified in the appropriate industry according to the service provided.

5612 Facilities Support Services

56121 Facilities Support Services

See industry description for 561210 below.

561210 Facilities Support Services

This industry comprises establishments primarily engaged in providing operating staff to perform a combination of support services within a client's facilities. Establishments in this industry typically provide a combination of services, such as janitorial; maintenance; trash disposal; guard and security; mail routing; reception; laundry; and related services to support operations within facilities. These establishments provide operating staff to carry out these support activities; but, are not involved with or responsible for the core business or activities of the client. Establishments providing facilities (except computer and/or data processing) opera-

US—United States industry only. CAN—United States and Canadian industries are comparable. MEX—United States and Mexican industries are comparable. Blank—Canadian, Mexican, and United States industries are comparable.

tion support services and establishments operating correctional facilities (i.e., jails) on a contract or fee basis are included in this industry.

Cross-References.

- Establishments primarily engaged in providing only one of the support services (e.g., janitorial services) that establishments in this industry provide are classified in the appropriate industry according to the service provided;
- Establishments primarily engaged in providing management and operating staff for the complete operation of a client's establishment, such as a hotel, restaurant, mine, or hospital, are classified according to the industry of the establishment operated;
- Establishments primarily engaged in providing on-site management and operation of a client's computer systems and/or data processing facilities are classified in U.S. Industry 541513, Computer Facilities Management Services; and
- Government correctional institutions are classified in Industry 922140, Correctional Institutions.

5613 Employment Services

56131 Employment Placement Agencies

See industry description for 561310 below.

561310 Employment Placement Agencies

This industry comprises establishments primarily engaged in listing employment vacancies and in referring or placing applicants for employment. The individuals referred or placed are not employees of the employment agencies.

Illustrative Examples:

Babysitting bureaus (i.e., registries)
Casting agencies or bureaus (i.e., motion picture, theatrical, video)
Employment agencies
Employment registries
Model registries

Cross-References. Establishments primarily engaged in—

- Providing executive search consulting services—are classified in U.S. Industry 541612, Human Resources and Executive Search Consulting Services;
- Supplying their own employees for limited periods of time to supplement the working force of a client's business—are classified in Industry 561320, Temporary Help Services;

US—United States industry only. CAN—United States and Canadian industries are comparable. MEX—United States and Mexican industries are comparable. Blank—Canadian, Mexican, and United States industries are comparable.

- Providing human resources and human resource management services to clients—are classified in Industry 561330, Professional Employer Organizations; and
- Representing models, entertainers, athletes, and other public figures as their agent or manager—are classified in Industry 711410, Agents and Managers for Artists, Athletes, Entertainers, and Other Public Figures.

56132 Temporary Help Services

See industry description for 561320 below.

561320 Temporary Help Services

This industry comprises establishments primarily engaged in supplying workers to clients' businesses for limited periods of time to supplement the working force of the client. The individuals provided are employees of the temporary help service establishment. However, these establishments do not provide direct supervision of their employees at the clients' work sites.

Illustrative Examples:

Help supply services
Labor (except farm) contractors (i.e., personnel suppliers)
Manpower pools
Model supply services
Temporary employment or temporary staffing services

Cross-References. Establishments primarily engaged in—

- Providing human resources and human resource management services to clients—are classified in Industry 561330, Professional Employer Organizations;
- Supplying farm labor—are classified in U.S. Industry 115115, Farm Labor Contractors and Crew Leaders;
- Providing operating staff to perform a combination of services to support operations within a client's facilities—are classified in Industry 561210, Facilities Support Services;
- Listing employment vacancies and referring or placing applicants for employment—are classified in Industry 561310, Employment Placement Agencies; and
- Representing models, entertainers, athletes, and other public figures as their agent or manager—are classified in Industry 711410, Agents and Managers for Artists, Athletes, Entertainers, and Other Public Figures.

US—United States industry only. CAN—United States and Canadian industries are comparable. MEX—United States and Mexican industries are comparable. Blank—Canadian, Mexican, and United States industries are comparable.

56133 Professional Employer Organizations

See industry description for 561330 below.

561330 Professional Employer Organizations

This industry comprises establishments primarily engaged in providing human resources and human resource management services to staff client businesses. Establishments in this industry operate in a coemployment relationship with client businesses or organizations and are specialized in performing a wide range of human resource and personnel management duties, such as payroll accounting, payroll tax return preparation, benefits administration, recruiting, and managing labor relations. Employee leasing establishments typically acquire and lease back some or all of the employees of their clients and serve as the employer of the leased employees for payroll, benefits, and related purposes. Employee leasing establishments exercise varying degrees of decisionmaking relating to their human resource or personnel management role, but do not have management accountability for the work of their clients' operations with regard to strategic planning, output, or profitability. Professional employer organizations (PEO) and establishments providing labor or staff leasing services are included in this industry.

Cross-References. Establishments primarily engaged in—

- Supplying their own employees for limited periods of time to supplement the working force of a client's business—are classified in Industry 561320, Temporary Help Services; and
- Listing employment vacancies and in referring or placing applicants for employment—are classified in Industry 561310, Employment Placement Agencies.

5614 Business Support Services

This industry group comprises establishments engaged in performing activities that are ongoing routine business support functions that businesses and organizations traditionally do for themselves.

56141 Document Preparation Services

See industry description for 561410 below.

561410 Document Preparation Services

This industry comprises establishments primarily engaged in one or more of the following: (1) letter or resume writing; (2) document editing or proofreading;

US—United States industry only. CAN—United States and Canadian industries are comparable. MEX—United States and Mexican industries are comparable. Blank—Canadian, Mexican, and United States industries are comparable.

(3) typing, word processing, or desktop publishing; and (4) stenographic (except court reporting or stenotype recording), transcription, and other secretarial services.

Cross-References. Establishments primarily engaged in—

- Providing verbatim reporting and stenotype recording of live legal proceedings and transcribing subsequent recorded materials—are classified in U.S. Industry 561492, Court Reporting and Stenotype Services;
- Performing prepress and postpress services in support of printing activities—are classified in Industry 32312, Support Activities for Printing;
- Providing document translation services—are classified in Industry 541930, Translation and Interpretation Services;
- Photocopying, duplicating, and other document copying services, with or without a range of other office support services (except printing)—are classified in U.S. Industry 561439, Other Business Service Centers (including Copy Shops); and
- Providing document copying services in combination with printing services, with or without a range of other office support services, and establishments known as quick or digital printers—are classified in Industry 32311, Printing.

56142 Telephone Call Centers

This industry comprises (1) establishments primarily engaged in answering telephone calls and relaying messages to clients and (2) establishments primarily engaged in providing telemarketing services on a contract or fee basis for others, such as promoting clients' products or services by telephone; taking orders for clients by telephone; and soliciting contributions or providing information for clients by telephone. Telemarketing establishments never own the product or provide the service that they are representing and generally can originate and/or receive calls for others.

Cross-References. Establishments primarily engaged in—

- Providing paging and beeper transmission services—are classified in Industry 51721, Wireless Telecommunications Carriers (except Satellite);
- Organizing and conducting fundraising campaigns on a contract or fee basis, that may include telephone solicitation services—are classified in Industry 56149, Other Business Support Services; and
- Gathering, recording, tabulating, and presenting marketing and public opinion data, that may include telephone canvassing services—are classified in Industry 54191, Marketing Research and Public Opinion Polling.

US—United States industry only. CAN—United States and Canadian industries are comparable. MEX—United States and Mexican industries are comparable. Blank—Canadian, Mexican, and United States industries are comparable.

561421 Telephone Answering Services[US]

This U.S. industry comprises establishments primarily engaged in answering telephone calls and relaying messages to clients.

Cross-References.

Establishments primarily engaged in providing paging or beeper transmission services are classified in Industry 517211, Paging.

561422 Telemarketing Bureaus[MEX]

This U.S. industry comprises establishments primarily engaged in providing telemarketing services on a contract or fee basis for others, such as: (1) promoting clients' products or services by telephone, (2) taking orders for clients by telephone, and (3) soliciting contributions or providing information for clients by telephone. These establishments never own the product or provide the services they are representing and generally can originate and/or receive calls for others.

Cross-References. Establishments primarily engaged in—

- Organizing and conducting fundraising campaigns on a contract or fee basis, that may include telephone solicitation services—are classified in U.S. Industry 561499, All Other Business Support Services; and
- Gathering, recording, tabulating, and presenting marketing and public opinion data, that may include telephone canvassing services—are classified in Industry 541910, Marketing Research and Public Opinion Polling.

56143 Business Service Centers

This industry comprises (1) establishments primarily engaged in providing mailbox rental and other postal and mailing services (except direct mail advertising); (2) establishments, generally known as copy centers or shops, primarily engaged in providing photocopying, duplicating, blueprinting, and other document copying services without also providing printing services (i.e., offset printing, quick printing, digital printing, prepress services); and (3) establishments that provide a range of office support services (except printing services), such as mailing services, document copying services, facsimile services, word processing services, on-site PC rental services, and office product sales.

Cross-References. Establishments primarily engaged in—

- Operating contract post offices—are classified in Industry 49111, Postal Service;

US—United States industry only. CAN—United States and Canadian industries are comparable. MEX—United States and Mexican industries are comparable. Blank—Canadian, Mexican, and United States industries are comparable.

- Delivering letters and parcels—are classified in Subsector 492, Couriers and Messengers;
- Providing voice mailbox services—are classified in Industry 56142, Telephone Call Centers;
- Providing direct mail advertising services—are classified in Industry 54186, Direct Mail Advertising;
- Providing document copying services in combination with printing services, with or without a range of other office support services, and establishments known as quick or digital printers—are classified in Industry 32311, Printing; and
- Providing only one of the support services (e.g., word processing services) that establishments in this industry provide—are classified in the appropriate industry according to the service provided.

561431 Private Mail Centers[US]

This U.S. industry comprises (1) establishments primarily engaged in providing mailbox rental and other postal and mailing (except direct mail advertising) services or (2) establishments engaged in providing these mailing services along with one or more other office support services, such as facsimile services, word processing services, on-site PC rental services, and office product sales.

Cross-References. Establishments primarily engaged in—

- Operating contract post offices—are classified in Industry 491110, Postal Service;
- Delivering letters and parcels—are classified in Subsector 492, Couriers and Messengers;
- Providing voice mailbox services—are classified in U.S. Industry 561421, Telephone Answering Services;
- Providing direct mail advertising services—are classified in Industry 541860, Direct Mail Advertising; and
- Providing only one of the support services (e.g., word processing services) that establishments in this industry provide—are classified in the appropriate industry according to the service provided.
- Establishments engaged in providing full service office space, whether on a lease or service contract basis—are classified in Industry 531120, Lessors of Nonresidential Buildings (except Miniwarehouses).

US—United States industry only. CAN—United States and Canadian industries are comparable. MEX—United States and Mexican industries are comparable. Blank—Canadian, Mexican, and United States industries are comparable.

561439 Other Business Service Centers (including Copy Shops)[US]

This U.S. industry comprises (1) establishments generally known as copy centers or shops primarily engaged in providing photocopying, duplicating, blueprinting, and other document copying services, without also providing printing services (e.g., offset printing, quick printing, digital printing, prepress services) and (2) establishments (except private mail centers) engaged in providing a range of office support services (except printing services), such as document copying services, facsimile services, word processing services, on-site PC rental services, and office product sales.

Cross-References.

- Establishments engaged in providing document copying services in combination with printing services, with or without a range of other office support services, and establishments known as quick or digital printers are classified in Industry 32311, Printing;
- Establishments engaged in providing mailbox rental and other postal and mailing services with or without one or more other office support services (except printing) are classified in U.S. Industry 561431, Private Mail Centers; and
- Establishments exclusively engaged in providing a single office support service (except document copying) to clients, but not the range of office support services that establishments in this industry may provide, are classified according to the service provided.
- Establishments engaged in providing full service office space, whether on a lease or service contract basis, are classified in Industry 531120, Lessors of Nonresidential Buildings (except Miniwarehouses).

56144 Collection Agencies

See industry description for 561440 below.

561440 Collection Agencies

This industry comprises establishments primarily engaged in collecting payments for claims and remitting payments collected to their clients.

Illustrative Examples:

Account or delinquent account collection services
Bill or debt collection services
Tax collection services on a contract or fee basis

US—United States industry only. CAN—United States and Canadian industries are comparable. MEX—United States and Mexican industries are comparable. Blank—Canadian, Mexican, and United States industries are comparable.

Cross-References. Establishments primarily engaged in—

- Repossessing tangible assets—are classified in U.S. Industry 561491, Repossession Services; and
- Providing financing to others by factoring accounts receivables (i.e., assuming the risk of collection and credit losses)—are classified in U.S. Industry 522298, All Other Nondepository Credit Intermediation.

56145 Credit Bureaus

See industry description for 561450 below.

561450 Credit Bureaus

This industry comprises establishments primarily engaged in compiling information, such as credit and employment histories on individuals and credit histories on businesses, and providing the information to financial institutions, retailers, and others who have a need to evaluate the creditworthiness of these persons and businesses.

Illustrative Examples:

Credit agencies
Credit investigation services
Credit rating services
Credit reporting bureaus

56149 Other Business Support Services

This industry comprises establishments primarily engaged in providing business support services (except secretarial and other document preparation services; telephone answering or telemarketing services; private mail services or document copying services conducted as separate activities or in conjunction with other office support services; monetary debt collection services; and credit reporting services).

Illustrative Examples:

Address bar coding services
Bar code imprinting services
Court reporting services
Fundraising organization services on a contract or fee basis
Mail presorting services
Real-time (i.e., simultaneous) closed captioning of live television performances, meetings, conferences
Repossession services

Cross-References. Establishments primarily engaged in—

- Providing secretarial and other document preparation services—are classified in Industry 56141, Document Preparation Services;

US—United States industry only. CAN—United States and Canadian industries are comparable. MEX—United States and Mexican industries are comparable. Blank—Canadian, Mexican, and United States industries are comparable.

- Providing telephone answering or telemarketing services—are classified in Industry 56142, Telephone Call Centers;
- Providing private mail services; document copying services (except printing services); and/or a range of office support services (except printing)—are classified in Industry 56143, Business Service Centers;
- Providing document copying services in combination with printing services, with or without a range of other office support services, and establishments known as quick or digital printers—are classified in Industry 32311, Printing;
- Providing monetary debt collection services—are classified in Industry 56144, Collection Agencies;
- Providing credit reporting services—are classified in Industry 56145, Credit Bureaus; and
- Providing film or tape captioning or subtitling services—are classified in Industry 51219, Postproduction Services and Other Motion Picture and Video Industries.

561491 Repossession Services[US]

This U.S. industry comprises establishments primarily engaged in repossessing tangible assets (e.g., automobiles, boats, equipment, planes, furniture, appliances) for the creditor as a result of delinquent debts.

Cross-References.

Establishments primarily engaged in providing monetary debt collection services are classified in Industry 561440, Collection Agencies.

561492 Court Reporting and Stenotype Services[US]

This U.S. industry comprises establishments primarily engaged in providing verbatim reporting and stenotype recording of live legal proceedings and transcribing subsequent recorded materials.

Illustrative Examples:

Court reporting or stenotype recording services
Public stenography services
Real-time (i.e., simultaneous) closed captioning of live television performances of meetings, conferences

---

US—United States industry only. CAN—United States and Canadian industries are comparable. MEX—United States and Mexican industries are comparable. Blank—Canadian, Mexican, and United States industries are comparable.

Cross-References. Establishments primarily engaged in—

- Providing stenotype recording of correspondence, reports, and other documents or in providing document transcription services—are classified in Industry 561410, Document Preparation Services; and
- Providing film or tape captioning or subtitling services—are classified in U.S. Industry 512191, Teleproduction and Other Postproduction Services.

561499 All Other Business Support Services[US]

This U.S. industry comprises establishments primarily engaged in providing business support services (except secretarial and other document preparation services; telephone answering and telemarketing services; private mail services or document copying services conducted as separate activities or in conjunction with other office support services; monetary debt collection services; credit reporting services; repossession services; and court reporting and stenotype recording services).

Illustrative Examples:

Address bar coding services
Bar code imprinting services
Fundraising organization services on a contract or fee basis
Mail presorting services

Cross-References. Establishments primarily engaged in—

- Providing secretarial and other document preparation services—are classified in Industry 561410, Document Preparation Services;
- Providing telephone answering or telemarketing services—are classified in Industry 56142, Telephone Call Centers;
- Providing private mail services, document copying services without printing services and/or a range of office support services—are classified in Industry 56143, Business Service Centers;
- Providing document copying services in combination with printing services (with or without one or more other office support services) and establishments known as quick or digital printers—are classified in Industry 32311, Printing;
- Providing monetary debt collection services—are classified in Industry 561440, Collection Agencies;
- Providing credit reporting services—are classified in Industry 561450, Credit Bureaus;

US—United States industry only. CAN—United States and Canadian industries are comparable. MEX—United States and Mexican industries are comparable. Blank—Canadian, Mexican, and United States industries are comparable.

- Providing repossession services—are classified in U.S. Industry 561491, Repossession Services; and
- Providing court reporting and stenotype services—are classified in U.S. Industry 561492, Court Reporting and Stenotype Services.

5615 Travel Arrangement and Reservation Services

56151 Travel Agencies

See industry description for 561510 below.

561510 Travel Agencies

This industry comprises establishments primarily engaged in acting as agents in selling travel, tour, and accommodation services to the general public and commercial clients.

Cross-References. Establishments primarily engaged in—

- Arranging and assembling tours that they generally sell through travel agencies or on their own account—are classified in Industry 561520, Tour Operators;
- Providing guide services, such as archeological, museum, tourist, hunting, or fishing—are classified in Industry 713990, All Other Amusement and Recreation Industries; and
- Providing reservation services (e.g., accommodations, entertainment events, travel)—are classified in U.S. Industry 561599, All Other Travel Arrangement and Reservation Services.

56152 Tour Operators

See industry description for 561520 below.

561520 Tour Operators

This industry comprises establishments primarily engaged in arranging and assembling tours. The tours are sold through travel agencies or tour operators. Travel or wholesale tour operators are included in this industry.

Cross-References. Establishments primarily engaged in—

- Acting as agents in selling travel, tour, and accommodation services to the general public and commercial clients—are classified in Industry 561510, Travel Agencies;

US—United States industry only. CAN—United States and Canadian industries are comparable. MEX—United States and Mexican industries are comparable. Blank—Canadian, Mexican, and United States industries are comparable.

- Conducting scenic and sightseeing tours—are classified in Subsector 487, Scenic and Sightseeing Transportation; and
- Providing guide services, such as archeological, museum, tourist, hunting, or fishing—are classified in Industry 713990, All Other Amusement and Recreation Industries.

56159 Other Travel Arrangement and Reservation Services

This industry comprises establishments (except travel agencies and tour operators) primarily engaged in providing travel arrangement and reservation services.

Illustrative Examples:

Condominium time-share exchange services
Convention or visitors bureaus
Reservation (e.g., airline, car rental, hotel, restaurant) services
Road and travel services automobile clubs
Ticket (e.g., airline, bus, cruise ship, sports, theatrical) offices
Ticket (e.g., amusement, sports, theatrical) agencies

Cross-References.

- Establishments primarily engaged in arranging the rental of vacation properties are classified in Industry 53121, Offices of Real Estate Agents and Brokers;
- Travel agencies are classified in Industry 56151, Travel Agencies;
- Tour operators are classified in Industry 56152, Tour Operators;
- Automobile clubs (i.e., enthusiasts' clubs) (except road and travel services) are classified in Industry 81341, Civic and Social Organizations; and
- Establishments primarily engaged in organizing, promoting, and/or managing events, such as business and trade shows, conventions, conferences, and meetings (whether or not they manage and provide the staff to operate the facilities in which these events take place), are classified in Industry 56192, Convention and Trade Show Organizers.

561591 Convention and Visitors Bureaus[US]

This U.S. industry comprises establishments primarily engaged in marketing and promoting communities and facilities to businesses and leisure travelers through a range of activities, such as assisting organizations in locating meeting and convention sites; providing travel information on area attractions, lodging accommodations, restaurants; providing maps; and organizing group tours of local historical, recreational, and cultural attractions.

US—United States industry only. CAN—United States and Canadian industries are comparable. MEX—United States and Mexican industries are comparable. Blank—Canadian, Mexican, and United States industries are comparable.

Cross-References.

Establishments primarily engaged in organizing, promoting, and/or managing events, such as business and trade shows, conventions, conferences, and meetings (whether or not they manage and provide the staff to operate the facilities in which these events take place), are classified in Industry 561920, Convention and Trade Show Organizers.

561599 All Other Travel Arrangement and Reservation Services[US]

This U.S. industry comprises establishments (except travel agencies, tour operators, and convention and visitors bureaus) primarily engaged in providing travel arrangement and reservation services.

Illustrative Examples:

Condominium time-share exchange services
Reservation (e.g., airline, car rental, hotel, restaurant) services
Road and travel services automobile clubs
Ticket (e.g., airline, bus, cruise ship, sports, theatrical) offices
Ticket (e.g., amusement, sports, theatrical) agencies

Cross-References.

- Establishments primarily engaged in arranging the rental of vacation properties are classified in Industry 531210, Offices of Real Estate Agents and Brokers;
- Travel agencies are classified in Industry 561510, Travel Agencies;
- Tour operators are classified in Industry 561520, Tour Operators;
- Convention and visitors bureaus are classified in U.S. Industry 561591, Convention and Visitors Bureaus;
- Establishments primarily engaged in organizing, promoting, and/or managing events, such as business and trade shows, conventions, conferences, and meetings (whether or not they manage and provide the staff to operate the facilities in which these events take place), are classified in Industry 561920, Convention and Trade Show Organizers; and
- Automobile clubs (i.e., enthusiasts' clubs) (except road and travel services) are classified in Industry 813410, Civic and Social Organizations.

5616 Investigation and Security Services

56161 Investigation, Guard, and Armored Car Services

This industry comprises establishments primarily engaged in providing one or more of the following: (1) investigation and detective services; (2) guard and patrol

US—United States industry only. CAN—United States and Canadian industries are comparable. MEX—United States and Mexican industries are comparable. Blank—Canadian, Mexican, and United States industries are comparable.

services; and (3) picking up and delivering money, receipts, or other valuable items with personnel and equipment to protect such properties while in transit.

Illustrative Examples:

Armored car services
Bodyguard services
Polygraph services
Private detective services
Security guard services

Cross-References. Establishments primarily engaged in—

- Providing credit checks—are classified in Industry 56145, Credit Bureaus; and
- Selling, installing, monitoring, and maintaining security systems and devices (e.g., burglar and fire alarm systems)—are classified in Industry 56162, Security Systems Services.

561611 Investigation Services[CAN]

This U.S. industry comprises establishments primarily engaged in providing investigation and detective services.

Illustrative Examples:

Fingerprinting services
Polygraph services
Private detective services
Private investigative services

Cross-References.

Establishments primarily engaged in providing credit checks are classified in Industry 561450, Credit Bureaus.

561612 Security Guards and Patrol Services[CAN]

This U.S. industry comprises establishments primarily engaged in providing guard and patrol services, such as bodyguard, guard dog, and parking security services.

Cross-References.

Establishments primarily engaged in selling, installing, monitoring, and maintaining security systems and devices, such as burglar and fire alarms and locking devices, are classified in Industry 56162, Security Systems Services.

US—United States industry only. CAN—United States and Canadian industries are comparable. MEX—United States and Mexican industries are comparable. Blank—Canadian, Mexican, and United States industries are comparable.

561613 Armored Car Services[CAN]

This U.S. industry comprises establishments primarily engaged in picking up and delivering money, receipts, or other valuable items. These establishments maintain personnel and equipment to protect such properties while in transit.

56162 Security Systems Services

This industry comprises establishments engaged in (1) selling security systems, such as burglar and fire alarms and locking devices, along with installation, repair, or monitoring services or (2) remote monitoring of electronic security alarm systems.

Cross-References. Establishments primarily engaged in—

- Selling security systems for buildings without installation, repair, or monitoring services—are classified in Sector 42, Wholesale Trade or Sector 44-45, Retail Trade;
- Retailing motor vehicle security systems with or without installation or repair services—are classified in Industry 44131, Automotive Parts and Accessories Stores; and
- Providing key duplication services—are classified in Industry 81149, Other Personal and Household Goods Repair and Maintenance.

561621 Security Systems Services (except Locksmiths)[CAN]

This U.S. industry comprises establishments primarily engaged in (1) selling security alarm systems, such as burglar and fire alarms, along with installation, repair, or monitoring services or (2) remote monitoring of electronic security alarm systems.

Cross-References. Establishments primarily engaged in—

- Selling security alarm systems for buildings, without installation, repair, or monitoring services—are classified in Sector 42, Wholesale Trade or Sector 44-45, Retail Trade; and
- Retailing motor vehicle security systems with or without installation or repair services—are classified in Industry 441310, Automotive Parts and Accessories Stores.

561622 Locksmiths[CAN]

This U.S. industry comprises establishments primarily engaged in (1) selling mechanical or electronic locking devices, safes, and security vaults, along with

---

US—United States industry only. CAN—United States and Canadian industries are comparable. MEX—United States and Mexican industries are comparable. Blank—Canadian, Mexican, and United States industries are comparable.

installation, repair, rebuilding, or adjusting services or (2) installing, repairing, rebuilding, and adjusting mechanical or electronic locking devices, safes, and security vaults.

Cross-References. Establishments primarily engaged in—

- Selling security systems, such as locking devices, safes, and vaults, without installation or maintenance services—are classified in Sector 42, Wholesale Trade or Sector 44-45, Retail Trade; and
- Providing key duplication services—are classified in Industry 811490, Other Personal and Household Goods Repair and Maintenance.

5617 Services to Buildings and Dwellings

56171 Exterminating and Pest Control Services

See industry description for 561710 below.

561710 Exterminating and Pest Control Services

This industry comprises establishments primarily engaged in exterminating and controlling birds, mosquitoes, rodents, termites, and other insects and pests (except for crop production and forestry production). Establishments providing fumigation services are included in this industry.

Cross-References.

Establishments primarily engaged in providing pest control for crop or forestry production are classified in Subsector 115, Support Activities for Agriculture and Forestry.

56172 Janitorial Services

See industry description for 561720 below.

561720 Janitorial Services[MEX]

This industry comprises establishments primarily engaged in cleaning building interiors, interiors of transportation equipment (e.g., aircraft, rail cars, ships), and/or windows.

Illustrative Examples:

Custodial services
Housekeeping (i.e., cleaning) services
Maid (i.e., cleaning) services
Service station cleaning and degreasing services
Washroom sanitation services

US—United States industry only. CAN—United States and Canadian industries are comparable. MEX—United States and Mexican industries are comparable. Blank—Canadian, Mexican, and United States industries are comparable.

Cross-References. Establishments primarily engaged in—

- Cleaning building exteriors (except sandblasting and window cleaning) or chimneys—are classified in Industry 561790, Other Services to Buildings and Dwellings; and
- Sandblasting building exteriors—are classified in Industry 238990, All Other Specialty Trade Contractors.

56173 Landscaping Services

See industry description for 561730 below.

561730 Landscaping Services

This industry comprises (1) establishments primarily engaged in providing landscape care and maintenance services and/or installing trees, shrubs, plants, lawns, or gardens and (2) establishments primarily engaged in providing these services along with the design of landscape plans and/or the construction (i.e., installation) of walkways, retaining walls, decks, fences, ponds, and similar structures.

Cross-References. Establishments primarily engaged in—

- Installing artificial turf or in constructing (i.e., installing) walkways, retaining walls, decks, fences, ponds, or similar structures—are classified in Sector 23, Construction;
- Planning and designing the development of land areas for projects, such as parks and other recreational areas; airports; highways; hospitals; schools; land subdivisions; and commercial, industrial, and residential areas (without also installing trees, shrubs, plants, lawns/gardens, walkways, retaining walls, decks, and similar items or structures)—are classified in Industry 541320, Landscape Architectural Services; and
- Retailing landscaping materials and providing the installation and maintenance of these materials—are classified in Industry 444220, Nursery, Garden Center, and Farm Supply Stores.

56174 Carpet and Upholstery Cleaning Services

See industry description for 561740 below.

561740 Carpet and Upholstery Cleaning Services

This industry comprises establishments primarily engaged in cleaning and dyeing used rugs, carpets, and upholstery.

US—United States industry only. CAN—United States and Canadian industries are comparable. MEX—United States and Mexican industries are comparable. Blank—Canadian, Mexican, and United States industries are comparable.

Cross-References. Establishments primarily engaged in—

- Rug repair not associated with rug cleaning—are classified in Industry 811490, Other Personal and Household Goods Repair and Maintenance; and
- Reupholstering and repairing furniture—are classified in Industry 811420, Reupholstery and Furniture Repair.

56179 Other Services to Buildings and Dwellings

See industry description for 561790 below.

561790 Other Services to Buildings and Dwellings[MEX]

This industry comprises establishments primarily engaged in providing services to buildings and dwellings (except exterminating and pest control; janitorial; landscaping care and maintenance; and carpet and upholstery cleaning).

Illustrative Examples:

Building exterior cleaning services (except sandblasting and window cleaning)
Chimney cleaning services
Drain or gutter cleaning services
Swimming pool cleaning and maintenance services
Ventilation duct cleaning services

Cross-References. Establishments primarily engaged in—

- Providing exterminating and pest control services—are classified in Industry 561710, Exterminating and Pest Control Services;
- Providing janitorial services—are classified in Industry 561720, Janitorial Services;
- Providing landscaping care and maintenance—are classified in Industry 561730, Landscaping Services;
- Providing carpet and upholstery cleaning services—are classified in Industry 561740, Carpet and Upholstery Cleaning Services; and
- Sandblasting building exteriors—are classified in Industry 238990, All Other Specialty Trade Contractors.

5619 Other Support Services

This industry group comprises establishments primarily engaged in providing day-to-day business and other organizational support services (except office administrative services; facilities support services; employment services; business support services; travel arrangement and reservation services; security and investigation services; and services to buildings and dwellings).

US—United States industry only. CAN—United States and Canadian industries are comparable. MEX—United States and Mexican industries are comparable. Blank—Canadian, Mexican, and United States industries are comparable.

56191 Packaging and Labeling Services

See industry description for 561910 below.

561910 Packaging and Labeling Services

This industry comprises establishments primarily engaged in packaging client-owned materials. The services may include labeling and/or imprinting the package.

Illustrative Examples:

Apparel and textile folding and packaging services
Blister packaging services
Gift wrapping services
Kit assembling and packaging services
Shrink-wrapping services

Cross-References. Establishments primarily engaged in—

- Processing client-owned materials into a different product, such as mixing water and concentrate to produce soft drinks—are classified in Sector 31-33, Manufacturing;
- Providing aerosol packaging services—are classified in U.S. Industry 325998, All Other Miscellaneous Chemical Product and Preparation Manufacturing;
- Providing packing and crating services incidental to transportation—are classified in U.S. Industry 488991, Packing and Crating;
- Providing warehousing services, as well as packaging or other logistics services—are classified in Industry Group 4931, Warehousing and Storage; and
- Providing packing and crating services for agricultural products—are classified in U.S. Industry 115114, Postharvest Crop Activities (except Cotton Ginning).

56192 Convention and Trade Show Organizers

See industry description for 561920 below.

561920 Convention and Trade Show Organizers

This industry comprises establishments primarily engaged in organizing, promoting, and/or managing events, such as business and trade shows, conventions, conferences, and meetings (whether or not they manage and provide the staff to operate the facilities in which these events take place).

US—United States industry only. CAN—United States and Canadian industries are comparable. MEX—United States and Mexican industries are comparable. Blank—Canadian, Mexican, and United States industries are comparable.

Cross-References.

Establishments primarily engaged in organizing, promoting, and/or managing live performing arts productions, sports events, and similar events, such as festivals (whether or not they manage and provide the staff to operate the facilities in which these events take place), are classified in Industry Group 7113, Promoters of Performing Arts, Sports, and Similar Events.

56199 All Other Support Services

See industry description for 561990 below.

561990 All Other Support Services

This industry comprises establishments primarily engaged in providing day-to-day business and other organizational support services (except office administrative services, facilities support services, employment services, business support services, travel arrangement and reservation services, security and investigation services, services to buildings and other structures, packaging and labeling services, and convention and trade show organizing services).

Illustrative Examples:

Bartering services
Bottle exchanges
Cloth cutting, bolting, or winding for the trade
Contract meter reading services
Diving services on a contract or fee basis
Flagging (i.e., traffic control) services
Float decorating services
Inventory taking services
Lumber grading services

Cross-References. Establishments primarily engaged in—

- Providing office administrative services—are classified in Industry 561110, Office Administrative Services;
- Providing facilities support services—are classified in Industry 561210, Facilities Support Services;
- Providing employment services—are classified in Industry Group 5613, Employment Services;
- Providing business support services—are classified in Industry Group 5614, Business Support Services;
- Providing travel arrangement and reservation services—are classified in Industry Group 5615, Travel Arrangement and Reservation Services;
- Providing security and investigation services—are classified in Industry Group 5616, Investigation and Security Services;

US—United States industry only. CAN—United States and Canadian industries are comparable. MEX—United States and Mexican industries are comparable. Blank—Canadian, Mexican, and United States industries are comparable.

- Providing services to buildings and other structures—are classified in Industry Group 5617, Services to Buildings and Dwellings;
- Providing packaging and labeling services—are classified in Industry 561910, Packaging and Labeling Services; and
- Organizing, promoting, and/or managing conferences, conventions, and trade shows (whether or not they manage and provide the staff to operate the facilities in which these events take place)—are classified in Industry 561920, Convention and Trade Show Organizers.

562 Waste Management and Remediation Services

Industries in the Waste Management and Remediation Services subsector group establishments engaged in the collection, treatment, and disposal of waste materials. This includes establishments engaged in local hauling of waste materials; operating materials recovery facilities (i.e., those that sort recyclable materials from the trash stream); providing remediation services (i.e., those that provide for the cleanup of contaminated buildings, mine sites, soil, or ground water); and providing septic pumping and other miscellaneous waste management services. There are three industry groups within the subsector that separate these activities into waste collection, waste treatment and disposal, and remediation and other waste management.

Excluded from this subsector are establishments primarily engaged in collecting, treating, and disposing waste through sewer systems or sewage treatment facilities that are classified in Industry 22132, Sewage Treatment Facilities and establishments primarily engaged in long-distance hauling of waste materials that are classified in Industry 48423, Specialized Freight (except Used Goods) Trucking, Long-Distance. Also, there are some activities that appear to be related to waste management, but that are not included in this subsector. For example, establishments primarily engaged in providing waste management consulting services are classified in Industry 54162, Environmental Consulting Services.

5621 Waste Collection[CAN]

56211 Waste Collection[CAN]

This industry comprises establishments primarily engaged in (1) collecting and/or hauling hazardous waste, nonhazardous waste, and/or recyclable materials within a local area and/or (2) operating hazardous or nonhazardous waste transfer stations. Hazardous waste collection establishments may be responsible for the identification, treatment, packaging, and labeling of waste for the purposes of transport.

US—United States industry only. CAN—United States and Canadian industries are comparable. MEX—United States and Mexican industries are comparable. Blank—Canadian, Mexican, and United States industries are comparable.

Cross-References. Establishments primarily engaged in—

- Long-distance trucking of waste—are classified in Industry 48423, Specialized Freight (except Used Goods) Trucking, Long-Distance;
- Operating facilities for separating and sorting recyclable materials from nonhazardous waste streams (i.e., garbage) and/or for sorting commingled recyclable materials, such as paper, plastics, and metal cans, into distinct categories—are classified in Industry 56292, Materials Recovery Facilities; and
- Collecting and/or hauling in combination with disposal of waste materials—are classified in Industry 56221, Waste Treatment and Disposal.

562111 Solid Waste Collection[US]

This U.S. industry comprises establishments primarily engaged in one or more of the following: (1) collecting and/or hauling nonhazardous solid waste (i.e., garbage) within a local area; (2) operating nonhazardous solid waste transfer stations; and (3) collecting and/or hauling mixed recyclable materials within a local area.

Cross-References. Establishments primarily engaged in—

- Long-distance trucking of waste—are classified in Industry 484230, Specialized Freight (except Used Goods) Trucking, Long-Distance;
- Collecting and/or hauling in combination with disposal of nonhazardous waste materials—are classified in Industry 56221, Waste Treatment and Disposal;
- Collecting and/or hauling hazardous waste within a local area and/or operating hazardous waste transfer stations—are classified in U.S. Industry 562112, Hazardous Waste Collection;
- Collecting and removing debris, such as brush or rubble, within a local area—are classified in U.S. Industry 562119, Other Waste Collection; and
- Operating facilities for separating and sorting recyclable materials from nonhazardous waste streams (i.e., garbage) and/or for sorting commingled recyclable materials, such as paper, plastics, and metal cans, into distinct categories—are classified in Industry 562920, Materials Recovery Facilities.

562112 Hazardous Waste Collection[US]

This U.S. industry comprises establishments primarily engaged in collecting and/or hauling hazardous waste within a local area and/or operating hazardous

---

US—United States industry only. CAN—United States and Canadian industries are comparable. MEX—United States and Mexican industries are comparable. Blank—Canadian, Mexican, and United States industries are comparable.

waste transfer stations. Hazardous waste collection establishments may be responsible for the identification, treatment, packaging, and labeling of waste for the purposes of transport.

Cross-References. Establishments primarily engaged in—

- Long-distance trucking of waste—are classified in Industry 484230, Specialized Freight (except Used Goods) Trucking, Long-Distance;
- Collecting and/or hauling in combination with disposal of hazardous waste materials—are classified in U.S. Industry 562211, Hazardous Waste Treatment and Disposal;
- Collecting and/or hauling nonhazardous solid waste (i.e., garbage) and/or recyclable materials within a local area and/or operating nonhazardous solid waste transfer stations—are classified in U.S. Industry 562111, Solid Waste Collection; and
- Collecting and removing debris, such as brush or rubble, within a local area—are classified in U.S. Industry 562119, Other Waste Collection.

562119 Other Waste Collection[US]

This U.S. industry comprises establishments primarily engaged in collecting and/or hauling waste (except nonhazardous solid waste and hazardous waste) within a local area. Establishments engaged in brush or rubble removal services are included in this industry.

Cross-References. Establishments primarily engaged in—

- Long-distance trucking of waste—are classified in Industry 484230, Specialized Freight (except Used Goods) Trucking, Long-Distance;
- Collecting and/or hauling in combination with disposal of waste materials—are classified in Industry Group 5622, Waste Treatment and Disposal;
- Collecting and/or hauling nonhazardous solid waste (i.e., garbage) or mixed recyclable materials within a local area or operating nonhazardous solid waste transfer stations—are classified in U.S. Industry 562111, Solid Waste Collection;
- Collecting and/or hauling hazardous waste within a local area or operating hazardous waste transfer stations—are classified in U.S. Industry 562112, Hazardous Waste Collection; and
- Operating facilities for separating and sorting recyclable materials from nonhazardous waste streams (i.e., garbage) and/or for sorting commingled

US—United States industry only. CAN—United States and Canadian industries are comparable. MEX—United States and Mexican industries are comparable. Blank—Canadian, Mexican, and United States industries are comparable.

recyclable materials, such as paper, plastics, and metal cans, into distinct categories—are classified in Industry 562920, Materials Recovery Facilities.

5622 Waste Treatment and Disposal[CAN]

56221 Waste Treatment and Disposal[CAN]

This industry comprises establishments primarily engaged in (1) operating waste treatment or disposal facilities (except sewer systems or sewage treatment facilities) or (2) the combined activity of collecting and/or hauling of waste materials within a local area and operating waste treatment or disposal facilities. Waste combustors or incinerators (including those that may produce byproducts, such as electricity), solid waste landfills, and compost dumps are included in this industry.

Cross-References. Establishments primarily engaged in—

- Collecting, treating, and disposing waste through sewer systems or sewage treatment facilities—are classified in Industry 22132, Sewage Treatment Facilities; and
- Manufacturing compost—are classified in Industry 32531, Fertilizer Manufacturing.

562211 Hazardous Waste Treatment and Disposal[US]

This U.S. industry comprises establishments primarily engaged in (1) operating treatment and/or disposal facilities for hazardous waste or (2) the combined activity of collecting and/or hauling of hazardous waste materials within a local area and operating treatment or disposal facilities for hazardous waste.

Cross-References. Establishments primarily engaged in—

- Operating landfills for the disposal of nonhazardous solid waste—are classified in U.S. Industry 562212, Solid Waste Landfill;
- Operating combustors and incinerators for the disposal of nonhazardous solid waste—are classified in U.S. Industry 562213, Solid Waste Combustors and Incinerators;
- Collecting, treating, and disposing waste through sewer systems or sewage treatment facilities—are classified in Industry 221320, Sewage Treatment Facilities; and
- Operating nonhazardous waste treatment and disposal facilities (except landfills, combustors, incinerators, and sewer systems or sewage treatment facili-

US—United States industry only. CAN—United States and Canadian industries are comparable. MEX—United States and Mexican industries are comparable. Blank—Canadian, Mexican, and United States industries are comparable.

ties)—are classified in U.S. Industry 562219, Other Nonhazardous Waste Treatment and Disposal.

562212 Solid Waste Landfill[US]

This U.S. industry comprises establishments primarily engaged in (1) operating landfills for the disposal of nonhazardous solid waste or (2) the combined activity of collecting and/or hauling nonhazardous waste materials within a local area and operating landfills for the disposal of nonhazardous solid waste.

Cross-References. Establishments primarily engaged in—

- Operating treatment and/or disposal facilities for hazardous waste—are classified in U.S. Industry 562211, Hazardous Waste Treatment and Disposal;
- Operating combustors and incinerators for the disposal of nonhazardous solid waste—are classified in U.S. Industry 562213, Solid Waste Combustors and Incinerators;
- Collecting, treating, and disposing waste through sewer systems or sewage treatment facilities—are classified in Industry 221320, Sewage Treatment Facilities;
- Operating nonhazardous waste treatment and disposal facilities (except landfills, combustors, incinerators, and sewer systems or sewage treatment facilities)—are classified in U.S. Industry 562219, Other Nonhazardous Waste Treatment and Disposal; and
- Manufacturing compost—are classified in U.S. Industry 325314, Fertilizer (Mixing Only) Manufacturing.

562213 Solid Waste Combustors and Incinerators[US]

This U.S. industry comprises establishments primarily engaged in operating combustors and incinerators for the disposal of nonhazardous solid waste. These establishments may produce byproducts, such as electricity and steam.

Cross-References. Establishments primarily engaged in—

- Operating treatment and/or disposal facilities for hazardous waste—are classified in U.S. Industry 562211, Hazardous Waste Treatment and Disposal;
- Operating landfills for the disposal of nonhazardous solid waste—are classified in U.S. Industry 562212, Solid Waste Landfill;

US—United States industry only. CAN—United States and Canadian industries are comparable. MEX—United States and Mexican industries are comparable. Blank—Canadian, Mexican, and United States industries are comparable.

- Collecting, treating, and disposing waste through sewer systems or sewage treatment facilities—are classified in Industry 221320, Sewage Treatment Facilities; and
- Operating nonhazardous waste treatment and disposal facilities (except landfills, combustors, incinerators, and sewer systems or sewage treatment facilities)—are classified in U.S. Industry 562219, Other Nonhazardous Waste Treatment and Disposal.

562219 Other Nonhazardous Waste Treatment and Disposal[US]

This U.S. industry comprises establishments primarily engaged in (1) operating nonhazardous waste treatment and disposal facilities (except landfills, combustors, incinerators and sewer systems or sewage treatment facilities) or (2) the combined activity of collecting and/or hauling of nonhazardous waste materials within a local area and operating waste treatment or disposal facilities (except landfills, combustors, incinerators and sewer systems, or sewage treatment facilities). Compost dumps are included in this industry.

Cross-References. Establishments primarily engaged in—

- Operating landfills for the disposal of nonhazardous solid waste—are classified in U.S. Industry 562212, Solid Waste Landfill;
- Operating combustors and incinerators for the disposal of nonhazardous solid waste—are classified in U.S. Industry 562213, Solid Waste Combustors and Incinerators;
- Collecting, treating, and disposing waste through sewer systems or sewage treatment facilities—are classified in Industry 221320, Sewage Treatment Facilities; and
- Manufacturing compost—are classified in U.S. Industry 325314, Fertilizer (Mixing Only) Manufacturing.

5629 Remediation and Other Waste Management Services[CAN]

This industry group comprises establishments primarily engaged in remediation and other waste management services (except waste collection, waste treatment and disposal, and waste management consulting services).

56291 Remediation Services[CAN]

See industry description for 562910 below.

US—United States industry only. CAN—United States and Canadian industries are comparable. MEX—United States and Mexican industries are comparable. Blank—Canadian, Mexican, and United States industries are comparable.

562910 Remediation Services[CAN]

This industry comprises establishments primarily engaged in one or more of the following: (1) remediation and cleanup of contaminated buildings, mine sites, soil, or ground water; (2) integrated mine reclamation activities, including demolition, soil remediation, waste water treatment, hazardous material removal, contouring land, and revegetation; and (3) asbestos, lead paint, and other toxic material abatement.

Cross-References. Establishments primarily engaged in—

- Developing remedial action plans—are classified in Industry 541620, Environmental Consulting Services;
- Excavating soil—are classified in Industry 238910, Site Preparation Contractors;
- Individual activities as part of a reclamation or remediation project—are classified according to the primary activity;
- Building modifications to alleviate radon gas—are classified in Industry 238990, All Other Specialty Trade Contractors; and
- Collecting, treating, and disposing waste water through sewer systems or sewage treatment facilities—are classified in Industry 221320, Sewage Treatment Facilities.

56292 Materials Recovery Facilities[CAN]

See industry description for 562920 below.

562920 Materials Recovery Facilities[CAN]

This industry comprises establishments primarily engaged in (1) operating facilities for separating and sorting recyclable materials from nonhazardous waste streams (i.e., garbage) and/or (2) operating facilities where commingled recyclable materials, such as paper, plastics, used beverage cans, and metals are sorted into distinct categories.

Cross-References.

Establishments primarily engaged in merchant wholesaling automotive, industrial, and other recyclable materials are classified in Industry 423930, Recyclable Material Merchant Wholesalers.

56299 All Other Waste Management Services[CAN]

This industry comprises establishments primarily engaged in waste management services (except waste collection, waste treatment and disposal, remediation, operation of materials recovery facilities, and waste management consulting services).

US—United States industry only. CAN—United States and Canadian industries are comparable. MEX—United States and Mexican industries are comparable. Blank—Canadian, Mexican, and United States industries are comparable.

Illustrative Examples:

Beach cleaning and maintenance services
Cesspool cleaning services
Portable toilet renting and/or servicing
Pumping (i.e., cleaning) cesspools, portable toilets, or septic tanks
Sewer cleaning and rodding services
Sewer or storm basin cleanout services

Cross-References. Establishments primarily engaged in—

- Collecting and/or hauling waste within a local area—are classified in Industry 56211, Waste Collection;
- Long-distance trucking of waste—are classified in Industry 48423, Specialized Freight (except Used Goods) Trucking, Long-Distance;
- Operating treatment or disposal facilities (except sewer systems or sewage treatment facilities) for waste—are classified in Industry 56221, Waste Treatment and Disposal;
- Collecting, treating, and disposing waste through sewer systems or sewage treatment facilities—are classified in Industry 22132, Sewage Treatment Facilities;
- Remediation and cleanup of contaminated buildings, mine sites, soil, or ground water—are classified in Industry 56291, Remediation Services;
- Operating facilities for separating and sorting recyclable materials from nonhazardous waste streams (i.e., garbage) or where commingled recyclable materials, such as paper, plastics, and metal cans—are sorted into distinct categories are classified in Industry 56292, Materials Recovery Facilities;
- Installing septic tanks—are classified in Industry 23822, Plumbing, Heating, and Air-Conditioning Contractors; and
- Providing waste management consulting services, such as developing remedial action plans—are classified in Industry 54162, Environmental Consulting Services.

562991 Septic Tank and Related Services[US]

This U.S. industry comprises establishments primarily engaged in (1) pumping (i.e., cleaning) septic tanks and cesspools and/or (2) renting and/or servicing portable toilets.

Cross-References. Establishments primarily engaged in—

- Installing septic tanks—are classified in Industry 23822, Plumbing, Heating, and Air-Conditioning Contractors; and

---

US—United States industry only. CAN—United States and Canadian industries are comparable. MEX—United States and Mexican industries are comparable. Blank—Canadian, Mexican, and United States industries are comparable.

- Cleaning and rodding sewers and catch basins—are classified in U.S. Industry 562998, All Other Miscellaneous Waste Management Services.

562998 All Other Miscellaneous Waste Management Services[US]

This U.S. industry comprises establishments primarily engaged in providing waste management services (except waste collection, waste treatment and disposal, remediation, operation of materials recovery facilities, septic tank pumping and related services, and waste management consulting services).

Illustrative Examples:

Beach cleaning and maintenance services
Catch basin cleaning services
Sewer cleaning and rodding services
Sewer or storm basin cleanout services
Tank cleaning and disposal services, commercial or industrial

Cross-References. Establishments primarily engaged in—

- Collecting and/or hauling waste within a local area—are classified in Industry 56211, Waste Collection;
- Long-distance trucking of waste—are classified in Industry 484230, Specialized Freight (except Used Goods) Trucking, Long-Distance;
- Operating treatment or disposal facilities (except sewer systems or sewage treatment facilities) for waste—are classified in Industry 56221 Waste Treatment and Disposal;
- Collecting, treating, and disposing waste through sewer systems or sewage treatment facilities—are classified in Industry 221320, Sewage Treatment Facilities;
- The remediation and cleanup of contaminated buildings, mine sites, soil, or ground water—are classified in Industry 562910, Remediation Services;
- Operating facilities for separating and sorting recyclable materials from nonhazardous waste streams (i.e., garbage) or for sorting commingled recyclable materials, such as paper, plastics, and metal cans, into distinct categories—are classified in Industry 562920, Materials Recovery Facilities;
- Pumping (i.e., cleaning) cesspools, portable toilets, and septic tanks or renting portable toilets—are classified in U.S. Industry 562991, Septic Tank and Related Services; and
- Providing waste management consulting services, such as developing remedial action plans—are classified in Industry 541620, Environmental Consulting Services.

US—United States industry only. CAN—United States and Canadian industries are comparable. MEX—United States and Mexican industries are comparable. Blank—Canadian, Mexican, and United States industries are comparable.

Sector 61—Educational Services

The Sector as a Whole

The Educational Services sector comprises establishments that provide instruction and training in a wide variety of subjects. This instruction and training is provided by specialized establishments, such as schools, colleges, universities, and training centers. These establishments may be privately owned and operated for profit or not for profit, or they may be publicly owned and operated. They may also offer food and accommodation services to their students.

Educational services are usually delivered by teachers or instructors that explain, tell, demonstrate, supervise, and direct learning. Instruction is imparted in diverse settings, such as educational institutions, the workplace, or the home through correspondence, television, or other means. It can be adapted to the particular needs of the students, for example sign language can replace verbal language for teaching students with hearing impairments. All industries in the sector share this commonality of process, namely, labor inputs of instructors with the requisite subject matter expertise and teaching ability.

611 Educational Services

Industries in the Educational Services subsector provide instruction and training in a wide variety of subjects. The instruction and training is provided by specialized establishments, such as schools, colleges, universities, and training centers.

The subsector is structured according to level and type of educational services. Elementary and secondary schools, junior colleges and colleges, universities, and professional schools correspond to a recognized series of formal levels of education designated by diplomas, associate degrees (including equivalent certificates), and degrees. The remaining industry groups are based more on the type of instruction or training offered and the levels are not always as formally defined. The establishments are often highly specialized, many offering instruction in a very limited subject matter, for example ski lessons or one specific computer software package. Within the sector, the level and types of training that are required of the instructors and teachers vary depending on the industry.

Establishments that manage schools and other educational establishments on a contractual basis are classified in this subsector if they both manage the operation and provide the operating staff. Such establishments are classified in the educational services subsector based on the type of facility managed and operated.

6111 Elementary and Secondary Schools

61111 Elementary and Secondary Schools[CAN]

See industry description for 611110 below.

US—United States industry only. CAN—United States and Canadian industries are comparable. MEX—United States and Mexican industries are comparable. Blank—Canadian, Mexican, and United States industries are comparable.

611110 Elementary and Secondary Schools[CAN]

This industry comprises establishments primarily engaged in furnishing academic courses and associated course work that comprise a basic preparatory education. A basic preparatory education ordinarily constitutes kindergarten through 12th grade. This industry includes school boards and school districts.

Illustrative Examples:

Elementary schools
High schools
Kindergartens
Military academies, elementary or secondary
Parochial schools, elementary or secondary
Primary schools
Schools for the physically disabled, elementary or secondary

Cross-References.

- Establishments primarily engaged in providing preschool or prekindergarten education are classified in Industry 624410, Child Day Care Services; and
- Military academies, college level are classified in Industry 611310, Colleges, Universities, and Professional Schools.

6112 Junior Colleges

61121 Junior Colleges

See industry description for 611210 below.

611210 Junior Colleges[CAN]

This industry comprises establishments primarily engaged in furnishing academic, or academic and technical, courses and granting associate degrees, certificates, or diplomas below the baccalaureate level. The requirement for admission to an associate or equivalent degree program is at least a high school diploma or equivalent general academic training. Instruction may be provided in diverse settings, such as the establishment's or client's training facilities, educational institutions, the workplace, or the home, and through correspondence, television, Internet, or other means.

6113 Colleges, Universities, and Professional Schools

61131 Colleges, Universities, and Professional Schools

See industry description for 611310 below.

US—United States industry only. CAN—United States and Canadian industries are comparable. MEX—United States and Mexican industries are comparable. Blank—Canadian, Mexican, and United States industries are comparable.

611310 Colleges, Universities, and Professional Schools[CAN]

This industry comprises establishments primarily engaged in furnishing academic courses and granting degrees at baccalaureate or graduate levels. The requirement for admission is at least a high school diploma or equivalent general academic training. Instruction may be provided in diverse settings, such as the establishment's or client's training facilities, educational institutions, the workplace, or the home, and through correspondence, television, Internet, or other means.

Illustrative Examples:

Colleges (except junior colleges)
Military academies, college level
Professional schools (e.g.,business administration, dental, law, medical)
Theological seminaries offering baccalaureate or graduate degrees
Universities

Cross-References.

Establishments primarily engaged in furnishing academic, or academic and technical, courses and granting associate degrees, certificates, or diplomas below the baccalaureate level are classified in Industry 611210, Junior Colleges.

6114 Business Schools and Computer and Management Training

61141 Business and Secretarial Schools

See industry description for 611410 below.

611410 Business and Secretarial Schools[CAN]

This industry comprises establishments primarily engaged in offering courses in office procedures and secretarial and stenographic skills and may offer courses in basic office skills, such as word processing. In addition, these establishments may offer such classes as office machine operation, reception, communications, and other skills designed for individuals pursuing a clerical or secretarial career. Instruction may be provided in diverse settings, such as the establishment's or client's training facilities, educational institutions, the workplace, or the home, and through correspondence, television, Internet, or other means.

Cross-References. Establishments primarily engaged in—

- Offering computer training (except computer repair)—are classified in Industry 611420, Computer Training;

US—United States industry only. CAN—United States and Canadian industries are comparable. MEX—United States and Mexican industries are comparable. Blank—Canadian, Mexican, and United States industries are comparable.

- Offering academic degrees (e.g., baccalaureate, graduate level) in business education—are classified in Industry 611310, Colleges, Universities, and Professional Schools; and
- Offering training in the maintenance and repair of computers—are classified in Industry 611519, Other Technical and Trade Schools.

61142 Computer Training

See industry description for 611420 below.

611420 Computer Training[CAN]

This industry comprises establishments primarily engaged in conducting computer training (except computer repair), such as computer programming, software packages, computerized business systems, computer electronics technology, computer operations, and local area network management. Instruction may be provided in diverse settings, such as the establishment's or client's training facilities, educational institutions, the workplace, or the home, and through correspondence, television, Internet, or other means.

Cross-References. Establishments primarily engaged in—

- Offering training in the maintenance and repair of computers—are classified in Industry 611519, Other Technical and Trade Schools; and
- Computer retailing, wholesaling, or computer system designing that may also provide computer training—are classified in their appropriate industries.

61143 Professional and Management Development Training

See industry description for 611430 below.

611430 Professional and Management Development Training[CAN]

This industry comprises establishments primarily engaged in offering an array of short duration courses and seminars for management and professional development. Training for career development may be provided directly to individuals or through employers' training programs; and courses may be customized or modified to meet the special needs of customers. Instruction may be provided in diverse settings, such as the establishment's or client's training facilities, educational institutions, the workplace, or the home, and through correspondence, television, Internet, or other means.

US—United States industry only. CAN—United States and Canadian industries are comparable. MEX—United States and Mexican industries are comparable. Blank—Canadian, Mexican, and United States industries are comparable.

Cross-References. Establishments primarily engaged in—

- Advising clients on human resource and training issues without providing the training—are classified in U.S. Industry 541612, Human Resources and Executive Search Consulting Services; and
- Offering academic degrees (e.g., baccalaureate, graduate level)—are classified in Industry 611310, Colleges, Universities and Professional Schools.

6115 Technical and Trade Schools

61151 Technical and Trade Schools

This industry comprises establishments primarily engaged in offering vocational and technical training in a variety of technical subjects and trades. The training often leads to job-specific certification. Instruction may be provided in diverse settings, such as the establishment's or client's training facilities, educational institutions, the workplace, or the home, and through correspondence, television, Internet, or other means.

Illustrative Examples:

Apprenticeship training programs
Aviation and flight training instruction schools
Computer repair training
Cosmetology schools
Electronic equipment repair training
Graphic arts schools
Modeling schools
Nursing schools (except academic)
Real estate schools
Truck driving schools

Cross-References. Establishments primarily engaged in—

- Offering courses in office procedures and secretarial and stenographic skills—are classified in Industry 61141, Business and Secretarial Schools;
- Offering computer training (except computer repair)—are classified in Industry 61142, Computer Training;
- Offering professional and management development training—are classified in Industry 61143, Professional and Management Development Training;
- Offering academic courses that may also offer technical and trade courses—are classified according to the type of school;
- Specialty air transportation services which may also provide flight training—are classified in Industry 48121, Nonscheduled Air Transportation; and
- Offering registered nursing training—are classified in Industry 61121, Junior Colleges or Industry 61131, Colleges, Universities and Professional Schools.

US—United States industry only. CAN—United States and Canadian industries are comparable. MEX—United States and Mexican industries are comparable. Blank—Canadian, Mexican, and United States industries are comparable.

611511 Cosmetology and Barber Schools[US]

This U.S. industry comprises establishments primarily engaged in offering training in barbering, hair styling, or the cosmetic arts, such as makeup or skin care. These schools provide job-specific certification.

611512 Flight Training[US]

This U.S. industry comprises establishments primarily engaged in offering aviation and flight training. These establishments may offer vocational training, recreational training, or both.

Cross-References.

Establishments primarily engaged in specialty air transportation services which may also provide flight training are classified in U.S. Industry 481219, Other Nonscheduled Air Transportation.

611513 Apprenticeship Training[US]

This U.S. industry comprises establishments primarily engaged in offering apprenticeship training programs. These programs involve applied training as well as course work.

611519 Other Technical and Trade Schools[US]

This U.S. industry comprises establishments primarily engaged in offering job or career vocational or technical courses (except cosmetology and barber training, aviation and flight training, and apprenticeship training). The curriculums offered by these schools are highly structured and specialized and lead to job-specific certification.

Illustrative Examples:

Bartending schools
Broadcasting schools
Computer repair training
Graphic arts schools
Modeling schools
Real estate schools
Truck driving schools

Cross-References. Establishments primarily engaged in—

- Offering courses in office procedures and secretarial and stenographic skills—are classified in Industry 611410, Business and Secretarial Schools;

US—United States industry only. CAN—United States and Canadian industries are comparable. MEX—United States and Mexican industries are comparable. Blank—Canadian, Mexican, and United States industries are comparable.

- Offering computer training (except computer repair)—are classified in Industry 611420, Computer Training;
- Offering professional and management development training—are classified in Industry 611430, Professional and Management Development Training;
- Offering registered nursing training with academic degrees (e.g., associate baccalaureate)—are classified in Industry 611210, Junior Colleges or Industry 611310, Colleges, Universities and Professional Schools;
- Offering aviation and flight training—are classified in U.S. Industry 611512, Flight Training;
- Offering cosmetology and barber training—are classified in U.S. Industry 611511, Cosmetology and Barber Schools;
- Offering academic courses that may also offer technical and trade courses—are classified according to the type of school; and
- Offering apprenticeship training programs—are classified in U.S. Industry 611513, Apprenticeship Training.

6116 Other Schools and Instruction

This industry group comprises establishments primarily engaged in offering or providing instruction (except academic schools, colleges, and universities; and business, computer, management, technical, or trade instruction). Instruction may be provided in diverse settings, such as the establishment's or client's training facilities, educational institutions, the workplace, or the home, and through correspondence, television, Internet, or other means.

61161 Fine Arts Schools

See industry description for 611610 below.

611610 Fine Arts Schools[CAN]

This industry comprises establishments primarily engaged in offering instruction in the arts, including dance, art, drama, and music.

Illustrative Examples:

Art (except commercial and graphic) instruction
Dance instruction
Dance studios
Drama schools (except academic)
Fine arts schools (except academic)
Music instruction (e.g., piano, guitar)
Music schools (except academic)
Performing arts schools (except academic)
Photography schools (except commercial photography)

US—United States industry only. CAN—United States and Canadian industries are comparable. MEX—United States and Mexican industries are comparable. Blank—Canadian, Mexican, and United States industries are comparable.

Cross-References.

- Establishments offering high school diplomas or academic degrees (i.e., even if they specialize in fine arts) are classified elsewhere in this subsector according to the type of school; and
- Establishments primarily engaged in offering courses in commercial and graphic arts and commercial photography are classified in U.S. Industry 611519, Other Technical and Trade Schools.

61162 Sports and Recreation Instruction

See industry description for 611620 below.

611620 Sports and Recreation Instruction[CAN]

This industry comprises establishments, such as camps and schools, primarily engaged in offering instruction in athletic activities to groups of individuals. Overnight and day sports instruction camps are included in this industry.

Illustrative Examples:

Camps, sports instruction
Cheerleading instruction
Gymnastics instruction
Martial arts instruction, camps or schools
Professional sports instructors (i.e., not participating in sporting events)
Riding instruction academies or schools
Sports (e.g., baseball, basketball, football, golf)
Swimming instruction

Cross-References.

- Establishments primarily engaged in operating overnight recreational camps that may offer some athletic instruction in addition to other activities are classified in U.S. Industry 721214, Recreation and Vacation Camps (except Campgrounds);
- Establishments primarily engaged in operating sports and recreation establishments that also offer athletic instruction are classified in Sector 71, Arts, Entertainment, and Recreation;
- Independent (i.e., freelance) athletes engaged in providing sports instruction and participating in spectator sporting events are classified in U.S. Industry 711219, Other Spectator Sports; and
- Offering academic courses that may also offer athletic instruction are classified according to the type of school.

61163 Language Schools

See industry description for 611630 below.

US—United States industry only. CAN—United States and Canadian industries are comparable. MEX—United States and Mexican industries are comparable. Blank—Canadian, Mexican, and United States industries are comparable.

611630 Language Schools[CAN]

This industry comprises establishments primarily engaged in offering foreign language instruction (including sign language). These establishments are designed to offer language instruction ranging from conversational skills for personal enrichment to intensive training courses for career or educational opportunities.

Cross-References. Establishments primarily engaged in—

- Offering academic courses that may also offer language instruction—are classified according to type of school; and
- Providing translation and interpretation services—are classified in Industry 541930, Translation and Interpretation Services.

61169 All Other Schools and Instruction

This industry comprises establishments primarily engaged in offering instruction (except business, computer, management, technical, trade, fine arts, athletic, and language instruction). Also excluded from this industry are academic schools, colleges, and universities.

Illustrative Examples:

Academic tutoring services
Automobile driving schools
Exam preparation services
Public speaking training
Speed reading instruction

Cross-References. Establishments primarily engaged in—

- Offering elementary and secondary school instruction—are classified in Industry 61111, Elementary and Secondary Schools;
- Offering junior college instruction—are classified in Industry 61121, Junior Colleges;
- Offering college, university, and professional school instruction with academic degrees (e.g., baccalaureate, graduate)—are classified in Industry 61131, Colleges, Universities and Professional Schools;
- Offering business, computer (except computer repair), and management training—are classified in Industry Group 6114, Business Schools and Computer and Management Training;
- Offering technical and trade school instruction (e.g., computer repair and maintenance)—are classified in Industry 61151, Technical and Trade Schools;

US—United States industry only. CAN—United States and Canadian industries are comparable. MEX—United States and Mexican industries are comparable. Blank—Canadian, Mexican, and United States industries are comparable.

- Offering fine arts instruction—are classified in Industry 61161, Fine Arts Schools;
- Offering sports and recreation instruction—are classified in Industry 61162, Sports and Recreation Instruction; and
- Offering language instruction—are classified in Industry 61163, Language Schools.

611691 Exam Preparation and Tutoring[US]

This U.S. industry comprises establishments primarily engaged in offering preparation for standardized examinations and/or academic tutoring services.

llustrative Examples:

Academic tutoring services
College board preparation centers
Learning centers offering remedial courses
Professional examination review instruction

611692 Automobile Driving Schools[US]

This U.S. industry comprises establishments primarily engaged in offering automobile driving instruction.

Cross-References.

Establishments primarily engaged in offering truck and bus driving instruction are classified in U.S. Industry 611519, Other Technical and Trade Schools.

611699 All Other Miscellaneous Schools and Instruction[US]

This U.S. industry comprises establishments primarily engaged in offering instruction (except business, computer, management, technical, trade, fine arts, athletic, language instruction, tutoring, and automobile driving instruction). Also excluded from this industry are academic schools, colleges, and universities.

Illustrative Examples:

Public speaking training
Speed reading instruction
Survival training

Cross-References. Establishments primarily engaged in—

- Offering elementary and secondary school instruction—are classified in Industry 611110, Elementary and Secondary Schools;

US—United States industry only. CAN—United States and Canadian industries are comparable. MEX—United States and Mexican industries are comparable. Blank—Canadian, Mexican, and United States industries are comparable.

- Offering junior college instruction—are classified in Industry 611210, Junior Colleges;
- Offering college, university, and professional school instruction with academic degrees (e.g., baccalaureate, graduate)—are classified in Industry 611310, Colleges, Universities and Professional Schools;
- Offering business, computer (except computer repair), and management training—are classified in Industry Group 6114, Business Schools and Computer and Management Training;
- Offering technical and trade school instruction (e.g., computer repair and maintenance)—are classified in Industry 61151, Technical and Trade Schools;
- Offering fine arts instruction—are classified in Industry 611610, Fine Arts Schools;
- Offering sports and recreation instruction—are classified in Industry 611620, Sports and Recreation Instruction;
- Offering language instruction—are classified in Industry 611630, Language Schools;
- Offering exam preparation and tutoring services—are classified in U.S. Industry 611691, Exam Preparation and Tutoring; and
- Offering automobile driving instruction—are classified in U.S. Industry 611692, Automobile Driving Schools.

6117 Educational Support Services

61171 Educational Support Services

See industry description for 611710 below.

611710 Educational Support Services

This industry comprises establishments primarily engaged in providing noninstructional services that support educational processes or systems.

Illustrative Examples:

Educational consultants
Educational guidance counseling services
Educational testing evaluation services
Educational testing services
Student exchange programs

Cross-References. Establishments primarily engaged in—

- Providing job training for the unemployed, underemployed, physically disabled, and persons who have a job market disadvantage because of lack

US—United States industry only. CAN—United States and Canadian industries are comparable. MEX—United States and Mexican industries are comparable. Blank—Canadian, Mexican, and United States industries are comparable.

of education or job skills—are classified in Industry 624310, Vocational Rehabilitation Services; and

- Conducting research and analyses in cognitive development—are classified in Industry 541720, Research and Development in the Social Sciences and Humanities.

US—United States industry only. CAN—United States and Canadian industries are comparable. MEX—United States and Mexican industries are comparable. Blank—Canadian, Mexican, and United States industries are comparable.

Sector 62—Health Care and Social Assistance

The Sector as a Whole

The Health Care and Social Assistance sector comprises establishments providing health care and social assistance for individuals. The sector includes both health care and social assistance because it is sometimes difficult to distinguish between the boundaries of these two activities. The industries in this sector are arranged on a continuum starting with those establishments providing medical care exclusively, continuing with those providing health care and social assistance, and finally finishing with those providing only social assistance. The services provided by establishments in this sector are delivered by trained professionals. All industries in the sector share this commonality of process, namely, labor inputs of health practitioners or social workers with the requisite expertise. Many of the industries in the sector are defined based on the educational degree held by the practitioners included in the industry.

Excluded from this sector are aerobic classes in Subsector 713, Amusement, Gambling and Recreation Industries and nonmedical diet and weight reducing centers in Subsector 812, Personal and Laundry Services. Although these can be viewed as health services, these services are not typically delivered by health practitioners.

621 Ambulatory Health Care Services

Industries in the Ambulatory Health Care Services subsector provide health care services directly or indirectly to ambulatory patients and do not usually provide inpatient services. Health practitioners in this subsector provide outpatient services, with the facilities and equipment not usually being the most significant part of the production process.

6211 Offices of Physicians

62111 Offices of Physicians

This industry comprises establishments of health practitioners having the degree of M.D. (Doctor of medicine) or D.O. (Doctor of osteopathy) primarily engaged in the independent practice of general or specialized medicine (e.g., anesthesiology, oncology, ophthalmology, psychiatry) or surgery. These practitioners operate private or group practices in their own offices (e.g., centers, clinics) or in the facilities of others, such as hospitals or HMO medical centers.

US—United States industry only. CAN—United States and Canadian industries are comparable. MEX—United States and Mexican industries are comparable. Blank—Canadian, Mexican, and United States industries are comparable.

Cross-References.

- Medical centers primarily engaged in providing emergency medical care for accident or trauma victims and ambulatory surgical centers primarily engaged in providing surgery on an outpatient basis are classified in Industry 62149, Other Outpatient Care Centers;
- Establishments of oral pathologists are classified in Industry 62121, Offices of Dentists; and
- Establishments of speech or voice pathologists are classified in Industry 62134, Offices of Physical, Occupational and Speech Therapists, and Audiologists.

621111 Offices of Physicians (except Mental Health Specialists)[US]

This U.S. industry comprises establishments of health practitioners having the degree of M.D. (Doctor of medicine) or D.O. (Doctor of osteopathy) primarily engaged in the independent practice of general or specialized medicine (except psychiatry or psychoanalysis) or surgery. These practitioners operate private or group practices in their own offices (e.g., centers, clinics) or in the facilities of others, such as hospitals or HMO medical centers.

Cross-References.

- Establishments of physicians primarily engaged in the independent practice of psychiatry or psychoanalysis are classified in U.S. Industry 621112, Offices of Physicians, Mental Health Specialists;
- Freestanding medical centers primarily engaged in providing emergency medical care for accident or catastrophe victims and freestanding ambulatory surgical centers primarily engaged in providing surgery on an outpatient basis are classified in U.S. Industry 621493, Freestanding Ambulatory Surgical and Emergency Centers;
- Establishments of oral pathologists are classified in Industry 621210, Offices of Dentists; and
- Establishments of speech or voice pathologists are classified in Industry 621340, Offices of Physical, Occupational and Speech Therapists, and Audiologists.

621112 Offices of Physicians, Mental Health Specialists[US]

This U.S. industry comprises establishments of health practitioners having the degree of M.D. (Doctor of medicine) or D.O. (Doctor of osteopathy) primarily

US—United States industry only. CAN—United States and Canadian industries are comparable. MEX—United States and Mexican industries are comparable. Blank—Canadian, Mexican, and United States industries are comparable.

engaged in the independent practice of psychiatry or psychoanalysis. These practitioners operate private or group practices in their own offices (e.g., centers, clinics) or in the facilities of others, such as hospitals or HMO medical centers.

6212 Offices of Dentists

62121 Offices of Dentists

See industry description for 621210 below.

621210 Offices of Dentists[CAN]

This industry comprises establishments of health practitioners having the degree of D.M.D. (Doctor of dental medicine), D.D.S. (Doctor of dental surgery), or D.D.Sc. (Doctor of dental science) primarily engaged in the independent practice of general or specialized dentistry or dental surgery. These practitioners operate private or group practices in their own offices (e.g., centers, clinics) or in the facilities of others, such as hospitals or HMO medical centers. They can provide either comprehensive preventive, cosmetic, or emergency care, or specialize in a single field of dentistry.

Cross-References.

- Establishments known as dental laboratories primarily engaged in making dentures, artificial teeth, and orthodontic appliances to order for dentists are classified U.S. Industry 339116, Dental Laboratories; and
- Establishments of dental hygienists primarily engaged in cleaning teeth and gums or establishments of denturists primarily engaged in taking impressions for and fitting dentures are classified in U.S. Industry 621399, Offices of All Other Miscellaneous Health Practitioners.

6213 Offices of Other Health Practitioners

This industry group comprises establishments of independent health practitioners (except physicians and dentists).

62131 Offices of Chiropractors

See industry description for 621310 below.

621310 Offices of Chiropractors[CAN]

This industry comprises establishments of health practitioners having the degree of D.C. (Doctor of chiropractic) primarily engaged in the independent practice of

US—United States industry only. CAN—United States and Canadian industries are comparable. MEX—United States and Mexican industries are comparable. Blank—Canadian, Mexican, and United States industries are comparable.

chiropractic. These practitioners provide diagnostic and therapeutic treatment of neuromusculoskeletal and related disorders through the manipulation and adjustment of the spinal column and extremities, and operate private or group practices in their own offices (e.g., centers, clinics) or in the facilities of others, such as hospitals or HMO medical centers.

62132 Offices of Optometrists

See industry description for 621320 below.

621320 Offices of Optometrists

This industry comprises establishments of health practitioners having the degree of O.D. (Doctor of optometry) primarily engaged in the independent practice of optometry. These practitioners provide eye examinations to determine visual acuity or the presence of vision problems and to prescribe eyeglasses, contact lenses, and eye exercises. They operate private or group practices in their own offices (e.g., centers, clinics) or in the facilities of others, such as hospitals or HMO medical centers, and may also provide the same service as opticians, such as selling and fitting prescription eyeglasses and contact lenses.

Cross-References. Establishments of—

- Opticians primarily engaged in selling and fitting prescription eyeglasses and contact lenses—are classified in Industry 446130, Optical Goods Stores; and
- Physicians primarily engaged in the independent practice of ophthalmology—are classified in U.S. Industry 621111, Offices of Physicians (except Mental Health Specialists).

62133 Offices of Mental Health Practitioners (except Physicians)

See industry description for 621330 below.

621330 Offices of Mental Health Practitioners (except Physicians)[CAN]

This industry comprises establishments of independent mental health practitioners (except physicians) primarily engaged in (1) the diagnosis and treatment of mental, emotional, and behavioral disorders and/or (2) the diagnosis and treatment of individual or group social dysfunction brought about by such causes as mental illness, alcohol and substance abuse, physical and emotional trauma, or stress. These practitioners operate private or group practices in their own offices (e.g., centers, clinics) or in the facilities of others, such as hospitals or HMO medical centers.

US—United States industry only. CAN—United States and Canadian industries are comparable. MEX—United States and Mexican industries are comparable. Blank—Canadian, Mexican, and United States industries are comparable.

Cross-References.

Establishments of psychiatrists, psychoanalysts, and psychotherapists having the degree of M.D. (Doctor of medicine) or D.O. (Doctor of osteopathy) are classified in U.S. Industry 621112, Offices of Physicians, Mental Health Specialists.

62134 Offices of Physical, Occupational and Speech Therapists, and Audiologists

See industry description for 621340 below.

621340 Offices of Physical, Occupational and Speech Therapists, and Audiologists[CAN]

This industry comprises establishments of independent health practitioners primarily engaged in one of the following: (1) administering medically prescribed physical therapy treatment for patients suffering from injuries or muscle, nerve, joint, and bone disease; (2) planning and administering educational, recreational, and social activities designed to help patients or individuals with disabilities, regain physical or mental functioning or to adapt to their disabilities; and (3) diagnosing and treating speech, language, or hearing problems. These practitioners operate private or group practices in their own offices (e.g., centers, clinics) or in the facilities of others, such as hospitals or HMO medical centers.

Illustrative Examples:

Audiologists' offices
Industrial therapists' offices
Recreational (e.g., art, dance, music) therapists' offices

62139 Offices of All Other Health Practitioners

This industry comprises establishments of independent health practitioners (except physicians; dentists; chiropractors; optometrists; mental health specialists; physical, occupational, and speech therapists; and audiologists). These practitioners operate private or group practices in their own offices (e.g., centers, clinics) or in the facilities of others, such as hospitals or HMO medical centers.

Illustrative Examples:

Acupuncturists' (except MDs or DOs) offices
Dental hygienists' offices
Denturists' offices
Dietitians' offices
Homeopaths' offices
Inhalation or respiratory therapists' offices
Midwives' offices
Naturopaths' offices
Podiatrists' offices
Registered or licensed practical nurses' offices

US—United States industry only. CAN—United States and Canadian industries are comparable. MEX—United States and Mexican industries are comparable. Blank—Canadian, Mexican, and United States industries are comparable.

Cross-References. Establishments primarily engaged in—

- The independent practice of medicine (i.e., physicians)—are classified in Industry 62111, Offices of Physicians;
- The independent practice of dentistry—are classified in Industry 62121, Offices of Dentists;
- The independent practice of chiropractic—are classified in Industry 62131, Offices of Chiropractors;
- The independent practice of optometry—are classified in Industry 62132, Offices of Optometrists;
- The independent practice of mental health (except physicians)—are classified in Industry 62133, Offices of Mental Health Practitioners (except Physicians); and
- The independent practice of physical, occupational, and speech therapy and audiology—are classified in Industry 62134, Offices of Physical, Occupational and Speech Therapists, and Audiologists.

621391 Offices of Podiatrists[US]

This U.S. industry comprises establishments of health practitioners having the degree of D.P. (Doctor of podiatry) primarily engaged in the independent practice of podiatry. These practitioners diagnose and treat diseases and deformities of the foot and operate private or group practices in their own offices (e.g., centers, clinics) or in the facilities of others, such as hospitals or HMO medical centers.

621399 Offices of All Other Miscellaneous Health Practitioners[US]

This U.S. industry comprises establishments of independent health practitioners (except physicians; dentists; chiropractors; optometrists; mental health specialists; physical, occupational, and speech therapists; audiologists; and podiatrists). These practitioners operate private or group practices in their own offices (e.g., centers, clinics) or in the facilities of others, such as hospitals or HMO medical centers.

Illustrative Examples:

Acupuncturists' (except MDs or DOs) offices
Hypnotherapists' offices
Dental hygienists' offices
Denturists' offices
Dietitians' offices
Homeopaths' offices
Inhalation or respiratory therapists' offices
Midwives' offices
Naturopaths' offices
Registered or licensed practical nurses' offices

US—United States industry only. CAN—United States and Canadian industries are comparable. MEX—United States and Mexican industries are comparable. Blank—Canadian, Mexican, and United States industries are comparable.

Cross-References. Establishments primarily engaged in—

- The independent practice of medicine (i.e., physicians)—are classified in Industry 62111, Offices of Physicians;
- The independent practice of dentistry—are classified in Industry 621210, Offices of Dentists;
- The independent practice of chiropractic—are classified in Industry 621310, Offices of Chiropractors;
- The independent practice of optometry—are classified in Industry 621320, Offices of Optometrists;
- The independent practice of mental health (except physicians)—are classified in Industry 621330, Offices of Mental Health Practitioners (except Physicians);
- The independent practice of physical, occupational, and speech therapy, and audiology—are classified in Industry 621340, Offices of Physical, Occupational and Speech Therapists, and Audiologists; and
- The independent practice of podiatry—are classified in U.S. Industry 621391, Offices of Podiatrists.

6214 Outpatient Care Centers

62141 Family Planning Centers

See industry description for 621410 below.

621410 Family Planning Centers[CAN]

This industry comprises establishments with medical staff primarily engaged in providing a range of family planning services on an outpatient basis, such as contraceptive services, genetic and prenatal counseling, voluntary sterilization, and therapeutic and medically indicated termination of pregnancy.

Illustrative Examples:

Birth control clinics	Fertility clinics
Childbirth preparation classes	Pregnancy counseling centers

62142 Outpatient Mental Health and Substance Abuse Centers

See industry description for 621420 below.

US—United States industry only. CAN—United States and Canadian industries are comparable. MEX—United States and Mexican industries are comparable. Blank—Canadian, Mexican, and United States industries are comparable.

621420 Outpatient Mental Health and Substance Abuse Centers[CAN]

This industry comprises establishments with medical staff primarily engaged in providing outpatient services related to the diagnosis and treatment of mental health disorders and alcohol and other substance abuse. These establishments generally treat patients who do not require inpatient treatment. They may provide a counseling staff and information regarding a wide range of mental health and substance abuse issues and/or refer patients to more extensive treatment programs, if necessary.

Illustrative Examples:

Outpatient alcoholism treatment centers and clinics (except hospitals)
Outpatient detoxification centers and clinics (except hospitals)
Outpatient drug addiction treatment centers and clinics (except hospitals)
Outpatient mental health centers and clinics (except hospitals)
Outpatient substance abuse treatment (except hospitals)

Cross-References.

- Establishments known and licensed as hospitals primarily engaged in the inpatient treatment of mental health and substance abuse illnesses with an emphasis on medical treatment and monitoring are classified in Industry 622210, Psychiatric and Substance Abuse Hospitals; and
- Establishments primarily engaged in the inpatient treatment of mental health and substance abuse illness with an emphasis on residential care and counseling rather than medical treatment are classified in Industry 623220, Residential Mental Health and Substance Abuse Facilities.

62149 Other Outpatient Care Centers

This industry comprises establishments with medical staff primarily engaged in providing general or specialized outpatient care (except family planning centers and outpatient mental health and substance abuse centers). Centers or clinics of health practitioners with different degrees from more than one industry practicing within the same establishment (i.e., Doctor of medicine and Doctor of dental medicine) are included in this industry.

Illustrative Examples:

Dialysis centers and clinics
Freestanding ambulatory surgical centers and clinics
Freestanding emergency medical centers and clinics
Health maintenance organization (HMO) medical centers and clinics
Outpatient community health centers and clinics
Outpatient biofeedback centers and clinics
Outpatient sleep disorder centers and clinics

US—United States industry only. CAN—United States and Canadian industries are comparable. MEX—United States and Mexican industries are comparable. Blank—Canadian, Mexican, and United States industries are comparable.

Cross-References.

- Physician walk-in centers are classified in Industry 62111, Offices of Physicians;
- Centers and clinics of health practitioners from the same industry primarily engaged in the independent practice of their profession are classified in Industry 62111, Offices of Physicians; Industry 62121, Offices of Dentists; and Industry Group 6213, Offices of Other Health Practitioners;
- Family planning centers are classified in Industry 62141, Family Planning Centers;
- Outpatient mental health and substance abuse centers are classified in Industry 62142, Outpatient Mental Health and Substance Abuse Centers;
- HMO establishments (except those providing health care services) primarily engaged in underwriting health and medical insurance policies are classified in Industry 52411, Direct Life, Health, and Medical Insurance Carriers; and
- Establishments known and licensed as hospitals that also perform ambulatory surgery and emergency room services are classified in Subsector 622, Hospitals.

621491 HMO Medical Centers[US]

This U.S. industry comprises establishments with physicians and other medical staff primarily engaged in providing a range of outpatient medical services to the health maintenance organization (HMO) subscribers with a focus generally on primary health care. These establishments are owned by the HMO. Included in this industry are HMO establishments that both provide health care services and underwrite health and medical insurance policies.

Cross-References.

- Health practitioners or health practitioner groups contracting to provide their services to subscribers of prepaid health plans are classified in Industry 62111, Offices of Physicians; Industry 621210, Offices of Dentists; and Industry Group 6213, Offices of Other Health Practitioners; and
- HMO establishments (except those providing health care services) primarily engaged in underwriting and administering health and medical insurance policies are classified in U.S. Industry 524114, Direct Health and Medical Insurance Carriers.

US—United States industry only. CAN—United States and Canadian industries are comparable. MEX—United States and Mexican industries are comparable. Blank—Canadian, Mexican, and United States industries are comparable.

621492 Kidney Dialysis Centers[US]

This U.S. industry comprises establishments with medical staff primarily engaged in providing outpatient kidney or renal dialysis services.

621493 Freestanding Ambulatory Surgical and Emergency Centers[US]

This U.S. industry comprises establishments with physicians and other medical staff primarily engaged in (1) providing surgical services (e.g., orthoscopic and cataract surgery) on an outpatient basis or (2) providing emergency care services (e.g., setting broken bones, treating lacerations, or tending to patients suffering injuries as a result of accidents, trauma, or medical conditions necessitating immediate medical care) on an outpatient basis. Outpatient surgical establishments have specialized facilities, such as operating and recovery rooms, and specialized equipment, such as anesthetic or X-ray equipment.

Illustrative Examples:

Freestanding ambulatory surgical centers and clinics
Freestanding emergency medical centers and clinics
Freestanding trauma centers except hospitals
Urgent medical care centers and clinics (except hospitals)

Cross-References.

- Physician walk-in centers are classified in U.S. Industry 621111, Offices of Physicians (except Mental Health Specialists); and
- Establishments known and licensed as hospitals that also perform ambulatory surgery and emergency room services are classified in Subsector 622, Hospitals.

621498 All Other Outpatient Care Centers[US]

This U.S. industry comprises establishments with medical staff primarily engaged in providing general or specialized outpatient care (except family planning centers, outpatient mental health and substance abuse centers, HMO medical centers, kidney dialysis centers, and freestanding ambulatory surgical and emergency centers). Centers or clinics of health practitioners with different degrees from more than one industry practicing within the same establishment (i.e., Doctor of medicine and Doctor of dental medicine) are included in this industry.

Illustrative Examples:

Outpatient biofeedback centers and clinics
Outpatient community health centers and clinics
Outpatient pain therapy centers and clinics
Outpatient sleep disorder centers and clinics

US—United States industry only. CAN—United States and Canadian industries are comparable. MEX—United States and Mexican industries are comparable. Blank—Canadian, Mexican, and United States industries are comparable.

Cross-References.

- Physician walk-in centers are classified in U.S. Industry 621111, Offices of Physicians (except Mental Health Specialists);
- Centers and clinics of health practitioners from the same industry primarily engaged in the independent practice of their profession are classified in Industry 62111, Offices of Physicians; Industry 621210, Offices of Dentists; and Industry Group 6213, Offices of Other Health Practitioners;
- Family planning centers are classified in Industry 621410, Family Planning Centers;
- Outpatient mental health and substance abuse centers are classified in Industry 621420, Outpatient Mental Health and Substance Abuse Centers;
- HMO medical centers are classified in U.S. Industry 621491, HMO Medical Centers;
- Dialysis centers are classified in U.S. Industry 621492, Kidney Dialysis Centers; and
- Freestanding ambulatory surgical and emergency centers are classified in U.S. Industry 621493, Freestanding Ambulatory Surgical and Emergency Centers.

6215 Medical and Diagnostic Laboratories

62151 Medical and Diagnostic Laboratories

This industry comprises establishments known as medical and diagnostic laboratories primarily engaged in providing analytic or diagnostic services, including body fluid analysis and diagnostic imaging, generally to the medical profession or to the patient on referral from a health practitioner.

Illustrative Examples:

Dental or medical X-ray laboratories
Diagnostic imaging centers
Medical forensic laboratories
Medical pathology laboratories
Medical testing laboratories

Cross-References.

Establishments, such as dental, optical, and orthopedic laboratories, primarily engaged in providing the following activities to the medical profession, respectively: making dentures, artificial teeth, and orthodontic appliances to prescription; grinding of lenses to prescription; and making orthopedic or prosthetic appliances to prescription are classified in Industry 33911, Medical Equipment and Supplies Manufacturing.

US—United States industry only. CAN—United States and Canadian industries are comparable. MEX—United States and Mexican industries are comparable. Blank—Canadian, Mexican, and United States industries are comparable.

621511 Medical Laboratories[US]

This U.S. industry comprises establishments known as medical laboratories primarily engaged in providing analytic or diagnostic services, including body fluid analysis, generally to the medical profession or to the patient on referral from a health practitioner.

Illustrative Examples:

Blood analysis laboratories
Medical bacteriological laboratories
Medical forensic laboratories
Medical pathology laboratories
Medical testing laboratories

Cross-References.

- Establishments known as dental laboratories primarily engaged in making dentures, artificial teeth, and orthodontic appliances to prescription are classified in U.S. Industry 339116, Dental Laboratories;
- Establishments known as optical laboratories primarily engaged in grinding of lenses to prescription are classified in U.S. Industry 339115, Ophthalmic Goods Manufacturing; and
- Establishments known as orthopedic laboratories primarily engaged in making orthopedic or prosthetic appliances to prescription are classified in U.S. Industry 339113, Surgical Appliance and Supplies Manufacturing.

621512 Diagnostic Imaging Centers[US]

This U.S. industry comprises establishments known as diagnostic imaging centers primarily engaged in producing images of the patient generally on referral from a health practitioner.

Illustrative Examples:

Computer tomography (CT-scan) centers
Dental or medical X-ray laboratories
Medical radiological laboratories
Magnetic resonance imaging (MRI) centers
Ultrasound imaging centers

6216 Home Health Care Services

62161 Home Health Care Services

See industry description for 621610 below.

US—United States industry only. CAN—United States and Canadian industries are comparable. MEX—United States and Mexican industries are comparable. Blank—Canadian, Mexican, and United States industries are comparable.

621610 Home Health Care Services

This industry comprises establishments primarily engaged in providing skilled nursing services in the home, along with a range of the following: personal care services; homemaker and companion services; physical therapy; medical social services; medications; medical equipment and supplies; counseling; 24-hour home care; occupation and vocational therapy; dietary and nutritional services; speech therapy; audiology; and high-tech care, such as intravenous therapy.

Illustrative Examples:

Home health care agencies
In-home hospice care services
Visiting nurse associations

Cross-References.

- In-home health services provided by establishments of health practitioners and others primarily engaged in the independent practice of their profession are classified in Industry 62111, Offices of Physicians; Industry 621210, Offices of Dentists; and Industry Group 6213, Offices of Other Health Practitioners; and U.S. Industry 621999, All Other Miscellaneous Ambulatory Health Care Services; and
- Establishments primarily engaged in renting or leasing products for home health care are classified in U.S. Industry 532291, Home Health Equipment Rental.

6219 Other Ambulatory Health Care Services

This industry group comprises establishments primarily engaged in providing ambulatory health care services (except offices of physicians, dentists, and other health practitioners; outpatient care centers; medical laboratories and diagnostic imaging centers; and home health care providers).

62191 Ambulance Services

See industry description for 621910 below.

621910 Ambulance Services[MEX]

This industry comprises establishments primarily engaged in providing transportation of patients by ground or air, along with medical care. These services are often provided during a medical emergency but are not restricted to emergencies. The vehicles are equipped with lifesaving equipment operated by medically trained personnel.

US—United States industry only. CAN—United States and Canadian industries are comparable. MEX—United States and Mexican industries are comparable. Blank—Canadian, Mexican, and United States industries are comparable.

Cross-References.

Establishments primarily engaged in providing transportation of the disabled or elderly (without medical care) are classified in U.S. Industry 485991, Special Needs Transportation.

62199 All Other Ambulatory Health Care Services

This industry comprises establishments primarily engaged in providing ambulatory health care services (except office physicians, dentists, and other health practitioners; outpatient care centers; medical and diagnostic laboratories; home health care providers; and ambulances).

Illustrative Examples:

Blood or body organ banks
Blood donor stations
Health screening services (except by health practitioner offices)
Hearing testing services (except by audiologist offices)
Pacemaker monitoring services
Physical fitness evaluation services (except by health practitioner offices)
Smoking cessation programs

Cross-References.

- Establishments primarily engaged in the independent practice of medicine are classified in Industry 62111, Offices of Physicians;
- Establishments primarily engaged in the independent practice of dentistry are classified in Industry 62121, Offices of Dentists;
- Establishments primarily engaged in the independent practice of health care (except offices of physicians and dentists) are classified in Industry Group 6213, Offices of Other Health Practitioners;
- Establishments primarily engaged in providing general or specialized outpatient care services are classified in Industry Group 6214, Outpatient Care Centers;
- Establishments primarily engaged in providing home health care services are classified in Industry 62161, Home Health Care Services;
- Establishments primarily engaged in transportation of patients by ground or air, along with medical care are classified in Industry 62191, Ambulance Services; and
- Establishments known as medical and diagnostic laboratories primarily engaged in providing analytic or diagnostic services are classified in Industry 62151, Medical and Diagnostic Laboratories.

US—United States industry only. CAN—United States and Canadian industries are comparable. MEX—United States and Mexican industries are comparable. Blank—Canadian, Mexican, and United States industries are comparable.

621991 Blood and Organ Banks[US]

This U.S. industry comprises establishments primarily engaged in collecting, storing, and distributing blood and blood products and storing and distributing body organs.

621999 All Other Miscellaneous Ambulatory Health Care Services[US]

This U.S. industry comprises establishments primarily engaged in providing ambulatory health care services (except offices of physicians, dentists, and other health practitioners; outpatient care centers; medical and diagnostic laboratories; home health care providers; ambulances; and blood and organ banks).

Illustrative Examples:

Health screening services (except by offices of health practitioners)
Hearing testing services (except by offices of audiologists)
Pacemaker monitoring services
Physical fitness evaluation services (except by offices of health practitioners)
Smoking cessation programs

Cross-References.

- Establishments primarily engaged in the independent practice of medicine are classified in Industry 62111, Offices of Physicians;
- Establishments primarily engaged in the independent practice of dentistry are classified in Industry 621210, Offices of Dentists;
- Establishments primarily engaged in the independent practice of health care (except offices of physicians and dentists) are classified in Industry Group 6213, Offices of Other Health Practitioners;
- Establishments primarily engaged in providing general or specialized outpatient care services are classified in Industry Group 6214, Outpatient Care Centers;
- Establishments primarily engaged in providing home health care services are classified in Industry 621610, Home Health Care Services;
- Establishments primarily engaged in the transportation of patients by ground or air, along with medical care are classified in Industry 621910, Ambulance Services;
- Establishments known as medical and diagnostic laboratories primarily engaged in providing analytic or diagnostic services are classified in Industry 62151, Medical and Diagnostic Laboratories; and

US—United States industry only. CAN—United States and Canadian industries are comparable. MEX—United States and Mexican industries are comparable. Blank—Canadian, Mexican, and United States industries are comparable.

- Blood and organ banks are classified in U.S. Industry 621991, Blood and Organ Banks.

622 Hospitals

Industries in the Hospitals subsector provide medical, diagnostic, and treatment services that include physician, nursing, and other health services to inpatients and the specialized accommodation services required by inpatients. Hospitals may also provide outpatient services as a secondary activity. Establishments in the Hospitals subsector provide inpatient health services, many of which can only be provided using the specialized facilities and equipment that form a significant and integral part of the production process.

6221 General Medical and Surgical Hospitals

62211 General Medical and Surgical Hospitals

See industry description for 622110 below.

622110 General Medical and Surgical Hospitals[US]

This industry comprises establishments known and licensed as general medical and surgical hospitals primarily engaged in providing diagnostic and medical treatment (both surgical and nonsurgical) to inpatients with any of a wide variety of medical conditions. These establishments maintain inpatient beds and provide patients with food services that meet their nutritional requirements. These hospitals have an organized staff of physicians and other medical staff to provide patient care services. These establishments usually provide other services, such as outpatient services, anatomical pathology services, diagnostic X-ray services, clinical laboratory services, operating room services for a variety of procedures, and pharmacy services.

6222 Psychiatric and Substance Abuse Hospitals

62221 Psychiatric and Substance Abuse Hospitals

See industry description for 622210 below.

622210 Psychiatric and Substance Abuse Hospitals[CAN]

This industry comprises establishments known and licensed as psychiatric and substance abuse hospitals primarily engaged in providing diagnostic, medical treat-

---

US—United States industry only. CAN—United States and Canadian industries are comparable. MEX—United States and Mexican industries are comparable. Blank—Canadian, Mexican, and United States industries are comparable.

ment, and monitoring services for inpatients who suffer from mental illness or substance abuse disorders. The treatment often requires an extended stay in the hospital. These establishments maintain inpatient beds and provide patients with food services that meet their nutritional requirements. They have an organized staff of physicians and other medical staff to provide patient care services. Psychiatric, psychological, and social work services are available at the facility. These hospitals usually provide other services, such as outpatient services, clinical laboratory services, diagnostic X-ray services, and electroencephalograph services.

Cross-References.

- Establishments primarily engaged in providing treatment of mental health and substance abuse illnesses on an exclusively outpatient basis are classified in Industry 621420, Outpatient Mental Health and Substance Abuse Centers;
- Establishments referred to as hospitals but are primarily engaged in providing inpatient treatment of mental health and substance abuse illness with the emphasis on counseling rather than medical treatment are classified in Industry 623220, Residential Mental Health and Substance Abuse Facilities; and
- Establishments referred to as hospitals but are primarily engaged in providing residential care for persons diagnosed with mental retardation are classified in Industry 623210, Residential Mental Retardation Facilities.

6223 Specialty (except Psychiatric and Substance Abuse) Hospitals

62231 Specialty (except Psychiatric and Substance Abuse) Hospitals

See industry description for 622310 below.

622310 Specialty (except Psychiatric and Substance Abuse) Hospitals[CAN]

This industry consists of establishments known and licensed as specialty hospitals primarily engaged in providing diagnostic and medical treatment to inpatients with a specific type of disease or medical condition (except psychiatric or substance abuse). Hospitals providing long-term care for the chronically ill and hospitals providing rehabilitation, restorative, and adjustive services to physically challenged or disabled people are included in this industry. These establishments maintain inpatient beds and provide patients with food services that meet their nutritional requirements. They have an organized staff of physicians and other medical staff to provide patient care services. These hospitals may provide other services, such

US—United States industry only. CAN—United States and Canadian industries are comparable. MEX—United States and Mexican industries are comparable. Blank—Canadian, Mexican, and United States industries are comparable.

as outpatient services, diagnostic X-ray services, clinical laboratory services, operating room services, physical therapy services, educational and vocational services, and psychological and social work services.

Cross-References.

- Establishments known and licensed as hospitals primarily engaged in providing diagnostic and therapeutic inpatient services for a variety of medical conditions, both surgical and nonsurgical, are classified in Industry 622110, General Medical and Surgical Hospitals;
- Establishments known and licensed as hospitals primarily engaged in providing diagnostic and treatment services for inpatients with psychiatric or substance abuse illnesses are classified in Industry 622210, Psychiatric and Substance Abuse Hospitals;
- Establishments referred to as hospitals but are primarily engaged in providing inpatient nursing and rehabilitative services to persons requiring convalescence are classified in Industry 623110, Nursing Care Facilities;
- Establishments referred to as hospitals but are primarily engaged in providing residential care of persons diagnosed with mental retardation are classified in Industry 623210, Residential Mental Retardation Facilities; and
- Establishments referred to as hospitals but are primarily engaged in providing inpatient treatment for mental health and substance abuse illnesses with the emphasis on counseling rather than medical treatment are classified in Industry 623220, Residential Mental Health and Substance Abuse Facilities.

623 Nursing and Residential Care Facilities

Industries in the Nursing and Residential Care Facilities subsector provide residential care combined with either nursing, supervisory, or other types of care as required by the residents. In this subsector, the facilities are a significant part of the production process and the care provided is a mix of health and social services with the health services being largely some level of nursing services.

6231 Nursing Care Facilities

62311 Nursing Care Facilities

See industry description for 623110 below.

623110 Nursing Care Facilities[CAN]

This industry comprises establishments primarily engaged in providing inpatient nursing and rehabilitative services. The care is generally provided for an extended

US—United States industry only. CAN—United States and Canadian industries are comparable. MEX—United States and Mexican industries are comparable. Blank—Canadian, Mexican, and United States industries are comparable.

period of time to individuals requiring nursing care. These establishments have a permanent core staff of registered or licensed practical nurses who, along with other staff, provide nursing and continuous personal care services.

Illustrative Examples:

Convalescent homes or convalescent hospitals (except psychiatric)
Homes for the elderly with nursing care
Inpatient care hospices
Nursing homes
Rest homes with nursing care

Cross-References.

- Assisted-living facilities with on-site nursing care facilities are classified in U.S. Industry 623311, Continuing Care Retirement Communities; and
- Psychiatric convalescent homes are classified in Industry 623220, Residential Mental Health and Substance Abuse Facilities.

6232 Residential Mental Retardation, Mental Health and Substance Abuse Facilities

This industry group comprises establishments primarily engaged in providing residential care (but not licensed hospital care) to people with mental retardation, mental illness, or substance abuse problems.

62321 Residential Mental Retardation Facilities

See industry description for 623210 below.

623210 Residential Mental Retardation Facilities[CAN]

This industry comprises establishments (e.g., group homes, hospitals, intermediate care facilities) primarily engaged in providing residential care services for persons diagnosed with mental retardation. These facilities may provide some health care, though the focus is room, board, protective supervision, and counseling.

Cross-References.

- Establishments primarily engaged in providing inpatient treatment of mental health and substance abuse illnesses with an emphasis on counseling rather than medical treatment are classified in Industry 623220, Residential Mental Health and Substance Abuse Facilities;
- Establishments primarily engaged in providing treatment of mental health and substance abuse illnesses on an exclusively outpatient basis are classified in Industry 621420, Outpatient Mental Health and Substance Abuse Centers; and

US—United States industry only. CAN—United States and Canadian industries are comparable. MEX—United States and Mexican industries are comparable. Blank—Canadian, Mexican, and United States industries are comparable.

- Establishments known and licensed as hospitals primarily engaged in providing inpatient treatment of mental health and substance abuse illnesses with an emphasis on medical treatment and monitoring are classified in Industry 622210, Psychiatric and Substance Abuse Hospitals.

62322 Residential Mental Health and Substance Abuse Facilities

See industry description for 623220 below.

623220 Residential Mental Health and Substance Abuse Facilities[US]

This industry comprises establishments primarily engaged in providing residential care and treatment for patients with mental health and substance abuse illnesses. These establishments provide room, board, supervision, and counseling services. Although medical services may be available at these establishments, they are incidental to the counseling, mental rehabilitation, and support services offered. These establishments generally provide a wide range of social services in addition to counseling.

Illustrative Examples:

Alcoholism or drug addiction rehabilitation facilities (except licensed hospitals)
Mental health halfway houses
Psychiatric convalescent homes or hospitals
Residential group homes for the emotionally disturbed

Cross-References.

- Establishments primarily engaged in providing treatment of mental health and substance abuse illnesses on an exclusively outpatient basis are classified in Industry 621420, Outpatient Mental Health and Substance Abuse Centers;
- Establishments primarily engaged in providing residential care for persons diagnosed with mental retardation are classified in Industry 623210, Residential Mental Retardation Facilities; and
- Establishments known and licensed as hospitals primarily engaged in providing inpatient treatment of mental health and substance abuse illnesses with an emphasis on medical treatment and monitoring are classified in Industry 622210, Psychiatric and Substance Abuse Hospitals.

6233 Community Care Facilities for the Elderly

62331 Community Care Facilities for the Elderly

This industry comprises establishments primarily engaged in providing residential and personal care services for (1) the elderly and other persons who are unable

US—United States industry only. CAN—United States and Canadian industries are comparable. MEX—United States and Mexican industries are comparable. Blank—Canadian, Mexican, and United States industries are comparable.

to fully care for themselves and/or (2) the elderly and other persons who do not desire to live independently. The care typically includes room, board, supervision, and assistance in daily living, such as housekeeping services. In some instances these establishments provide skilled nursing care for residents in separate on-site facilities.

Illustrative Examples:

Assisted-living facilities
Continuing care retirement communities
Homes for the elderly without nursing care
Rest homes without nursing care

Cross-References.

- Establishments primarily engaged in providing inpatient nursing and rehabilitative services are classified in Industry 62311, Nursing Care Facilities; and
- Apartment or condominium complexes where people live independently in rented housing units are classified in Industry 53111, Lessors of Residential Buildings and Dwellings.

623311 Continuing Care Retirement Communities[US]

This U.S. industry comprises establishments primarily engaged in providing a range of residential and personal care services with on-site nursing care facilities for (1) the elderly and other persons who are unable to fully care for themselves and/or (2) the elderly and other persons who do not desire to live independently. Individuals live in a variety of residential settings with meals, housekeeping, social, leisure, and other services available to assist residents in daily living. Assisted-living facilities with on-site nursing care facilities are included in this industry.

Cross-References.

- Establishments primarily engaged in providing inpatient nursing and rehabilitative services are classified in Industry 623110, Nursing Care Facilities;
- Assisted-living facilities without on-site nursing care facilities are classified in U.S. Industry 623312, Homes for the Elderly; and
- Apartment or condominium complexes where people live independently in rented housing units are classified in Industry 531110, Lessors of Residential Buildings and Dwellings.

623312 Homes for the Elderly[US]

This U.S. industry comprises establishments primarily engaged in providing residential and personal care services (i.e., without on-site nursing care facilities)

US—United States industry only. CAN—United States and Canadian industries are comparable. MEX—United States and Mexican industries are comparable. Blank—Canadian, Mexican, and United States industries are comparable.

for (1) the elderly or other persons who are unable to fully care for themselves and/or (2) the elderly or other persons who do not desire to live independently. The care typically includes room, board, supervision, and assistance in daily living, such as housekeeping services.

Illustrative Examples:

Assisted-living facilities without on-site nursing care facilities
Homes for the elderly without nursing care
Rest homes without nursing care

Cross-References.

- Assisted-living facilities with on-site nursing care facilities are classified in U.S. Industry 623311, Continuing Care Retirement Communities;
- Homes for the elderly with nursing care or rest homes with nursing care are classified in Industry 623110, Nursing Care Facilities; and
- Apartment or condominium complexes where people live independently in rented or owned housing units are classified in Industry 53111, Lessors of Residential Buildings and Dwellings.

6239 Other Residential Care Facilities

This industry group comprises establishments of residential care facilities (except residential mental retardation, mental health, and substance abuse facilities and community care facilities for the elderly).

62399 Other Residential Care Facilities

See industry description for 623990 below.

623990 Other Residential Care Facilities[US]

This industry comprises establishments primarily engaged in providing residential care (except residential mental retardation facilities, residential health and substance abuse facilities, continuing care retirement communities, and homes for the elderly). These establishments also provide supervision and personal care services.

Illustrative Examples:

Boot or disciplinary camps (except correctional) for delinquent youth
Child group foster homes
Delinquent youth halfway group homes
Group homes for the disabled without nursing care
Halfway group homes for delinquents or ex-offenders

US—United States industry only. CAN—United States and Canadian industries are comparable. MEX—United States and Mexican industries are comparable. Blank—Canadian, Mexican, and United States industries are comparable.

Group homes for the hearing or visually impaired
Homes for unwed mothers
Orphanages

Cross-References.

- Residential mental retardation facilities are classified in Industry 623210, Residential Mental Retardation Facilities;
- Continuing care retirement communities are classified in U.S. Industry 623311, Continuing Care Retirement Communities;
- Residential mental health and substance abuse facilities are classified in 623220, Residential Mental Health and Substance Abuse Facilities;
- Homes for the elderly without nursing care are classified in U.S. Industry 623312, Homes for the Elderly;
- Establishments primarily engaged in providing inpatient nursing and rehabilitative services are classified in Industry 623110, Nursing Care Facilities;
- Establishments primarily engaged in providing temporary shelter are classified in U.S. Industry 624221, Temporary Shelters; and
- Correctional camps are classified in Industry 922140, Correctional Institutions.

624 Social Assistance

Industries in the Social Assistance subsector provide a wide variety of social assistance services directly to their clients. These services do not include residential or accommodation services, except on a short stay basis.

6241 Individual and Family Services

62411 Child and Youth Services

See industry description for 624110 below.

624110 Child and Youth Services[CAN]

This industry comprises establishments primarily engaged in providing nonresidential social assistance services for children and youth. These establishments provide for the welfare of children in such areas as adoption and foster care, drug prevention, life skills training, and positive social development.

Illustrative Examples:

Adoption agencies
Child guidance organizations
Foster care placement services
Youth centers (except recreational only)
Youth self-help organizations

US—United States industry only. CAN—United States and Canadian industries are comparable. MEX—United States and Mexican industries are comparable. Blank—Canadian, Mexican, and United States industries are comparable.

Cross-References.

- Youth recreational centers are classified in Industry 713940, Fitness and Recreational Sports Centers;
- Youth recreational sports teams and leagues are classified in Industry 713990, All Other Amusement and Recreation Industries;
- Scouting organizations are classified in Industry 813410, Civic and Social Organizations; and
- Establishments primarily engaged in providing day care services for children are classified in Industry 624410, Child Day Care Services.

62412 Services for the Elderly and Persons with Disabilities

See industry description for 624120 below.

624120 Services for the Elderly and Persons with Disabilities[CAN]

This industry comprises establishments primarily engaged in providing nonresidential social assistance services to improve the quality of life for the elderly, persons diagnosed with mental retardation, or persons with disabilities. These establishments provide for the welfare of these of individuals in such areas as day care, nonmedical home care or homemaker services, social activities, group support, and companionship.

Cross-References. Establishments primarily engaged in—

- Providing job training for persons diagnosed with mental retardation or persons with disabilities—are classified in Industry 624310, Vocational Rehabilitation Services;
- Providing residential care for the elderly, persons diagnosed with mental retardation, or persons with disabilities—are classified in Subsector 623, Nursing and Residential Care Facilities; and
- Providing in-home health care services—are classified in Subsector 621, Ambulatory Health Care Services.

62419 Other Individual and Family Services

See industry description for 624190 below.

624190 Other Individual and Family Services[CAN]

This industry comprises establishments primarily engaged in providing nonresidential individual and family social assistance services (except those specifically

---

US—United States industry only. CAN—United States and Canadian industries are comparable. MEX—United States and Mexican industries are comparable. Blank—Canadian, Mexican, and United States industries are comparable.

directed toward children, the elderly, persons diagnosed with mental retardation, or persons with disabilities).

Illustrative Examples:

Community action services agencies
Crisis intervention centers
Family social services agencies
Family welfare services
Hotline centers
Marriage counseling services (except by offices of mental health practitioners)
Multipurpose social services centers
Self-help organizations (except for disabled persons, the elderly, persons diagnosed with mental retardation)
Suicide crisis centers
Telephone counseling services

Cross-References. Establishments primarily engaged in—

- Providing clinical psychological and psychiatric social counseling services—are classified in Industry 621330, Offices of Mental Health Practitioners (except Physicians);
- Providing child and youth social assistance services (except day care)—are classified in Industry 624110, Child and Youth Services;
- Providing child day care services—are classified in Industry 624410, Child Day Care Services;
- Providing social assistance services for the elderly, persons diagnosed with mental retardation, and persons with disabilities—are classified in Industry 624120, Services for the Elderly and Persons with Disabilities;
- Community action advocacy—are classified in U.S. Industry 813319, Other Social Advocacy Organizations; and
- Providing in-home health care services—are classified in Subsector 621, Ambulatory Health Care Services.

6242 Community Food and Housing, and Emergency and Other Relief Services

62421 Community Food Services

See industry description for 624210 below.

624210 Community Food Services[CAN]

This industry comprises establishments primarily engaged in the collection, preparation, and delivery of food for the needy. Establishments in this industry may also distribute clothing and blankets to the poor. These establishments may prepare and deliver meals to persons who by reason of age, disability, or illness

US—United States industry only. CAN—United States and Canadian industries are comparable. MEX—United States and Mexican industries are comparable. Blank—Canadian, Mexican, and United States industries are comparable.

are unable to prepare meals for themselves; collect and distribute salvageable or donated food; or prepare and provide meals at fixed or mobile locations. Food banks, meal delivery programs, and soup kitchens are included in this industry.

62422 Community Housing Services

This industry comprises establishments primarily engaged in providing one or more of the following community housing services: (1) short term emergency shelter for victims of domestic violence, sexual assault, or child abuse; (2) temporary residential shelter for the homeless, runaway youths, and patients and families caught in medical crises; (3) transitional housing for low-income individuals and families; (4) volunteer construction or repair of low cost housing, in partnership with the homeowner who may assist in construction or repair work; and (5) repair of homes for elderly or disabled homeowners. These establishments may operate their own shelter; or may subsidize housing using existing homes, apartments, hotels, or motels; or may require a low-cost mortgage or work (sweat) equity.

Cross-References.

Central offices of government housing programs are classified in Industry 92511, Administration of Housing Programs.

624221 Temporary Shelters[US]

This U.S. industry comprises establishments primarily engaged in providing (1) short term emergency shelter for victims of domestic violence, sexual assault, or child abuse and/or (2) temporary residential shelter for homeless individuals or families, runaway youth, and patients and families caught in medical crises. These establishments may operate their own shelters or may subsidize housing using existing homes, apartments, hotels, or motels.

Cross-References.

Establishments primarily engaged in providing emergency shelter for victims of domestic or international disasters or conflicts are classified in Industry 624230, Emergency and Other Relief Services.

624229 Other Community Housing Services[US]

This U.S. industry comprises establishments primarily engaged in providing one or more of the following community housing services: (1) transitional housing to

US—United States industry only. CAN—United States and Canadian industries are comparable. MEX—United States and Mexican industries are comparable. Blank—Canadian, Mexican, and United States industries are comparable.

low-income individuals and families; (2) volunteer construction or repair of low-cost housing, in partnership with the homeowner who may assist in the construction or repair work; and (3) the repair of homes for elderly or disabled homeowners. These establishments may subsidize housing using existing homes, apartments, hotels, or motels or may require a low-cost mortgage or sweat equity. These establishments may also provide low-income families with furniture and household supplies.

Cross-References.

Central offices of government housing programs are classified in Industry 925110, Administration of Housing Programs.

62423 Emergency and Other Relief Services

See industry description for 624230 below.

624230 Emergency and Other Relief Services[CAN]

This industry comprises establishments primarily engaged in providing food, shelter, clothing, medical relief, resettlement, and counseling to victims of domestic or international disasters or conflicts (e.g., wars).

6243 Vocational Rehabilitation Services

62431 Vocational Rehabilitation Services

See industry description for 624310 below.

624310 Vocational Rehabilitation Services[CAN]

This industry comprises (1) establishments primarily engaged in providing vocational rehabilitation or habilitation services, such as job counseling, job training, and work experience, to unemployed and underemployed persons, persons with disabilities, and persons who have a job market disadvantage because of lack of education, job skill, or experience and (2) establishments primarily engaged in providing training and employment to persons with disabilities. Vocational rehabilitation job training facilities (except schools) and sheltered workshops (i.e., work experience centers) are included in this industry.

Cross-References.

- Schools (except high schools) primarily engaged in providing vocational training are classified in Industry 61151, Technical and Trade Schools;

US—United States industry only. CAN—United States and Canadian industries are comparable. MEX—United States and Mexican industries are comparable. Blank—Canadian, Mexican, and United States industries are comparable.

- Vocational high schools are classified in Industry 611110, Elementary and Secondary Schools; and
- Establishments primarily engaged in providing career and vocational counseling (except rehabilitative) are classified in Industry 611710, Educational Support Services.

6244 Child Day Care Services

62441 Child Day Care Services

See industry description for 624410 below.

624410 Child Day Care Services[CAN]

This industry comprises establishments primarily engaged in providing day care of infants or children. These establishments generally care for preschool children, but may care for older children when they are not in school and may also offer prekindergarten educational programs.

Illustrative Examples:

Child day care babysitting services
Child or infant day care centers
Nursery schools
Preschool centers

Cross-References.

Establishments primarily engaged in offering kindergarten educational programs are classified in Industry 611110, Elementary and Secondary Schools.

US—United States industry only. CAN—United States and Canadian industries are comparable. MEX—United States and Mexican industries are comparable. Blank—Canadian, Mexican, and United States industries are comparable.

Sector 71—Arts, Entertainment, and Recreation

The Sector as a Whole

The Arts, Entertainment, and Recreation sector includes a wide range of establishments that operate facilities or provide services to meet varied cultural, entertainment, and recreational interests of their patrons. This sector comprises (1) establishments that are involved in producing, promoting, or participating in live performances, events, or exhibits intended for public viewing; (2) establishments that preserve and exhibit objects and sites of historical, cultural, or educational interest; and (3) establishments that operate facilities or provide services that enable patrons to participate in recreational activities or pursue amusement, hobby, and leisure-time interests.

Some establishments that provide cultural, entertainment, or recreational facilities and services are classified in other sectors. Excluded from this sector are: (1) establishments that provide both accommodations and recreational facilities, such as hunting and fishing camps and resort and casino hotels are classified in Subsector 721, Accommodation; (2) restaurants and night clubs that provide live entertainment in addition to the sale of food and beverages are classified in Subsector 722, Food Services and Drinking Places; (3) motion picture theaters, libraries and archives, and publishers of newspapers, magazines, books, periodicals, and computer software are classified in Sector 51, Information; and (4) establishments using transportation equipment to provide recreational and entertainment services, such as those operating sightseeing buses, dinner cruises, or helicopter rides are classified in Subsector 487, Scenic and Sightseeing Transportation.

711 Performing Arts, Spectator Sports, and Related Industries

Industries in the Performing Arts, Spectator Sports, and Related Industries subsector group establishments that produce or organize and promote live presentations involving the performances of actors and actresses, singers, dancers, musical groups and artists, athletes, and other entertainers, including independent (i.e., freelance) entertainers and the establishments that manage their careers. The classification recognizes four basic processes: (1) producing (i.e., presenting) events; (2) organizing, managing, and/or promoting events; (3) managing and representing entertainers; and (4) providing the artistic, creative and technical skills necessary to the production of these live events. Also, this subsector contains four industries for performing arts companies. Each is defined on the basis of the particular skills of the entertainers involved in the presentations.

The industry structure for this subsector makes a clear distinction between performing arts companies and performing artists (i.e., independent or freelance).

US—United States industry only. CAN—United States and Canadian industries are comparable. MEX—United States and Mexican industries are comparable. Blank—Canadian, Mexican, and United States industries are comparable.

Although not unique to arts and entertainment, freelancing is a particularly important phenomenon in this Performing Arts, Spectator Sports, and Related Industries subsector. Distinguishing this activity from the production activity is a meaningful process differentiation. This approach, however, is difficult to implement in the case of musical groups (i.e., companies) and artists, especially pop groups. These establishments tend to be more loosely organized and it can be difficult to distinguish companies from freelancers. For this reason, NAICS includes one industry that covers both musical groups and musical artists.

This subsector contains two industries for Industry Group 7113, Promoters of Performing Arts, Sports, and Similar Events, one for those that operate facilities and another for those that do not. This is because there are significant differences in cost structures between those promoters that manage and provide the staff to operate facilities and those that do not. In addition to promoters without facilities, other industries in this subsector include establishments that may operate without permanent facilities. These types of establishments include: performing arts companies, musical groups and artists, spectator sports, and independent (i.e., freelance) artists, writers, and performers.

Excluded from this subsector are nightclubs. Some nightclubs promote live entertainment on a regular basis and it can be argued that they could be classified in Industry Group 7113, Promoters of Performing Arts, Sports, and Similar Events. However, since most of these establishments function as any other drinking place when they do not promote entertainment and because most of their revenue is derived from sale of food and beverages, they are classified in Subsector 722, Food Services and Drinking Places.

7111 Performing Arts Companies

This industry group comprises establishments primarily engaged in producing live presentations involving the performances of actors and actresses, singers, dancers, musical groups and artists, and other performing artists.

71111 Theater Companies and Dinner Theaters

See industry description for 711110 below.

711110 Theater Companies and Dinner Theaters[US]

This industry comprises (1) companies, groups, or theaters primarily engaged in producing the following live theatrical presentations: musicals; operas; plays; and comedy, improvisational, mime, and puppet shows and (2) establishments, commonly known as dinner theaters, engaged in producing live theatrical productions and in providing food and beverages for consumption on the premises. Theater

US—United States industry only. CAN—United States and Canadian industries are comparable. MEX—United States and Mexican industries are comparable. Blank—Canadian, Mexican, and United States industries are comparable.

groups or companies may or may not operate their own theater or other facility for staging their shows.

Illustrative Examples:

Comedy troupes	Opera companies
Live theatrical production (except dance)	Theatrical stock or repertory companies
Musical theater companies	

Cross-References.

- Establishments, such as nightclubs, primarily engaged in providing food and beverages for consumption on the premises and that also present live nontheatrical entertainment, are classified in Subsector 722, Food Services and Drinking Places;
- Establishments primarily engaged in organizing, managing, and/or promoting performing arts productions without producing their own shows are classified in Industry Group 7113, Promoters of Performing Arts, Sports, and Similar Events;
- Companies, groups, or theaters primarily engaged in producing all types of live theatrical dance presentations are classified in Industry 711120, Dance Companies;
- Freelance producers and performing artists (except musicians and vocalists) primarily engaged in theatrical activities independent of a company or group are classified in Industry 711510, Independent Artists, Writers, and Performers; and
- Musicians and vocalists are classified in Industry 711130, Musical Groups and Artists.

71112 Dance Companies

See industry description for 711120 below.

711120 Dance Companies[CAN]

This industry comprises companies, groups, or theaters primarily engaged in producing all types of live theatrical dance (e.g., ballet, contemporary dance, folk dance) presentations. Dance companies or groups may or may not operate their own theater or other facility for staging their shows.

Cross-References.

- Establishments, such as exotic dance clubs, primarily engaged in providing food and beverages for consumption on the premises and that also present

US—United States industry only. CAN—United States and Canadian industries are comparable. MEX—United States and Mexican industries are comparable. Blank—Canadian, Mexican, and United States industries are comparable.

live dance entertainment, are classified in Subsector 722, Food Services and Drinking Places;

- Establishments primarily engaged in organizing, promoting, and/or managing dance productions without producing their own shows are classified in Industry Group 7113, Promoters of Performing Arts, Sports, and Similar Events; and
- Freelance producers and dancers primarily engaged in theatrical activities independent of a company or group are classified in Industry 711510, Independent Artists, Writers, and Performers.

71113 Musical Groups and Artists

See industry description for 711130 below.

711130 Musical Groups and Artists[CAN]

This industry comprises (1) groups primarily engaged in producing live musical entertainment (except theatrical musical or opera productions) and (2) independent (i.e., freelance) artists primarily engaged in providing live musical entertainment. Musical groups and artists may perform in front of a live audience or in a studio, and may or may not operate their own facilities for staging their shows.

Illustrative Examples:

Bands
Musical groups (except theatrical musical groups)
Drum and bugle corps (i.e., drill teams)
Independent musicians or vocalists
Orchestras

Cross-References.

- Establishments primarily engaged in organizing, promoting, and/or managing concerts and other musical performances without producing their own shows are classified in Industry Group 7113, Promoters of Performing Arts, Sports, and Similar Events;
- Companies, groups, or theaters primarily engaged in producing theatrical musicals and opera productions are classified in Industry 711110, Theater Companies and Dinner Theaters; and
- Freelance producers (except musical groups and artists) primarily engaged in musical activities independent of a company or group are classified in Industry 711510, Independent Artists, Writers, and Performers.

71119 Other Performing Arts Companies

See industry description for 711190 below.

US—United States industry only. CAN—United States and Canadian industries are comparable. MEX—United States and Mexican industries are comparable. Blank—Canadian, Mexican, and United States industries are comparable.

711190 Other Performing Arts Companies[CAN]

This industry comprises companies or groups (except theater companies, dance companies, musical groups, and artists) primarily engaged in producing live theatrical presentations.

Illustrative Examples:

Carnival traveling shows
Circuses
Ice skating companies
Magic shows

Cross-References.

- Establishments, such as comedy clubs or nightclubs, primarily engaged in providing food and beverages for consumption on the premises and that also present live nontheatrical entertainment are classified in Subsector 722, Food Services and Drinking Places;
- Establishments primarily engaged in organizing, promoting, and/or managing ice skating shows, circuses, and other live performing arts presentations without producing their own shows are classified in Industry Group 7113, Promoters of Performing Arts, Sports, and Similar Events;
- Theater companies and groups (except dance) or dinner theaters engaged in producing musicals; plays; operas; and comedy, improvisational, mime, and puppet shows are classified in Industry 711110, Theater Companies and Dinner Theaters;
- Dance companies or groups are classified in Industry 711120, Dance Companies;
- Freelance producers and performing artists (except musicians and vocalists) are classified in Industry 711510, Independent Artists, Writers, and Performers; and
- Musical groups and independent musicians and vocalists are classified in Industry 711130, Musical Groups and Artists.

7112 Spectator Sports

71121 Spectator Sports

This industry comprises (1) sports teams or clubs primarily participating in live sporting events before a paying audience; (2) establishments primarily engaged in operating racetracks; (3) independent athletes engaged in participating in live sporting or racing events before a paying audience; (4) owners of racing participants,

---

US—United States industry only. CAN—United States and Canadian industries are comparable. MEX—United States and Mexican industries are comparable. Blank—Canadian, Mexican, and United States industries are comparable.

such as cars, dogs, and horses, primarily engaged in entering them in racing events or other spectator sports events; and (5) establishments, such as sports trainers, primarily engaged in providing specialized services to support participants in sports events or competitions. The sports teams and clubs included in this industry may or may not operate their own arena, stadium, or other facility for presenting their games or other spectator sports events.

Cross-References.

- Establishments primarily engaged in promoting sporting events without participating in sporting events are classified in Industry Group 7113, Promoters of Performing Arts, Sports, and Similar Events;
- Establishments, such as youth league baseball teams, primarily engaged in participating in sporting events for recreational purposes without playing before a paying audience are classified in Industry 71399, All Other Amusement and Recreation Industries;
- Amateur, semiprofessional, or professional athletic associations or leagues are classified in Industry 81399, Other Similar Organizations (except Business, Professional, Labor, and Political Organizations);
- Establishments primarily engaged in representing or managing the careers of sports figures are classified in Industry 71141, Agents and Managers for Artists, Athletes, Entertainers, and Other Public Figures;
- Independent athletes engaged in providing sports instruction without participating in sporting events before a paying audience are classified in Industry 61162, Sports and Recreation Instruction;
- Independent athletes exclusively engaged in endorsing products or making speeches are classified in Industry 71151, Independent Artists, Writers, and Performers; and
- Establishments primarily engaged in raising horses, mules, donkeys, and other equines are classified in Industry 11292, Horses and Other Equine Production.

711211 Sports Teams and Clubs[CAN]

This U.S. industry comprises professional or semiprofessional sports teams or clubs primarily engaged in participating in live sporting events, such as baseball, basketball, football, hockey, soccer, and jai alai games, before a paying audience. These establishments may or may not operate their own arena, stadium, or other facility for presenting these events.

US—United States industry only. CAN—United States and Canadian industries are comparable. MEX—United States and Mexican industries are comparable. Blank—Canadian, Mexican, and United States industries are comparable.

Cross-References.

- Establishments primarily engaged in promoting sporting events without participating in sporting events are classified in Industry Group 7113, Promoters of Performing Arts, Sports, and Similar Events;
- Establishments, such as youth league baseball teams, primarily engaged in participating in sporting events for recreational purposes without playing before a paying audience are classified in Industry 713990, All Other Amusement and Recreation Industries; and
- Amateur, semiprofessional, or professional athletic associations or leagues are classified in Industry 813990, Other Similar Organizations (except Business, Professional, Labor, and Political Organizations).

711212 Racetracks[US]

This U.S. industry comprises establishments primarily engaged in operating racetracks. These establishments may also present and /or promote the events, such as auto, dog, and horse races, held in these facilities.

Cross-References.

Owners of racing participants, such as cars, dogs, and horses, primarily engaged in entering them in racing events; trainers of racing participants; and independent athletes, such as jockeys and race car drivers, primarily engaged in participating in racing events are classified in U.S. Industry 711219, Other Spectator Sports.

711219 Other Spectator Sports[US]

This U.S. industry comprises (1) independent athletes, such as professional or semiprofessional golfers, boxers, and race car drivers, primarily engaged in participating in live sporting or racing events before a paying audience; (2) owners of racing participants, such as cars, dogs, and horses, primarily engaged in entering them in racing events or other spectator events; and (3) establishments, such as sports trainers, primarily engaged in providing specialized services required to support participants in sports events or competitions.

Cross-References.

- Establishments primarily engaged in operating racetracks are classified in U.S. Industry 711212, Racetracks;
- Establishments primarily engaged in representing or managing the careers of sports figures are classified in Industry 711410, Agents and Managers for Artists, Athletes, Entertainers, and Other Public Figures;

US—United States industry only. CAN—United States and Canadian industries are comparable. MEX—United States and Mexican industries are comparable. Blank—Canadian, Mexican, and United States industries are comparable.

- Independent athletes engaged in providing sports instruction without participating in sporting events before a paying audience are classified in Industry 611620, Sports and Recreation Instruction;
- Independent athletes exclusively engaged in endorsing products or making speeches are classified in Industry 711510, Independent Artists, Writers, and Performers; and
- Establishments primarily engaged in raising horses, mules, donkeys, and other equines are classified in Industry 112920, Horses and Other Equine Production.

7113 Promoters of Performing Arts, Sports, and Similar Events

71131 Promoters of Performing Arts, Sports, and Similar Events with Facilities

See industry description for 711310 below.

711310 Promoters of Performing Arts, Sports, and Similar Events with Facilities[US]

This industry comprises establishments primarily engaged in (1) organizing, promoting, and/or managing live performing arts productions, sports events, and similar events, such as state fairs, county fairs, agricultural fairs, concerts, and festivals, held in facilities that they manage and operate and/or (2) managing and providing the staff to operate arenas, stadiums, theaters, or other related facilities for rent to other promoters.

Cross-References. Establishments primarily engaged in—

- Producing live performances (but may also promote the performances and/or operate the facilities where the performances take place)—are classified in Industry Group 7111, Performing Arts Companies;
- Operating racetracks (but may also promote the events held in these facilities)—are classified in U.S. Industry 711212, Racetracks;
- Presenting sporting events (but may also promote these sporting events and/or operate the stadiums or arenas where the sporting events take place)—are classified in U.S. Industry 711211, Sports Teams and Clubs;
- Organizing, promoting, and/or managing conventions, conferences, and trade shows (but may also operate the facilities where these events take place)—are classified in Industry 561920, Convention and Trade Show Organizers;

US—United States industry only. CAN—United States and Canadian industries are comparable. MEX—United States and Mexican industries are comparable. Blank—Canadian, Mexican, and United States industries are comparable.

- Organizing, promoting, and/or managing performing arts productions, sports events, and similar events in facilities managed and operated by others—are classified in Industry 711320 Promoters of Performing Arts, Sports, and Similar Events without Facilities; and
- Leasing stadiums, arenas, theaters, and other related facilities to others without operating the facilities—are classified in Industry 531120, Lessors of Nonresidential Buildings (except Miniwarehouses).

71132 Promoters of Performing Arts, Sports, and Similar Events without Facilities

See industry description for 711320 below.

711320 Promoters of Performing Arts, Sports, and Similar Events without Facilities[MEX]

This industry comprises promoters primarily engaged in organizing, promoting, and/or managing live performing arts productions, sports events, and similar events, such as state fairs, county fairs, agricultural fairs, concerts, and festivals, in facilities that are managed and operated by others. Theatrical (except motion picture) booking agencies are included in this industry.

Cross-References. Establishments primarily engaged in—

- Booking motion pictures or videos—are classified in U.S. Industry 512199, Other Motion Picture and Video Industries;
- Producing live performances (but may also promote the performances)—are classified in Industry Group 7111, Performing Arts Companies;
- Operating racetracks (but may also promote the events held in these facilities)—are classified in U.S. Industry 711212, Racetracks;
- Presenting sporting events (but may also promote these events)—are classified in U.S. Industry 711211, Sports Teams and Clubs;
- Organizing, promoting, and/or managing conventions, conferences, and trade shows (but may also operate the facilities where these events take place)—are classified in Industry 561920, Convention and Trade Show Organizers;
- Organizing, promoting, and/or managing performing arts, sports, and similar events in facilities they manage or operate—are classified in Industry 711310, Promoters of Performing Arts, Sports, and Similar Events with Facilities; and

US—United States industry only. CAN—United States and Canadian industries are comparable. MEX—United States and Mexican industries are comparable. Blank—Canadian, Mexican, and United States industries are comparable.

- Operating amateur, semiprofessional, or professional athletic associations or leagues—are classified in Industry 813990, Other Similar Organizations (except Business, Professional, Labor, and Political Organizations).

7114 Agents and Managers for Artists, Athletes, Entertainers, and Other Public Figures

71141 Agents and Managers for Artists, Athletes, Entertainers, and Other Public Figures

See industry description for 711410 below.

711410 Agents and Managers for Artists, Athletes, Entertainers, and Other Public Figures

This industry comprises establishments of agents and managers primarily engaged in representing and/or managing creative and performing artists, sports figures, entertainers, and other public figures. The representation and management includes activities, such as representing clients in contract negotiations; managing or organizing client's financial affairs; and generally promoting the careers of their clients.

Illustrative Examples:

Celebrity agents or managers
Literary agents
Modeling agents
Sports figure agents or managers
Talent agents

Cross-References.

- Establishments primarily engaged in supplying models to clients are classified in Industry 561320, Temporary Help Services; and
- Establishments known as model registries primarily engaged in recruiting and placing models for clients are classified in Industry 561310, Employment Placement Agencies.

7115 Independent Artists, Writers, and Performers

71151 Independent Artists, Writers, and Performers

See industry description for 711510 below.

711510 Independent Artists, Writers, and Performers

This industry comprises independent (i.e., freelance) individuals primarily engaged in performing in artistic productions, in creating artistic and cultural works

US—United States industry only. CAN—United States and Canadian industries are comparable. MEX—United States and Mexican industries are comparable. Blank—Canadian, Mexican, and United States industries are comparable.

or productions, or in providing technical expertise necessary for these productions. This industry also includes athletes and other celebrities exclusively engaged in endorsing products and making speeches or public appearances for which they receive a fee.

Illustrative Examples:

Independent actors or actresses
Independent art restorers
Independent artists (except musical, commercial, or medical)
Independent cartoonists
Independent dancers
Independent journalists
Independent producers
Independent recording technicians
Independent speakers
Independent theatrical costume designers
Independent theatrical lighting technicians

Cross-References.

- Freelance musicians and vocalists—are classified in Industry 711130, Musical Groups and Artists;
- Independent commercial artists and graphic designers—are classified in Industry 541430, Graphic Design Services; and
- Artisans and craftspersons—are classified in the Sector 31-33, Manufacturing.

712 Museums, Historical Sites, and Similar Institutions

Industries in the Museums, Historical Sites, and Similar Institutions subsector engage in the preservation and exhibition of objects, sites, and natural wonders of historical, cultural, and/or educational value.

7121 Museums, Historical Sites, and Similar Institutions

71211 Museums

See industry description for 712110 below.

712110 Museums[US]

This industry comprises establishments primarily engaged in the preservation and exhibition of objects of historical, cultural, and/or educational value.

Illustrative Examples:

Art galleries (except retail)
Art museums
Halls of fame
Planetariums
Science or technology museums
Wax museums

US—United States industry only. CAN—United States and Canadian industries are comparable. MEX—United States and Mexican industries are comparable. Blank—Canadian, Mexican, and United States industries are comparable.

Cross-References.

Commercial art galleries primarily engaged in selling art objects are classified in Industry 453920, Art Dealers.

71212 Historical Sites

See industry description for 712120 below.

712120 Historical Sites

This industry comprises establishments primarily engaged in the preservation and exhibition of sites, buildings, forts, or communities that describe events or persons of particular historical interest. Archeological sites, battlefields, historical ships, and pioneer villages are included in this industry.

71213 Zoos and Botanical Gardens

See industry description for 712130 below.

712130 Zoos and Botanical Gardens[CAN]

This industry comprises establishments primarily engaged in the preservation and exhibition of live plant and animal life displays.

Illustrative Examples:

Aquariums
Arboreta
Aviaries
Wild animal parks
Zoological gardens

71219 Nature Parks and Other Similar Institutions

See industry description for 712190 below.

712190 Nature Parks and Other Similar Institutions

This industry comprises establishments primarily engaged in the preservation and exhibition of natural areas or settings.

Illustrative Examples:

Bird or wildlife sanctuaries
Conservation areas
Natural wonder (e.g., cavern, waterfall) tourist attractions
Nature centers or preserves
National parks

US—United States industry only. CAN—United States and Canadian industries are comparable. MEX—United States and Mexican industries are comparable. Blank—Canadian, Mexican, and United States industries are comparable.

Cross-References.

Establishments primarily engaged in operating commercial hunting or fishing preserves (e.g., game farms) are classified in Industry 114210, Hunting and Trapping.

713 Amusement, Gambling, and Recreation Industries

Industries in the Amusement, Gambling, and Recreation Industries subsector (1) operate facilities where patrons can primarily engage in sports, recreation, amusement, or gambling activities and/or (2) provide other amusement and recreation services, such as supplying and servicing amusement devices in places of business operated by others; operating sports teams, clubs, or leagues engaged in playing games for recreational purposes; and guiding tours without using transportation equipment.

This subsector does not cover all establishments providing recreational services. Other sectors of NAICS also provide recreational services. Providers of recreational services are often engaged in processes classified in other sectors of NAICS. For example, operators of resorts and hunting and fishing camps provide both accommodation and recreational facilities and services. These establishments are classified in Subsector 721, Accommodation, partly to reflect the significant costs associated with the provision of accommodation services and partly to ensure consistency with international standards. Likewise, establishments using transportation equipment to provide recreational and entertainment services, such as those operating sightseeing buses, dinner cruises, or helicopter rides, are classified in Subsector 48-49, Transportation and Warehousing.

The industry groups in this subsector highlight particular types of activities: amusement parks and arcades, gambling industries, and other amusement and recreation industries. The groups, however, are not all inclusive of the activity. The Gambling Industries industry group does not provide for full coverage of gambling activities. For example, casino hotels are classified in Subsector 721, Accommodation; and horse and dog racing tracks are classified in Industry Group 7112, Spectator Sports.

7131 Amusement Parks and Arcades

This industry group comprises establishments primarily engaged in operating amusement parks and amusement arcades and parlors.

71311 Amusement and Theme Parks

See industry description for 713110 below.

US—United States industry only. CAN—United States and Canadian industries are comparable. MEX—United States and Mexican industries are comparable. Blank—Canadian, Mexican, and United States industries are comparable.

713110 Amusement and Theme Parks[CAN]

This industry comprises establishments, known as amusement or theme parks, primarily engaged in operating a variety of attractions, such as mechanical rides, water rides, games, shows, theme exhibits, refreshment stands, and picnic grounds. These establishments may lease space to others on a concession basis.

Cross-References. Establishments primarily engaged in—

- Operating mechanical or water rides on a concession basis in amusement parks, fairs, and carnivals or in operating a single attraction, such as a waterslide—are classified in Industry 713990, All Other Amusement and Recreation Industries;
- Operating refreshment stands on a concession basis—are classified in Industry Group 7222, Limited-Service Eating Places;
- Supplying and servicing coin-operated amusement (except gambling) devices in other's facilities—are classified in Industry 713990, All Other Amusement and Recreation Industries;
- Supplying and servicing coin-operated gambling devices (e.g., slot machines) in places of business operated by others—are classified in Industry 713290, Other Gambling Industries; and
- Organizing, promoting, and/or managing events, such as carnivals and fairs, with or without facilities—are classified in Industry Group 7113, Promoters of Performing Arts, Sports, and Similar Events.

71312 Amusement Arcades

See industry description for 713120 below.

713120 Amusement Arcades

This industry comprises establishments primarily engaged in operating amusement (except gambling, billiard, or pool) arcades and parlors.

Cross-References. Establishments primarily engaged in—

- Supplying and servicing coin-operated amusement (except gambling) devices in places of business operated by others or in operating billiard or pool parlors—are classified in Industry 713990, All Other Amusement and Recreation Industries;
- Operating bingo, off-track betting, or slot machine parlors or in supplying and servicing coin-operated gambling devices (e.g., slot machines or video

US—United States industry only. CAN—United States and Canadian industries are comparable. MEX—United States and Mexican industries are comparable. Blank—Canadian, Mexican, and United States industries are comparable.

gambling terminals) in places of business operated by others—are classified in Industry 713290, Other Gambling Industries;

- Operating casinos (except casino hotels)—are classified in Industry 713210, Casinos (except Casino Hotels); and
- Operating casino hotels—are classified in Industry 721120, Casino Hotels.

7132 Gambling Industries

This industry group comprises establishments (except casino hotels) primarily engaged in operating gambling facilities, such as casinos, bingo halls, and video gaming terminals, or in the provision of gambling services, such as lotteries and off-track betting. Casino hotels are classified in Industry 72112, Casino Hotels.

71321 Casinos (except Casino Hotels)

See industry description for 713210 below.

713210 Casinos (except Casino Hotels)

This industry comprises establishments primarily engaged in operating gambling facilities that offer table wagering games along with other gambling activities, such as slot machines and sports betting. These establishments often provide food and beverage services. Included in this industry are floating casinos (i.e., gambling cruises, riverboat casinos).

Cross-References. Establishments primarily engaged in—

- Operating bingo, off-track betting, or slot machine parlors or in supplying and servicing coin-operated gambling devices, such as slot machines and video gaming terminals in places of business operated by others—are classified in Industry 713290, Other Gambling Industries; and
- Operating casino hotels—are classified in Industry 721120, Casino Hotels.

71329 Other Gambling Industries

See industry description for 713290 below.

713290 Other Gambling Industries[US]

This industry comprises establishments primarily engaged in operating gambling facilities (except casinos or casino hotels) or providing gambling services.

US—United States industry only. CAN—United States and Canadian industries are comparable. MEX—United States and Mexican industries are comparable. Blank—Canadian, Mexican, and United States industries are comparable.

Illustrative Examples:

- Bingo, off-track betting, or slot machine parlors
- Bookmakers
- Card rooms (e.g., poker rooms)
- Coin-operated gambling device concession operators (i.e., supplying and servicing in other's facilities)
- Lottery ticket sales agents (except retail stores)

Cross-References. Establishments primarily engaged in—

- Operating casinos—are classified in Industry 713210, Casinos (except Casino Hotels);
- Operating casino hotels—are classified in Industry 721120, Casino Hotels;
- Operating facilities with coin-operated nongambling amusement devices—are classified in Industry 713120, Amusement Arcades;
- Supplying and servicing coin-operated nongambling amusement devices in places of business operated by others—are classified in Industry 713990, All Other Amusement and Recreation Industries; and
- Operating racetracks or presenting live racing or sporting events—are classified in Industry 71121, Spectator Sports.

7139 Other Amusement and Recreation Industries

71391 Golf Courses and Country Clubs

See industry description for 713910 below.

713910 Golf Courses and Country Clubs

This industry comprises (1) establishments primarily engaged in operating golf courses (except miniature) and (2) establishments primarily engaged in operating golf courses, along with dining facilities and other recreational facilities that are known as country clubs. These establishments often provide food and beverage services, equipment rental services, and golf instruction services.

Cross-References. Establishments primarily engaged in—

- Operating driving ranges and miniature golf courses—are classified in Industry 713990, All Other Amusement and Recreation Industries; and
- Operating resorts where golf facilities are combined with accommodations—are classified in Industry Group 7211, Traveler Accommodation.

US—United States industry only. CAN—United States and Canadian industries are comparable. MEX—United States and Mexican industries are comparable. Blank—Canadian, Mexican, and United States industries are comparable.

71392 Skiing Facilities

See industry description for 713920 below.

713920 Skiing Facilities

This industry comprises establishments engaged in (1) operating downhill, cross-country, or related skiing areas and/or (2) operating equipment, such as ski lifts and tows. These establishments often provide food and beverage services, equipment rental services, and ski instruction services. Four-season resorts without accommodations are included in this industry.

Cross-References.

Establishments primarily engaged in operating resorts where skiing facilities are combined with accommodations are classified in Industry Group 7211, Traveler Accommodation.

71393 Marinas

See industry description for 713930 below.

713930 Marinas

This industry comprises establishments, commonly known as marinas, engaged in operating docking and/or storage facilities for pleasure craft owners, with or without one or more related activities, such as retailing fuel and marine supplies; and repairing, maintaining, or renting pleasure boats.

Cross-References. Establishments primarily engaged in—

- Renting pleasure boats—are classified in U.S. Industry 532292, Recreational Goods Rental;
- Repairing pleasure boats—are classified in Industry 811490, Other Personal and Household Goods Repair and Maintenance;
- Retailing marine supplies—are classified in U.S. Industry 441222, Boat Dealers; and
- Retailing fuel for boats—are classified in Industry 447190, Other Gasoline Stations.

71394 Fitness and Recreational Sports Centers

See industry description for 713940 below.

US—United States industry only. CAN—United States and Canadian industries are comparable. MEX—United States and Mexican industries are comparable. Blank—Canadian, Mexican, and United States industries are comparable.

713940 Fitness and Recreational Sports Centers[CAN]

This industry comprises establishments primarily engaged in operating fitness and recreational sports facilities featuring exercise and other active physical fitness conditioning or recreational sports activities, such as swimming, skating, or racquet sports.

Illustrative Examples:

- Aerobic dance or exercise centers
- Gymnasiums
- Handball, racquetball, or tennis club facilities
- Ice or roller skating rinks
- Physical fitness centers
- Swimming or wave pools

Cross-References.

- Establishments primarily engaged in providing nonmedical services to assist clients in attaining or maintaining a desired weight are classified in U.S. Industry 812191, Diet and Weight Reducing Centers;
- Establishments primarily engaged in operating health resorts and spas where recreational facilities—are combined with accommodations are classified in Industry 721110, Hotels (except Casino Hotels) and Motels; and
- Recreational sports clubs (i.e., sports teams) not operating sports facilities—instructional) are classified in Industry 713990, All Other Amusement and Recreation Industries.

71395 Bowling Centers

See industry description for 713950 below.

713950 Bowling Centers

This industry comprises establishments engaged in operating bowling centers. These establishments often provide food and beverage services.

71399 All Other Amusement and Recreation Industries

See industry description for 713990 below.

713990 All Other Amusement and Recreation Industries[CAN]

This industry comprises establishments (except amusement parks and arcades; gambling industries; golf courses and country clubs; skiing facilities; marinas;

US—United States industry only. CAN—United States and Canadian industries are comparable. MEX—United States and Mexican industries are comparable. Blank—Canadian, Mexican, and United States industries are comparable.

fitness and recreational sports centers; and bowling centers) primarily engaged in providing recreational and amusement services.

Illustrative Examples:

Amusement ride or coin-operated nongambling amusement device concession operators (i.e., supplying or servicing in others facilities)
Archery or shooting ranges
Billiard or pool parlors
Boating clubs (without marinas)
Dance halls
Miniature golf courses
Recreational day camps (except instructional)
Recreational or youth sports teams and leagues
Recreational sports clubs (i.e., sports teams) not operating facilities
Riding stables

Cross-References.

- Establishments primarily engaged in operating amusement parks and arcades are classified in Industry Group 7131, Amusement Parks and Arcades;
- Establishments primarily engaged in operating gambling facilities (except casino hotels) or providing gambling services are classified in Industry Group 7132, Gambling Industries;
- Establishments primarily engaged in operating casino hotels are classified in Industry 721120, Casino Hotels;
- Establishments primarily engaged in operating golf courses (except miniature) and country clubs are classified in Industry 713910, Golf Courses and Country Clubs;
- Establishments primarily engaged in operating skiing facilities without hotel accommodation are classified in Industry 713920, Skiing Facilities;
- Establishments primarily engaged in operating resorts where recreational facilities are combined with lodging are classified in Industry Group 7211, Traveler Accommodation;
- Establishments primarily engaged in operating marinas are classified in Industry 713930, Marinas;
- Establishments primarily engaged in operating fitness and recreational sports centers are classified in Industry 713940, Fitness and Recreational Sports Centers;
- Establishments primarily engaged in operating bowling centers are classified in Industry 713950, Bowling Centers;
- Establishments primarily engaged in operating instructional camps, such as sports camps, fine arts camps, and computer camps, are classified in Sector 61, Educational Services, based on the nature of instruction;

US—United States industry only. CAN—United States and Canadian industries are comparable. MEX—United States and Mexican industries are comparable. Blank—Canadian, Mexican, and United States industries are comparable.

- Independent athletes engaged in participating in sporting events before a paying audience are classified in U.S. Industry 711219, Other Spectator Sports;
- Independent athletes engaged in providing sports instruction without participating in sporting events before a paying audience are classified in Industry 611620, Sports and Recreation Instruction;
- Independent athletes exclusively engaged in endorsing products or making speeches are classified in Industry 711510, Independent Artists, Writers, and Performers;
- Establishments primarily engaged in providing scenic and sightseeing transportation are classified in Subsector 487, Scenic and Sightseeing Transportation;
- Aviation clubs primarily engaged in providing specialty air and flying services are classified in U.S. Industry 481219, Other Nonscheduled Air Transportation;
- Aviation clubs primarily engaged in advocating social and political causes are classified in U.S. Industry 813319, Other Social Advocacy Organizations; and
- Amateur, semiprofessional, or professional athletic associations or leagues are classified in Industry 813990, Other Similar Organizations (except Business, Professional, Labor, and Political Organizations).

US—United States industry only. CAN—United States and Canadian industries are comparable. MEX—United States and Mexican industries are comparable. Blank—Canadian, Mexican, and United States industries are comparable.

Sector 72—Accommodation and Food Services

The Sector as a Whole

The Accommodation and Food Services sector comprises establishments providing customers with lodging and/or preparing meals, snacks, and beverages for immediate consumption. The sector includes both accommodation and food services establishments because the two activities are often combined at the same establishment.

Excluded from this sector are civic and social organizations; amusement and recreation parks; theaters; and other recreation or entertainment facilities providing food and beverage services.

721 Accommodation

Industries in the Accommodation subsector provide lodging or short-term accommodations for travelers, vacationers, and others. There is a wide range of establishments in these industries. Some provide lodging only; while others provide meals, laundry services, and recreational facilities, as well as lodging. Lodging establishments are classified in this subsector even if the provision of complementary services generates more revenue. The types of complementary services provided vary from establishment to establishment.

The subsector is organized into three industry groups: (1) traveler accommodation, (2) recreational accommodation, and (3) rooming and boarding houses. The Traveler Accommodation industry group includes establishments that primarily provide traditional types of lodging services. This group includes hotels, motels, and bed and breakfast inns. In addition to lodging, these establishments may provide a range of other services to their guests. The RV (Recreational Vehicle) Parks and Recreational Camps industry group includes establishments that operate lodging facilities primarily designed to accommodate outdoor enthusiasts. Included are travel trailer campsites, recreational vehicle parks, and outdoor adventure retreats. The Rooming and Boarding Houses industry group includes establishments providing temporary or longer-term accommodations, which for the period of occupancy, may serve as a principal residence. Board (i.e., meals) may be provided but is not essential.

Establishments that manage short-stay accommodation establishments (e.g., hotels and motels) on a contractual basis are classified in this subsector if they both manage the operation and provide the operating staff. Such establishments are classified based on the type of facility managed and operated.

7211 Traveler Accommodation

72111 Hotels (except Casino Hotels) and Motels

See industry description for 721110 below.

US—United States industry only. CAN—United States and Canadian industries are comparable. MEX—United States and Mexican industries are comparable. Blank—Canadian, Mexican, and United States industries are comparable.

721110 Hotels (except Casino Hotels) and Motels[US]

This industry comprises establishments primarily engaged in providing short-term lodging in facilities known as hotels, motor hotels, resort hotels, and motels. The establishments in this industry may offer food and beverage services, recreational services, conference rooms and convention services, laundry services, parking, and other services.

Cross-References. Establishments primarily engaged in—

- Providing short-term lodging with a casino on the premises—are classified in Industry 721120, Casino Hotels; and
- Providing short-term lodging in facilities known as bed-and-breakfast inns, youth hostels, housekeeping cabins and cottages, and tourist homes—are classified in Industry 72119, Other Traveler Accommodation.

72112 Casino Hotels

See industry description for 721120 below.

721120 Casino Hotels

This industry comprises establishments primarily engaged in providing short-term lodging in hotel facilities with a casino on the premises. The casino on premises includes table wagering games and may include other gambling activities, such as slot machines and sports betting. These establishments generally offer a range of services and amenities, such as food and beverage services, entertainment, valet parking, swimming pools, and conference and convention facilities.

Cross-References. Establishments primarily engaged in—

- Providing short-term lodging in facilities known as hotels and motels that provide limited gambling activities, such as slot machines, without a casino on the premises—are classified in Industry 721110, Hotels (except Casino Hotels) and Motels; and
- Operating as stand-alone casinos—are classified in Industry 713210, Casinos (except Casino Hotels).

72119 Other Traveler Accommodation

This industry comprises establishments primarily engaged in providing short-term lodging (except hotels, motels, and casino hotels).

US—United States industry only. CAN—United States and Canadian industries are comparable. MEX—United States and Mexican industries are comparable. Blank—Canadian, Mexican, and United States industries are comparable.

Illustrative Examples:

Bed-and-breakfast inns
Guest houses
Housekeeping cabins and cottages
Tourist homes
Youth hostels

Cross-References. Establishments primarily engaged in—

- Providing short-term lodging in facilities known as hotels without a casino on the premises—are classified in Industry 72111, Hotels (except Casino Hotels) and Motels; and
- Providing short-term lodging in facilities known as hotels with a casino on the premises—are classified in Industry 72112, Casino Hotels.

721191 Bed-and-Breakfast Inns[CAN]

This U.S. industry comprises establishments primarily engaged in providing short-term lodging in facilities known as bed-and-breakfast inns. These establishments provide short-term lodging in private homes or small buildings converted for this purpose. Bed-and-breakfast inns are characterized by a highly personalized service and inclusion of a full breakfast in a room rate.

721199 All Other Traveler Accommodation[US]

This U.S. industry comprises establishments primarily engaged in providing short-term lodging (except hotels, motels, casino hotels, and bed-and-breakfast inns).

Illustrative Examples:

Guest houses
Housekeeping cabins and cottages
Tourist homes
Youth hostels

Cross-References. Establishments primarily engaged in—

- Providing short-term lodging in facilities known as hotels without a casino on the premises—are classified in Industry 721110, Hotels (except Casino Hotels) and Motels;
- Providing short-term lodging in facilities known as hotels with a casino on the premises—are classified in Industry 721120, Casino Hotels; and
- Providing short-term lodging in establishments known as bed-and-breakfast inns—are classified in U.S. Industry 721191, Bed-and-Breakfast Inns.

US—United States industry only. CAN—United States and Canadian industries are comparable. MEX—United States and Mexican industries are comparable. Blank—Canadian, Mexican, and United States industries are comparable.

7212 RV (Recreational Vehicle) Parks and Recreational Camps

72121 RV (Recreational Vehicle) Parks and Recreational Camps

This industry comprises establishments primarily engaged in operating recreational vehicle parks and campgrounds and recreational and vacation camps. These establishments cater to outdoor enthusiasts and are characterized by the type of accommodation and by the nature and the range of recreational facilities and activities provided to their clients.

Illustrative Examples:

Fishing and hunting camps
Outdoor adventure retreats
Recreational vehicle parks
Travel trailer campsites
Vacation camps (except instructional, day)

Cross-References. Establishments primarily engaged in—

- Operating recreational facilities without accommodations—are classified in Subsector 713, Amusement, Gambling, and Recreation Industries;
- Operating instructional camps, such as sports camps, fine arts camps, and computer camps—are classified in Sector 61, Educational Services, based on the nature of instruction;
- Operating children's day camps (except instructional)—are classified in Industry 71399, All Other Amusement and Recreation Industries; and
- Acting as lessors of residential mobile home sites (i.e., trailer parks)—are classified in Industry 53119, Lessors of Other Real Estate Property.

721211 RV (Recreational Vehicle) Parks and Campgrounds[CAN]

This U.S. industry comprises establishments primarily engaged in operating sites to accommodate campers and their equipment, including tents, tent trailers, travel trailers, and RVs (recreational vehicles). These establishments may provide access to facilities, such as washrooms, laundry rooms, recreation halls and playgrounds, stores, and snack bars.

Cross-References. Establishments primarily engaged in—

- Operating recreational facilities without accommodations—are classified in Subsector 713, Amusement, Gambling, and Recreation Industries; and
- Acting as lessors of residential mobile home sites (i.e., trailer parks)—are classified in Industry 531190, Lessors of Other Real Estate Property.

US—United States industry only. CAN—United States and Canadian industries are comparable. MEX—United States and Mexican industries are comparable. Blank—Canadian, Mexican, and United States industries are comparable.

721214 Recreational and Vacation Camps (except Campgrounds)[US]

This U.S. industry comprises establishments primarily engaged in operating overnight recreational camps, such as children's camps, family vacation camps, hunting and fishing camps, and outdoor adventure retreats that offer trail riding, white-water rafting, hiking, and similar activities. These establishments provide accommodation facilities, such as cabins and fixed campsites, and other amenities, such as food services, recreational facilities and equipment, and organized recreational activities.

Illustrative Examples:

Fishing camps
Hunting camps
Outdoor adventure retreats
Vacation camps (except instructional, day)
Wilderness camps

Cross-References. Establishments primarily engaged in—

- Operating instructional camps, such as sports camps, fine arts camps, and computer camps—are classified in Sector 61, Educational Services, based on the nature of instruction; and
- Operating children's day camps (except instructional)—are classified in Industry 713990, All Other Amusement and Recreation Industries.

7213 Rooming and Boarding Houses

72131 Rooming and Boarding Houses

See industry description for 721310 below.

721310 Rooming and Boarding Houses[CAN]

This industry comprises establishments primarily engaged in operating rooming and boarding houses and similar facilities, such as fraternity houses, sorority houses, off-campus dormitories, residential clubs, and workers' camps. These establishments provide temporary or longer-term accommodations which, for the period of occupancy, may serve as a principal residence. These establishments also may provide complementary services, such as housekeeping, meals, and laundry services.

Illustrative Examples:

Dormitories (off campus)
Fraternity houses
Rooming houses
Sorority houses
Workers' camps

US—United States industry only. CAN—United States and Canadian industries are comparable. MEX—United States and Mexican industries are comparable. Blank—Canadian, Mexican, and United States industries are comparable.

722 Food Services and Drinking Places

Industries in the Food Services and Drinking Places subsector prepare meals, snacks, and beverages to customer order for immediate on-premises and off-premises consumption. There is a wide range of establishments in these industries. Some provide food and drink only; while others provide various combinations of seating space, waiter/waitress services and incidental amenities, such as limited entertainment. The industries in the subsector are grouped based on the type and level of services provided. The industry groups are full-service restaurants; limited-service eating places; special food services, such as food service contractors, caterers, and mobile food services; and drinking places.

Food services and drink activities at hotels and motels; amusement parks, theaters, casinos, country clubs, and similar recreational facilities; and civic and social organizations are included in this subsector only if these services are provided by a separate establishment primarily engaged in providing food and beverage services.

Excluded from this subsector are establishments operating dinner cruises. These establishments are classified in Subsector 487, Scenic and Sightseeing Transportation because those establishments utilize transportation equipment to provide scenic recreational entertainment.

7221 Full-Service Restaurants

This industry group comprises establishments primarily engaged in providing food services to patrons who order and are served while seated (i.e., waiter/waitress service) and pay after eating. Establishments that provide these types of food services to patrons with any combination of other services, such as takeout services, are classified in this industry.

72211 Full-Service Restaurants

See industry description for 722110 below.

722110 Full-Service Restaurants[CAN]

This industry comprises establishments primarily engaged in providing food services to patrons who order and are served while seated (i.e. waiter/waitress service) and pay after eating. These establishments may provide this type of food services to patrons in combination with selling alcoholic beverages, providing carry out services, or presenting live nontheatrical entertainment.

Cross-References. Establishments primarily engaged in—

- Providing food services where patrons generally order or select items and pay before eating—are classified in U.S. Industry 722211, Limited-Service Restaurants;

US—United States industry only. CAN—United States and Canadian industries are comparable. MEX—United States and Mexican industries are comparable. Blank—Canadian, Mexican, and United States industries are comparable.

- Selling a specialty snack or nonalcoholic beverage for consumption on or near the premises—are classified in U.S. Industry 722213, Snack and Nonalcoholic Beverage Bars;
- Preparing and serving alcoholic beverages and known as bars, taverns, or nightclubs—are classified in Industry 722410, Drinking Places (Alcoholic Beverages); and
- Presenting live theatrical productions and providing food and beverages for consumption on the premises—are classified in Industry 711110, Theater Companies and Dinner Theaters.

7222 Limited-Service Eating Places

This industry group comprises establishments primarily engaged in providing food services where patrons generally order or select items and pay before eating. Most establishments do not have waiter/waitress service, but some provide limited service, such as cooking to order (i.e., per special request), bringing food to seated customers, or providing off-site delivery.

72221 Limited-Service Eating Places

This industry comprises establishments primarily engaged in (1) providing food services where patrons generally order or select items and pay before eating or (2) selling a specialty snack or nonalcoholic beverage for consumption on or near the premises. Food and drink may be consumed on the premises, taken out, or delivered to the customer's location. Some establishments (except snack and nonalcoholic beverage bars) in this industry may provide these food services in combination with selling alcoholic beverages.

Illustrative Examples:

Cafeterias
Fast-food restaurants
Nonalcoholic beverage bars
Pizza delivery establishments
Snack bars (e.g., cookies, pretzels, popcorn)
Takeout eating places

Cross-References. Establishments primarily engaged in—

- Providing food services to patrons who order and are served while seated and pay after eating in combination with providing takeout service—are classified in Industry 72211, Full-Service Restaurants;
- Retailing confectionery goods and nuts not packaged for immediate consumption—are classified in Industry 44529, Other Specialty Food Stores;

US—United States industry only. CAN—United States and Canadian industries are comparable. MEX—United States and Mexican industries are comparable. Blank—Canadian, Mexican, and United States industries are comparable.

- Retailing baked goods (e.g., pretzels, doughnuts, cookies, and bagels) not baked on the premises and not for immediate consumption—are classified in Industry 44529, Other Specialty Food Stores;
- Retailing baked goods (e.g., doughnuts and bagels) and providing food services to patrons who order and are served while seated and pay after eating—are classified in Industry 72211, Full-Service Restaurants;
- Selling snacks and nonalcoholic beverages from mobile vehicles—are classified in Industry 72233, Mobile Food Services; and
- Preparing and serving alcoholic beverages and known as bars, taverns, or nightclubs—are classified in Industry 72241, Drinking Places (Alcoholic Beverages).

722211 Limited-Service Restaurants[US]

This U.S. industry comprises establishments primarily engaged in providing food services (except snack and nonalcoholic beverage bars) where patrons generally order or select items and pay before eating. Food and drink may be consumed on premises, taken out, or delivered to the customer's location. Some establishments in this industry may provide these food services in combination with selling alcoholic beverages.

Illustrative Examples:

Delicatessen restaurants
Family restaurants, limited service
Fast-food restaurants
Limited-service pizza parlors
Pizza delivery shops
Takeout eating places
Takeout sandwich shops

Cross-References. Establishments primarily engaged in—

- Preparing and serving meals for immediate consumption using cafeteria—style serving equipment, known as cafeterias—are classified in U.S. Industry 722212, Cafeterias;
- Providing food services to patrons who order and are served while seated and pay after eating—are classified in Industry 722110, Full-Service Restaurants;
- Selling a specialty snack (e.g., ice cream, frozen yogurt, candy, cookies) or nonalcoholic beverages, for consumption on or near the premises—are classified in U.S. Industry 722213, Snack and Nonalcoholic Beverage Bars;
- Retailing confectionery goods and nuts not packaged for immediate consumption—are classified in U.S. Industry 445292, Confectionery and Nut Stores;

US—United States industry only. CAN—United States and Canadian industries are comparable. MEX—United States and Mexican industries are comparable. Blank—Canadian, Mexican, and United States industries are comparable.

- Retailing baked goods (e.g., pretzels, doughnuts, cookies, and bagels) not baked on the premises and not for immediate consumption—are classified in U.S. Industry 445291, Baked Goods Stores;
- Preparing and serving alcoholic beverages, known as bars, taverns, or night-clubs—are classified in Industry 722410, Drinking Places (Alcoholic Beverages); and
- Selling baked goods (e.g., doughnuts and bagels) and providing food services to patrons who order and are served while seated and pay after eating—are classified in Industry 722110, Full-Service Restaurants.

722212 Cafeterias[US]

This U.S. industry comprises establishments, known as cafeterias, primarily engaged in preparing and serving meals for immediate consumption using cafeteria-style serving equipment, such as steam tables, a refrigerated area, and self-service nonalcoholic beverage dispensing equipment. Patrons select from food and drink items on display in a continuous cafeteria line.

Cross-References. Establishments primarily engaged in—

- Providing food services to patrons who order and are served while seated and pay after eating—are classified in Industry 722110, Full-Service Restaurants; and
- Providing food services where patrons generally order or select items and pay before eating—are classified in U.S. Industry 722211, Limited-Service Restaurants.

722213 Snack and Nonalcoholic Beverage Bars[US]

This U.S. industry comprises establishments primarily engaged in (1) preparing and/or serving a specialty snack, such as ice cream, frozen yogurt, cookies, or popcorn or (2) serving nonalcoholic beverages, such as coffee, juices, or sodas for consumption on or near the premises. These establishments may carry and sell a combination of snack, nonalcoholic beverage, and other related products (e.g., coffee beans, mugs, coffee makers) but generally promote and sell a unique snack or nonalcoholic beverage.

Illustrative Examples:

Beverage bars
Carryout service bagel shops with on-premises baking
Carryout service cookie shops with on-premises baking
Carryout service donut shops with on-premises baking
Carryout service pretzel shops with on-premises baking
Ice cream parlors

US—United States industry only. CAN—United States and Canadian industries are comparable. MEX—United States and Mexican industries are comparable. Blank—Canadian, Mexican, and United States industries are comparable.

Cross-References. Establishments primarily engaged in—

- Selling one or more of the following food specialties: hamburgers, hot dogs, pizza, chicken, specialty cuisines—are classified in U.S. Industry 722211, Limited-Service Restaurants or Industry 722110, Full-Service Restaurants, based on type of food services provided to patrons;
- Preparing and serving snacks and nonalcoholic beverages from mobile vehicles—are classified in Industry 722330, Mobile Food Services;
- Retailing confectionery goods and nuts not packaged for immediate consumption—are classified in U.S. Industry 445292, Confectionery and Nut Stores;
- Retailing baked goods (e.g., pretzels, doughnuts, cookies, and bagels) not baked on the premises and not for immediate consumption—are classified in U.S. Industry 445291, Baked Goods Stores; and
- Retailing baked goods (e.g., doughnuts and bagels) and providing food services to patrons who order and are served while seated and pay after eating—are classified in Industry 722110, Full-Service Restaurants.

7223 Special Food Services

This industry group comprises establishments primarily engaged in providing food services at one or more of the following: (1) the customer's location; (2) a location designated by the customer; or (3) from motorized vehicles or nonmotorized carts.

72231 Food Service Contractors

See industry description for 722310 below.

722310 Food Service Contractors

This industry comprises establishments primarily engaged in providing food services at institutional, governmental, commercial, or industrial locations of others based on contractual arrangements with these type of organizations for a specified period of time. The establishments of this industry provide food services for the convenience of the contracting organization or the contracting organization's customers. The contractual arrangement of these establishments with contracting organizations may vary from type of facility operated (e.g., cafeteria, restaurant, fast-food eating place), revenue sharing, cost structure, to providing personnel. Management staff is always provided by the food service contractors.

US—United States industry only. CAN—United States and Canadian industries are comparable. MEX—United States and Mexican industries are comparable. Blank—Canadian, Mexican, and United States industries are comparable.

Illustrative Examples:

Airline food service contractors
Cafeteria food service contractors (e.g., at schools, hospitals, government offices)
Food concession contractors (e.g., at sporting, entertainment, convention facilities)

Cross-References. Establishments primarily engaged in—

- Providing food services on a single-event basis—are classified in Industry 722320, Caterers; and
- Supplying and servicing food vending machines—are classified in Industry 454210, Vending Machine Operators.

72232 Caterers

See industry description for 722320 below.

722320 Caterers

This industry comprises establishments primarily engaged in providing single event-based food services. These establishments generally have equipment and vehicles to transport meals and snacks to events and/or prepare food at an off-premise site. Banquet halls with catering staff are included in this industry. Examples of events catered by establishments in this industry are graduation parties, wedding receptions, business or retirement luncheons, and trade shows.

Cross-References. Establishments primarily engaged in—

- Preparing and serving meals and snacks for immediate consumption from motorized vehicles or nonmotorized carts—are classified in Industry 722330, Mobile Food Services;
- Providing food services at institutional, governmental, commercial, or industrial locations of others (e.g., airline contractors, industrial caterers) or providing food services based on contractual arrangements for a specified period of time—are classified in Industry 722310, Food Service Contractors; and
- Renting out facilities without providing catering staff—are classified in Industry 531120, Lessors of Nonresidential Buildings (except Miniwarehouses).

72233 Mobile Food Services

See industry description for 722330 below.

US—United States industry only. CAN—United States and Canadian industries are comparable. MEX—United States and Mexican industries are comparable. Blank—Canadian, Mexican, and United States industries are comparable.

722330 Mobile Food Services

This industry comprises establishments primarily engaged in preparing and serving meals and snacks for immediate consumption from motorized vehicles or nonmotorized carts. The establishment is the central location from which the caterer route is serviced, not each vehicle or cart. Included in this industry are establishments primarily engaged in providing food services from vehicles, such as hot dog carts, and ice cream trucks.

Illustrative Examples:

Ice cream truck vendors
Mobile canteens
Mobile food carts
Mobile food concession stands
Mobile refreshment stands
Mobile snack stand

Cross-References. Establishments primarily engaged in—

- Providing food services where patrons generally order or select items and pay before eating—are classified in U.S. Industry 722211, Limited-Service Restaurants;
- Selling unprepared foods, such as vegetables, melons, and nuts or fruit from carts—are classified in Industry 454390, Other Direct Selling Establishments;
- Selling specialty snacks (e.g., ice cream, frozen yogurt, cookies, popcorn) or nonalcoholic beverages in nonmobile facilities for consumption on or near the premises—are classified in U.S. Industry 722213, Snack and Nonalcoholic Beverage Bars;
- Selling food specialties, such as hamburgers, hot dogs, chicken, pizza, or specialty cuisines from nonmobile facilities—are classified in U.S. Industry 722211, Limited-Service Restaurants or Industry 722110, Full-Service Restaurants based on type of food services provided to patrons; and
- Operating as street vendors (except food)—are classified in Industry 454390, Other Direct Selling Establishments.

7224 Drinking Places (Alcoholic Beverages)

This industry group comprises establishments primarily engaged in preparing and serving alcoholic beverages for immediate consumption.

72241 Drinking Places (Alcoholic Beverages)

See industry description for 722410 below.

US—United States industry only. CAN—United States and Canadian industries are comparable. MEX—United States and Mexican industries are comparable. Blank—Canadian, Mexican, and United States industries are comparable.

722410 Drinking Places (Alcoholic Beverages)[CAN]

This industry comprises establishments known as bars, taverns, nightclubs, or drinking places primarily engaged in preparing and serving alcoholic beverages for immediate consumption. These establishments may also provide limited food services.

Cross-References. Establishments primarily engaged in—

- Preparing and serving alcoholic beverages (i.e. not known as bars or taverns) and providing food services to patrons who order and are served while seated and pay after eating—are classified in Industry 722110, Full-Service Restaurants
- Preparing and serving alcoholic beverages (i.e. not known as bars or taverns) and providing food services to patrons who generally order or select items and pay before eating—are classified in Industry 722211, Limited-Service Restaurants
- Operating a civic or social association with a bar for the association members—are classified in Industry 81341, Civic and Social Organizations;
- Retailing packaged alcoholic beverages not for immediate consumption on the premises—are classified in Industry 445310, Beer, Wine, and Liquor Stores; and
- Operating discotheques or dance clubs without selling alcoholic beverages—are classified in Industry 713990, All Other Amusement and Recreation Industries.

US—United States industry only. CAN—United States and Canadian industries are comparable. MEX—United States and Mexican industries are comparable. Blank—Canadian, Mexican, and United States industries are comparable.

Sector 81—Other Services (except Public Administration)

The Sector as a Whole

The Other Services (except Public Administration) sector comprises establishments engaged in providing services not specifically provided for elsewhere in the classification system. Establishments in this sector are primarily engaged in activities, such as equipment and machinery repairing, promoting or administering religious activities, grantmaking, advocacy, and providing drycleaning and laundry services, personal care services, death care services, pet care services, photofinishing services, temporary parking services, and dating services.

Private households that engage in employing workers on or about the premises in activities primarily concerned with the operation of the household are included in this sector.

Excluded from this sector are establishments primarily engaged in retailing new equipment and also performing repairs and general maintenance on equipment. These establishments are classified in Sector 44-45, Retail Trade.

811 Repair and Maintenance

Industries in the Repair and Maintenance subsector restore machinery, equipment, and other products to working order. These establishments also typically provide general or routine maintenance (i.e., servicing) on such products to ensure they work efficiently and to prevent breakdown and unnecessary repairs.

The NAICS structure for this subsector brings together most types of repair and maintenance establishments and categorizes them based on production processes (i.e., on the type of repair and maintenance activity performed, and the necessary skills, expertise, and processes that are found in different repair and maintenance establishments). This NAICS classification does not delineate between repair services provided to businesses versus those that serve households. Although some industries primarily serve either businesses or households, separation by class of customer is limited by the fact that many establishments serve both. Establishments repairing computers and consumer electronics products are two examples of such overlap.

The Repair and Maintenance subsector does not include all establishments that do repair and maintenance. For example, a substantial amount of repair is done by establishments that also manufacture machinery, equipment, and other goods. These establishments are included in the Manufacturing sector in NAICS. In addition, repair of transportation equipment is often provided by or based at transportation facilities, such as airports, seaports, and these activities are included

US—United States industry only. CAN—United States and Canadian industries are comparable. MEX—United States and Mexican industries are comparable. Blank—Canadian, Mexican, and United States industries are comparable.

in the Transportation and Warehousing sector. A particularly unique situation exists with repair of buildings. Plumbing, electrical installation and repair, painting and decorating, and other construction-related establishments are often involved in performing installation or other work on new construction as well as providing repair services on existing structures. While some specialize in repair, it is difficult to distinguish between the two types and all have been included in the Construction sector.

Excluded from this subsector are establishments primarily engaged in rebuilding or remanufacturing machinery and equipment. These are classified in Sector 31-33, Manufacturing. Also excluded are retail establishments that provide after-sale services and repair. These are classified in Sector 44-45, Retail Trade.

8111 Automotive Repair and Maintenance

This industry group comprises establishments involved in providing repair and maintenance services for automotive vehicles, such as passenger cars, trucks, and vans, and all trailers. Establishments in this industry group employ mechanics with specialized technical skills to diagnose and repair the mechanical and electrical systems for automotive vehicles, repair automotive interiors, and paint or repair automotive exteriors.

81111 Automotive Mechanical and Electrical Repair and Maintenance

This industry comprises establishments primarily engaged in providing mechanical or electrical repair and maintenance services for automotive vehicles, such as passenger cars, trucks and vans, and all trailers. These establishments specialize in or may provide a wide range of these services.

Cross-References. Establishments primarily engaged in—

- Retailing automotive vehicles and automotive parts and accessories and also providing automotive repair services—are classified in Subsector 441, Motor Vehicle and Parts Dealers;
- Retailing motor fuels and also providing automotive vehicle repair services—are classified in Industry Group 4471, Gasoline Stations;
- Changing motor oil and lubricating the chassis of automotive vehicles—are classified in Industry 81119, Other Automotive Repair and Maintenance;
- Providing automotive vehicle air-conditioning repair—are classified in Industry 81119, Other Automotive Repair and Maintenance; and
- Motorcycle repair and maintenance services—are classified in Industry 81149, Other Personal and Household Goods Repair and Maintenance.

US—United States industry only. CAN—United States and Canadian industries are comparable. MEX—United States and Mexican industries are comparable. Blank—Canadian, Mexican, and United States industries are comparable.

811111 General Automotive Repair[CAN]

This U.S. industry comprises establishments primarily engaged in providing (1) a wide range of mechanical and electrical repair and maintenance services for automotive vehicles, such as passenger cars, trucks, and vans, and all trailers or (2) engine repair and replacement.

Illustrative Examples:

Automobile repair garages (except gasoline service stations)
Automotive engine repair and replacement shops
General automotive repair shops

Cross-References. Establishments primarily engaged in—

- Retailing new automotive parts and accessories and also providing automotive repair services—are classified in Industry 441310, Automotive Parts and Accessories Stores;
- Changing motor oil and lubricating the chassis of automotive vehicles—are classified in U.S. Industry 811191, Automotive Oil Change and Lubrication Shops;
- Replacing and repairing automotive vehicle exhaust systems—are classified in U.S. Industry 811112, Automotive Exhaust System Repair;
- Replacing and repairing automotive vehicle transmissions—are classified in U.S. Industry 811113, Automotive Transmission Repair;
- Retailing motor fuels and also providing automotive vehicle repair services—are classified in Industry Group 4471, Gasoline Stations;
- Retailing automobiles and light trucks for highway use and also providing automotive repair services—are classified in Industry Group 4411, Automobile Dealers; and
- Motorcycle repair and maintenance services—are classified in Industry 811490, Other Personal and Household Goods Repair and Maintenance.

811112 Automotive Exhaust System Repair[CAN]

This U.S. industry comprises establishments primarily engaged in replacing or repairing exhaust systems of automotive vehicles, such as passenger cars, trucks, and vans.

Illustrative Examples:

Automotive exhaust system replacement and repair shops
Automotive muffler replacement and repair shops

US—United States industry only. CAN—United States and Canadian industries are comparable. MEX—United States and Mexican industries are comparable. Blank—Canadian, Mexican, and United States industries are comparable.

Cross-References.

Establishments primarily engaged in motorcycle repair and maintenance services are classified in Industry 811490, Other Personal and Household Goods Repair and Maintenance.

811113 Automotive Transmission Repair[US]

This U.S. industry comprises establishments primarily engaged in replacing or repairing transmissions of automotive vehicles, such as passenger cars, trucks, and vans.

Cross-References.

Establishments primarily engaged in motorcycle repair and maintenance services are classified in Industry 811490, Other Personal and Household Goods Repair and Maintenance.

811118 Other Automotive Mechanical and Electrical Repair and Maintenance[US]

This U.S. industry comprises establishments primarily engaged in providing specialized mechanical or electrical repair and maintenance services (except engine repair and replacement, exhaust systems repair, and transmission repair) for automotive vehicles, such as passenger cars, trucks, and vans, and all trailers.

Illustrative Examples:

- Automotive brake repair shops
- Automotive electrical repair shops
- Automotive radiator repair shops
- Automotive tune-up shops

Cross-References. Establishments primarily engaged in—

- Providing a wide range of mechanical and electrical automotive vehicle repair or specializing in engine repair or replacement—are classified in U.S. Industry 811111, General Automotive Repair;
- Replacing and repairing automotive vehicle exhaust systems—are classified in U.S. Industry 811112, Automotive Exhaust System Repair;
- Replacing and repairing automotive vehicle transmissions—are classified in U.S. Industry 811113, Automotive Transmission Repair;
- Providing automotive vehicle air-conditioning repair—are classified in U.S. Industry 811198, All Other Automotive Repair and Maintenance; and
- Motorcycle repair and maintenance services—are classified in Industry 811490, Other Personal and Household Goods Repair and Maintenance.

US—United States industry only. CAN—United States and Canadian industries are comparable. MEX—United States and Mexican industries are comparable. Blank—Canadian, Mexican, and United States industries are comparable.

81112 Automotive Body, Paint, Interior, and Glass Repair

This industry comprises establishments primarily engaged in providing one or more of the following: (1) repairing or customizing automotive vehicles, such as passenger cars, trucks, and vans, and all trailer bodies and interiors; (2) painting automotive vehicle and trailer bodies; (3) replacing, repairing, and/or tinting automotive vehicle glass; and (4) customizing automobile, truck, and van interiors for the physically disabled or other customers with special requirements.

Illustrative Examples:

Automotive body shops
Automotive glass shops
Automotive paint shops

Cross-References. Establishments primarily engaged in—

- Manufacturing automotive vehicles and trailers or customizing these vehicles on an assembly-line basis—are classified in Subsector 336, Transportation Equipment Manufacturing;
- Motorcycle repair and maintenance services—are classified in Industry 81149, Other Personal and Household Goods Repair and Maintenance.

811121 Automotive Body, Paint, and Interior Repair and Maintenance[CAN]

This U.S. industry comprises establishments primarily engaged in repairing or customizing automotive vehicles, such as passenger cars, trucks, and vans, and all trailer bodies and interiors; and/or painting automotive vehicles and trailer bodies.

Illustrative Examples:

Automotive body shops
Automotive paint shops
Automotive upholstery shops

Cross-References. Establishments primarily engaged in—

- Automotive glass replacement, repair and/or tinting—are classified in U.S. Industry 811122, Automotive Glass Replacement Shops;
- Manufacturing automotive vehicles and trailers or customizing these vehicles on an assembly-line basis—are classified in Subsector 336, Transportation Equipment Manufacturing; and
- Motorcycle repair and maintenance services—are classified in Industry 811490, Other Personal and Household Goods Repair and Maintenance.

US—United States industry only. CAN—United States and Canadian industries are comparable. MEX—United States and Mexican industries are comparable. Blank—Canadian, Mexican, and United States industries are comparable.

811122 Automotive Glass Replacement Shops[CAN]

This U.S. industry comprises establishments primarily engaged in replacing, repairing, and/or tinting automotive vehicle, such as passenger car, truck, and van, glass.

Cross-References.

Establishments primarily engaged in motorcycle repair and maintenance service are classified in Industry 811490, Other Personal and Household Goods Repair and Maintenance.

81119 Other Automotive Repair and Maintenance

This industry comprises establishments primarily engaged in providing automotive repair and maintenance services (except mechanical and electrical repair and maintenance; transmission repair; and body, paint, interior, and glass repair) for automotive vehicles, such as passenger cars, trucks, and vans, and all trailers.

Illustrative Examples:

Automotive air-conditioning repair shops
Automotive oil change and lubrication shops
Automotive rustproofing and undercoating shops
Automotive tire repair shops
Car washes

Cross-References. Establishments primarily engaged in—

- Tire retreading or recapping—are classified in Industry 32621, Tire Manufacturing;
- Automotive vehicle mechanical and electrical repair and maintenance—are classified in Industry 81111, Automotive Mechanical and Electrical Repair and Maintenance;
- Automotive body, paint, interior, and glass repair—are classified in Industry 81112, Automotive Body, Paint, Interior, and Glass Repair; and
- Motorcycle repair and maintenance services—are classified in Industry 81149, Other Personal and Household Goods Repair and Maintenance.

811191 Automotive Oil Change and Lubrication Shops[US]

This U.S. industry comprises establishments primarily engaged in changing motor oil and lubricating the chassis of automotive vehicles, such as passenger cars, trucks, and vans.

US—United States industry only. CAN—United States and Canadian industries are comparable. MEX—United States and Mexican industries are comparable. Blank—Canadian, Mexican, and United States industries are comparable.

Cross-References.

Establishments primarily engaged in motorcycle repair and maintenance services are classified in Industry 811490, Other Personal and Household Goods Repair and Maintenance.

811192 Car Washes[CAN]

This U.S. industry comprises establishments primarily engaged in cleaning, washing, and/or waxing automotive vehicles, such as passenger cars, trucks, and vans, and trailers.

Illustrative Examples:

Automotive detail shops
Car washes
Mobile car and truck washes

811198 All Other Automotive Repair and Maintenance[US]

This U.S. industry comprises establishments primarily engaged in providing automotive repair and maintenance services (except mechanical and electrical repair and maintenance; body, paint, interior, and glass repair; motor oil change and lubrication; and car washing) for automotive vehicles, such as passenger cars, trucks, and vans, and all trailers.

Illustrative Examples:

Automotive air-conditioning repair shops
Automotive tire repair (except retreading) shops
Automotive rustproofing and undercoating shops

Cross-References. Establishments primarily engaged in—

- Tire retreading or recapping—are classified in U.S. Industry 326212, Tire Retreading;
- Providing a range of mechanical and electrical automotive vehicle repair or specializing in engine repair or replacement—are classified in U.S. Industry 811111, General Automotive Repair;
- Replacing and repairing automotive vehicle exhaust systems—are classified in U.S. Industry 811112, Automotive Exhaust System Repair;
- Replacing and repairing automotive vehicle transmissions—are classified in U.S. Industry 811113, Automotive Transmission Repair;

US—United States industry only. CAN—United States and Canadian industries are comparable. MEX—United States and Mexican industries are comparable. Blank—Canadian, Mexican, and United States industries are comparable.

- Repairing or customizing automotive vehicle bodies and interiors—are classified in U.S. Industry 811121, Automotive Body, Paint, and Interior Repair and Maintenance;
- Replacing, repairing, and/or tinting automotive glass—are classified in U.S. Industry 811122, Automotive Glass Replacement Shops;
- Changing motor oil and lubricating the chassis of automotive vehicles—are classified in U.S. Industry 811191, Automotive Oil Change and Lubrication Shops;
- Cleaning, washing, and/or waxing automotive vehicles and trailers—are classified in U.S. Industry 811192, Car Washes;
- Motorcycle repair and maintenance services—are classified in Industry 811490, Other Personal and Household Goods Repair and Maintenance; and
- Retailing and installing audio equipment—are classified in Industry 441310, Automotive Parts and Accessories Stores.

8112 Electronic and Precision Equipment Repair and Maintenance

This industry group comprises establishments primarily engaged in repairing electronic equipment, such as computers and communications equipment, and highly specialized precision instruments. Establishments in this industry group typically have staff skilled in repairing items having complex, electronic components.

81121 Electronic and Precision Equipment Repair and Maintenance

This industry comprises establishments primarily engaged in repairing and maintaining one or more of the following: (1) consumer electronic equipment; (2) computers; (3) office machines; (4) communication equipment; and (5) other electronic and precision equipment and instruments, without retailing these products as new. Establishments in this industry repair items, such as microscopes, radar and sonar equipment, televisions, stereos, video recorders, computers, fax machines, photocopying machines, two-way radios and other communications equipment, scientific instruments, and medical equipment.

Cross-References. Establishments primarily engaged in—

- Installing and monitoring home security systems—are classified in Industry 56162, Security Systems Services;
- Retailing new radios, televisions, and other consumer electronics and also providing repair services—are classified in Industry 44311, Appliance, Television, and Other Electronics Stores;

US—United States industry only. CAN—United States and Canadian industries are comparable. MEX—United States and Mexican industries are comparable. Blank—Canadian, Mexican, and United States industries are comparable.

- Retailing new computers and computer peripherals and also providing repair services—are classified in Industry 44312, Computer and Software Stores; and
- Rewinding armatures and rebuilding electric motors on a factory basis—are classified in Industry 33531, Electrical Equipment Manufacturing.

811211 Consumer Electronics Repair and Maintenance[MEX]

This U.S. industry comprises establishments primarily engaged in repairing and maintaining consumer electronics, such as televisions, stereos, speakers, video recorders, CD players, radios, and cameras, without retailing new consumer electronics.

Cross-References. Establishments primarily engaged in—

- Repairing computers and peripheral equipment—are classified in U.S. Industry 811212, Computer and Office Machine Repair and Maintenance;
- Installing and monitoring home security systems—are classified in U.S. Industry 561621, Security Systems Services (except Locksmiths);
- Retailing new radios, televisions, and other consumer electronics and also providing repair services—are classified in U.S. Industry 443112, Radio, Television, and Other Electronics Stores; and
- Repairing two-way radios—are classified in U.S. Industry 811213, Communication Equipment Repair and Maintenance.

811212 Computer and Office Machine Repair and Maintenance[US]

This U.S. industry comprises establishments primarily engaged in repairing and maintaining computers and office machines without retailing new computers and office machines, such as photocopying machines; and computer terminals, storage devices, printers; and CD-ROM drives.

Cross-References. Establishments primarily engaged in—

- Retailing new computers and computer peripherals and also providing repair services—are classified in Industry 443120, Computer and Software Stores; and
- Repairing and servicing fax machines—are classified in Industry 811213, Communication Equipment Repair and Maintenance.

811213 Communication Equipment Repair and Maintenance[US]

This U.S. industry comprises establishments primarily engaged in repairing and maintaining communications equipment without retailing new communication

US—United States industry only. CAN—United States and Canadian industries are comparable. MEX—United States and Mexican industries are comparable. Blank—Canadian, Mexican, and United States industries are comparable.

equipment, such as telephones, fax machines, communications transmission equipment, and two-way radios.

Cross-References. Establishments primarily engaged in—

- Retailing new telephones and also providing repair services—are classified in U.S. Industry 443112, Radio, Television, and Other Electronics Stores; and
- Repairing stereo and other consumer electronic equipment—are classified in U.S. Industry 811211, Consumer Electronics Repair and Maintenance.

811219 Other Electronic and Precision Equipment Repair and Maintenance[US]

This U.S. industry comprises establishments primarily engaged in repairing and maintaining (without retailing) electronic and precision equipment (except consumer electronics, computers and office machines, and communications equipment). Establishments in this industry repair and maintain equipment, such as medical diagnostic imaging equipment, measuring and surveying instruments, laboratory instruments, and radar and sonar equipment.

Cross-References. Establishments primarily engaged in—

- Rewinding armatures and rebuilding electric motors on a factory basis—are classified in U.S. Industry 335312, Motor and Generator Manufacturing;
- Repairing stereo and other consumer electronic equipment—are classified in U.S. Industry 811211, Consumer Electronics Repair and Maintenance;
- Repairing computers and office machines—are classified in U.S. Industry 811212, Computer and Office Machine Repair and Maintenance; and
- Repairing communications equipment—are classified in U.S. Industry 811213, Communication Equipment Repair and Maintenance.

8113 Commercial and Industrial Machinery and Equipment (except Automotive and Electronic) Repair and Maintenance

81131 Commercial and Industrial Machinery and Equipment (except Automotive and Electronic) Repair and Maintenance

See industry description for 811310 below.

811310 Commercial and Industrial Machinery and Equipment (except Automotive and Electronic) Repair and Maintenance[CAN]

This industry comprises establishments primarily engaged in the repair and maintenance of commercial and industrial machinery and equipment. Establish-

---

US—United States industry only. CAN—United States and Canadian industries are comparable. MEX—United States and Mexican industries are comparable. Blank—Canadian, Mexican, and United States industries are comparable.

ments in this industry either sharpen/install commercial and industrial machinery blades and saws or provide welding (e.g., automotive, general) repair services; or repair agricultural and other heavy and industrial machinery and equipment (e.g., forklifts and other materials handling equipment, machine tools, commercial refrigeration equipment, construction equipment, and mining machinery).

Cross-References. Establishments primarily engaged in—

- Automotive repair (except welding) and maintenance are—classified in Industry Group 8111, Automotive Repair and Maintenance;
- Repairing and maintaining electronic and precision equipment—are classified in Industry 81121, Electronic and Precision Equipment Repair and Maintenance;
- Repairing and servicing aircraft—are classified in Industry 488190, Other Support Activities for Air Transportation;
- Converting, rebuilding, and overhauling aircraft—are classified in Industry 336410, Aerospace Product and Parts Manufacturing;
- Repairing and servicing railroad cars and engines—are classified in Industry 488210, Support Activities for Rail Transportation;
- Rebuilding or remanufacturing railroad engines and cars—are classified in Industry 336510, Railroad Rolling Stock Manufacturing;
- Repairing and overhauling ships at floating dry docks—are classified in Industry 488390, Other Support Activities for Water Transportation;
- Repairing and overhauling ships at shipyards—are classified in U.S. Industry 336611, Ship Building and Repairing;
- Rewinding armatures or rebuilding electric motors on a factory basis—are classified in U.S. Industry 335312, Motor and Generator Manufacturing; and
- Repairing and maintaining home and garden equipment (e.g., sharpening or installing blades and saws)—are classified in Industry 811411, Home and Garden Equipment Repair and Maintenance.

8114 Personal and Household Goods Repair and Maintenance

81141 Home and Garden Equipment and Appliance Repair and Maintenance

This industry comprises establishments primarily engaged in repairing and servicing home and garden equipment and/or household-type appliances without retailing new equipment or appliances. Establishments in this industry repair and

US—United States industry only. CAN—United States and Canadian industries are comparable. MEX—United States and Mexican industries are comparable. Blank—Canadian, Mexican, and United States industries are comparable.

maintain items, such as lawnmowers, edgers, snow- and leaf-blowers, washing machines, clothes dryers, and refrigerators.

Cross-References. Establishments primarily engaged in—

- Retailing outdoor power equipment and also providing repair services—are classified in Industry 44421, Outdoor Power Equipment Stores;
- Retailing an array of new appliances and also providing repair services—are classified in Industry 44311, Appliance, Television, and Other Electronics Stores;
- Repairing, servicing, or installing central heating and air-conditioning equipment—are classified in Industry 23822, Plumbing, Heating, and Air-Conditioning Contractors; and
- Repairing commercial refrigeration equipment—are classified in Industry 81131, Commercial and Industrial Machinery and Equipment (except Automotive and Electronic) Repair and Maintenance.

811411 Home and Garden Equipment Repair and Maintenance[CAN]

This U.S. industry comprises establishments primarily engaged in repairing and servicing home and garden equipment without retailing new home and garden equipment, such as lawnmowers, handheld power tools, edgers, snow- and leaf-blowers, and trimmers.

Cross-References.

Establishments primarily engaged in retailing new outdoor power equipment and also providing repair services are classified in Industry 444210, Outdoor Power Equipment Stores.

811412 Appliance Repair and Maintenance[CAN]

This U.S. industry comprises establishments primarily engaged in repairing and servicing household appliances without retailing new appliances, such as refrigerators, stoves, washing machines, clothes dryers, and room air-conditioners.

Cross-References. Establishments primarily engaged in—

- Installing central heating and air-conditioning equipment—are classified in Industry 238220, Plumbing, Heating, and Air-Conditioning Contractors;
- Repairing commercial refrigeration equipment—are classified in Industry 811310, Commercial and Industrial Machinery and Equipment (except Automotive and Electronic) Repair and Maintenance; and

---

US—United States industry only. CAN—United States and Canadian industries are comparable. MEX—United States and Mexican industries are comparable. Blank—Canadian, Mexican, and United States industries are comparable.

- Retailing an array of new appliances and also providing repair services—are classified in U.S. Industry 443111, Household Appliance Stores.

81142 Reupholstery and Furniture Repair

See industry description for 811420 below.

811420 Reupholstery and Furniture Repair

This industry comprises establishments primarily engaged in one or more of the following: (1) reupholstering furniture; (2) refinishing furniture; (3) repairing furniture; and (4) repairing and restoring furniture.

Cross-References. Establishments primarily engaged in—

- Automotive vehicle and trailer upholstery repair—are classified in U.S. Industry 811121, Automotive Body, Paint, and Interior Repair and Maintenance; and
- The restoration of museum pieces—are classified in Industry 711510, Independent Artists, Writers, and Performers.

81143 Footwear and Leather Goods Repair

See industry description for 811430 below.

811430 Footwear and Leather Goods Repair

This industry comprises establishments primarily engaged in repairing footwear and/or repairing other leather or leather-like goods without retailing new footwear and leather or leather-like goods, such as handbags and briefcases.

Cross-References. Establishments primarily engaged in—

- Retailing new luggage and leather goods and also providing repair services—are classified in Industry 448320, Luggage and Leather Goods Stores;
- Shining shoes—are classified in Industry 812990, All Other Personal Services; and
- Repairing leather clothing—are classified in Industry 811490, Other Personal and Household Goods Repair and Maintenance.

81149 Other Personal and Household Goods Repair and Maintenance

See industry description for 811490 below.

US—United States industry only. CAN—United States and Canadian industries are comparable. MEX—United States and Mexican industries are comparable. Blank—Canadian, Mexican, and United States industries are comparable.

811490 Other Personal and Household Goods Repair and Maintenance[CAN]

This industry comprises establishments primarily engaged in repairing and servicing personal or household-type goods without retailing new personal and household-type goods (except home and garden equipment, appliances, furniture, and footwear and leather goods). Establishments in this industry repair items, such as garments; watches; jewelry; musical instruments; bicycles and motorcycles; motorboats, canoes, sailboats, and other recreational boats.

Cross-References. Establishments primarily engaged in—

- Repairing home and garden equipment—are classified in U.S. Industry 811411, Home and Garden Equipment Repair and Maintenance;
- Repairing appliances—are classified in U.S. Industry 811412, Appliance Repair and Maintenance;
- Reupholstering and repairing furniture—are classified in Industry 811420, Reupholstery and Furniture Repair;
- Repairing footwear and leather goods—are classified in Industry 811430, Footwear and Leather Goods Repair;
- Operating marinas and providing a range of other services including boat cleaning and repair—are classified in Industry 713930, Marinas; and
- Drycleaning garments—are classified in Industry Group 8123, Drycleaning and Laundry Services.

812 Personal and Laundry Services

Industries in the Personal and Laundry Services subsector group establishments that provide personal and laundry services to individuals, households, and businesses. Services performed include: personal care services; death care services; laundry and drycleaning services; and a wide range of other personal services, such as pet care (except veterinary) services, photofinishing services, temporary parking services, and dating services.

The Personal and Laundry Services subsector is by no means all-inclusive of the services that could be termed personal services (i.e., those provided to individuals rather than businesses). There are many other subsectors, as well as sectors, that provide services to persons. Establishments providing legal, accounting, tax preparation, architectural, portrait photography, and similar professional services are classified in Sector 54, Professional, Scientific, and Technical Services; those providing job placement, travel arrangement, home security, interior and exterior house cleaning, exterminating, lawn and garden care, and similar support services

US—United States industry only. CAN—United States and Canadian industries are comparable. MEX—United States and Mexican industries are comparable. Blank—Canadian, Mexican, and United States industries are comparable.

are classified in Sector 56, Administrative and Support, Waste Management and Remediation Services; those providing health and social services are classified in Sector 62, Health Care and Social Assistance; those providing amusement and recreation services are classified in Sector 71, Arts, Entertainment and Recreation; those providing educational instruction are classified in Sector 61, Educational Services; those providing repair services are classified in Subsector 811, Repair and Maintenance; and those providing spiritual, civic, and advocacy services are classified in Subsector 813, Religious, Grantmaking, Civic, Professional, and Similar Organizations.

8121 Personal Care Services[CAN]

This industry group comprises establishments, such as barber and beauty shops, that provide appearance care services to individual consumers.

81211 Hair, Nail, and Skin Care Services[CAN]

This industry comprises establishments primarily engaged in one or more of the following: (1) providing hair care services; (2) providing nail care services; and (3) providing facials or applying makeup (except permanent makeup).

Illustrative Examples:

Barber shops
Beauty salons
Cosmetology salons
Hair stylist shops
Nail salons

Cross-References. Establishments primarily engaged in—

- Offering training in barbering, hair styling, or the cosmetic arts—are classified in Industry 61151, Technical and Trade Schools;
- Providing massage, electrolysis (i.e., hair removal), permanent makeup, or tanning services—are classified in Industry 81219, Other Personal Care Services; and
- Providing medical skin care services (e.g., cosmetic surgery, dermatology)—are classified in Sector 62, Health Care and Social Assistance.

812111 Barber Shops[US]

This U.S. industry comprises establishments known as barber shops or men's hair stylist shops primarily engaged in cutting, trimming, and styling boys' and men's hair; and/or shaving and trimming men's beards.

US—United States industry only. CAN—United States and Canadian industries are comparable. MEX—United States and Mexican industries are comparable. Blank—Canadian, Mexican, and United States industries are comparable.

Cross-References. Establishments primarily engaged in—

- Offering training in barbering—are classified in U.S. Industry 611511, Cosmetology and Barber Schools; and
- Providing hair care services (except establishments known as barber shops or men's hair stylists)—are classified in U.S. Industry 812112, Beauty Salons.

812112 Beauty Salons[US]

This U.S. industry comprises establishments (except those known as barber shops or men's hair stylist shops) primarily engaged in one or more of the following: (1) cutting, trimming, shampooing, weaving, coloring, waving, or styling hair; (2) providing facials; and (3) applying makeup (except permanent makeup).

Illustrative Examples:

Beauty parlors or shops
Combined beauty and barber shops
Cosmetology salons or shops
Facial salons or shops
Hairdressing salons or shops
Unisex or women's hair stylist shops

Cross-References. Establishments primarily engaged in—

- Cutting, trimming, and styling men's and boys' hair (known as barber shops or men's hair stylist shops)—are classified in U.S. Industry 812111, Barber Shops;
- Offering training in hair styling or the cosmetic arts—are classified in U.S. Industry 611511, Cosmetology and Barber Schools;
- Providing nail care services—are classified in U.S. Industry 812113, Nail Salons;
- Providing massage, electrolysis (i.e., hair removal), permanent makeup, or tanning services—are classified in U.S. Industry 812199, All Other Personal Care Services; and
- Providing medical skin care services (e.g., cosmetic surgery, dermatology)—are classified in Sector 62, Health Care and Social Assistance.

812113 Nail Salons[US]

This U.S. industry comprises establishments primarily engaged in providing nail care services, such as manicures, pedicures, and nail extensions.

81219 Other Personal Care Services[CAN]

This industry comprises establishments primarily engaged in providing personal care services (except hair, nail, facial, or nonpermanent makeup services).

US—United States industry only. CAN—United States and Canadian industries are comparable. MEX—United States and Mexican industries are comparable. Blank—Canadian, Mexican, and United States industries are comparable.

Illustrative Examples:

Depilatory or electrolysis (i.e., hair removal) salons
Ear piercing services
Hair replacement (except by offices of physicians) or weaving services
Massage parlors
Nonmedical diet and weight reducing centers
Permanent makeup salons
Steam or turkish baths
Tanning salons
Tattoo parlors

Cross-References. Establishments primarily engaged in—

- Providing hair, nail, facial, or nonpermanent makeup services—are classified in Industry 81211, Hair, Nail, and Skin Care Services;
- Operating physical fitness facilities—are classified in Industry 71394, Fitness and Recreational Sports Centers;
- Operating health resorts and spas that provide lodging—are classified in Industry 72111, Hotels (except Casino Hotels) and Motels; and
- Providing medical or surgical hair replacement or weight reduction—are classified in Sector 62, Health Care and Social Assistance.

812191 Diet and Weight Reducing Centers[US]

This U.S. industry comprises establishments primarily engaged in providing nonmedical services to assist clients in attaining or maintaining a desired weight. The sale of weight reduction products, such as food supplements, may be an integral component of the program. These services typically include individual or group counseling, menu and exercise planning, and weight and body measurement monitoring.

Cross-References. Establishments primarily engaged in—

- Operating physical fitness facilities—are classified in Industry 713940, Fitness and Recreational Sports Centers;
- Operating health resorts and spas that provide lodging—are classified in Industry 721110, Hotels (except Casino Hotels) and Motels; and
- Providing medical or surgical weight reduction—are classified in Sector 62, Health Care and Social Assistance.

812199 Other Personal Care Services[US]

This U.S. industry comprises establishments primarily engaged in providing personal care services (except hair, nail, facial, nonpermanent makeup, or nonmedical diet and weight reducing services).

US—United States industry only. CAN—United States and Canadian industries are comparable. MEX—United States and Mexican industries are comparable. Blank—Canadian, Mexican, and United States industries are comparable.

Illustrative Examples:

Depilatory or electrolysis (i.e., hair removal) salons
Ear piercing services
Hair replacement (except by offices of physicians) or weaving services
Massage parlors
Permanent makeup salons
Saunas
Steam or turkish baths
Tanning salons
Tattoo parlors

Cross-References. Establishments primarily engaged in—

- Cutting, trimming, and styling men's and boys' hair (known as barber shops or men's hair stylist shops)—are classified in U. S. Industry 812111, Barber Shops;
- Providing hair, facial, or nonpermanent makeup services (except establishments known as barber shops or men's hair stylist shops)—are classified in U.S. Industry 812112, Beauty Shops;
- Nail care services—are classified in U.S. Industry 812113, Nail Salons;
- Providing nonmedical diet and weight reducing services—are classified in U.S. Industry 812191, Diet and Weight Reducing Centers; and
- Providing medical or surgical hair replacement or weight reduction services—are classified in Sector 62, Health Care and Social Assistance.

8122 Death Care Services [CAN]

81221 Funeral Homes and Funeral Services[CAN]

See industry description for 812210 below.

812210 Funeral Homes and Funeral Services[CAN]

This industry comprises establishments primarily engaged in preparing the dead for burial or interment and conducting funerals (i.e., providing facilities for wakes, arranging transportation for the dead, selling caskets and related merchandise). Funeral homes combined with crematories are included in this industry.

Cross-References.

Establishments (except funeral homes) primarily engaged in cremating the dead are classified in Industry 812220, Cemeteries and Crematories.

81222 Cemeteries and Crematories[CAN]

See industry description for 812220 below.

US—United States industry only. CAN—United States and Canadian industries are comparable. MEX—United States and Mexican industries are comparable. Blank—Canadian, Mexican, and United States industries are comparable.

812220 Cemeteries and Crematories[CAN]

This industry comprises establishments primarily engaged in operating sites or structures reserved for the interment of human or animal remains and/or cremating the dead.

Illustrative Examples:

- Cemetery associations (i.e., operators of cemeteries)
- Crematories (except combined with funeral homes)
- Mausoleums
- Memorial gardens (i.e., burial places)
- Pet cemeteries

Cross-References.

Crematories combined with funeral homes are classified in Industry 812210, Funeral Homes and Funeral Services.

8123 Drycleaning and Laundry Services[CAN]

81231 Coin-Operated Laundries and Drycleaners[CAN]

See industry description for 812310 below.

812310 Coin-Operated Laundries and Drycleaners[CAN]

This industry comprises (1) establishments primarily engaged in operating facilities with coin-operated or similar self-service laundry and drycleaning equipment for customer use on the premises and (2) establishments primarily engaged in supplying and servicing coin-operated or similar self-service laundry and drycleaning equipment for customer use in places of business operated by others, such as apartments and dormitories.

81232 Drycleaning and Laundry Services (except Coin-Operated)[CAN]

See industry description for 812320 below.

812320 Drycleaning and Laundry Services (except Coin-Operated)[CAN]

This industry comprises establishments primarily engaged in one or more of the following: (1) providing drycleaning services (except coin-operated); (2) providing laundering services (except linen and uniform supply or coin-operated); (3) providing dropoff and pickup sites for laundries and/or drycleaners; and

---

US—United States industry only. CAN—United States and Canadian industries are comparable. MEX—United States and Mexican industries are comparable. Blank—Canadian, Mexican, and United States industries are comparable.

(4) providing specialty cleaning services for specific types of garments and other textile items (except carpets and upholstery), such as fur, leather, or suede garments; wedding gowns; hats; draperies; and pillows. These establishments may provide all, a combination of, or none of the cleaning services on the premises.

Cross-References. Establishments primarily engaged in—

- Supplying laundered linens and uniforms on a rental or contract basis—are classified in Industry 81233, Linen and Uniform Supply;
- Operating coin-operated or similar self-service laundry or drycleaning facilities—are classified in Industry 812310, Coin-Operated Laundries and Drycleaners; and
- Cleaning used carpets and upholstery—are classified in Industry 561740, Carpet and Upholstery Cleaning Services.

81233 Linen and Uniform Supply[CAN]

This industry comprises establishments primarily engaged in supplying, on a rental or contract basis, laundered items, such as uniforms, gowns and coats, table linens, bed linens, towels, clean room apparel, and treated mops or shop towels.

812331 Linen Supply[US]

This U.S. industry comprises establishments primarily engaged in supplying, on a rental or contract basis, laundered items, such as table and bed linens; towels; diapers; and uniforms, gowns, or coats of the type used by doctors, nurses, barbers, beauticians, and waitresses.

Cross-References.

Establishments primarily engaged in supplying, on a rental or contract basis, laundered industrial work uniforms and related work clothing are classified in U.S. Industry 812332, Industrial Launderers.

812332 Industrial Launderers[US]

This U.S. industry comprises establishments primarily engaged in supplying, on a rental or contract basis, laundered industrial work uniforms and related work clothing, such as protective apparel (flame and heat resistant) and clean room apparel; dust control items, such as treated mops, rugs, mats, dust tool covers, cloths, and shop or wiping towels.

US—United States industry only. CAN—United States and Canadian industries are comparable. MEX—United States and Mexican industries are comparable. Blank—Canadian, Mexican, and United States industries are comparable.

Cross-References.

Establishments primarily engaged in supplying, on a rental or contract basis, laundered uniforms, gowns or coats of the type used by doctors, nurses, barbers, beauticians, and waitresses are classified in U.S. Industry 812331, Linen Supply.

8129 Other Personal Services[CAN]

The industry group comprises establishments primarily engaged in providing personal services (except personal care services, death care services, or drycleaning and laundry services).

81291 Pet Care (except Veterinary) Services[CAN]

See industry description for 812910 below.

812910 Pet Care (except Veterinary) Services[CAN]

This industry comprises establishments primarily engaged in providing pet care services (except veterinary), such as boarding, grooming, sitting, and training pets.

Cross-References. Establishments primarily engaged in—

- Practicing veterinary medicine—are classified in Industry 541940, Veterinary Services;
- Boarding horses—are classified in Industry 115210, Support Activities for Animal Production; and
- Transporting pets—are classified in U.S. Industry 485991, Special Needs Transportation.

81292 Photofinishing[CAN]

This industry comprises establishments primarily engaged in developing film and/or making photographic slides, prints, and enlargements.

Cross-References.

Establishments primarily engaged in processing motion picture film for the motion picture and television industries are classified in Industry 51219, Postproduction Services and Other Motion Picture and Video Industries.

US—United States industry only. CAN—United States and Canadian industries are comparable. MEX—United States and Mexican industries are comparable. Blank—Canadian, Mexican, and United States industries are comparable.

812921 Photofinishing Laboratories (except One-Hour)[CAN]

This U.S. industry comprises establishments (except those known as ''one-hour'' photofinishing labs) primarily engaged in developing film and/or making photographic slides, prints, and enlargements.

Cross-References.

- Establishments primarily engaged in processing motion picture film for the motion picture and television industries are classified in U.S. Industry 512199, Other Motion Picture and Video Industries; and
- Establishments known as ''one-hour'' photofinishing labs are classified in U.S. Industry 812922, One-Hour Photofinishing.

812922 One-Hour Photofinishing[CAN]

This U.S. industry comprises establishments known as ''one-hour'' photofinishing labs primarily engaged in developing film and/or making photographic slides, prints, and enlargements on a short turnaround or while-you-wait basis.

Cross-References.

Photofinishing laboratories (except those known as ''one-hour'' photofinishing labs) are classified in U.S. Industry 812921, Photofinishing Laboratories (except One-Hour).

81293 Parking Lots and Garages[CAN]

See industry description for 812930 below.

812930 Parking Lots and Garages[CAN]

This industry comprises establishments primarily engaged in providing parking space for motor vehicles, usually on an hourly, daily, or monthly basis and/or valet parking services.

Cross-References.

Establishments primarily engaged in providing extended or dead storage of motor vehicles are classified in Industry 493190, Other Warehousing and Storage.

81299 All Other Personal Services[CAN]

See industry description for 812990 below.

US—United States industry only. CAN—United States and Canadian industries are comparable. MEX—United States and Mexican industries are comparable. Blank—Canadian, Mexican, and United States industries are comparable.

812990 All Other Personal Services[CAN]

This industry comprises establishments primarily engaged in providing personal services (except personal care services, death care services, drycleaning and laundry services, pet care services, photofinishing services, or parking space and/or valet parking services).

Illustrative Examples:

Bail bonding or bondsperson services
Coin-operated personal services machine (e.g., blood pressure, locker, photographic, scale, shoeshine) concession operators
Consumer buying services
Dating services
Shoeshine services
Social escort services
Wedding planning services

Cross-References. Establishments primarily engaged in—

- Providing personal care services—are classified in Industry Group 8121, Personal Care Services;
- Providing death care services—are classified in Industry Group 8122, Death Care Services;
- Providing drycleaning and laundry services—are classified in Industry Group 8123, Drycleaning and Laundry Services;
- Providing pet care (except veterinary) services—are classified in Industry 812910, Pet Care (except Veterinary) Services;
- Practicing veterinary medicine—are classified in Industry 541940, Veterinary Services;
- Providing photofinishing services—are classified in Industry 81292, Photofinishing; and
- Providing parking space for motor vehicles and/or valet parking services—are classified in Industry 812930, Parking Lots and Garages.

813 Religious, Grantmaking, Civic, Professional, and Similar Organizations

Industries in the Religious, Grantmaking, Civic, Professional, and Similar Organizations subsector group establishments that organize and promote religious activities; support various causes through grantmaking; advocate various social and political causes; and promote and defend the interests of their members.

The industry groups within the subsector are defined in terms of their activities, such as establishments that provide funding for specific causes or for a variety of charitable causes; establishments that advocate and actively promote causes and

US—United States industry only. CAN—United States and Canadian industries are comparable. MEX—United States and Mexican industries are comparable. Blank—Canadian, Mexican, and United States industries are comparable.

beliefs for the public good; and establishments that have an active membership structure to promote causes and represent the interests of their members. Establishments in this subsector may publish newsletters, books, and periodicals for distribution to their membership.

8131 Religious Organizations[CAN]

81311 Religious Organizations[CAN]

See industry description for 813110 below.

813110 Religious Organizations[CAN]

This industry comprises (1) establishments primarily engaged in operating religious organizations, such as churches, religious temples, and monasteries and/or (2) establishments primarily engaged in administering an organized religion or promoting religious activities.

Illustrative Examples:

Churches
Monasteries (except schools)
Mosques, religious
Shrines, religious
Temples, religious
Synagogues

Cross-References.

- Schools, colleges, or universities operated by religious organizations are classified in Sector 61, Educational Services;
- Radio and television stations operated by religious organizations are classified in Subsector 515, Broadcasting (except Internet);
- Publishing houses operated by religious organizations are classified in Subsector 511, Publishing Industries (except Internet);
- Establishments operated by religious organizations primarily engaged in health and social assistance for individuals are classified in Sector 62, Health Care and Social Assistance; and
- Used merchandise stores operated by religious organizations are classified in Industry 453310, Used Merchandise Stores.

8132 Grantmaking and Giving Services[CAN]

81321 Grantmaking and Giving Services[CAN]

This industry comprises (1) establishments known as grantmaking foundations or charitable trusts and (2) establishments primarily engaged in raising funds for

US—United States industry only. CAN—United States and Canadian industries are comparable. MEX—United States and Mexican industries are comparable. Blank—Canadian, Mexican, and United States industries are comparable.

a wide range of social welfare activities, such as health, educational, scientific, and cultural activities.

Cross-References. Establishments primarily engaged in—

- Providing trust management services for others—are classified in Industry 52392, Portfolio Management;
- Organizing and conducting fundraising campaigns on a contract or fee basis—are classified in Industry 56149, Other Business Support Services;
- Providing telemarketing services for others—are classified in Industry 56142, Telephone Call Centers;
- Raising funds for political purposes—are classified in Industry 81394, Political Organizations;
- Advocating social causes or issues—are classified in Industry 81331, Social Advocacy Organizations; and
- Conducting health research—are classified in Industry 54171, Research and Development in the Physical, Engineering, and Life Sciences.

813211 Grantmaking Foundations[US]

This U.S. industry comprises establishments known as grantmaking foundations or charitable trusts. Establishments in this industry award grants from trust funds based on a competitive selection process or the preferences of the foundation managers and grantors; or fund a single entity, such as a museum or university.

Illustrative Examples:

Community foundations
Corporate foundations, awarding grants
Grantmaking foundations
Philanthropic trusts
Scholarship trusts

Cross-References.

Establishments primarily engaged in providing trust management services for others are classified in Industry 523920, Portfolio Management.

813212 Voluntary Health Organizations[US]

This U.S. industry comprises establishments primarily engaged in raising funds for health related research, such as disease (e.g., heart, cancer, diabetes) prevention, health education, and patient services.

US—United States industry only. CAN—United States and Canadian industries are comparable. MEX—United States and Mexican industries are comparable. Blank—Canadian, Mexican, and United States industries are comparable.

Illustrative Examples:

Disease awareness fundraising organizations
Disease research (e.g., heart, cancer) fundraising organizations
Health research fundraising organizations
Voluntary health organizations

Cross-References.

- Establishments primarily engaged in raising funds for a wide range of social welfare activities, such as educational, scientific, cultural, and health, are classified in U.S. Industry 813219, Other Grantmaking and Giving Services;
- Establishments primarily engaged in organizing and conducting fundraising campaigns on a contract or fee basis are classified in U.S. Industry 561499, All Other Business Support Services;
- Establishments primarily engaged in providing telemarketing services for others are classified in U.S. Industry 561422, Telemarketing Bureaus;
- Establishments known as grantmaking foundations or charitable trusts are classified in U.S. Industry 813211, Grantmaking Foundations; and
- Establishments primarily engaged in conducting health research are classified in Industry 541710, Research and Development in the Physical, Engineering, and Life Sciences.

813219 Other Grantmaking and Giving Services[US]

This U.S. industry comprises establishments (except voluntary health organizations) primarily engaged in raising funds for a wide range of social welfare activities, such as educational, scientific, cultural, and health.

Illustrative Examples:

Community chests
Federated charities
United fund councils
United funds for colleges

Cross-References.

- Establishments primarily engaged in raising funds for health related research are classified in U.S. Industry 813212, Voluntary Health Organizations;
- Establishments known as grantmaking foundations or charitable trusts are classified in U.S. Industry 813211, Grantmaking Foundations;
- Establishments primarily engaged in organizing and conducting fundraising campaigns on a contract or fee basis are classified in U.S. Industry 561499, All Other Business Support Services;

US—United States industry only. CAN—United States and Canadian industries are comparable. MEX—United States and Mexican industries are comparable. Blank—Canadian, Mexican, and United States industries are comparable.

- Establishments primarily engaged in providing telemarketing services for others are classified in U.S. Industry 561422, Telemarketing Bureaus;
- Establishments primarily engaged in raising funds for political purposes are classified in Industry 813940, Political Organizations; and
- Establishments primarily engaged in advocating social causes or issues are classified in Industry 81331, Social Advocacy Organizations.

8133 Social Advocacy Organizations[CAN]

81331 Social Advocacy Organizations[CAN]

This industry comprises establishments primarily engaged in promoting a particular cause or working for the realization of a specific social or political goal to benefit a broad or specific constituency. These organizations may solicit contributions and offer memberships to support these goals.

Illustrative Examples:

Conservation advocacy organizations
Community action advocacy organizations
Environmental advocacy organizations
Firearms advocacy organizations
Human rights advocacy organizations
Wildlife preservation organizations

Cross-References. Establishments primarily engaged in—

- Promoting the civic and social interests of their members—are classified in Industry 81341, Civic and Social Organizations;
- Promoting the interests of the organized labor and union employees—are classified in Industry 81393, Labor Unions and Similar Labor Organizations; and
- Providing legal services for social advocacy organizations—are classified in Industry Group 5411, Legal Services.

813311 Human Rights Organizations[US]

This U.S. industry comprises establishments primarily engaged in promoting causes associated with human rights either for a broad or specific constituency. Establishments in this industry address issues, such as protecting and promoting the broad constitutional rights and civil liberties of individuals and those suffering from neglect, abuse, or exploitation; promoting the interests of specific groups, such as children, women, senior citizens, or persons with disabilities; improving relations between racial, ethnic, and cultural groups; and promoting voter education

US—United States industry only. CAN—United States and Canadian industries are comparable. MEX—United States and Mexican industries are comparable. Blank—Canadian, Mexican, and United States industries are comparable.

and registration. These organizations may solicit contributions and offer memberships to support these causes.

Illustrative Examples:

Civil liberties organizations
Human rights advocacy organizations
Senior citizens' advocacy organizations
Veterans' rights organizations

Cross-References. Establishments primarily engaged in—

- Promoting the interests of organized labor and union employees—are classified in Industry 813930, Labor Unions and Similar Labor Organizations; and
- Providing legal services for human rights organizations—are classified in Industry Group 5411, Legal Services.

813312 Environment, Conservation and Wildlife Organizations[US]

This U.S. industry comprises establishments primarily engaged in promoting the preservation and protection of the environment and wildlife. Establishments in this industry address issues, such as clean air and water; global warming; conserving and developing natural resources, including land, plant, water, and energy resources; and protecting and preserving wildlife and endangered species. These organizations may solicit contributions and offer memberships to support these causes.

Illustrative Examples:

Animal rights organizations
Conservation advocacy organizations
Humane societies
Natural resource preservation organizations
Wildlife preservation organizations

Cross-References.

Establishments primarily engaged in providing legal services for environment, conservation, and wildlife organizations are classified in Industry Group 5411, Legal Services.

813319 Other Social Advocacy Organizations[US]

This U.S. industry comprises establishments primarily engaged in social advocacy (except human rights and environmental protection, conservation, and wildlife preservation). Establishments in this industry address issues, such as peace and international understanding; community action (excluding civic organizations); or advancing social causes, such as firearms safety, drunk driving prevention, drug

US—United States industry only. CAN—United States and Canadian industries are comparable. MEX—United States and Mexican industries are comparable. Blank—Canadian, Mexican, and United States industries are comparable.

abuse awareness. These organizations may solicit contributions and offer memberships to support these causes.

Illustrative Examples:

Community action advocacy organizations
Firearms advocacy organizations
Peace advocacy organizations
Substance abuse prevention advocacy organizations
Taxpayers' advocacy organizations

Cross-References. Establishments primarily engaged in—

- Advocating human rights issues—are classified in U.S. Industry 813311, Human Rights Organizations;
- Promoting the preservation and protection of the environment and wildlife—are classified in U.S. Industry 813312, Environment, Conservation and Wildlife Organizations;
- Promoting the civic and social interests of their members—are classified in Industry 813410, Civic and Social Organizations;
- Providing legal services for social advocacy organizations—are classified in Industry Group 5411, Legal Services; and
- Providing community action services, such as community action services agencies—are classified in Industry 624190, Other Individual and Family Services.

8134 Civic and Social Organizations[CAN]

81341 Civic and Social Organizations[CAN]

See industry description for 813410 below.

813410 Civic and Social Organizations[CAN]

This industry comprises establishments primarily engaged in promoting the civic and social interests of their members. Establishments in this industry may operate bars and restaurants for their members.

Illustrative Examples:

Alumni associations
Automobile clubs (except travel)
Booster clubs
Ethnic associations
Fraternal lodges
Granges
Parent-teacher associations
Scouting organizations
Social clubs
Veterans' membership organizations

US—United States industry only. CAN—United States and Canadian industries are comparable. MEX—United States and Mexican industries are comparable. Blank—Canadian, Mexican, and United States industries are comparable.

Cross-References.

- Establishments of insurance offices operated by fraternal benefit organizations are classified in Subsector 524, Insurance Carriers and Related Activities;
- Establishments primarily engaged in operating residential fraternity and sorority houses are classified in Industry 721310, Rooming and Boarding Houses; and
- Establishments primarily engaged in providing travel arrangements and reservation services, such as automobile travel clubs or motor travel clubs are classified in U.S. Industry 561599, All Other Travel Arrangement and Reservation Services.

8139 Business, Professional, Labor, Political, and Similar Organizations[CAN]

This industry group comprises establishments primarily engaged in promoting the interests of their members (except religious organizations, social advocacy organizations, and civic and social organizations). Examples of establishments in this industry are business associations, professional organizations, labor unions, and political organizations.

81391 Business Associations[CAN]

See industry description for 813910 below.

813910 Business Associations[CAN]

This industry comprises establishments primarily engaged in promoting the business interests of their members. These establishments may conduct research on new products and services; develop market statistics; sponsor quality and certification standards; lobby public officials; or publish newsletters, books, or periodicals for distribution to their members.

Illustrative Examples:

Agricultural organizations (except youth farming organizations, farm granges)
Chambers of commerce
Manufacturers' associations
Real estate boards
Trade associations

Cross-References.

- Establishments owned by their members but organized to perform a specific business function, such as common marketing of crops, joint advertising, or buying cooperatives, are classified according to their primary activity;

US—United States industry only. CAN—United States and Canadian industries are comparable. MEX—United States and Mexican industries are comparable. Blank—Canadian, Mexican, and United States industries are comparable.

- Establishments primarily engaged in promoting the professional interests of their members and the profession as a whole are classified in Industry 813920, Professional Organizations;
- Establishments primarily engaged in promoting the interests of organized labor and union employees, such as trade unions, are classified in Industry 813930, Labor Unions and Similar Labor Organizations; and
- Establishments primarily engaged in lobbying public officials (i.e., lobbyists) are classified in Industry 541820, Public Relations Agencies.

81392 Professional Organizations[CAN]

See industry description for 813920 below.

813920 Professional Organizations[CAN]

This industry comprises establishments primarily engaged in promoting the professional interests of their members and the profession as a whole. These establishments may conduct research; develop statistics; sponsor quality and certification standards; lobby public officials; or publish newsletters, books, or periodicals for distribution to their members.

Illustrative Examples:

Bar associations
Dentists' associations
Engineers' associations
Health professionals' associations
Learned societies
Peer review boards
Professional standards review boards
Scientists' associations

Cross-References. Establishments primarily engaged in—

- Promoting the business interests of their members—are classified in Industry 813910, Business Associations; and
- Lobbying public officials (i.e., lobbyists)—are classified in Industry 541820, Public Relations Agencies.

81393 Labor Unions and Similar Labor Organizations[CAN]

See industry description for 813930 below.

813930 Labor Unions and Similar Labor Organizations[CAN]

This industry comprises establishments primarily engaged in promoting the interests of organized labor and union employees.

US—United States industry only. CAN—United States and Canadian industries are comparable. MEX—United States and Mexican industries are comparable. Blank—Canadian, Mexican, and United States industries are comparable.

81394 Political Organizations[CAN]

See industry description for 813940 below.

813940 Political Organizations[CAN]

This industry comprises establishments primarily engaged in promoting the interests of national, state, or local political parties or candidates. Included are political groups organized to raise funds for a political party or individual candidates.

Illustrative Examples:

Campaign organizations, political
Political action committees (PACs)
Political campaign organizations
Political organizations or clubs
Political parties

Cross-References. Establishments primarily engaged in—

- Organizing and conducting fundraising campaigns on a contract or fee basis—are classified in U.S. Industry 561499, All Other Business Support Services; and
- Providing telemarketing services for others—are classified in U.S. Industry 561422, Telemarketing Bureaus.

81399 Other Similar Organizations (except Business, Professional, Labor, and Political Organizations)[CAN]

See industry description for 813990 below.

813990 Other Similar Organizations (except Business, Professional, Labor, and Political Organizations)[CAN]

This industry comprises establishments (except religious organizations, social advocacy organizations, civic and social organizations, business associations, professional organizations, labor unions, and political organizations) primarily engaged in promoting the interest of their members.

Illustrative Examples:

Athletic associations, regulatory or administrative
Condominium and homeowners' associations
Cooperative owners' associations
Property owners' associations
Tenant associations (except advocacy)

Cross-References. Establishments primarily engaged in—

- Operating religious organizations, such as churches, religious temples, and monasteries—are classified in Industry 813110, Religious Organizations;

US—United States industry only. CAN—United States and Canadian industries are comparable. MEX—United States and Mexican industries are comparable. Blank—Canadian, Mexican, and United States industries are comparable.

- Raising funds for a wide range of social welfare activities and establishments known as grantmaking foundations or charitable trusts—are classified in Industry 81321, Grantmaking and Giving Services;
- Advocating social causes or issues—are classified in Industry 81331, Social Advocacy Organizations;
- Promoting the civic and social interests of their members—are classified in Industry 813410, Civic and Social Organizations;
- Promoting the business interests of their members—are classified in Industry 813910, Business Associations;
- Promoting the professional interests of their members and the profession as a whole—are classified in Industry 813920, Professional Organizations;
- Promoting the interests of organized labor and union employees—are classified in Industry 813930, Labor Unions and Similar Labor Organizations;
- Promoting the interests of national, state, or local political parties or candidates—are classified in Industry 813940, Political Organizations; and
- Providing recreational and amusement services, such as recreational or youth sports teams and leagues—are classified in Industry 713990, All Other Amusement and Recreation Industries.

814 Private Households

Industries in the Private Households subsector include private households that engage in employing workers on or about the premises in activities primarily concerned with the operation of the household. These private households may employ individuals, such as cooks, maids, and butlers, and outside workers, such as gardeners, caretakers, and other maintenance workers.

8141 Private Households

81411 Private Households

See industry description for 814110 below.

814110 Private Households

This industry comprises private households primarily engaged in employing workers on or about the premises in activities primarily concerned with the operation of the household. These private households may employ individuals, such as cooks, maids, nannies, and butlers, and outside workers, such as gardeners, caretakers, and other maintenance workers.

US—United States industry only. CAN—United States and Canadian industries are comparable. MEX—United States and Mexican industries are comparable. Blank—Canadian, Mexican, and United States industries are comparable.

Sector 92—Public Administration

The Sector as a Whole

The Public Administration sector consists of establishments of federal, state, and local government agencies that administer, oversee, and manage public programs and have executive, legislative, or judicial authority over other institutions within a given area. These agencies also set policy, create laws, adjudicate civil and criminal legal cases, provide for public safety and for national defense. In general, government establishments in the Public Administration sector oversee governmental programs and activities that are not performed by private establishments. Establishments in this sector typically are engaged in the organization and financing of the production of public goods and services, most of which are provided for free or at prices that are not economically significant.

Government establishments also engage in a wide range of productive activities covering not only public goods and services but also individual goods and services similar to those produced in sectors typically identified with private-sector establishments. In general, ownership is not a criterion for classification in NAICS. Therefore, government establishments engaged in the production of private-sector-like goods and services should be classified in the same industry as private-sector establishments engaged in similar activities.

As a practical matter, it is difficult to identify separate establishment detail for many government agencies. To the extent that separate establishment records are available, the administration of governmental programs is classified in Sector 92, Public Administration, while the operation of that same governmental program is classified elsewhere in NAICS based on the activities performed. For example, the governmental administrative authority for an airport is classified in Industry 92612, Regulation and Administration of Transportation Programs, while operating the airport is classified in Industry 48811, Airport Operations. When separate records are not available to distinguish between the administration of a governmental program and the operation of it, the establishment is classified in Sector 92, Public Administration.

Examples of government-provided goods and services that are classified in sectors other than Public Administration include: schools, classified in Sector 61, Educational Services; hospitals, classified in Subsector 622, Hospitals; establishments operating transportation facilities, classified in Sector 48-49, Transportation and Warehousing; the operation of utilities, classified in Sector 22, Utilities; and the Government Printing Office, classified in Subsector 323, Printing and Related Support Activities.

921 Executive, Legislative, and Other General Government Support[US]

The Executive, Legislative, and Other General Government Support subsector groups offices of government executives, legislative bodies, public finance and general government support.

US—United States industry only. CAN—United States and Canadian industries are comparable. MEX—United States and Mexican industries are comparable. Blank—Canadian, Mexican, and United States industries are comparable.

9211 Executive, Legislative, and Other General Government Support[US]

92111 Executive Offices[US]

See industry description for 921110 below.

921110 Executive Offices[US]

This industry comprises government establishments serving as offices of chief executives and their advisory committees and commissions. This industry includes offices of the president, governors, and mayors, in addition to executive advisory commissions.

92112 Legislative Bodies[US]

See industry description for 921120 below.

921120 Legislative Bodies[US]

This industry comprises government establishments serving as legislative bodies and their advisory committees and commissions. Included in this industry are legislative bodies, such as Congress, state legislatures, and advisory and study legislative commissions.

92113 Public Finance Activities[US]

See industry description for 921130 below.

921130 Public Finance Activities[US]

This industry comprises government establishments primarily engaged in public finance, taxation and monetary policy. Included are financial administration activities, such as monetary policy; tax administration and collection; custody and disbursement of funds; debt and investment administration; auditing activities; and government employee retirement trust fund administration.

Cross-References. Government establishments primarily engaged in—

- Administering income maintenance programs—are classified in Industry 923130, Administration of Human Resource Programs (except Education, Public Health, and Veterans' Affairs Programs);
- Regulating insurance and banking institutions—are classified in Industry 926150, Regulation, Licensing, and Inspection of Miscellaneous Commercial Sectors; and

---

US—United States industry only. CAN—United States and Canadian industries are comparable. MEX—United States and Mexican industries are comparable. Blank—Canadian, Mexican, and United States industries are comparable.

- Performing central banking functions, such as issuing currency and acting as the fiscal agent for the central government—are classified in Industry 521110, Monetary Authorities-Central Bank.

92114 Executive and Legislative Offices, Combined[US]

See industry description for 921140 below.

921140 Executive and Legislative Offices, Combined[US]

This industry comprises government establishments serving as councils and boards of commissioners or supervisors and such bodies where the chief executive (e.g., county executive or city mayor) is a member of the legislative body (e.g., county or city council) itself.

Cross-References. Government establishments primarily engaged in—

- Serving as offices of chief executives—are classified in Industry 921110, Executive Offices; and
- Serving as legislative bodies—are classified in Industry 921120, Legislative Bodies.

92115 American Indian and Alaska Native Tribal Governments[US]

See industry description for 921150 below.

921150 American Indian and Alaska Native Tribal Governments[US]

This industry comprises American Indian and Alaska Native governing bodies. Establishments in this industry perform legislative, judicial, and administrative functions for their American Indian and Alaska Native lands. Included in this industry are American Indian and Alaska Native councils, courts, and law enforcement bodies.

Cross-References.

- Establishments primarily engaged in providing funding for American Indian and Alaska Native tribal programs through commercial activities, such as gaming, are classified in the industry of the commercial activity; and
- Government establishments providing public administration of American Indian and Alaska Native affairs are classified in Industry 921190, Other General Government Support.

US—United States industry only. CAN—United States and Canadian industries are comparable. MEX—United States and Mexican industries are comparable. Blank—Canadian, Mexican, and United States industries are comparable.

92119 Other General Government Support[US]

See industry description for 921190 below.

921190 Other General Government Support[US]

This industry comprises government establishments primarily engaged in providing general support for government. Such support services include personnel services, election boards, and other general government support establishments that are not classified elsewhere in public administration.

Illustrative Examples:

Civil rights commissions
Civil service commissions
General services departments, government
Personnel offices, government
Supply agencies, government

Cross-References.

- Government establishments primarily engaged in serving as offices of chief executives and their advisory committees and commissions are classified in Industry 921110, Executive Offices;
- Government establishments primarily engaged in serving as legislative bodies and their advisory committees and commissions are classified in Industry 921120, Legislative bodies;
- Government establishments primarily engaged in providing administration of public finance, tax collection, and monetary policy programs are classified in Industry 921130, Public Finance Activities;
- Government establishments primarily engaged in serving as combined executive and legislative offices are classified in Industry 921140, Executive and Legislative Offices, Combined; and
- Establishments primarily engaged in serving as American Indian or Alaska Native tribal leadership are classified in Industry 921150, American Indian and Alaska Native Tribal Governments.

922 Justice, Public Order, and Safety Activities[US]

The Justice, Public Order, and Safety Activities subsector groups government establishments engaged in the administration of justice, public order, and safety programs.

9221 Justice, Public Order, and Safety Activities[US]

92211 Courts[US]

See industry description for 922110 below.

US—United States industry only. CAN—United States and Canadian industries are comparable. MEX—United States and Mexican industries are comparable. Blank—Canadian, Mexican, and United States industries are comparable.

922110 Courts[US]

This industry comprises civilian courts of law (except Indian tribal and Alaska Native courts). Included in this industry are civilian courts, courts of law, and sheriffs' offices conducting court functions only.

Cross-References.

- Government establishments primarily engaged in operating military courts are classified in Industry 928110, National Security; and
- Establishments primarily engaged in operating Indian tribal or Alaska Native courts are classified in Industry 921150, American Indian and Alaska Native Tribal Governments.

92212 Police Protection[US]

See industry description for 922120 below.

922120 Police Protection[US]

This industry comprises government establishments primarily engaged in criminal and civil law enforcement, police, traffic safety, and other activities related to the enforcement of the law and preservation of order. Combined police and fire departments are included in this industry.

Cross-References.

- Government establishments primarily engaged in prosecution are classified in Industry 922130, Legal Counsel and Prosecution;
- Government establishments primarily engaged in collection of law enforcement statistics are classified in Industry 922190, Other Justice, Public Order, and Safety Activities;
- Government establishments primarily engaged in providing police service for the military or National Guard are classified in Industry 928110, National Security;
- Government establishments primarily engaged in providing police service for tribal governments are classified in Industry 921150, American Indian and Alaska Native Tribal Governments;
- Government establishments primarily engaged in enforcing immigration laws are classified in Industry 928120, International Affairs;
- Sheriffs' offices conducting court functions only are classified in Industry 922110, Courts; and

---

US—United States industry only. CAN—United States and Canadian industries are comparable. MEX—United States and Mexican industries are comparable. Blank—Canadian, Mexican, and United States industries are comparable.

- Private establishments primarily engaged in providing security and investigation services are classified in Industry 56161, Investigation, Guard, and Armored Car Services.

92213 Legal Counsel and Prosecution[US]

See industry description for 922130 below.

922130 Legal Counsel and Prosecution[US]

This industry comprises government establishments primarily engaged in providing legal counsel or prosecution services for the government.

Illustrative Examples:

Attorney generals' offices
District attorneys' offices
Public defenders' offices
Public prosecutors' offices

Cross-References.

Government establishments primarily engaged in collecting criminal justice statistics are classified in Industry 922190, Other Justice, Public Order, and Safety Activities.

92214 Correctional Institutions[US]

See industry description for 922140 below.

922140 Correctional Institutions[US]

This industry comprises government establishments primarily engaged in managing and operating correctional institutions. The facility is generally designed for the confinement, correction, and rehabilitation of adult and/or juvenile offenders sentenced by a court.

Illustrative Examples:

Correctional institutions, public administration
Detention centers, public administration
Jails, public administration
Penitentiaries, public administration
Prisons, public administration

Cross-References.

- Government establishments primarily engaged in operating half-way houses for ex-criminal offenders and delinquent youths are classified in Industry 623990, Other Residential Care Facilities; and

US—United States industry only. CAN—United States and Canadian industries are comparable. MEX—United States and Mexican industries are comparable. Blank—Canadian, Mexican, and United States industries are comparable.

- Establishments primarily engaged in managing or operating correctional facilities owned by others are classified in Industry 561210, Facilities Support Services.

92215 Parole Offices and Probation Offices[US]

See industry description for 922150 below.

922150 Parole Offices and Probation Offices[US]

This industry comprises government establishments primarily engaged in judicially administering probation offices, parole offices and boards, and pardon boards.

Cross-References.

Government establishments primarily engaged in providing probation, parole, and pardon activities as an integral part of a central administrative corrections' office are classified in Industry 922140, Correctional Institutions.

92216 Fire Protection[US]

See industry description for 922160 below.

922160 Fire Protection[US]

This industry comprises government establishments primarily engaged in fire fighting and other related fire protection activities. Government establishments providing combined fire protection and ambulance or rescue services are classified in this industry.

Cross-References. Government establishments primarily engaged in—

- Forest fire fighting—are classified in Industry 115310, Support Activities for Forestry;
- Providing combined police and fire protection services—are classified in Industry 922120, Police Protection;
- Providing fire fighting services as a commercial activity—are classified in Industry 561990, All Other Support Services; and
- Providing ambulance services without fire protection service—are classified in Industry 621910, Ambulance Services.

92219 Other Justice, Public Order, and Safety Activities[US]

See industry description for 922190 below.

US—United States industry only. CAN—United States and Canadian industries are comparable. MEX—United States and Mexican industries are comparable. Blank—Canadian, Mexican, and United States industries are comparable.

922190 Other Justice, Public Order, and Safety Activities[US]

This industry comprises government establishments primarily engaged in public order and safety (except courts, police protection, legal counsel and prosecution, correctional institutions, parole offices, probation offices, pardon boards, and fire protection). These establishments include the general administration of public order and safety programs. Government establishments responsible for the collection of statistics on public safety are included in this industry.

Illustrative Examples:

Consumer product safety commissions, public administration
Disaster preparedness and management offices, government
Emergency planning and management offices, government
Public safety bureaus and statistics centers, government

Cross-References. Government establishments primarily engaged in—

- Serving as civilian courts of law (except Indian tribal and Alaska Native)—are classified in Industry 922110, Courts;
- Criminal and civil law enforcement, police, traffic safety and similar activities related to the enforcement of law—are classified in Industry 922120, Police Protection;
- Providing legal counsel to or prosecution services for their governments—are classified in Industry 922130, Legal Counsel and Prosecution;
- The confinement, correction, and rehabilitation of adult and juvenile offenders sentenced by a court—are classified in Industry 922140, Correctional Institutions;
- Judicially administering probation offices, parole offices and boards, and pardon boards—are classified in Industry 922150, Parole Offices and Probation Offices; and
- Fire fighting and other related fire protection activities—are classified in Industry 922160, Fire Protection.

923 Administration of Human Resource Programs[US]

The Administration of Human Resource Programs subsector groups government establishments primarily engaged in the administration of human resource programs.

9231 Administration of Human Resource Programs[US]

92311 Administration of Education Programs[US]

See industry description for 923110 below.

US—United States industry only. CAN—United States and Canadian industries are comparable. MEX—United States and Mexican industries are comparable. Blank—Canadian, Mexican, and United States industries are comparable.

923110 Administration of Education Programs[US]

This industry comprises government establishments primarily engaged in the central coordination, planning, supervision and administration of funds, policies, intergovernmental activities, statistical reports and data collection, and centralized programs for educational administration. Government scholarship programs are included in this industry.

Illustrative Examples:

Education offices, nonoperating, public administration
Education statistics centers, government
State education departments
University regents or boards, government

Cross-References.

Schools and local school boards are classified in Subsector 611, Educational Services.

92312 Administration of Public Health Programs[US]

See industry description for 923120 below.

923120 Administration of Public Health Programs[US]

This industry comprises government establishments primarily engaged in the planning, administration, and coordination of public health programs and services, including environmental health activities, mental health, categorical health programs, health statistics, and immunization services. Government establishments primarily engaged in conducting public health-related inspections are included in this industry.

Illustrative Examples:

Communicable disease program administration, public administration
Coroners' offices, public administration
Health program administration, public administration
Mental health program administration, public administration
Public health program administration, nonoperating, public administration

Cross-References. Government establishments primarily engaged in—

- Operating hospitals (i.e., government or military)—are classified in Subsector 622, Hospitals;
- Providing health care in a clinical setting (i.e., military or government clinics)—are classified in Subsector 621, Ambulatory Health Care Services; and

US—United States industry only. CAN—United States and Canadian industries are comparable. MEX—United States and Mexican industries are comparable. Blank—Canadian, Mexican, and United States industries are comparable.

- Inspecting food, plants, animals, and other agriculture products—are classified in Industry 926140, Regulation of Agricultural Marketing and Commodities.

92313 Administration of Human Resource Programs (except Education, Public Health, and Veterans' Affairs Programs)[US]

See industry description for 923130 below.

923130 Administration of Human Resource Programs (except Education, Public Health, and Veterans' Affairs Programs)[US]

This industry comprises government establishments primarily engaged in the planning, administration, and coordination of programs for public assistance, social work, and welfare activities. The administration of Social Security, disability insurance, Medicare, unemployment insurance, and workers' compensation programs are included in this industry.

Cross-References. Government establishments primarily engaged in—

- Administering veterans' programs—are classified in Industry 923140, Administration of Veterans' Affairs;
- Operating state employment job service offices—are classified in Industry 561310, Employment Placement Agencies; and
- Operating programs for public assistance, social work, and welfare—are classified in Subsector 624, Social Assistance.

92314 Administration of Veterans' Affairs[US]

See industry description for 923140 below.

923140 Administration of Veterans' Affairs[US]

This industry comprises government establishments primarily engaged in the administration of programs of assistance, training, counseling, and other services to veterans and their dependents, heirs or survivors. Included in this industry are Veterans' Affairs offices that maintain liaison and coordinate activities with other service organizations and governmental agencies.

Cross-References.

- Government establishments operating veterans' hospitals are classified in Subsector 622, Hospitals;

US—United States industry only. CAN—United States and Canadian industries are comparable. MEX—United States and Mexican industries are comparable. Blank—Canadian, Mexican, and United States industries are comparable.

- Establishments providing veterans' insurance are classified in Subsector 524, Insurance Carriers and Related Activities; and
- Establishments operating civic and social organizations for veterans are classified in Industry 813410, Civic and Social Organizations.

924 Administration of Environmental Quality Programs[US]

The Administration of Environmental Quality Programs subsector groups government establishments primarily engaged in the administration of environmental quality.

9241 Administration of Environmental Quality Programs[US]

92411 Administration of Air and Water Resource and Solid Waste Management Programs[US]

See industry description for 924110 below.

924110 Administration of Air and Water Resource and Solid Waste Management Programs[US]

This industry comprises government establishments primarily engaged in one or more of the following: (1) the administration, regulation, and enforcement of air and water resource programs; (2) the administration and regulation of solid waste management programs; (3) the administration and regulation of water and air pollution control and prevention programs; (4) the administration and regulation of flood control programs; (5) the administration and regulation of drainage development and water resource consumption programs; (6) the administration and regulation of toxic waste removal and cleanup programs; and (7) coordination of these activities at intergovernmental levels.

Illustrative Examples:

Environmental protection program administration, public administration
Pollution control program administration, public administration
Waste management program (except sanitation districts), administration, public administration
Water control and quality program administration, public administration

Cross-References. Government establishments primarily engaged in—

- Operating water and irrigation systems—are classified in Industry 221310, Water Supply and Irrigation Systems;

US—United States industry only. CAN—United States and Canadian industries are comparable. MEX—United States and Mexican industries are comparable. Blank—Canadian, Mexican, and United States industries are comparable.

- Administering sanitation districts—are classified in Industry 926130, Regulation and Administration of Communications, Electric, Gas, and Other Utilities;
- Operating sewage treatment facilities—are classified in Industry 221320, Sewage Treatment Facilities; and
- Providing waste collection, treatment, disposal, and/or remediation—are classified in Subsector 562, Waste Management and Remediation Services.

92412 Administration of Conservation Programs[US]

See industry description for 924120 below.

924120 Administration of Conservation Programs[US]

This industry comprises government establishments primarily engaged in the administration, regulation, supervision and control of land use, including recreational areas; conservation and preservation of natural resources; erosion control; geological survey program administration; weather forecasting program administration; and the administration and protection of publicly and privately owned forest lands. Government establishments responsible for planning, management, regulation and conservation of game, fish, and wildlife populations, including wildlife management areas and field stations; and other administrative matters relating to the protection of fish, game, and wildlife are included in this industry.

Cross-References. Government establishments primarily engaged in—

- Operating parks—are classified in Industry 712190, Nature Parks and Other Similar Institutions;
- Operating forest property—are classified in Subsector 113, Forestry and Logging;
- Geophysical surveying and/or mapping—are classified in Industry 541360, Geophysical Surveying and Mapping Services;
- Surveying and/or mapping (except geophysical)—are classified in Industry 541370, Surveying and Mapping (except Geophysical) Services;
- Weather forecasting—are classified in Industry 541990, All Other Professional, Scientific and Technical Services;
- Operating fish and game preserves—are classified in Industry 712130, Zoos and Botanical Gardens; and
- Serving as urban planning commissions—are classified in Industry 925120, Administration of Urban Planning and Community and Rural Development.

US—United States industry only. CAN—United States and Canadian industries are comparable. MEX—United States and Mexican industries are comparable. Blank—Canadian, Mexican, and United States industries are comparable.

925 Administration of Housing Programs, Urban Planning, and Community Development[US]

The Administration of Housing Programs, Urban Planning, and Community Development subsector groups government establishments primarily engaged in the administration of housing, urban planning, and community development.

9251 Administration of Housing Programs, Urban Planning, and Community Development[US]

92511 Administration of Housing Programs[US]

See industry description for 925110 below.

925110 Administration of Housing Programs[US]

This industry comprises government establishments primarily engaged in the administration and planning of housing programs.

Cross-References. Government establishments primarily engaged in—

- Operating government rental housing—are classified in Subsector 531, Real Estate;
- Conducting building inspections and enforcing building codes and standards—are classified in Industry 926150, Regulation, Licensing, and Inspection of Miscellaneous Commercial Sectors; and
- Buying, pooling, and repackaging mortgages or home loans for sale to others on the secondary market—are classified in U.S. Industry 522294, Secondary Market Financing.

92512 Administration of Urban Planning and Community and Rural Development[US]

See industry description for 925120 below.

925120 Administration of Urban Planning and Community and Rural Development[US]

This industry comprises government establishments primarily engaged in the administration and planning of the development of urban and rural areas. Included in this industry are government zoning boards and commissions.

US—United States industry only. CAN—United States and Canadian industries are comparable. MEX—United States and Mexican industries are comparable. Blank—Canadian, Mexican, and United States industries are comparable.

Illustrative Examples:

Land redevelopment agencies, government
Regional planning and development program administration, public administration
Urban planning commissions, government
Zoning boards and commissions, public administration

926 Administration of Economic Programs[US]

This subsector comprises government establishments primarily engaged in the administration of economic programs.

9261 Administration of Economic Program[US]

92611 Administration of General Economic Programs[US]

See industry description for 926110 below.

926110 Administration of General Economic Programs[US]

This industry comprises government establishments primarily engaged in the administration, promotion and development of economic resources, including business, industry, and tourism. Included in this industry are government establishments responsible for the development of general statistical data and analyses and promotion of the general economic well-being of the governed area.

Illustrative Examples:

Consumer protection offices, public administration
Economic development agencies, government
General economics statistical agencies, public administration
Small business development agencies, public administration
Trade commissions, government

92612 Regulation and Administration of Transportation Programs[US]

See industry description for 926120 below.

926120 Regulation and Administration of Transportation Program[US]

This industry comprises government establishments primarily engaged in the administration, regulation, licensing, planning, inspection, and investigation of transportation services and facilities. Included in this industry are government

US—United States industry only. CAN—United States and Canadian industries are comparable. MEX—United States and Mexican industries are comparable. Blank—Canadian, Mexican, and United States industries are comparable.

establishments responsible for motor vehicle and operator licensing, the Coast Guard (except the Coast Guard Academy), and parking authorities.

Cross-References. Government establishments primarily engaged in—

- Operating airports, railroads, depots, ports, toll roads and bridges, and other transportation facilities—are classified in Sector 48-49, Transportation and Warehousing;
- Operating parking lots and parking garages—are classified in Industry 812930, Parking Lots and Garages;
- Operating automobile safety inspection and emission testing facilities—are classified in Industry Group 8111, Automotive Repair and Maintenance;
- Building and/or maintaining roads and highways—are classified in Industry 237310, Highway, Street and Bridge Construction;
- Providing air traffic control services—are classified in U.S. Industry 488111, Air Traffic Control; and
- Operating weigh stations—are classified in Industry 488490, Other Support Activities for Road Transportation.

92613 Regulation and Administration of Communications, Electric, Gas, and Other Utilities[US]

See industry description for 926130 below.

926130 Regulation and Administration of Communications, Electric, Gas, and Other Utilities[US]

This industry comprises government establishments primarily engaged in the administration, regulation, licensing and inspection of utilities, such as communications, electric power (including fossil, nuclear, solar, water, and wind), gas and water supply, and sewerage.

Cross-References.

Government establishments primarily engaged in operating utilities are classified in Subsector 221, Utilities.

92614 Regulation of Agricultural Marketing and Commodities[US]

See industry description for 926140 below.

926140 Regulation of Agricultural Marketing and Commodities[US]

This industry comprises government establishments primarily engaged in the planning, administration, and coordination of agricultural programs for production,

US—United States industry only. CAN—United States and Canadian industries are comparable. MEX—United States and Mexican industries are comparable. Blank—Canadian, Mexican, and United States industries are comparable.

marketing, and utilization, including educational and promotional activities. Included in this industry are government establishments responsible for regulating and controlling the grading and inspection of food, plants, animals, and other agricultural products.

Cross-References. Government establishments primarily engaged in—

- Administering programs for developing economic data about agricultural and trade in agricultural products—are classified in Industry 926110, Administration of General Economic Programs;
- Administering programs for the conservation of natural resources—are classified in Industry Group 9241, Administration of Environmental Quality Programs; and
- Administering food stamp programs—are classified in Industry 923130, Administration Human Resource Programs (except Education, Public Health, and Veterans' Affairs Programs).

92615 Regulation, Licensing, and Inspection of Miscellaneous Commercial Sectors[US]

See industry description for 926150 below.

926150 Regulation, Licensing, and Inspection of Miscellaneous Commercial Sectors[US]

This industry comprises government establishments primarily engaged in the regulation, licensing, and inspection of commercial sectors, such as retail trade, professional occupations, manufacturing, mining, construction, and services. Included in this industry are government establishments maintaining physical standards, regulating hazardous conditions not elsewhere classified, and enforcing alcoholic beverage control regulations.

Illustrative Examples:

Alcoholic beverage control boards, public administration
Banking regulatory agencies, public administration
Building inspections, government
Insurance commissions, government
Labor management negotiations boards, government
Licensing and permit issuance for professional occupations, government
Licensing and permit issuance for business operations, government
Securities regulation commissions, public administration

US—United States industry only. CAN—United States and Canadian industries are comparable. MEX—United States and Mexican industries are comparable. Blank—Canadian, Mexican, and United States industries are comparable.

Cross-References. Government establishments primarily engaged in—

- Regulating, administering, and inspecting transportation services and facilities—are classified in Industry 926120, Regulation and Administration of Transportation Programs; and
- Regulating, administering, and inspecting communications, electric, gas, and other utilities—are classified in Industry 926130, Regulation and Administration of Communications, Electric, Gas, and Other Utilities.

927 Space Research and Technology[US]

This subsector group comprises government establishments that conduct space research.

9271 Space Research and Technology[US]

92711 Space Research and Technology[US]

See industry description for 927110 below.

927110 Space Research and Technology[US]

This industry comprises government establishments primarily engaged in the administration and operations of space flights, space research, and space exploration. Included in this industry are government establishments operating space flight centers.

Cross-References.

- Private establishments primarily engaged in providing space freight transportation are classified in U.S. Industry 481212, Nonscheduled Chartered Freight Air Transportation;
- Government establishments primarily engaged in manufacturing aerospace vehicles and parts are classified in Industry 33641, Aerospace Product and Parts Manufacturing; and
- Government establishments primarily engaged in manufacturing space satellites are classified in Industry 334220, Radio and Television Broadcasting and Wireless Communications Equipment Manufacturing.

928 National Security and International Affairs[US]

This subsector comprises government establishments primarily engaged in national security and international affairs.

US—United States industry only. CAN—United States and Canadian industries are comparable. MEX—United States and Mexican industries are comparable. Blank—Canadian, Mexican, and United States industries are comparable.

9281 National Security and International Affairs[US]

92811 National Security[US]

See industry description for 928110 below.

928110 National Security[US]

This industry comprises government establishments of the Armed Forces, including the National Guard, primarily engaged in national security and related activities.

Illustrative Examples:

Air Force
Army
Marine Corps
Military courts
Military police
Military training schools (except military service academies)
National Guard
Navy

Cross-References. Government establishments primarily engaged in—

- Operating military service academies—are classified in Industry 611310, Colleges, Universities, and Professional Schools; and
- Regulating and administering water transportation, such as the U.S. Coast Guard and the Merchant Marine—are classified in Industry 926120, Regulation and Administration of Transportation Programs.

92812 International Affairs[US]

See industry description for 928120 below.

928120 International Affairs[US]

This industry comprises establishments of U.S. and foreign governments primarily engaged in international affairs and programs relating to other nations and peoples.

Cross-References.

- Private sector trade associations and councils are classified in Industry 813910, Business Associations; and
- Government establishments administering international trade, such as trade commissions and councils are classified in Industry 926110, Administration of General Economic Programs.

US—United States industry only. CAN—United States and Canadian industries are comparable. MEX—United States and Mexican industries are comparable. Blank—Canadian, Mexican, and United States industries are comparable.

Part II

List of Short Titles

List of Short Titles

Standard Short Titles for NAICS United States are shown below. They have been created for the use of those who find that space limitations preclude the use of the full title for the dissemination of data classified to NAICS. The adoptions of these titles is recommended in all cases when the full title cannot be used.

The standard short titles are limited to 45 spaces. If the official full title falls within 45 spaces it remains unchanged.

Note: For definitions of abbreviations and acronyms see page 964.

Code	Short title
11	**AGRICULTURE, FORESTRY, FISHING AND HUNTING**
111	**Crop production**
1111	Oilseed and grain farming
11111	Soybean farming
111110	Soybean farming
11112	Oilseed, except soybean, farming
111120	Oilseed, except soybean, farming
11113	Dry pea and bean farming
111130	Dry pea and bean farming
11114	Wheat farming
111140	Wheat farming
11115	Corn farming
111150	Corn farming
11116	Rice farming
111160	Rice farming
11119	Other grain farming
111191	Oilseed and grain combination farming
111199	All other grain farming
1112	Vegetable and melon farming
11121	Vegetable and melon farming
111211	Potato farming
111219	Other vegetable and melon farming
1113	Fruit and tree nut farming
11131	Orange groves
111310	Orange groves
11132	Citrus, except orange, groves
111320	Citrus, except orange, groves
11133	Noncitrus fruit and tree nut farming
111331	Apple orchards
111332	Grape vineyards
111333	Strawberry farming
111334	Berry, except strawberry, farming
111335	Tree nut farming
111336	Fruit and tree nut combination farming
111339	Other noncitrus fruit farming
1114	Greenhouse and nursery production
11141	Food crops grown under cover
111411	Mushroom production
111419	Other food crops grown under cover
11142	Nursery and floriculture production
111421	Nursery and tree production
111422	Floriculture production
1119	Other crop farming
11191	Tobacco farming
111910	Tobacco farming
11192	Cotton farming
111920	Cotton farming
11193	Sugarcane farming
111930	Sugarcane farming
11194	Hay farming
111940	Hay farming
11199	All other crop farming
111991	Sugar beet farming
111992	Peanut farming
111998	All other miscellaneous crop farming
112	**Animal production**
1121	Cattle ranching and farming
11211	Beef cattle ranching, farming, and feedlots
112111	Beef cattle ranching and farming
112112	Cattle feedlots
11212	Dairy cattle and milk production
112120	Dairy cattle and milk production
11213	Dual-purpose cattle ranching and farming
112130	Dual-purpose cattle ranching and farming
1122	Hog and pig farming
11221	Hog and pig farming
112210	Hog and pig farming
1123	Poultry and egg production
11231	Chicken egg production

Note: For definitions of abbreviations and acronyms see page 964.

Code	Short title
112310	Chicken egg production
11232	Broilers and meat type chicken production
112320	Broilers and meat type chicken production
11233	Turkey production
112330	Turkey production
11234	Poultry hatcheries
112340	Poultry hatcheries
11239	Other poultry production
112390	Other poultry production
1124	Sheep and goat farming
11241	Sheep farming
112410	Sheep farming
11242	Goat farming
112420	Goat farming
1125	Animal aquaculture
11251	Animal aquaculture
112511	Finfish farming and fish hatcheries
112512	Shellfish farming
112519	Other animal aquaculture
1129	Other animal production
11291	Apiculture
112910	Apiculture
11292	Horses and other equine production
112920	Horses and other equine production
11293	Fur-bearing animal and rabbit production
112930	Fur-bearing animal and rabbit production
11299	All other animal production
112990	All other animal production
113	**Forestry and logging**
1131	Timber tract operations
11311	Timber tract operations
113110	Timber tract operations
1132	Forest nursery and gathering forest products
11321	Forest nursery and gathering forest products
113210	Forest nursery and gathering forest products
1133	Logging
11331	Logging
113310	Logging
114	**Fishing, hunting and trapping**
1141	Fishing
11411	Fishing
114111	Finfish fishing
114112	Shellfish fishing
114119	Other marine fishing
1142	Hunting and trapping
11421	Hunting and trapping
114210	Hunting and trapping
115	**Agriculture and forestry support activities**
1151	Support activities for crop production
11511	Support activities for crop production
115111	Cotton ginning
115112	Soil preparation, planting, and cultivating
115113	Crop harvesting, primarily by machine
115114	Other postharvest crop activities
115115	Farm labor contractors and crew leaders
115116	Farm management services
1152	Support activities for animal production
11521	Support activities for animal production
115210	Support activities for animal production
1153	Support activities for forestry
11531	Support activities for forestry
115310	Support activities for forestry
21	**MINING**
211	**Oil and gas extraction**
2111	Oil and gas extraction
21111	Oil and gas extraction

Note: For definitions of abbreviations and acronyms see page 964.

Code	Short title
211111	Crude petroleum and natural gas extraction
211112	Natural gas liquid extraction
212	Mining, except oil and gas
2121	Coal mining
21211	Coal mining
212111	Bituminous coal and lignite surface mining
212112	Bituminous coal underground mining
212113	Anthracite mining
2122	Metal ore mining
21221	Iron ore mining
212210	Iron ore mining
21222	Gold ore and silver ore mining
212221	Gold ore mining
212222	Silver ore mining
21223	Copper, nickel, lead, and zinc mining
212231	Lead ore and zinc ore mining
212234	Copper ore and nickel ore mining
21229	Other metal ore mining
212291	Uranium-radium-vanadium ore mining
212299	All other metal ore mining
2123	Nonmetallic mineral mining and quarrying
21231	Stone mining and quarrying
212311	Dimension stone mining and quarrying
212312	Crushed and broken limestone mining
212313	Crushed and broken granite mining
212319	Other crushed and broken stone mining
21232	Sand, gravel, clay, and refractory mining
212321	Construction sand and gravel mining
212322	Industrial sand mining
212324	Kaolin and ball clay mining
212325	Clay, ceramic, and refractory minerals mining
21239	Other nonmetallic mineral mining
212391	Potash, soda, and borate mineral mining
212392	Phosphate rock mining
212393	Other chemical and fertilizer mineral mining
212399	All other nonmetallic mineral mining
213	**Support activities for mining**
2131	Support activities for mining
21311	Support activities for mining
213111	Drilling oil and gas wells
213112	Support activities for oil and gas operations
213113	Support activities for coal mining
213114	Support activities for metal mining
213115	Support activities for nonmetallic minerals
22	**UTILITIES**
221	**Utilities**
2211	Power generation and supply
22111	Electric power generation
221111	Hydroelectric power generation
221112	Fossil fuel electric power generation
221113	Nuclear electric power generation
221119	Other electric power generation
22112	Electric power transmission and distribution
221121	Electric bulk power transmission and control
221122	Electric power distribution
2212	Natural gas distribution
22121	Natural gas distribution
221210	Natural gas distribution
2213	Water, sewage and other systems
22131	Water supply and irrigation systems

Note: For definitions of abbreviations and acronyms see page 964.

Code	Short title
221310	Water supply and irrigation systems
22132	Sewage treatment facilities
221320	Sewage treatment facilities
22133	Steam and air-conditioning supply
221330	Steam and air-conditioning supply
23	**CONSTRUCTION**
236	**Construction of buildings**
2361	Residential building construction
23611	Residential building construction
236115	New single-family general contractors
236116	New multifamily general contractors
236117	New housing operative builders
236118	Residential remodelers
2362	Nonresidential building construction
23621	Industrial building construction
236210	Industrial building construction
23622	Commercial building construction
236220	Commercial building construction
237	**Heavy and civil engineering construction**
2371	Utility system construction
23711	Water and sewer system construction
237110	Water and sewer system construction
23712	Oil and gas pipeline construction
237120	Oil and gas pipeline construction
23713	Power and communication system construction
237130	Power and communication system construction

Code	Short title
2372	Land subdivision
23721	Land subdivision
237210	Land subdivision
2373	Highway, street, and bridge construction
23731	Highway, street, and bridge construction
237310	Highway, street, and bridge construction
2379	Other heavy construction
23799	Other heavy construction
237990	Other heavy construction
238	**Specialty trade contractors**
2381	Building foundation and exterior contractors
23811	Poured concrete structure contractors
238110	Poured concrete structure contractors
23812	Steel and precast concrete contractors
238120	Steel and precast concrete contractors
23813	Framing contractors
238130	Framing contractors
23814	Masonry contractors
238140	Masonry contractors
23815	Glass and glazing contractors
238150	Glass and glazing contractors
23816	Roofing contractors
238160	Roofing contractors
23817	Siding contractors
238170	Siding contractors
23819	Other building exterior contractors
238190	Other building exterior contractors
2382	Building equipment contractors
23821	Electrical contractors
238210	Electrical contractors
23822	Plumbing and HVAC contractors
238220	Plumbing and HVAC contractors

Note: For definitions of abbreviations and acronyms see page 964.

Code	Short title
23829	Other building equipment contractors
238290	Other building equipment contractors
2383	Building finishing contractors
23831	Drywall and insulation contractors
238310	Drywall and insulation contractors
23832	Painting and wall covering contractors
238320	Painting and wall covering contractors
23833	Flooring contractors
238330	Flooring contractors
23834	Tile and terrazzo contractors
238340	Tile and terrazzo contractors
23835	Finish carpentry contractors
238350	Finish carpentry contractors
23839	Other building finishing contractors
238390	Other building finishing contractors
2389	Other specialty trade contractors
23891	Site preparation contractors
238910	Site preparation contractors
23899	All other specialty trade contractors
238990	All other specialty trade contractors
31-33	**MANUFACTURING**
311	**Food manufacturing**
3111	Animal food manufacturing
31111	Animal food manufacturing
311111	Dog and cat food manufacturing
311119	Other animal food manufacturing
3112	Grain and oilseed milling
31121	Flour milling and malt manufacturing
311211	Flour milling
311212	Rice milling
311213	Malt manufacturing
31122	Starch and vegetable oil manufacturing
311221	Wet corn milling
311222	Soybean processing
311223	Other oilseed processing
311225	Fats and oils refining and blending
31123	Breakfast cereal manufacturing
311230	Breakfast cereal manufacturing
3113	Sugar and confectionery product manufacturing
31131	Sugar manufacturing
311311	Sugarcane mills
311312	Cane sugar refining
311313	Beet sugar manufacturing
31132	Confectionery manufacturing from cacao beans
311320	Confectionery manufacturing from cacao beans
31133	Confectionery mfg. from purchased chocolate
311330	Confectionery mfg. from purchased chocolate
31134	Nonchocolate confectionery manufacturing
311340	Nonchocolate confectionery manufacturing
3114	Fruit and vegetable preserving and specialty
31141	Frozen food manufacturing
311411	Frozen fruit and vegetable manufacturing
311412	Frozen specialty food manufacturing
31142	Fruit and vegetable canning and drying
311421	Fruit and vegetable canning
311422	Specialty canning
311423	Dried and dehydrated food manufacturing
3115	Dairy product manufacturing
31151	Dairy product, except frozen, manufacturing
311511	Fluid milk manufacturing
311512	Creamery butter manufacturing

Note: For definitions of abbreviations and acronyms see page 964.

Code	Short title
311513	Cheese manufacturing
311514	Dry, condensed, and evaporated dairy products
31152	Ice cream and frozen dessert manufacturing
311520	Ice cream and frozen dessert manufacturing
3116	Animal slaughtering and processing
31161	Animal slaughtering and processing
311611	Animal, except poultry, slaughtering
311612	Meat processed from carcasses
311613	Rendering and meat byproduct processing
311615	Poultry processing
3117	Seafood product preparation and packaging
31171	Seafood product preparation and packaging
311711	Seafood canning
311712	Fresh and frozen seafood processing
3118	Bakeries and tortilla manufacturing
31181	Bread and bakery product manufacturing
311811	Retail bakeries
311812	Commercial bakeries
311813	Frozen cakes and other pastries manufacturing
31182	Cookie, cracker, and pasta manufacturing
311821	Cookie and cracker manufacturing
311822	Mixes and dough made from purchased flour
311823	Dry pasta manufacturing
31183	Tortilla manufacturing
311830	Tortilla manufacturing
3119	Other food manufacturing
31191	Snack food manufacturing
311911	Roasted nuts and peanut butter manufacturing
311919	Other snack food manufacturing
31192	Coffee and tea manufacturing
311920	Coffee and tea manufacturing
31193	Flavoring syrup and concentrate manufacturing
311930	Flavoring syrup and concentrate manufacturing
31194	Seasoning and dressing manufacturing
311941	Mayonnaise, dressing, and sauce manufacturing
311942	Spice and extract manufacturing
31199	All other food manufacturing
311991	Perishable prepared food manufacturing
311999	All other miscellaneous food manufacturing
312	**Beverage and tobacco product manufacturing**
3121	Beverage manufacturing
31211	Soft drink and ice manufacturing
312111	Soft drink manufacturing
312112	Bottled water manufacturing
312113	Ice manufacturing
31212	Breweries
312120	Breweries
31213	Wineries
312130	Wineries
31214	Distilleries
312140	Distilleries
3122	Tobacco manufacturing
31221	Tobacco stemming and redrying
312210	Tobacco stemming and redrying
31222	Tobacco product manufacturing
312221	Cigarette manufacturing
312229	Other tobacco product manufacturing
313	**Textile mills**
3131	Fiber, yarn, and thread mills
31311	Fiber, yarn, and thread mills
313111	Yarn spinning mills

Note: For definitions of abbreviations and acronyms see page 964.

Code	Short title
313112	Yarn texturizing and twisting mills
313113	Thread mills
3132	Fabric mills
31321	Broadwoven fabric mills
313210	Broadwoven fabric mills
31322	Narrow fabric mills and schiffli embroidery
313221	Narrow fabric mills
313222	Schiffli machine embroidery
31323	Nonwoven fabric mills
313230	Nonwoven fabric mills
31324	Knit fabric mills
313241	Weft knit fabric mills
313249	Other knit fabric and lace mills
3133	Textile and fabric finishing mills
31331	Textile and fabric finishing mills
313311	Broadwoven fabric finishing mills
313312	Other textile and fabric finishing mills
31332	Fabric coating mills
313320	Fabric coating mills
314	**Textile product mills**
3141	Textile furnishings mills
31411	Carpet and rug mills
314110	Carpet and rug mills
31412	Curtain and linen mills
314121	Curtain and drapery mills
314129	Other household textile product mills
3149	Other textile product mills
31491	Textile bag and canvas mills
314911	Textile bag mills
314912	Canvas and related product mills
31499	All other textile product mills
314991	Rope, cordage, and twine mills
314992	Tire cord and tire fabric mills
314999	All other miscellaneous textile product mills

Code	Short title
315	**Apparel manufacturing**
3151	Apparel knitting mills
31511	Hosiery and sock mills
315111	Sheer hosiery mills
315119	Other hosiery and sock mills
31519	Other apparel knitting mills
315191	Outerwear knitting mills
315192	Underwear and nightwear knitting mills
3152	Cut and sew apparel manufacturing
31521	Cut and sew apparel contractors
315211	Men's cut and sew apparel contractors
315212	Women's cut and sew apparel contractors
31522	Men's cut and sew apparel manufacturing
315221	Men's underwear and nightwear manufacturing
315222	Men's suit, coat, and overcoat manufacturing
315223	Men's shirt, except work shirt, manufacturing
315224	Men's pants, except work pants, manufacturing
315225	Men's work clothing manufacturing
315228	Other men's outerwear manufacturing
31523	Women's cut and sew apparel manufacturing
315231	Women's lingerie and nightwear manufacturing
315232	Women's blouse and shirt manufacturing
315233	Women's dress manufacturing
315234	Women's suit, coat, jacket, and skirt mfg.
315239	Other women's outerwear manufacturing
31529	Other cut and sew apparel manufacturing
315291	Infants' cut and sew apparel manufacturing

Note: For definitions of abbreviations and acronyms see page 964.

Code	Short title
315292	Fur and leather apparel manufacturing
315299	All other cut and sew apparel manufacturing
3159	Accessories and other apparel manufacturing
31599	Accessories and other apparel manufacturing
315991	Hat, cap, and millinery manufacturing
315992	Glove and mitten manufacturing
315993	Men's and boys' neckwear manufacturing
315999	All other accessory and apparel manufacturing
316	**Leather and allied product manufacturing**
3161	Leather and hide tanning and finishing
31611	Leather and hide tanning and finishing
316110	Leather and hide tanning and finishing
3162	Footwear manufacturing
31621	Footwear manufacturing
316211	Rubber and plastics footwear manufacturing
316212	House slipper manufacturing
316213	Men's nonathletic footwear manufacturing
316214	Women's nonathletic footwear manufacturing
316219	Other footwear manufacturing
3169	Other leather product manufacturing
31699	Other leather product manufacturing
316991	Luggage manufacturing
316992	Women's handbag and purse manufacturing
316993	Other personal leather good manufacturing
316999	All other leather good manufacturing
321	**Wood product manufacturing**
3211	Sawmills and wood preservation
32111	Sawmills and wood preservation
321113	Sawmills
321114	Wood preservation
3212	Plywood and engineered wood product mfg.
32121	Plywood and engineered wood product mfg.
321211	Hardwood veneer and plywood manufacturing
321212	Softwood veneer and plywood manufacturing
321213	Engineered wood member manufacturing
321214	Truss manufacturing
321219	Reconstituted wood product manufacturing
3219	Other wood product manufacturing
32191	Millwork
321911	Wood window and door manufacturing
321912	Cut stock, resawing lumber, and planing
321918	Other millwork, including flooring
32192	Wood container and pallet manufacturing
321920	Wood container and pallet manufacturing
32199	All other wood product manufacturing
321991	Manufactured home, mobile home, manufacturing
321992	Prefabricated wood building manufacturing
321999	Miscellaneous wood product manufacturing
322	**Paper manufacturing**
3221	Pulp, paper, and paperboard mills
32211	Pulp mills
322110	Pulp mills

Note: For definitions of abbreviations and acronyms see page 964.

Code	Short title
32212	Paper mills
322121	Paper, except newsprint, mills
322122	Newsprint mills
32213	Paperboard mills
322130	Paperboard mills
3222	Converted paper product manufacturing
32221	Paperboard container manufacturing
322211	Corrugated and solid fiber box manufacturing
322212	Folding paperboard box manufacturing
322213	Setup paperboard box manufacturing
322214	Fiber can, tube, and drum manufacturing
322215	Nonfolding sanitary food container mfg.
32222	Paper bag and coated and treated paper mfg.
322221	Coated and laminated packaging materials mfg.
322222	Coated and laminated paper manufacturing
322223	Plastics, foil, and coated paper bag mfg.
322224	Uncoated paper and multiwall bag mfg.
322225	Flexible packaging foil manufacturing
322226	Surface-coated paperboard manufacturing
32223	Stationery product manufacturing
322231	Die-cut paper office supplies manufacturing
322232	Envelope manufacturing
322233	Stationery and related product manufacturing
32229	Other converted paper product manufacturing
322291	Sanitary paper product manufacturing
322299	All other converted paper product mfg.

Code	Short title
323	**Printing and related support activities**
3231	Printing and related support activities
32311	Printing
323110	Commercial lithographic printing
323111	Commercial gravure printing
323112	Commercial flexographic printing
323113	Commercial screen printing
323114	Quick printing
323115	Digital printing
323116	Manifold business forms printing
323117	Books printing
323118	Blankbook and looseleaf binder manufacturing
323119	Other commercial printing
32312	Support activities for printing
323121	Tradebinding and related work
323122	Prepress services
324	**Petroleum and coal products manufacturing**
3241	Petroleum and coal products manufacturing
32411	Petroleum refineries
324110	Petroleum refineries
32412	Asphalt paving and roofing materials mfg.
324121	Asphalt paving mixture and block mfg.
324122	Asphalt shingle and coating materials mfg.
32419	Other petroleum and coal products mfg.
324191	Petroleum lubricating oil and grease mfg.
324199	All other petroleum and coal products mfg.
325	**Chemical manufacturing**
3251	Basic chemical manufacturing
32511	Petrochemical manufacturing

Note: For definitions of abbreviations and acronyms see page 964.

Code	Short title
325110	Petrochemical manufacturing
32512	Industrial gas manufacturing
325120	Industrial gas manufacturing
32513	Synthetic dye and pigment manufacturing
325131	Inorganic dye and pigment manufacturing
325132	Synthetic organic dye and pigment mfg.
32518	Other basic inorganic chemical manufacturing
325181	Alkalies and chlorine manufacturing
325182	Carbon black manufacturing
325188	All other basic inorganic chemical mfg.
32519	Other basic organic chemical manufacturing
325191	Gum and wood chemical manufacturing
325192	Cyclic crude and intermediate manufacturing
325193	Ethyl alcohol manufacturing
325199	All other basic organic chemical mfg.
3252	Resin, rubber, and artificial fibers mfg.
32521	Resin and synthetic rubber manufacturing
325211	Plastics material and resin manufacturing
325212	Synthetic rubber manufacturing
32522	Artificial fibers and filaments manufacturing
325221	Cellulosic organic fiber manufacturing
325222	Noncellulosic organic fiber manufacturing
3253	Agricultural chemical manufacturing
32531	Fertilizer manufacturing
325311	Nitrogenous fertilizer manufacturing
325312	Phosphatic fertilizer manufacturing
325314	Fertilizer, mixing only, manufacturing
32532	Pesticide and other ag. chemical mfg.
325320	Pesticide and other ag. chemical mfg.
3254	Pharmaceutical and medicine manufacturing
32541	Pharmaceutical and medicine manufacturing
325411	Medicinal and botanical manufacturing
325412	Pharmaceutical preparation manufacturing
325413	In-vitro diagnostic substance manufacturing
325414	Other biological product manufacturing
3255	Paint, coating, and adhesive manufacturing
32551	Paint and coating manufacturing
325510	Paint and coating manufacturing
32552	Adhesive manufacturing
325520	Adhesive manufacturing
3256	Soap, cleaning compound, and toiletry mfg.
32561	Soap and cleaning compound manufacturing
325611	Soap and other detergent manufacturing
325612	Polish and other sanitation good mfg.
325613	Surface active agent manufacturing
32562	Toilet preparation manufacturing
325620	Toilet preparation manufacturing
3259	Other chemical product and preparation mfg.
32591	Printing ink manufacturing
325910	Printing ink manufacturing
32592	Explosives manufacturing
325920	Explosives manufacturing
32599	All other chemical preparation manufacturing

Note: For definitions of abbreviations and acronyms see page 964.

Code	Short title
325991	Custom compounding of purchased resins
325992	Photographic film and chemical manufacturing
325998	Other miscellaneous chemical product mfg.
326	**Plastics and rubber products manufacturing**
3261	Plastics product manufacturing
32611	Plastics packaging materials, film and sheet
326111	Plastics bag manufacturing
326112	Plastics packaging film and sheet mfg.
326113	Nonpackaging plastics film and sheet mfg.
32612	Plastics pipe, fittings, and profile shapes
326121	Unlaminated plastics profile shape mfg.
326122	Plastics pipe and pipe fitting manufacturing
32613	Laminated plastics plate, sheet, and shapes
326130	Laminated plastics plate, sheet, and shapes
32614	Polystyrene foam product manufacturing
326140	Polystyrene foam product manufacturing
32615	Urethane and other foam product manufacturing
326150	Urethane and other foam product manufacturing
32616	Plastics bottle manufacturing
326160	Plastics bottle manufacturing
32619	Other plastics product manufacturing
326191	Plastics plumbing fixture manufacturing
326192	Resilient floor covering manufacturing
326199	All other plastics product manufacturing

Code	Short title
3262	Rubber product manufacturing
32621	Tire manufacturing
326211	Tire manufacturing, except retreading
326212	Tire retreading
32622	Rubber and plastics hose and belting mfg.
326220	Rubber and plastics hose and belting mfg.
32629	Other rubber product manufacturing
326291	Rubber product mfg. for mechanical use
326299	All other rubber product manufacturing
327	**Nonmetallic mineral product manufacturing**
3271	Clay product and refractory manufacturing
32711	Pottery, ceramics, and plumbing fixture mfg.
327111	Vitreous china plumbing fixture manufacturing
327112	Vitreous china and earthenware articles mfg.
327113	Porcelain electrical supply manufacturing
32712	Clay building material and refractories mfg.
327121	Brick and structural clay tile manufacturing
327122	Ceramic wall and floor tile manufacturing
327123	Other structural clay product manufacturing
327124	Clay refractory manufacturing
327125	Nonclay refractory manufacturing
3272	Glass and glass product manufacturing
32721	Glass and glass product manufacturing
327211	Flat glass manufacturing
327212	Other pressed and blown glass and glassware

Note: For definitions of abbreviations and acronyms see page 964.

Code	Short title
327213	Glass container manufacturing
327215	Glass product mfg. made of purchased glass
3273	Cement and concrete product manufacturing
32731	Cement manufacturing
327310	Cement manufacturing
32732	Ready-mix concrete manufacturing
327320	Ready-mix concrete manufacturing
32733	Concrete pipe, brick, and block manufacturing
327331	Concrete block and brick manufacturing
327332	Concrete pipe manufacturing
32739	Other concrete product manufacturing
327390	Other concrete product manufacturing
3274	Lime and gypsum product manufacturing
32741	Lime manufacturing
327410	Lime manufacturing
32742	Gypsum product manufacturing
327420	Gypsum product manufacturing
3279	Other nonmetallic mineral products
32791	Abrasive product manufacturing
327910	Abrasive product manufacturing
32799	All other nonmetallic mineral products mfg.
327991	Cut stone and stone product manufacturing
327992	Ground or treated minerals and earths mfg.
327993	Mineral wool manufacturing
327999	Miscellaneous nonmetallic mineral products
331	**Primary metal manufacturing**
3311	Iron and steel mills and ferroalloy mfg.
33111	Iron and steel mills and ferroalloy mfg.

Code	Short title
331111	Iron and steel mills
331112	Ferroalloy and related product manufacturing
3312	Steel product mfg. from purchased steel
33121	Iron, steel pipe and tube from purchase steel
331210	Iron, steel pipe and tube from purchase steel
33122	Rolling and drawing of purchased steel
331221	Rolled steel shape manufacturing
331222	Steel wire drawing
3313	Alumina and aluminum production
33131	Alumina and aluminum production
331311	Alumina refining
331312	Primary aluminum production
331314	Secondary smelting and alloying of aluminum
331315	Aluminum sheet, plate, and foil manufacturing
331316	Aluminum extruded product manufacturing
331319	Other aluminum rolling and drawing
3314	Other nonferrous metal production
33141	Other nonferrous metal production
331411	Primary smelting and refining of copper
331419	Primary nonferrous metal, except Cu and Al
33142	Rolled, drawn, extruded, and alloyed copper
331421	Copper rolling, drawing, and extruding
331422	Copper wire, except mechanical, drawing
331423	Secondary processing of copper
33149	Nonferrous metal, except Cu and Al, shaping

Note: For definitions of abbreviations and acronyms see page 964.

Code	Short title
331491	Nonferrous metal, except Cu and Al, shaping
331492	Secondary processing of other nonferrous
3315	Foundries
33151	Ferrous metal foundries
331511	Iron foundries
331512	Steel investment foundries
331513	Steel foundries, except investment
33152	Nonferrous metal foundries
331521	Aluminum die-casting foundries
331522	Nonferrous, except Al, die-casting foundries
331524	Aluminum foundries, except die-casting
331525	Copper foundries, except die-casting
331528	Other nonferrous foundries, exc. die-casting
332	**Fabricated metal product manufacturing**
3321	Forging and stamping
33211	Forging and stamping
332111	Iron and steel forging
332112	Nonferrous forging
332114	Custom roll forming
332115	Crown and closure manufacturing
332116	Metal stamping
332117	Powder metallurgy part manufacturing
3322	Cutlery and handtool manufacturing
33221	Cutlery and handtool manufacturing
332211	Cutlery and flatware, except precious, mfg.
332212	Hand and edge tool manufacturing
332213	Saw blade and handsaw manufacturing
332214	Kitchen utensil, pot, and pan manufacturing

Code	Short title
3323	Architectural and structural metals mfg.
33231	Plate work and fabricated structural products
332311	Prefabricated metal buildings and components
332312	Fabricated structural metal manufacturing
332313	Plate work manufacturing
33232	Ornamental and architectural metal products
332321	Metal window and door manufacturing
332322	Sheet metal work manufacturing
332323	Ornamental and architectural metal work mfg.
3324	Boiler, tank, and shipping container mfg.
33241	Power boiler and heat exchanger manufacturing
332410	Power boiler and heat exchanger manufacturing
33242	Metal tank, heavy gauge, manufacturing
332420	Metal tank, heavy gauge, manufacturing
33243	Metal can, box, and other container mfg.
332431	Metal can manufacturing
332439	Other metal container manufacturing
3325	Hardware manufacturing
33251	Hardware manufacturing
332510	Hardware manufacturing
3326	Spring and wire product manufacturing
33261	Spring and wire product manufacturing
332611	Spring, heavy gauge, manufacturing
332612	Spring, light gauge, manufacturing
332618	Other fabricated wire product manufacturing
3327	Machine shops and threaded product mfg.

Note: For definitions of abbreviations and acronyms see page 964.

Code	Short title
33271	Machine shops
332710	Machine shops
33272	Turned product and screw, nut, and bolt mfg.
332721	Precision turned product manufacturing
332722	Bolt, nut, screw, rivet, and washer mfg.
3328	Coating, engraving, and heat treating metals
33281	Coating, engraving, and heat treating metals
332811	Metal heat treating
332812	Metal coating and nonprecious engraving
332813	Electroplating, anodizing, and coloring metal
3329	Other fabricated metal product manufacturing
33291	Metal valve manufacturing
332911	Industrial valve manufacturing
332912	Fluid power valve and hose fitting mfg.
332913	Plumbing fixture fitting and trim mfg.
332919	Other metal valve and pipe fitting mfg.
33299	All other fabricated metal product mfg.
332991	Ball and roller bearing manufacturing
332992	Small arms ammunition manufacturing
332993	Ammunition, except small arms, manufacturing
332994	Small arms manufacturing
332995	Other ordnance and accessories manufacturing
332996	Fabricated pipe and pipe fitting mfg.
332997	Industrial pattern manufacturing
332998	Enameled iron and metal sanitary ware mfg.
332999	Miscellaneous fabricated metal product mfg.

Code	Short title
333	**Machinery manufacturing**
3331	Ag., construction, and mining machinery mfg.
33311	Agricultural implement manufacturing
333111	Farm machinery and equipment manufacturing
333112	Lawn and garden equipment manufacturing
33312	Construction machinery manufacturing
333120	Construction machinery manufacturing
33313	Mining and oil and gas field machinery mfg.
333131	Mining machinery and equipment manufacturing
333132	Oil and gas field machinery and equipment
3332	Industrial machinery manufacturing
33321	Sawmill and woodworking machinery
333210	Sawmill and woodworking machinery
33322	Plastics and rubber industry machinery
333220	Plastics and rubber industry machinery
33329	Other industrial machinery manufacturing
333291	Paper industry machinery manufacturing
333292	Textile machinery manufacturing
333293	Printing machinery and equipment mfg.
333294	Food product machinery manufacturing
333295	Semiconductor machinery manufacturing
333298	All other industrial machinery manufacturing
3333	Commercial and service industry machinery

Note: For definitions of abbreviations and acronyms see page 964.

Code	Short title
33331	Commercial and service industry machinery
333311	Automatic vending machine manufacturing
333312	Commercial laundry and drycleaning machinery
333313	Office machinery manufacturing
333314	Optical instrument and lens manufacturing
333315	Photographic and photocopying equipment mfg.
333319	Other commercial and service machinery mfg.
3334	HVAC and commercial refrigeration equipment
33341	HVAC and commercial refrigeration equipment
333411	Air purification equipment manufacturing
333412	Industrial and commercial fan and blower mfg.
333414	Heating equipment, except warm air furnaces
333415	AC, refrigeration, and forced air heating
3335	Metalworking machinery manufacturing
33351	Metalworking machinery manufacturing
333511	Industrial mold manufacturing
333512	Metal cutting machine tool manufacturing
333513	Metal forming machine tool manufacturing
333514	Special tool, die, jig, and fixture mfg.
333515	Cutting tool and machine tool accessory mfg.
333516	Rolling mill machinery and equipment mfg.
333518	Other metalworking machinery manufacturing
3336	Turbine and power transmission equipment mfg.
33361	Turbine and power transmission equipment mfg.
333611	Turbine and turbine generator set units mfg.
333612	Speed changer, drive, and gear manufacturing
333613	Mechanical power transmission equipment mfg.
333618	Other engine equipment manufacturing
3339	Other general purpose machinery manufacturing
33391	Pump and compressor manufacturing
333911	Pump and pumping equipment manufacturing
333912	Air and gas compressor manufacturing
333913	Measuring and dispensing pump manufacturing
33392	Material handling equipment manufacturing
333921	Elevator and moving stairway manufacturing
333922	Conveyor and conveying equipment mfg.
333923	Overhead cranes, hoists, and monorail systems
333924	Industrial truck, trailer, and stacker mfg.
33399	All other general purpose machinery mfg.
333991	Power-driven handtool manufacturing
333992	Welding and soldering equipment manufacturing
333993	Packaging machinery manufacturing
333994	Industrial process furnace and oven mfg.
333995	Fluid power cylinder and actuator mfg.
333996	Fluid power pump and motor manufacturing
333997	Scale and balance, except laboratory, mfg.
333999	Miscellaneous general purpose machinery mfg.

Note: For definitions of abbreviations and acronyms see page 964.

Code	Short title
334	**Computer and electronic product manufacturing**
3341	Computer and peripheral equipment mfg.
33411	Computer and peripheral equipment mfg.
334111	Electronic computer manufacturing
334112	Computer storage device manufacturing
334113	Computer terminal manufacturing
334119	Other computer peripheral equipment mfg.
3342	Communications equipment manufacturing
33421	Telephone apparatus manufacturing
334210	Telephone apparatus manufacturing
33422	Broadcast and wireless communications equip.
334220	Broadcast and wireless communications equip.
33429	Other communications equipment manufacturing
334290	Other communications equipment manufacturing
3343	Audio and video equipment manufacturing
33431	Audio and video equipment manufacturing
334310	Audio and video equipment manufacturing
3344	Semiconductor and electronic component mfg.
33441	Semiconductor and electronic component mfg.
334411	Electron tube manufacturing
334412	Bare printed circuit board manufacturing
334413	Semiconductors and related device mfg.
334414	Electronic capacitor manufacturing

Code	Short title
334415	Electronic resistor manufacturing
334416	Electronic coils, transformers, and inductors
334417	Electronic connector manufacturing
334418	Printed circuit assembly manufacturing
334419	Other electronic component manufacturing
3345	Electronic instrument manufacturing
33451	Electronic instrument manufacturing
334510	Electromedical apparatus manufacturing
334511	Search, detection, and navigation instruments
334512	Automatic environmental control manufacturing
334513	Industrial process variable instruments
334514	Totalizing fluid meters and counting devices
334515	Electricity and signal testing instruments
334516	Analytical laboratory instrument mfg.
334517	Irradiation apparatus manufacturing
334518	Watch, clock, and part manufacturing
334519	Other measuring and controlling device mfg.
3346	Magnetic media manufacturing and reproducing
33461	Magnetic media manufacturing and reproducing
334611	Software reproducing
334612	Audio and video media reproduction
334613	Magnetic and optical recording media mfg.

Note: For definitions of abbreviations and acronyms see page 964.

Code	Short title
335	**Electrical equipment and appliance mfg.**
3351	Electric lighting equipment manufacturing
33511	Electric lamp bulb and part manufacturing
335110	Electric lamp bulb and part manufacturing
33512	Lighting fixture manufacturing
335121	Residential electric lighting fixture mfg.
335122	Nonresidential electric lighting fixture mfg.
335129	Other lighting equipment manufacturing
3352	Household appliance manufacturing
33521	Small electrical appliance manufacturing
335211	Electric housewares and household fan mfg.
335212	Household vacuum cleaner manufacturing
33522	Major appliance manufacturing
335221	Household cooking appliance manufacturing
335222	Household refrigerator and home freezer mfg.
335224	Household laundry equipment manufacturing
335228	Other major household appliance manufacturing
3353	Electrical equipment manufacturing
33531	Electrical equipment manufacturing
335311	Electric power and specialty transformer mfg.
335312	Motor and generator manufacturing
335313	Switchgear and switchboard apparatus mfg.
335314	Relay and industrial control manufacturing
3359	Other electrical equipment and component mfg.
33591	Battery manufacturing
335911	Storage battery manufacturing
335912	Primary battery manufacturing
33592	Communication and energy wire and cable mfg.
335921	Fiber optic cable manufacturing
335929	Other communication and energy wire mfg.
33593	Wiring device manufacturing
335931	Current-carrying wiring device manufacturing
335932	Noncurrent-carrying wiring device mfg.
33599	Other electrical equipment and component mfg.
335991	Carbon and graphite product manufacturing
335999	Miscellaneous electrical equipment mfg.
336	**Transportation equipment manufacturing**
3361	Motor vehicle manufacturing
33611	Automobile and light truck manufacturing
336111	Automobile manufacturing
336112	Light truck and utility vehicle manufacturing
33612	Heavy duty truck manufacturing
336120	Heavy duty truck manufacturing
3362	Motor vehicle body and trailer manufacturing
33621	Motor vehicle body and trailer manufacturing
336211	Motor vehicle body manufacturing
336212	Truck trailer manufacturing
336213	Motor home manufacturing
336214	Travel trailer and camper manufacturing
3363	Motor vehicle parts manufacturing
33631	Motor vehicle gasoline engine and parts mfg.

Note: For definitions of abbreviations and acronyms see page 964.

Code	Short title
336311	Carburetor, piston, ring, and valve mfg.
336312	Gasoline engine and engine parts mfg.
33632	Motor vehicle electric equipment
336321	Vehicular lighting equipment manufacturing
336322	Other motor vehicle electric equipment mfg.
33633	Motor vehicle steering and suspension parts
336330	Motor vehicle steering and suspension parts
33634	Motor vehicle brake system manufacturing
336340	Motor vehicle brake system manufacturing
33635	Motor vehicle power train components mfg.
336350	Motor vehicle power train components mfg.
33636	Motor vehicle seating and interior trim mfg.
336360	Motor vehicle seating and interior trim mfg.
33637	Motor vehicle metal stamping
336370	Motor vehicle metal stamping
33639	Other motor vehicle parts manufacturing
336391	Motor vehicle air-conditioning manufacturing
336399	All other motor vehicle parts manufacturing
3364	Aerospace product and parts manufacturing
33641	Aerospace product and parts manufacturing
336411	Aircraft manufacturing
336412	Aircraft engine and engine parts mfg.
336413	Other aircraft parts and equipment
336414	Guided missile and space vehicle mfg.
336415	Space vehicle propulsion units and parts mfg.
336419	Other guided missile and space vehicle parts
3365	Railroad rolling stock manufacturing
33651	Railroad rolling stock manufacturing
336510	Railroad rolling stock manufacturing
3366	Ship and boat building
33661	Ship and boat building
336611	Ship building and repairing
336612	Boat building
3369	Other transportation equipment manufacturing
33699	Other transportation equipment manufacturing
336991	Motorcycle, bicycle, and parts manufacturing
336992	Military armored vehicles and tank parts mfg.
336999	All other transportation equipment mfg.
337	**Furniture and related product manufacturing**
3371	Household and institutional furniture mfg.
33711	Wood kitchen cabinet and countertop mfg.
337110	Wood kitchen cabinet and countertop mfg.
33712	Other household and institutional furniture
337121	Upholstered household furniture manufacturing
337122	Nonupholstered wood household furniture mfg.
337124	Metal household furniture manufacturing
337125	Household furniture, exc. wood or metal, mfg.
337127	Institutional furniture manufacturing

Note: For definitions of abbreviations and acronyms see page 964.

Code	Short title
337129	Wood TV, radio, and sewing machine housings
3372	Office furniture and fixtures manufacturing
33721	Office furniture and fixtures manufacturing
337211	Wood office furniture manufacturing
337212	Custom architectural woodwork and millwork
337214	Office furniture, except wood, manufacturing
337215	Showcases, partitions, shelving, and lockers
3379	Other furniture related product manufacturing
33791	Mattress manufacturing
337910	Mattress manufacturing
33792	Blind and shade manufacturing
337920	Blind and shade manufacturing
339	**Miscellaneous manufacturing**
3391	Medical equipment and supplies manufacturing
33911	Medical equipment and supplies manufacturing
339111	Laboratory apparatus and furniture mfg.
339112	Surgical and medical instrument manufacturing
339113	Surgical appliance and supplies manufacturing
339114	Dental equipment and supplies manufacturing
339115	Ophthalmic goods manufacturing
339116	Dental laboratories
3399	Other miscellaneous manufacturing
33991	Jewelry and silverware manufacturing
339911	Jewelry, except costume, manufacturing
339912	Silverware and hollowware manufacturing

Code	Short title
339913	Jewelers' material and lapidary work mfg.
339914	Costume jewelry and novelty manufacturing
33992	Sporting and athletic goods manufacturing
339920	Sporting and athletic goods manufacturing
33993	Doll, toy, and game manufacturing
339931	Doll and stuffed toy manufacturing
339932	Game, toy, and children's vehicle mfg.
33994	Office supplies, except paper, manufacturing
339941	Pen and mechanical pencil manufacturing
339942	Lead pencil and art good manufacturing
339943	Marking device manufacturing
339944	Carbon paper and inked ribbon manufacturing
33995	Sign manufacturing
339950	Sign manufacturing
33999	All other miscellaneous manufacturing
339991	Gasket, packing, and sealing device mfg.
339992	Musical instrument manufacturing
339993	Fastener, button, needle, and pin mfg.
339994	Broom, brush, and mop manufacturing
339995	Burial casket manufacturing
339999	All other miscellaneous manufacturing
42	**WHOLESALE TRADE**
423	**Merchant wholesalers, durable goods**
4231	Motor vehicle and parts merchant wholesalers

Note: For definitions of abbreviations and acronyms see page 964.

Code	Short title
42311	Motor vehicle merchant wholesalers
423110	Motor vehicle merchant wholesalers
42312	New motor vehicle parts merchant wholesalers
423120	New motor vehicle parts merchant wholesalers
42313	Tire and tube merchant wholesalers
423130	Tire and tube merchant wholesalers
42314	Used motor vehicle parts merchant wholesalers
423140	Used motor vehicle parts merchant wholesalers
4232	Furniture and furnishing merchant wholesalers
42321	Furniture merchant wholesalers
423210	Furniture merchant wholesalers
42322	Home furnishing merchant wholesalers
423220	Home furnishing merchant wholesalers
4233	Lumber and const. supply merchant wholesalers
42331	Lumber and wood merchant wholesalers
423310	Lumber and wood merchant wholesalers
42332	Masonry material merchant wholesalers
423320	Masonry material merchant wholesalers
42333	Roofing and siding merchant wholesalers
423330	Roofing and siding merchant wholesalers
42339	Other const. material merchant wholesalers
423390	Other const. material merchant wholesalers
4234	Commercial equip. merchant wholesalers
42341	Photographic equip. merchant wholesalers
423410	Photographic equip. merchant wholesalers
42342	Office equipment merchant wholesalers
423420	Office equipment merchant wholesalers
42343	Computer and software merchant wholesalers
423430	Computer and software merchant wholesalers
42344	Other commercial equip. merchant wholesalers
423440	Other commercial equip. merchant wholesalers
42345	Medical equipment merchant wholesalers
423450	Medical equipment merchant wholesalers
42346	Ophthalmic goods merchant wholesalers
423460	Ophthalmic goods merchant wholesalers
42349	Other professional equip. merchant wholesaler
423490	Other professional equip. merchant wholesaler
4235	Metal and mineral merchant wholesalers
42351	Metal merchant wholesalers
423510	Metal merchant wholesalers
42352	Coal and other mineral merchant wholesalers
423520	Coal and other mineral merchant wholesalers
4236	Electric goods merchant wholesalers
42361	Elec. equip. and wiring merchant wholesalers
423610	Elec. equip. and wiring merchant wholesalers
42362	Electric appliance merchant wholesalers
423620	Electric appliance merchant wholesalers
42369	Other electronic parts merchant wholesalers

Note: For definitions of abbreviations and acronyms see page 964.

Code	Short title
423690	Other electronic parts merchant wholesalers
4237	Hardware and plumbing merchant wholesalers
42371	Hardware merchant wholesalers
423710	Hardware merchant wholesalers
42372	Plumbing equip. merchant wholesalers
423720	Plumbing equip. merchant wholesalers
42373	HVAC equip. merchant wholesalers
423730	HVAC equip. merchant wholesalers
42374	Refrigeration equip. merchant wholesalers
423740	Refrigeration equip. merchant wholesalers
4238	Machinery and supply merchant wholesalers
42381	Construction equipment merchant wholesalers
423810	Construction equipment merchant wholesalers
42382	Farm and garden equip. merchant wholesalers
423820	Farm and garden equip. merchant wholesalers
42383	Industrial machinery merchant wholesalers
423830	Industrial machinery merchant wholesalers
42384	Industrial supplies merchant wholesalers
423840	Industrial supplies merchant wholesalers
42385	Service estab. equip. merchant wholesalers
423850	Service estab. equip. merchant wholesalers
42386	Other transport. goods merchant wholesalers
423860	Other transport. goods merchant wholesalers
4239	Misc. durable goods merchant wholesalers
42391	Sporting goods merchant wholesalers
423910	Sporting goods merchant wholesalers
42392	Toy and hobby goods merchant wholesalers
423920	Toy and hobby goods merchant wholesalers
42393	Recyclable material merchant wholesalers
423930	Recyclable material merchant wholesalers
42394	Jewelry merchant wholesalers
423940	Jewelry merchant wholesalers
42399	All other durable goods merchant wholesalers
423990	All other durable goods merchant wholesalers
424	**Merchant wholesalers, nondurable goods**
4241	Paper and paper product merchant wholesalers
42411	Printing and writing paper merch. whls.
424110	Printing and writing paper merch. whls.
42412	Office supplies merchant wholesalers
424120	Office supplies merchant wholesalers
42413	Industrial paper merchant wholesalers
424130	Industrial paper merchant wholesalers
4242	Druggists' goods merchant wholesalers
42421	Druggists' goods merchant wholesalers
424210	Druggists' goods merchant wholesalers
4243	Apparel and piece goods merchant wholesalers
42431	Piece goods merchant wholesalers

Note: For definitions of abbreviations and acronyms see page 964.

Code	Short title	Code	Short title
424310	Piece goods merchant wholesalers	42449	Other grocery product merchant wholesalers
42432	Men's and boys' clothing merchant wholesalers	424490	Other grocery product merchant wholesalers
424320	Men's and boys' clothing merchant wholesalers	4245	Farm product raw material merch. whls.
42433	Women's and children's clothing merch. whls.	42451	Grain and field bean merchant wholesalers
424330	Women's and children's clothing merch. whls.	424510	Grain and field bean merchant wholesalers
42434	Footwear merchant wholesalers	42452	Livestock merchant wholesalers
424340	Footwear merchant wholesalers	424520	Livestock merchant wholesalers
4244	Grocery and related product wholesalers	42459	Other farm product raw material merch. whls.
42441	General line grocery merchant wholesalers	424590	Other farm product raw material merch. whls.
424410	General line grocery merchant wholesalers	4246	Chemical merchant wholesalers
42442	Packaged frozen food merchant wholesalers	42461	Plastics materials merchant wholesalers
424420	Packaged frozen food merchant wholesalers	424610	Plastics materials merchant wholesalers
42443	Dairy product merchant wholesalers	42469	Other chemicals merchant wholesalers
424430	Dairy product merchant wholesalers	424690	Other chemicals merchant wholesalers
42444	Poultry product merchant wholesalers	4247	Petroleum merchant wholesalers
424440	Poultry product merchant wholesalers	42471	Petroleum bulk stations and terminals
42445	Confectionery merchant wholesalers	424710	Petroleum bulk stations and terminals
424450	Confectionery merchant wholesalers	42472	Other petroleum merchant wholesalers
42446	Fish and seafood merchant wholesalers	424720	Other petroleum merchant wholesalers
424460	Fish and seafood merchant wholesalers	4248	Alcoholic beverage merchant wholesalers
42447	Meat and meat product merchant wholesalers	42481	Beer and ale merchant wholesalers
424470	Meat and meat product merchant wholesalers	424810	Beer and ale merchant wholesalers
42448	Fruit and vegetable merchant wholesalers	42482	Wine and spirit merchant wholesalers
424480	Fruit and vegetable merchant wholesalers	424820	Wine and spirit merchant wholesalers
		4249	Misc. nondurable goods merchant wholesalers

Note: For definitions of abbreviations and acronyms see page 964.

Code	Short title
42491	Farm supplies merchant wholesalers
424910	Farm supplies merchant wholesalers
42492	Book and periodical merchant wholesalers
424920	Book and periodical merchant wholesalers
42493	Nursery and florist merchant wholesalers
424930	Nursery and florist merchant wholesalers
42494	Tobacco and tobacco product merch. whls.
424940	Tobacco and tobacco product merch. whls.
42495	Paint and supplies merchant wholesalers
424950	Paint and supplies merchant wholesalers
42499	Other nondurable goods merchant wholesalers
424990	Other nondurable goods merchant wholesalers
425	**Electronic markets and agents and brokers**
4251	Electronic markets and agents and brokers
42511	Business to business electronic markets
425110	Business to business electronic markets
42512	Wholesale trade agents and brokers
425120	Wholesale trade agents and brokers
44-45	**RETAIL TRADE**
441	**Motor vehicle and parts dealers**
4411	Automobile dealers
44111	New car dealers
441110	New car dealers
44112	Used car dealers
441120	Used car dealers
4412	Other motor vehicle dealers
44121	Recreational vehicle dealers
441210	Recreational vehicle dealers
44122	Motorcycle, boat, and other vehicle dealers
441221	Motorcycle dealers
441222	Boat dealers
441229	All other motor vehicle dealers
4413	Auto parts, accessories, and tire stores
44131	Automotive parts and accessories stores
441310	Automotive parts and accessories stores
44132	Tire dealers
441320	Tire dealers
442	**Furniture and home furnishings stores**
4421	Furniture stores
44211	Furniture stores
442110	Furniture stores
4422	Home furnishings stores
44221	Floor covering stores
442210	Floor covering stores
44229	Other home furnishings stores
442291	Window treatment stores
442299	All other home furnishings stores
443	**Electronics and appliance stores**
4431	Electronics and appliance stores
44311	Appliance, TV, and other electronics stores
443111	Household appliance stores
443112	Radio, TV, and other electronics stores
44312	Computer and software stores
443120	Computer and software stores
44313	Camera and photographic supplies stores
443130	Camera and photographic supplies stores

Note: For definitions of abbreviations and acronyms see page 964.

Code	Short title
444	**Building material and garden supply stores**
4441	Building material and supplies dealers
44411	Home centers
444110	Home centers
44412	Paint and wallpaper stores
444120	Paint and wallpaper stores
44413	Hardware stores
444130	Hardware stores
44419	Other building material dealers
444190	Other building material dealers
4442	Lawn and garden equipment and supplies stores
44421	Outdoor power equipment stores
444210	Outdoor power equipment stores
44422	Nursery, garden, and farm supply stores
444220	Nursery, garden, and farm supply stores
445	**Food and beverage stores**
4451	Grocery stores
44511	Supermarkets and other grocery stores
445110	Supermarkets and other grocery stores
44512	Convenience stores
445120	Convenience stores
4452	Specialty food stores
44521	Meat markets
445210	Meat markets
44522	Fish and seafood markets
445220	Fish and seafood markets
44523	Fruit and vegetable markets
445230	Fruit and vegetable markets
44529	Other specialty food stores
445291	Baked goods stores
445292	Confectionery and nut stores
445299	All other specialty food stores
4453	Beer, wine, and liquor stores
44531	Beer, wine, and liquor stores
445310	Beer, wine, and liquor stores

Code	Short title
446	**Health and personal care stores**
4461	Health and personal care stores
44611	Pharmacies and drug stores
446110	Pharmacies and drug stores
44612	Cosmetic and beauty supply stores
446120	Cosmetic and beauty supply stores
44613	Optical goods stores
446130	Optical goods stores
44619	Other health and personal care stores
446191	Food, health, supplement stores
446199	All other health and personal care stores
447	**Gasoline stations**
4471	Gasoline stations
44711	Gasoline stations with convenience stores
447110	Gasoline stations with convenience stores
44719	Other gasoline stations
447190	Other gasoline stations
448	**Clothing and clothing accessories stores**
4481	Clothing stores
44811	Men's clothing stores
448110	Men's clothing stores
44812	Women's clothing stores
448120	Women's clothing stores
44813	Children's and infants' clothing stores
448130	Children's and infants' clothing stores
44814	Family clothing stores
448140	Family clothing stores
44815	Clothing accessories stores
448150	Clothing accessories stores
44819	Other clothing stores
448190	Other clothing stores
4482	Shoe stores
44821	Shoe stores

Note: For definitions of abbreviations and acronyms see page 964.

Code	Short title
448210	Shoe stores
4483	Jewelry, luggage, and leather goods stores
44831	Jewelry stores
448310	Jewelry stores
44832	Luggage and leather goods stores
448320	Luggage and leather goods stores
451	**Sporting goods, hobby, book and music stores**
4511	Sporting goods and musical instrument stores
45111	Sporting goods stores
451110	Sporting goods stores
45112	Hobby, toy, and game stores
451120	Hobby, toy, and game stores
45113	Sewing, needlework, and piece goods stores
451130	Sewing, needlework, and piece goods stores
45114	Musical instrument and supplies stores
451140	Musical instrument and supplies stores
4512	Book, periodical, and music stores
45121	Book stores and news dealers
451211	Book stores
451212	News dealers and newsstands
45122	Prerecorded tape, CD, and record stores
451220	Prerecorded tape, CD, and record stores
452	**General merchandise stores**
4521	Department stores
45211	Department stores
452111	Department stores, except discount
452112	Discount department stores
4529	Other general merchandise stores
45291	Warehouse clubs and supercenters

Code	Short title
452910	Warehouse clubs and supercenters
45299	All other general merchandise stores
452990	All other general merchandise stores
453	**Miscellaneous store retailers**
4531	Florists
45311	Florists
453110	Florists
4532	Office supplies, stationery, and gift stores
45321	Office supplies and stationery stores
453210	Office supplies and stationery stores
45322	Gift, novelty, and souvenir stores
453220	Gift, novelty, and souvenir stores
4533	Used merchandise stores
45331	Used merchandise stores
453310	Used merchandise stores
4539	Other miscellaneous store retailers
45391	Pet and pet supplies stores
453910	Pet and pet supplies stores
45392	Art dealers
453920	Art dealers
45393	Manufactured, mobile, home dealers
453930	Manufactured, mobile, home dealers
45399	All other miscellaneous store retailers
453991	Tobacco stores
453998	Store retailers not specified elsewhere
454	**Nonstore retailers**
4541	Electronic shopping and mail-order houses
45411	Electronic shopping and mail-order houses

Note: For definitions of abbreviations and acronyms see page 964.

Code	Short title
454111	Electronic shopping
454112	Electronic auctions
454113	Mail-order houses
4542	Vending machine operators
45421	Vending machine operators
454210	Vending machine operators
4543	Direct selling establishments
45431	Fuel dealers
454311	Heating oil dealers
454312	Liquefied petroleum gas, bottled gas, dealers
454319	Other fuel dealers
45439	Other direct selling establishments
454390	Other direct selling establishments
48-49	**TRANSPORTATION AND WAREHOUSING**
481	**Air transportation**
4811	Scheduled air transportation
48111	Scheduled air transportation
481111	Scheduled passenger air transportation
481112	Scheduled freight air transportation
4812	Nonscheduled air transportation
48121	Nonscheduled air transportation
481211	Nonscheduled air passenger chartering
481212	Nonscheduled air freight chartering
481219	Other nonscheduled air transportation
482	**Rail transportation**
4821	Rail transportation
48211	Rail transportation
482111	Line-haul railroads
482112	Short line railroads
483	**Water transportation**
4831	Sea, coastal, and Great Lakes transportation

Code	Short title
48311	Sea, coastal, and Great Lakes transportation
483111	Deep sea freight transportation
483112	Deep sea passenger transportation
483113	Coastal and Great Lakes freight transport.
483114	Coastal and Great Lakes passenger transport.
4832	Inland water transportation
48321	Inland water transportation
483211	Inland water freight transportation
483212	Inland water passenger transportation
484	**Truck transportation**
4841	General freight trucking
48411	General freight trucking, local
484110	General freight trucking, local
48412	General freight trucking, long-distance
484121	General freight trucking, long-distance TL
484122	General freight trucking, long-distance LTL
4842	Specialized freight trucking
48421	Used household and office goods moving
484210	Used household and office goods moving
48422	Other specialized trucking, local
484220	Other specialized trucking, local
48423	Other specialized trucking, long-distance
484230	Other specialized trucking, long-distance
485	**Transit and ground passenger transportation**
4851	Urban transit systems
48511	Urban transit systems
485111	Mixed mode transit systems
485112	Commuter rail systems
485113	Bus and other motor vehicle transit systems

Note: For definitions of abbreviations and acronyms see page 964.

Code	Short title
485119	Other urban transit systems
4852	Interurban and rural bus transportation
48521	Interurban and rural bus transportation
485210	Interurban and rural bus transportation
4853	Taxi and limousine service
48531	Taxi service
485310	Taxi service
48532	Limousine service
485320	Limousine service
4854	School and employee bus transportation
48541	School and employee bus transportation
485410	School and employee bus transportation
4855	Charter bus industry
48551	Charter bus industry
485510	Charter bus industry
4859	Other ground passenger transportation
48599	Other ground passenger transportation
485991	Special needs transportation
485999	All other ground passenger transportation
486	**Pipeline transportation**
4861	Pipeline transportation of crude oil
48611	Pipeline transportation of crude oil
486110	Pipeline transportation of crude oil
4862	Pipeline transportation of natural gas
48621	Pipeline transportation of natural gas
486210	Pipeline transportation of natural gas
4869	Other pipeline transportation
48691	Refined petroleum product pipeline transport.
486910	Refined petroleum product pipeline transport.
48699	All other pipeline transportation
486990	All other pipeline transportation
487	**Scenic and sightseeing transportation**
4871	Scenic and sightseeing transportation, land
48711	Scenic and sightseeing transportation, land
487110	Scenic and sightseeing transportation, land
4872	Scenic and sightseeing transportation, water
48721	Scenic and sightseeing transportation, water
487210	Scenic and sightseeing transportation, water
4879	Scenic and sightseeing transportation, other
48799	Scenic and sightseeing transportation, other
487990	Scenic and sightseeing transportation, other
488	**Support activities for transportation**
4881	Support activities for air transportation
48811	Airport operations
488111	Air traffic control
488119	Other airport operations
48819	Other support activities for air transport.
488190	Other support activities for air transport.
4882	Support activities for rail transportation
48821	Support activities for rail transportation
488210	Support activities for rail transportation
4883	Support activities for water transportation

Note: For definitions of abbreviations and acronyms see page 964.

Code	Short title
48831	Port and harbor operations
488310	Port and harbor operations
48832	Marine cargo handling
488320	Marine cargo handling
48833	Navigational services to shipping
488330	Navigational services to shipping
48839	Other support activities for water transport.
488390	Other support activities for water transport.
4884	Support activities for road transportation
48841	Motor vehicle towing
488410	Motor vehicle towing
48849	Other support activities for road transport.
488490	Other support activities for road transport.
4885	Freight transportation arrangement
48851	Freight transportation arrangement
488510	Freight transportation arrangement
4889	Other support activities for transportation
48899	Other support activities for transportation
488991	Packing and crating
488999	All other support activities for transport.
491	**Postal service**
4911	Postal service
49111	Postal service
491110	Postal service
492	**Couriers and messengers**
4921	Couriers
49211	Couriers
492110	Couriers
4922	Local messengers and local delivery
49221	Local messengers and local delivery
492210	Local messengers and local delivery
493	**Warehousing and storage**
4931	Warehousing and storage
49311	General warehousing and storage
493110	General warehousing and storage
49312	Refrigerated warehousing and storage
493120	Refrigerated warehousing and storage
49313	Farm product warehousing and storage
493130	Farm product warehousing and storage
49319	Other warehousing and storage
493190	Other warehousing and storage
51	**INFORMATION**
511	**Publishing industries, except Internet**
5111	Newspaper, book, and directory publishers
51111	Newspaper publishers
511110	Newspaper publishers
51112	Periodical publishers
511120	Periodical publishers
51113	Book publishers
511130	Book publishers
51114	Directory and mailing list publishers
511140	Directory and mailing list publishers
51119	Other publishers
511191	Greeting card publishers
511199	All other publishers
5112	Software publishers
51121	Software publishers
511210	Software publishers

Note: For definitions of abbreviations and acronyms see page 964.

Code	Short title
512	**Motion picture and sound recording industries**
5121	Motion picture and video industries
51211	Motion picture and video production
512110	Motion picture and video production
51212	Motion picture and video distribution
512120	Motion picture and video distribution
51213	Motion picture and video exhibition
512131	Motion picture theaters, except drive-ins
512132	Drive-in motion picture theaters
51219	Postproduction and other related industries
512191	Teleproduction and postproduction services
512199	Other motion picture and video industries
5122	Sound recording industries
51221	Record production
512210	Record production
51222	Integrated record production and distribution
512220	Integrated record production and distribution
51223	Music publishers
512230	Music publishers
51224	Sound recording studios
512240	Sound recording studios
51229	Other sound recording industries
512290	Other sound recording industries
515	**Broadcasting, except Internet**
5151	Radio and television broadcasting
51511	Radio broadcasting
515111	Radio networks
515112	Radio stations
51512	Television broadcasting
515120	Television broadcasting
5152	Cable and other subscription programming
51521	Cable and other subscription programming
515210	Cable and other subscription programming
516	**Internet publishing and broadcasting**
5161	Internet publishing and broadcasting
51611	Internet publishing and broadcasting
516110	Internet publishing and broadcasting
517	**Telecommunications**
5171	Wired telecommunications carriers
51711	Wired telecommunications carriers
517110	Wired telecommunications carriers
5172	Wireless telecommunications carriers
51721	Wireless telecommunications carriers
517211	Paging
517212	Cellular and other wireless carriers
5173	Telecommunications resellers
51731	Telecommunications resellers
517310	Telecommunications resellers
5174	Satellite telecommunications
51741	Satellite telecommunications
517410	Satellite telecommunications
5175	Cable and other program distribution
51751	Cable and other program distribution
517510	Cable and other program distribution
5179	Other telecommunications

Note: For definitions of abbreviations and acronyms see page 964.

Code	Short title
51791	Other telecommunications
517910	Other telecommunications
518	**ISPs, search portals, and data processing**
5181	ISPs and Web search portals
51811	ISPs and Web search portals
518111	Internet service providers
518112	Web search portals
5182	Data processing and related services
51821	Data processing and related services
518210	Data processing and related services
519	**Other information services**
5191	Other information services
51911	News syndicates
519110	News syndicates
51912	Libraries and archives
519120	Libraries and archives
51919	All other information services
519190	All other information services
52	**FINANCE AND INSURANCE**
521	**Monetary authorities—central bank**
5211	Monetary authorities—central bank
52111	Monetary authorities—central bank
521110	Monetary authorities—central bank
522	**Credit intermediation and related activities**
5221	Depository credit intermediation
52211	Commercial banking
522110	Commercial banking
52212	Savings institutions
522120	Savings institutions
52213	Credit unions
522130	Credit unions
52219	Other depository credit intermediation
522190	Other depository credit intermediation
5222	Nondepository credit intermediation
52221	Credit card issuing
522210	Credit card issuing
52222	Sales financing
522220	Sales financing
52229	Other nondepository credit intermediation
522291	Consumer lending
522292	Real estate credit
522293	International trade financing
522294	Secondary market financing
522298	All other nondepository credit intermediation
5223	Activities related to credit intermediation
52231	Mortgage and nonmortgage loan brokers
522310	Mortgage and nonmortgage loan brokers
52232	Financial transaction processing and clearing
522320	Financial transaction processing and clearing
52239	Other credit intermediation activities
522390	Other credit intermediation activities
523	**Securities, commodity contracts, investments**
5231	Securities and commodity contracts brokerage
52311	Investment banking and securities dealing
523110	Investment banking and securities dealing
52312	Securities brokerage
523120	Securities brokerage
52313	Commodity contracts dealing
523130	Commodity contracts dealing

Note: For definitions of abbreviations and acronyms see page 964.

Code	Short title
52314	Commodity contracts brokerage
523140	Commodity contracts brokerage
5232	Securities and commodity exchanges
52321	Securities and commodity exchanges
523210	Securities and commodity exchanges
5239	Other financial investment activities
52391	Miscellaneous intermediation
523910	Miscellaneous intermediation
52392	Portfolio management
523920	Portfolio management
52393	Investment advice
523930	Investment advice
52399	All other financial investment activities
523991	Trust, fiduciary, and custody activities
523999	Miscellaneous financial investment activities
524	**Insurance carriers and related activities**
5241	Insurance carriers
52411	Direct life and health insurance carriers
524113	Direct life insurance carriers
524114	Direct health and medical insurance carriers
52412	Direct insurers, except life and health
524126	Direct property and casualty insurers
524127	Direct title insurance carriers
524128	Other direct insurance carriers
52413	Reinsurance carriers
524130	Reinsurance carriers
5242	Insurance agencies and brokerages
52421	Insurance agencies and brokerages
524210	Insurance agencies and brokerages

Code	Short title
52429	Other insurance related activities
524291	Claims adjusting
524292	Third party administration of insurance funds
524298	All other insurance related activities
525	**Funds, trusts, and other financial vehicles**
5251	Insurance and employee benefit funds
52511	Pension funds
525110	Pension funds
52512	Health and welfare funds
525120	Health and welfare funds
52519	Other insurance funds
525190	Other insurance funds
5259	Other investment pools and funds
52591	Open-end investment funds
525910	Open-end investment funds
52592	Trusts, estates, and agency accounts
525920	Trusts, estates, and agency accounts
52593	Real estate investment trusts
525930	Real estate investment trusts
52599	Other financial vehicles
525990	Other financial vehicles
53	**REAL ESTATE AND RENTAL AND LEASING**
531	**Real estate**
5311	Lessors of real estate
53111	Lessors of residential buildings
531110	Lessors of residential buildings
53112	Lessors of nonresidential buildings
531120	Lessors of nonresidential buildings
53113	Miniwarehouse and self-storage unit operators
531130	Miniwarehouse and self-storage unit operators

Note: For definitions of abbreviations and acronyms see page 964.

Code	Short title
53119	Lessors of other real estate property
531190	Lessors of other real estate property
5312	Offices of real estate agents and brokers
53121	Offices of real estate agents and brokers
531210	Offices of real estate agents and brokers
5313	Activities related to real estate
53131	Real estate property managers
531311	Residential property managers
531312	Nonresidential property managers
53132	Offices of real estate appraisers
531320	Offices of real estate appraisers
53139	Other activities related to real estate
531390	Other activities related to real estate
532	**Rental and leasing services**
5321	Automotive equipment rental and leasing
53211	Passenger car rental and leasing
532111	Passenger car rental
532112	Passenger car leasing
53212	Truck, trailer, and RV rental and leasing
532120	Truck, trailer, and RV rental and leasing
5322	Consumer goods rental
53221	Consumer electronics and appliances rental
532210	Consumer electronics and appliances rental
53222	Formal wear and costume rental
532220	Formal wear and costume rental
53223	Video tape and disc rental
532230	Video tape and disc rental
53229	Other consumer goods rental
532291	Home health equipment rental
532292	Recreational goods rental
532299	All other consumer goods rental

Code	Short title
5323	General rental centers
53231	General rental centers
532310	General rental centers
5324	Machinery and equipment rental and leasing
53241	Heavy machinery rental and leasing
532411	Transportation equipment rental and leasing
532412	Other heavy machinery rental and leasing
53242	Office equipment rental and leasing
532420	Office equipment rental and leasing
53249	Other machinery rental and leasing
532490	Other machinery rental and leasing
533	**Lessors of nonfinancial intangible assets**
5331	Lessors of nonfinancial intangible assets
53311	Lessors of nonfinancial intangible assets
533110	Lessors of nonfinancial intangible assets
54	**PROFESSIONAL AND TECHNICAL SERVICES**
541	**Professional and technical services**
5411	Legal services
54111	Offices of lawyers
541110	Offices of lawyers
54112	Offices of notaries
541120	Offices of notaries
54119	Other legal services
541191	Title abstract and settlement offices
541199	All other legal services
5412	Accounting and bookkeeping services

Note: For definitions of abbreviations and acronyms see page 964.

Code	Short title
54121	Accounting and bookkeeping services
541211	Offices of certified public accountants
541213	Tax preparation services
541214	Payroll services
541219	Other accounting services
5413	Architectural and engineering services
54131	Architectural services
541310	Architectural services
54132	Landscape architectural services
541320	Landscape architectural services
54133	Engineering services
541330	Engineering services
54134	Drafting services
541340	Drafting services
54135	Building inspection services
541350	Building inspection services
54136	Geophysical surveying and mapping services
541360	Geophysical surveying and mapping services
54137	Other surveying and mapping services
541370	Other surveying and mapping services
54138	Testing laboratories
541380	Testing laboratories
5414	Specialized design services
54141	Interior design services
541410	Interior design services
54142	Industrial design services
541420	Industrial design services
54143	Graphic design services
541430	Graphic design services
54149	Other specialized design services
541490	Other specialized design services
5415	Computer systems design and related services
54151	Computer systems design and related services

Code	Short title
541511	Custom computer programming services
541512	Computer systems design services
541513	Computer facilities management services
541519	Other computer related services
5416	Management and technical consulting services
54161	Management consulting services
541611	Administrative management consulting services
541612	Human resource consulting services
541613	Marketing consulting services
541614	Process and logistics consulting services
541618	Other management consulting services
54162	Environmental consulting services
541620	Environmental consulting services
54169	Other technical consulting services
541690	Other technical consulting services
5417	Scientific research and development services
54171	Physical, engineering and biological research
541710	Physical, engineering and biological research
54172	Social science and humanities research
541720	Social science and humanities research
5418	Advertising and related services
54181	Advertising agencies
541810	Advertising agencies
54182	Public relations agencies
541820	Public relations agencies
54183	Media buying agencies
541830	Media buying agencies
54184	Media representatives

Note: For definitions of abbreviations and acronyms see page 964.

Code	Short title
541840	Media representatives
54185	Display advertising
541850	Display advertising
54186	Direct mail advertising
541860	Direct mail advertising
54187	Advertising material distribution services
541870	Advertising material distribution services
54189	Other services related to advertising
541890	Other services related to advertising
5419	Other professional and technical services
54191	Marketing research and public opinion polling
541910	Marketing research and public opinion polling
54192	Photographic services
541921	Photography studios, portrait
541922	Commercial photography
54193	Translation and interpretation services
541930	Translation and interpretation services
54194	Veterinary services
541940	Veterinary services
54199	All other professional and technical services
541990	All other professional and technical services
55	**MANAGEMENT OF COMPANIES AND ENTERPRISES**
551	**Management of companies and enterprises**
5511	Management of companies and enterprises
55111	Management of companies and enterprises
551111	Offices of bank holding companies
551112	Offices of other holding companies
551114	Managing offices
56	**ADMINISTRATIVE AND WASTE SERVICES**
561	**Administrative and support services**
5611	Office administrative services
56111	Office administrative services
561110	Office administrative services
5612	Facilities support services
56121	Facilities support services
561210	Facilities support services
5613	Employment services
56131	Employment placement agencies
561310	Employment placement agencies
56132	Temporary help services
561320	Temporary help services
56133	Professional employer organizations
561330	Professional employer organizations
5614	Business support services
56141	Document preparation services
561410	Document preparation services
56142	Telephone call centers
561421	Telephone answering services
561422	Telemarketing bureaus
56143	Business service centers
561431	Private mail centers
561439	Other business service centers
56144	Collection agencies
561440	Collection agencies
56145	Credit bureaus
561450	Credit bureaus
56149	Other business support services
561491	Repossession services
561492	Court reporting and stenotype services
561499	All other business support services

Note: For definitions of abbreviations and acronyms see page 964.

Code	Short title
5615	Travel arrangement and reservation services
56151	Travel agencies
561510	Travel agencies
56152	Tour operators
561520	Tour operators
56159	Other travel arrangement services
561591	Convention and visitors bureaus
561599	All other travel arrangement services
5616	Investigation and security services
56161	Security and armored car services
561611	Investigation services
561612	Security guards and patrol services
561613	Armored car services
56162	Security systems services
561621	Security systems services, except locksmiths
561622	Locksmiths
5617	Services to buildings and dwellings
56171	Exterminating and pest control services
561710	Exterminating and pest control services
56172	Janitorial services
561720	Janitorial services
56173	Landscaping services
561730	Landscaping services
56174	Carpet and upholstery cleaning services
561740	Carpet and upholstery cleaning services
56179	Other services to buildings and dwellings
561790	Other services to buildings and dwellings
5619	Other support services
56191	Packaging and labeling services
561910	Packaging and labeling services
56192	Convention and trade show organizers
561920	Convention and trade show organizers
56199	All other support services
561990	All other support services
562	**Waste management and remediation services**
5621	Waste collection
56211	Waste collection
562111	Solid waste collection
562112	Hazardous waste collection
562119	Other waste collection
5622	Waste treatment and disposal
56221	Waste treatment and disposal
562211	Hazardous waste treatment and disposal
562212	Solid waste landfill
562213	Solid waste combustors and incinerators
562219	Other nonhazardous waste disposal
5629	Remediation and other waste services
56291	Remediation services
562910	Remediation services
56292	Materials recovery facilities
562920	Materials recovery facilities
56299	All other waste management services
562991	Septic tank and related services
562998	Miscellaneous waste management services
61	**EDUCATIONAL SERVICES**
611	**Educational services**
6111	Elementary and secondary schools
61111	Elementary and secondary schools
611110	Elementary and secondary schools
6112	Junior colleges
61121	Junior colleges

Note: For definitions of abbreviations and acronyms see page 964.

Code	Short title
611210	Junior colleges
6113	Colleges and universities
61131	Colleges and universities
611310	Colleges and universities
6114	Business, computer and management training
61141	Business and secretarial schools
611410	Business and secretarial schools
61142	Computer training
611420	Computer training
61143	Management training
611430	Management training
6115	Technical and trade schools
61151	Technical and trade schools
611511	Cosmetology and barber schools
611512	Flight training
611513	Apprenticeship training
611519	Other technical and trade schools
6116	Other schools and instruction
61161	Fine arts schools
611610	Fine arts schools
61162	Sports and recreation instruction
611620	Sports and recreation instruction
61163	Language schools
611630	Language schools
61169	All other schools and instruction
611691	Exam preparation and tutoring
611692	Automobile driving schools
611699	Miscellaneous schools and instruction
6117	Educational support services
61171	Educational support services
611710	Educational support services
62	**HEALTH CARE AND SOCIAL ASSISTANCE**
621	**Ambulatory health care services**
6211	Offices of physicians
62111	Offices of physicians
621111	Offices of physicians, except mental health
621112	Offices of mental health physicians
6212	Offices of dentists
62121	Offices of dentists
621210	Offices of dentists
6213	Offices of other health practitioners
62131	Offices of chiropractors
621310	Offices of chiropractors
62132	Offices of optometrists
621320	Offices of optometrists
62133	Offices of mental health practitioners
621330	Offices of mental health practitioners
62134	Offices of specialty therapists
621340	Offices of specialty therapists
62139	Offices of all other health practitioners
621391	Offices of podiatrists
621399	Offices of miscellaneous health practitioners
6214	Outpatient care centers
62141	Family planning centers
621410	Family planning centers
62142	Outpatient mental health centers
621420	Outpatient mental health centers
62149	Other outpatient care centers
621491	HMO medical centers
621492	Kidney dialysis centers
621493	Freestanding emergency medical centers
621498	All other outpatient care centers
6215	Medical and diagnostic laboratories
62151	Medical and diagnostic laboratories
621511	Medical laboratories
621512	Diagnostic imaging centers
6216	Home health care services
62161	Home health care services
621610	Home health care services
6219	Other ambulatory health care services
62191	Ambulance services

Note: For definitions of abbreviations and acronyms see page 964.

Code	Short title
621910	Ambulance services
62199	All other ambulatory health care services
621991	Blood and organ banks
621999	Miscellaneous ambulatory health care services
622	**Hospitals**
6221	General medical and surgical hospitals
62211	General medical and surgical hospitals
622110	General medical and surgical hospitals
6222	Psychiatric and substance abuse hospitals
62221	Psychiatric and substance abuse hospitals
622210	Psychiatric and substance abuse hospitals
6223	Other hospitals
62231	Other hospitals
622310	Other hospitals
623	**Nursing and residential care facilities**
6231	Nursing care facilities
62311	Nursing care facilities
623110	Nursing care facilities
6232	Residential mental health facilities
62321	Residential mental retardation facilities
623210	Residential mental retardation facilities
62322	Residential mental and substance abuse care
623220	Residential mental and substance abuse care
6233	Community care facilities for the elderly
62331	Community care facilities for the elderly
623311	Continuing care retirement communities

Code	Short title
623312	Homes for the elderly
6239	Other residential care facilities
62399	Other residential care facilities
623990	Other residential care facilities
624	**Social assistance**
6241	Individual and family services
62411	Child and youth services
624110	Child and youth services
62412	Services for the elderly and disabled
624120	Services for the elderly and disabled
62419	Other individual and family services
624190	Other individual and family services
6242	Emergency and other relief services
62421	Community food services
624210	Community food services
62422	Community housing services
624221	Temporary shelters
624229	Other community housing services
62423	Emergency and other relief services
624230	Emergency and other relief services
6243	Vocational rehabilitation services
62431	Vocational rehabilitation services
624310	Vocational rehabilitation services
6244	Child day care services
62441	Child day care services
624410	Child day care services
71	**ARTS, ENTERTAINMENT, AND RECREATION**
711	**Performing arts and spectator sports**
7111	Performing arts companies

Note: For definitions of abbreviations and acronyms see page 964.

Code	Short title
71111	Theater companies and dinner theaters
711110	Theater companies and dinner theaters
71112	Dance companies
711120	Dance companies
71113	Musical groups and artists
711130	Musical groups and artists
71119	Other performing arts companies
711190	Other performing arts companies
7112	Spectator sports
71121	Spectator sports
711211	Sports teams and clubs
711212	Racetracks
711219	Other spectator sports
7113	Promoters of performing arts and sports
71131	Promoters with facilities
711310	Promoters with facilities
71132	Promoters without facilities
711320	Promoters without facilities
7114	Agents and managers for public figures
71141	Agents and managers for public figures
711410	Agents and managers for public figures
7115	Independent artists, writers, and performers
71151	Independent artists, writers, and performers
711510	Independent artists, writers, and performers
712	**Museums, historical sites, zoos, and parks**
7121	Museums, historical sites, zoos, and parks
71211	Museums
712110	Museums
71212	Historical sites
712120	Historical sites
71213	Zoos and botanical gardens
712130	Zoos and botanical gardens
71219	Nature parks and other similar institutions
712190	Nature parks and other similar institutions
713	**Amusements, gambling, and recreation**
7131	Amusement parks and arcades
71311	Amusement and theme parks
713110	Amusement and theme parks
71312	Amusement arcades
713120	Amusement arcades
7132	Gambling industries
71321	Casinos, except casino hotels
713210	Casinos, except casino hotels
71329	Other gambling industries
713290	Other gambling industries
7139	Other amusement and recreation industries
71391	Golf courses and country clubs
713910	Golf courses and country clubs
71392	Skiing facilities
713920	Skiing facilities
71393	Marinas
713930	Marinas
71394	Fitness and recreational sports centers
713940	Fitness and recreational sports centers
71395	Bowling centers
713950	Bowling centers
71399	All other amusement and recreation industries
713990	All other amusement and recreation industries
72	**ACCOMMODATION AND FOOD SERVICES**
721	**Accommodation**
7211	Traveler accommodation
72111	Hotels and motels, except casino hotels
721110	Hotels and motels, except casino hotels

Note: For definitions of abbreviations and acronyms see page 964.

Code	Short title
72112	Casino hotels
721120	Casino hotels
72119	Other traveler accommodation
721191	Bed-and-breakfast inns
721199	All other traveler accommodation
7212	RV parks and recreational camps
72121	RV parks and recreational camps
721211	RV parks and campgrounds
721214	Recreational and vacation camps
7213	Rooming and boarding houses
72131	Rooming and boarding houses
721310	Rooming and boarding houses
722	**Food services and drinking places**
7221	Full-service restaurants
72211	Full-service restaurants
722110	Full-service restaurants
7222	Limited-service eating places
72221	Limited-service eating places
722211	Limited-service restaurants
722212	Cafeterias
722213	Snack and nonalcoholic beverage bars
7223	Special food services
72231	Food service contractors
722310	Food service contractors
72232	Caterers
722320	Caterers
72233	Mobile food services
722330	Mobile food services
7224	Drinking places, alcoholic beverages
72241	Drinking places, alcoholic beverages
722410	Drinking places, alcoholic beverages

Code	Short title
81	**OTHER SERVICES, EXCEPT PUBLIC ADMINISTRATION**
811	**Repair and maintenance**
8111	Automotive repair and maintenance
81111	Automotive mechanical and electrical repair
811111	General automotive repair
811112	Automotive exhaust system repair
811113	Automotive transmission repair
811118	Other automotive mechanical and elec. repair
81112	Automotive body, interior, and glass repair
811121	Automotive body and interior repair
811122	Automotive glass replacement shops
81119	Other automotive repair and maintenance
811191	Automotive oil change and lubrication shops
811192	Car washes
811198	All other automotive repair and maintenance
8112	Electronic equipment repair and maintenance
81121	Electronic equipment repair and maintenance
811211	Consumer electronics repair and maintenance
811212	Computer and office machine repair
811213	Communication equipment repair
811219	Other electronic equipment repair
8113	Commercial machinery repair and maintenance
81131	Commercial machinery repair and maintenance
811310	Commercial machinery repair and maintenance

Note: For definitions of abbreviations and acronyms see page 964.

Code	Short title
8114	Household goods repair and maintenance
81141	Home and garden equip. and appliance repair
811411	Home and garden equipment repair
811412	Appliance repair and maintenance
81142	Reupholstery and furniture repair
811420	Reupholstery and furniture repair
81143	Footwear and leather goods repair
811430	Footwear and leather goods repair
81149	Other household goods repair and maintenance
811490	Other household goods repair and maintenance
812	**Personal and laundry services**
8121	Personal care services
81211	Hair, nail, and skin care services
812111	Barber shops
812112	Beauty salons
812113	Nail salons
81219	Other personal care services
812191	Diet and weight reducing centers
812199	Other personal care services
8122	Death care services
81221	Funeral homes and funeral services
812210	Funeral homes and funeral services
81222	Cemeteries and crematories
812220	Cemeteries and crematories
8123	Drycleaning and laundry services
81231	Coin-operated laundries and drycleaners
812310	Coin-operated laundries and drycleaners
81232	Drycleaning and laundry services
812320	Drycleaning and laundry services
81233	Linen and uniform supply
812331	Linen supply
812332	Industrial launderers
8129	Other personal services
81291	Pet care, except veterinary, services
812910	Pet care, except veterinary, services
81292	Photofinishing
812921	Photofinishing laboratories, except one-hour
812922	One-hour photofinishing
81293	Parking lots and garages
812930	Parking lots and garages
81299	All other personal services
812990	All other personal services
813	**Membership associations and organizations**
8131	Religious organizations
81311	Religious organizations
813110	Religious organizations
8132	Grantmaking and giving services
81321	Grantmaking and giving services
813211	Grantmaking foundations
813212	Voluntary health organizations
813219	Other grantmaking and giving services
8133	Social advocacy organizations
81331	Social advocacy organizations
813311	Human rights organizations
813312	Environment and conservation organizations
813319	Other social advocacy organizations
8134	Civic and social organizations
81341	Civic and social organizations
813410	Civic and social organizations

Note: For definitions of abbreviations and acronyms see page 964.

Code	Short title
8139	Professional and similar organizations
81391	Business associations
813910	Business associations
81392	Professional organizations
813920	Professional organizations
81393	Labor unions and similar labor organizations
813930	Labor unions and similar labor organizations
81394	Political organizations
813940	Political organizations
81399	Other similar organizations
813990	Other similar organizations
814	**Private households**
8141	Private households
81411	Private households
814110	Private households
92	**PUBLIC ADMINISTRATION**
921	**Executive, legislative and general government**
9211	Executive, legislative and general government
92111	Executive offices
921110	Executive offices
92112	Legislative bodies
921120	Legislative bodies
92113	Public finance activities
921130	Public finance activities
92114	Executive and legislative offices, combined
921140	Executive and legislative offices, combined
92115	Tribal governments
921150	Tribal governments
92119	Other general government support
921190	Other general government support
922	**Justice, public order, and safety activities**
9221	Justice, public order, and safety activities
92211	Courts
922110	Courts
92212	Police protection
922120	Police protection
92213	Legal counsel and prosecution
922130	Legal counsel and prosecution
92214	Correctional institutions
922140	Correctional institutions
92215	Parole offices and probation offices
922150	Parole offices and probation offices
92216	Fire protection
922160	Fire protection
92219	Other justice and safety activities
922190	Other justice and safety activities
923	**Administration of human resource programs**
9231	Administration of human resource programs
92311	Administration of education programs
923110	Administration of education programs
92312	Administration of public health programs
923120	Administration of public health programs
92313	Other human resource programs administration
923130	Other human resource programs administration
92314	Administration of veterans' affairs
923140	Administration of veterans' affairs
924	**Administration of environmental programs**
9241	Administration of environmental programs
92411	Air, water, and waste program administration

Note: For definitions of abbreviations and acronyms see page 964.

Code	Short title
924110	Air, water, and waste program administration
92412	Administration of conservation programs
924120	Administration of conservation programs
925	**Community and housing program administration**
9251	Community and housing program administration
92511	Administration of housing programs
925110	Administration of housing programs
92512	Urban and rural development administration
925120	Urban and rural development administration
926	**Administration of economic programs**
9261	Administration of economic programs
92611	Administration of general economic programs
926110	Administration of general economic programs
92612	Transportation program administration
926120	Transportation program administration
92613	Utility regulation and administration
926130	Utility regulation and administration
92614	Agricultural market and commodity regulation
926140	Agricultural market and commodity regulation
92615	Licensing and regulating commercial sectors
926150	Licensing and regulating commercial sectors
927	**Space research and technology**
9271	Space research and technology
92711	Space research and technology
927110	Space research and technology
928	**National security and international affairs**
9281	National security and international affairs
92811	National security
928110	National security
92812	International affairs
928120	International affairs

Note: For definitions of abbreviations and acronyms see page 964.

Abbreviations and Acronyms Used in Short Titles

Abbreviation/Acronym	Word
AC	air conditioning
ag.	agriculture
Al	aluminum
CD	compact disc
const.	construction
Cu	copper
elec.	electrical
equip.	equipment
estab.	establishment
exc.	except
HVAC	heating, ventilation, and air-conditioning
ISPs	Internet service providers
LTL	less than truckload
merch	merchant
mfg.	manufacturing
misc.	miscellaneous
RV	recreational vehicle
TL	truckload
transport.	transportation
TV	television
whls.	wholesalers

Part III

Appendixes

Appendixes A and B map the changes for 2002 NAICS to the 1997 NAICS in 2002 NAICS sequence (Appendix A) and 1997 NAICS sequence (Appendix B). The tables do not provide a comprehensive guide to all economic activities, but rather provide a map for the largest and most important changes from 1997 to 2002.

Full concordances for 1997 NAICS to 2002 NAICS and 1987 SIC to 2002 NAICS are available on the Census Bureau's Website at www.census.gov/naics.

Appendix A

2002 NAICS U.S. Matched to 1997 NAICS U.S.

	2002 NAICS Code	2002 NAICS U.S. Description	1997 NAICS Code	1997 NAICS U.S. Description
	236	Construction of Buildings		
	2361	Residential Building Construction		
	23611	Residential Building Construction		
US	236115	New Single-Family Housing Construction (except Operative Builders)	*233210	Single Family Housing Construction (except operative builders and remodeling contractors)
US	236116	New Multifamily Housing Construction (except Operative Builders)	*233220	Multifamily Housing Construction (except barrack and dormitory construction, operative builders, and remodeling contractors)
US	236117	New Housing Operative Builders	*233210	Single Family Housing Construction (operative builders)
			*233220	Multifamily Housing Construction (operative builders)
US	236118	Residential Remodelers	*233210	Single Family Housing Construction (remodeling contractors)
			*233220	Multifamily Housing Construction (remodeling contractors)
	2362	Nonresidential Building Construction		
	23621	Industrial Building Construction	*233310	Manufacturing and Industrial Building Construction (except grain elevators, dry cleaning plants, and manufacturing and industrial warehouses)

US—United States industry only. CAN—United States and Canadian industries are comparable. MEX—United States and Mexican industries are comparable. Blank—Canadian, Mexican, and United States industries are comparable. *—Part of.

2002 NAICS Code	2002 NAICS U.S. Description	1997 NAICS Code	1997 NAICS U.S. Description
		*234930	Industrial Nonbuilding Structure Construction (process batch plants, incinerators, industrial furnaces and kilns, mining appurtenance, and construction management of these projects)
		*234990	All Other Heavy Construction (waste disposal plant construction)
23622	Commercial and Institutional Building Construction	*233220	Multifamily Housing Construction (barrack and dormitory construction)
		*233310	Manufacturing and Industrial Building Construction (grain elevators, dry cleaning plants, and manufacturing and industrial warehouses)
		233320	Commercial and Institutional Building Construction
		*235990	All Other Special Trade Contractors (indoor swimming pools)
237	Heavy and Civil Engineering Construction		
2371	Utility System Construction		
23711	Water and Sewer Line and Related Structures Construction	*234910	Water, Sewer, and Pipeline Construction (water/sewer pumping stations, sewage collection and disposal lines, storm sewers, sewer/water mains and lines, water storage tanks and towers, and construction management of these projects)
		*234990	All Other Heavy Construction (irrigation systems, sewage treatment and water treatment plants, construction management of these projects)
		235810	Water Well Drilling Contractors

US—United States industry only. CAN—United States and Canadian industries are comparable. MEX—United States and Mexican industries are comparable. Blank—Canadian, Mexican, and United States industries are comparable. *—Part of.

2002 NAICS Code	2002 NAICS U.S. Description	1997 NAICS Code	1997 NAICS U.S. Description
23712	Oil and Gas Pipeline and Related Structures Construction	*213112	Support Activities for Oil and Gas Operations (construction of field gathering lines on a contract basis)
		*234910	Water, Sewer, and Pipeline Construction (gas and oil pumping stations, gas and oil pipeline construction, gas mains, gas and oil storage tank construction, and construction management of these projects)
		*234930	Industrial Nonbuilding Structure Construction (petrochemical plants, refineries, and construction management of these projects)
23713	Power and Communication Line and Related Structures Construction	234920	Power and Communication Transmission Line Construction
		*234930	Industrial Nonbuilding Structure Construction (power generation plants (excluding hydroelectric dams), transmission and distribution transformer stations, and construction management of these projects)
2372	Land Subdivision		
23721	Land Subdivision	233110	Land Subdivision and Land Development
2373	Highway, Street, and Bridge Construction		
23731	Highway, Street, and Bridge Construction	234110	Highway and Street Construction
		*234120	Bridge and Tunnel Construction (bridge construction)
		*235210	Painting and Wall Covering Contractors (highway and traffic line painting)
2379	Other Heavy and Civil Engineering Construction		

US—United States industry only. CAN—United States and Canadian industries are comparable. MEX—United States and Mexican industries are comparable. Blank—Canadian, Mexican, and United States industries are comparable. *—Part of.

	2002 NAICS Code	2002 NAICS U.S. Description	1997 NAICS Code	1997 NAICS U.S. Description
	23799	Other Heavy and Civil Engineering Construction	*234120	Bridge and Tunnel Construction (tunnel construction)
			*234990	All Other Heavy Construction (except waste disposal plant construction, irrigation systems, sewage treatment and water treatment plants, right-of-way clearing and line slashing, blasting, trenching, and equipment rental with operator)
			*235990	All Other Special Trade Contractors (anchored earth retention contractors)
	238	Specialty Trade Contractors		
	2381	Foundation, Structure, and Building Exterior Contractors		
	23811	Poured Concrete Foundation and Structure Contractors	*235710	Concrete Contractors (except residential and commercial asphalt, brick, and concrete paving)
	23812	Structural Steel and Precast Concrete Contractors	*235910	Structural Steel Erection Contractors (except curtain walls, metal furring installation, and cooling tower installation)
CAN	23813	Framing Contractors	*235510	Carpentry Contractors (framing carpentry)
CAN	23814	Masonry Contractors	235410	Masonry and Stone Contractors
			*235420	Drywall, Plastering, Acoustical, and Insulation Contractors (stucco contractors)
CAN	23815	Glass and Glazing Contractors	235920	Glass and Glazing Contractors
CAN	23816	Roofing Contractors	*235610	Roofing, Siding, and Sheet Metal Contractors (roofing contractors)
CAN	23817	Siding Contractors	*235610	Roofing, Siding, and Sheet Metal Contractors (siding contractors)
CAN	23819	Other Foundation, Structure, and Building Exterior Contractors	*235910	Structural Steel Erection Contractors (curtain walls and metal furring installation)

US—United States industry only. CAN—United States and Canadian industries are comparable. MEX—United States and Mexican industries are comparable. Blank—Canadian, Mexican, and United States industries are comparable. *—Part of.

2002 NAICS Code	2002 NAICS U.S. Description	1997 NAICS Code	1997 NAICS U.S. Description
		*235990	All Other Special Trade Contractors (forming contractors, ornamental metal work installation)
2382	Building Equipment Contractors		
23821	Electrical Contractors	*235110	Plumbing, Heating, and Air-Conditioning Contractors (environmental controls installation contractors)
		235310	Electrical Contractors
23822	Plumbing, Heating, and Air-Conditioning Contractors	*235110	Plumbing, Heating, and Air-Conditioning Contractors (except environmental controls installation contractors and septic tank, cesspool, and dry well construction)
		*235910	Structural Steel Erection Contractors (cooling tower installation)
		*235950	Building Equipment and Other Machinery Installation Contractors (scrubber, dust collection, and other industrial ventilation installation)
23829	Other Building Equipment Contractors	*235950	Building Equipment and Other Machinery Installation Contractors (except scrubber, dust collection, and other industrial ventilation installation)
		*235990	All Other Special Trade Contractors (service station equipment installation; boiler, duct, and pipe insulation; lightning rod installation; bowling alley installation; household-type antenna installation; church bell installation; and tower clock installation)
2383	Building Finishing Contractors		

US—United States industry only. CAN—United States and Canadian industries are comparable. MEX—United States and Mexican industries are comparable. Blank—Canadian, Mexican, and United States industries are comparable. *—Part of.

2002 NAICS Code	2002 NAICS U.S. Description	1997 NAICS Code	1997 NAICS U.S. Description
23831	Drywall and Insulation Contractors	*235420	Drywall, Plastering, Acoustical, and Insulation Contractors (except stucco contractors)
23832	Painting and Wall Covering Contractors	*235210	Painting and Wall Covering Contractors (except highway and traffic line painting)
23833	Flooring Contractors	235520	Floor Laying and Other Floor Contractors
23834	Tile and Terrazzo Contractors	235430	Tile, Marble, Terrazzo, and Mosaic Contractors
23835	Finish Carpentry Contractors	*235510	Carpentry Contractors (finish carpentry)
23839	Other Building Finishing Contractors	*235610	Roofing, Siding, and Sheet Metal Contractors (metal ceiling, panel, and shelving installation)
		*235990	All Other Special Trade Contractors (weather stripping and damp-proofing, modular furniture installation, bathtub refinishing, window covering fixture installation, trade show exhibit installation and dismantling, and spectator seating installation)
2389	Other Specialty Trade Contractors		
23891	Site Preparation Contractors	*213112	Support Activities for Oil and Gas Operations (site preparation and related construction activities on a contract basis)
		*213113	Support Activities for Coal Mining (site preparation and related construction activities on a contract basis)
		*213114	Support Activities for Metal Mining (site preparation and related construction activities on a contract basis)

US—United States industry only. CAN—United States and Canadian industries are comparable. MEX—United States and Mexican industries are comparable. Blank—Canadian, Mexican, and United States industries are comparable. *—Part of.

2002 NAICS Code	2002 NAICS U.S. Description	1997 NAICS Code	1997 NAICS U.S. Description
		*213115	Support Activities for Nonmetallic Minerals (except Fuels) (site preparation and related construction activities on a contract basis)
		*234990	All Other Heavy Construction (right-of-way clearing and line slashing, blasting, trenching, and equipment rental (except cranes) with operator)
		*235110	Plumbing, Heating, and Air-Conditioning Contractors (septic tank, cesspool, and dry well construction contractors)
		235930	Excavation Contractors
		235940	Wrecking and Demolition Contractors
		*235990	All Other Special Trade Contractors (dewatering contractors, core drilling for construction, and test drilling for construction)
23899	All Other Specialty Trade Contractors	*234990	All Other Heavy Construction (rental of cranes with operator)
		*235710	Concrete Contractors (residential and commercial asphalt, brick, and concrete paving)
		*235990	All Other Special Trade Contractors (except indoor swimming pools, earth retention contractors, forming contractors, ornamental metal work, building equipment contractors, building finishing contractors, dewatering contractors, core drilling for construction, and test boring for construction)
		*561720	Janitorial Services (cleaning buildings during and immediately after construction)

US—United States industry only. CAN—United States and Canadian industries are comparable. MEX—United States and Mexican industries are comparable. Blank—Canadian, Mexican, and United States industries are comparable. *—Part of.

	2002 NAICS Code	2002 NAICS U.S. Description	1997 NAICS Code	1997 NAICS U.S. Description
	42	Wholesale Trade		
US	423	Merchant Wholesalers, Durable Goods		
US	4231	Motor Vehicle and Motor Vehicle Parts and Supplies Merchant Wholesalers		
US	42311	Automobile and Other Motor Vehicle Merchant Wholesalers	*421110	Automobile and Other Motor Vehicle Wholesalers (merchant wholesalers)
US	42312	Motor Vehicle Supplies and New Parts Merchant Wholesalers	*421120	Motor Vehicle Supplies and New Parts Wholesalers (merchant wholesalers)
US	42313	Tire and Tube Merchant Wholesalers	*421130	Tire and Tube Wholesalers (merchant wholesalers)
US	42314	Motor Vehicle Parts (Used) Merchant Wholesalers	*421140	Motor Vehicle Parts (Used) Wholesalers (merchant wholesalers)
US	4232	Furniture and Home Furnishing Merchant Wholesalers		
US	42321	Furniture Merchant Wholesalers	*421210	Furniture Wholesalers (merchant wholesalers)
US	42322	Home Furnishing Merchant Wholesalers	*421220	Home Furnishing Wholesalers (merchant wholesalers)
US	4233	Lumber and Other Construction Materials Merchant Wholesalers		
US	42331	Lumber, Plywood, Millwork, and Wood Panel Merchant Wholesalers	*421310	Lumber, Plywood, Millwork, and Wood Panel Wholesalers (merchant wholesalers)
US	42332	Brick, Stone, and Related Construction Material Merchant Wholesalers	*421320	Brick, Stone, and Related Construction Material Wholesalers (merchant wholesalers)
US	42333	Roofing, Siding, and Insulation Material Merchant Wholesalers	*421330	Roofing, Siding, and Insulation Material Wholesalers (merchant wholesalers)
US	42339	Other Construction Material Merchant Wholesalers	*421390	Other Construction Material Wholesalers (merchant wholesalers)

US—United States industry only. CAN—United States and Canadian industries are comparable. MEX—United States and Mexican industries are comparable. Blank—Canadian, Mexican, and United States industries are comparable. *—Part of.

	2002 NAICS Code	2002 NAICS U.S. Description	1997 NAICS Code	1997 NAICS U.S. Description
US	4234	Professional and Commercial Equipment and Supplies Merchant Wholesalers		
US	42341	Photographic Equipment and Supplies Merchant Wholesalers	*421410	Photographic Equipment and Supplies Wholesalers (merchant wholesalers)
US	42342	Office Equipment Merchant Wholesalers	*421420	Office Equipment Wholesalers (merchant wholesalers)
US	42343	Computer and Computer Peripheral Equipment and Software Merchant Wholesalers	*421430	Computer and Computer Peripheral Equipment and Software Wholesalers (merchant wholesalers)
US	42344	Other Commercial Equipment Merchant Wholesalers	*421440	Other Commercial Equipment Wholesalers (merchant wholesalers)
US	42345	Medical, Dental, and Hospital Equipment and Supplies Merchant Wholesalers	*421450	Medical, Dental, and Hospital Equipment and Supplies Wholesalers (merchant wholesalers)
US	42346	Ophthalmic Goods Merchant Wholesalers	*421460	Ophthalmic Goods Wholesalers (merchant wholesalers)
US	42349	Other Professional Equipment and Supplies Merchant Wholesalers	*421490	Other Professional Equipment and Supplies Wholesalers (merchant wholesalers)
US	4235	Metal and Mineral (except Petroleum) Merchant Wholesalers		
US	42351	Metal Service Centers and Other Metal Merchant Wholesalers	*421510	Metal Service Centers and Offices (merchant wholesalers)
US	42352	Coal and Other Mineral and Ore Merchant Wholesalers	*421520	Coal and Other Mineral and Ore Wholesalers (merchant wholesalers)
US	4236	Electrical and Electronic Goods Merchant Wholesalers		
US	42361	Electrical Apparatus and Equipment, Wiring Supplies, and Related Equipment Merchant Wholesalers	*421610	Electrical Apparatus and Equipment, Wiring Supplies, and Construction Material Wholesalers (merchant wholesalers)

US—United States industry only. CAN—United States and Canadian industries are comparable. MEX—United States and Mexican industries are comparable. Blank—Canadian, Mexican, and United States industries are comparable. *—Part of.

	2002 NAICS Code	2002 NAICS U.S. Description	1997 NAICS Code	1997 NAICS U.S. Description
US	42362	Electrical and Electronic Appliance, Television, and Radio Set Merchant Wholesalers	*421620	Electrical Appliance, Television, and Radio Set Wholesalers (merchant wholesalers)
US	42369	Other Electronic Parts and Equipment Merchant Wholesalers	*421690	Other Electronic Parts and Equipment Wholesalers (merchant wholesalers)
US	4237	Hardware, and Plumbing and Heating Equipment and Supplies Merchant Wholesalers		
US	42371	Hardware Merchant Wholesalers	*421710	Hardware Wholesalers (merchant wholesalers)
US	42372	Plumbing and Heating Equipment and Supplies (Hydronics) Merchant Wholesalers	*421720	Plumbing and Heating Equipment and Supplies (Hydronics) Wholesalers (merchant wholesalers)
US	42373	Warm Air Heating and Air-Conditioning Equipment and Supplies Merchant Wholesalers	*421730	Warm Air Heating and Air-Conditioning Equipment and Supplies Wholesalers (merchant wholesalers)
US	42374	Refrigeration Equipment and Supplies Merchant Wholesalers	*421740	Refrigeration Equipment and Supplies Wholesalers (merchant wholesalers)
US	4238	Machinery, Equipment, and Supplies Merchant Wholesalers		
US	42381	Construction and Mining (except Oil Well) Machinery and Equipment Merchant Wholesalers	*421810	Construction and Mining (except Oil Well) Machinery and Equipment Wholesalers (merchant wholesalers)
US	42382	Farm and Garden Machinery and Equipment Merchant Wholesalers	*421820	Farm and Garden Machinery and Equipment Wholesalers (merchant wholesalers)
US	42383	Industrial Machinery and Equipment Merchant Wholesalers	*421830	Industrial Machinery and Equipment Wholesalers (merchant wholesalers)
US	42384	Industrial Supplies Merchant Wholesalers	*421840	Industrial Supplies Wholesalers (merchant wholesalers)

US—United States industry only. CAN—United States and Canadian industries are comparable. MEX—United States and Mexican industries are comparable. Blank—Canadian, Mexican, and United States industries are comparable. *—Part of.

	2002 NAICS Code	2002 NAICS U.S. Description	1997 NAICS Code	1997 NAICS U.S. Description
US	42385	Service Establishment Equipment and Supplies Merchant Wholesalers	*421850	Service Establishment Equipment and Supplies Wholesalers (merchant wholesalers)
US	42386	Transportation Equipment and Supplies (except Motor Vehicle) Merchant Wholesalers	*421860	Transportation Equipment and Supplies (except Motor Vehicle) Wholesalers (merchant wholesalers)
US	4239	Miscellaneous Durable Goods Merchant Wholesalers		
US	42391	Sporting and Recreational Goods and Supplies Merchant Wholesalers	*421910	Sporting and Recreational Goods and Supplies Wholesalers (merchant wholesalers)
US	42392	Toy and Hobby Goods and Supplies Merchant Wholesalers	*421920	Toy and Hobby Goods and Supplies Wholesalers (merchant wholesalers)
US	42393	Recyclable Material Merchant Wholesalers	*421930	Recyclable Material Wholesalers (merchant wholesalers)
US	42394	Jewelry, Watch, Precious Stone, and Precious Metal Merchant Wholesalers	*421940	Jewelry, Watch, Precious Stone, and Precious Metal Wholesalers (merchant wholesalers)
US	42399	Other Miscellaneous Durable Goods Merchant Wholesalers	*421990	Other Miscellaneous Durable Goods Wholesalers (merchant wholesalers)
US	424	Merchant Wholesalers, Nondurable Goods		
US	4241	Paper and Paper Product Merchant Wholesalers		
US	42411	Printing and Writing Paper Merchant Wholesalers	*422110	Printing and Writing Paper Wholesalers (merchant wholesalers)
US	42412	Stationary and Office Supplies Merchant Wholesalers	*422120	Stationary and Office Supplies Wholesalers (merchant wholesalers)
US	42413	Industrial and Personal Service Paper Merchant Wholesalers	*422130	Industrial and Personal Service Paper Wholesalers (merchant wholesalers)

US—United States industry only. CAN—United States and Canadian industries are comparable. MEX—United States and Mexican industries are comparable. Blank—Canadian, Mexican, and United States industries are comparable. *—Part of.

	2002 NAICS Code	2002 NAICS U.S. Description	1997 NAICS Code	1997 NAICS U.S. Description
US	4242	Drugs and Druggists' Sundries Merchant Wholesalers		
US	42421	Drugs and Druggists' Sundries Merchant Wholesalers	*422210	Drugs and Druggists' Sundries Wholesalers (merchant wholesalers)
US	4243	Apparel, Piece Goods, and Notions Merchant Wholesalers		
US	42431	Piece Goods, Notions, and Other Dry Goods Merchant Wholesalers	*422310	Piece Goods, Notions, and Other Dry Goods Wholesalers (merchant wholesalers)
US	42432	Men's and Boys' Clothing and Furnishings Merchant Wholesalers	*422320	Men's and Boys' Clothing and Furnishings Wholesalers (merchant wholesalers)
US	42433	Women's, Children's, and Infants' Clothing and Accessories Merchant Wholesalers	*422330	Women's, Children's, and Infants' Clothing and Accessories Wholesalers (merchant wholesalers)
US	42434	Footwear Merchant Wholesalers	*422340	Footwear Wholesalers (merchant wholesalers)
US	4244	Grocery and Related Product Merchant Wholesalers		
US	42441	General Line Grocery Merchant Wholesalers	*422410	General Line Grocery Wholesalers (merchant wholesalers)
US	42442	Packaged Frozen Food Merchant Wholesalers	*422420	Packaged Frozen Food Wholesalers (merchant wholesalers)
US	42443	Dairy Product (except Dried or Canned) Merchant Wholesalers	*422430	Dairy Product (except Dried or Canned) Wholesalers (merchant wholesalers)
US	42444	Poultry and Poultry Product Merchant Wholesalers	*422440	Poultry and Poultry Product Wholesalers (merchant wholesalers)
US	42445	Confectionery Merchant Wholesalers	*422450	Confectionery Wholesalers (merchant wholesalers)
US	42446	Fish and Seafood Merchant Wholesalers	*422460	Fish and Seafood Wholesalers (merchant wholesalers)

US—United States industry only. CAN—United States and Canadian industries are comparable. MEX—United States and Mexican industries are comparable. Blank—Canadian, Mexican, and United States industries are comparable. *—Part of.

	2002 NAICS Code	2002 NAICS U.S. Description	1997 NAICS Code	1997 NAICS U.S. Description
US	42447	Meat and Meat Product Merchant Wholesalers	*422470	Meat and Meat Product Wholesalers (merchant wholesalers)
US	42448	Fresh Fruit and Vegetable Merchant Wholesalers	*422480	Fresh Fruit and Vegetable Wholesalers (merchant wholesalers)
US	42449	Other Grocery and Related Products Merchant Wholesalers	*422490	Other Grocery and Related Products Wholesalers (merchant wholesalers)
US	4245	Farm Product Raw Material Merchant Wholesalers		
US	42451	Grain and Field Bean Merchant Wholesalers	*422510	Grain and Field Bean Wholesalers (merchant wholesalers)
US	42452	Livestock Merchant Wholesalers	*422520	Livestock Wholesalers (merchant wholesalers)
US	42459	Other Farm Product Raw Material Merchant Wholesalers	*422590	Other Farm Product Raw Material Wholesalers (merchant wholesalers)
US	4246	Chemical and Allied Products Merchant Wholesalers		
US	42461	Plastics Materials and Basic Forms and Shapes Merchant Wholesalers	*422610	Plastics Materials and Basic Forms and Shapes Wholesalers (merchant wholesalers)
US	42469	Other Chemical and Allied Products Merchant Wholesalers	*422690	Other Chemical and Allied Products Wholesalers (merchant wholesalers)
US	4247	Petroleum and Petroleum Products Merchant Wholesalers		
US	42471	Petroleum Bulk Stations and Terminals	422710	Petroleum Bulk Stations and Terminals
US	42472	Petroleum and Petroleum Products Merchant Wholesalers (except Bulk Stations and Terminals)	*422720	Petroleum and Petroleum Products Wholesalers (except Bulk Stations and Terminals) (merchant wholesalers)
US	4248	Beer, Wine, and Distilled Alcoholic Beverage Merchant Wholesalers		

US—United States industry only. CAN—United States and Canadian industries are comparable. MEX—United States and Mexican industries are comparable. Blank—Canadian, Mexican, and United States industries are comparable. *—Part of.

	2002 NAICS Code	2002 NAICS U.S. Description	1997 NAICS Code	1997 NAICS U.S. Description
US	42481	Beer and Ale Merchant Wholesalers	*422810	Beer and Ale Wholesalers (merchant wholesalers)
US	42482	Wine and Distilled Alcoholic Beverage Merchant Wholesalers	*422820	Wine and Distilled Alcoholic Beverage Wholesalers (merchant wholesalers)
US	4249	Miscellaneous Nondurable Goods Merchant Wholesalers		
US	42491	Farm Supplies Merchant Wholesalers	*422910	Farm Supplies Wholesalers (merchant wholesalers)
US	42492	Book, Periodical, and Newspaper Merchant Wholesalers	*422920	Book, Periodical, and Newspaper Wholesalers (merchant wholesalers)
US	42493	Flower, Nursery Stock, and Florists' Supplies Merchant Wholesalers	*422930	Flower, Nursery Stock, and Florists' Supplies Wholesalers (merchant wholesalers)
US	42494	Tobacco and Tobacco Product Merchant Wholesalers	*422940	Tobacco and Tobacco Product Wholesalers (merchant wholesalers)
US	42495	Paint, Varnish, and Supplies Merchant Wholesalers	*422950	Paint, Varnish, and Supplies Wholesalers (merchant wholesalers)
US	42499	Other Miscellaneous Nondurable Goods Merchant Wholesalers	*422990	Other Miscellaneous Nondurable Goods Wholesalers (merchant wholesalers)
US	425	Wholesale Electronic Markets and Agents and Brokers		
US	4251	Wholesale Electronic Markets and Agents and Brokers		
US	42511	Business to Business Electronic Markets	*421110	Automobile and Other Motor Vehicle Wholesalers (electronic markets)
			*421120	Motor Vehicle Supplies and New Parts Wholesalers (electronic markets)
			*421130	Tire and Tube Wholesalers (electronic markets)

US—United States industry only. CAN—United States and Canadian industries are comparable. MEX—United States and Mexican industries are comparable. Blank—Canadian, Mexican, and United States industries are comparable. *—Part of.

2002 NAICS Code	2002 NAICS U.S. Description	1997 NAICS Code	1997 NAICS U.S. Description
		*421140	Motor Vehicle Parts (Used) Wholesalers (electronic markets)
		*421210	Furniture Wholesalers (electronic markets)
		*421220	Home Furnishing Wholesalers (electronic markets)
		*421310	Lumber, Plywood, Millwork, and Wood Panel Wholesalers (electronic markets)
		*421320	Brick, Stone, and Related Construction Material Wholesalers (electronic markets)
		*421330	Roofing, Siding, and Insulation Material Wholesalers (electronic markets)
		*421390	Other Construction Material Wholesalers (electronic markets)
		*421410	Photographic Equipment and Supplies Wholesalers (electronic markets)
		*421420	Office Equipment Wholesalers (electronic markets)
		*421430	Computer and Computer Peripheral Equipment and Software Wholesalers (electronic markets)
		*421440	Other Commercial Equipment Wholesalers (electronic markets)
		*421450	Medical, Dental, and Hospital Equipment and Supplies Wholesalers (electronic markets)
		*421460	Ophthalmic Goods Wholesalers (electronic markets)
		*421490	Other Professional Equipment and Supplies Wholesalers (electronic markets)
		*421510	Metal Service Centers and Offices (electronic markets)

US—United States industry only. CAN—United States and Canadian industries are comparable. MEX—United States and Mexican industries are comparable. Blank—Canadian, Mexican, and United States industries are comparable. *—Part of.

2002 NAICS Code	2002 NAICS U.S. Description	1997 NAICS Code	1997 NAICS U.S. Description
		*421520	Coal and Other Mineral and Ore Wholesalers (electronic markets)
		*421610	Electrical Apparatus and Equipment, Wiring Supplies, and Construction Material Wholesalers (electronic markets)
		*421620	Electrical Appliance, Television, and Radio Set Wholesalers (electronic markets)
		*421690	Other Electronic Parts and Equipment Wholesalers (electronic markets)
		*421710	Hardware Wholesalers (electronic markets)
		*421720	Plumbing and Heating Equipment and Supplies (Hydronics) Wholesalers (electronic markets)
		*421730	Warm Air Heating and Air-Conditioning Equipment and Supplies Wholesalers (electronic markets)
		*421740	Refrigeration Equipment and Supplies Wholesalers (electronic markets)
		*421810	Construction and Mining (except Oil Well) Machinery and Equipment Wholesalers (electronic markets)
		*421820	Farm and Garden Machinery and Equipment Wholesalers (electronic markets)
		*421830	Industrial Machinery and Equipment Wholesalers (electronic markets)
		*421840	Industrial Supplies Wholesalers (electronic markets)
		*421850	Service Establishment Equipment and Supplies Wholesalers (electronic markets)

US—United States industry only. CAN—United States and Canadian industries are comparable. MEX—United States and Mexican industries are comparable. Blank—Canadian, Mexican, and United States industries are comparable. *—Part of.

2002 NAICS Code	2002 NAICS U.S. Description	1997 NAICS Code	1997 NAICS U.S. Description
		*421860	Transportation Equipment and Supplies (except Motor Vehicle) Wholesalers (electronic markets)
		*421910	Sporting and Recreational Goods and Supplies Wholesalers (electronic markets)
		*421920	Toy and Hobby Goods and Supplies Wholesalers (electronic markets)
		*421930	Recyclable Material Wholesalers (electronic markets)
		*421940	Jewelry, Watch, Precious Stone, and Precious Metal Wholesalers (electronic markets)
		*421990	Other Miscellaneous Durable Goods Wholesalers (electronic markets)
		*422110	Printing and Writing Paper Wholesalers (electronic markets)
		*422120	Stationary and Office Supplies Wholesalers (electronic markets)
		*422130	Industrial and Personal Service Paper Wholesalers (electronic markets)
		*422210	Drugs and Druggists' Sundries Wholesalers (electronic markets)
		*422310	Piece Goods, Notions, and Other Dry Goods Wholesalers (electronic markets)
		*422320	Men's and Boys' Clothing and Furnishings Wholesalers (electronic markets)
		*422330	Women's, Children's, and Infants' Clothing and Accessories Wholesalers (electronic markets)

US—United States industry only. CAN—United States and Canadian industries are comparable. MEX—United States and Mexican industries are comparable. Blank—Canadian, Mexican, and United States industries are comparable. *—Part of.

2002 NAICS Code	2002 NAICS U.S. Description	1997 NAICS Code	1997 NAICS U.S. Description
		*422340	Footwear Wholesalers (electronic markets)
		*422410	General Line Grocery Wholesalers (electronic markets)
		*422420	Packaged Frozen Food Wholesalers (electronic markets)
		*422430	Dairy Product (except Dried or Canned) Wholesalers (electronic markets)
		*422440	Poultry and Poultry Product Wholesalers (electronic markets)
		*422450	Confectionery Wholesalers (electronic markets)
		*422460	Fish and Seafood Wholesalers (electronic markets)
		*422470	Meat and Meat Product Wholesalers (electronic markets)
		*422480	Fresh Fruit and Vegetable Wholesalers (electronic markets)
		*422490	Other Grocery and Related Products Wholesalers (electronic markets)
		*422510	Grain and Field Bean Wholesalers (electronic markets)
		*422520	Livestock Wholesalers (electronic markets)
		*422590	Other Farm Product Raw Material Wholesalers (electronic markets)
		*422610	Plastics Materials and Basic Forms and Shapes Wholesalers (electronic markets)
		*422690	Other Chemical and Allied Products Wholesalers (electronic markets)

US—United States industry only. CAN—United States and Canadian industries are comparable. MEX—United States and Mexican industries are comparable. Blank—Canadian, Mexican, and United States industries are comparable. *—Part of.

	2002 NAICS Code	2002 NAICS U.S. Description	1997 NAICS Code	1997 NAICS U.S. Description
			*422720	Petroleum and Petroleum Products Wholesalers (except Bulk Stations and Terminals) (electronic markets)
			*422810	Beer and Ale Wholesalers (electronic markets)
			*422820	Wine and Distilled Alcoholic Beverage Wholesalers (electronic markets)
			*422910	Farm Supplies Wholesalers (electronic markets)
			*422920	Book, Periodical, and Newspaper Wholesalers (electronic markets)
			*422930	Flower, Nursery Stock, and Florists' Supplies Wholesalers (electronic markets)
			*422940	Tobacco and Tobacco Product Wholesalers (electronic markets)
			*422950	Paint, Varnish, and Supplies Wholesalers (electronic markets)
			*422990	Other Miscellaneous Nondurable Goods Wholesalers (electronic markets)
US	42512	Wholesale Trade Agents and Brokers	*421110	Automobile and Other Motor Vehicle Wholesalers (agents and brokers)
			*421120	Motor Vehicle Supplies and New Parts Wholesalers (agents and brokers)
			*421130	Tire and Tube Wholesalers (agents and brokers)
			*421140	Motor Vehicle Parts (Used) Wholesalers (agents and brokers)

US—United States industry only. CAN—United States and Canadian industries are comparable. MEX—United States and Mexican industries are comparable. Blank—Canadian, Mexican, and United States industries are comparable. *—Part of.

2002 NAICS Code	2002 NAICS U.S. Description	1997 NAICS Code	1997 NAICS U.S. Description
		*421210	Furniture Wholesalers (agents and brokers)
		*421220	Home Furnishing Wholesalers (agents and brokers)
		*421310	Lumber, Plywood, Millwork, and Wood Panel Wholesalers (agents and brokers)
		*421320	Brick, Stone, and Related Construction Material Wholesalers (agents and brokers)
		*421330	Roofing, Siding, and Insulation Material Wholesalers (agents and brokers)
		*421390	Other Construction Material Wholesalers (agents and brokers)
		*421410	Photographic Equipment and Supplies Wholesalers (agents and brokers)
		*421420	Office Equipment Wholesalers (agents and brokers)
		*421430	Computer and Computer Peripheral Equipment and Software Wholesalers (agents and brokers)
		*421440	Other Commercial Equipment Wholesalers (agents and brokers)
		*421450	Medical, Dental, and Hospital Equipment and Supplies Wholesalers (agents and brokers)
		*421460	Ophthalmic Goods Wholesalers (agents and brokers)
		*421490	Other Professional Equipment and Supplies Wholesalers (agents and brokers)
		*421510	Metal Service Centers and Offices (agents and brokers)
		*421520	Coal and Other Mineral and Ore Wholesalers (agents and brokers)

US—United States industry only. CAN—United States and Canadian industries are comparable. MEX—United States and Mexican industries are comparable. Blank—Canadian, Mexican, and United States industries are comparable. *—Part of.

2002 NAICS Code	2002 NAICS U.S. Description	1997 NAICS Code	1997 NAICS U.S. Description
		*421610	Electrical Apparatus and Equipment, Wiring Supplies, and Construction Material Wholesalers (agents and brokers)
		*421620	Electrical Appliance, Television, and Radio Set Wholesalers (agents and brokers)
		*421690	Other Electronic Parts and Equipment Wholesalers (agents and brokers)
		*421710	Hardware Wholesalers (agents and brokers)
		*421720	Plumbing and Heating Equipment and Supplies (Hydronics) Wholesalers (agents and brokers)
		*421730	Warm Air Heating and Air-Conditioning Equipment and Supplies Wholesalers (agents and brokers)
		*421740	Refrigeration Equipment and Supplies Wholesalers (agents and brokers)
		*421810	Construction and Mining (except Oil Well) Machinery and Equipment Wholesalers (agents and brokers)
		*421820	Farm and Garden Machinery and Equipment Wholesalers (agents and brokers)
		*421830	Industrial Machinery and Equipment Wholesalers (agents and brokers)
		*421840	Industrial Supplies Wholesalers (agents and brokers)
		*421850	Service Establishment Equipment and Supplies Wholesalers (agents and brokers)

US—United States industry only. CAN—United States and Canadian industries are comparable. MEX—United States and Mexican industries are comparable. Blank—Canadian, Mexican, and United States industries are comparable. *—Part of.

2002 NAICS Code	2002 NAICS U.S. Description	1997 NAICS Code	1997 NAICS U.S. Description
		*421860	Transportation Equipment and Supplies (except Motor Vehicle) Wholesalers (agents and brokers)
		*421910	Sporting and Recreational Goods and Supplies Wholesalers (agents and brokers)
		*421920	Toy and Hobby Goods and Supplies Wholesalers (agents and brokers)
		*421930	Recyclable Material Wholesalers (agents and brokers)
		*421940	Jewelry, Watch, Precious Stone, and Precious Metal Wholesalers (agents and brokers)
		*421990	Other Miscellaneous Durable Goods Wholesalers (agents and brokers)
		*422110	Printing and Writing Paper Wholesalers (agents and brokers)
		*422120	Stationary and Office Supplies Wholesalers (agents and brokers)
		*422130	Industrial and Personal Service Paper Wholesalers (agents and brokers)
		*422210	Drugs and Druggists' Sundries Wholesalers (agents and brokers)
		*422310	Piece Goods, Notions, and Other Dry Goods Wholesalers (agents and brokers)
		*422320	Men's and Boys' Clothing and Furnishings Wholesalers (agents and brokers)

US—United States industry only. CAN—United States and Canadian industries are comparable. MEX—United States and Mexican industries are comparable. Blank—Canadian, Mexican, and United States industries are comparable. *—Part of.

2002 NAICS Code	2002 NAICS U.S. Description	1997 NAICS Code	1997 NAICS U.S. Description
		*422330	Women's, Children's, and Infants' Clothing and Accessories Wholesalers (agents and brokers)
		*422340	Footwear Wholesalers (agents and brokers)
		*422410	General Line Grocery Wholesalers (agents and brokers)
		*422420	Packaged Frozen Food Wholesalers (agents and brokers)
		*422430	Dairy Product (except Dried or Canned) Wholesalers (agents and brokers)
		*422440	Poultry and Poultry Product Wholesalers (agents and brokers)
		*422450	Confectionery Wholesalers (agents and brokers)
		*422460	Fish and Seafood Wholesalers (agents and brokers)
		*422470	Meat and Meat Product Wholesalers (agents and brokers)
		*422480	Fresh Fruit and Vegetable Wholesalers (agents and brokers)
		*422490	Other Grocery and Related Products Wholesalers (agents and brokers)
		*422510	Grain and Field Bean Wholesalers (agents and brokers)
		*422520	Livestock Wholesalers (agents and brokers)
		*422590	Other Farm Product Raw Material Wholesalers (agents and brokers)
		*422610	Plastics Materials and Basic Forms and Shapes Wholesalers (agents and brokers)

US—United States industry only. CAN—United States and Canadian industries are comparable. MEX—United States and Mexican industries are comparable. Blank—Canadian, Mexican, and United States industries are comparable. *—Part of.

	2002 NAICS Code	2002 NAICS U.S. Description	1997 NAICS Code	1997 NAICS U.S. Description
			*422690	Other Chemical and Allied Products Wholesalers (agents and brokers)
			*422720	Petroleum and Petroleum Products Wholesalers (except Bulk Stations and Terminals) (agents and brokers)
			*422810	Beer and Ale Wholesalers (agents and brokers)
			*422820	Wine and Distilled Alcoholic Beverage Wholesalers (agents and brokers)
			*422910	Farm Supplies Wholesalers (agents and brokers)
			*422920	Book, Periodical, and Newspaper Wholesalers (agents and brokers)
			*422930	Flower, Nursery Stock, and Florists' Supplies Wholesalers (agents and brokers)
			*422940	Tobacco and Tobacco Product Wholesalers (agents and brokers)
			*422950	Paint, Varnish, and Supplies Wholesalers (agents and brokers)
			*422990	Other Miscellaneous Nondurable Goods Wholesalers (agents and brokers)
CAN	4521	Department Stores		
CAN	45211	Department Stores		
US	452111	Department Stores (except Discount Department Stores)	*452110	Department Stores (except discount department stores)
US	452112	Discount Department Stores	*452110	Department Stores (discount department stores)
CAN	4541	Electronic Shopping and Mail-Order Houses		
CAN	45411	Electronic Shopping and Mail-Order Houses		
US	454111	Electronic Shopping	*454110	Electronic Shopping and Mail-Order Houses (electronic shopping)

US—United States industry only. CAN—United States and Canadian industries are comparable. MEX—United States and Mexican industries are comparable. Blank—Canadian, Mexican, and United States industries are comparable. *—Part of.

	2002 NAICS Code	2002 NAICS U.S. Description	1997 NAICS Code	1997 NAICS U.S. Description
US	454112	Electronic Auctions	*454110	Electronic Shopping and Mail-Order Houses (Internet auctions)
US	454113	Mail-Order Houses	*454110	Electronic Shopping and Mail-Order Houses (except electronic shopping and Internet auctions)
	51	Information		
	511	Publishing Industries (except Internet)		
	5111	Newspaper, Periodical, Book, and Directory Publishers		
	51111	Newspaper Publishers	*511110	Newspaper Publishers (except Internet publishing)
	51112	Periodical Publishers	*511120	Periodical Publishers (except Internet publishing)
	51113	Book Publishers	*511130	Book Publishers (except Internet publishing)
			*511199	All Other Publishers (atlas and map publishing, except Internet publishing)
	51114	Directory and Mailing List Publishers	*511140	Database and Directory Publishers (except Internet publishing)
	51119	Other Publishers		
US	511191	Greeting Card Publishers	*511191	Greeting Card Publishers (except Internet publishing)
US	511199	All Other Publishers	*511199	All Other Publishers (except atlas and map publishing and Internet publishing)
	5112	Software Publishers		
	51121	Software Publishers	511210	Software Publishers
	512	Motion Picture and Sound Recording Industries		
	5121	Motion Picture and Video Industries		
	51211	Motion Picture and Video Production	512110	Motion Picture and Video Production
	51212	Motion Picture and Video Distribution	512120	Motion Picture and Video Distribution
	51213	Motion Picture and Video Exhibition		

US—United States industry only. CAN—United States and Canadian industries are comparable. MEX—United States and Mexican industries are comparable. Blank—Canadian, Mexican, and United States industries are comparable. *—Part of.

	2002 NAICS Code	2002 NAICS U.S. Description	1997 NAICS Code	1997 NAICS U.S. Description
US	512131	Motion Picture Theaters (except Drive-Ins)	512131	Motion Picture Theaters (except Drive-Ins)
US	512132	Drive-In Motion Picture Theaters	512132	Drive-In Motion Picture Theaters
	51219	Post Production Services and Other Motion Picture and Video Industries		
US	512191	Teleproduction and Other Postproduction Services	512191	Teleproduction and Other Postproduction Services
US	512199	Other Motion Picture and Video Industries	512199	Other Motion Picture and Video Industries
	5122	Sound Recording Industries		
	51221	Record Production	512210	Record Production
	51222	Integrated Record Production/Distribution	512220	Integrated Record Production/ Distribution
	51223	Music Publishers	512230	Music Publishers
	51224	Sound Recording Studios	512240	Sound Recording Studios
	51229	Other Sound Recording Industries	512290	Other Sound Recording Industries
	515	Broadcasting (except Internet)		
	5151	Radio and Television Broadcasting	51511	Radio Broadcasting
US	515111	Radio Networks	513111	Radio Networks
US	515112	Radio Stations	513112	Radio Stations
	51512	Television Broadcasting	513120	Television Broadcasting
	5152	Cable and Other Subscription Programming		
	51521	Cable and Other Subscription Programming	513210	Cable Networks
	516	Internet Publishing and Broadcasting		
	5161	Internet Publishing and Broadcasting		
	51611	Internet Publishing and Broadcasting	*511110	Newspaper Publishers (Internet newspaper publishers)

US—United States industry only. CAN—United States and Canadian industries are comparable. MEX—United States and Mexican industries are comparable. Blank—Canadian, Mexican, and United States industries are comparable. *—Part of.

	2002 NAICS Code	2002 NAICS U.S. Description	1997 NAICS Code	1997 NAICS U.S. Description
			*511120	Periodical Publishers (Internet periodical publishers)
			*511130	Book Publishers (Internet book publishers)
			*511140	Database and Directory Publishers (Internet directory publishers)
			*511191	Greeting Card Publishers (Internet greeting card publishers)
			*511199	All Other Publishers (All other Internet publishers)
			*514199	All Other Information Services (Internet broadcasting)
	517	Telecommunications		
	5171	Wired Telecommunications Carriers		
	51711	Wired Telecommunications Carriers	513310	Wired Telecommunications Carriers
	5172	Wireless Telecommunications Carriers (except Satellite)		
	51721	Wireless Telecommunications Carriers (except Satellite)		
US	517211	Paging	513321	Paging
US	517212	Cellular and Other Wireless Telecommunications	513322	Cellular and Other Wireless Telecommunications
	5173	Telecommunications Resellers		
	51731	Telecommunications Resellers	513330	Telecommunications Resellers
	5174	Satellite Telecommunications		
	51741	Satellite Telecommunications	513340	Satellite Telecommunications
	5175	Cable and Other Program Distribution		

US—United States industry only. CAN—United States and Canadian industries are comparable. MEX—United States and Mexican industries are comparable. Blank—Canadian, Mexican, and United States industries are comparable. *—Part of.

	2002 NAICS Code	2002 NAICS U.S. Description	1997 NAICS Code	1997 NAICS U.S. Description
	51751	Cable and Other Program Distribution	513220	Cable and Other Program Distribution
	5179	Other Telecommunications		
	51791	Other Telecommunications	513390	Other Telecommunications
	518	Internet Service Providers, Web Search Portals, and Data Processing Services		
	5181	Internet Service Providers and Web Search Portals		
	51811	Internet Service Providers and Web Search Portals		
US	518111	Internet Service Providers	514191	On-Line Information Services
US	518112	Web Search Portals	*514199	All Other Information Services (Internet search portals)
	5182	Data Processing, Hosting, and Related Services		
	51821	Data Processing, Hosting, and Related Services	514210	Data Processing Services
	519	Other Information Services		
	5191	Other Information Services		
	51911	News Syndicates	514110	News Syndicates
	51912	Libraries and Archives	514120	Libraries and Archives
	51919	All Other Information Services	*514199	All Other Information Services (except Internet search portals and Internet Broadcasting)

US—United States industry only. CAN—United States and Canadian industries are comparable. MEX—United States and Mexican industries are comparable. Blank—Canadian, Mexican, and United States industries are comparable. *—Part of.

Appendix B

1997 NAICS U.S. Matched to 2002 NAICS U.S.

1997 NAICS Code	1997 NAICS U.S. Description	2002 NAICS Code	2002 NAICS U.S. Description
213112	Support Activities for Oil and Gas Operations		
	Construction of Field Gathering Lines On A Contract Basis	237120	Oil and Gas Pipeline and Related Structures Construction (pt)
	Site Preparation and Related Construction Activities On A Contract Basis	238910	Site Preparation Contractors (pt)
	Support Activities For Oil and Gas Operations Except Site Preparation and Related Construction Activities	213112	Support Activities for Oil and Gas Operations
213113	Support Activities for Coal Mining		
	Site Preparation and Related Construction Activities On A Contract Basis	238910	Site Preparation Contractors (pt)
	Support Activities For Coal Mining Except Site Preparation and Related Construction Activities	213113	Support Activities for Coal Mining
213114	Support Activities for Metal Mining		
	Site Preparation and Related Construction Activities On A Contract Basis	238910	Site Preparation Contractors (pt)
	Support Activities For Metal Mining Except Site Preparation and Related Construction Activities	213114	Support Activities for Metal Mining
213115	Support Activities for Nonmetallic Minerals (except Fuels)		
	Site Preparation and Related Construction Activities On A Contract Basis	238910	Site Preparation Contractors (pt)

(pt)—Part of.

1997 NAICS Code	1997 NAICS U.S. Description	2002 NAICS Code	2002 NAICS U.S. Description
	Support Activities For Nonmetallic Mineral (Except Fuel) Mining Except Site Preparation and Related Construction Activities	213115	Support Activities for Nonmetallic Minerals (except Fuels)
233110	Land Subdivision and Land Development	237210	Land Subdivision
233210	Single Family Housing Construction		
	General Contractors	236115	New Single-Family Housing Construction (except Operative Builders)
	Operative Builders	236117	New Housing Operative Builders (pt)
	Remodeling Contractors	236118	Residential Remodelers (pt)
233220	Multifamily Housing Construction		
	General Contractors	236116	New Multifamily Housing Construction (except Operative Builders)
	Operative Builders	236117	New Housing Operative Builders (pt)
	Remodeling Contractors	236118	Residential Remodelers (pt)
	Barrack and Dormitory Construction	236220	Commercial and Institutional Building Construction (pt)
233310	Manufacturing and Industrial Building Construction		
	Grain Elevators, Dry Cleaning Plants, and Manufacturing and Industrial Warehouses	236220	Commercial and Institutional Building Construction (pt)
	Except Grain Elevators, Dry Cleaning Plants, and Manufacturing and Industrial Warehouses	236210	Industrial Building Construction (pt)
233320	Commercial and Institutional Building Construction	236220	Commercial and Institutional Building Construction (pt)
234110	Highway and Street Construction	237310	Highway, Street, and Bridge Construction (pt)
234120	Bridge and Tunnel Construction		
	Bridge Construction	237310	Highway, Street, and Bridge Construction (pt)
	Tunnel Construction	237990	Other Heavy and Civil Engineering Construction (pt)

(pt)—Part of.

1997 NAICS Code	1997 NAICS U.S. Description	2002 NAICS Code	2002 NAICS U.S. Description
234910	Water, Sewer, and Pipeline Construction		
	Water/Sewer Pumping Stations, Sewage Collection and Disposal Lines, Storm Sewers, Sewer/Water Mains and Lines, and Water Storage Tanks and Towers, and Construction Management of these Projects	237110	Water and Sewer Line and Related Structures Construction (pt)
	Gas and Oil Pumping Stations, Gas and Oil Pipeline Construction, Gas Mains, Gas and Oil Storage Tank Construction, and Construction Management of these Projects	237120	Oil and Gas Pipeline and Related Structures Construction (pt)
234920	Power and Communication Transmission Line Construction	237130	Power and Communication Line and Related Structures Construction (pt)
234930	Industrial Nonbuilding Structure Construction		
	Petrochemical Plants, Refineries, and Construction Management of these Projects	237120	Oil and Gas Pipeline and Related Structures Construction (pt)
	Power Generation Plants (excluding Hydroelectric Dams), Transmission and Distribution Transformer Stations, and Construction Management of these Projects	237130	Power and Communication Line and Related Structures Construction (pt)
	Process Batch Plants, Incinerators, Industrial Furnaces and Kilns, Mining Appurtenance, and Construction Management of these Projects	236210	Industrial Building Construction (pt)
234990	All Other Heavy Construction		
	Waste Disposal Plant Construction	236210	Industrial Building Construction (pt)
	Irrigation Systems, Sewage Treatment and Water Treatment Plants, Construction Management of these Projects	237110	Water and Sewer Line and Related Structures Construction (pt)

(pt)—Part of.

1997 NAICS Code	1997 NAICS U.S. Description	2002 NAICS Code	2002 NAICS U.S. Description
	Right-of-Way Clearing and Line Slashing, Blasting, Trenching, and Equipment Rental (except cranes) with Operator	238910	Site Preparation Contractors (pt)
	Crane Rental with Operator	238990	All Other Specialty Trade Contractors (pt)
	Except Waste Disposal Plant Construction, Irrigation Systems, Sewage Treatment and Water Treatment Plants, Right-of-Way Clearing and Line Slashing, Blasting, Trenching, and Equipment Rental with Operator	237990	Other Heavy and Civil Engineering Construction (pt)
235110	Plumbing, Heating, and Air-Conditioning Contractors		
	Environmental Controls Installation Contractors	238210	Electrical Contractors (pt)
	Septic Tank, Cesspool, and Dry Well Construction Contractors	238910	Site Preparation Contractors (pt)
	Except Environmental Controls Installation Contractors and Septic Tank, Cesspool, and Dry Well Construction Contractors	238220	Plumbing, Heating, and Air-Conditioning Contractors (pt)
235210	Painting and Wall Covering Contractors		
	Highway and Traffic Line Painting	237310	Highway, Street, and Bridge Construction (pt)
	Except Highway and Traffic Line Painting	238320	Painting and Wall Covering Contractors
235310	Electrical Contractors	238210	Electrical Contractors (pt)
235410	Masonry and Stone Contractors	238140	Masonry Contractors (pt)
235420	Drywall, Plastering, Acoustical, and Insulation Contractors		
	Stucco Contractors	238140	Masonry Contractors (pt)
	Except Stucco Contractors	238310	Drywall and Insulation Contractors
235430	Tile, Marble, Terrazzo, and Mosaic Contractors	238340	Tile and Terrazzo and Tile Contractors
235510	Carpentry Contractors		
	Framing Carpentry	238130	Framing Contractors

(pt)—Part of.

1997 NAICS Code	1997 NAICS U.S. Description	2002 NAICS Code	2002 NAICS U.S. Description
	Finish Carpentry	238350	Finish Carpentry Contractors
235520	Floor Laying and Other Floor Contractors	238330	Flooring Contractors
235610	Roofing, Siding, and Sheet Metal Contractors		
	Roofing Contractors	238160	Roofing Contractors
	Siding Contractors	238170	Siding Contractors
	Metal Ceiling, Panel, and Shelving Installation	238390	Other Building Finishing Contractors (pt)
235710	Concrete Contractors		
	Residential and Commercial Asphalt, Brick, and Concrete Paving	238990	All Other Specialty Trade Contractors (pt)
	Except Residential and Commercial Asphalt, Brick, and Concrete Paving	238110	Poured Concrete Foundation and Structure Contractors
235810	Water Well Drilling Contractors	237110	Water and Sewer Line and Related Structures Construction (pt)
235910	Structural Steel Erection Contractors		
	Curtain Walls and Metal Furring Installation	238190	Other Foundation, Structure, and Building Exterior Contractors (pt)
	Cooling Tower Installation	238220	Plumbing, Heating, and Air-Conditioning Contractors (pt)
	Except Curtain Walls, Metal Furring Installation, and Cooling Tower Installation	238120	Structural Steel and Precast Concrete Contractors
235920	Glass and Glazing Contractors	238150	Glass and Glazing Contractors
235930	Excavation Contractors	238910	Site Preparation Contractors (pt)
235940	Wrecking and Demolition Contractors	238910	Site Preparation Contractors (pt)
235950	Building Equipment and Other Machinery Installation Contractors		
	Scrubber, Dust Collection, and Other Industrial Ventilation Installation	238220	Plumbing, Heating, and Air-Conditioning Contractors (pt)
	Except Scrubber, Dust Collection, and Other Industrial Ventilation Installation	238290	Other Building Equipment Contractors (pt)

(pt)—Part of.

1997 NAICS Code	1997 NAICS U.S. Description	2002 NAICS Code	2002 NAICS U.S. Description
235990	All Other Special Trade Contractors		
	Indoor Swimming Pool Contractors	236220	Commercial and Institutional Building Construction (pt)
	Anchored Earth Retention Contractors	237990	Other Heavy and Civil Engineering Construction (pt)
	Forming Contractors, Ornamental Metal Work Installation	238190	Other Foundation, Structure, and Building Exterior Contractors (pt)
	Service Station Equipment Installation Contractors; Boiler, Duct, and Pipe Insulation; Lightning Rod Installation; Bowling Alley Installation; Household- Type Antenna Installation; Church Bell Installation; and Tower Clock Installation	238290	Other Building Equipment Contractors (pt)
	Weather Stripping and Damp-Proofing, Modular Furniture Installation, Bathtub Refinishing, Window Covering Fixture Installation, Trade Show Exhibit Installation and Dismantling, and Spectator Seating Installation	238390	Other Building Finishing Contractors (pt)
	Dewatering Contractors, Core Drilling For Construction, and Test Boring for Construction	238910	Site Preparation Contractors (pt)
	Except Indoor Swimming Pool Contractors, Anchored Earth Retention Contractors, Forming Contractors, Ornamental Metal Work Installation, Building Equipment Contractors, Building Finishing Contractors, Dewatering Contractors, Test Boring For Construction, and Core Drilling For Construction	238990	All Other Specialty Trade Contractors (pt)
421110	Automobile and Other Motor Vehicle Wholesalers		
	Merchant Wholesalers	423110	Automobile and Other Motor Vehicle Merchant Wholesalers

(pt)—Part of.

1997 NAICS Code	1997 NAICS U.S. Description	2002 NAICS Code	2002 NAICS U.S. Description
	Business to Business Electronic Markets	425110	Business to Business Electronic Markets (pt)
	Agents and Brokers	425120	Wholesale Trade Agents and Brokers (pt)
421120	Motor Vehicle Supplies and New Parts Wholesalers		
	Merchant Wholesalers	423120	Motor Vehicle Supplies and New Parts Merchant Wholesalers
	Business to Business Electronic Markets	425110	Business to Business Electronic Markets (pt)
	Agents and Brokers	425120	Wholesale Trade Agents and Brokers (pt)
421130	Tire and Tube Wholesalers		
	Merchant Wholesalers	423130	Tire and Tube Merchant Wholesalers
	Business to Business Electronic Markets	425110	Business to Business Electronic Markets (pt)
	Agents and Brokers	425120	Wholesale Trade Agents and Brokers (pt)
421140	Motor Vehicle Parts (Used) Wholesalers		
	Merchant Wholesalers	423140	Motor Vehicle Parts (Used) Merchant Wholesalers
	Business to Business Electronic Markets	425110	Business to Business Electronic Markets (pt)
	Agents and Brokers	425120	Wholesale Trade Agents and Brokers (pt)
421210	Furniture Wholesalers		
	Merchant Wholesalers	423210	Furniture Merchant Wholesalers
	Business to Business Electronic Markets	425110	Business to Business Electronic Markets (pt)
	Agents and Brokers	425120	Wholesale Trade Agents and Brokers (pt)
421220	Home Furnishing Wholesalers		
	Merchant Wholesalers	423220	Home Furnishing Merchant Wholesalers
	Business to Business Electronic Markets	425110	Business to Business Electronic Markets
	Agents and Brokers	425120	Wholesale Trade Agents and Brokers
421310	Lumber, Plywood, Millwork, and Wood Panel Wholesalers		

(pt)—Part of.

1997 NAICS Code	1997 NAICS U.S. Description	2002 NAICS Code	2002 NAICS U.S. Description
	Merchant Wholesalers	423310	Lumber, Plywood, Millwork, and Wood Panel Merchant Wholesalers
	Business to Business Electronic Markets	425110	Business to Business Electronic Markets (pt)
	Agents and Brokers	425120	Wholesale Trade Agents and Brokers (pt)
421320	Brick, Stone, and Related Construction Material Wholesalers		
	Merchant Wholesalers	423320	Brick, Stone, and Related Construction Material Merchant Wholesalers
	Business to Business Electronic Markets	425110	Business to Business Electronic Markets (pt)
	Agents and Brokers	425120	Wholesale Trade Agents and Brokers (pt)
421330	Roofing, Siding, and Insulation Material Wholesalers		
	Merchant Wholesalers	423330	Roofing, Siding, and Insulation Material Merchant Wholesalers
	Business to Business Electronic Markets	425110	Business to Business Electronic Markets (pt)
	Agents and Brokers	425120	Wholesale Trade Agents and Brokers (pt)
421390	Other Construction Material Wholesalers		
	Merchant Wholesalers	423390	Other Construction Material Merchant Wholesalers
	Business to Business Electronic Markets	425110	Business to Business Electronic Markets (pt)
	Agents and Brokers	425120	Wholesale Trade Agents and Brokers (pt)
421410	Photographic Equipment and Supplies Wholesalers		
	Merchant Wholesalers	423410	Photographic Equipment and Supplies Merchant Wholesalers
	Business to Business Electronic Markets	425110	Business to Business Electronic Markets (pt)
	Agents and Brokers	425120	Wholesale Trade Agents and Brokers (pt)
421420	Office Equipment Wholesalers		
	Merchant Wholesalers	423420	Office Equipment Merchant Wholesalers

(pt)—Part of.

1997 NAICS Code	1997 NAICS U.S. Description	2002 NAICS Code	2002 NAICS U.S. Description
	Business to Business Electronic Markets	425110	Business to Business Electronic Markets (pt)
	Agents and Brokers	425120	Wholesale Trade Agents and Brokers (pt)
421430	Computer and Computer Peripheral Equipment and Software Wholesalers		
	Merchant Wholesalers	423430	Computer and Computer Peripheral Equipment and Software Merchant Wholesalers
	Business to Business Electronic Markets	425110	Business to Business Electronic Markets (pt)
	Agents and Brokers	425120	Wholesale Trade Agents and Brokers (pt)
421440	Other Commercial Equipment Wholesalers		
	Merchant Wholesalers	423440	Other Commercial Equipment Merchant Wholesalers
	Business to Business Electronic Markets	425110	Business to Business Electronic Markets (pt)
	Agents and Brokers	425120	Wholesale Trade Agents and Brokers (pt)
421450	Medical, Dental, and Hospital Equipment and Supplies Wholesalers		
	Merchant Wholesalers	423450	Medical, Dental, and Hospital Equipment and Supplies Merchant Wholesalers
	Business to Business Electronic Markets	425110	Business to Business Electronic Markets (pt)
	Agents and Brokers	425120	Wholesale Trade Agents and Brokers (pt)
421460	Ophthalmic Goods Wholesalers		
	Merchant Wholesalers	423460	Ophthalmic Goods Merchant Wholesalers
	Business to Business Electronic Markets	425110	Business to Business Electronic Markets (pt)
	Agents and Brokers	425120	Wholesale Trade Agents and Brokers (pt)
421490	Other Professional Equipment and Supplies Wholesalers		
	Merchant Wholesalers	423490	Other Professional Equipment and Supplies Merchant Wholesalers

(pt)—Part of.

1997 NAICS Code	1997 NAICS U.S. Description	2002 NAICS Code	2002 NAICS U.S. Description
	Business to Business Electronic Markets	425110	Business to Business Electronic Markets (pt)
	Agents and Brokers	425120	Wholesale Trade Agents and Brokers (pt)
421510	Metal Service Centers and Offices		
	Merchant Wholesalers	423510	Metal Service Centers and Other Metal Merchant Wholesalers
	Business to Business Electronic Markets	425110	Business to Business Electronic Markets (pt)
	Agents and Brokers	425120	Wholesale Trade Agents and Brokers (pt)
421520	Coal and Other Mineral and Ore Wholesalers		
	Merchant Wholesalers	423520	Coal and Other Mineral and Ore Merchant Wholesalers
	Business to Business Electronic Markets	425110	Business to Business Electronic Markets (pt)
	Agents and Brokers	425120	Wholesale Trade Agents and Brokers (pt)
421610	Electrical Apparatus and Equipment, Wiring Supplies, and Construction Material Wholesalers		
	Merchant Wholesalers	423610	Electrical Apparatus and Equipment, Wiring Supplies, and Related Equipment Merchant Wholesalers
	Business to Business Electronic Markets	425110	Business to Business Electronic Markets (pt)
	Agents and Brokers	425120	Wholesale Trade Agents and Brokers (pt)
421620	Electrical Appliance, Television, and Radio Set Wholesalers		
	Merchant Wholesalers	423620	Electrical and Electronic Appliance, Television, and Radio Set Merchant Wholesalers
	Business to Business Electronic Markets	425110	Business to Business Electronic Markets (pt)
	Agents and Brokers	425120	Wholesale Trade Agents and Brokers (pt)
421690	Other Electronic Parts and Equipment Wholesalers		

(pt)—Part of.

1997 NAICS Code	1997 NAICS U.S. Description	2002 NAICS Code	2002 NAICS U.S. Description
	Merchant Wholesalers	423690	Other Electronic Parts and Equipment Merchant Wholesalers
	Business to Business Electronic Markets	425110	Business to Business Electronic Markets (pt)
	Agents and Brokers	425120	Wholesale Trade Agents and Brokers (pt)
421710	Hardware Wholesalers		
	Merchant Wholesalers	423710	Hardware Merchant Wholesalers
	Business to Business Electronic Markets	425110	Business to Business Electronic Markets (pt)
	Agents and Brokers	425120	Wholesale Trade Agents and Brokers (pt)
421720	Plumbing and Heating Equipment and Supplies (Hydronics) Wholesalers		
	Merchant Wholesalers	423720	Plumbing and Heating Equipment and Supplies (Hydronics) Merchant Wholesalers
	Business to Business Electronic Markets	425110	Business to Business Electronic Markets (pt)
	Agents and Brokers	425120	Wholesale Trade Agents and Brokers (pt)
421730	Warm Air Heating and Air-Conditioning Equipment and Supplies Wholesalers		
	Merchant Wholesalers	423730	Warm Air Heating and Air-Conditioning Equipment and Supplies Merchant Wholesalers
	Business to Business Electronic Markets	425110	Business to Business Electronic Markets (pt)
	Agents and Brokers	425120	Wholesale Trade Agents and Brokers (pt)
421740	Refrigeration Equipment and Supplies Wholesalers		
	Merchant Wholesalers	423740	Refrigeration Equipment and Supplies Merchant Wholesalers
	Business to Business Electronic Markets	425110	Business to Business Electronic Markets (pt)
	Agents and Brokers	425120	Wholesale Trade Agents and Brokers (pt)

(pt)—Part of.

1997 NAICS Code	1997 NAICS U.S. Description	2002 NAICS Code	2002 NAICS U.S. Description
421810	Construction and Mining (except Oil Well) Machinery and Equipment Wholesalers		
	Merchant Wholesalers	423810	Construction and Mining (except Oil Well) Machinery and Equipment Merchant Wholesalers
	Business to Business Electronic Markets	425110	Business to Business Electronic Markets (pt)
	Agents and Brokers	425120	Wholesale Trade Agents and Brokers (pt)
421820	Farm and Garden Machinery and Equipment Wholesalers		
	Merchant Wholesalers	423820	Farm and Garden Machinery and Equipment Merchant Wholesalers
	Business to Business Electronic Markets	425110	Business to Business Electronic Markets (pt)
	Agents and Brokers	425120	Wholesale Trade Agents and Brokers (pt)
421830	Industrial Machinery and Equipment Wholesalers		
	Merchant Wholesalers	423830	Industrial Machinery and Equipment Merchant Wholesalers
	Business to Business Electronic Markets	425110	Business to Business Electronic Markets (pt)
	Agents and Brokers	425120	Wholesale Trade Agents and Brokers (pt)
421840	Industrial Supplies Wholesalers		
	Merchant Wholesalers	423840	Industrial Supplies Merchant Wholesalers
	Business to Business Electronic Markets	425110	Business to Business Electronic Markets (pt)
	Agents and Brokers	425120	Wholesale Trade Agents and Brokers (pt)
421850	Service Establishment Equipment and Supplies Wholesalers		
	Merchant Wholesalers	423850	Service Establishment Equipment and Supplies Merchant Wholesalers
	Business to Business Electronic Markets	425110	Business to Business Electronic Markets (pt)

(pt)—Part of.

1997 NAICS Code	1997 NAICS U.S. Description	2002 NAICS Code	2002 NAICS U.S. Description
	Agents and Brokers	425120	Wholesale Trade Agents and Brokers (pt)
421860	Transportation Equipment and Supplies (except Motor Vehicle) Wholesalers		
	Merchant Wholesalers	423860	Transportation Equipment and Supplies (except Motor Vehicle) Merchant Wholesalers
	Business to Business Electronic Markets	425110	Business to Business Electronic Markets (pt)
	Agents and Brokers	425120	Wholesale Trade Agents and Brokers (pt)
421910	Sporting and Recreational Goods and Supplies Wholesalers		
	Merchant Wholesalers	423910	Sporting and Recreational Goods and Supplies Merchant Wholesalers
	Business to Business Electronic Markets	425110	Business to Business Electronic Markets (pt)
	Agents and Brokers	425120	Wholesale Trade Agents and Brokers (pt)
421920	Toy and Hobby Goods and Supplies Wholesalers		
	Merchant Wholesalers	423920	Toy and Hobby Goods and Supplies Merchant Wholesalers
	Business to Business Electronic Markets	425110	Business to Business Electronic Markets (pt)
	Agents and Brokers	425120	Wholesale Trade Agents and Brokers (pt)
421930	Recyclable Material Wholesalers		
	Merchant Wholesalers	423930	Recyclable Material Merchant Wholesalers
	Business to Business Electronic Markets	425110	Business to Business Electronic Markets (pt)
	Agents and Brokers	425120	Wholesale Trade Agents and Brokers (pt)
421940	Jewelry, Watch, Precious Stone, and Precious Metal Wholesalers		
	Merchant Wholesalers	423940	Jewelry, Watch, Precious Stone, and Precious Metal Merchant Wholesalers
	Business to Business Electronic Markets	425110	Business to Business Electronic Markets (pt)

(pt)—Part of.

1997 NAICS Code	1997 NAICS U.S. Description	2002 NAICS Code	2002 NAICS U.S. Description
	Agents and Brokers	425120	Wholesale Trade Agents and Brokers (pt)
421990	Other Miscellaneous Durable Goods Wholesalers		
	Merchant Wholesalers	423990	Other Miscellaneous Durable Goods Merchant Wholesalers
	Business to Business Electronic Markets	425110	Business to Business Electronic Markets (pt)
	Agents and Brokers	425120	Wholesale Trade Agents and Brokers (pt)
422110	Printing and Writing Paper Wholesalers		
	Merchant Wholesalers	424110	Printing and Writing Paper Merchant Wholesalers
	Business to Business Electronic Markets	425110	Business to Business Electronic Markets (pt)
	Agents and Brokers	425120	Wholesale Trade Agents and Brokers (pt)
422120	Stationary and Office Supplies Wholesalers		
	Merchant Wholesalers	424120	Stationary and Office Supplies Merchant Wholesalers
	Business to Business Electronic Markets	425110	Business to Business Electronic Markets (pt)
	Agents and Brokers	425120	Wholesale Trade Agents and Brokers (pt)
422130	Industrial and Personal Service Paper Wholesalers		
	Merchant Wholesalers	424130	Industrial and Personal Service Paper Merchant Wholesalers
	Business to Business Electronic Markets	425110	Business to Business Electronic Markets (pt)
	Agents and Brokers	425120	Wholesale Trade Agents and Brokers (pt)
422210	Drugs and Druggists' Sundries Wholesalers		
	Merchant Wholesalers	424210	Drugs and Druggists' Sundries Merchant Wholesalers
	Business to Business Electronic Markets	425110	Business to Business Electronic Markets (pt)
	Agents and Brokers	425120	Wholesale Trade Agents and Brokers (pt)
422310	Piece Goods, Notions, and Other Dry Goods Wholesalers		

(pt)—Part of.

1997 NAICS Code	1997 NAICS U.S. Description	2002 NAICS Code	2002 NAICS U.S. Description
	Merchant Wholesalers	424310	Piece Goods, Notions, and Other Dry Goods Merchant Wholesalers
	Business to Business Electronic Markets	425110	Business to Business Electronic Markets (pt)
	Agents and Brokers	425120	Wholesale Trade Agents and Brokers (pt)
422320	Men's and Boys' Clothing and Furnishings Wholesalers		
	Merchant Wholesalers	424320	Men's and Boys' Clothing and Furnishings Merchant Wholesalers
	Business to Business Electronic Markets	425110	Business to Business Electronic Markets (pt)
	Agents and Brokers	425120	Wholesale Trade Agents and Brokers (pt)
422330	Women's, Children's, and Infants' Clothing and Accessories Wholesalers		
	Merchant Wholesalers	424330	Women's, Children's, and Infants' Clothing and Accessories Merchant Wholesalers
	Business to Business Electronic Markets	425110	Business to Business Electronic Markets (pt)
	Agents and Brokers	425120	Wholesale Trade Agents and Brokers (pt)
422340	Footwear Wholesalers		
	Merchant Wholesalers	424340	Footwear Merchant Wholesalers
	Business to Business Electronic Markets	425110	Business to Business Electronic Markets (pt)
	Agents and Brokers	425120	Wholesale Trade Agents and Brokers (pt)
422410	General Line Grocery Wholesalers		
	Merchant Wholesalers	424410	General Line Grocery Merchant Wholesalers
	Business to Business Electronic Markets	425110	Business to Business Electronic Markets (pt)
	Agents and Brokers	425120	Wholesale Trade Agents and Brokers (pt)
422420	Packaged Frozen Food Wholesalers		
	Merchant Wholesalers	424420	Packaged Frozen Food Merchant Wholesalers

(pt)—Part of.

1997 NAICS Code	1997 NAICS U.S. Description	2002 NAICS Code	2002 NAICS U.S. Description
	Business to Business Electronic Markets	425110	Business to Business Electronic Markets (pt)
	Agents and Brokers	425120	Wholesale Trade Agents and Brokers (pt)
422430	Dairy Product (except Dried or Canned) Wholesalers		
	Merchant Wholesalers	424430	Dairy Product (except Dried or Canned) Merchant Wholesalers
	Business to Business Electronic Markets	425110	Business to Business Electronic Markets (pt)
	Agents and Brokers	425120	Wholesale Trade Agents and Brokers (pt)
422440	Poultry and Poultry Product Wholesalers		
	Merchant Wholesalers	424440	Poultry and Poultry Product Merchant Wholesalers
	Business to Business Electronic Markets	425110	Business to Business Electronic Markets (pt)
	Agents and Brokers	425120	Wholesale Trade Agents and Brokers (pt)
422450	Confectionery Wholesalers		
	Merchant Wholesalers	424450	Confectionery Merchant Wholesalers
	Business to Business Electronic Markets	425110	Business to Business Electronic Markets (pt)
	Agents and Brokers	425120	Wholesale Trade Agents and Brokers (pt)
422460	Fish and Seafood Wholesalers		
	Merchant Wholesalers	424460	Fish and Seafood Merchant Wholesalers
	Business to Business Electronic Markets	425110	Business to Business Electronic Markets (pt)
	Agents and Brokers	425120	Wholesale Trade Agents and Brokers (pt)
422470	Meat and Meat Product Wholesalers		
	Merchant Wholesalers	424470	Meat and Meat Product Merchant Wholesalers
	Business to Business Electronic Markets	425110	Business to Business Electronic Markets (pt)
	Agents and Brokers	425120	Wholesale Trade Agents and Brokers (pt)
422480	Fresh Fruit and Vegetable Wholesalers		

(pt)—Part of.

1997 NAICS Code	1997 NAICS U.S. Description	2002 NAICS Code	2002 NAICS U.S. Description
	Merchant Wholesalers	424480	Fresh Fruit and Vegetable Merchant Wholesalers
	Business to Business Electronic Markets	425110	Business to Business Electronic Markets (pt)
	Agents and Brokers	425120	Wholesale Trade Agents and Brokers (pt)
422490	Other Grocery and Related Products Wholesalers		
	Merchant Wholesalers	424490	Other Grocery and Related Products Merchant Wholesalers
	Business to Business Electronic Markets	425110	Business to Business Electronic Markets (pt)
	Agents and Brokers	425120	Wholesale Trade Agents and Brokers (pt)
422510	Grain and Field Bean Wholesalers		
	Merchant Wholesalers	424510	Grain and Field Bean Merchant Wholesalers
	Business to Business Electronic Markets	425110	Business to Business Electronic Markets (pt)
	Agents and Brokers	425120	Wholesale Trade Agents and Brokers (pt)
422520	Livestock Wholesalers		
	Merchant Wholesalers	424520	Livestock Merchant Wholesalers
	Business to Business Electronic Markets	425110	Business to Business Electronic Markets (pt)
	Agents and Brokers	425120	Wholesale Trade Agents and Brokers (pt)
422590	Other Farm Product Raw Material Wholesalers		
	Merchant Wholesalers	424590	Other Farm Product Raw Material Merchant Wholesalers
	Business to Business Electronic Markets	425110	Business to Business Electronic Markets (pt)
	Agents and Brokers	425120	Wholesale Trade Agents and Brokers (pt)
422610	Plastics Materials and Basic Forms and Shapes Wholesalers		
	Merchant Wholesalers	424610	Plastics Materials and Basic Forms and Shapes Merchant Wholesalers
	Business to Business Electronic Markets	425110	Business to Business Electronic Markets (pt)

(pt)—Part of.

1997 NAICS Code	1997 NAICS U.S. Description	2002 NAICS Code	2002 NAICS U.S. Description
	Agents and Brokers	425120	Wholesale Trade Agents and Brokers (pt)
422690	Other Chemical and Allied Products Wholesalers		
	Merchant Wholesalers	424690	Other Chemical and Allied Products Merchant Wholesalers
	Business to Business Electronic Markets	425110	Business to Business Electronic Markets (pt)
	Agents and Brokers	425120	Wholesale Trade Agents and Brokers (pt)
422710	Petroleum Bulk Stations and Terminals	424710	Petroleum Bulk Stations and Terminals
422720	Petroleum and Petroleum Products Wholesalers (except Bulk Stations and Terminals)		
	Merchant Wholesalers	424720	Petroleum and Petroleum Products Merchant Wholesalers (except Bulk Stations and Terminals)
	Business to Business Electronic Markets	425110	Business to Business Electronic Markets (pt)
	Agents and Brokers	425120	Wholesale Trade Agents and Brokers (pt)
422810	Beer and Ale Wholesalers		
	Merchant Wholesalers	424810	Beer and Ale Merchant Wholesalers
	Business to Business Electronic Markets	425110	Business to Business Electronic Markets (pt)
	Agents and Brokers	425120	Wholesale Trade Agents and Brokers (pt)
422820	Wine and Distilled Alcoholic Beverage Wholesalers		
	Merchant Wholesalers	424820	Wine and Distilled Alcoholic Beverage Merchant Wholesalers
	Business to Business Electronic Markets	425110	Business to Business Electronic Markets (pt)
	Agents and Brokers	425120	Wholesale Trade Agents and Brokers (pt)
422910	Farm Supplies Wholesalers		
	Merchant Wholesalers	424910	Farm Supplies Merchant Wholesalers
	Business to Business Electronic Markets	425110	Business to Business Electronic Markets (pt)
	Agents and Brokers	425120	Wholesale Trade Agents and Brokers (pt)

(pt)—Part of.

1997 NAICS Code	1997 NAICS U.S. Description	2002 NAICS Code	2002 NAICS U.S. Description
422920	Book, Periodical, and Newspaper Wholesalers		
	Merchant Wholesalers	424920	Book, Periodical, and Newspaper Merchant Wholesalers
	Business to Business Electronic Markets	425110	Business to Business Electronic Markets (pt)
	Agents and Brokers	425120	Wholesale Trade Agents and Brokers (pt)
422930	Flower, Nursery Stock, and Florists' Supplies Wholesalers		
	Merchant Wholesalers	424930	Flower, Nursery Stock, and Florists' Supplies Merchant Wholesalers
	Business to Business Electronic Markets	425110	Business to Business Electronic Markets (pt)
	Agents and Brokers	425120	Wholesale Trade Agents and Brokers (pt)
422940	Tobacco and Tobacco Product Wholesalers		
	Merchant Wholesalers	424940	Tobacco and Tobacco Product Merchant Wholesalers
	Business to Business Electronic Markets	425110	Business to Business Electronic Markets (pt)
	Agents and Brokers	425120	Wholesale Trade Agents and Brokers (pt)
422950	Paint, Varnish, and Supplies Wholesalers		
	Merchant Wholesalers	424950	Paint, Varnish, and Supplies Merchant Wholesalers
	Business to Business Electronic Markets	425110	Business to Business Electronic Markets (pt)
	Agents and Brokers	425120	Wholesale Trade Agents and Brokers (pt)
422990	Other Miscellaneous Nondurable Goods Wholesalers		
	Merchant Wholesalers	424990	Other Miscellaneous Nondurable Goods Merchant Wholesalers
	Business to Business Electronic Markets	425110	Business to Business Electronic Markets (pt)
	Agents and Brokers	425120	Wholesale Trade Agents and Brokers (pt)
452110	Department Stores		

(pt)—Part of.

1997 NAICS Code	1997 NAICS U.S. Description	2002 NAICS Code	2002 NAICS U.S. Description
	Department Stores (except Discount Department Stores)	452111	Department Stores (except Discount Department Stores)
	Discount Department Stores	452112	Discount Department Stores
454110	Electronic Shopping and Mail Order Houses		
	Electronic Shopping	454111	Electronic Shopping
	Electronic Auctions	454112	Electronic Auctions
	Mail-Order Houses	454113	Mail-Order Houses
511110	Newspaper Publishers		
	Newspaper Publishers (except Internet Publishers)	511110	Newspaper Publishers
	Internet Newspaper Publishers	516110	Internet Publishers (pt.)
511120	Periodical Publishers		
	Periodical Publishers (except Internet Publishers)	511120	Periodical Publishers
	Internet Periodical Publishers	516110	Internet Publishers (pt.)
511130	Book Publishers		
	Book Publishers (except Internet Publishers)	511130	Book Publishers
	Internet Book Publishers	516110	Internet Publishers (pt.)
511140	Database and Directory Publishers		
	Database and Directory Publishers (except Internet Publishers)	511140	Directory and Mailing List Publishers
	Internet Database and Directory Publishers	516110	Internet Publishers (pt.)
511191	Greeting Card Publishers		
	Greeting Card Publishers (except Internet Publishers)	511191	Greeting Card Publishers
	Internet Greeting Card Publishers	516110	Internet Publishers (pt.)
511199	All Other Publishers		
	Atlas and Map Publishers (except Internet Publishers)	511130	Book Publishers (pt.)
	All Other Publishers (except Internet Publishers)	511199	All Other Publishers
	Atlas and Map Publishers (Internet Publishers) and All Other Internet Publishers	516110	Internet Publishers (pt.)
511210	Software Publishers	511210	Software Publishers

(pt)—Part of.

1997 NAICS Code	1997 NAICS U.S. Description	2002 NAICS Code	2002 NAICS U.S. Description
512110	Motion Picture and Video Production	512110	Motion Picture and Video Production
512120	Motion Picture and Video Distribution	512120	Motion Picture and Video Distribution
512131	Motion Picture Theaters (except Drive-Ins)	512131	Motion Picture Theaters (except Drive-Ins)
512132	Drive-In Motion Picture Theaters	512132	Drive-In Motion Picture Theaters
512191	Teleproduction and Other Postproduction Services	512191	Teleproduction and other Postproduction Services
512199	Other Motion Picture and Video Industries	512199	Other Motion Picture and Video Industries
512210	Record Production	512210	Record Production
512220	Integrated Record Production/ Distribution	512220	Integrated Record Production/ Distribution
512230	Music Publishers	512230	Music Publishers
512240	Sound Recording Studios	512240	Sound Recording Studios
512290	Other Sound Recording Industries	512290	Other Sound Recording Industries
513111	Radio Networks	515111	Radio Networks
513112	Radio Stations	515112	Radio Stations
513120	Television Broadcasting	515120	Television Broadcasting
513210	Cable Networks	515210	Cable and Other Subscription Programming
513220	Cable and Other Program Distribution	517510	Cable and Other Program Distribution
513310	Wired Telecommunications Carriers	517110	Wired Telecommunications Carriers
513321	Paging	517211	Paging
513322	Cellular and Other Wireless Telecommunications	517212	Cellular and Other Wireless Telecommunications
513330	Telecommunications Resellers	517310	Telecommunications Resellers
513340	Satellite Telecommunications	517410	Satellite Telecommunications
513390	Other Telecommunications	517910	Other Telecommunications
514110	News Syndicates	519110	News Syndicates
514120	Libraries and Archives	519120	Libraries and Archives
514191	On-Line Information Services	518111	Internet Service Providers
514199	All Other Information Services		
	Internet Broadcasting	516110	Internet Publishing and Broadcasting (pt.)
	Web Search Portals	518112	Web Search Portals
	All Other Information Services	519190	All Other Information Services

(pt)—Part of.

1997 NAICS Code	1997 NAICS U.S. Description	2002 NAICS Code	2002 NAICS U.S. Description
514210	Data Processing Services	518210	Data Processing, Hosting, and Related Services
561720	Janitorial Services		
	Cleaning Buildings During and Immediately After Construction	238990	All Other Specialty Trade Contractors (pt)
	Except Cleaning Buildings During and Immediately After Construction	561720	Janitorial Services

(pt)—Part of.

Part IV

Alphabetic Index

Alphabetic Index

311611 Abattoirs
621410 Abortion clinics
334519 Abrasion testing machines manufacturing
339114 Abrasive points, wheels, and disks, dental, manufacturing
327910 Abrasive products manufacturing
212322 Abrasive sand quarrying and/or beneficiating
212399 Abrasive stones (e.g., emery, grindstones, hones, pumice) mining and/or beneficiating
423840 Abrasives merchant wholesalers
212399 Abrasives, natural, mining and/ or beneficiating
322121 Absorbent paper stock manufacturing
332420 Absorbers, gas, heavy gauge metal, manufacturing
334513 Absorption analyzers, industrial process type (e.g., infrared), manufacturing
237310 Abutment construction
611691 Academic tutoring services
611310 Academies, college or university
611110 Academies, elementary or secondary
611210 Academies, junior college
611310 Academies, military service (college)
611620 Academies, riding instruction
334511 Acceleration indicators and systems components, aerospace type, manufacturing
325199 Accelerators (i.e., basic synthetic chemical) manufacturing
334519 Accelerometers (except aerospace type) manufacturing
238330 Access flooring installation
813319 Accident prevention associations
524130 Accidental and health reinsurance carriers
524113 Accidental death and dismemberment insurance carriers, direct
524113 Accidental death and dismemberment insurance underwriting, direct
339992 Accordions and parts manufacturing
561440 Account collection services
541219 Accountants' (except CPAs) offices
541219 Accountants' (except CPAs) private practices
541211 Accountants' (i.e., CPAs) offices, certified public
541211 Accountants' (i.e., CPAs) private practices, certified public
813920 Accountants' associations
541211 Accounting (i.e., CPAs) services, certified public
423420 Accounting machines merchant wholesalers
541219 Accounting services (except CPAs)
332420 Accumulators, industrial pressure vessels, heavy gauge metal, manufacturing
325211 Acetal resins manufacturing
325199 Acetaldehyde manufacturing
325221 Acetate fibers and filaments manufacturing
325191 Acetate of lime, natural, made by distillation of wood
313111 Acetate spun yarns made from purchased fiber
325199 Acetates, not specified elsewhere by process, manufacturing
325199 Acetic acid manufacturing
325199 Acetic anhydride manufacturing
325199 Acetin manufacturing

325191 Acetone, natural, manufacturing
325199 Acetone, synthetic, manufacturing
332420 Acetylene cylinders, heavy gauge metal, manufacturing
325120 Acetylene manufacturing
325411 Acetylsalicylic acid manufacturing
325132 Acid dyes, synthetic organic, manufacturing
325199 Acid esters, not specified elsewhere by process, manufacturing
324110 Acid oils made in petroleum refineries
236210 Acid plant construction
562211 Acid waste disposal facilities
562211 Acid waste treatment facilities
334513 Acidity (i.e., pH) instruments, industrial process type, manufacturing
334516 Acidity (i.e., pH) measuring equipment, laboratory analysis-type, manufacturing
213112 Acidizing oil and gas field wells on a contract basis
311511 Acidophilus milk manufacturing
424690 Acids merchant wholesalers
325199 Acids, organic, not specified elsewhere by process, manufacturing
111219 Acorn squash farming, field, bedding plant and seed production
238310 Acoustical ceiling tile and panel installation
541330 Acoustical engineering consulting services
238310 Acoustical foam (i.e., sound barrier) installation
332323 Acoustical suspension systems, metal, manufacturing
541330 Acoustical system engineering design services
541380 Acoustics testing laboratories or services
325199 Acrolein manufacturing
325212 Acrylate rubber manufacturing
325212 Acrylate-butadiene rubber manufacturing
313112 Acrylic and modacrylic filament yarn throwing, twisting, texturizing, or winding purchased yarn
325222 Acrylic fibers and filaments manufacturing
326113 Acrylic film and unlaminated sheet (except packaging) manufacturing
325211 Acrylic resins manufacturing
325212 Acrylic rubber manufacturing
313111 Acrylic spun yarns made from purchased fiber
325222 Acrylonitrile fibers and filaments manufacturing
325199 Acrylonitrile manufacturing
325211 Acrylonitrile-butadiene-styrene (ABS) resins manufacturing
334519 Actinometers, meteorological, manufacturing
339931 Action figures manufacturing
325998 Activated carbon or charcoal manufacturing
624120 Activity centers for disabled persons, the elderly, and persons diagnosed with mental retardation
711510 Actors, independent
711510 Actresses, independent
541612 Actuarial consulting services
524298 Actuaries
333995 Actuators, fluid power, manufacturing
621399 Acupuncturists' (except MDs or DOs) offices (e.g., centers, clinics)
621111 Acupuncturists' (MDs or DOs) offices (e.g., centers, clinics)
325110 Acyclic hydrocarbons (e.g., butene, ethylene, propene) (except acetylene) made from refined petroleum or liquid hydrocarbons
332993 Adapters, bombcluster, manufacturing
333313 Adding machines manufacturing
236118 Addition, alteration and renovation (i.e., construction), multifamily building

236118 Addition, alteration and renovation (i.e., construction), residential building
236220 Addition, alteration and renovation general contractors, commercial and institutional building
236220 Addition, alteration and renovation general contractors, commercial warehouse
236220 Addition, alteration and renovation general contractors, hotel and motel
236220 Addition, alteration and renovation general contractors, industrial warehouse
236118 Addition, alteration and renovation of single-family dwellings
236220 Addition, alteration and renovation operative builders, commercial and institutional building
236220 Addition, alteration and renovation operative builders, commercial warehouse
236220 Addition, alteration and renovation operative builders, hotel and motel
236210 Addition, alteration and renovation operative builders, industrial building (except warehouses)
236220 Addition, alteration and renovation operative builders, industrial warehouse
236220 Addition, alteration and renovation, commercial and institutional building
236220 Addition, alteration and renovation, commercial warehouse
236210 Addition, alteration and renovation, general contractors, industrial building (except warehouses)
236220 Addition, alteration and renovation, hotel and motel
236210 Addition, alteration and renovation, industrial building (except warehouses)
236220 Addition, alteration and renovation, industrial warehouse
236118 Addition, alteration and renovation, multifamily building, general contractors
236118 Addition, alteration and renovation, multifamily building, operative builders
236118 Addition, alteration and renovation, residential building, general contractors
236118 Addition, alteration and renovation, residential building, operative builders
236118 Addition, alteration and renovation, single-family housing, general contractors
236118 Addition, alteration and renovation, single-family housing, operative builders
325998 Additive preparations for gasoline (e.g., antiknock preparations, detergents, gum inhibitors) manufacturing
561499 Address bar coding services
511140 Address list publishers (except exclusive Internet publishing)
511140 Address list publishers and printing combined
323112 Address lists flexographic printing without publishing
323111 Address lists gravure printing without publishing
323110 Address lists lithographic (offset) printing without publishing
323119 Address lists printing (except flexographic, gravure, lithographic, quick, screen) without publishing
323113 Address lists screen printing without publishing
423420 Addressing machines merchant wholesalers

322222 Adhesive tape (except medical) made from purchased materials
339113 Adhesive tape, medical, manufacturing
325520 Adhesives (except asphalt, dental, gypsum base) manufacturing
424690 Adhesives and sealants merchant wholesalers
325199 Adipic acid esters or amines manufacturing
325199 Adipic acid manufacturing
325199 Adiponitrile manufacturing
236220 Administration building construction
922110 Administrative courts
541611 Administrative management consulting services
561110 Administrative management services
523991 Administrators of private estates
327123 Adobe bricks manufacturing
624110 Adoption agencies
624110 Adoption services, child
325411 Adrenal derivatives, uncompounded, manufacturing
325412 Adrenal medicinal preparations manufacturing
611691 Adult literacy instruction
541810 Advertising agencies
541810 Advertising agency consulting services
541870 Advertising material (e.g., coupons, flyers, samples) direct distribution services
541860 Advertising material preparation services for mailing or other direct distribution
323110 Advertising materials (e.g., coupons, flyers) lithographic (offset) printing without publishing
541840 Advertising media representatives (i.e., independent of media owners)
511120 Advertising periodical publishers (except exclusive Internet publishing)
511120 Advertising periodical publishers and printing combined
516110 Advertising periodical publishers, exclusively on Internet
541850 Advertising services, indoor or outdoor display
541890 Advertising specialty (e.g., keychain, magnet, pen) distribution services
541850 Advertising, aerial
921110 Advisory commissions, executive government
921120 Advisory commissions, legislative
487990 Aerial cable car, scenic and sightseeing, operation
333315 Aerial cameras manufacturing
115112 Aerial dusting or spraying (i.e., using specialized or dedicated aircraft)
541360 Aerial geophysical surveying services
238910 Aerial or picker truck, construction, rental with operator
541370 Aerial surveying (except geophysical) services
487990 Aerial tramway, scenic and sightseeing, operation
333923 Aerial work platforms manufacturing
713940 Aerobic dance and exercise centers
423860 Aeronautical equipment and supplies merchant wholesalers
334511 Aeronautical systems and instruments manufacturing
325998 Aerosol can filling on a job order or contract basis
332431 Aerosol cans, light gauge metal, manufacturing
325998 Aerosol packaging services
332919 Aerosol valves manufacturing
332410 Aftercoolers (i.e., heat exchangers) manufacturing
325620 After-shave preparations manufacturing

325414 Agar culture media manufacturing
325411 Agar-agar grinding manufacturing
212399 Agate mining and/or beneficiating
111998 Agave farming
522293 Agencies of foreign banks (i.e., trade financing)
524210 Agencies, insurance
522310 Agencies, loan
531210 Agencies, real estate
531390 Agencies, real estate escrow
425120 Agents and brokers, durable goods, wholesale trade
425120 Agents and brokers, nondurable goods, wholesale trade
531390 Agents' offices, real estate escrow
711410 Agents, artists'
711410 Agents, authors'
711410 Agents, celebrities'
711410 Agents, entertainers'
812320 Agents, laundry and drycleaning
711410 Agents, modeling
711410 Agents, public figures'
531210 Agents, real estate
488510 Agents, shipping
711410 Agents, sports figures'
711410 Agents, talent
711410 Agents, theatrical talent
212210 Agglomerates, iron ore, beneficiating
333120 Aggregate spreaders manufacturing
325414 Aggressins (except in-vitro) manufacturing
551112 Agreement corporation (except international trade financing)
522293 Agreement corporations (i.e., international trade financing)
524126 Agricultural (i.e., crop, livestock) insurance carriers, direct
424910 Agricultural chemicals merchant wholesalers
541690 Agricultural consulting services
926140 Agricultural cooperative extension program administration
522298 Agricultural credit institutions, making loans or extending credit (except real estate, sales financing)
711320 Agricultural fair managers without facilities
711320 Agricultural fair organizers without facilities
711320 Agricultural fair promoters without facilities
332212 Agricultural handtools (e.g., hay forks, hoes, rakes, spades), nonpowered, manufacturing
423820 Agricultural implements merchant wholesalers
522298 Agricultural lending (except real estate, sales financing)
327410 Agricultural lime manufacturing
424910 Agricultural limestone merchant wholesalers
212312 Agricultural limestone mining and/or beneficiating
423820 Agricultural machinery and equipment merchant wholesalers
532490 Agricultural machinery and equipment rental or leasing
811310 Agricultural machinery and equipment repair and maintenance services
511120 Agricultural magazine and periodical publishers (except exclusive Internet publishing)
511120 Agricultural magazine and periodical publishers and printing combined
516110 Agricultural magazine and periodical publishers, exclusively on Internet
323112 Agricultural magazines and periodicals flexographic printing without publishing
323111 Agricultural magazines and periodicals gravure printing without publishing
323110 Agricultural magazines and periodicals lithographic (offset) printing without publishing

323119 Agricultural magazines and periodicals printing (except flexographic, gravure, lithographic, quick, screen) without publishing
323113 Agricultural magazines and periodicals screen printing without publishing
926140 Agricultural marketing services government
813910 Agricultural organizations (except youth farming organizations, farm granges)
926140 Agricultural pest and weed regulation, government
484220 Agricultural products trucking, local
531190 Agricultural property rental leasing
926140 Agriculture fair boards administration
115115 Agriculture production or harvesting crews
541710 Agriculture research and development laboratories or services
541690 Agrology consulting services
541690 Agronomy consulting services
624110 Aid to families with dependent children (AFDC)
621910 Air ambulance services
336399 Air bag assemblies manufacturing
336612 Air boat building
336340 Air brake systems and parts, automotive, truck, and bus, manufacturing
481212 Air cargo carriers (except air couriers), nonscheduled
481112 Air cargo carriers (except air couriers), scheduled
332439 Air cargo containers, light gauge metal, manufacturing
335313 Air circuit breakers manufacturing
481111 Air commuter carriers, scheduled
333912 Air compressors manufacturing
492110 Air courier services
332322 Air cowls, sheet metal (except stampings), manufacturing
336399 Air filters, automotive, truck, and bus, manufacturing
334512 Air flow controllers (except valves), air-conditioning and refrigeration, manufacturing
928110 Air Force
313230 Air laid nonwoven fabrics manufacturing
481211 Air passenger carriers, nonscheduled
481111 Air passenger carriers, scheduled
423730 Air pollution control equipment and supplies merchant wholesalers
335211 Air purification equipment, portable, manufacturing
333411 Air purification equipment, stationary, manufacturing
332420 Air receiver tanks, heavy gauge metal, manufacturing
333411 Air scrubbing systems manufacturing
711310 Air show managers with facilities
711320 Air show managers without facilities
711310 Air show organizers with facilities
711320 Air show organizers without facilities
711310 Air show promoters with facilities
711320 Air show promoters without facilities
238220 Air system balancing and testing
481211 Air taxi services
334511 Air traffic control radar systems and equipment manufacturing
611519 Air traffic control schools
488111 Air traffic control services (except military)
928110 Air traffic control, military
238220 Air vent installation
333411 Air washers (i.e., air scrubbers) manufacturing

487210 Airboat (i.e., swamp buggy) operation
334511 Airborne navigational systems manufacturing
334220 Airborne radio communications equipment manufacturing
532210 Air-conditioner rental
811412 Air-conditioner, window, repair and maintenance services
336391 Air-conditioners, motor vehicle, manufacturing
423620 Air-conditioners, room, merchant wholesalers
333415 Air-conditioners, unit (e.g., motor home, travel trailer, window), manufacturing
333415 Air-conditioning and warm air heating combination units manufacturing
333415 Air-conditioning compressors (except motor vehicle) manufacturing
333415 Air-conditioning condensers and condensing units manufacturing
333415 Air-conditioning equipment (except motor vehicle) manufacturing
423730 Air-conditioning equipment (except room units) merchant wholesalers
221330 Air-conditioning supply
238220 Air-conditioning system (except window) installation
331491 Aircraft and automotive wire and cable (except aluminum, copper) made from purchased nonferrous metals (except aluminum copper) in wire drawing plants
331422 Aircraft and automotive wire or cable made from purchased copper in wire drawing plants
332995 Aircraft artillery manufacturing
336413 Aircraft assemblies, subassemblies, and parts (except engines) manufacturing
336413 Aircraft auxiliary parts (e.g., crop dusting, external fuel tanks, inflight refueling equipment) manufacturing
333999 Aircraft carrier catapults manufacturing
481219 Aircraft charter services (i.e., general purpose aircraft used for a variety of specialty air and flying services)
481211 Aircraft charter services, passenger
336413 Aircraft control surface assemblies manufacturing
336411 Aircraft conversions (i.e., major modifications to system)
441229 Aircraft dealers
336412 Aircraft engine and engine parts (except carburetors, pistons, piston rings, valves) manufacturing
333924 Aircraft engine cradles manufacturing
334519 Aircraft engine instruments manufacturing
336412 Aircraft engine overhauling
336412 Aircraft engine rebuilding
423860 Aircraft engines and parts merchant wholesalers
423860 Aircraft equipment and supplies merchant wholesalers
488190 Aircraft ferrying services
334511 Aircraft flight instruments (except engine instruments) manufacturing
336413 Aircraft fuselage wing tail and similar assemblies manufacturing
488119 Aircraft hangar rental
332510 Aircraft hardware, metal, manufacturing
488190 Aircraft inspection services
926120 Aircraft inspection, government
561720 Aircraft janitorial services
336321 Aircraft lighting fixtures manufacturing
333924 Aircraft loading hoists manufacturing

488190 Aircraft maintenance and repair services (except factory conversion, factory overhaul, factory rebuilding)
336411 Aircraft manufacturing
423860 Aircraft merchant wholesalers
336411 Aircraft overhauling
488119 Aircraft parking service
336413 Aircraft propellers and parts manufacturing
336411 Aircraft rebuilding (i.e., restoration to original design specifications)
532411 Aircraft rental and leasing
336360 Aircraft seats manufacturing
488190 Aircraft testing services
314999 Aircraft tie down strap assemblies (except leather) manufacturing
326211 Aircraft tire manufacturing
336412 Aircraft turbines manufacturing
811420 Aircraft upholstery repair
333412 Aircurtains manufacturing
336413 Airframe assemblies (except for guided missiles) manufacturing
336419 Airframe assemblies for guided missiles manufacturing
334511 Airframe equipment instruments manufacturing
325612 Airfreshners manufacturing
722310 Airline food services contractors
561599 Airline reservation services
561599 Airline ticket offices
332313 Airlocks, fabricated metal plate work, manufacturing
481112 Airmail carriers, scheduled
532411 Airplane rental or leasing
488119 Airport baggage handling services
236220 Airport building construction
488119 Airport cargo handling services
531190 Airport leasing, not operating airport, rental or leasing
335311 Airport lighting transformers manufacturing
485999 Airport limousine services (i.e., shuttle)
488119 Airport operators (e.g., civil, international, national)
237310 Airport runway construction
238210 Airport runway lighting contractors
237310 Airport runway line painting (e.g., striping)
488119 Airport runway maintenance services
485999 Airport shuttle services
236220 Airport terminal construction
488119 Airports, civil, operation and maintenance
334511 Airspeed instruments (aeronautical) manufacturing
212399 Alabaster mining and/or beneficiating
423610 Alarm apparatus, electric, merchant wholesalers
334518 Alarm clocks manufacturing
238210 Alarm system (e.g., fire, burglar), electric, installation only
334290 Alarm system central monitoring equipment manufacturing
561621 Alarm system monitoring services
334290 Alarm systems and equipment manufacturing
561621 Alarm systems sales combined with installation, repair, or monitoring services
323118 Albums (e.g., photo, scrap) and refills manufacturing
424120 Albums, photo, merchant wholesalers
424690 Alcohol, industrial, merchant wholesalers
922120 Alcohol, tobacco, and firearms control
926150 Alcoholic beverage control boards
492210 Alcoholic beverage delivery service
722410 Alcoholic beverage drinking places
312140 Alcoholic beverages (except brandy) distilling
424810 Alcoholic beverages (except distilled spirits, wine) merchant wholesalers

312130 Alcoholic beverages, brandy, distilling
424820 Alcoholic beverages, wine and distilled spirits merchant wholesalers
624190 Alcoholism and drug addiction self-help organizations
624190 Alcoholism counseling (except medical treatment), nonresidential
623220 Alcoholism rehabilitation facilities (except licensed hospitals), residential
622210 Alcoholism rehabilitation hospitals
624190 Alcoholism self-help organizations
621420 Alcoholism treatment centers and clinics (except hospitals), outpatient
325199 Aldehydes manufacturing
312120 Ale brewing
424810 Ale merchant wholesalers
111940 Alfalfa hay farming
311119 Alfalfa meal, dehydrated, manufacturing
424910 Alfalfa merchant wholesalers
311119 Alfalfa prepared as feed for animals
111998 Alfalfa seed farming
111419 Alfalfa sprout farming, grown under cover
311119 Alfalfa, cubed, manufacturing
111998 Algae farming
325199 Alginates (e.g., calcium, potassium, sodium) manufacturing
325199 Alginic acid manufacturing
334519 Alidades, surveying, manufacturing
333319 Alignment equipment, motor vehicle, manufacturing
325110 Aliphatic (e.g., hydrocarbons) (except acetylene) made from refined petroleum or liquid hydrocarbons
324110 Aliphatic chemicals (i.e., acyclic) made in petroleum refineries
325181 Alkalies manufacturing
424690 Alkalies merchant wholesalers
335912 Alkaline cell primary batteries manufacturing
335911 Alkaline cell storage batteries (i.e., nickel-cadmium, nickel-iron, silver oxide-zinc) manufacturing
335912 Alkaline manganese primary batteries manufacturing
325211 Alkyd resins manufacturing
324110 Alkylates made in petroleum refineries
423110 All terrain vehicle (ATV's) merchant wholesalers
336999 All terrain vehicles (ATV's), wheeled or tracked, manufacturing
325414 Allergenic extracts (except diagnostic substances) manufacturing
325414 Allergens manufacturing
621111 Allergists' offices (e.g., centers, clinics)
112519 Alligator production, farm raising
331513 Alloy steel castings (except investment), unfinished, manufacturing
331314 Alloying purchased aluminum metals
331423 Alloying purchased copper
331423 Alloying purchased copper metals
331492 Alloying purchased nonferrous metals (except aluminum, copper)
441221 All-terrain vehicle (ATV) dealers
325211 Allyl resins manufacturing
323121 Almanac binding without printing
511130 Almanac publishers (except exclusive Internet publishing)
511130 Almanac publishers and printing combined
516110 Almanac publishers, exclusively on Internet
323117 Almanacs printing and binding without publishing

323117 Almanacs printing without publishing
111335 Almond farming
115114 Almond hulling and shelling
311999 Almond pastes manufacturing
111998 Aloe farming
112990 Alpaca production
721110 Alpine skiing facilities with accommodations (i.e., ski resort)
713920 Alpine skiing facilities without accommodations
237130 Alternative energy (e.g., geothermal, ocean wave, solar, wind) structure construction
334515 Alternator and generator testers manufacturing
336322 Alternators and generators for internal combustion engines manufacturing
334511 Altimeters, aeronautical, manufacturing
212391 Alum, natural, mining and/or beneficiating
327125 Alumina fused refractories manufacturing
327113 Alumina porcelain insulators manufacturing
331311 Alumina refining
327125 Aluminous refractory cement manufacturing
331312 Aluminum alloys made from bauxite or alumina producing primary aluminum and manufacturing
331314 Aluminum alloys made from scrap or dross
331316 Aluminum bar made by extruding purchased aluminum
331316 Aluminum bar made in integrated secondary smelting and extruding mills
331314 Aluminum billet made from purchased aluminum
331314 Aluminum billet made in integrated secondary smelting and rolling mills
332431 Aluminum cans, light gauge metal, manufacturing
331524 Aluminum castings (except die-castings), unfinished, manufacturing
325188 Aluminum chloride manufacturing
332812 Aluminum coating of metal products for the trade
325188 Aluminum compounds, not specified elsewhere by process, manufacturing
331521 Aluminum die-casting foundries
331521 Aluminum die-castings, unfinished, manufacturing
238350 Aluminum door and window, residential-type, installation
331314 Aluminum extrusion ingot (i.e., billet), secondary
331314 Aluminum flakes made from purchased aluminum
331315 Aluminum foil made by flat rolling purchased aluminum
331315 Aluminum foil made in integrated secondary smelting and flat rolling mills
332112 Aluminum forgings made from purchased metals, unfinished
331524 Aluminum foundries (except die-casting)
332999 Aluminum freezer foil not made in rolling mills
325188 Aluminum hydroxide (i.e., alumina trihydrate) manufacturing
331312 Aluminum ingot and other primary aluminum production shapes made from bauxite or alumina
331314 Aluminum ingot made from purchased aluminum
331314 Aluminum ingot, secondary smelting of aluminum and manufacturing
331314 Aluminum ingot, secondary, manufacturing
332999 Aluminum ladders manufacturing
327910 Aluminum oxide (fused) abrasives manufacturing
331311 Aluminum oxide refining

331316 Aluminum pipe made by extruding purchased aluminum
331316 Aluminum pipe made in integrated secondary smelting and extruding mills
236210 Aluminum plant construction
331315 Aluminum plate made by continuous casting purchased aluminum
331315 Aluminum plate made by flat rolling purchased aluminum
331315 Aluminum plate made in integrated secondary smelting and continuous casting mills
331315 Aluminum plate made in integrated secondary smelting and flat rolling mills
331312 Aluminum producing from alumina
331314 Aluminum recovering from scrap and making ingot and billet (except by rolling)
331316 Aluminum rod made by extruding purchased aluminum
331316 Aluminum rod made in integrated secondary smelting and extruding mills
331312 Aluminum shapes (e.g., bar, ingot, rod, sheet) made by producing primary aluminum and manufacturing
331315 Aluminum sheet made by flat rolling purchased aluminum
331315 Aluminum sheet made in integrated secondary smelting and flat rolling mills
238170 Aluminum siding installation
331314 Aluminum smelting, secondary, and making ingot and billet (except by rolling)
325188 Aluminum sulfate manufacturing
331316 Aluminum tube blooms made by extruding purchased aluminum
331316 Aluminum tube blooms made in integrated secondary smelting and extruding mills
331316 Aluminum tube made by drawing or extruding purchased aluminum
331316 Aluminum tube made in integrated secondary smelting and drawing plants
331316 Aluminum tube made in integrated secondary smelting and extruding mills
331315 Aluminum welded tube made by flat rolling purchased aluminum
331315 Aluminum welded tube made in integrated secondary smelting and flat rolling mills
813410 Alumni associations
813410 Alumni clubs
325188 Alums (e.g., aluminum ammonium sulfate, aluminum potassium sulfate) manufacturing
212393 Alunite mining and/or beneficiating
515112 AM radio stations
333131 Amalgamators (i.e., metallurgical and mining machinery) manufacturing
339114 Amalgams, dental, manufacturing
111998 Amaranth farming
713990 Amateur sports teams, recreational
325920 Amatols manufacturing
212393 Amblygonite mining and/or beneficiating
922160 Ambulance and fire service combined
336211 Ambulance bodies manufacturing
423110 Ambulance merchant wholesalers
621910 Ambulance services, air or ground
336211 Ambulances assembling on purchased chassis
621493 Ambulatory surgical centers and clinics, freestanding
921150 American Indian or Alaska Native tribal councils

921150 American Indian or Alaska Native tribal courts
921150 American Indian or Alaska Native, tribal chief's or chairman's office
212399 Amethyst mining and/or beneficiating
334516 Amino acid analyzers, laboratory-type, manufacturing
325211 Amino resins manufacturing
325211 Amino-aldehyde resins manufacturing
325192 Aminoanthraquinone manufacturing
325192 Aminoazobenzene manufacturing
325192 Aminoazotoluene manufacturing
325192 Aminophenol manufacturing
424690 Ammonia (except fertilizer material) merchant wholesalers
325311 Ammonia, anhydrous and aqueous, manufacturing
424910 Ammonia, fertilizer material, merchant wholesalers
325612 Ammonia, household-type, manufacturing
325188 Ammonium chloride manufacturing
325188 Ammonium compounds, not specified elsewhere by process, manufacturing
325188 Ammonium hydroxide manufacturing
325188 Ammonium molybdate manufacturing
325311 Ammonium nitrate manufacturing
325188 Ammonium perchlorate manufacturing
325312 Ammonium phosphates manufacturing
236210 Ammonium plant construction
325311 Ammonium sulfate manufacturing
325188 Ammonium thiosulfate manufacturing
423990 Ammunition (except sporting) merchant wholesalers
332993 Ammunition (i.e., more than 30 mm., more than 1.18 inch) manufacturing
321920 Ammunition boxes, wood, manufacturing
332439 Ammunition boxes, light gauge metal, manufacturing
332994 Ammunition carts (i.e., 30 mm or less, 1.18 inch or less) manufacturing
332995 Ammunition carts (i.e., more than 30 mm., more than 1.18 inch) manufacturing
332993 Ammunition loading and assembling plants
332992 Ammunition, small arms (i.e., 30 mm. or less, 1.18 inch or less), manufacturing
423910 Ammunition, sporting, merchant wholesalers
334515 Ampere-hour meters manufacturing
325411 Amphetamines, uncompounded, manufacturing
334310 Amplifiers (e.g., auto, home, musical instrument, public address) manufacturing
334220 Amplifiers, (e.g., RF power and IF), broadcast and studio equipment, manufacturing
335999 Amplifiers, magnetic, pulse, and maser, manufacturing
713120 Amusement arcades
713990 Amusement device (except gambling) concession operators (i.e., supplying and servicing in others' facilities)
713120 Amusement device (except gambling) parlors, coin-operated
713120 Amusement devices (except gambling) operated in own facilities
236220 Amusement facility construction
339999 Amusement machines, coin-operated, manufacturing
423850 Amusement park equipment merchant wholesalers
713110 Amusement parks (e.g., theme, water)

713990 Amusement ride concession operators (i.e., supplying and servicing in others' facilities)
325199 Amyl acetate manufacturing
325412 Analgesic preparations manufacturing
334111 Analog computers manufacturing
423490 Analytical instruments (e.g., chromatographic, photometers, spectrographs) merchant wholesalers
334515 Analyzers for testing electrical characteristics manufacturing
334513 Analyzers, industrial process control type, manufacturing
237990 Anchored earth retention contractors
114111 Anchovy fishing
212325 Andalusite mining and/or beneficiating
332999 Andirons manufacturing
339112 Anesthesia apparatus manufacturing
621111 Anesthesiologists' offices (e.g., centers, clinics)
325412 Anesthetic preparations manufacturing
325411 Anesthetics, uncompounded, manufacturing
325412 Angiourographic diagnostic preparations manufacturing
332999 Angle irons, metal, manufacturing
333515 Angle rings (i.e., a machine tool accessory) manufacturing
332911 Angle valves, industrial-type, manufacturing
334511 Angle-of-attack instrumentation manufacturing
334511 Angle-of-yaw instrumentation manufacturing
112420 Angora goat farming
325311 Anhydrous ammonia manufacturing
311512 Anhydrous butterfat manufacturing
325222 Anidex fibers and filaments manufacturing
325192 Aniline manufacturing
112519 Animal aquaculture (except finfish, shellfish)
325182 Animal black manufacturing
813910 Animal breeders' associations
812220 Animal cemeteries
712130 Animal exhibits, live
311611 Animal fats (except poultry and small game) produced in slaughtering plants
311613 Animal fats rendering
311119 Animal feed mills (except dog and cat) manufacturing
311111 Animal feed mills, dog and cat, manufacturing
424910 Animal feeds (except pet food) merchant wholesalers
311119 Animal feeds, prepared (except dog and cat), manufacturing
311111 Animal feeds, prepared, dog and cat, manufacturing
313112 Animal fiber yarn twisting or winding of purchased yarn
812910 Animal grooming services
424590 Animal hair merchant wholesalers
541940 Animal hospitals
311613 Animal oil rendering
926140 Animal quarantine service, government
813312 Animal rights organizations
712130 Animal safari parks
115210 Animal semen banks
236220 Animal shelter and clinic construction
812910 Animal shelters
114210 Animal trapping, commercial
332999 Animal traps, metal (except wire), manufacturing
813312 Animal welfare associations or leagues
336999 Animal-drawn vehicles and parts manufacturing
711510 Animated cartoon artists, independent
512120 Animated cartoon distribution
512110 Animated cartoon production
512110 Animated cartoon production and distribution
325998 Anise oil manufacturing

315119 Anklets, sheer hosiery or socks, knitting or knitting and finishing
325191 Annato extract manufacturing
332811 Annealing metals and metal products for the trade
332420 Annealing vats, heavy gauge metal, manufacturing
711510 Announcers, independent radio and television
524113 Annuities underwriting
332991 Annular ball bearings manufacturing
334513 Annunciators, relay and solid-state types, industrial display, manufacturing
333298 Anodizing equipment manufacturing
332813 Anodizing metals and metal products for the trade
423620 Answering machines, telephone, merchant wholesalers
561421 Answering services, telephone
325320 Ant poisons manufacturing
325412 Antacid preparations manufacturing
238290 Antenna, household-type, installation
423690 Antennas merchant wholesalers
334220 Antennas, satellite, manufacturing
334220 Antennas, transmitting and receiving, manufacturing
325412 Anthelmintic preparations manufacturing
325192 Anthracene manufacturing
212113 Anthracite beneficiating (e.g., crushing, screening, washing, cleaning, sizing)
213113 Anthracite mine tunneling on a contract basis
212113 Anthracite mining and/or beneficiating
213113 Anthracite mining services (except site preparation and related construction contractor activities) on a contract basis
325132 Anthraquinone dyes manufacturing
332995 Antiaircraft artillery manufacturing
325412 Antibacterial preparations manufacturing
325412 Antibiotic preparations manufacturing
424210 Antibiotics merchant wholesalers
325411 Antibiotics, uncompounded, manufacturing
325411 Anticholinergics, uncompounded, manufacturing
325411 Anticonvulsants, uncompounded, manufacturing
325412 Antidepressant preparations manufacturing
325411 Antidepressants, uncompounded, manufacturing
424690 Antifreeze merchant wholesalers
325998 Antifreeze preparations manufacturing
325414 Antigens manufacturing
325412 Antihistamine preparations manufacturing
325131 Antimony based pigments manufacturing
212299 Antimony concentrates mining and/or beneficiating
212299 Antimony ores mining and/or beneficiating
325188 Antimony oxide (except pigments) manufacturing
331419 Antimony refining, primary
325412 Antineoplastic preparations manufacturing
325620 Antiperspirants, personal, manufacturing
813319 Antipoverty advocacy organizations
325412 Antipyretic preparations manufacturing
811121 Antique and classic automotive restoration
441120 Antique auto dealers
424920 Antique book merchant wholesalers
453310 Antique dealers (except motor vehicles)
423210 Antique furniture merchant wholesalers

811420 Antique furniture repair and restoration shops
423220 Antique homefurnishing merchant wholesalers
423220 Antique houseware merchant wholesalers
423940 Antique jewelry merchant wholesalers
453310 Antique shops
332913 Antiscald bath and shower valves, plumbing, manufacturing
325998 Antiscaling compounds manufacturing
325412 Antiseptic preparations manufacturing
424210 Antiseptics merchant wholesalers
325414 Antiserums manufacturing
325412 Antispasmodic preparations manufacturing
332995 Antisubmarine projectors manufacturing
332995 Antitank rocket launchers manufacturing
325414 Antitoxins manufacturing
325414 Antivenoms manufacturing
236116 Apartment building construction general contractors
236117 Apartment building operative builders
531110 Apartment building rental or leasing
531110 Apartment hotel rental or leasing
531311 Apartment managers' offices
531110 Apartment rental or leasing
212392 Apatite mining and/or beneficiating
212325 Aplite mining and/or beneficiating
446110 Apothecaries
331491 Apparatus wire and cord (except aluminum, copper) made from purchased nonferrous metals (except aluminum, copper) in wire drawing plants
331422 Apparatus wire or cord made from purchased copper in wire drawing plants
331319 Apparatus wire or cord made in aluminum wire drawing plants
448150 Apparel accessory stores
314999 Apparel fillings (e.g., cotton mill waste, kapok) manufacturing
315999 Apparel findings and trimmings cut and sewn from purchased fabric (except apparel contractors)
561910 Apparel folding and packaging services
812320 Apparel pressing services
448130 Apparel stores, children's and infants' clothing
448110 Apparel stores, men's and boys' clothing
453310 Apparel stores, used clothing
448120 Apparel stores, women's and girls' clothing
315211 Apparel trimmings and findings, men's and boys', cut and sew apparel contractors
315212 Apparel trimmings and findings, women's, girls', and infants', cut and sew apparel contractors
424310 Apparel trimmings merchant wholesalers
313221 Apparel webbings manufacturing
315292 Apparel, fur (except apparel contractors), manufacturing
315211 Apparel, fur, men's and boys', cut and sew apparel contractors
315212 Apparel, fur, women's, girls', and infants', cut and sew apparel contractors
315211 Apparel, men's and boys', cut and sew apparel contractors
315212 Apparel, women's, girls', and infants', cut and sew contractors
111331 Apple orchards
312130 Applejack distilling

334512 Appliance controls manufacturing
335999 Appliance cords made from purchased insulated wire
332510 Appliance hardware, metal, manufacturing
334512 Appliance regulators (except switches) manufacturing
532210 Appliance rental
443111 Appliance stores, household-type
453310 Appliance stores, household-type, used
334518 Appliance timers manufacturing
811412 Appliance, household-type, repair and maintenance services without retailing new appliances
423720 Appliances, gas (except dryers, freezers, refrigerators), merchant wholesalers
423620 Appliances, household-type (except gas ranges, gas water heaters), merchant wholesalers
423450 Appliances, surgical, merchant wholesalers
518210 Application hosting
518210 Application service providers (ASPs)
541511 Applications software programming services, custom computer
511210 Applications software, computer, packaged
321999 Applicators, wood, manufacturing
315211 Appliqueing on men's and boys' apparel
314999 Appliqueing on textile products (except apparel)
315212 Appliqueing on women's, girls', and infants' apparel
323118 Appointment books and refills manufacturing
541990 Appraisal (except real estate) services
531320 Appraisal services, real estate
531320 Appraisers' offices, real estate
611513 Apprenticeship training programs
111339 Apricot farming
812331 Apron supply services
316999 Aprons for textile machinery, leather, manufacturing
316999 Aprons, leather (e.g., blacksmith's, welder's), manufacturing
315999 Aprons, waterproof (e.g., plastics, rubberized fabric), rubberizing fabric and manufacturing aprons
315212 Aprons, waterproof (including plastics, rubberized fabric), woman's, girls', and infants', cut and sew apparel contractors
315999 Aprons, waterproof (including rubberized fabric, plastics), cut and sewn from purchased fabric (except apparel contractors)
315211 Aprons, waterproof (including rubberized fabric, plastics), men's and boys', cut and sew apparel contractors
315211 Aprons, work (except leather), men's and boys, cut and sew apparel contractors
315212 Aprons, work (except leather), women's, girls', and infants', cut and sew apparel contractors
315225 Aprons, work (except leather, waterproof), men's and boys', cut and sewn from purchased fabric (except apparel contractors)
315239 Aprons, work (except waterproof, leather), women's, misses', and girls', cut and sewn from purchased fabric (except apparel contractors)
332999 Aquarium accessories, metal, manufacturing
712130 Aquariums
327215 Aquariums made from purchased glass
237110 Aqueduct construction

541990 Arbitration and conciliation services (except by attorney, paralegal)
333513 Arbor presses, metalworking, manufacturing
712130 Arboreta
712130 Arboretums
561730 Arborist services
333515 Arbors (i.e., a machine tool accessory) manufacturing
334510 Arc lamp units, electrotherapeutic (except infrared, ultraviolet), manufacturing
335129 Arc lighting fixtures (except electrotherapeutic), electric, manufacturing
333992 Arc welding equipment manufacturing
713120 Arcades, amusement
339113 Arch supports, orthopedic, manufacturing
541720 Archeological research and development services
712120 Archeological sites (i.e., public display)
339920 Archery equipment manufacturing
423910 Archery equipment merchant wholesalers
713990 Archery ranges
321213 Arches, glue laminated or pre-engineered wood, manufacturing
541310 Architects' (except landscape) offices
541310 Architects' (except landscape) private practices
813920 Architects' associations
423490 Architect's equipment and supplies merchant wholesalers
541320 Architects' offices, landscape
541320 Architects' private practices, landscape
541310 Architectural (except landscape) consultants' offices
541310 Architectural (except landscape) design services
541310 Architectural (except landscape) services
327331 Architectural block, concrete (e.g., fluted, ground face, screen, slump, split), manufacturing
325510 Architectural coatings (i.e., paint) manufacturing
332323 Architectural metalwork manufacturing
423390 Architectural metalwork merchant wholesalers
327112 Architectural sculptures, clay, manufacturing
327991 Architectural sculptures, stone, manufacturing
541320 Architectural services, landscape
327123 Architectural terra cotta manufacturing
327390 Architectural wall panels, precast concrete, manufacturing
337212 Architectural woodwork and fixtures (i.e., custom designed interiors) manufacturing
519120 Archives
316211 Arctics, plastics or plastics soled fabric upper, manufacturing
316211 Arctics, rubber or rubber soled fabric, manufacturing
335311 Arc-welding transformers, separate solid-state, manufacturing
335129 Area and sports luminaries (e.g., stadium lighting fixtures), electric, manufacturing
236220 Arena construction
711310 Arena operators
531120 Arena, no promotion of events, rental or leasing
212311 Argillite mining or quarrying
325120 Argon manufacturing
315999 Arm bands, elastic, cut and sewn from purchased fabric (except apparel contractors)
315211 Arm bands, elastic, men's and boys', cut and sew apparel contractors

315212 Arm bands, elastic, women's, girls', and infants', cut and sew apparel contractors
335314 Armature relays manufacturing
335312 Armature rewinding on a factory basis
811310 Armature rewinding services (except on an assembly line or factory basis)
335312 Armatures, industrial, manufacturing
928110 Armed forces
332993 Arming and fusing devices, missile, manufacturing
331111 Armor plate made in iron and steel mills
331422 Armored cable made from purchased copper in wire drawing plants
331422 Armored cable, copper, made in integrated secondary smelting and drawing plants
561613 Armored car services
336992 Armored military vehicles (except tanks) and parts manufacturing
236220 Armory construction
928110 Army
424690 Aromatic chemicals merchant wholesalers
113210 Aromatic wood gathering
488999 Arrangement of car pools and vanpools
335931 Arrestors and coils, lighting, manufacturing
325320 Arsenate insecticides manufacturing
325188 Arsenates (except insecticides) manufacturing
325131 Arsenic based pigments manufacturing
325188 Arsenic compounds, not specified elsewhere by process, manufacturing
212393 Arsenic mineral mining and/or beneficiating
325320 Arsenite insecticides manufacturing
325188 Arsenites manufacturing
611610 Art (except commercial or graphic) instruction
453920 Art auctions
453920 Art dealers
712110 Art galleries (except retail)
453920 Art galleries retailing art
327420 Art goods (e.g., gypsum, plaster of paris) manufacturing
424990 Art goods merchant wholesalers
712110 Art museums
315211 Art needlework contractors on men's and boys' apparel
315212 Art needlework contractors on women's, girls', and infants' apparel
314999 Art needlework on clothing for the trade
511199 Art print (except exclusive Internet publishing) publishers
323111 Art print gravure printing without publishing
511199 Art print publishers and printing combined
323112 Art prints flexographic printing without publishing
323110 Art prints lithographic (offset) printing without publishing
323119 Art prints printing (except flexographic, digital, gravure, lithographic, quick, screen) without publishing
323113 Art prints screen printing without publishing
511199 Art publishers (except exclusive Internet publishing)
516110 Art publishers, exclusively on Internet
711510 Art restorers, independent
611610 Art schools (except academic), fine
611519 Art schools, commercial or graphic
541430 Art services, commercial
541430 Art services, graphic
541430 Art studios, commercial
453998 Art supply stores
621340 Art therapists' offices (e.g., centers, clinics)
237110 Artesian well construction

111219 Artichoke farming, field, bedding plant and seed production
311421 Artichokes, canned, manufacturing
424990 Artificial Christmas trees merchant wholesalers
339999 Artificial flower arrangements assembled from purchased components
424930 Artificial flowers merchant wholesalers
334511 Artificial horizon instrumentation manufacturing
115210 Artificial insemination services for livestock
115210 Artificial insemination services for pets
339113 Artificial limbs manufacturing
238990 Artificial turf installation
312111 Artificially carbonated waters manufacturing
332993 Artillery ammunition (i.e., more than 30 mm., more than 1.18 inch) manufacturing
711510 Artists (except commercial, musical), independent
711510 Artists (i.e., painters), independent
711410 Artists' agents or managers
339942 Artist's paint manufacturing
339942 Artist's supplies (except paper) manufacturing
424990 Artists' supplies merchant wholesalers
541430 Artists, independent commercial
541430 Artists, independent graphic
541430 Artists, independent medical
926110 Arts and cultural program administration, government
711310 Arts event managers with facilities
711320 Arts event managers without facilities
711310 Arts event organizers with facilities
711320 Arts event organizers without facilities
711310 Arts event promoters with facilities
711320 Arts event promoters without facilities
711310 Arts festival managers with facilities
711320 Arts festival managers without facilities
711310 Arts festival organizers with facilities
711320 Arts festival organizers without facilities
711310 Arts festival promoters with facilities
711320 Arts festival promoters without facilities
562910 Asbestos abatement services
212399 Asbestos mining and/or beneficiating
327999 Asbestos products (except brake shoes and clutches) manufacturing
562910 Asbestos removal contractors
325411 Ascorbic acid (i.e., vitamin C), uncompounded, manufacturing
315211 Ascots, men's and boys', cut and sew apparel contractors
315993 Ascots, men's and boys', cut and sewn from purchased fabric (except apparel contractors)
562111 Ash collection services
562111 Ash hauling, local
212399 Ash, volcanic, mining and/or beneficiating
327215 Ashtrays made from purchased glass
327212 Ashtrays, glass, made in glass making plants
327112 Ashtrays, pottery, manufacturing
111219 Asparagus farming, field, bedding plant and seed production
324110 Asphalt and asphaltic materials made in petroleum refineries
423320 Asphalt and concrete mixtures merchant wholesalers
238990 Asphalt coating and sealing, residential and commercial parking lot and driveway

238330 Asphalt flooring, installation only
322121 Asphalt paper made in paper mills
237310 Asphalt paving (i.e., highway, road, street, public sidewalk)
324121 Asphalt paving blocks made from purchased asphaltic materials
324121 Asphalt paving mixtures made from purchased asphaltic materials
324110 Asphalt paving mixtures made in petroleum refineries
324121 Asphalt road compounds made from purchased asphaltic materials
212399 Asphalt rock mining and/or beneficiating
238160 Asphalt roof shingle installation
324122 Asphalt roofing cements made from purchased asphaltic materials
324122 Asphalt roofing coatings made from purchased asphaltic materials
333120 Asphalt roofing construction machinery manufacturing
423330 Asphalt roofing shingles merchant wholesalers
324122 Asphalt saturated boards made from purchased asphaltic materials
324122 Asphalt saturated mats and felts made from purchased asphaltic materials and paper
324122 Asphalt shingles made from purchased asphaltic materials
212399 Asphalt, native, mining and/or beneficiating
238990 Asphalting, residential and commercial driveway and parking area
518210 ASPs (Application Service Providers)
541380 Assaying services
336213 Assembly line conversions of purchased vans and mini-vans
336312 Assembly line rebuilding of automotive and truck gasoline engines
336350 Assembly line rebuilding of automotive, truck, and bus transmissions
333518 Assembly machines manufacturing
236210 Assembly plant construction
336120 Assembly plants, heavy trucks, and buses on chassis of own manufacture
336112 Assembly plants, light trucks on chassis of own manufacture
336112 Assembly plants, mini-vans on chassis of own manufacture
336111 Assembly plants, passenger car, on chassis of own manufacture
336112 Assembly plants, sport utility vehicles on chassis of own manufacture
921130 Assessor's offices, tax
325613 Assistants, textile and leather finishing, manufacturing
623311 Assisted-living facilities with on-site nursing facilities
623312 Assisted-living facilities without on-site nursing care facilities
813311 Associations for retired persons, advocacy
522120 Associations, savings and loan
325412 Astringent preparations manufacturing
812990 Astrology services
711219 Athletes, amateur, independent
711219 Athletes, independent (i.e., participating in live sports events)
813990 Athletic associations, regulatory
315228 Athletic clothing (except team athletic uniforms), men's, boys' and unisex (i.e., sized without regard to gender), cut and sewn from purchased fabric (except apparel contractors)

315239 Athletic clothing (except team athletic uniforms), women's, misses', and girls', cut and sewn from purchased fabric (except apparel contractors)
315191 Athletic clothing made in apparel knitting mills
315211 Athletic clothing, men's and boys', cut and sew apparel contractors
315212 Athletic clothing, women's, girls', and infants', cut and sew apparel contractors
713940 Athletic club facilities, physical fitness
713990 Athletic clubs (i.e., sports teams) not operating sports facilities, recreational
236220 Athletic court, indoor, construction
451110 Athletic equipment and supply stores (including uniforms)
237990 Athletic field (except stadium) construction
424340 Athletic footwear merchant wholesalers
339920 Athletic goods (except ammunition, clothing, footwear, small arms) manufacturing
423910 Athletic goods (except apparel, footwear, nonspecialty) merchant wholesalers
813990 Athletic leagues (i.e., regulating bodies)
448210 Athletic shoe (except bowling, golf, spiked) stores
316219 Athletic shoes (except rubber or plastics soled with fabric upper) manufacturing
316211 Athletic shoes, plastics or plastics soled fabric upper (except cleated), manufacturing
316211 Athletic shoes, rubber or rubber soled fabric uppers (except cleated), manufacturing
315119 Athletic socks, knitting or knitting and finishing
423910 Athletic uniforms merchant wholesalers
315299 Athletic uniforms, team, cut and sewn from purchased fabric (except apparel contractors)
315211 Athletic uniforms, team, men's and boys', cut and sew apparel contractors
315212 Athletic uniforms, team, women's, girls', and infants, cut and sew apparel contractors
511130 Atlas publishers (except exclusive Internet publishing)
511130 Atlas publishers and printing combined
516110 Atlas publishers, exclusively on Internet
323112 Atlases flexographic printing without publishing
323111 Atlases gravure printing without publishing
323110 Atlases lithographic (offset) printing without publishing
323119 Atlases printing (except flexographic, digital, gravure, lithographic, quick, screen) without publishing
323113 Atlases screen printing without publishing
238290 ATM (automated teller machine) installation
334119 ATM's (automatic teller machines) manufacturing
335999 Atom smashers (i.e., particle accelerators) manufacturing
339999 Atomizers (e.g., perfumes) manufacturing
325411 Atropine and derivatives manufacturing
316991 Attache cases, all materials, manufacturing
333112 Attachments, powered lawn and garden equipment, manufacturing
333412 Attic fans manufacturing
238310 Attic space insulating
922130 Attorney generals' offices
541110 Attorneys' offices
541110 Attorneys' private practices

453998 Auction houses (general merchandise)
424590 Auction markets, tobacco, horses, mules
561990 Auctioneers, independent
454112 Auctions, Internet retail
423990 Audio and video tapes and disks, prerecorded, merchant wholesalers
337129 Audio cabinets (i.e., housings), wood, manufacturing
238210 Audio equipment installation (except automotive) contractors
443112 Audio equipment stores (except automotive)
423620 Audio equipment, household-type, merchant wholesalers
512290 Audio recording of meetings or conferences
512240 Audio recording post-production services
532490 Audio visual equipment rental or leasing
334515 Audiofrequency oscillators manufacturing
334510 Audiological equipment, electromedical, manufacturing
621340 Audiologists' offices (e.g., centers, clinics)
334515 Audiometers (except medical) manufacturing
334613 Audiotape, blank, manufacturing
423690 Audiotapes, blank, merchant wholesalers
541211 Auditing accountants' (i.e., CPAs) offices
541211 Auditing accountants' (i.e., CPAs) private practices
541211 Auditing services (i.e., CPA services), accounts
236220 Auditorium construction
531120 Auditorium rental or leasing
541211 Auditors' (i.e., CPAs) offices, accounts
541211 Auditors' (i.e., CPAs) private practices, accounts
921190 Auditor's offices, government
213113 Auger coal mining services (except site preparation and related construction contractor activities) on a contract basis
333120 Augers (except mining-type) manufacturing
333131 Augers, mining-type, manufacturing
332212 Augers, nonpowered, manufacturing
711410 Authors' agents or managers
711510 Authors, independent
423120 Auto body shop supplies, merchant wholesalers
721110 Auto courts, lodging
441310 Auto supply stores
339114 Autoclaves, dental, manufacturing
332420 Autoclaves, industrial-type, heavy gauge metal, manufacturing
339111 Autoclaves, laboratory-type (except dental), manufacturing
336411 Autogiros manufacturing
238290 Automated and revolving door installation
334510 Automated blood and body fluid analyzers (except laboratory) manufacturing
522320 Automated clearinghouses, bank or check (except central bank)
518210 Automated data processing services
332911 Automatic (i.e., controlling-type, regulating) valves, industrial-type, manufacturing
334516 Automatic chemical analyzers, laboratory-type, manufacturing
238290 Automatic gate (e.g., garage, parking lot) installation
812310 Automatic laundries, coin-operated
454210 Automatic merchandising machine operators
333512 Automatic screw machines, metal cutting type, manufacturing
334119 Automatic teller machines (ATM) manufacturing

423420 Automatic teller machines (ATM) merchant wholesalers
336350 Automatic transmissions, automotive, truck, and bus, manufacturing
423120 Automobile accessories (except tires, tubes) merchant wholesalers
334220 Automobile antennas manufacturing
425120 Automobile auctions, wholesale
336211 Automobile bodies, passenger car, manufacturing
484220 Automobile carrier trucking, local
484230 Automobile carrier trucking, long-distance
813410 Automobile clubs (except road and travel services)
561599 Automobile clubs, road and travel services
721110 Automobile courts, lodging
493190 Automobile dead storage
441110 Automobile dealers, new only or new and used
441120 Automobile dealers, used only
611692 Automobile driving schools
522220 Automobile finance leasing companies
522220 Automobile financing
423120 Automobile glass merchant wholesalers
332510 Automobile hardware, metal, manufacturing
541420 Automobile industrial design services
524126 Automobile insurance carriers, direct
532112 Automobile leasing
333921 Automobile lifts (i.e., garage-type, service station) manufacturing
423110 Automobile merchant wholesalers
812930 Automobile parking garages or lots
441310 Automobile parts dealers
325612 Automobile polishes and cleaners manufacturing
541380 Automobile proving and testing grounds
711212 Automobile racetracks
611620 Automobile racing schools
711219 Automobile racing teams
334310 Automobile radio receivers manufacturing
532111 Automobile rental
485320 Automobile rental with driver (except shuttle service, taxis)
561491 Automobile repossession services
336360 Automobile seat covers manufacturing
336360 Automobile seat frames, metal, manufacturing
423120 Automobile service station equipment merchant wholesalers
561920 Automobile show managers
561920 Automobile show organizers
561920 Automobile show promoters
332618 Automobile skid chains made from purchased wire
335911 Automobile storage batteries manufacturing
332611 Automobile suspension springs, heavy gauge metal, manufacturing
336212 Automobile transporter trailers, multi-car, manufacturing
336214 Automobile transporter trailers, single car, manufacturing
336360 Automobile trimmings, textile, manufacturing
333923 Automobile wrecker (i.e., tow truck) hoists manufacturing
336211 Automobile wrecker truck bodies manufacturing
336211 Automobile wreckers assembling on purchased chassis
336111 Automobiles assembling on chassis of own manufacture
339932 Automobiles, children's, manufacturing
423730 Automotive air-conditioners merchant wholesalers
811198 Automotive air-conditioning repair shops

441310 Automotive audio equipment stores
811121 Automotive body shops
811118 Automotive brake repair shops
424690 Automotive chemicals (except lubricating greases, lubrication oils) merchant wholesalers
811192 Automotive detailing services (i.e., cleaning, polishing)
334515 Automotive electrical engine diagnostic equipment manufacturing
811118 Automotive electrical repair shops
335931 Automotive electrical switches manufacturing
334519 Automotive emissions testing equipment manufacturing
811198 Automotive emissions testing services
811111 Automotive engine repair and replacement shops
811112 Automotive exhaust system repair and replacement shops
811118 Automotive front end alignment shops
811122 Automotive glass shops
336322 Automotive harness and ignition sets manufacturing
335110 Automotive light bulbs manufacturing
336321 Automotive lighting fixtures manufacturing
336399 Automotive mirrors, framed, manufacturing
811191 Automotive oil change and lubrication shops
331319 Automotive or aircraft wire and cable made in aluminum wire drawing plants
811121 Automotive paint shops
441310 Automotive parts and supply stores
441310 Automotive parts dealers, used
423120 Automotive parts, new, merchant wholesalers
811118 Automotive radiator repair shops
423620 Automotive radios merchant wholesalers
811111 Automotive repair and replacement shops, general
811198 Automotive rustproofing and undercoating shops
811198 Automotive safety inspection services
334290 Automotive theft alarm systems manufacturing
441320 Automotive tire dealers
811198 Automotive tire repair (except retreading) shops
811113 Automotive transmission repair shops
811118 Automotive tune-up shops
811121 Automotive upholstery shops
811192 Automotive washing and polishing
336330 Automotive, truck and bus steering assemblies and parts manufacturing
336330 Automotive, truck and bus suspension assemblies and parts (except springs) manufacturing
339992 Autophones (organs with perforated music rolls) manufacturing
335311 Autotransformers for switchboards (except telephone switchboards) manufacturing
335311 Autotransformers manufacturing
237990 Avalanche protection, construction
712130 Aviaries
112990 Aviaries (i.e., raising birds for sale)
813319 Aviation advocacy organizations
481219 Aviation clubs providing a variety of air transportation activities to the general public
488119 Aviation clubs, primarily providing flying field services to the general public
713990 Aviation clubs, recreational
324110 Aviation fuels manufacturing
611512 Aviation schools
111339 Avocado farming
332212 Awls manufacturing
238190 Awning installation

423390 Awnings (except canvas) merchant wholesalers
314912 Awnings and canopies, outdoor, made from purchased fabrics
424990 Awnings, canvas, merchant wholesalers
326199 Awnings, rigid plastics or fiberglass, manufacturing
332322 Awnings, sheet metal (except stampings), manufacturing
332212 Axes manufacturing
336350 Axle bearings, automotive, truck, and bus, manufacturing
331111 Axles, rolled or forged, made in iron and steel mills
111421 Azalea farming
325920 Azides explosive materials manufacturing
325132 Azine dyes manufacturing
325132 Azo dyes manufacturing
325192 Azobenzene manufacturing
424330 Baby clothing merchant wholesalers
448130 Baby clothing shops
311422 Baby foods (including meats) canning
424490 Baby foods, canned, merchant wholesalers
311514 Baby formula, fresh, processed, and bottled, manufacturing
423210 Baby furniture merchant wholesalers
325620 Baby powder and baby oil manufacturing
333997 Baby scales manufacturing
812990 Baby shoe bronzing services
561310 Babysitting bureaus (i.e., registries)
624410 Babysitting services in provider's own home, child day care
624410 Babysitting services, child day care
238910 Backfilling, construction
332913 Backflow preventors, plumbing, manufacturing
112111 Backgrounding, cattle
238910 Backhoe rental with operator
333120 Backhoes manufacturing
311612 Bacon, slab and sliced, made from purchased carcasses
311611 Bacon, slab and sliced, produced in slaughtering plants
325414 Bacterial vaccines manufacturing
325414 Bacterins (i.e., bacterial vaccines) manufacturing
621511 Bacteriological laboratories, diagnostic
621511 Bacteriological laboratories, medical
541710 Bacteriological research and development laboratories or services
314999 Badges, fabric, manufacturing
332999 Badges, metal, manufacturing
326199 Badges, plastics, manufacturing
339920 Badminton equipment manufacturing
332313 Baffles, fabricated metal plate work, manufacturing
316110 Bag leather manufacturing
332993 Bag loading plants, ammunition, manufacturing
333993 Bag opening, filling, and closing machines manufacturing
722110 Bagel shops, full service
722213 Bagel shops, on premise baking and carryout service
311812 Bagels made in commercial bakeries
322223 Bags (except plastics only) made by laminating or coating combinations of purchased plastics, foil and paper
316991 Bags (i.e., luggage), all materials, manufacturing
313249 Bags and bagging fabric made in warp knitting mills
313241 Bags and bagging fabrics made in weft knitting mills
316991 Bags, athletic, manufacturing
322223 Bags, coated paper, made from purchased paper
322223 Bags, foil, made from purchased foil
339920 Bags, golf, manufacturing

313111 Bags, hemp, made from purchased fiber
322224 Bags, multiwall, made from purchased uncoated paper
424130 Bags, paper and disposable plastics, merchant wholesalers
322224 Bags, paper, uncoated, made from purchased paper
326111 Bags, plastics film, single wall or multiwall, manufacturing
314911 Bags, plastics, made from purchased woven plastics
339920 Bags, punching, manufacturing
314911 Bags, rubberized fabric, manufacturing
314999 Bags, sleeping, manufacturing
314911 Bags, textile, made from purchased woven or knitted materials
424990 Bags, textile, merchant wholesalers
322224 Bags, uncoated paper, made from purchased paper
812990 Bail bonding services
339920 Bait, artificial, fishing, manufacturing
423910 Bait, artificial, merchant wholesalers
424990 Bait, live, merchant wholesalers
112511 Baitfish production, farm raising
311422 Baked beans canning
311813 Baked goods (except bread, bread-type rolls), frozen, manufacturing
445210 Baked ham stores
311811 Bakeries with baking from flour on the premises, retailing not for immediate consumption
315211 Bakers' service apparel, washable, men's and boys', cut and sew apparel contractors
315225 Bakers' service apparel, washable, men's and boys', cut and sewn from purchased fabric (except apparel contractors)
315212 Bakers' service apparel, washable, women's, cut and sew apparel contractors
315239 Bakers' service apparel, washable, women's, misses', and girls, cut and sewn from purchased fabric (except apparel contractors)
333294 Bakery machinery and equipment manufacturing
423830 Bakery machinery and equipment merchant wholesalers
333294 Bakery ovens manufacturing
424490 Bakery products (except frozen) merchant wholesalers
311821 Bakery products, dry (e.g., biscuits, cookies, crackers), manufacturing
311812 Bakery products, fresh (i.e., bread, cakes, doughnuts, pastries), made in commercial bakeries
424420 Bakery products, frozen, merchant wholesalers
445291 Bakery stores, retailing only (except immediate consumption)
311320 Baking chocolate made from cacao beans
311330 Baking chocolate made from purchased chocolate
311999 Baking powder manufacturing
333997 Balances (except laboratory-type) manufacturing
423440 Balances and scales (except laboratory) merchant wholesalers
423490 Balances and scales, laboratory, merchant wholesalers
339111 Balances and scales, laboratory-type, manufacturing
333319 Balancing equipment, motor vehicle, manufacturing
332323 Balcony railings, metal, manufacturing
238190 Balcony, metal, installation
238120 Balcony, precast concrete, installation
333111 Bale throwers manufacturing
332618 Bale ties made from purchased wire

333111 Balers, farm-type (e.g., cotton, hay, straw), manufacturing
333999 Baling machinery (e.g., paper, scrap metal) manufacturing
332991 Ball bearings manufacturing
212324 Ball clay mining and/or beneficiating
333613 Ball joints (except aircraft, motor vehicle) manufacturing
339941 Ball point pens manufacturing
332911 Ball valves, industrial-type, manufacturing
335311 Ballasts (i.e., transformers) manufacturing
711120 Ballet companies
711510 Ballet dancers, independent
711120 Ballet productions, live theatrical
611610 Ballet schools (except academic)
316219 Ballet slippers manufacturing
453220 Balloon shops
812990 Balloon-o-gram services
326199 Balloons, plastics, manufacturing
326299 Balloons, rubber, manufacturing
713990 Ballrooms
339920 Balls, baseball, basketball, football, golf, tennis, pool, and bowling, manufacturing
339932 Balls, rubber (except athletic equipment), manufacturing
331111 Balls, steel, made in iron and steel mills
113210 Balsam needles gathering
111339 Banana farming
115114 Banana ripening
315299 Band uniforms cut and sewn from purchased fabric (except apparel contractors)
315211 Band uniforms, men's and boys', cut and sew apparel contractors
315212 Band uniforms, women's, girls', and infants', cut and sew apparel contractors
339113 Bandages and dressings, surgical and orthopedic, manufacturing
424210 Bandages merchant wholesalers
315212 Bandeaux, women's and girls', cut and sew apparel contractors
315231 Bandeaux, women's, misses', and girls', cut and sewn from purchased fabric (except apparel contractors)
711130 Bands
711130 Bands, dance
711130 Bands, musical
333210 Bandsaws, woodworking-type, manufacturing
339992 Banjos and parts manufacturing
334511 Bank and turn indicators and components (aeronautical instruments) manufacturing
236220 Bank building construction
531120 Bank building rental or leasing
332999 Bank chests, metal, manufacturing
522320 Bank clearinghouse associations
524128 Bank deposit insurance carriers, direct
332323 Bank fixtures, ornamental metal, manufacturing
551111 Bank holding companies (except managing)
523991 Bank trust offices
813910 Bankers' associations
926150 Banking regulatory agencies
611519 Banking schools (training in banking)
521110 Banking, central
523110 Banking, investment
525920 Bankruptcy estates
522110 Banks, commercial
522210 Banks, credit card
521110 Banks, Federal Reserve
522190 Banks, industrial (i.e., known as), depository
522298 Banks, industrial (i.e., known as), nondepository
522190 Banks, private (i.e., unincorporated)
522120 Banks, savings
522293 Banks, trade (i.e., international trade financing)
314999 Banners made from purchased fabrics

332323 Bannisters, metal, manufacturing
531120 Banquet hall rental or leasing
722320 Banquet halls with catering staff
327991 Baptismal fonts, cut stone, manufacturing
813920 Bar associations
561499 Bar code imprinting services
331316 Bar made by extruding purchased aluminum
331319 Bar made by rolling purchased aluminum
333516 Bar mill machinery, metalworking, manufacturing
325611 Bar soaps manufacturing
331316 Bar, aluminum, made in integrated secondary smelting and extruding mills
331319 Bar, aluminum, made in integrated secondary smelting and rolling mills
331421 Bar, copper and copper alloy, made from purchased copper or in integrated secondary smelting and rolling, drawing or extruding plants
331491 Bar, nonferrous metals (except aluminum, copper), made from purchased metals in wire drawing plants or in integrated secondary smelting and rolling, drawing, or extruding plants
311421 Barbecue sauce manufacturing
335221 Barbecues, grills, and braziers manufacturing
331222 Barbed and twisted wire made in wire drawing plants
332618 Barbed wire made from purchased wire
611511 Barber colleges
236220 Barber shop construction
423850 Barber shop equipment and supplies merchant wholesalers
812111 Barber shops
332211 Barber's scissors, manufacturing
315211 Barbers' service apparel, washable, men's and boys', cut and sew apparel contractors
315225 Barbers' service apparel, washable, men's and boys', cut and sewn from purchased fabric (except apparel contractors)
325412 Barbiturate preparations manufacturing
325411 Barbiturates, uncompounded, manufacturing
325411 Barbituric acid manufacturing
336611 Barge building
532411 Barge rental or leasing
332312 Barge sections, prefabricated metal, manufacturing
483211 Barge transportation, canal (freight)
483113 Barge transportation, coastal or Great Lakes (including St. Lawrence Seaway)
212393 Barite mining and/or beneficiating
327992 Barite processing beyond beneficiation
325188 Barium compounds, not specified elsewhere by process, manufacturing
325188 Barium hydroxide manufacturing
325412 Barium in-vivo diagnostic substances manufacturing
212393 Barium ores mining and/or beneficiating
327992 Barium processing beyond beneficiation
113210 Bark gathering
111199 Barley farming, field and seed production
311119 Barley feed, chopped, crushed or ground, manufacturing
311211 Barley flour manufacturing
311213 Barley, malt, manufacturing
332323 Barn stanchions and standards manufacturing
334519 Barographs manufacturing
334519 Barometers manufacturing
332410 Barometric condensers manufacturing
236220 Barrack construction
321920 Barrel heading and staves manufacturing

332994 Barrels, gun (i.e., 30 mm. or less, 1.18 inch or less), manufacturing
332995 Barrels, gun (i.e., more than 30 mm., more than 1.18 inch), manufacturing
332439 Barrels, light gauge metal, manufacturing
423840 Barrels, new and reconditioned, merchant wholesalers
321920 Barrels, wood, coopered, manufacturing
332999 Barricades, metal, manufacturing
541110 Barristers' offices
541110 Barristers' private practices
722410 Bars (i.e., drinking places), alcoholic beverage
331411 Bars made in primary copper smelting and refining mills
332312 Bars, concrete reinforcing, manufacturing
331111 Bars, iron, made in iron and steel mills
423510 Bars, metal (except precious), merchant wholesalers
331221 Bars, steel, made in cold rolling mills made from purchased steel
331111 Bars, steel, made in iron and steel mills
611519 Bartending schools
561990 Bartering services
325131 Barytes based pigments manufacturing
212393 Barytes mining and/or beneficiating
212319 Basalt crushed and broken stone mining and/or beneficiating
212311 Basalt mining or quarrying
561210 Base facilities operation support services
315211 Baseball caps (except plastics), men's and boys', cut and sew apparel contractors
315212 Baseball caps (except plastics), women's, girls', and infants', cut and sew apparel contractors
315991 Baseball caps cut and sewn from purchased fabric (except apparel contractors)
711211 Baseball clubs, professional or semiprofessional
713990 Baseball clubs, recreational
339920 Baseball equipment and supplies (except footwear, uniforms) manufacturing
423910 Baseball equipment and supplies merchant wholesalers
611620 Baseball instruction, camps, or schools
711211 Baseball teams, professional or semiprofessional
315299 Baseball uniforms cut and sewn from purchased fabric (except apparel contractors)
315211 Baseball uniforms, men's and boys', cut and sew apparel contractors
315212 Baseball uniforms, women's and girls', cut and sew apparel contractors
423730 Baseboard heaters, electric, non-portable, merchant wholesalers
333414 Baseboard heating equipment manufacturing
321918 Baseboards, floor, wood, manufacturing
332321 Baseboards, metal, manufacturing
711211 Basketball clubs, professional or semiprofessional
713990 Basketball clubs, recreational
339920 Basketball equipment and supplies (except footwear, uniforms) manufacturing
611620 Basketball instruction, camps, or schools
711211 Basketball teams, professional or semiprofessional
315299 Basketball uniforms cut and sewn from purchased fabric (except apparel contractors)
315211 Basketball uniforms, men's and boys', cut and sew apparel contractors

315212 Basketball uniforms, women's and girls', cut and sew apparel contractors
424990 Baskets merchant wholesalers
331222 Baskets, iron or steel, made in wire drawing plants
332618 Baskets, metal, made from purchased wire
321920 Baskets, wood (e.g., round stave, veneer), manufacturing
337125 Bassinets, reed and rattan, manufacturing
339992 Bassoons manufacturing
212299 Bastnaesite mining and/or beneficiating
335211 Bath fans with integral lighting fixture, residential, manufacturing
335211 Bath fans, residential, manufacturing
314110 Bath mats and bath sets made in carpet mills
326299 Bath mats, rubber, manufacturing
325620 Bath salts manufacturing
442299 Bath shops
238390 Bath tub refinishing on site
713990 Bathing beaches
315999 Bathing caps, rubber, manufacturing
315191 Bathing suits made in apparel knitting mills
315291 Bathing suits, infants', cut and sewn from purchased fabric (except apparel contractors)
315211 Bathing suits, men's and boys', cut and sew apparel contractors
315228 Bathing suits, men's and boys', cut and sewn from purchased fabric (except apparel contractors)
315212 Bathing suits, women's, girls', and infants', cut and sew apparel contractors
315239 Bathing suits, women's, misses', and girls', cut and sewn from purchased fabric (except apparel contractors)
315192 Bathrobes made in apparel knitting mills
315291 Bathrobes, infants', cut and sewn from purchased fabric (except apparel contractors)
315211 Bathrobes, men's and boys', cut and sew apparel contractors
315221 Bathrobes, men's and boys', cut and sewn from purchased fabric (except apparel contractors)
315212 Bathrobes, women's, girls', and infants', cut and sew apparel contractors
315231 Bathrobes, women's, misses', and girls', cut and sewn from purchased fabric (except apparel contractors)
423220 Bathroom accessories merchant wholesalers
327111 Bathroom accessories, vitreous china and earthenware, manufacturing
326199 Bathroom and toilet accessories, plastics, manufacturing
332998 Bathroom fixtures, metal, manufacturing
238220 Bathroom plumbing fixture and sanitary ware installation
333997 Bathroom scales manufacturing
337110 Bathroom vanities (except freestanding), stock or custom wood, manufacturing
812199 Baths, steam or turkish
332998 Bathtubs, metal, manufacturing
326191 Bathtubs, plastics, manufacturing
611620 Baton instruction
624221 Battered women's shelters
423610 Batteries (except automotive) merchant wholesalers
423120 Batteries, automotive, merchant wholesalers
335912 Batteries, primary, dry or wet, manufacturing
335911 Batteries, rechargeable, manufacturing
335911 Batteries, storage, manufacturing

311822 Batters, prepared, made from purchased flour
311211 Batters, prepared, made in flour mills
335999 Battery chargers, solid-state, manufacturing
334515 Battery testers, electrical, manufacturing
712120 Battlefields
314999 Batts and batting (except nonwoven fabrics) manufacturing
327125 Bauxite brick manufacturing
212299 Bauxite mining and/or beneficiating
325998 Bay oil manufacturing
454390 Bazaars (i.e., temporary stands)
332994 BB guns manufacturing
332992 BB shot manufacturing
532292 Beach chair rental
713990 Beach clubs, recreational
562998 Beach maintenance and cleaning services
316211 Beach sandals, plastics or plastics soled fabric upper, manufacturing
316211 Beach sandals, rubber or ruber soled fabric upper, manufacturing
532292 Beach umbrella rental
339999 Beach umbrellas manufacturing
713990 Beaches, bathing
315191 Beachwear made in apparel knitting mills
315291 Beachwear, infants', cut and sewn from purchased fabric (except apparel contractors)
315211 Beachwear, men's and boys', cut and sew apparel contractors
315228 Beachwear, men's and boys', cut and sewn from purchased fabric (except apparel contractors)
315212 Beachwear, women's, girls', and infants', cut and sew apparel contractors
315239 Beachwear, women's, misses', and girls', cut and sewn from purchased fabric (except apparel contractors)
333513 Beader machines, metalworking, manufacturing
314999 Beading on textile products (except apparel) for the trade
333292 Beaming machinery for yarn manufacturing
313112 Beaming yarn
321113 Beams, wood, made from logs or bolts
111219 Bean (except dry) farming, field and seed production
115114 Bean cleaning
111130 Bean farming, dry, field and seed production
111419 Bean sprout farming, grown under cover
311422 Beans, baked, canning
424510 Beans, dry, merchant wholesalers
332212 Bearing pullers, handtools, manufacturing
336312 Bearings (e.g., camshaft, crankshaft, connecting rod), automotive and truck gasoline engine, manufacturing
423840 Bearings merchant wholesalers
332991 Bearings, ball and roller, manufacturing
333613 Bearings, plain (except internal combustion engine), manufacturing
812112 Beautician services
611511 Beauty schools
812112 Beauty and barber shops, combined
711310 Beauty pageant managers with facilities
711320 Beauty pageant managers without facilities
711310 Beauty pageant organizers with facilities
711320 Beauty pageant organizers without facilities
711310 Beauty pageant promoters with facilities

711320 Beauty pageant promoters without facilities
423850 Beauty parlor equipment and supplies merchant wholesalers
812112 Beauty parlors
424210 Beauty preparations merchant wholesalers
236220 Beauty salon construction
812112 Beauty salons
812112 Beauty shops
424210 Beauty supplies merchant wholesalers
446120 Beauty supply stores
721191 Bed and breakfast inns
337122 Bed frames, wood household-type, manufacturing
812331 Bed linen supply services
442110 Bed stores, retail
335211 Bedcoverings, electric, manufacturing
111422 Bedding plant growing (except vegetable and melon bedding plants)
315212 Bedjackets, women's, girls' and infants', cut and sew apparel contractors
315231 Bedjackets, women's, misses', juniors', and girls', cut and sewn from purchased fabric (except apparel contractors)
337122 Bedroom furniture (except upholstered), wood household-type, manufacturing
337122 Beds (except hospital), wood household-type, manufacturing
337124 Beds (including cabinet and folding), metal household-type (except hospital), manufacturing
339111 Beds, hospital, manufacturing
423450 Beds, hospital, merchant wholesalers
337910 Beds, sleep-system ensembles (i.e., flotation, adjustable), manufacturing
337122 Beds, wood dormitory-type, manufacturing
337122 Beds, wood hotel-type, manufacturing
314129 Bedspreads and bed sets made from purchased fabrics
313249 Bedspreads and bed sets made in lace mills
313249 Bedspreads and bed sets made in warp knitting mills
313241 Bedspreads and bed sets made in weft knitting mills
112910 Bee production (i.e., apiculture)
311611 Beef carcasses, half carcasses, primal and sub-primal cuts, produced in slaughtering plants
112112 Beef cattle feedlots (except stockyards for transportation)
112111 Beef cattle ranching or farming
311611 Beef produced in slaughtering plants
311612 Beef stew made from purchased carcasses
311612 Beef, primal and sub-primal cuts, made from purchased carcasses
424910 Beekeeping supplies merchant wholesalers
517211 Beeper (i.e., radio pager) communication carriers
327213 Beer bottles, glass, manufacturing
312120 Beer brewing
332431 Beer cans, light gauge metal, manufacturing
333415 Beer cooling and dispensing equipment manufacturing
332439 Beer kegs, light gauge metal, manufacturing
424810 Beer merchant wholesalers
445310 Beer stores, packaged
325612 Beeswax polishes and waxes manufacturing
112910 Beeswax production
111219 Beet farming (except sugar beets), field, bedding plant and seed production
311313 Beet pulp, dried, manufacturing
311313 Beet sugar refining
541720 Behavioral research and development services
325412 Belladonna preparations manufacturing

332999 Bellows, hand, manufacturing
333999 Bellows, industrial type, manufacturing
339992 Bells (musical instruments) manufacturing
335999 Bells, electric, manufacturing
424310 Belt and buckle assembly kits merchant wholesalers
333922 Belt conveyor systems manufacturing
316999 Belt laces, leather, manufacturing
316110 Belting butts, curried or rough, manufacturing
313221 Belting fabrics, narrow woven
316999 Belting for machinery, leather, manufacturing
316110 Belting leather, manufacturing
314999 Belting made from purchased fabrics
423840 Belting, industrial, merchant wholesalers
326220 Belting, rubber (e.g., conveyor, elevator, transmission), manufacturing
482112 Beltline railroads
315999 Belts, apparel (e.g., fabric, leather, vinyl), cut and sewn from purchased fabric (except apparel contractors)
315211 Belts, apparel (e.g., fabric, leather, vinyl), men's and boys', cut and sew apparel contractors
315212 Belts, apparel (e.g., fabric, leather, vinyl), women's, girls', and infants', cut and sew apparel contractors
332618 Belts, conveyor, made from purchased wire
332618 Belts, drying, made from purchased wire
316999 Belts, leather safety, manufacturing
332994 Belts, machine gun (i.e., 30 mm. or less, 1.18 inch or less), manufacturing
332995 Belts, machine gun (i.e., more than 30 mm., more than 1.18 inch), manufacturing
315999 Belts, money, any material, cut and sewn from purchased fabric (except apparel contractors)
315211 Belts, money, any material, men's and boys', cut and sew apparel contractors
315212 Belts, money, any material, women's and girls', cut and sew apparel contractors
339111 Benches, laboratory-type, manufacturing
337127 Benches, park-type (except concrete, stone), manufacturing
337127 Benches, public building-type, manufacturing
337127 Benches, work, manufacturing
333513 Bending and forming machines, metalworking, manufacturing
332996 Bends, pipe, made from purchased metal pipe
541612 Benefit consulting services
111998 Bentgrass seed farming
212325 Bentonite mining and/or beneficiating
321999 Bentwood (steam bent) products (except furniture) manufacturing
325192 Benzaldehyde manufacturing
325320 Benzene hexachloride (BHC) insecticides manufacturing
325110 Benzene made from refined petroleum or liquid hydrocarbons
324110 Benzene made in petroleum refineries
325192 Benzoic acid manufacturing
311421 Berries, canned, manufacturing
424480 Berries, fresh, merchant wholesalers
115113 Berries, machine harvesting
111334 Berry (except strawberry) farming
321920 Berry crates, wood, wirebound, manufacturing
321920 Berry cups, veneer and splint, manufacturing
333111 Berry harvesting machines manufacturing

212299 Beryl mining and/or beneficiating
327113 Beryllia porcelain insulators manufacturing
331528 Beryllium castings (except die-castings), unfinished manufacturing
212299 Beryllium concentrates beneficiating
331522 Beryllium die-castings, unfinished, manufacturing
212299 Beryllium ores mining and/or beneficiating
325188 Beryllium oxide manufacturing
331419 Beryllium refining, primary
334517 Beta-ray irradiation equipment manufacturing
335999 Betatrons manufacturing
813910 Better business bureaus
722213 Beverage (e.g., coffee, juice, soft drink) bars, nonalcoholic, fixed location
311930 Beverage bases manufacturing
424490 Beverage bases merchant wholesalers
423830 Beverage bottling machinery merchant wholesalers
424490 Beverage concentrates merchant wholesalers
327213 Beverage containers, glass, manufacturing
423740 Beverage coolers, mechanical, merchant wholesalers
311930 Beverage flavorings (except coffee based) manufacturing
722330 Beverage stands, nonalcoholic, mobile
311930 Beverage syrups (except coffee based) manufacturing
424810 Beverages, alcoholic (except distilled spirits, wine), merchant wholesalers
312120 Beverages, beer, ale, and malt liquors, manufacturing
311514 Beverages, dietary, dairy and nondairy based
312111 Beverages, fruit and vegetable drinks, cocktails, and ades, manufacturing
311421 Beverages, fruit and vegetable juice, manufacturing
312140 Beverages, liquors (except brandies), manufacturing
311511 Beverages, milk based (except dietary), manufacturing
312112 Beverages, naturally carbonated bottled water, manufacturing
312111 Beverages, soft drink (including artificially carbonated waters), manufacturing
424820 Beverages, wine and distilled spirits, merchant wholesalers
312130 Beverages, wines and brandies, manufacturing
314999 Bias bindings made from purchased fabrics
313221 Bias bindings, woven, manufacturing
611699 Bible schools (except degree granting)
813110 Bible societies
315999 Bibs and aprons, waterproof (e.g., plastics, rubber, similar materials), cut and sewn from purchased fabric (except apparel contractors)
315211 Bibs and aprons, waterproof (e.g., plastics, rubber, similar materials), men's and boys', cut and sew apparel contractors
315999 Bibs and aprons, waterproof (e.g., plastics, rubber, similar materials), rubberizing fabric and manufacturing bibs and aprons
315212 Bibs and aprons, waterproof (e.g., plastics, rubber, similar materials), women's, girls', and infants', cut and sew apparel contractors
315212 Bibs, waterproof, cut and sew apparel contractors
451110 Bicycle (except motorized) shops
453310 Bicycle (except motorized) shops, used
492210 Bicycle courier
333912 Bicycle pumps manufacturing

532292 Bicycle rental
811490 Bicycle repair and maintenance shops without retailing new bicycles
441221 Bicycle shops, motorized
423110 Bicycle, motorized, merchant wholesalers
423910 Bicycles (except motorized) merchant wholesalers
336991 Bicycles and parts manufacturing
327111 Bidets, vitreous china, manufacturing
561440 Bill collection services
541850 Billboard display advertising services
238990 Billboard erection
339950 Billboards manufacturing
333516 Billet mill machinery, metalworking, manufacturing
331111 Billets, steel, made in iron and steel mills
316993 Billfolds, all materials, manufacturing
339920 Billiard equipment and supplies manufacturing
423910 Billiard equipment and supplies merchant wholesalers
713990 Billiard parlors
713990 Billiard rooms
541219 Billing services
322130 Binder's board manufacturing
424120 Binders, looseleaf, merchant wholesalers
333293 Bindery machinery manufacturing
314999 Binding carpets and rugs for the trade
333313 Binding equipment (i.e., plastics or tape binding), office-type, manufacturing
424310 Binding, textile, merchant wholesalers
314999 Bindings, bias, made from purchased fabrics
313221 Bindings, narrow woven, manufacturing
713290 Bingo halls
713290 Bingo parlors
316991 Binocular cases manufacturing
333314 Binoculars manufacturing
423460 Binoculars merchant wholesalers
332313 Bins, fabricated metal plate work, manufacturing
332439 Bins, light gauge metal, manufacturing
423390 Bins, storage, merchant wholesalers
621498 Biofeedback centers and clinics, outpatient
339113 Biohazard protective clothing and accessories manufacturing
541380 Biological (except medical, veterinary) testing laboratories or services
541690 Biological consulting services
621511 Biological laboratories, diagnostic
424210 Biologicals and allied products merchant wholesalers
541710 Biology research and development laboratories or services
334119 Biometrics system input device (e.g., retinal scan, iris pattern recognition, hand geometry) manufacturing
541710 Biotechnology research and development laboratories or services
311119 Bird feed, prepared, manufacturing
112990 Bird production (e.g., canaries, love birds, parakeets, parrots)
561710 Bird proofing services
712190 Bird sanctuaries
621410 Birth control clinics
326299 Birth control devices (i.e., diaphragms, prophylactics) manufacturing
325412 Birth control pills manufacturing
311812 Biscuits, bread-type, made in commercial bakeries
331419 Bismuth refining, primary
112990 Bison production
333515 Bits and knives for metalworking lathes, planers, and shapers manufacturing

333515 Bits, drill, metalworking, manufacturing
332212 Bits, edge tool, woodworking, manufacturing
333120 Bits, rock drill, construction and surface mining-type, manufacturing
333132 Bits, rock drill, oil and gas field-type, manufacturing
333131 Bits, rock drill, underground mining-type, manufacturing
212399 Bitumens, native, mining and/or beneficiating
212111 Bituminous coal and lignite surface mine site development for own account
212111 Bituminous coal cleaning plants
212111 Bituminous coal crushing
213113 Bituminous coal mining services (except site preparation and related construction contractor activities) on a contract basis
212111 Bituminous coal or lignite beneficiating (e.g., cleaning, crushing, screening, washing)
213113 Bituminous coal or lignite surface mine site development (except site preparation and related construction contractor activities) on a contract basis
212111 Bituminous coal screening plants
212111 Bituminous coal stripping (except on a contract, fee, or other basis)
213113 Bituminous coal stripping service on a contract basis
212111 Bituminous coal surface mining and/or beneficiating
212112 Bituminous coal underground mine site development for own account
212112 Bituminous coal underground mining or mining and beneficiating
212111 Bituminous coal washeries
212319 Bituminous limestone mining and/or beneficiating
213113 Bituminous or lignite auger mining service on a contract basis
212319 Bituminous sandstone mining and/or beneficiating
325131 Black pigments (except carbon black, bone black, lamp black) manufacturing
423510 Black plate merchant wholesalers
111334 Blackberry farming
423490 Blackboards merchant wholesalers
339942 Blackboards, framed, manufacturing
327991 Blackboards, unframed, slate, manufacturing
331111 Blackplate made in iron and steel mills
316999 Blacksmith's aprons, leather, manufacturing
311312 Blackstrap invert made from purchased raw cane sugar
311311 Blackstrap molasses made in sugarcane mill
238990 Blacktop work, residential and commercial driveway and parking area
811310 Blade sharpening, commercial and industrial machinery and equipment
423710 Blades (e.g., knife, saw) merchant wholesalers
333120 Blades for graders, scrapers, bulldozers, and snowplows manufacturing
332211 Blades, knife and razor, manufacturing
424210 Blades, razor, merchant wholesalers
332213 Blades, saw, all types, manufacturing
325131 Blanc fixe (i.e., barium sulfate, precipitated) manufacturing
332992 Blank cartridges (i.e., 30 mm. or less, 1.18 inch or less) manufacturing
423690 Blank diskette merchant wholesalers

334613 Blank tapes, audio and video, manufacturing
423690 Blank tapes, audio and video, merchant wholesalers
323118 Blankbooks and refills manufacturing
424120 Blankbooks merchant wholesalers
314911 Blanket bags manufacturing
314129 Blankets (except electric) made from purchased fabrics or felts
423220 Blankets (except electric) merchant wholesalers
313210 Blankets and bedspreads made in broadwoven fabric mills
335211 Blankets, electric, manufacturing
423620 Blankets, electric, merchant wholesalers
313230 Blankets, nonwoven fabric, manufacturing
327212 Blanks for electric light bulbs, glass, made in glass making plants
333515 Blanks, cutting tool, manufacturing
327215 Blanks, ophthalmic lens and optical glass, made from purchased glass
327212 Blanks, ophthalmic lens and optical glass, made in glass making plants
321912 Blanks, wood (e.g., bowling pins, handles, textile machinery accessories), manufacturing
311411 Blast freezing on a contract basis
236210 Blast furnace construction
327992 Blast furnace slag processing
331111 Blast furnaces
238910 Blast hole drilling (except mining)
212322 Blast sand quarrying and/or beneficiating
325920 Blasting accessories (e.g., caps, fuses, ignitors, squibbs) manufacturing
325920 Blasting powders manufacturing
213113 Blasting services, coal mining, on a contract basis
213114 Blasting services, metal mining, on a contract basis
213115 Blasting services, nonmetallic minerals mining (except fuels) on a contract basis
238910 Blasting, building demolition
238910 Blasting, construction site
238390 Bleacher installation
337127 Bleacher seating manufacturing
424690 Bleaches merchant wholesalers
325612 Bleaches, formulated for household use, manufacturing
325188 Bleaching agents, inorganic, manufacturing
325199 Bleaching agents, organic, manufacturing
313311 Bleaching broadwoven fabrics
212325 Bleaching clay mining and/or beneficiating
333292 Bleaching machinery for textiles manufacturing
313312 Bleaching textile products, apparel, and fabrics (except broadwoven)
212231 Blende (zinc) mining and/or beneficiating
311211 Blended flour made in flour mills
335211 Blenders, household-type electric, manufacturing
325620 Blending and compounding perfume bases
311119 Blending animal feed
312130 Blending brandy
312140 Blending distilled beverages (except brandy)
312130 Blending wines
336411 Blimps (i.e., aircraft) manufacturing
337920 Blinds (e.g., mini, venetian, vertical), all materials, manufacturing
423220 Blinds and shades, window, merchant wholesalers
331411 Blister copper manufacturing
561910 Blister packaging services
333923 Block and tackle manufacturing
312113 Block ice manufacturing

324121 Blocks, asphalt paving, made from purchased asphaltic materials
327331 Blocks, concrete and cinder, manufacturing
327124 Blocks, fire clay, manufacturing
327212 Blocks, glass, made in glass making plants
321999 Blocks, tackle, wood, manufacturing
321999 Blocks, tailors' pressing wood, manufacturing
621511 Blood analysis laboratories
334516 Blood bank process equipment manufacturing
621991 Blood banks
325413 Blood derivative in-vitro diagnostic substances manufacturing
325414 Blood derivatives manufacturing
424210 Blood derivatives merchant wholesalers
621991 Blood donor stations
325414 Blood fractions manufacturing
325413 Blood glucose test kits manufacturing
424210 Blood plasma merchant wholesalers
339112 Blood pressure apparatus manufacturing
621999 Blood pressure screening facilities
621999 Blood pressure screening services
812990 Blood pressure testing machine concession operators, coin-operated
339111 Blood testing apparatus, laboratory-type, manufacturing
339112 Blood transfusion equipment manufacturing
333516 Blooming and slabbing mill machinery, metalworking, manufacturing
331111 Blooms, steel, made in iron and steel mills
315191 Blouses made in apparel knitting mills
315291 Blouses, infants', manufacturing
315212 Blouses, women's, girls', and infants', cut and sew apparel contractors
315232 Blouses, women's, misses', and girls', cut and sewn from purchased fabric (except apparel contractors)
335211 Blow dryers, household-type electric, manufacturing
333220 Blow molding machinery for plastics manufacturing
332212 Blow torches manufacturing
238220 Blower and fan, cooling and dry heating, installation
333412 Blower filter units manufacturing
333111 Blowers, forage, manufacturing
423830 Blowers, industrial, merchant wholesalers
333112 Blowers, leaf, manufacturing
238310 Blown-in insulation (e.g., cellulose, vermiculite) installation
221210 Blue gas, carbureted, production and distribution
111334 Blueberry farming
114111 Bluefish fishing
111998 Bluegrass-Kentucky seed farming
541340 Blueprint drafting services
333315 Blueprint equipment manufacturing
423420 Blueprinting equipment merchant wholesalers
561439 Blueprinting services
212311 Bluestone mining or quarrying
325620 Blushes, face, manufacturing
921130 Board of Governors, Federal Reserve
321219 Board, bagasse, manufacturing
327420 Board, gypsum, manufacturing
321219 Board, particle, manufacturing
115210 Boarding horses
721310 Boarding houses
611110 Boarding schools, elementary or secondary
812910 Boarding services, pet
921120 Boards of supervisors, county and local
813910 Boards of trade

324122 Boards, asphalt saturated, made from purchased asphaltic materials
321999 Boards, bulletin, wood and cork, manufacturing
321999 Boards, wood (e.g., clip, ironing, meat, pastry), manufacturing
321113 Boards, wood, made from logs or bolts
321912 Boards, wood, resawing purchased lumber
336321 Boat and ship lighting fixtures manufacturing
441222 Boat dealers, new and used
541330 Boat engineering design services
484220 Boat hauling, truck, local
484230 Boat hauling, truck, long-distance
238990 Boat lift installation
333923 Boat lifts manufacturing
532411 Boat rental (except pleasure)
532411 Boat rental or leasing, commercial
532292 Boat rental, pleasure
332312 Boat sections, prefabricated metal, manufacturing
441222 Boat trailer dealers
336212 Boat transporter trailers, multi-unit, manufacturing
336214 Boat transporter trailers, single-unit, manufacturing
336612 Boat yards (i.e., boat manufacturing facilities)
487210 Boat, fishing charter, operation
811490 Boat, pleasure, repair and maintenance services without retailing new boats
713930 Boating clubs with marinas
713990 Boating clubs without marinas
423860 Boats (except pleasure) merchant wholesalers
336612 Boats (i.e., suitable or intended for personal use) manufacturing
326199 Boats, inflatable plastics, manufacturing
423910 Boats, pleasure (e.g., canoes, motorboats, sailboats), merchant wholesalers
321912 Bobbin blocks and blanks, wood, manufacturing
322214 Bobbins, fiber, made from purchased paperboard
333292 Bobbins, textile machinery, manufacturing
339920 Bobsleds manufacturing
812320 Bobtailers, laundry and drycleaning
713990 Boccie ball courts
423110 Bodies, motor vehicle, merchant wholesalers
713940 Body building studios, physical fitness
561612 Body guard services
811121 Body shops, automotive
315191 Body stockings made in apparel knitting mills
315212 Body stockings, women's, girls', and infants', cut and sew apparel contractors
315239 Body stockings, women's, misses', and girls', cut and sewn from purchased fabric (except apparel contractors)
332995 Bofors guns manufacturing
238290 Boiler and pipe insulation installation
332410 Boiler casings manufacturing
238220 Boiler chipping, cleaning and scaling
334513 Boiler controls, industrial, power, and marine-type, manufacturing
332919 Boiler couplings and drains, plumbing and heating-type, manufacturing
238290 Boiler covering installation
332911 Boiler gauge cocks, industrial-type, manufacturing
331210 Boiler tubes, wrought, made from purchased iron
238220 Boiler, heating, installation
423720 Boilers (e.g., heating, hot water, power, steam) merchant wholesalers
333414 Boilers, heating, manufacturing

332410 Boilers, power, manufacturing
311612 Bologna made from purchased carcasses
332722 Bolts, metal, manufacturing
326199 Bolts, nuts, and rivets, plastics, manufacturing
333924 Bomb lifts manufacturing
332993 Bomb loading and assembling plants
332993 Bombcluster adapters manufacturing
332993 Bombs manufacturing
523120 Bond brokerages
523110 Bond dealing (i.e., acting as a principal in dealing securities to investors)
322233 Bond paper made from purchased paper
322121 Bond paper made in paper mills
493190 Bonded warehousing (except farm products, general merchandise, refrigerated)
493130 Bonded warehousing, farm products (except refrigerated)
493110 Bonded warehousing, general merchandise
493120 Bonded warehousing, refrigerated
313230 Bonded-fiber fabrics manufacturing
332812 Bonderizing metal and metal products for the trade
524126 Bonding, fidelity or surety insurance, direct
812990 Bondsperson services
325182 Bone black manufacturing
327112 Bone china manufacturing
339112 Bone drills manufacturing
311119 Bone meal prepared as feed for animals and fowls
339999 Bone novelties manufacturing
339112 Bone plates and screws manufacturing
339112 Bone rongeurs manufacturing
311613 Bones, fat, rendering
511130 Book (e.g., hardback, paperback, tape) publishers (except exclusive Internet publishing)
323121 Book binding shops
323121 Book binding without printing
454113 Book clubs, not publishing, mail-order
813410 Book discussion clubs
332999 Book ends, metal, manufacturing
322222 Book paper made by coating purchased paper
322222 Book paper, coated, made from purchased paper
322121 Book paper, coated, made in paper mills
511130 Book publishers and printing combined
516110 Book publishers, exclusively on Internet
511130 Book publishers, university press (except exclusive Internet publishing)
451211 Book stores
453310 Book stores, used
316110 Bookbinder's leather manufacturing
333293 Bookbinding machines manufacturing
323121 Bookbinding without printing
337125 Bookcases (except wood and metal), household-type, manufacturing
337214 Bookcases (except wood), office-type, manufacturing
337124 Bookcases, metal household-type, manufacturing
337122 Bookcases, wood household-type, manufacturing
337211 Bookcases, wood office-type, manufacturing
713290 Bookies
512199 Booking agencies, motion picture
512199 Booking agencies, motion picture or video productions
711320 Booking agencies, theatrical (except motion picture)
541219 Bookkeepers' offices
541219 Bookkeepers' private practices
423420 Bookkeeping machines merchant wholesalers
541219 Bookkeeping services
713290 Bookmakers

519120 Bookmobiles
424920 Books merchant wholesalers
323117 Books printing and binding without publishing
323117 Books printing without publishing
424120 Books, sales or receipt, merchant wholesalers
323116 Books, sales, manifold, printing
339920 Boomerangs manufacturing
813410 Booster clubs
486990 Booster pumping station (except natural gas, petroleum)
486110 Booster pumping station, crude oil transportation
486210 Booster pumping station, natural gas transportation
486910 Booster pumping station, refined petroleum products transportation
332993 Boosters and bursters, artillery, manufacturing
335311 Boosters, feeder voltage (i.e., electrical transformers), manufacturing
423850 Boot and shoe cut stock and findings merchant wholesalers
316999 Boot and shoe cut stock and findings, leather, manufacturing
321999 Boot and shoe lasts, all materials, manufacturing
623990 Boot camps for delinquent youth
333298 Boot making and repairing machinery manufacturing
811430 Boot repair shops without retailing new boots
812990 Bootblack parlors
424340 Boots (e.g., hiking, western, work) merchant wholesalers
316219 Boots, dress and casual (except plastics, rubber), children's and infants', manufacturing
316213 Boots, dress and casual (except plastics, rubber), men's, manufacturing
316214 Boots, dress and casual (except plastics, rubber), women's, manufacturing
316219 Boots, hiking (except rubber, plastics), children's and infants', manufacturing
316213 Boots, hiking (except rubber, plastics), men's, manufacturing
316214 Boots, hiking (except rubber, plastics), women's, manufacturing
316211 Boots, plastics or plastics soled fabric upper, manufacturing
316211 Boots, rubber or rubber soled fabric upper, manufacturing
212391 Borate, natural, mining and/or beneficiating
325188 Borax (i.e., sodium borate) manufacturing
212391 Borax, crude, ground or pulverized, mining and/or beneficiating
325320 Bordeaux mixture insecticides manufacturing
325188 Boric acid manufacturing
333512 Boring machines, metalworking, manufacturing
213114 Boring test holes for metal mining on a contract basis
213115 Boring test holes for nonmetallic minerals mining (except fuels) on a contract basis
333512 Boring, drilling, and milling machine combinations, metalworking, manufacturing
238910 Boring, for building construction
212391 Boron compounds prepared at beneficiating plants
325188 Boron compounds, not specified elsewhere by process, manufacturing
212391 Boron mineral mining and/or beneficiating
325188 Borosilicate manufacturing
424210 Botanical drugs and herbs merchant wholesalers
325412 Botanical extract preparations (except in-vitro diagnostics) manufacturing
712130 Botanical gardens

325320 Botanical insecticides manufacturing
424210 Botanicals merchant wholesalers
541710 Botany research and development laboratories or services
326199 Bottle caps and lids, plastics, manufacturing
332115 Bottle caps and tops, metal, stamping
321999 Bottle corks manufacturing
321999 Bottle covers, willow, rattan, and reed, manufacturing
561990 Bottle exchanges
335211 Bottle warmers, household-type electric, manufacturing
333993 Bottle washers, packaging machinery, manufacturing
454312 Bottled gas dealers, direct selling
424490 Bottled water (except water treating) merchant wholesalers
454390 Bottled water providers, direct selling
423840 Bottles (except waste) merchant wholesalers
327213 Bottles (i.e., bottling, canning, packaging), glass, manufacturing
326160 Bottles, plastics, manufacturing
332439 Bottles, vacuum, light gauge metal, manufacturing
423930 Bottles, waste, merchant wholesalers
333993 Bottling machinery (e.g., capping, filling, labeling, sterilizing, washing) manufacturing
423830 Bottling machinery and equipment merchant wholesalers
335121 Boudoir lamp fixtures manufacturing
311422 Bouillon canning
311423 Bouillon made in dehydration plants
212319 Boulder crushed and broken mining and/or beneficiating
324199 Boulets (i.e., fuel bricks) made from refined petroleum
424590 Bovine semen merchant wholesalers
315211 Bow ties, men's and boys', cut and sew apparel contractors
315993 Bow ties, men's and boys', cut and sewn from purchased fabric (except apparel contractors)
238290 Bowling alley equipment installation
713950 Bowling alleys
337127 Bowling center furniture manufacturing
713950 Bowling centers
423910 Bowling equipment and supplies merchant wholesalers
451110 Bowling equipment and supply stores
611620 Bowling instruction
713990 Bowling leagues or teams, recreational
321912 Bowling pin blanks manufacturing
339920 Bowling pin machines, automatic, manufacturing
326199 Bowls and bowl covers, plastics, manufacturing
321999 Bowls, wood, turned and shaped, manufacturing
314999 Bows made from purchased fabrics
339920 Bows, archery, manufacturing
316999 Bows, shoe, leather, manufacturing
321920 Box cleats, wood, manufacturing
311991 Box lunches (for sale off premises) manufacturing
321920 Box shook manufacturing
337910 Box springs, assembled, made from purchased spring
316999 Box toes (i.e., shoe cut stock), leather, manufacturing
311612 Boxed beef made from purchased carcasses
311611 Boxed beef produced in slaughtering plants

311612 Boxed meat produced from purchased carcasses
311611 Boxed meats produced in slaughtering plants
711219 Boxers, independent professional
423840 Boxes and crates, industrial (except disposable plastics, paperboard, waste), merchant wholesalers
321920 Boxes, cigar, wood or part wood, manufacturing
322211 Boxes, corrugated and solid fiber, made from purchased paper or paperboard
335932 Boxes, electrical wiring (e.g., junction, outlet, switch), manufacturing
322212 Boxes, folding (except corrugated), made from purchased paperboard
316991 Boxes, hat (except paper or paperboard), manufacturing
321920 Boxes, jewelry, wood or part wood, manufacturing
316999 Boxes, leather, manufacturing
332439 Boxes, light gauge metal, manufacturing
424130 Boxes, paperboard and disposable plastics, merchant wholesalers
322215 Boxes, sanitary food (except folding), made from purchased paper or paperboard
322213 Boxes, setup (i.e., not shipped flat), made from purchased paperboard
322211 Boxes, shipping, laminated paper and paperboard, made from purchased paperboard
336211 Boxes, truck (e.g., cargo, dump, utility, van), assembled on purchased chassis
423930 Boxes, waste, merchant wholesalers
321920 Boxes, wood, manufacturing
321920 Boxes, wood, plain or fabric covered, nailed or lock corner, manufacturing
711211 Boxing clubs, professional or semiprofessional
713990 Boxing clubs, recreational
339920 Boxing equipment manufacturing
711310 Boxing event managers with facilities
711320 Boxing event managers without facilities
711310 Boxing event organizers with facilities
711320 Boxing event organizers without facilities
711310 Boxing event promoters with facilities
711320 Boxing event promoters without facilities
337215 Boxspring frames manufacturing
813410 Boy guiding organizations
623990 Boys' and girls' residential facilities (e.g., homes, ranches, villages)
721214 Boys' camps (except day, instructional)
611620 Boys' camps, sports instruction
611620 Boys' camps, sports instructor
713990 Boys' day camps (except instructional)
315119 Boys' socks manufacturing
111334 Boysenberry farming
339911 Bracelets, precious metal, manufacturing
115112 Bracing of orchard trees and vines
332510 Brackets (i.e., builder's hardware-type), metal, manufacturing
332618 Brackets made from purchased wire
321918 Brackets, wood, manufacturing
423710 Brads merchant wholesalers
331222 Brads, iron or steel, wire or cut, made in wire drawing plants
332618 Brads, metal, made from purchased wire
333292 Braiding machinery for textiles manufacturing
313221 Braiding narrow fabrics

336340 Brake and brake parts, automotive, truck, and bus, manufacturing
336340 Brake caliper assemblies, automotive, truck, and bus, manufacturing
336340 Brake cylinders, master and wheel, automotive, truck, and bus, manufacturing
336340 Brake discs (rotor), automotive, truck, and bus, manufacturing
336340 Brake drums, automotive, truck, and bus, manufacturing
325998 Brake fluid, synthetic, manufacturing
324191 Brake fluids, petroleum, made from refined petroleum
336340 Brake hose assemblies manufacturing
336340 Brake lining, automotive, truck, and bus, manufacturing
336340 Brake pads and shoes, automotive, truck, and bus, manufacturing
811118 Brake repair shops, automotive
333319 Brake service equipment (except mechanic's hand tools), motor vehicle, manufacturing
336340 Brake shoes and pads, asbestos, manufacturing
335314 Brakes and clutches, electromagnetic, manufacturing
336510 Brakes and parts for railroad rolling stock manufacturing
335314 Brakes, electromagnetic, manufacturing
333513 Brakes, press, metalworking, manufacturing
311212 Bran and other residues of milling rice
522110 Branches of foreign banks
521110 Branches, Federal Reserve Bank
533110 Brand name licensing
115210 Branding
339943 Branding irons (i.e., marking irons) manufacturing
424820 Brandy and brandy spirits merchant wholesalers
312130 Brandy distilling
315212 Bra-slips, women's and girls', cut and sew apparel contractors
315231 Bra-slips, women's, misses', and juniors', cut and sewn from purchased fabric (except apparel contractors)
331522 Brass die-castings, unfinished, manufacturing
331525 Brass foundries (except die-casting)
423720 Brass goods, plumbers', merchant wholesalers
325612 Brass polishes manufacturing
331421 Brass products, rolling, drawing, or extruding, made from purchased copper or in integrated secondary smelting and rolling, drawing or extruding plants
315212 Brassieres cut and sew apparel contractors
315231 Brassieres cut and sewn from purchased fabric (except apparel contractors)
332323 Brasswork, ornamental, manufacturing
335221 Braziers, barbecue, manufacturing
111335 Brazil nut farming
325191 Brazilwood extract manufacturing
332811 Brazing (i.e., hardening) metals and metal products for the trade
311822 Bread and bread-type roll mixes made from purchased flour
311812 Bread and bread-type rolls made in commercial bakeries
311999 Bread crumbs not made in bakeries
335211 Bread machines, household-type electric, manufacturing
333294 Bread slicing machinery manufacturing
333993 Bread wrapping machines manufacturing
212113 Breakers, anthracite mining and/ or beneficiating

333131 Breakers, coal, manufacturing
332919 Breakers, vacuum, plumbing, manufacturing
311340 Breakfast bars, nonchocolate covered, manufacturing
311230 Breakfast cereals manufacturing
424490 Breakfast cereals merchant wholesalers
237990 Breakwater construction
332313 Breechings, fabricated metal plate work, manufacturing
112990 Breeding of pets (e.g., birds, cats, dogs)
115210 Breeding, animal, services
312120 Breweries
311211 Brewers' and distillers' flakes and grits, corn, manufacturing
311213 Brewers' malt manufacturing
325191 Brewers' pitch made by distillation of wood
311212 Brewers' rice manufacturing
424490 Brewers' yeast merchant wholesalers
333294 Brewery machinery manufacturing
238990 Brick driveway contractors
238990 Brick paver (e.g., driveways, patios, sidewalks) installation
238140 Brick veneer, installation
238140 Bricklaying contractors
423320 Bricks (except refractory) merchant wholesalers
327121 Bricks (i.e., common, face, glazed, hollow, vitrified), clay, manufacturing
327123 Bricks, adobe, manufacturing
327124 Bricks, clay refractory, manufacturing
327331 Bricks, concrete, manufacturing
327215 Bricks, glass, made from purchased glass
327212 Bricks, glass, made in glass making plants
327125 Bricks, nonclay refractory, manufacturing
315233 Bridal dresses or gowns, custom made
315233 Bridal dresses or gowns, women's, misses', and girls', cut and sewn from purchased fabric (except apparel contractors)
315212 Bridal dresses or gowns, women's, misses', and juniors', apparel contractors
448190 Bridal gown shops (except custom)
532220 Bridal wear rental
333999 Bridge and gate lifting machinery manufacturing
611699 Bridge and other card game instruction
321114 Bridge and trestle parts, wood, treating
237310 Bridge approach construction
713990 Bridge clubs, recreational
237310 Bridge construction
237310 Bridge decking construction
238320 Bridge painting
332312 Bridge sections, prefabricated metal, manufacturing
488490 Bridge, tunnel, and highway operations
339116 Bridges, custom made in dental laboratories
334515 Bridges, electrical (e.g., Kelvin, megohm, vacuum tube, Wheatstone), manufacturing
316110 Bridle leather manufacturing
237990 Bridle path construction
316991 Briefcases, all materials, manufacturing
315291 Briefs, infants', cut and sewn from purchased fabric (except apparel contractors)
315192 Briefs, underwear, made in apparel knitting mills
315211 Briefs, underwear, men's and boys', cut and sew apparel contractors
315221 Briefs, underwear, men's and boys', cut and sewn from purchased fabric (except apparel contractors)
315231 Briefs, underwear, women's, misses', and girls', cut and sewn from purchased fabric (except apparel contractors)

315212 Briefs, women's, girls', and infants', cut and sew apparel contractors
212393 Brimstone mining and/or beneficiating
311421 Brining of fruits and vegetables
212210 Briquets, iron, mining and/or beneficiating
324199 Briquettes, petroleum, made from refined petroleum
424590 Bristles merchant wholesalers
322130 Bristols board stock manufacturing
322121 Bristols paper stock manufacturing
333515 Broaches (i.e., a machine tool accessory) manufacturing
333512 Broaching machines, metalworking, manufacturing
334220 Broadcast equipment (including studio), for radio and television, manufacturing
541910 Broadcast media rating services
423690 Broadcasting equipment merchant wholesalers
516110 Broadcasting exclusively on Internet, audio
516110 Broadcasting exclusively on Internet, video
515111 Broadcasting networks, radio
515120 Broadcasting networks, television
611519 Broadcasting schools
236220 Broadcasting station construction
515112 Broadcasting stations (except exclusively on Internet), radio
515120 Broadcasting stations, television
515112 Broadcasting studio, radio station
711110 Broadway theaters
313210 Broadwoven fabrics (except rugs, tire fabrics) weaving
313311 Broadwoven fabrics finishing
313210 Brocades weaving
111219 Broccoli farming, field, bedding plant and seed production
112320 Broiler chicken production
523140 Brokerages, commodity contracts
524210 Brokerages, insurance
522310 Brokerages, loan
522310 Brokerages, mortgage
531210 Brokerages, real estate
523120 Brokerages, securities
524210 Brokers' offices, insurance
522310 Brokers' offices, loan
522310 Brokers' offices, mortgage
531210 Brokers' offices, real estate
325188 Bromine manufacturing
325199 Bromochloromethane manufacturing
339112 Bronchoscopes (except electromedical) manufacturing
334510 Bronchoscopes, electromedical, manufacturing
331522 Bronze die-castings, unfinished, manufacturing
331525 Bronze foundries (except die-casting)
325910 Bronze printing inks manufacturing
331421 Bronze products, rolling, drawing, or extruding, made from purchased copper or in integrated secondary smelting and rolling, drawing or extruding plants
111199 Broomcorn farming
424590 Broomcorn merchant wholesalers
423220 Brooms and brushes, household-type, merchant wholesalers
339994 Brooms, hand and machine, manufacturing
311422 Broth (except seafood) canning
311313 Brown beet sugar refining
212111 Brown coal mining and/or beneficiating
212210 Brown ore mining and/or beneficiating
311313 Brown sugar made from beet sugar
311312 Brown sugar made from purchased raw cane sugar
311311 Brown sugar made in sugarcane mill
325411 Brucine manufacturing

212325 Brucite mining and/or beneficiating
335991 Brush blocks, carbon or molded graphite, manufacturing
321912 Brush blocks, wood, turned and shaped
562119 Brush collection services
562119 Brush hauling, local
562119 Brush removal services
335991 Brushes and brush stock contacts, electric, carbon and graphite, manufacturing
339942 Brushes, artists', manufacturing
339994 Brushes, household-type and industrial, manufacturing
339994 Brushes, paint (except artists'), manufacturing
326299 Brushes, rubber, manufacturing
333512 Brushing machines, metalworking, manufacturing
335991 Brushplates, carbon or graphite, manufacturing
111219 Brussel sprout farming, field, bedding plant and seed production
325620 Bubble bath preparations manufacturing
326199 Bubble packaging materials, plastics, manufacturing
333120 Bucket and scarifier teeth manufacturing
333922 Buckets, elevator or conveyor, manufacturing
333120 Buckets, excavating (e.g., clamshell, concrete, drag scraper, dragline, shovel), manufacturing
321920 Buckets, wood, coopered, manufacturing
339993 Buckles and buckle parts (including shoe) manufacturing
111199 Buckwheat farming
311211 Buckwheat flour manufacturing
921130 Budget agencies, government
112990 Buffalo production
722212 Buffet eating places
337122 Buffets (furniture), wood, manufacturing
333512 Buffing and polishing machines, metalworking, manufacturing
327910 Buffing and polishing wheels, abrasive and nonabrasive, manufacturing
325612 Buffing compounds manufacturing
333991 Buffing machines, handheld power-driven, manufacturing
332813 Buffing metals and metal products for the trade
316110 Buffings, russet, manufacturing
332510 Builder's hardware, metal, manufacturing
541310 Building architectural design services
238210 Building automation system installation contractors
423320 Building blocks (e.g., cinder, concrete) merchant wholesalers
423310 Building board (e.g., fiber, flake, particle) merchant wholesalers
561720 Building cleaning services, interior
561720 Building cleaning services, janitorial
238910 Building demolition
561790 Building exterior cleaning services (except sand blasting, window cleaning)
238390 Building fixture and fitting (except mechanical equipment) installation
238130 Building framing (except structural steel)
541350 Building inspection bureaus
541350 Building inspection services
926150 Building inspections, government
238310 Building insulation contractors
237210 Building lot subdividing
326199 Building materials (e.g., fascia, panels, siding, soffit), plastics, manufacturing
444190 Building materials supply dealers

423390 Building materials, fiberglass (except insulation, roofing, siding), merchant wholesalers
213112 Building oil and gas well foundations on a contract basis
326199 Building panels, corrugated and flat, plastics, manufacturing
423390 Building paper merchant wholesalers
322121 Building paper stock manufacturing
334512 Building services monitoring controls, automatic, manufacturing
925110 Building standards agencies, government
423320 Building stone merchant wholesalers
327121 Building tile, clay, manufacturing
531110 Building, apartment, rental or leasing
213112 Building, erecting, repairing, and dismantling oil and gas field rigs and derricks on a contract basis
531120 Building, nonresidential (except miniwarehouse), rental or leasing
236118 Building, residential, addition, alteration and renovation
531110 Building, residential, rental or leasing
321991 Buildings, mobile, commercial use, manufacturing
332311 Buildings, prefabricated metal, manufacturing
423390 Buildings, prefabricated nonwood, merchant wholesalers
423310 Buildings, prefabricated wood, merchant wholesalers
321992 Buildings, prefabricated, wood, manufacturing
238350 Built-in wood cabinets constructed on site
327999 Built-up mica manufacturing
335110 Bulbs, electric light, complete, manufacturing
311211 Bulgur (flour) manufacturing
424710 Bulk gasoline stations
484220 Bulk liquids trucking, local
484230 Bulk liquids trucking, long-distance
484110 Bulk mail truck transportation, contract, local
484121 Bulk mail truck transportation, contract, long-distance (TL)
493190 Bulk petroleum storage
424710 Bulk stations, petroleum
332420 Bulk storage tanks, heavy gauge metal, manufacturing
237990 Bulkhead wall construction
115210 Bull testing stations
532412 Bulldozer rental or leasing without operator
238910 Bulldozer rental with operator
333120 Bulldozers manufacturing
332992 Bullet jackets and cores (i.e., 30 mm. or less, 1.18 inch or less) manufacturing
321999 Bulletin boards, wood and cork, manufacturing
339113 Bulletproof vests manufacturing
212221 Bullion, gold, produced at the mine
212222 Bullion, silver, produced at the mine
336399 Bumpers and bumperettes assembled, automotive, truck, and bus, manufacturing
333313 Bundling machinery (e.g., box strapping, mail, newspaper) manufacturing
321999 Bungs, wood, manufacturing
236220 Bunkhouse construction
339111 Bunsen burners manufacturing
315212 Buntings, infants', cut and sew apparel contractors
315291 Buntings, infants', cut and sewn from purchased fabric (except apparel contractors)
334513 Buoyancy instruments, industrial process-type, manufacturing
321999 Buoys, cork, manufacturing
332313 Buoys, fabricated plate work metal, manufacturing

561621 Burglar alarm monitoring services
561621 Burglar alarm sales combined with installation, repair, or monitoring services
238210 Burglar alarm system, electric, installation only
334290 Burglar alarm systems and equipment manufacturing
524126 Burglary and theft insurance carriers, direct
339995 Burial caskets and cases manufacturing
423850 Burial caskets merchant wholesalers
315299 Burial garments cut and sewn from purchased fabric (except apparel contractors)
315211 Burial garments, men's and boys', cut and sew apparel contractors
315212 Burial garments, women's, girls' and infants', cut and sew apparel contractors
524128 Burial insurance carriers, direct
339995 Burial vaults (except concrete, stone) manufacturing
327390 Burial vaults, concrete and precast terrazzo, manufacturing
327991 Burial vaults, stone, manufacturing
424990 Burlap merchant wholesalers
711110 Burlesque companies
212325 Burley mining and/or beneficiating
313311 Burling and mending broadwoven fabrics
313312 Burling and mending fabrics (except broadwoven)
335311 Burner ignition transformers manufacturing
423720 Burners, fuel oil and distillate oil, merchant wholesalers
333414 Burners, heating, manufacturing
332811 Burning metals and metal products for the trade
333512 Burnishing machines, metalworking, manufacturing
321999 Burnt wood articles manufacturing
314999 Burnt-out laces manufacturing
112920 Burro production
212399 Burrstones, natural, mining and/or beneficiating
335313 Bus bar structures, switchgear-type, manufacturing
335931 Bus bars, electrical conductors (except switchgear-type), manufacturing
336211 Bus bodies assembling on purchased chassis
336211 Bus bodies manufacturing
541850 Bus card advertising services
485510 Bus charter services (except scenic, sightseeing)
541850 Bus display advertising services
611519 Bus driver training
485210 Bus line operation, intercity
485113 Bus line, local (except mixed mode)
423110 Bus merchant wholesalers
485410 Bus operation, school and employee
532120 Bus rental or leasing
485113 Bus services, urban and suburban (except mixed mode)
236220 Bus shelter construction
236220 Bus terminal construction
488490 Bus terminal operation, independent
561599 Bus ticket offices
485113 Bus transit systems (except mixed mode)
336120 Buses (except trackless trolley) assembling on chassis of own manufacture
487110 Buses, scenic and sightseeing operation
336510 Buses, trackless trolley, manufacturing
333613 Bushings, plain (except internal combustion engine), manufacturing
326199 Bushings, plastics, manufacturing
321999 Bushings, wood, manufacturing
813910 Business associations

541990 Business brokers (except real estate brokers)
611410 Business colleges or schools not offering academic degrees
611310 Business colleges or schools offering baccalaureate or graduate degrees
323112 Business directories flexographic printing without publishing
323111 Business directories gravure printing without publishing
323110 Business directories lithographic (offset) printing without publishing
323119 Business directories printing (except flexographic, gravure, lithographic, quick, screen) without publishing
323113 Business directories screen printing without publishing
511140 Business directory publishers (except exclusive Internet publishing)
511140 Business directory publishers and printing combined
516110 Business directory publishers, exclusively on Internet
323112 Business forms (except manifold) flexographic printing without publishing
323111 Business forms (except manifold) gravure printing without publishing
323110 Business forms (except manifold) lithographic printing
323119 Business forms (except manifold) printing (except flexographic, gravure, lithographic, quick, screen) without publishing
323113 Business forms (except manifold) screen printing without publishing
323116 Business forms, manifold, printing
423420 Business machines and equipment (except computers) merchant wholesalers
541611 Business management consulting services
561110 Business management services
541720 Business research and development services
611410 Business schools not offering academic degrees
561439 Business service centers (except private mail centers)
561439 Business service centers (except private mail centers) providing range of office support services (except printing)
541611 Business start-up consulting services
425110 Business to business electronic markets, durable goods, wholesale trade
425110 Business to business electronic markets, nondurable goods, wholesale trade
454111 Business to Consumer retail sales Internet sites
325211 Butadiene copolymers containing less than 50 percent butadiene manufacturing
325212 Butadiene copolymers containing more than 50 percent butadiene manufacturing
325199 Butadiene made from alcohol
325110 Butadiene made from refined petroleum or liquid hydrocarbons
325212 Butadiene rubber (i.e., polybutadiene) manufacturing
325110 Butane made from refined petroleum or liquid hydrocarbons
211112 Butane, natural, mining
445210 Butcher shops
332211 Butcher's knives manufacturing
311512 Butter manufacturing
424430 Butter merchant wholesalers
333294 Butter processing machinery manufacturing
311512 Butter, creamery and whey, manufacturing

332911 Butterfly valves, industrial-type, manufacturing
311511 Buttermilk manufacturing
111219 Butternut squash farming, field, bedding plant and seed production
335912 Button cells, primary batteries, manufacturing
333298 Buttonhole and eyelet machinery manufacturing
315211 Buttonhole making apparel contractors, men's and boys'
315212 Buttonhole making apparel contractors, women's, misses', girls', and infants' (except fur)
315212 Buttonhole making, fur goods, women's, girls', and infants', cut and sew apparel contractors
315211 Buttonholing and button covering apparel contractors, men's and boys'
315212 Buttonholing and button covering apparel contractors, women's, misses', and girls'
339993 Buttons (except precious metal, precious stones, semiprecious stones) manufacturing
339911 Buttons, precious metal, precious stones, semiprecious stones, manufacturing
325199 Butyl acetate manufacturing
325212 Butyl rubber manufacturing
324110 Butylene (i.e., butene) made in petroleum refineries
325110 Butylene made from refined petroleum or liquid hydrocarbons
531210 Buyers' agents, real estate, offices
531210 Buying agencies, real estate
531210 Buying real estate for others (i.e., agents, brokers)
485310 Cab (i.e., taxi) services
336112 Cab and chassis, light trucks and vans, manufacturing
111219 Cabbage farming, field, bedding plant and seed production
236115 Cabin construction general contractors
336612 Cabin cruiser
334511 Cabin environment indicators, transmitters, and sensors manufacturing
236117 Cabin operative builders
332510 Cabinet hardware, metal, manufacturing
444190 Cabinet stores, kitchen (except custom), to be installed
238350 Cabinet work performed at the construction site
238350 Cabinetry work performed at the construction site
337214 Cabinets (except wood), office-type, freestanding, manufacturing
337129 Cabinets (i.e., housings), wood (e.g., sewing machines, stereo, television), manufacturing
337110 Cabinets, kitchen (except freestanding), stock or custom wood, manufacturing
423310 Cabinets, kitchen, built in, merchant wholesalers
423210 Cabinets, kitchen, free standing, merchant wholesalers
337124 Cabinets, metal (i.e., bathroom, kitchen) (except freestanding), manufacturing
337124 Cabinets, metal household-type, freestanding, manufacturing
337124 Cabinets, metal, radio and television, manufacturing
238350 Cabinets, wood built-in, constructed on site
337122 Cabinets, wood household-type, freestanding, manufacturing
337211 Cabinets, wood office-type, freestanding, manufacturing
721199 Cabins, housekeeping
515210 Cable broadcasting networks
485119 Cable car systems (except mixed mode), commuter
487110 Cable car, land, scenic and sightseeing operation
334220 Cable decoders manufacturing
237130 Cable laying (e.g., cable television, electricity, marine, telephone), including underground

517510 Cable program distribution operators
238990 Cable splicing (except electrical or fiber optic)
238210 Cable splicing, electrical or fiber optic
238210 Cable television hookup contractors
515210 Cable television networks
334220 Cable television transmission and receiving equipment manufacturing
517510 Cable TV providers (except networks)
331422 Cable, copper (e.g., armored, bare, insulated), made from purchased copper in wire drawing plants
331422 Cable, copper (e.g., armored, bare, insulated), made in integrated secondary smelting and wire drawing plants
331222 Cable, iron or steel, insulated or armored, made in wire drawing plants
335929 Cable, nonferrous, insulated, or armored, made from purchased nonferrous wire
332618 Cable, noninsulated wire, made from purchased wire
423510 Cable, wire (except insulated), merchant wholesalers
333111 Cabs for agricultural machinery manufacturing
333120 Cabs for construction machinery manufacturing
333924 Cabs for industrial trucks manufacturing
111339 Cactus fruit farming
541512 CAD (computer-aided design) systems integration design services
541370 Cadastral surveying services
339920 Caddy carts manufacturing
331419 Cadmium refining, primary
541512 CAE (computer-aided engineering) systems integration design services
337215 Cafeteria fixtures manufacturing
722310 Cafeteria food services contractors (e.g., government office cafeterias, hospital cafeterias, school cafeterias)
337127 Cafeteria furniture manufacturing
337127 Cafeteria tables and benches manufacturing
722212 Cafeterias
325411 Caffeine and derivatives (i.e., basic chemicals) manufacturing
315291 Caftans, infants', cut and sewn from purchased fabric (except apparel contractors)
315211 Caftans, men's and boys', cut and sew apparel contractors
315223 Caftans, men's and boys', cut and sewn from purchased fabric (except apparel contractors)
315212 Caftans, women's, girls', and infants', cut and sew apparel contractors
315231 Caftans, women's, misses' and girls', cut and sewn from purchased fabric (except apparel contractors)
332618 Cages made from purchased wire
238910 Caisson (i.e., drilled building foundations) construction
237990 Caisson (i.e., marine or pneumatic structures) construction
332420 Caissons, underwater work, heavy gauge metal, manufacturing
311999 Cake frosting manufacturing
311999 Cake frosting mixes manufacturing
311822 Cake mixes made from purchased flour
311340 Cake ornaments, confectionery, manufacturing
311813 Cake, frozen, manufacturing
311812 Cakes, baking (except frozen), made in commercial bakeries
212231 Calamine mining and/or beneficiating

212221 Calaverite mining and/or beneficiating
212312 Calcareous tufa crushed and broken stone mining and/or beneficiating
212311 Calcareous tufa mining or quarrying
325510 Calcimines manufacturing
424950 Calcimines, merchant wholesalers
212392 Calcined phosphate rock mining and/or beneficiating
324199 Calcining petroleum coke from refined petroleum
212399 Calcite mining and/or beneficiating
325188 Calcium carbide, chloride, and hypochlorite manufacturing
325199 Calcium citrate manufacturing
327410 Calcium hydroxide (i.e., hydrated lime) manufacturing
325188 Calcium hypochlorite manufacturing
325188 Calcium inorganic compounds, not specified elsewhere by process, manufacturing
325199 Calcium organic compounds, not specified elsewhere by process, manufacturing
325199 Calcium oxalate manufacturing
327410 Calcium oxide (i.e., quicklime) manufacturing
423420 Calculators and calculating machines merchant wholesalers
333313 Calculators manufacturing
511199 Calendar publishers (except exclusive Internet publishing)
511199 Calendar publishers and printing combined
516110 Calendar publishers, exclusively on Internet
453998 Calendar shops
323112 Calendars flexographic printing without publishing
323111 Calendars gravure printing without publishing
323110 Calendars lithographic (offset) printing without publishing
323119 Calendars printing (except flexographic, digital, lithographic, gravure, quick, screen) without publishing
323113 Calendars screen printing without publishing
313311 Calendering broadwoven fabrics
333220 Calendering machinery for plastics manufacturing
333292 Calendering machinery for textiles manufacturing
313312 Calendering textile products, apparel, and fabrics (except broadwoven)
112111 Calf (e.g., feeder, stocker, veal) production
315119 Calf high sheer hosiery knitting or knitting and finishing
541380 Calibration and certification testing laboratories or services
332212 Calipers and dividers, machinists' precision tools, manufacturing
336340 Calipers, brake, automotive, truck, and bus, manufacturing
339992 Calliopes (steam organs) manufacturing
541512 CAM (computer-aided manufacturing) systems integration design services
532210 Camcorder rental
334310 Camcorders manufacturing
326211 Camelback (i.e., retreading material) manufacturing
333220 Camelback (i.e., retreading materials) machinery manufacturing
316991 Camera carrying bags, all materials, manufacturing
423410 Camera equipment and supplies, photographic, merchant wholesalers
333314 Camera lenses manufacturing
811211 Camera repair shops without retailing new cameras
443130 Camera shops, photographic
423410 Camera, television, merchant wholesalers

423410 Camera, video (except household-type) merchant wholesalers
711510 Cameramen, independent (freelance)
333315 Cameras (except digital, television, video) manufacturing
334220 Cameras, television, manufacturing
315212 Camisoles, women's and girls', cut and sew apparel contractors
315231 Camisoles, women's, misses' and girls', cut and sewn from purchased fabric (except apparel contractors)
337124 Camp furniture, metal, manufacturing
337125 Camp furniture, reed and rattan, manufacturing
337122 Camp furniture, wood, manufacturing
813940 Campaign organizations, political
441210 Camper dealers, recreational
532120 Camper rental
336214 Camper units, slide-in, for pick-up trucks, manufacturing
721211 Campgrounds
325191 Camphor, natural, manufacturing
325199 Camphor, synthetic, manufacturing
423910 Camping equipment and supplies merchant wholesalers
423110 Camping trailer merchant wholesalers
336214 Camping trailers and chassis manufacturing
721214 Camps (except day, instructional)
713990 Camps (except instructional), day
623990 Camps, boot or disciplinary (except correctional), for delinquent youth
611620 Camps, sports instruction
333515 Cams (i.e., a machine tool accessory) manufacturing
333513 Can forming machines, metalworking, manufacturing
332618 Can keys made from purchased wire
332431 Can lids and ends, light gauge metal, manufacturing
332212 Can openers (except electric) manufacturing
335211 Can openers, household-type electric, manufacturing
483211 Canal barge transportation (freight)
237990 Canal construction
488310 Canal maintenance services (except dredging)
488310 Canal operation
483212 Canal passenger transportation
221310 Canal, irrigation
333313 Canceling machinery, postal office-type, manufacturing
923120 Cancer detection program administration
622310 Cancer hospitals
541710 Cancer research laboratories or services
311340 Candied fruits and fruit peel manufacturing
713950 Candle pin bowling alleys
713950 Candle pin bowling centers
453998 Candle shops
339999 Candles manufacturing
424990 Candles merchant wholesalers
311320 Candy bars, chocolate (including chocolate covered), made from cacao beans
311340 Candy bars, nonchocolate, manufacturing
424450 Candy merchant wholesalers
311330 Candy stores, chocolate, candy made on premises not for immediate consumption
311340 Candy stores, nonchocolate, candy made on premises, not for immediate consumption
445292 Candy stores, packaged, retailing only
311320 Candy, chocolate, made from cacao beans
111930 Cane farming, sugar, field production

311312 Cane sugar made from purchased raw cane sugar
311311 Cane sugar made in sugarcane mill
424490 Cane sugar, refined, merchant wholesalers
311312 Cane syrup made from purchased raw cane sugar
311311 Cane syrup made in sugarcane mill
339999 Canes (except orthopedic) manufacturing
332993 Canisters, ammunition, manufacturing
424490 Canned foods (e.g., fish, meat, seafood, soups) merchant wholesalers
311611 Canned meats (except poultry) produced in slaughtering plants
311911 Canned nuts manufacturing
236210 Cannery construction
311711 Cannery, fish
311711 Cannery, shellfish
311421 Canning fruits and vegetables
311421 Canning jams and jellies
333993 Canning machinery manufacturing
311615 Canning poultry (except baby and pet food)
311422 Canning soups (except seafood)
423840 Canning supplies merchant wholesalers
311711 Canning, fish, crustacea, and molluscs
332995 Cannons manufacturing
339112 Cannulae manufacturing
532292 Canoe rental
713990 Canoeing, recreational
311225 Canola (rapeseed) oil, cake and meal, made from purchased oils
311223 Canola (rapeseed) oil, cake and meal, made in crushing mills
111120 Canola farming, field and seed production
332322 Canopies, sheet metal (except stampings), manufacturing
332431 Cans, aluminum, light gauge metal, manufacturing
332431 Cans, light guage metal, manufacturing
332431 Cans, steel, light gauge metal, manufacturing
111219 Cantaloupe farming, field, bedding plant and seed production
722213 Canteens, fixed location
722330 Canteens, mobile
321912 Cants, resawed (lumber), manufacturing
314911 Canvas bags manufacturing
339942 Canvas board, artist's, manufacturing
314912 Canvas products (except bags) made from purchased canvas or canvas substitutes
424990 Canvas products merchant wholesalers
316211 Canvas shoes, plastics soled fabric upper, manufacturing
316211 Canvas shoes, rubber soled fabric upper, manufacturing
339942 Canvas, artist's, prepared on frames, manufacturing
313210 Canvases weaving
454390 Canvassers (door-to-door), headquarters for retail sale of merchandise, direct selling
335999 Capacitors (except electronic), fixed and variable, manufacturing
334414 Capacitors, electronic, fixed and variable, manufacturing
423690 Capacitors, electronic, merchant wholesalers
315212 Capes (except fur), women's, girls' and infants', cut and sew apparel contractors
315234 Capes (except fur, waterproof), women's, misses', and girls', cut and sewn from purchased fabric (except apparel contractors)
315292 Capes, fur (except apparel contractors), manufacturing
315212 Capes, fur, women's, girls', and infants', cut and sew apparel contractors

315299 Capes, waterproof (e.g., plastics, rubber, similar materials), cut and sewn from purchased fabric (except apparel contractors)
237110 Capping of water wells
333993 Capping, sealing, and lidding packaging machinery manufacturing
325199 Caprolactam manufacturing
315991 Caps (except fur, leather) cut and sewn from purchased fabric (except apparel contractors)
315991 Caps (i.e., apparel accessory) cut and sewn from purchased fabric (except fur, leather, apparel contractors)
315211 Caps (i.e., apparel accessory), men's and boys', cut and sew apparel contractors
315212 Caps (i.e., apparel accessory), women's, girls', and infants', cut and sew apparel contractors
315299 Caps and gowns, academic, cut and sewn from purchased fabric (except apparel contractors)
315211 Caps and gowns, academic, men's and boys', cut and sew apparel contractors
315212 Caps and gowns, academic, women's and girls', cut and sew apparel contractors
335931 Caps and plugs, attachment, electric, manufacturing
332115 Caps and tops, bottle, metal, stamping
336214 Caps for pick-up trucks manufacturing
325998 Caps for toy pistols manufacturing
315191 Caps made in apparel knitting mills
325920 Caps, blasting and detonating, manufacturing
332993 Caps, bomb, manufacturing
315292 Caps, fur (except apparel contractors), manufacturing
316999 Caps, heel and toe, leather, manufacturing
315292 Caps, leather (except apparel contractors), manufacturing
315991 Caps, textiles, straw, fur-felt, and wool-felt, cut and sewn from purchased fabric (except apparel contractors)
315211 Caps, textiles, straw, fur-felt, and wool-felt, men's and boys', cut and sew apparel contractors
315212 Caps, textiles, straw, fur-felt, and wool-felt, women's, girls', and infants', cut and sew apparel contractors
325998 Capsules, gelatin, empty, manufacturing
334290 Car alarm manufacturing
336211 Car bodies, kit, manufacturing
811192 Car detailers
532112 Car leasing
483212 Car lighters (i.e., ferries), inland waters (except on Great Lakes system)
485999 Car pool operation
488999 Car pools, arrangement of
532111 Car rental
532111 Car rental agencies
561599 Car rental reservation services
811111 Car repair shops, general
332999 Car seals, metal, manufacturing
337125 Car seats, infant (except metal), manufacturing
334310 Car stereos manufacturing
423850 Car wash equipment and supplies merchant wholesalers
811192 Car washes
331111 Car wheels, rolled steel, made in iron and steel mills
325188 Carbides (e.g., boron, calcium, silicon, tungsten) manufacturing
332994 Carbines manufacturing
325199 Carbinol manufacturing
325211 Carbohydrate plastics manufacturing

334510 Carbon arc lamp units, electrotherapeutic (except infrared and ultraviolet), manufacturing
325182 Carbon black manufacturing
424690 Carbon black merchant wholesalers
327125 Carbon brick manufacturing
325120 Carbon dioxide manufacturing
325188 Carbon disulfide manufacturing
335991 Carbon electrodes and contacts, electric, manufacturing
325188 Carbon inorganic compounds manufacturing
334290 Carbon monoxide detectors manufacturing
423690 Carbon monoxide detectors, electronic, merchant wholesalers
325199 Carbon organic compounds, not specified elsewhere by process, manufacturing
339944 Carbon paper manufacturing
335991 Carbon specialties for aerospace use (except gaskets) manufacturing
335991 Carbon specialties for electrical use manufacturing
335991 Carbon specialties for mechanical use (except gaskets) manufacturing
325199 Carbon tetrachloride manufacturing
325998 Carbon, activated, manufacturing
312111 Carbonated soda manufacturing
312111 Carbonated soft drinks manufacturing
325188 Carbonic acid manufacturing
333292 Carbonizing equipment for processing wool manufacturing
313312 Carbonizing textile fibers
335991 Carbons, electric, manufacturing
335991 Carbons, lighting, manufacturing
325998 Carburetor cleaners manufacturing
336311 Carburetors, all types, manufacturing
316993 Card cases (except metal) manufacturing
339911 Card cases, precious metal, manufacturing
713290 Card rooms (e.g., poker rooms)
453220 Card shops, greeting
337122 Card table sets (furniture), wood, manufacturing
337124 Card table sets, metal, manufacturing
424130 Cardboard products merchant wholesalers
322130 Cardboard stock manufacturing
322226 Cardboard, laminated or surface coated, made from purchased paperboard
313230 Carded nonwoven fabrics manufacturing
313111 Carded yarn manufacturing
325412 Cardiac preparations manufacturing
333292 Carding machinery for textiles manufacturing
313312 Carding textile fibers
334510 Cardiodynameter manufacturing
334510 Cardiographs manufacturing
621111 Cardiologists' offices (e.g., centers, clinics)
334510 Cardiophone, electric, manufacturing
334510 Cardioscope manufacturing
334510 Cardiotachometer manufacturing
323119 Cards (e.g., business, greeting, playing, postcards, trading) engraving printing without publishing
323112 Cards (e.g., business, greeting, playing, postcards, trading) flexographic printing without publishing
323111 Cards (e.g., business, greeting, playing, postcards, trading) gravure printing without publishing
323119 Cards (e.g., business, greeting, playing, postcards, trading) letterpress printing without publishing

323110 Cards (e.g., business, greeting, playing, postcards, trading) lithographic (offset) printing without publishing
323119 Cards (e.g., business, greeting, playing, postcards, trading) printing (except flexographic, gravure, lithographic, quick, screen) without publishing
323113 Cards (e.g., business, greeting, playing, postcards, trading) screen printing without publishing
322299 Cards, die-cut (except office supply) made from purchased paper or paperboard
322231 Cards, die-cut office supply (e.g., index, library, time recording), made from purchased paper or paperboard
424120 Cards, greeting, merchant wholesalers
****** Cards, publishing—see specific product
481112 Cargo carriers, air, scheduled
488390 Cargo checkers, marine
488330 Cargo salvaging, marine
336611 Cargo ship building
488390 Cargo surveyors, marine
488490 Cargo surveyors, truck transportation
333319 Carnival and amusement park rides manufacturing
333319 Carnival and amusement park shooting gallery machinery manufacturing
423850 Carnival equipment merchant wholesalers
713990 Carnival ride concession operators (i.e., supplying and servicing in others' facilities)
711190 Carnival traveling shows
212291 Carnotite mining and/or beneficiating
333922 Carousel conveyors (e.g., luggage) manufacturing
333319 Carousels (i.e., merry-go-rounds) manufacturing
238350 Carpenters (except framing)
611513 Carpenters' apprenticeship training
332212 Carpenter's handtools, nonelectric (except saws), manufacturing
532490 Carpentry equipment rental or leasing
238350 Carpentry work (except framing)
238130 Carpentry, framing
333319 Carpet and floor cleaning equipment, electric commercial-type, manufacturing
335212 Carpet and floor cleaning equipment, household-type electric, manufacturing
532490 Carpet and rug cleaning equipment rental or leasing
313111 Carpet and rug yarn spinning
532299 Carpet and rug, residential, rental
561740 Carpet cleaning on customers' premises
561740 Carpet cleaning plants
561740 Carpet cleaning services
314999 Carpet cutting and binding
313210 Carpet linings (except felt) weaving
423220 Carpet merchant wholesalers
313230 Carpet paddings, nonwoven, manufacturing
442210 Carpet stores
333319 Carpet sweepers, mechanical, manufacturing
238330 Carpet, installation only
314110 Carpets and rugs made from textile materials
321999 Carpets, cork, manufacturing
332311 Carports, prefabricated metal, manufacturing
487110 Carriage, horse-drawn, operation
339932 Carriages, baby, manufacturing
339932 Carriages, doll, manufacturing
334210 Carrier equipment (i.e., analog, digital), telephone, manufacturing
111219 Carrot farming, field, bedding plant and seed production

311991 Carrots, cut, peeled or sliced fresh, manufacturing
722211 Carryout restaurants
336111 Cars, electric, for highway use, assembling on chassis of own manufacture
333131 Cars, mining, manufacturing
541370 Cartographic surveying services
333993 Carton filling machinery manufacturing
322299 Cartons, egg, molded pulp manufacturing
322212 Cartons, folding (except milk), made from purchased paperboard
322215 Cartons, milk, made from purchased paper or paperboard
424130 Cartons, paper and paperboard, merchant wholesalers
711510 Cartoonists, independent
333991 Cartridge (i.e., powder) handheld power-driven tools manufacturing
332992 Cartridge cases for ammunition (i.e., 30 mm.or less, 1.18 inch or less) manufacturing
331421 Cartridge cups, discs, and sheets, copper and copper alloy, made from purchased copper or in integrated secondary smelting and rolling, drawing or extruding plants
424120 Cartridge toner merchant wholesalers
332992 Cartridges (i.e., 30 mm. or less, 1.18 inch or less) manufacturing
339920 Carts, caddy, manufacturing
423860 Carts, golf, motorized passenger merchant wholesalers
333924 Carts, grocery, made from purchased wire
333112 Carts, lawn and garden-type, manufacturing
332211 Carving sets manufacturing
333319 Carwashing machinery manufacturing
111219 Casaba melon farming, field, bedding plant and seed production
316110 Case leather manufacturing
325222 Casein fibers and filaments manufacturing
325211 Casein plastics manufacturing
311514 Casein, dry and wet, manufacturing
332321 Casements, metal, manufacturing
316993 Cases, jewelry (except metal), manufacturing
339914 Cases, jewelry, metal (except precious), manufacturing
339911 Cases, jewelry, precious metal, manufacturing
316991 Cases, luggage, manufacturing
316991 Cases, musical instrument, manufacturing
321920 Cases, shipping, wood, wirebound, manufacturing
321920 Cases, wood packing, nailed or lock corner, manufacturing
321920 Cases, wood shipping, nailed or lock corner, manufacturing
332439 Cash boxes, light gauge metal, manufacturing
532420 Cash register rental or leasing
333313 Cash registers (except point of sales terminals) manufacturing
423420 Cash registers merchant wholesalers
111335 Cashew farming
211112 Casing-head butane and propane production
326121 Casings, sausage, nonrigid plastics, manufacturing
332313 Casings, scroll, fabricated metal plate work, manufacturing
332322 Casings, sheet metal (except stampings), manufacturing
236220 Casino construction
721120 Casino hotels
713210 Casinos (except casino hotels)
332510 Casket hardware, metal, manufacturing
339995 Caskets, burial, manufacturing
423850 Caskets, burial, merchant wholesalers

321920 Casks, wood, coopered, manufacturing
111219 Cassava farming, field and seed casava production
335211 Casseroles, household-type electric, manufacturing
334612 Cassette tapes, pre-recorded audio, mass reproducing
532230 Cassette, prerecorded video, rental
423990 Cassettes, prerecorded audio and video, merchant wholesalers
331511 Cast iron brake shoes, railroad, manufacturing
331511 Cast iron pipe and pipe fittings manufacturing
423510 Cast iron pipe merchant wholesalers
331511 Cast iron railroad car wheels manufacturing
331513 Cast steel railroad car wheels, unfinished, manufacturing
327390 Cast stone, concrete (except structural), manufacturing
327124 Castable refractories, clay, manufacturing
327125 Castable refractories, nonclay, manufacturing
332510 Casters, furniture, metal manufacturing
332510 Casters, industrial, metal, manufacturing
561310 Casting agencies (i.e., motion picture, theatrical, video)
561310 Casting agencies, motion picture or video
561310 Casting agencies, theatrical
561310 Casting bureaus (e.g., motion picture, theatrical, video)
561310 Casting bureaus, motion picture or video
561310 Casting bureaus, theatrical
331528 Castings (except die-castings), nonferrous metals (except aluminum, copper), unfinished manufacturing
331524 Castings (except die-castings), unfinished, aluminum, manufacturing
331525 Castings (except die-castings), unfinished, copper, manufacturing
331511 Castings, compacted graphite iron, unfinished, manufacturing
331511 Castings, malleable iron, unfinished, manufacturing
331513 Castings, steel (except investment), unfinished, manufacturing
331511 Castings, unfinished iron (e.g., ductile, gray, malleable, semisteel), manufacturing
311223 Castor oil and pomace made in crushing mills
316213 Casual shoes (except athletic, plastics, rubber), men's, manufacturing
316214 Casual shoes (except athletic, rubber, plastics), women's, manufacturing
316219 Casual shoes (except rubber, plastics), children's and infants', manufacturing
524126 Casualty insurance carriers, direct
621512 CAT (computerized axial tomography) scanner centers
311111 Cat food manufacturing
325998 Cat litter manufacturing
112990 Cat production
511199 Catalog (i.e., mail order, store merchandise) publishers (except exclusive Internet publishing)
511199 Catalog (i.e., mail order, store merchandise) publishers and printing combined
454113 Catalog (i.e., order taking) offices of mail-order houses
511140 Catalog of collections publishers (except exclusive Internet publishing)
511140 Catalog of collections publishers and printing combined
516110 Catalog of collections publishers, exclusively on Internet

452990 Catalog showrooms, general merchandise (except catalog mail-order)
323112 Catalogs flexographic printing without publishing
323111 Catalogs gravure printing without publishing
323110 Catalogs lithographic (offset) printing without publishing
323112 Catalogs of collections flexographic printing without publishing
323111 Catalogs of collections gravure printing without publishing
323110 Catalogs of collections lithographic (offset) printing without publishing
323119 Catalogs of collections printing (except flexographic, gravure, lithographic, quick, screen) without publishing
323113 Catalogs of collections screen printing without publishing
323119 Catalogs printing (except flexographic, gravure, lithographic, quick, screen) without publishing
323113 Catalogs screen printing without publishing
336399 Catalytic converters, engine exhaust, automotive, truck, and bus, manufacturing
332995 Catapult guns manufacturing
562998 Catch basin cleaning services
722320 Caterers
722320 Catering services, social
112511 Catfish production, farm raising
325412 Cathartic preparations manufacturing
339112 Catheters manufacturing
334411 Cathode ray tubes (CRT) manufacturing
335999 Cathodic protection equipment manufacturing
238190 Cathodic protection, installation
212399 Catlinite mining and/or beneficiating
424990 Cats merchant wholesalers
311421 Catsup manufacturing
112111 Cattle conditioning operations
112111 Cattle farming or ranching
333111 Cattle feeding and watering equipment manufacturing
112112 Cattle feedlots (except stockyards for transportation)
311119 Cattle feeds, supplements, concentrates, and premixes, manufacturing
424520 Cattle merchant wholesalers
115210 Cattle spraying
111219 Cauliflower farming, field, bedding plant and seed production
238390 Caulking (i.e., waterproofing) contractors
325520 Caulking compounds (except gypsum base) manufacturing
332212 Caulking guns, nonpowered, manufacturing
424690 Caulking materials merchant wholesalers
524291 Cause-of-loss investigators, insurance
237310 Causeway construction
325181 Caustic potash manufacturing
325181 Caustic soda (i.e., sodium hydroxide) manufacturing
424690 Caustic soda merchant wholesalers
712190 Caverns (i.e., natural wonder tourist attractions)
334220 CB (citizens band) radios manufacturing
332212 C-clamps manufacturing
334112 CD-ROM drives manufacturing
334611 CD-ROM, software, mass reproducing
337122 Cedar chests manufacturing
325998 Cedar oil manufacturing
238130 Ceiling beam, wood, installation
444190 Ceiling fan stores
335211 Ceiling fans with integral lighting fixture, residential, manufacturing
335211 Ceiling fans, residential, manufacturing
335122 Ceiling lighting fixtures, commercial, industrial, and institutional, manufacturing

335121 Ceiling lighting fixtures, residential, manufacturing
321912 Ceiling lumber, dressed, resawing purchased lumber
321113 Ceiling lumber, made from logs or bolts
238310 Ceiling tile installation
238390 Ceiling, metal, installation
334519 Ceilometers manufacturing
711410 Celebrities' agents or managers
711510 Celebrity spokespersons, independent
111219 Celery farming, field, bedding plant and seed production
212393 Celestite mining and/or beneficiating
325221 Cellophane film or sheet manufacturing
424120 Cellophane tape merchant wholesalers
339992 Cellos and parts manufacturing
237130 Cellular phone tower construction
517212 Cellular telephone communication carriers
517212 Cellular telephone services
443112 Cellular telephone stores
334220 Cellular telephones manufacturing
423690 Cellular telephones merchant wholesalers
325199 Cellulose acetate (except resins) manufacturing
325211 Cellulose acetate resins manufacturing
325211 Cellulose nitrate resins manufacturing
325211 Cellulose propionate resins manufacturing
325211 Cellulose resins manufacturing
325211 Cellulose xanthate (viscose) manufacturing
238310 Cellulosic fiber insulation installation
325221 Cellulosic fibers and filaments manufacturing
325221 Cellulosic filament yarn manufacturing
326113 Cellulosic plastics film and unlaminated sheet (except packaging) manufacturing
325221 Cellulosic staple fibers manufacturing
327310 Cement (e.g., hydraulic, masonry, portland, pozzolana) manufacturing
238140 Cement block laying
327310 Cement clinker manufacturing
333298 Cement kilns manufacturing
423320 Cement merchant wholesalers
236210 Cement plant construction
212312 Cement rock crushed and broken stone mining and/or beneficiating
327124 Cement, clay refractory, manufacturing
327420 Cement, Keene's (i.e., tiling plaster), manufacturing
325520 Cement, rubber, manufacturing
213112 Cementing oil and gas well casings on a contract basis
423830 Cement-making machinery merchant wholesalers
324122 Cements, asphalt roofing, made from purchased asphaltic materials
339114 Cements, dental, manufacturing
812220 Cemeteries
812220 Cemetery associations (i.e., operators)
812220 Cemetery management services
453998 Cemetery memorial dealers (e.g., headstones, markers, vaults)
561730 Cemetery plot care services
333512 Centering machines, metalworking, manufacturing
519120 Centers for documentation (i.e., archives)
624120 Centers, senior citizens'
238220 Central air-conditioning equipment installation
521110 Central bank, monetary authorities
238220 Central cooling equipment and piping installation
238220 Central heating equipment and piping installation

423730 Central heating equipment, warm-air, merchant wholesalers
325412 Central nervous system stimulant preparations manufacturing
334210 Central office and switching equipment, telephone, manufacturing
333319 Central vacuuming systems, commercial-type, manufacturing
335212 Central vacuuming systems, household-type, manufacturing
551114 Centralized administrative offices
327320 Central-mixed concrete manufacturing
333911 Centrifugal pumps manufacturing
333999 Centrifuges, industrial-type, manufacturing
325411 Cephalosporin, uncompounded, manufacturing
325131 Ceramic colors manufacturing
423320 Ceramic construction materials (except refractory) merchant wholesalers
327999 Ceramic fiber manufacturing
333994 Ceramic kilns and furnaces manufacturing
238340 Ceramic tile installation
444190 Ceramic tile stores
327122 Ceramic tiles, floor and wall, manufacturing
611610 Ceramics instruction
311211 Cereal grain flour manufacturing
311211 Cereal grain germ manufacturing
424490 Cereal products merchant wholesalers
541710 Cerebral palsy research laboratories or services
212299 Cerium concentrates mining and/or beneficiating
212299 Cerium ores mining and/or beneficiating
325188 Cerium salts manufacturing
523120 Certificate of deposit (CD) brokers' offices
923110 Certification of schools and teachers
541211 Certified accountants' offices
523930 Certified financial planners, customized, fees paid by client
541211 Certified public accountants' (CPAs) offices
212231 Cerussite mining and/or beneficiating
339113 Cervical collars manufacturing
325188 Cesium and cesium compounds, not specified elsewhere by process, manufacturing
562991 Cesspool cleaning services
238910 Cesspool construction
325199 Cetyl alcohol manufacturing
335211 Chafing dishes, household-type electric, manufacturing
332999 Chain fittings manufacturing
333923 Chain hoists manufacturing
332323 Chain ladders, metal, manufacturing
238990 Chain link fence installation
332618 Chain link fencing and fence gates made from purchased wire
331222 Chain link fencing, iron or steel, made in wire drawing plants
332618 Chain made from purchased wire
332213 Chain saw blades manufacturing
333991 Chain saws, handheld power-driven, manufacturing
332618 Chain, welded, made from purchased wire
339911 Chains or necklace, precious metal, manufacturing
333613 Chains, power transmission, manufacturing
334519 Chains, surveyor's, manufacturing
423830 Chainsaws merchant wholesalers
337121 Chair and couch springs, assembled, manufacturing
337215 Chair glides manufacturing

337215 Chair seats for furniture manufacturing
337122 Chairs (except upholstered), wood household-type, manufacturing
337214 Chairs (except wood), office-type, manufacturing
337127 Chairs, barber and beauty (i.e., hydraulic), manufacturing
337127 Chairs, barber, beauty shop (i.e., hydraulic), manufacturing
337125 Chairs, cane, wood household-type, manufacturing
339114 Chairs, dentist's, manufacturing
337124 Chairs, metal household-type (except upholstered), manufacturing
337127 Chairs, portable folding, auditorium-type, manufacturing
337127 Chairs, stacking, auditorium-type, manufacturing
337121 Chairs, upholstered household-type (except dining room, kitchen), manufacturing
337211 Chairs, wood office-type, manufacturing
212234 Chalcocite mining and/or beneficiating
212234 Chalcopyrite mining and/or beneficiating
339942 Chalk (e.g., artist's, blackboard, carpenter's, marking, tailor's), manufacturing
212312 Chalk crushed and broken stone mining and/or beneficiating
212312 Chalk, ground or otherwise treated, mining and/or beneficiating
339942 Chalkboards, framed, manufacturing
711130 Chamber musical groups
711130 Chamber orchestras
813910 Chambers of commerce
313210 Chambrays weaving
333512 Chamfering machines, metalworking, manufacturing
316110 Chamois leather manufacturing
424990 Chamois, leather, merchant wholesalers
312130 Champagne method sparkling wine, manufacturing
335122 Chandeliers, commercial, industrial, and institutional electric, manufacturing
335121 Chandeliers, residential, manufacturing
333311 Change making machines manufacturing
325182 Channel black manufacturing
237990 Channel construction
332323 Channels, furring metal, manufacturing
325191 Charcoal (except activated) manufacturing
325191 Charcoal briquettes, wood, manufacturing
424990 Charcoal merchant wholesalers
325998 Charcoal, activated, manufacturing
522210 Charge card issuing
813211 Charitable trusts, awarding grants
611699 Charm schools
481212 Charter air freight services
481211 Charter air passenger services
485510 Charter bus services (except scenic, sightseeing)
487210 Charter fishing boat operation
333515 Chasers (i.e., a machine tool accessory) manufacturing
212399 Chasers mining and/or beneficiating
332812 Chasing metals and metal products for the trade
336111 Chassis, automobile, manufacturing
336120 Chassis, heavy truck, with or without cabs, manufacturing
336112 Chassis, light truck and utility, manufacturing
423110 Chassis, motor vehicle, merchant wholesalers
561310 Chauffeur registries
611519 Chauffeur training
315991 Chauffeurs' hats and caps cut and sewn from purchased fabric (except apparel contractors)

315211 Chauffeurs' hats and caps, men's, cut and sew apparel contractors
315212 Chauffeurs' hats and caps, women's, cut and sew apparel contractors
522390 Check cashing services
521110 Check clearing activities of the central bank
522320 Check clearing services (except central banks)
522320 Check clearinghouse services (except central banks)
423420 Check handling machines merchant wholesalers
812990 Check room services
522320 Check validation services
332911 Check valves, industrial-type, manufacturing
333313 Check writing machines manufacturing
316993 Checkbook covers, (except metal), manufacturing
339911 Checkbook covers, precious metal, manufacturing
323116 Checkbooks and refills printing
339932 Checkers and checkerboards manufacturing
611620 Cheerleading instruction, camps, or schools
311513 Cheese (except cottage cheese) manufacturing
311513 Cheese analogs manufacturing
311941 Cheese based salad dressing manufacturing
424450 Cheese confections (e.g., curls, puffs) merchant wholesalers
311919 Cheese curls and puffs manufacturing
424430 Cheese merchant wholesalers
333294 Cheese processing machinery manufacturing
311513 Cheese products, imitation or substitute, manufacturing
311513 Cheese spreads manufacturing
311511 Cheese, cottage, manufacturing
311513 Cheese, imitation or substitute, manufacturing
311513 Cheese, natural (except cottage cheese), manufacturing
313210 Cheesecloths weaving
236210 Chemical (except petrochemical process type) plant construction
424690 Chemical additives (e.g., concrete, food, fuel, oil) merchant wholesalers
541690 Chemical consulting services
541330 Chemical engineering services
313311 Chemical finishing (e.g., fire, mildew, water resistance) broadwoven fabrics
313312 Chemical finishing (e.g., fire, mildew, water resistance) fabrics (except broadwoven and textile products)
424690 Chemical gases merchant wholesalers
423830 Chemical industries machinery and equipment merchant wholesalers
333298 Chemical kilns manufacturing
332710 Chemical milling job shops
333512 Chemical milling machines, metalworking, manufacturing
333298 Chemical processing machinery and equipment manufacturing
541710 Chemical research and development laboratories or services
327112 Chemical stoneware (i.e., pottery products) manufacturing
326191 Chemical toilets, plastics, manufacturing
115112 Chemical treatment of soil for crops
213112 Chemically treating oil and gas wells (e.g., acidizing, bailing, swabbing) on a contract basis
424690 Chemicals (except agriculture) (e.g., automotive, household, industrial, photographic) merchant wholesalers
424910 Chemicals, agricultural, merchant wholesalers
315191 Chemises made in apparel knitting mills

315212 Chemises, women's and girls', cut and sew apparel contractors
315231 Chemises, women's, misses' and girls', cut and sewn from purchased fabric (except apparel contractors)
111339 Cherry farming
113210 Cherry gum, gathering
339932 Chessmen and chessboards manufacturing
325191 Chestnut extract manufacturing
113210 Chestnut gum, gathering
321920 Chests for tools, wood, manufacturing
332999 Chests, fire or burglary resistive, metal, manufacturing
332999 Chests, money, metal, manufacturing
332999 Chests, safe deposit, metal, manufacturing
311340 Chewing gum base manufacturing
333294 Chewing gum machinery manufacturing
311340 Chewing gum manufacturing
424450 Chewing gum merchant wholesalers
312229 Chewing tobacco manufacturing
424940 Chewing tobacco merchant wholesalers
424440 Chicken and chicken products (except canned and packaged frozen) merchant wholesalers
333111 Chicken brooders manufacturing
321920 Chicken coops (i.e., crates), wood, wirebound for shipping poultry, manufacturing
321992 Chicken coops, prefabricated, wood, manufacturing
112310 Chicken egg production
112310 Chicken eggs (table, hatching) production
333111 Chicken feeders manufacturing
311119 Chicken feeds, prepared, manufacturing
112340 Chicken hatcheries
332618 Chicken netting made from purchased wire
112320 Chicken production (except egg laying)
311615 Chickens, processing, fresh, frozen, canned, or cooked (except baby and pet food)
311615 Chickens, slaughtering and dressing
424590 Chicks merchant wholesalers
111998 Chicory farming
624410 Child day care centers
624410 Child day care services
624410 Child day care services in provider's own home
624410 Child day care, before or after school, separate from schools
623990 Child group foster homes
624110 Child guidance agencies
624110 Child welfare services
621410 Childbirth preparation classes
622210 Children's hospitals, psychiatric or substance abuse
622310 Children's hospitals, specialty (except psychiatric, substance abuse)
721214 Children's camps (except day, instructional)
424330 Children's clothing merchant wholesalers
511199 Children's coloring book publishers (except exclusive Internet publishing)
516110 Children's coloring book publishers, exclusively on Internet
622110 Children's hospitals, general
316219 Children's shoes (except orthopedic extension, plastics, rubber) manufacturing
315119 Children's socks manufacturing
423920 Children's vehicles (except bicycles) merchant wholesalers
623990 Children's villages
311422 Chili con carne canning
311942 Chili pepper or powder manufacturing
311421 Chili sauce manufacturing
238220 Chilled water system installation

339992 Chimes and parts (musical instruments) manufacturing
335999 Chimes, electric, manufacturing
327390 Chimney caps, concrete, manufacturing
561790 Chimney cleaning services
238220 Chimney liner installation
561790 Chimney sweep (i.e., cleaning) services
238140 Chimney, brick, block or stone, contractors
238110 Chimney, concrete, construction
212324 China clay mining and/or beneficiating
337122 China closets, wood, manufacturing
327112 China cooking ware manufacturing
811490 China repair services
327112 China tableware, vitreous, manufacturing
442299 Chinaware stores
423440 Chinaware, commercial, merchant wholesalers
423220 Chinaware, household-type, merchant wholesalers
112930 Chinchilla production
311422 Chinese foods canning
311999 Chinese noodles, fried, manufacturing
111219 Chinese pea farming, bedding plant and seed production
313210 Chintzes weaving
333298 Chip placement machinery manufacturing
322130 Chipboard (i.e., paperboard) stock manufacturing
321219 Chipboard (i.e., particle core, wood chip face), manufacturing
322226 Chipboard, laminated or surface coated, made from purchased paperboard
321113 Chipper mills (except portable)
333112 Chippers (i.e., shredders), lawn and garden-type, manufacturing
333120 Chippers, portable, commercial (e.g., brush, limb, log), manufacturing
333291 Chippers, stationary (e.g., log), manufacturing
424450 Chips (e.g., corn, potato) merchant wholesalers
621310 Chiropractors' offices (e.g., centers, clinics)
332212 Chisels manufacturing
333991 Chissels, handheld power-driven, manufacturing
111219 Chive farming, field, bedding plant and seed production
325199 Chloral manufacturing
325320 Chlordane insecticides manufacturing
325188 Chloride of lime manufacturing
325212 Chlorinated rubber, synthetic, manufacturing
325188 Chlorine compounds, not specified elsewhere by process, manufacturing
325188 Chlorine dioxide manufacturing
325181 Chlorine manufacturing
325199 Chloroacetic acid manufacturing
325192 Chlorobenzene manufacturing
325120 Chlorodifluoromethane manufacturing
325120 Chlorofluorocarbon gases manufacturing
325199 Chloroform manufacturing
325192 Chloronaphthalene manufacturing
325192 Chlorophenol manufacturing
325199 Chloropicrin manufacturing
325212 Chloroprene rubber manufacturing
325212 Chlorosulfonated polyethylenes manufacturing
325188 Chlorosulfonic acid manufacturing
325192 Chlorotoluene manufacturing
311330 Chocolate (coating, instant, liquor, syrups) made from purchased chocolate
311320 Chocolate (e.g., coatings, instant, liquor, syrups) made from cacao beans
424490 Chocolate (except candy) merchant wholesalers
311320 Chocolate bars made from cocoa beans

424450 Chocolate candy merchant wholesalers
311330 Chocolate coatings and syrups made from purchased chocolate
311330 Chocolate covered candy bars made from purchased chocolate
311330 Chocolate covered granola bars made from purchased chocolate
311511 Chocolate drink (milk based) manufacturing
311511 Chocolate milk manufacturing
333294 Chocolate processing machinery manufacturing
311320 Chocolate, confectionery, made from cacao beans
711130 Choirs
334416 Chokes for electronic circuitry manufacturing
325414 Cholera serums manufacturing
325320 Cholinesterse inhibitors used as insecticides manufacturing
311412 Chop suey, frozen, manufacturing
115113 Chopping and silo filling
711510 Choreographers, independent
311412 Chow mein, frozen, manufacturing
311711 Chowders, fish and seafood, canning
311712 Chowders, frozen fish and seafood, manufacturing
621399 Christian Science practitioners' offices (e.g., centers, clinics)
424990 Christmas ornaments merchant wholesalers
453220 Christmas stores
333132 Christmas tree assemblies, oil and gas field-type, manufacturing
111421 Christmas tree growing
335129 Christmas tree lighting sets, electric, manufacturing
339999 Christmas tree ornaments (except electric, glass) manufacturing
327215 Christmas tree ornaments made from purchased glass
327212 Christmas tree ornaments, glass, made in glass making plants
424990 Christmas trees (e.g., artificial, cut) merchant wholesalers
339999 Christmas trees, artificial, manufacturing
454390 Christmas trees, cut, direct selling
334516 Chromatographic instruments, laboratory-type, manufacturing
334513 Chromatographs, industrial process-type, manufacturing
325131 Chrome pigments (e.g., chrome green, chrome orange, chrome yellow) manufacturing
332813 Chrome plating metals and metal products for the trade
325188 Chromic acid manufacturing
212299 Chromite mining and/or beneficiating
325188 Chromium compounds, not specified elsewhere by process, manufacturing
212299 Chromium concentrates beneficiating
212299 Chromium ore mining and/or beneficiating
325188 Chromium oxide manufacturing
331419 Chromium refining, primary
325188 Chromium salts manufacturing
622310 Chronic disease hospitals
334518 Chronographs manufacturing
334518 Chronometers manufacturing
334516 Chronoscopes manufacturing
333512 Chucking machines, automatic, metalworking, manufacturing
333515 Chucks (i.e., a machine tool accessory) manufacturing
238290 Church bell and tower clock installation
337127 Church furniture (except concrete, stone) manufacturing
423490 Church supplies (except plated ware, silverware) merchant wholesalers
813110 Churches
332313 Chutes, fabricated metal plate work, manufacturing
333294 Cider presses manufacturing
311941 Cider vinegar manufacturing

312130 Cider, alcoholic, manufacturing
311941 Cider, nonalcoholic, manufacturing
326199 Cigar and cigarette holders, plastics, manufacturing
321920 Cigar boxes, wood and part wood, manufacturing
316993 Cigar cases (except metal) manufacturing
339911 Cigar cases, precious metal, manufacturing
312229 Cigar manufacturing
453991 Cigar stores
316993 Cigarette cases (except metal) manufacturing
339911 Cigarette cases, precious metal, manufacturing
339999 Cigarette holders manufacturing
339999 Cigarette lighter flints manufacturing
339999 Cigarette lighters (except precious metal) manufacturing
424990 Cigarette lighters merchant wholesalers
333298 Cigarette making machinery manufacturing
322299 Cigarette paper made from purchased paper
322121 Cigarette paper made in paper mills
322299 Cigarette paper, book, made from purchased paper
453991 Cigarette stands, permanent
454390 Cigarette stands, temporary
325221 Cigarette tow, cellulosic fiber, manufacturing
333311 Cigarette vending machines manufacturing
312221 Cigarettes manufacturing
424940 Cigarettes merchant wholesalers
424940 Cigars merchant wholesalers
325411 Cinchona and derivatives (i.e., basic chemicals) manufacturing
327331 Cinder (clinker) block, concrete, manufacturing
238140 Cinder block installation
236220 Cinema construction
512131 Cinemas
711510 Cinematographers, independent
212299 Cinnabar mining and/or beneficiating
333298 Circuit board making machinery manufacturing
423690 Circuit boards merchant wholesalers
334412 Circuit boards, printed, bare, manufacturing
423610 Circuit breakers merchant wholesalers
335313 Circuit breakers, air, manufacturing
335313 Circuit breakers, power, manufacturing
922110 Circuit courts
334515 Circuit testers manufacturing
423690 Circuits, integrated, merchant wholesalers
313241 Circular (i.e., weft) fabrics knitting
541870 Circular direct distribution services
333292 Circular knitting machinery manufacturing
333991 Circular saws, handheld power-driven, manufacturing
333210 Circular saws, woodworking-type, stationary, manufacturing
519120 Circulating libraries
711190 Circus companies
711190 Circuses
334220 Citizens band (CB) radios manufacturing
325199 Citral manufacturing
325199 Citrates, not specified elsewhere by process, manufacturing
325199 Citric acid manufacturing
325998 Citronella oil manufacturing
325199 Citronellal manufacturing
115112 Citrus grove cultivation services
111320 Citrus groves (except orange)
311119 Citrus pulp, cattle feed, manufacturing
311411 Citrus pulp, frozen, manufacturing
921120 City and town councils
921110 City and town managers' offices
485113 City bus services (except mixed mode)
922110 City or county courts

541320 City planning services
813410 Civic associations
236220 Civic center construction
541330 Civil engineering services
813311 Civil liberties organizations
921190 Civil rights commissions
921190 Civil service commissions
524291 Claims adjusting, insurance
524292 Claims processing services, insurance, third-party
114112 Clam digging
112512 Clam production, farm raising
333515 Clamps (i.e., a machine tool accessory) manufacturing
339112 Clamps, surgical, manufacturing
339992 Clarinets and parts manufacturing
316999 Clasps, shoe (leather), manufacturing
813410 Classic car clubs
711120 Classical dance companies
711130 Classical musical artists, independent
711130 Classical musical groups
212325 Clay (except kaolin, ball) mining and/or beneficiating
327112 Clay and ceramic statuary manufacturing
212325 Clay bleaching
423320 Clay construction materials (except refractory) merchant wholesalers
327124 Clay refractories (e.g., mortar, brick, tile, block) manufacturing
212324 Clay, ball, mining and/or beneficiating
212325 Clay, ceramic and refractory minerals, mining and/or beneficiating
212325 Clay, fire, mining and/or beneficiating
339942 Clay, modeling, manufacturing
212324 Clay, natural, mining and/or beneficiating
333298 Clayworking and tempering machinery manufacturing
812332 Clean room apparel supply services
236210 Clean room construction
339113 Clean room suits and accessories manufacturing
812320 Cleaners, drycleaning and laundry service (except coin-operated)
335212 Cleaners, household-type electric vacuum, manufacturing
561790 Cleaning (e.g., power sweeping, washing) driveways and parking lots
332813 Cleaning and descaling metals and metal products for the trade
812320 Cleaning and dyeing plants (except rug cleaning plants)
311212 Cleaning and polishing rice
561790 Cleaning building exteriors (except sand blasting, window cleaning)
238990 Cleaning building interiors during and immediately after construction
561740 Cleaning carpets
424690 Cleaning compounds and preparations merchant wholesalers
335999 Cleaning equipment, ultrasonic (except dental, medical), manufacturing
561720 Cleaning homes
333131 Cleaning machinery, mining-type, manufacturing
238990 Cleaning new building interiors immediately after construction
561720 Cleaning offices
213112 Cleaning oil and gas field lease tanks on a contract basis
213112 Cleaning out (e.g., bailing out, steam cleaning, swabbing) wells on a contract basis
212113 Cleaning plants, anthracite coal
212111 Cleaning plants, bituminous coal
561740 Cleaning plants, carpet and rug
115210 Cleaning poultry houses
561740 Cleaning rugs
561740 Cleaning services, carpet and rug
561720 Cleaning shopping centers

561790 Cleaning swimming pools
213112 Cleaning wells on a contract basis
213112 Cleaning, repairing, and dismantling oil and gas field lease tanks on a contract basis
321918 Clear and finger joint wood moldings manufacturing
522320 Clearinghouses, bank or check
523999 Clearinghouses, commodity exchange or securities exchange
316219 Cleated athletic shoes manufacturing
332211 Cleavers manufacturing
315299 Clerical vestments cut and sewn from purchased fabric (except apparel contractors)
315191 Clerical vestments made in apparel knitting mills
315211 Clerical vestments, men's and boys, cut and sew apparel contractors
315212 Clerical vestments, women's and girls', cut and sew apparel contractors
316211 Climbing shoes, plastics or plastics soled fabric upper, manufacturing
316211 Climbing shoes, rubber or rubber soled fabric upper, manufacturing
236220 Clinic construction
621111 Clinical pathologists' offices (e.g., centers, clinics)
621330 Clinical psychologists' offices (e.g., centers, clinics)
****** Clinics, medical—see type
621498 Clinics/centers of health practitioners from more than one industry practicing within the same establishment
621498 Clinics/centers of health practitioners with multi-industry degrees
321999 Clipboards, wood, manufacturing
332212 Clippers for animal use, nonelectric, manufacturing
332211 Clippers, fingernail and toenail, manufacturing
519190 Clipping services, news
332994 Clips, gun (i.e., 30 mm. or less, 1.18 inch or less), manufacturing
332995 Clips, gun (i.e., more than 30 mm., more than 1.18 inch), manufacturing
334518 Clock materials and parts (except crystals) manufacturing
334518 Clock or watch springs, precision, made from purchased wire
334310 Clock radios manufacturing
811490 Clock repair shops without retailing new clocks
448310 Clock shops
334518 Clocks assembling
334518 Clocks assembling from purchased components
423940 Clocks merchant wholesalers
561492 Closed captioning services, real-time (i.e., simultaneous)
512191 Closed captioning services, taped material
517510 Closed circuit television (CCTV)
334220 Closed circuit television equipment manufacturing
525990 Closed-end investment funds (except REITs)
453998 Closet organizer stores
238390 Closet organizer system installation
332115 Closures, metal, stamping
424130 Closures, paper and disposable plastics, merchant wholesalers
327910 Cloth (e.g., aluminum oxide, garnet, emery, silicon carbide) coated manufacturing
561990 Cloth cutting, bolting, or winding for the trade
333292 Cloth spreading machinery manufacturing
321999 Cloth winding reels, wood
332618 Cloth, woven wire, made from purchased wire

334512 Clothes dryer controls, including dryness controls, manufacturing

423620 Clothes dryer, gas and electric, merchant wholesalers

811412 Clothes dryer, household-type, repair and maintenance services without retailing new clothes dryers

321999 Clothes dryers (clothes horses), wood manufacturing

424990 Clothes hangers merchant wholesalers

326199 Clothes hangers, plastics, manufacturing

321999 Clothes poles, wood, manufacturing

326199 Clothespins, plastics, manufacturing

321999 Clothespins, wood, manufacturing

448150 Clothing accessories stores

424330 Clothing accessories, women's, children's, and infants', merchant wholesalers

541490 Clothing design services

532220 Clothing rental (except industrial launderer, linen supply)

811490 Clothing repair shops, alterations only

448130 Clothing stores, children's and infants'

448140 Clothing stores, family

448110 Clothing stores, men's and boys'

453310 Clothing stores, used

448120 Clothing stores, women's and girls'

339931 Clothing, doll, manufacturing

315292 Clothing, fur (except apparel contractors), manufacturing

315211 Clothing, fur, men's and boys', cut and sew apparel contractors

315212 Clothing, fur, women's, girls', and infants', cut and sew apparel contractors

315292 Clothing, leather or sheep-lined (except apparel contractors), manufacturing

315211 Clothing, leather or sheep-lined, men's and boys', cut and sew apparel contractors

315212 Clothing, leather or sheep-lined, women's, girls', and infants', cut and sew apparel contractors

424320 Clothing, men's and boys', merchant wholesalers

315291 Clothing, water resistant, infants', cut and sewn from purchased fabric (except apparel contractors)

315211 Clothing, water resistant, men's and boy's, cut and sew apparel contractors

315228 Clothing, water resistant, not specified elsewhere, men's and boys', cut and sewn from purchased fabric (except apparel contractors)

315239 Clothing, water resistant, not specified elsewhere, women's, misses', and girls', cut and sewn from purchased fabric (except apparel contractors)

315212 Clothing, water resistant, women's, girls' and infants', cut and sew apparel contractors

315299 Clothing, waterproof, cut and sewn from purchased fabric (except apparel contractors)

315211 Clothing, waterproof, men's and boys', cut and sew apparel contractors

315212 Clothing, waterproof, women's, girls', and infants', cut and sew apparel contractors

315291 Clothing, water-repellent, infants', cut and sewn from purchased fabric (except apparel contractors)

315211 Clothing, water-repellent, men's and boys', cut and sew apparel contractors

315228 Clothing, water-repellent, not specified elsewhere, men's and boys', cut and sewn from purchased fabric (except apparel contractors)
315239 Clothing, water-repellent, not specified elsewhere, women's, misses', and girls', cut and sewn from purchased fabric (except apparel contractors)
315212 Clothing, water-repellent, women's, girls', and infants', cut and sew apparel contractors
424330 Clothing, women's, children's, and infants', merchant wholesalers
339994 Cloths (except chemically treated), dusting and polishing, manufacturing
325612 Cloths, dusting and polishing, chemically treated, manufacturing
325998 Clove oil manufacturing
111940 Clover hay farming
111998 Clover seed farming
721310 Clubs, residential
339920 Clubs, sporting goods (e.g., golf, Indian), manufacturing
336350 Clutches and clutch facings, asbestos, manufacturing
525990 CMOs (collateralized mortgage obligations)
325413 Coagulation in-vitro diagnostic substances manufacturing
325412 Coagulation in-vivo diagnostic substances manufacturing
333922 Coal and ore conveyors manufacturing
212113 Coal beneficiating plants, anthracite
212111 Coal beneficiating plants, bituminous or lignite (surface or underground)
333131 Coal breakers, cutters, and pulverizers manufacturing
332322 Coal chutes, sheet metal (except stampings), manufacturing
454319 Coal dealers, direct selling
211111 Coal gasification at mine site
484220 Coal hauling, truck, local
211111 Coal liquefaction at mine site
423520 Coal merchant wholesalers
213113 Coal mining services (except site preparation and related construction contractor activities)
213113 Coal mining support services (tunneling, blasting, training, overburden removal)(except site preparation and related construction contractor activities)
486990 Coal pipeline transportation
211111 Coal pyrolysis
325192 Coal tar distillates manufacturing
324121 Coal tar paving materials made from purchased coal tar
424690 Coal tar products, primary and intermediate, merchant wholesalers
325211 Coal tar resins manufacturing
212113 Coal, anthracite, mining and/or beneficiating
212111 Coal, bituminous, beneficiating
212112 Coal, bituminous, underground mining or mining and beneficiating
212111 Coal, brown, mining and/or beneficiating
926120 Coast Guard (except academy)
483113 Coastal freight transportation to and from domestic ports
483114 Coastal passenger transportation to and from domestic ports
483113 Coastal shipping of freight to and from domestic ports
812331 Coat (e.g., barber's, beautician's, doctor's, nurse's) supply services
332618 Coat hangers made from purchased wire
315292 Coat linings, fur (except apparel contractors), manufacturing
315211 Coat linings, fur, men's and boys', cut and sew apparel contractors

315212 Coat linings, fur, women's, girls', and infants', cut and sew apparel contractors
448190 Coat stores
315999 Coat trimmings fabric cut and sewn from purchased fabric (except apparel contractors)
315211 Coat trimmings, fabric, men's and boys', cut and sew apparel contractors
315212 Coat trimmings, fabric, women's, girls', and infants', cut and sew apparel contractors
322226 Coated board made from purchased paperboard
322130 Coated board made in paperboard mills
324122 Coating compounds, tar, made from purchased asphaltic materials
238390 Coating concrete structures with plastics
332812 Coating metals and metal products for the trade
332812 Coating of metal and metal products with plastics for the trade
335110 Coating purchased light bulbs
322222 Coating purchased papers for nonpackaging applications (except photosensitive paper)
322221 Coating purchased papers for packaging applications
311320 Coatings, chocolate, made from cacao beans
315239 Coats (except fur, leather, tailored, waterproof), women's, misses', and girls', cut and sewn from purchased fabric (except apparel contractors)
315228 Coats (except fur, leather, tailored, waterproof, work), men's and boys', cut and sewn from purchased fabric (except apparel contractors)
315292 Coats (including tailored), leather or sheep-lined (except apparel contractors), manufacturing
315212 Coats (including tailored, leather, or sheep-lined), women's, girls', and infants', cut and sew apparel contractors
315292 Coats, artificial leather, cut and sewn from purchased fabric (except apparel contractors)
315211 Coats, artificial leather, men's and boys', cut and sew apparel contractors
315212 Coats, artificial leather, women's, girls', and infants', cut and sew apparel contractors
315292 Coats, fur (except apparel contractors), manufacturing
315211 Coats, fur, men's and boys', cut and sew apparel contractors
315212 Coats, fur, women's, girls', and infants', cut and sew apparel contractors
315291 Coats, infants' (except waterproof), cut and sewn from purchased fabric (except apparel contractors)
315292 Coats, leather, (except apparel contractors)
315211 Coats, leather, men's and boys', cut and sew apparel contractors
315212 Coats, leather, women's, girls', and infants', cut and sew apparel contractors
315211 Coats, men's and boys', cut and sew apparel contractors
315211 Coats, nontailored service apparel (e.g., laboratory, mechanics', medical), men's and boys', cut and sew apparel contractors
315225 Coats, nontailored service apparel (e.g., laboratory, mechanics', medical), men's and boys', cut and sewn from purchased fabric (except apparel contractors)

315212 Coats, nontailored service apparel (e.g., laboratory, medical, mechanics'), women's and girls', cut and sew apparel contractors
315239 Coats, nontailored service apparel (e.g., laboratory, medical, mechanics'), women's, misses', and girls', cut and sewn from purchased fabric (except apparel contractors)
315222 Coats, tailored (except fur, leather), men's and boys', cut and sewn from purchased fabric (except apparel contractors)
315234 Coats, tailored (except fur, leather), women's, misses', and girls', cut and sewn from purchased fabric
315299 Coats, waterproof (e.g., plastics, rubberized fabric, similar materials) rubberizing fabric and manufacturing coats
315211 Coats, waterproof (i.e., plastic, rubberized fabric, similar materials), men's and boy's, cut and sew apparel contractors
315212 Coats, waterproof (i.e., plastics, rubberized fabric, similar materials), women's, girls', and infants', cut and sew apparel contractors
315299 Coats, waterproof, (e.g., plastics, rubberized fabric, similar materials) cut and sewn from purchased fabric (except apparel contractors)
315212 Coats, women's, girls', and infants', cut and sew apparel contractors
331319 Coaxial cable made in aluminum wire drawing plants
423610 Coaxial cable merchant wholesalers
331422 Coaxial cable, copper, made from purchased copper in wire drawing plants
331491 Coaxial cable, nonferrous metals (except aluminum, copper), made from purchased nonferrous metals (except aluminum, copper) in wire drawing plants
335929 Coaxial cable, nonferrous, made from purchased nonferrous wire
334417 Coaxial connectors manufacturing
339991 Coaxial mechanical face seals manufacturing
325188 Cobalt 60 (i.e., radioactive cobalt) manufacturing
325188 Cobalt chloride manufacturing
325188 Cobalt compounds, not specified elsewhere by process, manufacturing
212299 Cobalt concentrates beneficiating
212299 Cobalt ores mining and/or beneficiating
331419 Cobalt refining, primary
325188 Cobalt sulfate manufacturing
325411 Cocaine and derivatives (i.e., basic chemicals) manufacturing
332913 Cocks, drain, plumbing, manufacturing
722410 Cocktail lounges
311999 Cocktail mixes, dry, manufacturing
424820 Cocktails, alcoholic, premixed, merchant wholesalers
311320 Cocoa (e.g., instant, mix, mixed with other ingredients, powder drink, powdered) made from cacao beans
424590 Cocoa beans merchant wholesalers
311320 Cocoa butter made from cocoa beans
311330 Cocoa, powdered drink, prepared, made from purchased chocolate
311330 Cocoa, powdered, made from purchased chocolate

311330 Cocoa, powdered, mixed with other ingredients, made from purchased chocolate
311225 Coconut oil made from purchased oils
311223 Coconut oil made in crushing mills
111339 Coconut tree farming
311999 Coconut, desiccated and shredded, manufacturing
114111 Cod catching
114111 Cod fishing
311711 Cod liver oil extraction, crude, produced in a cannery
311712 Cod liver oil extraction, crude, produced in a fresh and frozen seafood plant
325411 Cod liver oil, medicinal, uncompounded, manufacturing
325411 Codeine and derivatives (i.e., basic chemicals) manufacturing
333993 Coding, dating, and imprinting packaging machinery manufacturing
445299 Coffee and tea (i.e., packaged) stores
722330 Coffee carts, mobile
311920 Coffee concentrates (i.e., instant coffee) manufacturing
311920 Coffee extracts manufacturing
111339 Coffee farming
322299 Coffee filters made from purchased paper
311920 Coffee flavoring and syrups (i.e., made from coffee) manufacturing
333319 Coffee makers and urns, commercial-type, manufacturing
335211 Coffee makers, household-type electric, manufacturing
424490 Coffee merchant wholesalers
311920 Coffee roasting
333294 Coffee roasting and grinding machinery (i.e., food manufacturing-type) manufacturing
722213 Coffee shops, on premise brewing
311920 Coffee substitute manufacturing
337122 Coffee tables, wood, manufacturing
311920 Coffee, blended, manufacturing
312111 Coffee, iced, manufacturing
311920 Coffee, instant and freeze dried, manufacturing
454390 Coffee-break service providers, direct selling
237990 Cofferdam construction
487110 Cog railway, scenic and sightseeing, operation
237130 Co-generation plant construction
541720 Cognitive research and development services
811310 Coil rewinding (except on an assembly line or factory basis)
333518 Coil winding and cutting machinery, metalworking, manufacturing
332612 Coiled springs (except clock, watch), light gauge, made from purchased wire or strip, manufacturing
332611 Coiled springs, heavy gauge metal, manufacturing
335312 Coils for motors and generators manufacturing
336322 Coils, ignition, internal combustion engines, manufacturing
332996 Coils, pipe, made from purchased metal pipe
333313 Coin counting machinery manufacturing
561990 Coin pick-up services, parking meter
316993 Coin purses (except metal) manufacturing
339911 Coin purses, precious metal, manufacturing
423420 Coin sorting machines merchant wholesalers
333313 Coin wrapping machines manufacturing
339999 Coin-operated amusement machines (except jukebox) manufacturing
812310 Coin-operated drycleaners and laundries

713290 Coin-operated gambling device concession operators (i.e., supplying and servicing in others' facilities)
339999 Coin-operated gambling devices manufacturing
423990 Coin-operated game machines merchant wholesalers
334310 Coin-operated jukebox manufacturing
812310 Coin-operated laundry and drycleaning routes (i.e., concession operators)
423440 Coin-operated merchandising machine merchant wholesalers
713990 Coin-operated nongambling amusement device concession operators (i.e., supplying and servicing in others' facilities)
812990 Coin-operated personal service machine (e.g., blood pressure, locker, photographic, scale, shoeshine) concession operators
423440 Coin-operated phonographs and vending machines merchant wholesalers
333311 Coin-operated vending machines manufacturing
423940 Coins merchant wholesalers
423520 Coke merchant wholesalers
221210 Coke oven gas, production and distribution
324199 Coke oven products (e.g., coke, gases, tars) made in coke oven establishments
331111 Coke oven products made in iron and steel mills
324110 Coke, petroleum, made in petroleum refineries
335110 Cold cathode fluorescent lamp tubes manufacturing
332111 Cold forgings made from purchased iron or steel, unfinished
332112 Cold forgings made from purchased nonferrous metals, unfinished
325412 Cold remedies manufacturing
333516 Cold rolling mill machinery, metalworking, manufacturing
331221 Cold rolling steel shapes (e.g., bar, plate, rod, sheet, strip) made from purchased steel
493120 Cold storage locker services
423740 Cold storage machinery merchant wholesalers
236220 Cold storage plant construction
493120 Cold storage warehousing
311991 Cole slaw, fresh, manufacturing
212391 Colemanite mining and/or beneficiating
311612 Collagen sausage casings made from purchased hides
332439 Collapsible tubes (e.g., toothpaste, glue), light gauge metal, manufacturing
315191 Collar and cuff sets made in apparel knitting mills
315212 Collar and cuff sets, women's, girls' and infants', cut and sew apparel contractors
315239 Collar and cuff sets, women's, misses' and girls', cut and sewn from purchased fabric (except apparel contractors)
316110 Collar leather, manufacturing
111219 Collard farming, field, bedding plant and seed production
333515 Collars (i.e., a machine tool accessory) manufacturing
316999 Collars and collar pads (i.e., harness) manufacturing
316999 Collars, dog, manufacturing
333613 Collars, shaft for power transmission equipment, manufacturing
525990 Collateralized mortgage obligations (CMOs)
333293 Collating machinery for printing and bookbinding manufacturing
333313 Collating machinery, office-type, manufacturing
453220 Collectible gift shops (e.g., crystal, pewter, porcelain)
812320 Collecting and distributing agents, laundry and drycleaning

561440 Collection agencies
561440 Collection agencies, accounts
221320 Collection, treatment, and disposal of waste through a sewer system
335312 Collector rings for motors and generators manufacturing
453998 Collector's items shops (e.g., autograph, card, coin, stamp)
454113 Collector's items, mail-order houses
611691 College board preparation centers
611691 College entrance exam preparation instruction
611710 College selection services
611310 Colleges (except junior colleges)
611511 Colleges, barber and beauty
611210 Colleges, community
611210 Colleges, junior
611310 Colleges, universities, and professional schools
333515 Collets (i.e., a machine tool accessory) manufacturing
325620 Colognes manufacturing
424210 Colognes merchant wholesalers
334510 Colonscopes, electromedical, manufacturing
812199 Color consulting services (i.e., personal care services)
325131 Color pigments, inorganic (except bone black, carbon black, lamp black), manufacturing
325132 Color pigments, organic (except animal black, bone black), manufacturing
323122 Color separation services, for the printing trade
334516 Colorimeters, laboratory-type, manufacturing
423920 Coloring books merchant wholesalers
316110 Coloring leather
332813 Coloring metals and metal products (except coating) for the trade
339113 Colostomy appliances manufacturing
812220 Columbariums
212299 Columbite mining and/or beneficiating
212299 Columbium ores mining and/or beneficiating
327420 Columns, architectural or ornamental plaster work, manufacturing
332420 Columns, fractionating, heavy gauge metal, manufacturing
321918 Columns, porch, wood, manufacturing
316993 Comb cases (except metal) manufacturing
339911 Comb cases, precious metal, manufacturing
334512 Combination limit and fan controls manufacturing
112990 Combination livestock farming (except dairy, poultry)
334512 Combination oil and hydronic controls manufacturing
333111 Combines (i.e., harvester-threshers) manufacturing
313312 Combing and converting top
333292 Combing machinery for textiles manufacturing
313312 Combing textile fibers
115113 Combining, agricultural
332999 Combs, metal, manufacturing
326199 Combs, plastics, manufacturing
326299 Combs, rubber, manufacturing
334513 Combustion control instruments (except commercial, household furnace-type) manufacturing
541330 Combustion engineering consulting services
562211 Combustors, hazardous waste
562213 Combustors, nonhazardous solid waste
711510 Comedians, independent
711110 Comedy troupes
812990 Comfort station operation
314129 Comforters made from purchased fabrics
511120 Comic book publishers (except exclusive Internet publishing)

511120 Comic book publishers and printing combined (except exclusive Internet publishing)
516110 Comic book publishers, exclusively on Internet
323112 Comic books flexographic printing without publishing
323111 Comic books gravure printing without publishing
323110 Comic books lithographic (offset) printing without publishing
323119 Comic books printing (except flexographic, gravure, lithographic, screen) without publishing
323113 Comic books screen printing without publishing
811310 Commercial and industrial machinery repair and maintenance services
541430 Commercial art services
541430 Commercial artists, independent
311812 Commercial bakeries
522110 Commercial banking
522110 Commercial banks
236220 Commercial building construction
236220 Commercial building construction general contractors
236220 Commercial building construction operative builders
531120 Commercial building rental or leasing
561450 Commercial credit reporting bureaus
323115 Commercial digital printing
323119 Commercial engraving printing
323112 Commercial flexographic printing
238220 Commercial freezer installation
323111 Commercial gravure printing
541430 Commercial illustration services
541430 Commercial illustrators, independent
238290 Commercial kitchen food preparation equipment (e.g., mixers, ovens, stoves) installation
323119 Commercial letterpress printing
335122 Commercial lighting fixtures, electric, manufacturing
323110 Commercial lithographic (offset) printing
523120 Commercial note brokers' offices
523110 Commercial paper dealing (i.e., acting as a principal in dealing securities to investors)
541922 Commercial photography services
323119 Commercial printing (except flexographic, digital, gravure, lithographic, quick, screen)
531312 Commercial property managing
323114 Commercial quick printing
531210 Commercial real estate agencies
531210 Commercial real estate agents' offices
531312 Commercial real estate property managers' offices
811310 Commercial refrigeration equipment repair and maintenance services
238220 Commercial refrigeration system installation
323113 Commercial screen printing
424120 Commercial stationery suppliers merchant wholesalers
334518 Commercial timing mechanisms manufacturing
512110 Commercials, television, production
238290 Commercial-type door installation
445110 Commissaries, primarily groceries
523130 Commodity contract trading companies
523140 Commodity contracts brokerages
523140 Commodity contracts brokers' offices
523130 Commodity contracts dealing (i.e., acting as a principal in dealing commodities to investors)
523210 Commodity contracts exchanges

523140 Commodity contracts floor brokers
523130 Commodity contracts floor traders (i.e., acting as a principal in dealing commodities to investors)
523130 Commodity contracts floor trading (i.e., acting as a principal in dealing commodities to investors)
523140 Commodity contracts options brokerages
523130 Commodity contracts options dealing (i.e., acting as a principal in dealing commodities to investors)
523130 Commodity contracts traders (i.e., acting as a principal in dealing commodities to investors)
522298 Commodity Credit Corporation
523140 Commodity futures brokerages
541990 Commodity inspection services
212325 Common clay mining and/or beneficiating
212321 Common sand quarrying and/or beneficiating
212325 Common shale mining and/or beneficiating
923120 Communicable disease program administration
237130 Communication antenna construction
541430 Communication design services, visual
238210 Communication equipment installation
811213 Communication equipment repair and maintenance services
237130 Communication tower construction
926130 Communications commissions
423690 Communications equipment merchant wholesalers
334220 Communications equipment, mobile and microwave, manufacturing
334210 Communications headgear, telephone, manufacturing
926130 Communications licensing commissions and agencies
335929 Communications wire and cable, nonferrous, made from purchased nonferrous wire
331319 Communications wire or cable made in aluminum wire drawing plants
331422 Communications wire or cable, copper, made from purchased copper in wire drawing plants
331491 Communications wire or cable, nonferrous metals (except aluminum, copper), made from purchased nonferrous metals (except aluminum, copper) in wire drawing plants
311812 Communion wafer manufacturing
813319 Community action advocacy organizations
624190 Community action service agencies
624120 Community centers (except recreational only), adult
624110 Community centers (except recreational only), youth
813219 Community chests
611210 Community colleges
611210 Community colleges offering a wide variety of academic and technical training
925120 Community development agencies, government
813211 Community foundations
621498 Community health centers and clinics, outpatient
923120 Community health programs administration
624210 Community meals, social services
712110 Community museums
924120 Community recreation programs, government
923130 Community social service program administration
711110 Community theaters
335312 Commutators, electric motor, manufacturing

481111 Commuter air carriers, scheduled
485113 Commuter bus operation (except mixed mode)
485112 Commuter rail systems (except mixed mode)
485111 Commuter transit systems, mixed mode (e.g., bus, commuter rail, subway combination)
334310 Compact disc players (e.g., automotive, household-type) manufacturing
423990 Compact discs (CDs), prerecorded, merchant wholesalers
334611 Compact discs (i.e., CD-ROM), software, mass reproducing
334612 Compact discs, prerecorded audio, mass reproducing
334613 Compact discs, recordable or rewritable, blank, manufacturing
335110 Compact fluorescent light bulbs manufacturing
339911 Compacts, precious metal, manufacturing
316993 Compacts, solid leather, manufacturing
112990 Companion animals production (e.g., cats, dogs, parakeets, parrots)
624120 Companion services for disabled persons, the elderly, and persons diagnosed with mental retardation
333314 Comparators, optical, manufacturing
334511 Compasses, gyroscopic and magnetic (except portable), manufacturing
334519 Compasses, portable magnetic-type, manufacturing
541612 Compensation consulting services
541612 Compensation planning services
525190 Compensation, workers, insurance funds
311119 Complete feed, livestock, manufacturing
711510 Composers, independent
322214 Composite cans (i.e., foil-fiber and other combinations) manufacturing
562219 Compost dumps
325314 Compost manufacturing
325120 Compressed and liquefied industrial gas manufacturing
332911 Compressed gas cylinder valves manufacturing
424690 Compressed gases (except LP gas) merchant wholesalers
321219 Compression modified wood manufacturing
333220 Compression molding machinery for plastics manufacturing
339991 Compression packings manufacturing
532490 Compressor, air and gas, rental or leasing
237120 Compressor, metering and pumping station, gas and oil pipeline, construction
423830 Compressors (except air-conditioning, refrigeration) merchant wholesalers
333912 Compressors, air and gas, general purpose-type, manufacturing
423730 Compressors, air-conditioning, merchant wholesalers
336391 Compressors, motor vehicle air-conditioning, manufacturing
423740 Compressors, refrigeration, merchant wholesalers
238210 Computer and network cable installation
541710 Computer and related hardware research and development laboratories or services
423430 Computer boards, loaded, merchant wholesalers
423690 Computer boards, unloaded, merchant wholesalers
334419 Computer cable (e.g., monitor, printer) manufacturing
423690 Computer chips merchant wholesalers

541519 Computer disaster recovery services
813410 Computer enthusiasts clubs
811212 Computer equipment repair and maintenance services without retailing new computers
443120 Computer equipment stores
238330 Computer flooring installation
323116 Computer forms (manifold or continuous) printing
337124 Computer furniture, metal household-type, manufacturing
337122 Computer furniture, wood household-type, manufacturing
541512 Computer hardware consulting services or consultants
518210 Computer input preparation services
334119 Computer input/output equipment (except terminals) manufacturing
611420 Computer operator training
424120 Computer paper supplies merchant wholesalers
322231 Computer paper, single layered continuous, die-cut, made from purchased paper
423430 Computer peripheral equipment merchant wholesalers
532420 Computer peripheral equipment rental or leasing
811212 Computer peripheral equipment repair and maintenance, without retailing new computer peripheral equipment
325992 Computer printer toner cartridges manufacturing
423430 Computer printers merchant wholesalers
541511 Computer program or software development, custom
611420 Computer programming schools
541511 Computer programming services, custom
532420 Computer rental or leasing
811212 Computer repair and maintenance services, without retailing new computers
611519 Computer repair training
334111 Computer servers manufacturing
541511 Computer software analysis and design services, custom
541512 Computer software consulting services or consultants
541511 Computer software programming services, custom
511210 Computer software publishers, packaged
511210 Computer software publishing and reproduction
541511 Computer software support services, custom
334613 Computer software tapes and disks, blank, rigid and floppy, manufacturing
611420 Computer software training
454113 Computer software, mail-order houses
423430 Computer software, packaged, merchant wholesalers
443120 Computer stores
541513 Computer systems facilities (i.e., clients' facilities) management and operation services
541512 Computer systems integration analysis and design services
541512 Computer systems integration design consulting services
541512 Computer systems integrator services
334113 Computer terminals manufacturing
518210 Computer time leasing
518210 Computer time rental
518210 Computer time sharing services
621512 Computer tomography (CT-SCAN) centers
611420 Computer training (except repair)
532230 Computer video game rental
541512 Computer-aided design (CAD) systems integration design services
541512 Computer-aided engineering (CAE) systems integration design services

541512 Computer-aided manufacturing (CAM) systems integration design services
334517 Computerized axial tomography (CT/CAT) scanners manufacturing
334512 Computerized environmental control systems for buildings manufacturing
334111 Computers manufacturing
423430 Computers merchant wholesalers
325411 Concentrated medicinal chemicals, uncompounded, manufacturing
311930 Concentrates, drink (except frozen fruit juice), manufacturing
311930 Concentrates, flavoring (except coffee based), manufacturing
311411 Concentrates, frozen fruit juice, manufacturing
423520 Concentrates, metallic, merchant wholesalers
333131 Concentration machinery, mining-type, manufacturing
711130 Concert artists, independent
711320 Concert booking agencies
711310 Concert hall operators
531120 Concert hall, no promotion of events, rental or leasing
711310 Concert managers with facilities
711320 Concert managers without facilities
711310 Concert organizers with facilities
711320 Concert organizers without facilities
711310 Concert promoters with facilities
711320 Concert promoters without facilities
713990 Concession operators, amusement device (except gambling) and ride
812990 Concierge services
926150 Conciliation and mediation services, government
325998 Concrete additive preparations (e.g., curing, hardening) manufacturing
424690 Concrete additives merchant wholesalers
327320 Concrete batch plants (including temporary)
238140 Concrete block laying
238910 Concrete breaking and cutting for demolition
423320 Concrete building products merchant wholesalers
238390 Concrete coating, glazing or sealing
238110 Concrete finishing
333120 Concrete finishing machinery manufacturing
238110 Concrete floor surfacing
238190 Concrete form contractors
332322 Concrete forms, sheet metal (except stampings), manufacturing
327390 Concrete furniture (e.g., benches, tables) manufacturing
333120 Concrete gunning equipment manufacturing
333120 Concrete mixing machinery, portable, manufacturing
238990 Concrete patio construction
237310 Concrete paving (i.e., highway, road, street, public sidewalk)
238990 Concrete paving, residential and commercial driveway and parking area
238110 Concrete pouring
423810 Concrete processing equipment merchant wholesalers
238120 Concrete product (e.g., structural precast, structural prestressed) installation
333298 Concrete products forming machinery manufacturing
327390 Concrete products, precast (except block, brick and pipe), manufacturing
238110 Concrete pumping (i.e., placement)
238120 Concrete reinforcement placement

332312 Concrete reinforcing bars manufacturing
423510 Concrete reinforcing bars merchant wholesalers
332618 Concrete reinforcing mesh made from purchased wire
238110 Concrete repair
238110 Concrete resurfacing
238990 Concrete sawing and drilling (except demolition)
327390 Concrete tanks manufacturing
327999 Concrete, dry mixture, manufacturing
211112 Condensate, cycle, natural gas production
333294 Condensed and evaporated milk machinery manufacturing
311514 Condensed milk manufacturing
311514 Condensed, evaporated or powdered whey, manufacturing
332410 Condenser boxes, metal, manufacturing
335999 Condensers (except electronic), fixed and variable, manufacturing
334414 Condensers, electronic, manufacturing
423690 Condensers, electronic, merchant wholesalers
332410 Condensers, steam, manufacturing
335312 Condensers, synchronous, electric, manufacturing
423830 Condensing units (except air-conditioning, refrigeration) merchant wholesalers
423730 Condensing units, air-conditioning, merchant wholesalers
423740 Condensing units, refrigeration, merchant wholesalers
326299 Condom manufacturing
813990 Condominium corporations
531312 Condominium managers' offices, commercial
531311 Condominium managers' offices, residential
236117 Condominium operative builders
813990 Condominium owners' associations
561599 Condominium time share exchange services
236116 Condominium, multifamily, construction general contractors
236115 Condominium, single-family, construction general contractors
335931 Conductor connectors, solderless connectors, sleeves, or soldering lugs, manufacturing
327123 Conduit, vitrified clay, manufacturing
331210 Conduit, welded and lock joint, made from purchased iron or steel
335932 Conduits and fittings, electrical, manufacturing
327332 Conduits, concrete, manufacturing
322214 Cones (e.g., winding yarn, string, ribbon, cloth), fiber, made from purchased paperboard
311821 Cones, ice cream, manufacturing
327112 Cones, pyrometric, earthenware, manufacturing
311313 Confectioner's beet sugar manufacturing
311312 Confectioner's powdered sugar made from purchased raw cane sugar
311320 Confectionery chocolate made from cacao beans
333294 Confectionery machinery manufacturing
424450 Confectionery merchant wholesalers
722213 Confectionery snack shops, made on premises with carryout services
445292 Confectionery stores, packaged, retailing only
311340 Confectionery, nonchocolate, manufacturing

531120 Conference center, no promotion of events, rental or leasing
322299 Confetti made from purchased paper
921120 Congress of the United States
336312 Connecting rods, automotive and truck gasoline engine, manufacturing
335931 Connectors and terminals for electrical devices manufacturing
335931 Connectors, electric cord, manufacturing
334417 Connectors, electronic (e.g., coaxial, cylindrical, printed circuit, rack and panel), manufacturing
423690 Connectors, electronic, merchant wholesalers
335313 Connectors, power, manufacturing
335931 Connectors, solderless (wiring devices), manufacturing
335931 Connectors, twist on wire (i.e., nuts), manufacturing
813312 Conservation advocacy organizations
924120 Conservation and reclamation agencies
712190 Conservation areas
611310 Conservatories of music (colleges or universities)
712130 Conservatories, botanical
711510 Conservators, independent
611610 Conservatory of music (except academic)
453310 Consignment shops, used
336350 Constant velocity joints, automotive, truck, and bus, manufacturing
813940 Constituencies' associations, political party
325520 Construction adhesives (except asphalt, gypsum base) manufacturing
813910 Construction associations
238990 Construction elevator (i.e., temporary use during construction) erection and dismantling
541330 Construction engineering services
238910 Construction equipment (except crane) rental with operator
532412 Construction form rental
522292 Construction lending
423810 Construction machinery and equipment merchant wholesalers
532412 Construction machinery and equipment rental or leasing without operator
811310 Construction machinery and equipment repair and maintenance services
333120 Construction machinery manufacturing
236220 Construction management, commercial and institutional building
237990 Construction management, dam
237310 Construction management, highway, road, street and bridge
236210 Construction management, industrial building (except warehouses)
237990 Construction management, marine structure
237990 Construction management, mass transit
236116 Construction management, multifamily building
237120 Construction management, oil and gas pipeline
237120 Construction management, oil refinery and petrochemical complex
237990 Construction management, outdoor recreation facility
237130 Construction management, power and communication transmission line
236118 Construction management, residential remodeling
236115 Construction management, single-family building
237990 Construction management, tunnel

237110 Construction management, water and sewage treatment plant
237110 Construction management, water and sewer line
423610 Construction materials, electrical, merchant wholesalers
322233 Construction paper, school and art, made from purchased paper
322121 Construction paper, school and art, made in paper mills
212321 Construction sand and gravel beneficiating (e.g., grinding, screening, washing)
212321 Construction sand or gravel dredging
238990 Construction site cleanup contractors
333120 Construction-type tractors and attachments manufacturing
928120 Consulates
****** Consultants—see specific activity
813920 Consultants' associations
531390 Consultants', real estate (except appraisers), offices
541330 Consulting engineers' offices
541330 Consulting engineers' private practices
812990 Consumer buying services
541990 Consumer credit counseling services
561450 Consumer credit reporting bureaus
423620 Consumer electronics merchant wholesalers
532210 Consumer electronics rental
811211 Consumer electronics repair and maintenance services without retailing new consumer electronics
522291 Consumer finance companies (i.e., unsecured cash loans)
522291 Consumer lending
922190 Consumer product safety commissions
926110 Consumer protection offices
443112 Consumer-type electronic stores (e.g., radio, television, video camera)
334514 Consumption meters (e.g., gas, water) manufacturing
524128 Contact lens insurance, direct
339115 Contact lenses manufacturing
423460 Contact lenses merchant wholesalers
335931 Contacts, electrical (except carbon and graphite), manufacturing
335991 Contacts, electrical, carbon and graphite, manufacturing
322130 Container board stock manufacturing
336611 Container ship building
484110 Container trucking services, local
484121 Container trucking services, long-distance (TL)
327213 Containers for packaging, bottling, and canning, glass, manufacturing
332439 Containers, air cargo, light gauge metal, manufacturing
332999 Containers, foil (except bags), manufacturing
423840 Containers, industrial, merchant wholesalers
332439 Containers, light gauge metal (except cans), manufacturing
424130 Containers, paper and disposable plastics, merchant wholesalers
321920 Containers, wood, manufacturing
712110 Contemporary art museums
711120 Contemporary dance companies
623311 Continuing care retirement communities
325412 Contraceptive preparations manufacturing
213112 Contract services (except site preparation and related construction contractor activities) for oil and gas fields
****** Contractors—see specific activity

813910 Contractors' associations
315211 Contractors, men's and boys', cut and sew apparel
315212 Contractors, women's, girls' and infants', cut and sew apparel
325412 Contrast media in-vivo diagnostic substances (e.g., iodine, barium) manufacturing
335314 Control circuit devices, magnet and solid-state, manufacturing
335314 Control circuit relays, industrial, manufacturing
335314 Control equipment, electric, manufacturing
335313 Control panels, electric power distribution, manufacturing
238210 Control system (e.g., environmental, humidity, temperature) installation
335311 Control transformers manufacturing
332912 Control valves, fluid power, manufacturing
332911 Control valves, industrial-type, manufacturing
921130 Controller's and comptrollers' offices, government
334513 Controllers for process variables (e.g., electric, electronic, mechanical, pneumatic operation) manufacturing
334290 Controlling equipment, street light, manufacturing
335314 Controls and control accessories, industrial, manufacturing
335314 Controls for adjustable speed drives manufacturing
334514 Controls, revolution and timing instruments, manufacturing
623110 Convalescent homes or convalescent hospitals (except psychiatric)
623220 Convalescent homes or hospitals for psychiatric patients
446199 Convalescent supply stores
335221 Convection ovens (including portable), household-type, manufacturing
445120 Convenience food stores
447110 Convenience food with gasoline stations
335931 Convenience outlets, electric, manufacturing
561591 Convention and visitors bureaus
561591 Convention bureaus
531120 Convention center, no promotion of events, rental or leasing
561920 Convention managers
561920 Convention organizers
561920 Convention promoters
561920 Convention services
813110 Convents (except schools)
424130 Converted paper (except stationery and office supplies) merchant wholesalers
313311 Converters, broadwoven piece goods
335312 Converters, phase and rotary, electrical equipment, manufacturing
337121 Convertible sofas (except futons) manufacturing
336399 Convertible tops for automotive, truck, and bus, manufacturing
313311 Converting textiles, broadwoven
313312 Converting textiles, narrow woven
316110 Convertors, leather
313312 Convertors, narrow woven piece goods
423830 Conveying equipment (except farm) merchant wholesalers
423820 Conveying equipment, farm, merchant wholesalers
326220 Conveyor belts, rubber, manufacturing
238290 Conveyor system installation
333922 Conveyors, farm-type, manufacturing
311612 Cooked meats made from purchased carcasses
311822 Cookie dough made from purchased flour

722213 Cookie shops, on premise baking and carryout service
311821 Cookies manufacturing
424490 Cookies merchant wholesalers
311821 Cookies, filled, manufacturing
335211 Cooking appliances (except convection, microwave ovens), household-type electric portable, manufacturing
311320 Cooking chocolate made from cacao beans
333319 Cooking equipment (i.e., fryers, microwave ovens, ovens, ranges), commercial-type, manufacturing
423440 Cooking equipment, commercial, merchant wholesalers
423620 Cooking equipment, electric household-type, merchant wholesalers
423720 Cooking equipment, gas, household-type, merchant wholesalers
424490 Cooking oils merchant wholesalers
611519 Cooking schools
331511 Cooking utensils, cast iron, manufacturing
332214 Cooking utensils, fabricated metal, manufacturing
327212 Cooking utensils, glass and glass ceramic, made in glass making plants
423220 Cooking utensils, household-type, merchant wholesalers
327112 Cooking ware (e.g., stoneware, coarse earthenware, pottery), manufacturing
327215 Cooking ware made from purchased glass
327212 Cooking ware made in glass making plants
327112 Cooking ware, china, manufacturing
327112 Cooking ware, fine earthenware, manufacturing
221330 Cooled air distribution
326199 Coolers or ice chests, plastics (except foam), manufacturing
326140 Coolers or ice chests, polystyrene foam, manufacturing
333415 Coolers, refrigeration, manufacturing
333415 Coolers, water, manufacturing
238220 Cooling tower installation
333415 Cooling towers manufacturing
321920 Cooperage manufacturing
321920 Cooperage stock (e.g., heading, hoops, staves) manufacturing
423840 Cooperage stock merchant wholesalers
321920 Cooperage stock mills
531311 Cooperative apartment managers' offices
236117 Cooperative apartment operative builders
236116 Cooperative apartment, construction general contractors
812331 Cooperative hospital laundries (i.e., linen supply services)
524113 Cooperative life insurance organizations
813990 Cooperative owners' associations
321920 Coopered tubs manufacturing
332212 Coordinate and contour measuring machines, machinists' precision tools, manufacturing
532420 Copier rental or leasing
327123 Coping, wall, clay, manufacturing
327390 Copings, concrete, manufacturing
331525 Copper alloy castings (except die-castings), unfinished, manufacturing
331423 Copper alloys (e.g., brass, bronze) made from purchased metal or scrap
331411 Copper alloys made in primary copper smelting and refining mills
331423 Copper and copper-based shapes (e.g., cake, ingot, slag, wire bar) made from purchased metal or scrap

325131 Copper base pigments manufacturing
212234 Copper beneficiating plants
325188 Copper chloride manufacturing
325612 Copper cleaners manufacturing
325188 Copper compounds, not specified elsewhere by process, manufacturing
331411 Copper concentrate refining
331522 Copper die-casting foundries
331522 Copper die-castings, unfinished, manufacturing
331421 Copper foil made from purchased metal or scrap
332999 Copper foil not made in rolling mills
332112 Copper forgings made from purchased metals, unfinished
331525 Copper foundries (except die-casting)
325188 Copper iodide manufacturing
212234 Copper ore concentrates recovery
212234 Copper ore mine site development for own account
212234 Copper ores mining and/or beneficiating
331423 Copper powder, flakes, and paste made from purchased copper
331421 Copper products (except communication wire, energy wire) made by drawing purchased copper
331421 Copper products (except communication wire, energy wire) made by rolling, drawing, or extruding purchased copper
331421 Copper products (except communication wire, energy wire) made in integrated secondary smelting and extruding mills
331421 Copper products (except communication wire, energy wire) made in integrated secondary smelting mills and drawing plants
238160 Copper roofing installation
331423 Copper secondary smelting and alloying
331423 Copper secondary smelting and refining from purchased metal or scrap
331411 Copper shapes (e.g., bar, billet, ingot, plate, sheet) made in primary copper smelting and refining mills
331411 Copper smelting and refining, primary
325188 Copper sulfate manufacturing
212234 Copper-water precipitates
561439 Copy centers (except combined with printing services)
561439 Copy shops (except combined with printing services)
423420 Copying machines merchant wholesalers
314991 Cord (except tire, wire) manufacturing
335931 Cord connectors, electric, manufacturing
314992 Cord for reinforcing rubber tires, industrial belting, and fuel cells manufacturing
331422 Cord sets, flexible, made from purchased copper in wire drawing plants
331319 Cord sets, flexible, made in aluminum wire drawing plants
331491 Cord sets, flexible, nonferrous metals (except aluminum, copper), made from purchased nonferrous metals (except aluminum, copper) in wire drawing plants
314991 Cordage (except wire) manufacturing
333292 Cordage and rope (except wire) making machines manufacturing
423840 Cordage merchant wholesalers
325920 Cordite explosive materials manufacturing
334210 Cordless telephones (except cellular) manufacturing
313221 Cords and braids, narrow woven, manufacturing
313210 Corduroys weaving

333994 Core baking and mold drying ovens manufacturing
213112 Core cutting in oil and gas wells, on a contract basis
238910 Core drilling and test boring for construction
213112 Core drilling, exploration services, oil and gas field
333131 Core drills, underground mining-type, manufacturing
322214 Cores (i.e., all-fiber, nonfiber ends of any material), fiber, made from purchased paperboard
332992 Cores, bullet (i.e., 30 mm. or less, 1.18 inch or less), manufacturing
332997 Cores, sand foundry, manufacturing
423840 Cork merchant wholesalers
321999 Cork products (except gaskets) manufacturing
321999 Corks, bottle, manufacturing
111421 Corms farming
311230 Corn breakfast foods manufacturing
311919 Corn chips and related corn snacks manufacturing
424450 Corn chips and related corn snacks merchant wholesalers
311340 Corn confections manufacturing
321992 Corn cribs, prefabricated, wood, manufacturing
311221 Corn dextrin manufacturing
115114 Corn drying
111150 Corn farming (except sweet corn), field and seed production
311211 Corn flour manufacturing
311221 Corn gluten feed manufacturing
311221 Corn gluten meal manufacturing
333111 Corn heads for combines manufacturing
311211 Corn meal made in flour mills
311221 Corn oil cake and meal manufacturing
311225 Corn oil made from purchased oils
311221 Corn oil mills
311221 Corn oil, crude and refined, made by wet milling corn
333111 Corn pickers and shellers manufacturing
335211 Corn poppers, household-type electric, manufacturing
333294 Corn popping machinery (i.e., food manufacturing-type) manufacturing
333319 Corn popping machines, commercial-type, manufacturing
339113 Corn remover and bunion pad manufacturing
115114 Corn shelling
311221 Corn starch manufacturing
311221 Corn sweeteners (e.g., dextrose, fructose, glucose) made by wet milling corn
311999 Corn syrups made from purchased sweeteners
311213 Corn, malt, manufacturing
339112 Corneal microscopes manufacturing
311612 Corned meats made from purchases carcasses
316999 Corners, luggage, leather, manufacturing
339992 Cornets and parts manufacturing
332322 Cornices, sheet metal (except stampings), manufacturing
321918 Cornices, wood, manufacturing
112320 Cornish hen production
424490 Cornmeal, edible, merchant wholesalers
212325 Cornwall stone mining and/or beneficiating
923120 Coroners' offices
522130 Corporate credit unions
813211 Corporate foundations, awarding grants
541430 Corporate identification (i.e., logo) design services
541110 Corporate law offices
551114 Corporate offices
115210 Corralling, drovers
332323 Corrals, metal, manufacturing
325998 Correction fluids (i.e., typewriter) manufacturing
922140 Correctional boot camps

561210 Correctional facility operation on a contract or fee basis
922140 Correctional institutions
237120 Corrosion protection, underground pipeline and oil storage tank
322211 Corrugated and solid fiber boxes made from purchased paper or paperboard
322211 Corrugated and solid fiberboard pads made from purchased paper or paperboard
238160 Corrugated metal roofing installation
322211 Corrugated paper made from purchased paper or paperboard
331221 Corrugating iron or steel in cold rolling mills made from purchased iron or steel
315212 Corselets cut and sew apparel contractors
315231 Corselets, women's, misses', and girls', cut and sewn from purchased fabric (except apparel contractors)
315212 Corsets and allied garments (except surgical), women's, cut and sew apparel contractors
315231 Corsets and allied garments (except surgical), women's, misses', and girls', cut and sewn from purchased fabric (except apparel contractors)
339113 Corsets, surgical, manufacturing
325411 Cortisone, uncompounded, manufacturing
212399 Corundum mining and/or beneficiating
316993 Cosmetic bags (except metal) manufacturing
339911 Cosmetic bags, precious metal, manufacturing
325620 Cosmetic creams, lotions, and oils manufacturing
561910 Cosmetic kit assembling and packaging services
424210 Cosmetics merchant wholesalers
446120 Cosmetics stores
812112 Cosmetology salons or shops
611511 Cosmetology schools
541490 Costume design services (except independent theatrical costume designers)
711510 Costume designers, independent theatrical
339914 Costume jewelry manufacturing
423940 Costume jewelry merchant wholesalers
448150 Costume jewelry stores
532220 Costume rental
448190 Costume stores (including theatrical)
315299 Costumes (e.g., lodge, masquerade, theatrical) cut and sewn from purchased fabric (except apparel contractors)
315212 Costumes (e.g., lodge, masquerade, theatrical) women's, girls' and infants', cut and sew apparel contractors
315211 Costumes (e.g., lodge, masquerade, theatrical), men's and boys', cut and sew apparel contractors
337121 Cot springs, assembled, manufacturing
337124 Cots, metal household-type, manufacturing
337122 Cots, wood household-type, manufacturing
311511 Cottage cheese manufacturing
236115 Cottage construction general contractors
236117 Cottage operative builders
531110 Cottage rental or leasing
721199 Cottages, housekeeping
332722 Cotter pins, metal, manufacturing
424990 Cotton (except raw) merchant wholesalers
339113 Cotton and cotton balls, absorbent, manufacturing
333111 Cotton balers and presses manufacturing
314999 Cotton battings (except nonwoven batting) manufacturing

313111 Cotton cordage spun yarns made from purchased fiber
313210 Cotton fabrics, broadwoven, weaving
313221 Cotton fabrics, narrow woven weaving
111920 Cotton farming, field and seed production
322121 Cotton fiber paper stock manufacturing
115111 Cotton ginning
333111 Cotton ginning machinery manufacturing
333111 Cotton picker and stripper harvesting machinery manufacturing
313111 Cotton spun yarns made from purchased fiber
313113 Cotton thread manufacturing
339113 Cotton tipped applicators manufacturing
115113 Cotton, machine harvesting
424590 Cotton, raw, merchant wholesalers
111920 Cottonseed farming
311225 Cottonseed oil made from purchased oils
311223 Cottonseed oil, cake and meal, made in crushing mills
337121 Couch springs, assembled, manufacturing
337121 Couches, upholstered, manufacturing
311340 Cough drops (except medicated) manufacturing
325412 Cough drops, medicated, manufacturing
325412 Cough medicines manufacturing
334513 Coulometric analyzers, industrial process-type, manufacturing
334516 Coulometric analyzers, laboratory-type, manufacturing
325199 Coumarin manufacturing
325211 Coumarone-indene resins manufacturing
926110 Councils of Economic Advisers
624190 Counseling services
621410 Counseling services, family planning
541110 Counselors' at law offices
541110 Counselors' at law private practices
334519 Count rate meters, nuclear radiation, manufacturing
238350 Counter top, residential-type, installation
334514 Counter type registers manufacturing
337215 Counter units (except refrigerated) manufacturing
333515 Counterbores (i.e., a machine tool accessory), metalworking, manufacturing
332212 Counterbores and countersinking bits, woodworking, manufacturing
334511 Countermeasure sets (e.g., active countermeasures, jamming equipment) manufacturing
334514 Counters (e.g., electrical, electronic, mechanical), totalizing, manufacturing
316999 Counters (i.e., shoe cut stock), leather, manufacturing
333415 Counters and display cases, refrigerated, manufacturing
334514 Counters, revolution, manufacturing
333515 Countersinks (i.e., a machine tool accessory) manufacturing
238390 Countertop and cabinet, metal (except residential-type), installation
337215 Countertops (except kitchen and bathroom), wood or plastics laminated on wood, manufacturing
337110 Countertops (i.e., kitchen, bathroom), wood or plastics laminated on wood, manufacturing
326199 Countertops, plastics, manufacturing
327991 Countertops, stone, manufacturing
337110 Countertops, wood, manufacturing
334514 Counting devices manufacturing

713910 Country clubs
711130 Country musical artists, independent
711130 Country musical groups
921120 County commissioners
925120 County development agencies
921110 County supervisors' and executives' offices
923110 County supervisors of education (except school boards)
332919 Couplings, hose, metal (except fluid power), manufacturing
333613 Couplings, mechanical power transmission, manufacturing
332996 Couplings, pipe, made from purchased metal pipe
541870 Coupon direct distribution services
561990 Coupon processing services
561990 Coupon redemption services (i.e., clearinghouse)
492110 Courier services (i.e., intercity network)
611410 Court reporting schools
561492 Court reporting services
922110 Courts of law, civilian (except American Indian or Alaska Native)
921150 Courts, American Indian or Alaska Native
922110 Courts, civilian (except American Indian or Alaska Native)
928110 Courts, military
922110 Courts, small claims
315211 Coveralls, work, men's and boys', cut and sew apparel contractors
315225 Coveralls, work, men's and boys', cut and sewn from purchased fabric (except apparel contractors)
315212 Coveralls, work, women's, girls', and infants', cut and sew apparel contractors
315239 Coveralls, work, women's, misses', and girls', cut and sewn from purchased fabric (except apparel contractors)
314912 Covers (e.g., boat, swimming pool, truck) made from purchased fabrics
332313 Covers, annealing, fabricated metal plate work, manufacturing
321999 Covers, bottle and demijohn, willow, rattan, and reed, manufacturing
332313 Covers, floating, fabricated metal plate work, manufacturing
332322 Cowls, sheet metal (except stampings), manufacturing
111219 Cowpea (except dry) farming, field and seed production
111130 Cowpea farming, dry, field and seed production
541211 CPAs' (certified public accountants) offices
611699 CPR (cardiac pulmonary resusitation) training and certification
332618 Crab traps made from purchased wire
114112 Crabbing
333294 Cracker making machinery manufacturing
311821 Crackers (e.g., graham, soda) manufacturing
333518 Cradle assembly machinery (i.e., wire making equipment) manufacturing
337122 Cradles, wood, manufacturing
453220 Craft (except craft supply) stores
339932 Craft and hobby kits and sets manufacturing
561920 Craft fair managers
561920 Craft fair organizers
561920 Craft fair promoters
423920 Craft kits merchant wholesalers
451120 Craft supply stores (except needlecraft)
611513 Craft union apprenticeship training programs
111334 Cranberry farming
335314 Crane and hoist controls, including metal mill, manufacturing

532412 Crane rental or leasing without operator
238990 Crane rental with operator
423810 Cranes (except industrial) merchant wholesalers
333120 Cranes, construction-type, manufacturing
333924 Cranes, industrial truck, manufacturing
423830 Cranes, industrial, merchant wholesalers
423810 Cranes, mining, merchant wholesalers
333923 Cranes, overhead traveling, manufacturing
325998 Crankcase additive preparations manufacturing
336312 Crankshaft assemblies, automotive and truck gasoline engine, manufacturing
333512 Crankshaft grinding machines metal cutting type, manufacturing
321920 Crates (e.g., berry, butter, fruit, vegetable) made of wood, wirebound, manufacturing
488991 Crating goods for shipping
112512 Crawfish production, farm raising
238910 Crawler tractor rental with operator
114112 Crayfish fishing
339942 Crayons manufacturing
311511 Cream manufacturing
424430 Cream merchant wholesalers
325199 Cream of tartar manufacturing
333111 Cream separators, farm-type, manufacturing
333294 Cream separators, industrial, manufacturing
424430 Cream stations merchant wholesalers
311514 Cream, dried and powdered, manufacturing
311512 Creamery butter manufacturing
424430 Creamery products (except canned) merchant wholesalers
424490 Creamery products, canned, merchant wholesalers
313311 Crease resistant finishing of broadwoven fabric
313312 Crease resistant finishing of fabrics (except broadwoven)
561450 Credit agencies
323119 Credit and identification card imprinting and embossing
326199 Credit and identification card stock, plastics, manufacturing
524126 Credit and other financial responsibility insurance carriers, direct
561450 Credit bureaus
522210 Credit card banks
522210 Credit card issuing
812990 Credit card notification services (i.e., lost or stolen card reporting)
522320 Credit card processing services
561450 Credit investigation services
524113 Credit life insurance carriers, direct
561450 Credit rating services
541990 Credit repair (i.e., counseling) services, consumer
561450 Credit reporting bureaus
522130 Credit unions
333999 Cremating ovens manufacturing
812220 Crematories (except combined with funeral homes)
111219 Crenshaw melon farming, field, bedding plant and seed production
325192 Creosote made by distillation of coal tar
325191 Creosote made by distillation of wood tar
321114 Creosoting of wood
322299 Crepe paper made from purchased paper
325211 Cresol resins manufacturing
325211 Cresol-furfural resins manufacturing
325192 Cresols made by distillation of coal tar
325192 Cresylic acids made from refined petroleum or natural gas
115115 Crew leaders, farm labor

315119 Crew socks knitting or knitting and finishing
237990 Cribbing (i.e., shore protection), construction
337124 Cribs (i.e., baby beds), metal, manufacturing
337122 Cribs (i.e., baby beds), wood, manufacturing
112990 Cricket production
922120 Criminal investigation offices, government
922190 Criminal justice statistics centers, government
541110 Criminal law offices
111998 Crimson cloves seed farming
624190 Crisis intervention centers
114111 Croaker fishing
313111 Crochet spun yarns (e.g., cotton, manmade fiber, silk, wool) made from purchased fiber
314999 Crochet ware made from purchased materials
335211 Crock pots, household-type electric, manufacturing
327112 Crockery manufacturing
311812 Croissants, baking, made in commercial bakeries
115114 Crop cleaning
333111 Crop driers manufacturing
115112 Crop dusting
524126 Crop insurance carrier, direct
423820 Crop preparation machinery (e.g., cleaning, conditioning, drying) merchant wholesalers
115112 Crop spraying
316999 Crops, riding, manufacturing
339920 Croquet sets manufacturing
713920 Cross country skiing facilities without accommodations
332911 Cross valves, industrial-type, manufacturing
321114 Crossties, treating
311812 Croutons and bread crumbs made in commercial bakeries
423840 Crowns and closures, metal, merchant wholesalers
332115 Crowns, metal (e.g., bottle, can), stamping
334411 CRT (cathode ray tube) manufacturing
327124 Crucibles, fire clay, manufacturing
327125 Crucibles, graphite, magnesite, chrome, silica, or other nonclay materials, manufacturing
311221 Crude corn oil manufacturing
424720 Crude oil merchant wholesalers (except bulk stations, terminals)
486110 Crude oil pipeline transportation
324110 Crude oil refining
424710 Crude oil terminals
211111 Crude petroleum from oil sand
211111 Crude petroleum from oil shale
211111 Crude petroleum production
324110 Crude petroleum refineries
424990 Crude rubber merchant wholesalers
336322 Cruise control mechanisms, electronic, automotive, truck, and bus, manufacturing
483114 Cruise lines (i.e., deep sea passenger transportation to and from domestic ports, including Puerto Rico)
483112 Cruise lines (i.e., deep sea passenger transportation to or from foreign ports)
561599 Cruise ship ticket offices
713210 Cruises, gambling
115310 Cruising timber
311812 Crullers (except frozen) made in commercial bakeries
311813 Crullers, frozen, made in a commercial bakery
423320 Crushed stone merchant wholesalers
333120 Crushing machinery, portable, manufacturing
333131 Crushing machinery, stationary, manufacturing
212111 Crushing plants, bituminous coal
333120 Crushing, pulverizing, and screening machinery, portable, manufacturing
112512 Crustacean production, farm raising

339113 Crutches and walkers manufacturing
423450 Crutches merchant wholesalers
532291 Crutches, invalid, rental
332420 Cryogenic tanks, heavy gauge metal, manufacturing
212399 Cryolite mining and/or beneficiating
311340 Crystallized fruits and fruit peel manufacturing
334419 Crystals and crystal assemblies, electronic, manufacturing
334517 CT/CAT (computerized axial tomography) scanners manufacturing
621512 CT-SCAN (computer tomography) centers
335313 Cubicles (i.e., electric switchboard equipment) manufacturing
111219 Cucumber farming (except under cover), field, bedding plant and seed production
111419 Cucumber farming, grown under cover
339993 Cuff links (except precious) manufacturing
339911 Cuff links, precious metal, manufacturing
332999 Cuffs, leg, iron, manufacturing
611519 Culinary arts schools
112310 Cull hen production
212113 Culm bank recovery, anthracite (except on a contract basis)
213113 Culm bank recovery, anthracite, on a contract basis
212111 Culm bank recovery, bituminous coal or lignite (except on a contract basis)
213113 Culm bank recovery, coal, on a contract basis
315212 Culottes, women's, girls' and infants', cut and sew apparel contractors
315239 Culottes, women's, misses', and girls', cut and sewn from purchased fabric (except apparel contractors)
111422 Cultivated florist greens growing
423820 Cultivating machinery and equipment merchant wholesalers
115112 Cultivation services
333111 Cultivators, farm-type, manufacturing
333112 Cultivators, powered, lawn and garden-type, manufacturing
926110 Cultural and arts development support program administration
325414 Culture media manufacturing
326191 Cultured marble plumbing fixtures manufacturing
326199 Cultured marble products (except plumbing fixtures) manufacturing
112512 Cultured pearl production, farm raising
326199 Cultured stone products (except plumbing fixtures) manufacturing
327332 Culvert pipe, concrete, manufacturing
238990 Culvert, concrete, residential and commercial paved area
332313 Culverts, fabricated metal plate work, manufacturing
237310 Culverts, highway, road and street, construction
332322 Culverts, sheet metal (except stampings), manufacturing
325110 Cumene made from refined petroleum or liquid hydrocarbons
324110 Cumene made in petroleum refineries
315999 Cummerbunds cut and sewn from purchased fabric (except apparel contractors)
315211 Cummerbunds, men's and boys', cut and sew apparel contractors
332313 Cupolas, fabricated metal plate work, manufacturing
212234 Cuprite mining and/or beneficiating
322299 Cups, molded pulp, manufacturing

424130 Cups, paper and disposable plastics, merchant wholesalers
423220 Cups, plastics (except disposable), merchant wholesalers
326199 Cups, plastics (except foam), manufacturing
326140 Cups, polystyrene foam, manufacturing
238990 Curb and gutter construction, residential and commercial driveway and parking area, concrete
327991 Curbing, granite and stone, manufacturing
237310 Curbs and street gutters, highway, road and street, construction
311513 Curds, cheese, made in a cheese plant, manufacturing
424460 Cured fish merchant wholesalers
311611 Cured hides and skins produced in slaughtering plants
311612 Cured meats (e.g., brined, dried, and salted) made from purchased carcasses
333111 Curers, tobacco, manufacturing
311711 Curing fish and seafood
453220 Curio shops
424990 Curios merchant wholesalers
326299 Curlers, hair, rubber, manufacturing
713990 Curling facilities
335211 Curling irons, household-type electric, manufacturing
111334 Currant farming
333313 Currency counting machinery manufacturing
423420 Currency handling machines merchant wholesalers
335311 Current limiting reactors, electrical, manufacturing
334515 Current measuring equipment manufacturing
335931 Current taps, attachment plug and screw shell types, manufacturing
423610 Current-carrying wiring devices merchant wholesalers
316110 Currying furs
316110 Currying leather
442291 Curtain and drapery stores, packaged
812320 Curtain cleaning services
337920 Curtain or drapery fixtures (e.g., poles, rods, rollers) manufacturing
337920 Curtain rods and fittings manufacturing
321999 Curtain stretchers, wood, manufacturing
238150 Curtain wall, glass, installation
238190 Curtain wall, metal, installation
332323 Curtain wall, metal, manufacturing
238120 Curtain wall, precast concrete, installation
313210 Curtains and draperies made in broadwoven fabric mills
314121 Curtains and draperies, window, made from purchased fabrics
313249 Curtains made in lace mills
313249 Curtains made in warp knitting mills
313241 Curtains made in weft knitting mills
423220 Curtains merchant wholesalers
337121 Cushion springs, assembled, manufacturing
314129 Cushions (except carpet, springs) made from purchased fabrics
326150 Cushions, carpet and rug, urethane and other foam plastics (except polystrene), manufacturing
311520 Custard, frozen, manufacturing
561720 Custodial services
337212 Custom architectural millwork and fixtures, manufacturing on a job shop basis
236116 Custom builders (except operative), multifamily buildings
236115 Custom builders (except operative), single-family home
236117 Custom builders, operative builders, multifamily buildings
236117 Custom builders, operative builders, single-family home

325991 Custom compounding (i.e., blending and mixing) of purchased plastics resins
337212 Custom design interiors (i.e., coordinated furniture, architectural woodwork, fixtures), manufacturing
311119 Custom milling of animal feed
442299 Custom picture frame shops
333513 Custom roll forming machines, metalworking, manufacturing
332114 Custom roll forming metal products
321113 Custom sawmills
311611 Custom slaughtering
315223 Custom tailors, men's and boys' dress shirts, cut and sewn from purchased fabric
315222 Custom tailors, men's and boys' suits, cut and sewn from purchased fabric
315233 Custom tailors, women's, misses' and girls' dresses cut and sewn from purchased fabric (except apparel contractors)
541613 Customer service management consulting services
488510 Customs brokers
921130 Customs bureaus
541614 Customs consulting services
327215 Cut and engraved glassware made from purchased glass
315211 Cut and sew apparel contractors, men's and boys'
315212 Cut and sew apparel contractors, women's, girls', and infants'
111422 Cut flower growing
111422 Cut rose growing
316999 Cut stock for boots and shoes manufacturing
321912 Cut stock manufacturing
327991 Cut stone bases (e.g., desk sets pedestals, lamps, plaques and similar small particles) manufacturing
327991 Cut stone products (e.g., blocks, statuary) manufacturing
811490 Cutlery (e.g., knives, scissors) sharpening, household-type
423710 Cutlery merchant wholesalers
332211 Cutlery, nonprecious and precious plated metal, manufacturing
339912 Cutlery, precious metal (except precious plated), manufacturing
333512 Cut-off machines, metalworking, manufacturing
335931 Cutouts, switch and fuse, manufacturing
333131 Cutters, coal, manufacturing
332212 Cutters, glass, manufacturing
333515 Cutters, metal milling, manufacturing
113310 Cutting and transporting timber
213112 Cutting cores in oil and gas wells on a contract basis
332212 Cutting dies (e.g., paper, leather, textile) manufacturing
332212 Cutting dies (except metal cutting) manufacturing
333514 Cutting dies, metalworking, manufacturing
315211 Cutting fabric owned by others for men's and boys' apparel
315212 Cutting fabric owned by others for women's, girls', and infants' apparel
339114 Cutting instruments, dental, manufacturing
333512 Cutting machines, metalworking, manufacturing
238910 Cutting new rights of way
316110 Cutting of leather
424470 Cutting of purchased carcasses (except boxed meat cut on an assembly-line basis) merchant wholesalers
324191 Cutting oils made from refined petroleum
325998 Cutting oils, synthetic, manufacturing
113310 Cutting timber
327215 Cutting, engraving, etching, painting or polishing purchased glass

111422 Cuttings farming
325188 Cyanides manufacturing
212325 Cyanite mining and/or beneficiating
211112 Cycle condensate production
325110 Cyclic aromatic hydrocarbons made from refined petroleum or liquid hydrocarbons
324110 Cyclic aromatic hydrocarbons made in petroleum refineries
424690 Cyclic crudes and intermediates merchant wholesalers
325192 Cyclic crudes made by distillation of coal tar
325212 Cyclo rubber, synthetic, manufacturing
325192 Cyclohexane manufacturing
332313 Cyclones, industrial, fabricated metal plate work, manufacturing
325192 Cyclopentane made from refined petroleum or natural gas
325192 Cyclopropane made from refined petroleum or natural gas
325412 Cyclopropane medicinal preparations manufacturing
325191 Cycloterpenes manufacturing
335999 Cyclotrons manufacturing
333512 Cylinder boring machines metal cutting type, manufacturing
336312 Cylinder heads, automotive and truck gasoline engine, manufacturing
327332 Cylinder pipe, prestressed concrete, manufacturing
332618 Cylinder wire cloth made from purchased wire
332994 Cylinders and clips, gun (i.e., 30 mm. or less, 1.18 inch or less), manufacturing
332995 Cylinders and clips, gun (i.e., more than 30 mm., more than 1.18 inch), manufacturing
333995 Cylinders, fluid power, manufacturing
336340 Cylinders, master brake (new and rebuilt), manufacturing
332420 Cylinders, pressure, heavy gauge metal, manufacturing
334417 Cylindrical connectors, electronic, manufacturing
332991 Cylindrical roller bearings manufacturing
339992 Cymbals and parts manufacturing
339112 Cystoscopes (except electromedical) manufacturing
334510 Cystoscopes, electromedical, manufacturing
325413 Cytology and histology in-vitro diagnostic substances manufacturing
621511 Cytology health laboratories
112120 Dairy cattle farming
311119 Dairy cattle feeds supplements, concentrates, and premixes, manufacturing
424430 Dairy depots merchant wholesalers
311514 Dairy food canning
112420 Dairy goat farming
112111 Dairy heifer replacement production
541690 Dairy herd consulting services
115210 Dairy herd improvement associations
445299 Dairy product stores
424430 Dairy products (except canned, dried) merchant wholesalers
424490 Dairy products, dried or canned, merchant wholesalers
424430 Dairy products, frozen, merchant wholesalers
112410 Dairy sheep farming
237990 Dam construction
332312 Dam gates, metal plate, manufacturing
334512 Damper operators (e.g., electric, pneumatic, thermostatic) manufacturing
332322 Dampers, sheet metal (except stampings), manufacturing
238390 Dampproofing contractors
711130 Dance bands
713940 Dance centers, aerobic
711120 Dance companies

711310 Dance festival managers with facilities
711320 Dance festival managers without facilities
711310 Dance festival organizers with facilities
711320 Dance festival organizers without facilities
711310 Dance festival promoters with facilities
711320 Dance festival promoters without facilities
531120 Dance hall rental or leasing
713990 Dance halls
611610 Dance instruction
711120 Dance productions, live theatrical
611610 Dance schools
611610 Dance studios
711120 Dance theaters
621340 Dance therapists' offices (e.g., centers, clinics)
711120 Dance troupes
711510 Dancers, independent
313113 Darning thread (e.g., cotton, manmade fibers, silk, wool) manufacturing
332994 Dart guns manufacturing
339932 Darts and dart games manufacturing
518210 Data capture imaging services
334210 Data communications equipment (e.g., bridges, gateways, routers) manufacturing
518210 Data entry services
334513 Data loggers, industrial process-type, manufacturing
518210 Data processing computer services
541513 Data processing facilities (i.e., clients' facilities) management and operation services
423430 Data processing machines, computer, merchant wholesalers
518210 Data processing services (except payroll services, financial transition processing services)
323112 Databases flexographic printing without publishing
323111 Databases gravure printing without publishing
323110 Databases lithographic (offset) printing without publishing
323119 Databases printing (except flexographic, gravure, lithographic, quick, screen) without publishing
323113 Databases screen printing without publishing
111339 Date farming
339943 Date stamps, hand operated, manufacturing
311423 Dates, dried, made in dehydration plant
311340 Dates, sugared and stuffed, manufacturing
334518 Dating devices and machines (except rubber stamps) manufacturing
812990 Dating services
333923 Davits manufacturing
****** Day camps, instructional—see type of instruction
624120 Day care centers for disabled persons, the elderly, and persons diagnosed with mental retardation
624120 Day care centers, adult
624410 Day care centers, child or infant
624410 Day care services, child or infant
621310 DCs' (doctors of chiropractic) offices (e.g., centers, clinics)
621210 DDSs' (doctors of dental surgery) offices (e.g., centers, clinics)
325320 DDT (dichlorodiphenyltrichloroethane) insecticides manufacturing
922120 DEA (Drug Enforcement Administration)
332510 Dead bolts, metal, manufacturing
****** Dealers—see type
561440 Debt collection services
333512 Deburring machines, metalworking, manufacturing

334515 Decade boxes (i.e., capacitance, inductance, resistance) manufacturing
325199 Decahydronaphthalene manufacturing
327112 Decalcomania on china and glass for the trade
339999 Decalcomania work (except on china, glass)
238190 Deck and grate (except roof), metal, installation
238350 Deck construction, residential-type
327215 Decorated glassware made from purchased glass
327112 Decorating china (e.g., encrusting gold, silver, other metal on china) for the trade
541410 Decorating consulting services, interior
335129 Decorative area lighting fixtures (except residential) manufacturing
335121 Decorative area lighting fixtures, residential, manufacturing
712110 Decorative art museums
238150 Decorative glass and mirror installation
327212 Decorative glassware made in glass making plants
335110 Decorative lamp bulbs manufacturing
238190 Decorative steel and wrought iron work installation
315211 Decorative stitching contractors on men's and boys' apparel
315212 Decorative stitching contractors on women's, misses', girls', and infants' apparel
314999 Decorative stitching on textile articles and apparel
321918 Decorative wood moldings (e.g., base, chair rail, crown, shoe) manufacturing
115114 Decorticating flax
483113 Deep sea freight transportation to or from domestic ports (including Puerto Rico)
483111 Deep sea freight transportation to or from foreign ports
483114 Deep sea passenger transportation to and from domestic ports (including Puerto Rico)
483112 Deep sea passenger transportation to or from foreign ports
333319 Deep-fat fryers, commercial-type, manufacturing
335211 Deep-fat fryers, household-type electric, manufacturing
112990 Deer production
334510 Defibrilators manufacturing
325312 Defluorinated phosphates manufacturing
325998 Defoamers and antifoaming agents manufacturing
325320 Defoliants manufacturing
325998 Degreasing preparations for machinery parts manufacturing
325612 Degreasing preparations, household-type, manufacturing
333415 Dehumidifiers (except portable electric) manufacturing
335211 Dehumidifiers, portable electric, manufacturing
311514 Dehydrated milk manufacturing
311423 Dehydrating fruits and vegetables
311423 Dehydrating potato products (e.g., flakes, granules)
325998 Deicing preparations manufacturing
322110 Deinking plants
322110 Deinking recovered paper
722211 Delicatessen restaurants
333997 Delicatessen scales manufacturing
445210 Delicatessens (except grocery store, restaurants)
445110 Delicatessens primarily retailing a range of grocery items and meats
561440 Delinquent account collection services
623990 Delinquent youth halfway group homes
115114 Delinting cottonseed

332618 Delivery cases made from purchased wire
492210 Delivery service (except as part of intercity carrier network, U.S. Postal Service)
334515 Demand meters, electric, manufacturing
541720 Demographic research and development services
238910 Demolition contractor
238910 Demolition, building and structure
541890 Demonstration services, merchandise
336212 Demountable cargo containers manufacturing
325193 Denatured alcohol manufacturing
313210 Denims weaving
321219 Densified wood manufacturing
333315 Densitometers (except laboratory analytical) manufacturing
334516 Densitometers, laboratory analytical, manufacturing
334513 Density and specific gravity instruments, industrial process-type, manufacturing
339114 Dental alloys for amalgams manufacturing
339114 Dental chairs manufacturing
423450 Dental chairs merchant wholesalers
339114 Dental equipment and instruments manufacturing
423450 Dental equipment and supplies merchant wholesalers
811219 Dental equipment repair and maintenance services
325620 Dental floss manufacturing
339114 Dental glues and cements manufacturing
339114 Dental hand instruments (e.g., forceps) manufacturing
611519 Dental hygienist schools
621399 Dental hygienists' offices (e.g., centers, clinics)
339114 Dental impression materials manufacturing
339114 Dental instrument delivery systems manufacturing
524114 Dental insurance carriers, direct
339116 Dental laboratories
339114 Dental laboratory equipment manufacturing
541710 Dental research and development laboratories or services
611310 Dental schools
621210 Dental surgeons' offices (e.g., centers, clinics)
611519 Dental technician schools
339114 Dental wax manufacturing
621512 Dental X-ray laboratories
325611 Dentifrices manufacturing
424210 Dentifrices merchant wholesalers
813920 Dentists' associations
621210 Dentists' offices (e.g., centers, clinics)
423450 Dentists' professional supplies merchant wholesalers
325620 Denture adhesives manufacturing
325620 Denture cleaners, effervescent, manufacturing
339114 Denture materials manufacturing
339116 Dentures, custom made in dental laboratories
621399 Denturists' offices (e.g., centers, clinics)
561720 Deodorant servicing of rest rooms
325612 Deodorants (except personal) manufacturing
424690 Deodorants (except personal) merchant wholesalers
325620 Deodorants, personal, manufacturing
424210 Deodorants, personal, merchant wholesalers
238290 Deodorization (i.e., air filtration) system installation
561720 Deodorizing services
452111 Department stores (except discount department stores)
452112 Department stores, discount

812199 Depilatory (i.e., hair removal) salons
325620 Depilatory preparations manufacturing
332813 Depolishing metals and metal products for the trade
523999 Deposit brokers
524128 Deposit or share insurance carriers, direct
522110 Depository trust companies
339113 Depressors, tongue, manufacturing
332995 Depth charge projectors manufacturing
332993 Depth charges manufacturing
325412 Dermatological preparations manufacturing
621111 Dermatologists' offices (e.g., centers, clinics)
213112 Derrick building, repairing, and dismantling at oil and gas fields on a contract basis
333132 Derricks, oil and gas field-type, manufacturing
325998 Desalination kits manufacturing
327992 Desiccants, activated clay, manufacturing
335211 Desk fans, electric, manufacturing
335122 Desk lamps, commercial, electric, manufacturing
335121 Desk lamps, residential, electric, manufacturing
316999 Desk sets, leather, manufacturing
337214 Desks (except wood), office-type, manufacturing
337122 Desks, wood household-type, manufacturing
337211 Desks, wood office-type, manufacturing
561410 Desktop publishing services (i.e., document preparation service)
424430 Desserts, dairy, merchant wholesalers
311520 Desserts, frozen (except bakery), manufacturing
311813 Desserts, frozen bakery, manufacturing
811192 Detailing services (i.e., cleaning and polishing), automotive
115112 Detasseling corn
561611 Detective agencies
334519 Detectors, scintillation, manufacturing
922140 Detention centers
325611 Detergents (e.g., dishwashing, industrial, laundry) manufacturing
424690 Detergents merchant wholesalers
331492 Detinning scrap (e.g., cans)
325920 Detonating caps, cord, fuses, and primers manufacturing
325920 Detonators (except ammunition) manufacturing
332993 Detonators, ammunition (i.e., more than 30 mm., more than 1.18 inch), manufacturing
621420 Detoxification centers and clinics (except hospitals), outpatient
622210 Detoxification hospitals
325188 Deuterium oxide (i.e., heavy water) manufacturing
325992 Developers, prepared photographic, manufacturing
336411 Developing and producing prototypes for aircraft
336412 Developing and producing prototypes for aircraft engines and engine parts
336413 Developing and producing prototypes for aircraft parts (except engines) and auxiliary equipment
336414 Developing and producing prototypes for complete guided missiles and space vehicles
336419 Developing and producing prototypes for guided missile and space vehicle components
336415 Developing and producing prototypes for guided missile and space vehicle engines
333315 Developing equipment, film, manufacturing

926110 Development assistance program administration
813311 Developmentally disabled advocacy organizations
238910 Dewatering contractors
111334 Dewberry farming
325520 Dextrin glues manufacturing
311221 Dextrin made by wet milling corn
212319 Diabase crushed and broken stone mining and/or beneficiating
212311 Diabase mining or quarrying
325412 Diagnostic biological preparations (except in-vitro) manufacturing
811198 Diagnostic centers without repair, automotive
334510 Diagnostic equipment, electromedical, manufacturing
423450 Diagnostic equipment, medical, merchant wholesalers
334510 Diagnostic equipment, MRI (magnetic resonance imaging), manufacturing
621512 Diagnostic imaging centers (medical)
811219 Diagnostic imaging equipment repair and maintenance services
424210 Diagnostic reagents merchant wholesalers
325413 Diagnostic substances, in-vitro, manufacturing
424210 Diagnostics, in-vitro and in-vivo, merchant wholesalers
332212 Dial indicators, machinists' precision tools, manufacturing
621492 Dialysis centers and clinics
334510 Dialysis equipment, electromedical, manufacturing
325312 Diammonium phosphates manufacturing
332618 Diamond cloths made from purchased wire
339913 Diamond cutting and polishing
333514 Diamond dies, metalworking, manufacturing
327910 Diamond dressing wheels manufacturing
423940 Diamonds (except industrial) merchant wholesalers
423840 Diamonds, industrial, merchant wholesalers
212399 Diamonds, industrial, mining and/or beneficiating
315212 Diaper covers, water resistant and waterproof, cut and sew apparel contractors
315291 Diaper covers, waterproof, infants', cut and sewn from purchased fabric (except apparel contractors)
812331 Diaper supply services
314999 Diapers (except disposable) made from purchased fabrics
424330 Diapers (except paper) merchant wholesalers
322291 Diapers, disposable, made from purchased paper or textile fiber
322121 Diapers, disposable, made in paper mills
424130 Diapers, paper, merchant wholesalers
326299 Diaphragms (i.e., birth control device), rubber, manufacturing
323118 Diaries manufacturing
511199 Diary and time scheduler publishers (except exclusive Internet publishing)
516110 Diary and time scheduler publishers, exclusively on Internet
212325 Diaspore mining and/or beneficiating
334510 Diathermy apparatus, electromedical, manufacturing
334510 Diathermy units manufacturing
212399 Diatomaceous earth mining and/or beneficitating
327992 Diatomaceous earth processing beyond beneficiation
212399 Diatomite mining and/or beneficiating
325992 Diazo (i.e., whiteprint) paper and cloth, sensitized, manufacturing
325120 Dichlorodifluoromethane manufacturing

325188 Dichromates manufacturing
315212 Dickeys, women's, girls', and infants', cut and sew apparel contractors
315239 Dickeys, women's, misses' and girls', cut and sewn from purchased fabric (except apparel contractors)
333313 Dictating machines manufacturing
423420 Dictating machines merchant wholesalers
561410 Dictation services
611699 Diction schools
323117 Dictionaries printing and binding without publishing
323117 Dictionaries printing without publishing
323121 Dictionary binding without printing
511130 Dictionary publishers (except exclusive Internet publishing)
511130 Dictionary publishers and printing combined
516110 Dictionary publishers, exclusively on Internet
325211 Dicyandiamine resins manufacturing
333514 Die sets for metal stamping presses manufacturing
333512 Die sinking machines, metalworking, manufacturing
333511 Die-casting dies manufacturing
333513 Die-casting machines, metalworking, manufacturing
331521 Die-castings, aluminum, unfinished, manufacturing
331522 Die-castings, nonferrous metals (except aluminum), unfinished, manufacturing
322299 Die-cut paper products (except for office use) made from purchased paper or paperboard
322231 Die-cut paper products for office use made from purchased paper or paperboard
333994 Dielectric industrial heating equipment manufacturing
333514 Dies and die holders for metal cutting and forming (except threading) manufacturing
333515 Dies and taps (i.e., a machine tool accessory) manufacturing
332212 Dies, cutting (except metal cutting), manufacturing
333514 Dies, metalworking (except threading), manufacturing
333514 Dies, plastics forming, manufacturing
332212 Dies, steel rule (except metal cutting), manufacturing
333514 Dies, steel rule, metal cutting, manufacturing
333618 Diesel and semidiesel engines manufacturing
324110 Diesel fuels manufacturing
812191 Diet centers, non-medical
812191 Diet workshops
311514 Dietary drinks, dairy and nondairy based, manufacturing
325192 Diethylcyclohexane manufacturing
325199 Diethylene glycol manufacturing
813920 Dietitians' associations
621399 Dietitians' offices (e.g., centers, clinics)
336350 Differential and rear axle assemblies, automotive, truck, and bus, manufacturing
334513 Differential pressure instruments, industrial process-type, manufacturing
334516 Differential thermal analysis instruments, laboratory-type, manufacturing
332420 Digesters, industrial-type, heavy gauge metal, manufacturing
325412 Digestive system preparations manufacturing
238910 Digging foundations
334119 Digital cameras manufacturing
334111 Digital computers manufacturing
334513 Digital displays of process variables manufacturing
334515 Digital panel meters, electricity measuring, manufacturing

323115 Digital printing (e.g., billboards, other large format graphic materials)
323115 Digital printing (e.g., graphics, high resolution)
333293 Digital printing presses manufacturing
334515 Digital test equipment (e.g., electronic and electrical circuits and equipment testing) manufacturing
334310 Digital video disc players manufacturing
325412 Digitalis medicinal preparations manufacturing
325411 Digitoxin, uncompounded, manufacturing
325211 Diisocyanate resins manufacturing
237990 Dike and other flood control structure construction
111219 Dill farming, field and seed production
321113 Dimension lumber, hardwood, made from logs or bolts
321912 Dimension lumber, hardwood, resawing purchased lumber
321113 Dimension lumber, made from logs or bolts
321912 Dimension lumber, resawing purchased lumber
321113 Dimension lumber, softwood, made from logs or bolts
321912 Dimension lumber, softwood, resawing purchased lumber
321912 Dimension stock, hardwood, manufacturing
321912 Dimension stock, softwood, manufacturing
321912 Dimension stock, wood, manufacturing
327991 Dimension stone dressing and manufacturing
327991 Dimension stone for buildings manufacturing
212311 Dimension stone mining or quarrying
325199 Dimethyl divinyl acetylene (di-isopropenyl acetylene) manufacturing
325199 Dimethylhydrazine manufacturing
335931 Dimmer switches, outlet box mounting-type, manufacturing
722110 Diners, full service
337124 Dinette sets, metal household-type, manufacturing
326299 Dinghies, inflatable rubber, manufacturing
336612 Dinghy (except inflatable rubber) manufacturing
337124 Dining room chairs (including upholstered), metal, manufacturing
337125 Dining room chairs (including upholstered), plastics manufacturing
337122 Dining room chairs (including upholstered), wood, manufacturing
337124 Dining room furniture, metal household-type, manufacturing
337122 Dining room furniture, wood household-type, manufacturing
487210 Dinner cruises
711110 Dinner theaters
311412 Dinners, frozen (except seafood-based), manufacturing
311712 Dinners, frozen seafood, manufacturing
424420 Dinners, frozen, merchant wholesalers
326199 Dinnerware, plastics (except polystyrene foam), manufacturing
326140 Dinnerware, polystyrene foam, manufacturing
334515 Diode and transistor testers manufacturing
423690 Diodes merchant wholesalers
334413 Diodes, solid-state (e.g., germanium, silicon), manufacturing
212313 Diorite crushed and broken stone mining and/or beneficiating
212311 Diorite mining or quarrying
325192 Diphenylamine manufacturing
928120 Diplomatic services

311941 Dips (except cheese and sour cream based) manufacturing
325320 Dips (i.e., pesticides), cattle and sheep, manufacturing
311513 Dips, cheese based, manufacturing
311511 Dips, sour cream based, manufacturing
334112 Direct access storage devices manufacturing
517510 Direct broadcast satellite (DBS)
325132 Direct dyes manufacturing
541860 Direct mail advertising services
541860 Direct mail or other direct distribution advertising campaign services
454113 Direct mailers (i.e., selling own merchandise)
331111 Direct reduction of iron ore
454390 Direct selling of merchandise (door-to-door)
213111 Directional drilling of oil and gas wells on a contract basis
812210 Director services, funeral
323112 Directories flexographic printing without publishing
323111 Directories gravure printing without publishing
323110 Directories lithographic (offset) printing without publishing
323119 Directories printing (except flexographic, gravure, lithographic, quick, screen) without publishing
323113 Directories screen printing without publishing
711510 Directors (i.e., film, motion picture, music, theatrical), independent
711510 Directors, independent motion picture
711510 Directors, independent music
511140 Directory and mailing list publishers (except exclusive Internet publishing)
511140 Directory and mailing list publishers and printing combined
511140 Directory publishers (except exclusive Internet publishing)
511140 Directory publishers and printing combined
516110 Directory publishers, exclusively on Internet
541870 Directory, telephone, distribution on a contract basis
517510 Direct-to-home satellite systems
238910 Dirt moving for construction
524113 Disability insurance carriers, direct
524113 Disability insurance underwriting, direct
624120 Disability support groups
623990 Disabled group homes without nursing care
922190 Disaster preparedness and management offices, government
624230 Disaster relief services
711510 Disc jockeys, independent
623990 Disciplinary camps for delinquent youth
713990 Discotheques (except those serving alcoholic beverages)
812990 Discount buying services
511199 Discount coupon book publishers (except exclusive Internet publishing)
511199 Discount coupon book publishers and printing combined
516110 Discount coupon book publishers, exclusively on Internet
323112 Discount coupon books flexographic printing without publishing
323111 Discount coupon books gravure printing without publishing
323110 Discount coupon books lithographic (offset) printing without publishing
323119 Discount coupon books printing (except flexographic, gravure, lithographic, quick, screen) without publishing
323113 Discount coupon books screen printing without publishing
452112 Discount department stores

813212 Disease awareness fundraising organizations
115112 Disease control for crops
813212 Disease research (e.g., cancer, heart) fundraising organizations
541940 Disease testing services, veterinary
313249 Dishcloths made in warp knitting mills
313241 Dishcloths made in weft knitting mills
423220 Dishes, household-type (except disposable plastics, paper), merchant wholesalers
424130 Dishes, paper and disposable plastics, merchant wholesalers
327112 Dishes, pottery, manufacturing
339932 Dishes, toy, manufacturing
321999 Dishes, wood, manufacturing
325611 Dishwasher detergents manufacturing
335228 Dishwashers, household-type, manufacturing
423620 Dishwashers, household-type, merchant wholesalers
423440 Dishwashing equipment, commercial-type, merchant wholesalers
333319 Dishwashing machines, commercial-type, manufacturing
335228 Dishwashing machines, household-type, manufacturing
325612 Disinfectants, household-type and industrial, manufacturing
518210 Disk and diskette conversion services
518210 Disk and diskette recertification services
332611 Disk and ring springs, heavy gauge metal, manufacturing
334112 Disk drives, computer, manufacturing
423430 Disk drives, computer, merchant wholesalers
334613 Diskettes, blank, manufacturing
423690 Diskettes, blank, merchant wholesalers
238910 Dismantling engineering structures (e.g., oil storage tank)
238290 Dismantling large-scale machinery and equipment
213112 Dismantling of oil well rigs on a contract basis
333913 Dispensing and measuring pumps (e.g., gasoline, lubricants) manufacturing
325132 Disperse dyes manufacturing
325510 Dispersions, pigment, manufacturing
541850 Display advertising services
423440 Display cases (except refrigerated) merchant wholesalers
337215 Display cases and fixtures (except refrigerated) manufacturing
333415 Display cases, refrigerated, manufacturing
423740 Display cases, refrigerated, merchant wholesalers
334513 Display instruments, industrial process control-type, manufacturing
541890 Display lettering services
339950 Displays (e.g., counter, floor, point-of-purchase) manufacturing
335912 Disposable flashlight batteries manufacturing
424130 Disposable plastics products (e.g., boxes, cups, cutlery, dishes, sanitary food containers) merchant wholesalers
334511 Distance measuring equipment (DME), aeronautical, manufacturing
325191 Distillates, wood, manufacturing
333994 Distillation ovens, charcoal and coke, manufacturing
424820 Distilled alcoholic beverages merchant wholesalers
325998 Distilled water manufacturing
312140 Distilleries
311213 Distiller's malt manufacturing

423830 Distillery machinery merchant wholesalers
312140 Distilling alcoholic beverages (except brandy)
312130 Distilling brandy
333298 Distilling equipment (except beverage) manufacturing
333294 Distilling equipment, beverage, manufacturing
312140 Distilling potable liquor (except brandy)
334515 Distortion meters and analyzers manufacturing
335313 Distribution boards, electric, manufacturing
335313 Distribution cutouts manufacturing
423610 Distribution equipment, electrical, merchant wholesalers
237120 Distribution line, gas and oil, construction
237110 Distribution line, sewer and water, construction
221330 Distribution of cooled air
221122 Distribution of electric power
221330 Distribution of heated air
221210 Distribution of manufactured gas
221210 Distribution of natural gas
221330 Distribution of steam heat
335311 Distribution transformers, electric, manufacturing
336322 Distributor cap and rotor for internal combustion engines manufacturing
813910 Distributors' associations
336322 Distributors for internal combustion engines manufacturing
551114 District and regional offices
922130 District attorneys' offices
333120 Ditchers and trenchers, self-propelled, manufacturing
325412 Diuretic preparations manufacturing
332212 Dividers, machinists' precision tools, manufacturing
451110 Diving equipment stores
561990 Diving services on a contract or fee basis
621210 DMDs' (doctors of dental medicine) offices (e.g., centers, clinics)
621511 DNA testing laboratories
531120 Dock and associated building rental or leasing
237990 Dock construction
488330 Docking and undocking marine vessel services
488310 Docking facility operations
621310 Doctors of chiropractic (DCs) offices (e.g., centers, clinics)
621210 Doctors of dental medicine (DMDs) offices (e.g., centers, clinics)
621210 Doctors of dental surgery (DDSs) offices (e.g., centers, clinics)
621320 Doctors of optometry (ODs) offices (e.g., centers, clinics)
621112 Doctors of osteopathy (DOs), mental health, offices (e.g., centers, clinics)
621111 Doctors of osteopathy (DOs, except mental health) offices (e.g., centers, clinics)
621391 Doctors of podiatry (DPs) offices (e.g., centers, clinics)
621330 Doctors of psychology offices (e.g., centers, clinics)
561439 Document copying services (except combined with printing services)
561439 Document duplicating services (except combined with printing services)
561410 Document preparation services
561990 Document shredding services
561410 Document transcription services
325110 Dodecene made from refined petroleum or liquid hydrocarbons
311111 Dog and cat food (e.g., canned, dry, frozen, semimoist), manufacturing
311111 Dog food manufacturing

316999 Dog furnishings (e.g., collars, harnesses, leashes, muzzles), manufacturing
711219 Dog owners, race (i.e., racing dogs)
812910 Dog pounds
112990 Dog production
711212 Dog racetracks
711219 Dog racing kennels
424990 Dogs merchant wholesalers
322299 Doilies, paper, made from purchased paper
339932 Doll carriages and carts manufacturing
339931 Doll clothing manufacturing
452990 Dollar stores
333924 Dollies manufacturing
423920 Dolls merchant wholesalers
339931 Dolls, doll parts, and doll clothing (except wigs) manufacturing
212312 Dolomite crushed and broken stone mining and/or beneficiating
212311 Dolomite mining or quarrying
327410 Dolomite, dead-burned, manufacturing
327410 Dolomitic lime manufacturing
212319 Dolomitic marble crushed and broken stone mining and/or beneficiating
212311 Dolomitic marble mining or quarrying
114111 Dolphin fishing
112920 Donkey production
332321 Door and jamb assemblies, metal, manufacturing
238350 Door and window frame construction
238350 Door and window, prefabricated, installation
332321 Door frames and sash, metal, manufacturing
321911 Door frames and sash, wood and covered wood, manufacturing
332322 Door hoods, sheet metal (except stampings), manufacturing
321911 Door jambs, wood, manufacturing
332510 Door locks, metal, manufacturing
332510 Door opening and closing devices (except electrical), metal, manufacturing
335999 Door opening and closing devices, electrical, manufacturing
321918 Door shutters, wood, manufacturing
444190 Door stores
321918 Door trim, wood molding, manufacturing
321911 Door units, prehung, wood and covered wood, manufacturing
238290 Door, commercial- or industrial-type, installation
238350 Door, folding, installation
314110 Doormats, all materials (except entirely of rubber or plastics), manufacturing
326199 Doormats, plastics, manufacturing
326299 Doormats, rubber, manufacturing
423310 Doors and door frames merchant wholesalers
326199 Doors and door frames, plastics, manufacturing
321911 Doors, combination screen-storm, wood, manufacturing
332321 Doors, metal, manufacturing
332999 Doors, safe and vault, metal, manufacturing
327215 Doors, unframed glass, made from purchased glass
321911 Doors, wood and covered wood, manufacturing
541870 Door-to-door distribution of advertising materials (e.g., coupons, flyers, samples)
454390 Door-to-door retailing of merchandise, direct selling
325510 Dopes, paint, and laquer, manufacturing
336612 Dories building
721310 Dormitories, off campus
236220 Dormitory construction

621112 DOs' (doctors of osteopathy), mental health, offices (e.g., centers, clinics)
621111 DOs' (doctors of osteopathy, except mental health) offices (e.g., centers, clinics)
334519 Dosimetry devices manufacturing
333294 Dough mixing machinery (i.e., food manufacturing-type) manufacturing
722110 Doughnut shops, full service
722213 Doughnut shops, on premise baking and carryout service
311812 Doughnuts (except frozen) made in commercial bakeries
311813 Doughnuts, frozen, manufacturing
424420 Doughs, frozen, merchant wholesalers
311211 Doughs, prepared, made in flour mills
311822 Doughs, refrigerated or frozen, made from purchased flour
333210 Dovetailing machines, woodworking-type, manufacturing
332722 Dowel pins, metal, manufacturing
321999 Dowels, wood, manufacturing
315291 Down-filled clothing, infants', cut and sewn from purchased fabric (except apparel contractors)
315211 Down-filled clothing, men's and boys', cut and sew apparel contractors
315228 Down-filled clothing, men's and boys', cut and sewn from purchased fabric (except apparel contractors)
315212 Down-filled clothing, women's, girls' and infants' cut and sew apparel contractors
315239 Down-filled clothing, women's, misses', and girls', cut and sewn from purchased fabric (except apparel contractors)
713920 Downhill skiing facilities without accommodations
238170 Downspout, gutter, and gutter guard installation
332322 Downspouts, sheet metal (except stampings), manufacturing
621391 DPs' (doctors of podiatry) offices (e.g., centers, clinics)
334513 Draft gauges, industrial process-type, manufacturing
334519 Drafting instruments manufacturing
423490 Drafting instruments merchant wholesalers
339942 Drafting materials (except instruments and tables) manufacturing
541340 Drafting services
337127 Drafting tables and boards manufacturing
423490 Drafting tables merchant wholesalers
541340 Draftsmen's offices
711212 Drag strips
333120 Draglines, crawler, manufacturing
325191 Dragon's blood manufacturing
333111 Drags, farm-type equipment, manufacturing
333120 Drags, road construction and road maintenance equipment, manufacturing
212399 Dragstones mining and/or beneficiating
561790 Drain cleaning services
332913 Drain cocks, plumbing, manufacturing
325612 Drain pipe cleaners manufacturing
332999 Drain plugs, magnetic, metal, manufacturing
327123 Drain tile, clay, manufacturing
238220 Drain, waste and vent system installation
237990 Drainage canal and ditch construction
237990 Drainage project construction
238910 Drainage system (e.g., cesspool, septic tank) installation

337110 Drainboards, wood or plastics laminated on wood, manufacturing
213113 Draining or pumping coal mines on a contract basis
213114 Draining or pumping of metal mines on a contract basis
213115 Draining or pumping of nonmetallic mineral mines (except fuels) on a contract basis
611610 Drama schools (except academic)
314121 Draperies made from purchased fabrics or sheet goods
423220 Draperies merchant wholesalers
812320 Drapery cleaning services
238390 Drapery fixture (e.g., hardware, rods, tracks) installation
339113 Drapes, surgical, disposable, manufacturing
333518 Draw bench machines manufacturing
315192 Drawers, apparel, made in apparel knitting mills
315211 Drawers, men's and boys', cut and sew apparel contractors
315221 Drawers, men's and boys', cut and sewn from purchased fabric (except apparel contractors)
315212 Drawers, women's, girls', and infants', cut and sew apparel contractors
315231 Drawers, women's, misses', and girls', cut and sewn from purchased fabric (except apparel contractors)
325998 Drawing inks manufacturing
331222 Drawing iron or steel wire from purchased iron or steel
331222 Drawing iron or steel wire from purchased iron or steel and fabricating wire products
333292 Drawing machinery for textiles manufacturing
337127 Drawing tables and boards, artist's, manufacturing
332212 Drawknives manufacturing
336611 Dredge building
237990 Dredging (e.g., canal, channel, ditch, waterway)
333120 Dredging machinery manufacturing
315992 Dress and semidress gloves cut and sewn from purchased fabric (except apparel contractors)
315191 Dress and semidress gloves made in apparel knitting mills
315211 Dress and semidress gloves, men's and boys', cut and sew apparel contractors
315212 Dress and semidress gloves, women's, girls', and infants', cut and sew apparel contractors
316219 Dress shoes, children's and infants', manufacturing
316213 Dress shoes, men's, manufacturing
316214 Dress shoes, women's, manufacturing
448190 Dress shops
532220 Dress suit rental
315999 Dress trimmings cut and sewn from purchased fabric (except apparel contractors)
315212 Dress trimmings, women's, girls', and infants', cut and sew apparel contractors
424990 Dressed furs and skins merchant wholesalers
337124 Dressers, metal, manufacturing
337122 Dressers, wood, manufacturing
315191 Dresses made in apparel knitting mills
424330 Dresses merchant wholesalers
315191 Dresses, hand-knit, manufacturing
315291 Dresses, infants', cut and sewn from purchased fabric (except apparel contractors)
315233 Dresses, women's, misses', and girls', cut and sewn from purchased fabric (except apparel contractors)
315212 Dresses, women's, misses', girls', and infants', cut and sew apparel contractors

316110 Dressing (i.e., bleaching, blending, currying, scraping, tanning) furs
315212 Dressing gowns, women's, girls', and infants', cut and sew apparel contractors
315231 Dressing gowns, women's, misses', and girls', cut and sewn from purchased fabric (except apparel contractors)
316110 Dressing hides
311615 Dressing small game
337124 Dressing tables, metal, manufacturing
337122 Dressing tables, wood, manufacturing
423450 Dressings, medical, merchant wholesalers
339113 Dressings, surgical, manufacturing
424490 Dried foods (e.g., fruits, milk, vegetables) merchant wholesalers
311612 Dried meats made from purchased carcasses
212392 Dried phosphate rock mining and/or beneficiating
325510 Driers, paint, and varnish, manufacturing
325992 Driers, photographic chemical, manufacturing
333315 Driers, photographic, manufacturing
334511 Driftmeters, aeronautical, manufacturing
333515 Drill bits, metalworking, manufacturing
332212 Drill bits, woodworking, manufacturing
333512 Drill presses, metalworking, manufacturing
333210 Drill presses, woodworking-type, manufacturing
332999 Drill stands, metal, manufacturing
238910 Drilled pier (i.e., for building foundations) contractors
238910 Drilled shaft (i.e., drilled building foundations) construction
339913 Drilling pearls
336611 Drilling and production platforms, floating, oil and gas, building
213111 Drilling directional oil and gas field wells on a contract basis
333132 Drilling equipment, oil and gas field-type, manufacturing
333131 Drilling equipment, underground mining-type, manufacturing
213111 Drilling for gas on a contract basis
213111 Drilling for oil on a contract basis
213111 Drilling gas and oil field wells on a contract basis
333512 Drilling machines, metalworking, manufacturing
325998 Drilling mud compounds, conditioners, and additives (except bentonites) manufacturing
424690 Drilling muds merchant wholesalers
213111 Drilling oil and gas field service wells on a contract basis
213112 Drilling rat holes and mouse holes at oil and gas fields on a contract basis
333132 Drilling rigs, oil and gas field-type, manufacturing
213113 Drilling services for coal mining on a contract basis
213114 Drilling services for metal mining on a contract basis
213115 Drilling services for nonmetallic mineral (except fuels) mining on a contract basis
213112 Drilling shot holes at oil and gas fields on a contract basis
213112 Drilling site preparation at oil and gas fields on a contract basis
213111 Drilling water intake wells, oil and gas field on a contract basis
237110 Drilling water wells (except water intake wells in oil and gas fields)

313210 Drills weaving
333131 Drills, core, underground mining-type, manufacturing
339114 Drills, dental, manufacturing
332212 Drills, hand held, nonelectric, manufacturing
333991 Drills, handheld power-driven (except heavy construction and mining type), manufacturing
333131 Drills, rock, underground mining-type, manufacturing
213112 Drill-stem testing in oil, gas, dry, and service well drilling on a contract basis
311999 Drink powder mixes (except chocolate, coffee, milk based, tea) manufacturing
311320 Drink powdered mixes, cocoa, made from cacao
311330 Drink powdered mixes, cocoa, made from purchased cocoa
311511 Drink, chocolate milk, manufacturing
238220 Drinking fountain installation
332998 Drinking fountains (except mechanically refrigerated), metal, manufacturing
326191 Drinking fountains (except mechanically refrigerated), plastics, manufacturing
333415 Drinking fountains, refrigerated, manufacturing
327111 Drinking fountains, vitreous china, non-refrigerated, manufacturing
722410 Drinking places (i.e., bars, lounges, taverns), alcoholic
312111 Drinks, fruit (except juice), manufacturing
333613 Drive chains, bicycle and motorcycle, manufacturing
336350 Drive shafts and half shafts, automotive, truck, and bus, manufacturing
512132 Drive-in motion picture theaters
237990 Drive-in movie facility construction
722211 Drive-in restaurants
611692 Driver education
611692 Driver training schools (except bus, heavy equipment, truck)
711219 Drivers, harness or race car
333612 Drives, high-speed industrial (except hydrostatic), manufacturing
561790 Driveway cleaning (e.g., power sweeping, washing) services
238990 Driveway paving or sealing
713990 Driving ranges, golf
488490 Driving services (e.g., automobile, truck delivery)
238310 Drop ceiling installation
332111 Drop forgings made from purchased iron or steel, unfinished
333513 Drop hammers, metal forging and shaping, manufacturing
812320 Drop-off and pick-up sites for laundries and drycleaners
813319 Drug abuse prevention advocacy organizations
623220 Drug addiction rehabilitation facilities (except licensed hospitals), residential
622210 Drug addiction rehabilitation hospitals
624190 Drug addiction self-help organizations
621420 Drug addiction treatment centers and clinics (except hospitals), outpatient
922120 Drug enforcement agencies and offices
424210 Drug proprietaries merchant wholesalers
446110 Drug stores
424210 Druggists' sundries merchant wholesalers
424210 Drugs merchant wholesalers
711130 Drum and bugle corps (i.e., drill teams)
333924 Drum cradles manufacturing
339992 Drums (musical instruments), parts, and accessories manufacturing
332439 Drums, light gauge metal, manufacturing
423840 Drums, new and reconditioned, merchant wholesalers

326199 Drums, plastics (i.e., containers), manufacturing
321920 Drums, plywood, manufacturing
321920 Drums, shipping, wood, wirebound, manufacturing
813319 Drunk driving prevention advocacy organizations
311422 Dry beans canning
424510 Dry beans merchant wholesalers
484230 Dry bulk carrier, truck, long-distance
484220 Dry bulk trucking (except garbage collection, garbage hauling), local
335912 Dry cell primary batteries, single and multiple cell, manufacturing
335912 Dry cells, primary (e.g., AAA, AA, C, D, 9V), manufacturing
236220 Dry cleaning plant construction
238220 Dry heating equipment installation
325120 Dry ice (i.e., solid carbon dioxide) manufacturing
424690 Dry ice merchant wholesalers
311514 Dry milk manufacturing
333294 Dry milk processing machinery manufacturing
311514 Dry milk products and mixture manufacturing
311514 Dry milk products for animal feed manufacturing
327999 Dry mix concrete manufacturing
311822 Dry mixes made from purchased flour
311823 Dry pasta manufacturing
311823 Dry pasta packaged with other ingredients made in dry pasta plants
335211 Dry shavers (i.e., electric razors) manufacturing
238910 Dry well construction
812320 Drycleaner drop-off and pick-up sites
812320 Drycleaners (except coin-operated)
335224 Drycleaning and laundry machines, household-type, manufacturing
333312 Drycleaning equipment and machinery manufacturing
423850 Drycleaning equipment and supplies merchant wholesalers
812310 Drycleaning machine routes (i.e., concession operators), coin-operated or similar self-service
812320 Drycleaning plants (except rug cleaning plants)
325612 Drycleaning preparations manufacturing
812320 Drycleaning services (except coin-operated)
812310 Drycleaning services, coin-operated or similar self-service
336611 Drydock, floating, building
488390 Drydocks, floating (i.e., routine repair and maintenance of ships)
423620 Dryer, clothes, gas and electric, merchant wholesalers
532210 Dryer, clothes, rental
335224 Dryers, clothes, household-type, gas and electric, manufacturing
423620 Dryers, hair, merchant wholesalers
335224 Dryers, household-type laundry, manufacturing
339111 Dryers, laboratory-type, manufacturing
333312 Dryers, laundry (except household-type), manufacturing
311711 Drying fish and seafood
333298 Drying kilns, lumber, manufacturing
333292 Drying machinery for textiles manufacturing
238310 Drywall contractors
238310 Drywall finishing (e.g., sanding, spackling, stippling, taping, texturing)
238310 Drywall hanging
238310 Drywall installation
423320 Drywall supplies merchant wholesalers
713950 Duck pin bowling alleys
713950 Duck pin bowling centers

112390 Duck production
313210 Ducks weaving
311615 Ducks, processing, fresh, frozen, canned, or cooked
311615 Ducks, slaughtering and dressing
561790 Duct cleaning services
238290 Duct insulation installation
322222 Duct tape made from purchased materials
238220 Duct work (e.g., cooling, dust collection, exhaust, heating, ventilation) installation
331511 Ductile iron castings, unfinished, manufacturing
331511 Ductile iron foundries
332313 Ducting, fabricated metal plate work, manufacturing
335313 Ducts for electrical switchboard apparatus manufacturing
332322 Ducts, sheet metal, manufacturing
721214 Dude ranches
339920 Dumbbells manufacturing
238290 Dumbwaiter installation
333921 Dumbwaiters manufacturing
212325 Dumortierite mining and/or beneficiating
336212 Dump trailer manufacturing
484220 Dump trucking (e.g., gravel, sand, top soil)
562119 Dump trucking of rubble or brush with collection or disposal
333131 Dumpers, mining car, manufacturing
562219 Dumps, compost
562212 Dumps, nonhazardous solid waste (e.g., trash)
336211 Dump-truck lifting mechanisms manufacturing
315291 Dungarees, infants', cut and sewn from purchased fabric (except apparel contractors)
315211 Dungarees, men's and boys', cut and sew apparel contractors
315224 Dungarees, men's and boys', cut and sewn from purchased fabric (except apparel contractors)
315212 Dungarees, women's girls' and infants', cut and sew apparel contractors
315239 Dungarees, women's, misses', and girls', cut and sewn from pruchased fabric (except apparel contractors)
236116 Duplex (i.e., one unit above the other), construction general contractors
236115 Duplex (i.e., side-by-side) construction general contractors
531110 Duplex houses (i.e., single family) rental or leasing
236117 Duplex operative builders
335931 Duplex receptacles, electrical, manufacturing
325910 Duplicating inks manufacturing
532420 Duplicating machine (e.g., copier) rental or leasing
333512 Duplicating machines (e.g., key cutting), metalworking, manufacturing
425120 Durable goods agents and brokers, wholesale trade
425110 Durable goods business to business electronic markets, wholesale trade
311211 Durum flour manufacturing
333411 Dust and fume collecting equipment manufacturing
314999 Dust cloths made from purchased fabrics
238220 Dust collecting and bag house equipment installation
423730 Dust collection equipment merchant wholesalers
812332 Dust control textile item (e.g., cloths, mats, mops, rugs, shop towels) supply services
315212 Dusters (i.e., apparel), women's and girls', cut and sew apparel contractors

315231 Dusters (i.e., apparel), women's, misses', and girls', cut and sewn from purchased fabric (except apparel contractors)
333111 Dusters, farm-type, manufacturing
115112 Dusting crops
445310 Duty free liquor shops
334112 DVD (digital video disc) drives, computer peripheral equipment, manufacturing
334310 DVD (digital video disc) players manufacturing
531110 Dwelling rental or leasing
332311 Dwellings, prefabricated metal, manufacturing
325998 Dye preparations, clothing, household-type, manufacturing
313311 Dyeing broadwoven fabrics
316110 Dyeing furs
313312 Dyeing gloves, woven or knit, for the trade
316110 Dyeing leather
333292 Dyeing machinery for textiles manufacturing
313312 Dyeing textile products and fabrics (except broadwoven fabrics)
424690 Dyes, industrial, merchant wholesalers
325131 Dyes, inorganic, manufacturing
325191 Dyes, natural, manufacturing
325132 Dyes, synthetic organic, manufacturing
424690 Dyestuffs merchant wholesalers
325920 Dynamite manufacturing
334519 Dynamometers manufacturing
335312 Dynamos, electric (except automotive), manufacturing
335312 Dynamotors manufacturing
812199 Ear piercing services
532412 Earth moving equipment rental or leasing without operator
237990 Earth retention system construction
334220 Earth station communications equipment manufacturing
517910 Earth stations (except satellite telecommunication carriers)
517410 Earth stations for satellite communication carriers
212399 Earth, diatomaceous, mining and/or beneficiating
212325 Earth, fuller's (e.g., all natural bleaching clays), mining and/or beneficiating
327112 Earthenware table and kitchen articles, coarse, manufacturing
327112 Earthenware, commercial and household, semivitreous, manufacturing
237990 Earth-filled dam construction
311119 Earthworm food and bedding manufacturing
112990 Earthworm hatcheries
339942 Easels, artists', manufacturing
424130 Eating utensils, disposable plastics, merchant wholesalers
332322 Eaves, sheet metal (except stampings), manufacturing
238170 Eavestrough installation
327112 Ecclesiastical statuary, clay, manufacturing
327420 Ecclesiastical statuary, gypsum, manufacturing
327999 Ecclesiastical statuary, paper mache, manufacturing
327991 Ecclesiastical statuary, stone, manufacturing
332999 Ecclesiastical ware, precious plated metal, manufacturing
541690 Economic consulting services
926110 Economic development agencies, government
928120 Economic development assistance (i.e., international), government
541720 Economic research and development services
332410 Economizers (i.e., power boiler accessory) manufacturing
522298 Edge Act corporations (except international trade financing)
522293 Edge Act corporations (i.e., international trade financing)
332212 Edge tools, woodworking (e.g., augers, bits, countersinks), manufacturing

333315 Editing equipment, motion picture (e.g., rewinders, splicers, titlers, viewers), manufacturing
561410 Editing services
923110 Education offices, nonoperating
923110 Education program administration
923110 Education statistics centers, government
236220 Educational building construction
611710 Educational consultants
611710 Educational guidance counseling services
611710 Educational support services
611710 Educational testing evaluation services
611710 Educational testing services
813211 Educational trusts, awarding grants
813920 Educators' associations
114111 Eel fishing
325412 Effervescent salts manufacturing
541614 Efficiency management (i.e., efficiency expert) consulting services
321920 Egg cases, wood, manufacturing
335211 Egg cookers, household-type electric, manufacturing
112340 Egg hatcheries, poultry
311823 Egg noodles, dry, manufacturing
311991 Egg noodles, fresh, manufacturing
112310 Egg production, chicken
112330 Egg production, turkey
311999 Egg substitutes manufacturing
312140 Eggnog, alcoholic, manufacturing
311514 Eggnog, canned, nonalcoholic, manufacturing
311511 Eggnog, fresh, nonalcoholic, manufacturing
311511 Eggnog, nonalcoholic (except canned), manufacturing
111219 Eggplant farming (except under cover), field, bedding plant and seed production
111419 Eggplant farming, grown under cover
424440 Eggs merchant wholesalers
112310 Eggs, chicken (table, hatching) production
311999 Eggs, processed, manufacturing
334515 Elapsed time meters, electronic, manufacturing
313210 Elastic fabrics, more than 12 inches in width, weaving
313221 Elastic fabrics, narrow woven, manufacturing
339113 Elastic hosiery, orthopedic, manufacturing
325222 Elastomeric fibers and filaments manufacturing
325211 Elastomers (except synthetic rubber) manufacturing
325212 Elastomers, synthetic rubber, manufacturing
332322 Elbows for conductor pipe, hot air ducts, and stovepipe, sheet metal (except stampings), manufacturing
332919 Elbows, pipe, metal (except made from purchased pipe), manufacturing
921190 Election boards
334512 Electric air cleaner controls, automatic, manufacturing
334513 Electric and electronic controllers, industrial process-type, manufacturing
336111 Electric automobiles for highway use manufacturing
335999 Electric bells manufacturing
335211 Electric blankets manufacturing
423620 Electric blankets merchant wholesalers
335211 Electric comfort heating equipment, portable, manufacturing
238210 Electric contracting
335999 Electric fence chargers manufacturing
335311 Electric furnace transformers manufacturing
334512 Electric heat proportioning controls, modulating controls, manufacturing

335110 Electric lamp bulb parts (except glass blanks) manufacturing
335110 Electric lamps (i.e., light bulbs) manufacturing
237130 Electric light and power plant (except hydroelectric) construction
335110 Electric light bulbs, complete, manufacturing
423610 Electric light fixtures merchant wholesalers
811310 Electric motor repair and maintenance services, commercial or industrial
423610 Electric motors, wiring supplies, and lighting fixtures merchant wholesalers
339992 Electric musical instruments manufacturing
333618 Electric outboard motors manufacturing
221122 Electric power brokers
221121 Electric power control
238210 Electric power control panel and outlet installation
221122 Electric power distribution systems
221119 Electric power generation, (except fossil fuel, hydroelectric, nuclear)
221112 Electric power generation, fossil fuel (e.g., coal, oil, gas)
221111 Electric power generation, hydroelectric
221113 Electric power generation, nuclear
221119 Electric power generation, solar
221119 Electric power generation, tidal
221119 Electric power generation, wind
237130 Electric power transmission line and tower construction
221121 Electric power transmission systems
334512 Electric space heater controls, automatic, manufacturing
335211 Electric space heaters, portable, manufacturing
333415 Electric warm air (i.e., forced air) furnaces manufacturing
238210 Electrical appliance installation
238210 Electrical contractors
541330 Electrical engineering services
811310 Electrical generating and transmission equipment repair and maintenance services
541360 Electrical geophysical surveying services
336322 Electrical ignition cable sets for internal combustion engines manufacturing
811219 Electrical measuring instrument repair and maintenance services
335932 Electrical metallic tube (EMTs) manufacturing
561990 Electrical meter reading services, contract
334515 Electrical network analyzers manufacturing
334515 Electrical power measuring equipment manufacturing
811118 Electrical repair shops, automotive
339950 Electrical signs manufacturing
423440 Electrical signs merchant wholesalers
444190 Electrical supply stores
541380 Electrical testing laboratories or services
238210 Electrical wiring contractors
238210 Electrical work
335211 Electrically heated bed coverings manufacturing
238210 Electrician
611513 Electricians' apprenticeship training
334515 Electricity and electrical signal measuring instruments manufacturing
334515 Electricity and electrical signal testing equipment manufacturing
237130 Electricity generating plant (except hydroelectric) construction
237990 Electricity generating plant, hydroelectric, construction
334510 Electrocardiographs manufacturing

335999 Electrochemical generators (i.e., fuel cells) manufacturing
333512 Electrochemical milling machines, metalworking, manufacturing
333512 Electrode discharge metal cutting machines manufacturing
333992 Electrode holders, welding, manufacturing
335991 Electrodes for thermal and electrolytic uses, carbon and graphite, manufacturing
334513 Electrodes used in industrial process measurement manufacturing
335110 Electrodes, cold cathode fluorescent lamp, manufacturing
333992 Electrodes, welding, manufacturing
334510 Electroencephalographs manufacturing
334510 Electrogastrograph manufacturing
332912 Electrohydraulic servo valves, fluid power, manufacturing
812199 Electrolysis (i.e., hair removal) salons
325412 Electrolyte in-vivo diagnostic substances manufacturing
334513 Electrolytic conductivity instruments, industrial process-type, manufacturing
334516 Electrolytic conductivity instruments, laboratory-type, manufacturing
333512 Electrolytic metal cutting machines manufacturing
334513 Electromagnetic flowmeters manufacturing
541360 Electromagnetic geophysical surveying services
334514 Electromechanical counters manufacturing
334510 Electromedical diagnostic equipment manufacturing
334510 Electromedical equipment manufacturing
423450 Electromedical equipment merchant wholesalers
334510 Electromedical therapy equipment manufacturing
331112 Electrometallurgical ferroalloy manufacturing
331111 Electrometallurgical steel manufacturing
334510 Electromyographs manufacturing
333992 Electron beam welding equipment manufacturing
335999 Electron linear accelerators manufacturing
334516 Electron microprobes, laboratory-type, manufacturing
334516 Electron microscopes manufacturing
334516 Electron paramagnetic spin-type apparatus manufacturing
333298 Electron tube machinery manufacturing
334411 Electron tube parts (e.g., bases, getters, guns) (except glass blanks) manufacturing
327215 Electron tube parts, glass blanks, made from purchased glass
327212 Electron tube parts, glass blanks, made in glass making plants
334515 Electron tube test equipment manufacturing
334411 Electron tubes manufacturing
333512 Electron-discharge metal cutting machines manufacturing
454112 Electronic auctions, retail
238210 Electronic containment fencing for pets, installation
238210 Electronic control installation and service
238210 Electronic control system installation
518210 Electronic data processing services
511140 Electronic directory publishers (except exclusive Internet publishing)
516110 Electronic directory publishers, exclusively on Internet

611519 Electronic equipment repair training
522320 Electronic financial payment services
522320 Electronic funds transfer services
713120 Electronic game arcades
423920 Electronic games merchant wholesalers
334511 Electronic guidance systems and equipment manufacturing
425110 Electronic markets, durable goods, business to business, wholesale trade
425110 Electronic markets, nondurable goods, business to business, wholesale trade
443112 Electronic part and component stores
423690 Electronic parts (e.g., condensers, connectors, switches) merchant wholesalers
323122 Electronic prepress services for the printing trade
541710 Electronic research and development laboratories or services
334515 Electronic test equipment for testing electrical characteristics manufacturing
541380 Electronic testing laboratories or services
334514 Electronic totalizing counters manufacturing
339932 Electronic toys and games manufacturing
423690 Electronic tubes (e.g., industrial, receiving, transmitting) merchant wholesalers
334516 Electrophoresis instruments manufacturing
333298 Electroplating machinery and equipment manufacturing
332813 Electroplating metals and formed products for the trade
238320 Electrostatic painting, on site, contractors
335999 Electrostatic particle accelerators manufacturing
333411 Electrostatic precipitation equipment manufacturing
334510 Electrotherapeutic apparatus manufacturing
335110 Electrotherapeutic lamp bulbs for ultraviolet and infrared radiation manufacturing
334510 Electrotherapy units manufacturing
323122 Electrotype plate preparation services
333293 Electrotyping machinery manufacturing
334516 Elemental analyzers manufacturing
611110 Elementary and secondary schools
611110 Elementary schools
237310 Elevated highway construction
332323 Elevator guide rails, metal, manufacturing
238290 Elevator installation
423830 Elevators merchant wholesalers
333921 Elevators, passenger and freight, manufacturing
112990 Elk production
325998 Embalming fluids manufacturing
812210 Embalming services
237990 Embankment construction
928120 Embassies
313311 Embossing broadwoven fabrics
316110 Embossing leather
323122 Embossing plate preparation services
339943 Embossing stamps manufacturing
313312 Embossing textile products and fabrics (except broadwoven)
313222 Embroideries, Schiffli machine, manufacturing
315211 Embroidering contractors on men's and boys' apparel
315212 Embroidering contractors on women's, misses', girls', and infants' apparel
314999 Embroidering on textile products (except apparel) for the trade
339932 Embroidery kits manufacturing

333292 Embroidery machinery manufacturing
424310 Embroidery products merchant wholesalers
313111 Embroidery spun yarns (e.g., cotton, manmade fiber, silk, wool) made from purchased fiber
313113 Embroidery thread (e.g., cotton, manmade fibers, silk, wool) manufacturing
335122 Emergency lighting (i.e., battery backup) manufacturing
621493 Emergency medical centers and clinics, freestanding
621910 Emergency medical transportation services, air or ground
922190 Emergency planning and management offices, government
453998 Emergency preparedness supply stores
624230 Emergency relief services
488410 Emergency road services (i.e., tow service)
624221 Emergency shelters (except for victims of domestic or international disasters or conflicts)
624230 Emergency shelters for victims of domestic or international disasters or conflicts
212399 Emery mining and/or beneficiating
811198 Emissions testing without repair, automotive
541612 Employee assessment consulting services
541612 Employee benefit consulting services
525110 Employee benefit pension plans
525120 Employee benefit plans (except pension)
524292 Employee benefit plans, third-party administrative processing services
485410 Employee bus services
541612 Employee compensation consulting services
561330 Employee leasing services
813930 Employees' associations for improvement of wages and working conditions
561310 Employment agencies
561310 Employment agencies, motion picture or video
561310 Employment agencies, radio or television
561310 Employment agencies, theatrical
561310 Employment placement agencies or services
561310 Employment referral agencies or services
561310 Employment registries
335932 EMTs (electrical metallic tube) manufacturing
112390 Emu production
325613 Emulsifiers (i.e., surface-active agents) manufacturing
325510 Enamel paints manufacturing
212322 Enamel sand quarrying and/or beneficiating
332214 Enameled metal cutting utensils
332812 Enameling metals and metal products for the trade
333994 Enameling ovens manufacturing
424950 Enamels merchant wholesalers
339114 Enamels, dental, manufacturing
323121 Encyclopedia binding without printing
511130 Encyclopedia publishers (except exclusive Internet publishing)
511130 Encyclopedia publishers and printing combined
516110 Encyclopedia publishers, exclusively on Internet
323117 Encyclopedias printing and binding without publishing
323117 Encyclopedias printing without publishing
337124 End tables, metal, manufacturing
337122 End tables, wood, manufacturing
111219 Endive farming (except under cover), field, bedding plant and seed production
111419 Endive farming, grown under cover

325411 Endocrine products, uncompounded, manufacturing
424210 Endocrine substances merchant wholesalers
621210 Endodontists' offices (e.g., centers, clinics)
334510 Endoscopic equipment, electromedical (e.g., bronchoscopes, colonoscopes, cystoscopes), manufacturing
325320 Endrin insecticides manufacturing
624229 Energy assistance programs
541690 Energy consulting services
334512 Energy cutoff controls, residential and commercial types, manufacturing
926110 Energy development and conservation agencies, nonoperating
926130 Energy development and conservation programs, government
334515 Energy measuring equipment, electrical, manufacturing
926110 Energy program administration
331319 Energy wire or cable made in aluminum wire drawing plants
331422 Energy wire or cable, copper, made from purchased copper in wire drawing plants
331491 Energy wire or cable, nonferrous metals (except aluminum, copper), made from purchased nonferrous metals (except aluminum, copper) in wire drawing plants
924110 Enforcement of environmental and pollution control regulations
336312 Engine block assemblies, automotive and truck gasoline, manufacturing
325998 Engine degreasers manufacturing
336311 Engine intake and exhaust valves manufacturing
811310 Engine repair (except automotive, small engine)
811111 Engine repair and replacement shops, automotive
811411 Engine repair, small engine
325998 Engine starting fluids manufacturing
423120 Engine testing equipment, motor vehicle, merchant wholesalers
541330 Engineering consulting services
541330 Engineering design services
541710 Engineering research and development laboratories or services
541330 Engineering services
238320 Engineering structure (e.g., oil storage tank, water tower) painting
813920 Engineers' associations
423490 Engineers' equipment and supplies merchant wholesalers
541330 Engineers' offices
541330 Engineers' private practices
336412 Engines and engine parts, aircraft (except carburetors, pistons, piston rings, valves), manufacturing
336312 Engines and parts (except diesel), automotive and truck, manufacturing
423860 Engines and parts, aircraft, merchant wholesalers
423120 Engines and parts, automotive, new, merchant wholesalers
423860 Engines and turbines, marine, merchant wholesalers
333618 Engines, diesel and semidiesel, manufacturing
333618 Engines, diesel locomotive, manufacturing
423830 Engines, internal combustion (except aircraft, automotive), merchant wholesalers
333618 Engines, internal combustion (except aircraft, nondiesel automotive), manufacturing
333618 Engines, natural gas, manufacturing
111219 English pea farming (except under cover), field, bedding plant and seed production

111419 English pea farming, grown under cover
332212 Engraver's handtools, nonpowered, manufacturing
339911 Engraving and etching precious metal (except precious plated) jewelry and flatware
339912 Engraving and etching precious metal flatware
339914 Engraving and/or etching costume jewelry
423830 Engraving machinery merchant wholesalers
332812 Engraving metals and metal products (except printing plates) for the trade
323122 Engraving printing plate, for the printing trade
333315 Enlargers, photographic, manufacturing
315191 Ensemble dresses made in apparel knitting mills
315212 Ensemble dresses, women's, girls', and infants', cut and sew apparel contractors
315233 Ensemble dresses, women's, misses', and girls', cut and sewn from purchased fabric (except apparel contractors)
711130 Ensembles, musical
926110 Enterprise development program administration
711410 Entertainers' agents or managers
711510 Entertainers, independent
516110 Entertainment sites, Internet
541710 Entomological research and development laboratories or services
115112 Entomological service, agricultural
541690 Entomology consulting services
333291 Envelope making machinery manufacturing
424110 Envelope paper, bulk, merchant wholesalers
333313 Envelope stuffing, sealing, and addressing machinery manufacturing
322232 Envelopes (i.e., mailing, stationery) made from any material
424120 Envelopes merchant wholesalers
813312 Environmental advocacy organizations
541620 Environmental consulting services
238210 Environmental control system installation
541330 Environmental engineering services
923120 Environmental health program administration
924110 Environmental protection program administration
562910 Environmental remediation services
541710 Environmental research and development laboratories or services
541380 Environmental testing laboratories or services
325413 Enzyme and isoenzyme in-vitro diagnostic substances manufacturing
325199 Enzyme proteins (i.e., basic synthetic chemicals) (except pharmaceutical use) manufacturing
325411 Enzyme proteins (i.e., basic synthetic chemicals), pharmaceutical use, manufacturing
325132 Eosin dyes manufacturing
325411 Ephedrine and derivatives (i.e., basic chemicals) manufacturing
325211 Epichlorohydrin bisphenol manufacturing
325211 Epichlorohydrin diphenol manufacturing
325212 Epichlorohydrin elastomers manufacturing
325520 Epoxy adhesives manufacturing
238190 Epoxy application contractors
325510 Epoxy coatings made from purchased resins
325211 Epoxy resins manufacturing

923130 Equal employment opportunity offices
115210 Equine boarding
522220 Equipment finance leasing
238910 Equipment rental (except crane), construction, with operator
326299 Erasers, rubber or rubber and abrasive combined, manufacturing
238120 Erecting structural steel
238190 Erection and dismantling, poured concrete form
325411 Ergot alkaloids (i.e., basic chemicals) manufacturing
541330 Erosion control engineering services
238290 Escalator installation
333921 Escalators manufacturing
423830 Escalators merchant wholesalers
111219 Escarole farming (except under cover), field, bedding plant and seed production
111419 Escarole farming, grown under cover
812990 Escort services, social
523991 Escrow agencies (except real estate)
531390 Escrow agencies, real estate
325998 Essential oils manufacturing
424690 Essential oils merchant wholesalers
325199 Essential oils, synthetic, manufacturing
541990 Estate assessment (i.e., appraisal) services
541110 Estate law offices
325211 Ester gum manufacturing
325199 Esters, not specified elsewhere by process, manufacturing
812112 Esthetician (i.e., skin care) services
115310 Estimating timber
454111 E-tailers
333295 Etching equipment, semiconductor, manufacturing
332812 Etching metals and metal products (except printing plates) for the trade
325110 Ethane made from refined petroleum or liquid hydrocarbons
211112 Ethane recovered from oil and gas field gases
325193 Ethanol, nonpotable, manufacturing
813410 Ethnic associations
711510 Ethnic dancers, independent
711320 Ethnic festival managers without facilities
711320 Ethnic festival organizers without facilities
711310 Ethnic festival promoters with facilities
711320 Ethnic festival promoters without facilities
325191 Ethyl acetate, natural, manufacturing
325199 Ethyl acetate, synthetic, manufacturing
424820 Ethyl alcohol merchant wholesalers
325193 Ethyl alcohol, nonpotable, manufacturing
312140 Ethyl alcohol, potable, manufacturing
325199 Ethyl butyrate manufacturing
325199 Ethyl cellulose (except resins) manufacturing
325199 Ethyl chloride manufacturing
325199 Ethyl ether manufacturing
325199 Ethyl formate manufacturing
325199 Ethyl nitrite manufacturing
325199 Ethyl perhydrophenanthrene manufacturing
325110 Ethylbenzene made from refined petroleum or liquid hydrocarbons
325211 Ethylcellulose plastics manufacturing
325199 Ethylene glycol ether manufacturing
325199 Ethylene glycol manufacturing
325110 Ethylene made from refined petroleum or liquid hydrocarbons

324110 Ethylene made in petroleum refineries
325199 Ethylene oxide manufacturing
325212 Ethylene-propylene rubber manufacturing
325212 Ethylene-propylene-nonconjugated diene (EPDM) rubber manufacturing
325211 Ethylene-vinyl acetate resins manufacturing
325998 Eucalyptus oil manufacturing
311514 Evaporated milk manufacturing
334519 Evaporation meters manufacturing
333415 Evaporative condensers (i.e., heat transfer equipment) manufacturing
611691 Exam preparation services
423810 Excavating machinery and equipment merchant wholesalers
213112 Excavating mud pits, slush pits, and cellars at oil and gas fields on a contract basis
238910 Excavating, earthmoving or land clearing, agricultural
238910 Excavating, earthmoving or land clearing, mining (except overburden removal at open pit mine sites or quarries)
238910 Excavating, earthmoving, or land clearing contractors
238910 Excavation contractors
333120 Excavators (e.g., power shovels) manufacturing
321999 Excelsior (e.g., pads, wrappers) manufacturing
523999 Exchange clearinghouses, commodities or securities
332410 Exchangers, heat, manufacturing
523210 Exchanges, commodity contracts
523210 Exchanges, securities
335312 Exciter assemblies, motor and generator, manufacturing
531210 Exclusive buyers' agencies
531210 Exclusive buyers' agents, offices of
487210 Excursion boat operation
921140 Executive and legislative office combinations
561110 Executive management services
921110 Executive offices, federal, state, and local (e.g., governor, mayor, president)
541612 Executive placement consulting services
541612 Executive search consulting services
531120 Executive suites (i.e., full service office space provision)
713940 Exercise centers
532292 Exercise equipment rental
451110 Exercise equipment stores
339920 Exercise machines manufacturing
621340 Exercise physiologists' offices (e.g., centers, clinics)
336399 Exhaust and tail pipes, automotive, truck, and bus, manufacturing
333412 Exhaust fans, industrial and commercial-type, manufacturing
238220 Exhaust system (e.g., kitchens, industrial work areas) installation
811112 Exhaust system repair and replacement shops, automotive
336399 Exhaust systems and parts, automotive, truck, and bus, manufacturing
531120 Exhibition hall, no promotion of events, rental or leasing
624190 Exoffender rehabilitation agencies
624190 Exoffender self-help organizations
316110 Exotic leathers manufacturing
332312 Expansion joints, metal, manufacturing
541710 Experimental farms
213113 Exploration services for coal (except geophysical surveying and mapping) on a contract basis
213114 Exploration services for metal (except geophysical surveying and mapping) on a contract basis

213115 Exploration services for nonmetallic minerals (except geophysical surveying and mapping) on a contract basis
213112 Exploration services for oil and gas (except geophysical surveying and mapping) on a contract basis
424690 Explosives (except ammunition, fireworks) merchant wholesalers
325920 Explosives manufacturing
522293 Export trading companies (i.e., international trade financing)
522293 Export-Import banks
333315 Exposure meters, photographic, manufacturing
622310 Extended care hospitals (except mental, substance abuse)
335999 Extension cords made from purchased insulated wire
321999 Extension ladders, wood, manufacturing
321999 Extension planks, wood, manufacturing
238310 Exterior insulation finish system installation
321918 Exterior wood shutters manufacturing
325320 Exterminating chemical products (e.g., fungicides, insecticides, pesticides) manufacturing
561710 Exterminating services
423990 Extinguishers, fire, merchant wholesalers
333120 Extractors, piling, manufacturing
311920 Extracts, essences and preparations, coffee, manufacturing
311920 Extracts, essences and preparations, tea, manufacturing
311942 Extracts, food (except coffee, meat), manufacturing
311942 Extracts, malt, manufacturing
325191 Extracts, natural dyeing and tanning, manufacturing
326291 Extruded, molded or lathe-cut rubber goods manufacturing
333220 Extruding machinery for plastics and rubber manufacturing
333292 Extruding machinery for yarn manufacturing
333513 Extruding machines, metalworking, manufacturing
331319 Extrusion billet made by rolling purchased aluminum
331319 Extrusion billet, aluminum, made in integrated secondary smelting and rolling mills
333514 Extrusion dies for use with all materials manufacturing
331319 Extrusion ingot made by rolling purchased aluminum
331319 Extrusion ingot, aluminum, made in integrated secondary smelting and rolling mills
331312 Extrusion ingot, primary aluminum, manufacturing
325412 Eye and ear preparations manufacturing
621991 Eye banks
339112 Eye examining instruments and apparatus manufacturing
325620 Eye make-up (e.g., eye shadow, eyebrow pencil, mascara) manufacturing
622310 Eye, ear, nose, and throat hospitals
316993 Eyeglass cases, all materials, manufacturing
339115 Eyeglass frames (i.e., fronts and temples), ophthalmic, manufacturing
423460 Eyeglasses merchant wholesalers
315211 Eyelet making contractors on men's and boys' apparel
315212 Eyelet making contractors on women's, misses', girls', and infants' apparel
339993 Eyelets, metal, manufacturing
339115 Eyes, glass and plastics, manufacturing
313312 Fabric (except broadwoven) finishing

451130 Fabric shops
325612 Fabric softeners manufacturing
238310 Fabric wall system, noise insulating, installation
332312 Fabricated bar joists manufacturing
332996 Fabricated pipe and pipe fittings made from purchased pipe
332313 Fabricated plate work manufacturing
314991 Fabricated rope products (e.g., nets, slings) made in cordage or twine mills
332312 Fabricated structural metal manufacturing
321213 Fabricated structural wood members (except trusses) manufacturing
238390 Fabrication, metal cabinet or countertop, on site
313210 Fabrics (except rug, tire fabrics), broadwoven, weaving
314992 Fabrics for reinforcing rubber tires, industrial belting, and fuel cells manufacturing
313311 Fabrics, broadwoven, finishing
313311 Fabrics, broadwoven, mercerizing
313249 Fabrics, knit, made in warp knit fabric mills
313241 Fabrics, knit, made in weft knit fabric mills
313249 Fabrics, lace, made in lace mills
313221 Fabrics, narrow woven, weaving
313230 Fabrics, nonwoven, manufacturing
424310 Fabrics, textile (except burlap, felt), merchant wholesalers
332618 Fabrics, woven wire, made from purchased wire
325620 Face creams (e.g., cleansing, moisturizing) manufacturing
335932 Face plates (i.e., outlet or switch covers) manufacturing
525990 Face-amount certificate funds
812112 Facial salons
424130 Facial tissue merchant wholesalers
322291 Facial tissues made from purchased paper
322121 Facial tissues made in paper mills
561210 Facilities (except computer operation) support services
541513 Facilities (i.e., clients' facilities) management and operation services, computer systems or data processing
541513 Facilities (i.e., clients' facilities) support services, computer systems or data processing
517110 Facilities-based telecommunication carriers (except wireless)
333512 Facing machines, metalworking, manufacturing
334210 Facsimile equipment, standalone, manufacturing
532420 Facsimile machine rental or leasing
811213 Facsimile machine repair and maintenance services
423690 Facsimile machines merchant wholesalers
325992 Facsimile toner cartridges manufacturing
522298 Factoring accounts receivable
236210 Factory construction
711310 Fair managers with facilities, agricultural
711320 Fair managers without facilities, agricultural
711310 Fair organizers with facilities, agricultural
711320 Fair organizers without facilities, agricultural
711310 Fair promoters with facilities
711310 Fair promoters with facilities, agricultural
711320 Fair promoters without facilities
711320 Fair promoters without facilities, agricultural
238190 Falsework construction
448140 Family clothing stores
621210 Family dentists' offices (e.g., centers, clinics)
713120 Family fun centers
541110 Family law offices
621111 Family physicians' offices (e.g., centers, clinics)

621410 Family planning centers
621410 Family planning counseling services
722110 Family restaurants, full service
722211 Family restaurants, limited-service
624190 Family social service agencies
624190 Family welfare services
326220 Fan belts, rubber or plastics, manufacturing
334512 Fan controls, temperature responsive, manufacturing
316110 Fancy leathers manufacturing
335211 Fans (except attic), household-type electric, manufacturing
336322 Fans, electric cooling, automotive, truck, and bus, manufacturing
335211 Fans, household-type kitchen, manufacturing
423620 Fans, household-type, merchant wholesalers
333412 Fans, industrial and commercial-type, manufacturing
423830 Fans, industrial, merchant wholesalers
334514 Fare collection equipment manufacturing
311211 Farina (except breakfast food) made in flour mills
311230 Farina, breakfast cereal, manufacturing
236220 Farm building construction
332311 Farm buildings, prefabricated metal, manufacturing
321992 Farm buildings, prefabricated wood, manufacturing
237990 Farm drainage tile installation
532490 Farm equipment rental or leasing
813410 Farm granges
115115 Farm labor contractors
423820 Farm machinery and equipment merchant wholesalers
811310 Farm machinery and equipment repair and maintenance services
115116 Farm management services
522292 Farm mortgage lending
493130 Farm product warehousing and storage (except refrigerated)
493120 Farm product warehousing and storage, refrigerated
484220 Farm products hauling, local
484230 Farm products trucking, long-distance
332420 Farm storage tanks, heavy gauge metal, manufacturing
424910 Farm supplies merchant wholesalers
444220 Farm supply stores
532490 Farm tractor rental or leasing
333111 Farm tractors and attachments manufacturing
333111 Farm wagons manufacturing
813910 Farmers' associations
813910 Farmers' unions
****** Farming—see type
531190 Farmland rental or leasing
333922 Farm-type conveyors manufacturing
115210 Farriers
112210 Farrow-to-finish operations
238170 Fascia and soffit installation
541490 Fashion design services
541490 Fashion designer services
423710 Fasteners (e.g., bolts, nuts, rivets, screws) merchant wholesalers
339993 Fasteners (e.g., glove, hook-and-eye, slide, snap) manufacturing
722211 Fast-food restaurants
334511 Fathometers manufacturing
334519 Fatigue testing machines, industrial, mechanical, manufacturing
311611 Fats, animal (except poultry, small game), produced in slaughtering plants
311613 Fats, animal, rendering
112112 Fattening cattle
325199 Fatty acid esters and amines manufacturing
325199 Fatty acids (e.g., margaric, oleic, stearic) manufacturing
325199 Fatty alcohols manufacturing

327111 Faucet handles, vitreous china and earthenware, manufacturing
332913 Faucets, plumbing, manufacturing
532420 Fax machine rental or leasing
811213 Fax machine repair and maintenance services
339999 Feather dusters manufacturing
315291 Feather-filled clothing, infants', cut and sewn from purchased fabric (except apparel contractors)
315239 Feather-filled clothing, jackets, and vests, women's, misses', and juniors', cut and sewn from purchased fabric (except apparel contractors)
315211 Feather-filled clothing, men's and boys', cut and sew apparel contractors
315228 Feather-filled clothing, men's and boys', cut and sewn from purchased fabric (except apparel contractors)
315212 Feather-filled clothing, women's, girls', and infants', cut and sew apparel contractors
424590 Feathers merchant wholesalers
339999 Feathers, preparing (i.e., for use in apparel and textile products)
519110 Feature syndicates (i.e., advice columns, comic, news)
522294 Federal Agricultural Mortgage Corporation
926120 Federal Aviation Administration (except air traffic control)
922120 Federal Bureau of Investigation (FBI)
926130 Federal Communications Commission (FCC)
522130 Federal credit unions
522298 Federal Home Loan Banks (FHLB)
522294 Federal Home Loan Mortgage Corporation (FHLMC)
522294 Federal Intermediate Credit Bank
522292 Federal Land Banks
522294 Federal National Mortgage Association (FNMA)
922120 Federal police services
521110 Federal Reserve Banks or Branches
921130 Federal Reserve Board of Governors
522120 Federal savings and loan associations (S&L)
522120 Federal savings banks
813219 Federated charities
813930 Federation of workers, labor organizations
813930 Federations of labor
424910 Feed additives merchant wholesalers
316999 Feed bags for horses manufacturing
314911 Feed bags made from purchased woven or knitted materials
311119 Feed concentrates, animal, manufacturing
311514 Feed grade dry milk products manufacturing
311119 Feed premixes, animal, manufacturing
333111 Feed processing equipment, farm-type, manufacturing
444220 Feed stores (except pet)
453910 Feed stores, pet
311119 Feed supplements, animal (except cat, dog), manufacturing
311111 Feed supplements, dog and cat, manufacturing
112112 Feed yards (except stockyards for transportation), cattle
112111 Feeder calf production
112210 Feeder pig farming
335311 Feeder voltage regulators and boosters (i.e., electrical transformers) manufacturing
423820 Feeders, animal, merchant wholesalers
333131 Feeders, mineral beneficiating-type, manufacturing
112112 Feedlots (except stockyards for transportation), cattle

112210 Feedlots (except stockyards for transportation), hog
112410 Feedlots (except stockyards for transportation), lamb
424910 Feeds (except pet) merchant wholesalers
311111 Feeds, prepared for dog and cat, manufacturing
311119 Feeds, prepared, for animals (except cat, dog) manufacturing
311119 Feeds, specialty (e.g., guinea pig, mice, mink), manufacturing
212325 Feldspar mining and/or beneficiating
327992 Feldspar processing beyond beneficiation
424990 Felt merchant wholesalers
339941 Felt tip markers manufacturing
322121 Felts, asphalt, made in paper mills
313210 Felts, broadwoven, weaving
313230 Felts, nonwoven, manufacturing
331222 Fence gates, posts, and fittings, iron or steel, made in wire drawing plants
238990 Fence installation (except electronic containment fencing for pets)
331111 Fence posts, iron or steel, made in iron and steel mills
332323 Fences and gates (except wire), metal, manufacturing
423390 Fencing (except wood) merchant wholesalers
332618 Fencing and fence gates made from purchased wire
423390 Fencing and fencing accessories, wire, merchant wholesalers
238990 Fencing contractors (except electronic containment fencing for pets)
444190 Fencing dealers
339920 Fencing equipment (sporting goods) manufacturing
321999 Fencing, prefabricated sections, wood, manufacturing
321999 Fencing, wood (except rough pickets, poles, and rails), manufacturing
423310 Fencing, wood, merchant wholesalers
212299 Ferberite ores and concentrates mining and/or beneficiating
333298 Fermentation equipment, chemical, manufacturing
424810 Fermented malt beverages merchant wholesalers
332420 Fermention tanks, heavy gauge metal tanks, manufacturing
212299 Ferroalloy ores (except vanadium) (e.g., chromium, columbium, molybdenum, tungsten) mining and/or beneficiating
325188 Ferric chloride manufacturing
325188 Ferric oxide manufacturing
325131 Ferric oxide pigments manufacturing
333319 Ferris wheels manufacturing
331112 Ferroalloys manufacturing
423510 Ferroalloys merchant wholesalers
331112 Ferrochromium manufacturing
325188 Ferrocyanides manufacturing
331112 Ferromanganese manufacturing
331112 Ferromolybdenum manufacturing
331112 Ferrophosphorus manufacturing
331112 Ferrosilicon manufacturing
331112 Ferrotitanium manufacturing
331112 Ferrotungsten manufacturing
332111 Ferrous forgings made from purchased iron or steel, unfinished
423510 Ferrous metals merchant wholesalers
331112 Ferrovanadium manufacturing
483114 Ferry passenger transportation, Great Lakes (including St. Lawrence Seaway)
336611 Ferryboat building
621410 Fertility clinics
424910 Fertilizer and fertilizer materials merchant wholesalers
115112 Fertilizer application for crops

212393 Fertilizer minerals, natural, mining and/or beneficiating
325314 Fertilizers, mixed, made in plants not manufacturing fertilizer materials
325311 Fertilizers, mixed, made in plants producing nitrogenous fertilizer materials
325312 Fertilizers, mixed, made in plants producing phosphatic fertilizer materials
325311 Fertilizers, natural organic (except compost), manufacturing
325311 Fertilizers, of animal waste origin, manufacturing
325311 Fertilizers, of sewage origin, manufacturing
561730 Fertilizing lawns
333111 Fertilizing machinery, farm-type, manufacturing
111998 Fescue seed farming
711310 Festival managers with facilities
711320 Festival managers without facilities
711310 Festival of arts managers with facilities
711320 Festival of arts managers without facilities
711310 Festival of arts organizers with facilities
711320 Festival of arts organizers without facilities
711310 Festival of arts promoters with facilities
711320 Festival of arts promoters without facilities
711310 Festival organizers with facilities
711320 Festival organizers without facilities
711310 Festival promoters with facilities
711320 Festival promoters without facilities
325412 Fever remedy preparations manufacturing
522294 FHLMC (Federal Home Loan Mortgage Corporation)
322214 Fiber cans and drums (i.e., all-fiber, nonfiber ends of any material) made from purchased paperboard
424130 Fiber cans and drums merchant wholesalers
322214 Fiber drums made from purchased paperboard
337125 Fiber furniture (except upholstered), household-type, manufacturing
313221 Fiberglasses, narrow woven, weaving
238210 Fiber optic cable (except transmission lines) installation
335921 Fiber optic cable manufacturing
237130 Fiber optic cable transmission line construction
334417 Fiber optic connectors manufacturing
322214 Fiber spools, reels, blocks made from purchased paperboard
322214 Fiber tubes made from purchased paperboard
314999 Fiber, textile recovery from textile mill waste and rags
321219 Fiberboard manufacturing
423310 Fiberboard merchant wholesalers
423390 Fiberglass building materials (except insulation, roofing, siding) merchant wholesalers
424310 Fiberglass fabrics merchant wholesalers
313210 Fiberglass fabrics weaving
327993 Fiberglass insulation products manufacturing
325221 Fibers and filaments, cellulosic, manufacturing and texturizing
325222 Fibers and filaments, noncellulosic, manufacturing and texturizing
335991 Fibers, carbon and graphite, manufacturing
327212 Fibers, glass, textile, made in glass making plants
424690 Fibers, manmade, merchant wholesalers
424590 Fibers, vegetable, merchant wholesalers

323121 Fiction book binding without printing
511130 Fiction book publishers (except exclusive Internet publishing)
511130 Fiction book publishers and printing combined
516110 Fiction book publishers, exclusively on Internet
323117 Fiction books printing and binding without publishing
323117 Fiction books printing without publishing
524126 Fidelity insurance carriers, direct
531390 Fiduciaries', real estate, offices
523991 Fiduciary agencies (except real estate)
332995 Field artillery manufacturing
315211 Field jackets, military, cut and sew apparel contractors
315228 Field jackets, military, men's and boys', cut and sewn from purchased fabric (except apparel contractors)
111421 Field nurseries (i.e., growing of flowers and shrubbery)
238140 Field stone (i.e., masonry) installation
334515 Field strength and intensity measuring equipment, electrical, manufacturing
336211 Fifth wheel assemblies manufacturing
111339 Fig farming
711219 Figure skaters, independent
335110 Filaments for electric lamp bulbs manufacturing
111335 Filbert farming
115114 Filbert hulling and shelling
424120 File cards and folders merchant wholesalers
322231 File folders (e.g., accordion, expanding, hanging, manila) made from purchased paper and paperboard
333515 Files (i.e., a machine tool accessory) manufacturing
332212 Files, handheld, manufacturing
337214 Filing cabinets (except wood), office-type, manufacturing
337211 Filing cabinets, wood, office type, manufacturing
333512 Filing machines, metalworking, manufacturing
212399 Fill dirt pits mining and/or beneficiating
325510 Fillers, wood (e.g., dry, liquid, paste), manufacturing
314999 Filling (except nonwoven textile), upholstery, manufacturing
311999 Fillings, cake or pie (except fruits, meat, vegetables), manufacturing
711510 Film actors, independent
519120 Film archives
541380 Film badge testing (i.e., radiation testing) laboratories or services
812921 Film developing and printing (except motion picture, one-hour)
812922 Film developing and printing, one hour
333315 Film developing equipment manufacturing
423410 Film developing equipment merchant wholesalers
512120 Film distribution agencies
512120 Film distribution, motion picture and video
512131 Film festivals exhibitors
512120 Film libraries, commercial distribution
512199 Film libraries, motion picture or video, stock footage
512191 Film or tape closed captioning
512191 Film or video transfer services
512199 Film processing laboratories, motion picture
711510 Film producers, independent
512110 Film studios producing films
423410 Film, photographic, merchant wholesalers
326113 Film, plastics (except packaging), manufacturing
326112 Film, plastics, packaging, manufacturing

325992 Film, sensitized (e.g., camera, motion picture, X-ray), manufacturing
512110 Films, motion picture production
512110 Films, motion picture production and distribution
424130 Filter papers merchant wholesalers
327112 Filtering media, pottery, manufacturing
336399 Filters (e.g., air, engine oil, fuel) automotive, truck, and bus, manufacturing
333411 Filters, air-conditioner, manufacturing
334419 Filters, electronic component-type, manufacturing
333411 Filters, furnace, manufacturing
333999 Filters, industrial and general line (except internal combustion engine, warm air furnace), manufacturing
322299 Filters, paper, made from purchased paper
221310 Filtration plant, water
212322 Filtration sand quarrying and/or beneficiating
332993 Fin assemblies, mortar, manufacturing
332993 Fin assemblies, torpedo and bomb, manufacturing
522291 Finance companies (i.e., unsecured cash loans)
523140 Financial futures brokerages
551112 Financial holding companies
523930 Financial investment advice services, customized, fees paid by client
511120 Financial magazine and periodical publishers (except exclusive Internet publishing)
511120 Financial magazine and periodical publishers and printing combined
516110 Financial magazine and periodical publishers, exclusively on Internet
323112 Financial magazines and periodicals flexographic printing without publishing
323111 Financial magazines and periodicals gravure printing without publishing
323110 Financial magazines and periodicals lithographic (offset) printing without publishing
323119 Financial magazines and periodicals printing (except flexographic, gravure, lithographic, quick, screen) without publishing
323113 Financial magazines and periodicals screen printing without publishing
541611 Financial management consulting (except investment advice) services
523930 Financial planning services, customized, fees paid by client
522320 Financial transactions processing (except central bank)
521110 Financial transactions processing of the central bank
522220 Financing, sales
522294 Financing, secondary market
316999 Findings, boot and shoe, manufacturing
339913 Findings, jeweler's, manufacturing
315212 Findings, suit and coat (e.g., coat fronts, pockets), women's, girls', and infants', cut and sew apparel contractors
315999 Findings, suit and coat (e.g., coat fronts, pockets), cut and sewn from purchased fabric (except apparel contractors)
315211 Findings, suit and coat (e.g., coat fronts, pockets), men's and boys', cut and sew apparel contractors
712110 Fine arts museums

611610 Fine arts schools (except academic)
722110 Fine dining restaurants, full service
424110 Fine paper, bulk, merchant wholesalers
114111 Finfish fishing (e.g., flounder, salmon, trout)
112511 Finfish production, farm raising
112511 Finfish, hatcheries
321213 Finger joint lumber manufacturing
561611 Fingerprint services
238350 Finish carpentry
314110 Finishing (e.g., dyeing) rugs and carpets
325613 Finishing agents, textile and leather, manufacturing
238310 Finishing drywall contractors
316110 Finishing hides and skins on a contract basis
316110 Finishing leather
333292 Finishing machinery for textile manufacturing
313311 Finishing plants, broadwoven fabric
611110 Finishing schools, secondary
561621 Fire alarm monitoring services
561621 Fire alarm sales combined with installation, repair, or monitoring services
238210 Fire alarm system, electric, installation only
236220 Fire and flood restoration of commercial and institutional buildings
236118 Fire and flood restoration, multifamily building, general contractors
236118 Fire and flood restoration, single-family housing, general contractors
922160 Fire and rescue service
212325 Fire clay mining and/or beneficiating
922160 Fire departments (e.g., government, volunteer (except private))
334290 Fire detection and alarm systems manufacturing
334519 Fire detector systems, nonelectric, manufacturing
332321 Fire doors, metal, manufacturing
238190 Fire escape installation
332323 Fire escapes, metal, manufacturing
325998 Fire extinguisher chemical preparations manufacturing
424690 Fire extinguisher preparations merchant wholesalers
423990 Fire extinguisher sales combined with rental and/or service, merchant wholesalers
423990 Fire extinguishers merchant wholesalers
339999 Fire extinguishers, portable, manufacturing
611519 Fire fighter training schools
561990 Fire fighting services as a commercial activity
314999 Fire hose, textile, made from purchased materials
237110 Fire hydrant installation
332911 Fire hydrant valves manufacturing
332911 Fire hydrants, complete, manufacturing
524126 Fire insurance carriers, direct
541380 Fire insurance underwriters' laboratories
524291 Fire investigators
922160 Fire marshals' offices
922160 Fire prevention offices, government
115310 Fire prevention, forest
325998 Fire retardant chemical preparations manufacturing
238220 Fire sprinkler system installation
236220 Fire station construction
423990 Firearms (except sporting) merchant wholesalers
813319 Firearms advocacy organizations
332994 Firearms, small, manufacturing
423910 Firearms, sporting, merchant wholesalers

336611 Fireboat building
327124 Firebrick, clay refractories, manufacturing
315211 Firefighters' dress uniforms, men's, cut and sew apparel contractors
315222 Firefighters' dress uniforms, men's, cut and sewn from purchased fabric (except apparel contractors)
315212 Firefighters' dress uniforms, women's, cut and sew apparel contractors
315234 Firefighters' dress uniforms, women's, cut and sewn from purchased fabric (except apparel contractors)
922160 Firefighting (except forest), government and volunteer (except private)
423850 Firefighting equipment and supplies merchant wholesalers
922160 Firefighting services (except forest and private)
339113 Firefighting suits and accessories manufacturing
115310 Firefighting, forest
332999 Fireplace fixtures and equipment manufacturing
333414 Fireplace inserts (i.e., heat directing) manufacturing
335129 Fireplace logs, electric, manufacturing
238140 Fireplace, masonry, installation
238220 Fireplace, natural gas, installation
423720 Fireplaces, gas, merchant wholesalers
238330 Fireproof flooring installation
238190 Fireproofing buildings
321999 Firewood and fuel wood containing fuel binder manufacturing
454319 Firewood dealers, direct selling
423990 Firewood merchant wholesalers
713990 Fireworks display services
325998 Fireworks manufacturing
423920 Fireworks merchant wholesalers
453998 Fireworks shops (i.e., permanent location)
327112 Firing china for the trade
321920 Firkins and kits, wood, coopered, manufacturing
611699 First aid instruction
339113 First aid, snake bite, or burn kits manufacturing
423450 First-aid kits merchant wholesalers
424210 First-aid supplies merchant wholesalers
424460 Fish (except canned, packaged frozen) merchant wholesalers
924120 Fish and game agencies
311711 Fish and marine animal oils produced in a cannery
311712 Fish and marine animal oils produced in a fresh and frozen seafood plant
311711 Fish and seafood chowder canning
924120 Fish and wildlife conservation program administration
311711 Fish egg bait canning
112511 Fish farms, finfish
112512 Fish farms, shellfish
334511 Fish finders (i.e., sonar) manufacturing
311119 Fish food for feeding fish manufacturing
311712 Fish freezing (e.g., blocks, fillets, ready-to-serve products)
325411 Fish liver oils, medicinal, uncompounded, manufacturing
445220 Fish markets
311711 Fish meal produced in a cannery
311712 Fish meal produced in a fresh and frozen seafood plant
236210 Fish processing plant construction
332212 Fish wire (i.e., electrical wiring tool) manufacturing
311711 Fish, canned and cured, manufacturing
424490 Fish, canned, merchant wholesalers
311711 Fish, curing, drying, pickling, salting, and smoking

311712 Fish, fresh or frozen, manufacturing
311712 Fish, fresh prepared, manufacturing
424420 Fish, packaged frozen, merchant wholesalers
424990 Fish, tropical, merchant wholesalers
541710 Fisheries research and development laboratories or services
114111 Fisheries, finfish
114112 Fisheries, shellfish
487210 Fishing boat charter operation
336611 Fishing boat, commercial, building
721214 Fishing camps with accommodation facilities
713990 Fishing clubs, recreational
423910 Fishing equipment and supplies (except commercial) merchant wholesalers
213112 Fishing for tools at oil and gas fields on a contract basis
713990 Fishing guide services
332211 Fishing knives manufacturing
314999 Fishing nets made from purchased materials
713990 Fishing piers
114210 Fishing preserves
451110 Fishing supply stores (e.g., bait)
339920 Fishing tackle and equipment (except lines, nets, seines) manufacturing
713940 Fitness centers
423910 Fitness equipment and supplies merchant wholesalers
713940 Fitness salons
713940 Fitness spas without accommodations
326122 Fittings and unions, rigid plastics pipe, manufacturing
423720 Fittings and valves, plumbers', merchant wholesalers
326122 Fittings, rigid plastics pipe, manufacturing
331511 Fittings, soil and pressure pipe, cast iron, manufacturing
713950 Five pin bowling centers
722213 Fixed location refreshment stands
325992 Fixers, prepared photographic, manufacturing
337920 Fixtures (e.g., poles, rods, rollers), curtain and drapery, manufacturing
423610 Fixtures, electric lighting, merchant wholesalers
423440 Fixtures, store (except refrigerated), merchant wholesalers
337215 Fixtures, store display, manufacturing
453998 Flag and banner shops
561990 Flagging (i.e., traffic control) services
238990 Flagpole installation
332323 Flagpoles, metal, manufacturing
321999 Flagpoles, wood, manufacturing
314999 Flags, textile (e.g., banners, bunting, emblems, pennants), made from purchased fabrics
212311 Flagstone mining or quarrying
327991 Flagstones cutting
321219 Flakeboard manufacturing
331221 Flakes made from purchased iron or steel
331314 Flakes, aluminum, made from purchased aluminum
331111 Flakes, iron or steel, made in iron and steel mills
334516 Flame photometers manufacturing
812332 Flame resistant clothing supply services
334512 Flame safety controls for furnaces and boilers manufacturing
332995 Flame throwers manufacturing
333512 Flange facing machines, metalworking, manufacturing
332991 Flange units, ball or roller bearing, manufacturing
332919 Flanges and flange unions, pipe, metal, manufacturing
315223 Flannel shirts (except work shirts), men's and boys', cut and sewn from purchased fabric (except apparel contractors)

315291 Flannel shirts, infants', cut and sewn from purchased fabric (except apparel contractors)
315211 Flannel shirts, men's and boys', cut and sew apparel contractors
315212 Flannel shirts, women's, girls', and infants', cut and sew apparel contractors
315232 Flannel shirts, women's, misses', and girls', cut and sewn from purchased fabric (except apparel contrctors)
315225 Flannel shirts, work, men's and boys', cut and sewn from purchased fabric (except apparel contractors)
313210 Flannels, broadwoven, weaving
325998 Flares manufacturing
333315 Flash apparatus, photographic, manufacturing
335110 Flash bulbs, photographic, manufacturing
238170 Flashing contractors
335912 Flashlight batteries, disposable, manufacturing
335110 Flashlight bulb manufacturing
335129 Flashlights manufacturing
423610 Flashlights merchant wholesalers
313249 Flat (i.e., warp) fabrics knitting
331221 Flat bright steel strip made in cold rolling mills made from purchased steel
327211 Flat glass (e.g., float, plate) manufacturing
423390 Flat glass merchant wholesalers
334119 Flat panel displays (i.e., complete units), computer peripheral equipment, manufacturing
332612 Flat springs (except clock, watch), light gauge, made from purchased wire or strip, manufacturing
332611 Flat springs, heavy gauge metal, manufacturing
336212 Flatbed trailers, commercial, manufacturing
484220 Flatbed trucking, local
484230 Flatbed trucking, long-distance
331111 Flats, iron or steel, made in iron and steel mills
321920 Flats, wood, greenhouse, manufacturing
423220 Flatware (except plated, precious) merchant wholesalers
332211 Flatware, nonprecious and precious plated metal, manufacturing
423940 Flatware, precious and plated, merchant wholesalers
311942 Flavor extracts (except coffee) manufacturing
311511 Flavored milk drinks manufacturing
312111 Flavored water manufacturing
311930 Flavoring concentrates (except coffee based) manufacturing
424490 Flavoring extracts (except for fountain use) merchant wholesalers
325199 Flavoring materials (i.e., basic synthetic chemicals such as coumarin) manufacturing
311930 Flavoring pastes, powders, and syrups for soft drink manufacturing
313111 Flax spun yarns made from purchased fiber
111120 Flaxseed farming, field and seed production
311225 Flaxseed oil made from purchased oils
311223 Flaxseed oil made in crushing mills
531190 Flea market space (except under roof) rental or leasing
531120 Flea market space, under roof, rental or leasing
454390 Flea markets, temporary location, direct selling
453310 Flea markets, used merchandise, permanent
325320 Flea powders or sprays manufacturing
532112 Fleet leasing, passenger vehicle
316110 Fleshers, leather (i.e., flesh side of split leather), manufacturing

334112 Flexible (i.e., floppy) magnetic disk drives manufacturing
332999 Flexible metal hose and tubing manufacturing
322221 Flexible packaging sheet materials (except foil-paper laminates) made by coating or laminating purchased paper
322225 Flexible packaging sheet materials made by laminating purchased foil
326112 Flexible packaging, plastics film, manufacturing
334412 Flexible wiring boards, bare, manufacturing
325910 Flexographic inks manufacturing
323122 Flexographic plate preparation services
323112 Flexographic printing (except books, manifold business forms, printing grey goods)
333293 Flexographic printing presses manufacturing
339920 Flies, artificial fishing, manufacturing
334511 Flight and navigation sensors, transmitters, and displays manufacturing
611519 Flight attendant schools
334511 Flight recorders (i.e., black boxes) manufacturing
333319 Flight simulation machinery manufacturing
611512 Flight training schools
212325 Flint clay mining and/or beneficiating
327992 Flint processing beyond beneficiation
339999 Flints, lighter, manufacturing
321113 Flitches (i.e., veneer stock) made in sawmills
334512 Float controls, residential and commercial types, manufacturing
561990 Float decorating services
541490 Float design services
327124 Floaters, glasshouse, clay, manufacturing
713210 Floating casinos (i.e., gambling cruises, riverboat casinos)
332313 Floating covers, fabricated metal plate work, manufacturing
311711 Floating factory ships seafood processing
332812 Flocking metals and metal products for the trade
237990 Flood control project construction
332312 Flood gates, metal plate, manufacturing
335129 Floodlights (i.e., lighting fixtures) manufacturing
237990 Floodway canal and ditch construction
321918 Floor baseboards, wood, manufacturing
442210 Floor covering stores (except wood or ceramic tile only)
444190 Floor covering stores, wood or ceramic tile only
423220 Floor coverings merchant wholesalers
326192 Floor coverings, linoleum, manufacturing
326192 Floor coverings, resilient, manufacturing
326192 Floor coverings, rubber, manufacturing
326192 Floor coverings, vinyl, manufacturing
332312 Floor jacks, metal, manufacturing
335121 Floor lamps (i.e., lighting fixtures), residential, manufacturing
238330 Floor laying, scraping, finishing and refinishing
423850 Floor maintenance equipment merchant wholesalers
326299 Floor mats (e.g., bath, door), rubber, manufacturing
325612 Floor polishes and waxes manufacturing
332312 Floor posts, adjustable metal, manufacturing
532490 Floor sanding machine rental or leasing

333319 Floor sanding, washing, and polishing machines, commercial-type, manufacturing
335212 Floor scrubbing and shampooing machines, household-type electric, manufacturing
335211 Floor standing fans, household-type electric, manufacturing
238330 Floor tile and sheets, installation only
327122 Floor tile, ceramic, manufacturing
321214 Floor trusses, wood, manufacturing
335212 Floor waxers and polishers, household-type electric, manufacturing
532490 Floor waxing equipment rental or leasing
332323 Flooring, open steel (i.e., grating), manufacturing
332322 Flooring, sheet metal (except stampings), manufacturing
321114 Flooring, wood block, treating
321918 Flooring, wood, manufacturing
423310 Flooring, wood, merchant wholesalers
334112 Floppy disk drives manufacturing
561422 Floral wire services (i.e., telemarketing services)
453110 Florists
327112 Florists' articles, red earthenware, manufacturing
424930 Florist's supplies merchant wholesalers
333131 Flotation machinery, mining-type, manufacturing
114111 Flounder fishing
314911 Flour bags made from purchased woven or knitted materials
424490 Flour merchant wholesalers
333294 Flour milling machinery manufacturing
311230 Flour mills, breakfast cereal, manufacturing
311211 Flour mills, cereals grains (except breakfast cereals, rice)
311211 Flour mixes made in flour mills
311822 Flour, blended or self-rising, made from purchased flour
311211 Flour, blended, prepared, or self-rising (except rice), made in flour mills
311213 Flour, malt, manufacturing
311212 Flour, rice, manufacturing
321999 Flour, wood, manufacturing
335314 Flow actuated electrical switches manufacturing
334513 Flow instruments, industrial process-type, manufacturing
327420 Flower boxes, plaster of paris, manufacturing
111421 Flower bulb growing
424910 Flower bulbs merchant wholesalers
111422 Flower growing
327112 Flower pots, red earthenware, manufacturing
111422 Flower seed production
453998 Flower shops, artificial or dried
453110 Flower shops, fresh
561920 Flower show managers
561920 Flower show organizers
561920 Flower show promoters
424930 Flowers merchant wholesalers
339999 Flowers, artificial (except glass, plastics), manufacturing
327123 Flue lining, clay, manufacturing
423320 Flue pipe and linings merchant wholesalers
332322 Flues, stove and furnace, sheet metal (except stampings), manufacturing
332439 Fluid milk shipping containers, light gauge metal, manufacturing
311511 Fluid milk substitutes processing
333995 Fluid power actuators manufacturing
332912 Fluid power aircraft subassemblies manufacturing
333995 Fluid power cylinders manufacturing

332912 Fluid power hose assemblies manufacturing
333996 Fluid power motors manufacturing
333996 Fluid power pumps manufacturing
332912 Fluid power valves and hose fittings manufacturing
334513 Fluidic devices, circuits, and systems for process control, manufacturing
423830 Fluid-power transmission equipment merchant wholesalers
332313 Flumes, fabricated metal plate work, manufacturing
332322 Flumes, sheet metal (except stampings), manufacturing
325188 Fluoboric acid manufacturing
335311 Fluorescent ballasts (i.e., transformers) manufacturing
325132 Fluorescent dyes manufacturing
335110 Fluorescent lamp tubes, electric, manufacturing
335122 Fluorescent lighting fixtures, commercial, institutional, and industrial electric, manufacturing
335121 Fluorescent lighting fixtures, residential, manufacturing
335311 Fluorescent lighting transformers manufacturing
325120 Fluorinated hydrocarbon gases manufacturing
325188 Fluorine manufacturing
212393 Fluorite mining and/or beneficiating
325212 Fluoro rubbers manufacturing
325212 Fluorocarbon derivative rubbers manufacturing
325222 Fluorocarbon fibers and filaments manufacturing
325120 Fluorocarbon gases manufacturing
325211 Fluorohydrocarbon resins manufacturing
325211 Fluoro-polymer resins manufacturing
334517 Fluoroscopes manufacturing
334517 Fluoroscopic X-ray apparatus and tubes manufacturing
212393 Fluorspar mining and/or beneficiating
335110 Fluroescent lamp electrodes, cold cathode, manufacturing
332998 Flush tanks, metal, manufacturing
332913 Flush valves, plumbing, manufacturing
339992 Flutes and parts manufacturing
325998 Fluxes (e.g., brazing, galvanizing, soldering, welding) manufacturing
325320 Fly sprays manufacturing
339999 Fly swatters manufacturing
541870 Flyer direct distribution (except direct mail) services
713990 Flying clubs, recreational
488119 Flying field operators
611512 Flying instruction
335129 Flytraps, electrical, manufacturing
336312 Flywheels and ring gears, automotive and truck gasoline engine, manufacturing
515112 FM radio stations
522294 FNMA (Federal National Mortgage Association)
238310 Foam insulation installation
326150 Foam plastics products (except polystrene) manufacturing
326140 Foam polystyrene products manufacturing
424990 Foam rubber merchant wholesalers
424610 Foam, plastics, resins and shapes, merchant wholesalers
322223 Foil bags made from purchased foil
332999 Foil containers (except bags) manufacturing
332999 Foil not made in rolling mills
322225 Foil sheet, laminating purchased foil sheets for packaging applications
331315 Foil, aluminum, made by flat rolling purchased aluminum

331315 Foil, aluminum, made in integrated secondary smelting and flat rolling mills
331421 Foil, copper, made from purchased metal or scrap
331491 Foil, gold, made by rolling purchased metals or scrap
331491 Foil, nickel, made by rolling purchased metals or scrap
331491 Foil, silver, made by rolling purchased metals or scrap
424120 Folders, file, merchant wholesalers
561910 Folding and packaging services, textile and apparel
322130 Folding boxboard stock manufacturing
322212 Folding boxes (except corrugated) made from purchased paperboard
322212 Folding paper and paperboard containers (except corrugated) made from purchased paperboard
111422 Foliage growing
711120 Folk dance companies
711510 Folk dancers, independent
445110 Food (i.e., groceries) stores
446191 Food (i.e., health) supplement stores
336999 Food (vendor) carts on wheels manufacturing
624210 Food banks
722330 Food carts, mobile
333294 Food choppers, grinders, mixers, and slicers (i.e., food manufacturing-type) manufacturing
325132 Food coloring, synthetic, manufacturing
311942 Food coloring, natural, manufacturing
722310 Food concession contractors (e.g., convention facilities, entertainment facilities, sporting facilities)
722330 Food concession stands, mobile
322299 Food containers made from molded pulp
326140 Food containers, polystyrene foam, manufacturing
322215 Food containers, sanitary (except folding), made from purchased paper or paperboard
322212 Food containers, sanitary, folding, made from purchased paperboard
333294 Food dehydrating equipment (except household-type) manufacturing
923130 Food distribution program administration, government
311942 Food extracts (except coffee, meat) manufacturing
926140 Food inspection agencies
811310 Food machinery repair and maintenance services
335211 Food mixers, household-type electric, manufacturing
333993 Food packaging machinery manufacturing
327213 Food packaging, glass, manufacturing
236210 Food processing plant construction
541710 Food research and development laboratories or services
722310 Food service contractors, airline
722310 Food service contractors, cafeteria
722310 Food service contractors, concession operator (e.g., convention facilities, entertainment facilities, sporting facilities)
423440 Food service equipment (except refrigerated), commercial, merchant wholesalers
923120 Food service health inspections
326111 Food storage bags, plastics film, single wall or multiwall, manufacturing
541380 Food testing laboratories or services
322299 Food trays, molded pulp, manufacturing
333319 Food warming equipment, commercial-type, manufacturing

335228 Food waste disposal units, household-type, manufacturing
311991 Food, prepared, perishable, packaged for individual resale
423830 Food-processing machinery and equipment merchant wholesalers
339113 Foot appliances, orthopedic, manufacturing
621391 Foot specialists' (podiatry) offices (e.g., centers, clinics)
711211 Football clubs, professional or semiprofessional
713990 Football clubs, recreational
339920 Football equipment and supplies (except footwear, uniforms) manufacturing
423910 Football equipment and supplies merchant wholesalers
611620 Football instruction, camps, or schools
711211 Football teams, professional or semiprofessional
316211 Footholds, plastics or plastics soled fabric upper, manufacturing
316211 Footholds, rubber or rubber soled fabric upper, manufacturing
315119 Footies, sheer, knitting or knitting and finishing
238110 Footing and foundation concrete contractors
451110 Footwear (e.g., bowling, golf, spiked), specialty sports, stores
316211 Footwear (except house slippers), plastics or plastics soled fabric uppers, manufacturing
333298 Footwear making or repairing machinery manufacturing
424340 Footwear merchant wholesalers
326199 Footwear parts (e.g., heels, soles), plastics, manufacturing
326299 Footwear parts (e.g., heels, soles, soling strips), rubber, manufacturing
316219 Footwear, athletic (except rubber or plastics soled with fabric upper), manufacturing
316219 Footwear, children's (except house slippers, orthopedic extension, plastics, rubber), manufacturing
316219 Footwear, children's, leather or vinyl upper with rubber or plastics soles, manufacturing
316213 Footwear, men's (except house slippers, athletic, orthopedic extension, plastics, rubber), manufacturing
316213 Footwear, men's leather or vinyl upper with rubber or plastics soles, manufacturing
316214 Footwear, women's (except house slippers, athletic, orthopedic extension, plastics, rubber) manufacturing
316214 Footwear, women's leather or vinyl upper with rubber or plastics soles, manufacturing
339112 Forceps, surgical, manufacturing
523130 Foreign currency exchange dealing (i.e., acting as a principal in dealing commodities to investors)
523130 Foreign currency exchange services (i.e., selling to the public)
928120 Foreign economic and social development services, government
928120 Foreign government service
611630 Foreign language schools
928120 Foreign missions
541380 Forensic (except medical) laboratories or services
621511 Forensic laboratories, medical
621111 Forensic pathologists' offices
531190 Forest land rental or leasing
115310 Forest management plans preparation
113210 Forest nurseries for reforestation, growing trees
423990 Forest products (except lumber) merchant wholesalers

484230 Forest products trucking, long-distance
423810 Forestry machinery and equipment merchant wholesalers
532412 Forestry machinery and equipment rental or leasing
811310 Forestry machinery and equipment repair and maintenance services
541710 Forestry research and development laboratories or services
115310 Forestry services
333513 Forging machinery and hammers manufacturing
332111 Forgings made from purchased iron or steel, unfinished
331111 Forgings, iron or steel, made in iron and steel mills
811310 Forklift repair and maintenance services
423830 Forklift trucks (except log) merchant wholesalers
333924 Forklifts manufacturing
332212 Forks, handtools (e.g., garden, hay, manure), manufacturing
332211 Forks, table, nonprecious and precious plated metal, manufacturing
331222 Form ties made in wire drawing plants
315211 Formal jackets, men's and boys', cut and sew apparel contractors
315222 Formal jackets, men's and boys', cut and sewn from purchased fabric (except apparel contractors)
532220 Formal wear rental
325199 Formaldehyde manufacturing
325199 Formalin manufacturing
325199 Formic acid manufacturing
238190 Forming contractor
333513 Forming machines (except drawing), metalworking, manufacturing
327112 Forms for dipped rubber products, pottery, manufacturing
238190 Forms for poured concrete, erecting and dismantling
423420 Forms handling machines merchant wholesalers
332322 Forms, concrete, sheet metal (except stampings), manufacturing
321999 Forms, display, boot and shoe, all materials, manufacturing
424120 Forms, paper (e.g., business, office, sales), merchant wholesalers
312130 Fortified wines manufacturing
812990 Fortune-telling services
624110 Foster care placement agencies
624110 Foster home placement services
238140 Foundation (e.g., brick, block, stone), building, contractors
238390 Foundation dampproofing (including installing rigid foam insulation)
238910 Foundation digging (i.e., excavation)
238910 Foundation drilling contractors
315212 Foundation garments, women's and girls', cut and sew apparel contractors
315231 Foundation garments, women's, misses', and girls', cut and sewn from purchased fabric (except apparel contractors)
238110 Foundation, building, poured concrete, contractors
238130 Foundation, building, wood, contractors
325620 Foundations (i.e., make-up) manufacturing
331528 Foundries (except die-casting), nonferrous metals (except aluminum, copper)
331524 Foundries, aluminum (except die-casting)
331525 Foundries, brass, bronze, and copper (except die-casting) manufacturing
331525 Foundries, copper (except die-casting)
331521 Foundries, die-casting, aluminum

331522 Foundries, die-casting, nonferrous metals (except aluminum)
331511 Foundries, iron (i.e., ductile, gray, malleable, semisteel)
331513 Foundries, steel (except investment)
331512 Foundries, steel investment
333511 Foundry casting molds manufacturing
236210 Foundry construction
325998 Foundry core oil, wash, and wax manufacturing
332997 Foundry cores manufacturing
423830 Foundry machinery and equipment merchant wholesalers
811310 Foundry machinery and equipment repair and maintenance services
332997 Foundry pattern making
423510 Foundry products merchant wholesalers
212322 Foundry sand quarrying and/or beneficiating
424450 Fountain fruits and syrups merchant wholesalers
335129 Fountain lighting fixtures manufacturing
339941 Fountain pens manufacturing
332999 Fountains (except drinking), metal, manufacturing
332998 Fountains, drinking (except mechanically refrigerated), metal, manufacturing
423720 Fountains, drinking (except refrigerated), merchant wholesalers
423740 Fountains, drinking, refrigerated, merchant wholesalers
327420 Fountains, plaster of paris, manufacturing
333415 Fountains, refrigerated drinking, manufacturing
713920 Four season ski resorts without accommodations
333291 Fourdrinier machinery manufacturing
332618 Fourdrinier wire cloth made from purchased wire
112930 Fox production
335312 Fractional horsepower electric motors manufacturing
333298 Fractionating equipment, chemical, manufacturing
211112 Fractionating natural gas liquids
333319 Frame and body alignment equipment, motor vehicle, manufacturing
332999 Frames and handles, handbag and luggage, metal, manufacturing
423220 Frames and pictures merchant wholesalers
339942 Frames for artist's canvases (i.e., stretchers) manufacturing
333292 Frames for textile making machinery manufacturing
332321 Frames, door and window, metal, manufacturing
321911 Frames, door and window, wood, manufacturing
332999 Frames, metal, lamp shade, manufacturing
332999 Frames, metal, umbrella and parasol, manufacturing
339999 Frames, mirror and picture, all materials, manufacturing
423460 Frames, ophthalmic, merchant wholesalers
238130 Framework, house, contractors
238130 Framing contractors
533110 Franchise agreements, leasing, selling or licensing, without providing other services
813410 Fraternal associations or lodges, social or civic
524113 Fraternal life insurance organizations
813410 Fraternal lodges
813410 Fraternal organizations
813410 Fraternities (except residential)
721310 Fraternity houses
621493 Freestanding ambulatory surgical centers and clinics
621493 Freestanding emergency medical centers and clinics

311423 Freeze-dried, food processing, fruits and vegetables
811310 Freezer, commercial, repair and maintenance services
335222 Freezers, chest and upright household-type, manufacturing
423620 Freezers, household-type, merchant wholesalers
333415 Freezing equipment, industrial and commercial-type, manufacturing
311712 Freezing fish (e.g., blocks, fillets, ready-to-serve products)
488210 Freight car cleaning services
481112 Freight carriers (except air couriers), air, scheduled
481212 Freight charter services, air
488510 Freight forwarding
482111 Freight railways, line-haul
482112 Freight railways, short-line or beltline
541614 Freight rate auditor services
541614 Freight rate consulting services
483113 Freight shipping on the Great Lakes system (including St. Lawrence Seaway)
541614 Freight traffic consulting services
481212 Freight transportation, air, charter services
481212 Freight transportation, air, nonscheduled
483113 Freight transportation, deep sea, to and from domestic ports
483111 Freight transportation, deep sea, to or from foreign ports
483211 Freight transportation, inland waters (except on Great Lakes system)
311411 French fries, frozen, pre-cooked, manufacturing
311412 French toast, frozen, manufacturing
335312 Frequency converters (i.e., electric generators) manufacturing
334515 Frequency meters (e.g., electrical, electronic, mechanical) manufacturing
334515 Frequency synthesizers manufacturing
238310 Fresco (i.e., decorative plaster finishing) contractors
424460 Fresh fish merchant wholesalers
424480 Fresh fruits, vegetables and berries merchant wholesalers
424470 Fresh meats merchant wholesalers
424440 Fresh poultry merchant wholesalers
424460 Fresh seafood merchant wholesalers
339992 Fretted instruments and parts manufacturing
313221 Fringes weaving
325510 Frit manufacturing
114119 Frog fishing
112519 Frog production, farm raising
331111 Frogs, iron or steel, made in iron and steel mills
811118 Front end alignment shops, automotive
423820 Frost protection machinery merchant wholesalers
311999 Frosting, prepared, manufacturing
311411 Frozen ades, drinks and cocktail mixes, manufacturing
311812 Frozen bread and bread-type rolls, made in commercial bakeries
311813 Frozen cake manufacturing
311411 Frozen citrus pulp manufacturing
311520 Frozen custard manufacturing
722213 Frozen custard stands, fixed location
311520 Frozen desserts (except bakery) manufacturing
311412 Frozen dinners (except seafood-based) manufacturing
311822 Frozen doughs made from purchased flour
424460 Frozen fish (except packaged) merchant wholesalers
454390 Frozen food and freezer plan providers, direct selling

326111 Frozen food bags, plastics film, single wall or multiwall, manufacturing
311412 Frozen food entrees (except seafood based), packaged, manufacturing
424420 Frozen foods, packaged (except dairy products), merchant wholesalers
311411 Frozen fruit and vegetable processing
311411 Frozen fruits, fruit juices, and vegetables, manufacturing
311612 Frozen meat pies (i.e., tourtires) made from purchased carcasses
445210 Frozen meat stores
424470 Frozen meats (except packaged) merchant wholesalers
311412 Frozen pizza manufacturing
311412 Frozen pot pies manufacturing
424440 Frozen poultry (except packaged) merchant wholesalers
311412 Frozen rice dishes manufacturing
424460 Frozen seafood (except packaged) merchant wholesalers
311412 Frozen side dishes manufacturing
311412 Frozen soups (except seafood) manufacturing
311412 Frozen waffles manufacturing
111336 Fruit and tree nut combination farming
445230 Fruit and vegetable stands, permanent
311423 Fruit and vegetables, dehydrating, manufacturing
321920 Fruit baskets, veneer and splint, manufacturing
311421 Fruit brining
311421 Fruit butters manufacturing
321920 Fruit crates, wood, wirebound, manufacturing
312111 Fruit drinks (except juice), manufacturing
311942 Fruit extracts manufacturing
111419 Fruit farming, grown under cover
311211 Fruit flour, meal, and powders, manufacturing
333111 Fruit harvesting machines manufacturing
311421 Fruit juice canning
311411 Fruit juice concentrates, frozen, manufacturing
311421 Fruit juices, fresh, manufacturing
445230 Fruit markets
311340 Fruit peel products (e.g., candied, crystallized, glace, glazed) manufacturing
311421 Fruit pickling
311421 Fruit pie fillings, canning
311520 Fruit pops, frozen, manufacturing
115114 Fruit precooling
115114 Fruit sorting, grading, and packing
445230 Fruit stands, permanent
454390 Fruit stands, temporary
111421 Fruit stock (e.g., plants, seedlings, trees) growing
311930 Fruit syrups, flavoring, manufacturing
115113 Fruit, machine harvesting
115114 Fruit, sun drying
115114 Fruit, vacuum cooling
311340 Fruits (e.g., candied, crystallized, glazed) manufacturing
326199 Fruits and vegetables, artificial, plastics, manufacturing
311423 Fruits dehydrating (except sun drying)
311421 Fruits pickling
339999 Fruits, artificial (except glass, plastics), manufacturing
327215 Fruits, artificial, made from purchased glass
327212 Fruits, artificial, made in glass making plants
311421 Fruits, canned, manufacturing
424490 Fruits, canned, merchant wholesalers

424480 Fruits, fresh, merchant wholesalers
311411 Fruits, frozen, manufacturing
424420 Fruits, frozen, merchant wholesalers
112320 Fryer chicken production
335211 Fryers, household-type electric, manufacturing
311320 Fudge, chocolate, made from cacao beans
311330 Fudge, chocolate, made from purchased chocolate
311340 Fudge, nonchocolate, manufacturing
326299 Fuel bladders, rubber, manufacturing
324199 Fuel briquettes or boulets made from refined petroleum
335999 Fuel cells, electrochemical generators, manufacturing
334413 Fuel cells, solid-state, manufacturing
334519 Fuel densitometers, aircraft engine, manufacturing
336312 Fuel injection systems and parts, automotive and truck gasoline engine, manufacturing
334519 Fuel mixture indicators, aircraft engine, manufacturing
454311 Fuel oil (i.e., heating) dealers, direct selling
424710 Fuel oil bulk stations and terminals
238220 Fuel oil burner installation
424720 Fuel oil merchant wholesalers (except bulk stations, terminals)
424720 Fuel oil truck jobbers
324110 Fuel oils manufacturing
325188 Fuel propellants, solid inorganic, not specified elsewhere by process, manufacturing
325199 Fuel propellants, solid organic, not specified elsewhere by process, manufacturing
336322 Fuel pumps, electric, automotive, truck, and bus, manufacturing
336312 Fuel pumps, mechanical, automotive and truck gasoline engine, manufacturing
334519 Fuel system instruments, aircraft, manufacturing
334519 Fuel totalizers, aircraft engine, manufacturing
423520 Fuel, coal and coke, merchant wholesalers
424720 Fueling aircraft (except on a contract or fee basis)
488190 Fueling aircraft on a contract or fee basis
324110 Fuels, jet, manufacturing
321113 Fuelwood made from sawmill waste
531120 Full service office space provision
722110 Full service restaurants
212325 Fuller's earth mining and/or beneficiating
327992 Fuller's earth processing beyond beneficiating
332313 Fumigating chambers, fabricated metal plate work, manufacturing
115114 Fumigating grain
561710 Fumigating services (except crop fumigating)
334515 Function generators manufacturing
561499 Fundraising campaign organization services on a contract or fee basis
334119 Funds transfer devices manufacturing
525110 Funds, employee benefit pension
525120 Funds, health and welfare
525990 Funds, mutual, closed-end
525910 Funds, mutual, open-ended
525110 Funds, pension
525190 Funds, self-insurance (except employee benefit funds)
812210 Funeral director services
812210 Funeral homes
812210 Funeral homes combined with crematories
524128 Funeral insurance carriers, direct
812210 Funeral parlors

325320 Fungicides manufacturing

315292 Fur accessories and trimings (except apparel contractors) manufacturing

315211 Fur accessories and trimings, men's and boys', cut and sew apparel contractors

315212 Fur accessories and trimings, women's, girls', and infants', cut and sew apparel contractors

315292 Fur apparel (e.g., capes, coats, hats, jackets, neckpieces) (except apparel contractors) manufacturing

315211 Fur apparel (e.g., capes, coats, hats, jackets, neckpieces), men's and boys', cut and sew apparel contractors

315212 Fur apparel (e.g., capes, coats, hats, jackets, neckpieces), women's, girls', and infants', cut and sew apparel contractors

448190 Fur apparel stores

112930 Fur bearing animal production

315292 Fur clothing (except apparel contractors) manufacturing

424330 Fur clothing merchant wholesalers

315211 Fur clothing, men's and boys', cut and sew apparel contractors

315212 Fur clothing, women's, girls', and infants', cut and sew apparel contractors

423930 Fur cuttings and scraps merchant wholesalers

541490 Fur design services

315211 Fur finishers, liners, and buttonhole makers, men's and boys', cut and sew apparel contractors

315212 Fur finishers, liners, and buttonhole makers, women's, girls', and infants', cut and sew apparel contractors

812320 Fur garment cleaning services

811490 Fur garment repair shops without retailing new fur garments

315292 Fur plates and trimmings (except apparel contractors) manufacturing

315211 Fur plates and trimmings, men's and boys', cut and sew apparel contractors

315212 Fur plates and trimmings, women's, girls', and infants', cut and sew apparel contractors

532220 Fur rental

493120 Fur storage warehousing for the trade

316110 Fur stripping

236210 Furnace (i.e., industrial plant structure) construction

325182 Furnace black manufacturing

332322 Furnace casings, sheet metal (except stampings), manufacturing

238220 Furnace conversion (i.e., from one fuel to another)

333411 Furnace filters manufacturing

332322 Furnace flues, sheet metal (except stampings), manufacturing

238220 Furnace humidifier installation

238220 Furnace installation

238220 Furnace, forced air, installation

333414 Furnaces (except forced air), heating, manufacturing

333994 Furnaces and ovens, semiconductor wafer, manufacturing

423720 Furnaces, (except forced air), heating, merchant wholesalers

339114 Furnaces, dental laboratory, manufacturing

333414 Furnaces, floor and wall, manufacturing

423830 Furnaces, industrial process, merchant wholesalers

333994 Furnaces, industrial-type, manufacturing

339111 Furnaces, laboratory-type (except dental), manufacturing

333415 Furnaces, warm air (i.e., forced air), manufacturing
423730 Furnaces, warm air (i.e., forced air), merchant wholesalers
333994 Furnances and ovens for drying and redrying, industrial process-type, manufacturing
424320 Furnishings (except shoes), men's and boys', merchant wholesalers
424330 Furnishings (except shoes), women's, girls' and infants', merchant wholesalers
448150 Furnishings stores, men's and boys'
448150 Furnishings stores, women's and girls'
423210 Furniture (except drafting tables, hospital beds, medical furniture) merchant wholesalers
337124 Furniture (except upholstered), metal household-type, manufacturing
337214 Furniture (except wood), office-type, padded, upholstered, or plain, manufacturing
337125 Furniture (except wood, metal, upholstered) indoor and outdoor household-type, manufacturing
532299 Furniture (i.e., residential) rental centers
442110 Furniture and appliance stores (i.e., primarily retailing furniture)
561740 Furniture cleaning on customers' premises
561740 Furniture cleaning services
541420 Furniture design services
321912 Furniture dimension stock, hardwood, unfinished, manufacturing
321912 Furniture dimension stock, softwood, unfinished, manufacturing
321912 Furniture dimension stock, unfinished wood, manufacturing
337215 Furniture frames and parts, metal, manufacturing
337215 Furniture frames, wood, manufacturing
332510 Furniture hardware, metal, manufacturing
321999 Furniture inlays manufacturing
484210 Furniture moving, used
423210 Furniture parts merchant wholesalers
337215 Furniture parts, finished metal, manufacturing
337215 Furniture parts, finished plastics, manufacturing
337215 Furniture parts, finished wood, manufacturing
325612 Furniture polishes and waxes manufacturing
811420 Furniture refinishing shops
811420 Furniture repair shops
811420 Furniture reupholstering shops
332612 Furniture springs, light gauge, unassembled, made from purchased wire or strip
321912 Furniture squares, unfinished hardwood, manufacturing
442110 Furniture stores (e.g., household, office, outdoor)
453310 Furniture stores, used
327215 Furniture tops, glass (e.g., beveled, cut, polished), made from purchased glass
314999 Furniture trimmings made from purchased fabrics
327991 Furniture, cut stone (i.e., benches, tables, church), manufacturing
337127 Furniture, factory-type (e.g., cabinets, stools, tool stands, work benches), manufacturing
532291 Furniture, home health, rental
339111 Furniture, hospital (e.g., hospital beds, operating room furniture), manufacturing
337121 Furniture, household-type, upholstered on frames of any material, manufacturing
532490 Furniture, institutional (i.e. public building), rental or leasing

337127 Furniture, institutional, manufacturing
339111 Furniture, laboratory-type (e.g., benches, cabinets, stools, tables), manufacturing
532420 Furniture, office, rental or leasing
337211 Furniture, office-type, padded, upholstered, or plain wood, manufacturing
337124 Furniture, outdoor metal household-type (e.g., beach, garden, lawn, porch), manufacturing
337122 Furniture, outdoor wood household-type (e.g., beach, garden, lawn, porch), manufacturing
337127 Furniture, public building (e.g., church, library, school, theater), manufacturing
532299 Furniture, residential, rental or leasing
337127 Furniture, restaurant-type, manufacturing
337122 Furniture, unassembled or knock-down wood household-type, manufacturing
337122 Furniture, unfinished wood household-type, manufacturing
337122 Furniture, wood household-type, not upholstered (except TV and radio housings, and sewing machine cabinets), manufacturing
448190 Furriers
332323 Furring channels, sheet metal, manufacturing
316110 Furs, dressed (e.g., bleached, curried, dyed, scraped, tanned), manufacturing
424990 Furs, dressed, merchant wholesalers
424590 Furs, raw, merchant wholesalers
335313 Fuse clips and blocks, electric, manufacturing
335931 Fuse cutouts manufacturing
335313 Fuse mountings, electric power, manufacturing
332993 Fuses ammunition (i.e., more than 30 mm., more than 1.18 inch) manufacturing
423610 Fuses, electric, merchant wholesalers
335313 Fuses, electrical, manufacturing
325191 Fustic wood extract manufacturing
337122 Futon frames manufacturing
523140 Futures commodity contracts brokerages
523140 Futures commodity contracts brokers' offices
523130 Futures commodity contracts dealing (i.e., acting as a principal in dealing commodities to investors)
523210 Futures commodity contracts exchanges
212319 Gabbro crushed and broken stone mining and/or beneficiating
212311 Gabbro mining or quarrying
237990 Gabion construction
316211 Gaiters, plastics or plastics soled fabric upper, manufacturing
316211 Gaiters, rubber or rubber soled fabric upper, manufacturing
212231 Galena mining and/or beneficiating
712110 Galleries, art (except retail)
453920 Galleries, art, retail
713990 Galleries, shooting
316211 Galoshes, plastics or plastics soled fabric upper, manufacturing
316211 Galoshes, rubber, or rubber soled fabric upper, manufacturing
238160 Galvanized iron roofing installation
333516 Galvanizing machinery manufacturing
331111 Galvanizing metals and metal formed products made in iron and steel mills
332812 Galvanizing metals and metal products for the trade

334515 Galvanometers (except geophysical) manufacturing
334519 Galvanometers, geophysical, manufacturing
325191 Gambier extract manufacturing
921130 Gambling control boards, nonoperating
713290 Gambling control boards, operating gambling activities
713210 Gambling cruises
713290 Gambling device arcades or parlors, coin-operated
713290 Gambling device concession operators (i.e., supplying and servicing in others' facilities), coin-operated
924120 Game and inland fish agencies
334611 Game cartridge software, mass reproducing
114210 Game preserves, commercial
114210 Game propagation
114210 Game retreats
516110 Game sites, Internet
423430 Game software merchant wholesalers
451120 Game stores (including electronic)
924120 Game wardens
339932 Games (except coin-operated), children's and adult, manufacturing
423920 Games (except coin-operated) merchant wholesalers
339999 Games, coin-operated, manufacturing
423990 Games, coin-operated, merchant wholesalers
334611 Games, computer software, mass reproducing
511210 Games, computer software, publishing
334517 Gamma ray irradiation equipment manufacturing
212319 Ganister crushed and broken stone mining and/or beneficiating
236220 Garage and service station, commercial, construction
444190 Garage door dealers
335999 Garage door openers manufacturing
238290 Garage door, commercial- or industrial-type, installation
238350 Garage door, residential-type, installation
332321 Garage doors, metal, manufacturing
321911 Garage doors, wood, manufacturing
812930 Garages, automobile parking
811198 Garages, do-it-yourself automotive repair
811111 Garages, general automotive repair (except gasoline service stations)
332311 Garages, prefabricated metal, manufacturing
321992 Garages, prefabricated wood, manufacturing
332439 Garbage cans, light gauge metal, manufacturing
562111 Garbage collection services
562213 Garbage disposal combustors or incinerators
562212 Garbage disposal landfills
236210 Garbage disposal plant construction
333319 Garbage disposal units, commercial-type, manufacturing
423440 Garbage disposal units, commercial-type, merchant wholesalers
335228 Garbage disposal units, household-type, manufacturing
423620 Garbage disposal units, household-type, merchant wholesalers
562212 Garbage dumps
562111 Garbage hauling, local
333994 Garbage incinerators (except precast concrete) manufacturing
327390 Garbage incinerators, precast concrete, manufacturing
562111 Garbage pick-up services
336211 Garbage truck bodies manufacturing

336120 Garbage trucks assembling on chassis of own manufacture
336211 Garbage trucks assembling on purchased chassis
111130 Garbanzo farming, dry, field and seed production
236116 Garden apartment construction general contractors
236117 Garden apartment operative builders
444220 Garden centers
813410 Garden clubs
811411 Garden equipment repair and maintenance services without retailing new garden equipment
327390 Garden furniture, precast concrete, manufacturing
327991 Garden furniture, stone, manufacturing
337122 Garden furniture, wood, manufacturing
326220 Garden hose, rubber or plastics, manufacturing
423820 Garden machinery and equipment merchant wholesalers
333112 Garden machinery and equipment, powered, manufacturing
561730 Garden maintenance services
541320 Garden planning services
327112 Garden pottery manufacturing
444210 Garden power equipment stores
424910 Garden supplies (e.g., fertilizers, pesticides) merchant wholesalers
811411 Garden tool sharpening and repair services
532490 Garden tractor rental or leasing
339999 Garden umbrellas manufacturing
712130 Gardens, zoological or botanical
111219 Garlic farming (except under cover), field, bedding plant and seed production
111419 Garlic farming, grown under cover
811490 Garment alteration and/or repair shops without retailing new garments
812320 Garment cleaning (e.g., fur, leather, suede) services
321999 Garment hangers, wood, manufacturing
316110 Garment leather manufacturing
314911 Garment storage bags manufacturing
315292 Garments, leather or sheep-lined (except apparel contractors), manufacturing
315211 Garments, leather or sheep-lined, men's and boys', cut and sew apparel contractors
315212 Garments, leather or sheep-lined, women's, girls', and infants', cut and sew apparel contractors
313320 Garments, oiling (i.e., waterproofing)
212399 Garnet mining and/or beneficiating
333292 Garnetting machinery for textiles manufacturing
314999 Garnetting of textile waste and rags
315212 Garter belts cut and sew apparel contractors
315231 Garter belts cut and sewn from purchased fabric (except apparel contractors)
315212 Garters, women's, cut and sew apparel contractors
315231 Garters, women's, misses', and girls', cut and sewn from purchased fabric (except apparel contractors)
334513 Gas analyzers, industrial process-type, manufacturing
334516 Gas analyzers, laboratory-type, manufacturing
334513 Gas and liquid analysis instruments, industrial process-type, manufacturing
334512 Gas burner automatic controls (except valves) manufacturing
333414 Gas burners, heating, manufacturing

334513 Gas chromatographic instruments, industrial process-type, manufacturing
334516 Gas chromatographic instruments, laboratory-type, manufacturing
333414 Gas fireplaces manufacturing
423720 Gas fireplaces merchant wholesalers
238220 Gas fitting contractor
334513 Gas flow instrumentation, industrial process-type, manufacturing
333999 Gas generating machinery, general purpose-type, manufacturing
423720 Gas hot water heaters merchant wholesalers
334519 Gas leak detectors manufacturing
523999 Gas lease brokers' offices
335129 Gas lighting fixtures manufacturing
423990 Gas lighting fixtures merchant wholesalers
238220 Gas line installation, individual hookup, contractors
333298 Gas liquefying machinery manufacturing
237120 Gas main construction
339113 Gas masks manufacturing
561990 Gas meter reading services, contract
423720 Gas ranges merchant wholesalers
333319 Gas ranges, commercial-type, manufacturing
335221 Gas ranges, household-type, manufacturing
333999 Gas separating machinery manufacturing
333414 Gas space heaters manufacturing
332420 Gas storage tanks, heavy gauge metal, manufacturing
336399 Gas tanks assembled, automotive, truck, and bus, manufacturing
333611 Gas turbine generator set units manufacturing
333611 Gas turbines (except aircraft) manufacturing
336412 Gas turbines, aircraft, manufacturing
332911 Gas valves, industrial-type, manufacturing
333992 Gas welding equipment manufacturing
333992 Gas welding rods, coated or cored, manufacturing
213111 Gas well drilling on a contract basis
333132 Gas well machinery and equipment manufacturing
213112 Gas well rig building, repairing, and dismantling on a contract basis
213112 Gas, compressing natural, in the field on a contract basis
221210 Gas, manufactured, production and distribution
221210 Gas, mixed natural and manufactured, production and distribution
211112 Gas, natural liquefied petroleum, extraction
221210 Gas, natural, distribution
211111 Gas, natural, extraction
211112 Gas, natural, liquids, extraction
486210 Gas, natural, pipeline operation
211112 Gas, residue, extraction
424690 Gases, compressed and liquefied (except liquefied petroleum gas), merchant wholesalers
325120 Gases, industrial (i.e., compressed, liquefied, solid), manufacturing
211112 Gases, petroleum, liquefied, extraction
339991 Gasket, packing, and sealing devices manufacturing
339991 Gaskets manufacturing
423840 Gaskets merchant wholesalers
334514 Gasmeters, consumption registering, manufacturing
334514 Gasmeters, large capacity, domestic and industrial, manufacturing
333414 Gas-oil burners, combination, manufacturing

424710 Gasoline bulk stations and terminals
334514 Gasoline dispensing meters (except pumps) manufacturing
336412 Gasoline engine parts (except carburetors, pistons, piston rings, valves), aircraft, manufacturing
336312 Gasoline engine parts (except carburetors, pistons, piston rings, valves), automotive and truck, manufacturing
333618 Gasoline engines (except aircraft, automotive, truck) manufacturing
336412 Gasoline engines, aircraft, manufacturing
336312 Gasoline engines, automotive and truck, manufacturing
324110 Gasoline made in petroleum refineries
423120 Gasoline marketing equipment merchant wholesalers
333913 Gasoline measuring and dispensing pumps manufacturing
424720 Gasoline merchant wholesalers (except bulk stations, terminals)
486910 Gasoline pipeline transportation
238290 Gasoline pump, service station, installation
423120 Gasoline service station equipment merchant wholesalers
447110 Gasoline stations with convenience stores
447190 Gasoline stations without convenience stores
447110 Gasoline with convenience stores
211112 Gasoline, natural, production
313312 Gassing yarn (i.e., singeing)
621111 Gastroenterologists' offices (e.g., centers, clinics)
339112 Gastroscopes (except electromedical) manufacturing
334510 Gastroscopes, electromedical, manufacturing
333999 Gate and bridge lifting machinery manufacturing
332911 Gate valves, industrial-type, manufacturing
332323 Gates, holding, sheet metal, manufacturing
332323 Gates, metal (except wire), manufacturing
237120 Gathering line, gas and oil field, construction
113210 Gathering of forest products (e.g., barks, gums, needles, seeds)
113210 Gathering, extracting, and selling tree seeds
332212 Gauge blocks, machinists' precision tools, manufacturing
334514 Gauges (e.g., oil pressure, water temperature, speedometer, tachometer), motor vehicle, manufacturing
334513 Gauges (i.e., analog, digital), industrial process-type, manufacturing
334514 Gauges for computing pressure-temperature corrections manufacturing
333314 Gauges, machinist's precision tool, optical, manufacturing
332212 Gauges, machinists' precision tools (except optical), manufacturing
424210 Gauze merchant wholesalers
339113 Gauze, surgical, made from purchased fabric
313210 Gauzes, surgical, made in broadwoven fabric mills
321999 Gavels, wood, manufacturing
333512 Gear cutting and finishing machines, metalworking, manufacturing
332212 Gear pullers, handtools, manufacturing
333513 Gear rolling machines, metalworking, manufacturing
333612 Gearmotors (i.e., power transmission equipment) manufacturing

336350 Gears (e.g., crown, pinion, spider), automotive, truck, and bus, manufacturing
333612 Gears, power transmission (except aircraft, motor vehicle), manufacturing
112390 Geese production
311615 Geese, processing, fresh, frozen, canned, or cooked
311615 Geese, slaughtering and dressing
334519 Geiger counters manufacturing
325998 Gelatin capsules, empty, manufacturing
311999 Gelatin dessert preparations manufacturing
311999 Gelatin for cooking manufacturing
424490 Gelatin, edible, merchant wholesalers
424690 Gelatin, inedible, merchant wholesalers
212399 Gem stone (e.g., amethyst, garnet, agate, ruby, sapphire, jade) mining and/or beneficiating
423940 Gem stones merchant wholesalers
333298 Gemstone processing machinery manufacturing
325414 Gene therapy preparations manufacturing
812990 Genealogical investigation services
921190 General accounting offices, government
811111 General automotive repair shops
112990 General combination animal farming
111998 General combination crop farming (except fruit and nut combinations, oilseed and grain, vegetable)
926110 General economics statistical agencies
484110 General freight trucking, local
484122 General freight trucking, long-distance, less-than-truckload (LTL)
484121 General freight trucking, long-distance, truckload (TL)
541611 General management consulting services
622110 General medical and surgical hospitals
423990 General merchandise, durable goods, merchant wholesalers
424990 General merchandise, nondurable goods, merchant wholesalers
921190 General public administration
532310 General rental centers
921190 General services departments, government
452990 General stores
493110 General warehousing and storage
424210 General-line drugs merchant wholesalers
424410 General-line groceries merchant wholesalers
423840 General-line industrial supplies merchant wholesalers
423930 General-line scrap merchant wholesalers
423830 General-purpose industrial machinery and equipment merchant wholesalers
336322 Generating apparatus and parts for internal combustion engines manufacturing
335312 Generating apparatus and parts, electrical (except internal combustion engine and welding), manufacturing
333992 Generating apparatus and parts, welding, electrical, manufacturing
335313 Generator control and metering panels, switchgear-type, manufacturing
532490 Generator rental or leasing
335312 Generator sets, prime mover (except turbine generator sets), manufacturing
333611 Generator sets, turbine (e.g., gas, hydraulic, steam), manufacturing

335311 Generator voltage regulators, electric induction and step-type (except engine electrical equipment), manufacturing
335312 Generators and sets, electric (except internal combustion engine, welding, turbine generator sets), manufacturing
335312 Generators for gas-electric and oil-electric vehicles, manufacturing
336322 Generators for internal combustion engines manufacturing
335312 Generators for storage battery chargers (except internal combustion engine and aircraft) manufacturing
423610 Generators, electrical (except motor vehicle), merchant wholesalers
423120 Generators, motor vehicle electrical, new, merchant wholesalers
423140 Generators, motor vehicle electrical, used, merchant wholesalers
332995 Generators, smoke, manufacturing
334517 Generators, X-ray, manufacturing
621511 Genetic testing laboratories
541710 Genetics research and development laboratories or services
541690 Geochemical consulting services
321992 Geodesic domes, prefabricated, wood, manufacturing
541370 Geodetic surveying services
541370 Geographic information system (GIS) base mapping services
541330 Geological engineering services
213112 Geological exploration (except surveying) for oil and gas on a contract basis
541710 Geological research and development laboratories or services
924120 Geological research program administration
541360 Geological surveying services
541330 Geophysical engineering services
213112 Geophysical exploration (except surveying) for oil and gas on a contract basis
334519 Geophysical instruments manufacturing
541360 Geophysical mapping services
541360 Geophysical surveying services
541370 Geospatial mapping services
541380 Geotechnical testing laboratories or services
237110 Geothermal drilling
221330 Geothermal steam production
325199 Geraniol manufacturing
331492 Germanium recovering from scrap and/or alloying purchased metals
331419 Germanium refining, primary
335931 GFCI (ground fault circuit interrupters) manufacturing
711510 Ghost writers, independent
453220 Gift shops
453220 Gift stands, permanent location
322222 Gift wrap made from purchased materials
424120 Gift wrapping paper merchant wholesalers
561910 Gift wrapping services
212399 Gilsonite mining and/or beneficiating
111219 Gingerroot farming (except under cover), field, bedding plant and seed production
111419 Gingerroot farming, grown under cover
115111 Ginning cotton
111219 Ginseng farming (except under cover), field, bedding plant and seed production
111419 Ginseng farming, grown under cover
113210 Ginseng gathering
327390 Girders and beams, prestressed concrete, manufacturing
327390 Girders, prestressed concrete, manufacturing

315192 Girdles and other foundation garments made in apparel knitting mills
315212 Girdles, women's, cut and sew apparel contractors
315231 Girdles, women's, misses', and girls', cut and sewn from purchased fabric (except apparel contractors)
813410 Girl guiding organizations
721214 Girls' camps (except day, instructional)
611620 Girls' camps, sports instruction
713990 Girls' day camps (except instructional)
315111 Girls' hosiery, sheer, full length or knee length, knitting and finishing
315119 Girls' socks manufacturing
325411 Glandular derivatives, uncompounded, manufacturing
325412 Glandular medicinal preparations manufacturing
325612 Glass and tile cleaning preparations manufacturing
327215 Glass blanks for electric light bulbs made from purchased glass
327212 Glass blanks for electric light bulbs made in glass making plants
238140 Glass block laying
334290 Glass breakage detection and signaling devices
313210 Glass broadwoven fabrics weaving
238150 Glass cladding (i.e., curtain wall), installation
238150 Glass coating and tinting (except automotive) contractors
313221 Glass fabrics, narrow woven weaving
238310 Glass fiber insulation installation
327212 Glass fiber, optical, made in glass making plants
327212 Glass fiber, textile type, made in glass making plants
238150 Glass installation (except automotive) contractors
811122 Glass installation, automotive repair
327212 Glass making and blowing by hand
333298 Glass making machinery (e.g., blowing, forming, molding) manufacturing
327213 Glass packaging containers manufacturing
238150 Glass partitions, installation
327215 Glass products (except packaging containers) made from purchased glass
327212 Glass products (except packaging containers) made in a glass making plants
212322 Glass sand quarrying and/or beneficiating
423930 Glass scrap merchant wholesalers
811122 Glass shops, automotive
444190 Glass stores
811122 Glass tinting, automotive
238140 Glass unit (i.e., glass block) masonry
811122 Glass work, automotive
327215 Glass, automotive, made from purchased glass
423120 Glass, automotive, merchant wholesalers
327211 Glass, plate, made in glass making plants
423390 Glass, plate, merchant wholesalers
333314 Glasses, field or opera, manufacturing
327124 Glasshouse refractories manufacturing
322299 Glassine wrapping paper made from purchased paper
322121 Glassine wrapping paper made in paper mills
327215 Glassware for industrial, scientific, and technical use made from purchased glass

327212 Glassware for industrial, scientific, and technical use made in glass making plants
327215 Glassware for lighting fixtures made from purchased glass
327212 Glassware for lighting fixtures made in glass making plants
442299 Glassware stores
327215 Glassware, art decorative and novelty, made from purchased glass
327212 Glassware, art, decorative, and novelty made in glass making plants
327215 Glassware, cutting and engraving, made from purchased glass
423220 Glassware, household-type, merchant wholesalers
423450 Glassware, medical, merchant wholesalers
325188 Glauber's salt manufacturing
212391 Glauber's salt mining and/or beneficiating
325510 Glaziers' putty manufacturing
238150 Glazing contractors
315292 Glazing furs
332812 Glazing metals and metal products for the trade
334511 Glide slope instrumentation manufacturing
487990 Glider excursions
336411 Gliders (i.e., aircraft) manufacturing
334220 Global positioning system (GPS) equipment manufacturing
511130 Globe cover publishers
511130 Globe cover publishers and printing combined
323112 Globe covers and maps flexographic printing without publishing
323111 Globe covers and maps gravure printing without publishing
323110 Globe covers and maps lithographic (offset) printing without publishing
323119 Globe covers and maps printing (except flexographic, digital, gravure, lithographic, quick, screen) without publishing
323113 Globe covers and maps screen printing without publishing
332911 Globe valves, industrial-type, manufacturing
339999 Globes, geographical, manufacturing
316110 Glove leather manufacturing
315992 Glove linings (except fur) manufacturing
315292 Glove linings, fur (except apparel contractors), manufacturing
315211 Glove linings, fur, men's and boys', cut and sew apparel contractors
315212 Glove linings, fur, women's, girls', and infants', cut and sew apparel contractors
315992 Gloves and mittens (except athletic), leather, fabric, fur, or combinations, cut and sewn from purchased fabric (except apparel contractors)
315211 Gloves and mittens (except athletic), leather, fabric, fur, or combinations, men's and boys', cut and sew apparel contractors
315212 Gloves and mittens (except athletic), leather, fabric, fur, or combinations, women's, girls', and infants', cut and sew apparel contractors
315992 Gloves and mittens, woven or knit, cut and sewn from purchased fabric (except apparel contractors), manufacturing
315212 Gloves and mittens, woven or knit, women's, girls', and infants', cut and sew apparel contractors
315191 Gloves, knit, made in apparel knitting mills

315211 Gloves, leather (except athletic), men's and boys', cut and sew apparel contractors
315212 Gloves, leather (except athletic), women's, girls', and infants', cut and sew apparel contractors
315992 Gloves, leather (except athletic, cut and sewn apparel contractors), manufacturing
424320 Gloves, men's and boys', merchant wholesalers
326199 Gloves, plastics, manufacturing
339113 Gloves, rubber (e.g., electrician's, examination, household-type, surgeon's), manufacturing
339920 Gloves, sport and athletic (e.g., baseball, boxing, racketball, handball), manufacturing
424330 Gloves, women's, children's, and infants', merchant wholesalers
335110 Glow lamp bulbs manufacturing
339114 Glue, dental, manufacturing
325520 Glues (except dental) manufacturing
424690 Glues merchant wholesalers
311221 Gluten feed, flour, and meal, made by wet milling corn
311221 Gluten manufacturing
325611 Glycerin (i.e., glycerol), natural, manufacturing
325199 Glycerin (i.e., glycerol), synthetic, manufacturing
325411 Glycosides, uncompounded, manufacturing
212313 Gneiss crushed and broken stone mining and/or beneficiating
212311 Gneiss mining or quarrying
522294 GNMA (Government National Mortgage Association)
112420 Goat farming (e.g., meat, milk, mohair production)
424520 Goats merchant wholesalers
713990 Gocart raceways (i.e., amusement rides)
713990 Gocart tracks (i.e., amusement rides)
336999 Gocarts (except children's) manufacturing
423910 Gocarts merchant wholesalers
339932 Go-carts, children's, manufacturing
339115 Goggles (e.g., industrial, safety, sun, underwater) manufacturing
331491 Gold and gold alloy bar, sheet, strip, and tubing made from purchased metals or scrap
332813 Gold and silver plating metals and metal products for the trade
332999 Gold beating (i.e., foil, leaf)
331419 Gold bullion or dore bar produced at primary metal refineries
332999 Gold foil and leaf not made in rolling mills
331491 Gold foil made by rolling purchased metals or scrap
212221 Gold lode mining and/or beneficiating
212221 Gold ore mine site development for own account
212221 Gold ore mining and/or beneficiating plants
212221 Gold ores, concentrates, bullion, and/or precipitates mining and/or beneficiating
212221 Gold placer mining and/or beneficiating
325910 Gold printing inks manufacturing
331492 Gold recovering from scrap and/or alloying purchased metals
331419 Gold refining, primary
331491 Gold rolling and drawing purchased metals or scrap
323121 Gold stamping books for the trade
813410 Golden age clubs
112511 Goldfish production, farm raising
713910 Golf and country clubs
441229 Golf cart dealers, powered
532292 Golf cart rental

423910 Golf carts (except motorized passenger) merchant wholesalers
336999 Golf carts and similar motorized passenger carriers manufacturing
423860 Golf carts, motorized passenger, merchant wholesalers
336999 Golf carts, powered, manufacturing
237990 Golf course construction
541320 Golf course design services
713910 Golf courses (except miniature, pitch-n-putt)
713990 Golf courses, miniature
713990 Golf courses, pitch-n-putt
713990 Golf driving ranges
423910 Golf equipment and supplies merchant wholesalers
611620 Golf instruction, camps, or schools
713990 Golf practice ranges
451110 Golf pro shops
316219 Golf shoes, men's cleated, manufacturing
316219 Golf shoes, women's cleated, manufacturing
711219 Golfers, independent professional (i.e., participating in sports events)
339920 Golfing equipment (e.g., bags, balls, caddy carts, clubs, tees) manufacturing
335999 Gongs, electric, manufacturing
111334 Gooseberry farming
332212 Gouges, woodworking, manufacturing
445299 Gourmet food stores
561210 Government base facilities operation support services
522294 Government National Mortgage Association (GNMA)
522294 Government-sponsored enterprises providing secondary market financing
336312 Governors for automotive gasoline engines manufacturing
921110 Governors' offices
333618 Governors, diesel engine, manufacturing
333618 Governors, gasoline engine (except automotive), manufacturing
333611 Governors, steam, manufacturing
812331 Gown (e.g., doctors, nurses, hospital, beauticians) supply services
532220 Gown rental
315299 Gowns (e.g., academic, choir, clerical) cut and sewn from purchased fabric (except apparel contractors)
315211 Gowns (e.g., academic, choir, clerical), men's and boys', cut and sew apparel contractors
315212 Gowns (e.g., academic, choir, clerical), women's, and girls', cut and sew apparel contractors
315212 Gowns, formal, women's and girls', cut and sew apparel contractors
315233 Gowns, formal, women's, misses', and girls', cut and sewn from purchased fabric (except apparel contractors)
315299 Gowns, hospital, surgical and patient, cut and sewn from purchased fabric (except apparel contractors)
315211 Gowns, hospital, surgical and patient, men's and boys', cut and sew apparel contractors
315212 Gowns, hospital, surgical and patient, women's, girls', and infants', cut and sew apparel contractors
315212 Gowns, wedding, women's, cut and sew apparel contractors
315233 Gowns, wedding, women's, misses', and girls', cut and sewn from purchased fabric (except apparel contractors)
334220 GPS (global positioning system) equipment manufacturing
333120 Grader attachments manufacturing

333120 Graders, road, manufacturing
238910 Grading construction sites
333294 Grading, cleaning, and sorting machinery (i.e., food manufacturing-type) manufacturing
333111 Grading, cleaning, and sorting machinery, farm-type, manufacturing
237310 Grading, highway, road, street and airport runway
334512 Gradual switches, pneumatic, manufacturing
532220 Graduation cap and gown rental
315299 Graduation caps and gowns cut and sewn from purchased fabric (except apparel contractors)
315211 Graduation caps and gowns, men's and boys', cut and sew apparel contractors
315212 Graduation caps and gowns, women's and girls', cut and sew apparel contractors
311211 Graham flour manufacturing
311821 Graham wafers manufacturing
212399 Grahamite mining and/or beneficiating
312140 Grain alcohol, beverage, manufacturing
325193 Grain alcohol, nonpotable, manufacturing
115114 Grain cleaning
333111 Grain drills manufacturing
115114 Grain drying
236220 Grain elevator construction
424510 Grain elevators merchant wholesalers grain
493130 Grain elevators, storage only
115114 Grain fumigation
115114 Grain grinding (except custom grinding for animal feed)
311119 Grain grinding, custom, for animal feed
484220 Grain hauling, local
484230 Grain hauling, long-distance
488210 Grain leveling and trimming in railroad cars
321999 Grain measures, wood, turned and shaped, manufacturing
424510 Grain merchant wholesalers
333294 Grain milling machinery manufacturing
311211 Grain mills (except animal feed, breakfast cereal, rice)
311119 Grain mills, animal feed
311230 Grain mills, breakfast cereal
311212 Grain mills, rice
333111 Grain stackers manufacturing
311230 Grain, breakfast cereal, manufacturing
312120 Grain, brewers' spent, manufacturing
115113 Grain, machine harvesting
327910 Grains, abrasive, natural and artificial, manufacturing
813410 Granges
212313 Granite beneficiating plants (e.g., grinding or pulverizing)
212313 Granite crushed and broken stone mining and/or beneficiating
212311 Granite mining or quarrying
238140 Granite, exterior, contractors
238340 Granite, interior, installation
311320 Granola bars and clusters, chocolate, made from cacao beans
311330 Granola bars and clusters, chocolate, made from purchased chocolate
311340 Granola bars and clusters, nonchocolate, manufacturing
311230 Granola, cereal (except bars and clusters), manufacturing
813211 Grantmaking foundations
311313 Granulated beet sugar manufacturing
311312 Granulated cane sugar made from purchased raw cane sugar
311311 Granulated cane sugar made from sugar cane
333220 Granulator and pelletizer machinery for plastics manufacturing
212319 Granules, slate, mining and/or beneficiating
312130 Grape farming and making wine

111332 Grape farming without making wine
111320 Grapefruit groves
325998 Grapefruit oil manufacturing
311423 Grapes, artificially drying
541430 Graphic art and related design services
541430 Graphic artists, independent
325992 Graphic arts plates, sensitized, manufacturing
611519 Graphic arts schools
541430 Graphic design services
334515 Graphic recording meters, electric, manufacturing
335991 Graphite electrodes and contacts, electric, manufacturing
212399 Graphite mining and/or beneficiating
335991 Graphite specialties for aerospace use (except gaskets) manufacturing
335991 Graphite specialties for electrical use manufacturing
335991 Graphite specialties for mechanical use (except gaskets) manufacturing
327992 Graphite, natural (e.g., ground, pulverized, refined, blended), manufacturing
111940 Grass hay farming
333111 Grass mowing equipment (except lawn and garden) manufacturing
332212 Grass mowing equipment, nonpowered lawn and garden, manufacturing
333112 Grass mowing equipment, powered lawn and garden, manufacturing
111998 Grass seed farming
332323 Gratings (i.e., open steel flooring) manufacturing
333314 Gratings, diffraction, manufacturing
238910 Grave excavation contractors
484220 Gravel hauling, local
484230 Gravel hauling, long-distance
212321 Gravel quarrying and/or beneficiating
423320 Gravel, construction, merchant wholesalers
541360 Gravity geophysical surveying services
325910 Gravure inks manufacturing
323122 Gravure plate and cylinder preparation services
323111 Gravure printing (except books, manifold business forms, printing grey goods)
333293 Gravure printing presses manufacturing
311422 Gravy canning
311942 Gravy mixes, dry, manufacturing
331511 Gray iron foundries
531190 Grazing land rental or leasing
311613 Grease rendering
339991 Grease seals manufacturing
562998 Grease trap cleaning
311225 Grease, inedible, animal and vegetable, refining and blending purchased oils
424990 Greases, inedible animal and vegetable, merchant wholesalers
324191 Greases, petroleum lubricating, made from refined petroleum
325998 Greases, synthetic lubricating, manufacturing
483113 Great Lakes freight transportation (including St. Lawrence Seaway)
483114 Great Lakes passenger transportation (including St. Lawrence Seaway)
111219 Green bean farming, field and seed production
111219 Green cowpea farming, field and seed production
111219 Green lima bean farming, field and seed production
111219 Green pea farming, field and seed production
332311 Greenhouses, prefabricated metal, manufacturing
212399 Greensand mining and/or beneficiating
212311 Greenstone mining or quarrying

511191 Greeting card publishers (except exclusive Internet publishing)
511191 Greeting card publishers and printing combined
516110 Greeting card publishers, exclusively on Internet
453220 Greeting card shops
323112 Greeting cards (e.g., birthday, holiday, sympathy) flexographic printing without publishing
323111 Greeting cards (e.g., birthday, holiday, sympathy) gravure printing without publishing
323110 Greeting cards (e.g., birthday, holiday, sympathy) lithographic (offset) printing without publishing
323119 Greeting cards (e.g., birthday, holiday, sympathy) printing (except flexographic, gravure, lithographic, quick, screen) without publishing
323113 Greeting cards (e.g., birthday, holiday, sympathy) screen printing without publishing
323119 Greeting cards engraving printing without publishing
323119 Greeting cards letterpress printing without publishing
424120 Greeting cards merchant wholesalers
332994 Grenade launchers manufacturing
332993 Grenades, hand or projectile, manufacturing
711212 Greyhound dog racetracks
335211 Griddles and grills, household-type portable electric, manufacturing
332618 Grilles and grillwork made from purchased wire
332323 Grills and grillwork, sheet metal, manufacturing
332323 Grillwork, ornamental metal, manufacturing
333991 Grinders, handheld power-driven, manufacturing
325411 Grinding and milling botanicals (i.e., for medicinal use)
327910 Grinding balls, ceramic, manufacturing
333512 Grinding machines, metalworking, manufacturing
332813 Grinding metal castings for the trade
324191 Grinding oils, petroleum, made from refined petroleum
212399 Grinding pebbles mining and/or beneficiating
212322 Grinding sand quarrying and/or beneficiating
311942 Grinding spices
327910 Grinding wheels manufacturing
212399 Grindstones mining and/or beneficiating
326299 Grips and handles, rubber, manufacturing
311211 Grits and flakes, corn brewer's, manufacturing
212319 Grits crushed and broken stone mining and/or beneficiating
424410 Groceries, general-line, merchant wholesalers
322224 Grocers' bags and sacks made from purchased uncoated paper
326111 Grocery bags, plastics film, single wall or multiwall, manufacturing
333924 Grocery carts made from purchased wire
492210 Grocery delivery services (i.e., independent service from grocery store)
445110 Grocery stores
423840 Grommets merchant wholesalers
326299 Grommets, rubber, manufacturing
812910 Grooming services, animal
335931 Ground clamps (i.e., electric wiring devices) manufacturing
335931 Ground fault circuit interrupters (GFCI) manufacturing
238910 Ground thawing for construction site digging
322122 Groundwood paper products (e.g., publication and printing paper, tablet stock, wallpaper base) made in newsprint mills

424110 Groundwood paper, bulk, merchant wholesalers
322121 Groundwood paper, coated, laminated, or treated in paper mills
322222 Groundwood paper, coated, made from purchased paper
322121 Groundwood paper, coated, made in paper mills
322122 Groundwood paper, newsprint, made in paper mills
322110 Groundwood pulp manufacturing
624410 Group day care centers, child or infant
623990 Group foster homes for children
623110 Group homes for the disabled with nursing care
623990 Group homes for the disabled without nursing care
623990 Group homes for the hearing impaired
623990 Group homes for the visually impaired
623210 Group homes, mental retardation
621491 Group hospitalization plans providing health care services
524114 Group hospitalization plans without providing health care services
114111 Grouper fishing
238110 Grouting (i.e., reinforcing with concrete)
335122 Grow light fixtures (except residential) manufacturing
335121 Grow light fixtures, residential, electric, manufacturing
813910 Growers' associations
212393 Guano mining and/or beneficiating
111998 Guar farming
524127 Guaranteeing titles
561612 Guard dog services
812910 Guard dog training services
561612 Guard services
237310 Guardrail construction
332322 Guardrails, highway, sheet metal (except stampings), manufacturing
332323 Guards, bannisters, and railings, sheet metal, manufacturing
332618 Guards, wire, made from purchased wire
111339 Guavas farming
721199 Guest houses
721214 Guest ranches with accommodation facilities
812910 Guide dog training services
713990 Guide services (i.e., fishing, hunting, tourist)
713990 Guide services, fishing
713990 Guide services, hunting
713990 Guide services, tourist
511130 Guide, street map, publishers (except exclusive Internet publishing)
511130 Guide, street map, publishers and printing combined
516110 Guide, street map, publishers, exclusively on Internet
336415 Guided missile and space vehicle engine manufacturing
541710 Guided missile and space vehicle engine research and development
336414 Guided missile and space vehicle manufacturing
336419 Guided missile and space vehicle parts (except engines) manufacturing
541710 Guided missile and space vehicle parts (except engines) research and development
423860 Guided missiles and space vehicles merchant wholesalers
336414 Guided missiles, complete, assembling
323112 Guides, street map, flexographic printing without publishing
323111 Guides, street map, gravure printing without publishing
323110 Guides, street map, lithographic (offset) printing without publishing
323119 Guides, street map, printing (except flexographic, digital, gravure, lithographic, quick, screen) without publishing

323113 Guides, street map, screen printing without publishing
339992 Guitars and parts, electric and nonelectric, manufacturing
113210 Gum (i.e., forest product) gathering
325191 Gum and wood chemicals manufacturing
424690 Gum and wood chemicals merchant wholesalers
311340 Gum, chewing, manufacturing
424450 Gum, chewing, merchant wholesalers
322222 Gummed paper products (e.g., labels, sheets, tapes) made from purchased paper
424130 Gummed tapes (except cellophane) merchant wholesalers
424120 Gummed tapes, cellophane, merchant wholesalers
332994 Gun barrels (i.e., 30 mm. or less, 1.18 inch or less) manufacturing
332995 Gun barrels (i.e., more than 30 mm., more than 1.18 inch) manufacturing
713990 Gun clubs, recreational
813319 Gun control organizations
332111 Gun forgings made from purchased iron or steel, unfinished
331111 Gun forgings made in iron and steel mills
332994 Gun magazines (i.e., 30 mm. or less, 1.18 inch or less) manufacturing
332995 Gun magazines (i.e., more than 30 mm., more than 1.18 inch) manufacturing
811490 Gun repair and maintenance shops without retailing new guns
451110 Gun shops
333314 Gun sighting and fire control equipment and instruments, optical, manufacturing
333314 Gun sights, optical, manufacturing
332612 Gun springs, light gauge, made from purchased wire or strip, manufacturing
321912 Gun stock blanks manufacturing
332510 Gun trigger locks, metal, manufacturing
332995 Gun turrets (i.e., more than 30 mm., more than 1.18 inch) manufacturing
238110 Gunite contractors
334413 Gunn effect devices manufacturing
238110 Gunning shotcrete
325920 Gunpowder manufacturing
423990 Guns (except sporting) merchant wholesalers
332994 Guns (i.e., 30 mm. or less, 1.18 inch or less) manufacturing
332995 Guns (i.e., more than 30 mm., more than 1.18 inch) manufacturing
332994 Guns, BB and pellet, manufacturing
332212 Guns, caulking, nonpowered, manufacturing
423910 Guns, sporting equipment, merchant wholesalers
451110 Gunsmith shops retailing new guns
811490 Gunsmith shops without retailing new guns
238170 Gutter and downspout contractors
561790 Gutter cleaning services
423330 Gutters and down spouts (except wood) merchant wholesalers
332114 Gutters and down spouts sheet metal, custom roll formed, manufacturing
326199 Gutters and down spouts, plastics, manufacturing
238170 Gutters, seamless roof, formed and installed on site
332322 Gutters, sheet metal (except custom roll formed), manufacturing
339920 Gymnasium and playground equipment, manufacturing

713940 Gymnasiums
611620 Gymnastics instruction, camps, or schools
339113 Gynecological supplies and appliances manufacturing
621111 Gynecologists' offices (e.g., centers, clinics)
212399 Gypsite mining and/or beneficiating
238310 Gypsum board installation
327420 Gypsum building products manufacturing
423390 Gypsum building products merchant wholesalers
212399 Gypsum mining and/or beneficiating
327420 Gypsum products (e.g., block, board, plaster, lath, rock, tile) manufacturing
334511 Gyrocompasses manufacturing
334511 Gyrogimbals manufacturing
334511 Gyroscopes manufacturing
624310 Habilitation job counseling and training, vocational
114111 Haddock fishing
212299 Hafnium mining and/or beneficiating
424310 Hair accessories merchant wholesalers
326299 Hair care products (e.g., combs, curlers), rubber, manufacturing
333111 Hair clippers for animal use, electric, manufacturing
332212 Hair clippers for animal use, nonelectric, manufacturing
335211 Hair clippers for human use, electric, manufacturing
332211 Hair clippers for human use, nonelectric, manufacturing
325620 Hair coloring preparations manufacturing
335211 Hair curlers, household-type electric, manufacturing
332999 Hair curlers, metal, manufacturing
335211 Hair driers, electric (except equipment designed for beauty parlor use), manufacturing
423620 Hair dryers merchant wholesalers
333319 Hair dryers, beauty parlor-type, manufacturing
339999 Hair nets made from purchased netting
325620 Hair preparations (e.g., conditioners, dyes, rinses, shampoos) manufacturing
424210 Hair preparations (except professional) merchant wholesalers
423850 Hair preparations, professional, merchant wholesalers
812199 Hair removal (i.e., dipilatory, electrolysis) services
812199 Hair replacement services (except by offices of physicians)
325620 Hair sprays manufacturing
812112 Hair stylist salons or shops, unisex or women's
812111 Hair stylist services, men's
812112 Hair stylist services, unisex or women's
812111 Hair stylist shops, men's
812199 Hair weaving services
339994 Hairbrushes manufacturing
424990 Hairbrushes merchant wholesalers
812112 Hairdresser services
812112 Hairdressing salons or shops, unisex or women's
339999 Hairpieces (e.g., toupees, wigs, wiglets) manufacturing
424990 Hairpieces (e.g., toupees, wigs, wiglets) merchant wholesalers
339993 Hairpins (except rubber) manufacturing
326299 Hairpins, rubber, manufacturing
332612 Hairsprings (except clock, watch), light gauge, made from purchased wire or strip, manufacturing
114111 Hake fishing
623990 Halfway group homes for delinquents and ex-offenders
623220 Halfway houses for patients with mental health illnesses
623220 Halfway houses, substance abuse (e.g., alcoholism, drug addiction)

114111 Halibut fishing
531120 Hall and banquet room, nonresidential, rental or leasing
334413 Hall effect devices manufacturing
531120 Hall, nonresidential, rental or leasing
339912 Hallowware, precious metal, manufacturing
712110 Halls of fame
335110 Halogen light bulbs manufacturing
325192 Halogenated aromatic hydrocarbon derivatives manufacturing
325199 Halogenated hydrocarbon derivatives (except aromatic) manufacturing
311340 Halvah manufacturing
332111 Hammer forgings made from purchased iron or steel, unfinished
332112 Hammer forgings made from purchased nonferrous metals, unfinished
333120 Hammer mill machinery (i.e., rock and ore crushing machines), portable, manufacturing
333131 Hammer mill machinery (i.e., rock and ore crushing machines), stationary, manufacturing
332212 Hammers, handtools, manufacturing
339992 Hammers, piano, manufacturing
321999 Hammers, wood, meat, manufacturing
314999 Hammocks, fabric, manufacturing
337124 Hammocks, metal framed, manufacturing
337122 Hammocks, wood framed, manufacturing
326199 Hampers, laundry, plastics, manufacturing
337125 Hampers, laundry, reed, wicker, rattan, manufacturing
332322 Hampers, laundry, sheet metal (except stampings), manufacturing
311611 Hams (except poultry) produced in slaughtering plants
311612 Hams, canned, made from purchased carcasses
311615 Hams, poultry, manufacturing
311612 Hams, preserved (except poultry), made from purchased carcasses
327215 Hand blowing purchased glass
334111 Hand held computers (e.g., PDAs) manufacturing
313249 Hand knitting lace or warp fabric products
812320 Hand laundries
325620 Hand lotions manufacturing
339943 Hand operated stamps (e.g., canceling, postmark, shoe, textile marking) manufacturing
325611 Hand soaps (e.g., hard, liquid, soft) manufacturing
334518 Hand stamps (e.g., date, time), timing mechanism operated, manufacturing
333924 Hand trucks manufacturing
313221 Hand weaving fabric, 12 inches or less (30cm)
313210 Hand weaving fabrics, more than 12 inches (30 cm) in width
316110 Handbag leather manufacturing
448150 Handbag stores
316993 Handbags (except metal), men's, manufacturing
424330 Handbags merchant wholesalers
339911 Handbags, precious metal, manufacturing
316992 Handbags, women's, all materials (except precious metal), manufacturing
713940 Handball club facilities
541870 Handbill direct distribution services
332999 Handcuffs manufacturing
332212 Handheld edge tools (except saws, scissors-type), nonelectric, manufacturing

485991 Handicapped passenger transportation services
611110 Handicapped, schools for, elementary or secondary
611610 Handicrafts instruction
315999 Handkerchiefs (except paper) cut and sewn from purchased fabric
315211 Handkerchiefs (except paper), men's and boys', cut and sew apparel contractors
315212 Handkerchiefs (except paper), women's, girls', and infants', cut and sew apparel contractors
322291 Handkerchiefs, paper, made from purchased paper
321912 Handle blanks, wood, manufacturing
321912 Handle stock, sawed or planed, manufacturing
321999 Handles (e.g., broom, mop, handtool), wood, manufacturing
424990 Handles (e.g., broom, mop, paint) merchant wholesalers
326199 Handles (e.g., brush, tool, umbrella), plastics, manufacturing
316999 Handles (e.g., luggage, whip), leather, manufacturing
332999 Handles (e.g., parasol, umbrella), metal, manufacturing
327111 Handles, faucet, vitreous china and earthenware, manufacturing
541420 Handtool industrial design services
332212 Handtool metal blades (e.g., putty knives, scrapers, screw drivers) manufacturing
423710 Handtools (except motor vehicle mechanics', machinists' precision) merchant wholesalers
332212 Handtools, machinists' precision, manufacturing
423830 Handtools, machinists' precision, merchant wholesalers
332212 Handtools, motor vehicle mechanics', manufacturing
423120 Handtools, motor vehicle mechanics', merchant wholesalers
333991 Handtools, power-driven, manufacturing
444130 Handtools, power-driven, repair and maintenance services retailing new power-driven handtools
811411 Handtools, power-driven, repair and maintenance services without retailing new power-driven handtools
541990 Handwriting analysis services
541990 Handwriting expert services
236220 Handyman construction service, commercial and institutional building
236118 Handyman construction service, residential building
336411 Hang gliders manufacturing
236220 Hangar construction
332321 Hangar doors, metal, manufacturing
488119 Hangar rental, aircraft
321999 Hangers, wooden, garment, manufacturing
111422 Hanging basket plant growing
237990 Harbor construction
488310 Harbor maintenance services (except dredging)
488310 Harbor operation
487210 Harbor sightseeing tours
488330 Harbor tugboat services
213112 Hard banding oil and gas field service on a contract basis
311340 Hard candies manufacturing
212113 Hard coal (i.e., anthracite) surface mining
212113 Hard coal (i.e., anthracite) underground mining
334112 Hard disk drives manufacturing
334613 Hard drive media manufacturing

313210 Hard fiber fabrics, broadwoven, weaving
313111 Hard fiber spun yarns made from purchased fiber
313113 Hard fiber thread manufacturing
313221 Hard fiber, narrow woven, weaving
339113 Hard hats manufacturing
321219 Hardboard manufacturing
332811 Hardening (i.e., heat treating) metals and metal products for the trade
334519 Hardness testing equipment manufacturing
423710 Hardware (except motor vehicle) merchant wholesalers
332618 Hardware cloth, woven wire, made from purchased wire
444130 Hardware stores
423120 Hardware, motor vehicle, merchant wholesalers
326199 Hardware, plastics, manufacturing
335932 Hardware, transmission pole and line, manufacturing
423610 Hardware, transmission pole and line, merchant wholesalers
321912 Hardwood dimension lumber and stock, resawing purchased lumber
325191 Hardwood distillates manufacturing
444190 Hardwood flooring dealers
238330 Hardwood flooring, installation only
321211 Hardwood plywood composites manufacturing
321211 Hardwood veneer or plywood manufacturing
339992 Harmonicas manufacturing
334419 Harness assemblies for electronic use manufacturing
711219 Harness drivers
424910 Harness equipment merchant wholesalers
316110 Harness leather manufacturing
332999 Harness parts, metal, manufacturing
711212 Harness racetracks
316999 Harnesses and harness parts, leather, manufacturing
316999 Harnesses, dog, manufacturing
339992 Harps and parts manufacturing
339992 Harpsichords manufacturing
333111 Harrows (e.g., disc, spring, tine) manufacturing
315991 Harvest hats, straw, manufacturing
113210 Harvesting berries or nuts from native and non-cultivated plants
333111 Harvesting machinery and equipment, agriculture, manufacturing
423820 Harvesting machinery and equipment, agriculture, merchant wholesalers
335211 Hassock fans, electric, manufacturing
448150 Hat and cap stores
339999 Hat blocks manufacturing
315991 Hat bodies (e.g., fur-felt, straw, wool-felt) cut and sewn from purchased fabric (except apparel contractors)
315211 Hat bodies (e.g., fur-felt, straw, wool-felt), men's and boys', cut and sew apparel contractors
315212 Hat bodies (e.g., fur-felt, straw, wool-felt), women's, girls', and infants', cut and sew apparel contractors
812320 Hat cleaning services
315999 Hat findings cut and sewn from purchased fabric (except apparel contractors)
315211 Hat findings, men's and boys', cut and sew apparel contractors
315212 Hat findings, women's, girls', and infants', cut and sew apparel contractors
315999 Hat linings and trimmings cut and sewn from purchased fabric (except apparel contractors)

315211 Hat linings and trimmings, men's and boys', cut and sew apparel contractors
315212 Hat linings and trimmings, women's, girls', and infants', cut and sew apparel contractors
112511 Hatcheries, finfish
112340 Hatcheries, poultry
112512 Hatcheries, shellfish
332212 Hatchets manufacturing
315991 Hats (except fur, knitting mill products, leather) cut and sewn from purchased fabric (except apparel contractors)
424320 Hats and caps, men's and boys', merchant wholesalers
424330 Hats and caps, women's, girls' and infants', merchant wholesalers
322299 Hats made from purchased paper
315191 Hats made in apparel knitting mills
315991 Hats, cloth, cut and sewn from purchased fabric (except apparel contractors)
315211 Hats, cloth, men's and boys', cut and sew apparel contractors
315212 Hats, cloth, women's, girls', and infants', cut and sew apparel contractors
315292 Hats, fur (except apparel contractors), manufacturing
315211 Hats, fur, men's and boys', cut and sew apparel contractors
315212 Hats, fur, women's, girls', and infants', cut and sew apparel contractors
315991 Hats, fur-felt, straw, and wool-felt, cut and sewn from purchased fabric (except apparel contractors)
315211 Hats, fur-felt, straw, and wool-felt, men's and boys', cut and sew apparel contractors
315212 Hats, fur-felt, straw, and wool-felt, women's, girls', and infants', cut and sew apparel contractors
315292 Hats, leather (except apparel contractors), manufacturing
315211 Hats, leather, men's and boys', cut and sew apparel contractors
315212 Hats, leather, women's, girls', and infants', cut and sew apparel contractors
315211 Hats, men's and boys', cut and sew apparel contractors
315991 Hats, trimmed, cut and sewn from purchased fabric (except apparel contractors)
315211 Hats, trimmed, men's and boys', cut and sew apparel contractors
315212 Hats, trimmed, women's, girls', and infants', cut and sew apparel contractors
315212 Hats, women's, girls', and infants', cut and sew apparel contractors
333111 Hay balers and presses manufacturing
111940 Hay farming (e.g., alfalfa hay, clover hay, grass hay)
424910 Hay merchant wholesalers
115113 Hay mowing, raking, baling, and chopping
111998 Hay seed farming
311119 Hay, cubed, manufacturing
333111 Haying machines manufacturing
423820 Haying machines merchant wholesalers
562112 Hazardous waste collection services
562211 Hazardous waste disposal facilities
562211 Hazardous waste disposal facilities combined with collection and/or local hauling of hazardous waste
562211 Hazardous waste material disposal facilities
562211 Hazardous waste material treatment facilities
562211 Hazardous waste treatment facilities

562211 Hazardous waste treatment facilities combined with collection and/or local hauling of hazardous waste
111335 Hazelnut farming
334613 Head cleaners for magnetic tape equipment, manufacturing
551114 Head offices
311212 Head rice manufacturing
624410 Head start programs, separate from schools
315999 Headbands, women's and girls', cut and sewn from purchased fabric (except apparel contractors)
315212 Headbands, women's, girls', and infants', cut and sew apparel contractors
337122 Headboards, wood, manufacturing
321920 Heading, barrel (i.e., cooperage stock), wood, manufacturing
334419 Heads (e.g., recording, read/write) manufacturing
334511 Heads-up display (HUD) systems, aeronautical, manufacturing
236220 Health and athletic club construction
525120 Health and welfare funds
713940 Health club facilities, physical fitness
424490 Health foods (except fresh fruits, vegetables) merchant wholesalers
424480 Health foods, fresh fruits and vegetables, merchant wholesalers
524114 Health insurance carriers, direct
335110 Health lamp bulbs, infrared and ultraviolet radiation, manufacturing
621491 Health maintenance organization (HMO) medical centers and clinics
923120 Health planning and development agencies, government
813920 Health professionals' associations
926150 Health professions licensure agencies
923120 Health program administration
541710 Health research and development laboratories or services
813212 Health research fundraising organizations
621999 Health screening services (except by offices of health practitioners)
621111 Health screening services in physicians' offices
721110 Health spas (i.e., physical fitness facilities) with accommodations
713940 Health spas without accommodations, physical fitness
923120 Health statistics centers, government
713940 Health studios, physical fitness
446199 Hearing aid stores
423450 Hearing aids merchant wholesalers
334510 Hearing aids, electronic, manufacturing
621999 Hearing testing services (except by offices of audiologists)
621340 Hearing testing services by offices of audiologists
336211 Hearse bodies manufacturing
532111 Hearse rental
485320 Hearse rental with driver
336111 Hearses assembling on chassis of own manufacture
336211 Hearses assembling on purchased chassis
334510 Heart-lung machine, manufacturing
332410 Heat exchangers manufacturing
238220 Heat pump installation
333415 Heat pumps manufacturing
423730 Heat pumps merchant wholesalers
325992 Heat sensitized (i.e., thermal) paper made from purchased paper
335991 Heat shields, carbon or graphite, manufacturing

332811 Heat treating metals and metal products for the trade
333994 Heat treating ovens, industrial process-type, manufacturing
221330 Heat, steam, distribution
221330 Heated air distribution
335211 Heaters, portable electric space, manufacturing
423620 Heaters, portable electric, merchant wholesalers
333414 Heaters, space (except portable electric), manufacturing
333414 Heaters, swimming pool, manufacturing
335211 Heaters, tape, manufacturing
333415 Heating and air conditioning combination units manufacturing
238220 Heating and cooling duct work installation
334512 Heating and cooling system controls, residential and commercial, manufacturing
238220 Heating and ventilation system component (e.g., air registers, diffusers, filters, grilles, sound attenuators) installation
238220 Heating boiler installation
423720 Heating boilers, steam and hot water, merchant wholesalers
238220 Heating contractors
541330 Heating engineering consulting services
238220 Heating equipment installation
333414 Heating equipment, hot water (except hot water heaters), manufacturing
423720 Heating equipment, hot water, merchant wholesalers
423730 Heating equipment, warm air (i.e. forced air), merchant wholesalers
333415 Heating equipment, warm air (i.e., forced air), manufacturing
454311 Heating oil dealers, direct selling
324110 Heating oils made in petroleum refineries
335211 Heating pads, electric, manufacturing
334512 Heating regulators manufacturing
221330 Heating steam (suppliers of heat) providers
335211 Heating units for electric appliances manufacturing
333414 Heating units, baseboard, manufacturing
238220 Heating, ventilation and air-conditioning (HVAC) contractors
532412 Heavy construction equipment rental without operator
611519 Heavy equipment operation schools
611519 Heavy equipment repair training
811310 Heavy machinery and equipment repair and maintenance services
336120 Heavy trucks assembling on chassis of own manufacture
336211 Heavy trucks assembling on purchased chassis
325188 Heavy water (i.e., deuterium oxide) manufacturing
332212 Hedge shears and trimmers, nonelectric, manufacturing
333112 Hedge trimmers, powered, manufacturing
316999 Heel caps, leather or metal, manufacturing
316999 Heel lifts, leather, manufacturing
321999 Heels, boot and shoe, finished wood, manufacturing
316999 Heels, boot and shoe, leather, manufacturing
332611 Helical springs, hot wound heavy gauge metal, manufacturing
332612 Helical springs, light gauge, made from purchased wire or strip, manufacturing
481212 Helicopter carriers, freight, nonscheduled
481112 Helicopter freight carriers, scheduled

481211 Helicopter passenger carriers (except scenic, sightseeing), nonscheduled
481111 Helicopter passenger carriers, scheduled
487990 Helicopter ride, scenic and sightseeing, operation
336411 Helicopters manufacturing
325120 Helium manufacturing
325120 Helium recovery from natural gas
339113 Helmets (except athletic), safety (e.g., motorized vehicle crash helmets, space helmets), manufacturing
339920 Helmets, athletic (except motorized vehicle crash helmets), manufacturing
561320 Help supply services
212210 Hematite mining and/or beneficiating
334516 Hematology instruments manufacturing
325413 Hematology in-vitro diagnostic substances manufacturing
325412 Hematology in-vivo diagnostic substances manufacturing
325414 Hematology products (except diagnostic substances) manufacturing
325191 Hemlock extract manufacturing
113210 Hemlock gum gathering
621492 Hemodialysis centers and clinics
313111 Hemp bags made from purchased fiber
313111 Hemp ropes made from purchased fiber
313111 Hemp spun yarns made from purchased fiber
315211 Hemstitching apparel contractors on men's and boys' apparel
315212 Hemstitching apparel contractors on women's, girls', and infants' apparel
325110 Heptanes made from refined petroleum or liquid hydrocarbons
325110 Heptenes made from refined petroleum or liquid hydrocarbons
111419 Herb farming, grown under cover
111998 Herb farming, open field
111421 Herbaceous perennial growing
621399 Herbalists' offices (e.g., centers, clinics)
712110 Herbariums
325320 Herbicides manufacturing
711310 Heritage festival managers with facilities
711320 Heritage festival managers without facilities
711310 Heritage festival organizers with facilities
711320 Heritage festival organizers without facilities
711310 Heritage festival promoters with facilities
711320 Heritage festival promoters without facilities
712120 Heritage villages
238150 Hermetically sealed window unit, commercial type, installation
238350 Hermetically sealed window unit, residential-type, installation
114111 Herring fishing
325199 Heterocyclic chemicals, not specified elsewhere by process, manufacturing
325199 Hexadecanol manufacturing
325199 Hexamethylenediamine manufacturing
325199 Hexamethylenetetramine manufacturing
325199 Hexanol manufacturing
311221 HFCS (high fructose corn syrup) manufacturing
311611 Hides and skins produced in slaughtering plants
316110 Hides and skins, finishing on a contract basis
424590 Hides merchant wholesalers
316110 Hides, tanning, currying, dressing, and finishing

337122 High chairs, wood, children's, manufacturing
311221 High fructose corn syrup (HFCS) manufacturing
335110 High intensity lamp bulbs manufacturing
331112 High percentage nonferrous alloying elements (i.e., ferroalloys) manufacturing
611110 High schools
611110 High schools offering both academic and technical courses
611110 High schools offering both academic and vocational courses
236116 High-rise apartment construction general contractors
236117 High-rise apartment operative builders
332312 Highway bridge sections, prefabricated metal, manufacturing
237310 Highway construction
332322 Highway guardrails, sheet metal (except stampings), manufacturing
333120 Highway line marking machinery manufacturing
237310 Highway line painting
922120 Highway patrols, police
336120 Highway tractors assembled on chassis of own manufacture
336211 Highway tractors assembling on purchased chassis
238210 Highway, street and bridge lighting and electrical signal installation
332510 Hinges, metal, manufacturing
813410 Historical clubs
712120 Historical forts
712110 Historical museums
712120 Historical ships
712120 Historical sites
336399 Hitches, trailer, automotive, truck, and bus, manufacturing
325413 HIV test kits manufacturing
621491 HMO (health maintenance organization) medical centers and clinics
451120 Hobby shops
339932 Hobbyhorses manufacturing
423920 Hobbyists' supplies merchant wholesalers
333515 Hobs (i.e., metal gear cutting tool) manufacturing
711211 Hockey clubs, professional or semiprofessional
713990 Hockey clubs, recreational
339920 Hockey equipment (except apparel) manufacturing
423910 Hockey equipment and supplies merchant wholesalers
611620 Hockey instruction, camps, or schools
339920 Hockey skates manufacturing
711211 Hockey teams, professional or semiprofessional
713990 Hockey teams, recreational
115112 Hoeing
332212 Hoes, garden and mason's handtools, manufacturing
112210 Hog and pig (including breeding, farrowing, nursery, and finishing activities) farming
333111 Hog feeding and watering equipment manufacturing
112210 Hog feedlots (except stockyards for transportation)
424520 Hogs merchant wholesalers
321920 Hogsheads, coopered wood, manufacturing
238290 Hoisting and placement of large-scale apparatus
333923 Hoists (except aircraft loading) manufacturing
423830 Hoists (except automotive) merchant wholesalers
333924 Hoists, aircraft loading, manufacturing
423120 Hoists, automotive, merchant wholesalers
551112 Holding companies (except bank, managing)
551114 Holding companies that manage

551111 Holding companies, bank (except managing)
333313 Holepunchers (except hand operated), office-type, manufacturing
339942 Holepunchers, hand operated, manufacturing
332999 Hollowware, precious plated metal, manufacturing
316999 Holsters, leather, manufacturing
452990 Home and auto supply stores
532310 Home and garden equipment rental centers
238210 Home automation system installation
236116 Home builders (except operative), multifamily
236115 Home builders (except operative), single-family
236117 Home builders, operative
332115 Home canning lids and rings, metal stamping
621610 Home care of elderly, medical
624120 Home care of elderly, non-medical
444110 Home centers, building materials
624229 Home construction organizations, work (sweat) equity
454390 Home delivery newspaper routes, direct selling
337124 Home entertainment centers, metal, manufacturing
337122 Home entertainment centers, wood, manufacturing
522292 Home equity credit lending
621610 Home health agencies
611519 Home health aid schools
621610 Home health care agencies
532291 Home health furniture and equipment rental
236118 Home improvement (e.g., adding on, remodeling, renovating)
236118 Home improvement (e.g., adding on, remodeling, renovating), multifamily building, general contractors
236118 Home improvement (e.g., adding on, remodeling, renovating), multifamily building, operative builders
236118 Home improvement (e.g., adding on, remodeling, renovating), single-family housing, general contractors
236118 Home improvement (e.g., adding on, remodeling, renovating), single-family housing, operative builders
444110 Home improvement centers
541350 Home inspection services
621610 Home nursing services (except private practices)
621399 Home nursing services, private practice
236118 Home renovation
453998 Home security equipment stores
561920 Home show managers
561920 Home show organizers
561920 Home show promoters
334310 Home stereo systems manufacturing
334310 Home tape recorders and players (e.g., cartridge, cassette, reel) manufacturing
334310 Home theater audio and video equipment manufacturing
238210 Home theater installation
333512 Home workshop metal cutting machine tools (except handtools, welding equipment) manufacturing
423220 Homefurnishings merchant wholesalers
442299 Homefurnishings stores
624221 Homeless shelters
624120 Homemaker's service for elderly or disabled persons, non-medical
621399 Homeopaths' offices (e.g., centers, clinics)
813990 Homeowners' associations
813990 Homeowners' associations, condominium
524126 Homeowners' insurance carriers, direct

524128 Homeowners' warranty insurance carriers, direct
623990 Homes for children with health care incidental
623220 Homes for emotionally disturbed adults or children
623110 Homes for the aged with nursing care
623312 Homes for the aged without nursing care
623110 Homes for the elderly with nursing care
623312 Homes for the elderly without nursing care
623990 Homes for unwed mothers
623210 Homes with or without health care, mental retardation
623220 Homes, psychiatric convalescent
311211 Hominy grits (except breakfast food), manufacturing
311230 Hominy grits, prepared as cereal breakfast food, manufacturing
311421 Hominy, canned, manufacturing
333294 Homogenizing machinery, food, manufacturing
311511 Homogenizing milk
212399 Hones mining and/or beneficiating
112910 Honey bee production
424490 Honey merchant wholesalers
311999 Honey processing
111219 Honeydew melon farming, field, bedding plant and seed production
333512 Honing and lapping machines, metal cutting type, manufacturing
333515 Honing heads (i.e., a machine tool accessory) manufacturing
922140 Honor camps, correctional
332313 Hoods, industrial, fabricated metal plate work, manufacturing
332322 Hoods, range (except household-type), sheet metal (except stampings), manufacturing
335211 Hoods, range, household-type, manufacturing
115210 Hoof trimming
339993 Hook and eye fasteners (i.e., sewing accessories) manufacturing
332722 Hook and eye latches, metal, manufacturing
313221 Hook and loop fastener fabric manufacturing
332722 Hooks (i.e., general purpose fasteners), metal, manufacturing
339920 Hooks, fishing, manufacturing
332212 Hooks, handtools (e.g., baling, bush, grass, husking), manufacturing
332722 Hooks, metal screw, manufacturing
331111 Hoops made in iron and steel mills
331111 Hoops, galvanized, made in iron and steel mills
332999 Hoops, metal (except wire), fabricated from purchased metal
321920 Hoops, sawed or split wood for tight or slack cooperage, manufacturing
311942 Hop extract manufacturing
424490 Hop extract merchant wholesalers
111998 Hop farming
333515 Hopper feed devices (i.e., a machine tool accessory) manufacturing
332313 Hoppers, fabricated metal plate work, manufacturing
332439 Hoppers, light gauge metal, manufacturing
424590 Hops merchant wholesalers
334511 Horizon situation instrumentation manufacturing
237990 Horizontal drilling (e.g., underground cable, pipeline, sewer installation)
325413 Hormone in-vitro diagnostic substances manufacturing
325412 Hormone preparations (except in-vitro diagnostics) manufacturing

325411 Hormones and derivatives, uncompounded, manufacturing
112920 Horse (including thoroughbreds) production
332999 Horse bits manufacturing
316999 Horse boots and muzzles manufacturing
711212 Horse racetracks
711219 Horse racing stables
713990 Horse rental services, recreational saddle
711310 Horse show managers with facilities
711320 Horse show managers without facilities
711310 Horse show organizers with facilities
711320 Horse show organizers without facilities
711310 Horse show promoters with facilities
711320 Horse show promoters without facilities
336214 Horse trailers (except fifth-wheel-type) manufacturing
336212 Horse trailers, fifth-wheel-type, manufacturing
713990 Horseback riding, recreational
487110 Horse-drawn carriage operation
311611 Horsemeat produced in slaughtering plants
311111 Horsemeat, processing, for dog and cat food
311421 Horseradish (except sauce) canning
311941 Horseradish, prepared sauce, manufacturing
115210 Horses (except racehorses), boarding
424590 Horses merchant wholesalers
115210 Horses, training (except racehorses)
331222 Horseshoe nails, iron or steel, made in wire drawing plants
115210 Horseshoeing
332111 Horseshoes, ferrous forged, made from purchased iron or steel
541690 Horticultural consulting services
332912 Hose assemblies for fluid power systems manufacturing
332722 Hose clamps, metal, manufacturing
332912 Hose couplings and fittings, fluid power, manufacturing
332919 Hose couplings, metal (except fluid power), manufacturing
313221 Hose fabrics, tubular, weaving
332999 Hose, flexible metal, manufacturing
423840 Hose, industrial, merchant wholesalers
326220 Hoses, reinforced, made from purchased rubber or plastics manufacturing
326220 Hoses, rubberized fabric, manufacturing
315119 Hosiery (except sheer), women's, girls' and infants', manufacturing
333292 Hosiery machines manufacturing
448190 Hosiery stores
424320 Hosiery, men's and boys', merchant wholesalers
339113 Hosiery, orthopedic support, manufacturing
315111 Hosiery, sheer, women's, misses', and girls' full-length and knee-length, knitting or knitting and finishing
424330 Hosiery, women's and girls', merchant wholesalers
424330 Hosiery, women's, children's, and infants', merchant wholesalers
621610 Hospice care services, in home
623110 Hospices, inpatient care
813920 Hospital administrators' associations
524114 Hospital and medical service plans, direct, without providing health care services
813910 Hospital associations
532291 Hospital bed rental and leasing (i.e. home use)
339111 Hospital beds manufacturing
423450 Hospital beds merchant wholesalers

236220 Hospital construction
423450 Hospital equipment and supplies merchant wholesalers
532291 Hospital equipment rental (i.e., home use)
339111 Hospital furniture (e.g., hospital beds, operating room furniture) manufacturing
532291 Hospital furniture and equipment rental (i.e., home use)
423450 Hospital furniture merchant wholesalers
926150 Hospital licensure agencies
611519 Hospital management schools (except academic)
611310 Hospital management schools offering baccalaureate or graduate degrees
315211 Hospital service apparel, washable, men's and boys', cut and sew apparel contractors
315225 Hospital service apparel, washable, men's and boys', cut and sewn from purchased fabric (except apparel contractors)
315212 Hospital service apparel, washable, women's and girls', cut and sew apparel contractors
315239 Hospital service apparel, washable, women's, misses', and girls', cut and sewn from purchased fabric (except apparel contractors)
611519 Hospitality management schools (except academic)
611310 Hospitality management schools offering baccalaureate or graduate degrees
524114 Hospitalization insurance carriers, direct, without providing health care services
****** Hospitals—see type
622210 Hospitals for alcoholics
622210 Hospitals, addiction
541940 Hospitals, animal
622110 Hospitals, general medical and surgical
622110 Hospitals, general pediatric
622210 Hospitals, mental (except mental retardation)
623210 Hospitals, mental retardation
622210 Hospitals, psychiatric (except convalescent)
623220 Hospitals, psychiatric convalescent
622210 Hospitals, psychiatric pediatric
622310 Hospitals, specialty (except psychiatric, substance abuse)
622210 Hospitals, substance abuse
721199 Hostels
487990 Hot air balloon ride, scenic and sightseeing, operation
333311 Hot beverage vending machines manufacturing
332812 Hot dip galvanizing metals and metal products for the trade
311612 Hot dogs (except poultry) made from purchased carcasses
311611 Hot dogs (except poultry) produced in slaughtering plants
311615 Hot dogs, poultry, manufacturing
332111 Hot forgings made from purchased iron or steel, unfinished
332112 Hot forgings made from purchased nonferrous metals, unfinished
213112 Hot oil treating of oil field tanks on a contract basis
213112 Hot shot service on a contract basis
333516 Hot strip mill machinery, metalworking, manufacturing
453998 Hot tub stores
423910 Hot tubs merchant wholesalers
321920 Hot tubs, coopered, manufacturing
326191 Hot tubs, plastics or fiberglass, manufacturing
326299 Hot water bottles, rubber, manufacturing

335228 Hot water heaters (including nonelectric), household-type, manufacturing
238220 Hot water heating system installation
238220 Hot water tank installation
531120 Hotel building, rental or leasing, not operating hotel
236220 Hotel construction
423440 Hotel equipment and supplies (except furniture) merchant wholesalers
423210 Hotel furniture merchant wholesalers
561110 Hotel management services (except complete operation of client's business)
721110 Hotel management services (i.e., providing management and operating staff to run hotel)
561599 Hotel reservation services
327112 Hotel tableware and kitchen articles, vitreous china, manufacturing
721110 Hotels (except casino hotels)
721110 Hotels (except casino hotels) with golf courses, tennis courts, and/or other health spa facilities (i.e., resorts)
721120 Hotels, casino
721110 Hotels, membership
721120 Hotels, resort, with casinos
721110 Hotels, resort, without casinos
721120 Hotels, seasonal, with casinos
721110 Hotels, seasonal, without casinos
624190 Hotline centers
333319 Hotplates, commercial-type, manufacturing
335211 Hotplates, household-type electric, manufacturing
331111 Hot-rolling iron or steel products in iron and steel mills
333516 Hot-rolling mill machinery, metalworking, manufacturing
331221 Hot-rolling purchased steel

238910 House demolishing
238130 House framing
238990 House moving (i.e., raising from one site, moving, and placing on a new foundation)
238320 House painting
111422 House plant growing
238910 House razing
812990 House sitting services
316212 House slippers manufacturing
316212 House slippers, plastics or plastics soled fabric upper, manufacturing
316212 House slippers, rubber or rubber soled fabric upper, manufacturing
532292 Houseboat rental
315191 Housecoats made in apparel knitting mills
315291 Housecoats, infants', cut and sewn from purchased fabric (except apparel contractors)
315212 Housecoats, women's, girls', and infants', cut and sew apparel contractors
315231 Housecoats, women's, misses', and girls', cut and sewn from purchased fabric (except apparel contractors)
315212 Housedresses, women's and girls', cut and sew apparel contractors
315233 Housedresses, women's, misses', and girls', cut and sewn from purchased fabric (except apparel contractors)
238220 Household oil storage tank installation
814110 Households, private, employing (e.g., cooks, maids, chauffeurs, gardeners)
814110 Households, private, employing domestic personnel
443111 Household-type appliance stores
423620 Household-type appliances, electrical, merchant wholesalers
327112 Household-type earthenware, semivitreous, manufacturing

423210 Household-type furniture merchant wholesalers
337121 Household-type furniture, upholstered, manufacturing
337122 Household-type furniture, wood, not upholstered (except TV and radio housings and sewing machine cabinets), manufacturing
325320 Household-type insecticides manufacturing
423620 Household-type laundry equipment (e.g., dryers, washers) merchant wholesalers
327112 Household-type tableware and kitchen articles, vitreous china, manufacturing
334518 Household-type timing mechanisms manufacturing
321999 Household-type woodenware manufacturing
721199 Housekeeping cabins
721199 Housekeeping cottages
561720 Housekeeping services (i.e., cleaning services)
922140 Houses of correction
531110 Houses rental or leasing
332311 Houses, prefabricated metal, manufacturing
321991 Houses, prefabricated mobile homes, manufacturing
321992 Houses, prefabricated, wood (except mobile homes), manufacturing
454390 House-to-house direct selling
423220 Housewares (except electric) merchant wholesalers
442299 Housewares stores
423620 Housewares, electric, merchant wholesalers
624229 Housing assistance agencies
531110 Housing authorities operating residential buildings
925110 Housing authorities, nonoperating
236117 Housing construction, merchant builder
236117 Housing construction, operative builder
922120 Housing police, government
925110 Housing programs, planning and development, government
624229 Housing repair organizations, volunteer
236116 Housing, multifamily, construction general contractors
236115 Housing, single-family, construction general contractors
336612 Hovercraft building
487210 Hovercraft sightseeing operation
332995 Howitzers manufacturing
321999 Hubs, wood, manufacturing
111334 Huckleberry farming
113210 Huckleberry greens, gathering of
334511 HUD (heads-up display) systems, aeronautical, manufacturing
212299 Huebnerite mining and/or beneficiating
115114 Hulling and shelling of nuts
333111 Hulling machinery, farm-type, manufacturing
712110 Human history museums
541612 Human resource consulting services
813311 Human rights advocacy organizations
921190 Human rights commissions, government
813312 Humane societies
541720 Humanities research and development services
423730 Humidifiers and dehumidifiers (except portable) merchant wholesalers
423620 Humidifiers and dehumidifiers, portable, merchant wholesalers
335211 Humidifiers, portable electric, manufacturing
333415 Humidifying equipment (except portable) manufacturing
334512 Humidistats (e.g., duct, skeleton, wall) manufacturing
238210 Humidity control system installation

334512 Humidity controls, air-conditioning-type, manufacturing
334519 Humidity instruments (except industrial process and air-conditioning type) manufacturing
334513 Humidity instruments, industrial process-type, manufacturing
212399 Humus, peat, mining and/or beneficiating
721214 Hunting camps with accommodation facilities
713990 Hunting clubs, recreational
315211 Hunting coats and vests, men's and boys', cut and sew apparel contractors
315228 Hunting coats and vests, men's and boys', cut and sewn from purchased fabric (except apparel contractors)
423910 Hunting equipment and supplies merchant wholesalers
713990 Hunting guide services
332211 Hunting knives manufacturing
114210 Hunting preserves
238220 HVAC (heating, ventilation and air-conditioning) contractors
334111 Hybrid computers manufacturing
334413 Hybrid integrated circuits manufacturing
112511 Hybrid striped bass production
327410 Hydrated lime (i.e., calcium hydroxide) manufacturing
332912 Hydraulic aircraft subassemblies manufacturing
333995 Hydraulic cylinders, fluid power, manufacturing
811310 Hydraulic equipment repair and maintenance services
324110 Hydraulic fluids made in petroleum refineries
324191 Hydraulic fluids, petroleum, made from refined petroleum
325998 Hydraulic fluids, synthetic, manufacturing
213112 Hydraulic fracturing wells on a contract basis
332912 Hydraulic hose fittings, fluid power, manufacturing
326220 Hydraulic hoses (without fitting), rubber or plastics, manufacturing
423830 Hydraulic power transmission equipment merchant wholesalers
423830 Hydraulic pumps and parts merchant wholesalers
333996 Hydraulic pumps, fluid power, manufacturing
336340 Hydraulic slave cylinders, automotive, truck, and bus clutch, manufacturing
333611 Hydraulic turbine generator set units manufacturing
333611 Hydraulic turbines manufacturing
332912 Hydraulic valves, fluid power, manufacturing
325188 Hydrazine manufacturing
325188 Hydrochloric acid manufacturing
325188 Hydrocyanic acid manufacturing
238910 Hydrodemolition (i.e., demolition with pressurized water) contractors
237990 Hydroelectric generating facility construction
221111 Hydroelectric power generation
325188 Hydrofluoric acid manufacturing
325188 Hydrofluosilicic acid manufacturing
336611 Hydrofoil vessel building and repairing in shipyard
325120 Hydrogen manufacturing
325188 Hydrogen peroxide manufacturing
325188 Hydrogen sulfide manufacturing
311225 Hydrogenating purchased oil
541370 Hydrographic mapping services
541370 Hydrographic surveying services
541690 Hydrology consulting services
334519 Hydrometers (except industrial process-type) manufacturing
334513 Hydrometers, industrial process-type, manufacturing

334512 Hydronic circulator control, automatic, manufacturing
423720 Hydronic heating equipment and supplies merchant wholesalers
333414 Hydronic heating equipment manufacturing
238220 Hydronic heating system installation
334512 Hydronic limit control manufacturing
334512 Hydronic limit, pressure, and temperature controls, manufacturing
334511 Hydrophones manufacturing
111419 Hydroponic crop farming
325192 Hydroquinone manufacturing
561730 Hydroseeding services (e.g., decorative, erosion control purposes)
333996 Hydrostatic drives manufacturing
541380 Hydrostatic testing laboratories or services
333996 Hydrostatic transmissions manufacturing
325188 Hydrosulfites manufacturing
339113 Hydrotherapy equipment manufacturing
334519 Hygrometers (except industrial process-type) manufacturing
334513 Hygrometers, industrial process-type, manufacturing
334519 Hygrothermographs manufacturing
621399 Hypnotherapists' offices (e.g., centers, clinics)
325411 Hypnotic drugs, uncompounded, manufacturing
325188 Hypochlorites manufacturing
339112 Hypodermic needles and syringes manufacturing
325188 Hypophosphites manufacturing
312113 Ice (except dry ice) manufacturing
424990 Ice (except dry ice) merchant wholesalers
238170 Ice apron, roof, installation
334512 Ice bank controls manufacturing
335222 Ice boxes, household-type, manufacturing
326199 Ice buckets, plastics (except foam), manufacturing
326140 Ice buckets, polystyrene foam, manufacturing
326150 Ice buckets, urethane or other plastics foam (except polystyrene), manufacturing
332439 Ice chests or coolers, light gauge metal, manufacturing
326199 Ice chests or coolers, plastics (except plastics foam) manufacturing
326140 Ice chests or coolers, polystyrene foam, manufacturing
326150 Ice chests or coolers, urethane or other plastics foam (except polystyrene) manufacturing
445299 Ice cream (i.e., packaged) stores
424430 Ice cream and ices merchant wholesalers
311821 Ice cream cones manufacturing
424490 Ice cream cones merchant wholesalers
333294 Ice cream making machinery manufacturing
311520 Ice cream manufacturing
424430 Ice cream merchant wholesalers
311514 Ice cream mix manufacturing
722213 Ice cream parlors
311520 Ice cream specialties manufacturing
722330 Ice cream truck vendors
333311 Ice cream vending machines manufacturing
335211 Ice crushers, household-type electric, manufacturing
333999 Ice crushers, industrial and commercial-type, manufacturing
711211 Ice hockey clubs, professional or semiprofessional
713990 Ice hockey clubs, recreational
334512 Ice maker controls manufacturing
333415 Ice making machinery manufacturing

423740 Ice making machines merchant wholesalers
311520 Ice milk manufacturing
311514 Ice milk mix manufacturing
311520 Ice milk specialties manufacturing
237990 Ice rink (except indoor) construction
236220 Ice rink, indoor, construction
339920 Ice skates manufacturing
711190 Ice skating companies
713940 Ice skating rinks
711190 Ice skating shows
312130 Ice wine
325120 Ice, dry, manufacturing
424690 Ice, dry, merchant wholesalers
312111 Iced coffee manufacturing
312111 Iced tea manufacturing
212399 Iceland spar (i.e., optical grade calcite), mining and/or beneficiating
311520 Ices, flavored sherbets, manufacturing
332999 Identification plates, metal, manufacturing
423410 Identity recorders merchant wholesalers
332993 Igniters, ammunition tracer (i.e., more than 30 mm., more than 1.18 inch), manufacturing
334512 Ignition controls for gas appliances and furnaces, automatic, manufacturing
336322 Ignition points and condensers for internal combustion engines manufacturing
334515 Ignition testing instruments manufacturing
336322 Ignition wiring harness for internal combustion engines manufacturing
321213 I-joists, wood, fabricating
335122 Illuminated indoor lighting fixtures (e.g., directional, exit) manufacturing
541430 Illustrators, independent commercial
212299 Ilmenite ores mining and/or beneficiating
327420 Images, small gypsum, manufacturing
327999 Images, small papier-mache, manufacturing
323122 Imagesetting services, prepress
312221 Imitation tobacco cigarettes, manufacturing
335211 Immersion heaters, household-type electric, manufacturing
624230 Immigrant resettlement services
928120 Immigration services
923120 Immunization program administration
621111 Immunologists' offices (e.g., centers, clinics)
334516 Immunology instruments, laboratory, manufacturing
333991 Impact wrenches, handheld power-driven, manufacturing
334515 Impedance measuring equipment manufacturing
334514 Impeller and counter driven flow meters manufacturing
339113 Implants, surgical, manufacturing
213112 Impounding and storing salt water in connection with petroleum production
221310 Impounding reservoirs, irrigation
339114 Impression material, dental, manufacturing
711110 Improvisational theaters
334512 In-built thermostats, filled system and bimetal types, manufacturing
335110 Incandescent filament lamp bulbs, complete, manufacturing
325998 Incense manufacturing
334512 Incinerator control systems, residential and commercial-type, manufacturing
236210 Incinerator, mass-burn type, construction
236210 Incinerator, municipal waste disposal, construction
333994 Incinerators (except precast concrete) manufacturing

238290 Incinerators, building equipment type, installation
562211 Incinerators, hazardous waste, operating
562213 Incinerators, nonhazardous solid waste
327390 Incinerators, precast concrete, manufacturing
541213 Income tax compilation services
541213 Income tax return preparation services
333313 Incoming mail handling equipment (e.g., opening, scanning, sorting) manufacturing
339113 Incubators, infant, manufacturing
339111 Incubators, laboratory-type, manufacturing
333111 Incubators, poultry, manufacturing
325998 Indelible inks manufacturing
488190 Independent pilot, air (except owner-operators)
488490 Independent truck driver (except owner-operators)
333515 Indexing, rotary tables (i.e., a machine tool accessory) manufacturing
325998 India inks manufacturing
921190 Indian affairs programs, government
334515 Indicating instruments, electric, manufacturing
334519 Indicator testers, turntable, manufacturing
334513 Indicators, industrial process control-type, manufacturing
325188 Indium chloride manufacturing
624190 Individual and family social services, multi-purpose
523910 Individuals investing in financial contracts on own account
541850 Indoor display advertising services
713120 Indoor play areas
236220 Indoor swimming pool construction
333994 Induction heating equipment, industrial process-type, manufacturing
334416 Inductors, electronic component-type (e.g., chokes, coils, transformers), manufacturing
813910 Industrial associations
522190 Industrial banks (i.e., known as), depository
522298 Industrial banks (i.e., known as), nondepository
314992 Industrial belting reinforcement, cord and fabric, manufacturing
236210 Industrial building (except warehouses) construction
236210 Industrial building (except warehouses) construction, general contractors
236210 Industrial building (except warehouses) construction, operative builders
531120 Industrial building rental or leasing
722310 Industrial caterers (i.e., providing food services on a contractural arrangement (except single-event basis))
424690 Industrial chemicals merchant wholesalers
423840 Industrial containers merchant wholesalers
335314 Industrial controls (e.g., push button, selector, and pilot switches, manufacturing
423610 Industrial controls, electrical, merchant wholesalers
541420 Industrial design consulting services
533110 Industrial design licensing
541420 Industrial design services
926110 Industrial development program administration
423840 Industrial diamonds merchant wholesalers
541330 Industrial engineering services
811310 Industrial equipment and machinery repair and maintenance services

315211 Industrial garments, men's and boys', cut and sew apparel contractors
315225 Industrial garments, men's and boys', cut and sewn from purchased fabric (except apparel contractors)
315212 Industrial garments, women's and girls', cut and sew apparel contractors
315239 Industrial garments, women's, misses', and girls', cut and sewn from purchased fabric (except apparel contractors)
325120 Industrial gases manufacturing
424690 Industrial gases merchant wholesalers
327212 Industrial glassware and glass products, pressed or blown, made in glass making plants
327215 Industrial glassware made from purchased glass
813930 Industrial labor unions
541320 Industrial land use planning services
812332 Industrial launderers
335122 Industrial lighting fixtures, electric, manufacturing
522298 Industrial loan companies, nondepository
336510 Industrial locomotives and parts manufacturing
423830 Industrial machinery and equipment (except electrical) merchant wholesalers
335122 Industrial mercury lighting fixtures, electric, manufacturing
333511 Industrial molds (except steel ingot) manufacturing
331511 Industrial molds, steel ingot, manufacturing
332997 Industrial pattern manufacturing
334513 Industrial process control instruments manufacturing
238220 Industrial process piping installation
325510 Industrial product finishes and coatings (i.e., paint) manufacturing
541710 Industrial research and development laboratories or services
423450 Industrial safety devices (e.g., eye shields, face shields, first-aid kits) merchant wholesalers
325998 Industrial salt manufacturing
424690 Industrial salts merchant wholesalers
212322 Industrial sand beneficiating (e.g., screening, washing)
212322 Industrial sand sandpits and dredging
333997 Industrial scales manufacturing
423840 Industrial supplies (except disposable plastics, paper) merchant wholesalers
424130 Industrial supplies, disposable plastics, paper, merchant wholesalers
541380 Industrial testing laboratories or services
621340 Industrial therapists' offices (e.g., centers, clinics)
811310 Industrial truck (e.g., forklifts) repair and maintenance services
532490 Industrial truck rental or leasing
333924 Industrial trucks and tractors manufacturing
423830 Industrial trucks, tractors, or trailers merchant wholesalers
812332 Industrial uniform supply services
423930 Industrial wastes to be reclaimed merchant wholesalers
311611 Inedible products (e.g., hides, skins, pulled wool, wool grease) produced in slaughtering plants
334511 Inertial navigation systems, aeronautical, manufacturing
311422 Infant and junior food canning
311230 Infant cereals, dry, manufacturing
624410 Infant day care centers
624410 Infant day care services
339113 Infant incubators manufacturing

315291 Infants' apparel cut and sewn from purchased fabric (except apparel contractors)
424330 Infants' clothing merchant wholesalers
315212 Infants' cut and sew apparel contractors
311514 Infant's formulas manufacturing
316219 Infant's shoes (except plastics, rubber), manufacturing
315291 Infants water resistant outerwear cut and sewn from purchased fabric (except apparel contractors)
518111 Information access services, on-line
541512 Information management computer systems integration design services
334516 Infrared analytical instruments, laboratory-type, manufacturing
334511 Infrared homing systems, aeronautical, manufacturing
334513 Infrared instruments, industrial process-type, manufacturing
335110 Infrared lamp bulbs manufacturing
335129 Infrared lamp fixtures manufacturing
333994 Infrared ovens, industrial, manufacturing
334413 Infrared sensors, solid-state, manufacturing
621498 Infusion therapy centers and clinics, outpatient
331319 Ingot made by rolling purchased aluminum
331111 Ingot made in iron and steel mills
331319 Ingot, aluminum, made in integrated secondary smelting and rolling mills
331492 Ingot, nonferrous metals (except aluminum, copper), secondary smelting and refining
331312 Ingot, primary aluminum, manufacturing
331419 Ingot, primary, nonferrous metals (except aluminum, copper), manufacturing
423510 Ingots (except precious) merchant wholesalers
423940 Ingots, precious, merchant wholesalers
621399 Inhalation therapists' offices (e.g., centers, clinics)
339112 Inhalation therapy equipment manufacturing
339112 Inhalators, surgical and medical, manufacturing
325998 Inhibitors (e.g., corrosion, oxidation, polymerization) manufacturing
454390 In-home sales of merchandise, direct selling
333220 Injection molding machinery for plastics manufacturing
325612 Ink eradicators manufacturing
424120 Ink, writing, merchant wholesalers
339944 Inked ribbons manufacturing
424120 Inked ribbons merchant wholesalers
325910 Inkjet cartridges manufacturing
325910 Inkjet inks manufacturing
325910 Inks, printing, manufacturing
423840 Inks, printing, merchant wholesalers
325998 Inks, writing, manufacturing
316999 Inner soles, leather, manufacturing
326211 Inner tubes manufacturing
337910 Innerspring cushions manufacturing
721191 Inns, bed and breakfast
424690 Inorganic chemicals merchant wholesalers
325131 Inorganic pigments (except bone black, carbon black, lamp black) manufacturing
334119 Input/output equipment, computer (except terminals), manufacturing
115112 Insect control for crops
335129 Insect lamps, electric, manufacturing
332618 Insect screening made from purchased wire
325320 Insecticides manufacturing

333515 Inserts, cutting tool, manufacturing
541350 Inspection bureaus, building
926150 Inspection for labor standards
488490 Inspection or weighing services, truck transportation
488190 Inspection services, aircraft
541350 Inspection services, building or home
213112 Installing production equipment at the oil or gas field on a contract basis
522220 Installment sales financing
311920 Instant coffee manufacturing
311230 Instant hot cereals manufacturing
323114 Instant printing (i.e., quick printing)
311920 Instant tea manufacturing
236220 Institutional building construction
236220 Institutional building construction general contractors
236220 Institutional building construction operative builders
337127 Institutional furniture manufacturing
335122 Institutional lighting fixtures, electric, manufacturing
522120 Institutions, savings
****** Instruction—see type of training
512110 Instructional video production
336322 Instrument control panels (i.e., assembling purchased gauges), automotive, truck, and bus, manufacturing
334511 Instrument landing system instrumentation, airborne or airport, manufacturing
333314 Instrument lenses manufacturing
334514 Instrument panels, assembling gauges made in the same establishment
334515 Instrument shunts manufacturing
332612 Instrument springs, precision (except clock, watch), light gauge, made from purchased wire or strip, manufacturing
335311 Instrument transformers (except complete instruments) for metering or protective relaying use manufacturing
334519 Instrumentation for reactor controls, auxiliary, manufacturing
423830 Instruments (except electrical) (e.g., controlling, indicating, recording) merchant wholesalers
334513 Instruments for industrial process control manufacturing
334515 Instruments for measuring electrical quantities manufacturing
334511 Instruments, aeronautical, manufacturing
334515 Instruments, electric (i.e., testing electrical characteristics), manufacturing
339112 Instruments, mechanical microsurgical, manufacturing
339992 Instruments, musical, manufacturing
423990 Instruments, musical, merchant wholesalers
423490 Instruments, professional and scientific, merchant wholesalers
331422 Insulated wire or cable made from purchased copper in wire drawing plants
331319 Insulated wire or cable made in aluminum wire drawing plants
423610 Insulated wire or cable merchant wholesalers
331422 Insulated wire or cable, copper, made in integrated secondary smelting and wire drawing plants
322299 Insulating batts, fills, or blankets made from purchased paper

327993 Insulating batts, fills, or blankets, fiberglass, manufacturing
327124 Insulating firebrick and shapes, clay, manufacturing
327215 Insulating glass, sealed units, made from purchased glass
327211 Insulating glass, sealed units, made in glass making plants
321999 Insulating materials, cork, manufacturing
325998 Insulating oils manufacturing
335929 Insulating purchased nonferrous wire
326150 Insulation and cushioning, foam plastics (except polystrene), manufacturing
326140 Insulation and cushioning, polystyrene foam plastics, manufacturing
321219 Insulation board, cellular fiber, manufacturing
238310 Insulation contractors
423330 Insulation materials (except wood) merchant wholesalers
238290 Insulation, boiler, duct and pipe, installation
335932 Insulators, electrical (except glass, porcelain), manufacturing
327113 Insulators, electrical porcelain, manufacturing
327215 Insulators, electrical, glass, made from purchased glass
327212 Insulators, electrical, glass, made in glass making plants
423610 Insulators, electrical, merchant wholesalers
325412 Insulin preparations manufacturing
325411 Insulin, uncompounded, manufacturing
524298 Insurance actuarial services
524298 Insurance advisory services
524210 Insurance agencies
524210 Insurance brokerages
531120 Insurance building rental or leasing
524113 Insurance carriers, disability, direct
524126 Insurance carriers, fidelity, direct
524114 Insurance carriers, health, direct
524113 Insurance carriers, life, direct
524126 Insurance carriers, property and casualty, direct
524126 Insurance carriers, surety, direct
524127 Insurance carriers, title, direct
524291 Insurance claims adjusting
524291 Insurance claims investigation services
524292 Insurance claims processing services, third party
926150 Insurance commissions, government
524298 Insurance coverage consulting services
524298 Insurance exchanges
524292 Insurance fund, third party administrative services (except claims adjusting only)
551112 Insurance holding companies
524298 Insurance investigation services (except claims investigation)
524298 Insurance loss prevention services
524292 Insurance plan administrative services (except claims adjusting only), third-party
524298 Insurance processing, contract or fee basis
524298 Insurance rate making services
524298 Insurance reporting services
524291 Insurance settlement offices
524298 Insurance underwriters laboratories and standards services
524113 Insurance underwriting, disability, direct
524114 Insurance underwriting, health and medical, direct
524113 Insurance underwriting, life, direct
524126 Insurance underwriting, property and casualty, direct
524127 Insurance underwriting, title, direct
813910 Insurers' associations
323111 Intaglio printing

335312 Integral horsepower electric motors manufacturing
423690 Integrated circuits merchant wholesalers
334413 Integrated microcircuits manufacturing
512220 Integrated record companies (i.e., releasing, promoting, distributing)
512220 Integrated record production and distribution
334515 Integrated-circuit testers manufacturing
334515 Integrating electricity meters manufacturing
334514 Integrating meters, nonelectric, manufacturing
712110 Interactive museums
485210 Intercity bus line operation
483113 Intercoastal freight transportation to and from domestic ports
483114 Intercoastal transportation of passengers to and from domestic ports
334290 Intercom systems and equipment manufacturing
238210 Intercommunication (intercom) system installation
332410 Intercooler shells manufacturing
333314 Interferometers manufacturing
541410 Interior decorating consultant services
541410 Interior decorating consulting services
541410 Interior design consulting services
541410 Interior design services
541410 Interior designer services
811121 Interior repair shops, automotive
238990 Interlocking brick and block installation
623210 Intermediate care facilities, mental retardation
334515 Internal combustion engine analyzers (i.e., testing electrical characteristics) manufacturing
333618 Internal combustion engines (except aircraft, nondiesel automotive, nondiesel truck) manufacturing
423830 Internal combustion engines (except aircraft, nondiesel automotive, nondiesel truck) merchant wholesalers
336412 Internal combustion engines, aircraft, manufacturing
336312 Internal combustion engines, automotive and truck gasoline, manufacturing
921130 Internal Revenue Service
928120 International Monetary Fund
522293 International trade financing
518111 Internet access providers
454112 Internet auctions, retail
516110 Internet book publishers
516110 Internet broadcasting
516110 Internet comic book publishing
516110 Internet entertainment sites
516110 Internet game sites
516110 Internet magazine publishing
516110 Internet news publishers
516110 Internet newsletter publishing
516110 Internet newspaper publishing
516110 Internet periodical publishers
516110 Internet radio stations
454111 Internet retail sales sites
518112 Internet search Web sites
518111 Internet service providers (ISP)
516110 Internet sports sites
516110 Internet video broadcast sites
621111 Internists' offices (e.g., centers, clinics)
541940 Internists' offices, veterinary
541930 Interpretation services, language
712190 Interpretive centers, nature
711120 Interpretive dance companies
711510 Interpretive dancers, independent
485210 Interstate bus line operation
485210 Interurban bus line operation
339113 Intra ocular lenses manufacturing
483211 Intracoastal transportation of freight
483212 Intracoastal transportation of passengers

339113 Intrauterine devices manufacturing
325412 Intravenous (IV) solution preparations manufacturing
812990 Introduction services, social
532291 Invalid equipment rental (i.e., home use)
561990 Inventory computing services
541614 Inventory planning and control management consulting services
561990 Inventory taking services
311312 Invert sugar made from purchased raw cane sugar
335312 Inverters, rotating electrical, manufacturing
335999 Inverters, solid-state, manufacturing
561611 Investigation services (except credit), private
561450 Investigation services, credit
561611 Investigators, private
523930 Investment advice consulting services, customized, fees paid by client
523930 Investment advice counseling services, customized, fees paid by client
523930 Investment advisory services, customized, fees paid by client
523110 Investment banking
331524 Investment castings, aluminum, unfinished, manufacturing
331525 Investment castings, copper (except die-castings), unfinished, manufacturing
331528 Investment castings, nonferrous metal (except alumninum, copper), unfinished, manufacturing
331512 Investment castings, steel, unfinished, manufacturing
523910 Investment clubs
525990 Investment funds, closed-end
525910 Investment funds, open-ended
523920 Investment management
325413 In-vitro diagnostic substances manufacturing
325412 In-vivo diagnostic substances manufacturing
325188 Iodides manufacturing
325412 Iodinated in-vivo diagnostic substances manufacturing
325188 Iodine, crude or resublimed, manufacturing
334519 Ion chambers manufacturing
325211 Ion exchange resins manufacturing
325211 Ionomer resins manufacturing
325199 Ionone manufacturing
331491 Iridium bar, rod, sheet, strip and tubing made from purchased metals or scrap
212299 Iridium mining and/or beneficiating
331492 Iridium recovering from scrap and/or alloying purchased metals
331419 Iridium refining, primary
423390 Iron and steel architectural shapes merchant wholesalers
325131 Iron based pigments manufacturing
331511 Iron castings, unfinished, manufacturing
325188 Iron compounds, not specified elsewhere by process, manufacturing
332111 Iron forgings made from purchased iron, unfinished
331511 Iron foundries
339113 Iron lungs manufacturing
212210 Iron ore (e.g., hematite, magnetite, siderite, taconite) mining and/or beneficiating
212210 Iron ore agglomerates mining and/or beneficiating
212210 Iron ore beneficiating plants (e.g., agglomeration, sintering)
212210 Iron ore mine site development for own account
331111 Iron ore recovery from open hearth slag
212210 Iron ore, blocked, mining and/or beneficiating
331111 Iron sinter made in iron and steel mills
325188 Iron sulphate manufacturing

238120 Iron work, structural, contractors
331111 Iron, pig, manufacturing
335224 Ironers and mangles, household-type (except portable irons), manufacturing
332999 Ironing boards, metal, manufacturing
321999 Ironing boards, wood, manufacturing
335211 Irons, household-type electric, manufacturing
334517 Irradiation apparatus and tubes (e.g., industrial, medical diagnostic, medical therapeutic, research, scientific), manufacturing
334517 Irradiation equipment manufacturing
115114 Irradiation of fruits and vegetables
926130 Irrigation districts, nonoperating
423820 Irrigation equipment merchant wholesalers
333111 Irrigation equipment, agriculture, manufacturing
327332 Irrigation pipe, concrete, manufacturing
332322 Irrigation pipe, sheet metal (except stampings), manufacturing
237110 Irrigation system construction
221310 Irrigation system operation
325110 Isobutane made from refined petroleum or liquid hydrocarbons
211112 Isobutane recovered from oil and gas field gases
325110 Isobutene made from refined petroleum or liquid hydrocarbons
325211 Isobutylene polymer resins manufacturing
325212 Isobutylene-isoprene rubber manufacturing
325212 Isocyanate rubber manufacturing
325192 Isocyanates manufacturing
335311 Isolation transformers manufacturing
211112 Isopentane recovered from oil and gas field gases
325110 Isoprene made from refined petroleum or liquid hydrocarbons
325199 Isopropyl alcohol manufacturing
518111 ISP (internet service providers)
522210 Issuing, credit card
311422 Italian foods canning
339112 IV apparatus manufacturing
333120 Jack hammers manufacturing
315191 Jackets made in apparel knitting mills
332992 Jackets, bullet (i.e., 30 mm. or less, 1.18 inch or less), manufacturing
315292 Jackets, fur (except apparel contractors), manufacturing
315211 Jackets, fur, men's and boys', cut and sew apparel contractors
315212 Jackets, fur, women's, girls', and infants', cut and sew apparel contractors
332313 Jackets, industrial, fabricated metal plate work, manufacturing
315291 Jackets, infants', cut and sewn from purchased fabric (except apparel contractors)
315292 Jackets, leather (except welders') or sheep-lined (except apparel contractors), manufacturing
315211 Jackets, leather (except welders') or sheep-lined, men's and boys', cut and sew apparel contractors
315212 Jackets, leather (except welders') or sheep-lined, women's, girls', and infants', cut and sew apparel contractors
315211 Jackets, men's and boys', cut and sew apparel contractors
315225 Jackets, nontailored work, men's and boys', cut and sewn from purchased fabric (except apparel contractors)

315239 Jackets, nontailored work, women's, misses', and girls', cut and sewn from purchased fabric (except apparel contractors)
315239 Jackets, nontailored, women's, misses', and girls', cut and sewn from purchased fabric (except apparel contractors)
315228 Jackets, not tailored (except work), men's and boys', cut and sewn from purchased fabric (except apparel contractors)
315211 Jackets, service apparel (e.g., laboratory, medical), men's and boys', cut and sew apparel contractors
315225 Jackets, service apparel (e.g., laboratory, medical), men's and boys', cut and sewn from purchased fabric (except apparel contractors)
315212 Jackets, service apparel (e.g., laboratory, medical), women's and girls', cut and sew apparel contractors
315239 Jackets, service apparel (e.g., laboratory, medical), women's, misses', and girls', cut and sewn from purchased fabric (except apparel contractors)
315291 Jackets, ski, infants', cut and sewn from purchased fabric (except apparel contractors)
315211 Jackets, ski, men's and boys', cut and sew apparel contractors
315228 Jackets, ski, men's and boys', cut and sewn from purchased fabric (except apparel contractors)
315212 Jackets, ski, women's, girls', and infants', cut and sew apparel contractors
315239 Jackets, ski, women's, misses', and girls', cut and sewn from purchased fabric (except apparel contractors)
315222 Jackets, tailored (except fur, leather, sheep-lined), men's and boys', cut and sewn from purchased fabric (except apparel contractors)
315234 Jackets, tailored (except fur, sheep-lined), women's, misses', and girls', cut and sewn from purchased fabric (except apparel contractors)
315211 Jackets, tailored, men's and boys', cut and sew apparel contractors
315212 Jackets, tailored, women's, girls', and infants', cut and sew apparel contractors
316999 Jackets, welder's, leather, manufacturing
315212 Jackets, women's, girls', and infants', cut and sew apparel contractors
332212 Jacks (except hydraulic, pneumatic) manufacturing
333999 Jacks, hydraulic and pneumatic, manufacturing
333292 Jacquard card cutting machinery manufacturing
313210 Jacquard woven fabrics weaving
212399 Jade mining and/or beneficiating
611620 Jai alai instruction, camps, or schools
711211 Jai alai teams, professional or semiprofessional
236220 Jail construction
561210 Jail operation on a contract or fee basis
922140 Jails (except private operation of)
561210 Jails, privately operated
332321 Jalousies, metal, manufacturing
424690 Janitorial chemicals merchant wholesalers
423850 Janitorial equipment and supplies merchant wholesalers
453998 Janitorial equipment and supplies stores
561720 Janitorial services
561720 Janitorial services, aircraft
332812 Japanning metals and metal products for the trade
316110 Japanning of leather
333994 Japanning ovens manufacturing

327213 Jars for packaging, bottling, and canning, glass, manufacturing
326199 Jars, plastics, manufacturing
711120 Jazz dance companies
711510 Jazz dancers, independent
711130 Jazz musical artists, independent
711130 Jazz musical groups
315211 Jean-cut casual slacks, men's and boys', cut and sew apparel contractors
315224 Jean-cut casual slacks, men's and boys', cut and sewn from purchased fabric (except apparel contractors)
315212 Jean-cut casual slacks, women's, girls, and infants', cut and sew apparel contractors
315239 Jean-cut casual slacks, women's, misses', and girls', cut and sewn from purchased fabric (except apparel contractors)
315291 Jeans, infants', cut and sewn from purchased fabric (except apparel contractors)
315211 Jeans, men's and boys', cut and sew apparel contractors
315239 Jeans, women's, misses', and girls', cut and sewn from purchased fabric (except apparel contractors)
315212 Jeans, women's, misses', girls', and infants', cut and sew apparel contractors
311421 Jellies and jams manufacturing
424490 Jellies and jams merchant wholesalers
311340 Jelly candies manufacturing
315191 Jerseys made in apparel knitting mills
315211 Jerseys, men's and boys', cut and sew apparel contractors
315223 Jerseys, men's and boys', cut and sewn from purchased fabric (except apparel contractors)
315212 Jerseys, women's, girls', and infants', cut and sew apparel contractors
315232 Jerseys, women's, misses', and girls', cut and sewn from purchased fabric (except apparel contractors)
324110 Jet fuels manufacturing
336412 Jet propulsion and internal combustion engines and parts, aircraft, manufacturing
332993 Jet propulsion projectiles (except guided missiles) manufacturing
237990 Jetty construction
339911 Jewel settings and mountings, precious metal, manufacturing
339913 Jeweler's findings and materials manufacturing
423940 Jewelers' findings merchant wholesalers
332212 Jeweler's handtools, nonelectric, manufacturing
424990 Jewelry boxes merchant wholesalers
541490 Jewelry design services
423940 Jewelry merchant wholesalers
811490 Jewelry repair shops without retailing new jewelry
448150 Jewelry stores, costume
448310 Jewelry stores, precious
339914 Jewelry, costume, manufacturing
339911 Jewelry, natural or cultured pearls, manufacturing
339911 Jewelry, precious metal, manufacturing
333514 Jigs (e.g., checking, gauging, inspection) manufacturing
333514 Jigs and fixtures for use with machine tools manufacturing
333991 Jigsaws, handheld power-driven, manufacturing
333210 Jigsaws, woodworking-type, stationary, manufacturing
624310 Job counseling, vocational rehabilitation or habilitation
323119 Job printing (except flexographic, digital, gravure, lithographic, quick, screen)

323119 Job printing, engraving
323112 Job printing, flexographic
323111 Job printing, gravure
323119 Job printing, letterpress
323110 Job printing, lithographic
323110 Job printing, offset
323113 Job printing, screen
336370 Job stampings, automotive, metal, manufacturing
624310 Job training, vocational rehabilitation or habilitation
711219 Jockeys, horse racing
339920 Jogging machines, manufacturing
315191 Jogging suits made in apparel knitting mills
315291 Jogging suits, infants', cut and sewn from purchased fabric (except apparel contractors)
315211 Jogging suits, men's and boys', cut and sew apparel contractors
315228 Jogging suits, men's and boys', cut and sewn from purchased fabric (except apparel contractors)
315212 Jogging suits, women's, girls', and infants', cut and sew apparel contractors
315239 Jogging suits, women's, misses', and girls', cut and sewn from purchased fabric (except apparel contractors)
325520 Joint compounds (except gypsum base) manufacturing
327420 Joint compounds, gypsum based, manufacturing
333210 Jointers, woodworking-type, manufacturing
333613 Joints, swivel (except aircraft, motor vehicle), manufacturing
333613 Joints, universal (except aircraft, motor vehicle), manufacturing
336413 Joints, universal, aircraft, manufacturing
336350 Joints, universal, automotive, truck, and bus, manufacturing
332312 Joists, fabricated bar, manufacturing
332322 Joists, sheet metal (except stampings), manufacturing
111998 Jojoba farming
711510 Journalists, independent (freelance)
334119 Joystick devices manufacturing
611620 Judo instruction, camps, or schools
326150 Jugs, vacuum, foam plastics (except polystyrene), manufacturing
332439 Jugs, vacuum, light gauge metal, manufacturing
326140 Jugs, vacuum, polystyrene foam plastics, manufacturing
333294 Juice extractors (i.e., food manufacturing-type) manufacturing
335211 Juice extractors, household-type electric, manufacturing
311520 Juice pops, frozen, manufacturing
424490 Juices, canned or fresh, merchant wholesalers
424420 Juices, frozen, merchant wholesalers
311411 Juices, fruit or vegetable concentrates, frozen, manufacturing
311421 Juices, fruit or vegetable, canned manufacturing
311421 Juices, fruit or vegetable, fresh, manufacturing
311411 Juices, fruit or vegetable, frozen, manufacturing
713990 Jukebox concession operators (i.e., supplying and servicing in others' facilities)
334310 Jukeboxes manufacturing
315212 Jumpsuits, women's, girls', and infants', cut and sew apparel contractors
315234 Jumpsuits, women's, misses', and girls', cut and sewn from purchased fabric (except apparel contractors)
335932 Junction boxes, electrical wiring, manufacturing
813910 Junior chambers of commerce
611210 Junior colleges

611210 Junior colleges
611210 Junior colleges offering a wide variety of academic and technical training
611110 Junior high schools
313210 Jute bags made in broadwoven mills
424310 Jute piece goods (except burlap) merchant wholesalers
337124 Juvenile furniture (except upholstered), metal manufacturing
337122 Juvenile furniture (except upholstered), wood, manufacturing
337125 Juvenile furniture, rattan and reed, manufacturing
337121 Juvenile furniture, upholstered, manufacturing
623990 Juvenile halfway group homes
511120 Juvenile magazine and periodical publishers (except exclusive Internet publishing)
511120 Juvenile magazine and periodical publishers and printing combined
516110 Juvenile magazine and periodical publishers, exclusively on Internet
323112 Juvenile magazines and periodicals flexographic printing without publishing
323111 Juvenile magazines and periodicals gravure printing without publishing
323110 Juvenile magazines and periodicals lithographic (offset) printing without publishing
323119 Juvenile magazines and periodicals printing (except flexographic, gravure, lithographic, quick, screen) without publishing
323113 Juvenile magazines and periodicals screen printing without publishing
111219 Kale farming, field, bedding plant and seed production
212324 Kaolin mining and/or beneficiating
327992 Kaolin, processing beyond beneficiation
611620 Karate instruction, camps or schools
713990 Kayaking, recreational
327420 Keene's cement manufacturing
321920 Kegs, wood, coopered, manufacturing
311119 Kelp meal and pellets, animal feed manufacturing
334515 Kelvin bridges (i.e., electrical measuring instruments) manufacturing
111998 Kenaf farming
112990 Kennels, breeding and raising stock for sale
711219 Kennels, dog racing
812910 Kennels, pet boarding
212391 Kernite mining and/or beneficiating
211111 Kerogen processing
324110 Kerosene manufacturing
333414 Kerosene space heaters manufacturing
311421 Ketchup manufacturing
325199 Ketone compounds, not specified elsewhere by process, manufacturing
332420 Kettles, heavy gauge metal, manufacturing
332510 Key blanks, metal, manufacturing
316993 Key cases (except metal) manufacturing
339911 Key cases, precious metal, manufacturing
333512 Key cutting machines, metal cutting type, manufacturing
811490 Key duplicating shops
332618 Key rings made from purchased wire
334119 Keyboards, computer peripheral equipment, manufacturing
339992 Keyboards, piano or organ, manufacturing
336322 Keyless entry systems, automotive, truck, and bus, manufacturing

423710 Keys and locks merchant wholesalers
334210 Keysets, telephone, manufacturing
621492 Kidney dialysis centers and clinics
236210 Kiln construction
321999 Kiln drying lumber
327124 Kiln furniture, clay, manufacturing
333994 Kilns (except cement, chemical, wood) manufacturing
333298 Kilns (i.e., cement, chemical, wood) manufacturing
423830 Kilns, industrial, merchant wholesalers
611110 Kindergartens
334519 Kinematic test and measuring equipment manufacturing
561910 Kit assembling and packaging services
336211 Kit car bodies manufacturing
423620 Kitchen appliances, household-type, electric, merchant wholesalers
327112 Kitchen articles, coarse earthenware, manufacturing
444190 Kitchen cabinet (except custom) stores
337110 Kitchen cabinets (except freestanding), stock or custom wood, manufacturing
238350 Kitchen cabinets and counters, constructed on site
423310 Kitchen cabinets, built in, merchant wholesalers
337122 Kitchen chairs (e.g., upholstered), wood, manufacturing
337124 Kitchen chairs (including upholstered), metal, manufacturing
337125 Kitchen chairs (including upholstered), plastics manufacturing
332211 Kitchen cutlery, nonprecious and precious plated metal, manufacturing
325612 Kitchen degreasing and cleaning preparations manufacturing
337124 Kitchen furniture, household-type, metal, manufacturing
337124 Kitchen furniture, metal household-type, manufacturing
337122 Kitchen furniture, wood household-type, manufacturing
238220 Kitchen sink and hardware installation
423440 Kitchen utensils, commercial, merchant wholesalers
332214 Kitchen utensils, fabricated metal (e.g., colanders, garlic presses, ice cream scoops, spatulas), manufacturing
423220 Kitchen utensils, household-type, merchant wholesalers
326199 Kitchen utensils, plastics, manufacturing
442299 Kitchenware stores
327112 Kitchenware, commercial and household-type, vitreous china, manufacturing
327112 Kitchenware, semivitreous earthenware, manufacturing
321999 Kitchenware, wood, manufacturing
339932 Kites manufacturing
111339 Kiwi fruit farming
334411 Klystron tubes manufacturing
314911 Knapsacks (e.g., backpacks, book bags) manufacturing
314911 Knapsacks, made from purchased woven or knitted materials
315211 Knickers, dress, men's and boys', cut and sew apparel contractors
315291 Knickers, infants', cut and sewn from purchased fabric (except apparel contractors)
315228 Knickers, men's and boys', cut and sewn from purchased fabric (except apparel contractors)
315212 Knickers, women's, girls', and infants', cut and sew apparel contractors
315239 Knickers, women's, misses', and girls', cut and sewn from purchased fabric (except apparel contractors)

337122 Knickknack shelves, wood, manufacturing
332211 Knife blades manufacturing
332211 Knife blanks manufacturing
335313 Knife switches, electric power switchgear-type, manufacturing
311812 Knishes (except frozen) made in commercial bakeries
311813 Knishes, frozen, manufacturing
315992 Knit gloves cut and sewn from purchased fabric (except apparel contractors)
315191 Knit gloves made in apparel knitting mills
315211 Knit gloves, men's and boys', cut and sew apparel contractors
315212 Knit gloves, women's, girls', and infants', cut and sew apparel contractors
313113 Knitting and crocheting thread manufacturing
313249 Knitting and finishing lace
313249 Knitting and finishing warp fabric
313241 Knitting and finishing weft fabric
313249 Knitting lace
333292 Knitting machinery manufacturing
313111 Knitting spun yarns (e.g., cotton, manmade fiber, silk, wool) made from purchased fiber
313249 Knitting warp fabric
313241 Knitting weft fabric
332211 Knives (e.g., hunting, pocket, table nonprecious, table precious plated) manufacturing
423710 Knives (except disposable plastics) merchant wholesalers
333515 Knives and bits for metalworking lathes, planers, and shapers manufacturing
332212 Knives and bits for woodworking lathes, planers, and shapers manufacturing
424130 Knives, disposable plastics, merchant wholesalers
335211 Knives, household-type electric carving, manufacturing
339112 Knives, surgical, manufacturing
339992 Knobs, organ, manufacturing
321999 Knobs, wood, manufacturing
333292 Knot tying machinery for textiles manufacturing
333513 Knurling machines, metalworking, manufacturing
322130 Kraft liner board manufacturing
322121 Kraft paper stock manufacturing
212325 Kyanite mining and/or beneficiating
339942 Label making equipment, handheld, manufacturing
333993 Labeling (i.e., packaging) machinery manufacturing
561910 Labeling services
323110 Labels, lithographic (offset) printing, on a job-order basis
424310 Labels, textile, merchant wholesalers
313221 Labels weaving
561320 Labor (except farm) contractors (i.e., personnel suppliers)
561320 Labor (except farm) pools
115115 Labor contractors, farm
813930 Labor federations
561330 Labor leasing services
926150 Labor management negotiations boards, government
541612 Labor relations consulting services
926110 Labor statistics agencies
813930 Labor unions (except apprenticeship programs)
Laboratories (see specific type)
621512 Laboratories, dental X-ray
621511 Laboratories, medical (except radiological, X-ray)
621512 Laboratories, medical radiological or X-ray
334516 Laboratory analytical instruments (except optical) manufacturing
333314 Laboratory analytical optical instruments (e.g., microscopes) manufacturing
311119 Laboratory animal feed manufacturing

112990 Laboratory animal production (e.g., guinea pigs, mice, rats)
315211 Laboratory coats, men's and boys', cut and sew apparel contractors
315225 Laboratory coats, men's and boys', cut and sewn from purchased fabric (except apparel contractors)
315212 Laboratory coats, women's, cut and sew apparel contractors
315239 Laboratory coats, women's, misses', and girls', cut and sewn from purchased fabric (except apparel contractors)
236220 Laboratory construction
423490 Laboratory equipment (except dental, medical, ophthalmic) merchant wholesalers
423450 Laboratory equipment, dental and medical, merchant wholesalers
238390 Laboratory furniture and equipment installation
327215 Laboratory glassware (e.g., beakers, test tubes, vials) made from purchased glass
327212 Laboratory glassware (e.g., beakers, test tubes, vials) made in glass making plants
811219 Laboratory instrument repair and maintenance services
512199 Laboratory services, motion picture
334515 Laboratory standards testing instruments (e.g., capacitance, electrical resistance, inductance) manufacturing
541380 Laboratory testing (except medical, veterinary) services
621511 Laboratory testing services, medical (except radiological, X-ray)
621512 Laboratory testing services, medical radiological or X-ray
541940 Laboratory testing services, veterinary
339111 Laboratory-type centrifuges manufacturing
339111 Laboratory-type distilling apparatus manufacturing
339111 Laboratory-type equipment (e.g., balances, centrifuges, furnaces) manufacturing
339111 Laboratory-type evaporation apparatus manufacturing
339111 Laboratory-type freezers manufacturing
339111 Laboratory-type furniture (e.g., benches, cabinets, stools, tables) (except dental) manufacturing
339111 Laboratory-type sample preparation apparatus manufacturing
333292 Lace and net making machinery manufacturing
316110 Lace leather manufacturing
313249 Lace manufacturing
313249 Lace products (except apparel) made in lace mills
314999 Lace, burnt-out, manufacturing
313221 Laces (e.g., shoe), textile, manufacturing
316999 Laces (e.g., shoe), leather, manufacturing
332812 Lacquering metals and metal products for the trade
333994 Lacquering ovens manufacturing
325510 Lacquers manufacturing
424950 Lacquers merchant wholesalers
325199 Lactic acid manufacturing
311514 Lactose manufacturing
332999 Ladder jacks, metal, manufacturing
321999 Ladder jacks, wood, manufacturing
321912 Ladder rounds or rungs, hardwood, manufacturing
423830 Ladders merchant wholesalers
321999 Ladders, extension, wood, manufacturing
326199 Ladders, fiberglass, manufacturing
332323 Ladders, metal chain, manufacturing
332323 Ladders, permanently installed, metal, manufacturing

332999 Ladders, portable metal, manufacturing
332313 Ladle bails, fabricated metal plate work, manufacturing
332313 Ladles, fabricated metal plate work, manufacturing
312120 Lager brewing
237110 Lagoon, sewage treatment construction
483211 Lake freight transportation (except on Great Lakes system)
483113 Lake freight transportation, Great Lakes (including St. Lawrence Seaway)
483212 Lake passenger transportation (except on Great Lakes system)
483114 Lake passenger transportation, Great Lakes (including St. Lawrence Seaway)
325132 Lakes (i.e., organic pigments) manufacturing
311611 Lamb carcasses, half carcasses, primal and sub-primal cuts, produced in slaughtering plants
112410 Lamb feedlots (except stockyards for transportation)
311612 Lamb, primal and sub-primal cuts, made from purchased carcasses
327215 Laminated glass made from purchased glass
327211 Laminated glass made in glass making plants
326130 Laminated plastics plate, rod, and sheet, manufacturing
321213 Laminated structural wood members (except trusses) manufacturing
321213 Laminated veneer lumber (LVL) manufacturing
322225 Laminating foil for flexible packaging applications
332813 Laminating metals and metal formed products without fabricating
322222 Laminating purchased foil sheets for nonpackaging applications
322226 Laminating purchased paperboard
322222 Laminating purchased papers for nonpackaging applications
322221 Laminating purchased papers for packaging applications
313320 Laminating purchased textiles
335311 Lamp ballasts manufacturing
327112 Lamp bases, pottery, manufacturing
325182 Lamp black manufacturing
335110 Lamp bulb parts (except glass blanks), electric, manufacturing
335110 Lamp bulbs and tubes, electric (i.e., fluorescent, incandescent filament, vapor), manufacturing
335110 Lamp bulbs and tubes, health, infrared and ultraviolet radiation, manufacturing
332618 Lamp frames, wire, made from purchased wire
335931 Lamp holders manufacturing
332999 Lamp shade frames, metal, manufacturing
335121 Lamp shades (except glass, plastics), residential, manufacturing
327215 Lamp shades made from purchased glass
327212 Lamp shades made in glass making plants
326199 Lamp shades, plastics, manufacturing
442299 Lamp shops, electric
335931 Lamp sockets and receptacles (i.e., electric wiring devices) manufacturing
423220 Lamps (i.e., lighting fixtures) merchant wholesalers
335122 Lamps (i.e., lighting fixtures), commercial, industrial, and institutional, manufacturing
335121 Lamps (i.e., lighting fixtures), residential, electric, manufacturing

335129 Lamps, insect, electric fixture, manufacturing
334517 Lamps, X-ray, manufacturing
237210 Land (except cemeteries) subdividers
237210 Land acquisition, assembling and subdividing
238910 Land clearing
237990 Land drainage contractors
238910 Land leveling contractors
924120 Land management program administration
423820 Land preparation machinery, agricultural, merchant wholesalers
333120 Land preparation machinery, construction, manufacturing
423810 Land preparation machinery, construction, merchant wholesalers
925120 Land redevelopment agencies, government
531190 Land rental or leasing
237210 Land subdividing and utility installation (e.g., electric, sewer and water)
541370 Land surveying services
335312 Land transportation motors and generators manufacturing
541320 Land use design services
541320 Land use planning services
562212 Landfills
332312 Landing mats, aircraft, metal, manufacturing
541320 Landscape architects' offices
541320 Landscape architects' private practices
541320 Landscape architectural services
561730 Landscape care and maintenance services
541320 Landscape consulting services
561730 Landscape contractors (except construction)
541320 Landscape design services
561730 Landscape installation services
541320 Landscape planning services
561730 Landscaping services (except planning)
541930 Language interpretation services
541720 Language research and development services
611630 Language schools
541930 Language services (e.g., interpretation, sign, translation)
541930 Language translation services
335129 Lanterns (e.g., carbide, electric, gas, gasoline, kerosene) manufacturing
339913 Lapidary work manufacturing
334111 Laptop computers manufacturing
311613 Lard made from purchased fat
424470 Lard merchant wholesalers
311611 Lard produced in slaughtering plants
333512 Laser boring, drilling, and cutting machines, metalworking, manufacturing
334413 Laser diodes manufacturing
532230 Laser disc, video, rental
334612 Laser disks, prerecorded video, mass reproducing
334510 Laser equipment, electromedical, manufacturing
621493 Laser surgery centers, freestanding
334510 Laser systems and equipment, medical, manufacturing
333992 Laser welding equipment manufacturing
316999 Lashes (i.e., whips) manufacturing
321999 Last sole patterns, all materials, manufacturing
212325 Laterite mining and/or beneficiating
326299 Latex foam rubber manufacturing
325510 Latex paint (i.e., water based) manufacturing
325212 Latex rubber, synthetic, manufacturing
332323 Lath, expanded metal, manufacturing
321219 Lath, fiber, manufacturing
327420 Lath, gypsum, manufacturing
321912 Lath, wood, manufacturing

333512 Lathes, metalworking, manufacturing
333210 Lathes, woodworking-type, manufacturing
238310 Lathing contractors
321912 Lathmills, wood
316110 Latigo leather manufacturing
812332 Laundered mat and rug supply services
812332 Launderers, industrial
812310 Launderettes
812320 Laundries (except coin-operated, linen supply, uniform supply)
812310 Laundries, coin-operated or similar self-service
812331 Laundries, linen and uniform supply
812310 Laundromats
812320 Laundry and drycleaning agents
314911 Laundry bags made from purchased woven or knitted materials
812320 Laundry drop-off and pick-up sites
335224 Laundry equipment (e.g., dryers, washers), household-type, manufacturing
333312 Laundry extractors manufacturing
332439 Laundry hampers, light gauge metal, manufacturing
337125 Laundry hampers, rattan, reed, wicker or willow, manufacturing
812310 Laundry machine routes (i.e., concession operators), coin-operated or similar self-service
333312 Laundry machinery and equipment (except household-type) manufacturing
423620 Laundry machinery and equipment, household-type (e.g., dryers, washers), merchant wholesalers
423850 Laundry machinery, equipment, and supplies, commercial, merchant wholesalers
314999 Laundry nets made from purchased materials
333312 Laundry pressing machines (except household-type) manufacturing
812320 Laundry services (except coin-operated, linen supply, uniform supply)
812310 Laundry services, coin-operated or similar self-service
812332 Laundry services, industrial
812331 Laundry services, linen supply
325611 Laundry soap, chips, and powder manufacturing
424690 Laundry soap, chips, and powder, merchant wholesalers
332998 Laundry tubs, metal, manufacturing
326191 Laundry tubs, plastics, manufacturing
325199 Lauric acid esters and amines manufacturing
332998 Lavatories, metal, manufacturing
327111 Lavatories, vitreous china, manufacturing
922190 Law enforcement statistics centers, government
541110 Law firms
541110 Law offices
541110 Law practices
611310 Law schools
333112 Lawn and garden equipment manufacturing
811411 Lawn and garden equipment repair and maintenance services without retailing new lawn and garden equipment
713990 Lawn bowling clubs
561730 Lawn care services (e.g., fertilizing, mowing, seeding, spraying)
424910 Lawn care supplies (e.g., chemicals, fertilizers, pesticides) merchant wholesalers
332212 Lawn edgers, nonpowered, manufacturing
333112 Lawn edgers, powered, manufacturing
561730 Lawn fertilizing services

337125 Lawn furniture (except concrete, metal, stone, wood) manufacturing
337124 Lawn furniture, metal, manufacturing
337122 Lawn furniture, wood, manufacturing
332919 Lawn hose nozzles and lawn sprinklers manufacturing
423820 Lawn maintenance machinery and equipment merchant wholesalers
561730 Lawn maintenance services
811411 Lawn mower repair and maintenance shops without retailing new lawn mowers
423820 Lawn mowers merchant wholesalers
561730 Lawn mowing services
444210 Lawn power equipment stores
561730 Lawn seeding services
561730 Lawn spraying services
238220 Lawn sprinkler system installation
444220 Lawn supply stores
532490 Lawnmower rental or leasing
333112 Lawnmowers (except agricultural-type), powered, manufacturing
333111 Lawnmowers, agricultural-type, powered, manufacturing
332212 Lawnmowers, nonpowered, manufacturing
541110 Lawyers' offices
541110 Lawyers' private practices
325412 Laxative preparations manufacturing
112310 Layer-type chicken production
334419 LCD (liquid crystal display) unit screens manufacturing
212291 Leaching of uranium, radium, or vanadium ores
335911 Lead acid storage batteries manufacturing
331491 Lead and lead alloy bar, pipe, plate, rod, sheet, strip, and tubing made from purchased metals or scrap
325131 Lead based pigments manufacturing
331528 Lead castings (except die-castings), unfinished, manufacturing
331522 Lead die-castings, unfinished, manufacturing
332999 Lead foil not made in rolling mills
238390 Lead lining walls for x-ray room contractors
212231 Lead ore mine site development for own account
212231 Lead ore mining and/or beneficiating
325188 Lead oxides (except pigments) manufacturing
562910 Lead paint abatement services
562910 Lead paint removal contractors
325131 Lead pigments manufacturing
331492 Lead recovering from scrap and/or alloying purchased metals
331491 Lead rolling, drawing, or extruding purchased metals or scrap
325188 Lead silicate manufacturing
331419 Lead smelting and refining, primary
327992 Lead, black (i.e., natural graphite), ground, refined, or blended, manufacturing
335110 Lead-in wires, electric lamp, made from purchased wire
212231 Lead-zinc ore mining and/or beneficiating
333112 Leaf blowers manufacturing
332212 Leaf skimmers and rakes, nonpowered swimming pool, manufacturing
332611 Leaf springs, heavy gauge metal, manufacturing
424590 Leaf tobacco merchant wholesalers
332999 Leaf, metal, manufacturing
334519 Leak detectors, water, manufacturing
813920 Learned societies
611691 Learning centers offering remedial courses
541720 Learning disabilities research and development services

211111 Lease condensate production
213112 Lease tank cleaning and repairing on a contract basis
316999 Leashes, dog, manufacturing
****** Leasing—see type of property or article being leased
522220 Leasing in combination with sales financing
315292 Leather apparel (e.g., capes, coats, hats, jackets) (except apparel contractors) manufacturing
315211 Leather apparel (e.g., capes, coats, hats, jackets), men's and boys', cut and sew apparel contractors
315212 Leather apparel (e.g., capes, coats, hats, jackets), women's, girls', and infants', cut and sew apparel contractors
316999 Leather belting manufacturing
315292 Leather clothing (except apparel contractors) manufacturing
315212 Leather clothing manufacturing, women's, girls', and infants', cut and sew apparel contractors
315211 Leather clothing, men's and boys', cut and sew apparel contractors
448190 Leather coat stores
316110 Leather coloring, cutting, embossing, and japanning
316110 Leather converters
424990 Leather cut stock (except boot, shoe) merchant wholesalers
316999 Leather cut stock for shoe and boot manufacturing
424340 Leather cut stock for shoe and boot merchant wholesalers
316219 Leather footwear (except house slippers, men's, women's) manufacturing
316213 Leather footwear, men's (except athletic, slippers), manufacturing
316212 Leather footwear, slippers, manufacturing
316214 Leather footwear, women's (except athletic, slippers), manufacturing
812320 Leather garment cleaning services
315211 Leather gloves or mittens (except athletic), men's and boys', cut and sew apparel contractors
315212 Leather gloves or mittens (except athletic), women's, girls', and infants', cut and sew apparel contractors
315992 Leather gloves or mittens (except athletic, cut and sewn apparel contractors) manufacturing
339920 Leather gloves, athletic, manufacturing
424990 Leather goods (except belting, footwear, handbags, gloves, luggage) merchant wholesalers
811430 Leather goods repair shops without retailing new leather goods
448320 Leather goods stores
316993 Leather goods, small personal (e.g., coin purses, eyeglass cases, key cases), manufacturing
316992 Leather handbags and purses manufacturing
316212 Leather house slippers manufacturing
316991 Leather luggage manufacturing
316110 Leather tanning, currying, and finishing
316219 Leather upper athletic footwear manufacturing
316999 Leather welting manufacturing
333298 Leather working machinery manufacturing
313320 Leather, artificial, made from purchased fabric
322226 Leatherboard (i.e., paperboard based) made from purchased paperboard
322130 Leatherboard (i.e., paperboard based) made in paperboard mills

311225 Lecithin made from purchased oils
311223 Lecithin, cottonseed, made in crushing mills
311222 Lecithin, soybean, made in crushing mills
334413 LED (light emitting diode) manufacturing
111219 Leek farming, field, bedding plant and seed production
541110 Legal aid services
922130 Legal counsel offices, government
315119 Leggings knitting or knitting and finishing
315291 Leggings, infants', cut and sewn from purchased fabric (except apparel contractors)
316999 Leggings, welder's, leather, manufacturing
315212 Leggings, women's, girls', and infants', cut and sew apparel contractors
315239 Leggings, women's, misses' and girls', cut and sewn from purchased fabric (except apparel contractors)
315239 Leggings, women's, misses', and girls', cut and sewn from purchased fabric (except apparel contractors)
921140 Legislative and executive office combinations
921120 Legislative assemblies
921120 Legislative bodies (e.g., federal, local, and state)
921120 Legislative commissions
111320 Lemon groves
325998 Lemon oil manufacturing
519120 Lending libraries
423460 Lens blanks, ophthalmic, merchant wholesalers
327215 Lens blanks, optical and ophthalmic, made from purchased glass
327212 Lens blanks, optical and ophthalmic, made in glass making plants
326199 Lens blanks, plastics ophthalmic or optical, manufacturing
333314 Lens coating (except ophthalmic)
339115 Lens coating, ophthalmic
333314 Lens grinding (except ophthalmic)
339115 Lens grinding, ophthalmic (except in retail stores)
446130 Lens grinding, ophthalmic, in retail stores
333315 Lens hoods, camera, manufacturing
333314 Lens mounting (except ophthalmic)
339115 Lens mounts, ophthalmic, manufacturing
333314 Lens polishing (except ophthalmic)
339115 Lens polishing, ophthalmic
333314 Lenses (except ophthalmic) manufacturing
339115 Lenses, ophthalmic, manufacturing
111130 Lentil farming, dry, field and seed production
315191 Leotards made in apparel knitting mills
315212 Leotards, women's, girls', and infants', cut and sew apparel contractors
315239 Leotards, women's, misses', and girls', cut and sewn from purchased fabric (except apparel contractors)
212393 Lepidolite mining and/or beneficiating
622310 Leprosy hospitals
****** Lessors—see specific type of asset or property being rented or leased
531130 Lessors of miniwarehouses
531120 Lessors of nonresidential buildings (except miniwarehouses)
531110 Lessors of residential buildings and dwellings
531130 Lessors of self storage units
333313 Letter folding, stuffing, and sealing machinery manufacturing

333515 Letter pins (e.g., gauging, measuring) manufacturing
561410 Letter writing services
325910 Letterpress inks manufacturing
323122 Letterpress plate preparation services
333293 Letterpress printing presses manufacturing
339950 Letters for signs manufacturing
322231 Letters, die-cut, made from purchased cardboard
111219 Lettuce farming, field, bedding plant and seed production
237990 Levee construction
334513 Level and bulk measuring instruments, industrial process-type, manufacturing
334519 Level gauges, radiation-type, manufacturing
334519 Levels and tapes, surveying, manufacturing
332212 Levels, carpenter's, manufacturing
524126 Liability insurance carriers, direct
519120 Libraries (except motion picture stock footage, motion picture commercial distribution)
512199 Libraries, motion picture stock footage film
512199 Libraries, videotape, stock footage
236220 Library construction
561990 License issuing services (except government), motor vehicle
621399 Licensed practical nurses' (LPNs) offices (e.g., centers, clinics)
926130 Licensing and inspecting of utilities
926150 Licensing and permit issuance for business operations, government
926150 Licensing and permit issuance for professional occupations, government
926120 Licensing of transportation equipment, facilities, and services
311340 Licorice candy manufacturing
332431 Lids and ends, can, light gauge metal, manufacturing
332115 Lids, jar, metal, stamping
561611 Lie detection services
334519 Lie detectors manufacturing
611699 Life guard training
524210 Life insurance agencies
524113 Life insurance carriers, direct
339113 Life preservers manufacturing
326199 Life rafts, inflatable plastics, manufacturing
326299 Life rafts, inflatable rubberized fabric, manufacturing
524130 Life reinsurance carriers
541710 Life sciences research and development laboratories or services
423830 Lift trucks, industrial, merchant wholesalers
316999 Lifts, heel, leather, manufacturing
333298 Light bulb and tube (i.e., electric lamp) machinery manufacturing
335110 Light bulbs manufacturing
423610 Light bulbs merchant wholesalers
335110 Light bulbs, sealed beam automotive, manufacturing
334413 Light emitting diodes (LED) manufacturing
333315 Light meters, photographic, manufacturing
336510 Light rail cars and equipment manufacturing
237990 Light rail system construction
485119 Light rail systems (except mixed mode), commuter
334511 Light reconnaissance and surveillance systems and equipment manufacturing
334512 Light responsive appliance controls manufacturing
441110 Light utility truck dealers, new only or new and used
441120 Light utility truck dealers, used only
336112 Light utility trucks assembling on chassis of own manufacture

325998 Lighter fluids (e.g., charcoal, cigarette) manufacturing
483211 Lighterage (i.e., freight transportation except vessel supply services)
339999 Lighters, cigar and cigarette (except motor vehicle, precious metal), manufacturing
339911 Lighters, cigar and cigarette, clad with precious metal, manufacturing
424990 Lighters, cigar and cigarette, merchant wholesalers
488310 Lighthouse operation
335991 Lighting carbons manufacturing
423990 Lighting equipment, gas, merchant wholesalers
444190 Lighting fixture stores
335129 Lighting fixtures, airport (e.g., approach, ramp, runway, taxi), manufacturing
335122 Lighting fixtures, commercial electric, manufacturing
423610 Lighting fixtures, electric, merchant wholesalers
335122 Lighting fixtures, industrial electric, manufacturing
335122 Lighting fixtures, institutional electric, manufacturing
335129 Lighting fixtures, nonelectric (e.g., propane, kerosene, carbide), manufacturing
335121 Lighting fixtures, residential electric, manufacturing
561790 Lighting maintenance services (e.g., bulb and fuse replacement and cleaning)
238210 Lighting system installation
711510 Lighting technicians, theatrical, independent
335311 Lighting transformers manufacturing
335311 Lighting transformers, street and airport, manufacturing
335931 Lightning arrestors and coils manufacturing
238290 Lightning protection equipment (e.g., lightning rod) installation
335931 Lightning protection equipment manufacturing
238290 Lightning rod and conductor installation
325211 Lignin plastics manufacturing
213113 Lignite mining services (except site preparation and related construction contractor activities) on a contract basis
212111 Lignite surface mining and/or beneficiating
111130 Lima bean farming, dry, field and seed production
339113 Limbs, artificial, manufacturing
423320 Lime (except agricultural) merchant wholesalers
111320 Lime groves
325998 Lime oil manufacturing
327410 Lime production
212312 Lime rock, ground, mining and/or beneficiating
424910 Lime, agricultural, merchant wholesalers
212312 Limestone (except bituminous) crushed and broken stone mining and/or beneficiating
212312 Limestone beneficiating plants (e.g., grinding or pulverizing)
212311 Limestone mining or quarrying
212319 Limestone, bituminous, mining and/or beneficiating
325320 Lime-sulfur fungicides manufacturing
334512 Limit controls (e.g., air-conditioning, appliance, heating) manufacturing
511199 Limited editions art print publishers (except exclusive Internet publishing)
452990 Limited price variety stores
212210 Limonite mining and/or beneficiating
532111 Limousine rental without driver
485320 Limousine services (except shuttle services)
485320 Limousines for hire with driver (except taxis)
325320 Lindane pesticides manufacturing

334512 Line or limit control for electric heat manufacturing
561730 Line slash (i.e., rights of way) maintenance services
238910 Line slashing or cutting (except maintenance)
335311 Line voltage regulators (i.e., electric transformers) manufacturing
335999 Linear accelerators manufacturing
332991 Linear ball bearings manufacturing
334514 Linear counters manufacturing
325222 Linear esters fibers and filaments manufacturing
332991 Linear roller bearings manufacturing
442299 Linen stores
812331 Linen supply services
423220 Linens (e.g., bath, bed, table) merchant wholesalers
314129 Linens made from purchased materials
327123 Liner brick and plates, vitrified clay, manufacturing
332313 Liners, industrial, fabricated metal plate work, manufacturing
114111 Lingcod fishing
424330 Lingerie merchant wholesalers
448190 Lingerie stores
315212 Lingerie, women's, cut and sew apparel contractors
315231 Lingerie, women's, misses', and girls', cut and sewn from purchased fabric (except apparel contractors)
316110 Lining leather manufacturing
316999 Linings, boot and shoe, leather, manufacturing
314999 Linings, casket, manufacturing
315211 Linings, hat, men's, cut and sew apparel contractors
315999 Linings, hat, men's, cut and sewn from purchased fabric (except apparel contractors)
314999 Linings, luggage, manufacturing
332999 Linings, metal safe and vault, manufacturing
332994 Links, ammunition (i.e., 30 mm. or less, 1.18 inch or less), manufacturing
332995 Links, ammunition (i.e., more than 30 mm., more than 1.18 inch), manufacturing
325199 Linoleic acid esters and amines manufacturing
326192 Linoleum floor coverings manufacturing
238330 Linoleum, installation only
333293 Linotype machines manufacturing
311225 Linseed oil made from purchased oils
311223 Linseed oil, cake and meal, made in crushing mills
327390 Lintels, concrete, manufacturing
325412 Lip balms manufacturing
325620 Lipsticks manufacturing
424690 Liquefied gases (except LP) merchant wholesalers
424710 Liquefied petroleum gas (LPG) bulk stations and terminals
332420 Liquefied petroleum gas (LPG) cylinders manufacturing
454312 Liquefied petroleum gas (LPG) dealers, direct selling
221210 Liquefied petroleum gas (LPG) distribution through mains
324110 Liquefied petroleum gas (LPG) made in refineries
424720 Liquefied petroleum gas (LPG) merchant wholesalers (except bulk stations, terminals)
211112 Liquefied petroleum gases (LPG), natural
325120 Liquid air manufacturing
334513 Liquid analysis instruments, industrial process-type, manufacturing
311313 Liquid beet syrup manufacturing
334516 Liquid chromatographic instruments, laboratory-type, manufacturing
334513 Liquid concentration instruments, industrial process-type, manufacturing

334514 Liquid flow meters manufacturing
211112 Liquid hydrocarbons recovered from oil and gas field gases
334512 Liquid level controls, residential and commercial heating-type, manufacturing
334513 Liquid level instruments, industrial process-type, manufacturing
332420 Liquid oxygen tanks manufacturing
311313 Liquid sugar made from beet sugar
311312 Liquid sugar made from purchased raw cane sugar
311311 Liquid sugar made in sugarcane mill
211112 Liquids, natural gas (e.g., ethane, isobutane, natural gasoline, propane) recovered from oil and gas field gases
445310 Liquor stores, package
311320 Liquor, chocolate, made from cacao beans
311330 Liquor, chocolate, made from purchased chocolate
424820 Liquors merchant wholesalers
312130 Liquors, brandy, distilling and blending
424820 Liquors, distilled, merchant wholesalers
312140 Liquors, distilling and blending (except brandy)
339942 List finders and roledex address files manufacturing
531390 Listing services, real estate
711410 Literary agents
325131 Litharge manufacturing
335912 Lithium batteries, primary, manufacturing
325188 Lithium compounds, not specified elsewhere by process, manufacturing
212393 Lithium mineral mining and/or beneficiating
325910 Lithographic inks manufacturing
323122 Lithographic plate preparation services
323110 Lithographic printing (except books, manifold business forms, printing grey goods, quick printing)
333293 Lithographic printing presses manufacturing
325131 Lithopone manufacturing
334510 Lithotripters manufacturing
711310 Live arts center operators
424990 Live bait merchant wholesalers
711310 Live theater operators
332995 Livens projectors (i.e., ordnance) manufacturing
541690 Livestock breeding consulting services
115210 Livestock breeding services (except consulting)
424910 Livestock feeds merchant wholesalers
311119 Livestock feeds, supplements, concentrates and premixes, manufacturing
541940 Livestock inspecting and testing services, veterinary
115210 Livestock spraying
484220 Livestock trucking, local
484230 Livestock trucking, long-distance
541940 Livestock veterinary services
337124 Living room furniture (except upholstered), metal, manufacturing
337122 Living room furniture (except upholstered), wood, manufacturing
337121 Living room furniture, upholstered, manufacturing
112990 Llama production
334418 Loaded computer boards manufacturing
423430 Loaded computer boards merchant wholesalers
333120 Loaders, shovel, manufacturing
332993 Loading and assembling bombs
488490 Loading and unloading at truck terminals
488320 Loading and unloading services at ports and harbors

488210 Loading and unloading services at rail terminals
333131 Loading machines, underground mining, manufacturing
334418 Loading printed circuit boards
522310 Loan brokerages
522310 Loan brokers' or agents' offices (i.e., independent)
522291 Loan companies (i.e., consumer, personal, small, student)
522292 Loan correspondents (i.e., lending funds with real estate as collateral)
522390 Loan servicing
541820 Lobbying services
541820 Lobbyists' offices
114112 Lobster fishing
334210 Local area network (LAN) communications equipment (e.g., bridges, gateways, routers) manufacturing
541512 Local area network (LAN) computer systems integration design services
611420 Local area network (LAN) management training
485113 Local bus services (except mixed mode)
492210 Local letter and parcel delivery services (except as part of intercity carrier network, U.S. Postal Service)
492110 Local letter and parcel delivery services as part of intercity courier network
485112 Local passenger rail systems (except mixed mode)
813940 Local political organizations
517110 Local telephone carriers (except wireless)
485111 Local transit systems, mixed mode (e.g., bus, commuter rail, subway combinations)
561990 Locating underground utility lines prior to digging
237990 Lock and waterway construction
332722 Lock washers, metal, manufacturing
454390 Locker meat provisioners, direct selling
337215 Lockers (except refrigerated) manufacturing
423440 Lockers (except refrigerated) merchant wholesalers
812990 Lockers, coin-operated, rental
333415 Lockers, refrigerated, manufacturing
423740 Lockers, refrigerated, merchant wholesalers
332510 Locks (except coin-operated, time locks), metal, manufacturing
333311 Locks, coin-operated, manufacturing
423710 Locks, security, merchant wholesalers
423850 Locksmith equipment and supplies merchant wholesalers
561622 Locksmith services
561622 Locksmith services with or without sales of locking devices, safes, and security vaults
561622 Locksmith shops
488210 Locomotive and rail car repair (except factory conversion, factory overhaul, factory rebuilding)
336321 Locomotive and railroad car light fixtures manufacturing
333923 Locomotive cranes manufacturing
333618 Locomotive diesel engines manufacturing
336510 Locomotives manufacturing
423860 Locomotives merchant wholesalers
336510 Locomotives rebuilding
212221 Lode gold mining and/or beneficiating
321992 Log cabins, prefabricated wood, manufacturing
333120 Log debarking machinery, portable, manufacturing
333291 Log debarking machinery, stationary, manufacturing
113310 Log harvesting
484220 Log hauling, local
484230 Log hauling, long-distance

236115 Log home construction general contractors
236117 Log home operative builders
333120 Log splitters, portable, manufacturing
333291 Log splitters, stationary, manufacturing
111334 Loganberry farming
113310 Logging
236220 Logging camp construction
541330 Logging engineering services
423810 Logging equipment merchant wholesalers
532412 Logging equipment rental or leasing without operator
482112 Logging railroads
237310 Logging road construction
336212 Logging trailers manufacturing
213112 Logging wells on a contract basis
334515 Logic circuit testers manufacturing
541614 Logistics management consulting services
333414 Logs, gas fireplace, manufacturing
325191 Logwood extract manufacturing
517310 Long-distance telecommunication resellers (except satellite)
517110 Long-distance telephone carriers (except wireless)
517410 Long-distance telephone satellite communication carriers
488320 Longshoremen services
333292 Loom bobbins manufacturing
333292 Loom reeds manufacturing
333292 Looms for textiles manufacturing
333292 Loopers for textiles manufacturing
323118 Looseleaf binders and devices manufacturing
424120 Looseleaf binders merchant wholesalers
322233 Looseleaf fillers and paper made from purchased paper
322121 Looseleaf fillers and paper made in paper mills
524291 Loss control consultants
325620 Lotions (e.g., body, face, hand) manufacturing
713290 Lottery control boards (i.e., operating lotteries)
921130 Lottery control boards, nonoperating
713290 Lottery corporations
713290 Lottery ticket sales agents (except retail stores)
334119 Lottery ticket sales terminal manufacturing
713290 Lottery ticket vendors (except retail stores)
334310 Loudspeakers manufacturing
722410 Lounges, cocktail
315192 Lounging robes and dressing gowns made in apparel knitting mills
315291 Lounging robes and dressing gowns, infants', cut and sewn from purchased fabric (except apparel contractors)
315211 Lounging robes and dressing gowns, men's and boys', cut and sew apparel contractors
315221 Lounging robes and dressing gowns, men's and boys', cut and sewn from purchased fabric (except apparel contractors)
315212 Lounging robes and dressing gowns, women's, girls', and infants', cut and sew apparel contractors
315231 Lounging robes and dressing gowns, women's, misses', and girls', cut and sewn from purchased fabric (except apparel contractors)
333314 Loupes (e.g., jewelers) manufacturing
321911 Louver windows and doors, made from purchased glass with wood frame
332321 Louver windows, metal, manufacturing
332322 Louvers, sheet metal (except stampings), manufacturing

236117 Low income housing construction operative builders
236116 Low income housing, multifamily, construction general contractors
236115 Low income housing, single-family, construction general contractors
238160 Low slope roofing installation
238210 Low voltage electrical work
335121 Low voltage lighting equipment, residential, electric, manufacturing
236116 Low-rise apartment construction general contractors
236117 Low-rise apartment operative builders
311340 Lozenges, nonmedicated, candy, manufacturing
621399 LPNs' (licensed practical nurses) offices (e.g., centers, clinics)
484122 LTL (less-than-truckload) long-distance freight trucking
424710 Lubricating oils and greases bulk stations and terminals
324110 Lubricating oils and greases made in petroleum refineries
424720 Lubricating oils and greases merchant wholesalers (except bulk stations, terminals)
324191 Lubricating oils and greases, petroleum, made from refined petroleum
325998 Lubricating oils and greases, synthetic, manufacturing
811191 Lubrication shops, automotive
336510 Lubrication systems, locomotive (except pumps), manufacturing
332510 Luggage hardware, metal, manufacturing
314999 Luggage linings manufacturing
423990 Luggage merchant wholesalers
336399 Luggage racks, car top, automotive, truck, and bus, manufacturing
811430 Luggage repair shops without retailing new luggage
448320 Luggage stores
316991 Luggage, all materials, manufacturing
335931 Lugs and connectors, electrical, manufacturing
423610 Lugs and connectors, electrical, merchant wholesalers
423310 Lumber (e.g., dressed, finished, rough) merchant wholesalers
321113 Lumber (i.e., rough, dressed) made from logs or bolts
561990 Lumber grading services
444190 Lumber retailing yards
493190 Lumber storage terminals
321113 Lumber, hardwood dimension, made from logs or bolts
321912 Lumber, hardwood dimension, resawing purchased lumber
321999 Lumber, kiln drying
321213 Lumber, parallel strand, manufacturing
321113 Lumber, softwood dimension, made from logs or bolts
321912 Lumber, softwood dimension, resawing purchased lumber
335122 Luminous panel ceilings, electric, manufacturing
335311 Luminous tube transformers manufacturing
332439 Lunch boxes, light gauge metal, manufacturing
722330 Lunch wagons
311612 Luncheon meat (except poultry) made from purchased carcasses
311611 Luncheon meat (except poultry) produced in slaughtering plants
311615 Luncheon meat, poultry, manufacturing
532111 Luxury automobile rental
485320 Luxury automobiles for hire with driver (except taxis)
321213 LVL (laminated veneer lumber) manufacturing
325612 Lye, household-type, manufacturing
111335 Macadamia farming
424490 Macaroni merchant wholesalers
311823 Macaroni, dry, manufacturing
311991 Macaroni, fresh, manufacturing

311412 Macaroni, frozen, manufacturing
332212 Machetes manufacturing
332999 Machine bases, metal, manufacturing
332322 Machine guards, sheet metal (except stampings), manufacturing
332994 Machine gun belts (i.e., 30 mm. or less, 1.18 inch or less) manufacturing
332995 Machine gun belts (i.e., more than 30 mm., more than 1.18 inch) manufacturing
332994 Machine guns (i.e., 30 mm. or less, 1.18 inch or less) manufacturing
332995 Machine guns (i.e., more than 30 mm., more than 1.18 inch) manufacturing
332722 Machine keys, metal, manufacturing
332212 Machine knives (except metal cutting) manufacturing
333515 Machine knives, metal cutting, manufacturing
238290 Machine rigging
332710 Machine shops
333515 Machine tool attachments and accessories manufacturing
335311 Machine tool transformers manufacturing
423830 Machine tools and accessories merchant wholesalers
811310 Machine tools repair and maintenance services
333512 Machine tools, metal cutting, manufacturing
333513 Machine tools, metal forming, manufacturing
238290 Machinery and equipment, large-scale, installation
522220 Machinery finance leasing
238910 Machinery, construction (except cranes), rental with operator
423420 Machines, office, merchant wholesalers
332212 Machinists' precision measuring tools (except optical) manufacturing
423830 Machinists' precision measuring tools merchant wholesalers
334511 Machmeters manufacturing
114111 Mackerel fishing
315291 Mackinaws, infants', cut and sewn from purchased fabric (except apparel contractors)
315211 Mackinaws, men's and boys', cut and sew apparel contractors
315228 Mackinaws, men's and boys', cut and sewn from purchased fabric (except apparel contractors)
315212 Mackinaws, women's, girls', and infants', cut and sew apparel contractors
315239 Mackinaws, women's, misses', and girls', cut and sewn from purchased fabric (except apparel contractors)
541840 Magazine advertising representatives (i.e., independent of media owners)
511120 Magazine publishers (except exclusive Internet publishing)
511120 Magazine publishers and printing combined
516110 Magazine publishers, exclusively on Internet
337122 Magazine racks, wood, manufacturing
451212 Magazine stands (i.e., permanent)
323112 Magazines and periodicals flexographic printing without publishing
323111 Magazines and periodicals gravure printing without publishing
323110 Magazines and periodicals lithographic (offset) printing without publishing
323119 Magazines and periodicals printing (except flexographic, gravure, lithographic, quick, screen) without publishing
323113 Magazines and periodicals screen printing without publishing

424920 Magazines merchant wholesalers
711190 Magic shows
451120 Magic supply stores
711510 Magicians, independent
327125 Magnesia refractory cement manufacturing
325411 Magnesia, medicinal, uncompounded, manufacturing
212325 Magnesite mining and/or beneficiating
327992 Magnesite, crude (e.g., calcined, dead-burned, ground), manufacturing
331491 Magnesium and magnesium alloy bar, rod, shape, sheet, strip, and tubing made from purchased metals or scrap
325188 Magnesium carbonate manufacturing
331528 Magnesium castings (except die-castings), unfinished, manufacturing
325188 Magnesium chloride manufacturing
325188 Magnesium compounds, not specified elsewhere by process, manufacturing
331522 Magnesium die-castings, unfinished, manufacturing
331491 Magnesium foil made by rolling purchased metals or scrap
332999 Magnesium foil not made in rolling mills
331492 Magnesium recovering from scrap and/or alloying purchased metals
331419 Magnesium refining, primary
331491 Magnesium rolling, drawing, or extruding purchased metals or scrap
331422 Magnet wire, insulated, made from purchased copper in wire drawing plants
331319 Magnet wire, insulated, made in aluminum wire drawing plants
331491 Magnet wire, nonferrous metals (except aluminum, copper), made from purchased nonferrous metals (except aluminum, copper) in wire drawing plants
334613 Magnetic and optical media, blank, manufacturing
334514 Magnetic counters manufacturing
334513 Magnetic flow meters, industrial process-type, manufacturing
333513 Magnetic forming machines, metalworking, manufacturing
541360 Magnetic geophysical surveying services
334119 Magnetic ink recognition devices, computer peripheral equipment, manufacturing
334613 Magnetic recording media for tapes, cassettes, and disks, manufacturing
621512 Magnetic resonance imaging (MRI) centers
334510 Magnetic resonance imaging (MRI) medical diagnostic equipment manufacturing
334516 Magnetic resonance imaging (MRI) type apparatus (except medical diagnostic) manufacturing
334613 Magnetic tapes, cassettes and disks, blank, manufacturing
423690 Magnetic tapes, cassettes, and disks, blank, merchant wholesalers
334112 Magnetic/optical combination storage units for computers manufacturing
334519 Magnetometers manufacturing
334411 Magnetron tubes manufacturing
327113 Magnets, permanent, ceramic or ferrite, manufacturing
332999 Magnets, permanent, metallic, manufacturing
339115 Magnifiers, corrective vision-type, manufacturing
333314 Magnifying glasses (except corrective vision-type) manufacturing

333314 Magnifying instruments, optical, manufacturing
114111 Mahimahi fishing
561310 Maid registries
561720 Maid services (i.e., cleaning services)
238990 Mail box units, outdoor, multiple box-type, erection
337215 Mail carrier cases and tables, wood, manufacturing
332322 Mail chutes, sheet metal (except stampings), manufacturing
333313 Mail handling machinery, post office-type, manufacturing
561499 Mail presorting services
561431 Mailbox rental centers, private
561431 Mailbox rental services combined with one or more other office support services, private
332439 Mailboxes, light gauge metal, manufacturing
322214 Mailing cases and tubes, paper fiber (i.e., all-fiber, nonfiber ends of any material), made from purchased paperboard
532420 Mailing equipment rental or leasing
511140 Mailing list publishers (except exclusive Internet publishing)
423420 Mailing machines merchant wholesalers
454113 Mail-order houses
334111 Mainframe computers manufacturing
488190 Maintenance and repair services, aircraft (except factory conversion, factory overhaul, factory rebuilding)
561730 Maintenance of plants and shrubs in buildings
488210 Maintenance of rights-of-way and structures, railway
488119 Maintenance services, runway
488310 Maintenance services, waterfront terminal (except dredging)
711211 Major league baseball clubs
812112 Make-up (except permanent) salons
325620 Make-up (i.e., cosmetics) manufacturing
812199 Make-up salons, permanent
523110 Making markets for securities
337125 Malacca furniture (except upholstered), household-type, manufacturing
325320 Malathion insecticides manufacturing
325192 Maleic anhydride manufacturing
531120 Mall property operation (i.e., not operating contained businesses) rental or leasing
331511 Malleable iron foundries
332212 Mallets (e.g., rubber, wood) manufacturing
321999 Mallets, wood, manufacturing
325199 Malonic dinitrile manufacturing
524126 Malpractice insurance carriers, direct
311942 Malt extract and syrups manufacturing
424490 Malt extract merchant wholesalers
311213 Malt flour manufacturing
312120 Malt liquor brewing
311213 Malt manufacturing
424490 Malt merchant wholesalers
333294 Malt milling machinery manufacturing
311213 Malt sprouts manufacturing
311514 Malted milk manufacturing
311213 Malting (germinating and drying grains)
311221 Maltodextrins manufacturing
621512 Mammogram (i.e., breast imaging) centers
711410 Management agencies for artists, entertainers, and other public figures
611430 Management development training
561110 Management services (except complete operation of client's business)
115116 Management services, farm
711310 Managers of agricultural fairs with facilities
711320 Managers of agricultural fairs without facilities

711310 Managers of arts events with facilities
711320 Managers of arts events without facilities
711310 Managers of festivals with facilities
711320 Managers of festivals without facilities
711310 Managers of live performing arts productions (e.g., concerts) with facilities
711320 Managers of live performing arts productions (e.g., concerts) without facilities
711310 Managers of sports events with facilities
711320 Managers of sports events without facilities
531312 Managers' offices, commercial condominium
531312 Managers' offices, commercial real estate
531312 Managers' offices, nonresidential real estate
531311 Managers' offices, residential condominium
531311 Managers' offices, residential real estate
711410 Managers, authors'
711410 Managers, celebrities'
561920 Managers, convention
711410 Managers, entertainers'
711410 Managers, pubic figures'
711410 Managers, sports figures'
561920 Managers, trade fair or show
531312 Managing commercial condominiums
531312 Managing commercial real estate
531311 Managing cooperative apartments
523920 Managing investment funds
523920 Managing mutual funds
561110 Managing offices of dentists
561110 Managing offices of physicians and surgeons
561110 Managing offices of professionals (e.g., dentists, physicians, surgeons)
523920 Managing personal investment trusts
531311 Managing residential condominiums
531311 Managing residential real estate
523920 Managing trusts
111320 Mandarin groves
339992 Mandolins manufacturing
333515 Mandrels (i.e., a machine tool accessory) manufacturing
212299 Manganese concentrates beneficiating
325188 Manganese dioxide manufacturing
331112 Manganese metal ferroalloys manufacturing
212299 Manganese ores mining and/or beneficiating
212210 Manganiferous ores valued for iron content, mining and/or beneficiating
212299 Manganiferousares ores (not valued for iron content) mining and/or beneficiating
212299 Manganite mining and/or beneficiating
111339 Mango farming
325191 Mangrove extract manufacturing
331511 Manhole covers, cast iron, manufacturing
812113 Manicure and pedicure salons
611511 Manicure and pedicure schools
325620 Manicure preparations manufacturing
812113 Manicurist services
323116 Manifold business forms printing
336312 Manifolds (i.e., intake and exhaust), automotive and truck gasoline engine, manufacturing
332996 Manifolds, pipe, made from purchased metal pipe
322231 Manila folders, die-cut, made from purchased paper or paperboard
325221 Manmade cellulosic fibers manufacturing
313221 Manmade fabric, narrow woven, weaving

313210 Manmade fabrics, broadwoven, weaving
313113 Manmade fiber thread manufacturing
325222 Manmade fibers and filaments (except cellulosic) manufacturing
424690 Man-made fibers merchant wholesalers
313111 Manmade staple spun yarns made from purchased fiber
541890 Mannequin decorating services
339999 Mannequins manufacturing
423440 Mannequins merchant wholesalers
325920 Mannitol hexanitrate explosive materials manufacturing
334513 Manometers, industrial process-type, manufacturing
561320 Manpower pools
238340 Mantel, marble or stone, installation
621399 Manual-arts therapists' offices (e.g., centers, clinics)
423390 Manufactured (i.e., mobile) homes merchant wholesalers
321991 Manufactured (mobile) buildings for commercial use (e.g., banks, offices) manufacturing
321991 Manufactured (mobile) classrooms manufacturing
453930 Manufactured (mobile) home dealers
531190 Manufactured (mobile) home parks
453930 Manufactured (mobile) home parts and accessory dealers
238990 Manufactured (mobile) home set up and tie down
531190 Manufactured (mobile) home sites rental or leasing
321991 Manufactured (mobile) homes manufacturing
221210 Manufactured gas production and distribution
813910 Manufacturers' associations
236210 Manufacturing building construction
531120 Manufacturing building rental or leasing
532490 Manufacturing machinery and equipment rental or leasing
541614 Manufacturing management consulting services
541614 Manufacturing operations improvement consulting services
511130 Map publishers (except exclusive Internet publishing)
511130 Map publishers and printing combined
516110 Map publishers, exclusively on Internet
111998 Maple sap concentrating (i.e., producing pure maple syrup in the field)
111998 Maple sap gathering
111998 Maple syrup (i.e., maple sap reducing)
311999 Maple syrup mixing into other products
541370 Mapping (except geophysical) services
541360 Mapping services, geophysical
424920 Maps (except globe, school, wall) merchant wholesalers
323112 Maps flexographic printing without publishing
323111 Maps gravure printing without publishing
323110 Maps lithographic (offset) printing without publishing
323119 Maps printing (except flexographic, digital, gravure, lithographic, quick, screen) without publishing
323113 Maps screen printing without publishing
212319 Marble crushed and broken stone mining and/or beneficiating
212311 Marble mining or quarrying
238140 Marble, granite and slate, exterior, contractors
238340 Marble, granite and slate, interior, contractors
339932 Marbles manufacturing

212393 Marcasite mining and/or beneficiating
325199 Margaric acid manufacturing
311221 Margarine and other corn oils made by wet milling corn
424490 Margarine merchant wholesalers
311225 Margarine-butter blend made from purchased fats and oils
311225 Margarines (including imitation) made from purchased fats and oils
713930 Marinas
335314 Marine and navy auxiliary controls, manufacturing
713930 Marine basins, operation of
488390 Marine cargo checkers and surveyors
488320 Marine cargo handling services
237990 Marine construction
928110 Marine Corps
541330 Marine engineering services
333618 Marine engines manufacturing
332510 Marine hardware, metal, manufacturing
332999 Marine horns, compressed air or steam, metal, manufacturing
524126 Marine insurance carriers, direct
712110 Marine museums
611519 Marine navigational schools
325510 Marine paints manufacturing
332410 Marine power boilers manufacturing
334220 Marine radio communications equipment manufacturing
524130 Marine reinsurance carriers
488330 Marine salvaging services
447190 Marine service stations
488510 Marine shipping agency
335911 Marine storage batteries manufacturing
423860 Marine supplies (except pleasure) merchant wholesalers
423910 Marine supplies, pleasure, merchant wholesalers
441222 Marine supply dealers
541990 Marine surveyor (i.e., ship appraiser) services
488330 Marine vessel traffic reporting services
339999 Marionettes (i.e., puppets) manufacturing
339942 Marker boards (i.e., whiteboards) manufacturing
523110 Market making for securities
541910 Marketing analysis services
541613 Marketing consulting services
541613 Marketing management consulting services
541910 Marketing research services
339943 Marking devices manufacturing
424120 Marking devices merchant wholesalers
333518 Marking machines, metal, manufacturing
212312 Marl crushed and broken stone mining and/or beneficiating
311421 Marmalade manufacturing
321999 Marquetry, wood, manufacturing
624190 Marriage counseling services (except by offices of mental health practitioners)
922120 Marshals' offices
311340 Marshmallow creme manufacturing
311340 Marshmallows manufacturing
611620 Martial arts instruction, camps, or schools
311340 Marzipan (i.e., candy) manufacturing
335999 Maser (i.e., microwave amplification by stimulated emission of radiation) amplifiers manufacturing
321999 Mashers, potato, wood, manufacturing
322222 Masking tape made from purchased paper
444190 Masonry (e.g., block, brick, stone) dealers
238140 Masonry contractors
238140 Masonry pointing, cleaning or caulking
332212 Mason's handtools manufacturing
423320 Mason's materials merchant wholesalers
334516 Mass spectrometers manufacturing

334516 Mass spectroscopy instrumentation manufacturing
335211 Massage machines, electric (except designed for beauty and barber shop use), manufacturing
812199 Massage parlors
611519 Massage therapist instruction
621399 Massage therapists' offices
512210 Master recording leasing and licensing
424690 Mastics (except construction) merchant wholesalers
321999 Masts, wood, manufacturing
812332 Mat and rug supply services
325998 Matches and match books manufacturing
424990 Matches and match books merchant wholesalers
238290 Materials handling equipment installation
811310 Materials handling equipment repair and maintenance services
423830 Materials handling machinery and equipment merchant wholesalers
532490 Materials handling machinery and equipment rental or leasing
541614 Materials management consulting services
562920 Materials recovery facilities (MRF)
236210 Materials recovery facility construction
923120 Maternity and child health program administration
315212 Maternity bras and corsets, women's, cut and sew apparel contractors
315231 Maternity bras and corsets, women's, misses', and girls', cut and sewn from purchased fabric (except apparel contractors)
622310 Maternity hospitals
448120 Maternity shops
541710 Mathematics research and development laboratories or services
332618 Mats and matting made from purchased wire
332212 Mattocks (i.e., handtools) manufacturing
326299 Mattress protectors, rubber, manufacturing
332612 Mattress springs and spring units, light gauge, made from purchased wire or strip
442110 Mattress stores (including waterbeds)
337910 Mattresses (i.e., box spring, innerspring, noninnerspring) manufacturing
337910 Mattresses made from felt, foam rubber, urethane and similar materials
423210 Mattresses merchant wholesalers
326199 Mattresses, air, plastics, manufacturing
326299 Mattresses, air, rubber, manufacturing
311812 Matzo baking made in commercial bakeries
332212 Mauls, metal, manufacturing
321999 Mauls, wood, manufacturing
236220 Mausoleum (i.e., building) construction
812220 Mausoleums
311941 Mayonnaise manufacturing
921110 Mayor's offices
321219 MDF (medium density fiberboard) manufacturing
621112 MDs' (medical doctors), mental health, offices (e.g., centers, clinics)
621111 MDs' (medical doctors, except mental health) offices (e.g., centers, clinics)
624210 Meal delivery programs
311119 Meal, alfalfa, manufacturing
311119 Meal, bone, prepared as feed for animals and fowls, manufacturing

311211 Meal, corn, for human consumption made in flour mills
423830 Measuring and testing equipment (except automotive) merchant wholesalers
333515 Measuring attachments (e.g., sine bars) for machine tool manufacturing
334515 Measuring equipment for electronic and electrical circuits and equipment manufacturing
811219 Measuring instrument repair and maintenance services
334515 Measuring instruments and meters, electric, manufacturing
334513 Measuring instruments, industrial process control-type, manufacturing
332212 Measuring tools, machinist's (except optical), manufacturing
334514 Measuring wheels manufacturing
311613 Meat and bone meal and tankage, produced in rendering plant
311612 Meat canning (except baby, pet food, poultry), made from purchased carcasses
311611 Meat canning (except poultry) produced in slaughtering plants
311422 Meat canning, baby food, manufacturing
311111 Meat canning, dog and cat, pet food, made from purchased carcasses
311615 Meat canning, poultry (except baby and pet food), manufacturing
311612 Meat extracts made from purchased carcasses
333294 Meat grinders, food-type, manufacturing
445210 Meat markets
311615 Meat products (e.g., hot dogs, luncheon meats, sausages) made from a combination of poultry and other meats
311612 Meat products canning (except baby, pet food, poultry) made from purchased carcasses
311111 Meat products, dog and cat, pet food, canning, made from purchased carcasses
311612 Meats (except poultry), cured or smoked, made from purchased carcasses
424470 Meats and meat products (except canned, packaged frozen) merchant wholesalers
311611 Meats fresh, chilled or frozen (except poultry and small game), produced in slaughtering plants
424490 Meats, canned, merchant wholesalers
424470 Meats, cured or smoked, merchant wholesalers
311611 Meats, cured or smoked, produced in slaughtering plants
311612 Meats, fresh or chilled (except poultry and small game), frozen, made from purchased carcasses
424470 Meats, fresh, merchant wholesalers
424470 Meats, frozen (except packaged), merchant wholesalers
424420 Meats, packaged frozen, merchant wholesalers
238220 Mechanical contractors
541330 Mechanical engineering services
238290 Mechanical equipment insulation
313311 Mechanical finishing of broadwoven fabrics
316110 Mechanical leather manufacturing
334513 Mechanical measuring instruments, industrial process-type, manufacturing
339942 Mechanical pencil refills manufacturing
339941 Mechanical pencils manufacturing

811310 Mechanical power transmission equipment repair and maintenance services
423840 Mechanical power transmission supplies (e.g., gears, pulleys, sprockets) merchant wholesalers
326291 Mechanical rubber goods (i.e., extruded, lathe-cut, molded) manufacturing
423840 Mechanical rubber goods merchant wholesalers
541380 Mechanical testing laboratories or services
611513 Mechanic's apprenticeship training
333924 Mechanic's creepers manufacturing
325611 Mechanic's hand soaps and pastes manufacturing
332212 Mechanic's handtools, nonpowered, manufacturing
611519 Mechanic's schools (except apprenticeship)
423120 Mechanic's tools merchant wholesalers
333311 Mechanisms for coin-operated machines manufacturing
334518 Mechanisms, clockwork operated device, manufacturing
541840 Media advertising representatives (i.e., independent of media owners)
541830 Media buying agencies
541830 Media buying services
541840 Media representatives (i.e., independent of media owners)
518210 Media streaming services
926150 Mediation and conciliation services, government
541990 Mediation product services (except by lawyer, attorney, paralegal offices, family and social services)
624190 Mediation, social service, family, agencies
811219 Medical and surgical equipment repair and maintenance services
541430 Medical art services
541430 Medical artists, independent
923130 Medical assistance programs administration, government
813920 Medical associations
531120 Medical building rental or leasing
334510 Medical cleaning equipment, ultrasonic, manufacturing
524298 Medical cost evaluation services
621112 Medical doctors' (MDs), mental health, offices (e.g. centers, clinics)
621111 Medical doctors' (MDs, except mental health) offices (e.g., centers, clinics)
423450 Medical dressings merchant wholesalers
532490 Medical equipment (except home health furniture and equipment) rental or leasing
446199 Medical equipment and supplies stores
423450 Medical equipment merchant wholesalers
423450 Medical furniture merchant wholesalers
327215 Medical glassware made from purchased glass
327212 Medical glassware made in glass making plants
423450 Medical glassware merchant wholesalers
541430 Medical illustration services
541430 Medical illustrators, independent
423450 Medical instruments merchant wholesalers
524114 Medical insurance carriers, direct
511120 Medical journal and periodical publishers (except exclusive Internet publishing)
511120 Medical journal and periodical publishers and printing combined
516110 Medical journal and periodical publishers, exclusively on Internet

621511 Medical laboratories (except radiological, X-ray)
621512 Medical laboratories, radiological or X-ray
541611 Medical office management consulting services or consultants
561110 Medical office management services
621511 Medical pathology laboratories
541922 Medical photography services
334517 Medical radiation therapy equipment manufacturing
621512 Medical radiological laboratories
524130 Medical reinsurance carriers
541710 Medical research and development laboratories or services
611310 Medical schools
315211 Medical service apparel, men's and boys', cut and sew apparel contractors
315225 Medical service apparel, men's and boys', cut and sewn from purchased fabric (except apparel contractors)
315212 Medical service apparel, women's, cut and sew apparel contractors
315239 Medical service apparel, women's, misses', and girls', cut and sewn from purchased fabric (except apparel contractors)
524114 Medical service plans without providing health care services
424210 Medical sundries, rubber, merchant wholesalers
423450 Medical supplies merchant wholesalers
611519 Medical technician schools
339112 Medical thermometers manufacturing
334510 Medical ultrasound equipment manufacturing
621512 Medical X-ray laboratories
923130 Medicare and Medicaid administration
325411 Medicinal chemicals, uncompounded, manufacturing
337110 Medicine cabinets (except freestanding), wood household-type, manufacturing
337124 Medicine cabinets, metal household-type, manufacturing
321219 Medium density fiberboard (MDF) manufacturing
212399 Meerschaum mining and/or beneficiating
531120 Meeting hall and room rental or leasing
325211 Melamine resins manufacturing
111219 Melon farming (e.g., cantaloupe, casaba, honeydew, watermelon), field, bedding plant and seed production
111419 Melon farming, grown under cover
313230 Melt blown nonwoven fabrics manufacturing
315291 Melton jackets, infants', cut and sewn from purchased fabric (except apparel contractors)
315211 Melton jackets, men's and boys', cut and sew apparel contractors
315228 Melton jackets, men's and boys', cut and sewn from purchased fabric (except apparel contractors)
315212 Melton jackets, women's, girls', and infants', cut and sew apparel contractors
315239 Melton jackets, women's, misses', and girls', cut and sewn from purchased fabric (except apparel contractors)
813410 Membership associations, civic or social
721110 Membership hotels
812220 Memorial gardens (i.e., burial places)
334418 Memory boards manufacturing
712130 Menageries
114111 Menhaden fishing
424320 Men's and boys' clothing merchant wholesalers

424320 Men's and boys' furnishings (except shoes) merchant wholesalers
315119 Men's socks knitting or knitting and finishing
623210 Mental retardation intermediate care facilities
622210 Mental (except mental retardation) hospitals
621420 Mental health centers and clinics (except hospitals), outpatient
623220 Mental health facilities, residential
623220 Mental health halfway houses
622210 Mental health hospitals
621112 Mental health physicians' offices (e.g., centers, clinics)
923120 Mental health program administration
623210 Mental retardation facilities (e.g., homes, hospitals, intermediate care facilities), residential
623210 Mental retardation homes
623210 Mental retardation hospitals
813311 Mentally retarded advocacy groups
561450 Mercantile credit reporting bureaus
313311 Mercerizing broadwoven fabrics
333292 Mercerizing machinery manufacturing
313312 Mercerizing narrow woven textile products and fabrics (except broadwoven)
326111 Merchandise bags, plastics film, single wall or multiwall, manufacturing
423440 Merchandising machines, coin-operated, merchant wholesalers
236117 Merchant builders (i.e., building on own land, for sale), residential
926120 Merchant Marine (except academy)
813910 Merchants' associations
335912 Mercuric oxide batteries manufacturing
212299 Mercury (quicksilver) mining and/or beneficiating
335999 Mercury arc rectifiers (i.e., electrical apparatus) manufacturing
325188 Mercury chloride manufacturing
325188 Mercury compounds, not specified elsewhere by process, manufacturing
325920 Mercury fulminate explosive materials manufacturing
335110 Mercury halide lamp bulbs manufacturing
212299 Mercury ores mining and/or beneficiating
325188 Mercury oxide manufacturing
332618 Mesh made from purchased wire
331422 Mesh, wire, made from purchased copper in wire drawing plants
331319 Mesh, wire, made in aluminum wire drawing plants
331111 Mesh, wire, made in iron and steel mills
331222 Mesh, wire, made in wire drawing mills
331491 Mesh, wire, nonferrous metals (except aluminum, copper), made from purchased nonferrous metals (except aluminum, copper) in wire drawing plants
561421 Message services, telephone answering
492210 Messenger service
325412 Metabolite in-vivo diagnostic substances manufacturing
332431 Metal cans, light gauge metal, manufacturing
333298 Metal casting machinery and equipment manufacturing
333512 Metal cutting machine tools manufacturing
332213 Metal cutting saw blades manufacturing
424690 Metal cyanides merchant wholesalers
333513 Metal deposit forming machines manufacturing

334519 Metal detectors manufacturing
339113 Metal fabric and mesh safety gloves manufacturing
332999 Metal foil containers (except bags) manufacturing
333513 Metal forming machine tools manufacturing
337121 Metal framed furniture, household-type, upholstered, manufacturing
238190 Metal furring contractors
339943 Metal hand stamps manufacturing
333994 Metal melting furnaces, industrial, manufacturing
213114 Metal mining support services (shaft sinking, tunneling, blasting) (except site preparation and related construction contractor activities)
336370 Metal motor vehicle body parts stamping
423520 Metal ores merchant wholesalers
334413 Metal oxide silicon (MOS) devices manufacturing
423510 Metal pipe merchant wholesalers
325612 Metal polishes (i.e., tarnish removers) manufacturing
331314 Metal powder and flake made from purchased aluminum
331423 Metal powder and flake made from purchased copper
331221 Metal powder and flake made from purchased iron or steel
331492 Metal powder and flake nonferrous (except aluminum, copper) made from purchased metal
236210 Metal processing plant construction
423510 Metal products (e.g., bars, ingots, plates, rods, shapes, sheets) merchant wholesalers
423930 Metal scrap and waste merchant wholesalers
238170 Metal siding installation
332116 Metal stampings (except automotive, cans, cooking, closures, crowns), unfinished, manufacturing
335991 Metal-graphite product manufacturing
423520 Metallic concentrates merchant wholesalers
325131 Metallic pigments, inorganic, manufacturing
325199 Metallic soap manufacturing
313320 Metallizing purchased textiles
541380 Metallurgical testing laboratories or services
423510 Metals sales offices
423510 Metals service centers
423510 Metals, ferrous and nonferrous, merchant wholesalers
423940 Metals, precious, merchant wholesalers
333512 Metalworking lathes manufacturing
423830 Metalworking machinery and equipment merchant wholesalers
532490 Metalworking machinery and equipment rental or leasing
334519 Meteorologic tracking systems manufacturing
811219 Meteorological instrument repair and maintenance services
334519 Meteorological instruments manufacturing
541990 Meteorological services
561990 Meter reading services, contract
334514 Metering devices (except electrical and industrial process control) manufacturing
335313 Metering panels, electric, manufacturing
334514 Meters (except electrical and industrial process control) manufacturing
423830 Meters (except electrical, parking) merchant wholesalers
334515 Meters, electrical (i.e., graphic recording, panelboard, pocket, portable), manufacturing

423610 Meters, electrical, merchant wholesalers
334513 Meters, industrial process control-type, manufacturing
334514 Meters, parking, manufacturing
423850 Meters, parking, merchant wholesalers
334515 Meters, power factor and phase angle, manufacturing
325320 Methoxychlor insecticides manufacturing
325191 Methyl acetone manufacturing
325211 Methyl acrylate resins manufacturing
325199 Methyl alcohol (i.e., methanol), synthetic, manufacturing
325191 Methyl alcohol (methanol), natural, manufacturing
325211 Methyl cellulose resins manufacturing
325199 Methyl chloride manufacturing
325211 Methyl methacrylate resins manufacturing
325199 Methyl perhydrofluorine manufacturing
325199 Methyl salicylate manufacturing
325132 Methyl violet toners manufacturing
325199 Methylamine manufacturing
325199 Methylene chloride manufacturing
311422 Mexican foods canning
311412 Mexican foods, frozen, manufacturing
212399 Mica mining and/or beneficiating
327992 Mica processing beyond beneficiation
327999 Mica products manufacturing
212319 Mica schist crushed and broken stone mining and/or beneficiating
212311 Mica schist mining or quarrying
311119 Micro and macro premixes, livestock, manufacturing
334516 Microbiology instruments manufacturing
325413 Microbiology, virology, and serology in-vitro diagnostic substances manufacturing
334111 Microcomputers manufacturing
334413 Microcontroller chip manufacturing
333315 Microfiche equipment (e.g., cameras, projectors, readers) manufacturing
518210 Microfiche recording and imaging services
333315 Microfilm equipment (e.g., cameras, projectors, readers) manufacturing
423420 Microfilm equipment and supplies merchant wholesalers
518210 Microfilm recording and imaging services
212299 Microlite mining and/or beneficiating
333295 Micro-lithography equipment, semiconductor, manufacturing
332212 Micrometers, machinist's precision tools, manufacturing
334310 Microphones manufacturing
334516 Microprobes (e.g., electron, ion, laser, X-ray) manufacturing
334413 Microprocessor chip manufacturing
333314 Microscopes (except electron, proton) manufacturing
334516 Microscopes, electron and proton, manufacturing
237990 Microtunneling contractors
334220 Microwave communications equipment manufacturing
334419 Microwave components manufacturing
811412 Microwave oven, household-type, repair and maintenance services, without retailing new microwave ovens
335221 Microwave ovens (including portable), household-type, manufacturing
333319 Microwave ovens, commercial-type, manufacturing
237130 Microwave relay tower construction
517310 Microwave telecommunication resellers
334515 Microwave test equipment manufacturing

326199 Microwaveware, plastics, manufacturing
315291 Middies, infants', cut and sewn from purchased fabric (except apparel contractors)
315212 Middies, women's, girls' and infants', cut and sew apparel contractors
315232 Middies, women's, misses', and girls', cut and sewn from purchased fabric (except apparel contractors)
611110 Middle schools
621399 Midwives' offices (e.g., centers, clinics)
721310 Migrant workers' camps
611310 Military academies, college level
611110 Military academies, elementary or secondary
928110 Military bases and camps
315211 Military dress uniforms, men's and boys', cut and sew apparel contractors
315222 Military dress uniforms, men's and boys', cut and sewn from purchased fabric (except apparel contractors)
315234 Military dress uniforms, tailored, women's, misses' and girls', cut and sewn from purchased fabric (except apparel contractors)
315212 Military dress uniforms, women's, cut and sew apparel contractors
332999 Military insignia, metal, manufacturing
314999 Military insignia, textile, manufacturing
712110 Military museums
928110 Military police
928110 Military reserve armories and bases
611310 Military service academies (college)
928110 Military training schools (except academies)
423860 Military vehicles (except trucks) merchant wholesalers
311511 Milk based drinks (except dietary) manufacturing
311514 Milk based drinks, dietary, manufacturing
322130 Milk carton board made in paperboard mills
322226 Milk carton board stock made from purchased paperboard
311511 Milk drink, chocolate, manufacturing
484220 Milk hauling, local
311511 Milk pasteurizing
311511 Milk processing (e.g., bottling, homogenizing, pasteurizing, vitaminizing) manufacturing
333294 Milk processing (except farm-type) machinery manufacturing
112120 Milk production, dairy cattle
311511 Milk substitutes manufacturing
115210 Milk testing for butterfat and milk solids
311511 Milk, acidophilus, manufacturing
424490 Milk, canned or dried, merchant wholesalers
311514 Milk, concentrated, condensed, dried, evaporated, and powdered, manufacturing
311511 Milk, fluid (except canned), manufacturing
424430 Milk, fluid (except canned), merchant wholesalers
311514 Milk, malted, manufacturing
311514 Milk, powdered, manufacturing
311514 Milk, ultra-high temperature, manufacturing
112120 Milking dairy cattle
112420 Milking dairy goat
112410 Milking dairy sheep
423820 Milking machinery and equipment merchant wholesalers
333111 Milking machines manufacturing
311514 Milkshake mixes manufacturing
314999 Mill menders, contract, woven fabrics
316999 Mill strapping for textile mills, leather, manufacturing

423840 Mill supplies merchant wholesalers
315991 Millinery cut and sewn from purchased fabric (except apparel contractors)
424330 Millinery merchant wholesalers
424310 Millinery supplies merchant wholesalers
315999 Millinery trimmings cut and sewn from purchased fabric (except apparel contractors)
315211 Millinery trimmings, men's and boys', cut and sew apparel contractors
315212 Millinery trimmings, women's, girls', and infants', cut and sew apparel contractors
315211 Millinery, men's and boys', cut and sew apparel contractors
315212 Millinery, women's, girls', and infants', cut and sew apparel contractors
333512 Milling machines, metalworking, manufacturing
311212 Milling rice
212399 Millstones mining and/or beneficiating
238350 Millwork installation
423310 Millwork merchant wholesalers
337212 Millwork, custom architectural, manufacturing
321114 Millwork, treating
238290 Millwrights
111199 Milo farming, field and seed production
711110 Mime theaters
333922 Mine conveyors manufacturing
213114 Mine development (except site preparation and related construction contractor activities) for metal mining on a contract basis
213115 Mine development for nonmetallic minerals mining (except fuels) on a contract basis
236210 Mine loading and discharging station construction
321114 Mine props, treating
562910 Mine reclamation services, integrated (e.g., demolition, hazardous material removal, soil remediation)
213113 Mine shaft sinking services for coal mining on a contract basis
213114 Mine shaft sinking services for metal mining on a contract basis
213115 Mine shaft sinking services for nonmetallic minerals (except fuels) on a contract basis
238910 Mine site preparation and related construction activities, construction contractors
321114 Mine ties, wood, treated, manufacturing
213113 Mine tunneling services for coal mining on a contract basis
213114 Mine tunneling services for metal mining on a contract basis
213115 Mine tunneling services for nonmetallic minerals (except fuels) on a contract basis
325131 Mineral colors and pigments manufacturing
311119 Mineral feed supplements (except cat, dog) manufacturing
311111 Mineral feed supplements, dog and cat, manufacturing
212393 Mineral pigments, natural, mining and/or beneficiating
333131 Mineral processing and beneficiating machinery manufacturing
523910 Mineral royalties or leases dealing (i.e., acting as a principal in dealing royalties or leases to investors)
311119 Mineral supplements, animal (except cat, dog), manufacturing
424910 Mineral supplements, animal, merchant wholesalers
311111 Mineral supplements, dog and cat, manufacturing

238310 Mineral wool insulation installation
327993 Mineral wool insulation materials manufacturing
327993 Mineral wool products (e.g., board, insulation, tile) manufacturing
423520 Minerals (except construction materials, petroleum) merchant wholesalers
335129 Miner's lamps manufacturing
332993 Mines, ammunition, manufacturing
713990 Miniature golf courses
337920 Miniblinds manufacturing
334111 Minicomputers manufacturing
331111 Mini-mills, steel
926150 Minimum wage program administration
****** Mining—see type
813910 Mining associations
333131 Mining cars manufacturing
423810 Mining cranes merchant wholesalers
541330 Mining engineering services
336510 Mining locomotives and parts manufacturing
423810 Mining machinery and equipment (except petroleum) merchant wholesalers
532412 Mining machinery and equipment rental or leasing
811310 Mining machinery and equipment repair and maintenance services
423830 Mining machinery and equipment, petroleum, merchant wholesalers
531190 Mining property leasing
336112 Minivans assembling on chassis of own manufacture
531130 Miniwarehouse rental or leasing
112930 Mink production
112511 Minnow production, farm raising
711211 Minor league baseball clubs
111998 Mint farming
238150 Mirror installation
423220 Mirrors (except automotive) merchant wholesalers
423120 Mirrors, automotive, merchant wholesalers
327215 Mirrors, framed (except automotive) or unframed, made from purchased glass
333314 Mirrors, optical, manufacturing
237990 Missile facility construction
332993 Missile warheads manufacturing
561611 Missing person tracing services
813110 Missions, religious organization
332212 Miter boxes manufacturing
315992 Mittens cut and sewn from purchased fabric (except apparel contractors)
315191 Mittens, knit, made in apparel knitting mills
315992 Mittens, leather (except apparel contractors), manufacturing
315211 Mittens, leather, men's and boys', cut and sew apparel contractors
315212 Mittens, leather, women's, girls', and infants', cut and sew apparel contractors
315211 Mittens, men's and boys', cut and sew apparel contractors
315212 Mittens, women's, girls', and infants', cut and sew apparel contractors
315992 Mittens, woven or knit, cut and sewn from purchased fabric (except apparel contractors)
315211 Mittens, woven or knit, men's and boys', cut and sew apparel contractors
315212 Mittens, woven or knit, women's, girls', and infants', cut and sew apparel contractors
311230 Mix grain breakfast manufacturing
311514 Mix, ice cream, manufacturing
312140 Mixed drinks, alcoholic, manufacturing
111940 Mixed hay farming
485111 Mixed mode transit systems (e.g., bus, commuter rail, subway combinations)
333120 Mixers, concrete, portable, manufacturing

424490 Mixes (e.g., cake, dessert, pie) merchant wholesalers
311211 Mixes, flour (e.g., biscuit, cake, doughnut, pancake) made in flour mills
311822 Mixes, flour (e.g., biscuit, cake, doughnut, pancake), made from purchased flour
325314 Mixing purchased fertilizer materials
531190 Mobile (manufactured) home parks
531190 Mobile (manufactured) home site rental or leasing
531110 Mobile (manufactured) home, on site, rental or leasing
621512 Mobile breast imaging centers
811192 Mobile car and truck washes
334220 Mobile communications equipment manufacturing
311119 Mobile feed mill
722330 Mobile food stands
453930 Mobile home dealers, manufactured
321991 Mobile home manufacturing
532120 Mobile home rental (except on site)
484220 Mobile home towing services, local
484230 Mobile home towing services, long-distance
712110 Mobile museums
624210 Mobile soup kitchens
333924 Mobile straddle carriers manufacturing
517212 Mobile telephone communication carriers
621512 Mobile X-ray facilities (medical)
316219 Moccasins manufacturing
325222 Modacrylic fibers and filaments manufacturing
313111 Modacrylic spun yarns made from purchased fiber
339932 Model kits manufacturing
423920 Model kits merchant wholesalers
339932 Model railroad manufacturing
561310 Model registries
561320 Model supply services
711410 Modeling agents
339942 Modeling clay manufacturing
611519 Modeling schools
711410 Models' agents or managers
339999 Models, anatomical, manufacturing
711510 Models, independent
339932 Models, toy and hobby (e.g., airplane, boat, ship), manufacturing
423690 Modems merchant wholesalers
334210 Modems, carrier equipment, manufacturing
711120 Modern dance companies
238390 Modular furniture system attachment and installation
337214 Modular furniture systems (except wood frame), office-type, manufacturing
337211 Modular furniture systems, wood frame office-type, manufacturing
236115 Modular house assembly on site by general contractors
236117 Modular housing, residential, assembled on site by operative builders
334518 Modules for clocks and watches manufacturing
112420 Mohair farming
313112 Mohair yarn twisting or winding of purchased yarn
424590 Mohair, raw, merchant wholesalers
334516 Moisture analyzers, laboratory-type, manufacturing
334513 Moisture meters, industrial process-type, manufacturing
311312 Molasses made from purchased raw cane sugar
311313 Molasses made from sugar beets
311311 Molasses made in sugarcane mill
424490 Molasses merchant wholesalers
311312 Molasses, blackstrap, made from purchased raw cane sugar

311311 Molasses, blackstrap, made in sugarcane mill
339991 Molded packings and seals manufacturing
322299 Molded pulp products (e.g., egg cartons, food containers, food trays) manufacturing
423310 Molding (e.g., sheet metal, wood) merchant wholesalers
332321 Molding and trim (except motor vehicle), metal, manufacturing
238350 Molding or trim, wood or plastic, installation
212322 Molding sand quarrying and/or beneficiating
336370 Moldings and trim, motor vehicle, stamping
321918 Moldings, clear and finger joint wood, manufacturing
321918 Moldings, wood and covered wood, manufacturing
333511 Molds (except steel ingot), industrial, manufacturing
331511 Molds for casting steel ingots manufacturing
333511 Molds for forming materials (e.g., glass, plastics, rubber) manufacturing
333511 Molds for metal casting (except steel ingot) manufacturing
333511 Molds for plastics and rubber working machinery manufacturing
331511 Molds, steel ingot, industrial, manufacturing
112512 Mollusk production, farm raising
212299 Molybdenite mining and/or beneficiating
331491 Molybdenum and molybdenum alloy bar, plate, pipe, rod, sheet, tubing, and wire made from purchased metals or scrap
212299 Molybdenum ores mining and/ or beneficiating
331491 Molybdenum rolling, drawing, or extruding purchased metals or scrap
331112 Molybdenum silicon ferroalloys manufacturing
212299 Molybdite mining and/or beneficiating
813110 Monasteries (except schools)
212299 Monazite mining and/or beneficiating
521110 Monetary authorities, central bank
332999 Money chests, metal, manufacturing
525990 Money market mutual funds, closed-end
525910 Money market mutual funds, open-ended
522390 Money order issuance services
334119 Monitors, computer peripheral equipment, manufacturing
325120 Monochlorodifluoromethane manufacturing
334516 Monochrometers, laboratory-type, manufacturing
334413 Monolithic integrated circuits (solid-state) manufacturing
325199 Monomethylparaminophenol sulfate manufacturing
237990 Monorail construction
333923 Monorail systems (except passenger-type) manufacturing
485119 Monorail transit systems (except mixed mode), commuter
487110 Monorail, scenic and sightseeing, operation
325199 Monosodium glutamate manufacturing
611110 Montessori schools, elementary or secondary
236220 Monument (i.e., building) construction
453998 Monument (i.e., burial marker) dealers
423990 Monuments and grave markers merchant wholesalers
327991 Monuments and tombstone, cut stone (except finishing or lettering to order only), manufacturing
333319 Mop wringers manufacturing
441221 Moped dealers
423110 Moped merchant wholesalers

532292 Moped rental
336991 Mopeds and parts manufacturing
339994 Mops, floor and dust, manufacturing
325132 Mordant dyes manufacturing
325613 Mordants manufacturing
325411 Morphine and derivatives (i.e., basic chemicals) manufacturing
522190 Morris Plans (i.e., known as), depository
522298 Morris Plans (i.e., known as), nondepository
333120 Mortar mixers, portable, manufacturing
332993 Mortar shells manufacturing
327125 Mortar, nonclay refractory, manufacturing
332995 Mortars manufacturing
327124 Mortars, clay refractory, manufacturing
522292 Mortgage banking (i.e., nondepository mortgage lending)
522310 Mortgage brokerages
522310 Mortgage brokers' or agents' offices (i.e., independent)
522292 Mortgage companies
524126 Mortgage guaranty insurance carriers, direct
812210 Mortician services
333210 Mortisers, woodworking-type, manufacturing
812210 Mortuaries
334413 MOS (metal oxide silicon) devices manufacturing
327122 Mosaic tile, ceramic, manufacturing
238340 Mosaic work
813110 Mosques, religious
926130 Mosquito eradication districts
561710 Mosquito eradication services
113210 Moss gathering
531120 Motel building, not operating motel, rental or leasing
236220 Motel construction
561110 Motel management services (except complete operation of client's business)
721110 Motels
325320 Moth repellants manufacturing
423430 Mother boards merchant wholesalers
334290 Motion alarms (e.g., swimming pool, perimeter) manufacturing
334290 Motion detectors, security system, manufacturing
512110 Motion picture and video production
512110 Motion picture and video production and distribution
512191 Motion picture animation, post-production
512199 Motion picture booking agencies
333315 Motion picture cameras manufacturing
423410 Motion picture cameras, equipment, and supplies merchant wholesalers
541690 Motion picture consulting services
711510 Motion picture directors, independent
512120 Motion picture distribution exclusive of production
532490 Motion picture equipment rental or leasing
512131 Motion picture exhibition
512131 Motion picture exhibitors for airlines
512131 Motion picture exhibitors, itinerant
512120 Motion picture film distributors
512199 Motion picture film laboratories
512120 Motion picture film libraries
519120 Motion picture film libraries, archives
512199 Motion picture film libraries, stock footage
325992 Motion picture film manufacturing
512199 Motion picture film reproduction for theatrical distribution
512199 Motion picture laboratories
512191 Motion picture or video editing services

512191 Motion picture or video post-production services
512191 Motion picture or video titling
711510 Motion picture producers, independent
512110 Motion picture production
512110 Motion picture production and distribution
512191 Motion picture production special effects, post-production
333315 Motion picture projectors manufacturing
512110 Motion picture studios, producing motion pictures
512132 Motion picture theaters, drive-in
512131 Motion picture theaters, indoor
532220 Motion picture wardrobe and costume rental
711510 Motivational speakers, independent
441221 Motor bike dealers
926120 Motor carrier licensing and inspection offices
485210 Motor coach operation, interurban and rural
335314 Motor control accessories (including overload relays) manufacturing
335314 Motor control centers, manufacturing
335314 Motor controls, electric, manufacturing
423610 Motor controls, electric, merchant wholesalers
721110 Motor courts
484110 Motor freight carrier, general, local
484122 Motor freight carrier, general, long-distance, less-than-truckload (LTL)
484121 Motor freight carrier, general, long-distance, truckload (TL)
484210 Motor freight carrier, used household goods
335312 Motor generator sets (except automotive, turbine generator sets) manufacturing
333611 Motor generator sets, turbo generators, manufacturing
441210 Motor home dealers
423110 Motor home merchant wholesalers
532120 Motor home rental
336213 Motor homes, self-contained, assembling on purchased chassis
336120 Motor homes, self-contained, mounted on heavy truck chassis of own manufacture
336112 Motor homes, self-contained, mounted on light duty truck chassis of own manufacture
721110 Motor hotels without casinos
721110 Motor inns
721110 Motor lodges
324191 Motor oils, petroleum, made from refined petroleum
325998 Motor oils, synthetic, manufacturing
811310 Motor repair and maintenance services, commercial or industrial
441221 Motor scooters dealers
336991 Motor scooters manufacturing
335314 Motor starters, contractors, and controllers, industrial, manufacturing
561599 Motor travel clubs
333997 Motor truck scales manufacturing
236210 Motor vehicle assembly plant construction
326220 Motor vehicle belts, rubber or plastics, manufacturing
238290 Motor vehicle garage and service station mechanical equipment (e.g., gasoline pumps, hoists) installation
332510 Motor vehicle hardware, metal, manufacturing
326220 Motor vehicle hoses, rubber or plastics, manufacturing
334514 Motor vehicle instruments (e.g., fuel level gauges, oil pressure, speedometers, tachometers, water temperature) manufacturing
423120 Motor vehicle instruments, electric, merchant wholesalers

336360 Motor vehicle interior systems (e.g., headliners, panels, seats, trims) manufacturing
561990 Motor vehicle license issuing services, private franchise
926120 Motor vehicle licensing offices, government
423110 Motor vehicle merchant wholesalers
336370 Motor vehicle metal bumper stampings
336370 Motor vehicle metal parts stamping
336370 Motor vehicle metal stampings (e.g., body parts, fenders, hub caps, tops, trim) manufacturing
326199 Motor vehicle moldings and extrusions, plastics, manufacturing
325510 Motor vehicle paints manufacturing
423120 Motor vehicle parts and accessories, new, merchant wholesalers
423140 Motor vehicle parts, used, merchant wholesalers
336360 Motor vehicle seats manufacturing
336360 Motor vehicle seats, metal framed, manufacturing
423130 Motor vehicle tire and tube merchant wholesalers
326211 Motor vehicle tires manufacturing
488410 Motor vehicle towing services
336360 Motor vehicle trimmings manufacturing
811490 Motorboat (i.e., inboard and outboard) repair and maintenance services
336612 Motorboat, inboard or outboard, building
441221 Motorcycle dealers
423110 Motorcycle merchant wholesalers
441221 Motorcycle parts and accessories dealers
423120 Motorcycle parts, new, merchant wholesalers
711212 Motorcycle racetracks
711219 Motorcycle racing teams
532292 Motorcycle rental
811490 Motorcycle repair shops without retailing new motorcycles
336991 Motorcycles and parts manufacturing
423860 Motorized passenger golf carts merchant wholesalers
335312 Motors, electric (except engine starting motors, gearmotors, outboard), manufacturing
423610 Motors, electric, merchant wholesalers
333996 Motors, fluid power, manufacturing
333612 Motors, gear, manufacturing
333618 Motors, outboard, manufacturing
423910 Motors, outboard, merchant wholesalers
336322 Motors, starter, for internal combustion engines, manufacturing
713990 Mountain hiking, recreational
561910 Mounting merchandise on cards
334119 Mouse devices, computer peripheral equipment, manufacturing
213112 Mouse hole and rat hole drilling at oil and gas fields on a contract basis
339992 Mouthpieces for musical instruments manufacturing
325620 Mouthwashes (except medicinal) manufacturing
325412 Mouthwashes, medicated, manufacturing
334518 Movements, watch or clock, manufacturing
512110 Movie production and distribution
512131 Movie theaters (except drive-in)
512132 Movie theaters, drive-in
238290 Moving sidewalk installation
561730 Mowing services (e.g., highway, lawn, road strip)
562920 MRF (materials recovery facilities)

621512 MRI (magnetic resonance imaging) centers
334510 MRI (magnetic resonance imaging) medical diagnostic equipment manufacturing
325520 Mucilage adhesives manufacturing
213112 Mud service for oil field drilling on a contract basis
238110 Mud-jacking contractors
811112 Muffler repair and replacement shops
336399 Mufflers and resonators, automotive, truck, and buses manufacturing
315191 Mufflers made in apparel knitting mills
423120 Mufflers, exhaust, merchant wholesalers
315211 Mufflers, men's and boys', cut and sew apparel contractors
315993 Mufflers, men's and boys', cut and sewn from purchased fabric (except apparel contractors)
315999 Mufflers, women's and girls', cut and sewn from purchased fabric (except apparel contractors)
315212 Mufflers, women's, girls', and infants', cut and sew apparel contractors
424910 Mulch merchant wholesalers
333112 Mulchers, lawn and garden-type, manufacturing
112920 Mule production
424590 Mules merchant wholesalers
114111 Mullet fishing
712110 Multidisciplinary museums
236116 Multifamily building construction general contractors
236117 Multifamily building operative builders
334515 Multimeters manufacturing
334210 Multiplex equipment, telephone, manufacturing
624190 Multiservice centers, neighborhood
212391 Muriate of potash, mining
325412 Muscle relaxant preparations manufacturing
212399 Muscovite mining and/or beneficiating
236220 Museum construction
712110 Museums
111411 Mushroom farming
111411 Mushroom spawn farming
311421 Mushrooms canning
519120 Music archives
711510 Music arrangers, independent
512230 Music book (i.e., bound sheet music) publishers
512230 Music book (i.e., bound sheet music) publishers and printing combined
323117 Music books printing or printing and binding without publishing
339999 Music boxes manufacturing
512230 Music copyright authorizing use
512230 Music copyright buying and licensing
711510 Music directors, independent
711310 Music festival managers with facilities
711320 Music festival managers without facilities
711310 Music festival organizers with facilities
711320 Music festival organizers without facilities
711310 Music festival promoters with facilities
711320 Music festival promoters without facilities
611610 Music instruction (e.g., guitar, piano)
515112 Music program distribution (except exclusively on Internet), radio
517510 Music program distribution, cable or satellite
512290 Music program distribution, pre-recorded
512230 Music publishers
339992 Music rolls, perforated, manufacturing
611610 Music schools (except academic)

451220 Music stores (e.g., cassette, compact disc, record, tape)
453310 Music stores (e.g., cassette, instrument, record, tape), used
451140 Music stores (i.e., instrument)
621340 Music therapists' offices (e.g., centers, clinics)
512110 Music video production
512110 Music video production and distribution
323112 Music, sheet, flexographic printing without publishing
323111 Music, sheet, gravure printing without publishing
323110 Music, sheet, lithographic (offset) printing without publishing
424990 Music, sheet, merchant wholesalers
323119 Music, sheet, printing (except flexographic, gravure, lithographic, quick, screen) without publishing
512230 Music, sheet, publishers and printing combined
323113 Music, sheet, screen printing without publishing
711130 Musical artists, independent
711130 Musical groups (except musical theater groups)
339992 Musical instrument accessories (e.g., mouthpieces, reeds, stands, traps) manufacturing
423990 Musical instrument accessories and supplies merchant wholesalers
316991 Musical instrument cases, all materials, manufacturing
532299 Musical instrument rental
811490 Musical instrument repair shops without retailing new musical instruments
451140 Musical instrument stores
339992 Musical instruments (except toy) manufacturing
423990 Musical instruments merchant wholesalers
339932 Musical instruments, toy, manufacturing
711130 Musical productions (except musical theater productions), live
512220 Musical recording, releasing, promoting, and distributing
423990 Musical recordings (e.g., compact discs, records, tapes) merchant wholesalers
711110 Musical theater companies or groups
711110 Musical theater productions, live
711130 Musicians, independent
111219 Muskmelon farming, field, bedding plant and seed production
114112 Mussel fishing
112512 Mussel production, farm raising
111120 Mustard seed farming, field and seed production
311941 Mustard, prepared, manufacturing
523120 Mutual fund agencies (i.e., brokerages)
523120 Mutual fund agents' (i.e., brokers') offices
523920 Mutual fund managing
525990 Mutual funds, closed-end
525910 Mutual funds, open-ended
522120 Mutual savings banks
621511 Mycology health laboratories
325191 Myrobalans extract manufacturing
333991 Nail guns, handheld power-driven, manufacturing
333513 Nail heading machines manufacturing
325620 Nail polish remover manufacturing
325620 Nail polishes manufacturing
812113 Nail salons
333991 Nailers and staplers, handheld power-driven, manufacturing
423510 Nails merchant wholesalers
331319 Nails, aluminum, made in wire drawing plants
332618 Nails, brads, and staples made from purchased wire
331222 Nails, iron or steel, made in wire drawing plants

331491 Nails, nonferrous metals (except aluminum, copper), made from purchased nonferrous metals (except aluminum, copper) in wire drawing plants
332999 Name plate blanks, metal, manufacturing
325998 Napalm manufacturing
325192 Naphtha made by distillation of coal tar
324110 Naphtha made in petroleum refineries
325192 Naphtha, solvent, made by distillation of coal tar
325192 Naphthalene made from refined petroleum or natural gas
325192 Naphthalenesulfonic acid manufacturing
325199 Naphthenic acid soaps manufacturing
325192 Naphthenic acids made from refined petroleum or natural gas
324110 Naphthenic acids made in petroleum refineries
325192 Naphthol, alpha and beta, manufacturing
325192 Naphtholsulfonic acids manufacturing
423220 Napkins (except paper) merchant wholesalers
314129 Napkins made from purchased fabrics
424130 Napkins, paper, merchant wholesalers
322291 Napkins, table, made from purchased paper
322121 Napkins, table, made in paper mills
313311 Napping broadwoven fabrics
333292 Napping machinery for textiles manufacturing
313312 Napping textile products and fabrics (except broadwoven fabrics)
313221 Narrow fabrics weaving
927110 National Aeronautics and Space Administration
522110 National commercial banks
522298 National Credit Union Administration (NCUA)
928110 National Guard
712190 National parks
926120 National Transportation Safety Board
311422 Nationality specialty foods canning
311412 Nationality specialty foods, frozen, manufacturing
212399 Native asphalt mining and/or beneficiating
327310 Natural (i.e., calcined earth) cement manufacturing
212399 Natural abrasives (e.g., emery, grindstones, hones, pumice) (except sand) mining and/or beneficiating
313113 Natural fiber (i.e., hemp, linen, ramie) thread manufacturing
313210 Natural fiber fabrics (i.e., jute, linen, hemp, ramie), broadwoven, weaving
313221 Natural fiber fabrics (i.e., jute, linen, hemp, ramie), narrow woven, weaving
313111 Natural fiber spun yarns (i.e., hemp, jute, ramie, flax) made from purchased fiber
221210 Natural gas brokers
221210 Natural gas distribution systems
333618 Natural gas engines manufacturing
211112 Natural gas liquids (e.g., ethane, isobutane, natural gasoline, propane) recovered from oil and gas field gases
486910 Natural gas liquids pipeline transportation
221210 Natural gas marketers
237120 Natural gas pipeline construction
486210 Natural gas pipeline transportation
238220 Natural gas piping installation
237120 Natural gas processing plant construction
211111 Natural gas production

486210 Natural gas transmission (i.e., processing plants to local distribution systems)
211111 Natural gas, offshore production
211112 Natural gasoline recovered from oil and gas field gases
712110 Natural history museums
325199 Natural nonfood coloring, manufacturing
813312 Natural resource preservation organizations
712110 Natural science museums
712190 Natural wonder tourist attractions (e.g., caverns, waterfalls)
312112 Naturally carbonated water, purifying and bottling
712190 Nature centers
712190 Nature parks
712190 Nature preserves
712190 Nature reserves
621399 Naturopaths' offices (e.g., centers, clinics)
334511 Nautical systems and instruments manufacturing
332995 Naval artillery manufacturing
336611 Naval ship building
325191 Naval stores, gum or wood, manufacturing
811219 Navigational instruments (e.g., radar, sonar) repair and maintenance services
423860 Navigational instruments (except electronic) merchant wholesalers
334511 Navigational instruments manufacturing
423690 Navigational instruments, electronic (e.g., radar, sonar), merchant wholesalers
928110 Navy
312120 Near beer brewing
311613 Neatsfoot oil rendering
315292 Neckpieces, fur (except apparel contractors), manufacturing
315211 Neckpieces, fur, men's and boys', cut and sew apparel contractors
315212 Neckpieces, fur, women's, girls', and infants', cut and sew apparel contractors
315191 Neckties made in apparel knitting mills
315211 Neckties, men's and boys', cut and sew apparel contractors
315993 Neckties, men's and boys', cut and sewn from purchased fabric (except apparel contractors)
424320 Neckties, men's and boys', merchant wholesalers
315999 Neckties, women's and girls', cut and sewn from purchased fabric (except apparel contractors)
315212 Neckties, women's, girls', and infants', cut and sew apparel contractors
315191 Neckwear made in a apparel knitting mills
448150 Neckwear stores
315993 Neckwear, men's and boys', cut and sewn from purchased fabric (except apparel contractors)
315211 Neckwear, men's and boys', cut and sew apparel contractors
315212 Neckwear, women's, girls' and infants', cut and sew apparel contractors
111339 Nectarine farming
332991 Needle roller bearings manufacturing
451130 Needlecraft sewing supply stores
339993 Needles (except hypodermic, phonograph, styli) manufacturing
333292 Needles for knitting machinery manufacturing
339112 Needles, hypodermic and suture, manufacturing
334419 Needles, phonograph and styli, manufacturing
424310 Needles, sewing, merchant wholesalers
315211 Needlework art contractors on men's and boys' apparel

315212 Needlework art contractors on women's, girls', and infants' apparel
315192 Negligees made in apparel knitting mills
315212 Negligees, women's, cut and sew apparel contractors
315231 Negligees, women's, misses', and girls', cut and sewn from purchased fabric (except apparel contractors)
813319 Neighborhood development advocacy organizations
325120 Neon manufacturing
339950 Neon signs manufacturing
325212 Neoprene manufacturing
212325 Nepheline syenite mining and/ or beneficiating
334516 Nephelometers (except meteorological) manufacturing
334519 Nephoscopes manufacturing
333292 Net and lace making machinery manufacturing
424310 Net goods merchant wholesalers
313210 Nets and nettings, more than 12 inches in width, weaving
313249 Netting made in warp knitting mills
313241 Netting made in weft knitting mills
313249 Netting made on a lace or net machine
326199 Netting, plastics, manufacturing
332618 Netting, woven, made from purchased wire
515111 Network broadcasting service, radio
515111 Network radio broadcasting
541512 Network systems integration design services, computer
515120 Network television broadcasting
515210 Networks, cable television
622310 Neurological hospitals
621111 Neurologists' offices (e.g., centers, clinics)
621111 Neuropathologists' offices (e.g., centers, clinics)
312140 Neutral spirit, beverages (except fruit), manufacturing
424820 Neutral spirits merchant wholesalers
334516 Neutron activation analysis instruments manufacturing
441110 New car dealers
541613 New product development consulting services
321918 Newel posts, wood, manufacturing
451212 News dealers
519110 News picture gathering and distributing services
519110 News reporting services
519110 News service syndicates
519110 News ticker services
511120 Newsletter publishers (except exclusive Internet publishing)
511120 Newsletter publishers and printing combined (except Internet)
516110 Newsletter publishers, exclusively on Internet
323112 Newsletters flexographic printing without publishing
323111 Newsletters gravure printing without publishing
323110 Newsletters lithographic (offset) printing without publishing
323119 Newsletters printing (except flexographic, gravure, lithographic, quick, screen) without publishing
323113 Newsletters screen printing without publishing
541840 Newspaper advertising representatives (i.e., independent of media owners)
424920 Newspaper agencies merchant wholesalers
511110 Newspaper branch offices
711510 Newspaper columnists, independent (freelance)
519110 Newspaper feature syndicates
333293 Newspaper inserting equipment manufacturing
511110 Newspaper publishers (except exclusive Internet publishing)
511110 Newspaper publishers and printing combined

516110 Newspaper publishing, exclusively on Internet
323112 Newspapers flexographic printing without publishing
323111 Newspapers gravure printing without publishing
323110 Newspapers lithographic (offset) printing without publishing
424920 Newspapers merchant wholesalers
323119 Newspapers printing (except flexographic, gravure, lithographic, quick, screen) without publishing
323113 Newspapers screen printing without publishing
424110 Newsprint merchant wholesalers
322122 Newsprint mills
322122 Newsprint paper, manufacturing
451212 Newsstands (i.e., permanent)
339941 Nibs (i.e., pen points) manufacturing
331522 Nickel alloy die-castings, unfinished, manufacturing
325188 Nickel ammonium sulfate manufacturing
331491 Nickel and nickel alloy pipe, plate, sheet, strip, and tubing made from purchased metals or scrap
335911 Nickel cadmium storage batteries manufacturing
325188 Nickel carbonate manufacturing
331528 Nickel castings (except die-castings), unfinished, manufacturing
325188 Nickel compounds, not specified elsewhere by process, manufacturing
212234 Nickel concentrates recovery
331522 Nickel die-castings, unfinished, manufacturing
332999 Nickel foil not made in rolling mills
212234 Nickel ore beneficiating plants
212234 Nickel ore mine site development for own account
212234 Nickel ores mining and/or beneficiating
331492 Nickel recovering from scrap and/or alloying purchased metals
331419 Nickel refining, primary
331491 Nickel rolling, drawing, or extruding purchased metals or scrap
325188 Nickel sulfate manufacturing
325411 Nicotine and derivatives (i.e., basic chemicals) manufacturing
325320 Nicotine insecticides manufacturing
713990 Nightclubs without alcoholic beverages
337122 Night stands, wood, manufacturing
333314 Night vision optical device manufacturing
722410 Nightclubs, alcoholic beverage
315192 Nightgowns made in apparel knitting mills
315291 Nightgowns, infants', cut and sewn from purchased fabric (except apparel contractors)
315211 Nightgowns, men's and boys', cut and sew apparel contractors
315221 Nightgowns, men's and boys', cut and sewn from purchased fabric (except apparel contractors)
315212 Nightgowns, women's, girls', and infants', cut and sew apparel contractors
315231 Nightgowns, women's, misses', and girls', cut and sewn from purchased fabric (except apparel contractors)
315192 Nightshirts made in apparel knitting mills
315291 Nightshirts, infants', cut and sewn from purchased fabric (except apparel contractors)
315211 Nightshirts, men's and boys', cut and sew apparel contractors
315221 Nightshirts, men's and boys', cut and sewn from purchased fabric (except apparel contractors)

315212 Nightshirts, women's, girls', and infants', cut and sew apparel contractors
315231 Nightshirts, women's, misses', and girls', cut and sewn from purchased fabric (except contractors)
315192 Nightwear made in apparel knitting mills
315291 Nightwear, infants', cut and sewn from purchased fabric (except apparel contractors)
315211 Nightwear, men's and boys', cut and sew apparel contractors
315221 Nightwear, men's and boys', cut and sewn from purchased fabric (except apparel contractors)
424320 Nightwear, men's and boys', merchant wholesalers
315212 Nightwear, women's, girls', and infants', cut and sew apparel contractors
315231 Nightwear, women's, misses', and girls', cut and sewn from purchased fabric (except apparel contractors)
331419 Niobium refining, primary
326299 Nipples and teething rings, rubber, manufacturing
332996 Nipples, metal, made from purchased pipe
325192 Nitrated hydrocarbon derivatives manufacturing
325311 Nitric acid manufacturing
325212 Nitrile rubber manufacturing
325212 Nitrile-butadiene rubber manufacturing
325212 Nitrile-chloroprene rubbers manufacturing
325192 Nitroaniline manufacturing
325192 Nitrobenzene manufacturing
325211 Nitrocellulose (i.e., pyroxylin) resins manufacturing
325920 Nitrocellulose explosive materials manufacturing
325221 Nitrocellulose fibers manufacturing
325120 Nitrogen manufacturing
325311 Nitrogenous fertilizer materials manufacturing
325314 Nitrogenous fertilizers made by mixing purchased materials
325920 Nitroglycerin explosive materials manufacturing
325192 Nitrophenol manufacturing
325192 Nitrosated hydrocarbon derivatives manufacturing
325132 Nitroso dyes manufacturing
325920 Nitrostarch explosive materials manufacturing
325199 Nitrous ether manufacturing
325120 Nitrous oxide manufacturing
325411 N-methylpiperazine manufacturing
924110 NOAA (National Oceanic and Atmospheric Administration)
339113 Noise protectors, personal, manufacturing
312120 Nonalcoholic beer brewing
312130 Nonalcoholic wines manufacturing
551112 Nonbank holding companies (except managing)
325222 Noncellulosic fibers and filaments manufacturing
325222 Noncellulosic filament yarn manufacturing
325222 Noncellulosic staple fibers and filaments manufacturing
111339 Noncitrus fruit farming
327125 Nonclay refractories (e.g., block, brick, mortar, tile) manufacturing
311514 Nondairy creamers, dry, manufacturing
311511 Nondairy creamers, liquid, manufacturing
541380 Non-destructive testing laboratories or services
425120 Nondurable goods agents and brokers, wholesale trade
425110 Nondurable goods business to business electronic markets, wholesale trade
325110 Nonene made from refined petroleum or liquid hydrocarbons
311514 Nonfat dry milk manufacturing

331522 Nonferrous (except aluminum) die-casting foundries
331492 Nonferrous alloys (except aluminum, copper) made from purchased nonferrous metals
331492 Nonferrous alloys (except aluminum, copper) made in integrated secondary smelting and alloying plants
331419 Nonferrous metal (except aluminum, copper) shapes made in primary nonferrous metal smelting and refining mills
331491 Nonferrous metal shapes (except aluminum, copper) made by rolling, drawing, or extruding purchased nonferrous metal
331491 Nonferrous metal shapes (except aluminum, copper) made in integrated secondary smelting and extruding mills
331491 Nonferrous metal shapes (except aluminum, copper) made in integrated secondary smelting and rolling mills
331491 Nonferrous metal shapes (except aluminum, copper) made in integrated secondary smelting mills and wire drawing plants
331528 Nonferrous metals (except aluminum, copper) foundries (except die-casting)
331419 Nonferrous metals (except aluminum, copper) made in primary nonferrous metal smelting and refining mills
331492 Nonferrous metals (except aluminum, copper) secondary smelting and refining
331419 Nonferrous metals (except aluminum, copper) smelting and refining, primary
331528 Nonferrous metals (except aluminum, copper) unfinished castings (except die-castings) manufacturing
423510 Nonferrous metals (except precious) merchant wholesalers
331491 Nonferrous wire (except aluminum, copper) made from purchased nonferrous metals (except aluminum, copper) in wire drawing plants
331491 Nonferrous wire (except aluminum, copper) made in integrated secondary smelting mills and wire drawing plants
323121 Nonfiction book binding without printing
511130 Nonfiction book publishers (except exclusive Internet publshing)
511130 Nonfiction book publishers and printing combined
516110 Nonfiction book publishers, exclusively on Internet
323117 Nonfiction books printing and binding without publishing
323117 Nonfiction books printing without publishing
562219 Nonhazardous waste treatment and disposal facilities (except combustors, incinerators, landfills, sewer systems, sewage treatment facilities)
423510 Noninsulated wire merchant wholesalers
423520 Nonmetallic minerals (except precious and semiprecious stones and minerals used in construction, such as sand and gravel)
213115 Nonmetallic minerals mining support services (e.g., blasting, shaft sinking, tunneling) (except site preparation and related construction contractor activities) on a contract basis
325412 Nonprescription drug preparations manufacturing
424210 Nonprescription drugs merchant wholesalers
531312 Nonresidential property managing

531120 Nonresidential building (except miniwarehouse) rental or leasing
481212 Nonscheduled air freight transportation
481211 Nonscheduled air passenger transportation
332214 Nonstick metal cooking utensils
337122 Nonupholstered, household-type, custom wood furniture, manufacturing
313230 Nonwoven fabric tapes manufacturing
313230 Nonwoven fabrics manufacturing
313230 Nonwoven felts manufacturing
311999 Noodle mixes made from purchased dry ingredients
311423 Noodle mixes made in dehydration plants
311823 Noodle mixes made in dry pasta plants
311823 Noodles, dry, manufacturing
311991 Noodles, fresh, manufacturing
311999 Noodles, fried, manufacturing
339113 Nose and ear plugs manufacturing
541199 Notary public services
541199 Notary publics' private practices
334111 Notebook computers manufacturing
322233 Notebooks (including mechanically bound by wire, or plastics) made from purchased paper
424120 Notebooks merchant wholesalers
332999 Novelties and specialties, nonprecious metal and precious plated, manufacturing
424990 Novelties merchant wholesalers
316999 Novelties, leather (e.g., cigarette lighter covers, key fobs), manufacturing
339999 Novelties, not specified elsewhere, manufacturing
339911 Novelties, precious metal (except precious plated), manufacturing
321999 Novelties, wood fiber, manufacturing
453220 Novelty shops
315211 Novelty stitching contractors on men's and boys' apparel
315212 Novelty stitching contractors on women's, girls', and infants' apparel
326199 Nozzles, aerosol spray, plastics, manufacturing
332919 Nozzles, fire fighting, manufacturing
332919 Nozzles, lawn hose, manufacturing
325212 N-type rubber manufacturing
332911 Nuclear application valves manufacturing
541690 Nuclear energy consulting services
926130 Nuclear energy inspection and regulation offices
325188 Nuclear fuel scrap reprocessing
325188 Nuclear fuels, inorganic, manufacturing
334519 Nuclear instrument modules manufacturing
334517 Nuclear irradiation equipment manufacturing
325412 Nuclear medicine (e.g., radioactive isotopes) preparations manufacturing
237130 Nuclear power plant construction
332410 Nuclear reactor steam supply systems manufacturing
332410 Nuclear reactors control rod drive mechanisms manufacturing
332410 Nuclear reactors manufacturing
332313 Nuclear shielding, fabricated metal plate work, manufacturing
332420 Nuclear waste casks, heavy gauge metal, manufacturing
237990 Nuclear waste disposal site construction
721214 Nudist camps with accommodation facilities
713990 Nudist camps without accommodations

335314 Numerical controls, manufacturing
333512 Numerically controlled metal cutting machine tools manufacturing
812990 Numerology services
621610 Nurse associations, visiting
561310 Nurse registries
113210 Nurseries for reforestation growing trees
444220 Nursery and garden centers without tree production
337122 Nursery furniture (except upholstered), wood, manufacturing
337124 Nursery furniture, metal, manufacturing
624410 Nursery schools
424930 Nursery stock (except plant bulbs, seeds) merchant wholesalers
111421 Nursery stock growing
111421 Nursery with tree production (except for reforestation)
611519 Nurse's aides schools
813920 Nurses' associations
621399 Nurses', licensed practical or registered, offices (e.g., centers, clinics)
621610 Nursing agencies, primarily providing home nursing services
623110 Nursing care facilities
623110 Nursing homes
611519 Nursing schools (except academic)
445292 Nut (i.e., packaged) stores
115114 Nut hulling and shelling
331221 Nut rods, iron or steel, made in cold rolling mills
331111 Nut rods, iron or steel, made in iron and steel mills
333111 Nut shellers, farm-type, manufacturing
446191 Nutrition (i.e., food supplement) stores
621399 Nutritionists' offices (e.g., centers, clinics)
424450 Nuts (e.g., canned, roasted, salted) merchant wholesalers
311320 Nuts, chocolate covered, made from cacao beans
311330 Nuts, chocolate covered, made from purchased chocolate
311340 Nuts, covered (except chocolate covered), manufacturing
311911 Nuts, kernels and seeds, roasting and processing
115113 Nuts, machine harvesting
332722 Nuts, metal, manufacturing
311911 Nuts, salted, roasted, cooked, canned, manufacturing
424590 Nuts, unprocessed or shelled only, merchant wholesalers
325222 Nylon fibers and filaments manufacturing
315111 Nylon hosiery, sheer, women's, misses', and girls' full-length and knee-length, knitting or knitting and finishing
325211 Nylon resins manufacturing
313111 Nylon spun yarns made from purchased fiber
313113 Nylon thread manufacturing
313112 Nylon yarn twisting or winding of purchased yarn
315111 Nylons, sheer, women's, misses', and girls' full-length and knee-length, knitting or knitting and finishing
325191 Oak extract manufacturing
321999 Oars, wood, manufacturing
111199 Oat farming, field and seed production
311211 Oat flour manufacturing
311230 Oatmeal (i.e., cereal breakfast food) manufacturing
311230 Oats, breakfast cereal, manufacturing
311230 Oats, rolled (i.e., cereal breakfast food), manufacturing
812910 Obedience training services, pet
339992 Oboes manufacturing
713990 Observation towers
712110 Observatories (except research institutions)
541710 Observatories, research institutions
622310 Obstetrical hospital

621111 Obstetricians' offices (e.g., centers, clinics)
339992 Ocarinas manufacturing
926150 Occupational safety and health administration
926150 Occupational safety and health standards agencies
813920 Occupational therapists' associations
621340 Occupational therapists' offices (e.g., centers, clinics)
541710 Oceanographic research and development laboratories or services
212393 Ocher mining and/or beneficiating
325131 Ocher pigments manufacturing
339992 Octophones manufacturing
114112 Octopus fishing
621320 ODs' (doctors of optometry) offices (e.g., centers, clinics)
332995 Oerlikon guns manufacturing
721310 Off campus dormitories
624190 Offender self-help organizations
336999 Off-highway tracked vehicles (except construction, armored military) manufacturing
333120 Off-highway trucks manufacturing
561110 Office administration services
541512 Office automation computer systems integration design services
236220 Office building construction
531120 Office building rental or leasing
561720 Office cleaning services
423420 Office equipment merchant wholesalers
337214 Office furniture (except wood), padded, upholstered, or plain (except wood), manufacturing
423210 Office furniture merchant wholesalers
532420 Office furniture rental or leasing
442110 Office furniture stores
238390 Office furniture, modular system, installation
337211 Office furniture, padded, upholstered, or plain wood, manufacturing
561320 Office help supply services
811212 Office machine repair and maintenance services (except communication equipment)
532420 Office machinery and equipment rental or leasing
423420 Office machines merchant wholesalers
561110 Office management services
322121 Office paper (e.g., computer printer, photocopy, plain paper) made in paper mills
322233 Office paper (e.g., computer printer, photocopy, plain paper), cut sheet, made from purchased paper
424120 Office supplies (except furniture, machines) merchant wholesalers
322231 Office supplies, die-cut paper, made from purchased paper or paperboard
561320 Office supply pools
453210 Office supply stores
336999 Off-road all terrain vehicles (ATV's), wheeled or tracked, manufacturing
441221 Off-road all-terrain vehicles (ATV), wheeled or tracked, dealers
325910 Offset inks manufacturing
323122 Offset plate preparation services
323110 Offset printing (except books, manifold business forms, printing grey goods)
333293 Offset printing presses manufacturing
211111 Offshore crude petroleum production
211111 Offshore natural gas production
713290 Off-track betting parlors
334515 Ohmmeters manufacturing
324110 Oil (i.e., petroleum) refineries
325998 Oil additive preparations manufacturing
324110 Oil additives made in petroleum refineries
424690 Oil additives merchant wholesalers

211111 Oil and gas field development for own account
237120 Oil and gas field distribution line construction
211111 Oil and gas field exploration for own account
213112 Oil and gas field services (except contract drilling, site preparation and related construction contractor activities) on a contract basis
333132 Oil and gas field-type drilling machinery and equipment (except offshore floating platforms) manufacturing
336611 Oil and gas offshore floating platforms manufacturing
213111 Oil and gas well drilling services (redrilling, spudding, tailing) on a contract basis
238220 Oil burner installation
333414 Oil burners, heating, manufacturing
423720 Oil burners, heating, merchant wholesalers
811191 Oil change and lubrication shops, automotive
424690 Oil drilling muds merchant wholesalers
213112 Oil field exploration (except surveying) on a contract basis
532412 Oil field machinery and equipment rental or leasing
237310 Oil field road construction
423120 Oil filters, automotive, merchant wholesalers
336399 Oil filters, automotive, truck, and bus, manufacturing
424590 Oil kernels merchant wholesalers
523999 Oil lease brokers' offices
211112 Oil line drip, natural gas liquid
333913 Oil measuring and dispensing pumps manufacturing
424590 Oil nuts merchant wholesalers
237120 Oil pipeline construction
237120 Oil refinery construction
533110 Oil royalty companies
523910 Oil royalty dealing (i.e., acting as a principal in dealing royalties to investors)
533110 Oil royalty leasing
213112 Oil sampling services on a contract basis
339991 Oil seals manufacturing
211111 Oil shale mining and/or beneficiating
562910 Oil spill cleanup services
332420 Oil storage tanks, heavy gauge metal, manufacturing
532412 Oil well drilling machinery and equipment rental or leasing
213111 Oil well drilling on a contract basis
213112 Oil well logging on a contract basis
423830 Oil well machinery and equipment merchant wholesalers
213112 Oil well rig building, repairing, and dismantling, on a contract basis
423830 Oil well supply houses merchant wholesalers
311613 Oil, animal, rendering
311221 Oil, corn crude and refined, made by wet milling corn
311225 Oil, olive, made from purchased oils
424710 Oil, petroleum, bulk stations and terminals
424720 Oil, petroleum, merchant wholesalers (except bulk stations, terminals)
311225 Oil, vegetable stearin, made from purchased oils
423930 Oil, waste, merchant wholesalers
324199 Oil-based additives made from refined petroleum
313320 Oilcloth manufacturing
313320 Oiling of purchased textiles and apparel
325998 Oils (e.g., cutting, lubricating), synthetic, manufacturing
325192 Oils made by distillation of coal tar

424490 Oils, cooking and salad, merchant wholesalers
324110 Oils, fuel, manufacturing
424990 Oils, inedible, animal or vegetable, merchant wholesalers
324191 Oils, lubricating petroleum, made from refined petroleum
325998 Oils, lubricating, synthetic, manufacturing
324191 Oils, petroleum lubricating, re-refining used
325613 Oils, soluble (i.e., textile finishing assistants), manufacturing
325411 Oils, vegetable and animal, medicinal, uncompounded, manufacturing
325191 Oils, wood, made by distillation of wood
111191 Oilseed and grain combination farming, field and seed production
424990 Oilseed cake and meal merchant wholesalers
333294 Oilseed crushing and extracting machinery manufacturing
111120 Oilseed farming (except soybean), field and seed production
424590 Oilseeds merchant wholesalers
212399 Oilstones mining and/or beneficiating
333911 Oil-well and oil-field pumps manufacturing
111219 Okra farming, field, bedding plant and seed production
623312 Old age homes without nursing care
923130 Old age survivors and disability programs
623312 Old soldiers' homes without nursing care
325222 Olefin fibers and filaments manufacturing
325110 Olefins made from refined petroleum or liquid hydrocarbons
325199 Oleic acid (i.e., red oil) manufacturing
325199 Oleic acid esters manufacturing
325188 Oleum (i.e., fuming sulfuric acid) manufacturing
111339 Olive farming
311225 Olive oil made from purchased oils
311223 Olive oil made in crushing mills
311421 Olives brined
311423 Olives, dried, made in dehydration plant
212325 Olivine, non-gem, mining and/or beneficiating
334511 Omnibearing instrumentation manufacturing
621111 Oncologists' offices (e.g., centers, clinics)
812922 One-hour photofinishing services
111219 Onion farming, field, bedding plant and seed production
311421 Onions pickled
518111 On-line access service providers
212319 Onyx marble crushed and broken stone mining and/or beneficiating
212311 Onyx marble mining or quarrying
512132 Open air motion picture theaters
711110 Opera companies
315991 Opera hats cut and sewn from purchased fabric (except apparel contractors)
315211 Opera hats, men's and boys', cut and sew apparel contractors
315212 Opera hats, women's, girls', and infants', cut and sew apparel contractors
711130 Opera singers, independent
927110 Operating and launching government satellites
339111 Operating room tables manufacturing
511210 Operating systems software, computer, packaged
541614 Operations research consulting services

236220 Operative builders (i.e., building on own land, for sale), commercial and institutional building
236210 Operative builders (i.e., building on own land, for sale), industrial building (except warehouses)
236117 Operative builders (i.e., building on own land, for sale), residential
236117 Operative builders (i.e., building on own land, for sale), single-family housing
325411 Ophthalmic agents, uncompounded, manufacturing
423460 Ophthalmic goods (except cameras) merchant wholesalers
339112 Ophthalmic instruments and apparatus (except laser surgical) manufacturing
621111 Ophthalmologists' offices (e.g., centers, clinics)
339112 Ophthalmometers and ophthalmoscopes manufacturing
541910 Opinion research services
325411 Opium and opium derivatives (i.e., basic chemicals) manufacturing
333314 Optical alignment and display instruments (except photographic) manufacturing
334112 Optical disk drives manufacturing
423460 Optical goods (except cameras) merchant wholesalers
446130 Optical goods stores (except offices of optometrists)
212399 Optical grade calcite mining and/or beneficiating
333314 Optical gun sighting and fire control equipment and instruments manufacturing
811219 Optical instrument repair and maintenance services (e.g. microscopes, telescopes)
333298 Optical lens making and grinding machinery manufacturing
334119 Optical readers and scanners manufacturing
518210 Optical scanning services
333314 Optical test and inspection equipment manufacturing
334413 Optoelectronic devices manufacturing
339112 Optometers manufacturing
423460 Optometric equipment and supplies merchant wholesalers
813920 Optometrists' associations
621320 Optometrists' offices (e.g., centers, clinics)
621210 Oral and maxillofacial surgeons' offices (e.g., centers, clinics)
325412 Oral contraceptive preparations manufacturing
621210 Oral pathologists' offices (e.g., centers, clinics)
111310 Orange groves
325998 Orange oil manufacturing
115112 Orchard cultivation services (e.g., bracing, planting, pruning, removal, spraying, surgery)
111998 Orchard grass seed farming
711510 Orchestra conductors, independent
711130 Orchestras
454113 Order taking offices of mail-order houses
561422 Order-taking for clients over the internet
423990 Ordnance and accessories merchant wholesalers
236210 Ore and metal refinery construction
423520 Ore concentrates merchant wholesalers
333131 Ore crushing, washing, screening, and loading machinery manufacturing
423520 Ores (e.g., gold, iron, lead, silver, zinc) merchant wholesalers
621991 Organ banks, body

621991 Organ donor centers, body
424690 Organic chemicals merchant wholesalers
325222 Organic fibers and filaments (except cellulosic) manufacturing
325132 Organic pigments, dyes, lakes, and toners manufacturing
541612 Organization development consulting services
928120 Organization for Economic Coperation and Development
928120 Organization of American States
326199 Organizers for closets, drawers, and shelves, plastics, manufacturing
711310 Organizers of agricultural fairs with facilities
711320 Organizers of agricultural fairs without facilities
711310 Organizers of arts events with facilities
711320 Organizers of arts events without facilities
711310 Organizers of festivals with facilities
711320 Organizers of festivals without facilities
711310 Organizers of live performing arts productions (e.g., concerts) with facilities
711320 Organizers of live performing arts productions (e.g., concerts) without facilities
711310 Organizers of sports events with facilities
711320 Organizers of sports events without facilities
325199 Organo-inorganic compound manufacturing
325320 Organo-phosphate based insecticides manufacturing
321219 Oriented strandboard (OSB) manufacturing
327420 Ornamental and architectural plaster work (e.g., columns, mantels, molding) manufacturing
112511 Ornamental fish production, farm raising
423390 Ornamental ironwork merchant wholesalers
238190 Ornamental metal work installation
332323 Ornamental metalwork manufacturing
111422 Ornamental plant growing
561730 Ornamental tree and shrub services
321918 Ornamental woodwork (e.g., cornices, mantels) manufacturing
339999 Ornaments, Christmas tree (except electric, glass), manufacturing
335129 Ornaments, Christmas tree, electric, manufacturing
327212 Ornaments, Christmas tree, glass, made in glass making plants
327215 Ornaments, Christmas tree, made from purchased glass
623990 Orphanages
325998 Orris oil manufacturing
325192 Orthodichlorobenzene manufacturing
339116 Orthodontic appliance, custom made in dental laboratories
339114 Orthodontic appliances manufacturing
621210 Orthodontists' offices (e.g., centers, clinics)
339113 Orthopedic canes manufacturing
339113 Orthopedic device manufacturing and sale in retail environment
339113 Orthopedic devices manufacturing
423450 Orthopedic equipment and supplies merchant wholesalers
339113 Orthopedic extension shoes manufacturing
339113 Orthopedic hosiery, elastic, manufacturing
622310 Orthopedic hospitals
621111 Orthopedic physicians' offices (e.g., centers, clinics)

327420 Orthopedic plaster, gypsum, manufacturing
316219 Orthopedic shoes (except extension shoes), children's, manufacturing
316213 Orthopedic shoes (except extension shoes), men's, manufacturing
316214 Orthopedic shoes (except extension shoes), women's, manufacturing
448210 Orthopedic shoes stores
621111 Orthopedic surgeons' offices (e.g., centers, clinics)
321219 OSB (oriented strandboard) manufacturing
334515 Oscillators (e.g., instrument type audiofrequency and radiofrequency) manufacturing
334515 Oscilloscopes manufacturing
212299 Osmium mining and/or beneficiating
334516 Osmometers manufacturing
325998 Ossein manufacturing
622110 Osteopathic hospitals
621111 Osteopathic physicians' (except mental health) offices (e.g., centers, clinics)
112390 Ostrich production
621111 Otolaryngologists' offices (e.g., centers, clinics)
334510 Otoscopes, electromedical, manufacturing
337121 Ottomans, upholstered, manufacturing
441222 Outboard motor dealers
811490 Outboard motor repair shops
333618 Outboard motors manufacturing
423910 Outboard motors merchant wholesalers
713990 Outdoor adventure operations (e.g., white water rafting) without accommodations
721214 Outdoor adventure retreats with accommodation facilities
541850 Outdoor display advertising services
423210 Outdoor furniture merchant wholesalers
237990 Outdoor recreation facility construction
451110 Outdoor sporting equipment stores
315191 Outerwear handknitted for the trade
424320 Outerwear, men's and boys', merchant wholesalers
424330 Outerwear, women's, children's, and infants', merchant wholesalers
335932 Outlet boxes, electrical wiring, manufacturing
335931 Outlets (i.e., receptacles), electrical, manufacturing
335931 Outlets, convenience, electrical, manufacturing
541850 Out-of-home media (i.e., display) advertising services
621420 Outpatient mental health centers and clinics (except hospitals)
621420 Outpatient treatment centers and clinics (except hospitals) for substance abuse (i.e., alcoholism, drug addiction)
621420 Outpatient treatment centers and clinics for alcoholism
621420 Outpatient treatment centers and clinics for drug addiction
541612 Outplacement consulting services
541990 Outplacement services
325612 Oven cleaners manufacturing
334512 Oven temperature controls, nonindustrial, manufacturing
811412 Oven, household-type, repair and maintenance services without retailing new ovens
236210 Oven, industrial plant, construction
423720 Ovens (except electric), household-type, merchant wholesalers
333294 Ovens, bakery, manufacturing
333319 Ovens, commercial-type, manufacturing
423440 Ovens, commercial-type, merchant wholesalers
423620 Ovens, electric household-type, merchant wholesalers

335221 Ovens, freestanding household-type, manufacturing
333994 Ovens, industrial process-type, manufacturing
423830 Ovens, industrial, merchant wholesalers
339111 Ovens, laboratory-type, manufacturing
335211 Ovens, portable household-type (except microwave and convection ovens), manufacturing
335221 Ovens, portable household-type convention and microwave, manufacturing
327215 Ovenware made from purchased glass
327212 Ovenware, glass, made in glass making plants
315211 Overall jackets, work, men's and boys', cut and sew apparel contractors
315225 Overall jackets, work, men's and boys', cut and sewn from purchased fabric (except apparel contractors)
315211 Overalls, work, men's and boys', cut and sew apparel contractors
315225 Overalls, work, men's and boys', cut and sewn from purchased fabric (except apparel contractors)
213113 Overburden removal for coal mining on a contract basis
213114 Overburden removal for metal mining on a contract basis
213115 Overburden removal for nonmetallic minerals mining (except fuels) on a contract basis
315211 Overcoats, men's and boys', cut and sew apparel contractors
315222 Overcoats, men's and boys', cut and sewn from purchased fabric (except apparel contractors)
315212 Overcoats, women's, girls', and infants', cut and sew apparel contractors
315234 Overcoats, women's, misses', and girls', cut and sewn from purchased fabric (except apparel contractors)
333922 Overhead conveyors manufacturing
238290 Overhead door, commercial- or industrial-type, installation
238350 Overhead door, residential-type, installation
333315 Overhead projectors (except computer peripheral) manufacturing
334119 Overhead projectors, computer peripheral-type, manufacturing
333923 Overhead traveling cranes manufacturing
237310 Overpass construction
316211 Overshoes, plastics or plastics soled fabric upper, manufacturing
316211 Overshoes, rubber, or rubber soled fabric, manufacturing
325199 Oxalates (e.g., ammonium oxalate, ethyl oxalate, sodium oxalate) manufacturing
325199 Oxalic acid manufacturing
532291 Oxygen equipment rental (i.e. home use)
325120 Oxygen manufacturing
339112 Oxygen tents manufacturing
114112 Oyster dredging
112512 Oyster production, farm raising
212399 Ozokerite mining and/or beneficiating
333319 Ozone machines for water purification manufacturing
621999 Pacemaker monitoring services
334510 Pacemakers manufacturing
326299 Pacifiers, rubber, manufacturing
713990 Pack trains (i.e., trail riding), recreational
445310 Package stores (i.e., liquor)
511210 Packaged computer software publishers
326112 Packaging film, plastics, single-web or multiweb, manufacturing
115114 Packaging fresh or farm-dried fruits and vegetables

541420 Packaging industrial design services
333993 Packaging machinery manufacturing
423840 Packaging material merchant wholesalers
561910 Packaging services (except packing and crating for transportation)
326150 Packaging, foam plastics (except polystyrene), manufacturing
326199 Packaging, plastics (e.g., blister, bubble), manufacturing
325998 Packer's fluids manufacturing
488991 Packing and preparing goods for shipping
321920 Packing cases, wood, nailed or lock corner, manufacturing
321920 Packing crates, wood, manufacturing
115114 Packing fruits and vegetables
423830 Packing machinery and equipment merchant wholesalers
423840 Packing materials merchant wholesalers
813940 PACs (Political Action Committees)
316211 Pacs, plastics or plastics soled fabric upper, manufacturing
316211 Pacs, rubber or rubber soled fabric upper, manufacturing
322232 Padded envelopes manufacturing
314999 Padding and wadding (except nonwoven fabric) manufacturing
424310 Paddings, apparel, merchant wholesalers
321999 Paddles, wood, manufacturing
332510 Padlocks, metal, manufacturing
314129 Pads and protectors (e.g., ironing board, mattress, table), textile, made from purchased fabrics or felts
313230 Pads and wadding, nonwoven, manufacturing
322211 Pads, corrugated and solid fiberboard, made from purchased paper or paperboard
322233 Pads, desk, made from purchased paper
321999 Pads, excelsior, wood, manufacturing
322291 Pads, incontinent and bed, manufacturing
332999 Pads, soap impregnated scouring, manufacturing
321999 Pads, table, rattan, reed, and willow, manufacturing
443112 Pager and mobile phone stores
334220 Pagers manufacturing
517211 Paging services
321920 Pails, coopered wood, manufacturing
326199 Pails, plastics, manufacturing
321920 Pails, plywood, manufacturing
321920 Pails, wood, manufacturing
621498 Pain therapy centers and clinics, outpatient
325510 Paint and varnish removers manufacturing
238320 Paint and wallpaper stripping
333994 Paint baking and drying ovens manufacturing
339994 Paint rollers manufacturing
424950 Paint rollers merchant wholesalers
811121 Paint shops, automotive
333991 Paint spray guns, handheld pneumatic, manufacturing
333912 Paint sprayers (i.e., compressor and spray gun unit) manufacturing
332999 Paint sticks, metal, manufacturing
326199 Paint sticks, plastics, manufacturing
321999 Paint sticks, wood, manufacturing
444120 Paint stores
325510 Paint thinner and reducer preparations manufacturing
325510 Paintbrush cleaners manufacturing
339994 Paintbrushes manufacturing

424950 Paintbrushes merchant wholesalers
711510 Painters (i.e., artists), independent
424950 Painter's supplies (except artists', turpentine) merchant wholesalers
238320 Painting (except roof) contractors
238320 Painting and wallpapering
237310 Painting lines on highways, streets and bridges
332812 Painting metals and metal products for the trade
711510 Painting restorers, independent
237310 Painting traffic lanes or parking lots
238160 Painting, spraying, or coating, roof
325510 Paints (except artist's) manufacturing
424950 Paints (except artists') merchant wholesalers
339942 Paints, artist's, manufacturing
424990 Paints, artist's, merchant wholesalers
325510 Paints, emulsion (i.e., latex paint), manufacturing
325510 Paints, oil and alkyd vehicle, manufacturing
315192 Pajamas made in apparel knitting mills
315291 Pajamas, infants', cut and sewn from purchased fabric (except apparel contractors)
315211 Pajamas, men's and boys', cut and sew apparel contractors
315221 Pajamas, men's and boys', cut and sewn from purchased fabric (except apparel contractors)
315231 Pajamas, women's and girls', cut and sewn from purchased fabric (except apparel contractors)
315212 Pajamas, women's, girls', and infants', cut and sew apparel contractors
339942 Palettes, artist's, manufacturing
212299 Palladium mining and/or beneficiating
321920 Pallet containers, wood or wood and metal combination, manufacturing
333924 Pallet movers manufacturing
333924 Pallet or skid jacks manufacturing
332999 Pallet parts, metal, manufacturing
321920 Pallet parts, wood, manufacturing
532490 Pallet rental or leasing
423830 Pallets and skids merchant wholesalers
322211 Pallets, corrugated and solid fiber, made from purchased paper or paperboard
332999 Pallets, metal, manufacturing
321920 Pallets, wood or wood and metal combination, manufacturing
812990 Palm reading services
325199 Palmitic acid esters and amines manufacturing
311225 Palm-kernel oil made from purchased oils
311223 Palm-kernel oil, cake, and meal made in crushing mills
323121 Pamphlet binding without printing
511130 Pamphlet publishers (except exclusive Internet publishing)
511130 Pamphlet publishers and printing combined
516110 Pamphlet publishers, exclusively on Internet
424920 Pamphlets merchant wholesalers
323117 Pamphlets printing and binding without publishing
323117 Pamphlets printing without publishing
315991 Panama hats cut and sewn from purchased fabric (except apparel contractors)
315211 Panama hats, men's and boys', cut and sew apparel contractors

315212 Panama hats, women's, girls', and infants', cut and sew apparel contractors
311822 Pancake mixes made from purchased flour
311999 Pancake syrups (except pure maple) manufacturing
311412 Pancakes, frozen, manufacturing
238310 Panel or rigid board insulation installation
321918 Panel work, wood millwork, manufacturing
238390 Panel, metal, installation
334513 Panelboard indicators, recorders, and controllers, receiver industrial process-type, manufacturing
335313 Panelboards, electric power distribution, manufacturing
423610 Panelboards, electric power distribution, merchant wholesalers
238350 Paneling installation
423310 Paneling merchant wholesalers
236117 Panelized housing, residential, assembled on site by operative builders
236116 Panelized multifamily housing assembled on site by general contractors
236117 Panelized multifamily housing assembled on site by operative builders
236115 Panelized single-family house assembly on site by general contractors
335313 Panels, generator control and metering, manufacturing
321211 Panels, hardwood plywood, manufacturing
332311 Panels, prefabricated metal building, manufacturing
321992 Panels, prefabricated wood building, manufacturing
321212 Panels, softwood plywood, manufacturing
315192 Panties made in apparel knitting mills
315291 Panties, infants', cut and sewn from purchased fabric (except apparel contractors)
315212 Panties, women's and girls', cut and sew apparel contractors
315231 Panties, women's, misses', and girls', cut and sewn from purchased fabric (except apparel contractors)
315239 Pants outfits (except pantsuits), women's, misses', and girls', cut and sewn from purchased fabric (except apparel contractors)
315212 Pants outfits, women's, girls', and infants', cut and sew apparel contractors
315211 Pants, althletic, men's and boys', cut and sew apparel contractors
315291 Pants, athletic, infants', cut and sewn from purchased fabric (except apparel contractors)
315191 Pants, athletic, made in apparel knitting mills
315228 Pants, athletic, men's and boys' (e.g., gymnastic, ski), cut and sewn from purchased fabric (except apparel contractors)
315212 Pants, athletic, women's, girls', and infants', cut and sew apparel contractors
315239 Pants, athletic, women's, misses', and girls', cut and sewn from purchased fabric (except apparel contractors)
315211 Pants, dress, men's and boys', cut and sew apparel contractors
315224 Pants, dress, men's and boys', cut and sewn from purchased fabric (except apparel contractors)
315291 Pants, infants' waterproof, cut and sewn from purchased fabric (except apparel contractors)
315212 Pants, infants', cut and sew apparel contractors

315291 Pants, infants', cut and sewn from purchased fabric (except apparel contractors)
315292 Pants, leather (except apparel contractors), manufacturing
315211 Pants, leather, men's and boys', cut and sew apparel contractors
315211 Pants, men's and boys', cut and sew apparel contractors
315191 Pants, outerwear, made in apparel knitting mills
315299 Pants, rubber and rubberized fabric, made in the same establishment as the basic material
315291 Pants, sweat, infant's, cut and sewn from purchased fabric (except apparel contractors)
315228 Pants, sweat, men's and boys', cut and sewn from purchased fabric (except apparel contractors)
315212 Pants, sweat, women's, girls', and infants', cut and sew apparel contractors
315239 Pants, sweat, women's, misses', and girls', cut and sewn from purchased fabric (except apparel contractors)
315211 Pants, unisex sweat, cut and sew apparel contractors
315228 Pants, unisex sweat, cut and sewn from purchased fabric (except apparel contractors)
315299 Pants, vulcanized rubber, manufacturing
315299 Pants, waterproof outerwear (except infants'), cut and sewn from purchased fabric (except apparel contractors)
315211 Pants, waterproof outerwear, men's and boys', cut and sew apparel contractors
315212 Pants, waterproof outerwear, women's, girls', and infants', cut and sew apparel contractors
315212 Pants, women's, girls', and infants', cut and sew apparel contractors
315239 Pants, women's, misses', and girls', cut and sewn from purchased fabric (except apparel contractors)
315211 Pants, work (except dungarees, jeans), men's and boys', cut and sew apparel contractors
315225 Pants, work (except dungarees, jeans), men's and boys', cut and sewn from purchased fabric (except apparel contractors)
315291 Pantsuits, infants', cut and sewn from purchased fabric (except apparel contractors)
315212 Pantsuits, women's, girls', and infants', cut and sew apparel contractors
315234 Pantsuits, women's, misses', and girls', cut and sewn from purchased fabric (except apparel contractors)
315212 Panty girdles cut and sew apparel contractors
315231 Panty girdles, women's, misses', and girls', cut and sewn from purchased fabric (except apparel contractors)
315111 Panty hose, women's and girls', knitting or knitting and finishing
111339 Papaya farming
327910 Paper (e.g., aluminum oxide, emery, garnet, silicon carbide), abrasive coated, made from purchased paper
424110 Paper (e.g., fine, printing, writing), bulk, merchant wholesalers
322121 Paper (except newsprint, uncoated groundwood) manufacturing
322121 Paper (except newsprint, uncoated groundwood) products made in paper mills

322121 Paper (except newsprint, uncoated groundwood), coated, laminated or treated, made in paper mills
424130 Paper (except office supplies, printing paper, stationery, writing paper) merchant wholesalers
333291 Paper and paperboard coating and finishing machinery manufacturing
333291 Paper and paperboard converting machinery manufacturing
333291 Paper and paperboard corrugating machinery manufacturing
333291 Paper and paperboard cutting and folding machinery manufacturing
333291 Paper and paperboard die-cutting and stamping machinery manufacturing
423830 Paper and pulp industries manufacturing machinery merchant wholesalers
333291 Paper bag making machinery manufacturing
424130 Paper bags merchant wholesalers
322223 Paper bags, coated, made from purchased paper
322224 Paper bags, uncoated, made from purchased paper
212324 Paper clay mining and/or beneficiating
332618 Paper clips made from purchased wire
331222 Paper clips, iron or steel, made in wire drawing plants
322215 Paper cups made from purchased paper or paperboard
339942 Paper cutters, office-type, manufacturing
322299 Paper dishes (e.g., cups, plates) made from molded pulp
322215 Paper dishes (e.g., cups, plates) made from purchased paper or paperboard
315212 Paper dresses, women's, girls', and infants', cut and sew apparel contractors
315233 Paper dresses, women's, misses, and girls', cut and sewn from purchased fabric (except apparel contractors)
313221 Paper fabric, narrow woven, weaving
313210 Paper fabrics, broadwoven, weaving
332618 Paper machine wire cloth made from purchased wire
333291 Paper making machinery manufacturing
811310 Paper making machinery repair and maintenance services
322121 Paper mills (except newsprint, uncoated groundwood paper mills)
322122 Paper mills, newsprint
322122 Paper mills, uncoated groundwood
322291 Paper napkins and tablecloths made from purchased paper
322299 Paper novelties made from purchased paper
236210 Paper or pulp mill construction
322215 Paper plates made from purchased paper or paperboard
322299 Paper products (except office supply), die-cut, made from purchased paper or paperboard
322231 Paper products, die-cut office supply, made from purchased paper or paperboard
332992 Paper shells (i.e., 30 mm. or less, 1.18 inch or less) manufacturing
322121 Paper stock for conversion into paper products (e.g., bag and sack stock, envelope stock, tissue stock, wallpaper stock) manufacturing
322291 Paper towels made from purchased paper
322121 Paper towels made in paper mills
313111 Paper yarn manufacturing

322121 Paper, asphalt, made in paper mills
423390 Paper, building, merchant wholesalers
339944 Paper, carbon, manufacturing
322211 Paper, corrugated, made from purchased paper or paperboard
523110 Paper, dealing of commercial (i.e., acting as principal in dealing securities to investors)
322122 Paper, newsprint and uncoated groundwood, manufacturing
424120 Paper, office (e.g., carbon, computer, copier, typewriter), merchant wholesalers
325992 Paper, photographic sensitized, manufacturing
423930 Paper, scrap, merchant wholesalers
339944 Paper, stencil, manufacturing
322130 Paperboard (e.g., can/drum stock, container board, corrugating medium, folding carton stock, linerboard, tube) manufacturing
424130 Paperboard and paperboard products (except office supplies) merchant wholesalers
333291 Paperboard box making machinery manufacturing
322130 Paperboard coating, laminating, or treating in paperboard mills
333291 Paperboard making machinery manufacturing
322130 Paperboard mills
322130 Paperboard products (e.g., containers) made in paperboard mills
322226 Paperboard, pasted, lined, laminated, or surface coated, made from purchased paperboard
238320 Paperhanging and removal contractors
238320 Paperhanging or removal contractors
327999 Papier-mache statuary and related art goods (e.g., urns, vases) manufacturing
713990 Para sailing, recreational
314999 Parachutes manufacturing
213112 Paraffin services, oil and gas field, on a contract basis
324110 Paraffin waxes made in petroleum refineries
325110 Paraffins made from refined petroleum or liquid hydrocarbons
541199 Paralegal services
321213 Parallel strand lumber manufacturing
621399 Paramedics' offices (e.g., centers, clinics)
325132 Pararosaniline dyes manufacturing
621511 Parasitology health laboratories
339999 Parasols manufacturing
325320 Parathion insecticides manufacturing
485991 Paratransit transportation services
561431 Parcel mailing services combined with one or more other office support services, private
561431 Parcel mailing services, private
333997 Parcel post scales manufacturing
316110 Parchment leather manufacturing
922150 Pardon boards and offices
624190 Parenting support services
813410 Parent-teachers' associations
325320 Paris green insecticides manufacturing
237990 Park and recreational open space improvement construction
922120 Park police
332812 Parkerizing metals and metal products for the trade
236220 Parking garage construction
812930 Parking garages, automobile
561790 Parking lot cleaning (e.g., power sweeping, washing) services
237310 Parking lot marking and line painting
238990 Parking lot paving and sealing

812930 Parking lots, automobile
334514 Parking meters manufacturing
561612 Parking security services
488119 Parking services, aircraft
812930 Parking services, valet
713110 Parks (e.g., theme, water), amusement
924120 Parks and recreation commission, government
712190 Parks, national
712190 Parks, nature
712130 Parks, wild animal
237310 Parkway construction
611310 Parochial schools, college level
611110 Parochial schools, elementary or secondary
922150 Parole offices
238330 Parquet flooring installation
321918 Parquet flooring, hardwood, manufacturing
321918 Parquetry, hardwood, manufacturing
111219 Parsley farming, field, bedding plant and seed production
111219 Parsnip farming, field, bedding plant and seed production
335999 Particle accelerators, high voltage, manufacturing
334516 Particle beam excitation instruments, laboratory-type, manufacturing
334516 Particle size analyzers manufacturing
321219 Particleboard manufacturing
423310 Particleboard merchant wholesalers
238390 Partition (e.g., office, washroom), metal, installation
238390 Partition, moveable and/or demountable, installation
337215 Partitions for floor attachment, prefabricated, manufacturing
423440 Partitions merchant wholesalers
322211 Partitions, corrugated and solid fiber, made from purchased paper or paperboard
337215 Partitions, freestanding, prefabricated, manufacturing
332323 Partitions, ornamental metal, manufacturing
441310 Parts and accessories dealers, automotive
423120 Parts, new, motor vehicle, merchant wholesalers
423140 Parts, used, motor vehicle, merchant wholesalers
453220 Party goods (e.g., paper supplies, decorations, novelties) stores
532299 Party (i.e., banquet) equipment rental
454390 Party plan merchandisers, direct selling
812990 Party planning services
532299 Party rental supply centers
481211 Passenger air transportation, nonscheduled
481111 Passenger air transportation, scheduled
333922 Passenger baggage belt loaders (except industrial truck) manufacturing
532112 Passenger car leasing
532111 Passenger car rental
481211 Passenger carriers, air, nonscheduled
481111 Passenger carriers, air, scheduled
485320 Passenger limousine rental with driver (except shuttle service, taxi)
482111 Passenger railways, line-haul
336611 Passenger ship building
483114 Passenger transportation, coastal or Great Lakes (including St. Lawrence Seaway)
483114 Passenger transportation, deep sea, to and from domestic ports (including Puerto Rico)
483112 Passenger transportation, deep sea, to or from foreign ports
483212 Passenger transportation, inland waters (except on Great Lakes system)
532112 Passenger van leasing
532111 Passenger van rental
532111 Passenger van rental agencies
485320 Passenger van rental with driver (except shuttle service, taxi)
532112 Passenger vehicle fleet leasing

111339 Passion fruit farming
928120 Passport issuing services
541921 Passport photography services
311422 Pasta based products canning
333294 Pasta making machinery (i.e., food manufacturing-type) manufacturing
311999 Pasta mixes made from purchased dry ingredients
311823 Pasta, dry, manufacturing
311991 Pasta, fresh, manufacturing
331314 Paste made from purchased aluminum
331423 Paste made from purchased copper
331221 Paste made from purchased iron or steel
331111 Paste, iron or steel, made in iron and steel mills
331492 Paste, nonferrous metals (except aluminum, copper), made from purchased metal
325520 Pastes, adhesive, manufacturing
311421 Pastes, fruit and vegetable, canning
333294 Pasteurizing equipment, food, manufacturing
311511 Pasteurizing milk
311612 Pastrami made from purchased carcasses
311812 Pastries (e.g., Danish, French), fresh, made in commercial bakeries
311813 Pastries (e.g., Danish, French), frozen, manufacturing
311822 Pastries, uncooked, manufacturing
321999 Pastry boards, wood, manufacturing
541199 Patent agent services (i.e., patent filing and searching services)
541110 Patent attorneys' offices
541110 Patent attorneys' private practices
541990 Patent broker services (i.e., patent marketing services)
533110 Patent buying and licensing
533110 Patent leasing
316110 Patent leather manufacturing
325412 Patent medicine preparations manufacturing
621511 Pathological analysis laboratories
621111 Pathologists' (except oral, speech, voice) offices (e.g., centers, clinics)
621111 Pathologists', forensic, offices (e.g., centers, clinics)
621111 Pathologists', neuropathological, offices (e.g., centers, clinics)
621210 Pathologists', oral, offices (e.g., centers, clinics)
621340 Pathologists', speech or voice, offices (e.g., centers, clinics)
621111 Pathologists', surgical, offices (e.g., centers, clinics)
621511 Pathology laboratories, medical
334510 Patient monitoring equipment (e.g., intensive care, coronary care unit) manufacturing
423450 Patient monitoring equipment merchant wholesalers
327331 Patio block, concrete, manufacturing
238990 Patio construction
336611 Patrol boat building
561612 Patrol services, security
541990 Patrolling (i.e., visual inspection) of electric transmission or gas lines
511199 Pattern and plan (e.g., clothing patterns) publishers (except exclusive Internet publishing)
511199 Pattern and plan (e.g., clothing patterns) publishers and printing combined
516110 Pattern and plan (e.g., clothing patterns) publishers, exclusively on Internet
332997 Patterns (except shoe), industrial, manufacturing
423830 Patterns (except shoe), industrial, merchant wholesalers
323112 Patterns and plans (e.g., clothing patterns) flexographic printing without publishing

323111 Patterns and plans (e.g., clothing patterns) gravure printing without publishing
323110 Patterns and plans (e.g., clothing patterns) lithographic (offset) printing without publishing
323119 Patterns and plans (e.g., clothing patterns) printing (except flexographic, gravure, lithographic, blueprinting, quick, screen) without publishing
323113 Patterns and plans (e.g., clothing patterns) screen printing without publishing
339999 Patterns, shoe, manufacturing
423850 Patterns, shoe, merchant wholesalers
237310 Pavement, highway, road, street, bridge or airport runway, construction
238990 Paver, brick (e.g., driveway, patio, sidewalk), installation
212399 Pavers mining and/or beneficiating
324121 Paving blocks and mixtures made from purchased asphaltic materials
327331 Paving blocks, concrete, manufacturing
327121 Paving brick, clay, manufacturing
333120 Paving machinery manufacturing
238990 Paving, residential and commercial driveway and parking lot
522298 Pawnshops
515210 Pay-per-view cable programming
812990 Pay telephone equipment concession operators
515210 Pay television networks
541214 Payroll processing services
334210 PBX (private branch exchange) equipment manufacturing
111219 Pea (except dry) farming, field and seed production
111130 Pea farming, dry, field and seed production
813319 Peace advocacy organizations
928120 Peace Corps
111339 Peach farming
325132 Peacock blue lake manufacturing
311911 Peanut butter blended with jelly manufacturing
311911 Peanut butter manufacturing
311223 Peanut cake, meal, and oil made in crushing mills
333111 Peanut combines (i.e., diggers, packers, threshers) manufacturing
111992 Peanut farming
311225 Peanut oil made from purchased oils
333294 Peanut roasting machines (i.e., food manufacturing-type) manufacturing
115114 Peanut shelling
115113 Peanut, machine harvesting
111339 Pear farming
339913 Pearl drilling, peeling, or sawing
325131 Pearl essence pigment, synthetic, manufacturing
331511 Pearlitic castings, malleable iron, unfinished, manufacturing
423940 Pearls merchant wholesalers
339914 Pearls, costume, manufacturing
212399 Peat grinding
212399 Peat humus mining and/or beneficiating
212399 Peat mining and/or beneficiating
327999 Peat pots, molded pulp, manufacturing
212321 Pebbles (except grinding) mining and/or beneficiating
212399 Pebbles grinding
111335 Pecan farming
115114 Pecan hulling and shelling
311942 Pectin manufacturing
621111 Pediatricians' (except mental health) offices (e.g., centers, clinics)
621112 Pediatricians', mental health, offices (e.g., centers, clinics)

812113 Pedicure and manicure salons
812113 Pedicurist services
115210 Pedigree (i.e., livestock, pets, poultry) record services
334514 Pedometers manufacturing
813920 Peer review boards
212325 Pegmatite, feldspar, mining and/ or beneficiating
316999 Pegs, leather shoe, manufacturing
332994 Pellet guns manufacturing
333131 Pellet mills machinery, mining-type, manufacturing
332992 Pellets, air rifle and pistol, manufacturing
316110 Pelts bleaching, currying, dyeing, scraping, and tanning
424590 Pelts, raw, merchant wholesalers
339112 Pelvimeters manufacturing
339941 Pen refills and cartridges manufacturing
339942 Pencil leads manufacturing
339942 Pencil sharpeners manufacturing
321999 Pencil slats, wood, manufacturing
339942 Pencils (except mechanical) manufacturing
424120 Pencils merchant wholesalers
339941 Pencils, mechanical, manufacturing
335122 Pendant lamps (except residential), electric, manufacturing
335121 Pendant lamps fixtures, residential electric, manufacturing
325613 Penetrants manufacturing
325998 Penetrating fluids, synthetic, manufacturing
325412 Penicillin preparations manufacturing
325411 Penicillin, uncompounded, manufacturing
922140 Penitentiaries
236220 Penitentiary construction
212113 Pennsylvania anthracite mining and/or beneficiating
339941 Pens manufacturing
424120 Pens, writing, merchant wholesalers
523920 Pension fund managing
524292 Pension fund, third party administrative services
525110 Pension funds
525110 Pension plans (e.g., employee benefit, retirement)
332313 Penstocks, fabricated metal plate, manufacturing
325192 Pentachlorophenol manufacturing
325199 Pentaerythritol manufacturing
325110 Pentanes made from refined petroleum or liquid hydrocarbons
325110 Pentenes made from refined petroleum or liquid hydrocarbons
325920 Pentolite explosive materials manufacturing
561330 PEO (professional employer organizations)
111219 Pepper (e.g., bell, chili, green, hot, red, sweet) farming
311942 Pepper (i.e., spice) manufacturing
325998 Peppermint oil manufacturing
313210 Percales weaving
114111 Perch fishing
325188 Perchloric acid manufacturing
325199 Perchloroethylene manufacturing
335211 Percolators, household-type electric, manufacturing
332992 Percussion caps (i.e., 30 mm. or less, 1.18 inch or less), ammunition, manufacturing
339992 Percussion musical instruments manufacturing
213112 Perforating oil and gas well casings on a contract basis
711510 Performers (i.e., entertainers), independent
711510 Performing artists, independent
711310 Performing arts center operators
611610 Performing arts schools (except academic)

325199 Perfume materials (i.e., basic synthetic chemicals, such as terpineol) manufacturing
446120 Perfume stores
325620 Perfumes manufacturing
424210 Perfumes merchant wholesalers
511120 Periodical publishers (except exclusive Internet publishing)
511120 Periodical publishers and printing combined
516110 Periodical publishers, exclusively on Internet
323112 Periodicals flexographic printing without publishing
323111 Periodicals gravure printing without publishing
323110 Periodicals lithographic (offset) printing without publishing
424920 Periodicals merchant wholesalers
323119 Periodicals printing (except flexographic, gravure, lithographic, quick, screen) without publishing
323113 Periodicals screen printing without publishing
621210 Periodontists' offices (e.g., centers, clinics)
334418 Peripheral controller boards manufacturing
423430 Peripheral equipment, computer, merchant wholesalers
333314 Periscopes manufacturing
327992 Perlite aggregates manufacturing
212399 Perlite mining and/or beneficiating
327992 Perlite, expanded, manufacturing
331524 Permanent mold castings, aluminum, unfinished, manufacturing
331525 Permanent mold castings, copper, unfinished, manufacturing
331528 Permanent mold castings, nonferrous metal (except alumninum, copper), unfinished, manufacturing
325620 Permanent wave preparations manufacturing
238130 Permanent wood foundation installation
325188 Peroxides, inorganic, manufacturing
325199 Peroxides, organic, manufacturing
325132 Persian orange lake manufacturing
111339 Persimmon farming
517212 Personal communication services (PCS) (i.e., communication carriers)
334418 Personal computer modems manufacturing
334111 Personal computers manufacturing
522291 Personal credit institutions (i.e., unsecured cash loans)
525920 Personal estates (i.e., managing assets)
522291 Personal finance companies (i.e., unsecured cash loans)
812990 Personal fitness trainer
339914 Personal goods, metal (except precious), manufacturing
551112 Personal holding companies
525920 Personal investment trusts
523991 Personal investments trust administration
523920 Personal investments trusts, managing
316993 Personal leather goods (e.g., coin purses, eyeglass cases, key cases), small, manufacturing
561612 Personal protection services (except security systems services)
339113 Personal safety devices, not specified elsewhere, manufacturing
424130 Personal sanitary paper products merchant wholesalers
812990 Personal shopping services
525920 Personal trusts
441221 Personal watercraft dealers
336999 Personal watercraft manufacturing

532292 Personal watercraft rental
561320 Personnel (e.g., industrial, office) suppliers
813920 Personnel management associations
541612 Personnel management consulting services
921190 Personnel offices, government
325320 Pest (e.g., ant, rat, roach, rodent) control poison manufacturing
561710 Pest control (except agricultural, forestry) services
926140 Pest control programs, agriculture, government
115112 Pest control services, agricultural
115310 Pest control services, forestry
424690 Pesticides (except agricultural) merchant wholesalers
325320 Pesticides manufacturing
424910 Pesticides, agricultural, merchant wholesalers
334510 PET (positron emission tomography) scanners manufacturing
812910 Pet boarding services
812220 Pet cemeteries
311119 Pet food (except cat, dog) manufacturing
424490 Pet food merchant wholesalers
311111 Pet food, dog and cat, manufacturing
812910 Pet grooming services
524128 Pet health insurance carriers, direct
541940 Pet hospitals
926150 Pet licensing
453910 Pet shops
812910 Pet sitting services
424990 Pet supplies (except pet food) merchant wholesalers
453910 Pet supply stores
812910 Pet training services
324110 Petrochemical feedstocks made in petroleum refineries
237120 Petrochemical plant construction
324110 Petrochemicals made in petroleum refineries
424710 Petroleum and petroleum products bulk stations and terminals
424720 Petroleum and petroleum products merchant wholesalers (except bulk stations, terminals)
425120 Petroleum brokers
324110 Petroleum coke made in petroleum refineries
324110 Petroleum cracking and reforming
324110 Petroleum distillation
541330 Petroleum engineering services
211112 Petroleum gases, liquefied, recovering from oil and gas field gases
324199 Petroleum jelly made from refined petroleum
324110 Petroleum jelly made in petroleum refineries
324191 Petroleum lubricating oils made from refined petroleum
324110 Petroleum lubricating oils made in petroleum refineries
486110 Petroleum pipelines, crude
486910 Petroleum pipelines, refined
325211 Petroleum polymer resins manufacturing
324110 Petroleum refineries
237120 Petroleum refinery construction
333298 Petroleum refining machinery manufacturing
332420 Petroleum storage tanks, heavy gauge metal, manufacturing
324199 Petroleum waxes made from refined petroleum
211111 Petroleum, crude, production (i.e., extraction)
424990 Pets merchant wholesalers
712130 Petting zoos
337127 Pews, church, manufacturing
339912 Pewter ware manufacturing
236210 Pharmaceutical manufacturing plant construction
325412 Pharmaceutical preparations (e.g., capsules, liniments, ointments, tablets) manufacturing

424210 Pharmaceuticals merchant wholesalers
446110 Pharmacies
813920 Pharmacists' associations
334515 Phase angle meters manufacturing
335312 Phase converters (i.e., electrical equipment) manufacturing
112390 Pheasant production
325192 Phenol manufacturing
325211 Phenol-formaldehyde resins manufacturing
325211 Phenol-furfural resins manufacturing
325211 Phenolic resins manufacturing
325211 Phenoxy resins manufacturing
813211 Philanthropic trusts, awarding grants
212399 Phlogopite mining and/or beneficiating
334510 Phonocardiographs manufacturing
334612 Phonograph records manufacturing
423990 Phonograph records merchant wholesalers
423440 Phonographs, coin-operated, merchant wholesalers
325199 Phosgene manufacturing
212392 Phosphate rock mining and/or beneficiating
325312 Phosphatic fertilizer materials manufacturing
325314 Phosphatic fertilizers made by mixing purchased materials
325132 Phosphomolybdic acid lakes and toners manufacturing
325199 Phosphoric acid esters manufacturing
325312 Phosphoric acid manufacturing
325188 Phosphorus compounds, not specified elsewhere by process, manufacturing
325188 Phosphorus oxychloride manufacturing
325132 Phosphotungstic acid lakes and toners manufacturing
323118 Photo albums and refills manufacturing
424120 Photo albums merchant wholesalers
711510 Photo journalists, independent (freelance)
323122 Photocomposition services, for the printing trade
424120 Photocopy supplies merchant wholesalers
811212 Photocopying machine repair and maintenance services without retailing new photocopying machines
333315 Photocopying machines manufacturing
561439 Photocopying services (except combined with printing services)
325992 Photocopying toner cartridges manufacturing
334413 Photoelectric cells, solid-state (e.g., electronic eye), manufacturing
333293 Photoengraving machinery manufacturing
323122 Photoengraving plate preparation services
423410 Photofinishing equipment merchant wholesalers
812921 Photofinishing labs (except one-hour)
812922 Photofinishing labs, one-hour
812921 Photofinishing services (except one-hour)
812922 Photofinishing services, one-hour
335110 Photoflash and photoflood lamp bulbs and tubes manufacturing
333315 Photoflash equipment manufacturing
541370 Photogrammetric mapping services
322299 Photograph folders, mats, and mounts manufacturing
541922 Photographers specializing in aerial photography
711510 Photographers, independent artistic
325992 Photographic chemicals manufacturing

333315 Photographic equipment (except lenses) manufacturing
423410 Photographic equipment and supplies merchant wholesalers
532210 Photographic equipment rental
811211 Photographic equipment repair shops without retailing new photographic equipment
423410 Photographic film merchant wholesalers
325992 Photographic film, cloth, paper, and plate, sensitized, manufacturing
333314 Photographic lenses manufacturing
812990 Photographic machine concession operators, coin-operated
443130 Photographic supply stores
326113 Photographic, micrographic, and X-ray plastics, sheet, and film (except sensitized), manufacturing
611610 Photography schools, art
611519 Photography schools, commercial
541922 Photography services, commercial
541921 Photography services, portrait (e.g., still, video)
541922 Photography studios, commercial
541921 Photography studios, portrait
327212 Photomask blanks, glass, made in glass making plants
325992 Photomasks manufacturing
334516 Photometers (except photographic exposure meters) manufacturing
334516 Photonexcitation analyzers manufacturing
325992 Photosensitized paper manufacturing
323122 Phototypesetting services
334413 Photovoltaic devices, solid-state, manufacturing
812990 Phrenology services
325199 Phthalate acid manufacturing
325211 Phthalic alkyd resins manufacturing
325192 Phthalic anhydride manufacturing
325211 Phthalic anhydride resins manufacturing
325132 Phthalocyanine pigments manufacturing
541614 Physical distribution consulting services
621340 Physical equestrian therapist offices (e.g., centers, clinics)
713940 Physical fitness centers
621999 Physical fitness evaluation services (except by offices of health practitioners)
713940 Physical fitness facilities
713940 Physical fitness studios
334519 Physical properties testing and inspection equipment manufacturing
622310 Physical rehabilitation hospitals
541710 Physical science research and development laboratories or services
621340 Physical therapists' offices (e.g., centers, clinics)
621340 Physical therapy offices (e.g., centers, clinics)
621340 Physical-integration practitioners' offices (e.g., centers, clinics)
621111 Physicians' (except mental health) offices (e.g., centers, clinics)
621399 Physicians' assistants' offices (e.g., centers, clinics)
621112 Physicians', mental health, offices (e.g., centers, clinics)
541690 Physics consulting services
541710 Physics research and development laboratories or services
621340 Physiotherapists' offices (e.g., centers, clinics)
339112 Physiotherapy equipment (except electrotherapeutic) manufacturing
325411 Physostigmine and derivatives (i.e., basic chemicals) manufacturing

332510 Piano hardware, metal, manufacturing
339992 Piano parts and materials (except piano hardware) manufacturing
532299 Piano rental
451140 Piano stores
339992 Piccolos and parts manufacturing
333292 Picker machinery for textiles manufacturing
333292 Picker sticks for looms manufacturing
311712 Picking crab meat
333516 Picklers and pickling machinery, metalworking, manufacturing
311421 Pickles manufacturing
311421 Pickling fruits and vegetables
332813 Pickling metals and metal products for the trade
332212 Picks (i.e., handtools) manufacturing
812320 Pickup and drop-off sites for drycleaners and laundries
336214 Pickup canopies, caps, or covers manufacturing
336112 Pick-up trucks, light duty, assembling on chassis of own manufacture
713990 Picnic grounds
326199 Picnic jugs, plastics (except foam), manufacturing
325920 Picric acid explosive materials manufacturing
334511 Pictorial situation instrumentation manufacturing
442299 Picture frame shops, custom
311822 Pie crust shells, uncooked, made from purchased flour
424310 Piece goods (except burlap, felt) merchant wholesalers
451130 Piece goods stores
424990 Piece goods, burlap and felt, merchant wholesalers
237990 Pier construction
531120 Piers and associated building rental or leasing
713110 Piers, amusement
424420 Pies (e.g., fruit, meat, poultry), frozen, merchant wholesalers
311812 Pies, fresh, made in commercial bakeries
311813 Pies, frozen, manufacturing
334419 Piezoelectric crystals manufacturing
334419 Piezoelectric devices manufacturing
112210 Pig farming
331111 Pig iron manufacturing
423510 Pig iron merchant wholesalers
325132 Pigment, scarlet lake, manufacturing
325132 Pigments (except animal black, bone black), organic, manufacturing
325131 Pigments (except bone black, carbon black, lamp black), inorganic, manufacturing
212393 Pigments, natural, mineral, mining and/or beneficiating
424950 Pigments, paint, merchant wholesalers
311612 Pig's feet, cooked and pickled, made from purchased carcasses
114111 Pilchard fishing
238910 Pile driving, building foundation
237990 Pile driving, marine
313249 Pile fabrics made in warp knitting mills
313241 Pile fabrics made in weft knitting mills
332313 Pile shells, fabricated metal plate, manufacturing
332322 Pile shells, sheet metal (except stampings), manufacturing
333120 Pile-driving equipment manufacturing
238910 Piling (i.e., bored, cast-in-place, drilled), building foundation, contractors
321114 Pilings, foundation and marine construction, treating
331111 Pilings, iron or steel plain sheet, made in iron and steel mills
321114 Pilings, round wood, cutting and treating

321114 Pilings, wood, treating
332991 Pillow blocks with ball or roller bearings manufacturing
812320 Pillow cleaning services
314129 Pillowcases, bed, made from purchased fabrics
314129 Pillows, bed, made from purchased materials
488490 Pilot car services (i.e., wide load warning services)
488330 Piloting services, water transportation
713120 Pinball arcades
713990 Pinball machine concession operators (i.e., supplying and servicing in others' facilities)
339999 Pinball machines, coin-operated, manufacturing
113210 Pine gum extracting
325191 Pine oil manufacturing
111339 Pineapple farming
325191 Pinene manufacturing
713990 Ping pong parlors
212325 Pinite mining and/or beneficiating
339993 Pins (except precious) manufacturing
339911 Pins and brooches, precious metal, manufacturing
712120 Pioneer villages
331210 Pipe (e.g., heavy riveted, lock joint, seamless, welded) made from purchased iron or steel
332996 Pipe and pipe fittings made from purchased metal pipe
331511 Pipe and pipe fittings, cast iron, manufacturing
333516 Pipe and tube rolling mill machinery, metalworking, manufacturing
332323 Pipe bannisters, metal, manufacturing
326299 Pipe bits and stems, tobacco, hard rubber, manufacturing
339999 Pipe cleaners manufacturing
332996 Pipe couplings made from purchased metal pipe
331511 Pipe couplings, cast iron, manufacturing
238290 Pipe covering
333512 Pipe cutting and threading machines, metalworking, manufacturing
332996 Pipe fabricating (i.e., bending, cutting, threading) made from purchased metal pipe
238220 Pipe fitting contractors
326122 Pipe fittings, rigid plastics, manufacturing
332323 Pipe guards, metal, manufacturing
332999 Pipe hangers and supports, metal, manufacturing
332996 Pipe headers made from purchased metal pipe
237120 Pipe lining (except thermal insulating) contractors
331316 Pipe made by extruding purchased aluminum
332323 Pipe railings, metal, manufacturing
325520 Pipe sealing compounds manufacturing
213112 Pipe testing services, oil and gas field, on a contract basis
424940 Pipe tobacco merchant wholesalers
312229 Pipe tobacco, prepared, manufacturing
331316 Pipe, aluminum, made in integrated secondary smelting and extruding mills
327332 Pipe, concrete, manufacturing
238290 Pipe, duct and boiler insulation
331421 Pipe, extruded and drawn, brass, bronze, and copper, made from purchased copper or in integrated secondary smelting and rolling, drawing or extruding plants
332313 Pipe, fabricated metal plate, manufacturing
331111 Pipe, iron or steel, made in iron and steel mills
423510 Pipe, metal, merchant wholesalers
331491 Pipe, nonferrous metals (except aluminum, copper), made from purchased metals or scrap

326122 Pipe, rigid plastics, manufacturing
332322 Pipe, sheet metal (except stampings), manufacturing
515112 Piped-in music services, radio transmitted
237990 Pipe-jacking contractors
237120 Pipeline construction on oil and gas field gathering lines to point of distribution on a contract basis
541990 Pipeline inspection (i.e., visual) services
423830 Pipeline machinery and equipment merchant wholesalers
237120 Pipeline rehabilitation contractors
488999 Pipeline terminal facilities, independently operated
486990 Pipeline transportation (except crude oil, natural gas, refined petroleum products)
486110 Pipeline transportation, crude oil
486910 Pipeline transportation, gasoline and other refined petroleum products
486210 Pipeline transportation, natural gas
237120 Pipeline wrapping contractors
237120 Pipeline, gas and oil, construction
339992 Pipes, organ, manufacturing
339999 Pipes, smoker's, manufacturing
212399 Pipestones mining and/or beneficiating
111335 Pistachio farming
332994 Pistols manufacturing
336311 Pistons and piston rings manufacturing
423830 Pistons, hydraulic and pneumatic, merchant wholesalers
325192 Pitch made by distillation of coal tar
324122 Pitch, roofing, made from purchased asphaltic materials
325191 Pitch, wood, manufacturing
212291 Pitchblende mining and/or beneficiating
334519 Pitometers manufacturing
325411 Pituitary gland derivatives, uncompounded, manufacturing
325412 Pituitary gland preparations manufacturing
722211 Pizza delivery shops
311822 Pizza doughs made from purchased flour
722110 Pizza parlors, full service
722211 Pizza parlors, limited-service
424490 Pizzas (except frozen) merchant wholesalers
311991 Pizzas, fresh, manufacturing
311412 Pizzas, frozen, manufacturing
424420 Pizzas, frozen, merchant wholesalers
722110 Pizzerias, full service
722211 Pizzerias, limited-service (e.g., take-out)
314129 Placemats, all materials, made from purchased materials
561310 Placement agencies or services, employment
621991 Placenta banks
212221 Placer gold mining and/or beneficiating
212222 Placer silver mining and/or beneficiating
813110 Places of worship
238120 Placing and tying reinforcing rod at a construction site
334417 Planar cable connectors manufacturing
333210 Planers woodworking-type, stationary, manufacturing
333120 Planers, bituminous, manufacturing
333991 Planers, handheld power-driven, manufacturing
333512 Planers, metalworking, manufacturing
332212 Planes, handheld, nonpowered, manufacturing
712110 Planetariums
321912 Planing mills (except millwork)
321918 Planing mills, millwork
321912 Planing purchased lumber

525120 Plans, health and welfare related employee benefit
522190 Plans, Morris (i.e., known as), depository
522298 Plans, Morris (i.e., known as), nondepository
525110 Plans, pension
561730 Plant and shrub maintenance in buildings
424990 Plant food merchant wholesalers
325311 Plant foods, mixed, made in plants producing nitrogenous fertilizer materials
325312 Plant foods, mixed, made in plants producing phosphatic fertilizer materials
325320 Plant growth regulants manufacturing
561730 Plant maintenance services
111422 Plant, ornamental, growing
111422 Plant, potted flower and foliage, growing
111339 Plantain farming
115112 Planting crops
423820 Planting machinery and equipment, farm-type, merchant wholesalers
333111 Planting machines, farm-type, manufacturing
333513 Plasma jet spray metal forming machines manufacturing
333512 Plasma process metal cutting machines (except welding equipment) manufacturing
333992 Plasma welding equipment manufacturing
621991 Plasmapheresis centers
325414 Plasmas manufacturing
424210 Plasmas, blood, merchant wholesalers
327420 Plaster and plasterboard, gypsum, manufacturing
423320 Plaster merchant wholesalers
327420 Plaster of paris manufacturing
327420 Plaster of paris products (e.g., columns, statuary, urns) manufacturing
327420 Plaster, gypsum, manufacturing
238310 Plastering (i.e., ornamental, plain) contractors
212325 Plastic fire clay mining and/or beneficiating
621111 Plastic surgeons' offices (e.g., centers, clinics)
325510 Plastic wood fillers manufacturing
325199 Plasticizers (i.e., basic synthetic chemicals) manufacturing
424610 Plasticizers merchant wholesalers
337125 Plastics (including fiberglass) furniture (except upholstered), household-type, manufacturing
326220 Plastics and rubber belts and hoses (without fittings) manufacturing
325211 Plastics and synthetic resins regenerating, precipitating, and coagulating
424130 Plastics bags merchant wholesalers
424610 Plastics basic shapes (e.g., film, rod, sheet, sheeting, tubing) merchant wholesalers
313320 Plastics coating of textiles and apparel
326113 Plastics film and unlaminated sheet (except packaging) manufacturing
424610 Plastics foam merchant wholesalers
423840 Plastics foam packing and packaging materials merchant wholesalers
424990 Plastics foam products (except disposable) merchant wholesalers
424130 Plastics foam products, disposable (except packaging, packing), merchant wholesalers
315299 Plastics gowns (except infants') cut and sewn from purchased fabric (except apparel contractors)
315291 Plastics gowns, infants', cut and sewn from purchased fabric (except apparel contractors)

315211 Plastics gowns, men's and boys', cut and sew apparel contractors
315212 Plastics gowns, women's, girls', and infants, cut and sew apparel contractors
423830 Plastics industries machinery, equipment, and supplies merchant wholesalers
337110 Plastics laminated over particleboard (e.g., fixture tops) manufacturing
424610 Plastics materials merchant wholesalers
315299 Plastics rainwear cut and sewn from purchased fabric (except apparel contractors)
315211 Plastics rainwear, men's and boys', cut and sewn apparel contractors
315212 Plastics rainwear, women's, girls', and infants', cut and sew apparel contractors
325991 Plastics resins compounding from recycled materials
424610 Plastics resins merchant wholesalers
325991 Plastics resins, custom compounding of purchased
423930 Plastics scrap merchant wholesalers
333220 Plastics working machinery manufacturing
325510 Plastisol coating compounds manufacturing
524126 Plate glass insurance carriers, direct
423390 Plate glass merchant wholesalers
333516 Plate rolling mill machinery, metalworking, manufacturing
332313 Plate work (e.g., bending, cutting, punching, shaping, welding), fabricated metal, manufacturing
331315 Plate, aluminum, made by continuous casting purchased aluminum
331315 Plate, aluminum, made by flat rolling purchased aluminum
331315 Plate, aluminum, made in integrated secondary smelting and continuous casting mills
331315 Plate, aluminum, made in integrated secondary smelting and flat rolling mills
331421 Plate, copper and copper alloy, made from purchased copper or in integrated secondary smelting and rolling, drawing or extruding plants
331111 Plate, iron or steel, made in iron and steel mills
326130 Plate, laminated plastics, manufacturing
331491 Plate, nonferrous metals (except aluminum, copper), made from purchased metals or scrap
332211 Plated metal cutlery manufacturing
423940 Plated metal cutlery or flatware merchant wholesalers
332211 Plated metal flatware manufacturing
332999 Plated ware (e.g., ecclesiastical ware, hollowware, toilet ware) manufacturing
335932 Plates (i.e., outlet or switch covers), face, manufacturing
322299 Plates, molded pulp, manufacturing
326140 Plates, polystyrene foam, manufacturing
332813 Plating metals and metal products for the trade
331491 Platinum and platinum alloy rolling, drawing, or extruding from purchased metals or scrap
331491 Platinum and platinum alloy sheet and tubing made from purchased metals or scrap
332999 Platinum foil and leaf not made in rolling mills
212299 Platinum mining and/or beneficiating
331492 Platinum recovering from scrap and/or alloying purchased metals

331419 Platinum refining, primary
237990 Play ground construction
423910 Playground equipment and supplies merchant wholesalers
238990 Playground equipment installation
423920 Playing cards merchant wholesalers
337124 Playpens, children's metal, manufacturing
337122 Playpens, children's wood, manufacturing
315291 Playsuits, infants', cut and sewn from purchased fabric (except apparel contractors)
315212 Playsuits, women's, girls', and infants', cut and sew apparel contractors
315239 Playsuits, women's, misses', and girls', cut and sewn from purchased fabric (except apparel contractors)
711510 Playwrights, independent
532292 Pleasure boat rental
336612 Pleasure boats manufacturing
423910 Pleasure boats merchant wholesalers
315211 Pleating contractors on men's and boys' apparel
315212 Pleating contractors on women's, girls', and infants' apparel
332212 Pliers, handtools, manufacturing
327331 Plinth blocks, precast terrazzo, manufacturing
334119 Plotters, computer, manufacturing
115112 Plowing
333120 Plows, construction (e.g., excavating, grading), manufacturing
423820 Plows, farm, merchant wholesalers
333111 Plows, farm-type, manufacturing
111422 Plug (i.e., floriculture products) growing
332911 Plug valves, industrial-type, manufacturing
213112 Plugging and abandoning wells on a contract basis
335931 Plugs, electric cord, manufacturing
332999 Plugs, magnetic metal drain, manufacturing
321999 Plugs, wood, manufacturing
111339 Plum farming
238220 Plumbers
611513 Plumbers' apprenticeship training
423720 Plumbers' brass goods merchant wholesalers
332212 plumbers' handtools, nonpowered, manufacturing
325520 plumbers' putty manufacturing
238220 Plumbing and heating contractors
332919 Plumbing and heating inline valves (e.g., check, cutoffs, stop) manufacturing
423720 Plumbing and heating valves merchant wholesalers
238220 Plumbing contractors
423720 Plumbing equipment merchant wholesalers
532490 Plumbing equipment rental or leasing
332913 Plumbing fittings and couplings (e.g., compression fittings, metal elbows, metal unions) manufacturing
332913 Plumbing fixture fittings and trim, all materials, manufacturing
238220 Plumbing fixture installation
326191 Plumbing fixtures (e.g., shower stalls, toilets, urinals), plastics or fiberglass, manufacturing
423720 Plumbing fixtures merchant wholesalers
332998 Plumbing fixtures, metal, manufacturing
327111 Plumbing fixtures, vitreous china, manufacturing
423720 Plumbing supplies merchant wholesalers
444190 Plumbing supply stores
423310 Plywood merchant wholesalers

321211 Plywood, faced with nonwood materials, hardwood, manufacturing

321212 Plywood, faced with nonwood materials, softwood, manufacturing

321211 Plywood, hardwood faced, manufacturing

321211 Plywood, hardwood, manufacturing

321212 Plywood, softwood faced, manufacturing

321212 Plywood, softwood, manufacturing

332912 Pneumatic aircraft subassemblies manufacturing

334513 Pneumatic controllers, industrial process type, manufacturing

238290 Pneumatic conveyance system installation

333995 Pneumatic cylinders, fluid power, manufacturing

326220 Pneumatic hose (without fittings), rubber or plastics, manufacturing

332912 Pneumatic hose fittings, fluid power, manufacturing

423830 Pneumatic pumps and parts merchant wholesalers

333996 Pneumatic pumps, fluid power, manufacturing

334512 Pneumatic relays, air-conditioning-type, manufacturing

333922 Pneumatic tube conveyors manufacturing

332912 Pneumatic valves, fluid power, manufacturing

322231 Pocket folders made from purchased paper or paperboard

332211 Pocket knives manufacturing

339911 Pocketbooks, precious metal, manufacturing

339911 Pocketbooks, precious metal, men's, manufacturing

339911 Pocketbooks, precious metal, women's, manufacturing

315211 Pockets (e.g., coat, suit), men's and boys', cut and sew apparel contractors

315212 Pockets (e.g., coat, suit), women's, girls', and infants', cut and sew apparel contractors

621391 Podiatrists' offices (e.g., centers, clinics)

813410 Poetry clubs

711510 Poets, independent

334119 Point of sale terminals manufacturing

423420 Point of sale terminals merchant wholesalers

334119 Pointing devices, computer peripheral equipment, manufacturing

315292 Pointing furs

339114 Points, abrasive dental, manufacturing

334516 Polariscopes manufacturing

334516 Polarizers manufacturing

334516 Polarographic equipment manufacturing

238990 Pole (e.g., telephone) removal

237130 Pole line construction

423610 Pole line hardware merchant wholesalers

327390 Poles, concrete, manufacturing

423510 Poles, metal, merchant wholesalers

321114 Poles, round wood, cutting and treating

321113 Poles, wood, made from log or bolts

321114 Poles, wood, treating

922120 Police academies

922120 Police and fire departments, combined

315991 Police caps and hats (except protective head gear) cut and sewn from purchased fabric (except apparel contractors)

315211 Police caps and hats (except protective head gear), men's, cut and sew apparel contractors

315212 Police caps and hats (except protective head gear), women's, cut and sew apparel contractors

922120 Police departments (except American Indian or Alaska Native)
315222 Police dress uniforms, men's, cut and sewn from purchased fabric (except apparel contractors)
315234 Police dress uniforms, women's, cut and sewn from purchased fabric (except apparel contractors)
453998 Police supply stores
611519 Police training schools
315211 Police uniforms, men's, cut and sew apparel contractors
315212 Police uniforms, women's, cut and sew apparel contractors
921150 Police, American Indian or Alaska Native tribal
311212 Polished rice manufacturing
333991 Polishers, handheld power-driven, manufacturing
325612 Polishes (e.g., automobile, furniture, metal, shoe) manufacturing
424690 Polishes (e.g., automobile, furniture, metal, shoe, stove) merchant wholesalers
333512 Polishing and buffing machines, metalworking, manufacturing
332813 Polishing metals and metal products for the trade
325612 Polishing preparations manufacturing
327910 Polishing wheels manufacturing
813940 Political action committees (PACs)
813940 Political campaign organizations
711510 Political cartoonists, independent
541820 Political consulting services
541910 Political opinion polling services
813940 Political organizations or clubs
813940 Political parties
115112 Pollinating
114111 Pollock fishing
423830 Pollution control equipment (except air) merchant wholesalers
423730 Pollution control equipment, air, merchant wholesalers
924110 Pollution control program administration
541380 Pollution testing (except automotive emissions testing) services
315191 Polo shirts made in apparel knitting mills
315211 Polo shirts, men's and boys', cut and sew apparel contractors
315223 Polo shirts, men's and boys', cut and sewn from purchased fabric (except apparel contractors)
315212 Polo shirts, women's, girls', and infants', cut and sew apparel contractors
315232 Polo shirts, women's, misses', and girls', cut and sewn from purchased fabric (except apparel contractors)
325211 Polyacrylonitrile resins manufacturing
325211 Polyamide resins manufacturing
325211 Polycarbonate resins manufacturing
325222 Polyester fibers and filaments manufacturing
313112 Polyester filament yarn throwing, twisting, texturizing, or winding of purchased yarn
326113 Polyester film and unlaminated sheet (except packaging) manufacturing
325211 Polyester resins manufacturing
313111 Polyester spun yarns made from purchased fiber
313113 Polyester thread manufacturing
326113 Polyethylene film and unlaminated sheet (except packaging) manufacturing
325211 Polyethylene resins manufacturing
325212 Polyethylene rubber manufacturing
325211 Polyethylene terephathalate (PET) resins manufacturing

325222 Polyethylene terephthalate (PET) fibers and filaments manufacturing
334519 Polygraph machines manufacturing
561611 Polygraph services
325211 Polyhexamethylenediamine adipamide resins manufacturing
325199 Polyhydric alcohol esters and amines manufacturing
325199 Polyhydric alcohols manufacturing
325211 Polyisobutylene resins manufacturing
325212 Polyisobutylene rubber manufacturing
325212 Polyisobutylene-isoprene rubber manufacturing
325211 Polymethacrylate resins manufacturing
325212 Polymethylene rubber manufacturing
325222 Polyolefin fibers and filaments manufacturing
313112 Polypropylene filament yarn throwing, twisting, texturizing, or winding of puchased yarn
326113 Polypropylene film and unlaminated sheet (except packaging) manufacturing
325211 Polypropylene resins manufacturing
313111 Polypropylene spun yarns made from purchased fiber
238310 Polystyrene board insulation installation
326140 Polystyrene foam packaging manufacturing
325211 Polystyrene resins manufacturing
325212 Polysulfide rubber manufacturing
325211 Polytetrafluoroethylene resins manufacturing
325510 Polyurethane coatings manufacturing
326150 Polyurethane foam products manufacturing
325211 Polyurethane resins manufacturing
325211 Polyvinyl alcohol resins manufacturing
325211 Polyvinyl chloride (PVC) resins manufacturing
325222 Polyvinyl ester fibers and filaments manufacturing
326113 Polyvinyl film and unlaminated sheet (except packaging) manufacturing
325211 Polyvinyl halide resins manufacturing
325211 Polyvinyl resins manufacturing
325222 Polyvinylidene chloride (i.e., saran) fibers and filaments manufacturing
111339 Pomegranate farming
315299 Ponchos and similar waterproof raincoats (except infants') cut and sewn from purchased fabric (except apparel contractors)
315291 Ponchos and similar waterproof raincoats, infants', cut and sewn from purchased fabric (except apparel contractors)
315211 Ponchos and similar waterproof raincoats, men's and boys', cut and sew apparel contractors
315212 Ponchos and similar waterproof raincoats, women's, girls', and infants', cut and sew apparel contractors
112920 Pony production
423910 Pool (billiards) supplies merchant wholesalers
423910 Pool (swimming) and equipment merchant wholesalers
713990 Pool halls
713990 Pool parlors
713990 Pool rooms
312111 Pop, soda, manufacturing
311919 Popcorn (except candy covered), popped, manufacturing
311999 Popcorn (except popped) manufacturing

311340 Popcorn balls manufacturing
111150 Popcorn farming, field and seed production
424450 Popcorn merchant wholesalers
335211 Popcorn poppers, household-type electric, manufacturing
311340 Popcorn, candy covered popped, manufacturing
313210 Poplins weaving
621391 Popopediatricians' offices (e.g., centers, clinics)
711130 Popular musical artists, independent
711130 Popular musical groups
532120 Popup camper rental
327113 Porcelain parts, electrical and electronic device, molded, manufacturing
327112 Porcelain, chemical, manufacturing
236118 Porch construction, residential-type
337122 Porch furniture (except upholstered), wood, manufacturing
337920 Porch shades, wood slat, manufacturing
337124 Porch swings, metal, manufacturing
321918 Porch work (e.g., columns, newels, rails, trellises), wood, manufacturing
114111 Porgy fishing
311422 Pork and beans canning
311611 Pork carcasses, half carcasses, and primal and sub-primal cuts produced in slaughtering plants
311919 Pork rinds manufacturing
311612 Pork, primal and sub-primal cuts, made from purchased carcasses
926120 Port authorities and districts, nonoperating
237990 Port facility construction
488310 Port facility operation
332311 Portable buildings, prefabricated metal, manufacturing
332998 Portable chemical toilets, metal, manufacturing
334111 Portable computers manufacturing
335211 Portable cooking appliances (except convection, microwave ovens), household-type electric, manufacturing
335211 Portable electric space heaters manufacturing
335211 Portable hair dryers, electric, manufacturing
335211 Portable humidifiers and dehumidifiers manufacturing
334290 Portable intrusion detection and signaling devices manufacturing
334310 Portable stereo systems manufacturing
334515 Portable test meters manufacturing
562991 Portable toilet pumping (i.e., cleaning) services
562991 Portable toilet renting and/or servicing
326191 Portable toilets, plastics, manufacturing
518112 Portals, web search
312120 Porter brewing
424810 Porter merchant wholesalers
812990 Porter services
523920 Portfolio fund managing
541921 Portrait photography services
541921 Portrait photography studios
621512 Positron emission tomography (PET) scanner centers
334511 Position indicators (e.g., for landing gear, stabilizers), airframe equipment, manufacturing
336312 Positive crankcase ventilation (PCV) valves, engine, manufacturing
334514 Positive displacement meters manufacturing
334510 Positron emission tomography (PET) scanners manufacturing
238130 Post frame contractors
332212 Post hole diggers, nonpowered, manufacturing
333120 Post hole diggers, powered, manufacturing

236220 Post office construction
333997 Post office-type scales manufacturing
333313 Postage meters manufacturing
423420 Postage meters merchant wholesalers
333311 Postage stamp vending machines manufacturing
491110 Postal delivery services, local, operated by U.S. Postal Service
491110 Postal delivery services, local, operated on a contract basis
337215 Postal service lock boxes manufacturing
491110 Postal services operated by U.S. Postal Service
491110 Postal stations operated by U.S. Postal Service
491110 Postal stations operated on a contract basis
511199 Postcard publishers (except exclusive Internet publishing)
511199 Postcard publishers and printing combined
516110 Postcard publishers, exclusively on Internet
323112 Postcards flexographic printing without publishing
323111 Postcards gravure printing without publishing
323110 Postcards lithographic (offset) printing without publishing
424120 Postcards merchant wholesalers
323119 Postcards printing (except flexographic, gravure, lithographic, quick, screen) without publishing
323113 Postcards screen printing without publishing
511199 Poster publishers (except exclusive Internet publishing)
511199 Poster publishers and printing combined
516110 Poster publishers, exclusively on Internet
323112 Posters flexographic printing without publishing
323111 Posters gravure printing without publishing
323110 Posters lithographic (offset) printing without publishing
323119 Posters printing (except flexographic, digital, gravure, lithographic, quick, screen) without publishing
323113 Posters screen printing without publishing
238990 Posthole digging
323121 Postpress services (e.g., beveling, bronzing, folding, gluing, edging, foil stamping, gilding) on printed materials
512191 Post-production facilities, motion picture or video
327390 Posts, concrete, manufacturing
321114 Posts, round wood, cutting and treating
321114 Posts, wood, treating
512191 Post-synchronization sound dubbing
311412 Pot pies, frozen, manufacturing
212391 Potash mining and/or beneficiating
325314 Potassic fertilizers made by mixing purchased materials
325188 Potassium aluminum sulfate manufacturing
325188 Potassium bichromate and chromate manufacturing
325199 Potassium bitartrate manufacturing
325188 Potassium bromide manufacturing
212391 Potassium bromide, natural, mining and/or beneficiating
325181 Potassium carbonate manufacturing
325188 Potassium chlorate manufacturing
325188 Potassium chloride manufacturing
212391 Potassium chloride mining and/ or beneficiating
212391 Potassium compounds prepared at beneficiating plants
212391 Potassium compounds, natural, mining and/or beneficiating
325188 Potassium cyanide manufacturing

325181 Potassium hydroxide manufacturing
325188 Potassium hypochlorate manufacturing
325188 Potassium inorganic compounds, not specified elsewhere by process, manufacturing
325188 Potassium iodide manufacturing
325188 Potassium nitrate manufacturing
325199 Potassium organic compounds, not specified elsewhere by process, manufacturing
325188 Potassium permanganate manufacturing
325188 Potassium salts manufacturing
212391 Potassium salts, natural, mining and/or beneficiating
325188 Potassium sulfate manufacturing
424450 Potato chips and related snacks merchant wholesalers
311919 Potato chips manufacturing
115114 Potato curing
333111 Potato diggers, harvesters, and planters manufacturing
111211 Potato farming, field and seed potato production
311211 Potato flour manufacturing
332214 Potato mashers manufacturing
311999 Potato mixes made from purchased dry ingredients
311423 Potato products (e.g., flakes, granules) dehydrating
311221 Potato starches manufacturing
311919 Potato sticks manufacturing
311991 Potatoes, peeled or cut, manufacturing
334515 Potentiometric instruments (except industrial process-type) manufacturing
334513 Potentiometric instruments (except X-Y recorders), industrial process-type, manufacturing
237310 Pothole filling, highway, road, street or bridge
339999 Potpourri manufacturing
332420 Pots (e.g., annealing, melting, smelting), heavy gauge metal, manufacturing
332214 Pots and pans, fabricated metal, manufacturing
327124 Pots, glass-house, clay refractory, manufacturing
311612 Potted meats made from purchased carcasses
327112 Pottery made and sold on site
327112 Pottery products (except plumbing fixtures and porcelain electrical goods) manufacturing
325314 Potting soil manufacturing
311615 Poultry (e.g., canned, cooked, fresh, frozen) manufacturing
311615 Poultry (e.g., canned, cooked, fresh, frozen) processing
424440 Poultry and poultry products (except canned, packaged frozen) merchant wholesalers
333111 Poultry brooders, feeders, and waterers manufacturing
311615 Poultry canning (except baby, pet food)
115210 Poultry catching services
445210 Poultry dealers
423820 Poultry equipment merchant wholesalers
311119 Poultry feeds, supplements, and concentrates manufacturing
112340 Poultry hatcheries
332618 Poultry netting made from purchased wire
311615 Poultry slaughtering, dressing, and packing
424490 Poultry, canned, merchant wholesalers
424440 Poultry, live and dressed, merchant wholesalers
424420 Poultry, packaged frozen, merchant wholesalers
333991 Powder actuated handheld power tools manufacturing
332812 Powder coating metals and metal products for the trade
325510 Powder coatings manufacturing
331221 Powder made from purchased iron or steel
331314 Powder made from purchased aluminum

331423 Powder made from purchased copper
333513 Powder metal forming presses manufacturing
332117 Powder metallurgy products manufactured on a job or order basis
314999 Powder puffs and mitts manufacturing
331111 Powder, iron or steel, made in iron and steel mills
331492 Powder, nonferrous metals (except aluminum, copper), made from purchased metal
311999 Powdered drink mixes (except chocolate, coffee, tea, milk based) manufacturing
311514 Powdered milk manufacturing
325620 Powders (e.g., baby, body, face, talcum, toilet) manufacturing
311999 Powders, baking, manufacturing
333912 Power (i.e., pressure) washer units manufacturing
441222 Power boat dealers
238290 Power boiler, installation only
332410 Power boilers manufacturing
335313 Power circuit breakers manufacturing
335313 Power connectors manufacturing
335999 Power converter units (i.e., AC to DC), static, manufacturing
444210 Power equipment stores, outdoor
334515 Power factor meters manufacturing
335313 Power fuses (i.e., 600 volts and over) manufacturing
238290 Power generating equipment installation
221119 Power generation, electric (except fossil fuel, hydroelectric, nonhazardous solid waste, nuclear)
221112 Power generation, fossil fuel (e.g., coal, gas, oil), electric
221111 Power generation, hydroelectric
562213 Power generation, nonhazardous solid waste combustor or incinerator electric
221113 Power generation, nuclear electric
221119 Power generation, solar electric
221119 Power generation, tidal electric
221119 Power generation, wind electric
335312 Power generators manufacturing
423710 Power handtools (e.g., drills, sanders, saws) merchant wholesalers
812320 Power laundries, family
541990 Power line inspection (i.e., visual) services
237130 Power line stringing
334515 Power measuring equipment, electrical, manufacturing
237130 Power plant (except hydroelectric) construction
237990 Power plant, hydroelectric, construction
238910 Power shovel, construction, rental with operator
336330 Power steering hose assemblies manufacturing
336330 Power steering pumps manufacturing
335999 Power supplies, regulated and unregulated, manufacturing
335313 Power switchboards manufacturing
335313 Power switching equipment manufacturing
335311 Power transformers, electric, manufacturing
423610 Power transmission equipment, electrical, merchant wholesalers
423840 Power transmission supplies (e.g., gears, pulleys, sprockets), mechanical, merchant wholesalers
333319 Power washer cleaning equipment manufacturing
532490 Power washer rental or leasing
561790 Power washing building exteriors
336322 Power window and door lock systems, automotive, truck, and bus, manufacturing

238910 Power, communication and pipe line right of way clearance (except maintenance)
333991 Power-driven handtools manufacturing
212399 Pozzolana mining and/or beneficiating
621399 Practical nurses' offices (e.g., centers, clinics), licensed
315299 Prayer shawls cut and sewn from purchased fabric (except apparel contractors)
315191 Prayer shawls made in apparel knitting mills
315211 Prayer shawls, men's and boys', cut and sew apparel contractors
315212 Prayer shawls, women's, girls', and infants', cut and sew apparel contractors
327331 Precast concrete block and brick manufacturing
238120 Precast concrete panel, slab, or form installation
327332 Precast concrete pipe manufacturing
327390 Precast concrete products (except brick, block, pipe) manufacturing
423940 Precious and semiprecious stones merchant wholesalers
423940 Precious and semiprecious stones merchant wholesalers
331491 Precious metal bar, rod, sheet, strip, and tubing made from purchased metals or scrap
423940 Precious metals merchant wholesalers
331492 Precious metals recovering from scrap and/or alloying purchased metals
331419 Precious metals refining, primary
212399 Precious stones mining and/or beneficiating
811219 Precision equipment calibration
332212 Precision tools, machinist's (except optical), manufacturing
332721 Precision turned product manufacturing
236117 Precut housing, residential, assembled on site by operative builders
236116 Precut multifamily housing assembled on site by general contractors
236115 Precut single-family housing assembly on site by general contractors
334514 Predetermined counters manufacturing
444190 Prefabricated building dealers
423390 Prefabricated buildings (except wood) merchant wholesalers
332311 Prefabricated buildings, metal, manufacturing
423310 Prefabricated buildings, wood, merchant wholesalers
236220 Prefabricated commercial building erection
321992 Prefabricated homes (except mobile homes), wood, manufacturing
332311 Prefabricated homes, metal, manufacturing
236210 Prefabricated industrial building (except warehouses) erection
236220 Prefabricated institutional building erection
238350 Prefabricated kitchen and bath cabinet, residential-type, installation
238350 Prefabricated sash and door installation
321992 Prefabricated wood buildings manufacturing
238130 Prefabricated wood frame component (e.g., trusses) installation
321211 Prefinished hardwood plywood manufacturing
321212 Prefinished softwood plywood manufacturing
621410 Pregnancy counseling centers
325413 Pregnancy test kits manufacturing

624410 Pre-kindergarten centers (except part of elementary school system)
334611 Prepackaged software, mass reproducing
424990 Pre-paid calling card distribution, merchant wholesalers
517310 Pre-paid calling cards, telecommunications resellers
213112 Preparation of oil and gas field drilling sites (except site preparation and related construction contractor activities) on a contract basis
212113 Preparation plants, anthracite
611110 Preparatory schools, elementary or secondary
311822 Prepared flour mixes made from purchased flour
311211 Prepared flour mixes made in flour mills
424490 Prepared foods (except frozen) merchant wholesalers
424420 Prepared foods, frozen (except dairy products), merchant wholesalers
424430 Prepared foods, frozen dairy, merchant wholesalers
311991 Prepared meals, perishable, packaged for individual resale
311941 Prepared sauces (except gravy, tomato based) manufacturing
488991 Preparing goods for transportation (i.e., crating, packing)
323122 Prepress printing services (e.g., color separation, imagesetting, photocomposition, typesetting)
541350 Prepurchase home inspection services
423990 Prerecorded audio and video tapes and discs merchant wholesalers
512220 Prerecorded audio tapes and compact discs integrated manufacture, release, and distribution
334612 Pre-recorded magnetic audio tapes and cassettes mass reproducing
454113 Prerecorded tape, compact disc, and record mail-order houses
624410 Preschool centers
424210 Prescription drugs merchant wholesalers
111421 Preseeded mat farming
311421 Preserves (e.g., imitation) canning
321114 Preserving purchased wood and wood products
313311 Preshrinking broadwoven fabrics
313312 Preshrinking textile products and fabrics (except broadwoven)
921110 President's office, United States
325611 Presoaks manufacturing
333513 Press brakes, metalworking, manufacturing
519190 Press clipping services
332111 Press forgings made from purchased iron or steel, unfinished
332112 Press forgings made from purchased nonferrous metals, unfinished
424130 Pressed and molded pulp goods (e.g., egg cartons, shipping supplies) merchant wholesalers
313230 Pressed felts manufacturing
321999 Pressed logs of sawdust and other wood particles, nonpetroleum binder, manufacturing
333513 Presses (e.g., bending, punching, shearing, stamping), metal forming, manufacturing
333294 Presses (i.e., food manufacturing-type) manufacturing
333210 Presses for making composite woods (e.g., hardboard, medium density fiberboard (MDF), particleboard, plywood) manufacturing

333111 Presses, farm-type, manufacturing
333999 Presses, metal baling, manufacturing
333293 Presses, printing (except textile), manufacturing
321999 Pressing blocks, wood, tailor's, manufacturing
336350 Pressure and clutch plate assemblies, automotive, truck, and bus, manufacturing
334519 Pressure and vacuum indicators, aircraft engine, manufacturing
332911 Pressure control valves (except fluid power), industrial-type, manufacturing
332912 Pressure control valves, fluid power, manufacturing
334512 Pressure controllers, air-conditioning system-type, manufacturing
332214 Pressure cookers, household-type, manufacturing
334513 Pressure gauges (e.g., dial, digital), industrial process-type, manufacturing
334513 Pressure instruments, industrial process-type, manufacturing
327332 Pressure pipe, reinforced concrete, manufacturing
322222 Pressure sensitive paper and tape (except medical) made from purchased materials
334519 Pressure transducers manufacturing
321113 Pressure treated lumber made from logs or bolts and treated
321114 Pressure treated lumber made from purchased lumber
561790 Pressure washing (e.g., buildings, decks, fences)
334512 Pressurestats manufacturing
238120 Prestressed concrete beam, slab or other component installation
327331 Prestressed concrete blocks or bricks manufacturing
327332 Prestressed concrete pipes manufacturing
327390 Prestressed concrete products (except blocks, bricks, pipes) manufacturing
722213 Pretzel shops, on premise baking and carryout service
424490 Pretzels (except frozen) merchant wholesalers
311919 Pretzels (except soft) manufacturing
424420 Pretzels, frozen, merchant wholesalers
311812 Pretzels, soft, manufacturing
335129 Prewired poles, brackets, and accessories for electric lighting, manufacturing
926150 Price control agencies
111339 Prickly pear farming
331312 Primary aluminum production and manufacturing aluminum alloys
331312 Primary aluminum production and manufacturing aluminum shapes (e.g., bar, ingot, rod, sheet)
335912 Primary batteries manufacturing
334513 Primary elements for process flow measurement (i.e., orifice plates) manufacturing
334512 Primary oil burner controls (e.g., cadmium cells, stack controls) manufacturing
334513 Primary process temperature sensors manufacturing
331312 Primary refining of aluminum
331411 Primary refining of copper
331419 Primary refining of nonferrous metals (except aluminum, copper)
611110 Primary schools
331312 Primary smelting of aluminum
331411 Primary smelting of copper
331419 Primary smelting of nonferrous metals (except aluminum, copper)
335312 Prime mover generator sets (except turbine generator sets) manufacturing
332993 Primers (i.e., more than 30 mm., more than 1.18 inch), ammunition, manufacturing

325510 Primers, paint, manufacturing
323115 Print shops, digital
323119 Print shops, engraving
323112 Print shops, flexographic
323111 Print shops, gravure
323119 Print shops, letterpress
323110 Print shops, lithographic (offset) (except grey goods, manifold business forms, printing books, quick printing)
323114 Print shops, quick
323113 Print shops, screen
334418 Printed circuit assemblies manufacturing
334418 Printed circuit boards loading
423690 Printed circuit boards merchant wholesalers
334412 Printed circuit boards, bare, manufacturing
334419 Printed circuit laminates manufacturing
334119 Printers, computer, manufacturing
423430 Printers, computer, merchant wholesalers
323117 Printing and binding books without publishing
323117 Printing books without publishing
313311 Printing broadwoven fabrics grey goods
561990 Printing brokers
313312 Printing fabric grey goods (except broadwoven)
325910 Printing inks manufacturing
423840 Printing inks merchant wholesalers
333292 Printing machinery for textiles manufacturing
323116 Printing manifold business forms
424120 Printing paper (except bulk) merchant wholesalers
424110 Printing paper, bulk, merchant wholesalers
236210 Printing plant construction
333293 Printing plate engraving machinery manufacturing
323122 Printing plate preparation services
333293 Printing plates, blank (except photosentive), manufacturing
323121 Printing postpress services (e.g., beveling, bronzing, folding, gluing, edging, foil stamping) to printed products (e.g., books, cards, paper)
323122 Printing prepress services (e.g., color separation, imagesetting, photocomposition, typesetting)
333293 Printing press rollers manufacturing
333293 Printing presses (except textile) manufacturing
313312 Printing textile products (except apparel)
811310 Printing trade machinery repair and maintenance services
423830 Printing trade machinery, equipment, and supplies merchant wholesalers
323115 Printing, digital (e.g., billboards, other large format graphical materials)
323115 Printing, digital (e.g., graphics, high resolution)
323119 Printing, engraving, on paper products
323112 Printing, flexographic (except books, grey goods, manifold business forms)
323111 Printing, gravure (except books, grey goods, manifold business forms)
323119 Printing, letterpress (except books, grey goods, manifold business forms)
323110 Printing, lithographic (except books, grey goods, manifold business forms, quick printing)
323110 Printing, photo-offset (except books, grey goods, manifold business forms, printing books)
323114 Printing, quick
323113 Printing, screen (except books, manifold business forms, grey goods)
333314 Prisms, optical, manufacturing

337127 Prison bed manufacturing
236220 Prison construction
922140 Prison farms
922140 Prisons
522190 Private banks (i.e., unincorporated)
334210 Private branch exchange (PBX) equipment manufacturing
611310 Private colleges (except community or junior college)
561611 Private detective services
238210 Private driveway or parking area lighting contractors
525920 Private estates (i.e., administering on behalf of beneficiaries)
814110 Private households employing domestic personnel
814110 Private households with employees
561611 Private investigation services (except credit)
561431 Private mail centers
561431 Private mailbox rental centers
624190 Private parole offices
624190 Private probation offices
611110 Private schools, elementary or secondary
561990 Private volunteer fire fighting
493190 Private warehousing and storage (except farm products, general merchandise, refrigerated)
493130 Private warehousing and storage, farm products (except refrigerated)
493110 Private warehousing and storage, general merchandise
493120 Private warehousing and storage, refrigerated
451110 Pro shops (e.g., golf, skiing, tennis)
922150 Probation offices
212391 Probertite mining and/or quarrying
334510 Probes, electric medical, manufacturing
339112 Probes, surgical, manufacturing
325411 Procaine and derivatives (i.e., basic chemicals) manufacturing
334513 Process control instruments, industrial, manufacturing
238220 Process piping installation
541199 Process server services
541199 Process serving services
311513 Processed cheeses manufacturing
424470 Processed meats (e.g., luncheon, sausage) merchant wholesalers
311612 Processed meats manufacturing
424440 Processed poultry (e.g., luncheon) merchant wholesalers
311615 Processed poultry manufacturing
522320 Processing financial transactions
314999 Processing of textile mill waste and recovering fibers
621111 Proctologists' offices (e.g., centers, clinics)
424910 Produce containers merchant wholesalers
445230 Produce markets
445230 Produce stands, permanent
454390 Produce stands, temporary
424480 Produce, fresh, merchant wholesalers
813910 Producers' associations
711510 Producers, independent
561910 Product sterilization and packaging services
541380 Product testing laboratories or services
524128 Product warranty insurance carriers, direct
334514 Production counters manufacturing
541614 Production planning and control consulting services
541614 Productivity improvement consulting services
813920 Professional associations
711219 Professional athletes, independent (i.e., participating in sports events)
711211 Professional baseball clubs
323121 Professional book binding without printing

511130 Professional book publishers (except exclusive Internet publishing)
511130 Professional book publishers and printing combined
516110 Professional book publishers, exclusively on Internet
323117 Professional books printing and binding without publishing
323117 Professional books printing without publishing
611430 Professional development training
561330 Professional employer organizations (PEO)
423490 Professional equipment and supplies (except dental, medical, ophthalmic) merchant wholesalers
611691 Professional examination review instructions
711211 Professional football clubs
423490 Professional instruments merchant wholesalers
511120 Professional magazine and periodical publishers (except exclusive Internet publishing)
511120 Professional magazine and periodical publishers and printing combined
516110 Professional magazine and periodical publishers, exclusively on Internet
323112 Professional magazines and periodicals flexographic printing without publishing
323111 Professional magazines and periodicals gravure printing without publishing
323110 Professional magazines and periodicals lithographic (offset) printing without publishing
323119 Professional magazines and periodicals printing (except flexographic, gravure, lithographic, quick, screen) without publishing
323113 Professional magazines and periodicals screen printing without publishing
813920 Professional membership associations
531120 Professional office building rental or leasing
611310 Professional schools (e.g., business administration, dental, law, medical)
315211 Professional service apparel, washable, men's and boys', cut and sew apparel contractors
315225 Professional service apparel, washable, men's and boys', cut and sewn from purchased fabric (except apparel contractors)
315212 Professional service apparel, washable, women's, cut and sew apparel contractors
315239 Professional service apparel, washable, women's, misses', and girls', cut and sewn from purchased fabric (except apparel contractors)
611620 Professional sports (e.g., golf, skiing, swimming, tennis) instructors (i.e., not participating in sporting events)
711211 Professional sports clubs
711310 Professional sports promoters with facilities
711320 Professional sports promoters without facilities
813920 Professional standards review boards
326130 Profile shapes (e.g., plate, rod, sheet), laminated plastics, manufacturing
326121 Profile shapes (e.g., rod, tube), nonrigid plastics, manufacturing
525990 Profit-sharing funds
512110 Program producing, television
334513 Programmers, process-type, manufacturing

511210 Programming language and compiler software publishers, packaged
541511 Programming services, custom computer
332993 Projectiles (except guided missile), jet propulsion, manufacturing
333315 Projection equipment (e.g., motion picture, slide), photographic, manufacturing
423410 Projection equipment (e.g., motion picture, slide), photographic, merchant wholesalers
333314 Projection lenses manufacturing
333315 Projection screens (i.e., motion picture, overhead, slide) manufacturing
334310 Projection television manufacturing
332995 Projectors (e.g., antisub, depth charge release, grenade, livens, rocket), ordnance, manufacturing
711310 Promoters of agricultural fairs with facilities
711320 Promoters of agricultural fairs without facilities
711310 Promoters of arts events with facilities
711320 Promoters of arts events without facilities
561920 Promoters of conventions with or without facilities
711310 Promoters of festivals with facilities
711320 Promoters of festivals without facilities
711310 Promoters of live performing arts productions (e.g., concerts) with facilities
711320 Promoters of live performing arts productions (e.g., concerts) without facilities
711310 Promoters of sports events with facilities
711320 Promoters of sports events without facilities
561920 Promoters of trade fairs or shows with or without facilities
561410 Proofreading services
111421 Propagation material farming
424710 Propane bulk stations and terminals
324110 Propane gases made in petroleum refineries
211112 Propane recovered from oil and gas field gases
333518 Propeller straightening presses manufacturing
334514 Propeller type meters with registers manufacturing
332999 Propellers, ship and boat, made from purchased metal
524126 Property and casualty insurance carriers, direct
524130 Property and casualty reinsurance carriers
524126 Property damage insurance carriers, direct
531312 Property managers' offices, commercial real estate
531312 Property managers' offices, nonresidential real estate
531311 Property managers' offices, residential real estate
531312 Property managing, commercial real estate
531312 Property managing, nonresidential real estate
531311 Property managing, residential real estate
813990 Property owners' associations
561612 Property protection services (except armored car, security systems)
921130 Property tax assessors' offices
326299 Prophylactics manufacturing
112910 Propolis production, bees
336415 Propulsion units and parts, guided missile and space vehicle, manufacturing
325199 Propylcarbinol manufacturing
324110 Propylene (i.e., propene) made in petroleum refineries
325199 Propylene glycol manufacturing

325110 Propylene made from refined petroleum or liquid hydrocarbons
325211 Propylene resins manufacturing
213113 Prospect and test drilling services for coal mining on contract basis
213114 Prospect and test drilling services for metal mining on contract basis
213115 Prospect and test drilling services for nonmetallic mineral mining (except fuels) on a contract basis
339113 Prosthetic appliances and supplies manufacturing
423450 Prosthetic appliances and supplies merchant wholesalers
446199 Prosthetic stores
621210 Prosthodontists' offices (e.g., centers, clinics)
561612 Protection services (except armored car, security systems), personal or property
812332 Protective apparel supply services
523999 Protective committees, security holders
316211 Protective footwear, plastics or plastics-soled fabric upper, manufacturing
316211 Protective footwear, rubber or rubber-soled fabric upper, manufacturing
561612 Protective guard services
339920 Protectors, sports (e.g., baseball, basketball, hockey), manufacturing
334516 Protein analyzers, laboratory-type, manufacturing
325222 Protein fibers and filaments manufacturing
325211 Protein plastics manufacturing
712190 Provincial parks
334511 Proximity warning (i.e., collision avoidance) equipment manufacturing
111339 Prune farming
332212 Pruners manufacturing
311423 Prunes, dried, made in dehydration plants
115112 Pruning of orchard trees and vines
561730 Pruning services, ornamental tree and shrub
325131 Prussian blue pigments manufacturing
332212 Pry (i.e., crow) bars manufacturing
212299 Psilomelane mining and/or beneficiating
621420 Psychiatric centers and clinics (except hospitals), outpatient
623220 Psychiatric convalescent homes or hospitals
622210 Psychiatric hospitals (except convalescent)
621112 Psychiatrists' offices (e.g., centers, clinics)
812990 Psychic services
621330 Psychoanalysts' (except MDs or DOs) offices (e.g., centers, clinics)
621112 Psychoanalysts' (MDs or DOs) offices (e.g., centers, clinics)
813920 Psychologists' associations
621330 Psychologists' offices (e.g., centers, clinics), clinical
541720 Psychology research and development services
621330 Psychotherapists' (except MDs or DOs) offices (e.g., centers, clinics)
621112 Psychotherapists' (MDs or DOs) offices (e.g., centers, clinics)
541211 Public accountants' (CPAs) offices, certified
541211 Public accountants' (CPAs) private practices, certified
541219 Public accountants' (except CPAs) offices
541219 Public accountants' (except CPAs) private practices
238210 Public address system installation
532490 Public address system rental or leasing

811213 Public address system repair and maintenance services
334310 Public address systems and equipment manufacturing
423690 Public address systems and equipment merchant wholesalers
423210 Public building furniture merchant wholesalers
922130 Public defenders' offices
711410 Public figures' agents or managers
923120 Public health program administration, nonoperating
541910 Public opinion polling services
541910 Public opinion research services
921190 Public property management services, government
922130 Public prosecutors' offices
541820 Public relations agencies
541820 Public relations consulting services
541820 Public relations services
813319 Public safety advocacy organizations
922190 Public safety bureaus and statistics centers, government
922190 Public safety statistics centers, government
926130 Public service (except transportation) commissions, nonoperating
813410 Public speaking improvement clubs
611699 Public speaking training
561492 Public stenography services
926120 Public transportation commissions, nonoperating
926130 Public utility (except transportation) commissions, nonoperating
813910 Public utility associations
551112 Public utility holding companies
236220 Public warehouse construction
493190 Public warehousing and storage (except farm products, general merchandise, refrigerated, self storage)
493110 Public warehousing and storage (except self storage), general merchandise
493130 Public warehousing and storage, farm products (except refrigerated)
493120 Public warehousing and storage, refrigerated
511130 Publishers (except exclusive Internet publishing), book
511140 Publishers (except exclusive Internet publishing), directory
511191 Publishers (except exclusive Internet publishing), greeting card
511120 Publishers (except exclusive Internet publishing), magazine
511130 Publishers (except exclusive Internet publishing), map
511120 Publishers (except exclusive Internet publishing), periodical
511199 Publishers (except exclusive Internet publishing), racing form
****** Publishers—see specific type
541840 Publishers' advertising representatives (i.e., independent of media owners)
****** Publishers and printing combined—see specific type of publisher
****** Publishers or publishing—see specific type
511130 Publishers, book, combined with printing
511191 Publishers, greeting card, combined with printing
516110 Publishers, Internet greeting card
516110 Publishers, Internet map
516110 Publishers, Internet racing form
511120 Publishers, magazine, combined with printing
512230 Publishers, music
511110 Publishers, newspaper (except exclusive Internet publishing)
511110 Publishers, newspaper, combined with printing
511210 Publishers, packaged computer software

511120 Publishers, periodical, combined with printing
311520 Pudding pops, frozen, manufacturing
311999 Puddings, canned dessert, manufacturing
311999 Puddings, dessert, manufacturing
333923 Pulleys (except power transmission), metal, manufacturing
333613 Pulleys, power transmission, manufacturing
321999 Pulleys, wood, manufacturing
213112 Pulling oil and gas field casings, tubes, or rods on a contract basis
621111 Pulmonary specialists' offices (e.g., centers, clinics)
322122 Pulp and newsprint combined manufacturing
322121 Pulp and paper (except groundwood, newsprint) combined manufacturing
322130 Pulp and paperboard combined manufacturing
333291 Pulp making machinery manufacturing
322110 Pulp manufacturing (i.e., chemical, mechanical, or semichemical processes) without making paper
322110 Pulp manufacturing (made from bagasse, linters, rags, straw, wastepaper, or wood) without making paper
322122 Pulp mills and groundwood paper, uncoated and untreated, manufacturing
322110 Pulp mills not making paper or paperboard
322122 Pulp mills producing newsprint paper
322121 Pulp mills producing paper (except groundwood, newsprint)
322130 Pulp mills producing paperboard
322299 Pulp products, molded, manufacturing
333291 Pulp, paper, and paperboard molding machinery manufacturing
212399 Pulpstones, natural, mining and/or beneficiating
113310 Pulpwood logging camps
423990 Pulpwood merchant wholesalers
334515 Pulse (i.e., signal) generators manufacturing
334519 Pulse analyzers, nuclear monitoring, manufacturing
327992 Pumice (except abrasives) processing beyond beneficiation
327910 Pumice and pumicite abrasives manufacturing
212399 Pumice mining and/or beneficiating
212399 Pumicite mining and/or beneficiating
562991 Pumping (i.e., cleaning) cesspools and septic tanks
562991 Pumping (i.e., cleaning) portable toilets
213112 Pumping oil and gas wells on a contract basis
213113 Pumping or draining coal mines on a contract basis
213114 Pumping or draining metal mines on a contract basis
213115 Pumping or draining nonmetallic mineral mines (except fuel) on a contract basis
237120 Pumping station, gas and oil transmission, construction
237110 Pumping station, water and sewage system, construction
238220 Pumping system, water, installation
111219 Pumpkin farming, field and seed production
423120 Pumps (e.g., fuel, oil, power steering, water), automotive, merchant wholesalers
336312 Pumps (e.g., fuel, oil, water), mechanical, automotive and truck gasoline engine (except power steering), manufacturing

333911 Pumps (except fluid power), general purpose, manufacturing
316214 Pumps (i.e., dress shoes) manufacturing
423830 Pumps and pumping equipment, industrial-type, merchant wholesalers
333911 Pumps for railroad equipment lubrication systems manufacturing
333996 Pumps, fluid power, manufacturing
333911 Pumps, industrial and commercial-type, general purpose, manufacturing
333913 Pumps, measuring and dispensing (e.g., gasoline), manufacturing
333911 Pumps, oil field or well, manufacturing
333911 Pumps, sump or water, residential-type, manufacturing
313230 Punched felts manufacturing
332212 Punches (except paper), nonpowered handtool, manufacturing
333514 Punches for use with machine tools manufacturing
333513 Punching machines, metalworking, manufacturing
711110 Puppet theaters
339999 Puppets manufacturing
921190 Purchasing and supply agencies, government
522298 Purchasing of accounts receivable
332323 Purlins, metal, manufacturing
316993 Purses (except precious metal), men's, manufacturing
316992 Purses (except precious metal), women's, manufacturing
339911 Purses, precious metal or clad with precious metal, manufacturing
333515 Pushers (i.e., a machine tool accessory) manufacturing
332212 Putty knives manufacturing
423920 Puzzles merchant wholesalers
326122 PVC pipe manufacturing
325320 Pyrethrin insecticides manufacturing
334519 Pyrheliometers manufacturing
212393 Pyrite concentrates mining and/or beneficiating
212393 Pyrite mining and/or beneficiating
325191 Pyroligneous acids manufacturing
212299 Pyrolusite mining and/or beneficiating
327112 Pyrometer tubes manufacturing
334513 Pyrometers, industrial process-type, manufacturing
327112 Pyrometric cones, earthenware, manufacturing
212399 Pyrophyllite mining and/or beneficiating
327992 Pyrophyllite processing beyond beneficiation
332994 Pyrotechnic pistols and projectors manufacturing
325998 Pyrotechnics (e.g., flares, flashlight bombs, signals) manufacturing
325211 Pyroxylin (i.e., nitrocellulose) resins manufacturing
212393 Pyrrhotite mining and/or beneficiating
112390 Quail production
611430 Quality assurance training
541990 Quantity surveyor services
327122 Quarry tiles, clay, manufacturing
333131 Quarrying machinery and equipment manufacturing
423810 Quarrying machinery and equipment merchant wholesalers
316999 Quarters (i.e., shoe cut stock), leather, manufacturing
212399 Quartz crystal, pure, mining and/or beneficiating
334419 Quartz crystals, electronic application, manufacturing
212319 Quartzite crushed and broken stone mining and/or beneficiating
212311 Quartzite dimension stone mining or quarrying

325191 Quebracho extracts manufacturing
112910 Queen bee production
325191 Quercitron extracts manufacturing
323114 Quick printing
327410 Quicklime (i.e., calcium oxide) manufacturing
811191 Quick-lube shops
212299 Quicksilver ores and metal mining and/or beneficiating
314999 Quilting of textiles
314129 Quilts made from purchased materials
111339 Quince farming
325411 Quinine and derivatives (i.e., basic chemicals) manufacturing
523999 Quotation services, securities
523999 Quotation services, stock
311119 Rabbit food manufacturing
112930 Rabbit production
311615 Rabbits processing (i.e., canned, cooked, fresh, frozen)
311615 Rabbits slaughtering and dressing
711219 Race car drivers
711219 Race car owners (i.e., racing cars)
336999 Race cars manufacturing
711219 Race dog owners (i.e., racing dogs)
711219 Racehorse owners (i.e., racing horses)
711219 Racehorse trainers
711219 Racehorse training
332991 Races, ball or roller bearings, manufacturing
511199 Racetrack program publishers (except Internet)
511199 Racetrack program publishers and printing combined
516110 Racetrack program publishers, exclusively on Internet
323112 Racetrack programs flexographic printing without publishing
323111 Racetrack programs gravure printing without publishing
323110 Racetrack programs lithographic (offset) printing without publishing
323119 Racetrack programs printing (except flexographic, gravure, lithographic, quick, screen) without publishing
323113 Racetrack programs screen printing without publishing
711212 Racetracks (e.g., automobile, dog, horse)
713990 Racetracks, slot car (i.e., amusement devices)
335932 Raceways manufacturing
713990 Raceways, gocart (i.e., amusement rides)
511199 Racing form publishers (except exclusive Internet publishing)
511199 Racing form publishers and printing combined
516110 Racing form publishers, exclusively on Internet
323112 Racing forms flexographic printing without publishing
323111 Racing forms gravure printing without publishing
323110 Racing forms lithographic (offset) printing without publishing
323119 Racing forms printing (except flexographic, gravure, lithographic, quick, screen) without publishing
323113 Racing forms screen printing without publishing
711219 Racing stables, horse
711219 Racing teams (e.g., automobile, motorcycle, snowmobile)
334417 Rack and panel connectors manufacturing
336330 Rack and pinion steering assemblies manufacturing
336399 Racks (e.g., bicycle, luggage, ski, tire), automotive, truck, and buses manufacturing
332313 Racks (e.g., trash), fabricated metal plate, manufacturing
332618 Racks, household-type, made from purchased wire
713940 Racquetball club facilities

811219 Radar and sonar equipment repair and maintenance services
334511 Radar detectors manufacturing
423690 Radar equipment merchant wholesalers
517910 Radar station operations
334511 Radar systems and equipment manufacturing
334515 Radar testing instruments, electric, manufacturing
334519 RADIAC (radioactivity detection, identification, and computation) equipment manufacturing
238220 Radiant floor heating equipment installation
334519 Radiation detection and monitoring instruments manufacturing
541380 Radiation dosimetry (i.e., radiation testing) laboratories or services
812332 Radiation protection garment supply services
339113 Radiation shielding aprons, gloves, and sheeting manufacturing
541380 Radiation testing laboratories or services
325998 Radiator additive preparations manufacturing
326220 Radiator and heater hoses, rubber or plastics, manufacturing
811118 Radiator repair shops, automotive
332322 Radiator shields and enclosures, sheet metal (except stampings), manufacturing
333414 Radiators (except motor vehicle, portable electric) manufacturing
336399 Radiators and cores manufacturing
423120 Radiators, motor vehicle, merchant wholesalers
335211 Radiators, portable electric, manufacturing
541840 Radio advertising representatives (i.e., independent of media owners)
236220 Radio and television broadcast studio construction
443112 Radio and television stores
332312 Radio and television tower sections, fabricated structural metal, manufacturing
488330 Radio beacon (i.e., ship navigation) services
515112 Radio broadcasting (except exclusively on Internet) stations (e.g., AM, FM, shortwave)
515111 Radio broadcasting network services
515111 Radio broadcasting networks
515111 Radio broadcasting syndicates
711510 Radio commentators, independent
541690 Radio consulting services
511120 Radio guide publishers (except exclusive Internet publishing)
511120 Radio guide publishers and printing combined
516110 Radio guide publishers, exclusively on Internet
323112 Radio guides flexographic printing without publishing
323111 Radio guides gravure printing without publishing
323110 Radio guides lithographic (offset) printing without publishing
323119 Radio guides printing (except flexographic, gravure, lithographic, quick, screen) without publishing
323113 Radio guides screen printing without publishing
334310 Radio headphones manufacturing
326199 Radio housings, plastics, manufacturing
334511 Radio magnetic instrumentation (RMI) manufacturing
517211 Radio paging services communication carriers

423690 Radio parts and accessories (e.g., transitors, tubes) merchant wholesalers
512290 Radio program tape production (except independent producers)
334310 Radio receiving sets manufacturing
811211 Radio repair and maintenance services without retailing new radios
811211 Radio repair, automotive, without retailing new
323111 Radio schedule gravure printing without publishing
511120 Radio schedule publishers (except exclusive Internet publishing)
511120 Radio schedule publishers and printing combined
516110 Radio schedule publishers, exclusively on Internet
323112 Radio schedules flexographic printing without publishing
323110 Radio schedules lithographic (offset) printing without publishing
323119 Radio schedules printing (except flexographic, gravure, lithographic, quick, screen) without publishing
323113 Radio schedules screen printing without publishing
236220 Radio station construction
515112 Radio stations (except exclusively on Internet)
561410 Radio transcription services
334220 Radio transmitting antennas and ground equipment manufacturing
237130 Radio transmitting tower construction
325188 Radioactive elements manufacturing
541360 Radioactive geophysical surveying services
325412 Radioactive in-vivo diagnostic substances manufacturing
325188 Radioactive isotopes manufacturing
424210 Radioactive pharmaceutical isotopes merchant wholesalers
562112 Radioactive waste collecting and/or local hauling
562211 Radioactive waste collecting and/or local hauling in combination with disposal and/or treatment facilities
562211 Radioactive waste disposal facilities
484230 Radioactive waste hauling, long-distance
562211 Radioactive waste treatment facilities
334519 Radioactivity detection, identification, and computation (RADIAC) equipment manufacturing
334515 Radiofrequency measuring equipment manufacturing
334515 Radiofrequency oscillators manufacturing
541380 Radiographic testing laboratories or services
541380 Radiographing welded joints on pipes and fittings
541380 Radiography inspection services
621512 Radiological laboratories, medical
621512 Radiological laboratory services, medical
621111 Radiologists' offices (e.g., centers, clinics)
423690 Radios (except household-type) merchant wholesalers
423620 Radios, household-type, merchant wholesalers
111219 Radish farming, field and seed production
325188 Radium chloride manufacturing
334517 Radium equipment manufacturing
325188 Radium luminous compounds manufacturing
212291 Radium ores mining and/or beneficiating
238990 Radon gas alleviation contractors
541380 Radon testing laboratories or services

326299 Rafts, rubber inflatable, manufacturing
423930 Rags merchant wholesalers
335931 Rail bonds, propulsion and signal circuit electric, manufacturing
331111 Rail joints and fastenings made in iron and steel mills
336510 Rail laying and tamping equipment manufacturing
485112 Rail transportation (except mixed mode), commuter
332323 Railings, metal, manufacturing
321918 Railings, wood stair, manufacturing
926120 Railroad and warehouse commissions, nonoperating
333613 Railroad car journal bearings, plain, manufacturing
532411 Railroad car rental and leasing
336510 Railroad cars and car equipment manufacturing
423860 Railroad cars merchant wholesalers
336510 Railroad cars, self-propelled, manufacturing
237990 Railroad construction
331111 Railroad crossings, iron or steel, made in iron and steel mills
423860 Railroad equipment and supplies merchant wholesalers
336510 Railroad locomotives and parts (except diesel engines) manufacturing
339932 Railroad models, hobby and toy, manufacturing
923130 Railroad Retirement Board
531190 Railroad right of way leasing
336510 Railroad rolling stock manufacturing
336360 Railroad seating manufacturing
334290 Railroad signaling equipment manufacturing
238210 Railroad signalling equipment installation
488210 Railroad switching services
488210 Railroad terminals, independent operation
561599 Railroad ticket offices
321114 Railroad ties (i.e., bridge, cross, switch) treating
423990 Railroad ties, wood, merchant wholesalers
333997 Railroad track scales manufacturing
482111 Railroad transportation, line-haul
487110 Railroad transportation, scenic and sightseeing
482112 Railroad transportation, short-line or beltline
487110 Railroad, scenic and sightseeing, operation
482111 Railroads, line-haul
482112 Railroads, short-line or beltline
321999 Rails (except rough), wood fence, manufacturing
423510 Rails and accessories, metal, merchant wholesalers
331319 Rails made by rolling or drawing purchased aluminum
331111 Rails rerolled or renewed in iron and steel mills
331319 Rails, aluminum, made in integrated secondary smelting and drawing plants
331319 Rails, aluminum, made in integrated secondary smelting and rolling mills
331111 Rails, iron or steel, made in iron and steel mills
113310 Rails, rough wood, manufacturing
332312 Railway bridge sections, prefabricated metal, manufacturing
237990 Railway construction (e.g., interlocker, roadbed, signal, track)
335312 Railway motors and control equipment, electric, manufacturing
237990 Railway roadbed construction
236220 Railway station construction
485112 Railway systems (except mixed mode), commuter
488210 Railway terminals, independent operation

482111 Railway transportation, line-haul
487110 Railway transportation, scenic and sightseeing
482112 Railway transportation, short-line or beltline
334519 Rain gauges manufacturing
315211 Raincoats water resistant, men's and boys', cut and sew apparel contractors
313320 Raincoats waterproofing (i.e., oiling)
315299 Raincoats, rubber or rubberized fabric, manufacturing
315291 Raincoats, water resistant, infants', cut and sewn from purchased fabric (except apparel contractors)
315228 Raincoats, water resistant, nontailored, men's and boys', cut and sewn from purchased fabric (except apparel contractors)
315239 Raincoats, water resistant, nontailored, women's, misses', and girls', cut and sewn from purchased fabric (except apparel contractors)
315222 Raincoats, water resistant, tailored, men's and boys', cut and sewn from purchased fabric (except apparel contractors)
315234 Raincoats, water resistant, tailored, women's, misses', and girls', cut and sewn from purchased fabric (except apparel contractors)
315212 Raincoats, water resistant, women's, girls', and infants', cut and sew apparel contractors
315299 Raincoats, waterproof (except infants'), cut and sewn from purchased fabric (except apparel contractors)
315291 Raincoats, waterproof, infants', cut and sewn from purchased fabric (except apparel contractors)
315211 Raincoats, waterproof, men's and boys', cut and sew apparel contractors
315212 Raincoats, waterproof, women's, girls', and infants', cut and sew apparel contractors
315291 Raincoats, water-repellent, infants', cut and sewn from purchased fabric (except apparel contractors)
315211 Raincoats, water-repellent, men's and boys', cut and sew apparel contractors
315228 Raincoats, water-repellent, nontailored, men's and boys', cut and sewn from purchased fabric (except apparel contractors)
315239 Raincoats, water-repellent, nontailored, women's, misses', and girls', cut and sewn from purchased fabric (except apparel contractors)
315222 Raincoats, water-repellent, tailored, men's and boys', cut and sewn from purchased fabric (except apparel contractors)
315234 Raincoats, water-repellent, tailored, women's, misses', and girls', cut and sewn from purchased fabric (except apparel contractors)
315212 Raincoats, water-repellent, women's, girls', and infants', cut and sew apparel contractors
111332 Raisin farming
112990 Raising swans, peacocks, flamingos, or other adornment birds
311423 Raisins made in dehydration plants
333111 Rakes, hay, manufacturing
332212 Rakes, nonpowered handtool, manufacturing
313111 Ramie spun yarns made from purchased fiber

316999 Rands (i.e., shoe cut stock), leather, manufacturing
333315 Range finders, photographic, manufacturing
335211 Range hoods with integral lighting fixtures, household-type, manufacturing
335211 Range hoods, household-type, manufacturing
333319 Ranges, commercial-type, manufacturing
335221 Ranges, household-type cooking, manufacturing
624190 Rape crisis centers
311225 Rapeseed (i.e., canola) oil made from purchased oils
311223 Rapeseed (i.e., canola) oil made in crushing mills
111120 Rapeseed farming, field and seed production
336510 Rapid transit cars and equipment manufacturing
325188 Rare earth compounds, not specified elsewhere by process, manufacturing
212299 Rare earth metal concentrates beneficiating
212299 Rare earth metal ores mining and/or beneficiating
325188 Rare earth salts manufacturing
453310 Rare manuscript stores
111334 Raspberry farming
332212 Rasps, handheld, manufacturing
332212 Ratchets, nonpowered, manufacturing
524298 Rate making services, insurance
334511 Rate-of-climb instrumentation manufacturing
213112 Rathole and mousehole drilling at oil and gas fields on a contract basis
112390 Ratite production
337125 Rattan furniture, household-type, manufacturing
321999 Rattan ware (except furniture) manufacturing
112990 Rattlesnake production
311313 Raw beet sugar manufacturing
424590 Raw farm products (except field beans, grains) merchant wholesalers
316110 Rawhide manufacturing
114111 Ray fishing
325221 Rayon fibers and filaments manufacturing
313111 Rayon spun yarns made from purchased fiber
313113 Rayon thread manufacturing
313112 Rayon yarn throwing, twisting, texturizing, or winding purchased filament
331221 Razor blade strip steel made in cold rolling mills
332211 Razor blades manufacturing
424210 Razor blades merchant wholesalers
316999 Razor strops manufacturing
332211 Razors (except electric) manufacturing
424210 Razors (except electric) merchant wholesalers
335211 Razors, electric, manufacturing
423620 Razors, electric, merchant wholesalers
332313 Reactor containment vessels, fabricated metal plate, manufacturing
332410 Reactors, nuclear, manufacturing
333315 Readers, microfilm or microfiche, manufacturing
327320 Ready-mix concrete manufacturing and distributing
336211 Ready-mix concrete trucks assembling on purchased chassis
531190 Real estate (except building) rental or leasing
237210 Real estate (except cemeteries) subdividers
531210 Real estate agencies
531210 Real estate agents' offices
531320 Real estate appraisal services
531320 Real estate appraisers' offices
531390 Real estate asset management services (except property management)
813910 Real estate boards

531210 Real estate brokerages
531210 Real estate brokers' offices
531390 Real estate consultants' (except agents, appraisers) offices
522292 Real estate credit lending
531390 Real estate escrow agencies
531390 Real estate escrow agents' offices
531390 Real estate fiduciaries' offices
525930 Real estate investment trusts (REITs)
541110 Real estate law offices
531390 Real estate listing services
525990 Real estate mortgage investment conduits (REMICs)
522294 Real estate mortgage investment conduits (REMICs) issuing, private
531312 Real estate property managers' offices, commercial
531311 Real estate property managers' offices, residential
531130 Real estate rental or leasing of miniwarehouses and self-storage units
531120 Real estate rental or leasing of nonresidential building (except miniwarehouse)
531110 Real estate rental or leasing of residential building
611519 Real estate schools
524127 Real estate title insurance carriers, direct
237210 Real property (except cemeteries) subdivision
561492 Real-time (i.e., simultaneous) closed captioning of live television performances, meetings, conferences, and so forth
333515 Reamers (i.e., a machine tool accessory) manufacturing
333512 Reaming machines, metalworking, manufacturing
238120 Rebar contractors
323121 Rebinding books, magazines, or pamphlets
515112 Rebroadcast radio stations (except exclusively on Internet)
336312 Rebuilding automotive and truck gasoline engines
326212 Rebuilding tires
326212 Recapping tires
424120 Receipt books merchant wholesalers
334220 Receiver-transmitter units (i.e., transceivers) manufacturing
335931 Receptacles (i.e., outlets), electrical, manufacturing
423610 Receptacles, electrical, merchant wholesalers
531120 Reception hall rental or leasing
335122 Recessed lighting housings and trim (except residential), electric, manufacturing
335121 Recessed lighting housings and trim, residential electric, manufacturing
335911 Rechargeable battery packs made from purchased battery cells and housings
335911 Rechargeable nickel cadmium (NICAD) batteries manufacturing
314999 Reclaimed wool processing
326299 Reclaiming rubber from waste or scrap
337121 Recliners, upholstered, manufacturing
332994 Recoil mechanisms (i.e., 30 mm. or less, 1.18 inch or less), gun, manufacturing
332995 Recoil mechanisms (i.e., more than 30 mm., more than 1.18 inch), gun, manufacturing
332995 Recoilless rifles manufacturing
423840 Reconditioned barrels and drums merchant wholesalers
213111 Reconditioning oil and gas field wells on a contract basis
811310 Reconditioning shipping barrels and drums
321219 Reconstituted wood panels manufacturing
321219 Reconstituted wood sheets and boards manufacturing
312229 Reconstituting tobacco
512210 Record producers (except independent)

711510 Record producers, independent
512210 Record production (except independent record producers) without duplication or distribution
512220 Record releasing, promoting, and distributing combined with mass duplication
451220 Record stores, new
453310 Record stores, used
423620 Recorders (e.g., tape, video), household-type, merchant wholesalers
334513 Recorders, industrial process control-type, manufacturing
334515 Recorders, oscillographic, manufacturing
512290 Recording books on tape or disc (except publishers)
512290 Recording seminars and conferences, audio
512240 Recording studios, sound, operating on a contract or fee basis
711510 Recording technicians, independent
541611 Records management consulting services
314999 Recovered fibers processing
331492 Recovering and refining of nonferrous metals (except aluminum, copper) from scrap
331492 Recovering silver from used photographic film or X-ray plates
237990 Recreation area, open space, construction
621340 Recreational (e.g., art, dance, music) therapists' offices (e.g., centers, clinics)
721214 Recreational camps with accommodation facilities (except campgrounds)
713990 Recreational camps without accommodations
713990 Recreational day camps (except instructional)
423910 Recreational equipment and supplies (except vehicles) merchant wholesalers
236220 Recreational facility building construction
532292 Recreational goods rental
924120 Recreational programs administration, government
713940 Recreational sports club facilities
713990 Recreational sports clubs (i.e., sports teams) not operating sports facilities
713990 Recreational sports teams and leagues
532120 Recreational trailer rental
441210 Recreational vehicle (RV) dealers
532120 Recreational vehicle (RV) rental or leasing
423110 Recreational vehicle merchant wholesalers
237990 Recreational vehicle park construction
721211 Recreational vehicle parks
441210 Recreational vehicle parts and accessories stores
335999 Rectifiers (except electronic component type, semiconductor) manufacturing
334419 Rectifiers, electronic component-type (except semiconductor), manufacturing
423690 Rectifiers, electronic, merchant wholesalers
334413 Rectifiers, semiconductor, manufacturing
333298 Rectifying equipment, chemical, manufacturing
562111 Recyclable material collection services
562111 Recyclable material hauling, local
484230 Recyclable material hauling, long-distance
423930 Recyclable materials (e.g., glass, metal, paper) merchant wholesalers
325612 Recycling drycleaning fluids
811212 Recycling inkjet cartridges

325998 Recycling services for degreasing solvents (e.g., engine, machinery) manufacturing
325199 Red oil (i.e., oleic acid) manufacturing
925120 Redevelopment land agencies, government
334516 Redox (i.e., oxidation-reduction potential) instruments manufacturing
333612 Reducers, speed, manufacturing
333612 Reduction gears and gear units (except aircraft power transmission equipment, automotive) manufacturing
337125 Reed furniture (except upholstered), household-type, manufacturing
212399 Reed peat mining and/or beneficiating
321999 Reed ware (except furniture) manufacturing
339992 Reeds, musical instrument, manufacturing
339920 Reels, fishing, manufacturing
332999 Reels, metal, manufacturing
326199 Reels, plastics, manufacturing
321999 Reels, plywood, manufacturing
321999 Reels, wood, manufacturing
711219 Referees and umpires
519120 Reference libraries
561310 Referral agencies or services, employment
624190 Referral services for personal and social problems
486910 Refined petroleum products pipeline transportation
324110 Refineries, petroleum
324110 Refinery gases made in petroleum refineries
423830 Refinery machinery and equipment merchant wholesalers
237120 Refinery, petroleum, construction
331312 Refining aluminum, primary
331314 Refining aluminum, secondary
331411 Refining copper, primary
331423 Refining copper, secondary
331419 Refining nonferrous metals and alloys (except aluminum, copper), primary
331492 Refining nonferrous metals and alloys (except aluminum, copper), secondary
335129 Reflectors for lighting equipment, metal, manufacturing
333314 Reflectors, optical, manufacturing
326199 Reflectors, plastics, manufacturing
115310 Reforestation
922140 Reformatories
325991 Reformulating plastics resins from recycled plastics products
334513 Refractometers, industrial process-type, manufacturing
334516 Refractometers, laboratory-type, manufacturing
327124 Refractories (e.g., block, brick, mortar, tile), clay, manufacturing
327125 Refractories (e.g., block, brick, mortar, tile), nonclay, manufacturing
238140 Refractory brick contractors
327125 Refractory cement, nonclay, manufacturing
423840 Refractory materials (e.g., block, brick, mortar, tile) merchant wholesalers
212325 Refractory minerals mining and/or beneficiating
722330 Refreshment stands, mobile
423740 Refrigerated display cases merchant wholesalers
311822 Refrigerated doughs made from purchased flour
333415 Refrigerated lockers manufacturing
484220 Refrigerated products trucking, local
484230 Refrigerated products trucking, long-distance
493120 Refrigerated warehousing
333415 Refrigeration compressors manufacturing

334512 Refrigeration controls, residential and commercial-type, manufacturing
423740 Refrigeration equipment and supplies, commercial-type, merchant wholesalers
811310 Refrigeration equipment repair and maintenance services, industrial and commercial-type
333415 Refrigeration equipment, industrial and commercial-type, manufacturing
238220 Refrigeration system (e.g., commercial, industrial, scientific) installation
334512 Refrigeration thermostats manufacturing
423740 Refrigeration units, motor vehicle, merchant wholesalers
333415 Refrigeration units, truck-type, manufacturing
334512 Refrigeration/air-conditioning defrost controls manufacturing
532210 Refrigerator rental
811412 Refrigerator, household-type, repair and maintenance services without retailing new refrigerators
335222 Refrigerator/freezer combinations, household-type, manufacturing
335222 Refrigerators (e.g., absorption, mechanical), household-type, manufacturing
423740 Refrigerators (e.g., reach-in, walk-in), commercial-type, merchant wholesalers
423620 Refrigerators, household-type, merchant wholesalers
624230 Refugee settlement services
562212 Refuse collecting and operating solid waste landfills
562111 Refuse collection services
562213 Refuse disposal combustors or incinerators
562212 Refuse disposal landfills
236210 Refuse disposal plant construction
562111 Refuse hauling, local
484230 Refuse hauling, long-distance
325221 Regenerated cellulosic fibers manufacturing
925120 Regional planning and development program administration
621399 Registered nurses' (RNs) offices (e.g., centers, clinics)
334514 Registers, linear tallying, manufacturing
332323 Registers, metal air, manufacturing
561310 Registries, employment
561310 Registries, teacher
335311 Regulating transformers, power system-type, manufacturing
926140 Regulation and inspection of agricultural products
926130 Regulation of utilities
335311 Regulators (i.e., electric transformers), feeder voltage, manufacturing
336322 Regulators, motor vehicle voltage for internal combustion engines manufacturing
335313 Regulators, power, manufacturing
423610 Regulators, voltage (except motor vehicle), merchant wholesalers
624190 Rehabilitation agencies for offenders
622310 Rehabilitation hospitals (except alcoholism, drug addiction)
622210 Rehabilitation hospitals, alcoholism and drug addiction
624310 Rehabilitation job counseling and training, vocational
922150 Rehabilitation services, correctional, government
332618 Reinforcing mesh, concrete, made from purchased wire
238120 Reinforcing rod, bar, mesh and cage installation
238120 Reinforcing steel contractors
524130 Reinsurance carriers
525930 REITs (real estate investment trusts)

334515 Relays (except electrical, electronic), instrument, manufacturing
423610 Relays merchant wholesalers
335314 Relays, electrical and electronic, manufacturing
624230 Relief services, disaster
624230 Relief services, emergency
323121 Religious book binding without printing
511130 Religious book publishers (except exclusive Internet publishing)
511130 Religious book publishers and printing combined
516110 Religious book publishers, exclusively on Internet
451211 Religious book stores
323117 Religious books printing and binding without publishing
323117 Religious books printing without publishing
236220 Religious building (e.g., church, synagogue, mosque, temple) construction
337127 Religious furniture manufacturing
423210 Religious furniture merchant wholesalers
453998 Religious goods (except books) stores
511120 Religious magazine and periodical publishers (except exclusive Internet publishing)
511120 Religious magazine and periodical publishers and printing combined
516110 Religious magazine and periodical publishers, exclusively on Internet
323112 Religious magazines and periodicals flexographic printing without publishing
323111 Religious magazines and periodicals gravure printing without publishing
323110 Religious magazines and periodicals lithographic (offset) printing without publishing
323119 Religious magazines and periodicals printing (except flexographic, gravure, lithographic, quick, screen) without publishing
323113 Religious magazines and periodicals screen printing without publishing
813110 Religious organizations
423490 Religious supplies merchant wholesalers
311421 Relishes canning
562910 Remediation and clean up of contaminated buildings, mine sites, soil, or ground water
562910 Remediation services, environmental
525990 REMICs (real estate mortgage investment conduits)
522294 REMICs (real estate mortgage investment conduits) issuing, private
424310 Remnants, piece goods, merchant wholesalers
236118 Remodeling and renovating general contractors, multifamily building
236118 Remodeling and renovating general contractors, residential
236118 Remodeling and renovating general contractors, single-family housing
236118 Remodeling and renovating operative builders
236118 Remodeling and renovating single-family housing
236118 Remodeling and renovating, residential building
334290 Remote control units (e.g., garage door, television) manufacturing
541360 Remote sensing geophysical surveying services
213112 Removal of condensate gasoline from field gathering lines on a contract basis
213113 Removal of overburden for coal mining on a contract basis

213114 Removal of overburden for metal mining on a contract basis
213115 Removal of overburden for nonmetallic minerals mining (except fuels) on a contract basis
562920 Removal of recyclable materials from a waste stream
621492 Renal dialysis centers and clinics
311613 Rendering animals (carrion) for feed
311613 Rendering fats
311613 Rendering plants
424990 Rennets merchant wholesalers
926150 Rent control agencies
****** Rental—see type of article or property being rented
532310 Rent-all centers
532490 Renting coin-operated amusement devices (except concession operators)
531210 Renting real estate for others (i.e., agents, brokers)
541611 Reorganizational consulting services
522294 Repackaging loans for sale to others (i.e., private conduits)
****** Repair—see type of article being repaired
237310 Repair, highway, road, street, bridge or airport runway
323121 Repairing books
334210 Repeater and transceiver equipment, carrier line, manufacturing
711110 Repertory companies, theatrical
322231 Report covers made from purchased paper or paperboard
711510 Reporters, independent (freelance)
561491 Repossession services
512199 Reproduction of motion picture films for theatrical distribution
115210 Reproductive flushing services for animals
621410 Reproductive health services centers
561439 Reprographic services
712130 Reptile exhibits, live
324191 Re-refining used petroleum lubricating oils
321912 Resawing purchased lumber
621910 Rescue services, air
621910 Rescue services, medical
517410 Resellers, satellite telecommunication
517310 Resellers, telecommunication (except satellite)
325411 Reserpines (i.e., basic chemicals) manufacturing
561599 Reservation (e.g., airline, car rental, hotel, restaurant) services
522320 Reserve and liquidity services (except central bank)
237110 Reservoir construction
721310 Residence clubs, organizational
531110 Residential building rental or leasing
561720 Residential cleaning services
721310 Residential clubs
236116 Residential construction, multifamily, general contractors
236115 Residential construction, single-family, general contractors
623220 Residential group homes for the emotionally disturbed
531110 Residential hotel rental or leasing
236117 Residential operative builders
531311 Residential property managing
531210 Residential real estate agencies
531210 Residential real estate agents' offices
531210 Residential real estate brokerages
531210 Residential real estate brokers' offices
531311 Residential real estate property managers' offices
531190 Residential trailer parks
211112 Residue gas production
326192 Resilient floor coverings (e.g., sheet, tile) manufacturing
238330 Resilient floor tile or sheet (e.g., linoleum, rubber, vinyl), installation only

325211 Resins, plastics (except custom compounding purchased resins), manufacturing
424610 Resins, plastics, merchant wholesalers
424690 Resins, synthetic rubber, merchant wholesalers
334515 Resistance measuring equipment manufacturing
334513 Resistance thermometers and bulbs, industrial process-type, manufacturing
333992 Resistance welding equipment manufacturing
334415 Resistors, electronic, manufacturing
423690 Resistors, electronic, merchant wholesalers
335312 Resolvers manufacturing
334516 Resonance instruments (i.e., laboratory-type) manufacturing
334419 Resonant reed devices, electronic, manufacturing
325192 Resorcinol manufacturing
721120 Resort hotels with casinos
721110 Resort hotels without casinos
334510 Respiratory analysis equipment, electromedical, manufacturing
339113 Respiratory protection mask manufacturing
621399 Respiratory therapists' offices (e.g., centers, clinics)
623110 Rest homes with nursing care
623312 Rest homes without nursing care
561720 Rest room cleaning services
812990 Rest room operation
813910 Restaurant associations
236220 Restaurant construction
423440 Restaurant equipment (except furniture) merchant wholesalers
337127 Restaurant furniture (e.g., carts, chairs, foodwagons, tables) manufacturing
423210 Restaurant furniture merchant wholesalers
561720 Restaurant kitchen cleaning services
611519 Restaurant management schools (except academic)
492210 Restaurant meals delivery services (i.e., independent delivery services)
722211 Restaurants, carryout
722211 Restaurants, fast food
722110 Restaurants, full service
811420 Restoration and repair of antique furniture
811121 Restoration shops, antique and classic automotive
339113 Restraints, patient, manufacturing
561410 Resume writing services
238330 Resurfacing hardwood flooring
237310 Resurfacing, highway, road, street, bridge or airport runway
****** Retail—see type of dealer, shop, or store
333997 Retail scales (e.g., butcher, delicatessen, produce) manufacturing
813910 Retailers' associations
238110 Retaining wall (except anchored earth), poured concrete, construction
238140 Retaining wall, masonry (i.e., block, brick, stone), construction
237990 Retaining walls, anchored (e.g., with piles, soil nails, tieback anchors), construction
325998 Retarders (e.g., flameproofing agents, mildewproofing agents) manufacturing
339112 Retinoscopes (except electromedical) manufacturing
334510 Retinoscopes, electromedical, manufacturing
813410 Retirement associations, social
623311 Retirement communities, continuing care
623110 Retirement homes with nursing care
623312 Retirement homes without nursing care
531110 Retirement hotel rental or leasing

525110 Retirement pension plans
332420 Retorts, heavy gauge metal, manufacturing
339112 Retractors, medical, manufacturing
326211 Retreading materials, tire, manufacturing
326212 Retreading tires
813110 Retreat houses, religious
115114 Retting flax
811420 Reupholstery shops, furniture
522292 Reverse mortgage lending
237990 Revetment construction
332994 Revolvers manufacturing
238290 Revolving door installation
811310 Rewinding armatures (except on an assembly line or factory basis)
213111 Reworking oil and gas wells on a contract basis
331419 Rhenium refining, primary
335931 Rheostats (i.e., dimmer switches), current carrying wiring device, manufacturing
334419 Rheostats, electronic, manufacturing
335314 Rheostats, industrial control, manufacturing
212299 Rhodium mining and/or beneficiating
212299 Rhodochrosite mining and/or beneficiating
111219 Rhubarb farming, field and seed production
111419 Rhubarb, grown under cover
339944 Ribbons (e.g., cash register, printer, typewriter), inked, manufacturing
314999 Ribbons made from purchased fabrics
313221 Ribbons made in narrow woven fabric mills
313230 Ribbons made in nonwoven fabric mills
339944 Ribbons, inked, manufacturing
424120 Ribbons, inked, merchant wholesalers
424310 Ribbons, textile, merchant wholesalers
111160 Rice (except wild rice) farming, field and seed production
311212 Rice bran, flour, and meals, manufacturing
311230 Rice breakfast foods manufacturing
311212 Rice cleaning and polishing
115114 Rice drying
311212 Rice flour manufacturing
311213 Rice malt manufacturing
311212 Rice meal manufacturing
311212 Rice milling
311999 Rice mixes (i.e., uncooked and packaged with other ingredients) made from purchased rice and dry ingredients
311423 Rice mixes (i.e., uncooked and packaged with other ingredients) made in dehydration plants
311212 Rice mixes (i.e., uncooked and packaged with other ingredients) made in rice mills
311221 Rice starches manufacturing
311212 Rice, brewer's, manufacturing
311212 Rice, brown, manufacturing
424490 Rice, polished, merchant wholesalers
424510 Rice, unpolished, merchant wholesalers
315211 Riding clothes, men's and boys', cut and sew apparel contractors
315228 Riding clothes, men's and boys', cut and sewn from purchased fabric (except apparel contractors)
315212 Riding clothes, women's and girls', cut and sew apparel contractors
315239 Riding clothes, women's, misses', and girls', cut and sewn from purchased fabric (except apparel contractors)
713990 Riding clubs, recreational
316999 Riding crops manufacturing
611620 Riding instruction academies or schools
713990 Riding stables

713990 Rifle clubs, recreational
332994 Rifles (except recoilless, toy) manufacturing
332994 Rifles, BB and pellet, manufacturing
332994 Rifles, pneumatic, manufacturing
332995 Rifles, recoilless, manufacturing
339932 Rifles, toy, manufacturing
333512 Rifling machines, metalworking, manufacturing
213112 Rig skidding, oil and gas field, on a contract basis
238290 Rigging large-scale equipment
238910 Right of way cutting (except maintenance)
336399 Rims, automotive, truck, and bus wheel, manufacturing
336311 Rings, piston, manufacturing
713940 Rinks, ice or roller skating
237990 Riprap installation
212319 Riprap (except granite, limestone) preparation plants
212319 Riprap (except limestone and granite) mining or quarrying
212313 Riprap, granite, mining or quarrying
212313 Riprap, granite, preparation plants
212312 Riprap, limestone, mining or quarrying
212312 Riprap, limestone, preparation plants
483211 River freight transportation
483212 River passenger transportation
713990 River rafting, recreational
713210 Riverboat casinos
333991 Riveting guns, handheld power-driven, manufacturing
333513 Riveting machines, metalworking, manufacturing
332722 Rivets, metal, manufacturing
621399 RNs' (registered nurses) offices (e.g., centers, clinics)
325320 Roach poisons manufacturing
711110 Road companies, theatrical
237310 Road construction
423810 Road construction and maintenance machinery merchant wholesalers
324199 Road oils made from refined petroleum
324110 Road oils made in petroleum refineries
311911 Roasted nuts and seeds manufacturing
112320 Roaster chicken production
335211 Roasters (i.e., cooking appliances), household-type electric, manufacturing
311920 Roasting coffee
333294 Roasting machinery manufacturing
315291 Robes, lounging, infants', cut and sewn from purchased fabric (except apparel contractors)
315192 Robes, lounging, made in apparel knitting mills
315211 Robes, lounging, men's and boys', cut and sew apparel contractors
315221 Robes, lounging, men's and boys', cut and sewn from purchased fabric (except apparel contractors)
315212 Robes, lounging, women's, girls', and infants', cut and sew apparel contractors
315231 Robes, lounging, women's, misses', and girls', cut and sewn from purchased fabric (except apparel contractors)
333120 Rock crushing machinery, portable, manufacturing
333131 Rock crushing machinery, stationary, manufacturing
333132 Rock drill bits, oil and gas field-type, manufacturing
333120 Rock drills, construction and surface mining-type, manufacturing
333131 Rock drills, underground mining-type, manufacturing
711130 Rock musical artists, independent
711130 Rock musical groups
237990 Rock removal, underwater
212393 Rock salt mining and/or beneficiating

336312 Rocker arms and parts, automotive and truck gasoline engine, manufacturing
337122 Rockers (except upholstered), wood, manufacturing
337121 Rockers, upholstered, manufacturing
332313 Rocket casings, fabricated metal work, manufacturing
336412 Rocket engines, aircraft, manufacturing
336415 Rocket engines, guided missile, manufacturing
332995 Rocket launchers manufacturing
336414 Rockets (guided missiles), space and military, complete, manufacturing
332993 Rockets, ammunition (except guided missiles, pyrotechnic), manufacturing
114111 Rockfish fishing
339932 Rocking horses manufacturing
331316 Rod made by extruding purchased aluminum
331319 Rod made by rolling purchased aluminum
333516 Rod rolling mill machinery, metalworking, manufacturing
331316 Rod, aluminum, made in integrated secondary smelting and extruding mills
331319 Rod, aluminum, made in integrated secondary smelting and rolling mills
331421 Rod, copper and copper alloy, made from purchased copper or in integrated secondary smelting and rolling, drawing or extruding plants
326130 Rod, laminated plastics, manufacturing
331491 Rod, nonferrous metals (except aluminum, copper), made from purchased metals or scrap
326121 Rod, nonrigid plastics, manufacturing
325320 Rodent poisons manufacturing
325320 Rodenticides manufacturing
711310 Rodeo managers with facilities
711320 Rodeo managers without facilities
711310 Rodeo organizers with facilities
711320 Rodeo organizers without facilities
711310 Rodeo promoters with facilities
711320 Rodeo promoters without facilities
339920 Rods and rod parts, fishing, manufacturing
326299 Rods, hard rubber, manufacturing
331111 Rods, iron or steel, made in iron and steel mills
423510 Rods, metal (except precious), merchant wholesalers
334519 Rods, surveyor's, manufacturing
238160 Roll roofing installation
332991 Roller bearings manufacturing
711211 Roller hockey clubs, professional or semiprofessional
316110 Roller leather manufacturing
339920 Roller skates manufacturing
713940 Roller skating rinks
333120 Rollers, road construction and maintenance machinery, manufacturing
321999 Rollers, wood, manufacturing
332321 Rolling doors for industrial buildings and warehouses, metal, manufacturing
333516 Rolling mill machinery and equipment, metalworking, manufacturing
333516 Rolling mill roll machines, metalworking, manufacturing
331511 Rolling mill rolls, iron, manufacturing
331513 Rolling mill rolls, steel, manufacturing
321999 Rolling pins, wood, manufacturing
336510 Rolling stock, railroad, rebuilding
311812 Rolls and buns (including frozen) made in commercial bakeries

326299 Rolls and roll coverings, rubber (e.g., industrial, papermill, painters', steelmill) manufacturing
111219 Romaine lettuce farming, field and seed production
315291 Rompers, infants', cut and sewn from purchased fabric (except apparel contractors)
315212 Rompers, women's, girls', and infants', cut and sew apparel contractors
332322 Roof deck, sheet metal (except stampings), manufacturing
238310 Roof insulation contractor
238160 Roof membrane installation
238160 Roof painting, spraying, or coating
238130 Roof truss installation
321214 Roof trusses, wood, manufacturing
326299 Roofing (i.e., single ply rubber membrane) manufacturing
324122 Roofing cements, asphalt, made from purchased asphaltic materials
324122 Roofing coatings made from purchased asphaltic materials
238160 Roofing contractors
324122 Roofing felts made from purchased asphaltic materials
444190 Roofing material dealers
423330 Roofing materials (except wood) merchant wholesalers
423310 Roofing materials, wood, merchant wholesalers
327123 Roofing tile, clay, manufacturing
327390 Roofing tile, concrete, manufacturing
238160 Roofing, built-up tar and gravel, installation
332322 Roofing, sheet metal (except stampings), manufacturing
333415 Room air-conditioners manufacturing
423620 Room air-conditioners merchant wholesalers
337122 Room dividers, wood household-type, manufacturing
333414 Room heaters (except portable electric) manufacturing
335211 Room heaters, portable electric, manufacturing
334512 Room thermostats manufacturing
721310 Rooming and boarding houses
325320 Root removing chemicals manufacturing
311221 Root starches manufacturing
332999 Rope fittings manufacturing
332618 Rope, wire, made from purchased wire
314991 Ropes (except wire rope) manufacturing
423840 Ropes (except wire rope) merchant wholesalers
313111 Ropes, hemp, made from purchased fiber
423510 Ropes, wire (except insulated), merchant wholesalers
339911 Rosaries and other small religious articles, precious metal, manufacturing
212291 Roscoelite (vanadium hydromica) mining and/or beneficiating
111421 Rose bush growing
325211 Rosins (i.e., modified resins) manufacturing
325191 Rosins made by distillation of pine gum or pine wood
424690 Rosins merchant wholesalers
333111 Rotary hoes manufacturing
333111 Rotary tillers, farm-type, manufacturing
334514 Rotary type meters, consumption registering, manufacturing
325320 Rotenone insecticides manufacturing
323111 Rotogravure printing
323122 Rotogravure printing plates and cylinders preparation services
335312 Rotor retainers and housings manufacturing
335312 Rotors (i.e., for motors) manufacturing
325620 Rouge, cosmetic, manufacturing

321920 Round stave baskets (e.g., fruit, vegetable) manufacturing
321912 Rounds or rungs, furniture, hardwood, manufacturing
331111 Rounds, tube, steel, made in iron and steel mills
423990 Roundwood merchant wholesalers
213112 Roustabout mining services, on a contract basis
333991 Routers, handheld power-driven, manufacturing
333292 Roving machinery for textiles manufacturing
236115 Row house (i.e., single-family type) construction general contractors
236117 Row house construction operative builders
532292 Rowboat rental
336612 Rowboats manufacturing
713990 Rowing clubs, recreational
112910 Royal jelly production, bees
326220 Rubber and plastics belts and hoses (without fittings) manufacturing
326299 Rubber bands manufacturing
325520 Rubber cements manufacturing
212324 Rubber clay mining and/or beneficiating
238290 Rubber door installation
326192 Rubber floor coverings manufacturing
326291 Rubber goods, mechanical (i.e., extruded, lathe-cut, molded), manufacturing
423840 Rubber goods, mechanical (i.e., extruded, lathe-cut, molded), merchant wholesalers
424210 Rubber goods, medical, merchant wholesalers
325998 Rubber processing preparations (e.g., accelerators, stabilizers) manufacturing
423930 Rubber scrap and scrap tires merchant wholesalers
339943 Rubber stamps manufacturing
424120 Rubber stamps, merchant wholesalers
313221 Rubber thread and yarns, fabric covered, manufacturing
333220 Rubber working machinery manufacturing
424990 Rubber, crude, merchant wholesalers
325212 Rubber, synthetic, manufacturing
313320 Rubberizing purchased capes
313320 Rubberizing purchased cloaks
313320 Rubberizing purchased clothing
313320 Rubberizing purchased coats
313320 Rubberizing purchased textiles and apparel
212399 Rubbing stones mining and/or beneficiating
562111 Rubbish (i.e., nonhazardous solid waste) hauling, local
562111 Rubbish collection services
562213 Rubbish disposal combustors or incinerators
562212 Rubbish disposal landfills
484220 Rubbish hauling without collection or disposal, truck, local
484230 Rubbish hauling without collection or disposal, truck, long-distance
562119 Rubble hauling, local
562119 Rubble removal services
212399 Ruby mining and/or beneficiating
532299 Rug and carpet rental
561740 Rug cleaning plants
325612 Rug cleaning preparations manufacturing
561740 Rug cleaning services
442210 Rug stores
314110 Rugs and carpets made from textile materials
423220 Rugs merchant wholesalers
321999 Rulers and rules (except slide), wood, manufacturing
332212 Rulers, metal, manufacturing
326199 Rulers, plastics, manufacturing
334519 Rules, slide, manufacturing
624221 Runaway youth shelters
488119 Runway maintenance services
237310 Runway, airport, line painting (e.g., striping)

485210 Rural bus services
324191 Rust arresting petroleum compounds made from refined petroleum
325998 Rust preventive preparations manufacturing
325612 Rust removers manufacturing
238320 Rustproofing (except automotive)
332812 Rustproofing metals and metal products for the trade
811198 Rustproofing shops, automotive
111219 Rutabaga farming, field and seed production
212299 Ruthenium ore mining and/or beneficiating
212299 Rutile mining and/or beneficiating
721211 RV (recreational vehicle) parks
532120 RV (recreational vehicle) rental or leasing
441210 RV dealers
111199 Rye farming, field and seed production
311211 Rye flour manufacturing
311213 Rye malt manufacturing
111998 Ryegrass seed farming
114111 Sablefish fishing
325199 Saccharin manufacturing
325620 Sachet, scented, manufacturing
322224 Sacks, multiwall, made from purchased uncoated paper
424130 Sacks, paper, merchant wholesalers
713990 Saddle horse rental services, recreational
325612 Saddle soaps manufacturing
321999 Saddle trees, wood, manufacturing
316110 Saddlery leather manufacturing
424910 Saddlery merchant wholesalers
332999 Saddlery parts, metal, manufacturing
811430 Saddlery repair shops without retailing new saddlery
451110 Saddlery stores
316999 Saddles and parts, leather, manufacturing
332999 Safe deposit boxes and chests, metal, manufacturing
332999 Safe doors and linings, metal, manufacturing
332999 Safes, metal, manufacturing
423420 Safes, security, merchant wholesalers
332911 Safety (i.e., pop-off) valves, industrial-type, manufacturing
316999 Safety belts, leather, manufacturing
541690 Safety consulting services
325920 Safety fuses, blasting, manufacturing
327215 Safety glass (including motor vehicle) made from purchased glass
238990 Safety net system, erecting and dismantling at construction site
339993 Safety pins manufacturing
332211 Safety razor blades manufacturing
332211 Safety razors manufacturing
111120 Safflower farming, field and seed production
311225 Safflower oil made from purchased oils
311223 Safflower oil made in crushing mills
441222 Sail boat dealers
339920 Sailboards manufacturing
336612 Sailboat building, not done in shipyards
532292 Sailboat rental
713930 Sailing clubs with marinas
713990 Sailing clubs without marinas
336611 Sailing ships, commercial, manufacturing
314912 Sails made from purchased fabrics
325181 Sal soda (i.e., washing soda) manufacturing
311423 Salad dressing mixes, dry, made in a dehydration plant
311942 Salad dressing mixes, dry, manufacturing
311941 Salad dressings manufacturing
424490 Salad dressings merchant wholesalers
424490 Salad oils merchant wholesalers

311991 Salads, fresh or refrigerated, manufacturing
424120 Sales books merchant wholesalers
323116 Sales books, manifold, printing
522220 Sales financing
541613 Sales management consulting services
325199 Salicylic acid (except medicinal) manufacturing
325411 Salicylic acid, medicinal, uncompounded, manufacturing
212391 Salines (except common salt) mining and/or beneficiating
114111 Salmon fishing
236220 Salon construction
311421 Salsa canning
325998 Salt (except table) manufacturing
311942 Salt substitute manufacturing
213112 Salt water disposal systems, oil and gas field, on a contract basis
212393 Salt, common, mining and/or beneficiating
212393 Salt, rock, mining and/or beneficiating
311942 Salt, table, manufacturing
424490 Salt, table, merchant wholesalers
311612 Salted meats made from purchased carcasses
311821 Saltines manufacturing
424210 Salts, bath, merchant wholesalers
424690 Salts, industrial, merchant wholesalers
334516 Sample analysis instruments (except medical) manufacturing
316991 Sample cases, all materials, manufacturing
334519 Sample changers, nuclear radiation, manufacturing
541870 Sample direct distribution services
323121 Samples mounting
541910 Sampling services, statistical
423320 Sand (except industrial) merchant wholesalers
212321 Sand and gravel quarrying (i.e., construction grade) and/or beneficiating
213112 Sand blasting pipelines on lease, oil and gas field on a contract basis
331524 Sand castings, aluminum, unfinished, manufacturing
331525 Sand castings, copper and copper-base alloy, unfinished, manufacturing
331528 Sand castings, nonferrous metals (except aluminum, copper), unfinished, manufacturing
484220 Sand hauling, local
484230 Sand hauling, long-distance
333120 Sand mixers manufacturing
212322 Sand, blast, quarrying and/or beneficiating
212321 Sand, construction grade, quarrying and/or beneficiating
212322 Sand, industrial (e.g., engine, filtration, glass grinding), quarrying and/or beneficiating
423840 Sand, industrial, merchant wholesalers
316219 Sandals, children's (except rubber, plastics), manufacturing
316213 Sandals, men's footwear (except rubber, plastics), manufacturing
316211 Sandals, plastics or plastics soled fabric upper, manufacturing
316211 Sandals, rubber or rubber soled fabric upper, manufacturing
316214 Sandals, women's footwear (except rubber, plastics), manufacturing
332813 Sandblasting metals and metal products for the trade
238990 Sandblasting, building exterior
333991 Sanders, handheld power-driven, manufacturing
333319 Sanding machines, floor, manufacturing

333210 Sanding machines, woodworking-type, stationary, manufacturing
333291 Sandpaper making machines manufacturing
327910 Sandpaper manufacturing
212319 Sandstone crushed and broken stone mining
212311 Sandstone mining or quarrying
212399 Sandstone, bituminous, mining and/or beneficiating
722211 Sandwich shops, limited-service
311612 Sandwich spreads, meat, made from purchased carcasses
311941 Sandwich spreads, salad dressing based, manufacturing
335211 Sandwich toasters and grills, household-type electric, manufacturing
424490 Sandwiches merchant wholesalers
311991 Sandwiches, fresh (i.e., assembled and packaged for wholesale market), manufacturing
322212 Sanitary food container, folding, made from purchased paperboard
424130 Sanitary food containers (e.g., disposable plastics, paper, paperboard) merchant wholesalers
322215 Sanitary food containers (except folding) made from purchased paper or paperboard
562212 Sanitary landfills
322291 Sanitary napkins and tampons made from purchased paper or textile fiber
322121 Sanitary napkins and tampons made in paper mills
322121 Sanitary paper products (except newsprint, uncoated groundwood) made in paper mills
424130 Sanitary paper products merchant wholesalers
322121 Sanitary paper stock manufacturing
322291 Sanitary products made from purchased sanitary paper stock
322121 Sanitary products made in paper mills
237110 Sanitary sewer construction
332998 Sanitary ware (e.g., bathtubs, lavatories, sinks), metal, manufacturing
238220 Sanitary ware installation
423720 Sanitary ware, china or enameled iron, merchant wholesalers
541620 Sanitation consulting services
926130 Sanitation districts, nonoperating
924110 Sanitation engineering agencies, government
212399 Sapphire mining and/or beneficiating
325222 Saran (i.e., polyvinylidene chloride) fibers and filaments manufacturing
332612 Sash balance springs, light gauge, made from purchased wire or strip
332321 Sash, door and window, metal, manufacturing
321911 Sash, door and window, wood and covered wood, manufacturing
316991 Satchels, all materials, manufacturing
334220 Satellite antennas manufacturing
334220 Satellite communications equipment manufacturing
238290 Satellite dish, household-type, installation
517510 Satellite master antenna television service (SMATV)
515111 Satellite radio networks
237130 Satellite receiving station construction
517410 Satellite telecommunication carriers
517410 Satellite telecommunication resellers
517910 Satellite telemetry operations on a contract or fee basis
517510 Satellite television distribution systems

515210 Satellite television networks
517910 Satellite tracking stations on a contract or fee basis
325131 Satin white pigments manufacturing
335311 Saturable transformers manufacturing
324122 Saturated felts made from purchased paper
322121 Saturated felts made in paper mills
311423 Sauce mixes, dry, made in dehydration plants
311942 Sauce mixes, dry, manufacturing
311941 Sauces (except tomato based) manufacturing
311941 Sauces for meat (except tomato based) manufacturing
311941 Sauces for seafood (except tomato based) manufacturing
311941 Sauces for vegetable (except tomato based) manufacturing
311421 Sauces, tomato-based, canning
311421 Sauerkraut manufacturing
335211 Sauna heaters, electric, manufacturing
321992 Sauna rooms, prefabricated, wood, manufacturing
812199 Saunas
311612 Sausage and similar cased products made from purchased carcasses
424490 Sausage casings merchant wholesalers
311612 Sausage casings, collagen, made from purchased hides
311611 Sausage casings, natural, produced in slaughtering plant
326121 Sausage casings, plastics, manufacturing
522120 Savings and loan associations (S&L)
524113 Savings bank life insurance carriers, direct
522120 Savings banks
522120 Savings institutions
332213 Saw blades, all types, manufacturing
811411 Saw repair and maintenance (except sawmills) without retailing new saws
321113 Sawdust and shavings (i.e., sawmill byproducts) manufacturing
424990 Sawdust merchant wholesalers
321999 Sawdust, regrinding
321113 Sawed lumber made in sawmills
321912 Sawed lumber, resawing purchased lumber
333512 Sawing machines, metalworking, manufacturing
333210 Sawmill equipment manufacturing
532490 Sawmill machinery rental or leasing
423830 Sawmill machinery, equipment, and supplies merchant wholesalers
321113 Sawmills
333210 Saws, bench and table, power-driven, woodworking-type, manufacturing
332213 Saws, hand, nonpowered, manufacturing
333991 Saws, handheld power-driven, manufacturing
339112 Saws, surgical, manufacturing
339992 Saxophones and parts manufacturing
238990 Scaffold erecting and dismantling
423810 Scaffolding merchant wholesalers
532490 Scaffolding rental or leasing
332323 Scaffolds, metal, manufacturing
334519 Scalers, nuclear radiation, manufacturing
333997 Scales (except laboratory-type) manufacturing
339111 Scales and balances, laboratory-type, manufacturing
339111 Scales, laboratory, manufacturing
114112 Scallop fishing
812199 Scalp treating services
518210 Scanning services, optical

333210 Scarfing machines, woodworking-type, manufacturing
333516 Scarfing units, rolling mill machinery, metalworking, manufacturing
333120 Scarifiers, road, manufacturing
325132 Scarlet 2 R lake manufacturing
315191 Scarves made in apparel knitting mills
315211 Scarves, men's and boys', cut and sew apparel contractors
315993 Scarves, men's and boys', cut and sewn from purchased fabric (except apparel contractors)
315212 Scarves, women's, girls', and infants', cut and sew apparel contractors
315999 Scarves, women's, misses', and girls', cut and sewn from purchased fabric (except apparel contractors)
336350 Scattershield, engine, manufacturing
711510 Scenery designers, independent theatrical
532490 Scenery, theatrical, rental or leasing
487990 Scenic and sightseeing excursions, aerial
487110 Scenic and sightseeing excursions, land
487210 Scenic and sightseeing excursions, water
481112 Scheduled air freight carriers
481112 Scheduled air freight transportation
481111 Scheduled air passenger carriers
481111 Scheduled air passenger transportation
212299 Scheelite mining and/or beneficiating
313222 Schiffli machine embroideries manufacturing
333292 Schiffli machinery manufacturing
212319 Schist, mica, crushed and broken stone, mining and/or beneficiating
212311 Schist, mica, mining or quarrying
511120 Scholarly journal publishers (except exclusive Internet publishing)
511120 Scholarly journal publishers and printing combined
516110 Scholarly journal publishers, exclusively on Internet
323112 Scholarly journals flexographic printing without publishing
323111 Scholarly journals gravure printing without publishing
323110 Scholarly journals lithographic (offset) printing without publishing
323119 Scholarly journals printing (except flexographic, gravure, lithographic, quick, screen) without publishing
323113 Scholarly journals screen printing without publishing
813211 Scholarship trusts (i.e., grantmaking, charitable trust foundations)
511120 Scholastic magazine and periodical publishers (except exclusive Internet publishing)
511120 Scholastic magazine and periodical publishers and printing combined
516110 Scholastic magazine and periodical publishers, exclusively on Internet
323112 Scholastic magazines and periodicals flexographic printing without publishing
323111 Scholastic magazines and periodicals gravure printing without publishing
323110 Scholastic magazines and periodicals lithographic (offset) printing without publishing
323119 Scholastic magazines and periodicals printing (except flexographic, gravure, lithographic, quick, screen) without publishing

323113 Scholastic magazines and periodicals screen printing without publishing
611110 School boards, elementary and secondary
511130 School book publishers (except exclusive Internet publishing)
511130 School book publishers and printing combined
516110 School book publishers, exclusively on Internet
323117 School books printing and binding without publishing
323117 School books printing without publishing
236220 School building construction
611710 School bus attendant services
423110 School bus merchant wholesalers
532120 School bus rental or leasing
485410 School bus services
336211 School buses assembling on purchased chassis
611110 School districts, elementary or secondary
423490 School equipment and supplies (except books, furniture) merchant wholesalers
337127 School furniture manufacturing
423210 School furniture merchant wholesalers
541921 School photography (i.e., portrait photography) services
453210 School supply stores
511130 School textbook publishers (except exclusive Internet publishing)
511130 School textbook publishers and printing combined
516110 School textbook publishers, exclusively on Internet
323121 School textbooks binding without printing
448190 School uniform stores
611110 Schools for the handicapped, elementary or secondary
611110 Schools for the mentally retarded (except preschool, job training, vocational rehabilitation)
611110 Schools for the physically disabled, elementary or secondary
611512 Schools, aviation
611511 Schools, barber
611511 Schools, beauty
611410 Schools, business, not offering academic degrees
611310 Schools, correspondence, college level
611511 Schools, cosmetology
611610 Schools, drama (except academic)
611110 Schools, elementary
611210 Schools, junior college
611210 Schools, junior college vocational
611630 Schools, language
611310 Schools, medical
611610 Schools, music (except academic)
611310 Schools, professional (colleges or universities)
611110 Schools, secondary
611620 Schools, sports instruction
712110 Science and technology museums
339932 Science kits (e.g., chemistry sets, microscopes, natural science sets) manufacturing
327215 Scientific apparatus glassware made from purchased glass
813920 Scientific associations
327215 Scientific glassware made from purchased glass
327212 Scientific glassware, pressed or blown, made in glass making plants
423490 Scientific instruments merchant wholesalers
511120 Scientific journal and periodical publishers (except exclusive Internet publishing)
511120 Scientific journal and periodical publishers and printing combined
516110 Scientific journal and periodical publishers, exclusively on Internet

423490 Scientific laboratory equipment merchant wholesalers
334519 Scintillation detectors manufacturing
335211 Scissors, electric, manufacturing
332211 Scissors, nonelectric, manufacturing
332212 Scoops, metal (except kitchen-type), manufacturing
321999 Scoops, wood, manufacturing
339932 Scooters, children's, manufacturing
339950 Scoreboards manufacturing
212399 Scoria mining and/or beneficiating
313312 Scouring and combing textile fibers
325611 Scouring cleansers (e.g., pastes, powders) manufacturing
332999 Scouring pads, soap impregnated, manufacturing
813410 Scouting organizations
423930 Scrap materials (e.g., automotive, industrial) merchant wholesalers
323118 Scrapbooks and refills manufacturing
424120 Scrapbooks merchant wholesalers
333131 Scraper loaders, underground mining-type, manufacturing
333120 Scrapers, construction-type, manufacturing
332321 Screen doors, metal frame, manufacturing
323122 Screen for printing, preparation services
323113 Screen printing (except books, manifold business forms, grey goods)
323113 Screen printing apparel and textile products (e.g. caps, napkins, placemats, T-shirts, towels) (except grey goods)
313311 Screen printing broadwoven fabric grey goods
325910 Screen process inks manufacturing
333999 Screening and sifting machinery for general industrial use manufacturing
333120 Screening machinery, portable, manufacturing
333131 Screening machinery, stationary, manufacturing
212399 Screening peat
212113 Screening plants, anthracite
212111 Screening plants, bituminous coal or lignite
326199 Screening, window, plastics, manufacturing
711510 Screenplay writers, independent
313312 Screenprinting fabric grey goods (except broadwoven) and textile products (except apparel)
334419 Screens for liquid crystal display (LCD) manufacturing
332321 Screens, door and window, metal frame, manufacturing
321911 Screens, door and window, wood framed, manufacturing
333315 Screens, projection (i.e., motion picture, overhead, slide), manufacturing
423310 Screens, window and door, merchant wholesalers
333512 Screw and nut slotting machines, metalworking, manufacturing
333922 Screw conveyors manufacturing
332212 Screw drivers, nonelectric, manufacturing
332722 Screw eyes, metal, manufacturing
333518 Screwdowns and boxes machinery, metal, manufacturing
333991 Screwdrivers and nut drivers, handheld power-driven, manufacturing
333518 Screwdriving machines manufacturing
332212 Screwjacks manufacturing
332722 Screws, metal, manufacturing
711510 Script writers, independent
238220 Scrubber, air purification, installation

339920 Scuba diving equipment manufacturing
611620 Scuba instruction, camps, or schools
711510 Sculptors, independent
611610 Sculpture instruction
327420 Sculptures (e.g., gypsum, plaster of paris) manufacturing
327112 Sculptures, architectural, clay, manufacturing
332212 Scythes manufacturing
212399 Scythestones mining and/or beneficiating
114111 Sea bass fishing
114111 Sea herring fishing
713990 Sea kayaking, recreational
111998 Sea plant agriculture
114111 Sea trout fishing
114112 Sea urchin fishing
424460 Seafood (except canned, packaged frozen) merchant wholesalers
311711 Seafood and seafood products canning
311711 Seafood and seafood products curing
311712 Seafood dinners, frozen, manufacturing
445220 Seafood markets
311712 Seafood products, fresh prepared, manufacturing
311712 Seafood products, frozen, manufacturing
424490 Seafood, canned, merchant wholesalers
311712 Seafood, fresh prepared, manufacturing
311712 Seafood, frozen, manufacturing
424420 Seafoods, packaged frozen, merchant wholesalers
339943 Seal presses (e.g., notary), hand operated, manufacturing
424690 Sealants merchant wholesalers
335110 Sealed beam automotive light bulbs manufacturing
325520 Sealing compounds for pipe threads and joints manufacturing
423840 Seals merchant wholesalers
339991 Seals, grease or oil, manufacturing
333992 Seam welding equipment manufacturing
334511 Search and detection systems and instruments manufacturing
518112 Search portals, Internet
335129 Searchlights, electric and nonelectric, manufacturing
453220 Seasonal and holiday decoration stores
721110 Seasonal hotels without casinos
561730 Seasonal property maintenance services (i.e., snow plowing in winter, landscaping during other seasons)
311942 Seasoning salt manufacturing
336360 Seat belts, motor vehicle and aircraft, manufacturing
423120 Seat covers, automotive, merchant wholesalers
321999 Seat covers, rattan, manufacturing
326150 Seat cushions, foam plastics (except polystyrene), manufacturing
316999 Seatbelts, leather, manufacturing
336360 Seats for public conveyances, manufacturing
336360 Seats, railroad, manufacturing
321999 Seats, toilet, wood, manufacturing
237990 Seawall, wave protection, construction
488310 Seaway operation
111998 Seaweed farming
114119 Seaweed gathering
311711 Seaweed processing (e.g., dulse)
325199 Sebacic acid esters manufacturing
325199 Sebacic acid manufacturing
611630 Second language instruction
522294 Secondary market financing (i.e., buying, pooling, repackaging loans for sale to others)
331492 Secondary refining of nonferrous metals (except aluminum, copper)

611110 Secondary schools offering both academic and technical courses
331492 Secondary smelting of nonferrous metals (except aluminum, copper)
453310 Second-hand merchandise stores
611410 Secretarial schools
561410 Secretarial services
332311 Sections for prefabricated metal buildings manufacturing
321992 Sections, prefabricated wood building, manufacturing
523120 Securities brokerages
523120 Securities brokers' offices
523991 Securities custodians
523110 Securities dealers (i.e., acting as a principal in dealing securities to investors)
523110 Securities dealing (i.e., acting as a principal in dealing securities to investors)
523110 Securities distributing (i.e., acting as a principal in dealing securities to investors)
523210 Securities exchanges
523120 Securities floor brokers
523110 Securities floor traders (i.e., acting as a principal in dealing securities to investors)
523110 Securities flotation companies
523999 Securities holders' protective services
523110 Securities originating (i.e., acting as a principal in dealing securities to investors)
926150 Securities regulation commissions
523110 Securities trading (i.e., acting as a principal in dealing securities to investors)
523999 Securities transfer agencies
523110 Securities underwriting
561621 Security alarm systems sales combined with installation, repair, or monitoring services
238210 Security and fire system, installation only
541690 Security consulting services
561612 Security guard services
611519 Security guard training
561612 Security patrol services
423420 Security safes merchant wholesalers
561621 Security system monitoring services
423610 Security systems merchant wholesalers
325412 Sedative preparations manufacturing
212399 Sedge peat mining and/or beneficiating
237990 Sediment control system construction
333131 Sedimentary mineral machinery manufacturing
314911 Seed bags made from purchased woven or knitted materials
115112 Seed bed preparing
115114 Seed cleaning
322232 Seed packets made from purchased paper
541380 Seed testing laboratories or services
325320 Seed treatment preparations manufacturing
333111 Seeders, farm-type, manufacturing
333112 Seeders, lawn and garden-type, manufacturing
115112 Seeding crops
561730 Seeding lawns
424450 Seeds (e.g., canned, roasted, salted) merchant wholesalers
424910 Seeds (e.g., field, flower, garden) merchant wholesalers
311911 Seeds, snack (e.g., canned, cooked, roasted, salted) manufacturing
541360 Seismic geophysical surveying services
213112 Seismograph exploration (except surveying) for oil and gas on a contract basis
334519 Seismographs manufacturing
334519 Seismometers manufacturing
334519 Seismoscopes manufacturing
212399 Selenite mining and/or beneficiating

331491 Selenium bar, rod, sheet, strip, and tubing made from purchased metals or scrap
325188 Selenium compounds, not specified elsewhere by process, manufacturing
325188 Selenium dioxide manufacturing
331492 Selenium recovering from scrap and/or alloying purchased metals
331419 Selenium refining, primary
611699 Self defense (except martial arts) instruction
624190 Self-help organizations (except for disabled persons, the elderly, persons diagnosed with mental retardation)
624120 Self-help organizations for disabled persons, the elderly, and persons diagnosed with mental retardation
624110 Self-help organizations, youth
525190 Self-insurance funds (except employee benefit funds)
811192 Self-service carwash
812310 Self-service drycleaners and laundries
531130 Self-storage unit rental or leasing
531130 Self-storage warehousing
531210 Selling real estate for others (i.e., agents, brokers)
115210 Semen collection
424590 Semen, bovine, merchant wholesalers
212111 Semianthracite surface mining and/or beneficiating
212112 Semianthracite underground mining or mining and beneficiating
212111 Semibituminous coal surface mining and/or beneficiating
212112 Semibituminous coal underground mining or mining and beneficiating
333295 Semiconductor assembly and packaging machinery manufacturing
335999 Semiconductor battery chargers manufacturing
334413 Semiconductor circuit networks (i.e., solid-state integrated circuits) manufacturing
334413 Semiconductor devices manufacturing
423690 Semiconductor devices merchant wholesalers
334413 Semiconductor dice and wafers manufacturing
335999 Semiconductor high-voltage power supplies manufacturing
333295 Semiconductor making machinery manufacturing
334413 Semiconductor memory chips manufacturing
334515 Semiconductor test equipment manufacturing
333618 Semidiesel engines manufacturing
423510 Semi-finished metal products merchant wholesalers
611110 Seminaries, below university grade
611310 Seminaries, theological, offering baccalaureate or graduate degrees
212399 Semiprecious stones mining and/or beneficiating
711211 Semiprofessional baseball clubs
711211 Semiprofessional football clubs
711211 Semiprofessional sports clubs
331511 Semisteel foundries
336212 Semi-trailer manufacturing
532120 Semi-trailer rental or leasing
311211 Semolina flour manufacturing
624120 Senior citizens activity centers
813311 Senior citizens advocacy organizations
813410 Senior citizens' associations, social
624120 Senior citizens centers
623312 Senior citizens' homes without nursing care
485991 Senior citizens transportation services
325992 Sensitized cloth or paper (e.g., blueprint, photographic) manufacturing
333315 Sensitometers, photographic, manufacturing

334510 Sentinel, cardiac, manufacturing
238910 Septic system contractors
238910 Septic tank and weeping tile installation
562991 Septic tank cleaning services
562991 Septic tank pumping (i.e., cleaning) services
423390 Septic tanks (except concrete) merchant wholesalers
423320 Septic tanks, concrete, merchant wholesalers
332420 Septic tanks, heavy gauge metal, manufacturing
326199 Septic tanks, plastics or fiberglass, manufacturing
334512 Sequencing controls for electric heating equipment manufacturing
335999 Series capacitors (except electronic) manufacturing
212319 Serpentine crushed and broken stone mining and/or beneficiating
212311 Serpentine mining or quarrying
325414 Serums (except diagnostic substances) manufacturing
315211 Service apparel, washable, men's and boys', cut and sew apparel contractors
315225 Service apparel, washable, men's and boys', cut and sewn from purchased fabric (except apparel contractors)
315212 Service apparel, washable, women's, cut and sew apparel contractors
315239 Service apparel, washable, women's, misses' and girls', cut and sewn from purchased fabric (except apparel contractors)
423850 Service establishment equipment and supplies merchant wholesalers
813910 Service industries associations
237120 Service line, gas and oil, construction
811310 Service machinery and equipment repair and maintenance services
561720 Service station cleaning and degreasing services
236220 Service station construction
447190 Service stations, gasoline
213111 Service well drilling on a contract basis
213112 Servicing oil and gas wells on a contract basis
337124 Serving carts, metal household-type, manufacturing
337122 Serving carts, wood household-type, manufacturing
335312 Servomotors manufacturing
111120 Sesame farming, field and seed production
711510 Set designers, independent theatrical
541191 Settlement offices, real estate
322213 Setup (i.e., not shipped flat) boxes made from purchased paperboard
322130 Setup boxboard stock manufacturing
237110 Sewage collection and disposal line construction
237110 Sewage disposal plant construction
221320 Sewage disposal plants
333319 Sewage treatment equipment manufacturing
237110 Sewage treatment plant construction
221320 Sewage treatment plants or facilities
562998 Sewer cleaning and rodding services
562998 Sewer cleanout services
237110 Sewer construction
238220 Sewer hook-up and connection, building
237110 Sewer main, pipe and connection, construction
327123 Sewer pipe and fittings, clay, manufacturing
331511 Sewer pipe, cast iron, manufacturing

327332 Sewer pipe, concrete, manufacturing
221320 Sewer systems
424310 Sewing accessories merchant wholesalers
339999 Sewing and mending kits assembling
316993 Sewing cases (except metal) manufacturing
339911 Sewing cases, precious metal, manufacturing
315211 Sewing fabric owned by others for men's and boys' apparel
315212 Sewing fabric owned by others for women's, girls' and infants' apparel
337129 Sewing machine cabinets, wood, manufacturing
443111 Sewing machine stores, household-type
811412 Sewing machine, household-type, repair shops without retailing new sewing machines
333298 Sewing machines (including household-type) manufacturing
423620 Sewing machines, household-type, merchant wholesalers
423830 Sewing machines, industrial, merchant wholesalers
451130 Sewing supply stores
313113 Sewing threads manufacturing
334511 Sextants (except surveying) manufacturing
334519 Sextants, surveying, manufacturing
337920 Shade pulls, window, manufacturing
335121 Shades, lamp (except glass, plastics), residential-type, manufacturing
337920 Shades, window (except outdoor canvas awnings), manufacturing
213113 Shaft sinking for coal mines on a contract basis
213114 Shaft sinking for metal mines on a contract basis
238160 Shake and shingle, roof, installation
321113 Shakes (i.e., hand split shingles) manufacturing
212325 Shale (except oil shale) mining and/or beneficiating
327992 Shale, expanded, manufacturing
211111 Shale, oil, mining and/or beneficiating
111219 Shallot farming, field and seed production
325620 Shampoos and conditioners, hair, manufacturing
316999 Shanks, shoe, leather, manufacturing
333210 Shapers, woodworking-type, manufacturing
114111 Shark fishing
339994 Shaving brushes manufacturing
333512 Shaving machines, metalworking, manufacturing
325620 Shaving preparations (e.g., creams, gels, lotions, powders) manufacturing
424210 Shaving preparations merchant wholesalers
333513 Shearing machines, metal forming, manufacturing
316110 Shearling (i.e., prepared sheepskin) manufacturing
333991 Shears and nibblers, handheld power-driven, manufacturing
332211 Shears, nonelectric, household-type (e.g., kitchen, barber, tailor) manufacturing
332212 Shears, nonelectric, tool-type (e.g., garden, pruners, tinsnip), manufacturing
333111 Shears, powered, for use on animals, manufacturing
322121 Sheathing paper (except newsprint, uncoated groundwood) made in paper mills
324122 Sheathing, asphalt saturated, made from refined petroleum
238130 Sheathing, wood, installation
333613 Sheaves, mechanical power transmission, manufacturing
332311 Sheds, (e.g., garden, storage, utility) prefabricated metal, manufacturing

321992 Sheds, (e.g., garden, storage, utility) prefabricated wood, manufacturing
115210 Sheep dipping and shearing
112410 Sheep farming (e.g., meat, milk, wool production)
424520 Sheep merchant wholesalers
333111 Sheep shears, powered, manufacturing
326140 Sheet (i.e., board), polystyrene foam insulation, manufacturing
238220 Sheet metal duct work installation
333513 Sheet metal forming machines manufacturing
238160 Sheet metal roofing installation
423330 Sheet metal roofing materials merchant wholesalers
332322 Sheet metal work (except stampings) manufacturing
611513 Sheet metal workers' apprenticeship training
323112 Sheet music flexographic printing without publishing
323111 Sheet music gravure printing without publishing
323110 Sheet music lithographic (offset) printing without publishing
424990 Sheet music merchant wholesalers
323119 Sheet music printing (except flexographic, gravure, lithographic, qiuck, screen) without publishing
512230 Sheet music publishers
512230 Sheet music publishers and printing combined
323113 Sheet music screen printing without publishing
451140 Sheet music stores
331111 Sheet pilings, plain, iron or steel, made in iron and steel mills
331315 Sheet, aluminum, made by flat rolling purchased aluminum
331315 Sheet, aluminum, made in integrated secondary smelting and flat rolling mills
331421 Sheet, copper and copper alloy, made from purchased copper or in integrated secondary smelting and rolling, drawing or extruding plants
326130 Sheet, laminated plastics (except flexible packaging), manufacturing
326113 Sheet, plastics, unlaminated (except packaging), manufacturing
326299 Sheeting, rubber, manufacturing
314129 Sheets and pillowcases made from purchased fabrics
313210 Sheets and pillowcases made in broadwoven fabric mills
331111 Sheets, steel, made in iron and steel mills
311119 Shell crushing and grinding for animal feed
311119 Shell crushing for feed
332993 Shell loading and assembly plants
212399 Shell mining and/or beneficiating
339999 Shell novelties
331111 Shell slugs, steel, made in iron and steel mills
325510 Shellac manufacturing
424950 Shellac merchant wholesalers
311711 Shellfish and shellfish products canning
311711 Shellfish curing
114112 Shellfish fishing (e.g., clam, crab, oyster, shrimp)
112512 Shellfish hatcheries
311712 Shellfish products, fresh prepared, manufacturing
311712 Shellfish products, frozen, manufacturing
311712 Shellfish, fresh prepared, manufacturing
311712 Shellfish, frozen, manufacturing
332993 Shells, artillery, manufacturing
332992 Shells, small arms (i.e., 30 mm. or less, 1.18 inch or less), manufacturing

624310 Sheltered workshops (i.e., work experience centers)
624221 Shelters (except for victims of domestic or international disasters or conflicts), emergency
624230 Shelters for victims of domestic or international disasters or conflicts, emergency
624221 Shelters, battered women's
624221 Shelters, homeless
624221 Shelters, runaway youth
624221 Shelters, temporary (e.g., battered women's, homeless, runaway youth)
337215 Shelving (except wire) manufacturing
423440 Shelving, commercial, merchant wholesalers
238390 Shelving, metal, constructed on site
332618 Shelving, wire, made from purchased wire
238350 Shelving, wood, constructed on site
332812 Sherardizing of metals and metal products for the trade
311520 Sherbets manufacturing
922120 Sheriffs' offices (except court functions only)
922110 Sheriffs' offices, court functions only
332999 Shims, metal, manufacturing
321113 Shingle mills, wood
423330 Shingles (except wood) merchant wholesalers
324122 Shingles made from purchased asphaltic materials
423310 Shingles, wood, merchant wholesalers
321113 Shingles, wood, sawed or hand split, manufacturing
331525 Ship and boat propellers, cast brass, bronze and copper (except die-casting), unfinished, manufacturing
424990 Ship chandler merchant wholesalers
483113 Ship chartering with crew, coastal or Great Lakes freight transportation (including St. Lawrence Seaway)
483114 Ship chartering with crew, coastal or Great Lakes passenger transportation (including St. Lawrence Seaway)
483111 Ship chartering with crew, deep sea freight transportation to or from foreign ports
483112 Ship chartering with crew, deep sea passenger transportation to or from foreign ports
483211 Ship chartering with crew, freight transportation, inland waters (except on Great Lakes system)
483212 Ship chartering with crew, passenger transportation, inland waters (except on Great Lakes system)
333923 Ship cranes and derricks manufacturing
561310 Ship crew employment agencies
561310 Ship crew registries
423930 Ship dismantling (except at floating drydocks and shipyards) merchant wholesalers
488390 Ship dismantling at floating drydock
336611 Ship dismantling at shipyards
337127 Ship furniture manufacturing
488320 Ship hold cleaning services
238350 Ship joinery contractors
238320 Ship painting contractors
532411 Ship rental or leasing without operators
336611 Ship repair done in a shipyard
336611 Ship scaling services done at a shipyard
488390 Ship scaling services not done at a shipyard
332312 Ship sections, prefabricated metal, manufacturing
331422 Shipboard cable made from purchased copper in wire drawing plants

331319 Shipboard cable made in aluminum wire drawing plants
488510 Shipping agents (freight forwarding)
314911 Shipping bags made from purchased woven or knitted materials
332439 Shipping barrels, drums, kegs, and pails, light gauge metal, manufacturing
321920 Shipping cases and drums, wood, wirebound, manufacturing
321920 Shipping cases, wood, nailed or lock corner, manufacturing
813910 Shipping companies' associations
423840 Shipping containers (except disposable plastics, paper) merchant wholesalers
322211 Shipping containers made from purchased paperboard
322211 Shipping containers, corrugated, made from purchased paper or paperboard
321920 Shipping crates, wood, manufacturing
483113 Shipping freight to and from domestic ports (i.e., coastal, deep sea (including Puerto Rico), Great Lakes system (including St. Lawrence Seaway))
483111 Shipping freight to or from foreign ports, deep sea
483211 Shipping freight, inland waters (except on Great Lakes system)
326150 Shipping pads and shaped cushioning, foam plastics (except polystyrene), manufacturing
326140 Shipping pads and shaped cushioning, polystyrene foam, manufacturing
423840 Shipping pails, metal, merchant wholesalers
323112 Shipping registers flexographic printing without publishing
323111 Shipping registers gravure printing without publishing
323110 Shipping registers lithographic (offset) printing without publishing
323113 Shipping registers screen printing without publishing
424130 Shipping supplies, paper and disposable plastics, merchant wholesalers
336611 Ships (i.e., not suitable or intended for personal use) manufacturing
423860 Ships merchant wholesalers
517212 Ship-to-shore broadcasting communication carriers (except satellite)
336611 Shipyard (i.e., facility capable of building ships)
315223 Shirts, outerwear (except work shirts), men's and boys', cut and sewn from purchased fabric (except apparel contractors)
315225 Shirts, outerwear work, men's and boys', cut and sewn from purchased fabric (except apparel contractors)
315291 Shirts, outerwear, infants', cut and sewn from purchased fabric (except apparel contractors)
315191 Shirts, outerwear, made in apparel knitting mills
315211 Shirts, outerwear, men's and boys', cut and sew apparel contractors
315223 Shirts, outerwear, unisex (i.e., sized without regard to gender), cut and sewn from purchased fabric (except apparel contractors)
315212 Shirts, outerwear, women's, girls', and infants', cut and sew apparel contractors
315232 Shirts, outerwear, women's, misses', and girls', cut and sewn from purchased fabric (except apparel contractors)

315291 Shirts, underwear, infants', cut and sewn from purchased fabric (except apparel contractors)
315192 Shirts, underwear, made in apparel knitting mills
315211 Shirts, underwear, men's and boys', cut and sew apparel contractors
315221 Shirts, underwear, men's and boys', cut and sewn from purchased fabric (except apparel contractors)
315212 Shirts, underwear, women's, girls', and infants', cut and sew apparel contractors
315231 Shirts, underwear, women's, misses', and girls', cut and sewn from purchased fabric (except apparel contractors)
111411 Shitake mushroom farming
336330 Shock absorbers, automotive, truck, and bus, manufacturing
448210 Shoe (except bowling, golf, spiked) stores
326299 Shoe and boot parts (e.g., heels, soles, soling strips), rubber, manufacturing
322212 Shoe boxes, folding, made from purchased paperboard
322213 Shoe boxes, setup, made from purchased paperboard
541490 Shoe design services
321999 Shoe display forms, all materials, manufacturing
316991 Shoe kits (i.e., cases), all materials, manufacturing
333298 Shoe making and repairing machinery manufacturing
423830 Shoe manufacturing and repairing machinery merchant wholesalers
326199 Shoe parts (e.g., heels, soles), plastics, manufacturing
335211 Shoe polishers, household-type electric, manufacturing
325612 Shoe polishes and cleaners manufacturing
423850 Shoe repair materials merchant wholesalers
811430 Shoe repair shops without retailing new shoes
316999 Shoe soles, leather, manufacturing
448210 Shoe stores, orthopedic
451110 Shoe stores, specialty sports footwear (e.g., bowling, golf, spiked)
321999 Shoe stretchers manufacturing
321999 Shoe trees manufacturing
424340 Shoes merchant wholesalers
316219 Shoes, athletic (except rubber or plastics soled with fabric upper), manufacturing
316219 Shoes, ballet, manufacturing
316219 Shoes, children's and infant's (except house slippers, orthopedic extension, plastics, rubber), manufacturing
316219 Shoes, cleated or spiked, all materials, manufacturing
316213 Shoes, men's (except house slippers, athletic, rubber, orthopedic extension), manufacturing
339113 Shoes, orthopedic extension, manufacturing
316211 Shoes, plastics or plastics soled fabric upper (except cleated athletic), manufacturing
316211 Shoes, rubber or rubber soled fabric upper (except cleated athletic), manufacturing
316219 Shoes, theatrical, manufacturing
316214 Shoes, women's (except house slippers, athletic, orthopedic extension, plastic, rubber), manufacturing
316219 Shoes, wooden, manufacturing
812990 Shoeshine parlors
812990 Shoeshine services
321920 Shook, box, manufacturing
713990 Shooting clubs, recreational
713990 Shooting galleries
713990 Shooting ranges
423120 Shop equipment, service station, merchant wholesalers

424130 Shopping bags, paper and plastics, merchant wholesalers
531120 Shopping center (i.e., not operating contained businesses) rental or leasing
236220 Shopping center construction
236220 Shopping mall construction
812990 Shopping services, personal
****** Shops—see type
238990 Shoring, construction
111421 Short rotation woody tree growing (i.e., growing and harvesting cycle 10 years or less)
311223 Shortening (except soybean) made in crushing mills
311222 Shortening, soybean, made in crushing mills
311225 Shortening made from purchased fats and oils
424490 Shortening, vegetable, merchant wholesalers
482112 Short-line railroads
315291 Shorts, outerwear, infants', cut and sewn from purchased fabric (except apparel contractors)
315191 Shorts, outerwear, made in apparel knitting mills
315211 Shorts, outerwear, men's and boys', cut and sew apparel contractors
315228 Shorts, outerwear, men's and boys', cut and sewn from purchased fabric (except apparel contractors)
315212 Shorts, outerwear, women's, girls', and infants', cut and sew apparel contractors
315239 Shorts, outerwear, women's, misses', and girls', cut and sewn from purchased fabric (except apparel contractors)
315192 Shorts, underwear, made in apparel knitting mills
315211 Shorts, underwear, men's and boys', cut and sew apparel contractors
315221 Shorts, underwear, men's and boys', cut and sewn from purchased fabric (except apparel contractors)
522298 Short-term inventory credit lending
213112 Shot hole drilling, oil and gas field, on a contract basis
332811 Shot peening metal and metal products for the trade
332992 Shot, BB, manufacturing
332992 Shot, lead, manufacturing
332992 Shot, pellet, manufacturing
332992 Shot, steel, manufacturing
238110 Shotcrete contractors
332992 Shotgun shells manufacturing
332994 Shotguns manufacturing
333120 Shovel loaders manufacturing
332212 Shovels, handheld, manufacturing
333120 Shovels, power, manufacturing
337215 Showcases (except refrigerated) manufacturing
423440 Showcases (except refrigerated) merchant wholesalers
333415 Showcases, refrigerated, manufacturing
314129 Shower and bath curtains, all materials, made from purchased fabric or sheet goods
332913 Shower heads, plumbing, manufacturing
332998 Shower receptors, metal, manufacturing
332999 Shower rods, metal, manufacturing
316211 Shower sandals or slippers, rubber, manufacturing
332998 Shower stalls, metal, manufacturing
326191 Shower stalls, plastics or fiberglass, manufacturing
115210 Showing of cattle, hogs, sheep, goats, and poultry
333111 Shredders, farm-type, manufacturing
212399 Shredding peat mining and/or beneficiating
114112 Shrimp fishing

112512 Shrimp production, farm raising
813110 Shrines, religious
561910 Shrink wrapping services
313311 Shrinking broadwoven fabrics
313312 Shrinking textile products and fabrics (except broadwoven)
561730 Shrub services (e.g., bracing, planting, pruning, removal, spraying, surgery, trimming)
111421 Shrubbery farming
311712 Shucking and packing fresh shellfish
488490 Shunting of trailers in truck terminals
488210 Shunting trailers in rail terminals
334515 Shunts, instrument, manufacturing
238190 Shutter installation
332321 Shutters, door and window, metal, manufacturing
321918 Shutters, door and window, wood and covered wood, manufacturing
326199 Shutters, plastics, manufacturing
321918 Shutters, wood, manufacturing
485999 Shuttle services (except employee bus)
333292 Shuttles for textile weaving machinery manufacturing
446199 Sick room supply stores
332212 Sickles manufacturing
212210 Siderite mining and/or beneficiating
238990 Sidewalk construction, residential and commercial
237310 Sidewalk, public, construction
238170 Siding (e.g., vinyl, wood, aluminum) installation
423330 Siding (except wood) merchant wholesalers
238170 Siding contractors
444190 Siding dealers
324122 Siding made from purchased asphaltic materials
321113 Siding mills, wood
321113 Siding, dressed lumber, manufacturing
326199 Siding, plastics, manufacturing
332322 Siding, sheet metal (except stampings), manufacturing
423310 Siding, wood, merchant wholesalers
212393 Sienna mining and/or beneficiating
325131 Sienna pigment manufacturing
333294 Sieves and screening equipment (i.e., food manufacturing-type) manufacturing
333298 Sieves and screening equipment, chemical preparation-type, manufacturing
333999 Sieves and screening equipment, general purpose-type, manufacturing
333131 Sieves and screening equipment, mineral beneficiating, manufacturing
332618 Sieves, made from purchased wire, manufacturing
333294 Sifting machine (i.e., food manufacturing-type) manufacturing
333314 Sights, telescopic, manufacturing
487210 Sightseeing boat operation
487110 Sightseeing bus operation
487110 Sightseeing operation, human-drawn vehicle
238990 Sign (except on highways, streets, bridges and tunnels) erection
237310 Sign erection, highway, roads street or bridge
611630 Sign language instruction
611630 Sign language schools
541930 Sign language services
541890 Sign lettering and painting services
238990 Sign, building, erection
331422 Signal and control cable made from purchased copper in wire drawing plants
331319 Signal and control cable made in aluminum wire drawing plants
334515 Signal generators and averagers manufacturing

423610 Signal systems and devices merchant wholesalers
335311 Signaling transformers, electric, manufacturing
334290 Signals (e.g., highway, pedestrian, railway, traffic) manufacturing
423990 Signs (except electrical) merchant wholesalers
339950 Signs and signboards (except paper, paperboard) manufacturing
423440 Signs, electrical, merchant wholesalers
325188 Silica gel manufacturing
212322 Silica mining and/or beneficiating
212322 Silica sand quarrying and/or beneficiating
325188 Silica, amorphous, manufacturing
325188 Silicofluorides manufacturing
331112 Silicomanganese ferroalloys manufacturing
327910 Silicon carbide abrasives manufacturing
334413 Silicon wafers, chemically doped, manufacturing
327992 Silicon, ultra high purity, manufacturing
325199 Silicone (except resins) manufacturing
325211 Silicone resins manufacturing
325212 Silicone rubber manufacturing
313210 Silk fabrics, broadwoven, weaving
541430 Silk screen design services
333292 Silk screens for textile fabrics manufacturing
313111 Silk spun yarns made from purchased fiber
313113 Silk thread manufacturing
313112 Silk throwing, spooling, twisting, or winding of puchased yarn
424590 Silk, raw, merchant wholesalers
212325 Sillimanite mining and/or beneficiating
327390 Sills, concrete, manufacturing
236220 Silo construction
327390 Silos, prefabricated concrete, manufacturing
332311 Silos, prefabricated metal, manufacturing
331491 Silver and silver alloy bar, rod, sheet, strip, and tubing made from purchased metals or scrap
332999 Silver beating (i.e., foil, leaf)
325188 Silver bromide manufacturing
331419 Silver bullion or dore bar produced at primary metal refineries
325188 Silver chloride manufacturing
325188 Silver compounds, not specified elsewhere by process, manufacturing
332999 Silver foil and leaf not made in rolling mills
331491 Silver foil made by rolling purchased metals or scrap
325188 Silver nitrate manufacturing
212222 Silver ores mining and/or beneficiating
325612 Silver polishes manufacturing
331492 Silver recovering from scrap and/or alloying purchased metals
331492 Silver recovering from used photographic film or X-ray plates
331419 Silver refining, primary
331491 Silver rolling, drawing, or extruding purchased metals or scrap
532299 Silverware rental
423940 Silverware, precious and plated, merchant wholesalers
333515 Sine bars (i.e., a machine tool accessory) manufacturing
711130 Singers, independent
813410 Singing societies
812990 Singing telegram services
531110 Single family house rental or leasing
621512 Single photon emission computerized tomography (SPECT) centers

236115 Single-family attached housing construction general contractors
236115 Single-family detached housing construction general contractors
236115 Single-family homes built on land owned by others, general contractors of
236115 Single-family house construction by general contractors
236117 Single-family housing built on own land for sale (i.e., operative builders)
236117 Single-family housing construction operative builders
213113 Sinking shafts for coal mining on a contract basis
213114 Sinking shafts for metal mining on a contract basis
332998 Sinks, metal, manufacturing
326191 Sinks, plastics, manufacturing
327111 Sinks, vitreous china, manufacturing
212210 Sintered iron ore produced at the mine
212392 Sintered phosphate rock mining and/or beneficiating
334290 Sirens (e.g., air raid, industrial, marine, vehicle) manufacturing
541611 Site location consulting services
541620 Site remediation consulting services
562910 Site remediation services
541611 Site selection consulting services
812990 Sitting services, house
812910 Sitting services, pet
313311 Sizing of broadwoven fabrics
313312 Sizing of fabric (except broadwoven)
339920 Skateboards manufacturing
339920 Skates and parts, ice and roller, manufacturing
713990 Skeet shooting facilities
331111 Skelp, iron or steel, made in iron and steel mills
711510 Sketch artists, independent
321999 Skewers, wood, manufacturing
541320 Ski area design services
541320 Ski area planning services
532292 Ski equipment rental
713920 Ski lift and tow operators
721110 Ski lodges and resorts with accommodations
315191 Ski pants made in apparel knitting mills
315291 Ski pants, infants', cut and sewn from purchased fabric (except apparel contractors)
315211 Ski pants, men's and boys', cut and sew apparel contractors
315228 Ski pants, men's and boys', cut and sewn from purchased fabric (except apparel contractors)
315212 Ski pants, women's, girls', and infants', cut and sew apparel contractors
315239 Ski pants, women's, misses', and girls', cut and sewn from purchased fabric (except apparel contractors)
713920 Ski resorts without accommodations
315191 Ski suits made in apparel knitting mills
315291 Ski suits, infants', cut and sewn from purchased fabric (except apparel contractors)
315211 Ski suits, men's and boys', cut and sew apparel contractors
315228 Ski suits, men's and boys', cut and sewn from purchased fabric (except apparel contractors)
315212 Ski suits, women's, girls', and infants', cut and sew apparel contractors
315239 Ski suits, women's, misses', and girls', cut and sewn from purchased fabric (except apparel contractors)
237990 Ski tow construction
532490 Skid rental or leasing
213112 Skidding of rigs, oil and gas field, on a contract basis

321920 Skids and pallets, wood or wood and metal combination, manufacturing
332999 Skids, metal, manufacturing
711219 Skiers, independent (i.e., participating in sports events)
423910 Skiing equipment and supplies merchant wholesalers
713920 Skiing facilities, cross country, without accommodations
713920 Skiing facilities, downhill, without accommodations
611620 Skiing instruction, camps, or schools
623110 Skilled nursing facilities
561910 Skin blister packaging services
611620 Skin diving instruction, camps, or schools
339112 Skin grafting equipment manufacturing
424990 Skins, dressed, merchant wholesalers
424590 Skins, raw, merchant wholesalers
316110 Skins, tanning, currying and finishing
561611 Skip tracing services
316110 Skirting leather manufacturing
315234 Skirts (except tennis skirts), women's, misses', and girls', cut and sewn from purchased fabric (except apparel contractors)
315191 Skirts made in apparel knitting mills
315291 Skirts, infants', cut and sewn from purchased fabric (except apparel contractors)
315239 Skirts, tennis, women's, misses', and girls', cut and sewn from purchased fabric (except apparel contractors)
315212 Skirts, women's, misses', girls', and infants', cut and sew apparel contractors
339920 Skis and skiing equipment (except apparel) manufacturing
316110 Skivers, leather, manufacturing
611620 Sky diving instruction, camps, or schools
238160 Skylight installation
332321 Skylights, sheet metal, manufacturing
331419 Slab, nonferrous metals (except aluminum, copper), primary
331312 Slab, primary aluminum, manufacturing
331111 Slab, steel, made in iron and steel mills
315191 Slacks made in apparel knitting mills
315291 Slacks, infants', cut and sewn from purchased fabric (except apparel contractors)
315291 Slacks, jean-cut casual, infants', cut and sewn from purchased fabric (except apparel contractors)
315191 Slacks, jean-cut casual, made in apparel knitting mills
315211 Slacks, jean-cut casual, men's and boys', cut and sew apparel contractors
315224 Slacks, jean-cut casual, men's and boys', cut and sewn from purchased fabric (except apparel contractors)
315212 Slacks, jean-cut casual, women's, girls', and infants', cut and sew apparel contractors
315239 Slacks, jean-cut casual, women's, misses', and girls', cut and sewn from purchased fabric (except apparel contractors)
315211 Slacks, men's and boys', cut and sew apparel contractors
315224 Slacks, men's and boys', cut and sewn from purchased fabric (except apparel contractors)
315212 Slacks, women's, girls', and infants', cut and sew apparel contractors
315239 Slacks, women's, misses', and girls', cut and sewn from purchased fabric (except apparel contractors)

333120 Slag mixers, portable, manufacturing
238140 Slate (i.e., masonry) contractors
212319 Slate crushed and broken stone mining and/or beneficiating
212311 Slate mining or quarrying
327991 Slate products manufacturing
238340 Slate, interior, installation
311611 Slaughtering, custom
311991 Slaw, cole, fresh, manufacturing
332212 Sledgehammers manufacturing
339932 Sleds, children's, manufacturing
621498 Sleep disorder centers and clinics, outpatient
337215 Sleeper mechanisms, convertible bed, manufacturing
314999 Sleeping bags manufacturing
316999 Sleeves, welder's, leather, manufacturing
333294 Slicing machinery (i.e., food manufacturing-type) manufacturing
339993 Slide fasteners (i.e., zippers) manufacturing
332618 Slings, lifting, made from purchased wire
212324 Slip clay mining and/or beneficiating
335312 Slip rings for motors and generators manufacturing
423220 Slipcovers merchant wholesalers
314129 Slipcovers, all materials, made from purchased materials
316212 Slipper socks made from purchased socks
315119 Slipper socks made in sock mills
424340 Slippers merchant wholesalers
316219 Slippers, ballet, manufacturing
316212 Slippers, house, manufacturing
315192 Slips made in apparel knitting mills
315212 Slips, women's and girls', cut and sew apparel contractors
315231 Slips, women's, misses', and girls', cut and sewn from purchased fabric (except apparel contractors)
522294 SLMA (Student Loan Marketing Association)
713990 Slot car racetracks (i.e., amusement devices)
713290 Slot machine concession operators (i.e., supplying and servicing in others' facilities)
713290 Slot machine parlors
339999 Slot machines manufacturing
333512 Slotting machines, metalworking, manufacturing
562212 Sludge disposal sites
333999 Sludge tables manufacturing
327331 Slumped brick manufacturing
486990 Slurry pipeline transportation
213112 Slush pits and cellars, excavation of, on a contract basis
541940 Small animal veterinary services
332992 Small arms ammunition (i.e., 30 mm. or less, 1.18 inch or less) manufacturing
926110 Small business development agencies
811411 Small engine repair and maintenance shops
311615 Small game, processing, fresh, frozen, canned or cooked
311615 Small game, slaughtering, dressing and packing
522291 Small loan companies (i.e., unsecured cash loans)
236210 Smelter construction
331492 Smelting and refining of nonferrous metals (except aluminum, copper), secondary
423830 Smelting machinery and equipment merchant wholesalers
331492 Smelting nonferrous metals (except aluminum, copper), secondary
331419 Smelting of nonferrous metals (except aluminum, copper), primary
333994 Smelting ovens manufacturing
332420 Smelting pots and retorts manufacturing
212231 Smithsonite mining and/or beneficiating

238210 Smoke detection system, installation only
334290 Smoke detectors manufacturing
423620 Smoke detectors, household-type, merchant wholesalers
332995 Smoke generators manufacturing
311612 Smoked meats made from purchased carcasses
424990 Smokers' supplies merchant wholesalers
453991 Smokers' supply stores
332313 Smokestacks, fabricated metal boiler plate, manufacturing
621999 Smoking cessation programs
312229 Smoking tobacco (e.g., cigarette, pipe) manufacturing
333311 Snack and confection vending machines manufacturing
722213 Snack bars (e.g., cookies, popcorn, pretzels), fixed location
722330 Snack stands, mobile
111219 Snap bean farming (i.e., bush and pole), field and seed production
335931 Snap switches (i.e., electric wiring devices) manufacturing
114111 Snapper fishing
488490 Snow clearing, highways and bridges, road transportation
321912 Snow fence lath manufacturing
321999 Snow fence, sections or rolls, manufacturing
333415 Snow making machinery manufacturing
238210 Snow melting cable, electric, installation
238220 Snow melting system (e.g., hot water, glycol) installation
111219 Snow pea farming, field and seed production
333120 Snow plow attachments (except lawn, garden-type) manufacturing
333112 Snow plow attachments, lawn and garden-type, manufacturing
561790 Snow plowing driveways and parking lots (i.e., not combined with any other service)
561730 Snow plowing services combined with landscaping services (i.e., seasonal property maintenance services)
423810 Snow plows merchant wholesalers
488490 Snow removal, highway
532292 Snow ski equipment rental
423810 Snowblowers (except household-type) merchant wholesalers
333112 Snowblowers and throwers, residential-type, manufacturing
423820 Snowblowers, household-type, merchant wholesalers
441229 Snowmobile dealers
423110 Snowmobile merchant wholesalers
711212 Snowmobile racetracks
711219 Snowmobile racing teams
336999 Snowmobiles and parts manufacturing
713990 Snowmobiling, recreational
339920 Snowshoes manufacturing
315191 Snowsuits made in apparel knitting mills
315291 Snowsuits, infants', cut and sewn from purchased fabric (except apparel contractors)
315211 Snowsuits, men's and boys', cut and sew apparel contractors
315228 Snowsuits, men's and boys', cut and sewn from purchased fabric (except apparel contractors)
315212 Snowsuits, women's, girls', and infants', cut and sew apparel contractors
315239 Snowsuits, women's, misses', and girls', cut and sewn from purchased fabric (except apparel contractors)
312229 Snuff manufacturing
424940 Snuff merchant wholesalers
327111 Soap dishes, vitreous china and earthenware, manufacturing

332999 Soap dispensers, metal, manufacturing
325611 Soaps (e.g., bar, chip, powder) manufacturing
212399 Soapstone mining and/or beneficiating
711211 Soccer clubs, professional or semiprofessional
713990 Soccer clubs, recreational
611620 Soccer instruction, camps, or schools
711211 Soccer teams, professional or semiprofessional
923130 Social assistance cost-sharing, government
813319 Social change advocacy organizations
813410 Social clubs
812990 Social escort services
813410 Social organizations, civic and fraternal
541720 Social science research and development services
923130 Social Security Administration (SSA), federal
813319 Social service advocacy organizations
624190 Social service agencies, family
624190 Social service centers, multipurpose
424120 Social stationery merchant wholesalers
813920 Social workers' associations
621330 Social workers' offices (e.g., centers, clinics)
541720 Sociological research and development services
541720 Sociology research and development services
332212 Sockets and socket sets manufacturing
335931 Sockets, electric, manufacturing
315119 Socks knitting or knitting and finishing
315119 Socks, men's and boy's, manufacturing
316212 Socks, slipper, made from purchased socks
315119 Socks, slipper, made in sock mills
111421 Sod farming
333111 Sod harvesting machines manufacturing
561730 Sod laying services
325181 Soda ash manufacturing
212391 Soda ash mining and/or beneficiating
212391 Soda ash, natural, mining and/ or beneficiating
327213 Soda bottles, glass, manufacturing
312111 Soda carbonated, manufacturing
311821 Soda crackers manufacturing
333415 Soda fountain cooling and dispensing equipment manufacturing
423440 Soda fountain fixtures (except refrigerated) merchant wholesalers
311930 Soda fountain syrups manufacturing
312111 Soda pop manufacturing
325199 Sodium acetate manufacturing
325199 Sodium alginate manufacturing
325188 Sodium aluminate manufacturing
325188 Sodium aluminum sulfate manufacturing
325188 Sodium antimoniate manufacturing
325320 Sodium arsenite insecticides manufacturing
325188 Sodium arsenite (except insecticides) manufacturing
325199 Sodium benzoate manufacturing
325181 Sodium bicarbonate manufacturing
325188 Sodium bichromate and chromate manufacturing
325188 Sodium borate manufacturing
212391 Sodium borates, natural, mining and/or beneficiating
325188 Sodium borohydride manufacturing
325188 Sodium bromide manufacturing
325181 Sodium carbonate (i.e., soda ash) manufacturing
212391 Sodium carbonates, natural, mining and/or beneficiating
325188 Sodium chlorate manufacturing

325412 Sodium chloride pharmaceutical preparations manufacturing
212393 Sodium chloride, rock salt, mining and/or beneficiating
212391 Sodium compounds prepared at beneficiating plants
212391 Sodium compounds, natural (except common salt), mining and/or beneficiating
325188 Sodium cyanide manufacturing
325199 Sodium glutamate manufacturing
325188 Sodium hydrosulfite manufacturing
325181 Sodium hydroxide (i.e., caustic soda) manufacturing
325188 Sodium hypochlorite manufacturing
325188 Sodium inorganic compounds, not specified elsewhere by process, manufacturing
325188 Sodium molybdate manufacturing
325199 Sodium organic compounds, not specified elsewhere by process, manufacturing
325199 Sodium pentachlorophenate manufacturing
325188 Sodium perborate manufacturing
325188 Sodium peroxide manufacturing
325188 Sodium phosphate manufacturing
325188 Sodium polyphosphate manufacturing
325412 Sodium salicylate preparations manufacturing
325188 Sodium silicate (i.e., water glass) manufacturing
325188 Sodium silicofluoride manufacturing
325188 Sodium stannate manufacturing
325188 Sodium sulfate manufacturing
212391 Sodium sulfate, natural, mining and/or beneficiating
325199 Sodium sulfoxalate formaldehyde manufacturing
325188 Sodium tetraborate manufacturing
325188 Sodium thiosulfate manufacturing
325188 Sodium tungstate manufacturing
325188 Sodium uranate manufacturing
335110 Sodium vapor lamp bulbs manufacturing
337121 Sofa beds and chair beds, upholstered, manufacturing
337121 Sofas, convertible (except futons), manufacturing
337121 Sofas, upholstered, manufacturing
722213 Soft drink beverage bars, nonalcoholic, fixed location
332431 Soft drink cans manufacturing
311930 Soft drink concentrates (i.e., syrup) manufacturing
445299 Soft drink stores, bottled
333311 Soft drink vending machines manufacturing
312111 Soft drinks manufacturing
424490 Soft drinks merchant wholesalers
311812 Soft pretzels made in a commercial bakery
325613 Softeners, leather or textile, manufacturing
541511 Software analysis and design services, custom computer
611420 Software application training
511210 Software computer, packaged, publishers
541519 Software installation services, computer
541511 Software programming services, custom computer
511210 Software publishers
511210 Software publishers, packaged
443120 Software stores, computer
423430 Software, computer, packaged, merchant wholesalers
334611 Software, packaged, mass reproducing
321912 Softwood dimension lumber and stock, resawing purchased lumber
325191 Softwood distillates manufacturing
321212 Softwood plywood composites manufacturing

321212 Softwood veneer or plywood manufacturing
238910 Soil compacting
924120 Soil conservation services, government
331511 Soil pipe, cast iron, manufacturing
562910 Soil remediation services
238910 Soil test drilling
325998 Soil testing kits manufacturing
541380 Soil testing laboratories or services
334413 Solar cells manufacturing
423690 Solar cells merchant wholesalers
926130 Solar energy regulation
333414 Solar energy heating equipment manufacturing
238220 Solar heating equipment installation
423720 Solar heating panels and equipment merchant wholesalers
333414 Solar heating systems manufacturing
335122 Solar lighting fixtures (except residential), electric, manufacturing
335121 Solar lighting fixtures, residential, electric, manufacturing
237130 Solar power structure construction
238160 Solar reflecting coating, roof, application
423330 Solar reflective film merchant wholesalers
334519 Solarimeters manufacturing
331491 Solder wire, nonferrous metals (except aluminum, copper), made from purchased metals or scrap
333992 Soldering equipment (except hand held) manufacturing
332212 Soldering guns and irons, handheld (including electric), manufacturing
332212 Soldering iron tips and tiplets manufacturing
335931 Solderless connectors (electric wiring devices) manufacturing
316110 Sole leather manufacturing
335314 Solenoid switches, industrial, manufacturing
332911 Solenoid valves (except fluid power), industrial-type, manufacturing
332912 Solenoid valves, fluid power, manufacturing
334419 Solenoids for electronic applications manufacturing
316999 Soles, boot and shoe, leather, manufacturing
541110 Solicitors' offices, private
922130 Solicitors' offices, government
541110 Solicitors' private practices
325188 Solid fuel propellants, inorganic, not specified elsewhere by process, manufacturing
562213 Solid waste combustors or incinerators, nonhazardous
562212 Solid waste landfills combined with collection and/or local hauling of nonhazardous waste materials
562212 Solid waste landfills, nonhazardous
711130 Soloists, independent musical
325132 Solvent dyes manufacturing
324110 Solvents made in petroleum refineries
334511 Sonabuoys manufacturing
423690 Sonar equipment merchant wholesalers
334511 Sonar fish finders manufacturing
334511 Sonar systems and equipment manufacturing
512230 Song publishers
512230 Song publishers and printing combined
711510 Song writers, independent
325612 Soot removing chemicals manufacturing
325199 Sorbitol manufacturing
111199 Sorghum farming, field and seed production
311211 Sorghum flour manufacturing
111998 Sorghum sudan seed farming

311999 Sorghum syrup manufacturing
813410 Sororities (except residential)
721310 Sorority houses
115114 Sorting, grading, cleaning, and packing of fruits and vegetables
532490 Sound and lighting equipment rental or leasing
512191 Sound dubbing services, motion picture
238210 Sound equipment installation
423330 Sound insulation merchant wholesalers
512240 Sound recording studios (except integrated record companies)
512220 Sound recording, integrated production, reproduction, release, and distribution
512220 Sound recording, releasing, promoting, and distributing
238310 Soundproofing contractors
332431 Soup cans, light gauge metal, manufacturing
624210 Soup kitchens
311423 Soup mixes made in a dehydration plant
311999 Soup mixes, dry, made from purchased dry ingredients
424490 Soups (except frozen) merchant wholesalers
311422 Soups (except seafood) canning
311711 Soups, fish and seafood, canning
311412 Soups, frozen (except seafood), manufacturing
311712 Soups, frozen fish and shellfish, manufacturing
424420 Soups, frozen, merchant wholesalers
311511 Sour cream manufacturing
311511 Sour cream substitutes manufacturing
453220 Souvenir shops
311941 Soy sauce manufacturing
311222 Soybean cakes and meal manufacturing
311225 Soybean cooking oil made from purchased oils
111110 Soybean farming, field and seed production
325222 Soybean fibers and filaments manufacturing
311222 Soybean flour and grits manufacturing
311222 Soybean millfeed made in oil mills
311222 Soybean oil mills
311222 Soybean oil, cake, and meal, made in crushing mills
311222 Soybean oil, crude, manufacturing
311222 Soybean oil, deodorized, made in oil mills
311222 Soybean oil, refined, made in crushing mills
325211 Soybean plastics manufacturing
311222 Soybean protein concentrates made in crushing mills
311222 Soybean protein isolates made in crushing mills
424510 Soybeans merchant wholesalers
336419 Space capsules manufacturing
927110 Space flight operations, government
333414 Space heaters (except portable electric) manufacturing
334220 Space satellites, communications, manufacturing
332313 Space simulation chambers, fabricated metal plate work, manufacturing
339113 Space suits manufacturing
481212 Space transportation, freight, nonscheduled
334511 Space vehicle guidance systems and equipment manufacturing
336414 Space vehicles, complete, manufacturing
332212 Spades and shovels, handheld, manufacturing
311422 Spaghetti canning
424490 Spaghetti merchant wholesalers
311421 Spaghetti sauce canning
111219 Spaghetti squash farming, field, bedding plant and seed production
311823 Spaghetti, dry, manufacturing
313210 Spandex broadwoven fabrics

325222 Spandex fiber, filaments, and yarn manufacturing
113210 Spanish moss gathering
212399 Spar, iceland, mining and/or beneficiating
327113 Spark plug insulators, porcelain, manufacturing
334515 Spark plug testing instruments, electric, manufacturing
336322 Spark plugs for internal combustion engines manufacturing
312130 Sparkling wines manufacturing
321999 Spars, wood, manufacturing
713940 Spas without accommodations, fitness
316999 Spats, leather, manufacturing
326299 Spatulas, rubber, manufacturing
337129 Speaker cabinets (i.e., housings), wood, manufacturing
813410 Speakers' clubs
334310 Speaker systems manufacturing
711410 Speakers' bureaus
711510 Speakers, independent
325998 Spearmint oil manufacturing
711510 Special effect technicians, independent
512191 Special effects for motion picture production, post-production
516110 Special interest portals (e.g., parents sharing information about child rearing, etc.), Internet
485991 Special needs passenger transportation services
336211 Special purpose highway vehicle (e.g., firefighting vehicles) assembling on purchased chassis
336211 Special purpose highway vehicle (e.g., firefighting vehicles) bodies manufacturing
336120 Special purpose highway vehicles (e.g., firefighting vehicles) assembling on heavy chassis of own manufacture
423830 Special purpose industrial machinery and equipment merchant wholesalers
525990 Special purpose financial vehicles
445299 Specialty food stores
316110 Specialty leathers manufacturing
515210 Specialty television (e.g., music, sports, news) cable networks
335311 Specialty transformers, electric, manufacturing
424210 Specialty-line pharmaceuticals merchant wholesalers
334516 Specific ion measuring instruments, laboratory-type, manufacturing
238390 Spectator seating installation
334516 Spectrofluorometers manufacturing
334516 Spectrographs manufacturing
334516 Spectrometers (e.g., electron diffraction, mass, NMR, Raman) manufacturing
334519 Spectrometers (e.g., liquid scintillation, nuclear) manufacturing
334516 Spectrophotometers (e.g., atomic absorption, atomic emission, flame, fluorescence, infrared, Raman, visible) manufacturing
334515 Spectrum analyzers manufacturing
236220 Speculative builders (i.e., building on own land, for sale), commercial and institutional building
236210 Speculative builders (i.e., building on own land, for sale), industrial building (except warehouses)
236117 Speculative builders (i.e., building on own land, for sale), multifamily housing
236117 Speculative builders (i.e., building on own land, for sale), residential
236117 Speculative builders (i.e., building on own land, for sale), single-family housing
339112 Speculums manufacturing

541930 Speech (i.e., language) interpretation services
621340 Speech clinicians' offices (e.g., centers, clinics)
621340 Speech defect clinics
621340 Speech pathologists' offices (e.g., centers, clinics)
621340 Speech therapists' offices (e.g., centers, clinics)
333612 Speed changers (i.e., power transmission equipment) manufacturing
611699 Speed reading instruction
333612 Speed reducers (i.e., power transmission equipment) manufacturing
441310 Speed shops
334511 Speed, pitch, and roll navigational instruments and systems manufacturing
711212 Speedways
621991 Sperm banks, human
113210 Sphagnum moss gathering
212231 Sphalerite mining and/or beneficiating
339112 Sphygmomanometers manufacturing
111998 Spice farming
111419 Spice farming, grown under cover
311942 Spice grinding and blending
311942 Spice mixtures manufacturing
445299 Spice stores
311942 Spices and spice mix manufacturing
424490 Spices merchant wholesalers
331112 Spiegeleisen ferroalloys manufacturing
332913 Spigots, plumbing fixture fitting, manufacturing
321999 Spigots, wood, manufacturing
331111 Spike rods made in iron and steel mills
332618 Spikes made from purchased wire
331222 Spikes, iron or steel, made in wire drawing plants
423510 Spikes, metal, merchant wholesalers
237990 Spillway, floodwater, construction
111219 Spinach farming, field, bedding plant and seed production
333292 Spindles for textile machinery manufacturing
313111 Spinning carpet and rug yarn from purchased fiber
333292 Spinning machinery for textiles manufacturing
333513 Spinning machines, metalworking, manufacturing
332116 Spinning unfinished metal products
313111 Spinning yarn from purchased fiber
332618 Spiral cloth made from purchased wire
312140 Spirits, distilled (except brandy), manufacturing
424820 Spirits, distilled, merchant wholesalers
333513 Spline rolling machines, metalworking, manufacturing
321920 Splint baskets for fruits and vegetables, manufacturing
339113 Splints manufacturing
316110 Splits, leather, manufacturing
212393 Spodumene mining and/or beneficiating
321999 Spokes, wood, manufacturing
114119 Sponge gathering
331111 Sponge iron
424990 Sponges merchant wholesalers
332999 Sponges, metal scouring, manufacturing
326199 Sponges, plastics, manufacturing
326299 Sponges, rubber, manufacturing
313311 Sponging broadwoven fabrics
313312 Sponging textile products and fabrics (except broadwoven)
313112 Spooling of yarn
313112 Spooling of yarns for the trade
321999 Spools (except for textile machinery), wood, manufacturing
333292 Spools for textile machinery manufacturing

332211 Spoons, table, nonprecious and precious plated metal, manufacturing
315222 Sport coats (except fur, leather), men's and boys', cut and sewn from purchased fabric (except apparel contractors)
315292 Sport coats, fur (except apparel contractors), manufacturing
315211 Sport coats, fur, men's and boys', cut and sew apparel contractors
315292 Sport coats, leather (including artificial and tailored) (except apparel contractors), manufacturing
315211 Sport coats, leather (including artificial and tailored), men's and boys', cut and sew apparel contractors
315211 Sport coats, men's and boys', cut and sew apparel contractors
315211 Sport shirts, men's and boys', cut and sew apparel contractors
315223 Sport shirts, men's and boys', cut and sewn from purchased fabric (except apparel contractors)
532112 Sport utility vehicle leasing
423110 Sport utility vehicle merchant wholesalers
532111 Sport utility vehicle rental
336112 Sport utility vehicles assembling on chassis of own manufacture
811490 Sporting equipment repair and maintenance without retailing new sports equipment
423910 Sporting firearms and ammunition merchant wholesalers
339920 Sporting goods (except ammunition, clothing, footwear, small arms) manufacturing
423910 Sporting goods and supplies merchant wholesalers
532292 Sporting goods rental
451110 Sporting goods stores
453310 Sporting goods stores, used
711510 Sports announcers, independent
711310 Sports arena operators
611620 Sports camps (e.g., baseball, basketball, football), instructional
315228 Sports clothing (except team uniforms), men's and boys', cut and sewn from purchased fabric (except apparel contractors)
315239 Sports clothing (except team uniforms), women's, misses', and girls', cut and sewn from purchased fabric (except apparel contractors)
315191 Sports clothing made in apparel knitting mills
315211 Sports clothing, men's and boys', cut and sew apparel contractors
315299 Sports clothing, team uniforms, cut and sewn from purchased fabric (except apparel contractors)
315212 Sports clothing, women's and girls', cut and sew apparel contractors
713940 Sports club facilities, physical fitness
713990 Sports clubs (i.e., sports teams) not operating sports facilities, recreational
711211 Sports clubs, professional or semiprofessional
423910 Sports equipment and supplies merchant wholesalers
532292 Sports equipment rental
711310 Sports event managers with facilities
711320 Sports event managers without facilities
711310 Sports event organizers with facilities
711320 Sports event organizers without facilities
711310 Sports event promoters with facilities

711320 Sports event promoters without facilities
237990 Sports field construction
711410 Sports figures' agents or managers
451110 Sports gear stores (e.g., outdoors, scuba, skiing)
813990 Sports governing bodies
712110 Sports halls of fame
611620 Sports instruction, camps, or schools
611620 Sports instructors, independent (i.e., not participating in sporting events)
813990 Sports leagues (i.e., regulating bodies)
621340 Sports physical therapists' offices (e.g., centers, clinics)
711219 Sports professionals, independent (i.e., participating in sports events)
315191 Sports shirts made in apparel knitting mills
711310 Sports stadium operators
713990 Sports teams and leagues, recreational or youth
711211 Sports teams, professional or semiprofessional
561599 Sports ticket offices
711219 Sports trainers, independent
424320 Sportswear, men's and boys', merchant wholesalers
325612 Spot removers (except laundry presoaks) manufacturing
333992 Spot welding equipment manufacturing
335129 Spotlights (except vehicular) manufacturing
336321 Spotlights, vehicular, manufacturing
332322 Spouts, sheet metal (except stampings), manufacturing
424950 Spray painting equipment (except industrial-type) merchant wholesalers
423830 Spray painting equipment, industrial-type, merchant wholesalers
333111 Sprayers and dusters, farm-type, manufacturing
423820 Sprayers, farm-type, merchant wholesalers
333912 Sprayers, manual pump, general purpose-type, manufacturing
115112 Spraying crops
561730 Spraying lawns
811198 Spray-on bedliner installation for trucks
333111 Spreaders, farm-type, manufacturing
423820 Spreaders, fertilizer, merchant wholesalers
333112 Spreaders, lawn and garden-type, manufacturing
115112 Spreading lime for crops
311513 Spreads, cheese, manufacturing
332722 Spring pins, metal, manufacturing
332722 Spring washers, metal, manufacturing
312112 Spring waters, purifying and bottling
333513 Spring winding and forming machines, metalworking, manufacturing
332612 Springs and spring units for seats, light gauge, made from purchased wire or strip
337910 Springs, assembled bed and box, made from purchased springs
334518 Springs, clock and watch, made from purchased wire
332611 Springs, heavy gauge metal, manufacturing
332612 Springs, light gauge (except clock, watch), made from purchased wire or strip
332612 Springs, precision (except clock, watch), light gauge, made from purchased wire or strip
423510 Springs, steel, merchant wholesalers
238220 Sprinkler system, building, installation
333999 Sprinkler systems, automatic fire, manufacturing
423850 Sprinkler systems, fire, merchant wholesalers

423820 Sprinklers, agricultural, merchant wholesalers
332919 Sprinklers, lawn, manufacturing
333613 Sprockets, power transmission equipment, manufacturing
113210 Spruce gum gathering
213111 Spudding in oil and gas wells on a contract basis
313230 Spunbonded fabrics manufacturing
332212 Squares, carpenters', metal, manufacturing
713940 Squash club facilities
339920 Squash equipment (except apparel) manufacturing
111219 Squash farming, field, bedding plant and seed production
114112 Squid fishing
332999 Stabilizing bars, cargo, metal, manufacturing
711219 Stables, horse racing
713990 Stables, riding
423830 Stackers, industrial, merchant wholesalers
333924 Stackers, industrial, truck-type, manufacturing
333924 Stackers, portable (except farm), manufacturing
236220 Stadium and arena construction
711310 Stadium operators
337127 Stadium seating manufacturing
531120 Stadium rental or leasing without promotion of events
561330 Staff leasing services
335129 Stage lighting equipment manufacturing
711510 Stage set (e.g., concert, motion picture, television) erecting and dismantling, independent
327211 Stained glass and stained glass products made in glass making plants
238150 Stained glass installation
327215 Stained glass products made from purchased glass
331513 Stainless steel castings (except investment), unfinished, manufacturing
331111 Stainless steel made in iron and steel mills
325510 Stains (except biological) manufacturing
424950 Stains merchant wholesalers
325132 Stains, biological, manufacturing
332323 Stair railings, metal, manufacturing
321918 Stair railings, wood, manufacturing
332323 Stair treads, metal, manufacturing
326299 Stair treads, rubber, manufacturing
332323 Staircases, metal, manufacturing
332323 Stairs, metal, manufacturing
238190 Stairway, metal, installation
238120 Stairway, precast concrete, installation
238350 Stairway, wood, installation
333921 Stairways, moving, manufacturing
321918 Stairwork (e.g., newel posts, railings, staircases, stairs), wood, manufacturing
321999 Stakes, surveyor's, wood, manufacturing
333111 Stalk choppers (i.e., shredders) manufacturing
332323 Stalls, metal, manufacturing
325998 Stamp pad ink manufacturing
339943 Stamp pads manufacturing
339943 Stamping devices, hand operated, manufacturing
333513 Stamping machines, metalworking, manufacturing
336370 Stamping metal motor vehicle body parts
336370 Stamping metal motor vehicle moldings and trims
332116 Stampings (except automotive, cans, cooking, closures, crowns), metal, unfinished, manufacturing
713210 Stand alone casinos (except slot machine parlors)
334515 Standards and calibration equipment for electrical measuring manufacturing
813920 Standards review committees, professional

926150 Standards, setting and management, agencies, government
334515 Standing wave ratio measuring equipment manufacturing
337215 Stands (except wire), merchandise display, manufacturing
711510 Standup comedians, independent
325188 Stannic and stannous chloride manufacturing
339942 Staple removers manufacturing
333991 Staplers and nailers, handheld power-driven, manufacturing
339942 Staplers manufacturing
332618 Staples made from purchased wire
423710 Staples merchant wholesalers
331222 Staples, iron or steel, made in wire drawing plants
325520 Starch glues manufacturing
311221 Starches (except laundry) manufacturing
325612 Starches, laundry, manufacturing
112310 Started pullet production
336322 Starter and starter parts for internal combustion engines manufacturing
522110 State commercial banks
522130 State credit unions
928120 State Department
923110 State education departments
561310 State operated employment job services offices
922120 State police
522120 State savings and loan associations
522120 State savings banks
921130 State tax commissions
334413 Static converters, integrated circuits, manufacturing
334512 Static pressure regulators manufacturing
332410 Stationary power boilers manufacturing
327112 Stationery articles, pottery, manufacturing
323112 Stationery, flexographic printing, on a job-order basis
323111 Stationery, gravure printing, on a job-order basis
323110 Stationery, lithographic (offset) printing, on a job-order basis
322233 Stationery made from purchased paper
323114 Stationery, quick printing, on a job-order basis
323113 Stationery, screen printing, on a job-order basis
453210 Stationery stores
424120 Stationery supplies merchant wholesalers
335312 Stators for motors manufacturing
327420 Statuary (e.g., gypsum, plaster of paris) manufacturing
424990 Statuary goods (except religious) merchant wholesalers
327112 Statuary, clay and ceramic, manufacturing
327991 Statuary, marble, manufacturing
327999 Statuary, vases, and urns, papier-mache, manufacturing
238990 Statue erection
212399 Staurolite mining and/or beneficiating
321920 Staves, barrel, sawed or split, manufacturing
316999 Stays, shoe, leather, manufacturing
722110 Steak houses, full service
722211 Steak houses, limited-service
812199 Steam baths
561790 Steam cleaning building exteriors
213112 Steam cleaning oil and gas wells on a contract basis
332410 Steam condensers manufacturing
333319 Steam cookers, commercial-type, manufacturing
335211 Steam cookers, household-type, manufacturing
611513 Steam fitters' apprenticeship training
238220 Steam fitting contractors

332919 Steam fittings, metal, manufacturing
221330 Steam heat distribution
333414 Steam heating equipment manufacturing
221330 Steam heating systems (i.e., suppliers of heat)
334512 Steam pressure controls, residential and commercial heating-type, manufacturing
221330 Steam production and distribution
333999 Steam separating machinery manufacturing
221330 Steam supply systems, including geothermal
333319 Steam tables manufacturing
487110 Steam train excursions
332911 Steam traps, industrial-type, manufacturing
333611 Steam turbine generator set units manufacturing
333611 Steam turbines manufacturing
532411 Steamship rental or leasing without operator
325199 Stearic acid esters manufacturing
325199 Stearic acid manufacturing
325199 Stearic acid salts manufacturing
311613 Stearin, animal, rendering
212399 Steatite mining and/or beneficiating
327113 Steatite porcelain insulators manufacturing
331111 Steel balls made in iron and steel mills
332431 Steel cans, light gauge metal, manufacturing
331513 Steel castings (except investment), unfinished, manufacturing
332111 Steel forgings made from purchased steel, unfinished
331513 Steel foundries (except investment)
238130 Steel framing contractors
331512 Steel investment castings, unfinished, manufacturing
331512 Steel investment foundries
332312 Steel joists manufacturing
331111 Steel manufacturing
423510 Steel merchant wholesalers
236210 Steel mill construction
331111 Steel mill products (e.g., bar, plate, rod, sheet, structural shapes) manufacturing
331111 Steel mills
332312 Steel railroad car racks manufacturing
238120 Steel reinforcing contractors
327910 Steel shot abrasives manufacturing
332999 Steel wool manufacturing
423510 Steel wool merchant wholesalers
331111 Steel, from pig iron, manufacturing
238160 Steep slope roofing installation
238990 Steeplejack work
311221 Steepwater concentrate manufacturing
336330 Steering boxes, manual and power assist, manufacturing
336330 Steering columns, automotive, truck, and bus, manufacturing
336330 Steering wheels, automotive, truck, and bus, manufacturing
327215 Stemware made from purchased glass
327212 Stemware, glass, made in glass making plants
325910 Stencil inks manufacturing
339944 Stencil paper manufacturing
339943 Stencils for painting and marking (e.g., cardboard, metal) manufacturing
561410 Stenographic services (except court or stenographic reporting)
333313 Stenography machinery manufacturing
561492 Stenography services, public
561492 Stenotype recording services
332999 Stepladders, metal, manufacturing
321999 Stepladders, wood, manufacturing
337129 Stereo cabinets (i.e., housings), wood, manufacturing
423620 Stereo equipment merchant wholesalers

532210 Stereo equipment rental
811211 Stereo equipment repair shops without retailing new stereo equipment
325212 Stereo rubber manufacturing
443112 Stereo stores (except automotive)
441310 Stereo stores, automotive
339114 Sterilizers, dental, manufacturing
339113 Sterilizers, hospital and surgical, manufacturing
339111 Sterilizers, laboratory-type (except dental), manufacturing
332313 Sterilizing chambers, fabricated metal plate work, manufacturing
325411 Steriods, uncompounded, manufacturing
339112 Stethoscopes manufacturing
488320 Stevedoring services
339920 Sticks, sports (e.g., hockey, lacrosse), manufacturing
325132 Stilbene dyes manufacturing
324110 Still gases made in petroleum refineries
332420 Stills, heavy gauge metal, manufacturing
333293 Stitchers and trimmers book binding equipment manufacturing
315211 Stitching, decorative and novelty, contractors on men's and boys' apparel
315212 Stitching, decorative and novelty, contractors on women's, girls', and infants' apparel
314999 Stitching, decorative and novelty, on textile articles and apparel
523120 Stock brokerages
523120 Stock brokers' offices
711212 Stock car racetracks
711219 Stock car racing teams
711110 Stock companies, theatrical
523210 Stock exchanges
512199 Stock footage film libraries
512290 Stock music and other audio services
523120 Stock options brokerages
523110 Stock options dealing (i.e., acting as a principal in dealing securities to investors)
523210 Stock or commodity options exchanges
519190 Stock photo agencies
523999 Stock quotation services
512290 Stock sound library (e.g., general background sounds, stock music)
523999 Stock transfer agencies
321912 Stock, chair, unfinished hardwood, manufacturing
112111 Stocker calf production
315111 Stockings (except socks), sheer, manufacturing
315111 Stockings, sheer, women's, misses', and girls', full-length and knee-length, knitting or knitting and finishing
488999 Stockyards (i.e., not for fattening or selling livestock), transportation
212319 Stone (except limestone and granite) beneficiating plants (e.g., grinding)
212311 Stone, dimension, mining or quarrying
333131 Stone beneficiating machinery manufacturing
332213 Stone cutting saw blades manufacturing
238340 Stone flooring installation
313311 Stone washing broadwoven fabrics
313312 Stone washing textile products, apparel, and fabrics (except broadwoven)
333298 Stone working machinery manufacturing
423320 Stone, building or crushed, merchant wholesalers
212319 Stone, crushed and broken (except granite or limestone), mining and/or beneficiating
332212 Stonecutters' handtools, nonpowered, manufacturing

212399 Stones, abrasive (e.g., emery, grindstones, hones, pumice), mining and/or beneficiating
423940 Stones, precious and semiprecious, merchant wholesalers
327999 Stones, synthetic, for gem stones and industrial use, manufacturing
327112 Stoneware (i.e., pottery products) manufacturing
212325 Stoneware clay mining and/or beneficiating
238140 Stonework (i.e., masonry) contractors
337124 Stools, metal household-type (except upholstered), manufacturing
337122 Stools, wood household-type (except upholstered), manufacturing
621999 Stop smoking clinics
332911 Stop valves, industrial-type, manufacturing
332913 Stopcock drains, plumbing, manufacturing
321999 Stoppers, cork, manufacturing
326299 Stoppers, rubber, manufacturing
423610 Storage batteries (except automotive) merchant wholesalers
335911 Storage batteries manufacturing
335312 Storage battery chargers (except internal combustion engine-type) manufacturing
423390 Storage bins merchant wholesalers
334112 Storage devices, computer, manufacturing
236220 Storage elevator construction
486210 Storage of natural gas
237120 Storage tank, natural gas or oil, tank farm or field construction
332420 Storage tanks, heavy gauge metal, manufacturing
423510 Storage tanks, metal, merchant wholesalers
236220 Store construction
541850 Store display advertising services
337215 Store display fixtures manufacturing
423440 Store equipment (except furniture) merchant wholesalers
423440 Store fixtures (except refrigerated) merchant wholesalers
238190 Store front, metal or metal frame, installation
423210 Store furniture merchant wholesalers
****** Stores—see type
562998 Storm basin cleanout services
332321 Storm doors and windows, metal, manufacturing
321911 Storm doors and windows, wood framed, manufacturing
237110 Storm sewer construction
711510 Storytellers, independent
312120 Stout brewing
332322 Stove boards, sheet metal (except stampings), manufacturing
327123 Stove lining, clay, manufacturing
332322 Stove pipes and flues, sheet metal (except stampings), manufacturing
811412 Stove, household-type, repair and maintenance services without retailing new stoves
335221 Stoves, ceramic disk element, household-type, manufacturing
333319 Stoves, commercial-type, manufacturing
423720 Stoves, cooking and heating (except electric), household-type, merchant wholesalers
335221 Stoves, household-type cooking, manufacturing
333924 Straddle carriers, mobile, manufacturing
332211 Straight razors manufacturing
332911 Straightway (i.e., Y-type) valves, industrial-type, manufacturing

333999 Strainers, pipeline, manufacturing
321219 Strandboard, oriented, manufacturing
332618 Stranded wire, uninsulated, made from purchased wire
316110 Strap leather manufacturing
332999 Strappings, metal, manufacturing
316999 Straps (except watch), leather, manufacturing
316993 Straps, watch (except metal), manufacturing
339911 Straps, watch, precious metal, manufacturing
541611 Strategic planning consulting services
213112 Stratigraphic drilling, oil and gas field exploration on a contract basis
321999 Straw baskets manufacturing
315991 Straw hats manufacturing
424910 Straw merchant wholesalers
111333 Strawberry farming
488490 Street cleaning service
237310 Street construction
335129 Street lighting fixtures (except traffic signals) manufacturing
516110 Street map and guide publishers, exclusively on Internet
511130 Street map guide publishers (except exclusive Internet publishing)
485119 Street railway systems (except mixed mode), commuter
423810 Street sweeping and cleaning equipment merchant wholesalers
454390 Street vendors (except food)
722330 Street vendors, food
238990 Street, interlocking brick (i.e., not mortared), installation
237990 Streetcar line construction
336510 Streetcars and car equipment, urban transit, manufacturing
713940 Strength development centers
336211 Stretch limousines assembling on purchased chassis
321999 Stretchers, curtain, wood, manufacturing
339113 Stretchers, medical, manufacturing
333513 Stretching machines, metalworking, manufacturing
111219 String bean farming, field and seed production
314991 Strings (except musical instrument) manufacturing
339992 Strings, musical instrument, manufacturing
212113 Strip mining, anthracite, on own account
212111 Strip mining, bituminous coal or lignite, on own account
212111 Strip mining, lignite, on own account
331421 Strip, copper and copper alloy, made from purchased copper or in integrated secondary smelting and rolling, drawing or extruding plants
331111 Strip, galvanized iron or steel, made in iron and steel mills
331111 Strip, iron or steel, made in iron and steel mills
331491 Strip, nonferrous metals (except aluminum, copper), made from purchased metals or scrap
211111 Stripper well production
213113 Stripping overburden services for coal mining on a contract basis
213114 Stripping overburden services for metal mining on a contract basis
213115 Stripping overburden services for nonmetallic minerals mining (except fuels) on a contract basis
334515 Stroboscopes manufacturing
335110 Strobotrons manufacturing
339932 Strollers, baby, manufacturing
212393 Strontianite mining and/or beneficiating
325188 Strontium carbonate manufacturing

325188 Strontium compounds, not specified elsewhere by process, manufacturing
212393 Strontium mineral mining and/or beneficiating
325188 Strontium nitrate manufacturing
423510 Structural assemblies, metal, merchant wholesalers
423390 Structural assemblies, prefabricated (except wood), merchant wholesalers
423310 Structural assemblies, prefabricated wood, merchant wholesalers
423320 Structural clay tile (except refractory) merchant wholesalers
327121 Structural clay tile manufacturing
321114 Structural lumber and timber, treating
321213 Structural members, glue laminated or pre-engineered wood, manufacturing
333516 Structural rolling mill machinery, metalworking, manufacturing
331319 Structural shapes made by rolling purchased aluminum
331319 Structural shapes, aluminum, made in integrated secondary smelting and rolling mills
331111 Structural shapes, iron or steel, made in iron and steel mills
238120 Structural steel contractors
332312 Structural steel, fabricated, manufacturing
339932 Structural toy sets manufacturing
321213 Structural wood members (except trusses), fabricated, manufacturing
336330 Struts, automotive, truck, and bus, manufacturing
325411 Strychnine and derivatives (i.e., basic chemicals) manufacturing
327999 Stucco and stucco products manufacturing
238140 Stucco contractors
321113 Stud mills
115210 Stud services
238130 Stud wall (e.g., wood, steel) installation
813410 Student clubs
611710 Student exchange programs
522291 Student loan companies
522294 Student Loan Marketing Association (SLMA)
813410 Students' associations
813410 Students' unions
334220 Studio equipment, radio and television broadcasting, manufacturing
541430 Studios, commercial art
321912 Studs, resawing purchased lumber
332322 Studs, sheet metal (except stampings), manufacturing
921120 Study commissions, legislative
339931 Stuffed toys (including animals) manufacturing
333294 Stuffer, sausage machinery, manufacturing
113310 Stump removing in the field
325212 S-type rubber manufacturing
325920 Styphnic acid explosive materials manufacturing
325110 Styrene made from refined petroleum or liquid hydrocarbons
324110 Styrene made in petroleum refineries
325211 Styrene resins manufacturing
325211 Styrene-acrylonitrile resins manufacturing
325212 Styrene-butadiene rubber containing less than 50 percent styrene manufacturing
325212 Styrene-chloroprene rubber manufacturing
325212 Styrene-isoprene rubber manufacturing
238310 Styrofoam insulation installation
212111 Subbituminous coal surface mining and/or beneficiating
212112 Subbituminous coal underground mining or mining and beneficiating
237210 Subdividers, real estate

237210 Subdividing real estate
332994 Submachine guns manufacturing
336611 Submarine building
333514 Subpresses, machine tool, manufacturing
334210 Subscriber loop equipment, telephone, manufacturing
515210 Subscription television networks
551114 Subsidiary management offices
623220 Substance abuse (i.e., alcoholism, drug addiction) halfway houses
623220 Substance abuse facilities, residential
813319 Substance abuse prevention advocacy organizations
621420 Substance abuse treatment centers and clinics (except hospitals), outpatient
237130 Substation and switching station, power transmission line, construction
335311 Substation transformers, electric power distribution, manufacturing
512191 Subtitling of motion picture film or video
485113 Suburban bus line services (except mixed mode)
485112 Suburban commuter rail systems (except mixed mode)
485111 Suburban transit systems, mixed mode (e.g., bus, commuter rail, subway combinations)
541850 Subway card display advertising services
336510 Subway cars manufacturing
423860 Subway cars merchant wholesalers
237990 Subway construction
485119 Subway systems (except mixed mode), commuter
339112 Suction therapy apparatus manufacturing
812320 Suede garment cleaning services
313311 Sueding broadwoven fabrics
313312 Sueding textile products and fabrics (except broadwoven)
111991 Sugar beet farming
115113 Sugar beets, machine harvesting
311221 Sugar made by wet milling corn
333294 Sugar refining machinery manufacturing
325998 Sugar substitutes (i.e., synthetic sweeteners blended with other ingredients) made from purchased synthetic sweeteners
325199 Sugar substitutes (i.e., synthetic sweeteners blended with other ingredients) made in synthetic sweetener establishments
311312 Sugar, cane, made from purchased raw cane sugar
311311 Sugar, clarified, granulated, and raw, made in sugarcane mill
311312 Sugar, confectionery, made from purchased raw cane sugar
311313 Sugar, confectionery, made from sugar beets
311311 Sugar, confectionery, made in sugarcane mill
311312 Sugar, granulated, made from purchased raw cane sugar
311313 Sugar, granulated, made from sugar beets
311311 Sugar, granulated, made in sugarcane mill
311312 Sugar, invert, made from purchased raw cane sugar
311313 Sugar, invert, made from sugar beets
311311 Sugar, invert, made in sugarcane mill
311313 Sugar, liquid, made from sugar beets
311311 Sugar, raw, made in sugarcane mill
424590 Sugar, raw, merchant wholesalers
311312 Sugar, refined, made from purchased raw cane sugar
424490 Sugar, refined, merchant wholesalers
111930 Sugarcane farming, field production
311311 Sugarcane mills
311311 Sugarcane refining
115113 Sugarcane, machine harvesting

624190 Suicide crisis centers
532220 Suit rental
315999 Suit trimmings cut and sewn from purchased fabric (except apparel contractors)
315211 Suit trimmings, men's and boys', cut and sew apparel contractors
332510 Suitcase hardware, metal, manufacturing
316991 Suitcases, all materials, manufacturing
315211 Suits (i.e., nontailored, tailored, work), men's and boys', cut and sew apparel contractors
315212 Suits (i.e., nontailored, tailored, work), women's, misses', girls', and infants', cut and sew apparel contractors
315191 Suits made in apparel knitting mills
339113 Suits, firefighting, manufacturing
315291 Suits, infants' (e.g., warm-up, jogging, snowsuits), cut and sewn from purchased fabric (except apparel contractors)
424320 Suits, men's and boys', merchant wholesalers
315239 Suits, nontailored (e.g., jogging, snowsuit, warm-up), women's, misses', and girls', cut and sewn from purchased fabric (except apparel contractors)
315228 Suits, nontailored (e.g., jogging, snow, ski, warm-up), men's and boys', cut and sewn from purchased fabric (except apparel contractors)
339113 Suits, space, manufacturing
315222 Suits, tailored, men's and boys', cut and sewn from purchased fabric (except apparel contractors)
315234 Suits, tailored, women's, misses', and girls', cut and sewn from purchased fabric (except apparel contractors)
325411 Sulfa drugs, uncompounded, manufacturing
212391 Sulfate, sodium, mining and/or beneficiating
325188 Sulfides and sulfites manufacturing
325188 Sulfocyanides manufacturing
325411 Sulfonamides, uncompounded, manufacturing
325188 Sulfur and sulfur compounds, not specified elsewhere by process, manufacturing
325188 Sulfur chloride manufacturing
325188 Sulfur dioxide manufacturing
325188 Sulfur hexafluoride gas manufacturing
325320 Sulfur insecticides manufacturing
212393 Sulfur mining and/or beneficiating
211112 Sulfur recovered from natural gas
325188 Sulfur recovering or refining (except from sour natural gas)
212393 Sulfur, native, mining and/or beneficiating
325188 Sulfuric acid manufacturing
424690 Sulfuric acid merchant wholesalers
325192 Sulphonated derivatives manufacturing
311423 Sulphured fruits and vegetables manufacturing
325191 Sumac extract manufacturing
721214 Summer camps (except day, instructional)
713990 Summer day camps (except instructional)
721110 Summer resort hotels without casinos
711110 Summer theaters
238220 Sump pump installation
333911 Sump pumps, residential-type, manufacturing
115114 Sun drying of dates, prunes, raisins, and olives
115114 Sun drying of fruits and vegetables
115114 Sun drying of tomatoes
812199 Sun tanning salons

111120 Sunflower farming, field and seed production
311223 Sunflower seed oil, cake and meal, made in crushing mills
446130 Sunglass stores
339115 Sunglasses and goggles manufacturing
423460 Sunglasses merchant wholesalers
336399 Sunroofs and parts, automotive, truck, and bus, manufacturing
236118 Sun-room additions, residential
325620 Sunscreen lotions and oils manufacturing
315291 Sunsuits, infants', cut and sewn from purchased fabric (except apparel contractors)
325620 Suntan lotions and oils manufacturing
331111 Superalloys, iron or steel, manufacturing
331492 Superalloys, nonferrous based, made from purchased metals or scrap
445110 Supermarkets
325312 Superphosphates manufacturing
452910 Superstores (i.e., food and general merchandise)
921190 Supply agencies, government
332913 Supply line assemblies, plumbing (i.e., flexible hose with fittings), manufacturing
624190 Support group services
339113 Supports, orthopedic (e.g., abdominal, ankle, arch, kneecap), manufacturing
325412 Suppositories manufacturing
524126 Surety insurance carriers, direct
325613 Surface active agents manufacturing
424690 Surface active agents merchant wholesalers
334516 Surface area analyzers manufacturing
334512 Surface burner controls, temperature, manufacturing
322226 Surface coating purchased paperboard
333120 Surface mining machinery (except drilling) manufacturing
333295 Surface mount machinery for making printed circuit boards manufacturing
237310 Surfacing, highway, road, street, bridge or airport runway
532292 Surfboard rental
339920 Surfboards manufacturing
335999 Surge suppressors manufacturing
621111 Surgeons' (except dental) offices (e.g., centers, clinics)
541940 Surgeons' offices, veterinary
621210 Surgeons', dental, offices (e.g., centers, clinics)
115112 Surgery on trees and vines
541940 Surgery services, veterinary
423450 Surgical appliances merchant wholesalers
339112 Surgical clamps manufacturing
339113 Surgical dressings manufacturing
339113 Surgical implants manufacturing
811219 Surgical instrument repair and maintenance services
423450 Surgical instruments and apparatus merchant wholesalers
339112 Surgical knife blades and handles manufacturing
621111 Surgical pathologists' offices (e.g., centers, clinics)
339112 Surgical stapling devices manufacturing
339113 Surgical supplies (except medical instruments) manufacturing
423450 Surgical supplies merchant wholesalers
334510 Surgical support systems (e.g., heart-lung machines) (except iron lungs) manufacturing
423450 Surgical towels merchant wholesalers
311711 Surimi canning
311712 Surimi, fresh and frozen, manufacturing

238210 Surveillance system, installation only
213112 Surveying (except seismographic) oil or gas wells on a contract basis
541370 Surveying and mapping services (except geophysical)
423490 Surveying equipment and supplies merchant wholesalers
811219 Surveying instrument repair and maintenance services
334519 Surveying instruments manufacturing
541360 Surveying services, geophysical
321999 Surveyor's stakes, wood, manufacturing
611699 Survival training instruction
238310 Suspended ceiling installation
315999 Suspenders cut and sewn from purchased fabric (except apparel contractors)
315211 Suspenders, men's and boys', cut and sew apparel contractors
315212 Suspenders, women's, girls', and infants', cut and sew apparel contractors
811118 Suspension repair shops, automotive
339113 Sutures, surgical, manufacturing
213112 Swabbing oil or gas wells on a contract basis
333513 Swaging machines, metalworking, manufacturing
487210 Swamp buggy operation
323121 Swatches and samples, mounting for the trade
332999 Swatters, fly, metal, manufacturing
315299 Sweat bands cut and sewn from purchased fabric (except apparel contractors)
315191 Sweat bands made in apparel knitting mills
315211 Sweat bands, men's and boys', cut and sew apparel contractors
315212 Sweat bands, women's, girls', and infants', cut and sew apparel contractors
315191 Sweat pants made in apparel knitting mills
315291 Sweat pants, infants', cut and sewn from purchased fabric (except apparel contractors)
315228 Sweat pants, men's, boys', and unisex (i.e., sized without regard to gender), cut and sewn from purchased fabric (except apparel contractors)
315211 Sweat pants, men's, boys', and unisex, cut and sew apparel contractors
315212 Sweat pants, women's, girls', and infants', cut and sew apparel contractors
315239 Sweat pants, women's, misses', and girls', cut and sewn from purchased fabric (except apparel contractors)
315191 Sweat suits made in apparel knitting mills
315291 Sweat suits, infants', cut and sewn from purchased fabric (except apparel contractors)
315211 Sweat suits, men's and boys', cut and sew apparel contractors
315228 Sweat suits, men's and boys', cut and sewn from purchased fabric (except apparel contractors)
315212 Sweat suits, women's, girls', and infants', cut and sew apparel contractors
315239 Sweat suits, women's, misses', and girls', cut and sewn from purchased fabric (except apparel contractors)
316110 Sweatband leather manufacturing
315191 Sweater jackets made in apparel knitting mills
315291 Sweater jackets, infants', cut and sewn from purchased fabric (except apparel contractors)
315211 Sweater jackets, men's and boys', cut and sew apparel contractors

315228 Sweater jackets, men's and boys', cut and sewn from purchased fabric (except apparel contractors)
315212 Sweater jackets, women's, girls', and infants', cut and sew apparel contractors
315239 Sweater jackets, women's, misses', and girls', cut and sewn from purchased fabric (except apparel contractors)
315191 Sweater vests made in apparel knitting mills
315291 Sweater vests, infants', cut and sewn from purchased fabric (except apparel contractors)
315211 Sweater vests, men's and boys', cut and sew apparel contractors
315228 Sweater vests, men's and boys', cut and sewn from purchased fabric (except apparel contractors)
315212 Sweater vests, women's, girls', and infants', cut and sew apparel contractors
315239 Sweater vests, women's, misses', and girls', cut and sewn from purchased fabric (except apparel contractors)
315191 Sweaters made in apparel knitting mills
315291 Sweaters, infants', cut and sewn from purchased fabric (except apparel contractors)
315211 Sweaters, men's and boys', cut and sew apparel contractors
315228 Sweaters, men's and boys', cut and sewn from purchased fabric (except apparel contractors)
315212 Sweaters, women's, and girls', and infants', cut and sew apparel contractors
315239 Sweaters, women's, misses', and girls', cut and sewn from purchased fabric (except apparel contractors)
315191 Sweatshirts made in apparel knitting mills
315291 Sweatshirts, infants', cut and sewn from purchased fabric (except apparel contractors)
315211 Sweatshirts, men's and boys', cut and sew apparel contractors
315223 Sweatshirts, men's and boys', cut and sewn from purchased fabric (except apparel contractors)
315223 Sweatshirts, outerwear, unisex (sized without regard to gender), cut and sewn from purchased fabric (except apparel contractors)
315212 Sweatshirts, women's, girls', and infants', cut and sew apparel contractors
315232 Sweatshirts, women's, misses', and girls', cut and sewn from purchased fabric (except apparel contractors)
334515 Sweep generators manufacturing
334515 Sweep oscillators manufacturing
335212 Sweepers, household-type electric vacuum, manufacturing
325612 Sweeping compounds, absorbent, manufacturing
111219 Sweet corn farming, field and seed production
111219 Sweet pepper farming, field, bedding plant and seed production
115114 Sweet potato curing
111219 Sweet potato farming, field and seed potato production
311812 Sweet yeast goods (except frozen) manufacturing
311813 Sweet yeast goods, frozen, manufacturing
311999 Sweetening syrups (except pure maple) manufacturing
611620 Swimming instruction
325998 Swimming pool chemical preparations manufacturing
561790 Swimming pool cleaning and maintenance services
326199 Swimming pool covers and liners, plastics, manufacturing

333319 Swimming pool filter systems manufacturing
333414 Swimming pool heaters manufacturing
335129 Swimming pool lighting fixtures manufacturing
238990 Swimming pool screen enclosure construction
453998 Swimming pool supply stores
236220 Swimming pool, indoor, construction
238990 Swimming pool, outdoor, construction
713940 Swimming pools
423910 Swimming pools and equipment merchant wholesalers
339920 Swimming pools, above ground, manufacturing
326199 Swimming pools, fiberglass, manufacturing
315191 Swimsuits made in apparel knitting mills
315291 Swimsuits, infants', cut and sewn from purchased fabric (except apparel contractors)
315211 Swimsuits, men's and boys', cut and sew apparel contractors
315228 Swimsuits, men's and boys', cut and sewn from purchased fabric (except apparel contractors)
315212 Swimsuits, women's, girls', and infants', cut and sew apparel contractors
315239 Swimsuits, women's, misses', and girls', cut and sewn from purchased fabric (except apparel contractors)
448190 Swimwear stores
424320 Swimwear, men's and boys', merchant wholesalers
424330 Swimwear, women's, children's, and infants', merchant wholesalers
311119 Swine feed, complete, manufacturing
311119 Swine feed, supplements, concentrates, and premixes, manufacturing
424520 Swine merchant wholesalers
335932 Switch boxes, electrical wiring, manufacturing
335931 Switch cutouts manufacturing
335313 Switchboards and parts, power, manufacturing
423610 Switchboards, electrical distribution, merchant wholesalers
335931 Switches for electrical wiring (e.g., pressure, pushbutton, snap, tumbler) manufacturing
334419 Switches for electronic applications manufacturing
335313 Switches, electric power (except pushbotton, snap, solenoid, tumbler), manufacturing
423610 Switches, electrical, merchant wholesalers
423690 Switches, electronic, merchant wholesalers
335931 Switches, outlet box mounting-type, manufacturing
334512 Switches, pneumatic positioning remote, manufacturing
334512 Switches, thermostatic, manufacturing
335313 Switchgear and switchgear accessories manufacturing
335313 Switching equipment, power, manufacturing
334210 Switching equipment, telephone, manufacturing
488210 Switching services, railroad
114111 Swordfish fishing
332211 Swords, nonprecious and precious plated metal, manufacturing
212313 Syenite (except nepheline) crushed and broken stone mining and/or beneficiating
212311 Syenite (except nepheline) mining or quarrying
212325 Syenite, nepheline, mining and/or beneficiating
212221 Sylvanite mining and/or beneficiating
711130 Symphony orchestras
813110 Synagogues

335312 Synchronous condensers and timing motors, electric, manufacturing
335312 Synchronous motors manufacturing
334515 Synchroscopes manufacturing
519110 Syndicates, news
339992 Synthesizers, music, manufacturing
311340 Synthetic chocolate manufacturing
325212 Synthetic rubber (i.e., vulcanizable elastomers) manufacturing
424690 Synthetic rubber merchant wholesalers
327999 Synthetic stones, for gem stones and industrial use, manufacturing
325199 Synthetic sweeteners (i.e., sweetening agents) manufacturing
339112 Syringes, hypodermic, manufacturing
424490 Syrup (except fountain) merchant wholesalers
311313 Syrup made from sugar beets
311930 Syrup, beverage, manufacturing
311312 Syrup, cane, made from purchased raw cane sugar
311311 Syrup, cane, made in sugarcane mill
311320 Syrup, chocolate, made from cacao beans
311330 Syrup, chocolate, made from purchased chocolate
311999 Syrup, corn (except wet milled), manufacturing
311221 Syrup, corn, made by wet milling
311930 Syrup, flavoring (except coffee based), manufacturing
311920 Syrup, flavoring, coffee based, manufacturing
424450 Syrup, fountain, merchant wholesalers
111998 Syrup, pure maple (i.e., maple syrup reducing)
311999 Syrup, sweetening (except pure maple), manufacturing
311999 Syrup, table, artificially flavored, manufacturing
541512 Systems integration design consulting services, computer
541512 Systems integration design services, computer
532299 Table and banquet accessory rental
327112 Table articles, coarse earthenware, manufacturing
327112 Table articles, earthenware, manufacturing
327112 Table articles, fine earthenware (i.e., whiteware), manufacturing
327112 Table articles, vitreous china, manufacturing
332211 Table cutlery, nonprecious and precious plated metal, manufacturing
339912 Table cutlery, precious metal, manufacturing
335121 Table lamps (i.e., lighting fixtures) manufacturing
812331 Table linen supply services
311225 Table oil made from purchased oils
311221 Table oil, corn, made by wet milling
311942 Table salt manufacturing
327991 Table tops, marble, manufacturing
337110 Table tops, wood, manufacturing
314129 Tablecloths (except paper) made from purchased materials
313210 Tablecloths made in broadwoven fabric mills
313249 Tablecloths made in lace mills
313249 Tablecloths made in warp knitting mills
313241 Tablecloths made in weft knitting mills
322291 Tablecloths, paper, made from purchased paper
337214 Tables (except wood), office-type, manufacturing
337124 Tables, metal household-type, manufacturing

337122 Tables, wood household-type, manufacturing
337211 Tables, wood, office-type, manufacturing
322233 Tablets (e.g., memo, note, writing) made from purchased paper
322121 Tablets (e.g., memo, note, writing) made in paper mills
332999 Tablets, metal, manufacturing
423220 Tableware (except disposable, plated, precious) merchant wholesalers
327215 Tableware made from purchased glass
327212 Tableware made in glass making plants
532299 Tableware rental
424130 Tableware, disposable, merchant wholesalers
423940 Tableware, precious and plated, merchant wholesalers
327112 Tableware, vitreous china, manufacturing
334515 Tachometer generators manufacturing
451110 Tack shops
321999 Tackle blocks, wood, manufacturing
451110 Tackle shops (i.e., fishing)
339920 Tackle, fishing (except line, nets, seines), manufacturing
423710 Tacks merchant wholesalers
331222 Tacks, iron or steel, made in wire drawing plants
332618 Tacks, metal, made from purchased wire
212210 Taconite concentrates or agglomerates beneficiating
212210 Taconite ores mining and/or beneficiating
334511 Taffrail logs manufacturing
213111 Tailing in oil and gas field wells on a contract basis
811490 Tailor shops, alterations only
315211 Tailored dress and sport coats, men's and boys', cut and sew apparel contractors
315222 Tailored dress and sport coats, men's and boys', cut and sewn from purchased fabric (except apparel contractors)
332211 Tailors' scissors, nonelectric, manufacturing
423850 Tailors' supplies merchant wholesalers
****** Tailors—see specific apparel manufacturing
722211 Take out eating places
212399 Talc mining and/or beneficiating
327992 Talc processing beyond beneficiation
325620 Talcum powders manufacturing
711410 Talent agencies
711410 Talent agents
541214 Talent payment services
325191 Tall oil (except skimmings) manufacturing
311611 Tallow produced in a slaughtering plant
311613 Tallow produced in rendering plant
334514 Tally counters manufacturing
334514 Tallying meters (except clocks, electricity meters, watches) manufacturing
333120 Tampers, powered, manufacturing
332995 Tampion guns manufacturing
111320 Tangelo groves
111320 Tangerine groves
332995 Tank artillery manufacturing
336211 Tank bodies for trucks manufacturing
562998 Tank cleaning and disposal services, commercial or industrial
562991 Tank cleaning services, septic
238990 Tank lining contractors
315291 Tank tops, infants', cut and sewn from purchased fabric (except apparel contractors)
315211 Tank tops, men's and boys', cut and sew apparel contractors
315191 Tank tops, outerwear, made in apparel knitting mills

315223 Tank tops, outerwear, men's and boys', cut and sewn from purchased fabric (except apparel contractors)
315232 Tank tops, outerwear, women's, misses', and girls', cut and sewn from purchased fabric (except apparel contractors)
315192 Tank tops, underwear, made in apparel knitting mills
315221 Tank tops, underwear, men's and boys', cut and sewn from purchased fabric (except apparel contractors)
315231 Tank tops, underwear, women's, misses', and girls', cut and sewn from purchased fabric (except apparel contractors)
315212 Tank tops, women's, girls', and infants', cut and sew apparel contractors
336212 Tank trailer, liquid and dry bulk, manufacturing
334514 Tank truck meters manufacturing
336211 Tank trucks (e.g., fuel oil, milk, water) assembling on purchased chassis
532411 Tanker rental or leasing
484220 Tanker trucking (e.g., chemical, juice, milk, petroleum), local
484230 Tanker trucking (e.g., chemical, juice, milk, petroleum), long-distance
327390 Tanks, concrete, manufacturing
327111 Tanks, flush, vitreous china, manufacturing
332420 Tanks, heavy gauge metal, manufacturing
336992 Tanks, military (including factory rebuilding), manufacturing
333315 Tanks, photographic developing, fixing, and washing, manufacturing
423510 Tanks, storage metal, merchant wholesalers
326199 Tanks, storage, plastics or fiberglass, manufacturing
321920 Tanks, wood, coopered, manufacturing
316110 Tannery leather manufacturing
333298 Tannery machinery manufacturing
325191 Tannic acid (i.e., tannins) manufacturing
325188 Tanning agents, inorganic, manufacturing
325199 Tanning agents, synthetic organic, manufacturing
316110 Tanning and currying furs
325191 Tanning extracts and materials, natural, manufacturing
812199 Tanning salons
212299 Tantalite mining and/or beneficiating
212299 Tantalum ores mining and/or beneficiating
331419 Tantalum refining, primary
711120 Tap dance companies
339942 Tape dispensers manufacturing
512120 Tape distribution for television
332212 Tape measures, metal, manufacturing
334310 Tape players and recorders, household-type, manufacturing
423620 Tape players and recorders, household-type, merchant wholesalers
532210 Tape recorder rental
561990 Tape slitting (e.g., cutting plastic or leather into widths) for the trade
334112 Tape storage units (e.g., drive backups), computer peripheral equipment, manufacturing
512191 Tape transfer service
332991 Tapered roller bearings manufacturing
322231 Tapes (e.g., adding machine, calculator, cash register) made from purchased paper
322222 Tapes (e.g., cellophane, masking, pressure sensitive), gummed, made from purchased paper or other materials
313221 Tapes weaving

423690 Tapes, blank, audio and video, merchant wholesalers
424120 Tapes, cellophane, merchant wholesalers
334613 Tapes, magnetic recording (i.e., audio, data, video), blank, manufacturing
339113 Tapes, medical adhesive, manufacturing
423450 Tapes, medical and surgical, merchant wholesalers
313230 Tapes, nonwoven fabric, manufacturing
423990 Tapes, prerecorded, audio or video, merchant wholesalers
334519 Tapes, surveyor's, manufacturing
424310 Tapes, textile, merchant wholesalers
313320 Tapes, varnished and coated (except magnetic), made from purchased fabric
238310 Taping and finishing drywall
311221 Tapioca manufacturing
333512 Tapping machines, metalworking, manufacturing
333515 Taps and dies (i.e., a machine tool accessory) manufacturing
335931 Taps, current, attachment plug and screw shell types, manufacturing
316999 Taps, shoe, leather, manufacturing
325211 Tar acid resins manufacturing
324121 Tar and asphalt paving mixtures made from purchased asphaltic materials
325191 Tar and tar oils made by distillation of wood
325192 Tar made by distillation of coal tar
324110 Tar made in petroleum refineries
324122 Tar paper made from purchased asphaltic materials and paper
324122 Tar paper, building and roofing, made from purchased paper
322121 Tar paper, building and roofing, made in paper mills
324122 Tar roofing cements and coatings made from purchased asphaltic materials
211111 Tar sands mining
336411 Target drones, aircraft, manufacturing
336413 Targets, trailer type, aircraft, manufacturing
541614 Tariff rate consulting services
541614 Tariff rate information services
111219 Taro farming, field and seed production
314912 Tarpaulins made from purchased fabrics
423330 Tarred felts merchant wholesalers
237310 Tarring roads
311941 Tartar sauce manufacturing
325199 Tartaric acid manufacturing
325199 Tartrates, not specified elsewhere by process, manufacturing
812199 Tattoo parlors
722410 Taverns (i.e., drinking places)
561440 Tax collection services on a contract or fee basis
541110 Tax law attorneys' offices
541110 Tax law attorneys' private practices
523910 Tax liens dealing (i.e., acting as a principal in dealing tax liens to investors)
541213 Tax return preparation services
921130 Taxation departments
541850 Taxicab card advertising services
485310 Taxicab dispatch services
485310 Taxicab fleet operators
423110 Taxicab merchant wholesalers
485310 Taxicab organizations
485310 Taxicab owner-operators
485310 Taxicab services
711510 Taxidermists, independent
423850 Taxidermy supplies merchant wholesalers
334514 Taximeters manufacturing
813319 Taxpayers' advocacy organizations
311920 Tea (except herbal) manufacturing

445299 Tea and coffee (i.e., packaged) stores
311920 Tea blending
111998 Tea farming
424490 Tea merchant wholesalers
311920 Tea, herbal, manufacturing
312111 Tea, iced, manufacturing
311920 Tea, instant, manufacturing
113210 Teaberries gathering
923110 Teacher certification bureaus
561310 Teacher registries
333319 Teaching machines (e.g., flight simulators) manufacturing
423490 Teaching machines (except computers), electronic, merchant wholesalers
332214 Teakettles and coffee pots, fabricated metal (except electric, glass), manufacturing
335211 Teakettles, electric, manufacturing
327212 Teakettles, glass and glass ceramic, made in glass making plants
315299 Team athletic uniforms cut and sewn from purchased fabric (except apparel contractors)
315211 Team athletic uniforms, men's and boys', cut and sew apparel contractors
315212 Team athletic uniforms, women's and girls', cut and sew apparel contractors
325199 Tear gas manufacturing
313311 Teaseling broadwoven fabrics
313312 Teaseling fabrics (except broadwoven)
325412 Technetium medicinal preparations manufacturing
327212 Technical glassware and glass products, pressed or blown, made in glass making plants
327215 Technical glassware made from purchased glass
511120 Technical magazine and periodical publishers (except exclusive Internet publishing)
511120 Technical magazine and periodical publishers and printing combined
516110 Technical magazine and periodical publishers, exclusively on Internet
323112 Technical magazines and periodicals flexographic printing without publishing
323111 Technical magazines and periodicals gravure printing without publishing
323110 Technical magazines and periodicals lithographic (offset) printing without publishing
323119 Technical magazines and periodicals printing (except flexographic, gravure, lithographic, quick, screen) without publishing
323113 Technical magazines and periodicals screen printing without publishing
511130 Technical manual and paperback book publishers (except exclusive Internet publishing)
511130 Technical manual and paperback book publishers and printing combined
323121 Technical manual paper (books) binding without printing
511130 Technical manual publishers (except exclusive Internet publishing)
516110 Technical manual publishers, exclusively on Internet
323117 Technical manuals and papers (books) printing and binding without publishing
323117 Technical manuals and papers (books) printing without publishing
711510 Technical writers, independent
315212 Teddies, women's, cut and sew apparel contractors
315231 Teddies, women's, misses', and girls', cut and sewn from purchased fabric (except apparel contractors)
624110 Teen outreach services

339114 Teeth (except customized) manufacturing
339116 Teeth, custom made in dental laboratories
423450 Teeth, dental, merchant wholesalers
517212 Telecommunications carriers, cellular telephone
517110 Telecommunications carriers, wired
238210 Telecommunications equipment and wiring (except transmission line) installation contractors
532490 Telecommunications equipment rental or leasing
541618 Telecommunications management consulting services
517110 Telecommunications networks, wired
517310 Telecommunications resellers
561499 Teleconferencing services
517110 Telegram services (except wireless)
812990 Telegram services, singing
423690 Telegraph equipment merchant wholesalers
561422 Telemarketing bureaus
561422 Telemarketing services on a contract or fee basis
334513 Telemetering instruments, industrial process-type, manufacturing
517910 Telemetry and tracking system operations on a contract or fee basis
334416 Telephone and telegraph transformers, electronic component-type, manufacturing
334210 Telephone answering machines manufacturing
423620 Telephone answering machines merchant wholesalers
561421 Telephone answering services
337215 Telephone booths manufacturing
561422 Telephone call centers
334210 Telephone carrier line equipment manufacturing
334210 Telephone carrier switching equipment manufacturing
517110 Telephone carriers, facilities-based (except wireless)
517410 Telephone communications carriers, satellite
517212 Telephone communications carriers, wireless (except satellite)
517310 Telephone communications resellers (except satellite)
624190 Telephone counseling services
323112 Telephone directories flexographic printing without publishing
323111 Telephone directories gravure printing without publishing
323110 Telephone directories lithographic (offset) printing without publishing
323119 Telephone directories printing (except flexographic, gravure, lithographic, quick, screen) without publishing
323113 Telephone directories screen printing without publishing
541870 Telephone directory distribution services, door-to-door
511140 Telephone directory publishers (except exclusive Internet publishing)
511140 Telephone directory publishers and printing combined
516110 Telephone directory publishers, exclusively on Internet
238210 Telephone equipment and building wiring installation
423690 Telephone equipment merchant wholesalers
811213 Telephone equipment repair and maintenance services without retailing new telephone equipment
517110 Telephone installation by telecommunications carriers, wired
238210 Telephone installation contractors

237130 Telephone line construction
237130 Telephone line stringing
561422 Telephone solicitation services on a contract or fee basis
443112 Telephone stores (including cellular)
519190 Telephone-based recorded information services
334210 Telephones (except cellular telephone) manufacturing
423690 Telephones merchant wholesalers
334220 Telephones, cellular, manufacturing
334210 Telephones, coin-operated, manufacturing
334113 Teleprinters (i.e., computer terminals) manufacturing
512191 Teleproduction services
333314 Telescopes manufacturing
334310 Television (TV) sets manufacturing
541840 Television advertising representatives (i.e., independent of media owners)
443112 Television and radio stores
515120 Television broadcasting networks
515120 Television broadcasting stations
337129 Television cabinets (i.e., housings), wood, manufacturing
423410 Television cameras merchant wholesalers
512110 Television commercial production
561310 Television employment agencies
511120 Television guide publishers (except exclusive Internet publishing)
511120 Television guide publishers and printing combined
516110 Television guide publishers, exclusively on Internet
323112 Television guides flexographic printing without publishing
323111 Television guides gravure printing without publishing
323110 Television guides lithographic (offset) printing without publishing
323119 Television guides printing (except flexographic, gravure, lithographic, quick, screen) without publishing
323113 Television guides screen printing without publishing
326199 Television housings, plastics, manufacturing
517510 Television operations multichannel multipoint distribution services (MMDS)
517510 Television operations, closed circuit
517510 Television operations, multipoint distribution system
454113 Television order, home shopping
334411 Television picture tubes manufacturing
711510 Television producers, independent
532210 Television rental
811211 Television repair services without retailing new televisions
423620 Television sets merchant wholesalers
512110 Television show production
512120 Television show syndicators
236220 Television station construction
515210 Television subscription services
332312 Television tower sections, fabricated structural metal, manufacturing
334220 Television transmitting antennas and ground equipment manufacturing
237130 Television transmitting tower construction
334220 Television, closed-circuit equipment, manufacturing
212221 Telluride (gold) mining and/or beneficiating
331419 Tellurium refining, primary
813319 Temperance organizations
238210 Temperature control system installation

334512 Temperature controls, automatic, residential and commercial-types, manufacturing
334513 Temperature instruments, industrial process-type (except glass and bimetal thermometers), manufacturing
334512 Temperature sensors for motor windings manufacturing
327215 Tempered glass made from purchased glass
332811 Tempering metals and metal products for the trade
331111 Template, made in iron and steel mills, manufacturing
334519 Templates, drafting, manufacturing
339115 Temples and fronts (i.e., eyeglass frames), ophthalmic, manufacturing
813110 Temples, religious
561320 Temporary employment services
561320 Temporary help services
624221 Temporary housing for families of medical patients
624221 Temporary shelters (e.g., battered women's, homeless, runaway youth)
561320 Temporary staffing services
713950 Ten pin bowling alleys
713950 Ten pin bowling centers
813319 Tenants' advocacy associations
813990 Tenants' associations (except advocacy)
813319 Tenants' associations, advocacy
713940 Tennis club facilities
236220 Tennis court, indoor, construction
713940 Tennis courts
237990 Tennis courts, outdoor, construction
423910 Tennis equipment and supplies merchant wholesalers
339920 Tennis goods (e.g., balls, frames, rackets) manufacturing
611620 Tennis instruction, camps, or schools
711219 Tennis professionals, independent (i.e., participating in sports events)
315191 Tennis shirts made in apparel knitting mills
315291 Tennis shirts, infants', cut and sewn from purchased fabric (except apparel contractors)
315211 Tennis shirts, men's and boys', cut and sew apparel contractors
315223 Tennis shirts, men's and boys', cut and sewn from purchased fabric (except apparel contractors)
315212 Tennis shirts, women's, girls', and infants', cut and sew apparel contractors
315239 Tennis shirts, women's, misses', and girls', cut and sewn from purchased fabric (except apparel contractors)
315191 Tennis skirts made in apparel knitting mills
315212 Tennis skirts, women's and girls', cut and sew apparel contractors
315239 Tennis skirts, women's, misses', and girls', cut and sewn from purchased fabric (except apparel contractors)
334510 TENS (transcutaneous electrical nerve stimulator) manufacturing
334519 Tensile strength testing equipment manufacturing
321999 Tent poles, wood, manufacturing
336214 Tent trailers (hard top and soft top) manufacturing
532292 Tent, camping, rental
532299 Tent, party, rental
314912 Tents made from purchased fabrics
335931 Terminals and connectors for electrical devices manufacturing
334113 Terminals, computer, manufacturing
424710 Terminals, petroleum

561710 Termite control services
325320 Termite poisons manufacturing
331111 Terneplate made in iron and steel mills
423510 Terneplate merchant wholesalers
331111 Ternes, iron or steel, long or short, made in iron and steel mills
325199 Terpineol manufacturing
114119 Terrapin fishing
238340 Terrazzo and tile refinishing
238340 Terrazzo contractors
327390 Terrazzo products, precast (except brick, block and pipe), manufacturing
313210 Terry broadwoven fabrics weaving
325199 Tert-butylated bis (p-phenoxyphenyl) ether fluid manufacturing
238910 Test boring for construction
611710 Test development and evaluation services, educational
213114 Test drilling for metal mining on a contract basis
213115 Test drilling for nonmetallic minerals mining (except fuel) on a contract basis
334515 Test equipment for electronic and electrical circuits and equipment manufacturing
334515 Test sets, ignition harness, manufacturing
525920 Testamentary trusts
334519 Testers for checking hydraulic controls on aircraft manufacturing
423830 Testing and measuring equipment, electrical (except automotive), merchant wholesalers
334519 Testing equipment (e.g., abrasion, shearing strength, tensile strength, torsion) manufacturing
541380 Testing laboratories (except medical, veterinary)
621511 Testing laboratories, medical
541940 Testing laboratories, veterinary
541940 Testing services for veterinarians
488190 Testing services, aircraft
611710 Testing services, educational
333993 Testing, weighing, inspecting, packaging machinery manufacturing
325199 Tetrachloroethylene manufacturing
325411 Tetracycline, uncompounded, manufacturing
325199 Tetraethyl lead manufacturing
325920 Tetryl explosive materials manufacturing
323117 Textbooks printing and binding without publishing
323117 Textbooks printing without publishing
314911 Textile bags made from purchased woven or knitted materials
424990 Textile bags merchant wholesalers
313210 Textile broadwoven fabrics mills
561990 Textile cutting services
541490 Textile design services
325613 Textile finishing assistants manufacturing
333292 Textile finishing machinery (e.g., bleaching, dyeing, mercerizing, printing) manufacturing
314999 Textile fire hose made from purchased material
561910 Textile folding and packaging services
327212 Textile glass fibers made in glass making plants
327112 Textile guides, porcelain, manufacturing
316999 Textile leathers (e.g., apron picker leather, mill strapping) manufacturing
423830 Textile machinery and equipment merchant wholesalers
532490 Textile machinery rental or leasing

811310 Textile machinery repair and maintenance services
333292 Textile making machinery (except sewing machines) manufacturing
236210 Textile mill construction
313210 Textile mills, broadwoven fabrics
313221 Textile mills, narrow woven fabric
313221 Textile narrow woven fabric mills
325910 Textile printing inks manufacturing
333292 Textile printing machinery manufacturing
313210 Textile products (except apparel) made in broadwoven fabric mills
313249 Textile products (except apparel) made in lace mills
313221 Textile products (except apparel) made in narrow woven fabric mills
313249 Textile products (except apparel) made in warp knitting mills
313241 Textile products (except apparel) made in weft knitting mills
313312 Textile products finishing
325613 Textile scouring agents manufacturing
423930 Textile waste merchant wholesalers
313320 Textile waterproofing
424310 Textiles (except burlap, felt) merchant wholesalers
325221 Texturizing cellulosic yarn made in the same establishment
333292 Texturizing machinery for textiles manufacturing
325222 Texturizing noncellulosic yarn made in the same establishment
313112 Texturizing purchased yarn
212299 Thallium mining and/or beneficiating
711110 Theater companies (except dance)
711110 Theater companies (except dance), amateur
711120 Theater companies, dance
236220 Theater construction
423410 Theater equipment (except seats) merchant wholesalers
711310 Theater festival managers with facilities
711320 Theater festival managers without facilities
711310 Theater festival organizers with facilities
711320 Theater festival organizers without facilities
711310 Theater festival promoters with facilities
711320 Theater festival promoters without facilities
711310 Theater operators
611610 Theater schools
337127 Theater seating manufacturing
423210 Theater seats merchant wholesalers
531120 Theater, property operation, rental or leasing
711120 Theaters, dance
711110 Theaters, dinner
711110 Theaters, live theatrical production (except dance)
512131 Theaters, motion picture (except drive-in)
512132 Theaters, motion picture, drive-in
512131 Theaters, motion picture, indoor
711110 Theaters, musical
512132 Theaters, outdoor motion picture
711320 Theatrical booking agencies (except motion picture)
315299 Theatrical costumes cut and sewn from purchased fabric (except apparel contractors)
315211 Theatrical costumes, men's and boys', cut and sew apparel contractors
315212 Theatrical costumes, women's, girls', and infants', cut and sew apparel contractors

711120 Theatrical dance productions, live
561310 Theatrical employment agencies
532490 Theatrical equipment (except costumes) rental or leasing
711310 Theatrical production managers with facilities
711320 Theatrical production managers without facilities
711310 Theatrical production organizers with facilities
711320 Theatrical production organizers without facilities
711310 Theatrical production promoters with facilities
711320 Theatrical production promoters without facilities
711110 Theatrical repertory companies
711110 Theatrical road companies
339999 Theatrical scenery manufacturing
711110 Theatrical stock companies
711410 Theatrical talent agents
561599 Theatrical ticket offices
532220 Theatrical wardrobe and costume rental
334290 Theft prevention signaling devices (e.g., door entrance annunciation, holdup signaling devices, personal duress signaling devices), manufacturing
713110 Theme parks, amusement
325411 Theobromine and derivatives (i.e., basic chemicals) manufacturing
333314 Theodolites manufacturing
334519 Theodolites, surveying, manufacturing
611310 Theological seminaries offering baccalaureate or graduate degrees
334517 Therapeutic X-ray apparatus and tubes (e.g., medical, industrial, research) manufacturing
****** Therapists' offices—see type
423450 Therapy equipment merchant wholesalers
334516 Thermal analysis instruments, laboratory-type, manufacturing
334516 Thermal conductivity instruments and sensors manufacturing
334513 Thermal conductivity instruments, industrial process-type, manufacturing
326140 Thermal insulation, polystyrene foam, manufacturing
237130 Thermal power plant construction
541380 Thermal testing laboratories or services
334415 Thermistors manufacturing
334513 Thermistors, industrial process-type, manufacturing
334519 Thermocouples (except industrial process, aircraft type, glass vacuum) manufacturing
334512 Thermocouples, glass vacuum, manufacturing
334513 Thermocouples, industrial process-type, manufacturing
335999 Thermoelectric generators manufacturing
333993 Thermoform, blister, and skin packaging machinery manufacturing
333220 Thermoforming machinery for plastics manufacturing
334516 Thermogravimetric analyzers manufacturing
334519 Thermometer, liquid-in-glass and bimetal types (except medical), manufacturing
423450 Thermometers merchant wholesalers
334513 Thermometers, filled system industrial process-type, manufacturing
339112 Thermometers, medical, manufacturing
325211 Thermoplastic resins and plastics materials manufacturing
325211 Thermosetting plastics resins manufacturing

325212 Thermosetting vulcanizable elastomers manufacturing
332911 Thermostatic traps, industrial-type, manufacturing
334512 Thermostats (e.g., air-conditioning, appliance, comfort heating, refrigeration) manufacturing
336399 Thermostats, automotive, truck, and bus, manufacturing
334519 Thickness gauging instruments, ultrasonic, manufacturing
332999 Thimbles for wire rope manufacturing
334413 Thin film integrated circuits manufacturing
333295 Thin layer deposition equipment, semiconductor, manufacturing
115112 Thinning of crops, mechanical and chemical
325188 Thiocyanate manufacturing
325199 Thioglycolic acid manufacturing
325212 Thiol rubber manufacturing
212299 Thorite mining and/or beneficiating
212299 Thorium ores mining and/or beneficiating
711212 Thoroughbred racetracks
424310 Thread (except industrial) merchant wholesalers
333515 Thread cutting dies (i.e., a machine tool accessory) manufacturing
313312 Thread finishing
333292 Thread making machinery manufacturing
313113 Thread mills
333513 Thread rolling machines, metalworking, manufacturing
313113 Thread, all fibers, manufacturing
423840 Thread, industrial, merchant wholesalers
326299 Thread, rubber (except fabric covered), manufacturing
333512 Threading machines, metalworking, manufacturing
115113 Threshing service
453310 Thrift shops, used merchandise
333298 Through-hole machinery, printed circuit board loading, manufacturing
325221 Throwing cellulosic yarn made in the same establishment
325222 Throwing noncellulosic yarn made in the same establishment
313112 Throwing purchased yarn
334519 Thrust power indicators, aircraft engine, manufacturing
332991 Thrust roller bearings manufacturing
334413 Thyristors manufacturing
325412 Thyroid preparations manufacturing
325320 Tick powders or sprays manufacturing
561599 Ticket (e.g., airline, bus, cruise ship, sports, theatrical) offices
561599 Ticket (e.g., airline, bus, cruise ship, sports, theatrical) sales offices
561599 Ticket (e.g., amusement, sports, theatrical) agencies
561599 Ticket (e.g., amusement, sports, theatrical) sales agencies
561599 Ticket agencies, amusement
561599 Ticket agencies, sports
561599 Ticket agencies, theatrical
561599 Ticket offices for foreign cruise ship companies
331111 Tie plates, iron or steel, made in iron and steel mills
448150 Tie shops
331222 Tie wires made in wire drawing plants
315191 Ties made in apparel knitting mills
327390 Ties, concrete, railroad, manufacturing
315993 Ties, men's and boys' hand sewn (except apparel contractors), manufacturing
315211 Ties, men's and boys' hand sewn, cut and sew apparel contractors
321113 Ties, railroad, made from logs or bolts

321114 Ties, wood railroad bridge, cross, and switch, treating
321113 Ties, wood, made from logs or bolts
423990 Ties, wood, merchant wholesalers
315119 Tights knitting or knitting and finishing
112511 Tilapia production
238340 Tile (except resilient) contractors
238340 Tile (except resilient) laying and setting
325520 Tile adhesives manufacturing
333298 Tile making machinery (except kilns) manufacturing
444190 Tile stores, ceramic
327122 Tile, ceramic wall and floor, manufacturing
327124 Tile, clay, refractory, manufacturing
327121 Tile, clay, structural, manufacturing
321999 Tile, cork, manufacturing
327123 Tile, roofing and drain, clay, manufacturing
327123 Tile, sewer, clay, manufacturing
423320 Tile, structural clay (except refractory), merchant wholesalers
114111 Tilefish fishing
333994 Tilemaking kilns manufacturing
326192 Tiles, floor (i.e., linoleum, rubber, vinyl), manufacturing
423820 Tillers, farm and garden, merchant wholesalers
333112 Tillers, lawn and garden-type, manufacturing
423990 Timber and timber products (except lumber) merchant wholesalers
113310 Timber piling
113310 Timber pole cutting
237990 Timber removal, underwater
113110 Timber tract operations
115310 Timber valuation
321114 Timber, structural, treating
321113 Timbers, made from logs or bolts
321213 Timbers, structural, glue laminated or pre-engineered wood, manufacturing
334518 Time clocks and time recording devices manufacturing
334513 Time cycle and program controllers, industrial process-type, manufacturing
334518 Time locks manufacturing
323118 Time planners/organizers and refills manufacturing
334512 Time program controls, air-conditioning systems, manufacturing
423420 Time recording machines merchant wholesalers
561599 Time share exchange services, condominium
334518 Time stamps containing clock mechanisms manufacturing
335313 Time switches, electrical switchgear apparatus, manufacturing
334518 Timers for industrial use, clockwork mechanism, manufacturing
236115 Time-share condominium construction general contractors
236117 Time-share condominium construction operative builders
326220 Timing belt, rubber or plastics, manufacturing
335314 Timing devices, mechanical and solid-state (except clockwork), manufacturing
336312 Timing gears and chains, automotive and truck gasoline engine, manufacturing
334518 Timing mechanisms, clockwork, manufacturing
335312 Timing motors, synchronous, electric, manufacturing
331491 Tin and tin alloy bar, pipe, rod, sheet, strip, and tubing made from purchased metals or scrap
331419 Tin base alloys made in primary tin smelting and refining mills
325188 Tin chloride manufacturing

325188 Tin compounds, not specified elsewhere by process, manufacturing
212299 Tin metal concentrates beneficiating
212299 Tin metal ores mining and/or beneficiating
325188 Tin oxide manufacturing
332431 Tin plate cans, light gauge metal, manufacturing
423510 Tin plate merchant wholesalers
331492 Tin recovering from scrap and/ or alloying purchased metals
331419 Tin refining, primary
331491 Tin rolling, drawing, or extruding purchased metals or scrap
325188 Tin salts manufacturing
325412 Tincture of iodine preparations manufacturing
332999 Tinfoil not made in rolling mills
331111 Tin-free steel made in iron and steel mills
332212 Tinners' snips manufacturing
331111 Tinplate made in iron and steel mills
339999 Tinsel manufacturing
325998 Tint and dye preparations, household-type (except hair), manufacturing
325620 Tints, dyes, and rinses, hair, manufacturing
212111 Tipple operation, bituminous coal mining and/or beneficiating
236210 Tipple, mining, construction
316999 Tips, shoe, leather, manufacturing
423130 Tire and tube repair materials merchant wholesalers
332618 Tire chains made from purchased wire
314992 Tire cord and fabric, all materials, manufacturing
336360 Tire covers made from purchased fabric
441320 Tire dealers, automotive
325998 Tire inflators, aerosol, manufacturing
333220 Tire making machinery manufacturing
333319 Tire mounting machines, motor vehicle, manufacturing
333220 Tire recapping machinery manufacturing
423830 Tire recapping machinery merchant wholesalers
326211 Tire repair materials manufacturing
811198 Tire repair shops (except retreading), automotive
326212 Tire retreading, recapping or rebuilding
333220 Tire shredding machinery manufacturing
423130 Tire tubes, motor vehicle, merchant wholesalers
326211 Tires (e.g., pneumatic, semi-pneumatic, solid rubber) manufacturing
423130 Tires, new, motor vehicle, merchant wholesalers
326199 Tires, plastics, manufacturing
423930 Tires, scrap, merchant wholesalers
423130 Tires, used (except scrap), merchant wholesalers
111421 Tissue culture farming
322121 Tissue paper stock manufacturing
424130 Tissue paper, toilet and facial, merchant wholesalers
327113 Titania porcelain insulators manufacturing
212299 Titaniferous-magnetite ores, valued chiefly for titanium content, mining and/or beneficiating
331491 Titanium and titanium alloy bar, billet, rod, sheet, strip, and tubing made from purchased metals or scrap
325131 Titanium based pigments manufacturing
331528 Titanium castings (except die-castings), unfinished, manufacturing
212299 Titanium concentrates beneficiating

331522 Titanium die-castings, unfinished, manufacturing
325188 Titanium dioxide manufacturing
332112 Titanium forgings made from purchased metals, unfinished
212299 Titanium ores mining and/or beneficiating
331419 Titanium refining, primary
331491 Titanium rolling, drawing, or extruding purchased metals or scrap
541191 Title abstract companies, real estate
541191 Title companies, real estate
524127 Title insurance carriers, real estate, direct
541191 Title search companies, real estate
519190 Title search services (except real estate)
512191 Titling of motion picture film or video
334516 Titrimeters manufacturing
325920 TNT (trinitrotoluene) manufacturing
335211 Toaster ovens, household-type electric, manufacturing
423620 Toasters, electric, merchant wholesalers
335211 Toasters, household-type electric, manufacturing
424940 Tobacco (except leaf) merchant wholesalers
111910 Tobacco farming, field and seed production
115114 Tobacco grading
333111 Tobacco harvester machines manufacturing
321920 Tobacco hogshead stock, manufacturing
321920 Tobacco hogsheads, manufacturing
312210 Tobacco leaf processing and aging
339999 Tobacco pipes manufacturing
316993 Tobacco pouches (except metal) manufacturing
339911 Tobacco pouches, precious metal, manufacturing
333298 Tobacco processing machinery (except farm-type) manufacturing
312229 Tobacco products (e.g., chewing, smoking, snuff) manufacturing
424940 Tobacco products merchant wholesalers
312229 Tobacco products, imitation (except cigarettes) manufacturing
312229 Tobacco sheeting services
312210 Tobacco stemming and redrying
453991 Tobacco stores
424590 Tobacco, leaf, merchant wholesalers
339920 Toboggans manufacturing
316999 Toe caps, leather, manufacturing
311340 Toffee manufacturing
311991 Tofu (i.e., bean curd) (except frozen desserts) manufacturing
311520 Tofu frozen desserts manufacturing
332722 Toggle bolts, metal, manufacturing
325612 Toilet bowl cleaners manufacturing
332998 Toilet fixtures, metal, manufacturing
326191 Toilet fixtures, plastics, manufacturing
327111 Toilet fixtures, vitreous china, manufacturing
316993 Toilet kits and cases (except metal) manufacturing
339911 Toilet kits and cases, precious metal, manufacturing
322291 Toilet paper made from purchased paper
322121 Toilet paper made in paper mills
325620 Toilet preparations (e.g., cosmetics, deodorants, perfumes) manufacturing
424210 Toilet preparations merchant wholesalers
562991 Toilet renting and/or servicing, portable

321999 Toilet seats, wood, manufacturing
325611 Toilet soaps manufacturing
424210 Toilet soaps merchant wholesalers
424130 Toilet tissue merchant wholesalers
332999 Toilet ware, precious plated metal, manufacturing
325620 Toilet water manufacturing
424210 Toiletries merchant wholesalers
334210 Toll switching equipment, telephone, manufacturing
325110 Toluene made from refined petroleum or liquid hydrocarbons
324110 Toluene made in petroleum refineries
325192 Toluidines manufacturing
111219 Tomato farming (except under cover), field, bedding plant and seed production
111419 Tomato farming, grown under cover
333111 Tomato harvesting machines manufacturing
325992 Toner cartridges manufacturing
424120 Toner cartridges merchant wholesalers
325992 Toner cartridges rebuilding
325132 Toners (except electrostatic, photographic) manufacturing
325992 Toners, electrostatic and photographic, manufacturing
339113 Tongue depressors manufacturing
316999 Tongues, boot and shoe, leather, manufacturing
339112 Tonometers, medical, manufacturing
332439 Tool boxes, light gauge metal, manufacturing
321920 Tool chests, wood, manufacturing
321999 Tool handles, wood, turned and shaped, manufacturing
541420 Tool industrial design services
337127 Tool stands, factory, manufacturing
331111 Tool steel made in iron and steel mills
444130 Tool stores, power and hand (except outdoor)
333515 Toolholders (i.e., a machine tool accessory) manufacturing
333515 Tools and accessories for machine tools manufacturing
423120 Tools and equipment, motor vehicle, merchant wholesalers
339114 Tools, dentists', manufacturing
423710 Tools, hand (except motor vehicle, machinists' precision tools), merchant wholesalers
332212 Tools, hand, metal blade (e.g., putty knives, scrapers, screwdrivers)
333991 Tools, handheld power-driven, manufacturing
332212 Tools, handheld, nonpowered (except kitchen-type), manufacturing
423830 Tools, machinists' precision, merchant wholesalers
332212 Tools, woodworking edge (e.g., augers, bits, countersinks), manufacturing
339994 Toothbrushes (except electric) manufacturing
424210 Toothbrushes (except electric) merchant wholesalers
335211 Toothbrushes, electric, manufacturing
423620 Toothbrushes, electric, merchant wholesalers
325611 Toothpastes, gels, and tooth powders manufacturing
321999 Toothpicks, wood, manufacturing
316999 Top lifts, boot and shoe, leather, manufacturing
212325 Topaz, non-gem, mining and/or beneficiating
315211 Topcoats, men's and boys', cut and sew apparel contractors
315222 Topcoats, men's and boys', cut and sewn from purchased fabric (except apparel contractors)
541370 Topographic mapping services

541370 Topographic surveying services
424490 Toppings (except fountain) merchant wholesalers
336399 Tops, convertible automotive, manufacturing
484220 Top-soil hauling, local
332995 Torpedo tubes manufacturing
332993 Torpedoes manufacturing
336350 Torque converters, automotive, truck, and bus, manufacturing
335312 Torque motors, electric, manufacturing
332611 Torsion bar, heavy gauge metal, manufacturing
334519 Torsion testing equipment manufacturing
311919 Tortilla chips manufacturing
311830 Tortillas manufacturing
334514 Totalizing fluid meters manufacturing
334514 Totalizing meters (except aircraft), consumption registering, manufacturing
339999 Toupees manufacturing
424990 Toupees merchant wholesalers
487110 Tour bus, scenic and sightseeing, operation
561520 Tour operators (i.e., arranging and assembling tours)
561591 Tourism bureaus
926110 Tourism development offices, government
713990 Tourist guide services
721199 Tourist homes
561591 Tourist information bureaus
721110 Tourist lodges
336413 Tow targets, aircraft, manufacturing
488410 Tow truck services
336211 Tow trucks (including tilt and load) assembling on purchased chassis
336611 Towboat building and repairing
532411 Towboat rental or leasing
812331 Towel (except shop, wiping) supply services
327111 Towel bar holders, vitreous china and earthenware, manufacturing
812332 Towel supply services, shop or wiping
325620 Towelettes, premoistened, manufacturing
313210 Towels and washcloths made in broadwoven fabric mills
313249 Towels and washcloths made in warp knitting mills
313241 Towels and washcloths made in weft knitting mills
423220 Towels and washcloths merchant wholesalers
314129 Towels or washcloths made from purchased fabrics
423840 Towels, industrial, merchant wholesalers
322291 Towels, paper, made from purchased paper
322121 Towels, paper, made in paper mills
423450 Towels, surgical, merchant wholesalers
237130 Tower, power distribution and communication, construction
336399 Towing bars and systems manufacturing
483211 Towing service, inland waters (except on Great Lakes system)
488410 Towing services, motor vehicle
236115 Town house (i.e., single-family type) construction by general contractors
236117 Town house construction operative builders
531110 Town house rental or leasing
541320 Town planners' offices
541320 Town planning services
562910 Toxic material abatement services
562910 Toxic material removal contractors
621511 Toxicology health laboratories
325414 Toxoids (e.g., diphtheria, tetanus) manufacturing
339932 Toy furniture and household-type equipment manufacturing
451120 Toy stores
339932 Toys (except dolls, stuffed toys) manufacturing

423920 Toys (including electronic) merchant wholesalers
339931 Toys, doll, manufacturing
339931 Toys, stuffed, manufacturing
333515 Tracer and tapering machine tool attachments manufacturing
332993 Tracer igniters, ammunition (i.e., more than 30 mm., more than 1.18 inch), manufacturing
339920 Track and field athletic equipment (except apparel, footwear) manufacturing
335121 Track lighting fixtures and equipment, residential, electric, manufacturing
484220 Tracked vehicle freight transportation, local
484230 Tracked vehicle freight transportation, long-distance
487110 Tracked vehicle sightseeing operation
339113 Traction apparatus manufacturing
811310 Tractor, farm or construction equipment repair and maintenance services
532490 Tractor, farm, rental or leasing
532490 Tractor, garden, rental or leasing
333120 Tractors and attachments, construction-type, manufacturing
333111 Tractors and attachments, farm-type, manufacturing
333112 Tractors and attachments, lawn and garden-type, manufacturing
333120 Tractors, crawler, manufacturing
423820 Tractors, farm and garden, merchant wholesalers
423110 Tractors, highway, merchant wholesalers
333924 Tractors, industrial, manufacturing
423830 Tractors, industrial, merchant wholesalers
811411 Tractors, lawn and garden repair and maintenance services without retailing new lawn and garden tractors
336120 Tractors, truck for highway use, assembled on chassis of own manufacture
813910 Trade associations
522293 Trade banks (i.e., international trade financing)
323121 Trade binding services
926110 Trade commissions, government
926110 Trade development program administration
561920 Trade fair managers
561920 Trade fair organizers
561920 Trade fair promoters
522293 Trade financing, international
511120 Trade journal publishers (except exclusive Internet publishing)
511120 Trade journal publishers and printing combined
516110 Trade journal publishers, exclusively on Internet
323112 Trade journals flexographic printing without publishing
323111 Trade journals gravure printing without publishing
323110 Trade journals lithographic (offset) printing without publishing
323119 Trade journals printing (except flexographic, gravure, lithographic, quick, screen) without publishing
323113 Trade journals screen printing without publishing
511120 Trade magazine and periodical publishers (except exclusive Internet publishing)
511120 Trade magazine and periodical publishers and printing combined
516110 Trade magazine and periodical publishers, exclusively on Internet
323112 Trade magazines and periodicals flexographic printing without publishing
323111 Trade magazines and periodicals gravure printing without publishing

323110 Trade magazines and periodicals lithographic (offset) printing without publishing
323119 Trade magazines and periodicals printing (except flexographic, gravure, lithographic, quick, screen) without publishing
323113 Trade magazines and periodicals screen printing without publishing
238390 Trade show exhibit installation and dismantling contractors
561920 Trade show managers
561920 Trade show organizers
561920 Trade show promoters
611513 Trade union apprenticeship training programs
813930 Trade unions (except apprenticeship programs)
813930 Trade unions, local
533110 Trademark licensing
523130 Trading companies, commodity contracts
452990 Trading posts, general merchandise
523110 Trading securities (i.e., acting as a principal in dealing securities to investors)
561990 Trading stamp promotion and sale to stores
561990 Trading stamp redemption services
334290 Traffic advisory and signalling systems manufacturing
922110 Traffic courts
541330 Traffic engineering consulting services
237310 Traffic lane painting
519110 Traffic reporting services
238210 Traffic signal installation
334290 Traffic signals manufacturing
237990 Trail construction
721214 Trail riding camps with accommodation facilities
713990 Trail riding, recreational
336399 Trailer hitches, motor vehicle, manufacturing
531190 Trailer park or court, residential
423120 Trailer parts, new, merchant wholesalers
532120 Trailer rental or leasing
336214 Trailers for transporting horses (except fifth-wheel-type) manufacturing
336214 Trailers, camping, manufacturing
336212 Trailers, fifth-wheel type, for transporting horses, manufacturing
423830 Trailers, industrial, merchant wholesalers
423110 Trailers, motor vehicle, merchant wholesalers
115210 Training horses (except racehorses)
315212 Training pants (i.e., underwear), infants', cut and sew apparel contractors
315291 Training pants (i.e., underwear), infants', cut and sewn from purchased fabric (except apparel contractors)
711219 Training race dogs
711219 Training racehorses
339932 Trains and equipment, toy, electric or mechanical, manufacturing
713990 Trampoline facilities, recreational
485119 Tramway systems (except mixed mode), commuter
487990 Tramway, aerial, scenic and sightseeing operation
332994 Tranquilizer guns, manufacturing
325412 Tranquilizer preparations manufacturing
336350 Transaxles, automotive, truck, and bus, manufacturing
334220 Transceivers (i.e., transmitter-receiver units) manufacturing
561410 Transcription services
334510 Transcutaneous electrical nerve stimulators (TENS) manufacturing
334419 Transducers (except pressure) manufacturing

334519 Transducers, pressure, manufacturing
484110 Transfer (trucking) services, general freight, local
523999 Transfer agencies, securities
237130 Transformer station and substation, electric power, construction
423610 Transformers (except electronic) merchant wholesalers
335311 Transformers, electric power, manufacturing
334416 Transformers, electronic component-types, manufacturing
423690 Transformers, electronic, merchant wholesalers
335311 Transformers, ignition, for use on domestic fuel burners, manufacturing
335311 Transformers, reactor, manufacturing
335311 Transformers, separate solid-state arc-welding, manufacturing
335912 Transistor radio batteries manufacturing
334413 Transistors manufacturing
423690 Transistors merchant wholesalers
541850 Transit advertising services
922120 Transit police
926120 Transit systems and authorities, nonoperating
485111 Transit systems, mixed mode (e.g., bus, commuter rail, subway combinations)
624229 Transitional housing agencies
327320 Transit-mixed concrete manufacturing
334519 Transits, surveying, manufacturing
541930 Translation services, language
237130 Transmission and distribution line construction
335311 Transmission and distribution voltage regulators manufacturing
316999 Transmission belting, leather, manufacturing
326220 Transmission belts, rubber, manufacturing
336399 Transmission coolers manufacturing
423610 Transmission equipment, electrical, merchant wholesalers
324191 Transmission fluids, petroleum, made from refined petroleum
325998 Transmission fluids, synthetic, manufacturing
221121 Transmission of electric power
486210 Transmission of natural gas via pipeline (i.e., processing plants to local distribution systems)
335932 Transmission pole and line hardware manufacturing
811113 Transmission repair shops, automotive
332312 Transmission tower sections, fabricated structural metal, manufacturing
336350 Transmissions and parts, automotive, truck, and bus, manufacturing
423690 Transmitters merchant wholesalers
334513 Transmitters, industrial process control-type, manufacturing
333111 Transplanters, farm-type, manufacturing
115112 Transplanting services
****** Transportation—see mode
481212 Transportation by spacecraft, freight
926120 Transportation departments, nonoperating
423860 Transportation equipment and supplies (except marine pleasure craft, motor vehicles) merchant wholesalers
336360 Transportation equipment seating manufacturing
541614 Transportation management consulting services
926120 Transportation regulatory agencies
926120 Transportation safety programs, government

483111 Transporting freight to or from foreign ports, deep sea
483112 Transporting passengers to or from foreign ports, deep sea
212319 Trap rock crushed and broken stone mining and/or beneficiating
212311 Trap rock mining or quarrying
332618 Traps, animal and fish, made from purchased wire
332913 Traps, water, manufacturing
423910 Trapshooting equipment and supplies merchant wholesalers
713990 Trapshooting facilities, recreational
333319 Trash and garbage compactors, commercial-type, manufacturing
335228 Trash and garbage compactors, household-type, manufacturing
326111 Trash bags, plastics film, single wall or multiwall, manufacturing
562111 Trash collection services
326199 Trash containers, plastics, manufacturing
562213 Trash disposal combustors or incinerators
562212 Trash disposal landfills
562111 Trash hauling, local
484230 Trash hauling, long-distance
332313 Trash racks, fabricated metal plate work, manufacturing
621493 Trauma centers (except hospitals), freestanding
561510 Travel agencies
511130 Travel guide book publishers (except exclusive Internet publishing)
511130 Travel guide book publishers and printing combined
516110 Travel guide book publishers, exclusively on Internet
323117 Travel guide books printing and binding without publishing
323117 Travel guide books printing without publishing
561520 Travel tour operators
423110 Travel trailer (e.g., tent trailers) merchant wholesalers
721211 Travel trailer campsites
441210 Travel trailer dealers
336214 Travel trailers, recreational, manufacturing
624190 Travelers' aid centers
522390 Travelers' check issuance services
316991 Traveling bags, all materials, manufacturing
712110 Traveling museum exhibits
711190 Traveling shows, carnival
334411 Traveling wave tubes manufacturing
212312 Travertine crushed and broken stone mining and/or beneficiating
212311 Travertine mining or quarrying
337127 Tray trucks, restaurant, manufacturing
321920 Trays, carrier, wood, manufacturing
322299 Trays, food, molded pulp, manufacturing
333315 Trays, photographic printing and processing, manufacturing
332618 Trays, wire, made from purchased wire
321999 Trays, wood, wicker, and bagasse, manufacturing
326211 Tread rubber (i.e., camelback) manufacturing
332323 Treads, metal stair, manufacturing
921130 Treasurers' offices, government
321114 Treating purchased wood and wood products
238160 Treating roofs (by spraying, painting or coating)
321114 Treating wood products with creosote or other preservatives
561730 Tree and brush trimming, overhead utility line
113310 Tree chipping in the field
111421 Tree crop farming (except forestry), short rotation growing and harvesting cycle
111335 Tree nut farming
311225 Tree nut oils (e.g., tung, walnut) made from purchased oils

311223 Tree nut oils (e.g., tung, walnut) made in crushing mill
561730 Tree pruning services
561730 Tree removal services
113210 Tree seed extracting
113210 Tree seed gathering
113210 Tree seed growing for reforestation
561730 Tree services (e.g., bracing, planting, pruning, removal, spraying, surgery, trimming)
333111 Tree shakers (e.g., citrus, nut, soft fruit) manufacturing
561730 Tree surgery services
561730 Tree trimming services
339999 Trees and plants, artificial, manufacturing
424930 Trees merchant wholesalers
321918 Trellises, wood, manufacturing
238910 Trenching (except underwater)
333120 Trenching machines manufacturing
237990 Trenching, underwater
237310 Trestle construction
321114 Trestle parts, wood, treating
325221 Triacetate fibers and yarns manufacturing
921150 Tribal chief's or chairman's office, American Indian or Alaska Native
921150 Tribal councils, American Indian or Alaska Native
921150 Tribal courts, American Indian or Alaska Native
325199 Trichloroethylene manufacturing
325199 Trichlorophenoxyacetic acid manufacturing
325199 Tricresyl phosphate manufacturing
339932 Tricycles (except metal) manufacturing
336991 Tricycles, metal, adult and children's, manufacturing
325199 Tridecyl alcohol manufacturing
238350 Trim and finish carpentry contractors
332321 Trim and molding (except motor vehicle), metal, manufacturing
332321 Trim, metal, manufacturing
321918 Trim, wood and covered wood, manufacturing
333112 Trimmers, hedge, electric, manufacturing
332212 Trimmers, hedge, nonelectric, manufacturing
333112 Trimmers, string, lawn and garden-type, manufacturing
315292 Trimmings, fur (except apparel contractors), manufacturing
315211 Trimmings, fur, men's and boys', cut and sew apparel contractors
315212 Trimmings, fur, women's, girls', and infants', cut and sew apparel contractors
316999 Trimmings, shoe, leather, manufacturing
325920 Trinitrotoluene (TNT) manufacturing
325199 Triphenyl phosphate manufacturing
333315 Tripods, camera and projector, manufacturing
212399 Tripoli mining and/or beneficiating
339112 Trocars manufacturing
485119 Trolley systems (except mixed mode), commuter
487110 Trolley, scenic and sightseeing, operation
339992 Trombones and parts manufacturing
212391 Trona mining and/or beneficiating
423940 Trophies merchant wholesalers
332999 Trophies, nonprecious and precious plated metal, manufacturing
339912 Trophies, precious metal, (except precious plated) manufacturing
453998 Trophy (including awards and plaques) shops
321999 Trophy bases, wood, manufacturing
424990 Tropical fish merchant wholesalers
112511 Tropical fish production, farm raising

561730 Tropical plant maintenance services
335129 Trouble lights manufacturing
332322 Troughs, elevator, sheet meta (except stampings), manufacturing
332313 Troughs, industrial, fabricated metal plate work, manufacturing
335211 Trouser pressers, household-type electric, manufacturing
315191 Trousers made in apparel knitting mills
315211 Trousers, men's and boys', cut and sew apparel contractors
315224 Trousers, men's and boys', cut and sewn from purchased fabric (except apparel contractors)
114111 Trout fishing
112511 Trout production, farm raising
332212 Trowels manufacturing
532120 Truck (except industrial) rental or leasing
811192 Truck and bus washes
336211 Truck bodies and cabs manufacturing
336211 Truck bodies assembling on purchased chassis
336214 Truck campers (i.e., slide-in campers) manufacturing
441310 Truck cap stores
611519 Truck driving schools
111219 Truck farming, field, bedding plant and seed production
522220 Truck finance leasing
423120 Truck parts, new, merchant wholesalers
811310 Truck refrigeration repair and maintenance services
811111 Truck repair shops, general
447190 Truck stops
236220 Truck terminal construction
532120 Truck tractor rental or leasing
336120 Truck tractors for highway use, assembling on chassis of own manufacture
336211 Truck tractors for highway use, assembling on purchased chassis
423110 Truck tractors, road, merchant wholesalers
811121 Truck trailer body shops
336212 Truck trailer manufacturing
423110 Truck trailer merchant wholesalers
811121 Truck trailer paint and body repair
488490 Truck weighing station operation
532490 Truck, industrial, rental or leasing
488490 Trucking terminals, independently operated
484210 Trucking used household, office, or institutional furniture and equipment
484110 Trucking, general freight, local
484122 Trucking, general freight, long-distance, less-than-truckload (LTL)
484121 Trucking, general freight, long-distance, truckload (TL)
484220 Trucking, specialized freight (except used goods), local
484230 Trucking, specialized freight (except used goods), long-distance
327320 Truck-mixed concrete manufacturing
336120 Trucks, heavy, assembling on chassis of own manufacture
333924 Trucks, industrial, manufacturing
423830 Trucks, industrial, merchant wholesalers
336112 Trucks, light duty, assembling on chassis of own manufacture
333120 Trucks, off-highway, manufacturing
423110 Trucks, road, merchant wholesalers
111419 Truffles farming, grown under cover
339992 Trumpets and parts manufacturing
316991 Trunks (i.e., luggage), all materials, manufacturing

332313 Truss plates, metal, manufacturing
321214 Trusses, glue laminated or pre-engineered wood, manufacturing
321214 Trusses, wood roof or floor, manufacturing
321214 Trusses, wood, glue laminated or metal connected, manufacturing
523991 Trust administration, personal investment
523991 Trust companies, nondepository
813211 Trusts, charitable, awarding grants
813211 Trusts, educational, awarding grants
525920 Trusts, estates, and agency accounts
813211 Trusts, religious, awarding grants
448190 T-shirt shops, custom printed
315291 T-shirts, outerwear, infants', cut and sewn from purchased fabric (except apparel contractors)
315191 T-shirts, outerwear, made in apparel knitting mills
315223 T-shirts, outerwear, men's and boys', cut and sewn from purchased fabric (except apparel contractors)
315211 T-shirts, outerwear, men's, boys' and unisex, cut and sew apparel contractors
315223 T-shirts, outerwear, unisex (i.e., sized without regard to gender), cut and sewn from purchased fabric (except apparel contractors)
315212 T-shirts, outerwear, women's, girls', and infants', cut and sew apparel contractors
315232 T-shirts, outerwear, women's, misses', and girls', cut and sewn from purchased fabric (except apparel contractors)
315291 T-shirts, underwear, infants', cut and sewn from purchased fabric (except apparel contractors)
315192 T-shirts, underwear, made in apparel knitting mills
315211 T-shirts, underwear, men's and boys', cut and sew apparel contractors
315221 T-shirts, underwear, men's and boys', cut and sewn from purchased fabric (except apparel contractors)
315231 T-shirts, underwear, women's, misses', and girls', cut and sewn from purchased fabric (except apparel contractors)
315212 T-shirts, underwear, women's, misses', girls', and infants', cut and sew apparel contractors
334519 T-squares (drafting) manufacturing
325612 Tub and tile cleaning preparations manufacturing
331210 Tube (e.g., heavy riveted, lock joint, seamless, welded) made from purchased iron or steel
332912 Tube and hose fittings, fluid power, manufacturing
331316 Tube blooms made by extruding purchased aluminum
331316 Tube blooms, aluminum, made in integrated secondary smelting and extruding mills
331316 Tube made by drawing or extruding purchased aluminum
333516 Tube rolling mill machinery, metalworking, manufacturing
331111 Tube rounds, iron or steel, made in iron and steel mills
331316 Tube, aluminum, made in integrated secondary smelting and drawing plants
331316 Tube, aluminum, made in integrated secondary smelting and extruding mills
331111 Tube, iron or steel, made in iron and steel mills
326121 Tube, nonrigid plastics, manufacturing
331315 Tube, welded, aluminum, made by flat rolling purchased aluminum

331315 Tube, welded, aluminum, made in integrated secondary smelting and flat rolling mills
325414 Tuberculin (i.e., tuberculo-protein derived) manufacturing
622310 Tuberculosis and other respiratory illness hospitals
332996 Tubes made from purchased metal pipe
334411 Tubes, cathode ray, manufacturing
334411 Tubes, electron, manufacturing
423690 Tubes, electronic (e.g., industrial, receiving, transmitting), merchant wholesalers
334411 Tubes, electronic, manufacturing
334411 Tubes, klystron, manufacturing
334517 Tubes, X-ray, manufacturing
331421 Tubing, copper and copper alloy, made from purchased copper or in integrated secondary smelting and rolling, drawing or extruding plants
332999 Tubing, flexible metal, manufacturing
331210 Tubing, mechanical and hypodermic sizes, cold-drawn stainless steel, made from purchased steel
423510 Tubing, metal, merchant wholesalers
331491 Tubing, nonferrous metals (except aluminum, copper), made from purchased metals or scrap
326299 Tubing, rubber (except extruded, molded, lathe-cut), manufacturing
331111 Tubing, seamless steel, made in iron and steel mills
331111 Tubing, wrought iron or steel, made in iron and steel mills
332998 Tubs, laundry and bath, metal, manufacturing
238140 Tuck pointing contractors
212312 Tufa, calcareous, crushed and broken stone, mining and/or beneficiating
212311 Tufa, calcareous, mining or quarrying
333292 Tufting machinery for textiles manufacturing
336611 Tugboat building
532411 Tugboat rental or leasing
488330 Tugboat services, harbor operation
326199 Tumblers, plastics, manufacturing
332813 Tumbling (i.e., cleaning and polishing) metal and metal products for the trade
114111 Tuna fishing
811118 Tune-up shops, automotive
325188 Tungstates (e.g., ammonium tungstate, sodium tungstate) manufacturing
331491 Tungsten bar, rod, sheet, strip, and tubing made by rolling, drawing, or extruding purchased metals or scrap
331492 Tungsten carbide powder made by metallurgical process
325188 Tungsten compounds, not specified elsewhere by process, manufacturing
212299 Tungsten concentrates beneficiating
212299 Tungsten ores mining and/or beneficiating
811490 Tuning and repair of musical instruments
339992 Tuning forks manufacturing
237990 Tunnel construction
238210 Tunnel lighting contractors
332313 Tunnel lining, fabricated metal plate work, manufacturing
213113 Tunneling services for coal mining on a contract basis
332313 Tunnels, wind, fabricated metal plate work, manufacturing
334513 Turbidity instruments, industrial process-type, manufacturing
334516 Turbidometers, laboratory-type, manufacturing

334513 Turbine flow meters, industrial process-type, manufacturing
333611 Turbine generator set units manufacturing
334514 Turbine meters, consumption registering, manufacturing
333611 Turbines (except aircraft) manufacturing
423830 Turbines (except transportation) merchant wholesalers
423860 Turbines, transportation, merchant wholesalers
561730 Turf (except artificial) installation services
238990 Turf, artificial, installation
424440 Turkey and turkey products (except canned and packaged frozen) merchant wholesalers
112330 Turkey egg production
311119 Turkey feeds, prepared, manufacturing
112340 Turkey hatcheries
112330 Turkey production
311615 Turkeys, processing, fresh, frozen, canned, or cooked
311615 Turkeys, slaughtering and dressing
812199 Turkish bathhouses
812199 Turkish baths
332722 Turnbuckles, metal, manufacturing
333512 Turning machines (i.e., lathes), metalworking, manufacturing
321912 Turnings, furniture, unfinished wood, manufacturing
111219 Turnip farming, field, bedding plant and seed production
325191 Turpentine made by distillation of pine gum or pine wood
424690 Turpentine merchant wholesalers
212399 Turquoise mining and/or beneficiating
333512 Turret lathes, metalworking, manufacturing
332995 Turrets, gun, manufacturing
114119 Turtle fishing
112519 Turtle production, farm raising
611691 Tutoring, academic
532220 Tuxedo rental
315222 Tuxedos cut and sewn from purchased fabric (except apparel contractors)
315211 Tuxedos, cut and sew apparel contractors
334310 TV (television) sets manufacturing
443112 TV (television) stores
532490 TV broadcasting and studio equipment rental or leasing
337124 TV stands and similar stands for consumer electronics, metal, manufacturing
337125 TV stands and similar stands for consumer electronics, plastics, manufacturing
337122 TV stands and similar stands for consumer electronics, wood, manufacturing
313210 Twills weaving
423840 Twine merchant wholesalers
314991 Twines manufacturing
423830 Twist drills merchant wholesalers
517211 Two-way paging communication carriers
323122 Typesetting (i.e., computer controlled, hand, machine)
333293 Typesetting machinery manufacturing
424120 Typewriter paper merchant wholesalers
811212 Typewriter repair and maintenance services
339944 Typewriter ribbons manufacturing
333313 Typewriters manufacturing
423420 Typewriters merchant wholesalers
561410 Typing services
212291 Tyuyamunite mining and/or beneficiating
922130 U. S. attorneys' offices
522320 U.S. Central Credit Union
311514 UHT (ultra high temperature) milk manufacturing
339992 Ukuleles and parts manufacturing
212391 Ulexite mining and/or beneficiating

531130 U-lock storage
336411 Ultra light aircraft manufacturing
325131 Ultramarine pigments manufacturing
333512 Ultrasonic boring, drilling, and cutting machines, metalworking, manufacturing
335999 Ultrasonic cleaning equipment (except dental, medical) manufacturing
339114 Ultrasonic dental equipment manufacturing
335999 Ultrasonic generators sold separately for inclusion in tools and equipment manufacturing
339113 Ultrasonic medical cleaning equipment manufacturing
334510 Ultrasonic medical equipment manufacturing
333513 Ultrasonic metal forming machines manufacturing
334510 Ultrasonic scanning devices, medical, manufacturing
334519 Ultrasonic testing equipment (except medical) manufacturing
333992 Ultrasonic welding equipment manufacturing
621512 Ultrasound imaging centers
335110 Ultraviolet lamp bulbs manufacturing
335129 Ultraviolet lamp fixtures manufacturing
334516 Ultraviolet-type analytical instruments manufacturing
325131 Umber manufacturing
212393 Umber mining and/or beneficiating
339999 Umbrellas manufacturing
424320 Umbrellas, men's and boys', merchant wholesalers
322122 Uncoated groundwood paper mills
811198 Undercoating shops, automotive
237130 Underground cable (e.g., cable television, electricity, telephone) laying
333131 Underground mining machinery manufacturing
238910 Underground tank (except hazardous material) removal
237310 Underpass construction
238990 Underpinning, construction
812210 Undertaker services
423850 Undertakers' equipment and supplies merchant wholesalers
335129 Underwater lighting fixtures manufacturing
334511 Underwater navigational systems manufacturing
315192 Underwear made in apparel knitting mills
315192 Underwear shirts made in apparel knitting mills
315291 Underwear shirts, infants', cut and sewn from purchased fabric (except apparel contractors)
315211 Underwear shirts, men's and boys', cut and sew apparel contractors
315221 Underwear shirts, men's and boys', cut and sewn from purchased fabric (except apparel contractors)
315212 Underwear shirts, women's, girls', and infants', cut and sew apparel contractors
315231 Underwear shirts, women's, misses', and girls', cut and sewn from purchased fabric (except apparel contractors)
315192 Underwear shorts made in apparel knitting mills
315291 Underwear shorts, infants', cut and sewn from purchased fabric (except apparel contractors)
315211 Underwear shorts, men's and boys', cut and sew apparel contractors
315221 Underwear shorts, men's and boys', cut and sewn from purchased fabric (except apparel contractors)

315212 Underwear shorts, women's, girls', and infants', cut and sew apparel contractors
315231 Underwear shorts, women's, misses', and girls', cut and sewn from purchased fabric (except apparel contractors)
315291 Underwear, infants', cut and sewn from purchased fabric (except apparel contractors)
315211 Underwear, men's and boys', cut and sew apparel contractors
315221 Underwear, men's and boys', cut and sewn from purchased fabric (except apparel contractors)
424320 Underwear, men's and boys', merchant wholesalers
424330 Underwear, women's, children's, and infants', merchant wholesalers
315231 Underwear, women's, misses', and girls', cut and sewn from purchased fabric (except apparel contractors)
315212 Underwear, women's, misses', girls', and infants', cut and sew apparel contractors
523110 Underwriting securities
923130 Unemployment insurance program administration
812331 Uniform (except industrial) supply services
315991 Uniform hats and caps cut and sewn from purchased fabric (except apparel contractors)
315211 Uniform hats and caps, men's and boys', cut and sew apparel contractors
315212 Uniform hats and caps, women's, and girls', cut and sew apparel contractors
315232 Uniform shirts (except team athletic), women's, misses', and girls', cut and sewn from purchased fabric (except apparel contractors)
315223 Uniform shirts (except team athletic, work), men's and boys', cut and sewn from purchased fabric (except apparel contractors)
315211 Uniform shirts, men's and boys', cut and sew apparel contractors
315299 Uniform shirts, team athletic, cut and sewn from purchased fabric (except apparel contractors)
315212 Uniform shirts, women's and girls', cut and sew apparel contractors
315225 Uniform shirts, work, men's and boys', cut and sewn from purchased fabric (except apparel contractors)
448190 Uniform stores (except athletic)
451110 Uniform stores, athletic
812332 Uniform supply services, industrial
315299 Uniforms, band, cut and sewn from purchased fabric (except apparel contractors)
315211 Uniforms, band, men's and boys', cut and sew apparel contractors
315212 Uniforms, band, women's, girls', and infants', cut and sew apparel contractors
315211 Uniforms, dress (e.g., fire fighter, military, police), men's, cut and sew apparel contractors
315222 Uniforms, dress (e.g., fire fighter, military, police), men's, cut and sewn from purchased fabric (except apparel contractors)
315212 Uniforms, dress (e.g., military, police, fire fighter), women's, cut and sew apparel contractors

315234 Uniforms, dress, tailored (e.g., fire fighter, military, police), women's, misses', and girls', cut and sewn from purchased fabric (except apparel contractors)
315228 Uniforms, nontailored (except work), men's and boys', cut and sewn from purchased fabric (except apparel contractors)
315225 Uniforms, nontailored work, men's, cut and sewn from purchased fabric (except apparel contractors)
315191 Uniforms, nontailored, made in apparel knitting mills
315211 Uniforms, nontailored, men's and boys', cut and sew apparel contractors
315212 Uniforms, nontailored, women's and girls', cut and sew apparel contractors
315239 Uniforms, nontailored, women's, misses', and girls', cut and sewn from purchased fabric (except team athletic, apparel contractors)
315299 Uniforms, team athletic, cut and sewn from purchased fabric (except apparel contractors)
315211 Uniforms, team athletic, men's and boys', cut and sew apparel contractors
315212 Uniforms, team athletic, women's and girls', cut and sew apparel contractors
335999 Uninterruptible power supplies (UPS) manufacturing
525120 Union health and welfare funds
525110 Union pension funds
315192 Union suits made in apparel knitting mills
315291 Union suits, infants', cut and sewn from purchased fabric (except apparel contractors)
315211 Union suits, men's and boys', cut and sew apparel contractors
315221 Union suits, men's and boys', cut and sewn from purchased fabric (except apparel contractors)
315212 Union suits, women's, girls', and infants', cut and sew apparel contractors
315231 Union suits, women's, misses', and girls', cut and sewn from purchased fabric (except apparel contractors)
813930 Unions (except apprenticeship programs), labor
522130 Unions, credit
332919 Unions, pipe, metal (except made from purchased pipe), manufacturing
424330 Unisex clothing merchant wholesalers
448140 Unisex clothing stores
812112 Unisex hair stylist shops
333414 Unit heaters (except portable electric) manufacturing
335211 Unit heaters, portable electric, manufacturing
525990 Unit investment trust funds
323116 Unit set forms (e.g., manifold credit card slips) printing
813219 United fund councils
813219 United funds for colleges
928120 United Nations
333613 Universal joints (except aircraft, motor vehicle) manufacturing
336413 Universal joints, aircraft, manufacturing
336350 Universal joints, automotive, truck, and bus, manufacturing
611310 Universities
813410 University clubs
511130 University press publishers (except exclusive Internet publishing)
516110 University press publishers, exclusively on Internet
923110 University regents or boards, government
311812 Unleavened bread made in commercial bakeries
423690 Unloaded computer board merchant wholesalers

337121 Upholstered furniture, household-type, custom, manufacturing
337121 Upholstered furniture, household-type, on frames of any material, manufacturing
423850 Upholsterers' equipment and supplies (except fabrics) merchant wholesalers
314999 Upholstering filling (except nonwoven fabric) manufacturing
811420 Upholstery (except motor vehicle) repair services
561740 Upholstery cleaning on customers' premises
561740 Upholstery cleaning services
316110 Upholstery leather manufacturing
451130 Upholstery materials stores
811121 Upholstery shops, automotive
332612 Upholstery springs and spring units, light gauge, made from purchased wire or strip
316110 Upper leather manufacturing
316999 Uppers (i.e., shoe cut stock), leather, manufacturing
335999 UPS (uninterruptible power supplies) manufacturing
332111 Upset forgings made from purchased iron or steel, unfinished
332112 Upset forgings made from purchased nonferrous metals, unfinished
333513 Upsetters (i.e., forging machines) manufacturing
212291 Uraninite (pitchblende) mining and/or beneficiating
325188 Uranium compounds, not specified elsewhere by process, manufacturing
212291 Uranium ores mining and/or beneficiating
325188 Uranium oxide manufacturing
331419 Uranium refining, primary
325188 Uranium, enriched, manufacturing
212291 Uranium-radium-vanadium ore mine site development for own account
212291 Uranium-radium-vanadium ores mining and/or beneficiating
485113 Urban bus line services (except mixed mode)
485112 Urban commuter rail systems (except mixed mode)
541320 Urban planners' offices
925120 Urban planning commissions, government
541320 Urban planning services
485111 Urban transit systems, mixed mode (e.g., bus, commuter rail, subway combinations)
325311 Urea manufacturing
325211 Urea resins manufacturing
325211 Urea-formaldehyde resins manufacturing
238310 Urethane foam insulation application
326150 Urethane foam products manufacturing
325212 Urethane rubber manufacturing
621493 Urgent medical care centers and clinics (except hospitals), freestanding
332998 Urinals, metal, manufacturing
326191 Urinals, plastics, manufacturing
327111 Urinals, vitreous china, manufacturing
621511 Urinalysis laboratories
327420 Urns (e.g., gypsum, plaster of paris) manufacturing
335211 Urns, household-type electric, manufacturing
621111 Urologists' offices (e.g., centers, clinics)
441229 Used aircraft dealers
441310 Used automotive parts stores
441320 Used automotive tire dealers
453310 Used bicycle (except motorized) shops
441222 Used boat dealers
441120 Used car dealers
423110 Used car merchant wholesalers
484210 Used household and office goods moving

453930 Used manufactured (mobile) home dealers
453310 Used merchandise dealers (except motor vehicles and parts)
453310 Used merchandise stores
441221 Used motorcycle dealers
423140 Used parts, motor vehicle, merchant wholesalers
441210 Used recreational vehicle (RV) dealers
441320 Used tire dealers
423130 Used tires, motor vehicle, merchant wholesalers
441229 Used utility trailer dealers
541618 Utilities management consulting services
332311 Utility buildings, prefabricated metal, manufacturing
326199 Utility containers (e.g., baskets, bins, boxes, buckets, dishpans, pails), plastics (except foam), manufacturing
237130 Utility line (i.e., communication, electric power), construction
237110 Utility line (i.e., sewer, water), construction
511210 Utility software, computer, packaged
441229 Utility trailer dealers
423110 Utility trailer merchant wholesalers
532120 Utility trailer rental or leasing
336214 Utility trailers manufacturing
531190 Vacant lot rental or leasing
531190 Vacation and recreation land rental or leasing
721214 Vacation camps (except campgrounds, day instructional)
236115 Vacation home, single-family, construction by general contractors
236117 Vacation housing construction operative builders
115210 Vaccinating livestock (except by veterinarians)
541940 Vaccination services, veterinary
325414 Vaccines (i.e., bacterial, virus) manufacturing
424210 Vaccines merchant wholesalers
332439 Vacuum bottles and jugs, light gauge metal, manufacturing
336340 Vacuum brake booster, automotive, truck, and bus, manufacturing
326220 Vacuum cleaner belts, rubber or plastics, manufacturing
443111 Vacuum cleaner stores, household-type
335212 Vacuum cleaners (e.g., canister, handheld, upright) household-type electric, manufacturing
335212 Vacuum cleaners and sweepers, household-type electric, manufacturing
423620 Vacuum cleaners, household-type, merchant wholesalers
333319 Vacuum cleaners, industrial and commercial-type, manufacturing
238290 Vacuum cleaning system, built-in, installation
333912 Vacuum pumps (except laboratory) manufacturing
339111 Vacuum pumps, laboratory-type, manufacturing
335314 Vacuum relays manufacturing
332420 Vacuum tanks, heavy gauge metal, manufacturing
327215 Vacuum tube blanks, glass, made from purchased glass
327212 Vacuum tube blanks, glass, made in glass making plants
334411 Vacuum tubes manufacturing
488119 Vacuuming of airport runways
333112 Vacuums, yard, manufacturing
812930 Valet parking services
316991 Valises, all materials, manufacturing
325191 Valonia extract manufacturing
333512 Valve grinding machines, metalworking, manufacturing
423840 Valves (except hydraulic, plumbing, pneumatic) merchant wholesalers
332911 Valves for nuclear applications manufacturing

332911 Valves for water works and municipal water systems manufacturing
336311 Valves, engine, intake and exhaust, manufacturing
332912 Valves, hydraulic and pneumatic, fluid power, manufacturing
423830 Valves, hydraulic and pneumatic, merchant wholesalers
332911 Valves, industrial-type (e.g., check, gate, globe, relief, safety), manufacturing
332919 Valves, inline plumbing and heating (e.g., cutoffs, stop), manufacturing
423720 Valves, plumbing and heating, merchant wholesalers
316999 Vamps, leather, manufacturing
532120 Van (except passenger) rental or leasing without driver
532112 Van (passenger) leasing
532111 Van (passenger) rental
336213 Van and minivan conversions on purchased chassis
811121 Van conversion shops (except on assembly line or factory basis)
484210 Van lines, moving and storage services
212291 Vanadium ores mining and/or beneficiating
325199 Vanillin, synthetic, manufacturing
337110 Vanities (except freestanding), stock or custom wood, manufacturing
337122 Vanities, freestanding, wood, manufacturing
337124 Vanities, metal household-type, manufacturing
316993 Vanity cases, leather, manufacturing
337110 Vanity tops, wood or plastics laminated on wood, manufacturing
485999 Vanpool operation
488999 Vanpools, arrangement of
336112 Vans, commercial and passenger light duty, assembling on chassis of own manufacture
334512 Vapor heating controls manufacturing
335110 Vapor lamps, electric, manufacturing
333999 Vapor separating machinery manufacturing
335211 Vaporizers, household-type electric, manufacturing
334513 Variable control instruments, industrial process-type, manufacturing
311612 Variety meats, edible organs, made from purchased meats
311611 Variety meats, edible organs, made in slaughtering plants
452990 Variety stores
334415 Varistors manufacturing
325510 Varnishes manufacturing
424950 Varnishes merchant wholesalers
332812 Varnishing metals and metal products for the trade
313320 Varnishing purchased textiles and apparel
327420 Vases (e.g., gypsum, plaster of paris) manufacturing
327215 Vases, glass, made from purchased glass
327212 Vases, glass, made in glass making plants
327112 Vases, pottery (e.g., china, earthenware, stoneware), manufacturing
325132 Vat dyes, synthetic, manufacturing
332420 Vats, heavy gauge metal, manufacturing
332439 Vats, light gauge metal, manufacturing
711110 Vaudeville companies
332999 Vault doors and linings, metal, manufacturing
238290 Vault, safe and banking machine installation
332999 Vaults (except burial), metal, manufacturing

339995 Vaults (except concrete) manufacturing
326220 V-belts, rubber or plastics, manufacturing
334310 VCR (video cassette recorder) manufacturing
112111 Veal calf production
311611 Veal carcasses, half carcasses, primal and sub-primal cuts, produced in slaughtering plants
311612 Veal, primal and sub-primal cuts, made from purchased carcasses
325411 Vegetable alkaloids (i.e., basic chemicals) (e.g., caffeine, codeine, morphine, nicotine), manufacturing
111211 Vegetable and melon farming, potato dominant crop, field and seed production
111219 Vegetable and melon farming, vegetable (except potato) and melon dominant crops, field, bedding plants and seed production
111211 Vegetable and potato farming, potato dominant crop, field and seed potato production
111219 Vegetable and potato farming, vegetable (except potato) dominant crops, field, bedding plants and seed production
321920 Vegetable baskets, veneer and splint, manufacturing
311421 Vegetable brining
424990 Vegetable cake and meal merchant wholesalers
311421 Vegetable canning
321920 Vegetable crates, wood, wirebound, manufacturing
424910 Vegetable dusts and sprays merchant wholesalers
111419 Vegetable farming, grown under cover
311211 Vegetable flour manufacturing
311211 Vegetable flour, meal, and powders, made in flour mills
311411 Vegetable juice concentrates, frozen, manufacturing
311421 Vegetable juices canning
311421 Vegetable juices, fresh, manufacturing
445230 Vegetable markets
333294 Vegetable oil processing machinery manufacturing
311223 Vegetable oils (except soybean) made in crushing mills
311225 Vegetable oils made from purchased oils
115114 Vegetable precooling
115114 Vegetable sorting, grading, and packing
311221 Vegetable starches manufacturing
115114 Vegetable sun drying
115114 Vegetable vacuum cooling
311423 Vegetables dehydrating
311421 Vegetables pickling
424490 Vegetables, canned, merchant wholesalers
311991 Vegetables, cut or peeled, fresh, manufacturing
424480 Vegetables, fresh, merchant wholesalers
311411 Vegetables, frozen, manufacturing
424420 Vegetables, frozen, merchant wholesalers
115113 Vegetables, machine harvesting
238290 Vehicle lift installation
333997 Vehicle scales manufacturing
321912 Vehicle stock, hardwood, manufacturing
336991 Vehicle, children's, metal manufacturing
339932 Vehicles, children's (except bicycles and metal tricycles), manufacturing
423920 Vehicles, children's (except bicycles), merchant wholesalers
423110 Vehicles, recreational, merchant wholesalers
336321 Vehicular lighting fixtures manufacturing
316110 Vellum leather manufacturing
313210 Velvets, manmade fiber and silk, weaving
238290 Vending machine installation

454210 Vending machine merchandisers, sale of products
532490 Vending machine rental
333311 Vending machines manufacturing
423440 Vending machines merchant wholesalers
333210 Veneer and plywood forming machinery manufacturing
321920 Veneer baskets, for fruits and vegetables, manufacturing
321211 Veneer mills, hardwood
321212 Veneer mills, softwood
321999 Veneer work, inlaid, manufacturing
811490 Venetian blind repair and maintenance shops without retailing new venetian blinds
321918 Venetian blind slats, wood, manufacturing
337920 Venetian blinds manufacturing
238390 Ventilated wire shelving (i.e., closet organizing-type) installation
238220 Ventilating contractors
423730 Ventilating equipment and supplies (except household-type fans) merchant wholesalers
333412 Ventilating fans, industrial and commercial-type, manufacturing
335211 Ventilating kitchen fans, household-type electric, manufacturing
335211 Ventilation and exhaust fans (except attic fans), household-type, manufacturing
561790 Ventilation duct cleaning services
561790 Ventilation duct cleaning services
332322 Ventilators, sheet metal (except stampings), manufacturing
523910 Venture capital companies
212319 Verde' antique crushed and broken stone mining and/or beneficiating
212311 Verde' antique mining or quarrying
212399 Vermiculite mining and/or beneficiating
327992 Vermiculite, exfoliated, manufacturing
325412 Vermifuge preparations manufacturing
325131 Vermilion pigments manufacturing
312130 Vermouth manufacturing
337920 Vertical blinds manufacturing
488390 Vessel supply services
332420 Vessels, heavy gauge metal, manufacturing
315299 Vestments, academic and clerical, cut and sewn from purchased fabric (except apparel contractors)
315211 Vestments, academic and clerical, men's and boys', cut and sew apparel contractors
315212 Vestments, academic and clerical, women's and girls', cut and sew apparel contractors
315292 Vests, leather, fur, or sheep-lined (except apparel contractors), manufacturing
315211 Vests, leather, fur, or sheep-lined, men's and boys', cut and sew apparel contractors
315212 Vests, leather, fur, or sheep-lined, women's, girls', and infants', cut and sew apparel contractors
315211 Vests, men's and boys', cut and sew apparel contractors
315228 Vests, nontailored, men's and boys', cut and sewn from purchased fabric (except apparel contractors)
315239 Vests, nontailored, women's, misses', and girls', cut and sewn from purchased fabric (except apparel contractors)
315222 Vests, tailored, men's and boys', cut and sewn from purchased fabric (except apparel contractors)

315234 Vests, tailored, women's, misses', and girls', cut and sewn from purchased fabric
315212 Vests, women's, girls', and infants', cut and sew apparel contractors
813410 Veterans' membership organizations
923140 Veterans' affairs offices
923140 Veterans' benefits program administration, government
813311 Veterans' rights organizations
423490 Veterinarians' equipment and supplies merchant wholesalers
339112 Veterinarians' instruments and apparatus manufacturing
424210 Veterinarians' medicines merchant wholesalers
541940 Veterinarians' offices
541940 Veterinarians' practices
541940 Veterinary clinics
325412 Veterinary medicinal preparations manufacturing
541710 Veterinary research and development laboratories or services
541940 Veterinary services
541940 Veterinary services, livestock
541940 Veterinary services, pets and other animal specialties
541940 Veterinary testing laboratories
523910 Viatical settlement companies
339992 Vibraphones manufacturing
238390 Vibration isolation contractors
334519 Vibration meters, analyzers, and calibrators, manufacturing
541380 Vibration testing laboratories or services
333120 Vibrators, concrete, manufacturing
516110 Video broadcasting, exclusively on Internet
334220 Video camera (except household-type, television broadcast) manufacturing
423410 Video cameras (except household-type) merchant wholesalers
334310 Video cameras, household-type, manufacturing
423620 Video cameras, household-type, merchant wholesalers
811211 Video cassette recorder (VCR) repair services without retailing new video cassette recorders
532210 Video cassette recorder rental
334310 Video cassette recorders (VCR) manufacturing
334613 Video cassettes, blank, manufacturing
334612 Video cassettes, pre-recorded, mass reproducing
512191 Video conversion services (i.e., between formats)
532210 Video disc player rental
532230 Video disc rental for home electronic equipment (e.g., VCR)
713290 Video gambling device concession operators (i.e., supplying and servicing in others' facilities)
713120 Video game arcades (except gambling)
339932 Video game machines (except coin-operated) manufacturing
532230 Video game rental
713290 Video gaming device concession operators (i.e., supplying and servicing in others' facilities)
541921 Video photography services, portrait
512191 Video post-production services
512110 Video production
512110 Video production and distribution
532210 Video recorder rental
334612 Video tape or disk mass reproducing
532210 Video tape player rental
532230 Video tape rental for home electronic equipment (e.g., VCR)
532230 Video tape rental stores
451220 Video tape stores
334613 Video tapes, blank, manufacturing

423690 Video tapes, blank, merchant wholesalers
423990 Video tapes, prerecorded, merchant wholesalers
541922 Video taping services for legal depositions
541921 Video taping services, special events (e.g., birthdays, weddings)
561499 Videoconferencing services
512199 Videotape libraries, stock footage
311941 Vinegar manufacturing
115112 Vineyard cultivation services
325199 Vinyl acetate (except resins) manufacturing
325211 Vinyl acetate resins manufacturing
326113 Vinyl and vinyl copolymer film and unlaminated sheet (except packaging) manufacturing
325211 Vinyl chloride resins manufacturing
313320 Vinyl coated fabrics manufacturing
325222 Vinyl fibers and filaments manufacturing
326192 Vinyl floor coverings manufacturing
238330 Vinyl flooring contractors
325211 Vinyl resins manufacturing
423330 Vinyl siding merchant wholesalers
238170 Vinyl siding, soffit and fascia, installation
316219 Vinyl upper athletic footwear manufacturing
325222 Vinylidene chloride fiber and filament manufacturing
325211 Vinylidene resins manufacturing
339992 Violas and parts manufacturing
339992 Violins and parts manufacturing
325413 Viral in-vitro diagnostic test substances manufacturing
325414 Virus vaccines manufacturing
325221 Viscose fibers, bands, strips, and yarn manufacturing
334519 Viscosimeters (except industrial process type) manufacturing
334513 Viscosimeters, industrial process-type, manufacturing
332212 Vises (except machine tool attachments) manufacturing
621610 Visiting nurse associations
561591 Visitors bureaus
325412 Vitamin preparations manufacturing
446191 Vitamin stores
424210 Vitamins merchant wholesalers
325411 Vitamins, uncompounded, manufacturing
711130 Vocalists, independent
611513 Vocational apprenticeship training
624310 Vocational habilitation job counseling
624310 Vocational habilitation job training facilities (except schools)
624310 Vocational rehabilitation agencies
624310 Vocational rehabilitation job counseling
624310 Vocational rehabilitation job training facilities (except schools)
624310 Vocational rehabilitation or habilitation services (e.g., job counseling, job training, work experience)
611610 Voice instruction
561421 Voice mailbox services
621340 Voice pathologists' offices (e.g., centers, clinics)
212399 Volcanic ash mining and/or beneficiating
212319 Volcanic rock crushed and broken stone mining and/or beneficiating
212311 Volcanic rock, mining or quarrying
335311 Voltage regulating transformers, electric power, manufacturing
423610 Voltage regulators (except motor vehicle) merchant wholesalers
336322 Voltage regulators for internal combustion engines manufacturing

334413 Voltage regulators, integrated circuits, manufacturing
335311 Voltage regulators, transmission and distribution, manufacturing
334515 Voltmeters manufacturing
813212 Voluntary health organizations
624229 Volunteer housing repair organizations
333313 Voting machines manufacturing
423850 Voting machines merchant wholesalers
322214 Vulcanized fiber products made from purchased paperboard
325212 Vulcanized oils manufacturing
333220 Vulcanizing machinery manufacturing
332992 Wads, ammunition, manufacturing
333295 Wafer processing equipment, semiconductor, manufacturing
321219 Waferboard manufacturing
334413 Wafers (semiconductor devices) manufacturing
335211 Waffle irons, household-type electric, manufacturing
311412 Waffles, frozen, manufacturing
926150 Wage control agencies, government
339932 Wagons, children's (e.g., coaster, express, and play), manufacturing
333111 Wagons, farm-type, manufacturing
333112 Wagons, lawn and garden-type, manufacturing
321918 Wainscots, wood, manufacturing
561421 Wakeup call services
532291 Walker, invalid, rental
339932 Walkers, baby (vehicles), manufacturing
621111 Walk-in physicians' offices (e.g., centers, clinics)
333921 Walkways, moving, manufacturing
238310 Wall cavity and attic space insulation installation
334518 Wall clocks manufacturing
238130 Wall component (i.e., exterior, interior), prefabricated, installation
238320 Wall covering or removal contractors
424950 Wall coverings (e.g., fabric, plastics) merchant wholesalers
335122 Wall lamps (i.e., lighting fixtures), commercial, institutional, and industrial electric, manufacturing
335121 Wall lamps (i.e., lighting fixtures), residential electric, manufacturing
327122 Wall tile, ceramic, manufacturing
423310 Wallboard merchant wholesalers
327420 Wallboard, gypsum, manufacturing
316993 Wallets (except metal) manufacturing
339911 Wallets, precious metal, manufacturing
444120 Wallpaper and wall coverings stores
325612 Wallpaper cleaners manufacturing
238320 Wallpaper hanging and removal contractors
322222 Wallpaper made from purchased papers or other materials
424950 Wallpaper merchant wholesalers
238320 Wallpaper stripping
111335 Walnut farming
115114 Walnut hulling and shelling
712110 War museums
316991 Wardrobe bags (i.e., luggage) manufacturing
532220 Wardrobe rental
337124 Wardrobes, metal household-type, manufacturing
337122 Wardrobes, wood household-type, manufacturing
452910 Warehouse clubs (i.e., food and general merchandise)
236220 Warehouse construction (e.g., commercial, industrial, manufacturing, private)
238220 Warehouse refrigeration system installation

236220 Warehouse, commercial and institutional, construction
236220 Warehouse, industrial, construction
332311 Warehouses, prefabricated metal, manufacturing
493190 Warehousing (except farm products, general merchandise, refrigerated)
493110 Warehousing (including foreign trade zones), general merchandise
493110 Warehousing and storage, general merchandise
813910 Warehousing associations
493130 Warehousing, farm products (except refrigerated)
493120 Warehousing, refrigerated
531130 Warehousing, self storage
334511 Warfare countermeasures equipment manufacturing
423730 Warm air heating equipment merchant wholesalers
238220 Warm air heating system installation
335211 Warming trays, electric, manufacturing
315191 Warmup suits made in apparel knitting mills
315291 Warmup suits, infants', cut and sewn from purchased fabric (except apparel contractors)
315211 Warmup suits, men's and boys', cut and sew apparel contractors
315228 Warmup suits, men's and boys', cut and sewn from purchased fabric (except apparel contractors)
315212 Warmup suits, women's, girls', and infants', cut and sew apparel contractors
315239 Warmup suits, women's, misses', and girls', cut and sewn from purchased fabric (except apparel contractors)
313249 Warp fabrics knitting
333292 Warping machinery manufacturing
524128 Warranty insurance carriers (e.g., appliance, automobile, homeowners, product), direct
315211 Washable service apparel (e.g., barbers', hospital, professional), men's and boys', cut and sew apparel contractors
315225 Washable service apparel (e.g., barbers', hospital, professional), men's and boys', cut and sewn from purchased fabric (except apparel contractors)
315212 Washable service apparel, women's and girls', cut and sew apparel contractors
315239 Washable service apparel, women's, misses', and girls', cut and sewn from purchased fabric (except apparel contractors)
321999 Washboards, wood and part wood, manufacturing
532210 Washer, clothes, rental
212113 Washeries, anthracite
212111 Washeries, bituminous coal or lignite
333131 Washers, aggregate and sand, stationary, manufacturing
332722 Washers, metal, manufacturing
236210 Washery, mining, construction
811412 Washing machine, household-type, repair and maintenance services without retailing new washing machine
335224 Washing machines, household-type, manufacturing
333312 Washing machines, laundry (except household-type), manufacturing
561720 Washroom sanitation services
562219 Waste (except sewage) treatment facilities, nonhazardous
562119 Waste (except solid and hazardous) collection services
562119 Waste (except solid and hazardous) hauling, local

562112 Waste collection services, hazardous
562111 Waste collection services, nonhazardous solid
221320 Waste collection, treatment, and disposal through a sewer system
562213 Waste disposal combustors or incinerators, nonhazardous solid
562211 Waste disposal facilities, hazardous
562212 Waste disposal landfills, nonhazardous solid
236210 Waste disposal plant (except sewage treatment) construction
484230 Waste hauling, hazardous, long-distance
562112 Waste hauling, local, hazardous
562111 Waste hauling, local, nonhazardous solid
484230 Waste hauling, nonhazardous, long-distance
924110 Waste management program administration
423930 Waste materials merchant wholesalers
562920 Waste recovery facilities
562112 Waste transfer stations, hazardous
562111 Waste transfer stations, nonhazardous solid
562211 Waste treatment facilities, hazardous
562211 Waste treatment plants, hazardous
322214 Wastebaskets, fiber made from purchased paperboard
316993 Watch bands (except metal) manufacturing
339914 Watch bands, metal (except precious), manufacturing
339911 Watch bands, precious metal, manufacturing
335912 Watch batteries manufacturing
327215 Watch crystals made from purchased glass
326199 Watch crystals, plastics, manufacturing
334518 Watch jewels manufacturing
811490 Watch repair shops without retailing new watches
448310 Watch shops
334518 Watchcase manufacturing
334518 Watches and parts (except crystals) manufacturing
423940 Watches and parts merchant wholesalers
333415 Water (i.e., drinking) coolers, mechanical, manufacturing
325412 Water (i.e., drinking) decontamination or purification tablets manufacturing
337124 Water bed frames, metal, manufacturing
337122 Water bed frames, wood, manufacturing
337910 Water bed mattresses manufacturing
327111 Water closet bowls, vitreous china, manufacturing
332998 Water closets, metal, manufacturing
339942 Water colors, artist's, manufacturing
924110 Water control and quality program administration
423740 Water coolers, mechanical, merchant wholesalers
237110 Water desalination plant construction
221310 Water distribution (except irrigation)
221310 Water distribution for irrigation
237110 Water filtration plant construction
221310 Water filtration plant operation
334512 Water heater controls manufacturing
238220 Water heater installation
811412 Water heater repair and maintenance services without retailing new water heaters
333319 Water heaters (except boilers), commercial-type, manufacturing
423720 Water heaters (except electric) merchant wholesalers

335228 Water heaters (including nonelectric), household-type, manufacturing
423620 Water heaters, electric, merchant wholesalers
326220 Water hoses, rubber or plastics, manufacturing
213111 Water intake well drilling, oil and gas field on a contract basis
334519 Water leak detectors manufacturing
237110 Water main and line construction
238220 Water meter installation
713110 Water parks, amusement
238290 Water pipe insulating
331511 Water pipe, cast iron, manufacturing
335211 Water pulsating devices, household-type electric, manufacturing
237110 Water pumping or lift station construction
333319 Water purification equipment manufacturing
334513 Water quality monitoring and control systems manufacturing
325510 Water repellant coatings for wood, concrete and masonry manufacturing
315211 Water resistant apparel, men's and boys', cut and sew apparel contractors
315228 Water resistant jackets and windbreakers, nontailored, men's and boys', cut and sewn from purchased fabric (except apparel contractors)
315239 Water resistant jackets and windbreakers, not tailored, women's, misses' and girls', cut and sewn from purchased fabric (except apparel contractors)
315228 Water resistant outerwear (except overcoats), men's and boys', cut and sewn from purchased fabric (except apparel contractors)
315239 Water resistant outerwear (except overcoats), women's, misses', and girls', cut and sewn from purchased fabric (except apparel contractors)
315291 Water resistant outerwear infants', cut and sewn from purchased fabric (except apparel contractors)
315212 Water resistant outerwear, women's, girls', and infants', cut and sew apparel contractors
315222 Water resistant overcoats, men's and boys', cut and sewn from purchased fabric (except apparel contractors)
315234 Water resistant overcoats, women's, misses', and girls', cut and sewn from purchased fabric (except apparel contractors)
316211 Water shoes, plastics or plastics soled fabric upper, manufacturing
316211 Water shoes, rubber or rubber soled fabric upper, manufacturing
532292 Water ski rental
238220 Water softener installation
454390 Water softener service providers, direct selling
423720 Water softening and conditioning equipment merchant wholesalers
424690 Water softening compounds merchant wholesalers
333319 Water softening equipment manufacturing
237110 Water system storage tank and tower construction
445299 Water stores, bottled
221310 Water supply systems
238220 Water system balancing and testing contractors
332420 Water tanks, heavy gauge metal, manufacturing
483212 Water taxi services
332913 Water traps manufacturing
221310 Water treatment and distribution

333319 Water treatment equipment manufacturing
423830 Water treatment equipment, industrial, merchant wholesalers
423850 Water treatment equipment, municipal, merchant wholesalers
237110 Water treatment plant construction
221310 Water treatment plants
333611 Water turbines manufacturing
333132 Water well drilling machinery manufacturing
237110 Water well drilling, digging, boring or sinking (except water intake wells in oil and gas fields)
237110 Water well pump and well piping system installation
312111 Water, artificially carbonated, manufacturing
424490 Water, bottled (except water treating), merchant wholesalers
325998 Water, distilled, manufacturing
312111 Water, flavored, manufacturing
312112 Water, naturally carbonated, purifying and bottling
712190 Waterfalls (i.e., natural wonder tourist attractions)
488310 Waterfront terminal operation (e.g., docks, piers, wharves)
326199 Watering cans, plastics, manufacturing
325611 Waterless hand soaps manufacturing
111219 Watermelon farming, field, bedding plant and seed production
334514 Watermeters, consumption registering, manufacturing
315299 Waterproof outerwear cut and sewn from purchased fabric (except apparel contractors)
315211 Waterproof outerwear, men's and boys', cut and sew apparel contractors
315299 Waterproof outerwear, rubberizing fabric and manufacturing outerwear
315212 Waterproof outerwear, women's, girls', and infants', cut and sew apparel contractors
313320 Waterproofing apparel, fabrics and textile products (e.g., oiling, rubberizing, waxing, varnishing)
238390 Waterproofing contractors
315228 Water-repellent outerwear (except overcoats), men's and boys', cut and sewn from purchased fabric (except apparel contractors)
315239 Water-repellent outerwear (except overcoats), women's, misses', and girls', cut and sewn from purchased fabric (except apparel contractors)
315291 Water-repellent outerwear, infants', cut and sewn from purchased fabric (except apparel contractors)
315211 Water-repellent outerwear, men's and boys', cut and sew apparel contractors
315212 Water-repellent outerwear, women's, girls', and infants', cut and sew apparel contractors
315222 Water-repellent overcoats, men's and boys', cut and sewn from purchased fabric (except apparel contractors)
315234 Water-repellent overcoats, women's, misses', and girls', cut and sewn from purchased fabric (except apparel contractors)
713990 Waterslides (i.e., amusement rides)
332911 Waterworks and municipal water system valves manufacturing
334515 Watt-hour and demand meters, combined, manufacturing

334515 Watt-hour and time switch meters, combined, manufacturing
334515 Watt-hour meters, electric, manufacturing
325191 Wattle extract manufacturing
334515 Wattmeters manufacturing
713940 Wave pools
334515 Waveform measuring and/or analyzing equipment manufacturing
339999 Wax figures (i.e., mannequins) manufacturing
712110 Wax museums
325612 Wax removers manufacturing
322222 Waxed paper for nonpackaging applications made from purchased paper
322221 Waxed paper for packaging applications made from purchased paper
424130 Waxed paper merchant wholesalers
424690 Waxes (except petroleum) merchant wholesalers
324199 Waxes, petroleum, made from refined petroleum
324110 Waxes, petroleum, made in petroleum refineries
325612 Waxes, polishing (e.g., floor, furniture), manufacturing
313320 Waxing purchased textiles and apparel
115114 Waxing, fruits or vegetables
112210 Weaning pig operations
336992 Weapons, self-propelled, manufacturing
541990 Weather forecasting services
924120 Weather research program administration
321918 Weather strip, wood, manufacturing
238390 Weather stripping installation
423330 Weather stripping merchant wholesalers
334519 Weather tracking equipment manufacturing
333999 Weather vanes manufacturing
331422 Weatherproof wire or cable made from purchased copper in wire drawing plants
331319 Weatherproof wire or cable made in aluminum wire drawing plants
238390 Weatherproofing concrete
332321 Weatherstrip, metal, manufacturing
314999 Weatherstripping made from purchased textiles
313221 Weaving and finishing narrow fabrics
313210 Weaving and finishing of broadwoven fabrics (except rugs, tire fabric)
313210 Weaving broadwoven fabrics (except rugs, tire fabrics)
313210 Weaving broadwoven felts
313221 Weaving fabric less than 12 inches (30cm)
313210 Weaving fabrics more than 12 inches (30cm) in width
333292 Weaving machinery manufacturing
313221 Weaving narrow fabrics
314110 Weaving rugs, carpets, and mats
541511 WEB (i.e., Internet) page design services, custom
516110 Web broadcasting
516110 Web communities (except Web search portals)
518210 Web hosting
454111 Web retailers
518112 Web search portals
313221 Webbing weaving
321999 Webbing, cane, reed, and rattan, manufacturing
812990 Wedding chapels (except churches)
315212 Wedding dresses, women's, cut and sew apparel contractors
315233 Wedding dresses, women's, misses', and girls', cut and sewn from purchased fabric (except apparel contractors)
541921 Wedding photography services
812990 Wedding planning services
561730 Weed control and fertilizing services (except crop)

115112 Weed control services for crops
926140 Weed control, agriculture, government
333111 Weeding machines, farm-type, manufacturing
238910 Weeping tile installation
313241 Weft fabrics knitting
811219 Weighing equipment (e.g., balance, scales) repair and maintenance services
812191 Weight loss centers, non-medical
812191 Weight reducing centers, non-medical
713940 Weight training centers
541890 Welcoming services (i.e., advertising services)
331222 Welded iron or steel wire fabric made in wire drawing plants
316999 Welders' aprons, leather, manufacturing
339113 Welder's hoods manufacturing
316999 Welders' jackets, leggings, and sleeves, leather, manufacturing
333992 Welding equipment manufacturing
532412 Welding equipment rental or leasing
424690 Welding gases merchant wholesalers
423830 Welding machinery and equipment merchant wholesalers
333514 Welding positioners (i.e., jigs) manufacturing
811310 Welding repair services (e.g., automotive, general)
331491 Welding rod, uncoated, nonferrous metals (except aluminum, copper), made from purchased metals or scrap
423840 Welding supplies (except welding gases) merchant wholesalers
333992 Welding wire or rods (i.e., coated, cored) manufacturing
238190 Welding, on site, contractors
332313 Weldments manufacturing
923130 Welfare administration, nonoperating
923130 Welfare programs administration
624190 Welfare service centers, multi-program
213112 Well casing running, cutting and pulling, oil and gas field on a contract basis
331210 Well casings (e.g., heavy riveted, lock joint, welded, wrought) made from purchased iron or steel
331111 Well casings, iron or steel, made in iron and steel mills
213111 Well drilling (i.e., oil, gas, water intake wells) on a contract basis
532412 Well drilling machinery and equipment rental or leasing
333132 Well logging equipment manufacturing
213112 Well logging, oil and gas field, on a contract basis
213112 Well plugging, oil and gas field, on a contract basis
213112 Well pumping, oil and gas field, on a contract basis
213112 Well servicing, oil and gas field, on a contract basis
213112 Well surveying, oil and gas field, on a contract basis
332322 Wells, light, sheet metal (except stampings), manufacturing
316110 Welting leather manufacturing
448140 Western wear stores
316110 Wet blues manufacturing
313230 Wet laid nonwoven fabrics manufacturing
322130 Wet machine board mills
311221 Wet milling corn and other vegetables
339920 Wet suits manufacturing
325613 Wetting agents manufacturing
487210 Whale watching excursions
237990 Wharf construction
488310 Wharf operation
311211 Wheat bran manufacturing
311230 Wheat breakfast cereal manufacturing

111140 Wheat farming, field and seed production
311211 Wheat flour manufacturing
311211 Wheat germ manufacturing
311213 Wheat malt manufacturing
334515 Wheatstone bridges (i.e., electrical measuring instruments) manufacturing
811118 Wheel alignment shops, automotive
532291 Wheel chair rental
334511 Wheel position indicators and transmitters, aircraft, manufacturing
332212 Wheel pullers, handtools, manufacturing
333924 Wheelbarrows manufacturing
339113 Wheelchairs manufacturing
423450 Wheelchairs merchant wholesalers
336399 Wheels (i.e., rims), automotive, truck, and bus, manufacturing
327910 Wheels, abrasive, manufacturing
331111 Wheels, car and locomotive, iron or steel, made in iron and steel mills
423120 Wheels, motor vehicle, new, merchant wholesalers
327910 Wheels, polishing and grinding, manufacturing
336330 Wheels, steering, automotive, truck, and bus, manufacturing
327910 Whetstones manufacturing
212399 Whetstones mining and/or beneficiating
311512 Whey butter manufacturing
311514 Whey, condensed, dried, evaporated, and powdered, manufacturing
311513 Whey, raw, liquid, manufacturing
311511 Whipped topping (except dry mix, frozen) manufacturing
311514 Whipped topping, dry mix, manufacturing
311412 Whipped topping, frozen, manufacturing
335211 Whippers, household-type electric, manufacturing
311511 Whipping cream manufacturing
316999 Whips, horse, manufacturing
316999 Whipstocks manufacturing
339113 Whirlpool baths (i.e., hydrotherapy equipment) manufacturing
423450 Whirlpool baths merchant wholesalers
493190 Whiskey warehousing
325131 White extender pigments (e.g., barytes, blanc fixe, whiting) manufacturing
331528 White metal castings (except die-castings), unfinished, manufacturing
713990 White water rafting, recreational
238320 Whitewashing contractors
212312 Whiting crushed and broken stone, mining and/or beneficiating
114111 Whiting fishing
325131 Whiting manufacturing
334519 Whole body counters, nuclear, manufacturing
****** Wholesale—see type of product
561520 Wholesale tour operators
813910 Wholesalers' associations
337125 Wicker furniture (except upholstered), household-type, manufacturing
313221 Wicks manufacturing
334210 Wide area network communications equipment (e.g., bridges, gateways, routers) manufacturing
448150 Wig and hairpiece stores
424990 Wigs merchant wholesalers
339999 Wigs, wiglets, toupees, hair pieces, manufacturing
712130 Wild animal parks
111199 Wild rice farming, field and seed production
721214 Wilderness camps
711510 Wildlife artists, independent
924120 Wildlife conservation agencies
813312 Wildlife preservation organizations
712190 Wildlife sanctuaries
212231 Willemite mining and/or beneficiating

337125 Willow furniture (except upholstered), household-type, manufacturing
321999 Willow ware (except furniture) manufacturing
333923 Winches manufacturing
423830 Winches merchant wholesalers
924120 Wind and water erosion control agencies, government
334519 Wind direction indicators manufacturing
926130 Wind generated electrical power regulation
237130 Wind power structure construction
333611 Wind powered turbine generator sets manufacturing
333611 Wind turbines (i.e., windmill) manufacturing
315291 Windbreakers, infants', cut and sewn from purchased fabric (except apparel contractors)
315211 Windbreakers, men's and boys', cut and sew apparel contractors
315228 Windbreakers, men's and boys', cut and sewn from purchased fabric (except apparel contractors)
315212 Windbreakers, women's, girls', and infants', cut and sew apparel contractors
315239 Windbreakers, women's, misses', and girls', cut and sewn from purchased fabric (except apparel contractors)
333292 Winding machinery for textiles manufacturing
313112 Winding purchased yarn
313112 Winding, spooling, beaming and rewinding of purchased yarn
333611 Windmills, electric power, generation-type, manufacturing
333111 Windmills, farm-type, manufacturing
238350 Window and door (residential-type) of any material, prefabricated, installation
325612 Window cleaning preparations manufacturing
561720 Window cleaning services
541890 Window dressing or trimming services, store
332321 Window frames and sash, metal, manufacturing
321911 Window frames and sash, wood and covered wood, manufacturing
238350 Window installation
238150 Window pane or sheet installation
332618 Window screening, woven, made from purchased wire
332321 Window screens, metal frame, manufacturing
321911 Window screens, wood framed, manufacturing
238390 Window shade and blind installation
811490 Window shade repair and maintenance shops
337920 Window shade rollers and fittings manufacturing
337920 Window shades (except awnings) manufacturing
423220 Window shades and blinds merchant wholesalers
444190 Window stores
811122 Window tinting, automotive
442291 Window treatment stores
321918 Window trim, wood and covered wood moldings, manufacturing
321911 Window units, wood and covered wood, manufacturing
238350 Window, metal-frame residential-type, installation
238350 Window, wood, installation
423310 Windows and window frames merchant wholesalers
326199 Windows and window frames, plastics, manufacturing
321911 Windows, louver, wood, manufacturing
332321 Windows, metal, manufacturing
321911 Windows, wood and covered wood, manufacturing

336322 Windshield washer pumps, automotive, truck, and bus, manufacturing
336399 Windshield wiper blades and refills manufacturing
336322 Windshield wiper systems, automotive, truck, and bus, manufacturing
326199 Windshields, plastics, manufacturing
312130 Wine coolers manufacturing
424820 Wine coolers, alcoholic, merchant wholesalers
445310 Wine shops, packaged
312130 Wineries
312130 Wines manufacturing
424820 Wines merchant wholesalers
312130 Wines, cooking, manufacturing
325998 Wintergreen oil manufacturing
336399 Wipers, windshield, automotive, truck, and bus, manufacturing
313230 Wipes, nonwoven fabric, manufacturing
423840 Wiping cloths merchant wholesalers
423510 Wire (except insulated) merchant wholesalers
423510 Wire and cable (except electrical) merchant wholesalers
333298 Wire and cable insulating machinery manufacturing
331222 Wire cages, iron or steel, made in wire drawing plants
331222 Wire carts (e.g., grocery, household, industrial), iron or steel, made in wire drawing plants
331422 Wire cloth made from purchased copper in wire drawing plants
331319 Wire cloth made in aluminum wire drawing plants
331422 Wire cloth, copper, made in integrated secondary smelting and wire drawing plants
331222 Wire cloth, iron or steel, made in wire drawing plants
331491 Wire cloth, nonferrous metals (except aluminum, copper), made from purchased metals or scrap
423390 Wire fencing and fencing accessories merchant wholesalers
331222 Wire garment hangers, iron or steel, made in wire drawing plants
519110 Wire photo services
331111 Wire products, iron or steel, made in iron and steel mills
331222 Wire products, iron or steel, made in wire drawing plants
423510 Wire rope (except insulated) merchant wholesalers
333923 Wire rope hoists manufacturing
423510 Wire screening merchant wholesalers
331319 Wire screening, aluminum, made in integrated secondary smelting and drawing plants
331491 Wire screening, nonferrous metals (except aluminum, copper), made from purchased nonferrous metals (except aluminum, copper) in wire drawing plants
561422 Wire services (i.e., telemarketing services), floral
519110 Wire services, news
331319 Wire, armored, made in aluminum wire drawing plants
331319 Wire, bare, made in aluminum wire drawing plants
331422 Wire, copper (except mechanical) (e.g., armored, bare, insulated), made from purchased copper in wire drawing plants
331422 Wire, copper (except mechanical) (e.g., armored, bare, insulated), made in integrated secondary smelting and wire drawing plants
331221 Wire, flat, rolled strip, made in cold rolling mills
331319 Wire, insulated, made in aluminum wire drawing plants

423610 Wire, insulated, merchant wholesalers
331222 Wire, iron or steel (e.g., armored, bare, insulated), made in wire drawing plants
331421 Wire, mechanical, copper and copper alloy, made from purchased copper or in integrated secondary smelting and rolling, drawing or extruding plants
331491 Wire, nonferrous metals (except aluminum, copper), made from purchased nonferrous metals (except aluminum, copper) in wire drawing plants
331491 Wire, nonferrous metals (except aluminum, copper), made in integrated secondary smelting mills and wire drawing plants
517310 Wired telecommunication resellers
333518 Wiredrawing and fabricating machinery and equipment (except dies) manufacturing
333514 Wiredrawing and straightening dies manufacturing
517212 Wireless data communication carriers (except satellite)
517310 Wireless telecommunication resellers (except satellite)
517212 Wireless telephone communications carriers (except satellite)
213112 Wireline services, oil and gas field, on a contract basis
336322 Wiring harness and ignition sets for internal combustion engines manufacturing
423610 Wiring supplies merchant wholesalers
325191 Witch hazel extract manufacturing
212299 Wolframite mining and/or beneficiating
212399 Wollastonite mining and/or beneficiating
424330 Women's and children's clothing accessories merchant wholesalers
813410 Women's auxiliaries
923130 Women's bureaus
424330 Women's clothing merchant wholesalers
813410 Women's clubs
624221 Women's shelters, battered
325191 Wood alcohol, natural, manufacturing
325199 Wood alcohol, synthetic, manufacturing
424990 Wood carvings merchant wholesalers
113310 Wood chipping in the field
321113 Wood chips made in sawmills
332213 Wood cutting saw blades manufacturing
325191 Wood distillates manufacturing
321911 Wood door frames and sash manufacturing
333298 Wood drying kilns manufacturing
321114 Wood fence (i.e., pickets, poling, rails), treating
423310 Wood fencing merchant wholesalers
325510 Wood fillers manufacturing
238330 Wood floor finishing (e.g., coating, sanding)
321918 Wood flooring manufacturing
423310 Wood flooring merchant wholesalers
238330 Wood flooring, installation only
321999 Wood flour manufacturing
238130 Wood frame component (e.g., truss) fabrication on site
337121 Wood framed furniture, upholstered, household-type, manufacturing
321999 Wood heel blocks manufacturing
321999 Wood heels, finished, manufacturing
321213 Wood I-joists manufacturing
321918 Wood moldings (e.g., pre-finished, unfinished), clear and finger joint, manufacturing
325191 Wood oils manufacturing
423990 Wood products (e.g., chips, posts, shavings, ties) merchant wholesalers

321114 Wood products, creosoting purchased wood products
322110 Wood pulp manufacturing
424990 Wood pulp merchant wholesalers
423310 Wood shingles merchant wholesalers
321918 Wood shutters manufacturing
423310 Wood siding merchant wholesalers
238170 Wood siding, installation
333414 Wood stoves manufacturing
424690 Wood treating preparations merchant wholesalers
333210 Wood verneer laminating and gluing machines manufacturing
321911 Wood window frames and sash manufacturing
321999 Wood wool (excelsior) manufacturing
442299 Wood-burning stove stores
321999 Woodenware, kitchen and household, manufacturing
532490 Woodworking machinery and equipment rental or leasing
423830 Woodworking machinery merchant wholesalers
333210 Woodworking machines (except handheld) manufacturing
333292 Wool and worsted finishing machinery manufacturing
313210 Wool fabrics, broadwoven, weaving
313221 Wool fabrics, narrow woven, weaving
313111 Wool spun yarn made from purchased fiber
313312 Wool tops and noils manufacturing
424590 Wool tops and noils merchant wholesalers
314999 Wool waste processing
313112 Wool yarn, twisting or winding of purchased yarn
424590 Wool, raw, merchant wholesalers
311941 Worcestershire sauce manufacturing
333313 Word processing equipment, dedicated, manufacturing
561410 Word processing services
624229 Work (sweat) equity home construction organizations
337127 Work benches manufacturing
812332 Work clothing and uniform supply services, industrial
424320 Work clothing, men's and boys', merchant wholesalers
315211 Work coats and jackets, men's and boys', cut and sew apparel contractors
315225 Work coats and jackets, men's and boys', cut and sewn from purchased fabric (except apparel contractors
624310 Work experience centers (i.e., sheltered workshops)
315191 Work gloves and mittens, knit, made in apparel knitting mills
315992 Work gloves, leather (except apparel contractors), manufacturing
315211 Work gloves, leather, men's and boys', cut and sew apparel contractors
315212 Work gloves, leather, women's and girls', cut and sew apparel contractors
315225 Work pants (except dungarees, jeans), men's and boys', cut and sewn from purchased fabric (except apparel contractors)
315211 Work pants, men's and boys', cut and sew apparel contractors
315211 Work shirts, men's and boys', cut and sew apparel contractors
315225 Work shirts, men's and boys', cut and sewn from purchased fabric (except apparel contractors)
316213 Work shoes, men's (except rubber or plastics protective footwear), manufacturing
721310 Workers' camps

525190 Workers' compensation insurance funds
524126 Workers' compensation insurance underwriting
923130 Workers' compensation program administration
721310 Workers' dormitories
213111 Workover of oil and gas wells on a contract basis
624310 Workshops for persons with disabilities
334111 Workstations, computer, manufacturing
928120 World Bank
813319 World peace and understanding advocacy organizations
112990 Worm production
424990 Worms merchant wholesalers
313210 Worsted fabrics weaving
321999 Wrappers, excelsior, manufacturing
333993 Wrapping (i.e., packaging) machinery manufacturing
424130 Wrapping paper (except giftwrap) merchant wholesalers
339999 Wreaths, artificial, manufacturing
488410 Wrecker services (i.e., towing services), motor vehicle
238910 Wrecking, building or other structure
332212 Wrenches, handtools, nonpowered, manufacturing
333991 Wrenches, impact, handheld power-driven, manufacturing
711219 Wrestlers, independent professional
711310 Wrestling event managers with facilities
711320 Wrestling event managers without facilities
711310 Wrestling event organizers with facilities
711320 Wrestling event organizers without facilities
711310 Wrestling event promoters with facilities
711320 Wrestling event promoters without facilities
711510 Writers of advertising copy, independent
711510 Writers, independent (freelance)
813410 Writing clubs
325998 Writing inks manufacturing
424120 Writing paper (except bulk) merchant wholesalers
322233 Writing paper and envelopes, boxed sets, made from purchased paper
322121 Writing paper made in paper mills
322233 Writing paper, cut sheet, made from purchased paper
337124 Wrought iron furniture (except upholstered), household-type, manufacturing
332996 Wrought iron or steel pipe and tubing made from purchased metal pipe
331111 Wrought iron or steel pipe and tubing made in iron and steel mills
212299 Wulfenite mining and/or beneficiating
212399 Wurtzilite mining and/or beneficiating
325320 Xanthone insecticides manufacturing
335110 X-mas tree light bulbs manufacturing
334517 X-ray apparatus and tubes (e.g., control, industrial, medical, research) manufacturing
325992 X-ray film and plates, sensitized, manufacturing
334517 X-ray generators manufacturing
541380 X-ray inspection services
334517 X-ray irradiation equipment manufacturing
621512 X-ray laboratories, medical or dental
423450 X-ray machines and parts, medical and dental, merchant wholesalers
334517 X-ray tubes manufacturing
334515 X-Y recorders (i.e., plotters (except computer peripheral equipment)) manufacturing

325110 Xylene made from refined petroleum or liquid hydrocarbons
324110 Xylene made in petroleum refineries
339992 Xylophones and parts manufacturing
713930 Yacht basins
336612 Yacht building, not done in shipyards
713930 Yacht clubs with marinas
713990 Yacht clubs without marinas
532292 Yacht rental without crew
336611 Yachts built in shipyards
111219 Yam farming, field and seed production
424310 Yard goods, textile (except burlap, felt), merchant wholesalers
335121 Yard Lights, residential electric, manufacturing
332212 Yardsticks, metal, manufacturing
321999 Yardsticks, wood, manufacturing
313111 Yarn spinning mills
313111 Yarn spun from purchased fiber
333292 Yarn texturizing machines manufacturing
313112 Yarn throwing, twisting, and winding of purchased yarn
313111 Yarn, carpet and rug, spun from purchased fiber
325221 Yarn, cellulosic filament, manufacturing
325221 Yarn, cellulosic filament, manufacturing and texturizing
327212 Yarn, fiberglass, made in glass making plants
325222 Yarn, noncellulosic fiber and filament, manufacturing
325222 Yarn, noncellulosic fiber and filament, manufacturing and texturizing
424310 Yarns (except industrial), merchant wholesalers
424990 Yarns, industrial, merchant wholesalers
511199 Yearbook (e.g., high school, college, university) publishers (except exclusive Internet publishing)
511199 Yearbook (e.g., high school, college, university) publishers and printing combined
516110 Yearbook (e.g., high school, college, university) publishers, exclusively on Internet
323112 Yearbooks flexographic printing without publishing
323111 Yearbooks gravure printing without publishing
323110 Yearbooks lithographic (offset) printing without publishing
323119 Yearbooks printing (except flexographic, gravure, lithographic, quick, screen) without publishing
323113 Yearbooks screen printing without publishing
311999 Yeast manufacturing
424490 Yeast merchant wholesalers
611699 Yoga instruction, camps, or schools
311511 Yogurt (except frozen) manufacturing
424430 Yogurt merchant wholesalers
311514 Yogurt mix manufacturing
311520 Yogurt, frozen, manufacturing
111334 Youngberry farming
624110 Youth centers (except recreational only)
813410 Youth civic clubs
813410 Youth clubs (except recreational only)
813410 Youth farming organizations
624110 Youth guidance organizations
721199 Youth hostels
813410 Youth scouting organizations
624110 Youth self-help organizations
813410 Youth social clubs
713990 Youth sports leagues or teams
325222 Zein fibers and filaments manufacturing
325188 Zinc ammonium chloride manufacturing

331491 Zinc and zinc alloy bar, plate, pipe, rod, sheet, tubing, and wire made from purchased metals or scrap
325131 Zinc based pigments manufacturing
335912 Zinc carbon batteries manufacturing
331528 Zinc castings (except die-castings), unfinished, manufacturing
325188 Zinc chloride manufacturing
325188 Zinc compounds, not specified elsewhere by process, manufacturing
331522 Zinc die-castings, unfinished, manufacturing
331492 Zinc dust reclaiming
332999 Zinc foil and leaf not made in rolling mills
325188 Zinc hydrosulfite (i.e., zinc dithionite) manufacturing
212231 Zinc ore mine site development for own account
212231 Zinc ores mining and/or beneficiating
325188 Zinc oxide (except pigments) manufacturing
325412 Zinc oxide medicinal preparations manufacturing
331492 Zinc recovering from scrap and/or alloying purchased metals
331419 Zinc refining, primary
331491 Zinc rolling, drawing, or extruding purchased metals or scrap
325188 Zinc sulfide manufacturing
212231 Zinc-blende (sphalerite) mining and/or beneficiating
212231 Zincite mining and/or beneficiating
333298 Zipper making machinery manufacturing
313221 Zipper tape weaving
339993 Zippers (i.e., slide fasteners) manufacturing
424310 Zippers merchant wholesalers
331491 Zirconium and zirconium alloy bar, rod, billet, sheet, strip, and tubing made from purchased metals or scrap
212299 Zirconium concentrates beneficiating
212299 Zirconium ores mining and/or beneficiating
331419 Zirconium refining, primary
331491 Zirconium rolling, drawing, or extruding purchased metals or scrap
339992 Zithers and parts manufacturing
925120 Zoning boards and commissions
712130 Zoological gardens
712130 Zoos
111219 Zucchini farming, field, bedding plant and seed production